THE OXFORD COMPANION TO

Politics
IN INDIA

'This is a landmark publication. In thirty-eight sweeping essays some of the world's leading scholars describe, dissect and analyse the many-layered polity that is India. At a time when every aspect of India is getting rapidly and intricately inter-woven with the global, this book is an invaluable guide to not just political scientists but also economists, sociologists and anybody interested in the strategic analysis of India's international relations and domestic policymaking.'

—Kaushik Basu,
Chief Economic Adviser, Ministry of Finance,
Government of India

'This splendid collection shows that the study of Indian politics is essential for comparative politics and political theory. Jayal and Mehta have assembled a stunning group of authors, the best that can be imagined today, and have designed the volume in an impressively thoughtful way, covering institutions, political processes, social groups, and the politics of class, religion, gender, caste and region. Written with flair and fully accessible to non-experts, the essays put the study of India where it belongs, in the forefront of political science.'

—Martha C. Nussbaum,
The University of Chicago

'This companion really does justice to its subject, covering a range of issues from social cleavages at one end of the spectrum to the problems of applying quantitative techniques to the masses of raw data on Indian political life at the other. It is built on firm historical foundations and is extremely sophisticated about the ways in which India is and is not an "exceptional" case among modern democracies. It will be immensely useful to readers both within India and beyond.'

—Alan Ryan,
Princeton University

'This companion is undoubtedly indispensable to academic research on Indian politics as well as compulsory reading on university courses. It is also an invaluable introductory resource for the study of comparative international politics, with India now a subject of scholarly enquiry as successful democracy, amidst persistent inequality and social and cultural diversity. With growing interest in India as a global power in the twenty-first century, the book is of relevance to a worldwide audience of lay readers, policymakers and economic analysts, seeking to understand the complexities of Indian politics.'

—Nandini Gooptu,
University of Oxford

THE OXFORD COMPANION TO
Politics
IN INDIA

STUDENTedition

with a New Preface

edited by
NIRAJA GOPAL JAYAL
PRATAP BHANU MEHTA

OXFORD
UNIVERSITY PRESS

OXFORD

UNIVERSITY PRESS

Oxford University Press is a department of the University of Oxford.
It furthers the University's objective of excellence in research, scholarship,
and education by publishing worldwide. Oxford is a registered trademark of
Oxford University Press in the UK and in certain other countries

Published in India by
Oxford University Press
22 Workspace, 2nd Floor, 1/22 Asaf Ali Road, New Delhi 110002, India

First Edition published in 2010
Oxford India Paperbacks 2011
Eighteenth impression 2020

ISBN-13: 978-0-19-807592-9
ISBN-10: 0-19-807592-8

Typeset in Arno Pro 11/14
by Eleven Arts, Keshav Puram, Delhi 110 035
Printed in bound in India by Thomson Press India Ltd.

Contents

Tables and Appendices

TABLES

Appendix Tables

APPENDICES

Abbreviations

ABLTC	Akhil Bharatiya Loktantrik Congress	AUDF	Assam United Democratic Front
ABPS	Akhil Bharatiya Pratinidhi Sabha	AVARD	Association of Voluntary Agencies for Rural Development
ABVP	Akhil Bharatiya Vidyarthi Parishad	BADP	Border Area Development Programme
AC	Arunachal Congress		
AGP	Asom Gana Parishad	BDF	Bodoland Democratic Front
AIADMK	All India Anna Dravida Munnetra Kazhagam	BGVS	Bharat Gyan Vigyan Samithi
		BIFR	Board of Industrial and Financial Reconstruction
AICCWW	All India Coordination Committee for Working Women		
		BJD	Biju Janata Dal
AIDWA	All India Democratic Women's Association	BJP	Bharatiya Janata Party
		BJS	Bharatiya Jan Sangh
AIFB	All India Forward Bloc	BKD	Bharatiya Kranti Dal
AIKSC	All India Kisan Sabha Conference	BKS	Bharatiya Kisan Sangh
AIMIM	All India Majlis Ittehadual Muslimeen	BKU	Bharatiya Kisan Union
		BLD	Bharatiya Lok Dal
AITC	All India Trinamool Congress	BOP	Balance of Payment
AITUC	All India Trade Union Congress	BPL	Below Poverty Line
AIWC	All India Women's Conference	BMS	Bharatiya Mazdoor Sangh
AP	Andhra Pradesh	BSMC	Bodoland State Movement Committee
ASSOCHAM	Associated Chambers of Commerce and Industry		
		BSP	Bahujan Samaj Party

BVA	Bahujan Vikas Aghadi	FERA	Foreign Exchange Regulation Act
CAD	*Constituent Assembly Debates*	FICCI	Federation of Indian Chambers of
CAG	Comptroller and Auditor General		Commerce and Industry
CAPART	Council for Advancement of People's	FMCT	Fissile Material Cut-off Treaty
	Action and Rural Technology	FNWO	Forum of National Women's
CASI	Center for Advanced Study of India		Organization
CBI	Central Bureau of Investigation	FPTP	First-past-the-post
CBO	Community Based Organization	FSRI	Fiscal Self Reliance Indicator
CDP	Community Development	FWP	Forum for Women and Politics
	Programme	GATS	General Agreement on Trade and
CDS	Centre for Development Studies		Services
CEI	Confederation of Engineering	GATT	General Agreement on Tariffs and
	Industry		Trade
CIA	Central Intelligence Agency	GDP	Gross Domestic Product
CII	Confederation of Indian Industry	GNP	Gross National Product
COVA	Confederation of Voluntary	GOI	Government of India
	Associations	GRO	Grassroots Organization
CPI	Communist Party of India	GST	Goods and Service Tax
CPI(M)	Communist Part of India (Marxist)	HJC	Haryana Janhit Congress
CPR	Centre for Policy Research	HLD(R)	Haryana Lok Dal (Rashtriya)
CrPC	Criminal Procedure Code	HP	Himachal Pradesh
CSDS	Centre for the Study of Developing	HVC	Himachal Vikas Congress
	Societies	HVP	Haryana Vikas Party
CSS	Central Sector Schemes	IAS	Indian Administrative Service
CSSS	Centre for the Study of Society	ICHR	Indian Council of Historical
	and Secularism		Research
CSSSC	Centre for Studies in Social	ICS	Indian Civil Service
	Sciences, Calcutta	ICSSR	Indian Council of Social Science
CSWI	Committee on the Status of		Research
	Women in India	IDS	Institute of Development Studies
CTBT	Comprehensive Test Ban Treaty	IEG	Institute of Economic Growth
CWDS	Centre for Women's Development	IES	Indian Educational Service
	Studies	IFDP	Indian Federal Democratic Party
DFID	Department for International	IFS	Indian Foreign Service
	Development	IIBC	India International Business Council
DMK	Dravida Munnetra Kazhagam	IMF	International Monetary Fund
ECI	Election Commission of India	INA	Indian National Army
EGS	Employment Guarantee Scheme	INC	Indian National Congress
EVM	Electronic Voting Machine	INCO	Indian National Congress
FAOW	Forum Against Oppression of		(Organization)
	Women	INCU	Indian National Congress (Urs)
FBL	Forward Bloc	IND	Independent
FCI	Food Corporation of India	INLD	Indian National Lok Dal
FCRA	Foreign Contribution Regulation Act	INTUC	Indian National Trade Union
FDI	Foreign Direct Investment		Congress
FEMA	Foreign Exchange Management Act	IOU	Index of Opposition Unity

IPA	Institute of Public Administration	MLA	Member of Legislative Assembly
IPC	Indian Penal Code	MNC	Multinational Company
IPKF	Indian Peace-Keeping Force	MNF	Mizo National Front
IPS	Indian Police Service	MP	Madhya Pradesh/Member of Parliament
IRDA	Insurance Regulatory and Development Authority	MPLB	Muslim Personal Law Board
IRDP	Integrated Rural Development Programme	MRTP	Monopolies and Restrictive Trade Practices
ISEC	Institute of Social and Economic Change	MSCP	Manipur State Congress Party
ISI	Import Substituting Industrialization	MTCR	Missile Technology Control Regime
ISS	Institute of Social Sciences	MUL	Muslim League
IT	Information Technology	NAC	National Advisory Council
JD(S)	Janata Dal (Secular)	NASSCOM	National Association of Software and Services Companies
JD(U)	Janata Dal (United)	NBA	Narmada Bachao Andolan
JDS(Left)	Janata Dal (Secular) (Left)	NCAER	National Council of Applied Economic Research
J&K	Jammu and Kashmir		
JKNC	Jammu and Kashmir National Conference	NCERT	National Council for Educational Research and Training
JMM	Jharkhand Mukti Morcha	NCMP	National Common Minimum Programme
JP	Janata Party		
JPS	Janata Party Secular	NCP	Nationalist Congress Party
JVM(P)	Jharkhand Vikas Morcha (Pragatisheel)	NCRWC	National Commission to Review the Workings of the Constitution
JWP	Joint Women's Programme	NCWI	National Council for Women in India
KCM	Kerala Congress (Mani)		
KEC	Kerala Congress	NDA	National Democratic Alliance
KMPP	Kisan Mazdoor Praja Party	NFIW	National Federation of Indian Women
KRRS	Karnataka Rajya Ryot Sangha		
KSSP	Kerala Sasthra Sahithya Parishad	NGO	Non-governmental Organization
LCP	Loktantrik Congress	NPF	Nagaland People's Front
LGBT	Indian Lesbian, Gay, Bisexual and Transgender Movement	NREGA	National Rural Employment Guarantee Act
LJNP	Lok Janshakti Party	NREGS	National Rural Employment Guarantee Scheme
LKS	Lok Shakti		
LSD	*Lok Sabha Debates*	NRF	National Renewal Fund
LTTE	Liberation Tigers of Tamil Eelam	NRI	Non-resident Indian
MADMK	MGR Anna Dravida Munnetra Kazhagam	NSS	National Sample Survey
		NSSO	National Sample Survey Organization
MDGs	Millennium Development Goals		
MDMK	Marumalarchi Dravida Munnetra Kazhagam	NWS	Nuclear Weapon State
		OBC	Other Backward Class
MDS	Mahila Dakshita Samiti	ODI	Overseas Development Institute
MISA	Maintenance of Internal Security Act	OPEC	Organization of Petroleum Exporting Countries
MKSS	Mazdoor Kisan Shakti Sangathan		

PBGMS	Paschim Banga Ganatantrik Mahila Samiti	SEWA	Self-Employed Women's Association
PDP	People's Democratic Party	SEZ	Special Economic Zone
PDS	Public Distribution System/Party for Democratic Socialism	SHS	Shiv Sena
		SJP	Samajwadi Janata Party
PEO	Programme Evaluation Organization	SMT	Samata Party
		SNDP Yogam	Shree Narayana Dharma Paripalana Yogam
PIL	Public Interest Litigation		
PMK	Pattali Makkal Katchi	SNEP	Subterranean Nuclear Explosions Project
PR	Proportional Representation		
PRBP	People's Republican Party	SOC	Socialist Party
PRIA	Participatory Research in Asia	SP	Samajwadi Party
PSP	Praja Socialist Party	SS	Shetkari Sangathan
PUCL	People's Union of Civil Liberties	SSP	Samyukta Socialist Party
PUDR	Peoples Union for Democratic Rights report	ST	Scheduled Tribe
		SVD	Samyukta Vidhayak Dal
RBI	Reserve Bank of India	SWA	Swatantra Party
REER	Real Effective Exchange Rate	SWRC	Social Work and Research Centre
RJD	Rashtriya Janata Dal	TDP	Telugu Desam Party
RJP (Anand Mohan)	Rashtriya Janata Party (Anand Mohan)	TLG	Trade-led Deficit
		TMC	Tamil Manila Congress
RLD	Rashtriya Lok Dal	TNAA	Tamil Nadu Agriculturalist Association
RPA	Representation of the People Act		
RPI	Republican Party of India	TRC	Tamizhaga Rajiv Congress
RPI(A)	Republican Party of India (Athavale)	TRS	Telangana Rashtra Samiti
		UCC	Uniform Civil Code
RSP	Revolutionary Socialist Party	UN	United Nations
RSS	Rashtriya Swayamsevak Sangh	UP	Uttar Pradesh
RTI	Right to Information	UPA	United Progressive Alliance
SAARC	South Asian Association of Regional Cooperation	VAT	Value Added Tax
		VCK	Viduthalai Chiruthaigal Katchi
SAD	Shiromani Akali Dal	VHP	Vishwa Hindu Parishad
SAD(B)	Shiromani Akali Dal (Badal)	WEF	World Economic Forum
SAP	Structural Adjustment Programme	WMD	Weapons of Mass Destruction
SC	Scheduled Caste	WSF	World Social Forum
SCF	Scheduled Caste Federation	WTO	World Trade Organization
SDF	Sikkim Democratic Front	YIP	Young India Movement
SEBI	Securities and Exchange Board of India	YWCA	Young Women's Christian Association

Preface to the Student Edition

The *Oxford Companion to Politics in India* (or OCPI) is meant to be a wide-ranging, analytical introduction to the study of politics in India. We were fortunate enough to be able to put together the finest assembly of scholars possible to write essays that would introduce students, specialist scholars, and the general reader alike to various facets of Indian politics. The idea was to provide not merely an account of the major developments, but also to provide frameworks for understanding these developments. The orientation of the volume was methodologically pluralist: the essays were written from different methodological perspectives. Our hope was that taken together the volume would be a comprehensive *tour d'horizon* of the enduring debates in the study of Indian politics.

We are delighted that the volume is now coming out in paperback. But the occasion of its republication also warrants a little reflection. The single biggest challenge for anyone writing about Indian politics is the fact that the subject seems like such a rapidly moving target. The volume had tried to convey the sense that India is undergoing a rapid transformation. While a broad commitment to the institutions of democracy endures, almost everything else seems up for deeper contestation. If anything, the couple of years since the publication of this volume have heightened that sense of uncertainty. But on reflection, it is remarkable that so many of our authors provided the analytical tools through which to understand these rapid changes. This brief introduction simply recapitulates some of the major dimensions of these changes and how we might think about them. It lays out, without being exhaustive, some threads that students of Indian politics will have to pursue in years to come.

INSTITUTIONS

The OCPI opens with a section on the major institutions of democracy: the legislature, the judiciary, the President's office, etc. The premise of Indian democracy has always been that power needs to be divided amongst several institutions. This thicket of institutions provides a series of checks and balances, which ensures that the infirmities of one institution can be compensated for by the actions of another. At some level, all democracies have to strike a balance between two things. On the one hand, a multiplicity of institutions provides a necessary insurance against monopolies of power. Many of these institutions, like the Election Commission, for example, have played an important role in ensuring that the basic rules of democracy endure. On the other hand, the existence of a large number of institutions also poses a special challenge. How will the boundaries of power between them be defined? Will not each institution compete to secure more and more space for itself? Arguably recent trends in Indian politics have only exacerbated the urgency of these questions. For example, the division of authority between courts and the Parliament has always been a matter of contestation. This contest has extended not only to claims to be the supreme arbiter of the constitution; it now extends to issues of governance as well. There is a palpable sense that the authority of the Parliament is in decline. How enduring this decline will be is an open question. But the fundamental point about Indian democracy is that it is constituted by a thicket of institutions, which, together, provide the basic framework of governance. These institutions, however, are not necessarily in harmony in two different ways. First, sometimes internal processes and incentives within any of these institutions diminish their effectiveness or functioning. Second, as some institutions rise or decline, others try and step in to fill the vacuum, and they compete for legitimacy. If anything, the number of institutions is vastly increasing. This dynamic has two implications. The analytical implication is that the study of institutions will remain absolutely central to understanding Indian politics. The substantive implication is that the politics of checks and balances will remain deeply open ended. The range of institutions and actors even *within* the state makes it more and more difficult for any institution to monopolize power. For governance this means that decision-making is necessarily complex though it also ensures that capturing democracy is extremely difficult.

This institutional competition is taking place within a rapidly altering context in the domain of both the state and civil society. As several of the essays in this volume pointed out, the accountability models within the Indian state were premised on two features: hierarchy and secrecy. It was always assumed that there will be a hierarchy of power in the major institutions of the state, and that offices higher up in the hierarchy can hold lower offices to account. Clearly a hierarchy of offices will remain central to any system of government. But it can be argued that there is much more of a lateral fragmentation of power now in the Indian political system, which makes it more difficult for power to be exercised from the top down. This lateral fragmentation has many dimensions to it. Power is exercised at different levels and in different institutions; the nature of political formations makes it very difficult for any single party to dominate; the balance between different levels of government—central, state, and local—is also open to contestation. And the sheer complexity of government makes it more and more implausible to believe that authority from the top can be easily exercised.

The fragmentation of power has been accompanied by another trend. While India was always a robust electoral democracy, the access its citizens had to the state, particularly information, was relatively limited. One of the most remarkable trends of the last few years has been the opening up of the government. The Right to Information Act that allows citizens to access information is just one manifestation of this phenomenon. Citizens and civil society engagement in the pre-legislative process, social audits, and information campaigns, have all, albeit haltingly and incompletely, taken deeper root in Indian politics. In some ways India is at a transitional point. The normative validity of these new norms of accountability is growing, while the practices of the state continue to try and hold on to an equilibrium premised on control and secrecy. In many ways the struggle between transparency and control has now become a more prominent feature of Indian politics. However, this struggle is increasingly occurring, not within the space of politics, but outside it. Although it is a bit of a caricature, this struggle is often described as the struggle between civil society and the state. Civil society is a complex technical term; at the current conjuncture it has come to simply mean actors mobilizing outside of the rubrics of electoral and party politics, and even traditional interest group-based associations to hold the government accountable.

The Right to Information Movement and the recent anti-corruption movement are examples of this trend showing that the power of society to mobilize outside of the arenas of politics will continue to increase. While this civil society will remain deeply inflected by other social divisions like caste, class, and region, it is a phenomenon that is here to stay. This means that any form of governance will have to take into account the fact that governance premised on 'secrecy' is likely to be more difficult, and the state will have to take into account and negotiate with a range of non-state actors. We seem to be in the midst of a 'Great Churning' in governance, where the old norms are being contested by civil society. Whether this will lead to the institutionalization of new norms of accountability, or simply more heightened contestation, is an open question. The central question of how power will be organized institutionally will remain important for Indian politics.

SOCIAL CLEAVAGES

The focus on institutions does not by any means imply that traditional concerns that focus on class conflict or caste cleavages are about to disappear. The last few years have vindicated a point several of the authors have made in this volume: the increasing complexity of these cleavages. Caste remains a vital axis for political mobilization in India. But recent politics suggests that caste politics will be increasingly modified by two things. First, it is likely that there will be an involution of caste politics. The involution means that mobilization will be less around broad categories of Scheduled Caste (SC)/Scheduled Tribe (ST) and Other Backward Class (OBC), but rather around creative coalitions of subgroups within them. Many state politicians from Bihar to Andhra Pradesh have crafted political coalitions by focusing on the subgroups within these classes. In Bihar, for instance, the category of extremely backward classes has become a new fulcrum of mobilization; in Uttar Pradesh (UP) it is very likely that there will be a split between 'Chamars' and other groups within the SC community. These new political cleavages are also being reflected in new policy demands such as the demand for reservation by subgroups. So while caste

will remain important, there is a possibility of several new and shifting coalitions emerging.

We also know that caste identities are fundamentally shaped by forms of knowledge that describe them. The census created new forms identity at the turn of the century; and state-sanctioned categories like SC and OBC became salient forms of self-identification. With all kinds of new knowledge emerging about caste, it is also likely that these identities will undergo a further mutation. The caste census underway may, for example, reveal new axes of privilege and discrimination. We do not yet know quite how these forms of knowledge are going to transform identities or indeed what the normative implications of these new forms of knowledge will be. But, much in line with the claims in this volume, it is very clear that caste identities will continue to mutate in new and unexpected forms.

Something similar is likely to happen to notions of class. Class will continue to be a salient driver of politics and will interact in complex ways with other forms of identity, including caste and gender. But the nature of class politics is likely to be profoundly transformed for two reasons. First, the major economic transformation of our time is also going to change class compositions profoundly. The middle class, notwithstanding its uneven rates of political participation, is very likely to become a more assertive actor in Indian politics, though it is unclear what the character of this middle-class assertion will be. The position of other classes in the economy is also becoming increasingly complex. For example, both rural-to-rural and rural-to-urban migration is intensifying. Large-scale migration is often accompanied by changing forms of class consciousness, and a different menu of issues. For example, one thing the OCPI probably underemphasized is the fact that urbanization has a profound influence on the character of politics. It may generate new contradictions. But these contradictions will probably defy easy characterization. Occupational structures in both rural and urban India are becoming increasingly complex. These occupational structures will have influence on varieties of class mobilization. The link between urban and rural economies will also become more complex. In some instances, the ecological footprint of cities will profoundly affect the possibilities for agriculture. Conflicts over water are prime examples of such a conflict. On the other hand the demand linkages between urban and rural economies may create new forms of interdependence that attenuate old-style agrarian mobilization. But it is clear that new forms of politics will emerge that reflect the challenges of a transition from rural to an urban economy. Or there is the palpable fact that politics in various parts of India is being centred around what we might call the 'right to cities', where migrants want to access cities at the same time as cities become increasingly hostile to the poor. So the manifestations of class conflict will be varied, but no less intense for that reason.

POLITICAL ECONOMY

The student edition of the OCPI is coming out when the ongoing process of India's 'Great Transformation'—to use Karl Polyani's phrase—is still underway. The essence of this transformation is that the market, rather than the state, will command the leading heights of the economy. But the state will remain an important actor. State power will be used to restructure society to make it more hospitable to market relations. An entire gamut of legal regimes that govern property, labour, and natural resources will have to be restructured to make them hospitable to capital. We are already seeing the ways in which the state is 'facilitating' the creation of land markets, or *de facto* transforming labour regimes. Land, for example, has become a major axis of violent conflict in this restructuring, as has mining. This has transformed India's political economy. The very process of the state's attempts to restructure relationships to facilitate a market generates opportunities for rents. It is perhaps not an accident that the major instances of rent-seeking in recent times have been in sectors where the state not only exercises control, but actively uses that control to shape markets: land, natural resources, mining, etc. This transformation has, therefore, created new and collusive relationships between state and capital. It has also generated the possibilities of a violent backlash. Tribals in mining areas protest against this collusion that shuts them out. Farmers

often protest against this collusion that shortchanges them of their rights. Admittedly these protests often have an ambiguous character: sometimes they are acts of resistance against state restructuring on behalf of capital; often they are protests to more fully share the gains of that restructuring. But the process of making society more hospitable to markets will remain conflictual. There is also the larger issue of the impact that various forms of collusion between state and capital have had on the legitimacy of the state itself. It is fair to say that this collusion has deeply corroded the legitimacy of the state. It has also changed the incentives for politicians. Politicians often think they can derive their power from access to large-scale rents and resources, and convert this power into electoral success. To be sure there are signs of backlash. The institutional and civil society assertion referred to above are emerging as counterweights to this trend. At the state level, the newly found assertion of the electorate is also rewarding and punishing government performance. What will be the balance between these two trends? Will the legitimacy corroding collusion of state and capital triumph? Or will the new institutional and political assertion successfully overcome this collusion? Various essays in the OCPI dealt with these issues. But in coming years the mechanisms that affect the outcome of this important tension will have to be studied more carefully.

THE NEW POLITICS OF WELFARE

In theory India's Great Transformation is founded on a social contract. We are told that the rationale of the state making way for the market and capital is growth generation. This growth in turn generates greater resources, which are then deployed by the state to prepare more citizens for participation in this growth or to help those who are unable to participate. To a certain extent, we are living through this story. India's growth record is impressive by global standards; and government revenues are increasing. This has made it *possible* for the state to potentially expand a whole series of programmes from education to health to employment. One of the features of these programmes is that they are being increasingly articulated in terms of *rights*. We now have, *inter alia*, the right to food, employment, education, and so forth. Much of this rights-based assertion has had salutary benefits. It has underscored the point that citizens are entitled to participate in the gains of growth simply by virtue of their being citizens. It has also underscored the fact that any welfare measures by the state need mechanisms of accountability.

But beyond this articulation of rights, the question of actually designing effective systems of welfare remains the subject of debate. Many essays in the OCPI had analytically documented the failures of the state, some of which led to search for new models of welfare delivery. The appropriate architecture for the delivery of these services is not easy to design. Many of the existing models are beset with challenges of elite capture, leakage, improper targeting, and outright theft. Many of the most interesting and contentious debates are going to centre on designing better models. Should the state continue to strengthen the Public Distribution System (PDS) for food, or should it go for cash transfers instead? Should the state invest in public schools or rely on public–private partnerships and voucher systems? What should be the architecture of a health care system? What should be the wage levels in Employment Guarantee Schemes? Many of the most deeply contested issues of our time centre around questions like these. What makes these issues tricky is that often parties can share the same objective, but differ widely in the analytical design of architectures, and these fissures run all the way down to the state level. One of the remarkable things about contemporary India is the range of experimentation going on with rival delivery mechanisms. But what kind of welfare architecture will emerge in India a decade from now? How the stakes in this architecture will transform our politics remains an analytically challenging question.

IDEOLOGICAL DIVISIONS

In some ways the trends referred to above suggest one thing. Old distinctions between Left and Right are no longer very easy to map either onto class formations, or political parties, or even issues. Some state governments—such as that in Bihar, with its roots in Lohiate socialism—are surprisingly keen to

experiment with cash transfers. Other governments that are prime examples of collusion between capital and state like Tamil Nadu have been very successful at traditional institutions of welfare like PDS. Similarly, issues of environmental devastation also cut across boundaries of Left and Right. The very nature of policy choices and judgements in contemporary politics do not lend themselves to easy ideological categorization. This is not to say that ideology does not matter. It matters at two levels. First, at the macro level the choice of models of development clearly makes various ideological assumptions. What our pathways to growth, prosperity, and equity should be will remain contested. But it is not a foregone conclusion which parties or groups will adopt which pathways. The 'Left–Right' distinction often runs within major political parties as it runs between them. Often policy responses are shaped by circumstances and opportunities rather than neat ideological templates. But it is clear that no society can avoid a politics of privilege versus a politics of dispossession. No matter how successful an economy is, there will be ideological tendencies that try and make sense of those who are disaffected or are unable to participate. In this sense, ideological contestation will remain quite widespread. But it is likely to remain fragmented and beset by cross-cutting cleavages. The big challenge for the state will be to negotiate these forms of contestation.

It is perhaps fair to say that for several essays in this volume, the biggest ideological fissure haunting Indian politics was Hindu Nationalism versus its critics. Many had feared that while all other forms of ideological contestation will be episodic, fragmentary, and often local, this fissure could come to permanently define Indian politics. Many of the essays in the OCPI had also pointed out that it was not going to be easy for an ideological formation like Hindu Nationalism to dominate Indian politics for a variety of reasons. First, that ideology was itself a product of a period of great national anxiety in the late 1980s and early 1990s. That moment of anxiety may have receded. Despite the fragmentation of political power, India is much more consolidated as a nation state now than it was two decades ago. India's growth story has, for the time being, assuaged that sense of insecure resentment that had characterized that ideology. This is not to say that there are not active organizations peddling the ideology. Nor is it to claim that the prejudices and resentment that fed into it have disappeared. But the political salience of that ideology has receded significantly. The second reason that it was thought unlikely that Hindu Nationalism could dominate Indian politics for long was that the movement would diminish under the weight of its own contradictions. On the one hand, the imperatives of securing power would move it towards a more centrist position. On the other hand, the politics of regional and caste accommodation would make holding onto ideological unity very difficult. To a great extent both of these reasons have proved perceptive. While Hindu Nationalism will remain a shadow on Indian politics, the general assumption that Indian politics will remain broadly centrist is likely to hold.

INDIA AND THE WORLD

Many of the essays in the OCPI have gestured at the fact that India will now increasingly see itself as an actor on the world stage. Perhaps even more so than the domestic economy, the pace of change in world politics since the OCPI was published has been even more remarkable. India's integration into the world economy has only deepened. The balance of power in international politics has shifted in unexpected ways. The economic difficulties of the West have opened up strategic options for the rest of the world. Challenges around global public goods like climate change have generated the need for new norms and coalitions. Perhaps these have occasioned the need for India to play an even more of a leadership role in global affairs. It was initially thought that India would, inevitably, gravitate towards the United States in a new world order. But, in keeping with historical patterns, India has kept its options open, and not let any single alliance system or ideology constrict its strategic options. For a political science student the fascinating question will be: How will India think of its strategic options? How will it ensure that it preserves strategic economy, space for its own development, and yet contribute to a norm-based international system? India's role as an emerging power will provide interesting analytical challenges.

CONCLUSION

The OCPI was assembled on the premise that Indian democracy was an extraordinarily consequential and exciting phenomenon. The spirit in which it was written was exploratory: to explore the many different facets of this profound historical drama. In many ways India is beginning another decade of great change. We do not yet know where all the chips will fall. But we remain confident that the OCPI remains an invaluable guide to understanding where India came from, what it is currently undergoing, and where it might be headed.

efflorescence- blooming
scholarship-academic study
scaffolding-

Introduction

Niraja Gopal Jayal and Pratap Bhanu Mehta

The last decade has seen an unparalleled efflorescence of scholarship on Indian politics. While *The Oxford Companion to Politics in India* is part of a prestigious series of companions from the Oxford University Press, it is also an opportunity to bring together—for a wider and even non-academic readership—a smorgasbord of the knowledge generated on different aspects of Indian politics.

Much of the recent popular interest in India's political institutions and processes is fundamentally an interest in its democracy. The essays in this anthology provide insights into different dimensions of the Indian democratic experiment, for the study of Indian politics is, in many ways, the study of India's democracy understood in the most expansive sense. The constitutional scaffolding and the institutional foundations on which the architecture of India's polity rests are also the bases of democracy in India. If therefore the reader observes the absence of an essay on Indian democracy, so named, in this volume, it is because the idea of democracy suffuses almost everything that is central to the Indian political experience, from its institutional arrangements and political processes, to public policies and ideological contestations. It is, as such, the unwritten subtext of this volume.

In discussions of democracy and authoritarianism, India has in many ways been something of a curiosity. It has certainly remained an outlier by the lights of most theories of democracy that look at structural variables—such as class structure, extent of ethnic diversity, level of income, and education—to predict the prospects of a country instituting and remaining a democracy. The sense of intellectual surprise at Indian democracy was captured at a conference when one of the participants, paraphrasing Groucho Marx, said about India: 'It looks like democracy. It talks like a democracy. But don't be fooled by that. It really is a democracy.'

Even as the longevity and strengthening of democracy in India has been remarked upon and admired, it has remained a puzzle. The default explanation has been that it is a *sui generis* phenomenon, a case of Indian exceptionalism. But its existence gives rise to a whole host of other questions.

Why, despite being a democracy, is India's capacity to deliver material well-being to a large number of its citizens often in doubt? Why is its increasingly more representative system not responsive? What is the capacity of this democracy to create a sense of national identity without conflict? What is its capacity to manage social tensions arising out of the process of development? Even as these remain deeply puzzling questions, a slide into an authoritarian system of governance is not high on the list of anxieties about India. India does well on most other measures of success in a democracy: voter turnouts, turnover of incumbents, the empowering of new groups, the maintaining of a core set of liberal freedoms, civilian control over armed forces, and political contestation. Democracy in India is as much of an established fact as its success is a matter of surprise to political scientists.

How does one think about the Indian democratic experience? The usefulness of a collection such as this is that it is not premised on a single interpretive or explanatory framework within which to think about Indian democracy. Rather than looking for a single *theory* explaining Indian democracy, the focus of the papers, taken together, is to examine the myriad *mechanisms* by which this democracy has been sustained. These narratives of Indian democracy, rather than emphasizing one or two variables—a propitious class structure, or cultural norms, for instance—indicate the extent to which a whole host of factors, from the colonial legacy to the character of India's inherited institutions, from the beliefs of its leaders to the character of social divisions interact with each other to sustain democratic institutions.

This volume will, we hope, give readers the ability to navigate two different perspectives on politics. On the one hand, politics is clearly shaped by the long-term structural features of a society. Social hierarchies, economic possibilities, and historical legacies influence the nature and character of a political society. These long-range influences impact democracy. But they are also in turn modified by the working of democracy. For instance, there is very little doubt that deep-seated structures of social and economic inequality have had a profound influence on the way in which Indian democracy has functioned. Indeed, their persistence has been a constant reminder

of the imperfections of Indian democracy. But there is also little doubt that these hierarchies have been modified and reconfigured in a democratic context. Many of the essays in this volume draw attention to the relationship between democracy and abiding structural inheritances.

On the other hand, Indian democracy is also an ongoing exercise in *political improvisation*. Its trajectory has not been determined only by structural conditions, but has, at each step, been shaped by a number of contingent political choices. It is often said that modern India is a creation of politics; arguably the same is true of Indian democracy. An explanation of its success and limitations does not lie outside of the space of politics. The weakness of much of the earlier literature on Indian democracy was that it was united in its impulse to explain Indian democracy in terms outside of the space of politics, rather than through politics itself and the concrete and contingent choices made by the myriad actors who make up Indian democracy. We hope that these essays will allow readers to come to their own judgment about the relationship between structure and political choice when thinking about Indian democracy.

This Companion brings together some of the finest minds in political science, as well as some from other disciplines. The objective of the essays was three-fold: first, to introduce the kinds of theoretical and analytical questions that need to be asked about a particular theme; second, to give some sense of how the literature has discussed these questions; and third, to enable the authors to bring their own distinctive perspectives to bear upon a subject. The balance between these objectives varies somewhat. But the authors have endeavoured, for the most part, to provide accessible introductions to a subject without effacing their own individuality as social scientists. In doing so, they were asked to produce essays that would be accessible to a non-specialist, but would also benefit a specialist audience.

As with India's political architecture, this volume is also designed to begin with the constitutional and institutional foundations of the Indian state. As Partha Chatterjee records, the study of the state in India moved from early accounts in which the inseparability of the political system from the Congress Party was aptly captured in Rajni Kothari's term the 'Congress system', to political economy perspectives, both Marxist and other, which sought to explain the nature of the Indian state in terms of dominant classes and social groups. The macro-theorization of class interests and class coalitions was complemented by empirical studies of particular sectors of India's political economy and their relationship to the state. From the influential writings of Pranab Bardhan (1984) and Sudipta Kaviraj (1989) to those of Lloyd and Susanne Rudolph (1987), the focus was on how powerful classes sought to control the state or on the relative autonomy or capacity of the state to negotiate with and between these groups. The landed elites and 'bullock capitalists' of the Rudolphs' description, who successfully transformed their social dominance into political and economic power (Frankel and Rao 1990), have arguably been overtaken and outranked by the corporate class in the wake of economic reform.

Even as the influence of capital over the state has become more manifest, it is notable that the study of the state and classes is no longer confined to dominant classes and class coalitions, but is as much about the relationship of the state to subaltern groups: about how the state 'sees' the poor and their poverty, but also about how the poor see the state. A range of recent studies, many of them drawing upon the resources of anthropology (Chatterjee 2004; Gupta 1999, 2006; Fuller and Bénéï 2001), have opened up a whole new world of understanding about how the state is perceived, received (Corbridge et al. 2005) and even desired (Chandhoke 2005). If the earlier focus was on the state and high politics, it is supplemented now by studies of governmentalities, practices, and discourses not traditionally associated with doing politics. This, if nothing else, underlines the fact, as Chatterjee argues in this volume, that the state remains the overarching framework within which the oppositions between social classes are played out. Despite the withdrawal of the state from certain sectors of economic activity and its outsourcing of welfare functions to non-governmental organizations, Chatterjee persuasively contests the cliché about the separation between state and non-state domains by pointing to the way in which different state agencies have become the sites of a variety of tactical engagements and withdrawals. The law courts, for example, have 'emerged as defenders of a normative and homogeneous civil society of equal citizens'. (Chatterjee, p. 13 in this volume)

The interpretive endeavours of the courts have, of course, been anchored in judicial understandings of the Indian Constitution. Early scholarship on the Indian Constitution was substantively historical, as with Granville Austin's two works on the making of the Constitution and on its working (Austin 1972, 2003). More recently, detailed attention to particular themes in the *Constituent Assembly Debates* have yielded a number of excellent studies, many of which may be found in Bhargava (2008), and most of which are broadly internalist in their attempt to interpret the discursive landscape of the participants in these debates, especially as they wrestled with questions of cultural diversity in Indian society. There has however been little interpretation so far of the Indian Constitution as a *political* document, much less in a comparative perspective. Uday S. Mehta's essay presents a view of the Indian Constitution that is simultaneously externalist and internalist. All constitutions represent new beginnings: what, Mehta asks, does the constitutional moment in India represent? Do the apparent continuities with colonial constitutional arrangements disguise a more important discontinuity, even radical rupture? Unlike other constitutions—such as that of the United States—which were formulated after an antecedent moment of liberation, often associated with revolution and rebellion, the Indian Constitution, argues Mehta, in itself constitutes the truly revolutionary moment of rupture. It disrupts the relationship of politics with time and history, making historical practices—such as those of caste and religion—the subjects of political power, to be transformed by it. The preoccupation with national unity and the centrality of politics suggests, Mehta provocatively argues, that political power is implicitly conceived as unlimited, in ways that make it possible to view Hobbes as the intellectual mentor of the Indian Constitution.

Arguably the most dramatic Hobbesian moment in Indian politics since Independence was the Emergency of 1975–7, and three institutions— Parliament, the Supreme Court and the Election

Commission—bear the scars of that period, with the latter two having substantially reversed the trend. Vernon Hewitt and Shirin M. Rai locate the important shifts in parliamentary functioning in a narrative that contrasts the era of single-party rule with that of coalition government. Coalition government is seen to have produced many important impacts, not least among them being the enhanced role of the Speaker, the decline of rule by ordinances, and greater parliamentary capacity for oversight vis-à-vis the executive. This has also been a period in which Parliament has become more socially representative, and Hewitt and Rai discuss the consequences of this shift for policy. The apparently less 'orderly' quality of parliamentary practice, as indicated by the phenomenon of delays and disruptions in parliamentary proceedings, is explained with reference to the historical legacy of protest in the national movement revived in an earlier period of unreceptive majority governments.

In a widely-cited essay, Lloyd and Susanne Rudolph (2001) had noted the shift from an interventionist to a regulatory state in India. They had then identified the Supreme Court and the Election Commission as two of the three institutional forums in which this change was occurring. For both these, the Emergency was a watershed in terms of institutional emasculation. Subsequently, chiefly through the instrumentality of Public Interest Litigation, the Supreme Court emerged as that branch of the state to which citizens could appeal on matters as diverse as the environment and primary school admissions. The Court came to be popularly perceived, especially by the urban middle classes, as the only branch of the state that could be trusted to govern. This tendency to step into the breach created by legislative lassitude and executive inertia, has however generated concerns about the dangers of judicial overreach. In their comprehensive and detailed analysis of the Supreme Court—encompassing its exercise of legislative and executive powers—Lavanya Rajamani and Arghya Sengupta provide a nuanced account of the achievements as well as limitations of Public Interest Litigation; the tendency of judges' predilections to prevail over principles; and the Court's reliance on technical

experts that compromises both participation and equity, and potentially also legitimacy.

Like the Supreme Court, the relationship of the Election Commission to the government of the day has been significant in defining its institutional integrity. Alistair McMillan's article documents the transition of the Election Commission from a politically pliable agency to one that has claimed and jealously guarded its autonomy. Unlike the Supreme Court, which is limited by inadequate technical expertise, the Election Commission's innovations in the technical details of electoral administration—from the appointment of Block Level Officers to Vulnerability Mapping of constituencies—are counted as among its more important accomplishments.

Survey data shows that the Election Commission enjoys considerable legitimacy and trust in the electorate. It also shows that the federal norm has been internalized by the electorate, such that both Centre and state are perceived as legitimate, and not mutually exclusive, arenas of political action. Citing this data, Subrata K. Mitra and Malte Pehl show that the region has emerged as the nursery of the nation, with positive results for the cohesion and legitimacy of the Indian nation. Starting out as a quasi-federation—in the well-worn and no longer serviceable description of K.C. Wheare—Indian federalism has, in recent times, become a key feature of the Indian political system, and its recent performance is assessed here in relation to both coalition politics and economic liberalization.

It is only in the last fifteen years or so that the Indian federal experiment has been formally expanded to embrace sub-state levels of governance from the village to the district. It is curious that the study of Indian federalism and that of decentralization should not be more closely linked than it is. Certainly, the performance of India's decentralization programme, especially in its most recent phase following the constitutional amendments of 1993, suggests that variations across the Indian states are pronounced. While some have performed rather well, most have not and, drawing upon a mass of state-level evidence, as also upon comparative international experience, James Manor provides an explanation for the achievements and failures, identifying the conditions under which the poor and excluded sections of rural society, including women, are most likely to gain from democratic decentralization.

The final essay in this section on the institutional setting of Indian politics is E. Sridharan's discussion of the party system, a rigorous and empirically-informed evaluation of seven competing explanations for the fragmentation of the Indian party system. Rejecting the social cleavage theories of party systems, Sridharan provides an explanation grounded in the systemic attributes and imperatives of the first-past-the-post electoral system.

At Independence, the project of building a national civic identity, transcending the particularistic identities of caste, tribe, language, religion, and region, was recognized as the most important challenge facing the new nation. The social cleavages and identities of Indian society proved to be resilient in unexpected ways, and to be articulated and reproduced through the very language and processes of democratic politics that were intended to render them redundant. In Part II of this volume, Sunil Khilnani reflects on the two dominant forms in which a national identity has been sought to be constructed. Khilnani draws our attention to the fact that, in the founding moment of the Indian nation, Jawaharlal Nehru refused to give nationalism a primarily culturalist definition, giving it a developmental content instead. But simultaneously, the markers of cultural identity came to be treated as fluid, reversible and therefore provisional. This project of constructing a nation in the popular imagination subsequently came to be attacked and challenged by, among others, regionalist and secessionist movements, majoritarian politics and the claims of minorities alleging exclusion and/or unfair absorption in an assimilative conception of national identity. Some of these tensions are explored in the essays in Part II of this volume.

The challenges of regionalism have been with the Indian polity since the inauguration of the republic. Adopting a constructivist view of regions and regionalism, Sanjib Baruah argues that regional constructions are invariably contested since the territorialization of political life involves not only the state, which has the highest stake in the territorial stabilization of the nation, but also non-state actors. In his view, the challenge of regionalism has been largely domesticated, in part by the fact that regional parties are eager to participate in mainstream national politics by joining coalition governments at the Centre, and in part by the use of counter-insurgency methods by the state to quell secessionist movements such as that in Punjab.

A constructivist approach is also adopted by Christophe Jaffrelot in his essay on majoritarian politics, focusing on the organizational history, ideology, and politics of the Sangh Parivar. Jaffrelot demonstrates the use, by the Sangh Parivar, of a consciously instrumentalist strategy of reactivating the collective inferiority complex of the Hindu majority. While this led to electoral success for the BJP, the party's leadership of a coalition government introduced political constraints that in turn generated tensions between the BJP and the RSS. Meanwhile, even as the Sangh Parivar continues to face a structural dilemma, another structural issue—that of the discrimination and disadvantages of religious minorities—remains unresolved. This is the subject of Bishnu N. Mohapatra's contextualized theorization of the minority question, in which he argues that the positing of the identity and secular-developmental concerns as mutually exclusive is profoundly mistaken. It is not entirely clear whether the contemporary search for new modes of governing minorities—in conformity with the recommendations of the Sachar Committee, for instance—will promote the democratic agency of minorities. Mohapatra proposes that the identity and developmental concerns of minorities may be harmoniously united under the umbrella of the constitutional provision for the right to life.

In the often bewildering labyrinth of identitarian assertions, observers of Indian politics have, over the last two decades, tended to agree on two basic assumptions: one, that class politics is dead; and two, that caste politics is the dominant and enduring mode of politics in India. Both these assumptions are contested here, by John Harriss and Surinder S. Jodhka respectively. Jodhka makes the provocative claim that caste politics is weaker than before, while Harriss discusses the resilience of class in politics, including the 'new politics' of urban middle-class activism.

Jodhka argues that alliances between caste-based political parties provide space for individual political entrepreneurs, whose politics is conducted in the vocabulary of caste, thus giving the impression that caste politics is in the ascendant. The reality however is that ongoing processes of social and economic differentiation within caste groups, as also the migration and dispersion of populations, actually weakens the possibilities of caste solidarity and therefore caste politics.

As the study of class in Indian politics came to be marginalized, a range of important questions also diminished in significance. John Harriss reflects on questions such as does class consciousness arise spontaneously or is it made by powerful charismatic leaders? Why does class politics emerge in some states and not in others? Harriss underscores the importance of analysing the relationships between different fragments of the capitalist class, as also relationships between the working class in the formal and informal sectors. It could be argued that the two most compelling forms of class politics in the present are the problem of widespread Maoist violence in a large swathe of central India, and the new politics of urban middle-class activism. Harriss signals the first and discusses the second at some length. Civil society is stratified by class, and middle class activism is exercising a new hegemony over civil society, generating a 'new politics' of neighbourhood associations which tends to exclude the lower classes in the informal sector and so to perpetuate inequality rather than interrogate it.

This middle-class abhorrence of politics as dirty and corrupt is echoed also in women's perception of politics, as Amrita Basu's discussion of the deterrents to women's participation suggests. Basu highlights the paradoxes of democracy as political parties and social movements simultaneously enable and constrain participation by women, and support certain rights for women even as they maintain conservative positions on gender issues. Her analysis ranges widely over the diversity of positions held by political parties of different ideological persuasions; their electoral strategies for women candidates and women voters; the relationship, in political parties, between women leaders and women's representation more generally; and the role of social movements in influencing political parties to a greater commitment to gender equality. Basu cautions us that civil society may nurture movements that are hostile to women's rights, and that democratization and the political mobilization of women do not necessarily guarantee the advancement of women's interests.

Political processes, as we have seen, are central to the articulation of social cleavages as politically salient identities. Part III of this volume is about the political processes themselves, encompassing the workings of political parties, political mobilization, and political leadership, as well as local politics and the complex relationship of culture and politics. Zoya Hasan reflects on the puzzling phenomenon that political parties that have been responsible for the consolidation and deepening of democracy are themselves scarcely respectful of democratic norms in their internal organization or functioning. As the pragmatism of office-seeking rather than policy-orientation informs the strategies of parties, the polity is marked by ideological depolarization. The imperatives of coalition government only reinforce this tendency. The fundamental malaise, of course, remains the absence of internal democracy, the functioning of political parties as family fiefdoms, and their dependence on largely unregulated corporate funding.

This narrative of strategic politics is buttressed by Arun R. Swamy's conceptualization and survey of alliance-building strategies as the dominant mode of political mobilization in Indian politics across the twentieth century. Political mobilization occurs around social cleavages which are shaped by government policies and elected politicians. There are, Swamy argues, two recurrent patterns in the formation of such cleavages: the anti-hegemonic coalition and the sandwich tactic. The first, as its name suggests, unites intermediate powers against those that exercise hegemony; the second seeks to unite the extremes at either end of the power hierarchy against those in the middle. Sandwich tactics are also sometimes used in policy-formulation, as when anti-poverty policies of the past, such as the Integrated Rural Development Programme or the Employment Guarantee Scheme, took the modest form of social insurance instead of frontally addressing the structural aspects of poverty.

Anirudh Krishna's essay on local politics draws our attention to the gulf that separates the state from ordinary rural citizens and the need therefore for these interactions to be mediated. The intermediaries are no longer the upper-caste landlords characteristic of older forms of clientelism, but *naya netas,* new political entrepreneurs—younger and more educated intermediaries whose ability to negotiate with the state makes their caste irrelevant to the role they perform. Despite this change, and despite the more equal relationships between citizens and intermediaries, the absence of district- and sub-district level institutionalized mechanisms for citizens to access public institutions keeps the state at a lofty distance from the local.

The nature of local leadership is of course very different from leadership at the regional or national levels. In spite of the considerable degree to which the contingencies of Indian politics have been determined by leadership, this has strangely long been an unfashionable field of study, not least because of its association with behavioural political science in the 1950s and 1960s. Other than a couple of early scholarly contributions and a surprisingly small number of political biographies, this has remained a wholly neglected area. In this volume, Ramachandra Guha revisits the subject, surveying political leadership in India in terms of its representational claims (a caste/a region/the nation); its idiom (e.g., modern, traditional, charismatic, populist, authoritarian) and modes of political action, showing how political leadership has often acted to strengthen India's democracy but also sometimes to undermine it.

It could be argued that at no time did political leadership play a more defining role in shaping the contours of Indian politics than in the Nehruvian period. Stuart Corbridge elaborates the cultural assumptions of 'politics as reason' in the Nehruvian model of secularism and developmentalism, and the critique of these in the work of Ashis Nandy and Partha Chatterjee among others, as the project of ostensibly non-cultural elite politics to silence non-elite cultural politics. In a rigorous engagement with these influential writings, Corbridge constructs an alternative account of upper-caste militant Hinduism as a form of elite politics in opposition to the claims of

subaltern caste groups as well as religious minorities, and also proposes a challenging research agenda for the future study of politics and culture.

Indeed, secularism is, along with nationalism, representation, and social justice, one of the four most central ideological contestations in Indian politics since Independence, which form the subject of Part IV of this collection. All the contributors provide highly nuanced historical accounts and interpretations of the concept, and all signal their discomfort with the banality or thinning or unexpected appropriations of the meaning with which the concept was originally endowed. Sudipta Kaviraj's essay on nationalism points to the internal complexities of Indian nationalism in the colonial period. While the difficulties posed by internal diversity to nationalism were united and submerged in the political struggle against colonialism they were to resurface, Kaviraj argues, in the period when the triumphant version of Nehruvian nationalism sank into banality. This banal nationalism has been contested not only by lower-caste assertions and Hindu nationalism but also by regionalism. Kaviraj however sees India's capitalist economy, strong interventionist state, and modern professional class as sources of support for nationalism, not least because both the state and the market need to operate on a national scale.

Neera Chandhoke's narrative of the history of the concept of secularism enters into a substantive engagement with critics of secularism like Ashis Nandy and T.N. Madan, pointing to the consequences of their arguments for the politics of the period, inaugurated in the 1980s, when secularism appears as a beleaguered political project in the face of majoritarian intolerance. Chandhoke's argument links secularism and equality, suggesting that the state's attitude of formal equality towards all religious groups may not provide adequate guarantees to minorities, and proposing that attention to substantive equality is also required. This, after all, is the faultline of disagreement between the proponents of secular democracy, on the one hand, and those of the religious right, on the other.

With respect to the concept of representation, similarly, Yogendra Yadav suggests that a deepening of descriptive representation has been paralleled by a thinning of substantive representation. He explores the meaning of elections as the prime mechanism of representation, including for subaltern groups whose participation constitutes a conferment of dignity, on the one hand, and a conferment of legitimacy, on the other. Yadav however points to several limitations of electoral democracy, among them the routine oscillation between parties without meaningful political change; the reduced political salience of the Centre; the dilution of state representation in the upper house of Parliament; the domination of populism over substantive politics; and, above all, their failed promise for challenging entrenched elites.

The exclusive control of the state over the definition as well as the policy agenda of social justice lies at the core of Gopal Guru's essay on social justice. The 'struggle' concept of social justice articulated before Independence was, Guru argues, incorporated in the Indian constitutional vision and became therefore a 'sponsored' notion of social justice, the responsibility of the state. Offering a critical appreciation of the sponsored idea of social justice, he explores the question of why justice is social, and queries the idea of compensation, generated by the principle of co-responsibility for historical wrongs. Guru argues the necessity for the idea of democracy to be privileged over modernity, and for the latter to be viewed as an interim condition on the path to social justice. He defends the concept of quotas against the meritocratic idea of institutional well-being, even as he brings out the many complexities inherent in the quota question.

The contestations over secularism, representation, and social justice have been expressed not only in mainstream party politics, but also through a range of civil society assertions on these and many other issues including development. Under the broad rubric of Social Movements and Civil Society, Part V of this volume brings together two broad-sweep essays on social movements and non-governmental organizations and two essays about specific movements—those of women and farmers. All four essays highlight the difficulties of characterizing civil society in India. This is only partially because of the lack of a consensus on the concept of civil society

(Chatterjee 2004; Chandhoke 2003), but also because of the enormously differentiated nature of what is commonly acknowledged as civil society and of its constituent parts. Amita Baviskar and Rob Jenkins discuss the two sectors that are generally assumed to form the core of civil society: social movements and non-governmental organizations. Baviskar's article on social movements surveys the theoretical trends in social movement studies in general and the perspectives that have influenced the study of social movements in India in particular. She highlights the complex relationship of social movements in India to the state in ways not anticipated by Rajni Kothari's formulation of non-party political formations. Baviskar also emphasizes the recent tendency to study social movements ethnographically, whether in Ramachandra Guha's study of the Chipko movement (1989) or the studies that formed part of the Subaltern Studies collective. Looking forward, she signals three important research questions: the impact on social movements of institutionalized campaigns and NGOs; the impact, on the dynamics and discourses of social movements, of articulating their concerns in collaboration with transnational networks; and the emergence of new forms of revolutionary activity in recent years.

Non-governmental organizations are indeed commonly viewed as the moral and conceptual 'other' of social movements, lacking the virtue that the latter possess. Rob Jenkins's empirical account of the debates around NGOs and the controversies surrounding external funding is complemented by his spirited discussion of the academic debates on the place of NGOs in civil society. Most centrally, Jenkins interrogates the conventional assumption of a faultline between NGOs and social movements. He questions the assumption that social movements are ideologically pure, financially untainted, and invariably participatory, all the qualities that NGOs are accused of not possessing. This artificial dichotomy, he suggests, is sustained by the need to claim authenticity and legitimacy by demonstrating proximity to the people and distance from the state.

The two essays on specific movements similarly draw our attention to the multi-layered and highly differentiated quality of social movements. Sudha Pai's essay observes the absence of a farmers' movement in contemporary times, in the context of deepening agricultural crisis under conditions of globalization. Pai identifies three distinct phases in agrarian mobilization beginning with an anti-feudal phase in the early post-independence period. In the second phase, in the 1970s and 1980s, such mobilizations were led by rich farmers who also gained political power. However, it is in the 1990s that Pai perceives a split between the big capitalist farmers linked to global capital and the poor peasantry and landless agricultural labour who are increasingly vulnerable but unable to organize themself politically.

The women's movement too has been differentiated both historically as well as in terms of its identity-orientation. Anupama Roy's narrative of the women's movement highlights the opposition that emerged, in the 1980s, between those who believed that women's struggles should be affiliated to mass organizations like Trades Unions and political parties and those for whom the specific nature of women's oppressions suggested an autonomous women's movement. By the 1990s, the questions of identity—especially caste and religion—in the wider polity caused the women's movement to recognize difference, but simultaneously also introduced disagreements such as on the question of religious personal law. The fundamental question of whether a unified women's movement overriding differences of identity is possible and desirable, or whether other axes of social differentiation must inflect the women's movement(s), is, of course, reflected in debates on the repeatedly unlegislated Women's Reservation Bill. Is there a unified feminist political subject, Roy asks, or do feminist spaces get configured differently in different locations of domination?

Politics and policy is the theme of Part VI of this Companion. The essays in this section provide insights into the political economy of the state and of economic reform; into the relationship between the state and business, on the one hand, and state policies for redistribution and poverty reduction, on the other. Evaluating the changing role of the state in the context of India's recent successes in economic growth,

Devesh Kapur observes that the performance of the Indian state at the macro-level is much superior to that at the micro-level, and better at the federal than the state level. At the micro-level, the state's continued failure to address poverty leads the author to ask why, despite the widely-acknowledged leakages in anti-poverty programmes, such programmes repeatedly flounder on the rock of local public administration. Anti-incumbency, leading to frequent turnovers and coalition governments, encourages the proliferation of anti-poverty programmes, as each government wants to reinvent and re-launch programmes to bear their own imprint. Kapur argues that the Indian state is over-bureaucratized but understaffed, with huge unspent budgets and unfilled jobs. Given that the implementation of programmes is ultimately to be done at the local level, inadequate decentralization means lower incentives for local governments to engage in experimentation and innovation, and higher incentives for state governments to use their grip on local administration as a means of controlling the central transfers of funds.

Kapur's emphasis on implementation failures is echoed in Jean Drèze's essay on the Right to Work. The National Rural Employment Guarantee programme, unlike other anti-poverty programmes—or 'schemes'—was enacted into law thus placing an obligation on the state to provide employment and creating a legally enforceable right that could be claimed by those seeking it. In some states, social audits and strict enforcement of transparency safeguards helped to limit leakages though these are not entirely obviated. Effective implementation will, Drèze argues, require more efforts on the demand side, viz., higher levels of awareness among labour, more organizational work, and stronger mechanisms for grievance redressal.

Do the new mechanisms of accountability help to improve implementation and state responsiveness? Dilip Mookherjee identifies the diverse mechanisms of accountability in India—from decentralization to the local level to civic decentralization and competition, and patterns of political participation and awareness. His survey of recent empirical research findings from different regions of India suggests that government response and disaster relief efforts were superior in states with a wider readership of newspapers and that increased local democracy increased state responsiveness. Socio-economic inequality, such as caste and wealth, does not matter significantly for accountability, while gender and education matter more.

In a state where, as Atul Kohli argues, the ruling alliance is an alliance between the state and capital oriented towards growth, the future of redistributive politics may well require mobilization by the poor. States which have witnessed a decline in poverty, Kohli writes, are states in which the government has broadened its political base, by minimizing the hold of the upper classes on the state, consolidating the middle and lower strata into a power bloc and using this to channel resources to the poor. The big question continues to be whether and to what extent democracy can be a force for moderating inequalities.

The redistributive aspect of the state is, in general, much less in evidence than its close association with business. Aseema Sinha explores the changing business-politics relationship from the pre-reform to the post-reform era, arguing persuasively that the reforms impacted different sections of business differently, and that regional business often developed as state governments acted entrepreneurially, sometimes circumventing the Centre. Sinha emphasizes the greater mutual dependence of business and state since globalization in the 1990s, not least around negotiations related to the multilateral trade regime. Her discussion of the relationship between business and politics encompasses the seeking of policy inputs from firms and business associations and the higher representation of businesspersons in Parliament. Among the future trends she identifies is the transformation of agrarian capitalism through closer links with industry, including multinationals.

The common narrative of external factors compelling India to embark on economic reforms is interrogated by Rahul Mukherji, who examines the role played by the domestic as well as international economy in the reforms. He argues that the Indian executive's reformist orientation was independent of global economic constraints, and that the reforms

could have gone in two distinct possible directions, with the chosen direction being substantially influenced by the strategic situation between domestic actors. The Indian experience, says Mukherji, holds lessons for the design of IMF conditionality: to promote home-grown reforms based on country ownership of these.

Part VII of this volume—India and the World— takes forward this discussion of the interplay between the domestic and the international, in two papers: one on the dominant strategic paradigms in Indian foreign policy and the other on India's defence policy. Kanti Bajpai identifies three central strategic paradigms vying for dominance in India's strategic culture— Nehruvianism neo-liberalism and hyper-realism—and elaborates their assumptions about the role of war, the nature of adversaries, and the utility of force. While Nehruvians and neo-liberals believe that international relations can be transformed by better understanding and free market economic reforms respectively, hyperrealists argue the importance of military power for achieving peace and stability, and therefore its pre-eminence over economic power. Detailing the differences in the perspectives of these three schools on nuclear weapons, non-proliferation, and regional security, Bajpai argues that these differences should be seen as a strength rather than a weakness, insofar as they help to check the extremes of other positions and can prevent the installation of orthodoxy.

It may well be these checks that have contributed to the generally consensual approach to defence policy that Sumit Ganguly describes. Changes, Ganguly argues, have been slow, limited, and incremental and have not varied greatly across different party regimes. The major challenges, in his view, stem from internal conflicts (chiefly in Assam, Nagaland, and Kashmir) and from China. The bigger policy challenges are, first, the integration of India's nuclear forces into its overall military strategy and, second, the evolution of a long-term strategic vision with skilled professionals contributing to enhanced capability in areas of budgeting, acquisitions, and policy.

The final section of this volume is about ways of looking at Indian politics. In their essay, Susanne and Lloyd Rudolph chronicle the story of Indian political science from its early beginnings after Independence to the present; document and interpret the methodological shifts from early institutionalist writings through behaviouralism and its backlash, to postcolonial studies. They also provide a rich account of the chief fields tilled by political scientists—such as identity politics and postcolonial studies—which have seen innovative contributions being made by scholars of Indian politics. They reflect, finally, on the state of academic political science as taught in Indian universities, and the absence of professional standards. This is arguably the first and also the most definitive history of the discipline of political science in India.

While there has been an enormous expansion, even explosion, in the availability of data, including online, Steven I. Wilkinson alerts the reader to issues of quality and reliability in all types of data—from crime to development spending—and offers suggestions for checking data reliability. This is again an essay that breaks new ground in its reflections upon the contested nature of what constitutes, apparently uncontroversially, the grist to the political scientist's mill.

The list of topics covered in this Companion is by no means exhaustive. For instance, while there is a good deal of coverage of social conflict, there is no separate essay on violence. Similarly, civil society is a theme that emerges in many essays, but is not exhaustively conceptualized. What seem like absences in this instance are really an artifact of classification: the issues have been touched on without being named as such. There are other areas where there is admittedly less coverage. For example, there is no systematic consideration of political theory in modern India and its relationship to politics, though several categories of political theory like justice, representation, and constitutionalism appear in several essays. One can of course list more institutions and social movements that could have been covered. But we hope that the essays in this volume will contribute to thinking about subjects that are not explicitly covered.

The authors of these essays are amongst the finest scholars working on Indian politics. They come from many different disciplines—political

science, international relations, economics, sociology, history—and bring to their essays distinct theoretical and methodological perspectives. Taken together, the authors also represent a cross-section of different generations: some are at the beginning of their academic careers, while others are legendary eminences already. The institutional locations of the contributors are spread across several different countries: India, Canada, France, Germany, Singapore, the United Kingdom and the United States. These various diversities of authorship yield, we hope, a kaleidoscopic perspective on Indian politics.

As is invariably the case with mammoth undertakings of this kind, there are many scholars we would have liked to include but could not, either due to limitations of space or because they were, for various reasons, unable to contribute to this endeavour. Their inclusion must await a second edition. We are nevertheless confident that, read together, these essays will add up to a robust multifaceted conversation about Indian politics.

We would like to thank all our contributors. Coordinating the activities of close to forty authors has often posed challenges. But we hope this volume will give a sense that despite our different styles, we are a community of scholars trying to make sense of Indian politics. And we feel privileged to be part of that community.

The scale of this project has meant that this volume has been a while in the making, and has passed through many pairs of competent hands at OUP. We would like to thank the team at Oxford University Press for their perseverance in ensuring that the volume finally acquired tangible form.

REFERENCES

Austin, Granville. 2003. *Working a Democratic Constitution: The Indian Experience.* New Delhi: Oxford University Press.

———. 1972. *The Indian Constitution: Cornerstone of a Nation.* New Delhi: Oxford University Press.

Bardhan, Pranab. 1984. *The Political Economy of Development in India.* New Delhi: Oxford University Press.

Bhargava, Rajeev (ed.). 2008. *Politics and Ethics of the Indian Constitution.* New Delhi: Oxford University Press.

Chandhoke, Neera. 2005. '"Seeing" the State in India'
Economic and Political Weekly, XL(11), pp. 1033–9.
———. 2003. *The Conceits of Civil Society*. New Delhi:
Oxford University Press.

Chatterjee, Partha. 2004. *The Politics of the Governed:
Reflections on Political Society in Most of the World*. New
York: Columbia University Press.

Corbridge, Stuart, G. Williams, M. Srivastava, and R. Veron.
2005. *Seeing the State: Governance and Governmentality
in India*. Cambridge: Cambridge University Press.

Frankel, Francine and M.S.A. Rao (eds). 1990. *Dominance
and State Power in India: Decline of a Social Order*. New
Delhi: Oxford University Press.

Fuller, C.J. and Véronique Bénéï (eds). 2001. *Everyday
State and Society in Modern India*. New Delhi: Social
Sciences Press.

Gupta, Akhil. 2006. 'Blurred Boundaries: The Discourse of
Corruption, the Culture of Politics and the Imagined
State', in Aradhana Sharma and Akhil Gupta (eds). *The
Anthropology of the State: A Reader*. Oxford: Blackwell
Publishing Ltd.

Gupta, Akhil. 1999. *Postcolonial Developments: Agriculture
in the Making of Modern India*. New Delhi: Oxford
University Press.

Kaviraj, Sudipta. 1989. 'A Critique of the Passive
Revolution', *Economic and Political Weekly*, XXIII(45–
7), pp. 2429–44.

Rudolph, Lloyd I. and Susanne Hoeber Rudolph. 2001.
'Redoing the Constitutional Design: From an
Interventionist to a Regulatory State', in Atul Kohli
(ed.). *The Success of India's Democracy*. Cambridge.
Cambridge University Press.

———. 1987. *In Pursuit of Lakshmi: The Political Economy of
the Indian State*. Delhi: Orient Longman.

I The Institutional Setting

1 The State

Partha Chatterjee

THE STATE STRUCTURE AFTER INDEPENDENCE

An interesting historical question to ask is: how much of the structure of the Indian state after Independence was inherited from late colonial times? It is true that the Partition of the country into India and Pakistan and the integration of the princely states within India meant a significant reconfiguration of the territorial boundaries drawn in the period of British India. More significantly, the inauguration of the constitutional republic in 1950 introduced some radically new features into the state structure. First, there was a sovereign legislature elected by direct universal suffrage without communal representation, but with reservations for the Scheduled Castes (SCs) and Scheduled Tribes (STs). Second, there was a constitutionally guaranteed set of fundamental rights of all citizens. The Constitution provided for a parliamentary system of government of the British type with an executive responsible to Parliament, but with an indirectly elected President as head of state. It also provided for an independent judiciary with certain powers pertaining to the judicial review of laws made by Parliament. The Constitution was also federal, with state governments responsible to directly elected state legislatures, but with a distribution of powers between the Union and the states that was heavily inclined towards the Union. As a federal system, the Indian state was more centralized than most federations elsewhere.

However, other than these institutional changes, the basic apparatus of governmental administration in independent India was inherited from the colonial period, despite the huge increase in size. The administration consisted of a small elite cadre belonging to the all-India services and a much larger corps of functionaries organized in the provincial services. The Indian members of the Indian Civil Service (ICS), the much acclaimed 'steel frame' of the British Raj, were retained after Independence, but a new Indian Administrative Service (IAS), modelled on the ICS, was constituted as its successor. The crucial unit of the governmental apparatus was the district administration which, under the charge of the district officer, was principally responsible as in colonial times for maintaining law and order, but was soon also to become the agency for developmental work.

The basic structure of civil and criminal law as well as of its administration was also inherited from the colonial period. The major difference, of course, was the creation of a Supreme Court and its position within the new constitutional system. However, apart from the new issues that arose regarding relations between the legislature and the judiciary, the working of the high courts and district courts maintained an unbroken history from colonial times, continuing the same practices of legal tradition and precedent.

The Indian armed forces, too, maintained a continuing history from the colonial period. The British tradition of a professional army strictly under the control of the political leadership was successfully maintained in the period after Independence, and unlike most other countries, there was not even a joint command of the army, navy, and air forces except in the office of the political head of government.

STATE AND POLITICS, 1947–67

Politics in India from 1947 to 1967 is usually characterized as 'the Congress system'. The Congress party ran governments at the Centre as well as in the states. The provincial party units enjoyed considerable autonomy in relation to the central party leadership. This was also the period of the formation of a developmental state which intervened in the economy, planning and guiding its growth and trying directly to promote the welfare of the population. This was perhaps the principal governmental function that legitimized the postcolonial state. It meant considerable state intervention in the economy through the progressive taxation of personal and corporate incomes, and the provision by the state of public services such as education, health, and transport. In addition, the state in India in the Nehru period consciously chose elements from socialist systems such as that of the Soviet Union in order to create a planned economy, albeit within the framework of a mixed and not a socialist economy, where the state sector would control 'the commanding heights of the economy'. The idea was to industrialize rapidly by setting up new public enterprises in heavy

industries, while confining the private sector to consumer and intermediate goods. Rapid industrial growth was seen to be the key to the removal of poverty and the provision of welfare for the people.

The shortcomings of the strategy became clear by the middle of the 1960s, when there was an acute food shortage in the country, making it necessary for the government to import large quantities of foodgrains. There was also a severe foreign exchange crisis, exacerbated by the hugely increased defence expenditures in the wake of the wars with China and Pakistan. Soon after its formation in 1966, Indira Gandhi's government was forced to devalue the rupee. With high food prices and slowing down of growth, economic hardship was at its peak. This was reflected in massive, and often violent, agitations all over the country. The 1967 elections saw a sharp fall in Congress votes, and as many as nine states had non-Congress governments. This brought in a completely new situation in Indian politics, not only because the Congress lost its overwhelming dominance at the Centre, but also because the federal structure was now called upon to deal with relations between a Congress government at the Centre and several non-Congress governments in the states.

ANALYSING THE STATE: THE FIRST TWO DECADES

Early attempts to present a systematic account of the Indian state, such as those by Palmer (1962) and Morris-Jones (1964) were usually framed within a liberal modernization theory, and, more often than not, were celebratory in tone. Key institutions of the state were shown to have been put in place in the period of British rule. It was believed that with a liberal democratic constitutional system and universal suffrage, the Indian political system would gradually develop its own processes of democratic decision-making, rational administration, and modern citizenship. Features such as patronage relations based on caste, or religious loyalties and solidarities based on ethnicity were regarded as vestiges of underdevelopment that would go away. Later, more complex variants of the modernization theory were produced, most notably by Rudolph and Rudolph

(1967) and in the collection on *Caste and Indian Politics* (1970b) edited by Rajni Kothari, in which it was argued that elements of 'tradition' such as caste or religion could infiltrate a modern system of political institutions, adapt to it, and, by transforming themselves, find an enduring place within it as aspects of political modernity.

An influential account of the Indian state, operating within a democratic process, was the one proposed by Rajni Kothari (1970a). Using a structural-functional framework, he described the political system as working around a 'dynamic core' of institutions characterized by the dominance of the Congress party. It was a differentiated system functioning along the organizational structure of the party, from village or town to district to provincial to national levels, but connecting at each level with the parallel structure of government. This allowed for the dominance of a political centre as well as dissent from the peripheries, with opposition parties functioning as continuations of dissident Congress groups. The emphasis was on coalition building and consensus-making. Hence, while the political centre consisting of the modernizing elite tried to use the powers of the state to transform society, the pressures of consensus-making through an electoral system set many constraints on this modernizing project. Kothari's account was criticized at the time for overvaluing the consensual character of 'the Congress system', for overestimating the autonomy of the elite, and for taking far too gradualist a view of economic and social change. The usefulness of Kothari's account was overtaken by the events of the 1970s. The rise of militant opposition movements and the increasing use of the repressive apparatus of the state, culminating in the Emergency of 1975–7, were phenomena that could not be explained by Kothari's consensus model.

Marxist accounts were better able to explain conflicts and the repressive use of state power as systemic features of Indian democracy. However, much of the literature, especially from theorists working within rigid frameworks laid down by party programmes, was dominated by a sterile debate over what was called the class character of the state. More nuanced accounts, which tried not only to describe enduring structures of class power but also specific changes in political processes and institutional practices, began to emerge only in the 1970s. The key idea was that of a coalition of dominant class interests. Even though the constitutional form of the new Indian republic was that of a liberal democracy, its character was necessarily different from that of the advanced capitalist democracies of Europe or North America. This was because the Indian capitalist class did not have the social power to exercise hegemony. Hence, it had to share power with other dominant classes, including the traditional landed elites. An essay by K.N. Raj (1973) and the collections of essays by Gough and Sharma (1973) and Mathew Kurian (1975) contain good examples of Marxist accounts of the Indian state in its early decades.

STATE AND POLITICS IN THE 1970s

Following an internal crisis in the Congress party that led to a split in 1969, Indira Gandhi's Congress went into the 1971 elections with a stridently populist campaign under the slogan *garibi hatao* (remove poverty). Her party emerged victorious with a huge majority in Parliament. The structure of Congress dominance in the 1970s was, however, different from that of the 'Congress system' of the Nehru era. First of all, the idea was now firmly established that the state was the principal, and in many instances the sole, agent of bettering the condition of the people and providing relief in times of adversity. The performance of particular parties and leaders came to be judged by how much they had 'done' for their respective constituents. Second, the public-sector undertakings launched in earlier decades continued to grow rapidly, and the urban middle class and a large section of the working class became dependent upon its further expansion. However, there was also a massive food crisis in the 1960s, to tackle which a strategy for the quick increase in foodgrain production through state subsidy of irrigation, seeds and fertilizers, and government support for minimum foodgrain prices was formulated. Known as the 'green revolution', this strategy relied heavily on the enterprise of larger farmers, and was first tried out in the better irrigated zones of Punjab, Haryana, and western Uttar Pradesh (UP). This meant, however, that a new organized class interest—that of the rich farmer—would now become a player in national politics.

The restoration of the Congress under Indira Gandhi relied on several new political strategies. Following the split, her section of the Congress derived its identity from its leader. This was not merely symbolic, because even in its organization, the Congress now became strongly centralized, with power flowing directly from the central high command. Second, the developmental ideology of the Nehru era was now purveyed in a new rhetoric of state socialism, with the central executive structures of government playing the pivotal role. Other structures of government, such as the judiciary, or the local bureaucracy, or local political leaders, were frequently criticized for being conservative, corrupt, and acting as a hindrance to development. Third, welfare packages were now targeted towards specific groups of the population, such as SC/STs, workers, women, or minorities, and delivered in such a way as to produce the impression that they were a gift of the central leadership, Indira Gandhi in particular.

In spite of the 'green revolution', however, economic hardships continued to affect most sections of people. Agitations spread throughout the country in 1974–5, leading to repeated use of state repression through special laws such as the Maintenance of Internal Security Act and the deployment of central security forces. The repressive phase culminated in the state of Emergency in 1975–7. The end of the Emergency regime was marked by the stunning defeat of the Congress all over northern India, and the formation of the Janata government. The Janata experiment was, however, short-lived, and Indira Gandhi's Congress came back to power in 1980.

ANALYSING THE STATE: 1970s AND 1980s

The dominant class coalition model offered by Marxist scholars as a means to analyse the Indian state was refined and sharpened in the 1980s, following the experience of the Emergency. Pranab Bardhan (1984) identified the capitalists, the rich farmers, and the bureaucracy as the three dominant classes, competing and aligning with one another within a political space supervised by a relatively autonomous state.

Achin Vanaik (1990) also endorsed the dominant coalition model, emphasizing in particular the relative political strength of the agrarian bourgeoisie which, he stressed, was far greater than its economic importance—a strength that could be ascribed to its ability to mobilize rural electoral support. He also insisted that even though India had never had a classical bourgeois revolution, its political system was nevertheless a bourgeois democracy that enjoyed a considerable degree of legitimacy not only with the dominant classes, but also with the mass of the people. Several scholars writing about the 1980s, for instance, Rudolph and Rudolph (1987) and Varshney (1995), emphasized the growing political clout of the rich farmers or agrarian capitalists within the dominant coalition.

Marxist, or more generally political economic, accounts were often strong in describing the central structures of state power and their relations with dominant organized forces in Indian society, but when it came to connecting such an account with local societal institutions and micro-level political practices, they were on much less sure ground. Rudolph and Rudolph (1987), who took organized interest groups as the principal actors in the system, tried to periodize Indian politics in terms of the tussle between a 'demand polity', in which societal demands expressed as electoral pressure dominates over the state, and a 'command polity', where state hegemony prevails over society. Frankel and Rao (1990) made a distinction between public institutions such as the bureaucracy and organized industry and political institutions such as legislatures and political parties. The history of politics in independent India, they argued, was one of the rising power of formerly low-status groups such as the lower castes and the poorer classes in the political institutions, and the attempt by upper-caste and middle-class groups to protect their privileges in the public institutions. Atul Kohli (1991) described the story of the state in the 1980s as one in which, by surrendering to immediate electoral pressures exerted by various social groups, democratic state institutions were allowed to decay, leading to an all-round crisis of governability.

The dominant class coalition model was given a robust theoretical shape in a widely discussed essay by Sudipta Kaviraj (1989) in which, by using Antonio Gramsci's idea of the 'passive revolution' as a blocked dialectic, he was able to ascribe to the process of class domination in postcolonial India its own dynamic. Power had to be shared between the dominant classes because no one class had the ability to exercise hegemony on its own. However, 'sharing' was a process of ceaseless push and pull, with one class gaining a relative ascendancy at one point, only to lose it at another. Kaviraj provided a synoptic political history of the relative dominance and decline of the industrial capitalists, the rural elites, and the bureaucratic-managerial elite within the framework of the passive revolution of capital.

The characteristic features of the passive revolution in India were the relative autonomy of the state as a whole from the bourgeoisie and the landed elites; the supervision of the state by an elected political leadership, a permanent bureaucracy, and an independent judiciary; the negotiation of class interests through a multi-party electoral system; a protectionist regime discouraging the entry of foreign capital and promoting import substitution; the leading role of the state sector in heavy industry, infrastructure, transport and telecommunications; mining, banking, and insurance; state control over the private manufacturing sector through a regime of licensing; and the relatively greater influence of industrial capitalists over the Central government and that of the landed elites on the state governments. Passive revolution was a form marked by its difference from classical bourgeois democracy. But to the extent that capitalist democracy as established in Western Europe or North America served as the normative standard of bourgeois revolution, discussions of passive revolution in India carried with them the sense of a transitional system— from pre-colonial and colonial regimes to some yet-to-be-defined authentic modernity.

TRANSFORMED STRUCTURES OF POLITICAL POWER

The 1980s was a decade of Congress (I) dominance. It was marked by the centralization of control of the central leadership over the Congress party. But it was also the period of violent agitations in Punjab, Assam,

and Kashmir, and there was a distinct deterioration in the communal situation all over the country. Indira Gandhi was assassinated in 1984. The Congress (I) government of Rajiv Gandhi was defeated in the elections of 1989, and was succeeded by a short-lived National Front government. The Congress (I) then formed a minority government under P.V. Narasimha Rao in 1991, and began a set of structural economic reforms that were to change the character of the economy and society.

These changes also transformed the state of the passive revolution described earlier. The crucial difference consisted in the dismantling of the licence regime; greater entry of foreign capital and foreign consumer goods; and the opening up of sectors such as telecommunications, transport, infrastructure, mining, banking, insurance, and the like, to private capital. This led to a change in the very composition of the capitalist class. Instead of the earlier dominance of a few 'monopoly' houses drawn from traditional merchant backgrounds and protected by the licence and import substitution regime, there were now many more entrants into the capitalist class at all levels, and much greater mobility within its formation. Unlike the earlier fear of foreign competition, there appears to be much greater confidence among Indian capitalists to make use of the opportunities opened up by global flows of capital, goods and services, including, in recent times, significant exports of capital. The most dramatic event was the rise of the Indian information technology industry. Domestic manufacturing and services also received a major spurt, leading to annual growth rates of 8 or 9 per cent for the economy as a whole in the last few years.

There have been several political changes as a result. First, there is a distinct ascendancy in the relative power of the corporate capitalist class as compared to the landed elites. The political means by which this recent dominance has been achieved needs to be investigated more carefully, because it was not achieved through the mechanism of electoral mobilization (which used to be the source of the political power of the landed elites). Indeed, one study has described the economic reforms as having been carried out 'by stealth' (Jenkins 1999). Second, the dismantling of the licence regime has opened up a new field of competition between state governments to woo capitalist investment, both domestic and foreign. This has resulted in the involvement of state-level political parties and leaders with the interests of national and international corporate capital in unprecedented ways. Third, although the state continues to be the most important mediating apparatus in negotiating between conflicting class interests, the autonomy of the state in relation to the dominant classes appears to have been redefined. Crucially, the earlier role of the bureaucratic-managerial class, or more generally of the urban middle classes, in leading and operating, both socially and ideologically, the autonomous interventionist activities of the developmental state has significantly weakened. There is a strong ideological tendency among the urban middle classes today to view the state apparatus as ridden with corruption, inefficiency, and populist political venality, and a much greater social acceptance of the professionalism and commitment to growth and efficiency of the corporate capitalist sector. The urban middle class, which once played such a crucial role in producing and running the autonomous developmental state of the passive revolution, appears now to have largely come under the moral-political sway of the bourgeoisie.

It would be a mistake, however, to think that the result is a convergence of the Indian political system with the classical models of capitalist democracy. The critical difference has been produced, as described in Chatterjee (2004), by a split in the field of the political between a domain of a properly constituted *civil society* and a more ill-defined and contingently activated domain of *political society*. Civil society in India today, peopled largely by the urban middle classes, is the sphere that seeks to be congruent with the normative models of bourgeois civil society and represents the domain of capitalist hegemony. If this were the only relevant political domain, then India today would probably be indistinguishable from other Western capitalist democracies. But there is the other domain of what I have called political society, which includes large sections of the rural population and the urban poor. These people do, of course, have the formal status of citizens and can exercise their franchise as an instrument of political

bargaining. But they do not relate to the organs of the state in the same way that the middle classes do, nor do governmental agencies treat them as proper citizens belonging to civil society. Those in political society make their claims on government, and in turn are governed, not within the framework of stable constitutionally defined rights and laws, but rather through temporary, contextual, and unstable arrangements arrived at through direct political negotiations. The latter domain, which represents the vast bulk of democratic politics in India, is not under the moral-political leadership of the capitalist class.

Hence, it could be argued that the framework of passive revolution is still valid for India. But its structure and dynamic have undergone a change. The capitalist class has come to acquire a position of moral-political hegemony over civil society, which consists principally of the urban middle classes. It exercises its considerable influence over both the Central and the state governments not through the electoral mobilization of political parties and movements, but largely through the bureaucratic-managerial class, the increasingly influential print and visual media, and the judiciary and other independent regulatory bodies. The dominance of the capitalist class within the state structure as a whole can be inferred from the virtual consensus among all major political parties about the priorities of rapid economic growth led by private investment, both domestic and foreign. It is striking that even the Communist Party of India (Marxist), the CPI(M), in West Bengal and, slightly more ambiguously, in Kerala, has, in practice if not in theory, joined this consensus. This means that as far as the party system is concerned, it does not matter which particular combination of parties comes to power at the Centre or even in most of the states; state support for rapid economic growth is guaranteed to continue. This is evidence of the current success of the passive revolution.

However, the practices of the state also include the large range of governmental activities in political society. Here are found the locally dominant interests, such as those of landed elites, small producers, and local traders, who are able to exercise political influence through their powers of electoral mobilization. In the old understanding of the passive revolution, these interests would have been seen as potentially opposed to those of the industrial bourgeoisie; the conflicts would have been temporarily resolved through a compromise worked out within the party system and the autonomous apparatus of the state. Now, there is a new dynamic logic that ties the operations of political society with the hegemonic role of the bourgeoisie in civil society and its dominance over the state structure as a whole. This logic is supplied by the requirement of reversing the effects of primitive accumulation of capital, which must inevitably accompany the process of rapid industrial growth.

POLITICAL SOCIETY AND THE MANAGEMENT OF NON-CORPORATE CAPITAL

Let us consider a couple of familiar examples. Most of us are familiar with the phenomenon of street vendors in Indian cities. They occupy street space, usually violating municipal laws; they often erect permanent stalls, use municipal services such as water and electricity, and do not pay taxes. To carry on their trade under these conditions, they usually organize themselves into associations to deal with the municipal authorities, the police, credit agencies such as banks, and corporate firms that manufacture and distribute the commodities they sell on the streets. These associations are often large, and the volume of business they encompass can be quite considerable. Obviously, operating within a public and anonymous market situation, the vendors are subject to the standard conditions of profitability of their businesses. But to ensure that everyone is able to meet their livelihood needs, the association will usually try to limit the number of vendors who can operate in a given area and prevent the entry of newcomers. On the other hand, there are many examples where, if the businesses are doing particularly well, the vendors do not, like corporate capitalists, continue to accumulate on an expanded scale, but rather agree to extend their membership and allow new entrants. To cite another example, in most cities and towns of India, the transport system depends heavily on private operators who run buses and auto-rickshaws. Here too, there

is frequent violation of regulations such as licences, safety standards, and pollution norms—violations that allow these units to survive economically. Although most operators own only one or two vehicles each, they form associations to negotiate with transport authorities and the police over fares and routes, and control the frequency of services and entry of new operators to ensure that a minimum income, and not much more than a minimum income, is guaranteed to all.

In my book *The Politics of the Governed*, I have described the form of governmental regulation of population groups such as street vendors, illegal squatters and others, whose habitation or livelihood verge on the margins of legality, as *political society*. In political society, I have argued, people are not regarded by the state as proper citizens possessing rights and belonging to the properly constituted civil society. Rather, they are seen as belonging to particular population groups with specific empirically established and statistically described characteristics, which are targets of particular governmental policies. Since dealing with many of these groups implies the tacit acknowledgement of various illegal practices, governmental agencies will often treat such cases as exceptions, justified by very specific and special circumstances, so that the structure of general rules and principles is not compromised. Thus, illegal squatters may be given water supply or electricity connections, but on exceptional grounds so as not to club them with regular customers who secure legal titles to their property; or street vendors may be allowed to trade under specific conditions that distinguish them from regular shops and businesses which comply with the laws and pay taxes. All of this makes the claims of people in political society a matter of constant political negotiation, and the results are never secure or permanent. Their entitlements, even when recognized, never quite become rights. These features of the everyday practices of the state are now coming under scholarly attention in works such as Gupta (1998), Tarlo (2003), and Fuller and Bénéï (2001).

We may now advance the following proposition: civil society is where corporate capital is hegemonic, whereas political society is the space of management of non-corporate capital. We have seen that since the 1990s, corporate capital and along with it the class of corporate capitalists, have achieved a hegemonic position over civil society in India. This means that the logic of accumulation, expressed this time in the demand that national economic growth be maintained at a very high rate and that the requirements of corporate capital be given priority, holds sway over civil society—that is to say, over the urban middle classes. It also means that the educational, professional, and social aspirations of the middle classes have become tied with the fortunes of corporate capital. There is now a powerful tendency to insist on the legal rights of proper citizens, to impose civic order in public places and institutions, and to treat the messy world of the informal sector and political society with a degree of intolerance. A vague but powerful feeling seems to prevail among the urban middle classes that rapid growth will solve all problems of poverty and unequal opportunities.

The informal sector, which does not have a corporate structure and does not function principally according to the logic of accumulation, does not, however, lack organization. As we have seen from our examples, those who function in the informal sector often have large, and in many cases quite powerful and effective, organizations. They need to organize precisely to function in the modern market and governmental spaces. Traditional organizations of peasant and artisan societies are not adequate for the task. This organization is as much of a *political* activity as it is an economic one. Given the logic of non-corporate capital described above, the function of these organizations is precisely to successfully operate within the rules of the market and governmental regulations in order to ensure the livelihood needs of its members. Most of those who provide leadership in organizing people, both owners and workers, operating in the informal sector, are actually or potentially political leaders. Many such leaders are prominent local politicians, and many such organizations are directly or indirectly affiliated to political parties. Thus, it is not incorrect to say that the management of non-corporate capital under such conditions is a political function carried out by political leaders. The existence and survival of the vast

assemblage of so-called informal units of production in India today, including peasant production, is directly dependent on the successful operation of certain *political* functions. These are crucially facilitated by the process of democracy.

The organizations that can carry out these political functions have to be innovative—necessarily so, because neither the history of the cooperative movement nor that of socialist collective organization provides any model that can be copied by these non-corporate organizations of capital in India. What is noticeable here is a strong sense of attachment to small-scale private property and, at the same time, a willingness to organize and cooperate in order to protect the fragile basis of livelihood that is constantly under threat from the advancing forces of corporate capital. However, it appears that these organizations of non-corporate capital are stronger, at least at this time, in the non-agricultural informal sectors in cities and towns, and less so among the rural peasantry. This means that while the organization of non-corporate capital in urban areas has developed relatively stable and effective forms and is able, by mobilizing governmental support through the activities of political society, to sustain the livelihood needs of the urban poor in the informal sector, the rural poor, consisting of small peasants and rural labourers, are still dependent on direct governmental support for their basic needs, and are less able to make effective organized use of the market in agricultural commodities. This challenge lies at the heart of the recent controversies over 'farmer suicides' as well as the ongoing debates over the acquisition of agricultural land for industry. It is clear that in the face of rapid changes in agricultural production in the near future, Indian democracy will soon have to invent new forms of organization to ensure the survival of a vast rural population that is increasingly dependent on the operations of non-corporate forms of capital.

We have mentioned before that state agencies, or governmental agencies generally, including non-governmental organizations (NGOs) that carry out governmental functions, are no longer an external entity in relation to peasant society. This has had several implications. First, because various welfare and developmental functions are now widely recognized to be necessary tasks of the government in relation to the poor, which includes large sections of peasants, these functions in the fields of health, education, basic inputs for agricultural production, and the provision of basic necessities of life are now demanded from governmental agencies as a matter of legitimate claims by poor people. This means that government officials and political representatives in rural areas are constantly besieged by demands for various welfare and developmental benefits. It also means that poor people, including peasants, are learning to operate the levers of the governmental system, to apply pressure at the right places or negotiate for better terms. This is where the everyday operations of democratic politics, organization, and leadership come into play. Second, the response of state agencies to such demands is usually flexible, based on calculations of costs and returns. In most cases, the strategy is to break up the benefit seekers into smaller groups, defined by specific demographic or social characteristics, so that there can be a flexible policy that does not regard the entire rural population as a single homogeneous mass, but rather breaks it up into smaller target populations. The intention is precisely to fragment the benefit seekers and hence divide the potential opposition to the state. Third, this field of negotiations opened up by flexible policies of seeking and delivering benefits creates a new competitive spirit among benefit seekers. Since peasants now confront, not landlords or traders as direct exploiters, but rather governmental agencies from whom they expect benefits, the state is blamed for perceived inequalities in the distribution of benefits. Thus, peasants will accuse officials and political representatives of favouring cities at the cost of the countryside, or particular sections of peasants will complain of having been deprived while other sections belonging to other regions or ethnic groups or castes or political loyalties have been allegedly favoured. The charge against state agencies is not one of exploitation, but discrimination. This has given a completely new quality to peasant politics, one that was missing in the earlier understandings of peasant society.

Fourth, unlike the old forms of peasant insurgency, there is a quite different quality to the role of violence in contemporary rural politics. While subaltern peasant revolts of the old kind had their own notions of strategy and tactics, they were characterized by strong community solidarity on the one side and negative opposition to perceived exploiters on the other. Today, the use of violence in peasant agitations seems to have a far more calculative, almost utilitarian, logic, designed to draw attention to specific grievances with a view to seeking appropriate governmental benefits. A range of deliberate tactics are followed to elicit the right responses from officials, political leaders, and especially the media. This is probably the most significant change in the nature of peasant politics over the last two decades.

It is important to emphasize that contrary to what is suggested by the depoliticized idea of governmentality, the quality of politics in the domain of political society is by no means a mechanical transaction of benefits and services. Even as state agencies try, by constantly adjusting their flexible policies, to break up large combinations of claimants, the organization of demands in political society can adopt highly emotive resources of solidarity and militant action. Democratic politics in India is daily marked by passionate and often violent agitations to protest discrimination and to secure claims. The fact that the objectives of such agitations are framed by conditions of governmentality is no reason to believe that they cannot arouse considerable passion and affective energy. Collective actions in political society cannot be depoliticized by framing them within the grid of governmentality because the activities of governmentality affect the very conditions of livelihood and social existence of the groups they target.

Interestingly, even though the claims made by different groups in political society are for governmental benefits, these cannot often be met by the standard application of rules, and frequently require the declaration of an exception. Thus, when a group of people living or cultivating on illegally occupied land or selling goods on the street claim the right to continue with their activities, or demand compensation for moving somewhere else, they are in fact inviting the state to declare their case as an exception to the universally applicable rule. They do not demand that the right to private property in land be abolished or that the regulations on trade licences and sales taxes be set aside. Rather, they demand that their cases be treated as exceptions. When the state acknowledges these demands, it too must do so not by the simple application of administrative rules, but rather by a political decision to declare an exception. The governmental response to demands in political society is also, therefore, irreducibly political rather than merely administrative.

However, the underside of political society is the utter marginalization of those groups that do not even have the strategic leverage of electoral mobilization. In every region of India, there exist marginal groups of people who are unable to gain access to the mechanisms of political society. They are often marked by their exclusion from peasant society, such as low-caste groups who do not participate in agriculture, or tribal peoples who depend more on forest products or pastoral occupations than on agriculture. Political society and electoral democracy have not given these groups the means to make effective claims on the state. In this sense, these marginalized groups represent an outside beyond the boundaries of political society.

The unity of the state system as a whole is now maintained by relating civil society to political society through the logic of reversal of the effects of primitive accumulation. Once this logic is recognized by the bourgeoisie as a *necessary political condition* for the continued rapid growth of corporate capital, the state, with its mechanisms of electoral democracy, becomes the field for the political negotiation of demands for the transfer of resources, through fiscal and other means, from the accumulation economy to governmental programmes aimed at providing the livelihood needs of the poor and the marginalized. The autonomy of the state, and that of the bureaucracy, now lies in their power to adjudicate the quantum and form of transfer of resources to the so-called 'social sector of expenditure'. Ideological differences, such as those between the Right and the Left, for instance, are largely about the amount and modalities of social sector expenditure, such as poverty removal programmes. These differences do not question the dynamic logic that binds civil society to political society under the dominance of capital.

Thus, with the continuing rapid growth of the Indian economy, the hegemonic hold of corporate capital over the domain of civil society is likely to continue. This will inevitably mean continued primitive accumulation. That is to say, there will be more and more primary producers, that is, peasants, artisans, and petty manufacturers who will lose their means of production. However, most of these victims of primitive accumulation are unlikely to be absorbed in the new growth sectors of the economy. They will be marginalized and rendered useless as far as the sectors dominated by corporate capital are concerned. But the passive revolution under conditions of electoral democracy makes it unacceptable and illegitimate for the state to leave these marginalized populations without the means of labour to simply fend for themselves. That carries the risk of turning them into the 'dangerous classes'. Hence, a whole series of governmental policies are being, and will be, devised to reverse the effects of primitive accumulation. This is the field in which poor people, especially peasants, are having to redefine their relations with both the state and with capital. Thus far, it appears that whereas many new practices have been developed by peasants, using the mechanisms of democratic politics, to claim and negotiate benefits from the state, their ability to deal with the world of capital is still unsure and inadequate.

BETWEEN STATE AND SOCIETY

A strong theme in current discussions about state institutions in India is that of decline. From law-making to administration, policymaking to public services, the charge is that standards of accountability and probity have been allowed to deteriorate. The most proximate reason for this is the constant pressure on state authorities, exerted mainly through the electoral process, to satisfy the immediate demands of this or that organized popular group. The recent comprehensive history of Indian politics since Independence by Ramachandra Guha (2007) also adopts this narrative line. The decline argument assumes, of course, that the norms of state practice established in the early decades of the Indian republic, when mobilized demands were restricted to a very small section of the electorate and policy was decided by a handful of patrician politicians, should also have proved adequate in an age when democratic mobilizations are both wider and deeper. Clearly, this assumption is mistaken. While the normative view of the state required that society, consisting of equal citizens, be treated as homogeneous, the evolving practices of democratic politics required the recognition and identification of a heterogeneous social. This is reflected in the conceptual distinction between civil and political society.

One implication of economic liberalization since the 1990s is the withdrawal of the state from several sectors of economic activity. Even in areas where the state continues to be primarily responsible for providing services, it has preferred to outsource the job to NGOs and private agencies. This has happened at the same time that political mobilizations have produced electoral majorities led by lower castes and other hitherto subordinated communities. Thus, while the pressures have increased on state institutions to provide more direct benefits, including reservations in government employment and educational institutions, for backward groups, there is a contrary pressure on the state, exerted through fiscal, judicial, and other regulatory institutions, to curtail the range of its activities and allow those sectors to be operated by the supposedly more efficient and prudent private organizations.

Moreover, another significant recent development is the emergence of one branch of the state as a self-conscious check on the perceived excesses of the others. Thus, while Central and state executives and legislatures have been accused of violating norms of equality, rationality, and probity in order to satisfy various electoral constituencies, the law courts have taken it upon themselves to reassert those norms and direct the governmental agencies to undo the alleged damage. One particularly controversial instrument in this regard is the public interest litigation (PIL), by which the Supreme Court can take cognizance of any matter it deems to be in the public interest, investigate it, and issue orders to government agencies. While government authorities may be said to be acting in response to various mobilized demands in a heterogeneous political society, the courts have emerged as defenders of a normative and homogeneous civil society of equal citizens.

As early as Frankel and Rao (1990), the argument was made that democratic politics in India was heading towards a split between public institutions, where privileged groups such as the upper middle classes were entrenched, and political institutions, which were being taken over by representatives of the lower castes and hitherto underprivileged groups. More recently, it is often remarked that the split is between the private corporate sector, dominated by the upper-caste, urban, upper-middle classes, and the state sector, which is increasingly dominated by middle and lower castes and the upwardly mobile rural middle classes. More careful analysis shows that both these accounts are simplistic. While the reforms since the 1990s have undoubtedly led to the withdrawal of the state from many sectors in which it was previously the dominant or even the sole player, the importance of the state as the chief regulator, facilitator, arbiter, and even allocator of resources for society as a whole has by no means diminished. As we have argued earlier, the restructured state of the passive revolution, in which corporate capital has assumed a position of hegemony in civil society and dominance in the state structure as a whole, is still the framework within which all dominant social classes and most organized democratic forces are engaged in their political struggles. Hence, it is by no means true that the urban middle classes have abandoned the state or the democratic political institutions.

What is true, however, is that various institutions and processes within the state structure are being selectively used by dominant minority groups, such as corporate capitalists or the urban middle classes, to curtail the sway of governmental agencies operating as representatives of democratic majorities. These could be courts of law or particular bureaucratic offices, often projected in the public domain through the print and visual media. Further, there is also a certain spatial withdrawal of such dominant minority groups from territories generally administered by local institutions of the state. Thus, upper-class housing estates often prefer to reduce their dependence on local municipal services to a bare minimum so as to not have to deal with the messy politics of urban neighbourhoods. It is thought that the new Special Economic Zones, which are meant to contain entire townships, may become enclaves lying outside the normal jurisdiction of state agencies. Thus, instead of a split between state and non-state domains, the emergent social oppositions are being played out between different branches of the state, as well as through tactical and spatial engagements and withdrawals.

REFERENCES

Bardhan, Pranab. 1984. *The Political Economy of Development*. New Delhi: Oxford University Press.

Chatterjee, Partha. 2004. *The Politics of the Governed: Reflections on Political Society in Most of the World*. New York: Columbia University Press.

Frankel, Francine and M.S.A. Rao (eds). 1990. *Dominance and State Power in India: Decline of a Social Order*. New Delhi: Oxford University Press.

Fuller, C.J. and Véronique Bénéï (eds). 2001. *Everyday State and Society in Modern India*. London: Hurst.

Gough, Kathleen and Hari P. Sharma (eds). 1973. *Imperialism and Revolution in South Asia*. New York: Monthly Review Press.

Guha, Ramachandra. 2007. *India After Gandhi: The History of the World's Largest Democracy*. New Delhi: Picador India.

Gupta, Akhil. 1998. *Postcolonial Developments: Agriculture in the Making of Modern India*. Durham, N.C.: Duke University Press.

Jenkins, Rob. 1999. *Democratic Politics and Economic Reform in India*. Cambridge: Cambridge University Press.

Kaviraj, Sudipta. 1989. 'A Critique of the Passive Revolution', *Economic and Political Weekly*, XXIII (45–7), pp. 2429–44.

Kohli, Atul. 1991. *Democracy and Discontent: India's Growing Crisis of Governability*. Cambridge: Cambridge University Press.

Kothari, Rajni. 1970a. *Politics in India*. Boston: Little, Brown and New Delhi: Orient Longman.

———. (ed.) 1970b. *Caste and Indian Politics*. New Delhi: Orient Longman.

Kurian, K. Mathew (ed.). 1975. *India—State and Society: A Marxian Approach*. Madras: Orient Longman.

Morris-Jones, W.H. 1964. *The Government and Politics of India*. London: Hutchinson University Library.

Palmer, Norman. 1962. *The Indian Political System*. Boston: Houghton Mifflin.

Raj, K.N. 1973. 'The Politics and Economics of Intermediate Regimes', *Economic and Political Weekly*, VIII (27), pp. 1189–98.

Rudolph, Lloyd I. and Susanne H. Rudolph. 1987. *In Pursuit of Lakshmi: The Political Economy of the Indian State*. Chicago: University of Chicago Press.

———. 1967. *The Modernity of Tradition: Political Development in India*. Chicago: University of Chicago Press.

Tarlo, Emma. 2003. *Unsettling Memories: Narratives of the Emergency in India*. Berkeley: University of California Press.

Vanaik, Achin. 1990. *The Painful Transition: Bourgeois Democracy in India*. London: Verso.

Varshney, Ashutosh. 1995. *Democracy, Development and the Countryside: Urban-Rural Struggles in India*. Cambridge: Cambridge University Press.

2 Constitutionalism

Uday S. Mehta

We are here not to function for one party or one group, but always to think of India as a whole and always to think of the welfare of the four hundred million that comprise India....The time comes when we have to rise above party and think of the Nation, think sometimes even of the world at large of which our nation is a great part. When I think of the work of this Constituent Assembly, it seems to me,...[we] have to rise above our ordinary selves and party disputes and think of the great problem before us in the widest and most tolerant and most effective manner so that, whatever we may produce, should be worthy of India as a whole and should be such that the world should recognize that we have functioned, as we should have functioned, in this high adventure.

(Jawaharlal Nehru, *CAD* 1999, Book 1, vol. I, p. 60)

Constitutions profess to create what they allege already exists; to be a beginning in a stream of time, and to be authorized by an authority that they also claim to sanction. In this sense, constitutional beginnings are convolutions, which wager on the future to secure their legitimacy and to resolve the conundrum that attends all absolute moments. They are occasions when the dramatic and the literal cannot be precisely separated because both are buffeted by a monumental foreground that envelops the convulsive birth of nations. However, in a lower key, constitutions are scripts in which a people inscribe the text of their professed collective destiny. They write down who they think they are, what they want to be, and the principles that will guide their interaction along that path in the future. But at the moment of inception, none of these claims is anything more than a solemn wager. The people and the nation, on whose behalf the Constitution speaks, are not yet 'a people' or a unified nation; the state and the government that it authorizes are not yet stable entities; the principles that it articulates are abstract, and not yet backed by precedent or interpretive specificity; and the history that it professes to demarcate itself from still crowds in on the present. Precisely for these reasons, constitutional moments give us a clear view of the vision that informs them.

This chapter considers the Indian Constitution and the Constituent Assembly Debates (1946–9) that led to its adumbration with an eye to understanding the vision of India at a time when, politically speaking, there was little else other than that vision. During those critical years, the past could not be an alibi for the present, the way it had been during the Independence struggle. And the present could not represent the future because it was riven by uncertainty, factionalism, and Partition. As Nehru's famous inaugural address on the night of 14 August 1947 made clear, the only temporal register in which the nation could be spoken of was the future, and the vision associated with it. It was a moment when, as he said, 'we step out from the old to the new, when an age ends', and when 'the future beckons us' (*CAD* 1999: 4–5). The fact that the Constitution was to realize a beckons from the future is understandable; however, it was equally, and more vexingly, burdened with the challenge of bringing an age to an end and drawing a curtain on the past. In many ways, as the subsequent politics of India has made clear, this was a far greater challenge because the past had a momentum, which no constitutional bookend could simply exhaust or bring to a sudden halt. It has a tenacity to live on in the patterns of everyday life.

What did that mean, and why was the first act of Independence to invoke a temporality resonant with imperial associations? Why did Nehru and his cohorts in the Constituent Assembly view the present as the disjuncture between the past and the future, rather than the connecting tissue that linked the two? How was the past conceptualized so that its end could be envisioned? Why, from almost the very first instance, was India's Independence such a fraught event, even for those who had struggled valiantly to achieve it, such that the jubilation that accompanied it had to be muffled by solemnity and the prospect of long national ardour?

In the voluminous writings, debates, and speeches that inform constitutional reflections in India during the late 1940s and onwards, three issues have an unmistakable salience. First is an overriding concern with national unity; second, a deep and anxious preoccupation with social issues such as poverty, illiteracy, economic development, and many other similar foes; and finally, there is an intense concern with India's standing in the world and with foreign affairs more generally. Beyond the salience that these three issues have in constitutional reflection, they also constitute the template for much of the subsequent politics of the country; in fact, it seems fair to say that they characterize the general contours of the politics of many newly independent countries in the second half of the twentieth century.

This chapter is a series of reflections on these issues, on what underlies their salience, and on some of their enduring implications. In the course of it, I point to some similarities and contrasts with American constitutionalism in the late eighteenth century, primarily to help illustrate the claims I make, and also because the American case was, and remains, an exemplary instance of postcolonial nationalism, modern constitutionalism, and democratic federalism. My focus will be on the first two of these issues.

In the Indian case, each of these three concerns had obvious exigent reasons that explain their prominence. It is plain that a country on the verge of Independence, marked by dizzying, often fractious, and potentially centrifugal diversity—not to mention a diversity that had long been used to justify imperial subjection, and one in which the prospect, and then the reality, of Partition had loomed for many years—would be vigilant, indeed, obsessed with national unity. Similarly, under the depressing extant conditions of near ubiquitous social despair, illiteracy, and many other forms of destitution, the concern with such matters could hardly have been anything other than anxious and urgent. And finally, given the long history during which national identity had been denied, distorted, and disparaged, and the struggle for Independence during which it had been asserted as having a historical and objective warrant, it is only to be expected that a pressing and guiding feature of national idealism would have it alloyed with the question of recognition and standing in the international arena. If, as was the case, the claims of Western empires had been underwritten by a normative universality which vouched for themselves in terms of some amplified conception of Reason, nationalism in its opposition to empire had to assert an alternative universality in which the nation was the agential exemplar. No doubt nationalism had its particularistic and cultural anchors; however, at least among its more thoughtful advocates—figures such as Nehru and Fanon—nationalism was also always alloyed to an ideology whose transformative political and spiritual energies were thoroughly universal. Gandhi's claim that 'the attainment of Independence for me is the search for truth' had political and spiritual analogues in the thought of Nehru, and Tagore. Hence the claim of Independence, not unlike that of imperial authority and imperial subjection, had to be, at least partially, vindicated by a referent beyond itself. As it turns out, a concern with that referent anticipated what is now a plain fact, namely that nationalism, far from being the antithesis of globalization, can only fully affirm itself under those very conditions.

The three issues thus drew on urgencies and imperatives that were both historical and contemporaneous. They had an obvious logic that was both conceptual and material. Moreover, in their centrality, they explicitly signalled to a tradition of political thinking that extended back to the American War of Independence and the constitutionalism that followed it, along with the French and Russian revolutions. The three issues also anticipated many of the constitutional reflections that were to follow in the second half of the twentieth century. A conspicuous feature of constitutionalism in the twentieth century was the emphasis it placed on national unity and identity, on social uplift and equality, and on international standing.

Notwithstanding these informing urgencies, there is a revealing irony in the emphasis that these issues assume. Much of democratic constitutionalism, and more generally anti-colonial nationalism, conceived of their provenance as a response to tyranny, and to the umbrage to collective freedom provoked by imperial subjection. In political terms, the response to tyranny and subjection could only have been an insistence on freedom. In the Indian and other colonial contexts, this meant freedom *from* the tyranny of imperial subjection. Yet issues of national unity, social uplift, and recognition—and this is the irony—make that freedom conditional on an uncertain period of gestation, through which alone unity can be secured; on resources and extended effort, which are the requisites for social transformation; and on the vagaries of an international context, in which the assertions and recognition of sovereignty are at best conditionally secure. As a response to the temporizing with which empires

typically opposed the demand for national freedom, it is ironic that newly independent nations, such as India, should themselves have made the assertion of freedom conditional on achievements which could at best only be prospective (Mehta 1999: 77–114). In temporal terms, one might say that having vouched for the nation as having a warrant from the past, following Independence the constitutional moment could only point to the nation's future, without fully affirming the present as something in which freedom was realized. Nothing in the immanent condition of the nation appeared to support the idea of being free.

The terms in which new states conceived of freedom once Independence was secured made its affirmation into a capacious *project*, a sort of *promissory note* that was issued not just to all members of the nation itself, but also to the world at large. The nation was now conceived as a *project*; it was one in which one could not, at any given point or through any particular act or set of conditions, securely anchor the sentiment and singularity of national being on which the nationalist struggle had wagered so much. The nation and its freedom, following Independence, could only be a projection onto the future. Independence, one might say, illuminated— revealingly, in the Indian case, in the twilight of a 'midnight' hour—a condition of inadequacy. The irony is that the successful culmination to free oneself from imperial subjection led almost immediately to freedom itself becoming a subsidiary concern; that is, subsidiary to national unity, social uplift, and a concern with recognition. To paraphrase and extend Homi Bhabha's insight regarding agency under conditions of imperial subjection, one might say that Independence turned on a sly continuance of the ideology and practice of the empire (Bhabha 1994).

Where national purposefulness was associated with unity, social uplift, and recognition, freedom became a single strand of a larger tapestry. It could not stand alone as something secured through Independence itself. In such a view, freedom is never in the moment, never singular because it cannot be thought of as tangential to the national and collective purposes with which it is braided. Moreover, it cannot be associated with the conditions of everyday life. The quotidian materiality of life, in which Gandhi had invested his transformative energies and hopes, simply represented, in the more familiar nationalist and constitutional perspective, the deficient conditions for which national idealism offers a compensatory promise. The social conditions, the terms in which life was lived—that is, matters defined by religion, caste, economic opportunity, and prescribed identities—all get imbued with the presumption of being antithetical to freedom. Even individual freedom is vouched for primarily to the extent that the individual bears the imprimatur of being a citizen, and hence can be conceived of as a part of a unitary whole. Indeed, the enfranchisement of the individual as citizen becomes necessary not because he or she is 'ready' or 'educated', or 'free' from sedimented parochial social identities—as classical liberal theory would have required (Mill 1975a; 1975b)—but because citizenship is a category through which the nation can ratify its own purposefulness as an entity that will deliver on the promise of freedom.

Freedom, in this view, exists as a future prospect, as the distant culmination of a plan, and which can only be realized through the choices and resolution of that plan.[1] It becomes freighted with the seriousness and responsibility of pursuing an arduous collective journey. This is most clearly evident in Nehru's speeches from the period shortly prior to and following Independence. In their tone and content they are like a solemn dirge to the exacting, capacious and, strangely, even to the inescapable burdens that India's Independence imposes on her. They are unremittingly freighted by a sense of necessity and foreboding.[2]

What is clear is that the idea of being free, despite everything that the nationalist movement had wagered on this prospect, does not adequately capture that moment that extends roughly from the mid-1940s through at least the late 1960s, because freedom itself is just an appealing lure of a future condition. The vision that the Constitution articulates is not illuminated by the idea of an extant domain of public freedom, which comes into being through the evacuation of imperial governance. One must therefore ask: how should one conceive of that specific and very distinctive energy that marks constitutional reflection in India—and, as it turns out, elsewhere in the second half of the twentieth century?

A POLITICAL AND REVOLUTIONARY VISION

What is it about the language of unity and social uplift that allows it to serve as a caption for a broader national endeavour, in a way in which the securing of public freedom had served as the caption for American constitutionalism in the eighteenth century (Shklar 1998)? Does the compulsive talk about unity and social questions conceal, or rather only hint at, something else, which might in fact be its motive force and to which the Constitution gives expression?

I want to urge that it is in this language, for which, as I have already suggested, there are of course obvious and exigent reasons and explanations, that something else resides, in virtue of which the Constitution can be seen as doing something quite radical; indeed, as connecting Indian constitutionalism with that other constitutional moment of the eighteenth century, namely the French revolutionary tradition. Unity and social uplift, I want to suggest, are the terms through which a purely political vision is articulated and other forms of power and authority eclipsed, or, at least, rendered secondary. Politics becomes the ground for national unity, and the redressing of social issues the central venue through which this ground and unity are constantly reaffirmed.

In the modern Western tradition, Thomas Hobbes was the theorist who most closely identified the securing of life and living well (in his terms, self-preservation and felicity) with political power and national unity. It is with him that politics becomes the despositive and singular currency of order and progress, where all other forms of unity and distinction, to the extent that they survive, exist at the mercy of political power. Hobbes' response to the religious and other forms of diversity and sectarianism that had characterized English history during the sixteenth and seventeenth centuries, and which had issued in the tumult of the civil war, was a diagnosis in which death and anarchy could only be avoided through a unitary form of power. That power, and the authority that sanctioned it, had to be political. It was predicated on the premise of human equality and the rational priority of corporeal life. This new form of power—new on account of its priority and reach—

had to displace the extant social and religious order by associating them with a hierarchical and divisive form of existence, which in its inherent logic could not escape the *bellum omnium contra omnes*. A crucial insight of Hobbes' thought and its legacy was the degree to which he was successful in discrediting the social as a self-sustaining domain of life and freedom.

The fact that Hobbes endorses a form of political absolutism with a unified conception of power and authority has understandably led to the familiar view in which his ideas are presumed to be orthogonal to democratic politics. This is of course true, but it does nevertheless obscure an important point of overlap pertaining to the centrality of politics itself and the corresponding suspicion regarding the social. Democratic constitutions like the Indian Constitution expressly eschew the absolutism that is featured in Hobbes' thought. However, that fact does not by itself settle the question of whether such constitutions can—given their commitments to unity and social uplift—secure a principled and practical distinction with the form of power Hobbes advocates. Notwithstanding the often-touted liberal credentials of figures such as Nehru and Rajendra Prasad, Hobbes may be the largely unacknowledged mentor of Indian constitutionalism. The Indian Constitution authorizes a conception of power that articulates a vision that is, in fact, revolutionary; precisely because of the way it conceptualizes the question of national unity and its relationship with extant forms of social order. Its deep concern with the social is part of a piece with an equally deep worry regarding the diversity of the social order and its viability as an alternative nexus of power and authority—an alternative, that is, to the purely political vision, which the Constitution attempted to inscribe.

The claim that the Indian Constitution does something revolutionary, akin to the manner of Hobbes' thought, requires justification because it appears to fly in the face of the obvious facts about the Constitution, the debates that led to its adumbration, and to the relevant aspects of Independence itself. It is a familiar and often repeated fact that Indian Independence, the event that occurred on 15 August 1947, was marked not so much by metaphors of novelty and revolutionary rupture as by those of transference and continuity. This, of course, is not merely a metaphorical claim. It was literally, that is to say politically and juridically, the case. An extant 'interim' government, of which Nehru had been the executive head, became the Government of India, and of which, following Independence, he remained the head. Technically, King George VI, who had been the titular sovereign prior to August 1947, remained sovereign until 1949. In terms of governmental and administrative machinery, the 'transfer of power', as it was called, was just that, because it represented the simple succession of 'personnel'. Similarly, the Constituent Assembly and the Constitution that it produced were anchored in strict legislative precedent, because they were husbanded by the 1935 Government of India Act along with the additional guidance of the Viceroy and Cabinet Mission's Statement of May 1946 (Austin 1966; Rao 1960; Seervai 1999).

All these facts and circumstances suggest that the constitutional moment was anything but revolutionary. It was, after all, braced by clear judicial precedent, legislative authorization, and a deference to political convention. As the distinguished constitutional scholar Subhash Kashyap has pointed out, 'The founding fathers made it very clear that they were not writing on a clean slate. They took a conscious decision not to make a complete departure from the past, but to build on the existing structure and experience of institutions already established', and that 'nearly 75 per cent of the Constitution can be said to be reproduction of the Government of India Act, 1935.... The basic structure of the polity and the provisions regulating union-state relations, declaration of Emergency etc. were largely based on the 1935 Act' (Kashyap 2004: 4–5).

Moreover, unlike the French Revolution, and instead more akin to the American Revolution, in the Indian case the constitutional moment was not burdened by an inheritance of absolutism. Whatever one might say about British imperial governance, at least by the mid-1940s it bore no resemblance to the Bourbon absolutism of the late eighteenth century. To the important extent that revolutions are predetermined by the regimes they overthrow, the inheritance of a responsible and limited government might further vitiate the idea that Indian constitutionalism represented something revolutionary. And finally, one might add, again as in the American case, Indian constitutionalism plainly occurred in a context, which Burke had celebrated in the Hastings trial, where there existed a complex social skein of power and authority, and where, therefore, neither anarchy nor the void of power were present to escalate revolutionary demands.

However, along with these familiar facts is another set of facts pertaining to the Indian Constitution. Here was a document which granted universal adult franchise in a country that was overwhelmingly illiterate; where, moreover, the conditionality of acquiring citizenship made no reference to race, caste, religion, or creed, and in which, it is worth mentioning, there were no additional or more stringent conditions for the former British rulers to become citizens; which committed the state to being secular in a land that was by any reckoning deeply religious; which evacuated as a matter of law every form of prescribed social hierarchy under extant conditions marked by a dense plethora of entrenched hierarchies; that granted a raft of fundamental individual rights in the face of a virtually total absence of such rights. Here was a Constitution which, in its Preamble, committed the state to the most capacious conception of justice, including thereby 'social, economic, and political' justice, 'liberty of thought, expression, belief, faith, and worship', equality understood to include that of 'status and opportunity', and in which, under the heading of 'fraternity', it professed to insure 'the dignity of the individual and the unity and integrity of the Nation'. Most importantly, the Constitution created a federal democracy with all the juridical and political instruments of individual, federal, local, and provisional self-governance, where the nearest experience had been of imperial and princely authority.

A lot can be said about this document, which has aptly been called the 'cornerstone of a nation'. For one thing, it points to a truly remarkable self-confidence on the part of the framers and the Indian elite as they envisioned the future of this nation. When one considers, for example, the Directive Principles of the Constitution or the 'strivings' of the state, they include a fulsome engagement with matters of health, education, individual and communal safety, equality, and prosperity. One cannot but be awed by the extent and reach of such a political and social agenda. This constitutionally enshrined vision of the future is what has often been seen as implying an activist and capacious state, responsible for the eradication of poverty, undoing the stigmas of casteism, improving public health and education, building large industry, facilitating communication, fostering national unity, and, most broadly, creating conditions for the exercising of freedom.

It is this second set of facts about the Constitution that I wish to suggest constitutes the grounds of sovereignty in a rather interesting and distinct way. And again, it is these facts that I want to argue articulate a revolutionary agenda, including in the familiar sense that implies an attempt at a radical disjunction and rupture with the past. There are obvious similarities here with the American constitutional founding. Despite the frequency with which ancient authors and examples are invoked and Montesquieu in particular praised, the consensus of opinion among the *Federalists* suggests a decisive distancing from any exemplary past. The first three words of the American Constitution, 'We the People' (words which it shares with the first utterances of the Indian Constitution), alone suggest that break. They referred, as Judith Shklar has pointed out, neither to the plebs of Rome nor to the 'commons' of England, but rather to everyone (Shklar 1998). They summarized what Benjamin Franklin had said at the Convention:

> We have gone back to ancient history for models of Government, and examined the different forms of those Republics...we have viewed Modern States all around Europe, but find none of their Constitutions suitable to our circumstances'. (quoted in Farrand 1966: 397)

In both the Indian and the American cases, the forswearing of a past was part of a piece with the denial of extant social conditions as the basis of democratic citizenship. And in both cases, the vote and the terms of franchise were crucial grounds for authorizing a new kind of power and unity. In the Indian case, there was a clearly conceived sense that the vote and citizenship would create a new network of linkages that was specifically political, and as such, relatively free from long entrenched and crowded social identities (*Report of the Indian*

Franchise Committee 1932). Voting did not stem from a historical entitlement, but rather from a natural right in which neither poverty, caste, gender, educational disadvantage, nor the absence of property were disqualifications. As Alladi Krishnaswamy Ayyar, one of the leading lights of the Constituent Assembly, made clear,

> The principle of adult-suffrage was adopted in no light-hearted mood but with the full realization of its implications. If democracy is to be broad based and the system of government that is to function is to have the sanction of the people as a whole, in a country where the large mass of the people are illiterate and the people owning property are so few, the introduction of any property or educational qualifications for the exercise of the franchise would be a negation of the principles of democracy....The only alternative to adult suffrage was some kind indirect election based upon village communities and local bodies. (*CAD* 1999, vol. XI: 834)

In the American case, of course, the specific European fear of the property-less armed with the vote was absent, largely because mass poverty itself was absent and the plight of slaves and Native Americans ignored. However, in the Indian case, where one might have expected the elites to have such a fear, that worry is clearly compensated for by the consolation that universal franchise would work to the advantage of a new kind of state power. What Ayyar and others like Sardar Patel were fully aware of was that universal adult franchise was a way 'to demonstrate to the world, to the class of people who have...been nurtured on communal claims, our genuine faith in the fundamental principles of democracy and in the establishment of a secular state without distinction of caste, creed or class' (ibid.).

The same argument in favour of political power also addressed a familiar and long-standing colonial objection to Independence. That argument had been a claim that countries such as India had not articulated themselves into that specific form of society that could represent itself politically. Whatever forms of collective action they might be capable of, they were not capable of political self-representation. They were caught between anarchy, despotism, or, as J.S. Mill emphasized regarding India and the East, a surfeit of social norms and customary mores. They lacked, and

were as yet incapable of, a political will of which a state was the only evidence. They had no state which in effect could claim to be authorized by 'We the People'.

There were only two ways to disable this argument. There was the Gandhian alternative in which political agency, to the extent that it required a monopoly on the means of violence, was not in any case celebrated, and where, moreover, agency did not turn on the authorization of a central and unified state. Rather, agency rested on an adherence to universal ethical principles that were free from the instrumental logic of modern politics, and which were largely nested in extant social relationships. Gandhi was in effect challenging the very conception of politics and agency that underwrote the colonial claim, including the argument that required the transcending of the social and the diversity implied by it. The issue of the requisite unity of politics and representation was thus disabled through the universality of ethics and the inherent diversity of the social.

The second alternative was the constitutional and democratic alternative, in which the answer to the colonial question, 'Is there a political order and whom does it represent?' could only be 'first that we have an order which is vouched for by a corresponding unity and it is one in which everyone is represented'.[3] The answer, of course, was itself largely wishful, especially under conditions in which social identities were deeply entrenched, and where the very issue of the representation of minorities was particularly hardly felicitous. Yet it was an answer, which, if nothing else, indicated a clear constitutional orientation in which politics was to be the ground for a prospective unity.[4]

In the familiar distinction between the conditions of liberation and the conditions of freedom, the former are typically associated with the culmination of a period of rebellion and revolutionary activity, while freedom is likened to the quieter stage of framing constitutions, which become its foundation. Perhaps the most famous example of this mapping is the American case, where the War of Independence culminating in 1776 is known as the Revolutionary War, and the Constitutional Convention in Philadelphia, which issued the Constitution of 1787, is known for its more deliberative energy or, as John Adams expressed it, through the regulative image of the uniformity of time—as he said, 'Thirteen clocks struck as one'. This is not the appropriate context in which to discuss why Constitution-making has not been recognized as a truly revolutionary political moment. I hope it suffices to say that in the modern Western tradition of political theory, revolutions have been associated with that dramatic and tumultuous moment when individuals, in, for example, John Locke's understanding, contracted with each other to leave the state of nature and form a new 'body politic'. In contrast, constitutions have been associated with that orderly act where the body politic 'entrusted' its power in a particular form of government.

The Indian case is the reverse of what one has come to understand through this archetypal Lockean narrative, of which the American example is taken as paradigmatic. In India, it is the constitutional moment that is revolutionary and rupturing. However, this claim obviously provokes the question, revolutionary with respect to what and rupturing of what? What does the Indian Constitution rupture? I think the answer is that it ruptures the particular relationship with time and with history, and in doing so transforms the status of the social as the ground of lived experience. It's from this rupture or distancing of history that sovereignty, and the political, as an expression of a capacious public will, comes to be formed. To put the point somewhat polemically, the Indian Constitution, along with the conception of the political that it puts in place, does not so much emerge from history as it emerges in opposition to history and with a firm view of the future. If political absolutism in Europe had defined itself, following Bodin and Hobbes, as *potestas legibus soluta,* that is, power absolved from laws, one might say that in India, following the Constitution, the political became power absolved from history.

The relationship of power to history is fraught with imperial associations. In the nineteenth century, every major expression of European political thought had made history the evidentiary ground of political and even moral development. In Hegel, Marx, and J.S. Mill, notwithstanding their differing accounts of historical development, history was the register

through which alone a society's political condition and political future could be assessed. Hegel's articulation of the state as the embodiment of a concrete ethical rationality represented the realization of a journey of Reason that originated in the distant recesses of the East. Marx's vision of a proletarian future had its explanatory and political credence in overcoming the contrarian forces that fetter and spur historical movement. J.S. Mill's ideal of a liberalism that secured the conditions for the flourishing of individuality again explicitly rests on having reached a point of civilizational progress 'when mankind have become capable of being improved by free and equal discussion' (Mill 1975a: 16).

These arguments had a specifically imperial inflection. In J.S. Mill, who was by far the most influential liberal advocate of the empire, the argument went broadly along the following lines: political institutions such as a representative democracy are dependent on societies' having reached a historical maturation, or, in the language of the times, a particular level of civilization. Such civilizational maturation, however, was differentially achieved. That is, progress in history itself occurs differentially. Hence, those societies in which the higher accomplishments of civilization had not occurred plainly did not satisfy the conditions for a representative government. Under such conditions, liberalism, in the form of the empire, serviced the deficiencies of the past for societies that had been stunted through history. This, in brief, was the liberal justification of the empire. Its normative force rested squarely on a claim about history. It is what Dipesh Chakrabarty has called the 'waiting room' version of history (Chakrabarty 2000), the idea being that societies such as India had to wait until they were present in contemporary time, or what amounts to the same timing in contemporary history. They had to wait because their history made it clear that they were not 'as yet' ready for political self-governance. The denial of an autonomous political realm was the debt paid by the present on behalf of a deficient and recalcitrant past.

The nationalist response to this historically anchored waiting room model was to agree with the idea and the logic of the argument, but to disagree with the particulars of its application. Here, as elsewhere, Gandhi is the exception, because his conception of civilization and its cognate progress was never historically driven. When Gandhi speaks of civilization, it is invariably as an ethical relationship that an individual or community has with itself, with others, and with its deities.[5] Whatever else this does, it cuts through any reliance on history as the register from which alone progress can be read, evaluated, and directed. However, the more typical nationalist response, including among social reformers of the nineteenth century, was to concur with the claim that progress was historical, but to demur on the point that India was not 'as yet' ready. The nationalist claim instead was that India was in fact ready, that it had paid its debt on behalf of a 'backward' past through two centuries of tutelage. Its claim to political autonomy was simply the other side of the claim that it was present in contemporary time, and thus freed from the residual vestiges of historical time.

THE ABSOLUTE REACH OF POLITICAL POWER

But what did it concretely mean to be freed from history? And to be present in what I am calling contemporary time? It did not mean that India was not affected or influenced by its past, or that the problems of poverty, caste, and numerous other social and economic woes were without an historical dimension. That would have been rank stupidity; however, the framers of the Constitution and the members of the Constituent Assembly were not fools.

Instead, what I think it meant was that the historical aspect of these problems is taken as part of their social scientific and political nature, but not as an inheritance that limited the potential of political power. All historical issues are automatically translated in the language of politics, and in that translation they lose any temporal dimension of the past. History is brought to a threshold where, to recall Nehru's famous words, 'an age ends'. The instrument through which this temporal sequestration is effected is political power. History becomes a social and contemporary fact on which politics does its work. By this, I mean that history gets translated into a medium where it

is available for political modification. To make the point perhaps overly starkly, the challenge of caste injustice becomes analogous to that of building industry or large dams. They are both challenges in which the state draws upon and leans on the guiding primacy of science and social science. This conception of the political is nothing if not presentist; it loses an element of temporality that one associates with notions such as inheritance. It is anchored in the amplitude of choice; everything becomes an issue of choosing by reference to the larger purposes of the nation, because the conception of politics that it belongs to is supremely about choosing and realizing those purposes.

It is in this context that the concern with social issues, which is such a conspicuous feature of the Constituent Assembly debates and the Constitution, becomes relevant for two reasons. First, issues such as mass poverty and illiteracy and near ubiquitous destitution belong to the realm of necessity because they place human beings under the pressing dictates of their bodies. To the extent that political power concerns itself with—and under modern conditions it has to—this dimension of human life, it too becomes subject to a necessity. It can only represent freedom as something prospective. Its immediate ambit is dictated by the intensity of 'mere life'. And with regard to this ambit, political power can have no limiting bounds. Under such conditions, a simple logic transforms power from a traditional concern with establishing the conditions for freedom to a concern with life and its necessities. The power of the state is thus always underwritten by an elemental imperative to sustain life—the corporeal life of the citizen, and the unitary and corporate life of the nation. Neither the Fundamental Rights of citizens, with regard to which the Indian Constitution was famously expansive, nor the rights of the states and the communities that make up the federation have a warrant independent of the larger purposes of the nation. As the constitutional text (Part III) makes clear, the very enunciation of fundamental individual rights was immediately conjoined with the textual clarification of the ways in which such rights did not limit the power of the state in realizing a broader national and political vision. Ambedkar's statement to the Constituent Assembly on 4 November 1948 made the subsidiary priority of fundamental rights perfectly explicit, '... fundamental rights are the gifts of the law. Because fundamental rights are the gift of the state it does not follow that the state cannot qualify them' (*CAD* 1999, vol. VIII: 40).

The second aspect of the social, which explains its prominence, relates to its fundamental diversity in the Indian context. The diversity of India, of its religions, languages, castes, mores, and 'minor' traditions, had been the leitmotif of colonial and nationalist ethnography and historiography, dating back to William Jones, Edmund Burke, James Mill, Henry Maine, J.R. Seeley, and numerous others from the late eighteenth century onwards. It referred to a fact, which variously supported the view of India's cultural and civilizational richness, her history of confederation, her *sabhas*, *samitis* and panchayats, and the traditions of decentralized accountability; however, this very diversity was taken to be, in many of these narratives, the ground for India's political backwardness, her lack of national coherence, her easy resort to internecine conflict, and her fundamentally anti-modern orientation. Nationalists had, of course, also weighed in on these debates, whose stakes they knew pertained not just to their anti-imperial claims, but also to the period that was to follow. India, as both Gandhi and Nehru concurred, lived in her villages, and her villages, in being worlds unto themselves, tended to live in benign isolation from the rest of the world. For Gandhi, village India furnished the basic social integuments for resisting the lure of a vicarious existence, a feature that troubled him most about modernity. For Nehru, as a general matter, villages entrenched practices that were archaic, anti-rational, and sectarian in their prejudices. They represented everything to which his vision of the democratic nation offered a redemptive redress.

The constitutional vision, which in the main sidelined Gandhi's views, saw in the social diversity of India a profound challenge. It was variously coded as a resistance to the professed unity of the nation, and a support to the sectarian and inegalitarian norms that sustained and promoted the social. But, perhaps most importantly, the social with its essential diversity represented a resistance to the political vision, which

the Constitution attempted to put in place. Rajendra Prasad's words to the Constituent Assembly make this amply clear.

> After all, a constitution like machine is a lifeless thing. It acquires life because men who control it and operate it, and India needs today nothing more than a set of honest men who will have the interest of the country before them. There is fissiparous tendency arising out of various elements in our life. We have communal differences, caste differences, language difference, provincial differences and so forth. It requires men of strong character, men of vision, men who will not sacrifice the interests of the country at large for the sake of smaller groups and areas and who will rise over the prejudices which are born of these differences. (*CAD* 1999, vol. I: xvii)

Here we have all the familiar contrasts and binaries. On one side stands the Constitution, the unified nation, the men of honest character and integrity, the interests of the country, the ability to control and guide it; and on the other side, the diverse languages, castes, communal differences, prejudices, and the 'various elements of life' with their 'fissiparous tendency'.

This is a casting of India in the very terms in which Hobbes had viewed English history in the seventeenth century in his study of the English Civil War. The social domain was divisive, the political, unifying. The constitutional vision was meant to eviscerate or, at a minimum, trump these social and fissiparous tendencies by fixing them within a unified political frame. In fact, for Ambedkar, even the idea of India's being a federation was troubling, because it suggested the existence of parts or states that had, as in the American case, come to an 'agreement' to form a federation. For him, the constitutional vision was one in which the 'Union' was not at the mercy of any such agreement with its constituent parts:

> The federation is a Union because it is indestructible. Though the country and the people may be divided into different States for convenience of administration, the country is one integral whole, its people a single people living under a single imperium derived from a single source. (*CAD* 1999, vol. II: 42)

Not surprisingly, the text of the Constitution never uses the terms federal or federation.

For Nehru, Prasad, and others, the social diversity of India was a real—even if awkward—fact, which simultaneously provoked pride in India's civilizational fecundity and plurality, and a fear in its centrifugal potential. With Ambedkar, the diversity—to the extent that it was even acknowledged—existed solely as an administrative 'convenience' on the way to realizing an expressively political vision. For Ambedkar, the social did not even represent what Prasad called the 'elements of life', because the presumption in favour of a unitary political perspective was total. It is a perspective that is revealingly (and certainly wishfully) described as appropriate to 'a single people living under a single *imperium* derived from a single source'. Hobbes would have marvelled with envy at such propitious foundations—if only they had been true.

CONCLUSION

In *On Revolution,* Hannah Arendt makes the following claim, '...every attempt to solve the social question by political means leads to terror'(Arendt 1990: 112). By the social question, Arendt meant issues of material destitution and inequality. Arendt's view is an especially trenchant perspective on the consequences of attempting to address or redress social inequities by political means. The claim was itself one of the central planks by which Arendt distinguished the American and French Revolutions, and the constitutional settlements that followed them. For her, the singular calamity of the French Revolution, on account of which it led to terror and constitutional instability, lay in the fact that it attempted to address questions of destitution and social inequality solely within a political framework. In contrast, in the American case, by substantially ignoring the social questions of the day, the Constitution was able to limit the ambit of political power, and hence secure the domain of public freedom. Arendt admitted and was well aware that the question of slavery, the material plight of slaves, and the treatment of Native Americans were also largely ignored at that founding moment. To her these were judicious choices. The fact that mass poverty was substantially absent in late eighteenth century America was just a singular good fortune of the

Americans, in contrast with the French, who faced a more dire situation.

It is a central feature of Arendt's political vision that for power to be chastened and public freedom secured, political institutions must be exempt, and must exempt themselves, from shouldering the burden of redressing material and social inequities. It was the intermingling of political power with social issues that led the former to become absolute, and exact a heavy price on freedom. Indeed, Arendt even saw the reference to 'the pursuit of happiness' in the Declaration of Independence as an embryonic form of this intermingling, and hence the potential compromising of an autonomous political domain. Nevertheless, for Arendt, the American Constitution served as an ideal in which political power was limited, public freedom secured, and national unity anchored in the structures of political institutions—and all this was possible only because social questions were kept at bay. However, it was the French example that was the much more influential model for revolutions in the nineteenth and twentieth centuries. It was the one in which political power was constitutionally braided with issues of social uplift, and in which, moreover, French national unity was grounded on the shared material destitution of the French peasant. Citizenship was thus from the very outset a response to a social predicament, and the power of the state was similarly a promissory rejoinder to redress that predicament.

Whatever one might say in response to Arendt's neo-Aristotelian conception of politics as an agonistic public domain for the expression of ideas and ideals, substantially relieved of social pressures—and clearly a lot can be said of this rather pristine conception, including the claim, most often associated with the work of Amartya Sen, in which freedom, far from being secured through a disassociation with issues of development, is in fact conditional on the success of such a linkage (Sen 2000). Nevertheless, what cannot be disputed is Arendt's claim that it has been the French legacy that has been overwhelmingly influential in the subsequent history of revolutions and constitutionalism. With the short-lived exception of the Hungarian Constitution of 1956, which Arendt herself draws attention to, in the founding of new nations and the writing of new constitutions and thus in the articulation of the powers of the state, the commitment to social uplift and equality has in fact been at the front and centre of such enterprises.

Hannah Arendt may be wrong in identifying politics that concerns itself with social questions as leading to terror. Here, absolutism does not refer to the capriciousness of the Prince or the Leviathan who can take his will as a synonym for right and power. That aspect of absolutism constitutionalism clearly checks. The prophecy regarding terror has not been borne out in democratic countries like India. But absolutism understood as something in which there are no substantive limits on the domain of the political is a feature of power that is committed to alleviating the pressing exigencies of life. Perhaps, not surprisingly, this form of power is especially evident in contemporary India among parties and groups that speak on behalf of those who were historically discriminated against. It is also the very pressing concerns of life that become a central mechanism for conceiving of and emphasizing the unity of the nation. Not unlike the Jacobin projection of *le people, toujour malheureux,* which served as a ground for French unity, poverty, illiteracy, and destitution serve as a constitutional warrant for Indian unity.

It is tempting to think of the perspective that proffers the generality of the *suffering people* as stemming from compassion. However, that would be to mistake a central feature of its underlying motive. Compassion, in the face of suffering, has as its operative modality a commitment to co-suffering, to put oneself in the position of the sufferer or minimally to share in the suffering. It is tethered to a logic of exemplarity, that is, taking the place of the sufferer. Compassion repudiates the perspectival distance required to produce a conception of a whole people, let alone a way of redressing the plight of a whole people. And, finally, compassion, as Martha Nussbaum and Roberto Unger have insightfully pointed out, is deeply, even if not essentially, wedded to an epistemic and ontological uncertainty, that is, to the question of whether the suffering was adequately appraised and fully shared (Nussbaum 2003; Unger 1984). For these reasons, compassion for the most part has been

politically mute, though of course in rare instances, such as with Gandhi, it has profoundly affected the political realm—but even then it typically manifests a philosophical and temperamental reluctance towards the ordinary rationale of national politics.

In contrast, the perspective of pity faces no such obstacles. Since pity maintains a distance from its object, it can conceive of the object as embodying an abstraction, or representing a type, such as the poverty-stricken or the disadvantaged castes or the people of India. And because it is not limited by the injunction to share in the plight of those it perceives, it can imagine a redress to their condition that corresponds to the generality of its perspective. The perspective of pity is replete with the potential for solidarity, and hence unity. There is an important and still grossly under-explored relationship that links pity with the politics of modern nationalism.

The main point that I have been exploring can be made by way of a contrast. Whatever else American constitutionalism in the eighteenth century might have been, it stemmed from a deep distrust of power—in which a distrust of the absolutist prince was just a single instance. The first impulse of this constitutionalism was thus to limit political power, to be suspicious of it, and to constrain its reach. This was one of the things that most struck Tocqueville as he reflected on democracy in America, namely that the Central government was virtually absent and, at best, severely limited in the power at its disposal. In this view, the happiness and freedom of the individual could never be assigned to a distant prospective hope. Perhaps because the American Founding Fathers did not have to contend with the problem of mass poverty and had little concern with the issue of slavery, or perhaps because they were the last adherents to the idea that politics was about freedom and not the pressing necessities of life and the body, they could still articulate a constitutional vision in which political power was not absolute. When John Adams announced, 'Power had to be opposed by power', he meant that power, specifically political power, had to be limited. A central part of that limitation was that it would not redress the sufferings of the body, and would not allow its vision to be guided by that goal. Of course, in our own times, it has become clear that there is indeed an inhumanity to that limitation on power and the conception of the public interest that it can fashion.

Such a chastened conception of power and politics is plainly not the case with constitutionalism in much of the twentieth century, and in India in particular. This constitutionalism must and does constitute power, and increases and celebrates its ambit. It is only through politics and the specific kind of power it sanctions that the nation can be imagined, administered, and made just. However, it must be added that in that vision, freedom is recessed, and the tendency for political power to operate without limits deeply ingrained.

NOTES

1. 'For a long time we have had various plans for a free India in our minds, but now, when we are beginning the actual work, I hope, you will be one with me when I say, that we should present a clear picture of this plan to ourselves, to the people of India and the world at large. The resolution that I am placing before you defines our aims, describes an outline of the plan and points the way which we are going to tread' (Jawaharlal Nehru, *CAD* 1999, p. 57).

2. '...India after being dominated for a long period has emerged as a free sovereign democratic independent country, and that is a fact that changes and is changing history.... That is a tremendous responsibility. Freedom brings responsibility; of course, there is no such thing as freedom without responsibility.... Therefore, we have to be conscious of this tremendous burden of this responsibility which freedom has brought: the discipline of freedom and the organized way of working freedom. But there is something even more than that. The freedom that has come to India by virtue of many things, history, tradition, resources, our geographical position, our great potential and all that, inevitably leads India to play an important part in world affairs. It is not a question of our choosing this or that; it is an inevitable consequence of what India is and what a free India must be. And because we have to play that inevitable part in world affairs, that brings another and greater responsibility' (Jawaharlal Nehru, *CAD* 1999, Book 2, vol. VII, pp. 319–20).

3. 'We cannot say that the republican tradition is foreign to the genius of this country. We have had it from the beginning of our history...Panini, Megasthenes and Kautilya refer to the Republics of Ancient India. The Great Buddha belonged to the Republic of Kapilavastu' (Sarvepalli Radhakrishnan's speech to the Constituent Assembly, 20 January 1947, *CAD* vol. 1, p. 272). Also see Chakrabarty (2000, pp. 9–11).

4. I am indebted to an unpublished paper by Pratap Bhanu Mehta for some of the formulations in this and the previous paragraph.

5. For Gandhi's views on civilization and history, see Parel (1997, pp. 66–71).

REFERENCES

Arendt, Hannah. 1990. *On Revolution*. London: Penguin Books.

Austin, Granville. 1966. *The Indian Constitution: Cornerstone of a Nation*. Oxford: Clarendon Press.

Bhabha, Homi. 1994. *The Location of Culture*. London: Routledge.

Chakrabarty, Dipesh. 2000. *Provincializing Europe*. Princeton: Princeton University Press.

Constituent Assembly Debates. 1999. New Delhi: Lok Sabha Secretariat.

Farrand Max (ed.). 1966. *The Records of the Federal Convention of 1787*. New Haven, CT: Yale University Press.

Gandhi, M.K. 1984. *Collected Works of Mahatma Gandhi*. Publications Division, Ministry of Information and Broadcasting, Govt. of India, vol. 55, p. 426.

Kashyap, Subhash C. 2004. *Our Constitution: An Introduction to India's Constitution and Constitutional Law*. New Delhi: National Book Trust.

Mehta, Uday S. 1999. *Liberalism and Empire*. Chicago: The University of Chicago Press.

Mill, J.S. 1975a. 'On Liberty', in J.S. Mill, *Three Essays*. Oxford and New York: Oxford University Press.

———. 1975b. 'Considerations on Representative Government', in J.S. Mill, *Three Essays*. Oxford and New York: Oxford University Press.

Nussbaum, Martha. 2003. *Upheavals of Thought*. Cambridge: Cambridge University Press.

Parel, Anthony J. (ed.). 1997. *Hind Swaraj and Other Writings*. Cambridge: Cambridge University Press.

Rao, Sir B.N. 1960. *India's Constitution in the Making*. Calcutta: Orient Longman.

Report of the Indian Franchise Committee. 1932. Calcutta: Government of India.

Seervai, H.M. 1999. *Constitutional Law of India*. New Delhi: Universal Book Traders.

Sen, Amartya. 2000. *Freedom as Development*. New York: Anchor Edition.

Shklar, Judith N. 1998.*Redeeming American Political Thought*. Chicago: University of Chicago Press.

Unger, Roberto. 1984. *Passion*. New York: Free Press.

3 Parliament

Vernon Hewitt and Shirin M. Rai

India is a bicameral parliamentary democracy. The lower house is called the Lok Sabha (House of the People) and has 545 members. The upper house is called the Rajya Sabha (House of the States) with 250 members. Representatives are elected on a first-past-the-post (FPTP) basis by single-member constituencies for the lower house, and mostly by proportional representation from state assemblies for the upper. Fifteen per cent of all seats in the lower house are reserved for candidates drawn from the Scheduled Castes (SCs) (lower castes, called SCs after the Ninth Schedule of the Indian Constitution in which this provision was made; also known as Dalits) and 7.5 per cent for Scheduled Tribes (STs) (Jayal 2006: 118). Both of these groups benefit from such affirmative action on the basis of their long-standing material deprivation and social and economic discrimination.

Independent India has long claimed, and with much justification, to be the world's largest democracy. With the exception of the Internal Emergency between June 1975 and March 1977, and subject to varying incidents of socio-economic violence (Jalal 1995; Brass 2006) India has witnessed functioning Parliaments

in which government legislation has been amended or withdrawn through opposition participation, and in which opposition parties have regularly defeated incumbent governments. More political parties are present in the national Parliament than at any time since Independence—seven national and forty-five state registered parties contested elections in 2009 (Election Commission, 2009: http://eci.nic.in/eci_main/ElectoralLaws/OrdersNotifications/symbols170309.pdf). In 2004, 1,351 candidates stood from six nationally recognized parties, 801 candidates from thirty-six recognized state parties, and 2,385 individuals stood as independent candidates. In 2004, an average of ten candidates stood per constituency, up from 3.8 in 1952, but down from 1996's extraordinary 25.6 candidates per constituency—a reduction brought about by legislation aimed at eliminating frivolous candidates (Election Commission). Any Indian citizen who is registered as a voter and is over 25 years of age is allowed to contest elections to the Lok Sabha or State Legislative Assemblies. For the Rajya Sabha, the age limit is 30 years (Election Commission of India, http://www.eci.gov.in/ElectoralSystem/elecsys_fs.htm). In the previous, fourteenth, Lok Sabha, there

were forty-five women MPs—about 8.5 per cent of
the total. The increase in women's representation in
the Indian political system has therefore been relatively
small. Electoral turnouts for the national Parliament
are robust by international standards, as high as 77
per cent, although the turnout in 2004 was 59 per
cent, with the state turnout for Jammu and Kashmir
the lowest at 35.2 per cent (http://www.eci.gov.
in/StatisticalReports/LS_2004/vol_1_ls_2004_
pdf. accessed on 17 February 2009). Broader still,
Parliament is reported on and debated in a vibrant,
multilingual press and media, and is the subject of both
satire and humour (Mitra and Singh 1999).

This chapter will focus on the formal institutions
of Parliament, predominantly at the national level.
It will examine the changing socio-economic and
cultural backgrounds of the representatives who
sit in the legislatures, and examine how and in
what ways they 'mirror' India's highly pluralistic
social order. It will examine not just the procedures
through which Parliament seeks to check executive
powers and influence policy, but will also seek to
evaluate its effectiveness in translating representation
into policy (Jayal 2006). The essay will also assess
the interaction between the differing levels of
the parliamentary system inasmuch as the Indian
Constitution privileges the Union government to
act in the face of political breakdown in the states,
as well as the relationship between parliamentary
representation, the judiciary, and the wider electoral
and party system itself (Jayal 1999).

The institutions of parliamentary government
are an established element in Indian political culture,
structuring the forms and idioms of social and cultural
activity and, by definition, profoundly influencing the
nature of extra-parliamentary protest. Parliament is part
of a wider political process. It was once fashionable to
discuss politics and society without reference to the
formal institutions of state and government at all, a
habit rightly discarded (Bose and Jalal 1996; Corbridge
and Harriss 2000/2001). Yet, it would be equally
remiss to concentrate on these institutions to the
exclusion of the wider sociological and anthropological
perspectives established by recent scholarship,
especially with regard to subaltern historiographies
(Pandey 2006; Tarlo 2003; Gould 2002). An adequate

analysis of Parliament requires a synergy of these
various approaches and methodologies (Chatterjee
2004). Social protests are often aimed at influencing
parliamentary representation as opposed to removing
or abolishing it, and they have often been successful
in influencing parliamentary institutions and the party
system (Hewitt 1994; Mitra 1992).

The dynamics of parliamentary representation
have thus played a crucial role in structuring the
emergence of new types of political identity and
responding to the rise of broader social interests,
thus ensuring Parliament's long-term legitimacy
(Brown 1999; Jaffrelot 2003). The 1990s arguably
saw the most dramatic change in the composition of
Members of Parliament (MPs) in the Lok Sabha since
Independence, with an increase in the so-called 'Other
Backward Classes' (OBCs)[1] returning MPs from a
number of parties. Moreover, social categories that
identify elites and non-elites continue to fragment,
complicating debates in representation and how to
ensure its effectiveness. Together with the increasing
presence of the OBCs, Parliament has also, during
this period, fiercely debated the issue of gender-
based quotas for parliamentary seats—without any
resolution yet in sight (Rai 1997). The 1990s also saw
Parliament accommodate coalition politics, with many
different state-based parties becoming prominent in
the legislative debates and processes. Furthermore,
issues of corruption and increasing intra-institutional
competition from such agencies as the Supreme Court
and the lower judiciary have added to concerns over
a palpable democratic deficit in India, which belie its
otherwise remarkable success story (Singh 2002).

However, as Jayal has noted, while Parliament has
'certainly changed, as many non-elite groups that were
not formally part of the political process now are', it is
not clear to what extent this inclusion has led to the
policy initiatives that have significantly improved the
lot of the poor and disadvantaged that such MPs claim
to represent (2006: 2).

PARLIAMENTARY ORIGINS

The genesis of India's Parliament can be traced back
to the British response to the crisis of 1857, and
the passage of the Government of India Act 1858,

which created a Council for India to advise the newly constituted office of Viceroy and Secretary of State (Moore 1999). Colonial conceptions of good government were not about representation and accountability, but about consultation and efficiency (Hewitt 2006). However, between 1861 and 1892 and the passing of various Indian Councils Acts, an emergent English-speaking elite brought sufficient pressure to bear on the British authorities to make these bodies more accountable, and widen their scope of deliberation.

Thus, by the eve of World War I, Indians were sitting on a whole series of legislatures, had some token presence within the executive, could debate budget issues, and local and self-governing bodies could elect members as representatives of municipal interests (Brown 1999; Raychaudhuri 1999). British insistence on the links between colonial reform, representation, and Parliament, however ethnocentric and confined by racism, nevertheless ensured that emergent legislative bodies were seen by elites as valuable conduits for political patronage and influence. It would also, in the long term, familiarize India's political elite with the peculiarities of parliamentary forms of government, both as an arena of practical politics and as a political ideal worth striving for. As early as 1907, and during the expulsion of extremists from the Congress at Surat, legislative reforms were sufficiently important to sideline more extremist forms of anti-British protest (Sarkar 1989).

As Brown notes, 'Parliamentary institutions in India evolved in a context of rapid socio-economic and cultural change', and a culture marked by political protest that both pressurized and responded to the scale of constitutional reform on offer (Brown 1999). The experience of this dialectic between parliamentary and extra-parliamentary pressure led to the demand for universal franchise being made an integral demand in the nationalist protest, as well as one that defined its shape and content, even if it did not question the broader structures of representative government itself (Jayal 2006: 7). India's elite was committed to inheriting a British political system, essentially premised on Westminster and the idiosyncrasies of 'independent' representation, as opposed to a mandated and referenda-based

decision-making (Birch 1971; Birch 2001). Despite arguments that such a system was inappropriate for an ethnically diverse country marked by significant degrees of social, cultural, and religious differences, (Rueschmeyer *et al.* 1992) debates on proportional representation and local government initiatives were sidelined in favour of FPTP (Austin 2003).

The Indian Constitution moderated British parliamentarianism only with reference to affirmative action for specifically identified social groups, which were deemed to have been materially disadvantaged to a degree that would act as a barrier to entering the Parliament. Discrimination was applied to manipulate parliamentary representation to promote 'effective equality', and was initially perceived as a temporary measure (Brass 1994). Committed to the idea that Parliament should mirror societal plurality, little thought was given at the time of Independence to the problematic relationship between 'the represented and the representative', especially in the context of the changing outlines of multiple social identity, and wider disparities between parliamentary legislation and their effective implementation. At the same time, the history of the nationalist movement meant that provisions for reservations for the Dalits were not extended to Muslims and other minorities, resulting in substantial inequities in representation (Justice Sachar 2006).

PARLIAMENTARY STRUCTURES

The Indian Prime Minister is the head of the executive, and his or her position rests on being the head of a political party with the largest number of MPs sitting in the Lok Sabha. The Lok Sabha is made up of representatives elected from single-member constituencies, including the Speaker, and two nominated members from the Anglo-Indian community (under Article 331 of the Constitution). The day-to-day functioning of parliamentary government, the ordering of business, and the finessing of procedures rely on the role of the Speaker and the Deputy Speaker of the house. Indian Prime Ministers have predominantly been members of the Indian National Congress, but with the onset of coalitions since the 1990s, Prime Ministers have come from a number of political parties, some quite small. Between 1996 and 1998, for example, the Janata Dal party formed a government despite holding a mere 46 seats, less than a tenth of the entire lower chamber (Jayal 2006: 19).

Ultimately, however, governments retain office so long as they can command a working majority (half the membership of the house plus one). In the case of a premature dissolution, the President acts on the advice of the outgoing Prime Minister, advice from his own office, and, if necessary, the Supreme Court, to either reconstitute a leader who can command a majority or call for fresh elections. Presidential discretion—the extent to which prime ministerial advice is binding—has been controversial, especially when the Prime Minister's position is insecure. Such discretion was first seen during the Janata Party collapse of 1979, when the President dissolved the Lok Sabha on the advice of a leader who had failed to secure a majority of the House (the late Charan Singh), and without calling the leader of the opposition to form a government (Austin 2003: 471).

Lok Sabha seats have been historically revised in light of the 10-year census to ensure that each constituency represents roughly the same number of people. However, following a Constitutional Amendment in 1976, constituency boundary revisions were suspended until the 2001 census, ostensibly to prevent family planning targets distorting the seats of very large states. Although a Delimitation Committee was appointed in 2003 to adjust boundaries, the 2004 elections took place in constituencies drawn up nearly 30 years earlier. This has led to some wide discrepancies in the number of voters per constituency, some with as many as 25,000,000 and some as small as 50,000. Variations also exist in terms of geographical area; the largest constituency in India is Ladakh, 173 m, 227 square km in size, while the smallest is Chandni Chowk in New Delhi, a mere 10.59 square km (Electoral Commission).

Bicameralism is a significant feature of Indian parliamentary practice. The Rajya Sabha is a smaller body, with staggered indirect elections and members serving a period of six years and a third of its body up for election every two years. As such, the Rajya Sabha cannot be dissolved. The legislatures of the 27 Indian states and remaining Union Territories vote for 223

MPs. A further 12 are nominated by the President on the grounds of outstanding national service in a wide range of professions. Prime Ministers advise the President over the nomination of likely candidates, but the convention has long been established that such nominations ought not to reflect party loyalties; rather, individuals drawn from the professions and whose wider political experience will be of benefit to parliamentary decisions generally should be nominated. The Rajya Sabha has limits to its ability to check and frustrate legislation emanating from the directly elected lower chamber. It cannot vote on a money bill, nor can it filibuster on it, and the number of times it can return legislation passed by the Lok Sabha is limited. It can, however, initiate legislation. The Rajya Sabha has a Chairperson who conducts its business. Manmohan Singh is the first Indian Prime Minister to sit in the Rajya Sabha.

The President, whose address sets out the government's agenda following a successful election, opens the formal parliamentary year, neatly substituting the Monarch's Speech at the beginning of the British Parliament. Traditionally, Parliament sits in three sessions, the relatively lengthy winter session, the budget session, starting in January, and the short monsoon session. Governments timetable their legislative programmes through the Leader of the House, in conjunction with the Cabinet and Prime Minister's Secretariat, and the Business Advisory Committee. Such programmes reflect the manifesto commitments made by the parties, as well as the pressures brought to bear by such processes as opposition pressure and private member initiatives.

One of the most under-researched areas of Indian parliamentary practice concerns its committee structure, both as bodies in their own right and as constituting a distinct phase in the passing and consolidation of legislation that adds to the effectiveness of Parliament (Thakur 1995). An effective committee structure is one that, regardless of the brute majority of the House, is able to bring diverse party opinion to scrutinize proposed legislation as it evolves, and to inform debate to improve policy effectiveness (Kyle and Peacey 2002). Historically, the committee structures of the Indian Parliament have been weak, reflecting large government majorities, weak party discipline amongst the opposition, and a scrutiny process that is voluntary, and therefore largely under the control of the government. If wider consultations with the opposition are deemed appropriate or necessary, the government can refer legislation to standing committees after the second reading, or convene an ad hoc committee specifically for the purpose.

The decline in single-party governments since the 1990s has stimulated the role and function of committees, and increased the need for governments to use them in managing broad coalitions. As the number of parties has increased in the House, the committee structure has become more representative of parliamentary membership, and this has enhanced their function when dealing with proposed government legislation. New committees have been formed recently, in such areas as parliamentary security and issues of ethics, and the behaviour of members. Parliament also set up a Committee for Women's Empowerment in 1997, the remit of which is to consider government legislation in light of the National Commission for Women and its recommendations concerning affirmative action. As of 2004, there are 19 committees, all but four of which are required to table their reports to Parliament. A majority of them do not allow members to remain if they become ministers. As of 2004–5, there were seven ad hoc committees. The most significant committees are the Public Undertakings Committee, the Estimates Committee, the Public Accounts Committee, and the Business Advisory Committee. Interestingly, currently a member of the opposition chairs Public Accounts Committee, which was set up in 1923 and, as such, is one of the oldest committees in the Indian Parliament.

The Privileges Committee is an important body, deciding on issues of parliamentary conduct, with limited powers of investigation. This is one of the most active committees in Parliament (Thakur 1995). The Committee on Assurances is significant in that it follows up matters arising during question time and the various calling attention motions wherein ministers, unable to respond immediately, promise to bring answers to the House at a later date. The committee scrutinizes these promises, and investigates whether information was provided within a specified time frame. Committee reports frequently deal with requests from government ministers to be excluded from various assurances for a whole variety of reasons, many of which are found to be specious. The memberships of committees are largely nominated, some voted on through a PR system and a single transferable vote, and some consisting of members from the Rajya Sabha.

The Speaker, usually through consensus, convenes ad hoc committees, although votes have taken place in some cases. The Estimates Committee, made up of thirty members elected each year from the Lok Sabha, has the crucial job of scrutinizing government department estimates and recommending economies (Thakur 1995: 15). It was this Joint parliamentary Committee that, in 1991, unearthed a 1.3 billion dollar scam in the Ministry of Petroleum, and censured the then minister responsible.

One of the most significant types of ad hoc committees is the Parliamentary Committee of Enquiry, set up under the auspices of the Speaker, to look into and report on a particular issue of concern, and lay a report before the House. There is also the Commission of Enquiry Act (loosely based on the British Royal Commission of Enquiry Acts), which involves the appointment by the government of a broader-based enquiry into an issue of national interest. Such a commission is in the gift of the government, and has a broader remit in calling and cross-examining witnesses, but has the advantage of being a statutory document with a mandatory parliamentary debate attached to it.

Finally, the Indian Constitution provides for the promulgation of Presidential ordinances, in which the President passes legislation into immediate effect under the advice of the Prime Minister, and subject to parliamentary approval, within a specified time period (usually thirty days). Ordinances can only be issued when Parliament is not in session. Ordinances were devised to deal with issues such as national emergencies and the breakdown in state governments throughout the federal system. Wider ordinance powers were consciously shaped on elements of the 1935 Government of India Act, and on the role of emergency legislation in other countries (Austin

2003). They remain controversial in that they allow the executive a route to bypass Parliament, ignore the committee structure, and present the House with what is, in effect, a *fait accompli*.

PARLIAMENTARY MEMBERSHIP

Derived from a British discourse of liberal reform, parliamentary legitimacy claims to stem from its representativeness of society as a whole, its ability to 'mirror' wider social diversity, and to allow non-elites or subalterns access to the political process through their individual right to a free and fair vote. Until the 1990s, with one or two notable exceptions, Indian MPs reflected the dominance of a political, forward caste elite, constituting a middle class formed from the late nineteenth century onwards, and presiding over a profoundly hierarchical and unequal social order (Brass 1994; Jaffrelot 2003). And even though this is now changing, the 'poor and the dispossessed' are still under-represented.

Unlike the British case, issues of liberty in India are complicated by the imbrications of group and individual rights, and by the extent to which social plurality in India creates overlapping identities between religion, and cultural and material deprivation (Harriss-White 2004; Jayal 2006). The attempts to redress the under-representation of some groups began under the British government, which introduced quotas for a range of minorities under the Government of India Act of 1935, and a series of separate electorates for differing religious communities to ensure their presence within the legislatures. Separate electorates were abolished at Independence, and the Constitution set out to create a secular state in which religion, by itself, was not subject to separate treatment (Smith 1968). The Dalit leader Babasaheb Ambedkar, member of the Constituent Assembly of India, first articulated the need for quotas for the lowest castes and tribes on the grounds of poverty and exclusion, which would otherwise prevent them from exercising their individual rights as citizens of India (Baxi and Parekh 1998).

Such a commitment was enshrined in the Constitution and called 'reservations' or quotas under the Ninth Schedule (Articles 330 and 331).[2] They

were in the first instance provided for fifty years, but under the Sixty-second Amendment Act 1989 extended for another 40 years, pointing to the political sensitivity of removal of quotas once they have been established. Moreover, once established, reservations for SCs and STs while improving their presence within the Lok Sabha, have arguably led to the reproduction of sub-elites[3] within these groups, which does not necessarily benefit from the politics of the group as a whole. Moreover, as noted above, other disadvantaged groups such as OBCs and, recently, Most Backward Castes, politically active since the 1990s, had sought to extend quotas to ensure access to Parliament despite the fluidity of such identity politics, and the difficulties of extending quotas without eventually compromising the principle of equality.

Indian Muslims, for example, do not benefit from a separate quota, on the grounds that theirs is a religious category. Nonetheless, Muslims remain amongst the poorest of India's citizens and as such, suffer from material deprivation. Muslims make up just over 12 per cent of the Indian population, but in 2004, they made up a mere 6.44 per cent of the lower house. The figure has ranged from 4.4 per cent in 1952 to over 9 per cent in 1980. Some Muslims have recently called for quotas to redress this issue (Jayal 2006; Justice Sachar 2006).

Also, while 22 per cent of parliamentary seats were reserved for the SCs, no reservation was made for women. When the issue of women's under-representation was discussed in the Constituent Assembly, the women's movement came out strongly against quotas on the grounds of equal citizenship rights (Rai and Sharma 2000). The demand for greater representation of women in political institutions in India was not taken up in a systematic way until the setting up of the Committee on the Status of Women in India (CSWI), which published its report in 1976. In 1988, the National Perspective Plan for Women again focused on the political representation of women, and suggested that a 30 per cent quota for women be introduced at all levels of elective bodies. While a quota of 33 per cent was introduced at the level of village governing councils (panchayats), a Bill to introduce a quota at the national level has not yet been passed, despite many attempts and bitter debates (Rai 1999; Bates and Basu 2005). One of the issues blocking this Bill has been that concerning the elite profile of women who are elected to Parliament. There were 45 women members in the fourteenth Indian Parliament, a mere 8.9 per cent in the Lok Sabha and 11.9 per cent in the Rajya Sabha. If we examine the profile of women MPs, we find that women representatives in the Indian Parliament are mostly middle-class professionals, with few or no links with the women's movement. A significant number of them accessed politics through their families, some through various student and civil rights movements, and some because of state initiatives to increase representation from the lower castes. This selective inclusion of women into mainstream politics has tended to maintain divisions within the women's movement, posing difficult questions for representation of and by women.

More generally, the consequences of the quota approach to under-representation have been problematic. It has led to the allegation of exacerbating unequal rights, not on the basis of principle, but of political opportunism (Kothari 1994), and to the argument that through affirmative action based on material deprivation, religious identities have proliferated within a secular polity (Madan 1998).

PARLIAMENTARY PRACTICE

The efficacy of Parliament is not only a function of the access disadvantaged and marginal groups have to Parliament, it is also a function of their presence within the specific parties working inside Parliament to represent social interests and advocate policies on their behalf. W.H. Morris-Jones once candidly observed that 'the way in which parliamentary democracy works, depends more than we might like to admit on the balance of powers between political parties'(Morris-Jones 1957: 113). In the context of colonial reform, the Congress converted itself from an elite-led social movement into a political party, seeking to gain office and inherit the *Raj* as much as transform it. Although it retained a broad organizational wing after Independence, the parliamentary wing soon eclipsed this (Morris-Jones 1957). Candidates for high office were outstanding nationalists, not so much

the stuff of party politics as of nation-building and political emancipation. As such, Congress dominated the national Parliament, with Nehru dominating the party until his death in 1964, and the elections of 1967. Any diversity of opinion within Parliament at this time was as much a function of the diversity of the Congress itself. This has had a profound effect on the evolution of Parliament since Independence, and as the Congress atrophied, it was to have an impact on the workings of the Parliament itself (Brass 1994).

The presence of a formal opposition in the Lok Sabha has been, until relatively recently, marginal, with a significant number of non-Congress MPs being independents, and many parties being effectively dominated by personalities and families. Nonetheless, opposition parties have been able to obtain from the Speaker adequate parliamentary time in the form of calling attention notices, debates under Rule 184, half-hour debates, and privilege motions. Between 1971 and 1975, and again during 1980–9, there were a record number of privilege motions granted against the Prime Minister. These, as well as formal no-confidence motions, have been frequently allowed, and in exceptional circumstances have produced salutary effects even on governments with large majorities. In the wake of the 1962 Indo-China War, for example, Nehru faced the only no-confidence motion in his long parliamentary career and, despite his majority, the 'mood of the house' demanded the resignation of his Minister of Foreign Affairs and a public recognition of the failure of the government's foreign policy in general (Brown 2003).

Yet, Nehru was to some extent an exception. Despite the scale of his parliamentary majorities, he sought to create an atmosphere of trust and consultation with the opposition, at least at the national level (Khilnani 1997). For Nehru, Parliament was almost a moral institution, an emblem of India's modernity (Chandra *et al.* 1999). For other Prime Ministers it was something to be endured or, at worst, curtailed. Bequeathed by colonialism, redefined in the context of nationalist agitation, and consolidated during a time of large one-party majorities, Parliament and the conventions of parliamentary procedures *alone* often proved ineffective in controlling the executive or holding specific Prime Ministers to account, no matter how generous the Speaker is with parliamentary time (see below).

Governments with the will to mislead and manipulate Parliament have often had the majorities to do so. The worst cases come from the Emergency period and the passing of the Forty-second Amendment in 1976, which ironically, sought to extend the scope of parliamentary amendment over the Constitution as a whole, but in the interests of a centralized, unrepresentative party structure (Austin 2003; Hewitt 2008). There are other, less dramatic examples of the manipulation of Parliament by the executive. For example, in 1983, Mrs Gandhi convened the Sarkaria Commission to look into the vexed question of centre-state relations (following unprecedented activity by the opposition parties outside of Parliament), but did so without reference to the Commissions of Enquiry Act in the legislation. As such, she would not be obliged to lay such a report before the House if it made any unfavourable recommendations, which is exactly what she did (Austin 2003). Rajiv Gandhi sought to use his large parliamentary majority between 1984 and 1989 to amend the Commission of Enquiries Act so as to circumvent laying a specifically controversial report before Parliament (Hewitt 1994).

Given their numerical weakness, and faced with a Prime Minister who saw them either as a nuisance or as a threat to national security, the opposition could rarely defeat government legislation. In this context, the opposition devised extensive extra-parliamentary protests and disruptive behaviour to try and frustrate the government from automatically converting a bill into law. Such policies complemented and did not eclipse parliamentary institutions, and such behaviour would become an established part of opposition politics in India right to the present day. Such forms of protest take place both inside and outside Parliament, and again rely on an extensive and independent print and visual media to report events and inform members as much as the public.

Disrupting parliamentary activity through walkouts, the staging of dharnas and gheraos of ministers are specific idioms of protest that date back to the political culture of the freedom struggle (Sarkar 1989). At times they have been potentially violent, but

incidents of assault or abductions of elected members have been confined in the main to the state assemblies. During the Ninth Lok Sabha (1985–9, a period in which the then Congress government had the largest majority ever), there were on an average three walkouts per parliamentary session, usually following a ruling by the Speaker against the opposition, or in protest over some specific piece of legislation or a particular minister. In most cases, the Speaker and the Privileges Committee have resolved the matter, and so such events, when reported, tend to distort their overall significance on parliamentary procedure. Such forms of protest have continued to take place in the era of coalition governments and dramatically reduced majorities, where they can be used alongside formal calling attention notices or no-confidence motions to telling effect. Again, the emphasis here is not on the tension between 'acceptable' and 'unacceptable' forms of behaviour as such, but on the synergy between the two. Walkouts and disruptions overwhelmed the Lok Sabha in the wake of the demolition of the Ayodhya mosque in 1992, and also caused considerable difficulties for the National Front governments in 1996–8 during debates over the Uniform Civil Code (UCC), and during the readings of the Bill to introduce reservation of seats for women in parliamentary elections (Hewitt 2000; Rai 1997).

The frequency of such incidents can, especially during the budget session, have a serious effect on parliamentary business and the overall efficiency of the house. As the Speaker noted in 2002:

> It is with some satisfaction that I can say that from 15th July to 2nd August, 2002, only seven hours and 22 minutes of the time of the House were lost due to interruptions, which is mere 6.10 per cent of the total time as compared to 30.04 per cent during the previous Session...I am...concerned at the national waste caused by the adjournment of the House day after day without transacting any business. (*LSD* 2001)

The source of the ongoing conflict referred to petroleum licensing and allegations of government corruption. In the end the Speaker dissolved the house *sine die*, in the hope that MPs could return to their constituencies and 'reflect on the merit of their conduct'. Some MPs interviewed by one of us blamed the televising of parliamentary sessions for such disruption—'any chance of being seen on TV, however unseemly, is considered good publicity'. This also feeds into the discourse around the falling quality of MPs as the upper-class/caste bias dilutes. While there might be some truth in both these propositions, it is also true that disruption of parliamentary business by the opposition has a longer history than the televising of debates or the widening profile of MPs. Most of the women MPs interviewed by Rai suggested that, contrary to expectation, they did not find it difficult to either witness or even occasionally participate in such disruptive behaviour—'I am surprised at myself when I find myself in the well of the house,' said one MP.

Opposition parties have often coordinated their protests with wider demonstrations of popular support 'outside' Parliament, through well-tried Gandhian techniques as well as forms of protest and peaceful demonstration that are well known in any wider democratic context. One of the most dramatic uses of Gandhian-style forms of pressure on elected governments was levied against Indira Gandhi in 1975, when Morarji Desai, her former Finance Minister, threatened to fast unto death until Mrs Gandhi allowed state elections to be held in the state of Gujarat, and also repealed the notorious Maintenance of Internal Security Act (MISA). Mrs Gandhi objected to what she saw as an 'irrational' form of protest, but nonetheless called state elections (Frankel 2005). During the 1990s, the Bharatiya Janata Party (BJP) proved remarkably effective in combining extra-parliamentary protests to pressurize the government over the Ayodhya issue. Where such tactics are used widely and in areas of acute social tension, the ability to retain and direct peaceful protest is limited. Many commentators seek to respect the cultural roots of this type of protest, but condemn the irresponsibility of deploying it so indiscriminately (Chandra et al. 1999: 473).

Others note the context in which it has proved to be effective and in the wider interests of retaining representative institutions. Agitations in Gujarat and Bihar in the 1970s showed how effective extra-parliamentary protests can be in forcing parliamentary elections in situations of widespread social unrest. In the specific case of the Jayaprakash Narayan movement, widespread irregularities, ministerial corruption, and gratuitous Central intervention were cited as justifying the recourse to such measures, and in both cases such movements converted themselves into political actors contesting seats in subsequent elections. However, the balance here is a fine one. In extreme cases Parliament is bypassed by such action, and the entire basis of representative government appears undermined.

One other form of protest that has emerged in the context of large majorities is quite different from those touched upon above. It constitutes a sort of excessive legalism, almost a caricature of the parliamentary process itself. Such protests involve the opposition calling a proposed legislation into question because of the form in which it is submitted, drafted, or even time-tabled. In 1970, Mrs Gandhi's then minority government tabled a bill to abolish Princes Privy Purses—in effect a pension granted to India's former ruling princely houses—as a Government 'Money' Bill. This reduced the majority needed to secure its passage into law, and prevented the Rajya Sabha from voting on it. The opposition argued that it in fact constituted a Constitutional Amendment Bill, which would allow the upper house to vote on it. The Speaker agreed, and the bill was defeated in the upper house, much to Mrs Gandhi's outrage. In May 1975 the non-CPI opposition, led by two very experienced parliamentarians (Atal Bihari Vajpayee and Morarji Desai), persuaded the Speaker to withdraw a Bill aimed at extending preventive detention because the Ministry of Law had drafted it poorly. In 1986, an opposition attempt to get Rajiv Gandhi's Post Offices (Amendment) Bill defined as a Constitutional Amendment Bill on the grounds that it authorized the interception of personal mail and was thus an issue of fundamental rights, was less successful. In 1989, the non-Congress opposition was able to force the government to withdraw its crucial Panchayati Raj Constitutional Amendment Bill on the grounds that the preamble to the proposed Bill contained anomalies. In 2000, the National Democratic Alliance's (NDA) introduction of the Freedom of Information Act was subject to disputes over the way it had been drafted, with reference to its credibility and coherence, calling it, in effect, a charter for lawyers, since it could arguably not be easily implemented or understood (Adeney 2005).

Taken together, these forms of protest and procedure have usually ensured that Parliament has performed its functions in ways that its founders would find unusual. In 1988, Rajiv Gandhi's attempt to limit press freedom—critical to his government's survival in light of the ongoing Bofors scandal—had already cleared its first reading in the Lok Sabha when the government announced that the bill was being withdrawn. Amid parliamentary walkouts, protests to the Speaker, and an orchestrated campaign throughout metropolitan India by the press itself, it would be comforting to see this as the outcome of successful opposition within Parliament. While given the four-fifths majority enjoyed by Congress at the time, such a view needs careful qualification, such forms of protest continue today, with coalition governments now having to negotiate opposition within and outside Parliament.

COALITION GOVERNMENT AND THE ENHANCED ROLE OF THE SPEAKER

Within the Westminster tradition, the Speaker sits at the heart of Parliament, as mediator between government and opposition and as the sole authority over what types of procedures are adopted and when, and whether specific types of behaviour are acceptable or not. The Speaker rules on the validity and placing of calling attention notices, special mentions, motions of parliamentary privilege, half-hour debates, and questions to the ministers, which take place at the onset of parliamentary business each day.

Since the defeat of the Rajiv Gandhi government in 1989 and the rise of coalition governments containing an increasing number of parties (or parties supporting government 'from outside', that is, on the floor of Parliament, but not holding any government office), governments have become more vulnerable to adverse rulings by the Speaker (McMillan 2005). There was a notable increase in the number of Private Members' Bills initiated by the opposition during the Narasimha Rao government of 1991–6, with three in 1993 alone, all of them sponsored by the BJP, on the

issue of the UCC (Hewitt 2000). In the winter session of 2006 alone, a total of 66 Private Members' Bills were introduced in the Lok Sabha (Indian Parliament, http://164.100.24.208/ls/Bills/main_bill_ls.htm, accessed on 17 February 2009).

The Speaker has adapted to these changes with remarkable success. Speakers have never, with one notable exception, been craven to the executive. Only during the Emergency period has a Speaker capitulated entirely to the government. At the beginning of the 1975 monsoon session, the then Speaker accepted the Congress (R) Law Minister's proposal that, for the duration of the Emergency, only government bills could be debated, and all other forms of parliamentary process such as calling attention notices and short debates stood suspended. In less serious times, Speakers have sided with the government against a rowdy, order-paper throwing opposition, and been accused of complicity. In 1987, however, the Speaker actually allowed a privilege motion against himself, tabled by the opposition, for siding with the government on what was then the sensitive and vexed issue of the relationship between the President and the Prime Minister, disallowing a privilege motion that the Prime Minister had misled the House. Chaired by the Deputy Speaker, it was defeated by a large majority.

In the context of coalitions, the prospect of a Speaker and a Prime Minister finding themselves at odds is a real possibility. A dramatic example comes from the minority government of Chandra Shekhar in 1990–1, following the split within the Janata Dal party, which had deprived V.P. Singh of his majority. One of the factions, the Janata Dal (S) headed by Chandra Shekhar, went on to form the government with support from Congress (I). As the January budget session got underway, the Speaker dismissed five cabinet members under the terms of India's Anti-Defection Bill, which specified that if less than a third of the members from a political party defect to join another party, they must resign their seats and seek re-election under their new affiliation. This was a controversial ruling, since the Janata Dal party had been as much a 'forum' as a party, and if the ruling of the Speaker was correct, then in effect the whole government ought to have resigned. The Prime

Minister accepted the ruling, but delayed the resulting by-elections for the maximum six months allowed for a minister to hold office without a seat in Parliament, by which time the government had lost its majority. Interestingly, the then Law Minister threatened to lock the Speaker up, but later apologized to the House for his behaviour.

The visible transformation in the role of the Speaker involves him/her acting as a conciliator and facilitator of government–opposition dialogue. During the violence in Gujarat in 2002, the Speaker became central in trying to broker a deal between the government and the opposition that would enable the issues to be debated in the Lok Sabha to their mutual benefit, and allow the normal business of Parliament to proceed. After much negotiation, a debate was allowed under Rule 184 (a matter of urgent public interest), much to the obvious irritation of the treasury benches. The resulting censure motion condemning the government was defeated by 276 votes to 182, but with a significant number of abstentions, most notably the Telugu Desam party (Adeney 2005). The Speaker regularly convenes meetings with leaders of the opposition parties to work out particular issues, and to try and finesse the use of parliamentary time. This Indian version of the Westminster practice of 'meeting behind the Speaker's chair' is frequently used. As a result, the number of walkouts has declined, and where they have taken place, they have often been explicitly combined with no-confidence motions or the threat to withdraw support from the government in the Lok Sabha itself. With the general exception of the Rao government (1992–6), debates in the lower house have often led to formal divisions through the voting lobbies, to government legislation being defeated or heavily amended, sent back by the Rajya Sabha or referred back by the President.

THE PARLIAMENT: ITS FUTURE ROLE AND POTENTIAL OBSTACLES

With the onset of coalition governments containing significant numbers of small parties, the business of piloting legislation through India's Parliaments has become a fine balancing act, with parliamentary time-tabling frequently derailed over the need for consultations and compromise. The experience of increased representation in Parliaments has often been, paradoxically, one of frustration and delay, wherein lie new dangers and new temptations. One concern is that coalition governments may try and rule by fiat, where constitutionally possible, for fear of seeing proposed legislation mauled by political allies, the committee structure, and opposition voting.

Mention has already been made of the centralizing elements of the Indian Constitution that provide Central governments with recourse to ordinances with reference to government business at the Centre, when Parliament is not in session, and with reference to the breakdown of constitutional authority at the state level. The use of ordinances has long been a controversial one for the opposition, especially during the Indira Gandhi minority government of 1969–71. Ordinances involving President's Rule alone have been the subject of various inquiries and reports, most notably the Sarkaria Commission, and recently the BJP–NDA government's National Commission to Review the Workings of the Constitution (NCRWC) (Adeney 2005).

In circumstances where the Union President is unable or unwilling to refuse Prime Ministerial advice (a subject of great constitutional controversy over the years and itself the subject of two specific Constitutional Amendment Bills, the Forty-second and the Forty-fourth), ordinances have turned what were supposed to be exceptional powers into a procedural device to outmanoeuvre Parliament. When Mrs Gandhi's Law Minister accepted the Speaker's ruling that the Abolition of Princely Purses (amendment) Bill was indeed a constitutional one (see above), and when it was subsequently defeated by three votes in the upper house, the opposition sought assurances that the Prime Minister would not show contempt for Parliament by passing it as an ordinance once the parliamentary session ended. This is exactly what she did, however, as she had done with other important pieces of legislation such as a Banking and Insurance Nationalization Bill, which had been promulgated two days before Parliament reconvened. In 1973 four ordinances were issued, 14 in 1974, and 25 in 1975, distorted somewhat by the Emergency (Austin 2003).

Recent coalition governments have used ordinances to avoid debating legislation with their partners as much as with the opposition, as with V.P. Singh's surprise decision to implement the findings of the Mandal Commission on caste reservation through a Presidential ordinance in August 1990, allegedly without consulting members of his own cabinet. Following widespread social unrest, the government was forced in these circumstances to refer the matter to the Supreme Court, which upheld the decision, although a later ruling, as a consequence of the *Indra Sawhney vs Union of India* verdict in 1992, created a maximum ceiling of reservations at 50 per cent (Jayal 2006: 65). Attempts by V.P. Singh to use an ordinance to compulsorily purchase land in the vicinity of the Ayodhya mosque in order to frustrate plans to build a temple were foiled when it became clear that the government would fail to get it through the Lok Sabha.

Ordinances provide minority governments with a useful device, but one that is now increasingly difficult to convert into legislation once Parliament has convened. The number of ordinances issued in the last Parliament show an appreciable decline with the recent assertion of the authority of the President, whose refusal of some has seemed to act as a deterrent. Likewise, the Supreme Court has been proactive in questioning the legality of ordinances, especially President's Rule, when used for purely partisan purposes or to punish political parties, such as the wholesale dismissal of state governments in the wake of the demolition of the Babri Masjid in 1992 (Austin 2003). In the emerging context where electoral victory at the Centre requires cooperation between regionally-based parties in the states, incidents of President's Rule have declined dramatically. Since Independence, Article 356 has been declared 115 times, often in circumstances where it was perfectly clear that a breakdown in constitutional authority had not taken place, and in many cases before the governor issued a report to the President (Adeney 2005: 10). Yet, in 1997 and 1998, the then Union President refused to allow the Central government to impose President's Rule. He cited an earlier ruling of the Supreme Court in 1994 that extended the principle of judicial review to the circumstances surrounding the use of Article 356, and

reiterated that the executive could only use President's Rule once the state legislature in question had been given the opportunity to prove its majority in a vote. Interestingly enough, the only recent controversy involving Article 356 concerns the failure of the national government to use it in Gujarat in 2002 (Ruparelia 2005).

The end of the Congress era[4] has made Parliament more representative, and has increased its institutional abilities to oversee the executive. The cost of a more fragmented Lok Sabha has been to increase the time needed to pass government bills, an increase in the number of Private Members' Bills, and a dramatic increase in the parliamentary time for debates, questions, and the various calling attention motions. Governments now face increased demands to refer government bills to committees, and the subsequent impact this has on parliamentary time. The period 1999–2004 also saw an enhanced role for the Rajya Sabha in failing to ratify legislation, or where unable to do so, proposing amendments that in some cases were taken up in the third stage of reading in legislation (Austin 2003). While potentially encouraging governments to use ordinances for short-term gains, the evidence is that this merely delays the inevitability of either rethinking the subsequent bill in consultation with Parliament, or facing defeat. In procedural terms, this situation shows a marked improvement over the 1970s, the nadir of constitutionalism, and indeed over the 1980s.

This transformation in Parliament's place within India's system of government is part of wider changes witnessed during the 1990s, reflecting changes in the social milieu brought about by social movements as well as the ongoing political mobilization throughout India's electoral system, and changes to the balance of parties within Parliament (Jaffrelot 2003). The issue of parliamentary representativeness has also widened to include a discussion of how the various social groups represented in Indian society are appropriately reflected in Parliament. The two key and ongoing tensions resulting from this discussion are those around the representation of OBCs and that of women. The various modalities of addressing the representation of these two groups have challenged the way in which Parliament conducts business (the uproar regarding the Women's Bill, for instance), as well as the way it accommodates (or not) the competing interests of a newly developing social and political agenda. The fact that the Women's Bill is still pending will continue to challenge parliamentary practice in the near future.

While many applaud the increasing institutional complexity and interaction within and between state institutions as evidence of credible checks and balances, others are concerned that such trends can prove dangerous to the primacy of Parliament within the Indian political system. Ironically, the rights of Parliament can—and frequently have—been as much curtailed as advanced by the intervention of Presidents and those of the Supreme Court. A President can frustrate the role of a sovereign Parliament merely by delaying legislation or refusing to give it assent. The Supreme Court can, by itself under the power of judicial review, strike down legislation, with significant repercussions for governments and wide areas of social policy. Given the length of time needed for legal opinion to be reached, an enhanced role for the courts risks introducing further delays (Burnell 2002).

Recently, the higher judiciary has not only nagged governments (as in the wake of the Shah Bano case, where the Court blamed the mess on the failure of previous national governments to implement a UCC), it has also threatened to act unilaterally. In contrast to the dialectics of the 1950s–70s, in which the courts opposed the executive's attempts to allow parliamentary amendment over property rights, the role of the courts in the 1990s concerns protecting and extending civil liberties and the concept of political rights. Such social activism threatens to marginalize the legislature in that it exposes the gap between 'representation' within Parliament (the politics of presence) and the actual policy outcomes that such representation generates (Austin 2003; Jayal 2006). Paradoxically, it adds to a palpable democratic deficit by implying that, within Parliament as a whole, 'the politics of recognition have tended to eclipse the politics of redistribution' (Jayal 2006:17) and furthermore, that it is unable to police and reform itself on matters of corruption.

In 2002, for example, the Indian Election Commission ruled that candidates standing for parliamentary elections must declare evidence of criminal records for public scrutiny. The Vajpayee government overturned this decision, and re-wrote the Election Commission's charter through a Presidential Ordinance. When passed, the ordinance was converted into an Amendment Bill to the Representation of the People's Act, showing a remarkable, if worrying, consensus within Parliament over their own need for secrecy (Singh 2002: 140). In 2003, this amendment was struck down by the Supreme Court on the grounds that Parliament was incapable of investigating itself on matters of corruption. While clearly in the public interest, an unelected body intervening to restore the rights of another unelected body is peculiar—if not exceptional. The implications of such advocacy were of some concern to the centrality of Parliament as a law-making institution, and the practicality of having the Supreme Court draft legislation instead of Parliament. This was not an isolated incident. In 2003, the Supreme Court bluntly told Parliament that further delays to the passing of the Freedom of Information Act (introduced in 2000) would not be tolerated, and would lead to the required legislation being passed by the court itself (Singh 2002)!

While many commentators support this stance, especially on matters of political corruption, it risks emasculating Parliament, or diverting the political debate to issues of confrontation and not cooperation. Corruption is one of the key concerns throughout the Indian political system and is in urgent need of attention, but it is not clear that the courts are the best place to initiate policy implementation as opposed to overseeing the constitutional implications of legislation. Yet, if Parliament fails to address the issue itself and to ignore the findings of the Electoral Commission, have not the courts the right to act? Other concerns that underline threats to Parliament's ability to 'know and to act' lie in the recent trends of Prime Ministers to appoint special advisors with the ability to 'spin and obscure' as well as long-standing concerns about the powers of the Prime Minister's Office.

In sharp contrast to most postcolonial societies, Parliament has flourished in India, in part due to its longevity, and in part its ability to absorb and innovate on wider social and cultural practices. While significant aspects of Indian society remain under-represented, the 1990s have seen an important transformation in the socio-economic and cultural backgrounds of MPs sitting in the Lok Sabha. While protest has not always been effectively institutionalized and has surfaced with appalling results as recently as 2002, it has not overwhelmed Parliament or emasculated its ability to censure and criticize, even though it has arguably failed to direct.

Attempts have surfaced, from time to time, to change Parliament or review its place in the Constitution. The most recent, the NCRWC set up in 2000 by the NDA government, was surprisingly uncontroversial. It made practical recommendations to the workings of the government (including a limit to the size of the council of ministers in proportion to the overall size of the legislatures), but left some of the old chestnuts alone—Article 356—an indication of the change in the parliamentary and political climate since the mid-1990s, and showing that the new balance of power between the formal institutions of state had resolved the old grievances. Even amidst what some took to be the rise of a Hindu nation, articulated by cultural forces in complex association with a political party, no alternative vision of Parliament has emerged to command either consensus or enthusiasm (Ruparelia 2005). Co-opted by elites, widely disseminated by a popular press, aired on the radio and the television (and effectively and impressively through the web), Indians have come to cherish their Parliament, and to show pride and respect for it. And yet, while they have often laughed at it, caricatured, and ridiculed it, even at times *despaired* over it, they have never contemplated living without it. Apart from the principle of representation itself, the efficacy of Parliament must ultimately lie in its ability to legislate and implement social policy aimed at satisfying the principles of the Indian Constitution as set out in 1950. In this regard, Parliament has yet to live up to the hopes and aspirations of its founding fathers.

NOTES

1. Socially disadvantaged 'non-elite' groups other than those recognized as SCs and STs, as such, without 'reservation'.

2. Article 331 stipulated a reservation of seats for the Anglo-Indian community for two years if the President considered it under-represented in Parliament.

3. Called the 'creamy layer' by the Supreme Court recently.

4. Mulayam Singh Yadav was said to have declared on 18 April 2007: 'Recalling Mahatma Gandhi's view that the Congress must cease to exist once it achieved its aim of Independence, Mr Singh said this would become a reality at the end of the ongoing poll, which he sought to project as a battle between his Samajwadi Party and the Bharatiya Janata Party' (*The Hindu*, available at www.hindu.com; http://www.hindu.com/2007/04/18/stories/2007041805231400.htm last accessed on 17 February 2009).

REFERENCES

Adeney, K. 2005. 'Hindu Nationalists and Federal Structures in an Era of Regionalism', in K. Adeney and L. Saez (eds), *Coalition Politics and Hindu Nationalism*. London: Routledge, pp. 97–115.

Austin, Granville. 2003. *Working a Democratic Constitution: A History of the Indian Experience*. New Delhi: Oxford University Press.

Bates, C. and S. Basu (eds). 2005. *Rethinking Indian Political Institutions*. London: Anthem Press.

Baxi, Upendra and Bhikhu Parekh (eds). 1998. *Crisis and Change in Contemporary India*. New Delhi: Sage Publications.

Birch, A.H. 2001. *Concepts and Theories of Modern Democracy*, 2nd edn. London: Routledge.

———. 1971. *Representation*. London: Routledge and Kegan Paul.

Bose, S. and A. Jalal (eds). 1996. *Modern South Asia: History, Culture, Political Economy*. New Delhi: Oxford University Press.

Brass, Paul, R. 2006. *Forms of Collective Violence, Riots, Pogroms and Genocide in Modern India*. New Delhi: Three Essays Collective.

———. 1994. *The Politics of India since Independence*, 2nd edn. Cambridge: Cambridge University Press.

Brown, J. 2003. *Nehru: A Political Life*. New Haven: Yale University Press.

———. 1999. 'India', in Judith Brown and W.H. Roger Louis (eds). *The Oxford History of the British Empire: The Twentieth Century*. Oxford: Oxford University Press, pp. 421–46.

Chandra, B., M. Mukherjee, and A. Mukherjee. 1999. *India After Independence*. New Delhi: Viking.

Chatterjee, P. 2004. *The Politics of the Governed: Reflections on Popular Politics in Most of the World*. New York: Columbia University Press.

Corbridge, S. and J. Harriss. 2000/2001. *Reinventing India: Liberalization, Hindu Nationalism and Popular Democracy*. Cambridge: Polity Press.

Frankel, F.R. 2005. *India's Political Economy, 1947–2004: the Gradual Revolution*, 2nd edn. New Delhi: Oxford University Press.

Gould, Jeremy. 2002. 'Anthropology', in Peter J. Burnell (ed.), *Democratization through the Looking Glass*. Manchester: Manchester University Press, pp. 23–40.

Harriss-White, B. 2004. *India Working: Essays on Society and Economy*. New Delhi: Foundation Books.

Hewitt, V. 2008. *Political Mobilisation and Democracy in India: States of Emergency*. Abingdon: Routledge.

———. 2006. 'A Cautionary Tale: Colonial and Post-Colonial Conceptions of Good Government and Democratisation in Africa', *Commonwealth & Comparative Politics*, 44(1), pp. 32–48.

———. 2000. 'Containing Shiva? India, Non-proliferation, and the Comprehensive Test Ban', *Contemporary South Asia*, 9(1), pp. 25–39.

———. 1994. 'Prime Minister and the President', in J. Manor (ed.), *Nehru to the Nineties: The Changing Office of Prime Minister in India*. London: Hurst and Company.

Jaffrelot, C. 2003. *India's Silent Revolution: The Rise of the Low Castes in North Indian Politics*. New Delhi: Permanent Black.

Jalal, A. 1995. *Democracy and Authoritarianism in South Asia: A Comparative and Historical Perspective*. Cambridge: Cambridge University Press.

Jayal, Niraja Gopal. 2006. *Representing India: Ethnic Diversity and the Governance of Public Institutions*. Basingstoke: Palgrave MacMillan.

———. (ed.). 2001. *Democracy in India*. New Delhi: Oxford University Press.

———. 1999. *Democracy and the State: Welfare, Secularism and Development in Contemporary India*. New Delhi: Oxford University Press.

Khilnani, S. (1997) *The Idea of India*. London: Penguin.

Kothari, R. 1994. 'Rise of the Dalits and the Renewed Debate on Caste', *Economic and Political Weekly*, XXIX(26), pp. 1589–94.

Kyle, C.R. and J. Peacey (eds). 2002. *Parliament at Work: Parliamentary Committees, Political Power and Public Access in Early Modern England*. Woodbridge: Boydell Press.

Lok Sabha Debates. 2001. *Lok Sabha Debatee, Thirteenth Lok Sabha Tenth Session, 12th August 2002*. New Delhi: Lok Sabha.

Madan, T.N. 1998. 'Secularism in its Place', in R. Bhargava (ed.), *Secularism and its Critics*. New Delhi: Oxford University Press, pp. 297–320.

McMillan, A. 2005. 'The BJP Coalition: Partisanship and Power-sharing in Government', in K. Adeney and L. Saez (eds), *Coalition Politics and Hindu Nationalism*. London: Routledge, pp. 13–35.

Mitra, S.K. 1992. *Power, Protest and Participation: Local Elites and the Politics of Development in India*. London: Routledge.

Mitra, S.K. and J. Chiriyankandath. 1992. *Electoral Politics in India: A Changing Landscape*. New Delhi: Segment Books.

Mitra, S. and V.B. Singh. 1999. *Democracy and Social Change in India: A Cross Sectional Analysis of the Indian Electorate*. New Delhi: Sage Publications.

Moore, R.J. 1999. 'India in the 1940s', in Robin Winks (ed.), *The Oxford History of the British Empire, Volume V, Historiography*. Oxford: Oxford University Press, pp. 231–42.

Morris-Jones, W.H. 1957. *Parliament in India*. London: Longmans.

Pandey, G. 2006. *The Construction of Communalism in Colonial North India*, 2nd edn. New Delhi: Oxford University Press.

Rai, S.M. 1999. 'Democratic Institutions, Political Representation and Women's Empowerment: The Quota Debate in India', *Democratization*, 6 (3), pp. 84–99.

———. 1997. 'Women in the Indian Parliament', in A.M. Goetz (ed.), *Getting Institutions Right for Women in Development*. London: Zed Press, pp. 104–22.

Rai, S.M. and Kumud Sharma. 2000. 'Democratising the Indian Parliament: The "Reservation for Women" Debate' (with Kumud Sharma) in S. Rai (ed.), *International Perspectives on Gender and Democratisation*. Basingstoke: Macmillan, pp. 149–65.

Raychaudhuri, T. 1999. 'India 1858 to the 1930s' in Robin Winks (ed.), *Oxford History of the British Empire*, Oxford and New York: Oxford University Press, pp. 214–30.

Rueschmeyer, D., E.H. Stephens, and J.D. Stephens. 1992. *Capitalist Development and Democracy*. Cambridge: Polity Press.

Ruparelia, S. 2005. 'The Temptations of Presidentialism: An Explanation of the Evolving Strategy of the BJP', in C. Bates and S. Basu (eds), *Rethinking Indian Political Institutions*. London: Anthem Press, pp. 21–38.

Sachar, Justice Rajindar. 2006. *The Social, Economic and Educational Status of the Muslim Community in India*. The Prime Minister's High Level Committee, Government of India, New Delhi.

Sarkar, S. 1989. *Modern India: 1885–1947*, 2nd edn. Basingstoke: Macmillan.

Singh, Gurharpal. 2002. 'South Asia', in Peter Burnell (ed.), *Democratisation Through the Looking Glass*. Manchester: Manchester University Press, pp. 216–30.

Smith, D.E. 1968. *India as a Secular State*. Princeton: Princeton University Press.

Tarlo, E. 2003. *Unsettling Memories: Narratives of India's 'Emergency'*. New Delhi: Permanent Black.

Thakur, R. 1995. *Government and Politics of India*. Basingstoke: MacMillan.

4 Federalism*

Subrata K. Mitra and Malte Pehl

ederalism is best understood as a method of promoting self-rule and shared rule and of balancing the interests of a nation with that of its regions. Typically, this is done for a dual purpose—that of limiting the possibility of a tyranny of the majority, and of generating strength through union. A durable federal design thus aims at the contradictory goals of reconciling freedom with cohesion, and a diversity of political cultures and identities with effective collective action. Usually, one can assume such a design to be the product of a context with a tradition of political bargaining among autonomous units, and of a political culture leavened with a history of a social contract. None of these *a priori* conditions prepares the student of comparative federalism for the Indian case. With its history of colonial subjecthood and a constitution that is more the result of a transfer of power than of a concerted, organized, violent quest for independent

statehood, based on a contract, India stands apart from the world's major federations. The history of the evolution of India's federalism is a striking contrast to the union of pre-existing political units jealous of their identity, as in the case of the USA. India, not least with its more recent, ambiguous history of crisis government (*State of Emergency* and *President's Rule*), is hardly a model candidate for an optimal path towards a robust federal system. This chapter will show how in India, though it is not among the world's oldest federal political systems, federalism is nevertheless steadily emerging as a key feature of its political system, and as an interesting example of the innovative potential of federalism more generally. The success of India's federal arrangement, as argued in this chapter, derives from a combination of sometimes diverging factors such as its constitution, other institutional arrangements, political practice, and public opinion on these matters.

With a formally relatively clear, constitutionally guaranteed division of power between the Central government and the constituent states,[1] nowadays

*The authors would like to thank the editors of the volume for valuable feedback on an earlier draft of this chapter. All remaining errors are, of course, those of the authors alone.

effectively policed by an independent Supreme Court, separate, direct elections to the Central and regional legislatures, monitored by an independent Election Commission, and the capacity of the political process to sustain a dynamic balance between the jurisdictions of the two sets of governments, India exhibits many of the features of federalism. However, India's membership of this exclusive club remains a matter of some dispute.[2] Indians themselves, as the findings of surveys ranging from 1967 to 1999 indicate,[3] do not appear to share these doubts about the existence and effectiveness of a federal government along with regional and local governments. The political evidence with regard to the characteristics of a federal process[4] is present, and appears to support the conjectures based on the survey data, as shown later in this chapter. Scholarly scepticism persists, nevertheless, and surfaces as part of a larger question: with her multi-ethnic society, structural asymmetry of constituent units, mass illiteracy and poverty, and the uphill task of state-formation and nation-building, why does federalism not lead to a disintegration of the political community and system as a whole?[5] This chapter addresses some of these issues through its analysis of the innovative character of Indian federalism.

Since the indiscriminate use of the concepts of federalism, federal systems, and the federal process might lead to confusion, following Watts and building on notions from Elazar (Watts 1998; Elazar 1994; Elazar 1987), the terms will be defined at the outset. Federalism, for the purpose of this inquiry, and thus differing slightly from Watts' definition, is both a descriptive and a normative category, implying the opposite of unitary rule, and embodying the normative ideal of a division of substantive areas over which power is exercised between at least two sets of governments. A federal system is the constitutional arrangement that gives federalism its institutional form. It is typically identified with the existence of four institutional characteristics. First, there should be two sets of governments, each with its independent spheres of administrative and legislative competence; second, each set of governments should have

independent tax bases; third, there should be a written constitution from which each side derives its legislative power; and finally, in case of conflict, there should be a system of independent judicial courts to arbitrate between the Centre and the constituent units. The federal process, then, is the ensemble of actual participatory, legislative, and policy interactions that relate the structure of the federal system to the dynamics of everyday political life.

This chapter describes the features of India's federal system and process, and seeks to explain their effectiveness in terms of their symbiosis with the projects of nation-building and state-formation in India. This is done through a presentation of the basic structure of federalism in India and its political constraints. Next, the main role that the federal system and process have played in transforming a mere collection of disjointed British-administered territories and former princely states, set free to follow their destiny by their British 'allies' at the end of colonial rule, and the Indian provinces into an effective 'Union of States' is discussed.[6] The flexibility of the federal process has made it possible for the state in India to accommodate ethno-national movements in the form of new regions, thus gradually increasing both the number of states and the governability of the Union. In addition, the vertical expansion of the federal structure, to which a third tier was added through the constitutionally mandated authority and some financial autonomy accorded to village-level political institutions by the Seventy-third and Seventy-fourth Constitutional Amendment Acts of 1993, along with a mandatory quota of 33 per cent of seats for women in bodies of local self-government, deserves careful attention. This has turned the federal process into a major source of legitimization and democratization of power in India, even though some might argue that it has made governing unnecessarily complex and that policy performance did not clearly improve. However, as the example of Kashmir indicates, this success story has its limitations, for the juxtaposition of religion and geopolitics defines the limits of the integrative potential of federalism in India.

THE FEDERAL PROCESS: THREE PHASE OF DEVELOPMENT SINCE INDEPENDENCE

The framers of the Indian Constitution, as we saw above, were keen on federalism as a functional instrument for the creation of an Indian nation and a strong, cohesive state. The leading politicians of the immediate post-Independence state were besieged by threats to India's security both from outside and inside, and faced the challenge of development through having perceived and chosen centralized economic planning as an optimal method by which to reach that objective. Thus, both for constitutional and political reasons, the institutionalization of a strong federalism in the Indian system appears to have been seriously compromised from the outset. Nonetheless, the political process has been able to adapt to this design, and in many, though not all, cases mollify it when necessary to safeguard regional interests.

The first phase of federalization of the political process extended from the time of Independence to the mid-1960s. Prime Minister Jawaharlal Nehru took democracy seriously enough to face the enormously expanded Indian electorate (in 1951, in the first general election held both to the national Parliament and the provincial assemblies), providing for full and free participation in the election. He took the chief ministers (all of whom, with rare exceptions, were members of the Indian National Congress (INC), the party of which he was for part of this period the President and, of all this period, leader of the parliamentary party) seriously enough to write to each of them every month in an effort to keep them informed of the state of the nation and the world, and to solicit their opinion in an attempt to build a national consensus.[7] The INC, which had already embraced the federal principle back in the 1920s by organizing itself on the basis of Provincial Congress Committees based on linguistic regions, institutionalized the principle of consultation, accommodation, and consensus through a delicate balancing of the factions within the 'Congress System' (Kothari 1970). It also practised the co-optation of local and regional leaders in the national power

structure,[8] and the system of sending out Congress 'observers' from the Centre to mediate between warring factions in the provinces, thus simultaneously ensuring the legitimacy of the provincial power structure in running its own affairs as well as the role of Central mediation.

The second phase of the development of Indian federalism began with the fourth general elections (1967), which drastically reduced the overwhelming strength of the Congress party in the national Parliament to a simple majority and saw nearly half the states moving out of Congress control and into the hands of opposition parties or coalitions, and led to a radical change in the nature of centre–state relations. No longer could an imperious Congress Prime Minister afford to 'dictate' benevolently to a loyal Congress Chief Minister. However, even as the tone became more contentious, the essential principles of accommodation and consultation held between the crucial 1967–9 period of transition. The Congress-dominated Centre began cohabiting with opposition parties at the regional level. The balance was lost once the Congress party split (1969), and Prime Minister Indira Gandhi took to the strategy of radical rhetoric and strong centralized personal leadership. In consequence, the regional accommodation, which had been possible by way of the internal federalization of the Congress party, was subsequently eroded. However, after the authoritarian interlude of 1975–7, which, in both law and fact, reduced India's federal system to pretty much a unitary state, the system reverted to the earlier stage of tenuous cooperation between the Centre and the states.

With the prolonged period of coalition governments at the Centre, the third phase in the federalization of Indian politics began at the end of the 1980s. Regional parties, such as the Dravida Munnetra Kazhagam (DMK) of Tamil Nadu or the Rashtriya Janata Dal (RJD) of Bihar, have asserted their interests more openly over the past one-and-a-half decades of coalition and minority governments. This increased assertion on the part of regional parties at the Central level had forced even the Hindu nationalist Bharatiya Janata Party, which led the ruling coalition in the thirteenth Lok Sabha until 2004, to

be solicitous in its, at least symbolic, adherence to
the norms of centre–state relations established by
its predecessors, including such hallowed principles
of the Indian Union as the three-language formula,
in spite of its advocacy of Hindi as India's national
language during its long years in the opposition.[9]

INSTITUTIONAL DESIGN: STRENGTHS AND WEAKNESSES

When compared to the relatively longer existence
of four key federal states, namely the United States
(1789), Switzerland (1848), Canada (1867/1931),
and Australia (1901), their comparative ethnic and
cultural homogeneity during long periods of their
existence, and the high literacy and standards of living
considered necessary for the sophisticated power-
sharing that a federal system requires, India presents
a set of apparently insurmountable obstacles against
a likely federal solution. Wheare, reflecting this and
other reservations, describes the Indian case as '[...]a
quasi-federation—a unitary state with subsidiary
federal features rather than a federal state with
subsidiary unitary features'.[10]

The Institutional Set-up of Indian Federalism

The fact that academic debates have arisen over
time around the question of the character of Indian
federalism is rooted in the very constitutional framework
that constitutes its basis. While this framework at
first glance meets the basic normative requirements
of federalism, a number of additional provisions have
the potential of diluting their effects in reality and
transforming the system into a unitary one instead.

India's system of government is divided between
the Central level and the federal units (currently
twenty-eight states and seven Union Territories,
including the National Capital Territory of Delhi).[11]
The Constitution of India provides for a relatively
clear *vertical* division of powers between the Central
legislature (referred to in Indian usage as the Union
government) and the state legislatures, both constituted
through direct elections, respectively, in the Seventh
Schedule (see Table 4.1). The Union controls the
'Union list', consisting of areas that involve inter-state

relations, national security, and foreign affairs. Subjects
of primary interest to the regions, called the 'State list',
encompassing law and order, culture and education, are
under the jurisdiction of the states. The 'Concurrent list'
holds subjects of overlapping interest, like land reform
laws or issues relating to cultural or religious minorities,
where both Centre and state can make laws with the
understanding that in case of conflict, the Central
laws will take precedence. Subjects not specifically
mentioned in the Constitution, called the residuary
subjects, come under Central legislation. Each list also
mentions how the two governments can raise income
through taxation. In case of a conflict of jurisdiction,
the Centre or the state can move the Supreme Court to
have the point of law authoritatively interpreted.

A number of formally constituted organizational
units execute the responsibilities allocated to them
under this constitutional framework, sharing power
over the affairs of a political territory in two senses,
namely having joint or competing powers over the
same matters on the one hand, and having separate
powers over separate matters on the other. Ideal
typically, in a multi-level system of government such
as a federal political system, the sharing of powers of
this kind can be conceived of as involving three types
of sharing (in the sense of separation, but also fusion):
vertical power-sharing, horizontal power-sharing, and
transversal power-sharing. The term *vertical power-
sharing* describes the allocation of certain issue areas
and competences in decision-making to be handled
by either the Central, sub-national or the local level
of government, denoting the division aspect of the
allocation of powers, rather than the fusion aspect.
Thus, the vertical division of powers is depicted in
Table 4.1, allocating specific matters to either one of
the three levels of government. The term *horizontal
power-sharing* describes the sharing of competences at
the Central and the sub-national levels between the
branches of government, denoting the fusion as well as
the separation-aspect of sharing mechanisms, as well
as the sharing of powers between sub-units in a federal
political system in its separation and fusion variants.
By *transversal power-sharing* is meant, among other
things, a structural and processual sharing of powers
between levels of government, such that it involves, in
addition to the superior-level unit, one or more or all

Table 4.1: Important Legislative Competences

LEVEL	COMPETENCES	ENABLING PROVISION
Centre	Defence, Atomic Energy, Foreign Affairs, Citizenship, Transport Infrastructure, Currency, Postal Service, Banking/Insurance, Electoral Laws, Organization of the Supreme Court, Taxation in various areas, Natural Resources, Union Territory matters, Residual Competences	Art. 246 + Seventh Schedule (List I), Constitution of India
State	Public Order/Police, Public Health, Local Government, Agriculture, Water, Land, State Public Services, Taxes (on agricultural income, on land, etc.)	Art. 246 + Seventh Schedule (List II), Constitution of India
Local	Economic Development, Social Justice (subject to state laws allocating powers of local self-government to village councils)	Art. 243 G + respective State legislation
Centre + States (Concurrently)	Criminal Law/Criminal Procedure Law, Marriage and Divorce Law, Transfer of Non-agricultural Property, Civil and Commercial Law, Economic/Social/Family Planning	Art. 246 + Seventh Schedule (List III), Constitution of India

Source: GoI 1991.

lower-level units (such as the states in the Indian case) in its fusion-variant. The non-hierarchical and informal modes of joining levels and units through coordinating mechanisms are part of the phenomenon that has been described in another regional context as 'political interlocking' in cooperative federalism.[12] These three types of power-sharing involve, respectively, both hierarchical and non-hierarchical modes of coordination of action, as represented in Table 4.2, and also both formal and informal institutions.

At the Union level, a tripartite sharing out of power, referred to here as a *horizontal* allocation of powers, allocates different functions of government to the executive (President and Council of Ministers/Prime Minister), the legislative (Union Parliament, consisting of Lok Sabha and Rajiya Sabha), and the judicial branches of government (Supreme Court of India), although there is significant overlap in personnel between the legislative and the executive branches, with the requirement being that the Prime Minister and all other ministers must be members of either House of Parliament or lose their office after a period of six months (Article 75, Constitution of India). This division is mirrored to some extent at the state level with the institutions of chief ministers and their cabinets, state legislatures (unicameral in most, bicameral in some states) and the respective high courts (although high courts apply Union, as well as state laws, and their organization is highly centralized).

Another set of units, such as the Finance Commission, the Inter-state Council, the Inter-state

Table 4.2: Typology of Power-sharing Arrangements in Multi-level Systems

TYPE	MODE OF COORDINATION	LEVELS/UNITS INVOLVED
Vertical	Non-hierarchical	Centre-State levels State-Local levels
Horizontal	Non-hierarchical	Centre (branches) States
Transversal	Hierarchical and Non-hierarchical	Centre-State levels

Source: Authors' depiction

Tribunals, the National Development Council, and a number of informal fora serve as bridging mechanisms between the levels of government and between states, thus enabling *transversal* as well as *horizontal* power-sharing. The *Inter-state Council*, which was set up for the first time in accordance with Article 263 in 1990, is a body that aims, despite not having legislative or administrative powers, at enabling consultation between governments at the state and the Union levels. It is constituted according to the Presidential Order of 1990, under which it was set up by the Prime Minister, chief ministers of states and those Union Territories which have legislative assemblies, governors of states under President's rule, and eight Union cabinet ministers.[13] Although its primary function to date has been the debate on reforming centre–state relations, the Inter-state Council also functions as an important policy forum for informal discussions on other political issues affecting the states.

The *Finance Commission* is an organizational unit performing the task of providing recommendations to the President of India regarding the distribution of taxes between the Centre and the states, and between the states (Article 280, Section 1, Constitution of India). It is appointed regularly by the President of India every five years and consists of five members. Its importance in the process of regulating inter-governmental fiscal relations is enhanced by the fact that the recommendations, although not formally binding, have a quasi-binding character, and by the fact that many of the most expensive tasks of government, such as social matters or public orders are, directly or indirectly (through local government programmes financed from state funds), state-level matters. This issue will be taken up once more in a later section. The *Inter-state Tribunals* are ad hoc bodies infrequently constituted under the Inter-

state Water Disputes Act of 1956 in order to solve disputes over the use of water resources that cross the boundaries between states, such as rivers. In the past, these tribunals had been slow in their decision-making and ineffective in the area of implementation of decisions. With the Amendment Act of 2002, the period within which decisions now have to be reached has been shortened to a combined maximum of six years. Due to the increase in the need for, and the depletion of, freshwater resources on account of increasingly rapid agricultural and industrial expansion as well as urbanization, and the more frequent disputes arising from inter-state competition for this resource, these bodies can be expected to acquire increasing importance and visibility in the future.

Another institution which served informally as a mechanism for the coordination of political action between the central and sub-national levels

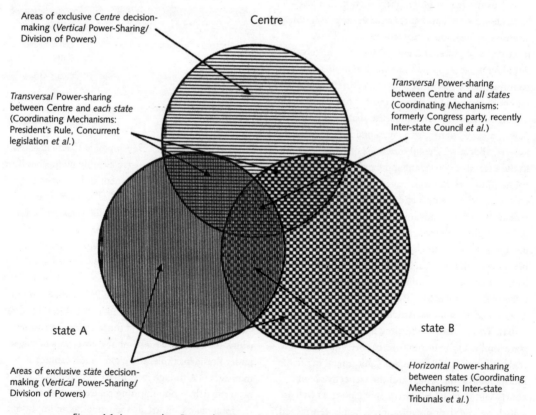

Figure 4.1: Issue-overlap, Power-sharing, and Coordination of Action of Centre and States

Source: Own depiction

of government in the past was the *Indian National Congress*, during the period of its electoral and administrative dominance.[14] Through its internal processes of decision-making and channels of communication, this system facilitated coordination between the leading politicians at the Centre and in the regions until the second half of the 1960s, thus joining decision-making elites at the national and state levels and enabling some degree of *transversal power-sharing*. Figure 4.1 illustrates the areas of issue-overlap in decision-making by the Union and the state governments, and the location of the various formal and informal institutions and coordinating mechanisms serving as instruments of policy coordination.

Nonetheless, doubts about the authenticity of Indian federalism arise from the constraints placed upon it by a number of institutions. These constraints are in part elements of the transversal type of power-sharing, which employ a hierarchical mode of coordination of action. One of these features, which has repeatedly come under intense criticism, is the role played by the Governors within India's states, and the use of *President's Rule*.[15] While the framers of the Indian Constitution intended the Governors to play a rather minimal role in the political process, mainly confined to extreme crisis situations, they have often intervened at the behest of the Central government in the political affairs of states.[16] The institution of the Governor has added a veto player to the democratic set-up of state politics, one who is appointed by the President on the advice of the Union Cabinet (Article 155), and is not accountable to any legislature either at the state or at the Central level. In essence, the Governor occupies the same constitutional position as the President at the Central level, as the Indian Supreme Court noted in *Ram Jawaya Kapoor vs State of Punjab*.[17] The influence of the Union within the constitutional framework of Indian politics is comparatively strong, and this fact has led to claims of Governors acting as the 'long arm' of the Centre and their neglect of state interests, especially in the area of decisions which the Governor takes at his discretion and not on the advice of the respective state's Council of Ministers. One arena in which this double-edged sword—of the formal obligation to uphold constitutional government in the states on the one hand and the accountability to the Centre on the other—has played out is that of President's Rule in the Indian states, that is, the supplanting of state governments by rule of the Central government in certain crisis situations in accordance with Article 356 of the Constitution of India. This issue will later resurface as part of the discussion on the interaction of institutional design and the political process.

Another constitutional peculiarity that has attracted commendation and scepticism alike with regard to India's federal character is the issue of the territorial integrity of the constituent units of the Indian Union, the states. Early authors such as Wheare (1964) noted that the fact that the constituent units within India did not enjoy a guarantee of territorial integrity, which could be waived only with their express consent, was one of the reasons why India was merely a 'quasi-federation'. This now dated assessment invites scrutiny of this particular arrangement among the constituent units. As Articles 2 and 3 of the Indian Constitution stipulate, the power to form, alter or dissolve states lies with the Parliament of India. The states' indirect role in this process is therefore confined to the vote in the Rajya Sabha, where debate ensues, in particular at the initiation of members from the respective regions in question, and to the expression of non-binding opinion on the issue of alteration of boundaries by the state Assemblies to the President (Article 3). On the other hand, however, the Indian Supreme Court, vindicating the claims of Watts (1998: 126) regarding the importance of an institutional arrangement to guarantee the autonomy of the constituent units, declared that 'the fact that under the scheme of our Constitution greater power is conferred upon the Centre vis-à-vis the states does not mean that states are mere appendages of the Centre. Within the sphere allotted to them, states are supreme. The Centre cannot tamper with their powers.'[18] It also confirmed the status of Indian federalism as part of the basic structure of the Indian Constitution. A different arrangement can be found in the German Constitution (the *Grundgesetz* or Basic Law), which does not specify the number of states that constitute Germany and also allows for the alteration of boundaries, albeit only with the consent of the people living in the territory concerned (Article 29), but declares the abolition of federalism, that is, the division of the country into constituent units as such, as beyond the scope of parliamentary amendment power (Article 79, Sec. 3, Grundgesetz).[19] Thus, this institutional designing, which was not expressly laid out in the Constitution of India, has been done procedurally by the Supreme Court. Nonetheless, the alterations of boundaries, not least in the cases of the creation of the state of Jharkhand out of Bihar, or Uttaranchal out of Uttar Pradesh, have invited protest on several occasions; and this instrument, while creating opportunities for greater autonomy to be afforded to certain ethnic or linguistic groups, has also placed constraints on the political process.

Institutional Design and the Political Process

The ambivalent legal position that the Indian Constitution accords to the constituent states of the Union must appear startling to the federalist. Not only did the construction of the Union not follow from a decision by a group of independent political units to shed parts of their sovereign powers out of mutual interest and create a federal state, but the Union and the states were also formally a simultaneous creation of the Constituent Assembly, in which the provinces did not have any special representation. Further, the Central government gradually dissolved the political character of the units that existed at the time of Independence, and started creating new units. The first major redesigning of state boundaries was undertaken in 1956–7 through the States' Reorganization Act, 1956, after prolonged agitation in some regions, notably in south India, for a reorganization of states along linguistic and cultural boundaries.[20] The process has continued unabated, facilitated by the fact that the consent of the states, especially those forced to cede territory, is not required for alteration of the names or boundaries of the states.

Further, even though in normal times the states have the exclusive power to make laws in the areas allocated to them (which are far less numerous than those given to the Centre), the Central Parliament has an extraordinary power of legislation on state subjects in the national interest when authorized by the Rajya Sabha, the Upper House of the Parliament, to do so

(Article 249). The Rajya Sabha, which was meant to be the states' representative at the Centre, is far from being the equal of the Lok Sabha, the Lower House. It has fewer legislative functions, particularly with regard to finance. Traditionally, the Prime Minister and other important members of the national Cabinet are members of the Lok Sabha. In view of its size, which is less than half of that of the Lok Sabha, it runs the risk of being outvoted in a joint session, that is, the prescribed method of decision-making in case of a serious difference of opinion between the two Houses. Nor does the composition of the Rajya Sabha reflect the equality and dignity that is accorded to all members of a federation which are, in the cases of many other federal systems, treated as equals. This is because the number of seats allocated to the states, in spite of the weighting added to the smaller members of the Union, still reflects the inequality that flows from the fact that the population of Uttar Pradesh is now nearly 170 million, compared to three million for Nagaland.

There are other points that continue to question the trust of those who believe in states' rights. The Governor of each state, head of state under the Constitution and the ceremonial head, is an appointee of the President of India, most of the time acting on the advice of the Prime Minister. The Governors of India, invariably political appointees of the ruling party at the Centre, have continued to act as the Centre's eyes and ears. Their role becomes crucial if no majority party or coalition emerges from the election, in which case the Governor is obliged to organize a viable government coalition. In the event of a loss of support of the majority for the state government in the legislature, in the past often due to defection or splits, or if law and order declines precipitously, the Governor's report becomes the basis of the declaration of President's Rule. The modes of emergency government (Articles 352, 356, 360, Constitution of India), if and when employed, can hold the federal character of the division of powers in temporary abeyance. However, a distinction needs to be made between (a) the breakdown of constitutional government in a state leading to President's Rule and what President's rule implies—that is, administration by the Centre rather than by a popularly elected state government, and (b) a national emergency.

As outlined above, President's Rule at the state level can be declared by the President at the recommendation of the Governor (again, Central appointee and not, as in the United States, a political leader elected by the voting population of the respective state) under Article 356. The same article authorizes the President to dismiss the government of a state and dissolve or suspend its legislature when he receives a report from the state Governor, or in any other way, that 'the government of the state cannot be carried on in accordance with the provisions of the Constitution'. He may then 'assume all or any of the powers' vested in the government of the state with the exception of the function of the state legislature, which is then exercised by the Union Parliament, which in turn can delegate this power to the President in accordance with Article 357. As far as federalism is concerned, the negative implications of this article became clear as early as 1959, when the elected Communist government of Kerala was dismissed by the Congress-ruled Central government. Once again, safeguards such as approval of the national Parliament are provided for, but the use of this power under the prime ministership of Indira Gandhi, which drastically reduced the autonomy of the states, serves as a reminder of the potential threat to federalism from this angle. The instrument of a declaration of President's Rule in the states was used 10 times between 1951 and 1966, 65 times between 1967 and 1988, and on 13 occasions between 1989 and 1997.[21] This means that on an average, President's Rule in the states was declared 1.5 times per year between 1951 and 1966, 3.1 times per year between 1967 and 1988, and on an average 2.3 times between 1989 and 1997, the latter being the period of minority and coalition governments at the Union level.

The proclamation of President's Rule, and also a national state of Emergency as a form of exceptional or crisis government, used to hang above the heads of India's regional governments like the sword of Damocles in the early decades of independent India.[22] The national Emergency of 1975–7 deeply scarred India's democratic and federal record. Once proclaimed by the President under Article 352, it can in principle reduce India to a unitary state with an authoritarian government. If the President is satisfied that the security of India or any part of India is threatened by war or

external aggression or armed rebellion, and issues a declaration to this effect, the Emergency provisions are applicable to the whole of India or any part (Article 352).[23] Article 353 specifies the implications of a national state of Emergency, of which two are relevant to federalism. During the state of Emergency 'the executive power of the Union shall extend to the giving of directions to any state or as to the manner in which the executive power thereof is to be exercised'. Further, 'the power of Parliament to make laws with respect to any matter includes the power to make laws conferring powers and imposing duties, or authorizing the conferring of powers and the imposition of duties, upon the Union or officers and authorities of the Union, notwithstanding the fact that it is one that is not enumerated in the Union List' (Article 353).

The Constitution now provides safeguards against the abuse of this provision. Thus, after the constitutional revisions in the second half of the 1970s, the President may act only at the written recommendation of the Cabinet, and the proclamation of Emergency needs to be approved by the Parliament. Still, the experience of 1975 continues to be a reminder of the potential threat. Ultimately, however, this institutional feature, as well as the instrument of President's Rule, as means of Central intervention in times of crisis, are in themselves not sufficient to warrant the claim that India is merely a 'quasi-federation', since similar provisions exist in many countries' constitutions. It is the process of employment of this instrument that calls the federal arrangement into question at certain times, when it is used for apparently party political considerations rather than crisis management.[24]

Finally, the problem of structural asymmetry, implying a great difference in the size of the members of a federation, is a key feature of the Indian case, affecting the political process. In terms of their presence in the Lok Sabha, for example, the contingent from Uttar Pradesh, with 85 Members of Parliament (MPs), is a much more significant presence than tiny Tripura with just two. Many of the Prime Ministers of India and many important members of the Central Cabinet have come in the past from Uttar Pradesh. Watts mentions India along with Spain, Belgium, Malaysia, and Russia as a federation that shows the presence of structural asymmetry either in its constitution or in political practices. Drawing on the work of Tarlton (1965), who first drew attention to the phenomenon of structural asymmetry in federations, Watts shows how 'political asymmetry, arising from the impact of cultural, economic, demographic and social conditions [could affect] the relative power and influence of different constituent units, as well as their relations with each other and with the federative institution'.[25] The dominance of some groups in the political systems of neighbouring South Asian countries, both in terms of language and area of origin, are enough evidence of the potential consequences of structural asymmetry in terms of relativizing the federal quality of the Union.

FISCAL AND DEVELOPMENTAL FEDERALIZATION AND CENTRE–STATE RELATIONS

Another characteristic of Indian federalism is the fact that the Central government possesses superior financial powers. The more lucrative sources of revenue in the past and of the future like import or export duties, non-agricultural income tax, and corporate taxes are allocated to the Centre (Part XII, Constitution of India). The revenue of the states, on the other hand, constitutes a shrinking base in some of the states because, under pressure of populism, they have done away with or drastically reduced the taxation on land and income from agriculture. In addition to this, the Indian states' capacity to collect taxes has traditionally been rather weak. This compounds the problems, especially at the state level.

States' revenues mainly accrue from four sources: tax and expenditure assignments derived from the Constitution of India (Seventh Schedule), transfers allocated by the Finance Commission (Article 275), transfers from the Planning Commission, and transfers from Central ministry budgets to the states. The transfers take the form of grants and loans to the states. Over the decades, the capacity of states to finance both revenue and capital expenditure from their own tax-based resources has declined substantially. Only 42 per cent of the states' total expenditure was covered by their own revenue receipts in 2000–1 (Singh 2004: 7–8). At the same time, a marked increase in the share of loans and advances in the total amounts of capital receipts of states from the Central government has also contributed, among other factors, to a further increase in the indebtedness of states (Saez 2002: 145).

The Union government alone, on the other hand, is empowered to regulate the money supply, contract foreign loans, charge income tax on non-agricultural income and on services, or collect import and export duties. Depending on the composition of the Central government of the day and its political inclinations vis-à-vis state autonomy, revenue centralization and subsequent decentralization have taken place during the first decades after Independence (Rao 2001: 2741–5). Also, compared to other federal systems, India's states had a relatively low level of revenue, which they could generate themselves (as opposed to the total revenue of states, which includes transfers from the Centre to the states) when measured against the total revenue of the states and Central government combined (ibid.: 2751–6). Part of the revenue levied at the Central level is of course redistributed among states, on the basis of the advice of the organizationally independent Finance Commission or through the Planning Commission, and constitutes a significant source of income for them. However, the impression that is thus created is one of profligate states, and a more careful and sophisticated Central financial management. The superior financial powers of the Centre are further reinforced by other functions relating to financial management that are allocated to it. For it is the Central leadership that appoints the Planning Commission as well as the Finance Commission, which generally set the priorities for the national government, allocate resources to the states, and act as a clearing house of economic policy.

Nevertheless, as studies have shown, since the liberalization of economic policies and the decentralization of policymaking to states from the early 1990s onwards[26] (and even before then[27]), states have been able to exercise some autonomy in regulating their own development trajectory. While this has increased the scope for competition among states and provided incentives for reform-oriented policies, disparities between states that are more and those that are less successful at coping with this changed policy environment have become apparent.[28]

While some states such as Andhra Pradesh, Karnataka, Tamil Nadu, and Kerala have shown signs of catching up as compared to early developers such as Gujarat, other states like Uttar Pradesh, Madhya Pradesh, Rajasthan, and Bihar have lost further ground when compared to the leading states. Thus, the trends of economic liberalization at the Centre, sub-national policy differentiation, and federalization of the overall political process have enabled some actors to use these new opportunities to their advantage, while others have fallen behind, compromising the relative comparability of living conditions for all Indian citizens. The picture today, then, is one of increasing differentiation among India's states in terms of their fiscal capabilities as well as their developmental potential, and a need for reform of inter-state mechanisms of coordination and equalization.[29]

THE FEDERAL PROCESS: PERCEPTION IN INDIA

It can be argued that the Indian political elite has demonstrated its trust in the Indian Union through participation in its electoral and everyday politics. Yet, the question raised by both Harrison and Moore (Harrison 1960; Moore 1966)[9] about the acceptance of the democratic and federal rule of the polity by ordinary people still remains. To measure the interest of the electorate in the political system at the Central, regional, and local levels, as well as the loyalty to the respective political arenas, questions were asked in the different National Election Studies of the Indian electorate.[30] The answers are presented in Tables 4.3 and 4.4.

Table 4.3: Interest in Central and State Government (in per cent)

	1971	1996	1999
Neither	24.9	39.7	26.0
Central Govt.	21.0	11.0	14.8
Both	14.5	20.9	26.7
State Govt.	18.9	23.0	25.6
DK, NA, Other	20.7	5.4	6.9

Source: Centre for the Study of Developing Societies (New Delhi), National Election Studies 1971, 1996, and 1999
Note: DK = Don't Know
     NA = Not Available

Table 4.4: Loyalty to Region First and Then to India (in per cent)

	1967	1996	1999
Agree	67.1	53.4	50.7
Disagree	22.3	21.0	21.4
DK/No Opinion	8.4	25.6	27.8

Source: Centre for the Study of Developing Societies (New Delhi), National Election Studies, 1967, 1996, and 1999
Note: DK = Don't Know

An analysis of these findings reveals, first, a growing interest in regional matters from 1971 to 1999 (Table 4.3). After the peak in 1996, the group of respondents who expressed no interest in either state or Central governments' work reverted approximately to the same level as that of 1971. A notable and steady increase can be seen, however, in the group of respondents who express an equal interest in both levels of government.

Thus, while the Central government seems more remote from many respondents, the regionalization conjecture also requires caveats. While the concern for the politics of regional matters conducted by state governments has certainly grown, so has, in an even larger measure, the group of people who view both as equally important. This can be interpreted as evidence of the internalization of the federal norm in that section of the electorate that appears to view the power-sharing arrangement as a natural given.

Based on the results presented in Table 4.4, one could infer that loyalty first and foremost to the regions is in steady decline. This is a fairly safe assumption to make. Yet, the findings from the 1967 survey need to be viewed in light of the emergence of regional politics as a separate political sphere for the first time in the 1967 elections and the political campaigning of that year. Increasingly, however, it does indeed seem that a growing number of citizens no longer perceive national and regional politics, conducted in the states, as a trade-off. From both Tables 4.3 and 4.4 it becomes relatively clear that both arenas are being increasingly perceived as legitimate arenas of political action that need not be mutually exclusive. Regional political forces, having established themselves in the states as well as at the Central level, can be assumed to have turned the issue of the relationship of national and regional identity from one of transcendence and an either-or type of choice into one that exists in the realm of transactional politics of the day in the eyes of respondents.

COALITIONS AND THE FEDERALIZATION OF NATIONAL POLITICS

The supportive empirical evidence concerning the overall functioning of the federal process that one gets from the opinion data presented in Tables 4.1 and 4.2, and the negative predictions of Harrison (1960) and Wheare (1964) suggest that India's federal system constitutes a puzzle. One is entitled to ask: if it 'works' relatively well in comparison with other postcolonial states, why does it do so? Drawing on the works of Friedrich (1968), Riker (1975), Dikshit (1975), and Hesse and Wright (1996), Watts suggests four general conditions to explain why federal processes work. The first and foremost, of course, is 'elite accommodation'. Next, reflecting the democratic trends of our times, comes 'public involvement', though it may 'complicate the patterns of negotiation for the establishment of a federal system' (Watts 1998: 128). An atmosphere of 'competition and collusion' between inter-governmental agencies is mentioned as a third condition (ibid.: 130). In the fourth place, drawing on Riker, Watts mentions 'the role and impact of political parties, including their number, their character, and the relations among federal, state and local branches' as helpful in explaining the dynamism of federal processes (ibid.).

Looking at the pattern of elite recruitment employed by the Congress party during the period of its hegemony (1952–67), where local and regional talent rose to prominence by rising within the party organization and moving horizontally to government, and the subsequent practice which saw new, upwardly-mobile social groups enter the electoral arena directly in the form of political parties organized under their own names, one could see a steady expansion of the social base of leadership in India. That satisfies the first two conditions mentioned by Watts. The competition among Indian states for scarce resources such as river waters, where the Centre often plays the role of mediator, involving bureaucrats and political leaders from competing regions, is a good example of the third

condition at work. However, with the decline of the Congress party as the main party in the states and at the Centre, one of the main mechanisms, namely the fourth condition mentioned by Watts as an explanatory variable in the analysis of the federal process, intra-party federalization, has been supplanted by an entirely different intra-party and inter-party system. The Congress system encapsulated the expressions of local and regional interests and symbols at lower levels of the internally federalized system; the new element in Indian politics makes these processes of consultation a systematic way of bringing out bits of India's outlying areas and peoples, and weaves them into different ways of defining what the nation is about and who has the legitimate right to speak in its name. As Table 4.5 shows, even at the Centre, regional parties have gained

Table 4.5: National Parties in Lok Sabha Elections: Seats and Votes

ELECTION YEARS	SEATS (IN PER CENT)[a]	VOTES (IN PER CENT)[b]
1952	82.6	67.8
1957	85.2	73.0
1962	89.0	78.4
1967	84.6	76.3
1971	85.1	77.8
1977	88.7	84.6
1980	91.7	85.1
1984	85.4	77.8
1989	89.0	79.3
1991	89.5	80.8
1996	76.6	69.6
1998	71.2	68.0
1999	68.0	67.1
2004	67.5	63.1
2009	69.4	n.a.

Notes: [a] Years 1952 to 1998 based on Butler *et al.* (1995) and the Election Commission of India, quoted in Mitra and Singh (1999). Years 1999 and 2004 are calculated based on figures supplied by the Press Information Bureau of India. Results for 2009 calculated on the basis of Election Commission of India (http://eci.gov.in/results/From Party Wise Trends And Results as pxi). accessed on 17 May 2009.
[b] Years 1952 to 1998 based on Butler *et al.* (1995) and the Election Commission of India, quoted in Mitra and Singh (1999). Years 1999 and 2004 based on figures supplied by the Press Information Bureau of India.

an ever increasing share of influence in comparison with national parties, as measured in the seat share in the successive Lok Sabha elections.

Nevertheless, just as regional parties emerge as champions of special and exclusive interests in the states, the next step on the career ladder of these leaders, which is aimed at Delhi, encourages them to place the region within the larger context of the nation. Eventually, as members of national coalitions of regional parties, they start striking the postures of national leaders, ready to bargain with and conciliate conflicting regional interests. Thus, even with the decline of the Congress as the once dominant party, the multi-party system that has replaced it has produced a similar institutionalized method of regional conflict resolution within a national framework.

Overall, the data from Lok Sabha electoral results and survey findings indicate the presence of a keen awareness of 'region' as an important level of the Indian political system. That the region is present in a distinctive way, in terms of support for regional parties even in national elections, does not of course suggest that it is exclusive, or that 'regionalists' necessarily pit the region and nation as polar opposites, separated by a chasm of distrust and conflict of loyalties. While the survey data support the existence of the two as separate and distinct entities on the basis of popular perceptions, the relationship of the two emerges as much more complex than is commonly supposed. The bark of regional chauvinists is louder than their bite: political scientists measuring the depth of national integration can accept the separatist rhetoric of regional leaders as an indicator of the imminent dissolution of national unity only with a number of caveats.

As one can see from the 1999 as well as the 2004 and 2009 Lok Sabha elections and the subsequent government coalitions,[31] regional parties have become part and parcel of government formation processes even at the level of the Central government. As in the case of the 2004 government formation process, however, some regional politicians have been able to secure more than their fair share of influence at the Central level, unlike what some key tenets of coalition theory would have led us to expect. While the twenty-one members strong RJD secured only two

Cabinet-rank ministries, the DMK, despite its limited strength of only sixteen MPs, was allocated three Cabinet ministries. At the same time, the RJD was able to secure a first tentative success in the form of the inclusion of the idea of a 'Backward States Grant Fund' in the Common Minimum Programme of the government after the 2004 elections, of which Bihar would be the main beneficiary.[32] This points to the ambiguous nature of the federal bargaining process, where office means influence and a say above and beyond the limits of the portfolio which a politician is allocated. While some regions can thus hope to have their interests represented through regional power brokers at the Central government level, other states have to fear being left behind whenever regional parties from their respective states are not included in the national government coalition.

The political process of the 1990s shows the internalization of federal norms in the game plans of local and regional political leaders. Rather than taking a mechanical, anti-Delhi stance as their only *raison d'etre*, the new breed of ambitious, upwardly-mobile leaders of India have learnt to play by the rules even as they challenge them, and thus have developed for themselves a new federal space in which the nation and the region can coexist. However, as Mitra and Lewis (1996) show, the integrative power of this model is at its best in Tamil Nadu, where a federal 'deal' can be struck with a specific group of actors, such as the DMK. When, however, the actors themselves are fragmented, and some of the distant actors are not a part of the negotiation (as in Kashmir, Assam, or Nagaland), the effectiveness of this model in producing a legitimate federal solution is limited.[33]

INDIAN FEDERALISM: CHALLENGES AND ADAPTATIONS

With remarkable prescience, the framers of the Indian Constitution have equipped the Indian state to respond to the demands for autonomy through the double mechanism of individual and group rights, as well as the federal construction of political power. During the first phase of India's constitutional development, some of these instruments were useful in empowering political majorities below the level of the national state through the effective enactment of provincial administrations. The second phase of constitutional development through the states' reorganization of 1956–7, which created linguistically homogeneous states and counterbalanced the likely chauvinism through the promotion of the three-language formula, requiring the use of Hindi, English, and the regional language, made it possible to institutionalize the multicultural nature of the Indian state, albeit with regional divergences of successes and failures in its implementation. In its third phase, the same process of constitutional development of federalism in the 1990s, India has witnessed the deepening of the principle of power-sharing by the constitutional and statutory powers accorded to village councils after 1993.[34]

These normative developments of the federal principle and their adaptation to India's cultural and historical context have been complemented by the political process. During the critical years of transition from British rule and the consolidation of popular democracy in India, the Congress party provided the link between the modern state and traditional society. Congress rule, both at the Centre and in the states, provided informal channels of communication, and a balancing of national, regional, and sectional interests. The politics of coalitions that has replaced Congress hegemony has given a public articulation to the process of integration of the local and regional for the purpose of launching a new debate on the nature of the nation, and for identifying the variable boundaries of the nation and the region. In consequence, looking for regional allies has now become an imperative for all national parties.

The new group of regional leaders of India, drawing on their power bases in the states, often consisting of people from India's periphery (in terms of religion, elite caste status, or geographic distance from the Centre), are able to generate a different and new construction of the Indian nation-state. In terms of the actual policies of the state, the regionalists are much more willing and (in view of their social base) able to listen to the minorities, to regions with historical grievances, to sections of society that entered post-Independence politics with unsolved, pre-Independence (in some cases, pre-modern) grievances.

It is thanks to some of these 'regionalists' that the emerging multi-party democracy of India is not merely an anomic battle for power and short-term gain, but the releasing of pent-up creativity and visions that provide a fertile and cohesive backdrop to the realignment of social forces. Far from being its antithesis, region has actually emerged as a nursery of the nation. The rules of the federal system, rather than being exogenous to the federal process, have become endogenous to it.

Finally, the horizontal and vertical expansion of the federal process has brought greater legitimacy to the Indian state and cohesion to the Indian nation. Rather than grand design, the process has been based on a series of ad hoc decisions, based on the perceived benefits of the respective political actors of the day, sometimes against the advice of specialists who have made the conventional arguments based on the imperatives of modernization and the logic of economic viability.

One important weakness of institutional design and the federal process is clearly the lack of effective mechanisms for a coordinated interest aggregation of states versus the Central government. Coordination mechanisms, such as the informal conference of Chief Ministers and, to some extent, also the Inter-state Council,[35] have largely proven to be limited in their effectiveness. Nevertheless, coordination among Chief Ministers belonging to parties not included in the Central government coalition has taken place, as have collusion and coordination between the Central government and many of those Chief Ministers belonging to parties which support the Central government in the Lok Sabha. In its own way, therefore, the Indian experience with the unprecedented and unconventional expansion of the federal principle serves to enrich the theory of federalism in confirming or disconfirming received knowledge about the strengths and weaknesses of federal systems the world over.

NOTES

1. The constituent units of the Indian federation will be called states and State will refer to the Central state.

2. Watts, in his comprehensive study of federal systems (Watts 1998, p. 121), counts 23 states as full federal states;

however, one senses a certain reluctance to admit India as a full member of this club. 'India and Malaysia, marked by deep-rooted multilingual, multicultural and multiracial diversity, have nevertheless managed to cohere for half and a third of a century respectively, but are at a critical phase in their development' (ibid., p. 118).

3. The national opinion survey of 1996, in the course of which a sample of 10,000 men and women representing the Indian electorate was interviewed by trained investigators from the Centre for the Study of Developing Societies during May–June 1996, on the basis of a questionnaire designed by the Lokchintan, a group of scholars based at various Indian research institutes and universities. Financial assistance for this project extended by the Konrad Adenauer Foundation, the Indian Council for Social Science Research, and *The Hindu* (Delhi) is hereby gratefully acknowledged.

4. Following the usage of Watts (1998, p. 117), federal process is used in this chapter as a descriptive category referring to the presence of a 'broad genus of federal arrangements' in a political system. These characteristics, which could in principle be composed into a scale, are drawn from the definition of a federation as 'a compound polity combining constituent units and a general government, each possessing powers delegated to it by the people through a constitution, each empowered to deal directly with the citizens in the exercise of a significant portion of its legislative, administrative, and taxing powers, and each directly elected by its citizens' (ibid., p. 121).

5. Wheare (1951 [1964]) is the main source of such contestation of India's federal status. Watts (1998, p. 131) mentions India's multi-ethnicity as a possible factor in why federalism might be diffcult to sustain. Indian writing on the theme (Bose 1986) pleads for more decentralization, but such arguments are based on the fact that a federation already exists, and has the necessary capacity to decentralize even further.

6. Article 1, Constitution of India, describes the Indian federation as follows: 'India that is Bharat shall be a Union of States'.

7. These letters are now available in the form of four volumes (Nehru 1985), which are a veritable treasure trove on the politics of the early post-Independence decades.

8. See Lijphart (1996, pp. 258–68) for a theoretical exploration of this consociational strategy.

9. See the telling quotation by the then President of the BJP, Atal Bihari Vajpayee, regarding this strategy of moving towards the middle of the political spectrum for the sake of recruiting coalition partners, quoted in Arora, 2000, p. 206, fn 54.

10. Wheare (1964, p. 28), cited in Basu (1985, p. 58).

11. See Appendix for a list and key characteristics of the states. The difference between state and Union

Territories is the stronger control exercised by the Union government over the (mostly comparatively small) Union Territories. Although some Union Territories have an elected assembly, the executive function is exercised by an appointed Governor and not an elected Chief Minister, as would be the case in the states. Delhi was conferred a special status by the amendment of the Indian Constitution in 1991, being jointly administered by the Union, the three local municipal corporations, and the elected NCT government as the National Capital Territory of Delhi. Jammu and Kashmir enjoys a special status among the states in accordance with Article 370 of the Constitution of India, in that it is guaranteed its own constitution, and Article 356 regarding the imposition of President's Rule does not apply to it.

12. Scharpf *et al.* (1976) has thus described the German political system as one of political interlocking (German: *Politikverflechtung*) between levels of federal government and separate units at the same level by virtue of more or less non-hierarchical and informal coordinating institutions.

13. Ministry of Home Affairs, New Delhi, http://mha.nic.in/AR01CHP7.htm (accessed on 4 December 2006).

14. See Kothari (1964, pp. 1161–73) for a description of the 'Congress system' and its working until the mid-1960s.

15. See Brass (1994, pp. 117–18) for a further discussion on this issue in the context of regional–national relations.

16. See Iyer (2000) for a discussion of crisis government in India.

17. AIR 1955 SC 549, at p. 556.

18. *S.R. Bommai vs Union of India,* 1994 (3) SCC 1, 216.

19. See F.W. Scharpf *et al.,* as the *locus classicus* for the description of German-style cooperative federalism, and Pehl (2003, pp. 173–95) for a discussion of the German federal system in connection with the accommodation of diversity.

20. See Mitra 2001, p. 55, for an assessment of linguistic and cultural diversity and its impact on federalism in India.

21. The data are based on the Government of India report on President's Rule in the states and Union Territories, quoted in Iyer (2000, p. 349 seq). Exact figures were unavailable for the period following 1997.

22. Three national emergencies were declared in accordance with Article 352 in India: in 1962 (revoked only in 1968) on account of the Sino-Indian Border War; in 1971 (revoked in 1977) ostensibly on account of the Indo-Pakistani war over the Independence of Bangladesh; and in 1975 (revoked in 1977) on account of internal disturbances connected with popular unrest in two states.

23. The term 'armed rebellion' was inserted for 'internal disturbance' by the Forty-fourth and Forty-fifth Constitution of India (Amendment) Acts, 1978, after this ground had

been used as the basis for the declaration of Emergency in 1975, and had subsequently been found to be too vague and to be inviting abuse by the Union government.

24. For a critical assessment of Article 356 of the Indian Constitution and its use, refer also to the *Final Report of the National Commission for the Reworking of the Constitution* (2001), vol. II, book 2. The group of commissioners inquiring into this issue was headed by R.S. Sarkaria, who had previously also headed the Commission on centre–state relations, termed the Sarkaria Commission, in 1988.

25. See Tarlton (1965, pp. 861–74), in Watts (1998, p. 123).

26. Jenkins (1999) provides valuable insights into the political management of the economic reform process by virtue of employing India's federal structure as an institutional framework for a quasi-laboratory of competing policies, and as an enabling structure aiming at providing incentives for policy innovation. Saez (2000) argues, in a similar vein in his assessment of the transformation, of cooperative federalism in India to a system of inter-jurisdictional competition after liberalization.

27. See Sinha (2005) for an overview of policy differentiation between states even during the era of more centralized economic planning, and its impact on the differential development of India's regions.

28. See Montek Singh Ahluwalia (2000), quoted in Drèze and Sen (2002, p. 321), for evidence of this trend.

29. For the latter point, see Rao and Singh (2004). This issue is additionally problematic because, as survey results have shown, the Indian public looks especially to state-level governments for the solution to developmental problems, reflecting an awareness of the responsibility on the part of states in this area, and assigns the blame for failure in these areas accordingly. See Chibber *et al.* 2004, p. 350.

30. For details, refer to Mitra and Singh (1999).

31. The BJP-led NDA coalition under Prime Minister Atal Bihari Vajpayee consisted initially of sixteen parties in the Lok Sabha, out of which only the BJP was a national party, and the Cabinet included many veteran regional politicians. In the fourteenth Lok Sabha, the ten-party coalition led by the Congress party under the name United Progressive Alliance (UPA), supported by the Left parties, included only two national parties, INC and NCP. Of the Cabinet ministers, two key portfolios, IT (Dayanidhi Maran) and Railways (Laloo Prasad Yadav), were allocated to regional figureheads.

32. *The Hindu*, 28 May 2004, www.thehindu. com/2004/05/28/stories/2004052807371200.htm (last accessed 8 June 2004).

33. See, for example, the discussions on Kashmir in Mathew (2002), and on India's Northeast in Bhattacharyya (2003) and Chattopadhyay (2006).

34. See the chapter on local governance in this volume.

35. See Saez (2002, pp. 128–9), for a detailed assessment of inter-governmental mechanisms, and the extent and limits of their achievements under the conditions of party-system fragmentation at the national and state levels, coalition governance, and the increased impact of disparities in socio-economic development with the advent of globalization and liberalization in India.

REFERENCES

Ahluwalia, Montek Singh. 2000. 'Economic Performance of States in Post-Reforms Period', *Economic and Political Weekly*, XXXV(19), pp. 1637–48.

Arora, Balveer. 2000. 'Negotiating Differences: Federal Coalitions and National Cohesion', in Francine R. Frankel, Zoya Hasan, and Balveer Arora (eds), *Transforming India: Social and Political Dynamics of Democracy*. New Delhi: Oxford University Press, pp. 176–206.

Basu, Durga Das. 1985. *Introduction to the Constitution of India*. New Delhi: Prentice-Hall, rpt 2003.

Bhattacharyya, Harihar. 2003. 'Indian Federalism and Tribal Self-rule', *Federations*, 3(3), pp. 11–12.

Bose, T.C. (ed.). 1986. *Indian Federalism: Problems and Issues*. Calcutta: K.P. Bagchi.

Brass, Paul R. 1994. *The Politics of India since Independence*, 2nd edn. Cambridge: Cambridge University Press.

Butler, David, Ashok Lahiri, and Prannoy Roy. 1995. *India Decides: Elections 1952–1995*. New Delhi: Books and Things.

Chattopadhyay, Rupak. 2006. 'The Challenge of Peace in Nagaland', *Federations*, 5(2), pp. 13–14.

Chibber, Pradeep, Sandeep Shastri, and Richard Sisson. 2004. 'Federal Arrangements and the Provision of Public Goods in India', *Asian Survey*, 44 (3), pp. 339–52.

Dikshit, R.D. 1975. *The Political Geography of Federalism*. Delhi: Macmillan.

Drèze, Jean and Amartya K. Sen. 2002. *India: Development and Participation*. New Delhi: Oxford University Press.

Elazar, Daniel J. 1994. *Federalism and the Way to Peace*. Kingston, Ont.: Institute in Intergovernmental Relations, Queen's University.

———. 1987. *Exploring Federalism*. Tuscaloosa: University of Alabama Press.

Friedrich, Carl J. 1968. *Trends of Federalism in Theory and Practice*. New York: Praeger.

GoI (Government of India). 1991. *The Constitution of India*. New Delhi: Government of India.

Harrison, Selig. 1960. *India: The Most Dangerous Decades*. Princeton: Princeton University Press.

Hesse, J.J. and V. Wright (eds). 1996. *Federalizing Europe: The Costs, Benefits and Conditions of Federal Political Systems*. Oxford: Oxford University Press.

Iyer, Venkat. 2000. *States of Emergency: The Indian Experience*. New Delhi: Butterworths India.

Jenkins, Rob. 1999. *Democratic Politics and Economic Reform in India*. Cambridge: Cambridge University Press.

Kothari, Rajni. 1970. *Politics in India*. New Delhi: Orient Longman.

———. 1964. 'The Congress System in India', *Asian Survey*, 4(12), pp. 1161–73.

Lijphart, Arendt. 1996. 'The Puzzle of Indian Democracy: A Consociational Interpretation', *American Political Science Review*, 90 (2), pp. 258–68.

Mathew, George. 2002. 'The Conflict in Kashmir challenges Indian federalism', *Federations*, 2 (3) available online at: http://www.forumfed.org/en/pubs/ vol. 2_no30_apr_2002.pdf, accessed on 1 February 2009.

Mitra, Subrata K. and R. Alison Lewis (eds). 1996. *Subnational Movements in South Asia*. Boulder, CO: Westview Press.

Mitra, Subrata K. and V.B. Singh. 1999. *Democracy and Social Change in India*. New Delhi: Sage Publications.

Mitra, Subrata K. 2001. 'Language and Federalism: The Multi-ethnic Challenge', *International Social Science Journal*, 167, pp. 157–60.

Moore, Barrington. 1966. *Social Origins of Dictatorship and Democracy: Lord and Peasant in the Making of the Modern World*. Boston: Beacon Press.

Nehru, Jawaharlal. 1985. *Letters to Chief Ministers, 1947–1964*. New Delhi: Oxford University Press.

Pehl, Malte. 2003. 'The Equal Right to Special Treatment? Territory, Identity and Minority Rights Protection in Germany's Federal Political System' in Institut du Federalisme (ed.), *Federalism, Decentralisation and Good Governance in Multicultural Societies*. Fribourg: Institut du Federalisme, pp. 173–95.

Rao, M. Govinda and Nirvikar Singh. 2004. 'The Political Economy of India's Federal System and Its Reform', Working Paper, Department of Economics, University of California, Santa Cruz. http://econ.ucsc.edu/ faculty/boxjenk/wp/rao_singh_apr2004.pdf (last accessed on 12 December 2006)

Rao, Rokkam S. 2001. 'Federalism and Fiscal Autonomy of States: The Indian Experience' in Ian Copland and John Rickard (eds), *Federalism: Comparative Perspectives from India and Australia*. New Delhi: Manohar, pp. 269–83.

Riker, William H. 1975. 'Federalism', in F. Greenstein, N.W. Polsby (eds), *Handbook of Political Science, Vol. 5: Governmental Institutions and Processes.*) Reading, MA: Addison-Wesley, pp. 93–172.

Saez, Lawrence. 2002. *Federalism without a Centre: The Impact of Political and Economic Reform on India's Federal System*. New Delhi: Sage Publications.

Scharpf, Fritz W., Bernd Beissert, and Fritz Schnabel (eds). 1976. *Politikverflechtung. Theorie und Empirie des Kooperativen Föderalismus in der Bundesrepublik Deutschland*. Kronberg: Scriptor.

Singh, Nirvikar. 2004. 'India's System of Intergovernmental Fiscal Relations', Working Paper, Santa Cruz: Department of Economics, University of California., http://econ.ucsc.edu/faculty/boxjenk/wp/ FFCSouthAfrica_Aug04.pdf (last accessed on 12 December 2006).

Sinha, Aseema. 2005. *The Regional Roots of Developmental Politics in India: A Divided Leviathan*. Bloomington: Indiana University Press.

Tarlton, C.D. 1965. 'Symmetry and Asymmetry as Elements of Federalism: A Theoretical Speculation', *Journal of Politics*, 27 (4), pp. 861–74.

Watts, Ronald L. 1998. 'Federalism, Federal Political Systems and Federations', *Annual Review of Political Science*, vol. I, pp. 117–37.

Wheare, K.C. 1964 [1951]. *Federal Government*, 4th edn. New York: Oxford University Press.

Appendix 4.1: A Profile of Indian States and Union Territories (arranged by population size)

NAME	CAPITAL	TYPE[a]	YEAR[b]	POPULATION ('000)[c]	AREA (KM²)[c]	NSDP (RS BILLION)[d]
Uttar Pradesh	Lucknow	State	1950	190,891	240,928	2412.0
Maharashtra	Mumbai	State	1950	106,894	307,713	3862.4
Bihar	Patna	State	1950	93,823	94,163	710.1
West Bengal	Kolkata	State	1950	87,869	88,752	2140.0
Andhra Pradesh	Hyderabad	State	1956	82,180	275,045	2106.6
Madhya Pradesh	Bhopal	State	1950	69,279	308,245	1031.3
Tamil Nadu	Chennai	State	1956	66,396	130,058	1945.3
Rajasthan	Jaipur	State	1956	64,641	342,239	1106.7
Karnataka	Bangalore	State	1956	57,399	191,791	1528.0
Gujarat	Gandhinagar	State	1960	56,408	196,024	1866.4
Orissa	Bhubaneswar	State	1950	39,899	155,707	671.0
Kerala	Thiruvanantha-puram	State	1956	34,232	38,863	1025.1
Jharkhand	Ranchi	State	2000	30,010	79,714	555.1
Assam	Dispur	State	1950	29,929	78,438	525
Punjab	Chandigarh	State	1950	26,591	50,362	925.4
Haryana	Chandigarh	State	1966	23,772	44,212	898.6
Chhattisgarh	Raipur	State	2000	23,646	135,191	457.4
National Capital Territory of Delhi	Delhi	NCT	1992	17,076	1,483	978.4
Jammu and Kashmir	Srinagar/Jammu	State	1957	12,366	222,236	n.a.
Uttarakhand	Dehradun	State	2000	9,497	53,483	225.2
Himachal Pradesh	Shimla	State	1971	6,550	55,673	224.0
Tripura	Agartala	State	1972	3,510	10,486	83.8
Meghalaya	Shillong	State	1972	2,536	22,429	57.6
Manipur	Imphal	State	1972	2,627	22,327	51.2
Nagaland	Kohima	State	1963	2,187	16,579	n.a.
Goa	Panaji	State	1987	1,628	3,702	109.5
Arunachal Pradesh	Itanagar	State	1987	1,200	83,743	27.7
Puducherry	Pondicherry	UT	1963	1,074	479	51.5
Chandigarh	Chandigarh	UT	1966	1,063	114	94.3
Mizoram	Aizawl	State	1987	980	21,081	n.a.
Sikkim	Gangtok	State	1975	594	7,096	15.3
Andaman and Nicobar Islands	Port Blair	UT	1956	411	8,249	14.4
Dadra and Nagar Haveli	Silvassa	UT	1961	262	491	n.a.
Daman and Diu	Daman	UT	1987	188	112	n.a.
Lakshadweep	Kavaratti	UT	1956	69	32	n.a.

Notes: [a] Type refers to the current constitutionally defined status of the respective political territory as a state, Union Territory (UT), or the National Capital Territory (NCT).

[b] Year refers to the year in which the respective unit acquired its current status as a separate state, Union Territory or National Capital Territory, which may or may not coincide with its last territorial revision or name change.

[c] Population figures are the projected March 2008 figures based on an extrapolation of the 2001 Census of India and were taken from the Census of India website (http://www.censusindia.gov.in/Census_Data_2001/Projected_Population/Projected_population. aspx). Figures for the states' geographic areas were compiled from state profiles on the Ministry of Health and Famil Welfare's website (http://www.mohfw.nic.in/NRHM.htm, accessed on 17 May 2009).

[d] NSDP is the 2005–6 Net State Domestic Product at current prices and was taken from the Goverment of India's Union Budget and Economic Survey 2008–9, http://indiabudget.nic.in/es2007–08/chapt2008/tab17.pdf (accessed 13 May 2009).

5 Local Governance

James Manor

Evidence from several Indian states indicates that India is better able to make democratic local government work well than are most other countries. This is true because India can offer several helpful preconditions: long prior experience of democracy; a well-developed capacity to conduct free and fair elections; extensive experience of bureaucrats yielding some influence to elected representatives; and a broad popular understanding that elections do not yield winner-take-all outcomes—so that opposition forces within India's elected councils are not utterly ignored or crushed as they are in some other cases (notably in Africa). Although democratic decentralization has limitations, when it works well (as it can in India), it yields substantial benefits, in terms of both development and of political renewal. Despite this, however, only a small minority of India's state governments have provided elected local bodies with enough powers and resources to enable them to work well. That paradox lies at the core of this analysis of local governance in India.

There are two main strands to the Indian story: remarkable achievements in a few states, and missed opportunities in most. The achievements have been extraordinary by any standard. Hard empirical evidence from many countries in Asia, Africa, and Latin America indicates that India's successes have been matched by only a handful of other countries— Bolivia, the Philippines, and perhaps two or three more.[1] However, since the Indian states in which opportunities have been missed greatly outnumber the high achievers, there is a sobering side to this story as well.

It is impossible in just a chapter to provide comprehensive details on democratic decentralization in India, because we are dealing not with a single case or system, but with twenty-eight—one for each state. Indeed, because rural (*panchayati*) and urban systems differ within individual states, it is arguable that we are dealing with fifty-six. Others have provided these details in great abundance, as we shall see. So this chapter concentrates on several important overarching themes that emerge from the details, and from the literature on democratic decentralization[2] internationally, since it yields insights into Indian cases that a focus on India alone would not reveal.

This chapter departs from patterns set by many other studies of the same topic in two ways. First, it avoids a detailed discussion of formal (constitutional and legal) policy blueprints and changes, of which there is no shortage. It does so partly because space is at a premium, but also because the *informalities* of politics are more important in determining outcomes—and they make for more interesting reading.

Second, it offers no analyses of the pre-Independence period. It therefore omits reference to decentralization in the British period, and to the familiar claims that panchayats flourished in India down through the centuries. British initiatives (which this writer has studied) appear to have little relevance to the post-Independence story. Claims that panchayats extended back into the mists of time (which he has not studied) appear debatable. This is true mainly because such panchayats as actually existed were bound up with caste dominance, and therefore operated on very different principles from those which—in theory at least—apply to recent experiments with democratic decentralization.

This chapter is divided into five parts. Part I examines the recent history of democratic decentralization, in India and internationally, because the Indian story diverges somewhat from patterns elsewhere in interesting ways. Part II assesses the promise and limitations of democratic decentralization. Both are important in their own right, but that discussion will also develop a fuller understanding both of the achievements in some Indian states and of the missed opportunities in others. Part III considers the pre-conditions that are *essential* to the success of democratic decentralization, and other factors that are merely *helpful*. That discussion will show why India is better able than most other countries to make decentralized systems work well. Part IV addresses variations from state to state within India, in order to move the analysis beyond an excessively general discussion. Finally, Part V considers the implications of democratic decentralization for poverty, inequality, and social exclusion. It examines well-founded concerns that it may offer little promise on these fronts, while

also presenting fresh evidence to suggest that the prevailing pessimism in the literature may have overstated the problem.

DECENTRALIZATION IN RECENT HISTORY: INTERNATIONALLY AND IN INDIA

Democratic decentralization is one of the fashions of our times. More than sixty governments across the world have experimented with it since the late 1970s. This has happened because decentralization fits logically into a broader trend in recent international history. So let us briefly consider the grand narrative which sums this up—and India's place within it. We will encounter certain singular aspects of the Indian case which indicate that the narrative oversimplifies.[3] That is the way with grand narratives. They are accurate up to a point, but when they are applied to specific cases, distinctive features arise.

The grand narrative goes like this. In nearly every part of the world, the period between World War II and the mid-1970s witnessed greater confidence in the centralized state as an instrument for managing society's business than any other era in modern history.[4] In the West and in the Soviet bloc, this confidence was inspired by the success that had been achieved by centralized modes of governance in coping with the problems of the Great Depression and in winning World War II. But it was also shared by most of the leaders of the emergent nations of Asia, Africa, and Latin America.

Then the mood changed, quite dramatically. After the oil shocks of the mid-1970s, and for complex reasons,[5] confidence in centralized modes of governance and development plummeted. This triggered a surge of enthusiasm for alternatives to the centralized state. These included (among other things) market forces, civil society, human rights, bottom-up participatory approaches to development—and democratic decentralization. Not all of these things sat comfortably alongside one another, so they should not be seen as a harmonious package. But as a result of this change—and of many other more specific things such as the success achieved by certain decentralizing state governments in India—a huge number of governments across the world (which differ greatly in their character and motivations) have experimented in various ways with democratic decentralization.

This narrative does not entirely fit the patterns of change that we find in India. It leads us to expect little interest in democratic decentralization there in the years before the late 1970s, and then a surge of interest in it. This is not exactly how things went. There *was* a surge after 1977, when the West Bengal government, and then the Karnataka government, began taking panchayats seriously. However, in the period before 1977, powerful people in India were not invariably and utterly disinterested in democratic decentralization.

This is partly explained by the influence of Gandhi's ideas. He was deeply sceptical about the concentration of power in a centralized state. His interest in the self-sufficiency of local arenas lent itself to calls to empower panchayats at the grassroots. His views did not, of course, go unchallenged. Ambedkar famously distrusted village-level hierarchies. And Nehru and Patel spent much of their time taking charge of, adapting, and sustaining the institutions of the Central government.

Much of Patel's work after Independence focused on establishing formidable central institutions and informal understandings that would maintain their pre-eminence. Witness his successful efforts to achieve the accession of India's princes to the new national order, and his reassurances to civil servants that they would retain something very like their crucial role in governing the country. Nehru was much enamoured of the Soviet model of development, led by a centralized state machinery. It was only possible to introduce a diluted version of that model in the new, democratic India.[6] But he still—for example—gave the state the leading role in promoting industrialization, and established a Planning Commission which in his day played a far more potent role than it has in recent years.

And yet it is inaccurate to conclude from this that Nehru was hostile to democratic decentralization. As early as 1949, he was urging Chief Ministers to pay attention to the Etawah project—an initiative in selected villages in Uttar Pradesh—which, among other things, sought to promote the idea of self-government through panchayats. He spoke of 'definite

and promising results' (Nehru [edited by Parthasarthi] 1985, vol. I: 402–3). Three years later, he was telling them of 'the great importance I attach to...community projects...' for agricultural extension, which were in much the same vein (ibid., vol. II: 556). And in the early 1960s, Rajni Kothari found him sympathetic to panchayats. Kothari had been drawn into a national study of democratic decentralization, and into a discussion group that met periodically with the Prime Minister. His experiences led him to conclude of panchayati raj that 'few beyond Nehru and S.K. Dey were convinced of it' (Kothari 1989, vol. I: xxx). It is no surprise that Dey was enthusiastic—he is well known as India's pre-eminent advocate of panchayats. But Nehru emerges here as a far more complex figure than we might expect. The principal custodian of the machinery of the Central government was also capable of seeing the limitations of centralized governance, and the utility of bottom-up influence on political and policy processes.

So in India—in contrast to the grand narrative—democratic decentralization enjoyed support from the apex of the political system between 1947 and the mid-1960s. There then followed a rather arid spell until interest was rekindled in West Bengal in the late 1970s.

In most countries and in many international development agencies, the reaction against the centralized state ran to excess, just as the earlier confidence in it had done. But in India, the reaction was less intense. There was (and is) enough inertia in the political system, and there were (and are) enough powerful people who favour centralized approaches to ensure that. We find them (of course) in the Central government, but there are also plenty of leaders at the state level who were (and are) also inclined towards centralized modes of governance within their states.

There were also, however, some leaders at the state level who took a different view—in two senses. In general terms, they sympathized with the reaction against over-centralization—especially those who had grown impatient with Indira Gandhi's attempts to concentrate power in her own hands. More specifically, in two key state governments, ruling parties that opposed Mrs Gandhi's Congress saw democratic decentralization as a means of demonstrating that they could do something imaginatively different from the national leadership, which would make government more open and responsive to ordinary people.

The first of these was the Communist Party of India (Marxist)-led government in West Bengal, which came to power in 1977 and breathed new life into existing panchayati raj legislation. It showed that it could achieve substantial change, which the Janata government in New Delhi advocated but did little about—partly for lack of time (Franda 1979: 116–46)—and which Mrs Gandhi's Congress government after 1980 opposed. The second was Ramakrishna Hegde's Janata government in Karnataka after 1983, which sought to demonstrate that it could be more adventurous and constructive than the governments of Indira and then Rajiv Gandhi.

When we consider Rajiv Gandhi, we encounter further ambiguities. Early in his premiership, in 1985, he expressed a tentative interest in decentralization, and then held consultations on this issue during 1987 and 1988 with bureaucrats posted at the district level. The opposition parties, not surprisingly, regarded these as inappropriate attempts to bypass state-level political leaders—and in part, they were correct. But these discussions appear to have helped persuade the Prime Minister that democratic decentralization made sense.

However, it was not until early 1989, a year which would end with a general election, that he began seeking support for the idea in earnest, with a series of sammelans attended by large numbers of elected members of panchayats. In May of that year, this led to the introduction of a bill to amend the Constitution, to ensure the creation of panchayats with substantial responsibilities at district, block, and local levels in rural areas, plus fair and regular elections to them. When introducing it, Rajiv Gandhi mentioned—as something of 'an afterthought'—that a second amendment would be proposed dealing with elected bodies in urban areas. Another round of sammelans with urban representatives was hastily organized, and a second Constitutional Amendment Bill then emerged (Sivaramakrishnan 2000: 5–7, 23).

Rajiv Gandhi appears by this point to have been genuinely committed to decentralization, but there is also no doubt that as the 1989 election approached, he needed ideas that might appeal to voters. Little

had been achieved during his time in power. He had done U-turns on most of his initial policy initiatives, so fresh proposals were necessary. This one appealed to Congressmen, since it cleverly poached an idea from opposition parties in West Bengal and Karnataka. The opposition, though, was not about to hand him a success, and the two bills failed to get the required support in the Rajya Sabha. Congress still made much of a slogan on decentralization during the 1989 election campaign. But by stressing this promise rather than past achievements, they suggested that there were all too few of the latter. They did poorly at the election.

The V.P. Singh government, which succeeded them, introduced a single bill to serve similar purposes. But it was overtaken by the Mandal and mandir controversies, which led to the government's fall in late 1990. Roughly the same two amendment bills that had been drawn up in 1989 were submitted to Parliament soon after the Congress, now led by P.V. Narasimha Rao, took power in 1991. This was done partly to pay homage to the late Rajiv Gandhi. But Narasimha Rao had long been a genuine enthusiast for democratic decentralization.[7] When the Hegde government in Karnataka wanted a Union minister to inaugurate its new panchayati raj programme in 1987, it invited Narasimha Rao (then Minister of Human Resource Development) to do so. To a huge crowd of panchayat members in Bangalore, he said, 'Mr Hegde may belong to the Janata Party and I may belong to the Congress party, but we both belong to the panchayati raj party.'

With cross-party support, the Seventy-third and Seventy-fourth Amendments—in support of democratic decentralization in the rural and urban sectors respectively—were passed, and came into force in March 1993. But despite the broad support and the enthusiasm of the Prime Minister, they could not require state governments to be generous in devolving powers and funds onto elected local bodies. Local government is a state subject under the Constitution, so the amendments had to suggest more things than they required of the states. Since then various state governments have responded to the amendments in diverse ways. The result has been a curious mixture of significant achievements and missed opportunities.

DEMOCRATIC DECENTRALIZATION: PROMISE AND LIMITATIONS

When it works well, democratic decentralization has numerous virtues. It never produces spectacular changes, and it is often attended by ambiguities and disappointments. It also has significant limitations (as we shall see later). But it tends strongly to change things for the better on several fronts.[8]

It almost always makes the business of government more transparent—because decisions are taken in open forums and close enough to the grassroots to be visible to ordinary people. It also enhances the accountability of government, and makes it more responsive, in three senses. The *speed* of responses (decisions, actions, projects, and so on) usually increases because empowered councils at lower levels need not wait for approval—often for long periods—from higher authorities. The *quantity* of responses also increases because those councils strongly prefer many small development projects, rather than a smaller number of big projects which appeal to politicians higher up. And, most crucially, the *quality* of government responses also increases—if 'quality' is measured by the degree to which responses conform to popular preferences. And since citizens gain some influence over decisions about development projects and thus get projects that they prefer, they acquire a sense of ownership vis-à-vis them. They therefore tend to maintain those projects more enthusiastically, so that they become more sustainable.

Information flows between government and citizens improve markedly—in both directions. Civil servants are empowered by a massive increase in the number of reports flowing *upward* from the grassroots through elected councillors. They receive early warnings—which were often unavailable before decentralization—of problems in remote places such as outbreaks of disease, flooding, or droughts, so that action can be taken before these mushroom into full-blown disasters. And the empowerment of local councils at lower levels often enables those bodies to take prompt action themselves (Manor 1993: 1019–20).

The *downward* flow of information about government programmes also increases. To cite one crucial example, the uptake on government health programmes—not least ante- and post-natal care schemes—tends to increase. This occurs because elected councillors are far better than government employees at explaining the value of such schemes in terms that ordinary folk can grasp.

Absenteeism by primary school teachers and local health workers (a significant problem in India) tends strongly to decline—not spectacularly as some claim, but often significantly—because citizens inform elected councillors of non-attendance, and the latter have the power to discipline absentees.

Democratic decentralization almost always stimulates increased political participation.[9] This happens because it gives ordinary people significant new opportunities to influence decisions that affect their lives. They naturally respond by becoming more active in public affairs than they were before, when decisions were made high up in the political system by people beyond their reach.

It also almost always causes associational activity to increase, so that civil society (voluntary organizations with some autonomy from the state) grows and becomes more vibrant. Old associations gain more members and become more active, and new associations form. And associations engage in a broader array of activities in the public sphere.

Democratic decentralization also tends to strengthen the integrative capacity of governments, both *horizontally* and *vertically*. It helps to achieve horizontal coordination of different sectors (health, education, agriculture, and so on). Elected councillors often insist on exercising coordination, both to enhance their own importance and to produce better development outcomes. If, for example, a small irrigation project is undertaken, they insist on involving bureaucrats who understand water use, agriculture, fisheries, sanitation, and engineering. Coordination is thereby strengthened. Decentralization also helps in 'scaling up' (vertically)—that is, the upward transmission of lessons from successes in isolated localities. Since each elected council is part of a state-wide network, if one council succeeds with a particular project, the network makes it possible for information about this to travel vertically to higher levels and horizontally to other councils, which might then try the same thing.

In some parts of India, the overall amount of money corruptly diverted from government programmes has declined as a result of democratic decentralization. The chairman of a local panchayat in Karnataka explained how this happens.[10] Before decentralization, he was a powerful figure at the sub-district or block level, where he and three bureaucrats would meet each year behind closed doors. They would steal 40 per cent of the block's development budget and divide it among themselves, and they would then present the remaining 60 per cent to the people as if it were 100 per cent of the budget. Since this process was opaque, they were never found out. After democratic decentralization, so many people knew how much money was coming down through the system—the process was so transparent—that, even though he chaired the local panchayat, he could only rake off a small fraction of his earlier profits. Democratic decentralization always causes the *number* of people involved in corruption to increase—because so many more people have a little influence to peddle—but it tends to reduce the *overall amount* of money stolen.

Democratic decentralization can renew the democratic political process in several ways. It creates opportunities for talented local residents, who previously remained out of public affairs, to hold political office and contribute to the democratic and development processes. It also brings new blood—plus talent, ideas, and energy—into parties that may have gone stale. Networks of elected councils at lower levels also provide parties with frameworks through which to extend the reach of their organizations.[11]

The creation of a huge number of elected posts close to the local level also eases the potentially dangerous resentments of ambitious people who, before decentralization, could not find a role in political life. In Karnataka, before 1987, there were just 224 elected posts that provided real influence (in the state assembly). After the creation of strong panchayats there, the number increased to over 50,000. Many ordinary people who had previously felt apathetic or cynical towards governments—because over-centralized structures provided them with

little influence and few benefits—discovered that they could make their preferences felt through their elected representatives. This eases popular apathy and cynicism, and causes the legitimacy of decentralizing governments to increase.

Finally, democratic decentralization can make governments seem adventurous, and perhaps even a little exciting. The thing that politicians hate most is to appear *boring*. And yet in this era of tight fiscal constraints, they often appear boring to citizens because they lack the funds to do exciting things. Democratic decentralization offers politicians a way out of this problem, because it is not particularly expensive and it makes leaders look innovative, and maybe even a little heroic and exciting. It can thus enhance not just the legitimacy, but also the popularity of decentralizing governments.[12]

We also need to recognize, however, that democratic decentralization has significant limitations on several fronts—even when it works well. It cannot encourage unified efforts by all sections of local communities to pursue development projects in a spirit of solidarity, because it causes competition (of a democratic nature, but competition nonetheless) to quicken between groups within the locality. It cannot help to reduce the overall amount of government expenditure. Governments which think that it can, and off-load tasks onto councils without providing enough funds to perform them, simply destroy the councils' capacity to operate constructively.

It cannot do much to increase the amounts of local resources that state institutions can mobilize, because elected councillors are seldom given strong revenue-raising powers, and even when they have them, they have good democratic reasons to use them sparingly. It cannot achieve anything close to what the literature suggests in promoting planning from below. Elected councillors again have good democratic reasons for hesitancy about planning—because it prevents them from responding flexibly to unexpected problems and changes in conditions.

Nor can democratic decentralization—except in major conurbations—do much to accelerate economic growth. It can produce changes in local arrangements that enable local economies to operate somewhat—

but *only* somewhat—more productively. But this cannot make much contribution to the nation's or any single Indian state's gross domestic product.[13]

Democratic decentralization has other limitations as well.[14] The most crucial of these has to do with its capacity to reduce poverty, inequality, and social exclusion. That is a matter serious enough to receive a detailed analysis here, in the fifth part of this chapter. This limitation will understandably persuade some readers that it matters little whether democratic decentralization works well. But evidence from various parts of India indicates that quite substantial gains for local residents in general are possible—as the discussion above on its promise indicated. Some of these gains benefit poor, disadvantaged groups as well as others (see Part V). These things imply that it is in the interests of India's state governments—and of their residents—to seek to make it work well.

DEMOCRATIC DECENTRALIZATION: THE INDIAN STORY

To understand why India is better able to make democratic decentralization work well—and how numerous state governments have prevented it from working well—we need to identify the things that enable it to flourish. We need to distinguish here between factors that are *essential*, and merely *helpful*. We shall see that India is well-equipped to make it work well because '*helpful*' things are present in abundance in nearly all parts of the country. But most state governments have been reluctant to provide *essential* things in sufficient measure to enable democratic local government to achieve its potential.

'*Helpful' things*: Some writers claim that a number of things which are merely 'helpful' to democratic decentralization are in fact 'essential', but they are mistaken. High literacy rates, good Human Development Index scores, and high per capita incomes are all helpful. So is extensive prior experience with democratic politics—which, among other things, acquaints bureaucrats with the process of working with elected representatives. So too is a lively, free press. It also helps if multi-party politics is well established.

It is helpful if enlightened civil society organizations are well developed and actively engaged in development activities, and that is true (to varying degrees) across much of India. It is especially helpful if such organizations work among poor and socially excluded groups, to build their capacity to engage effectively with elected councils at lower levels, and to provide them with information on the workings of the system and on specific government programmes to which they might gain access. Once again, in many parts of India such civil society organizations are present. More crucially, across much of India we find networks of such organizations, extending from New Delhi down to the regional and local levels.[15] It should be stressed that the list of developing countries where such networks exist is extremely short. Brazil is the only such country in Latin America, there are none in Africa. In Asia, this is true only of India, Bangladesh, and the Philippines.[16] Some Indians take these organizations for granted, but they are actually quite remarkable.

Some people (mainly those on the Right) argue that the prior existence of a middle class is essential to the successful working of democratic decentralization. There is clear evidence (see below) that this is *not* essential, and powerful middle-class interests may actually create problems by capturing many of the benefits that flow from decentralized bodies. But in many places, the existence of a middle class has helped decentralized systems to work well. Other people (mainly on the Left) argue that prior land reform is essential. There is again solid evidence to show that such systems can work well in the absence of this, but it plainly helps if it has occurred.

It also helps if—before the creation and empowerment of elected councils at lower levels— administrative deconcentration to those levels has occurred, so that bureaucrats from various development ministries are present at those levels. If administrative deconcentration takes place at the same time as democratic decentralization, the process is far more complicated and likely to misfire. Consider, for example, the decisions of the Bangladeshi and the Karnataka governments in the 1980s to attempt democratic decentralization. Bangladesh devolved powers onto the sub-district level, where bureaucrats from development ministries had previously been substantially absent. In India, such bureaucrats had long been present in strength at that level. This meant that the task which faced state governments in India was far less difficult than in Bangladesh. Prior deconcentration is helpful.

For evidence that these things are 'helpful' but not 'essential', consider the example of Mozambique. Several years ago, local councils in roughly one-third of that country were given significant powers and resources, and accountability mechanisms were put in place within decentralized institutions. The result was a quite successful new system, which enhanced local development and delivered projects that local residents preferred—in radical contrast to the stagnant, unresponsive, over-centralized system which had preceded it. *And yet*, Mozambique possessed almost none of the 'helpful' things listed above. It had low literacy, poor human development indicators, almost no prior experience of democracy, only a tiny middle class, a frail civil society, no functioning multi-party system, a tame press, and so on.[17] But despite all of that, success has been achieved in Mozambique because all of the 'essentials' to the effective working of democratic decentralization were present. It is to these that we now turn.

'Essential' things: Only three things are essential if democratic decentralization is to work well:

1. adequate powers must be provided to elected councils;
2. adequate resources (especially financial resources) must be provided; and
3. adequate accountability mechanisms must be provided—to ensure the accountability of bureaucrats to elected representatives, and the accountability of elected representatives to ordinary people.

Evidence from a large number of countries that have experimented with democratic decentralization indicates that if these three things are *present in strength*, the experiments will work *well*. If any one of them is *absent*, they will *fail*. If one or more of them are *present* but *weak*, the experiments will work *less than well*—either badly, or only somewhat well.[18]

With a few notable exceptions, state governments in India have tended to provide one or more of these essentials in *in*adequate measure. This has caused their

decentralized systems to work less than well, and often badly. Given the presence in nearly all parts of India of most of the things which are 'helpful' to the workings of democratic decentralization, these decisions by so many state governments represent a large number of sadly missed opportunities.

SUCCESSES AND MISSED OPPORTUNITIES: VARIATIONS AMONG STATES

The story of democratic decentralization in India in recent years is extremely complex—not least because we are dealing with twenty-eight different states. It is impossible in a chapter-length study to deal with all or even most of them. Readers who seek that sort of detail should turn to the splendid efforts at documentation by Indian non-governmental organizations.[19] This discussion distils their findings, and identifies important patterns across various states.

Most state governments have denied elected councils (urban and rural) sufficient powers and resources to enable them to work well, as they clearly can in the Indian context. The policies of most state governments have conformed to one or both of two broad trends:

1. most governments have refused from the outset to devolve adequate powers and resources onto elected councils at lower levels, and
2. many governments—whether they were reluctant or generous about devolution at first—have clawed back powers and resources over time.
   Let us consider these in turn.

Many state governments have refused to give elected councils responsibility for all—or even for very many—of the twenty-nine subjects listed in the Eleventh Schedule of the Constitution. Consider, for example, Aarthi Dhar's report on panchayati raj institutions in mid-2003. Karnataka was the only state that has delegated all the subjects, followed by Kerala at twenty-six. Jammu and Kashmir was yet to adopt the provisions of the Seventy-third Amendment while Andhra Pradesh, Arunachal Pradesh, Bihar, Goa, Gujarat, Maharashtra, Meghalaya, Mizoram, Nagaland, Tripura, Chandigarh, Delhi, and Pondicherry were yet to constitute District Planning Committees to facilitate the devolution of power. This violated the letter of the Seventy-third Amendment, but no action had been taken against these governments. The refusal of the Uttar Pradesh authorities to constitute such district committees was a violation of a law which that government itself had passed. In Haryana and Tamil Nadu, bureaucrats had been made chairs of these committees, and in Madhya Pradesh ministers had been put in charge of them—in violation of the amendment's spirit (Datta 2003). In other states, these committees were deprived of meaningful powers.

These things have persuaded India's Ministry of Rural Development to introduce a Constitutional Amendment Bill to make it mandatory to give greater financial and administrative powers to panchayats.[20] But we should not conclude from this that the Central government has been consistently sympathetic to decentralization. That same ministry has strengthened District Rural Development Agencies with substantial funds so they can bypass panchayats, and District Vigilance and Monitoring Committees chaired by Members of Parliament (MPs) and containing only nominated members which oversee development without giving panchayats a significant voice (Datta 2003).

Many state governments have also refused to give councils enough funds to perform tasks assigned to them, so that councils often face unfunded mandates which inspire popular cynicism about decentralization. Some—Andhra Pradesh under Chandrababu Naidu was an example—have illegally diverted funds to which councils were entitled to other programmes (Manor 2002). Some state governments have even delayed meeting their legal responsibility to conduct elections to councils. The Bihar government dragged its feet in holding initial panchayat elections, and the Andhra Pradesh government sought to delay the process of re-electing panchayats that were completing a previous term. The latter effort was only thwarted when a public interest litigation (PIL) led to a court order to proceed with a fresh election. In Gujarat, the government tried to offer Rs 1 lakh to any panchayat that would hold elections by consensus, in a clear effort to undermine the electoral process (ibid.). And so the many-faceted story goes on.[21]

Let us now examine the second broad trend, the tendency of governments to claw back powers and/or resources previously given to elected councils at lower levels. This afflicts democratic decentralization not just in India, but in many other countries. Claw-backs happen in several different ways, but as we consider them, we should note one factor that is almost always present—internationally and in India—although it is seldom the only cause. This is the demand that arises from politicians (ministers and especially legislators) and from some civil servants for a restoration of powers, and sometimes funds, that they have had to cede to elected councils.

This demand does not always produce results. An example from Karnataka in the late 1980s illustrates this. When the Hegde government formulated plans to devolve virtually every development task onto panchayats, the main architect of the initiative, Abdul Nazirsab, anticipated objections from legislators and ministers to such generosity. He therefore prepared a fallback position that would provide objectors with one minor concession—a reversal of the initial decision to place cooperatives under panchayats—while leaving all other development tasks in the hands of elected councils. In the event, this concession sufficed—thanks to firm backing from the Chief Minister—and panchayats were very substantially empowered.

This did not prevent ministers and legislators from grumbling thereafter. One powerful and very enlightened minister, B. Rachaiah, complained that 'I am the Minister of Education and I cannot even decide on the location of a school in my own constituency. The panchayats have that power, and I can only make high policy.'[22] But his pleas for a restoration of his former powers went unheeded.

On many occasions, however, the demand for claw-backs *has* succeeded. That happens when other factors reinforce the demand. How has this happened? We need to consider four scenarios.

The first occurs when demands from legislators and politicians are reinforced by anxieties among senior leaders about how decentralized systems are working. In 2000, the Madhya Pradesh government— which had originally been extremely generous to panchayats—faced pressure from jealous legislators and ministers to curb their power. At the same time, Chief Minister Digvijay Singh had become dismayed by the substantial power which *sarpanche*s (the chairpersons of panchayats) had begun to wield at all levels within the system. It was therefore decided to introduce something called 'District Governments', which had the effect of giving legislators and especially ministers—working in close collaboration with senior bureaucrats and police officers—control over the district level. The *zilla panchayats* (district councils) were stripped of many of their powers. (This prevented the Chief Minister from receiving the support and vital political intelligence of the members and leaders of zilla panchayats—and that was the single most important reason for his party's defeat at the state election in December 2003 [Manor 2004c].)

In the second scenario, senior leaders reckon that opposition parties may win control of too many elected councils at lower levels, and take back powers as a result. A senior civil servant in one state government once told this writer that the government's decision on whether to claw-back or increase the powers of panchayats depended on the number which the ruling party captured at an upcoming election. In some states, even when the ruling party wins control of *most* panchayats, leaders still divert powers and resources away from panchayats to other bodies over which they can exercise near-total control. This was true of, for example, the *Janmabhoomi* programme in Andhra Pradesh.

A third scenario entails a change in the ruling party at the state level, when the outgoing government has been generous to panchayats. The new government may (often erroneously) believe that panchayats are thus closely aligned with the former ruling party, and claw back powers from them as a result. Or the new ruling party may be less sympathetic to democratic decentralization. A few parties (the Dravida Munnetra Kazhagam in Tamil Nadu is an example) operate on ideological principles that cause them to be suspicious of decentralization. Much more often, parties which have little genuine ideology take back powers because they prefer centralized approaches.

A fourth scenario flows not from a change of ruling parties, but of ministers responsible for decentralization. The perceptions of a minister can trigger efforts to take powers away from elected councils at the lower level. These perceptions are

not always the same. Consider, for example, two Congress ministers in Karnataka. In the early 1990s, B. Basavalingappa served there as Minister for Rural Development and Panchayati Raj. He was a member of the Scheduled Castes (SCs), and he shared Ambedkar's view that villages were arenas in which prejudice against Dalits were more marked than at higher levels in the political system. He therefore sought to take back some of the powers which panchayats, especially *gram panchayats*, were exercising.[23] His Congress successor in that post, M.Y. Ghorpade, did not share Basavalingappa's views of villages. But he regarded panchayats as mere conduits for state government development programmes, rather than as institutions of local self-government which should have substantial decision-making powers. He therefore continued to curtail their powers,[24] but for reasons that differed from his predecessor.

We often hear enthusiasts for democratic decentralization claim that once powers are bestowed on elected councils at lower levels, they will never be taken back because citizens who resent this will protest and prevent it. However, all of the available evidence from numerous cases—in several Indian states and internationally—indicates that this never happens. Protests often arise, but they do not thwart recentralization.

One other trend is worth mentioning. It is less important than those discussed above, but it has still had a powerful impact in some Indian states. This is the tendency of state governments to *delegate* power to 'user committees' or 'stakeholder committees'— sometimes called 'parallel bodies'—at lower levels in the system. These bodies are sometimes unelected (appointed by bureaucrats). More often, they are elected through processes that are less reliably democratic than elections to local councils. That carries with it the danger that they may be largely controlled by bureaucrats and/or by the state's ruling party. These parallel bodies usually operate within single sectors— joint forest management committees, water user committees, health committees, and so on—in contrast to local councils, which deal with many different sectors. And since these committees often play a role in programmes funded by donors, they are sometimes provided with such substantial funds that they cannot manage them effectively—even though local councils in the same place may be crippled by a lack of resources. So we sometimes find—in a single locality—user committees with *excessively funded mandates* alongside local councils with *unfunded mandates*. Either of these things would be a recipe for trouble, but the combination is disastrous.[25] Among other things, it tends to inspire popular cynicism towards elected local councils—because without funds, they seem so useless alongside these other, lavishly funded parallel bodies. There is evidence that some state governments—Andhra Pradesh under Chandrababu Naidu was an example—actively seek this outcome.

This combination arises less often in India than in most of Africa, where it is doing great damage. But it exists in enough places in India to warrant concern. The delegation of powers and funds to parallel bodies that are often less rooted in local democracy than are local councils is another example of state government decisions that undermine democratic decentralization. And it is of a piece with a more general trend towards delegation in India's political system—which has some promise, but also inspires serious worries (Mehta 2003).

There is a way to overcome the difficulties posed by delegation to parallel bodies at lower levels. They can be placed under the control, or at least the substantial influence, of properly elected local councils—a policy which Digvijay Singh (among others) calls 'convergence'. That approach would address any shortfall in the democratic character of parallel bodies, while simultaneously tackling the funding shortfalls that afflict local councils. It would also ensure better coordination between various sectors (health, sanitation, irrigation, agriculture, among others), which become rather isolated when single-sector committees stand alone. Coordination is one thing that local councils do rather well. But most state governments are disinclined to adopt this approach.

This review of the various ways in which elected council at lower levels either never receive adequate powers and funds—which are essential if they are to work well—or lose them once they have been devolved, indicates how opportunities have been missed in so many Indian states.

DEMOCRATIC DECENTRALIZATION AND SOCIAL JUSTICE

In India and throughout the world, democratic decentralization tends *not* to trigger dramatic social change, but to reflect and reproduce existing power relations and patterns of inequity—while at the same time facilitating their gradual erosion. The discussion that follows considers two issues: social exclusion, and then the promise and limitations of democratic decentralization for poverty reduction.

Social Exclusion: One key aspect of social exclusion is exclusion from the public sphere. This problem has long been faced at the local level by Adivasis, Dalits, and women, for whom reserved seats on elected councils have been provided. In considering this issue, we face two difficulties. First, despite a number of fine studies (Meenakshisundaram 1994; Aziz and Arnold 1996; Maheshwari 1994; Lieten and Srivastava 1999), there are so many widely dispersed local councils—and so many different systems in the 28 states—that we lack sufficient evidence from empirical studies to draw firm general conclusions. So what follows should be seen as somewhat tentative. Second, in a chapter-length study, it is impossible to examine this immensely complex matter thoroughly. So let us concentrate on what—on present evidence at least—appears to be the main problem under the broad heading of 'social exclusion'.

It may surprise some readers, but that problem is gender. Adivasis often comprise substantial majorities on panchayats, which appears to ease their exclusion not only from the public sphere, but also from influence on local councils. Dalits—or at least Dalit men—have long had seats reserved for them on all types of public bodies. This has enabled them to overcome the problem of utter exclusion from the public sphere, and while many remain excluded from *influence* within it, their difficulties on that front appear—again, on present evidence—to be less severe than those faced by most women members of local councils.

This writer has repeatedly been told by hundreds of non-Dalit male villagers in seven quite varied Indian states that they view reservations for women on panchayats as far more 'shocking' and 'objectionable' than reservations for Dalits. There are four main explanations for this. First, reservations for Dalits have been common practice for decades—so they are accepted, if not necessarily welcomed. Second, in most localities, women greatly outnumber Dalits—so that if they become a coherent force, they pose a greater threat to the prevailing local power structure. Third, as many sociologists and anthropologists have been telling us, the power of caste hierarchies even in rural areas has declined quite substantially over time—so that in many localities, the issue of Dalit influence is less salient than it once was (although in some, it has intensified caste conflict). Finally, the power of patriarchy (gender inequity) has declined less, and women have often remained more thoroughly excluded from the public sphere than have male Dalits—so that the reservation of seats and headships on local councils for them is more unsettling to traditionally influential groups.

Most of the available evidence comes from studies of rural areas and thus of panchayats[26]—and in a chapter on 'local governance', our focus is mainly on village or gram panchayats, the lowest of the three tiers in the Indian system. We need to consider, first, the extent to which women have achieved a *presence* on these elected bodies, and second, the degree to which they have been able to exert *influence* there.[27] Their presence would seem to be guaranteed by the constitutional requirement that a minimum of one-third of seats and chairpersons' posts on panchayats be reserved for them. But in practice, in a sometimes significant minority of cases, male relatives or patrons often attend council meetings in their place[28]—although this practice appears to be on the wane (Kaushik 1998: 21). So even this most minimal of gains—mere presence—has been less than fully achieved.

The exercise of influence is a far more difficult task. Numerous impediments restrict it. The attitudes of male members of panchayats are a potent problem. For a taste of this, consider the reply of a village panchayat chairman in Karnataka when this writer asked him how male councillors' treatment of women members had changed in the early years after the Hegde government had created a strong panchayati system in 1987.

At first, when we gathered for meetings, we did not acknowledge their presence in the room. After five years, we would say to them, 'Hello, how are you', and then get on with making decisions.[29]

Male councillors frequently conspire with village panchayat secretaries and with bureaucrats who work just above the local level—who are overwhelmingly male—to deny women members information. They often prevent them from speaking, and sometimes even from voting in council meetings. They often refuse to listen or respond when women members bring concerns to them outside of meetings. It is a testament to the fortitude of women councillors that this tends not to discourage them from attending panchayat meetings,[30] but it severely undermines their capacity to exert influence.

A further set of impediments has arisen from men outside the panchayats. Women councillors frequently face scornful laughter, abuse, and even sexual violence (Jayal 2006: 25) from male residents of their localities for having the temerity to expect to play a role in public life. And to make matters far worse, women members of panchayats often face resistance from males at home—from their husbands and close relatives. These men may regard it as less than respectable for a woman to go unaccompanied to the council office or the offices of bureaucrats. They may accuse them of sexual impropriety, and react with jealousy to any activity independent of home and husband.[31] This is not always a problem. There is clear evidence that some male relatives of women councillors believe that their roles on panchayats have enhanced the status of the family, so they welcome this change and support them (Jayal 2006: 22). But this trend appears to be outweighed by negative cases.

Further impediments arise from institutional arrangements, some of which are rooted in constitutional amendments, but most of which have largely been crafted by state governments. The refusal of many of those governments to provide adequate powers and resources to panchayats deprives *all* members—women and men—of influence (a point to which we return below), but two more specific problems need to be noted.

Constituencies reserved for women change—rotate—at each election, and so do the chairpersons' posts on panchayats. As a result, a woman elected once to a reserved seat has little or no chance of being re-elected, since (except in a small number of states) it is highly unusual for women to win unreserved seats. This guarantees that the vast majority of women councillors will be inexperienced at any given time. A woman who has gradually acquired awareness, confidence, skills, and connections in five years as a councillor is usually denied the chance to serve a second term. This seriously undermines their capacity to influence events.

Still more serious is the rotation of chairpersons' posts. These provide women with much more significant opportunities than mere seats on councils, so that the principle is far more invidious here. To make matters worse, in some states, women are permitted to hold these posts for quite restricted periods—20 months in Karnataka, for example—rather than for their full five-year term.[32] It takes many women nearly that long to learn how to operate within the system. But then, no sooner do they do so than they are legally required to step down. And to reiterate, even where women chairpersons can serve a full five years, the women who hold those posts have virtually no chance to continue beyond five years. The policy of 'rotation' cries out for reconsideration.

There are also provisions (the particulars of which vary from state to state) to permit no-confidence motions to oust chairpersons of councils. This has been repeatedly abused by male councillors to remove women (or members of the SCs and Scheduled Tribes [STs]) who prove too assertive, or merely competent, for their liking.

Two counterweights to these tendencies deserve comment. First, a few state governments have sought to support women in panchayats. In a tiny number of states, progressive ruling parties have actively sought to promote social transformation through elected councils, and have made this one element of their strategies (Lieten 1996). Additionally, in Andhra Pradesh under Chandrababu Naidu, the government sought systematically to encourage women to play a more assertive role in public affairs—since women had always been strong supporters of the Telugu Desam Party. Unfortunately, Naidu was among the most hostile Chief Ministers in India to panchayati raj—

since he could exert less-than-total control over it—so his government's efforts did little for women members of panchayats. Sadly, the number of states to which the comments in this paragraph apply has been so limited as to yield little benefit for women councillors.

The other counterweight is the work of enlightened civil society organizations in a great many states, to enhance the political capacity of women members by providing them with crucial information, training, and connections beyond the village.[33] These associations include small community-based organizations at the local level, somewhat larger but sub-regional organizations, and much more formidable organizations with state-wide or inter-state impact. As we noted above, India is one of only four countries in Asia, Africa, and Latin America where the claims of national-level civil society organizations to penetrate to the grassroots are accurate. But despite the unusual strength of civil society in India—although it varies markedly from state to state—the 'reach' of these organizations is rather limited. They usually fail to engage with more than a minority (and often a small minority) of women at the village level. So, as this counterweight has not yet made a major contribution, it remains unusual for women to gain from it.

The impediments discussed above have not always sufficed to prevent women from exercising some influence in decentralized bodies. There is an abundance of credible stories to indicate that women councillors have had the determination to assert themselves (often facilitated by civil society organizations), and that they have acted collectively as a lobby for women's welfare (see just below). Competition among male leaders has—more often than is recognized in the literature—helped women to gain some limited leverage, since the men need the votes of women to obtain majorities on councils. But taken overall, the picture is depressing—at best, ambiguous. Women appear to be controlled by male relatives or patrons, or co-opted by the latter, more often than they assert themselves. As almost always happens with democratic decentralization, change has occurred at a painfully slow rate.

Despite this, however, there are more than one million women members of rural panchayats and urban councils across India (out of a total of three

million, half a million of which come from the SCs
and STs). They are beginning to acquire some limited
awareness, skills, connections, and confidence, to rival
male councillors, who usually possess these things
from the outset. They sometimes band together—
across caste, class, party, and factional lines—to
address issues of vital concern to women. They stress
women's needs for accessible sources of clean water,
food security, access to benefits, education for girls,
and their need for employment by way of assistance to
self-help groups at the grassroots, and opportunities
for poor women to obtain employment and fair pay
on public works projects (Jayal 2006).

They also do one vastly important thing which
has received far less attention from analysts than it
deserves. Women panchayat members often facilitate
an increase in the uptake—especially by female
villagers—on vital public services, especially in the
health sector. This is crucial because in villages, women
are usually the gatekeepers between the household
and the wider world when health issues arise.
Women councillors are far better able than are health
professionals or bureaucrats (or men in general) to
explain the need for health services to ordinary female
villagers—because they are their neighbours and their
peers. They can explain why ante- and post-natal care is
useful, and why inoculations from health professionals
who use intimidating needles can prevent illness
and even death. Their explanations often persuade
female villagers to come forward for health care in
greater numbers. This is the main reason why health
department bureaucrats and health professionals at the
district and sub-district levels in India tend to favour
democratic decentralization, once it has had a chance
to function for a time.[34] Amid all of the ambiguities
and disappointments that attend the role of women in
councils, there are *some* encouraging signs.

One further issue deserves especially careful
consideration. In most, though not all, states, it
appears that a majority of the women elected to
panchayats were illiterate or scarcely literate. This has
naturally inspired anxiety among some analysts that
this has thwarted these women's efforts to exercise
influence within panchayats. It has certainly limited
their capacity to do so, as a great many women
councillors themselves have consistently testified

to numerous investigators (Jayal 2006: 20, 24).
And recent, as yet unpublished, research by Anirudh
Krishna has found that a person's level of education is
a more powerful determinant than caste of his or her
capacity to operate effectively in the public sphere. But
one unusually reliable study in Karnataka (Stephen
and Sekaran 2001: 74) and most (though not all)
encounters with women councillors by this writer
in seven states suggest that illiterate or barely literate
women members of panchayats from low-status
groups have been *more* successful at influencing events
than have women from higher-status groups—in
part because they are less socialized to behave in
restrained ways that are the latter. This thesis needs to
be tested in studies in a diversity of states because, if
it were corroborated, it would fundamentally alter our
assessment of women's roles in panchayats.

However, despite some encouraging evidence,
we must take care not to stress positive aspects too
strongly. Many commentaries do so, since they describe
the system not as it is, but as analysts wish it to be. In
most places, the overall picture is still quite depressing.
To illustrate this, let us conclude by considering one of
the most scrupulous, systematic, and objective studies
yet to emerge. It was undertaken by a civil society
organization that has long done impressive work not
only in supporting women members of panchayats, but
also in analysing the workings of local governance—
SEARCH in Karnataka (Stephen and Sekaran 2001).
The study is particularly discouraging because that
is a state where panchayats have long had significant
powers and resources, so that elected members of local
councils—of both genders—have not been thwarted by
state government policies, as is common in many other
regions. Karnataka is also a state in which enlightened
civil society organizations have been present in strength,
and are very active among women councillors.

We might therefore expect plenty of good news
from this study, but that is not the main message. This
wide-ranging analysis found that 'some' women—
but '(v)ery few' were able to 'emerge victorious due
to their determination and perseverance', and to
inspire similar efforts among other women in
village panchayats. In general, they encountered
'more stumbling blocks than building blocks'(Stephen
and Sekaran 2001: 171, 174).

Nearly half the women councillors had contested elections against their will, at the insistence of males seeking to manipulate them to control the panchayats. 'Very few...could identify the problems/needs of the people in their respective villages or had contacted... government officials in order to solve them.' Male councillors, panchayat secretaries, and even villagers refused to cooperate with them, and the secretaries 'deliberately withheld information'. 'Most families...lent them no support.' When some women sought to assert themselves, they were 'ill treated by the same...relatives who had supported them originally'. Younger women—who in most states comprise a sizeable majority of female panchayat members[35]—suffered unusually strong prejudices, often became 'victims of gossip' when their official duties required them to interact with men, and found that the burdens of bearing and rearing children undercut their effectiveness in the public sphere. Women older than fifty felt 'too old to attend meetings'. A number of low-status women councillors 'faced threats to their lives...' (Stephen and Sekaran 2001: 171–7). And so it goes on.

The broad picture that emerges from this and other similarly objective, realistic analyses indicates that India's admirably bold attempt to give women substantial influence in the public sphere has only begun to make headway against the invidious influence of patriarchy. As Jayal has argued (Jayal 2006: 19), in most states democratic decentralization has made politics more *inclusive* of women, SCs, and STs, but has done far less to *empower* them.[36]

Poverty: Can democratic decentralization help to reduce poverty? Here again, the answers are complex and ambiguous.

As this writer has argued elsewhere (Manor 1999)[37] there are good reasons to expect democratic decentralization to reduce poverty that arises from inequalities *between* sub-regions or localities within Indian states. Decentralized systems tend strongly to provide more adequate representation and resources to remote, impoverished arenas that have previously been starved of both. They can also reduce urban bias. And they sometimes include provisions to channel extra resources to deprived areas.

However, democratic decentralization is less likely to reduce the poverty that arises from

inequalities *within* sub-regions or localities—and that type of poverty is usually the *main* problem, in India and everywhere else. It is even possible that decentralization can make things worse—if elite prejudices against poorer groups are stronger at lower levels in a political system than at higher ones. (If there is no difference between elite perceptions at various levels, then the impact of decentralization on poverty is likely to be neutral.) Democratic decentralization may result in elite capture of newly empowered bodies at lower levels. Other analyses have reached even more pessimistic conclusions, although the most cogent of these[38] is based mainly on evidence from Africa, where conditions and politicians' habits of mind are less promising than in India.

It is now apparent, however, that these earlier analyses (including this writer's) may have been a little too negative. More recent evidence indicates that poor and previously marginalized groups in Indian states may gain significantly from democratic decentralization when one or more of four conditions exist. They are as follows:

1. when the ruling party in a state is pro-poor,
2. when the vast majority of the people living within the arena served by an elected council are poor,
3. when poor and/or formerly excluded groups gain enough seats on decentralized bodies to make it necessary for leaders to create alliances with some of their representatives, or
4. when rival parties and/or elites in the larger political system and/or at lower levels compete to appeal to poor voters.

We need to consider each of these points in turn.

1. It is very unusual to find ruling parties that are ideologically committed to favouring the poor. But the Communist Party of India (Marxist)-led governments in West Bengal and Kerala qualify—although *objective* evidence on Kerala is still scarce and in West Bengal, the strong rural bias of the ruling alliance appears to have limited its capacity to assist the *urban* poor.
2. When the vast majority of people living in an arena served by a decentralized body are poor, then poor people are more likely to dominate—or loom large within—elected councils. In some parts of the world—most notably Africa—the

vast majority of the population in many countries is extremely poor, so that this condition exists very widely. In India, this is far less common, but such conditions exist in a number of sub-regions and localities.

3. The numbers of reserved seats on decentralized councils are almost always too limited to give poorer groups significant leverage. But when a very large number of citizens within an arena served by a council qualify as 'poor' and/or 'excluded', many or perhaps most elected representatives may come from those groups. Politicians who seek to become leaders on such bodies (who often come from more prosperous groups) may therefore feel compelled to forge alliances with some representatives of poor, previously excluded groups. That does not guarantee that such bodies will promote poverty reduction—prosperous leaders may simply co-opt members from disadvantaged groups. But it opens up that possibility, and an impact has been made on inequality in some arenas as a result.

4. More common, and therefore more promising as a source of pro-poor efforts, are situations in which political parties and/or local elites feel compelled to compete for the support of poorer groups—especially where the competing groups have roughly equal strength. Such competition almost always occurs not because local politicians are philosophically committed to poverty reduction, but for pragmatic reasons—because the votes of the poor can make the difference between victory and defeat at elections.

The four items above have been presented in order of the likelihood that they will arise in India—from the least to the most likely. Item (1) applies only in West Bengal and (at times) in Kerala. Item (2) is rather unusual in India, but it is not unheard of. Item (3) tends to apply in arenas where item (2) also applies, but not only there. Item (4) applies—and is likely to apply more often, over time (see below)—in far more places than do the first three.

These comments do not justify a surge in optimism about the promise of democratic decentralization as a force for social justice. But they mitigate somewhat the pessimism that is often expressed about this. We also need to consider a few other, mildly encouraging, points.

In some countries, and in some places within India, democratic decentralization produces such substantial benefits to *all* sections of society so that everyone—including the poor—gains. This is especially true when the political system prior to decentralization was decidedly ineffective and unresponsive to people at lower levels. In such systems, many ordinary people see even *modest* new opportunities to participate in open politics and to influence decisions about development projects as significant steps forward.[39] In such circumstances, poorer groups seldom gain more than prosperous ones. So we cannot argue that greater *equity* is an outcome. But poorer groups can, like everyone else, gain significantly when such changes occur.

We saw in the discussion of gender just above that democratic decentralization, especially in India, tends to increase the uptake on certain vital services—especially in the health sector, but in others as well. And democratic decentralization can reduce (not radically, but somewhat) absenteeism by teachers and health professionals in local government schools and health centres—because elected councillors easily learn of this and sometimes have the authority to press absentees to perform their duties.

When these things happen, the poor gain disproportionately. This is true of increased uptakes, because prosperous people who have higher levels of education and better connections with the wider world seldom need to be convinced of the utility of, for example, ante- and post-natal care programmes. Poor people, however, often need to be persuaded. This is true of reduced absenteeism in local government schools and health centres because the poor depend heavily upon them—unlike prosperous groups, who turn to the private sector.

Some programmes targeted specifically at the poor can also be linked effectively to decentralized councils. This plainly happened with the Education Guarantee Scheme under Digvijay Singh in Madhya Pradesh, and what is now Chhattisgarh. His government saw that civil society was weakly developed among poorer groups at the grassroots, so it had to find ways to stimulate demands for basic services from the poor, and to respond to them. To achieve this, it gave panchayats in villages that lacked primary schools the right to demand schools and teachers with rudimentary training. Most of the communities which demanded and received new schools were so poor that they contained very few prosperous people who might capture and misuse the benefits from the scheme. So elite capture was not a serious danger.[40]

This programme recruited residents of poor villages who had at least a secondary education to provide primary-level teaching to students, as para-professionals. The teachers were given more limited basic training than their counterparts in conventional government schools, but the training was quite intense. They were paid less than conventional teachers, and elected councils at lower levels were the agency that provided them with payment—with financial input from the state government. This ensured that the new schools, the buildings for which were also funded by the government, were affordable amid tight fiscal constraints. Since the panchayats paid the teachers, strong ties of accountability existed between them and the teachers. Over a six-year period, 26,571 impoverished localities demanded and received new schools and teachers, so that 1,233,000 children gained opportunities for an education, most of whom had *none* before. When such demand-driven programmes—which are exclusively targeted at poor villages—are linked to local councils, benefits clearly reach the poor (and the socially excluded, since a huge number of such schools were founded in Adivasi areas).

Finally, it is likely that *over time*—if decentralized systems are allowed to retain substantial powers and resources, which is sometimes a big 'if'—poorer groups will in most cases become better able to gain from decentralization. They will become better organized and connected, and more politically aware, self-confident, active, and skilled. Where that happens— and it has begun to happen in many parts of India— there is, again, less reason to be pessimistic about decentralization serving the goal of greater equity.

One last sobering comment needs to be made, however. It is very difficult for elected local councils which are weak, and which are denied powers and resources by politicians at higher levels, to achieve

much—in providing greater influence to women, SCs, and STs; in reducing poverty; or in any other vein.[41] Most state governments in India have been reluctant to empower and fund elected councils at lower levels, even though it would serve the interests of ruling parties to do so. So, despite a few splendid exceptions which stand as models to the rest of the world, Indian states' approaches to democratic decentralization may be chiefly remembered as sad examples of what might have been.

NOTES

1. Indeed, we can go further. India's achievements with democratic decentralization exceed those of a number of industrialized countries—especially, but not only, in eastern, central, and southern Europe.

2. The term 'democratic decentralization' is used here in preference to *'panchayati raj'* because the latter refers only to the rural sector. Most Indians live in rural areas, but the Seventy-fourth Amendment to the Constitution sought to promote democratic decentralization in urban centres. So a focus only on panchayats would be inadequate.

3. This is not an example of *Indian* exceptionalism. Other specific cases—that is, other countries—also tend to diverge from the pattern set out in the grand narrative.

4. I am grateful to Geoffrey Hawthorn for stressing this point.

5. The process entailed much more than a reaction to the oil shocks and resource constraints. It is discussed in detail in Manor (1999).

6. For a splendid and little noted analysis of this, see Nayar (1976, pp. 135–59).

7. Interview with P.V. Narasimha Rao, New Delhi, 11 February 1992.

8. The discussion which follows is set out in far greater detail in Manor (1999, Chapter 6). There is evidence from India to support all of the points made in this discussion.

9. Here, 'participation' means voting in elections, attending election meetings, and taking part in election campaigns. But between elections, people also contact their elected representatives and low-level bureaucrats and take part in demonstrations—to make demands, and to express themselves about things that they like or dislike. And they seek to obtain information from government bodies about programmes and projects that can make important differences to them. Democratic decentralization nearly always causes an increase in these activities.

10. Interview, Mandya district, 8 April 1993.

11. This was clearly understood by leaders of the Communist Party of India–Marxist in West Bengal, and of

the Janata Party/Dal in Karnataka when they decentralized. Interview with Ramakrishna Hegde and Abdul Nazirsab, Bangalore, 14 March 1986.

12. For much more in this vein, with India being assessed in comparative perspective, see Crook and Manor (1998).

13. This is worth remembering when we read that, for example, India's Empowered Sub-committee on the Financial and Administrative Powers of Panchayati Raj Institutions emphasized that in order to achieve a growth rate of 8 per cent in the Tenth Plan, it was essential to feed district plans into state- and national-level planning. *The Hindu*, 19 August 2003.

14. These are discussed at some length in Manor (1999, Chapter 6).

15. See, for example, the work of Participatory Research in Asia (PRIA) and its regional partners.

16. These comments are based on my discussions with civil society specialists at the Ford Foundation and the World Bank in 2002.

17. These comments are based on the research of Fidelx Kulipossa

18. It is impossible, in a chapter of this length, to explain the complex reasoning and evidence behind these statements, but see Manor (1999) especially Part IV.

19. The most comprehensive single survey was conducted by the Institute of Social Sciences, Mathew and Buch (2000). See also the monthly publication by that Institute, *Panchayati Raj Update*, which provides better documentation than is available on any other country, and a volume by another non-governmental organization, PRIA (2001).

20. *The Hindu,* 19 August 2003.

21. The vast number of examples of all these tactics are well-documented in the publications listed in note 19 above.

22. Interview, Bangalore, 12 March 1988.

23. Interview with the minister, Bangalore, 2 March 1993.

24. These comments are based on interviews in Bangalore in 1998 and 2000 with civil servants who were very familiar with Mr Ghorpade's approach.

25. These issues are examined in much more detail in Manor (2004b, pp. 192–213).

26. In addition to sources cited below, see also Palanithurai (2002, pp. 37–50), Stephen (1997, pp. 4–13), Athreya and Rajeswari (1998), Mathew and Nayak (1996), Pai (1998), Srinivas (1998), Verma (1998), Vidya (1997), and Hust (2004).

27. See in this connection, Phillips (1996). I am also grateful to Anne-Marie Goetz for numerous insights on these issues. She and some others use somewhat more elaborate modes of analysis than the one that appears here,

but the need for clarity and constraints of space require a more simplified approach.

28. N.G. Jayal has made this point (2006, pp. 15–35), and evidence seen by this writer supports this and her other arguments. See also, Jayal's 'Gender and Decentralisation', Background Paper for the United Nations Development Programme, New Delhi, typescript.

29. Interview, Mandya district, 26 March 1993.

30. See the evidence in Buch (1999), and Kaushik (1998).

31. I am grateful for the points in this paragraph to Gayathri, an anthropologist at the National Institute of Advanced Study, Bangalore. She has lived in the home of a woman councillor in Kodagu, and analysed these problems with insight.

32. I am grateful to Anand Inbanathan for calling attention to this point.

33. This writer has developed a detailed comparison (forthcoming) of the work of two such organizations— PRIA in Andhra Pradesh and *Samarthan* (a PRIA partner) in Madhya Pradesh—with similar, less formidable organizations in Ghana.

34. This insight was first put to me by a doctor in Dharwar district of Karnataka in 1993. Subsequent enquiries in six other states have yielded similar comments.

35. Buch (1999) and Kaushik (1998)—both cited by Jayal (2006).

36. Many of these issues are discussed in much greater detail in Manor (2004a).

37. For a detailed study of these issues in Karnataka, see Crook and Manor (1998, Ch. 2).

38. This is Crook and Sverrisson (2001). See also Johnson (2002, pp. 3–36).

39. This comment is based on the research of Fidelx Kulipossa on Mozambique.

40. This and the strong system of panchayats in Madhya Pradesh under Digvijay Singh are analysed in far greater detail in Melo *et al.* (forthcoming).

41. Jayal also makes this point (2006, p. 27).

REFERENCES

Athreya, V.B. and K.S. Rajeswari. 1998. *Women's Participation in Panchayati Raj: A Case Study from Tamil Nadu.* Chennai: M.S. Swaminathan Foundation.

Aziz, A. and D. Arnold (eds). 1996. *Decentralised Governance in Asian Countries.* New Delhi: Sage Publications.

Buch, N. 1999. *From Oppression to Assertion: A Study of Panchayats and Women in Madhya Pradesh, Rajasthan and Uttar Pradesh.* New Delhi: Centre for Women's Development Studies.

Crook, R. and A.S. Sverrisson. 2001. 'Decentralisation

and Poverty Alleviation in Developing Countries: A Comparative Analysis or, Is West Bengal Unique?', *IDS Working Paper 130,* Brighton.

Crook, R. and J. Manor. 1998. *Democracy and Decentralisation in South Asia and West Africa: Participation, Accountability and Performance.* Cambridge: Cambridge University Press.

Datta, P. 2003. 'Panchayati Raj', *Frontline,* 19 July–1 August.

Franda, M.F. 1979. *India's Rural Development: An Assessment of Alternatives.* Bloomington: Indiana University Press.

Hust, E. 2004. *Women's Political Representation and Empowerment in India: A Million Indiras Now?* New Delhi: Manohar.

Jayal, N.G. 2006. 'Engendering Local Democracy: The Impact of Quotas for Women in India's *Panchayats'*, *Democratization,* 13(1), pp. 15–35.

————. 'Gender and Decentralisation', Background Paper for the United Nations Development Programme, New Delhi, typescript.

Johnson, C. 2002. 'Decentralisation and Poverty: Exploring the Contradictions', *Indian Journal of Political Science,* 63(1), pp. 3–36.

Kaushik, S. 1998. *Participation of Women in Panchayati Raj in India: A Stock Taking.* New Delhi: National Commission for Women.

Kothari, R. 1989. *Politics and the People: In Search of a Humane India,* vol. I. New Delhi: Ajanta Publications.

Lieten, G.K. 1996. *Development, Devolution and Democracy: Village Discourse in West Bengal.* New Delhi: Sage Publications.

Lieten, G.K. and R. Srivastava. 1999. *Unequal Partners: Power Relations, Devolution and Development in Uttar Pradesh.* New Delhi: Sage Publications.

Maheshwari, S.R. 1994. *Local Government in India.* Agra: L.N. Agarwal Publications.

Manor, J. 2004a. 'Democratisation with Inclusion: Political Reforms and People's Empowerment at the Grassroots', *The Journal of Human Development,* 5(1), pp. 5–29.

————. 2004b. 'User Committees: A Potentially Damaging Second Wave of Decentralisation?' *European Journal of Development Research,* 16(1), pp. 192–213.

————. 2004c. 'The Congress Defeat in Madhya Pradesh', *Seminar,* vol. 534, pp. 21–2.

————. 2002. 'Democratic Decentralisation in Two Indian States: Past and Present', *Indian Journal of Political Science,* 63(1), pp. 51–72.

————. 1999. *The Political Economy of Democratic Decentralisation.* Washington: World Bank.

————. 1993. 'Panchayati Raj and Early Warnings of Disasters', *Economic and Political Weekly,* XXVIII(20), pp. 1019–20.

Mathew, G. and R.C. Nayak. 1996. 'Panchayats at Work: What It Means for the Oppressed', *Economic and Political Weekly,* XXXI(27), pp. 17565–73.

Mathew, G. and N. Buch (eds). 2000. *Status of Panchayati Raj in the States and Union Territories of India.* New Delhi: Concept Publishers and Co.

Meenakshisundaram, S.S. 1994. *Decentralisation in Developing Countries.* New Delhi: Concept.

Mehta, P.B. 2003. 'Towards a Post-Democratic Age?', *The Hindu,* 8 October.

Melo, M., N. Ng'ethe, and J. Manor. Forthcoming, *Against the Odds: Politicians, Institutions and the Struggle against Poverty.*

Nayar, B.R. 1976. 'Political Mobilization in a Market Polity: Goals, Capabilities and Performance in India' in R.I Crane (ed.), *Aspects of Political Mobilization in South Asia, Federalism without a Centre.* Syracuse: Maxwell School of Citizenship and Public Affairs, pp. 135–59.

Nehru, Jawaharlal.1985. *Letters to Chief Ministers 1947–1964,* vols. I and II edited by G. Parthasarathi. New Delhi: Oxford University Press.

Pai, S. 1998. 'Pradhanis in New Panchayats', *Economic and Political Weekly,* XXXIII(18), pp. 1009–10.

Palanithurai, G. 2002. 'Impediments to Empowerment of Women: Experiences of Elected Women Representatives in Panchayats in Tamil Nadu', *Indian Journal of Political Science,* 63(1), pp. 37–50.

Panda, S. 'Emerging Pattern of Leadership among Rural Women in Orissa', *Indian Journal of Public Administration,* 42(3–4).

Phillips, A. 1996. *The Politics of Presence.* Oxford: Oxford University Press.

PRIA (Participatory Research in Asia). 2001. *The State of Panchayats.* New Delhi: PRIA.

Sivaramakrishnan, K.C. 2000. *Power to the People? The Politics and Progress of Decentralisation.* New Delhi: Konark.

Srinivas, B. 1998. 'Panchayati Raj, Patriarchy and Challenges', in L. Raj Sebasti and E. Mathias (eds), *People Power and Panchayati Raj.* New Delhi: Indian Social Institute.

Stephen, F. 1997. 'Women's Empowerment: A Process of Reconstructing Power Relations', *SEARCH Bulletin,* July–September, pp. 4–13.

Stephen, F. and N. Raja Sekaran. 2001. *Sheep and Lambs: An Empirical Study of Women in Local Self Governance in Karnataka.* Bangalore: SEARCH.

Verma, B. 1998. *Participation of Women in Panchayati Raj: Garhwal Region.* New Delhi: Centre for Development Studies and Action.

Vidya, K.C. 1997. *Political Empowerment of Women at the Grassroots.* New Delhi: Kanishka Publishers.

6 The Supreme Court

Lavanya Rajamani and Arghya Sengupta

In a country in which representative institutions are widely perceived as failing in their core tasks, the Supreme Court of India has come to assume the mantle of a 'Supreme Court *for Indians*' (Baxi 2000: 156–7). In the past few decades, the Court[1] has opened its doors to public-spirited citizens, expanded the frontiers of fundamental rights, and even 'rewritten parts of the Constitution' (Bhagwati 1985). The Court has over time transformed itself into an arena in which political, social, and economic battles are fought, and socio-economic justice is delivered (Pillai 1984). This expansive judicial role in modern India has been welcomed in some quarters as 'chemotherapy for the carcinogenic body politic' (Baxi 2003), and treated in others with increasing concern.

This chapter traces the evolution of the Court from a modest institution seeking to find its place in a newly independent India to a powerful, dynamic actor that shapes law, evolves policy, and plays a central determinative role in the governance of modern India. Over the years, through progressive and far-reaching decisions, the Court has demonstrated a commitment to preserving constitutional liberty, and expanding and protecting human rights. It has also demonstrated an ability to keep the executive in check, and to adapt and respond to the demands placed on it as a consequence of the inaction or ineffectiveness of other wings of government. There are signs of overreach by the Court however, and this essay explores the early signs and dangers of such overreach and examines in particular the concerns that arise with the policy evolution role the Court is regularly called upon to play. It could be argued that the Court is ill-equipped to play this role, and in seeking to do so, it compromises on the role that it is equipped and required to play. Three likely consequences are discussed—the creation of a corpus of case law marked by rhetoric, imprecision, and intellectual fuzziness; the substitution of principle by predilection in shaping judgments and reaching decisions; and issues of access, participation, and equity raised by the Court's efforts to equip itself to play the expansive policy evolution role that it does. This chapter concludes that notwithstanding the fact that the Court has delivered several progressive judgments over the years, it needs to tap into a vein of self criticism and restraint if it is to continue to command popular legitimacy, and to contribute to a healthy functional balance between the wings of the government.

POWER, PROMISE, AND REACH

Apolitical Beginnings: Power and Promise

'[D]ifferent parts of the Constitution will act and react on each other and the [Supreme] Court will have to decide questions arising from such a situation... discharging its duties as perhaps no other Court has so far been called upon to do'.[2]

Chief Justice Kania's seemingly innocuous, albeit powerful words set the tone for the functioning of the Supreme Court as the ultimate dispenser of constitutional justice in India. Much like his statement, the Court in its early years was understated yet potent, using the restricted confines of the judicial space to act as an effective check on legislative pronouncements. This check, exercised through the power of judicial review, was used judiciously by the court in the early years. As illustrative examples—it denied procedural fairness to a detenu, detained under a preventive detention law, presumed constitutionality of statutes till proved otherwise, and refused to strike down legislation 'in a crusader's spirit'.[3] At the same time, it regularly found several land reform laws to be unconstitutional, invalidated curbs on free speech, and ruled against reservation of seats in medical colleges.

Three key aspects stand out in the early years of the Supreme Court. First, its strict adherence to the constitutional text; second, as a consequence of this, refusing to give in to lofty governmental ideologies if express warrant for it was not constitutionally provided for; third, an unequivocal concession of the plenary power of the Parliament to amend the Constitution. Landmark decisions of the Court in this period bear testimony to these propositions. In *A.K. Gopalan vs State of Madras*,[4] the constitutional question was whether the procedure for detention, contained in the law which permitted preventive detention, could be challenged for violating the fundamental freedoms of the petitioner under Article 19. In addition, whether the procedure established by law for enforcing preventive detention, which

deprived the detenu of his right to personal liberty under Article 21, would have to be a fair procedure was also at issue. The detenu was a Communist leader, and detention infringes a fundamental political liberty; hence this decision had considerable political charge. The Court, undeterred by the likely political repercussions of the decision, held that the law could not be judged on the basis of Article 19 as the provision applied to free persons and not to those in detention. Further, guarantees in Article 19 could not be used to curtail the government's power to lay down a procedure under Article 21 as each of the articles should be read separately. Finally, the procedure for detention did not need to incorporate any abstract standard of fairness and would be valid as long as it was contained in a validly enacted law. The constitutionality of the law was thus upheld, subject to the caveat that the grounds for such detention must be communicated to the detenu.

But *Gopalan* did not necessarily signal the Court's willingness to read fundamental rights restrictively. In the same year, the Court gave an expansive construction to freedom of speech in *Romesh Thapar vs State of Madras*,[5] severely constricting governmental leeway in imposing restrictions on free speech. Shortly after, in *State of Madras vs Srimathi Champakam Dorairajan and another*,[6] it held equality amongst communities in the question of admission to educational institutions to be sacrosanct under Articles 15 and 29 of the Constitution and struck down a provision for community-specific distribution of seats in medical colleges.

These seemingly divergent decisions suggest that the Court, at the outset, was engaged in a positivist interpretation of constitutional provisions rather than the pursuit of a particular ideology. Article 21 expressly used the term 'procedure established by law' in preference to 'due process established by law'.[7] The *Gopalan* Court viewed this omission as evidence of a clear intention to exclude fairness as a touchstone for testing the constitutionality of the procedure established by the law. Similarly, in *Romesh Thapar*, the Court refused to permit any restriction on the freedom of speech and expression that was not sanctioned by the constitutional text. And in *Champakam*, even though the law in question was directed at promoting social justice, the Court was wary of carving out an exception to the constitutional diktat of absolute equality in admission to educational institutions.

These early salvos fired by the Court forced the government into action. The view had gained ground that if the Constitution, which the Court was faithfully interpreting, stood in the way of governmental legislation in furtherance of social justice 'then surely it is time to change the Constitution'.[8] Thus, within two years of the Constitution having come into force, the First Amendment was introduced which widened the scope of restrictions on the freedom of speech, and facilitated admission of backward classes into educational institutions.[9]

The most controversial provision in the First Amendment however related to land reforms. Social justice—in particular, *zamindari* abolition—was a significant political issue for Congress governments at the Centre and the states. However, the decision of the Patna High Court, striking down the Bihar Land Reforms Act for being violative of the fundamental right to property,[10] and the possibility of a further potential reversal at the Supreme Court, put the land reforms programme in jeopardy. The government sought to address this through Article 31A which inter alia saved all laws on zamindari abolition from being invalidated on the singular ground that they violate fundamental rights, and Article 31B, which immunized all laws placed in the Ninth Schedule from judicial review. It was this aspect of the First Amendment and the constitutional amendments it spawned relating to land reforms which provided the central theatre of conflict between the legislature and the judiciary on who would ultimately hold the keys to the Constitution.

In *Sankari Prasad vs Union of India*,[11] the Supreme Court held that the power of amendment belongs to the Parliament, and this power was an unlimited one. In upholding the validity of Article 31A, the Court refused to read any rights-based limitations into the power to amend, as this was neither evident from the text of the Constitution nor could it have been said to be the intention of its drafters. While judicial review of legislative acts was a fundamental part of the constitutional scheme, the notion that courts would

strike down constitutional amendments for being unconstitutional, was not contemplated.[12]

Despite this ringing declaration of parliamentary supremacy, it was not ideological sympathy with the land reforms programme of the government that was at the root of the decision as much as a literal reading of the constitutional provisions coupled with a traditionalist understanding of the limitations of the judicial review. If any doubts persisted, those were quickly dispelled in *State of West Bengal vs Bela Banerjee and others*.[13] In this case, a law which sought to acquire land for the purpose of resettlement of refugees from East Pakistan was declared unconstitutional, and the Court held compensation under Article 31(2) to mean 'a just equivalent'. Hence, the government's scheme to provide compensation at rates which prevailed in 1946 was found to be violative of Article 31(2).

Paying compensation at rates which were 'a just equivalent' was deemed impossible by the government of the time. Social justice required land redistribution but the coffers prevented land acquisition at market rates. Bolstered by *Sankari Prasad* and the fact that a constitutional amendment would be beyond judicial scrutiny, the government passed the Fourth Amendment which inter alia made adequacy of compensation in a measure designed to promote a public purpose non-justiciable. Comparable quietus descended on the issue as a consequence. Though the Supreme Court reaffirmed its authority to determine whether the matter did pertain to a public purpose, and if it did not, whether the principles on which compensation were payable were germane,[14] the authority of Parliament to amend the Constitution in this manner, excluding judicial review, was not challenged for a considerable length of time.

Such a challenge however arose in *Sajjan Singh vs State of Rajasthan*.[15] Through the Seventeenth Amendment in 1964, the government had amended the Ninth Schedule and placed forty-four Acts therein, thereby excluding judicial review of these laws. The Amendment however was upheld, with the Court affirming *Sankari Prasad* and categorically conceding to Parliament the unfettered authority to amend the Constitution, even if such an amendment was to expressly overrule a court decision. It is interesting to note however that in *Sajjan Singh* for the first time, in a matter relating to the amendability of the Constitution, a nuanced position was adopted. Justice Mudholkar, in a revealing opinion, suggested that the Constitution has certain 'basic features' which function as limitations on the power of the Parliament to amend.[16] These features, he believed, were contained in the Preamble and any attempt to amend those would be an 'invalid amendment'. Not only was this opinion prescient, it marked for the first time, the inclination of a Supreme Court justice to go beyond the letter of the constitutional text, and creatively seek a doctrine which could limit the Parliament's power to amend the Constitution. However, it was a minority view and the government's land reform laws remained immune from judicial scrutiny. The Court's counter-majoritarian wings had been clipped by a series of constitutional amendments, a process which the courts acquiesced in, as being permissible in the constitutional schema envisaged by the drafters.

The common thread running through these decisions—which were both pro-state and anti-state—was an underlying adherence to the letter of the Constitution. The Court appeared aware of its significance in the Indian polity as an anti-majoritarian institution and assumed the role with aplomb, justifying its decisions and deflecting any criticisms with the argument that their decisions were in keeping with the constitutional mandate. Its legitimacy, hence, was not based on popular support, but was constitutional. As a result, though the Court was a significant political institution, capable of striking down governmental programmes and upholding citizens' rights or alternatively providing a constitutional seal of approval to governmental acts, neither did it consider itself political, nor was it perceived expressly as being so. It perceived itself as an institution discharging a function that the drafters of the Constitution envisaged for it; its allegiance owed solely to the constitutional text. Thus, when the Constitution itself was amended, the power of the Court was accordingly whittled down. Its supporters viewed the Court as an institution performing a crucial anti-majoritarian function in a constitutional democracy, whereas its critics felt it was impervious to the concerns of the masses and had sidetracked the government's promise of social

justice.[17] Few however doubted its motivations, fewer still the bona fides and the integrity of the judges. Even Nehru, frustrated by the Court's decisions derailing the government's programmes of social justice, maintained a relationship of healthy respect with the judiciary, cognizant of the necessity of such an institution in a constitutional democracy.

Thus, although the Court kept its head above the hurly-burly of quotidian politics, in the first fifteen years of India's Independence, it was a controversial institution, its decisions generating fierce and bitterly contested public debates. This was no surprise given the matters it was called upon to adjudicate. Civil liberties, free speech, caste discrimination, and most notably land reforms were matters central to the ideals, aspirations, and lived realities of people in the new republic. And with these matters the political odyssey of the Court began, an odyssey in which both the Court and the Parliament changed in ways few could have predicted.

Increasing Politicization: Reach

The argument that the Supreme Court, in its first phase, perceived itself and was publicly recognized as an apolitical institution concerned with politically significant issues was advanced on the strength of the fact that the Court respected, and was seen as respecting, Parliament's supremacy over the Constitution. With *Golak Nath*,[18] this perception changed dramatically. In this case, the Supreme Court reconsidered the constitutionality of the Seventeenth Amendment and by a majority of 6–5 held it invalid, thereby overruling *Sankari Prasad* and *Sajjan Singh*. It held the amending power of the Parliament to be subject to the fundamental rights enshrined in the Constitution. By creating this zone of legislative non-interference, the Court replaced popular sovereignty with constitutional sovereignty and arrogated to itself the power to rule on the validity of constitutional amendments. With one stroke the Court had denuded Parliament of its supremacy over the Constitution and given itself a determinative role in Indian politics.[19] Ideologically, this struck a body blow for the Directive Principles of State Policy, in pursuance of which most governmental reform measures had been instituted, with the Court considering fundamental rights to be sacrosanct, for all times to come, subject only to the unlikely possibility of a fresh Constituent Assembly being convened. In terms of perception, the Court was no longer seen as an institution which merely dealt with politically significant issues—it was seen as assuming political salience in its own right. The fact that the prime mover of the decision, Chief Justice Subba Rao resigned from the post of Chief Justice two months later to contest for the post of President of India with support from the pro-property Swatantra Party, created further public outcry against the decision and the motivations of the Court.

Two major reverses for the government ensued after *Golak Nath*. In *R.C. Cooper vs Union of India*,[20] Indira Gandhi's much-touted scheme of bank nationalization was struck down by the Court for being violative of Article 31(2), having specified principles of compensation which were irrelevant, rendering the compensation actually paid illusory. In *Madhavrao Scindia and others vs Union of India*,[21] the Presidential order de-recognizing the erstwhile princes as rulers and thereby abolishing their privy purses was struck down for violating the fundamental and legal rights of the princes. Though in the first phase the Supreme Court had similarly struck down major governmental reform measures, there were two crucial differences this time. First, coming as it did after *Golak Nath*, the government was wary of the Court and its tendency to use its constitutional power to strike down popular reform measures. Second, the government was no longer under the secure stewardship of Nehru who, despite some misgivings, maintained a great degree of respect for the judiciary, but led by Indira Gandhi, fresh into power on a populist plank, needing discernible political success to strengthen her hold over the Congress party and the country.

The change of guard, coupled with a growing suspicion of judicial intentions led to two consequences. First, the Constitution was amended with a broad political consensus to restore the supremacy of the Parliament. It is interesting to note that unlike other instances in which amendments sought only to protect certain classes of laws from judicial review, the Twenty-fourth Amendment went further and explicitly overruled *Golak Nath*, underlining the Parliament's general power to amend the Constitution, including the chapter on fundamental rights. The second consequence was more clandestine. Not content with eroding the Supreme Court's constitutional power, the government began a process of creating, what it termed as a 'committed judiciary'(Austin 1999b). By hoping to pack the Supreme Court with appointees who would rule in favour of the government in contentious matters, Indira Gandhi looked to leave no stone unturned to restore parliamentary supremacy, or as critics would contend, *her* supremacy over the Constitution.[22]

As expected, the constitutionality of the Twenty-fourth, Twenty-fifth (which further immunized certain land reform measures from judicial review), and the Twenty-ninth Amendment (which inserted the Kerala Land Reforms Act, the impugned law as a result of which the petitioner was an aggrieved party, into the Ninth Schedule) were challenged in *Kesavananda Bharati vs State of Kerala*,[23] arguably the most significant constitutional case in the history of the Supreme Court. At this time, Indira Gandhi's government was in power with a significant majority and hence the possibility of using the power of amendment to rewrite large portions of the Constitution was imminent. Instead of curtailing the power completely, as *Golak Nath* had sought, the majority in *Kesavananda* relying heavily on the natural and constitutional connotations of the word 'amend' held that the power of amendment cannot be used to abrogate the identity of the Constitution. This identity was characterized as the 'basic structure', a phrase which has since been the epicentre of the Supreme Court's constitutional jurisprudence. Thus, the Twenty-fourth Amendment by which the Parliament gave itself the unfettered power to amend the Constitution was held valid, subject to the basic structure limitation. The different opinions supporting this view had varying ideas of what the content of the basic structure doctrine would be. In any event, it was clear that henceforth it would be the prerogative of the Court to decide the constitutionality of an amendment on the ground that it violated the basic structure. *Golak Nath* had been overruled and the keys to the Constitution had once again been seized, albeit by a more astute and less belligerent Court.

The government read the eleven cross-cutting opinions spread over 1,300 pages in *Kesavananda* with alacrity and within a day of its pronouncement responded by superseding Justices Shelat, Hegde, and Grover who were next in line for the post of Chief Justice of India according to the established seniority convention, in favour of Justice A.N. Ray, whose political views were perceived as being similar to those of the government of the day.[24] Unlike in the 1950s when Nehru had offered the Chief Justiceship to B.K. Mukherjea superseding Justice Mahajan at a time when the seniority convention had still not been established, and faced a threat of en masse resignation by the Court, inconvenient moral pangs and intra-judicial solidarity were not in vogue during Indira Gandhi's time.

This process of politicization of the Supreme Court culminated in the Emergency declared by the President in June 1975.[25] A few days earlier, the Allahabad High Court had set aside Indira Gandhi's election to the Lok Sabha for having engaged in corrupt electoral practices. Much of her political career at the time hinged on her election result and to avoid the possibility of an adverse ruling by the Supreme Court to which she had appealed, a retrospective constitutional amendment was introduced which scuttled judicial review of the elections involving a sitting Prime Minister or a person appointed as a Prime Minister subsequent to the election in question. A five-judge bench of the Supreme Court with Chief Justice Ray presiding invalidated the constitutional amendment inter alia by extending the doctrine of basic structure to include the rule of law and judicial review. At the same time, the Court upheld Indira Gandhi's election by nullifying the charge of her having engaged in corrupt electoral practices. The decision was nuanced; it was not the unconditional genuflection before the government that many expected and in the face of a 'naked abuse of power'(Ramachandran 2000) the Court had withstood pressure from within and without and advanced the law of the land.

The resistance of the Court, however, crumbled in *ADM Jabalpur vs Shivkant Shukla*.[26] During the Emergency, the Maintenance of Internal Security Act (MISA) conferred extraordinary powers on the executive to detain persons without trial. In addition,

a Presidential Order under Article 359 had suspended the right to move the Court for violations of Article 14, 21, and 22. The question before the Supreme Court, in this case, was whether a habeas corpus petition could be maintained to ascertain whether an order of detention was in compliance with the Act; if it could be maintained, then what would the scope of judicial scrutiny be? Several high courts had heard such petitions and held the legality of the grounds for detention subject to judicial review. Four out of five judges of the Supreme Court, however, held that such a petition could not be maintained; that both legislations and executive actions were immune from judicial scrutiny; and most startlingly, that the right to life and personal liberty were bounties given to citizens by the state and hence could be withdrawn in times of Emergency. It was only Justice Khanna, who, despite governmental pressure to conform, held inter alia that the rule of law requires that life and personal liberty cannot be suspended under any circumstances and the legality of the detention can certainly be questioned by the detenu. He ended the judgment with the stirring words—'A dissent in a court of last resort...is an appeal to the brooding spirit of the law; to the intelligence of a future day, when a later decision may possibly correct the error into which the dissenting judge believes the court to have been betrayed'.[27]

At this moment in India's constitutional history, however, the brooding spirit of the law was dead. Justice Khanna was superseded for his principled opposition and the Forty-second Amendment was passed, substantially rewriting the Constitution and securing the supremacy of the executive. Unlike the first phase of the Supreme Court's functioning characterized by a healthy respect between the wings of the government and a constitutional belief of parliamentary supremacy shared unanimously by the Supreme Court judges, this phase was marked by a questioning Court challenging Parliament's authority to amend the Constitution and an executive which was seemingly willing to go to any lengths in its quest for unbridled power. Conventions of seniority were disregarded, judicial loyalty to government rewarded, and opposition punished. The net effect of these developments was a growing awareness among the judges of their political role, and a sense of betrayal felt by the public at the judicial surrender in *ADM Jabalpur*. The Court had gained considerable political clout as the guardian of the Constitution and had just as quickly lost it, by proving susceptible to executive pressure both with regard to appointment of the judges as well as decision-making. It had become both politicized and unpopular, facing a crisis of legitimacy. For its survival as an independent counter-majoritarian institution, it would have to make hard choices failing which its credibility amongst the people, that is, the consumers of justice, would be dissipated.

The World's Most Powerful Judiciary

Indira Gandhi's defeat in the elections in March 1977, coupled with the Forty-fourth Amendment to the Constitution passed by the new Janata government in power, gave a new lease of life to the Supreme Court. Collective repentance over the judicial surrender in the Emergency required atonement. This came in the form of two landmark decisions. The first widened the ambit of Article 21 thereby allowing laws to be tested on the grounds of procedural and substantive fairness,[28] and the second struck down key provisions of Indira Gandhi's Forty-second Amendment, including S. 55 of the said amendment which excluded judicial review of all constitutional amendments for violating the basic structure of the Constitution, of which judicial review was held to be an integral part.[29] But so deep was the sense of betrayal, that the Court felt constitutional correction itself was insufficient to regain the trust of the masses. Thus, constitutional legitimacy was replaced by a quest for popular legitimacy. There were two distinctive trends in this phase—a gradual expansion of fundamental rights through the vehicle of public interest litigation (PIL) and second, a concomitant process of self-correction with regard to the appointments process. Over the next two decades, these trends came together to make the Supreme Court a powerful and independent institution of governance in modern India.

The Growth of Public Interest Litigation

Public interest litigation broadly refers to the institutional changes engineered by the Supreme Court, in the early 1980s, to facilitate access to the Court. In the emancipatory aftermath of the Emergency, the groundwork for the growth of PIL was laid in a series of cases bristling with procedural innovation and doctrinal creativity. The most significant of these cases is *S.P. Gupta vs President of India and others*[30] in which Justice Bhagwati, the doyen of the activist judges in that period, relaxed the rule of locus standi, and opened up the doors of the judiciary to public-spirited citizens—both those wishing to espouse the cause of the poor and oppressed and those wishing to enforce performance of public duties.

The traditional rule of *locus standi* permitted only an aggrieved person, that is, a person who had suffered a specific legal injury to bring an action for judicial redress.[31] As a first step, in *Sunil Batra (II) vs Delhi Administration*,[32] the Court recognized a departure from the strict rule of locus standi in the service of the poor, oppressed, and voiceless. It permitted members of the public to move the Court for enforcement of constitutional or legal rights in cases where those whose constitutional or legal rights were violated were, by reason of social or economic disadvantage, unable to approach the Court for judicial redress. As illustrative examples, the Court has heard a non-governmental organization (NGO) seeking judicial assistance to direct the state of Haryana to implement constitutional and statutory prohibitions on bonded labour,[33] a public-spirited citizen approaching the Court seeking safeguards in relation to unregulated inter-country adoption of Indian babies,[34] and has even recognized what has come to be termed as epistolary jurisdiction, the jurisdiction to treat letters from public-minded citizens as writ petitions.[35]

In *S.P. Gupta*, the Court authorized a further departure from the rule of locus standi, this time in the service of strengthening performance of public duties. The Court permitted public-spirited citizens to claim judicial redress for public injury arising from breach of public duty(Mehta 2007a: 158, 167). The liberalization of locus standi and the recognition of citizen and representative standing created a new form of legal action—PIL[36]—and heralded the arrival of a new constitutional locus of power—the activist Court.

Today, three decades on, a vast range and number of PILs have graced the portals of the judiciary, and through them and in their continuing activist avatar, the courts have fashioned a legal creature that has shed the constraints of traditional judicial proceedings.[37] Public interest litigation has come to be characterized by a collaborative approach, procedural flexibility, judicially-supervised interim orders, and forward-looking relief. And, they typically involve numerous parties and stakeholders, amicus curiae, and fact-finding/expert/monitoring/policy-evolution committees. Once an issue catches the attention of the Court, the judicial machinery kicks into play. Given the inherent powers[38] and procedural innovations the Court has in its arsenal, it will take immediate steps to address the problem, and simultaneously set in motion an investigative and policy evolution process. This process may take several years or even decades, but in this period, it will continuously monitor administrative action and ensure compliance with the Court's orders. The Court typically passes a series of interim orders in the nature of 'continuing mandamus'—that is, it keeps an issue under the judicial gaze and passes orders tailored to the demands of a continually evolving situation.[39] It is in essence a technique designed to monitor the functioning of the Executive, and it is a characteristic element of the judicial approach to PIL.[40] In some public interest cases, the Court has passed over 200 orders in two decades.[41] At the conclusion of this process, the Court can and usually will pass a forward-looking and wide-reaching decree, whose enforcement it may well continue to monitor through the relevant committees.

The Expansion of Protected Rights

For PIL to be truly effective, the breadth of substantive rights protected under the Constitution would also need to be comprehensive. The activist Court and its descendants proceeded therefore to expand in tandem the substantive rights protected under the Indian Constitution. The chosen vehicle for this expansion was Article 21.[42] The fundamental right to life and liberty under Article 21 was gradually extended to cover unarticulated but implicit rights such as the right to live with human dignity,[43] the right to livelihood,[44] the right to education,[45] the right to health and medical care of workers,[46] and the right to enjoyment of pollution-free water and air.[47]

The Court in its Legislative Avatar

Since it had widened the scope of its jurisdiction as well as the breadth of substantive rights it was seeking to protect, the Court had to proportionately widen the nature and extent of the remedies that it could provide for such violations. In constitutional litigation, in India and elsewhere, the dominant remedy awarded by courts thus far had been declaratory in nature. But given the nature of violations the Court was now enquiring into, declaratory remedies would be of little or no consequence. For example, in *Laxmi Kant Pandey vs Union of India*[48] the Court was approached for regulating a hitherto unregulated area of law—inter-country adoptions. The relief sought was hence essentially legislative. But the Court, seizing on years of legislative inaction on this front, heard a broad spectrum of parties, allowed child welfare agencies and NGOs to file intervening applications, and laid down a series of guidelines in the best interests of the child, deriving from relevant international law conventions. In *Vishaka vs State of Rajasthan*[49] the Court, 'in the absence of enacted law', laid down guidelines defining sexual harassment in the workplace, and providing procedures and machinery for investigation and redress. It did so 'in exercise of the power available under Article 32 of the Constitution for enforcement of the fundamental rights'.[50] And, it 'emphasised that this would be treated as the law declared by this Court under Article 141 of the Constitution'.[51] It is worth noting that the Court's power under Article 141 of the Constitution[52] is to 'declare law', a power which only binds courts and tribunals throughout India. The Court does not have the power, as it has here assumed, to 'make law' binding upon all citizens of India.[53]

The Court in its Executive Avatar

If *Laxmi Kant Pandey* and *Vishaka* saw the Court in its legislative avatar, *Vineet Narain vs Union of India*[54] provides a striking example of a court functioning as an executive. This case involved a series of writ petitions that arose out of the arrest of a terrorist, which led to the discovery of a notebook containing details of payments made to prominent politicians and bureaucrats. The writ alleged that the terrorist–politician nexus was making an impartial investigation impossible, and sought the Court's intervention to make the CBI more independent and consequently, the investigation more effective. Using the remedy of 'continuing mandamus', the Court addressed the systemic deficiencies in the Indian investigation machinery. It gave the government a series of policy directions, including conferment of statutory status on the Central Vigilance Commission, manner of its selection, transfer and minimum tenure, procedure for the appointment of officers of the CBI and the Enforcement Directorate, and ordered the creation of several agencies for carrying out the said directions.[55] The Court has also used the device of 'continuing mandamus' to perform a similar role in environmental matters. At the behest of public-spirited individuals, the Court has passed (and continues to pass) orders inter alia to protect the Taj Mahal from corrosive air pollution,[56] rid the river Ganges of trade effluents,[57] address air pollution in Delhi and other metropolitan cities,[58] protect the forests and wildlife of India,[59] and clear cities of their garbage.[60] The phenomenon of potentially endless judicial oversight in public interest cases cannot but lead to the conclusion that the judiciary is merely substituting judicial governance for executive governance in areas highlighted by public interest litigants, a phenomenon some scholars would contend is 'judicial excessivism' or judicial over-activism.[61]

It is interesting to note that unlike in earlier phases of the functioning of the Court, where any curtailment of the government's powers was swiftly followed by a constitutional amendment restoring *status quo ante*, no such responses from the government ensued in this phase. Two reasons perhaps best explain this transformation in institutional politics. First, the Court derived its legitimacy for PIL from the moral high ground of rights jurisprudence. By expansively interpreting fundamental rights, especially the right to life, the Court garnered considerable popular support thereby rendering any opposition a politically risky proposition for the government. Successive governments considered it politic to co-operate with rather than confront the Court. Second, the nature of governments had changed. Unlike the Nehruvian years or the time Indira Gandhi was in power, the decade of the 1990s, when the Court became an

increasingly prominent institution in everyday governance, was characterized largely by coalition governments and unstable majorities. Lack of concrete action by these governments gave the Court the space to play a more active role in governance (Shankar forthcoming). The ineffectiveness and incoherence which marred their functioning also ensured that the public perception of the Court was one of a powerful dynamic institution that righted wrongs and granted remedies. The legitimacy for PIL and the expansive rights jurisprudence was thus not just constitutional; it was also popular, deriving strength from the laudatory public opinion it generated.

Appointments

The second broad trend discernible in this phase of a truly powerful judiciary has been the movement towards self-selection of judges in the higher courts. The Constitution in Article 124 (for the Supreme Court) and Article 217 (for the High Courts) provides for a hybrid method of judicial appointments. All appointments are to be made by the President, that is, the executive being the primary authority, after consultation with the Chief Justice of India, an authority whose role was deemed crucial to ensure impartiality in selection and competence in the composition of the Supreme Court.[62] A plurality of high functionaries, it was thus believed, would guard against human failings of bias and favouritism which could arise if power was concentrated in a single authority. It is revealing to note that a process of appointment of judges by a collegium of the Supreme Court itself, as is the practice today, was not discussed as a potential method for selection by the Constituent Assembly.

Since the President is mandated to act on the aid and advice of the Council of Ministers in appointing judges, executive appointments in accordance with the constitutional schema were not uncontroversial, especially since the requirement of consultation with the Chief Justice of India was often not given appropriate weight.[63] Appointments on communal, casteist, and parochial grounds were not unknown.[64] Following the fears of a 'committed judiciary' in the Indira Gandhi years and further executive assertion on the issue of particular judicial appointments thereafter, the situation was considered sufficiently grave to warrant a rethink. In *S.P. Gupta vs President of India*,[65] the Court while upholding the role of executive appointment of judges, added the caveat that consultation with the Chief Justice of India was mandatory to certify the antecedents of the judge and in case of High Court judges, also with the Chief Justice of the respective High Court to certify his or her competence and character.[66] Subsequently, in *Supreme Court Advocates-on-Record Association vs Union of India (SCAORA)*,[67] the Constitution was effectively rewritten by judicial diktat, rendering the opinion of the Chief Justice of India determinative in the process of selection. This was further clarified in the *Third Judges* case[68] which reiterated that in presenting his opinion, the Chief Justice of India would consult the four seniormost puisne judges of the Supreme Court for Supreme Court appointments and two seniormost puisne judges for high court appointments. It would be this collegium of judges whose opinion would be determinative insofar as appointments to the higher judiciary were concerned. Thus, the spirit of the original constitutional scheme of plurality of functionaries in appointment of the judges was affirmed by the *Third Judges* case; crucially however, this plurality was effectively limited to the institution of the judiciary, thereby presenting a curious case of the letter, albeit not the spirit of the Constitution, being violated.

This judicial rewriting of the Constitution, ostensibly aimed at securing judicial independence, had its genesis in a constant fear of an executive takeover of the Supreme Court. While such fears were not entirely unwarranted, the current system is also not uncontroversial.[69] Apart from the tenuous reasoning which led to the institution of the collegium,[70] the process is closed; no published criteria for appointments exist. Neither are there established procedures nor mechanisms for investigating malpractices in appointments.[71] Increasing opacity in appointments coupled with vast powers of governance has ensured that the Supreme Court lives up to its epithet of being 'the world's most powerful judiciary' (Godbole 2009: 22). The convergence of these trends has resulted in a Court that has been characterized as a 'deeply paradoxical institution'[72]—an institution

with tremendous power, but limited accountability. It is this combination of processes which has resulted in the Court wielding immense power; power, which as the next part demonstrates, has not always been judiciously exercised.

OVERREACH

The Court as a Policy Evolution Forum: Cause and Consequence

The Court thus, playing to a largely worshipful gallery in the 1980s and 1990s, has developed into a forum for policy evolution. As George Gadbois notes, political, social, and economic questions, not usually presented to judges in other countries, are decided as a matter of course by the Indian Supreme Court (Gadbois Jr. 1985: 250, 257). And, indeed the Court has come to be viewed as a forum 'to voice the grievances of the community'.[73] The Court, however, is arguably ill-equipped to play this role, and in seeking to do so, it compromises on the role that it is equipped and required to play, in some instances with perverse results. This refers not to the oft-cited backlog of cases, although that is of concern,[74] but to three specific consequences—the creation of a corpus of case law, with a few exceptions, marked by rhetoric, imprecision, and intellectual fuzziness; the substitution of principle by predilection in shaping judgments and reaching decisions; and issues of access, participation, and equity raised by the Court's efforts to equip itself to play the expansive policy evolution role that it does.

A Jurisprudence of Sorts

Pratap Bhanu Mehta, in his writings on the judiciary, argues that jurisprudence is 'completely moribund' in India (Mehta 2005) and that many judges engage in what he characterizes as the 'jurisprudence of exasperation'—where the function of law is to express frustration with the state of affairs (ibid.). Sadly, the evidence for this claim is easy to divine in the case law of the Court. Judges, confronted with the messy reality of governance in India, frequently respond with exasperation, express impatience, and pass orders directed to achieve predetermined ends. And, while the body of law that these orders form may, by definition, be characterized as jurisprudence, for the most part, it is a jurisprudence of sorts, not one that shapes, augments, and foments public reason and instructs and elevates debate. By way of illustration, case law in the area of environmental law offers key insights.

The Court has passed far-reaching orders in hundreds of environmental cases, through which it is believed to have 'fostered an extensive and innovative jurisprudence on environmental rights'.[75] Although the Indian judiciary is universally acclaimed for its proactive stance on environmental protection, its judgments, taken together, do not articulate a coherent philosophy of environmental law. The case law on the constitutionally-guaranteed environmental right, the chosen vehicle for the Court's justification for its activism, is a case in point.[76] The Court offers many different formulations of the constitutionally-protected environmental right. An oft-repeated one is that the right is to 'environmental protection and conservation of natural resources'.[77] This formulation raises more questions than it answers. To what level must the environment be protected in India—to the level that it is in the industrialized world or to a unique level based on its developmental needs and priorities? Levels of environmental protection vary across the world based on economic constraints, environmental factors, and developmental priorities. The Court has dealt with the environment— development tension in numerous cases, and while it recognizes the need to strike a delicate balance, it has not offered any markers to determine how this delicate balance has to be struck.[78] A right to environmental protection, without an accompanying explanation of what precisely that entails, namely, the substance of the right, what is at the core of the entitlement, what trumps it, what does not, and in what circumstances, is of limited doctrinal value. Where the Court has attempted to define or characterize the environmental right, the definitions have often done 'little definitional work, and end up begging the question'.[79] Instead of defining the environmental right in question, by drawing its boundaries, and laying down principles to guide its application, the Court appears to have moulded, and in some cases expanded, the right to fit the case before it. The imprecision of the

right as well as the case-by-case approach the Court favours, combine to create intellectual fuzziness in this area. As a result, the case law offers limited guidance in making the difficult value-laden judgments at the core of this right, such as—the relative worth of eco-centric and anthropocentric values when they conflict; the 'relative moral significance of different private and public costs' (du Bois 1996: 153, 163) the relative worth of different rights; the positioning of the environmental right in the hierarchy of rights; the markers to be used in striking a balance between development and environment; and the criteria to be used in establishing the rights of different generations (ibid.). The intellectual fuzziness in this area does not also lend itself to the identification of clearly identifiable rights and obligations. This is particularly true in relation to the state's obligations. In the words of the Court, '[t]he state has a duty ... to shed its extravagant unbridled sovereign power and to forge in its policy to maintain ecological balance and hygienic environment'.[80] This is a strongly worded call to action, but scarcely an enforceable legal obligation. Since no coherent philosophy of environmental law is evident from the Court's judgments, much is left to the discretion of the judge, and little is offered in the way of consistency, predictability, and certainty. This situation is merely illustrative and applies well beyond the field of environmental law as well.[81]

Predilection over Principle

Increased discretionary space, imprecise rights, unclear obligations, and fuzzy principles lend themselves to judgments based on predilections rather than principle. And, the Court's predilections are arguably discernible. The Court, given the kinds of issues it interests itself in and takes ownership of, is perceived as consisting of middle-class intellectuals, and therefore as more receptive to others of their ilk, certain social and value preferences (for instance, the right to a clean environment rather than the right to livelihood), and certain modes of argumentation over others (technical rather than social). The perception of the judiciary as middle-class intellectuals with middle-class preferences for fewer slums, cleaner air, cattle and garbage-free streets at any cost (to others), has in itself silenced certain voices. The courts are unlikely to be moved by or on behalf of the poor on urban poverty, or livelihood issues, for the outcomes are predictable and unfavourable, but they are likely to be moved on nursery school admissions, preservation of public parks, protection of monuments, treatment of the monkey menace in Lutyens' Delhi, and the like.[82] This is indeed ironic given the origins of judicial activism and PIL in India. The Court opened its doors and liberalized locus standi in the late 1970s to address the 'problems of the poor'. Yet today, several decades on, it is the problems of the middle class that are most likely to be viewed sympathetically by the Courts. The fact that predilection may prevail over principle, even if it does not do so for the most part, in itself is deeply troubling, as it casts a shadow over the functioning of the Court and the legitimacy of its judgments.

It is inevitable that a judge's social and value preferences play a role in the decision-making process.[83] Two factors, however, serve to limit such preferences from translating directly into law—the law itself, and judicial self-restraint. The former is a weak reed to rely on given the manufactured lack of clarity on first principles, and the latter only exhibits itself in fits and starts.[84] A recent example is *Divisional Manager, Aravalli Golf Club and Anr vs Chander Hass*,[85] where Justices Mathur and Katju tapped into a rare judicial vein of critical self-awareness, chastized the judiciary for overreach, and advocated judicial self-restraint.

Information, Access, and Participation

The Court's role in policy-making places acute informational demands on the system; something that a traditionally structured judicial system is not equipped to handle. The Court has addressed this informational and knowledge deficit by using its inherent powers to create a variety of bodies to assist it. In some cases, the need is for fact verification, as for instance where the practice of bonded labour is alleged;[86] in others, the need is for expert opinions, as for instance where the deleterious impact of a particular hazardous chemical plant on a neighbourhood is at issue.[87] The Court has created socio-legal commissions to assist it in fact verification and gathering. These have included, depending on the needs of the case, district judges, journalists, lawyers, mental health professionals, and bureaucrats. The Court has also created expert committees[88] or drawn on pre-existing expert bodies[89] to provide it with expert advice. On occasions the Court has appointed monitoring committees to supervise enforcement of its orders, but most of these have a fact-finding component to their allocated tasks as well.

In addition to the fact-gathering, expert advice, and monitoring commissions/committees, there is increasingly in use a hybrid creature which can best be characterized as a 'policy evolution' committee/body. It consists of a mix of experts and stakeholders and is charged with the task of both examining existing practices and laws and suggesting improvements, including where appropriate modifications to the law. The Asim Burman Committee constituted by the Court in the *Almitra Patel Case*[90] and the Bhure Lal Committee in the *Delhi Vehicular Pollution Case*[91] are both examples of such committees. The reports of these committees are predictive, insofar as they are concerned with modifying a course of conduct currently in train, and legislative, for they evolve policy consensus around a particular solution. Powerful as these committees are, their constitution, practice, and functioning is determined on an ad hoc rather than a principled basis, and this in itself creates inconsistencies and potential inequities. The nature and degree of access they permit to the stake holders, given the lack of guidelines from the Court, depends on the nature and composition of the committees. Few offer adequate avenues for public participation in the resolution of issues with critical implications for certain groups, and wider implications for all. If the processes used to arrive at a resolution of the issues are less than participatory, the solutions devised may be open to the criticism that they are less than equitable, that is, less than fair, just, and impartial—just a few of the hazards of entering into the terrain of policy-making.

The Folly of Overreach

Many hackles have been raised at the repeated judicial incursions into the arena of policy-making.[92] And, there are increasingly critical and vocal voices even within the judiciary. There are clear reasons for such disaffection. Ronald Dworkin in *Taking Rights Seriously* drew a persuasive distinction between principle (involving moral rights against the state) and policy (involving utilitarian calculations of the public good)(Dworkin 1977: 22). The former is the legitimate domain of judges and the latter that of the legislature and its agents (ibid.: 82–6). Each branch of the government is best confined to the exercise of its own function (Vile 1998: 14).[93] Indeed in the case of the judiciary, lack of institutional competence and democratic accountability would suggest that it exercise caution in entering into the policy-making arena.[94] A philosophy that the Indian courts have recognized in the past, the reason, in the words of Justice Chandrachud, is that 'the concentration of power in any one organ may...by upsetting that fine balance between the three organs, destroy the fundamental premises of a democratic government to which we are pledged.'[95] In the exercise of its public interest jurisdiction, the judiciary may reach the limits of its constitutional competence, and begin dabbling in policy-making, the exclusive domain of the democratically elected legislature. Indeed, this danger was recognized as early as in *Bandhua Mukti Morcha* where Justice Pathak noted—

> In the process of correcting executive error or removing legislative omission the Court can so easily find itself involved in policy making of a quality and degree characteristic of political authority, and indeed run the risk of being mistaken for one. An excessively political role identifiable with political governance betrays the court into functions alien to its fundamental character, and tends to destroy the delicate balance envisaged in our constitutional system between its three basic institutions.[96]

Today, however, unelected judges appear to have laid claim to what has been characterized as 'formal judicial supremacy' (Mehta 2007b). And, this is a cause for concern. While court interventions have led to desirable outcomes in many cases, overall the more capacious the ambit of judicial intervention, the more capricious the judiciary is perceived to be, and the less likely it is to foster a robust constitutional culture that imposes principled limits on the behaviour of governments and individuals (ibid.: 81).

Policy must emerge from a socio political process and must be considered in a legislative forum, not a judicial one. Many of the problems brought before the Court are, what L.L. Fuller would term,

'polycentric disputes,...(involving) many affected parties and a somewhat fluid state of affairs.'[97] This is certainly the case with many PIL cases. There are usually 'complex repercussions' to intervention in such situations,[98] as not all affected parties are readily identifiable and therefore before the Court. Given the limited participation of those affected by the disputes the Court cannot be sure of the extent of repercussions or of their legal irrelevance.[99] The Court would be well advised to exercise restraint in such cases. An argument often deployed to justify judicial intervention in ever-expanding arenas is that the judiciary is constrained to govern, and even to legislate, as the executive and legislature are incapable or unable to exercise their functions in a satisfactory manner. The Court, the argument goes, is merely filling the gaping vacuum. While it is true that neither the legislature nor the executive have distinguished themselves, a similar charge could be levelled against the judiciary. As Pratap Bhanu Mehta has noted, although the Court engages in headline grabbing PIL cases, routine access to justice remains elusive.[100] The judicial system has a backlog of approximately three crore cases,[101] and this backlog is set to continue unless existing vacancies in the judiciary are filled up. Further, it is arguable that the practice and continuing spectre of endless judicial oversight has in itself contributed to the dysfunctionality of the executive. Judicial governance becomes a crutch for the authorities. Indeed, some argue that judicial activism may have restricted the growth of a responsible and independent bureaucracy (Divan 1992). In the circumstances, judges may be well advised, as Justices Mathur and Katju recommended, to exercise restraint. In their words, 'judicial restraint complements the twin, overarching values of the independence of the judiciary and the separation of powers.'[102]

CONCLUSION

No essay can do justice to the extraordinary institution that is the Indian Supreme Court. The Court's history is replete with contradictions—strong counter-majoritarian stances followed by abject surrender to popular government; judicious use of judicial review going hand in hand with assertions of legislative and executive power. The Court began its career as an institution committed to the constitutional text, it veered cloyingly towards pro-government stances in the 1970s, before finally carving a niche for itself as a powerful independent institution of governance in the Indian polity. Today, the most contested political issues in the country are brought to and resolved by the Court. The Court possesses not just immense decision-making power but also wields considerable powers of implementation through a plethora of committees which work at its behest. Needless to say, it has played and continues to play a critical role in shaping India's constitutional democracy far beyond that which the drafters of the Constitution envisaged or what courts in other countries play. And, in playing this role, the Indian Supreme Court has delivered numerous progressive decisions and pulled off the 'epic legal accomplishment' of 'sustaining a regime of constitutional liberty with vigorous judicial protection of human rights in a very large, very poor and very diverse society...' (Galanter and Krishnan 2003).

Yet the Court is moving perilously close to becoming an 'imperium in imperio', the creation of which, the drafters of the Constitution specifically wished to avoid.[103] Three consequences of the exercise of such immense power are evident. The first is the folly of overreach, with the Court adjudicating matters beyond its legitimacy and competence, resulting in turn in jurisprudence without intellectual depth or rigour; the dominance of predilection over principle; and a host of concerns relating to access, equity, and participation. The second is the increasing disquiet over the composition of the Court and the calls for transparency and accountability in the process of judicial appointments. The third is the possibility of inter-institutional friction between an assertive court and a legislature smarting from the expansion of judicial power without requisite accountability. The fiery debate in the Parliament leading to the lapse of the Judges (Declaration of Assets and Liabilities) Bill 2009[104] is a warning sign that the respect that the judiciary enjoys in India both from its co-ordinate wings of the government as well as from the people could wane unless the Court sets its house, both procedurally in terms of its composition, and substantively, in terms of the power it wields, in order.

At the inauguration of the Supreme Court, the Attorney General M.C. Setalvad expressed hope that '[l]ike all human institutions, the Supreme Court... will earn reverence through truth.'[105] Today, a certain amount of reflection about its role in India's constitutional democracy, cognizant of the challenges which it faces, and the possible need for self-restraint and correction when such restraint is warranted, are critical, if the Court is to continue this professed quest for truth which it undertook sixty years ago. It is this introspection, a check against a movement towards unrestrained exercise of judicial power, which will ensure that the Court continues earning the reverence of the people and remains a key, albeit not the only pivot, in India's constitutional democracy.

NOTES

1. All instances of the term 'the Court' refer to the Supreme Court of India.

2. Chief Justice Harilal Kania, on the occasion of the inaugural sitting of the Supreme Court of India, 28 January 1950. See 1950 Bom. L.R. (Vol. LII.) 19, 20.

3. Per Patanjali Sastri CJ., *State of Madras vs V.G. Row*, AIR 1952 SC 196, 199.

4. AIR 1950 SC 27.

5. AIR 1950 SC 124.

6. AIR 1951 SC 226.

7. The rationale for the use of the former term in preference over the latter is attributable to the influence of US Supreme Court judge Felix Frankfurter on Constitutional Advisor B.N. Rau. See Austin (1999a).

8. Letter dated 1 February 1951, *NLTCM*, vol. 2, p. 325 as cited in Austin (1999b).

9. For the text of the First Amendment see http://indiacode.nic.in/coiweb/amend/amend1.htm.

10. *Kameshwar Singh vs State of Bihar*, AIR 1951 Patna 91.

11. (1952) 1 SCR 89.

12. For an analysis of the idea of an unconstitutional constitutional amendment, see Jacobsohn (2006).

13. AIR 1954 SC 170.

14. *P. Vajravelu Mudaliar vs Special Deputy Collector, Madras*, AIR 1965 SC 1017.

15. AIR 1965 SC 845.

16. Per Mudholkar J., at para 55.

17. For a trenchant critique of the early pro-property decisions of the Supreme Court, see Reddy (2008).

18. AIR 1967 SC 1643.

19. For a rich analysis of the opinions in the decision, see Dhavan (1976).

20. AIR 1969 SC 1126.

21. AIR 1971 SC 530.

22. For a scathing critique of the amendments to the Constitution introduced during Indira Gandhi's leadership and picking 'a judiciary made to measure', see Palkhivala (1974).

23. AIR 1973 SC 1461.

24. For a defence of this supersession and the need to have Chief Justices who shared 'the spirit of the times', see Kumaramangalam (1973).

25. For a critical and comprehensive discussion on the role of the Supreme Court and the judiciary, more generally during the Emergency, see Seervai (2008: Appendix Part I).

26. (1976) 2 SCC 521.

27. Per Khanna J., at para 594.

28. *Maneka Gandhi vs Union of India*, (1978) 1 SCC 248.

29. *Minerva Mills vs Union of India*, AIR 1980 SC 1789.

30. (1981) Supp (1) SCC 87.

31. *In Re Sidebottam* 1880, 14 Ch. Div. 458. James L.J. defined an aggrieved person as 'a man who has suffered a legal grievance, a man against whom a decision has been pronounced which wrongly deprived him of something, or wrongly affected his title to something'. Ibid., at 465.

32. (1980) 3 SCC 488.

33. *Bandhua Mukti Morcha vs Union of India*, (1984) 3 SCC 161.

34. *Laxmi Kant Pandey vs Union of India*, (1984) 2 SCC 244.

35. *Sunil Batra (II) vs Delhi Administration*, (1980) 3 SCC 488 at paras 4, 25, and 50.

36. PIL in India can be pursued either in the High Court or the Supreme Court. If the complaint is of a legal wrong; Article 226 of The Constitution of India 1950, permits recourse to the high court of the state. If the complaint alleges a violation of fundamental rights, Article 32 of the Constitution permits direct recourse to the Supreme Court.

37. In the context of public law litigation in the US, Abram Chayes observed that this new phenomenon 'is recognizable as a lawsuit only because it takes place in a courtroom before an official called a judge'. Chayes (1976).

38. The Supreme Court has extensive powers under Article 142 of the Constitution of India. It is empowered to 'make such order as is necessary for doing complete justice in any cause or matter pending before it'.

39. The Court, according to Rule 9 'may, if it thinks fit, grant such ad interim relief to the petitioner, as the justice of the case may require, upon such terms, if any as it may consider just and proper'. The Supreme Court Rules, 1966. Available at http://www.supremecourtofindia.nic.in/ruleshtml.htm

40. Upendra Baxi describes the phenomenon as 'creeping jurisdiction', which he argues 'typically consists of taking over the direction of administration in a particular arena from the executive'. See Baxi (1985a: 289, 298–300).

41. See e.g., *M.C. Mehta vs Union of India (Delhi Vehicular Pollution Case)*, Writ Petition Number 13029 of 1985 (ongoing).

42. Article 21 reads 'No person shall be deprived of his life or personal liberty except according to procedure established by law'.

43. *Francis Coralie Mullin vs The Administrator, Union Territory of Delhi*, (1981) 1 SCC 608, paras 7 and 8.

44. *Olga Tellis vs Bombay Municipal Corporation*, (1985) 3 SCC 545, para 32.

45. *Mohini Jain vs State of Karnataka*, (1992) 3 SCC 666, para 12, and *J.P. Unni Krishnan vs State of Andhra Pradesh*, (1993) 1 SCC 645, para 166, both of which preceded the introduction of Article 21A guaranteeing free and compulsory education for all children between the ages of 6 and 14 (Constitutional Amendment, Eighty-sixth Amendment Act, 2002).

46. *Consumer Education and Research Centre vs Union of India*, (1995) 3 SCC 42, paras 24 and 25.

47. *Subash Kumar vs State of Bihar*, (1991) 1 SCC 598, para 7. See also, *M.C. Mehta vs Union of India*, (1992) 3 SCC 256, para 2, and *Virender Gaur vs State of Haryana*, (1995) 2 SCC 577, para 7.

48. *Laxmi Kant Pandey vs Union of India*, (1984) 2 SCC 244.

49. *Vishaka vs State of Rajasthan*, (1997) 6 SCC 241.

50. Ibid., at para 16.

51. Ibid.

52. Article 141 reads—'The law declared by the Supreme Court shall be binding on all courts within the territory of India'.

53. Baxi 2000, pp. 156, 204.

54. (1998) 1 SCC 226.

55. Ibid., per Verma J., para 65.

56. The Court, in a series of directives spanning over two decades, responded by banning coal-based industries in the Taj Mahal's immediate vicinity, closing 230 other factories, requiring 300 factories to install pollution control devices, and ordering the creation of a traffic bypass and a tree belt to insulate the Taj Mahal. *M.C. Mehta vs Union of India (Taj Trapezium Case)*, Writ Petition Number 13381 of 1984.

57. *M.C. Mehta vs Union of India (Ganga Pollution Case)*, Writ Petition Number 3727 of 1985.

58. This order mandated conversion of Delhi's public transport system from conventional fuel to Compressed Natural Gas. *M.C. Mehta vs Union of India (Delhi Vehicular Pollution Case)*, Writ Petition Number 13029 of 1985, and ordered the closure and/or relocation of hazardous and noxious industries operating within Delhi, *M.C. Mehta*

vs Union of India (Delhi Industrial Relocation Case), Writ Petition Number 4677 of 1985.

59. In *T.N. Godavarman Thirumulpad vs Union of India and Ors*, Writ Petition Number 202 of 1995, the Court has undertaken the mammoth task of protecting the forests and wildlife of India.

60. *Almitra Patel vs Union of India*, Writ Petition Number 888 of 1996.

61. S.P. Sathe argues that '[Judicial] activism... is excessivism when a court undertakes responsibilities normally discharged by other co-ordinate organs of the government'. Sathe (2001).

62. Per B.R. Ambedkar, 24th May 1949, (CAD [2003]. p. 258).

63. Austin 1999b, chapters 5 and 12.

64. 14th Report of the Law Commission of India, Vol. I (September 1958) available at lawcommissionofindia.nic.in

65. (1981) Supp 1 SCC 87.

66. For a criticism of this decision and why it was an attempt at accommodating various interests without a principled consideration of the issues involved, see Baxi (1985b: 23–63).

67. (1993) 4 SCC 441.

68. AIR 1999 SC 1.

69. Illustrative of recent controversies are the confirmation of Justice Ashok Kumar as a permanent judge of the Madras High Court and the appointment of Justice Soumitra Sen as a judge of the Calcutta High Court, despite questionable antecedents (see Bhushan 2009).

70. The suspect reasoning employed in the *SCAORA* case and the *Third Judges* case was part of the reason which led the Law Commission to recommend a return to the previous system of executive appointments. See 214th Report of the Law Commission of India (November 2008) available at lawcommissionofindia.nic.in.

71. Most recently, in the controversy surrounding the appointment of Justice P.D. Dinakaran to the Supreme Court, an *ad hoc* procedure was adopted which would involve a 'discreet inquiry' by the Chief Justice of India, the results of which would be placed before the collegium for a final decision. This would, in effect, mean that representations against the nomination would be ultimately considered by the collegium, that is, the nominating body itself. For a criticism of the collegium appointment process, specifically with regard to the appointment of Justice Dinakaran, see Iyer (2009).

72. Mehta 2007a, p. 158.

73. *Dr P. Nalla Thampy vs Union of India*, (1983) 4 SCC 598, 603.

74. As of July 2009, 52,592 cases were pending in the Supreme Court, 40,18,914 cases across the High Courts and over 2.7 crore cases in the lower courts. See *Court News*, IV(3), New Delhi: Supreme

Court of India, September 2009, available at http://www.supremecourtofindia.nic.in/courtnews/court%20news%20jul-sept-09.pdf. For a classic study on 'docket explosion' and the underlying reasons for it, see Baxi (1982: 58–83).

75. Anderson (1996, p. 199). The Supreme Court of India was one of the first to embrace an environmental right. The Court traces in *A.P. Pollution Control Board vs M.V. Nayadu*, (2001) 2 SCC 62, para 6, the origins of the environmental right in India to *Bandhua Mukti Morcha vs Union of India*, (1984) 3 SCC 161, para 10.

76. This argument is developed in Rajamani (2007a, p. 274).

77. See e.g., *Intellectuals Forum, Tirupathi vs State of AP*, (2006) 3 SCC 549.

78. See e.g., *Vellore Citizen's Welfare Forum vs Union of India*, (1996) 5 SCC 647; *Karnataka Industrial Areas Development Board vs C. Kenchappa and Ors*, (2006) 6 SCC 371; and *Bombay Dyeing & Mfg. Co. Ltd. (3) vs Bombay Environmental Action Group and Ors*, (2006) 3 SCC 434, para 200.

79. Anderson (1996, p. 11).

80. *Virender Gaur vs State of Haryana*, (1995) 2 SCC 577, para 7.

81. For example, in the field of socio-economic rights, courts have variously held rights to housing, food, and health as part of Article 21 of the Constitution. However, the exact connotations of the said rights and what entitlements they lead to are less than clear. For a discussion on cases presenting different understandings of the said rights, see Kothari (2004).

82. This argument is developed more fully in Rajamani (2007b).

83. Justice Chandrachud noted that 'it is an accepted fact of constitutional interpretation that the content of justiciability changes according to how the Judge's value preferences respond to the multi-dimensional problems of the day'. *State of Rajasthan vs Union of India* (1977) 3 SCC 592, 648.

84. But, judges need to exercise restraint in the extent to which these value preferences will play a role. In the words of Justice Patanjali Sastri, 'the limit to their [judiciary's] interference with legislative judgment in such cases can only be dictated by their sense of responsibility and self-restraint and the sobering reflection that the Constitution is meant not only for people of their way of thinking but for all'. *State of Madras vs V.G. Row*. After V.G. Row, in place of *supra* should read: AIR 1952 SC 196.

85. (2008) 1 SCC 683.

86. *Bandhua Mukti Morcha vs Union of India*, (1984) 3 SCC 161.

87. *M.C. Mehta vs Union of India (Shriram Gas Leak Case)*, AIR 1987 SC 965, 969.

88. See for example the constitution of the Nilay Choudhary Committee in *M.C. Mehta vs Union of India (Shriram Gas Leak Case)* AIR 1987 SC 965.

89. See for example *M.C. Mehta vs Union of India (Calcutta Tanneries Case)*, 1997 (2), SCALE 411.

90. *Almitra Patel vs Union of India*, (1998) 2 SCC 416, 417.

91. See eg. *M.C. Mehta vs Union of India (Delhi Vehicular Pollution Case)*, Writ Petition Number 13029 of 1985 (ongoing).

92. A lapsed private member's bill, entitled Public Interest Litigation (Regulation) Bill, 1996, tabled before the Rajya Sabha, argued that PILs were placing a heavy burden on judicial time and resources, and were being misused. See Desai and Muralidhar (2000: 159).

93. Although there is no rigid separation of powers in the Indian Constitution, there is broad separation of functions and 'a system of salutary checks and balances'. The reason for this broad separation of power is that "the concentration of power in any one of organ may... by upsetting that fine balance between the three organs, destroy the fundamental premises of a democratic government to which we are pledged'. *See Indira Nehru Gandhi vs Raj Narain* (1975) Supp SCC 1, 260.

94. Dworkin 1977, p. 85 (arguing that 'policy decisions must...be made through the operation of some political process designed to produce an accurate expression of the different interests that should be taken into account. The political system of representative democracy may work only indifferently in this respect, but it works better than a system that allows non-elected judges, who have no mailbag or lobbyists or pressure groups, to compromise competing interests in their chambers').

95. See *Indira Nehru Gandhi vs Raj Narain*, (1975) Supp SCC 1, 260.

96. *Bandhua Mukti Morcha vs Union of India,* (1984) 3 SCC 161.

97. See Fuller (1978). Fuller illustrates this concept through the analogy of a spider's web: 'A pull on one strand will distribute tensions after a complicated pattern throughout the web as a whole. Doubling the original pull will, in all likelihood, not simply double each of the resulting tensions but will rather create a different complicated pattern of tensions. This would certainly occur, for example, if the doubled pull caused one or more of their weaker strands to snap. This is a "polycentric" situation because it is "many centered"—each crossing of strands is a distinct center for distributing tensions'. See also Allison (1994).

98. See Fuller (1978, pp. 394–5); see also *Steadman vs Steadman*, (1976) A.C. 536, 542 (Lord Reid arguing that 'Judges ought not to develop the law because it would be impracticable to foresee all the consequences of tampering with it').

99. See Fuller (1978, pp. 394–5).

100. Mehta 2007b.

101. See *Court News,* IV(3), New Delhi, Supreme Court of India, September 2009, available ews%20jul-sept-09.pdf" http://www.supremecourtofindia.nic.in/courtnews/court%20news%20jul-sept-09.pdf.

102. (2008) 1 SCC 683, para 35.

103. T.T. Krishnamachari, 2003. 27 May 1949, *Constituent Assembly Debates,* Vol. VIII, Book 3, New Delhi: Lok Sabha Secretariat, p. 389.

104. Available at: http://www.judicialreforms.org/files/Judges%20(Declaration%20of%20Assets%20and%20Liabilities)%20Bill%202009.pdf

105. 1950 Bom.L.R. (Vol. LII.) 18.

REFERENCES

Allison, J.W.F. 1994. 'Fuller's Analysis of Polycentric Disputes and the Limits of Adjudication', *Cambridge Law Journal*, 53(2), p. 367.

Anderson, Michael R. 1996. 'Individual Rights to Environmental Protection in India', in Alan Boyle and Michael R. Anderson (eds), *Human Rights Approaches to Environmental Protection.* Oxford: Clarendon Press, p. 199.

Austin, Granville. 1999a. *The Indian Constitution: Cornerstone of a Nation.* New Delhi: Oxford University Press.

———. 1999b. *Working a Democratic Constitution: The Indian Experience.* New Delhi: Oxford University Press.

Baxi, Upendra. 2003. 'Preface' in S.P. Sathe (ed.), *Judicial Activism in India.* New Delhi: Oxford University Press.

———. 2000. 'The Avatars of Indian Judicial Activism: Explorations in the Geography of (In)justice', in S.K. Verma and Kusum (eds), *Fifty Years of the Supreme Court of India: Its Grasp and Reach.* New Delhi: Oxford University Press, pp. 156–7.

———. 1985a. 'Taking Suffering Seriously: Social Action Litigation in the Supreme Court of India', in Rajeev Dhavan, V.R. Krishna Iyer, R. Sundarshan, Salman Khurshid (eds), *Judges and the Judicial Power: Essays in Honour of Justice V.R. Krishna Iyer.* Bombay: N.M. Tripathi Pvt. Ltd, pp. 289, 298–300.

———. 1985b. *Courage, Craft and Contention: The Indian Supreme Court in the Eighties,* Lecture 2. Bombay: N.M. Tripathi Pvt. Ltd.

———. 1982. *The Crisis in the Indian Legal System.* New Delhi: Vikas Publishing House.

Bhagwati, P.N. 1985. 'Judicial Activism and Public Interest Litigation', 23 *Colum. J. Trans. L.* 561, 567.

Bhushan, Prashant. 2009. 'Judging the Judges', 21 January,

available at http://www.outlookindia.com/printarticle. aspx?239534. Accessed on 7 September 2009.

Chayes, Abram. 1976. 'The Role of a Judge in Public Law Litigation' 89 *Harv. L. Rev.* 1281, 1302.

Constituent Assembly Debates. 2003. Vol. VIII, Book 3, New Delhi: Lok Sabha Secretariat.

Desai, Ashok H. and S. Muralidhar. 2000. 'Public Interest Litigation: Potential and Problems', in B.N. Kirpal and Ashok H. Desai (eds), *Supreme but not Infallible: Essays in Honour of the Supreme Court of India*. New Delhi: Oxford University Press, p. 159.

Dhavan, Rajeev. 1976. *The Supreme Court of India and Parliamentary Sovereignty*. New Delhi: Sterling Publishers Pvt. Ltd

Divan, Shyam. 1992. 'A Mistake of Judgment', *Down to Earth*, vol. 51.

du Bois, Francois. 1996. 'Social Justice and the Judicial Enforcement of Environmental Rights and Duties', in Alan Boyle and Michael R. Anderson (eds), *Human Rights Approaches to Environmental Protection*. Oxford: Clarendon Press, pp. 153, 163.

Dworkin, Ronald. 1977. *Taking Rights Seriously*. London: Duckworth Publishers.

Fuller, L.L. 1978. 'The Forms and Limits of Adjudication', 92, *Harvard Law Review* 353, 395, 397.

Gadbois Jr., George H. 1985. 'The Supreme Court of India as a Political Institution', in V.R Krishna Iyer, Rajeev Dhavan, R Sudarshan, and Salman Khurshid (eds), *Judges and the Judicial Power: Essays in Honour of Justice V.R. Krishna Iyer*. Bombay: N.M. Tripathi Pvt. Ltd, pp. 250, 257.

Galanter, Marc and Jayanth Krishnan. 2003. 'Debased Informalism: Lok Adalats and Legal Rights in Modern India', in Erik G. Jensen and Thomas C. Heller (eds), *Beyond Common Knowledge: Empirical Approaches to The Rule Of Law*. Stanford: Stanford University Press, pp. 96–141.

Godbole, Madhav. 2009. *The Judiciary and Governance in India*. New Delhi: Rupa & Co.

Iyer, V.R. Krishna. 2009. 'Issues Raised by L'affaire Dinakaran', *The Hindu*, 17 September 2009.

Jacobsohn, Gary Jeffrey. 2006. 'An Unconstitutional Constitution? A Comparative Perspective' *International Journal of Constitutional Law*, 4(3): 460–87.

Kothari, Jayna. 2004. 'Social Rights and the Indian Constitution', 2, *Law, Social Justice & Global Development Journal* available at http://www.

go.warwick.ac.uk/ elj/lgd/2004_2/Kothari. Accessed on 10 September 2009.

Kumaramangalam, Mohan. 1973. *Judicial Appointments*. New Delhi: Oxford and IBH Publishing Co.

Mehta, Pratap Bhanu. 2007a. 'India's Judiciary: The Promise of Uncertainty', in Pratap Bhanu Mehta and Devesh Kapur (eds), *Public Institutions in India: Performance and Design*. New Delhi: Oxford University Press, pp. 158, 167

———. 2007b. 'The Rise of Judicial Sovereignty', *Journal of Democracy*, 18(2), pp. 70–83.

———. 2005. 'Just Impatient: Can a Jurisprudence of Exasperation of Sustain the Court's Authority?', *The Telegraph*, 17 October 2005.

Palkhivala, Nani. 1974. *Our Constitution Defaced and Defiled*. New Delhi: Macmillan Publishers.

Pillai, K. Chandrasekharan. 1984. 'Role of Teachers and Students of law in Public Interest Litigation', 8 *Cochin University Law Review* 503.

Rajamani, Lavanya. 2007a. 'The Right to Environmental Protection in India: Many a Slip between the Cup and the Lip?', *Review of European Community and International Environmental Law*, 16(3), p. 274.

———. 2007b. 'Public Interest Environmental Litigation in India: Exploring Issues of Access, Participation, Equity, Effectiveness and Sustainability', *Journal of Environmental Law*, 19(3), pp. 293–321.

Ramachandran, Raju. 2000. 'The Supreme Court and the Basic Structure Doctrine', in B.N. Kirpal and Ashok H. Desai (eds), *Supreme but not Infallible: Essays in Honour of the Supreme Court of India*. New Delhi: Oxford University Press, p. 107.

Reddy, O. Chinappa. 2008. *The Court and the Constitution of India: Summits and Shallows*. New Delhi: Oxford University Press.

Sathe, S.P. 2001. 'Judicial Activism: The Indian Experience', WASH. U.J.L. & POL'Y 29, 40.

Seervai, H.M. 2008. *Constitutional Law of India Vol. 2*, 4th edn, (Appendix Part I). New Delhi: Universal Law Publishing Co.

Shankar, Shyalshri. forthcoming. 'India's Judiciary: Imperium in Imperio?', in Paul R. Brass (ed.), *Routledge Handbook of South Asian Politics: India, Pakistan, Bangladesh, Sri Lanka, and Nepal*. Routledge.

Vile, M.J.C. 1998. *Constitutionalism and the Separation of Powers*. Indianapolis: Liberty Fund.

7 The Election Commission

Alistair McMillan

he Election Commission was established
under the Constitution of India, which
provided the structure of government for
the independent state. The Commission
began functioning in January 1950 and organized
the framework within which elections have been
carried out from then through to the present day.
The Election Commission has performed effectively
as an independent body which is responsible for the
conduct of free and fair elections. It has overseen
the political development of India from a nascent
postcolonial state into an established multi-party
parliamentary democracy.

The successful operation of a democracy
necessarily involves some tension between the
institutions which govern and the voice of the
electorate. The Election Commission was established
in order to prevent the electoral process being
corrupted by interests which sought to subvert the
democratic process, and as such is caught between
the roles of democratic protector and being part of
the institutional establishment. It has been forced
to tread a fine line between the pressures exerted

by party politicians and what is perceived as the
national interest. Where these interests worked in
general conformity, notably in the early years of
Independence, the Election Commission can be seen
to have been successful. However, from the late 1960s,
when party politics became more clearly distinguished
from national priorities, and an entrenched
bureaucratic structure became the subject of executive
interference, the role of the Election Commission has
become more controversial.

Administrative bodies such as the Election
Commission play an important role in the successful
operation of democracy. Alongside institutions such
as the judiciary and the civil service, the Election
Commission has an administrative remit, but with
outcomes that have important political consequences.
Rudolph and Rudolph (2002: 59) note that the
Election Commission has a key position at the heart
of the new regulatory centrism of the Indian state,
as an institution (alongside the Presidency and the
Supreme Court) which acts as an enforcer of 'rules
that safeguard the democratic legitimacy of the
political system'. In terms of the general role of the

Election Commission, as Mozaffar and Schedler (2002: 6) suggest, 'good elections are impossible without effective electoral governance'. For Robert A. Pastor (1999), the significance of the institutional process for electoral management has been a much neglected factor in explaining the success or failure of the democratization process. Whilst most of the duties of the Election Commission are technical, the process of electoral administration can have decisive partisan implications, and decisions have to be made where political bias, or the perception of bias, can undermine the legitimacy of electoral politics. The Election Commission of India has certainly played a central part in the consolidation of democratic politics.

The history of the Election Commission can be seen to have gone through three periods: one of establishment in the post-Independence period, when it instituted the running of the electoral process based on a universal franchise; second, a period of quiescence, when it failed to react to fundamental challenges to the democratic process; and third, a period of activism, when it began to engage with a fluid party system and new aspects of political mobilization. Throughout these periods the basic constitutional structure and role has remained the same, although the operational structure and remit of the Election Commission has changed according to the political situation and the personalities holding the office.

This chapter first looks at the constitutional establishment of the Election Commission, and the role which was envisaged for the commissioners by the framers of the Constitution. It goes on to outline the Commission's structure and functions, and examines these in the light of its performance over the period since Independence. The chapter concludes by examining some of the controversial aspects of the operations of the Election Commission and its relation to the democratic politics of India.

THE CONSTITUTION AND THE ELECTION COMMISSION

Unlike much of the constitutional structure, which was based upon the existing British colonial model of government and the Westminster system, or influenced by the United States' Bill of Rights, the Election Commission was a new development.[1] The British had provided for no such body—the running of elections was left to the Central and Provincial governments—reflecting the subsidiary and ad hoc role given to elections under the colonial system. The emergence of the Election Commission was left to the drafters of the Indian Constitution, who had little recourse to precedent or institutional antecedents.

The Constituent Assembly envisaged an independent Election Commission which would organize and implement the wider electoral framework upon which the democratic state was built. However, it was not clear how to entrench this independence, or the range of powers which the institution would wield. Initial debate centred around how such a body would be integrated into the federal system, and whether separate institutions would be organized within each state (either independent or under the control of the Governor) feeding into a central system, or the direction coming from a centralized focus.[2] In accordance with much of the rest of the constitutional structure, the Chairman of the Drafting Committee, Dr B.R. Ambedkar, favoured a centralized body, although at a distance from the government:

> Many people felt that if the elections were conducted under the auspices of the Executive authority and if the Executive Authority did have power, as it must have, of transferring officers from one area to another with the object of gaining support for a particular candidate who was a favourite with the party in office or with the Government of the day that will certainly vitiate the free election which we all wanted. It was therefore unanimously resolved by the members of the Fundamental Rights Committee that the greatest safeguard for purity of election, for fairness in election, was to take away the matter from the hands of the Executive authority and to hand it over to some independent authority (29 July 1947, *Constituent Assembly Debates* ([henceforth *CAD*] IV: 973).

This was in line with Ambedkar's concern that decentralization would threaten minority rights, expressed in his view that state governments might try and subvert the electoral process: 'instructing and managing things in such a manner that those people who do not belong to them either racially, culturally or linguistically, are being excluded from being brought on to the electoral rolls' (Shiva Rao 1968: 465). The fact that such considerations mitigated against a federal principle of government, and would allow control by the Central government, was raised in debate, but rejected.[3]

The framers of the Indian Constitution appeared to have very little expectation that the workload of the Election Commission would be a demanding one: 'it may be at times heavy and at other times it may have no work' (Ambedkar, 15 June 1949, CAD VIII: 906). The Drafting Committee considered whether the body should be permanent, or whether it should be created as an ad hoc agency when elections were due. In the end, a compromise was struck whereby the only office provided for was that of the Chief Election Commissioner who would provide a continuous presence, buttressed by further appointments of commissioners when necessary (see speech by Ambedkar, 15 June 1949, CAD VIII: 905). For some members of the Constituent Assembly, the proposed framework of the Election Commission was too sketchy. Shibban Lal Saksena thought that a larger Election Commission was required, realizing that there would, in time, be a steady procession of state and national elections rather than a five-yearly cycle. He also proposed that the Chief Election Commissioner should be ratified by a two-thirds majority of the Parliament (CAD VIII: 907). Instead of this legislative entrenchment, Ambedkar forced through a less stringent structure which could be amended by future Parliaments (CAD VIII: 929). Whilst he recognized that there was some justification in these concerns, Ambedkar stressed the danger of time-consuming and administratively complex entrenchment, and favoured more flexible constitutional prescriptions. As he noted at the end of the debate on the Election Commission—'You cannot deal with a constitution on technical points. Too many technicalities will destroy constitution-making' (CAD VIII: 930).

Further entrenchment of the structure, and the danger of partisan nomination of the Chief Election Commissioner by a governing party, was deemed to be too prescriptive; set against a body which could be influenced by the Parliament and the needs of the evolving democratic system.

The final wording of Article 324 of the Constitution[4] stated that:

(1) The superintendence, direction and control of the preparation of the electoral rolls for, and the conduct of, all elections to Parliament and to the Legislature of every state and of elections to the offices of President and Vice-President held under this Constitution ... shall be vested in a Commission (referred to in this Constitution as the Election Commission).

(2) The Election Commission shall consist of the Chief Election Commissioner and such number of other Election Commissioners, if any, as the President may from time to time fix and the appointment of the Chief Election Commissioner and other Election Commissioners shall, subject to the provisions of any law made in that behalf by Parliament, be made by the President ...

The Article went on to assert the primacy of the Chief Election Commissioner whose position would be on the same grounds as a judge of the Supreme Court, and who would be provided with regional commissioners and administrative support sufficient to carry out the responsibilities outlined.

The wider responsibilities of the Election Commission were constitutionally delineated through a variety of Articles, including Articles 54–71 which set out the mode of presidential and vice-presidential elections; Articles 79–104 which outlined the parliamentary structure; and Articles 168–93 stating the composition and electoral basis of the state legislatures. This constitutional framework was consolidated through the Representation of the People Acts (RPA) of 1950 and 1951, which provided the detailed provisions for the delimitation of constituencies, administrative details of the electoral process, and basis of the electoral system.

The constitutional provisions for an Election Commission were an innovative response to the desire to have a democratic process that was institutionally entrenched and yet at an arms-length from party-political or governmental interference. It provided for a centralized structure, although one which was flexible enough to develop according to the demands that would emerge and the responsibilities of carrying out the functions which were ascribed. The constitutional basis of the Election Commission has been admirably robust, since Independence, although not without contentious aspects. However, these were an essential consequence of the desire, expressed by Ambedkar and shared by other influential figures in the drafting of the Constitution, that it should not be an overly prescriptive document.

THE ELECTION COMMISSION: STRUCTURE AND FUNCTIONS

The functions of the Election Commission, as set out in Article 324(1) were remarkably broad. The responsibility for the conduct of all major elections in such a large democracy—one which previously had only a partial franchise, and an electoral system and machinery controlled by a colonial administration—was a huge undertaking. The core duties of the Election Commission can be broken down into a number of separate undertakings—the delimitation of constituencies, the drawing-up of electoral rolls, the supervision of the nomination of candidates, the administration of the electoral process, and the surveillance of the probity of electoral conduct. In order to carry out these duties, the Election Commission was provided with a minimal executive structure, and had to rely on the general goodwill of the administrative and governmental machinery to carry out its tasks.

The authority of the Election Commission was invested in a Chief Election Commissioner. Whilst provision was made for the appointment of additional commissioners, for most of the post-Independence period the responsibility for the conduct of elections was vested in a single person. The list of Chief Election Commissioners is shown in Table 7.1.

The question of whether the authority of the Election Commission should be vested in a multi-member body has long been an issue in the debate over electoral reform. In 1972, the Joint Parliamentary Committee on reform of electoral law suggested that the Chief Election Commissioner should be supported by the appointment of other Election Commissioners, as allowed by Article 324 of the Constitution (Ali 2001: 41). The Tarkunde Committee on Electoral Reform (1975), (appointed by the Citizens for Democracy) suggested a multi-member body, and

Table 7.1: Chief Election Commissioners

CHIEF ELECTION COMMISSIONER	TENURE		
Sukumar Sen	21/3/1950	to	19/12/1958
K.V.K. Sundaram	20/12/1958	to	30/9/1967
S.P. Sen Verma	1/10/1967	to	30/9/1972
Nagendra Singh	1/10/1972	to	6/2/1973
T. Swaminathan	7/2/1973	to	17/6/1977
S.L. Shakdhar	18/6/1977	to	17/6/1982
R.K. Trivedi	18/6/1982	to	31/12/1985
R.V.S. Peri Sastri	1/1/1986	to	25/11/1990
V.S. Ramadevi	26/11/1990	to	11/12/1990
T.N. Seshan	12/12/1990	to	11/12/1996
M.S. Gill	12/12/1996	to	13/6/2001
J.M. Lyngdoh	14/6/2001	to	7/2/2004
T.S. Krishnamurthy	8/2/2004	to	15/5/2005
B.B. Tandon	16/5/2005	to	29/6/2006
N. Gopalaswami	29/6/2006	to	20/4/2009
N.B. Chawla	21/4/2009	to	date

proposed that the selection of commissioners, rather than being in the hands of the President alone, should be put in the hands of a committee consisting of the Prime Minister, Leader of Opposition in the Lok Sabha, and the Chief Justice. A similar proposal was made by the all-party Goswami Committee on Election Reforms in 1990. The Chief Election Commissioner, Peri Sastri, thought the issue worthy of consideration in the late 1980s but was not prepared for the sudden nomination of two extra commissioners instigated by the Rajiv Gandhi government, in October 1989. The change was seen as an attempt to undermine the independence of the Election Commission, in the run-up to the Lok Sabha elections, and the two new commissioners (S.S. Dhanoa and V.S. Seigal) were removed by the incoming government of V.P. Singh (Fadia 1992: 86; Ali 2001: 30).

A more determined attempt to temper the influence of the Chief Election Commissioner was instigated in October 1993, when a Presidential Ordinance re-established a three-member commission. Two new Election Commissioners, M.S. Gill and G.V.G. Krishnamurthy, were appointed to sit alongside the Chief Election Commissioner, T.N. Seshan. The decision was made with the implied backing of the Supreme Court, which had stated in 1991 that—'when an institution like the Election Commission is entrusted with vital functions and is armed with exclusive and uncontrolled powers to execute them, it is both necessary and desirable that the powers are not exercised by one individual, however wise he may be' (S.S. Dhanoa vs Union of India, AIR 1991 SC 1745, quoted in Ali 2001: 36).

Whilst the then Chief Election Commissioner, T.N. Seshan, challenged the change in the structure of the Election Commission, the decision was bolstered by the passage of the Chief Election Commissioner and other Election Commissioners (Conditions of Service) Act in 1991, which gave the Election Commissioners the same statutory basis as the Chief Election Commissioner. The attempt by Seshan to have these appointments declared unconstitutional was denied by the Supreme Court in 1995. Despite this rebuff, the Chief Election Commissioner developed a working relationship with the two other Election Commissioners, and a three-member commission became established, with decisions ostensibly taken on a unanimous basis.

Although the weak constitutional provisions for the structure of the Election Commission have caused controversy, the establishment of a three-member body, with a Chief Election Commissioner supported by two Election Commissioners, has been widely accepted. Whilst the possibility remains of a government (with the consent of the President) packing the Election Commission with favourable commissioners, this has to be balanced with the over-riding importance of the Election Commission as a guarantor of electoral legitimacy. Overt manipulation of the institution would be seen to be threatening the legitimacy of any democratic government. As such, whilst the move from a Chief Election Commissioner-led body to a multi-member body has been contentious, it has managed to evolve without seriously undermining the perceived fairness of the electoral system.

The first two Chief Election Commissioners, Sukumar Sen and K.V.K. Sundaram, were initially appointed for a period of five years and their term was extended by three years. In 1972, the rules were changed to limit this tenure to five years or attaining the age of sixty-five, whichever came first. This was changed to six years under the Chief Election Commissioner and Election Commissioners (conditions of service) Act 1991 (Ali 2001: 25).[5] This Act also further entrenched the position of the Chief Election Commissioner, who can only be removed by impeachment.[6]

The issue of partisan influence over appointments emerged in a blaze of controversy in January 2009, when the (soon to be retiring) Chief Election Commissioner Gopalaswami wrote a letter to the President recommending the removal of Election Commissioner Navin Chawla (then in line to replace Gopalaswami as Chief Election Commissioner). Gopalaswami accused Chawla of partisanship, reflecting complaints made to the President from the BJP, alleging that Chawla favoured the Congress party. The President, Pratibha Patil, declined to act on the recommendation. The controversy highlighted two institutional weaknesses in the structure of the Election Commission: the potential for partisan appointments by a government and the difference in security of tenure for the Chief Election Commissioner and Election Commissioners.

The events of 2009 reawakened interest in the ideas of the Tarkunde Committee (1975) and the Goswami Committee (1990) that Election Commissioners should be selected by a committee, including a representative of opposition parties. These recommendations sought to weaken the influence of government over the President's choice of Election Commissioners. The relative weakness of tenure for Election Commissioners, who legally could be seen to be serving at the behest of the Chief Election Commissioner, had been raised by the Election Commission in 2004, when a proposal was made to entrench the Election Commissioners in the same way as the Chief Election Commissioner (Katju 2009: 10).

At the inception of the Election Commission, it was supported by a remarkably meagre administrative staff. When the Election Commission started functioning on 25 January 1950 there was 'one Secretary, one Assistant Secretary, one Superintendent, five Assistants, ten Clerks, two stenographers and eight Class IV employees recruited on an ad hoc basis mostly from amongst the employees who were rendered surplus in the Constituent Assembly of India when that Assembly concluded its labours' (Bhalla 1973: 20).[7] As the institution settled, recruitment expanded and became more formal. The number of gazetted posts increased from thirteen in 1952 to forty-one in 1971; and the non-gazetted staff grew from 119 in 1952 to 241 in 1971 (Bhalla 1973: 21). By 2004, the Election Commission had over 300 officials, housed in the impressive Nirvachan Sadan headquarters, with an administrative budget of Rs 11.5 crore (Union Budget 2004–5). Expenditure incurred running Lok Sabha elections since 1967 is shown in Table 7.2.

Table 7.2: Election Expenditure, Lok Sabha Elections: 1952 to 1999

YEAR	EXPENDITURE (RS)
1951–2	10,45,47,099
1957	5,90,21,786
1962	7,31,58,000
1967	10,95,33,772
1971	11,60,87,450
1977	23,03,68,000
1980	54,77,39,000
1984	81,51,34,000
1989	1,54,22,00,000
1991	3,59,10,24,679
1996	5,97,34,41,000
1998	6,66,22,16,000
1999	8,80,00,00,000
2004	13,00,00,00,000

Source: Election Commission (series of reports on general elections) and http://www.eci.gov.in/miscellaneous_statistics/expenditurel_loksabha.asp (accessed October 2008). Expenditure figures for 1999 and 2004 are provisional.

The Central Commission is supported by state Election Commissions, run by a Chief Electoral Officer, appointed after consultation with state governments. There is an extensive network of state and district election officials, responsible for carrying out the duties of the Election Commission.[8] This core network is supplemented during the run-up to the elections with a huge contingent of government and associated officials, who are co-opted to the Election Commission to administer the electoral process. The 1999 Lok Sabha elections involved nearly five million personnel, in administrative and security capacities, temporarily in the charge of the Election Commission. At the time of the formation of the Election Commission, it was recognized that the temporary nature of this attachment could lead to a conflict of interest amongst these staff,[9] but Ambedkar felt that it would be administratively complex and wasteful to set up an elaborate machinery on a permanent basis (Bhalla 1973: 26).

The right of the Election Commissioner to censure government officials who have been co-opted to carry out election duties has been a source of controversy. In 1992, the Commission cancelled the appointment of the Chief Electoral Officer in West Bengal, and in 1993 a number of officials deputed from the Tripura government to administer the Vidhan Sabha elections were accused by the Commission of being 'contaminated' (Ali 2001: 60). The Election Commission has also sought to transfer government officials not directly engaged in work on elections, but whom it felt were acting in such a way as to threaten the fairness of the electoral process. During the 1996 Lok Sabha elections, the Uttar Pradesh government was ordered to transfer two Indian Police Service (IPS) officers accused of acting in a biased manner and the Election Commissioner forced transfers of a District Magistrate and Superintendent of Police in Uttar Pradesh and Rajasthan (Ali 2001: 61). As well as requesting transfers, the Election Commission has asserted the right to prevent the transfers of officials during an election campaign, if it feels that such transfers are likely to impede the fairness of the elections.

The central duties of the Election Commission can appear somewhat mundane, covering the general administration of the electoral process. The drawing-up of electoral rolls is an 'important but tedious function of the Election Commission', according to Fadia (1992: 82).[10] The accuracy of the registration of the electorate can play a crucial role, both in enabling voters to exercise their democratic rights, and preventing corruption. At the first general election, held in 1951–2, the Election Commission was faced with the problem that there was no precise definition of who was a citizen of India, a problem particularly acute after the huge migration following Partition. A flexible approach was adopted, enrolling any person who declared their intention to reside permanently in India (Election Commission 1955: 63).[11] Concerns about the accuracy of the electoral roll have continued to be raised. In 1999, the Election Commission was embarrassed when it was discovered that one of the Election Commissioners was not on the electoral roll (Venkatesan 2000).[12] As Sanjay Kumar argues—'Only those who might have experienced, can tell how difficult it is at the moment to get yourself enrolled as a voter ... Once we ensure an updated electoral role, half the battle on electoral reforms is won' (Kumar 2002: 3491).

A study in Andhra Pradesh by the Lok Satta movement, following the Lok Sabha elections of 1999, showed the administrative complexity and inaccuracy of methods developed for drawing-up and correcting the electoral rolls (Narayan 2001). This showed that the electoral register contained large numbers of ineligible names (due to changes of address, death, or being under the legal voting age). As a consequence of this study, the Election Commission in 2004 removed 93.42 lakh voters from the electoral rolls in Andhra Pradesh—reducing the total number of 'voters' by 7 per cent (Kumar 2004).[13]

For much of the 1990s, the Election Commission embarked on a quixotic campaign to solve the problems of voter registration, personation, and electoral corruption through the technocratic and expensive provision of voter identity cards. This was a personal crusade mounted by the Chief Election Commissioner T.N. Seshan, who raised the issue to a fundamental facet of the democratic process. Seshan was willing to postpone the holding of elections where full implementation of the photo identity cards was not complete. His campaign got mired in the administrative complexity of the process, which was a costly and bureaucratic distraction.[14] A more practical application of technology is the computerization of the electoral roll, which should lead to improvements in the accuracy and transparency of the registration process. Such technical innovation (whilst not solving the problems faced by potential voters with poor access to computers) would facilitate a continuous process of updating the electoral rolls, rather than the periodic updating of the electoral register.

A central function of the Election Commission has been the running of the polling process and vote counting. This has involved a huge logistical and administrative operation. The production and issuing of ballot papers and the organization of the counting of votes has generally been carried out efficiently and helped maintain the legitimacy of the electoral process. One attempt by the Election Commission to simplify and speed up the casting and counting of votes has been through the introduction of electronic voting machines (EVMs). The first experiment was carried out in 1982, but their use was disallowed by the Supreme Court in 1984,[15] on the grounds that the RPA (1951) included the words 'votes shall be given by ballots' (Butler *et al.* 1989: 16). An amendment to the RPA (1951) enabled the Election Commission to reintroduce EVMs. They were used in sixteen assembly constituencies in state elections held in November 1998, and for the complete voting in the Goa Vidhan Sabha elections of 1999. In the 1999 Lok Sabha elections over sixty million voters used EVMs (Election Commission 2000: 6). All voting for the 2004 and 2009 general elections was carried out using EVMs, and they have been used in all state Assembly elections and by-elections from 2003.

The Election Commission is responsible for the time-tabling of the electoral process; setting dates on which elections will be held, and overseeing the candidate nomination and vote counting process. In the case of dissolution of the Lok Sabha or state Assemblies, the notification of elections is issued by the President or Governor in consultation with the Election Commission. In the case of death, resignation, or disqualification of an MP or MLA, the RPA (1951) charged the Commission with holding a by-election as promptly as possible. This function was not always discharged effectively; in some cases, a delay of over two years occurred before a legislative vacancy was filled (Ali 2001: 46). In 1997, the Lok Sabha passed a law, with the support of the Election Commission, which set a six-month time limit for holding by-elections.

The Commission has considerable discretion over these aspects of electoral time-tabling,[16] and at times they can lead to political controversy. In 1995, T.N. Seshan, the Chief Election Commissioner, refused to set a timetable for Vidhan Sabha elections in the state of Jammu and Kashmir, stating that the security situation was too precarious, and undermined the possibility of free and fair elections. This was against the Union government's view that prolonging President's rule was harmful to the running of the state and elections should be held. After a judicial challenge, the Supreme Court ruled that the Chief Election Commissioner had exceeded his authority in rejecting the government's request to initiate elections and had behaved 'irresponsibly' (Ali 2001: 48–50). Also in 1995, Seshan delayed elections in Bihar, arguing that the failure to implement a scheme of voters' identity cards would endanger the fairness of the election. Again, the Supreme Court was forced to intervene to over-ride the Election Commission's decision to delay polling. In 1993 and 1994, the Election Commission delayed a series of by-elections in Tamil Nadu, Haryana, Uttar Pradesh, and Punjab, after allegations of electoral malpractice (Ali 2001: 51). In the aftermath of the communal massacres in Gujarat in the spring of 2002, the Election Commission resisted pressure from the Bharatiya Janata Party (BJP) government to hold early elections, arguing that circumstances would not allow free and fair elections.

The Election Commission's desire to ensure that polling is carried out within a secure law-and-order situation has tended to extend the period over which polling is held. Security forces from outside a state (considered to be less susceptible to political interference) have been used to counter violent conduct during elections. In order to concentrate the deployment of security forces, the Election Commission has held polling within a state in a number of separate phases, often over a number of weeks.

Whilst the first Lok Sabha elections was held over a period of four months, from October 1951 to February 1952, the Election Commission gradually speeded up the polling process—in 1957, polling was over seventeen days between 24 February and 14 March, and in 1962, polling lasted ten days (16 to 25 February). Between 1967 and 1977, polling was conducted in less than a week, and in 1980, polling was on just two days (3 and 6 January). In 1991, the Election Commission time-tabled most of the polling for 20 to 26 May, although the security situation in Punjab and Assam meant elections were scheduled in June. This schedule was upset by the shocking assassination of Rajiv Gandhi on 21 May 1991. The second round of polling was postponed, and took place on 15 June.[17] In 1996, the election was held in three phases, between 7 April and 7 May; in 1998, four phases, from 16 February to 7 March; and in 1999, in five phases, from 5 September to 3 October. In 2004, polling was held over four phases, between 20 April and 10 May; and in 2009, there were five phases, between 16 April and 13 May.

Concern over security has lengthened the electoral process in the 1990s, but the Election Commission has also tried to shorten the period over which active party political campaigning is allowed. Under the 1996 Representation of the People (Amendment) Act, passed by the United Front government with the concurrence of the Election Commission, the campaign period was reduced from twenty-one to fourteen days. This, alongside a more rigorous control of campaign spending, has changed the character of Indian elections—exchanging a vibrant campaigning period for a shorter campaign followed by a longer period of polling where partisan appeals are supposed to be muted. Whilst this has enabled the law and order situation surrounding polls to be tightened up, and the dangers of corruption and booth capture countered, it can be seen as having reduced the vibrancy of political debate. The interests of the bureaucratic administration of the elections have to be placed against a vibrant campaign in which policy issues and candidate performance can be fully examined.

The Election Commission has the authority (under the RPA 1951(58)) to countermand an election, order a re-poll within a particular area, or demand a recount of votes. This is designed to ensure that elections are free and fair, and to counter corruption and booth-capturing (which was codified through a 1989 Amendment to the RPA 1951). The strongest exercise of this power occurred in the Lok Sabha elections of 1991, when the Commission countermanded the result in five constituencies in Bihar and Uttar Pradesh.

The Election Commission has a role in the regulation and registration of political parties. The original function of the Commission was to allocate the symbols which appeared on a ballot paper next to a candidate's name. For the first Lok Sabha elections the Commission designated parties as national or state parties; national parties had a symbol reserved exclusively for its candidates across the country, and state parties had a symbol reserved for use within the state. In 1968, the Election Commission issued the Election Symbols (Reservation and Allotment) Order, which required political parties to be registered in order to gain recognition. In the case of (the very frequent) splits in party organizations, the Election Commission has to decide which (if any) party grouping should retain the party symbol and designation.[18] These developments gave the Commission a more interventionist role in the regulation of party politics.

The registering of political parties (under Section 29A of the RPA 1951) requires the provision of a copy of the party constitution, which should conform to the spirit of the Constitution. The Election Commission has attempted to strengthen this provision, through an amendment to the Electoral Symbols Order in 1994, which proposed that the Commission could withdraw registration and right to a symbol from any party deemed guilty of electoral malpractice (violating the 'model code of conduct'). The Chief Election Commissioner, T. N. Seshan, announced that any party which did not conform to its declared constitutional structure and practices would be deregistered. This proved to be an empty threat although it was reiterated by Seshan's replacement as Chief Election Commissioner in 1997 (Ali 2001: 59). In December 1997, Election Commissioner G.V.G. Krishnamurthy threatened the Shiv Sena with derecognition as a political party if organizational elections were not held. He was forced to back down, after the intervention of Chief Election Commissioner and the President, and the prospect that the decision would be challenged as unconstitutional (India Today, 29 December 1997).

The Election Commission plays an important role in the delimitation process, by which constituency boundaries are drawn up and states are allocated seats in the national Parliament. However, whilst providing most of the resources and expertise which underpin the process, the Election Commission is kept at a legal remove from control over the process; which is vested in Parliament. The Indian Constitution lays down certain ground rules for delimitation (Articles 81 and 82), but leaves the actual practical details for Parliament to decide. Both the underlying principles and the practical measures have been the subject of much debate and reform since Independence, although there has been a hiatus since 1976 when the delimitation process was put on hold (see McMillan 2000; McMillan 2008). The Constitution (Eighty-fourth) Amendment Act (2001) provided for a limited redrawing of constituency boundaries; restricting future delimitation to intra-state reallocation of seats, and keeping the number of seats allocated to each state at the existing level. A limited delimitation exercise on these lines was completed in 2008.

The first delimitation was carried out under the office of the President, with the groundwork being done by the Election Commission, whose proposals were then laid before Parliament. The process was seen as unsatisfactory; the Union Minister of Law, C.C. Biswas, commented that—'The President's Orders which were laid before the Parliament, were simply torn into pieces by Parliament, whose decisions seems to have been actuated more by the convenience of individual Members of the House rather than by considerations of general interest' (Jha 1963: 132).

The Delimitation Commission Act 1952 provided for a three-member Delimitation Commission made up of two judges (or ex-judges) and the Chairman of Election Commission (ex-officio). This was an attempt to 'judicialize' the process, but was tempered by the provision of two to seven associate members for each state; MLAs who were to be appointed by the Speaker of the state Legislative Assembly. Whilst the system worked much more smoothly than before, the setting up of the Delimitation Commission did not completely remove doubts about the independence of the process. As R.P. Bhalla notes—'It was regarded as a familiar device of giving an unbiased colouring to the biased proposals of the government' (Bhalla 1973: 61). The First Delimitation Commission carried out the apportionment of seats for the 1957 elections, taking into account the population figures from the 1951 census. The Second Delimitation Commission was established under the Delimitation Act 1962. The Act increased the number of Associate Members to nine for each state—four from the Lok Sabha and five from the Legislative Assembly. The change suggests that the MPs wanted to keep a close eye on changes in their own constituencies. The Third Delimitation Commission, and the last one before the 2001 census, was set up under the Delimitation Act 1972. The basic structure of a three-member Commission with two judicial members and the Chairman of the Election Commission was retained, although the number of Associate members for each state was increased to ten (five MPs and five MLAs), appointed by the speaker of the Lok Sabha or Vidhan Sabha.[19]

The Election Commission has played a key role in supporting the work of Delimitation Commissions, and has the expertise and resource base necessary for the effective application of delimitation. As such, the Election Commission's role as the organizational force behind delimitation should be recognized in law. Whether the Election Commission takes over the whole process of delimitation depends on two considerations. The first concerns the perceived benefits of having periodic judicial appointments which, whilst perhaps adding a veneer of independence, could disturb the application of what are technical (although highly politicized) procedures. The second consideration relates to the vagueness of the rules laid down for delimitation, which at the moment allow for significant political influence. The need for the Election Commission to maintain its reputation for neutrality and legitimacy may mean that it is better placed at a statutory distance from responsibility for the delimitation process.

The Election Commission holds a supervisory role in the nomination of the candidates for election, under Part V of the RPA 1951. This involves checking that a candidate has paid the appropriate deposit and has the requisite number of nominations. In 1997, at the request of the Election Commission, the government promulgated an Ordinance which increased the requirements for candidate nomination, raising the security deposit of candidates (in 'General'

seats from Rs 500 to 10,000) and increasing the number of nominations from ten to fifty. This was part of an attempt to reduce the number of candidates contesting elections, and succeeded in lowering the number of contestants significantly.[20] In the 2001 Tamil Nadu State Assembly elections, the candidature of the ex-Chief Minister, J. Jayalalitha, was rejected on the grounds of multiple candidature and (more controversially) her conviction (suspended by the Madras High Court) on corruption charges. This intervention was not enough to stop Jayalalitha from becoming Chief Minister once again (Kumar 2001).

Election of the President and Vice President is by indirect election, with the electorate made up of an electoral college consisting of the Lok Sabha and Vidhan Sabha membership. Votes are weighted so that states with large legislatures are not over-represented. The President and Vice President are chosen under a Single Transferable Vote system. The process of these elections (if not always the outcome) has been largely uncontroversial,[21] and so the role of the Election Commission has not been an issue at any time. Elections to the Rajya Sabha (with a third of the house being re-elected every two years) are based on the same electoral college. The House was established to protect state interests in the Parliament, and the key area of contention has been the extent to which its members actually represent the states. The residence requirement for election has been abused, and attempts by the Election Commission to tighten up the process have been unsuccessful.[22]

The statutory rules regarding election expenses are laid down in Section 77 of the RPA (1951). Until 1975, every candidate was required to keep a record of any expenditure in connection with the election incurred or authorized by him or by his election agent, over the period of the campaign. From the first Lok Sabha elections, the very low levels of authorized expenditure meant that most candidates were forced to understate their expenses. The Election Commission commented that the system was unworkable, and recommended that the expenditure limits be raised appreciably, and greater discretion given to the Returning Officer and the Commission in determining malpractice (Election Commission 1955: 174–5). Minor changes were introduced by the 1956

Representation of the People (Second Amendment) Act; raising the limit of candidate expenditure, and relaxing the regulations regarding spending by a candidate's party and supporters (provided such expenditure was not authorized by the candidate). The system was still not functioning satisfactorily, and the Report on the Third General Election stated—'The Commission is of the view that the legal provisions relating to election expenses as they stand at present are of no use and call for drastic amendment or total repeal' (Election Commission 1966: 124). The Commission was joined by the Supreme Court in expressing discontent with the statutory control of election expenditure (*R.K. Birla vs Megh Raj Patodia*, 1970, quoted in Bhalla 1973: 321).

However, in the 1970s, when the issue of election expenses caused the criminal conviction of Prime Minister Indira Gandhi, and was instrumental in her decision to declare an Emergency, the Election Commission was remarkably quiescent. The Indira Gandhi Election Case was sparked in 1971, when her opponent in the Rae Bareli constituency at the Lok Sabha elections, Raj Narain (of the Samyukta Socialist Party) claimed his defeat was due to the corrupt and extravagant election campaign run by the Prime Minister. He took the case to court, arguing that this violated the RPA, and its limitations on candidate expenses (for a more detailed account, see Austin 1999: chapter 14).

Raj Narain's persistence forced Indira Gandhi into further and more extreme attempts to twist the law and Constitution to protect her position. In another election expenses case,[23] the Court ruled that expenses incurred without consent in a candidate's advantage should be included in election expenses. Mrs Gandhi and the Law Ministry reacted by retrospectively altering the law. The Representation of the People (Amendment) Ordinance was passed in October 1974, stating that expenditure by parties and individuals other than the candidate or agent was not to be taken as part of the candidate's election expenses. The Election Laws (Amendment) Act 1975, separated acts and services provided by government officials in the course of their duty from counting towards election expenditure, and removed the provision for automatic disqualification

of a candidate found to have exceeded the statutory expenditure limits from contesting an election for six years (Election Commission 1978: 126–7). Indira Gandhi was forced to appear in court, and in June 1975 the Supreme Court ruled that although the amendment of the RPA in 1974 was legal, Mrs Gandhi's election was void because she exploited the services of state and Central government to such an extent that it was a 'corrupt practice'. The decision was stayed unconditionally (allowing Indira Gandhi to appear, although not vote, in Lok Sabha, and remain Prime Minister) by Krishna Iyer in a decision seen as judicially illiterate and verging on corruption. This stay allowed Parliament time to pass the Election Laws Amendment Act and the Thirty-ninth Amendment, which sought to retrospectively protect the position of the Prime Minister.

The Thirty-ninth Amendment, preventing Supreme Court from interfering in a Prime Minister's election, was passed after a two-hour 'debate' in the Lok Sabha. This put regulation on the election of the Prime Minister and speaker in charge of Parliament, rather than the Supreme Court. Mohan Dharia, an MP described it as 'a surrender of parliamentary democracy to the coming dictatorship' (Austin 1999: 320). On top of this, the Forty-first Amendment Bill prevented any criminal proceedings against President, Prime Minister, or Governor for acts 'done by him, whether before he entered upon his office or during his term of office'. Whilst the Supreme Court struck down the attempt to amend the Constitution so as to retrospectively protect the Prime Minister, these actions did give sufficient legislative backing to prevent the disqualification of Indira Gandhi, and allowed her to stand for future elections.

Accounts of the role of the Election Commission over this unhappy period in India's democratic history are remarkably thin. Whilst Indira Gandhi's Congress government ensured that the postponement of Lok Sabha elections after 1971 was constitutionally valid, the underlying principles of the Constitution were stretched to unacceptable levels. The impartiality of the Election Commission became a part of Jayaprakash Narayan's challenge to government performance. Although the Election Commission had expressed its dissatisfaction over the statutory regulation of election finance in the 1960s, it did not play a significant part in the debates of the 1970s which contributed to the collapse of Indira Gandhi's government. The impression remains that the Election Commission had become absorbed into the Congress system of government and lost sight of its broader remit to maintain the democratic structure of the Indian political system.

The issue of electoral finance has continued to play a major part in the perception of the role of the Election Commission and the conduct of elections. The impression that 'black money' (unofficial donations and pay-offs) dominated political campaigns has persisted, despite attempts at reform. Company donations to political parties were banned in 1969, but the Companies Act (1985) overturned this as long as there was full disclosure. From 1979, political parties were exempted from income and wealth taxes, provided they filed annual returns including audited accounts and the identities of donors. The disclosure of political funding was given force in 1996, when the Supreme Court (acting after a public interest litigation [PIL]) ordered parties to file returns required by Income Tax and Wealth Tax Acts (Sridharan 2001: 32). The Supreme Court, ruling in *Y.K. Gadak vs Balasaheb Vikhe Patil* (November 1993) observed that the 'prescription of ceiling on expenditure by a candidate is a mere eyewash and there is no practical check on election expenses for which it was enacted to attain a meaningful democracy' (Godbole 2002: 4003).

The role of the Election Commission in regulating spending by political parties on election campaigns has been hampered by the inadequacies of the legal structure laid down by Parliament. This inadequacy reflects an ambiguity about the nature of spending by political parties, which has tended to be associated with corrupt practices rather than effective promotion of a policy programme.[24] However, the issue of electoral finance illustrates the changing role and attitude of the Election Commission. In the 1950s and 1960s, the Commission was vocal in its criticism of the legal framework, whereas in the 1970s, it stood aside from the legal and constitutional maelstrom which engulfed the entire political system. In the 1990s, the Commission began to use the ambiguities of the statutory regulation in order to curb the excesses of the political parties, stretching its remit to the limit (and occasionally beyond) of its constitutional role.

The Election Commission's broad constitutional remit over the conduct of elections, laid down in Article 324, has been operationalized through a number of directives negotiated with the political parties. A model code of conduct for parties and candidates contesting elections was first used in Kerala prior to the Assembly Elections of February 1960, and circulated nationally in 1968 on the eve of State Assembly elections. It provided general rules for electoral conduct; setting norms regarding the notification and conduct of public meetings, standards of decency and decorum in political debate, and condemning campaigning based on appeals to violence or communal hostility. The code was publicized by the Election Commission prior to the Lok Sabha elections in 1971, and over the years has been revised and extended.[25] However, the lack of any legal sanction has meant that the code is a toothless weapon against electoral corruption and campaign malpractice.

An attempt to give such a code a legislative basis was made following the Goswami Committee Report, when it was included in the Representation of the People (Amendment) Bill of 1990. However, the National Front government collapsed before the Bill could be passed. The Chief Election Commissioner, T.N. Seshan, used the model code of conduct as a weapon in his crusade against electoral malpractice, backed up by the threat of postponement of elections and the countermanding of results. Such enforcement was seen as 'a patent abuse of power' (*The Statesman*, 11 August 1999). Seshan's replacement as Chief Election Commissioner, M.S. Gill, continued to use the model code of conduct as an instrument with which to exert influence on the election campaign, and argued that it was not necessary to give statutory basis to the code. According to the Commission—'The Model Code is a unique document and regarded by many democratic countries across the world as singular contribution by the Election Commission of India to the cause of free and fair elections' (Election Commission 2000: 4). In 1999, the Commission forced the Telugu Desam Party (TDP) government in Andhra Pradesh to suspend a number of government initiatives, which it felt were being used by the state government for political advantage. In 2009, the Election Commission censured Varun Gandhi, BJP candidate for the Pilibhit Lok Sabha constituency, suggesting that he had breached the Moral Code of Conduct by making speeches including 'highly derogatory references and seriously provocative language of a wholly unacceptable nature against a certain community'.[26] However, the Commission stopped short of taking any action against either the candidate or the party and Varun Gandhi won the seat.

In 1997, the Election Commission began a campaign against the 'criminalization' of politics, arguing that no candidate should be allowed to contest an election if they had been convicted of an offence, even if the conviction was under appeal. Then Commissioner, G.V.G. Krishnamurthy, pithily noted that 'no law-breaker should ever be a law-maker' (Ali 2001: 72). As with the attempt to impose the model code of conduct, it was seen as exceeding the powers of the Commission. Sanjay Kumar notes that:

> While criminalisation of politics is an issue of great concern, it should be noted that there are no authentic records about how many MLAs or MPs at present or in the recent past were criminals ... A person can be criminal in the eyes of the law since he had been involved in public activities defined to be unlawful, but those acts at times are applauded by the common people. Agitations, gheraos, demonstration on issues which concern people at large are a routine thing for people in politics. (2002: 3490)

In a country where special recognition is given to 'freedom fighters', who fought and were gaoled in a struggle against one regime for the establishment of Independence, the issue of civil disobedience should not be subsumed so easily in a dialogue of criminality of politics.

In a further attempt to counter 'criminalization', the Election Commission issued an order in June 2002, which laid down that each candidate for the Rajya Sabha, Lok Sabha, or State Assembly should submit an affidavit along with nomination papers. This affidavit would detail any involvement with a criminal prosecution, details of assets and property ownership, and educational qualifications (Venkatesan 2002). This followed a directive from the Supreme

Court, which suggested that, in the absence of legislative guidance, it was within the Commission's constitutional remit to seek such information. parliamentary attempts to codify the limits of disclosure of candidates' background were declared unsatisfactory by the Supreme Court, giving the Election Commission freedom to impose its own rules of disclosure (Venkatesan 2003).[27]

As part of its overview of the conduct of elections, the Election Commission has been drawn into issues of media regulation and reporting, and the relationship between political parties and media conduct. As early as 1950, the Election Commission tried to establish a scheme for allocating broadcasting time for political parties during the campaign. The attempts were unsuccessful, first due to governmental indifference (in 1956), and then due to inter-party wrangling over the distribution of broadcasting time (1961, 1966, and 1971) (Bhalla 1973: 210–20). Over time, the Election Commission did forge an arrangement, whereby registration and recognition as a political party was reflected in access to the national broadcaster, Doordarshan. However, the Election Commission was not able to check what was seen as a lack of independence in Doordarshan's news reporting. According to Victoria Farmer, the 1980s saw an 'erosion of the credibility of [Doordarshan] news programming, through blatant use of the medium for publicizing Congress party leaders and initiatives' (Farmer 2000: 268). In 1998, the provisions for public service broadcasting during the election campaign were extended, after an arrangement was negotiated between the Election Commission and the Prasar Bharati Corporation (Election Commission 2000: 7).

In January 1998, the Election Commission imposed a code of conduct on the electronic media, extending the forty-eight hour hiatus in the campaign imposed on candidates in the run-up from polling to broadcasting. The Commission also proposed that there should be restrictions on election speeches inciting violence or communal discord and that coverage of any constituency should not concentrate on one candidate (Ali 2001: 156). An attempt was also made to prevent exit or opinion polls being published or broadcasted prior to polling. This was challenged by the publishers of *The Hindu* and *Frontline*, and a Supreme Court ruling dismissed the Election Commission order in September 1999. In a triumphant editorial, *The Hindu* (29 August 1999) lambasted the Commission's heavy-handed attempt to control media reporting of the election campaign, arguing that 'the result is all-round confusion and an impression that the Commission is exceeding its brief'. This did not stop the Election Commission attempting to block the publication's opinion and exit polls during subsequent general elections, again unsuccessfully in 2004, but with the backing of the Supreme Court in 2009.

THE ELECTION COMMISSION: ASSESSING ITS ROLE AND PERFORMANCE

The Election Commission was established as an institution which would enhance and entrench the democratic character of the state. Its success in performing this role is a credit, both to the wisdom of those members of the Constituent Assembly who laid the foundations for its establishment, and the officials and commissioners who were charged with its operation. The constitutional basis of the Election Commission was designed to be flexible, since the demands which would be put upon the institution were not easy to predict. Scope was allowed for Parliament to adjust the remit and composition of the Commission. The lack of prescription in the constitutional structure and scope laid down for the Election Commission could be criticized as being vague and leaving the institution open to party-political manipulation.

In the event, the Election Commission has evolved within the constraints of the wider constitutional structure. It has responded to the changing legislative framework imposed by the Parliament, and where Parliament has been slow to give guidance, it has attempted to fulfil its broad constitutional remit regarding the conduct of elections. In doing so, it has been constrained (and sometimes facilitated) by the rulings of the Supreme Court. From its inception, with no significant institutional antecedents, and with the job of establishing a democracy based on universal franchise in a huge

and diverse country with only a limited experience of elections, it set up an effective electoral process which gave a solid grounding and enhanced the legitimacy of the democratic Indian government.

The first Chief Election Commissioner, Sukumar Sen 'built up an institution which became an example to the newly free countries in the 50s and 60s' (Fadia 1992: 85). The diligence of Sukumar Sen, operating with a minimal administrative organization, was essential to the formation of the institution. He resisted the temptation to instigate elections before the newly-formed governmental institutions were prepared, visiting every state to gauge electoral preparations, and meeting with political parties and the press (Election Commission 1955: 24–5). Delaying elections which were scheduled for 1950 meant that the process of constituency delimitation and drawing-up of electoral rolls was adequate, if not perfect. By example he set a standard of democratic performance which future Chief Election Commissioners had to emulate. The Election Commission Report on the Second Lok Sabha Elections of 1957 (somewhat immodestly) includes an anecdotal report:

> In Madras, a voter refused to exercise his franchise in favour of any person other than 'Shri Sukumar Sen', the Chief Election Commissioner. The voter is said to have remarked 'I want to vote for Shri Sukumar Sen only and not for the candidate of any of the parties. All these parties have been harassing me with their election propaganda for over a month'. (Election Commission 1959: 225)

Throughout the 1950s and 1960s, the Election Commission built on this legacy and established a tradition of effectiveness in conducting elections. It was not a high-profile institution, which possibly reflects its adequacy—'In the past the commission used to be considered a wing of the administration to complete the formalities of the election. Nobody even knew the name of the Election Commissioner, or gave any importance to this institution or even took notice of its activities' (Roy 1999: 2633).

The Election Commission did not function as an uncritical element of the government administration, and voiced its objection to certain aspects of the electoral system, notably the regulation of election expenses. It also recognized its own inadequacies in drawing-up accurate electoral rolls. The Election Commission was working within a wider political and governmental atmosphere which appreciated the benefits of a quasi-independent body which legitimized the electoral process.

As the Congress hegemony over Indian politics waned, from the late 1960s, the position of the Election Commission became more precarious. Under Indira Gandhi, the policy and behaviour of the Congress party and the national government became more strident, and was willing to undermine any institution which threatened to destabilize the Prime Minister's position. In such circumstances, the Election Commission appears to have entered a period of quiescence. The Election Commission played no visible role in the debate over election expenses sparked by Raj Narain's challenge to the election result of 1971. More damningly, there is no evidence of the Election Commission resisting the abrogation of democracy through the imposition of the Emergency in 1975. Whilst this was carried out with a veneer of legitimacy under special provisions of the Constitution, and with the complicity of a Congress-dominated Lok Sabha which was willing to push through any constitutional amendment necessary to protect the Prime Minister, it reflects little (or no) credit on the Election Commission.

The failure of the Janata Party government, and the reassertion of the Gandhi-dominated Congress after 1980, offered little scope for an independent Election Commission, and it was only in the late 1980s that the Election Commission began to make its presence known. Rajiv Gandhi's crude attempt to pack the Election Commission in 1989, just before the Lok Sabha elections, signalled that the institution may have an important role to play in the political arena.

The appointment of T.N. Seshan as Chief Election Commissioner in December 1990 proved to be a watershed for the Commission. Seshan might be seen as a partisan appointment (and was regarded at the time as a Congress sympathizer) if he hadn't (almost systematically) antagonized every major party.[28] Seshan's popularist posturing against a corrupt political culture gave the Election

Commission a public profile that it had never before enjoyed, and should, perhaps, have not attained. He attempted to extend limited powers of the Election Commission over the administration of elections to wage a battle against the political parties, and too often was found to have exceeded his remit. His recourse to election postponement, interventions in the conduct of elections, and threats to countermand elections were open to accusations of political manipulation, and devalued both the functioning of the Election Commission and the democratic process. Seshan's attempts to develop a positive role for the Commission were centred around glamorous but ineffective programmes, most notably the scheme for voter identity cards, which turned out to be an expensive and inefficient measure. As M.S. Gill commented (during the period when he held the position of Election Commissioner, but was sidelined by Seshan's challenge to the appointment in the Supreme Court)—'Seshan's directives are like bubbles of the day. They won't make any lasting contribution to strengthen the Commission. Only changes made in the structure of the Commission can be effective' (Venkatesan 1994).

Whilst fitting more easily into the structure of a three-member Election Commission, Gill proved almost as susceptible to the power and profile which attended the Commission after the Seshan era. His interventions to impose a model code of conduct, expose the criminalization of politics, and constrain media reporting of the election campaign have displayed the same easy popularism and desire to extend the ambit of the Election Commission that Seshan displayed (although without the egotism and faculty for self-promotion). Meanwhile, the tendency to extend the period of polling in elections, whilst restricting the period of campaigning, shows a preference for bureaucratic order over the messiness of democratic dialogue.

The Election Commission is primarily an administrative institution. Its core functions are important, but often mundane in their execution. Attempting to extend the executive functions of the Commission, without the guidance of Parliament or, failing this, the Supreme Court, has tended to leave the Commission isolated. At times, the

Election Commission can be seen to have pursued a bureaucratic agenda which leads to a tension with the democratic process—the desire to regulate electoral enrolment through the provision of voter identity cards, intervention in the organization of political parties, and control over the nomination of candidates. These interventions can be seen as undemocratic; preventing the people from voting for the candidates they wish to (even though they may be criminal, corrupt, and otherwise disreputable). Similarly, the role of the Election Commission in limiting the scope of election campaigning and media reporting can be seen as restricting the freedom of speech.

Often the technical details of electoral administration have a more practical impact on the democratic process than the high profile rhetorical interventions. More sophisticated planning of the sequence of elections across the country has led to improved security and more peaceful conduct of polling. The introduction of Booth Level Officers responsible for voter registration has improved the accuracy of the electoral rolls. A process of 'Vulnerability Mapping' has been used to identify areas where voter intimidation might occur, allowing election officials to be proactive in responding to the threat of violence or misconduct.[29] Such innovations show an awareness of the effect that good electoral administration at the grassroots level can have on voters' engagement with electoral politics.

Evidence of public perceptions of the performance of the Electoral Commission suggests that it has been successful in carrying out its duties whilst maintaining public trust. Mitra and Singh (1999: 260) report that the Election Commission has the highest level of public trust/confidence of the main political institutions; higher than the judiciary, government, political parties, and the police. The *State of Democracy in South Asia* report showed 51 per cent of respondents in India have a 'great deal' or 'some' trust in the Election Commission, compared to just 14 per cent with 'not very much' or 'none at all'.[30] More importantly, the view that elections are conducted in a free and fair manner is supported by over 80 per cent of respondents to the 2004 National Election Study, across the political spectrum.[31]

There is often tension between the institution of the Election Commission and the functioning of political parties, who often profess their desire to have a free and fair electoral system but benefit from illegal party funding and the involvement of criminal elements in their party organizations. Their interest is in a weak regulatory body which maintains the legitimacy of the system without preventing the running of the party machine. The Election Commission has a role in improving the transparency of the electoral process, but it has occasionally overstretched its competency, and extended its executive role. The difficulty lies in maintaining neutrality and independence, whilst providing a democratic structure that is run for, but not by, the political parties. The Commission is dependent on its constitutional position, rather than through any popular mandate, which is the arena in which political parties and the Parliament operate.

The Election Commission has an important constitutional role in maintaining the legitimacy of the democratic process which it has, to a large extent, performed successfully. In upholding the integrity of the electoral process, the Commission has contributed to the consolidation of democracy in India. At times, the Commission has been too quiescent, undermining its reputation as a non-partisan body when dealing with government; at times, the Chief Election Commissioner has pushed the demands of electoral probity to an extent when it threatens the vibrancy of the democratic process. The strength and independence of the Election Commission is crucial, but has to be exercised with some restraint. The real test of the Election Commission is in the legitimacy of a democratic government, and the public's faith in free and fair elections.

NOTES

1. The only similar institution alluded to in the Constituent Assembly was the body set up in Canada, under the Dominion Elections Act of 1920 (see debate on 15 and 16 June 1949, *Constituent Assembly Debates* ([CAD] VIII, pp. 903–30).

2. Whilst initially seen as of such importance that it was placed within the Fundamental Rights section of the Constitution, it was later moved to a separate section (Bhalla 1973, p. 3).

3. An amendment providing for separately constituted State Election Commissions, proposed by H.V. Pataskar (29 July 1947, *CAD* IV: 971), was initially accepted, but then overruled in subsequent redrafting (*CAD* VIII, pp. 910–912).

4. Referred to in the Constituent Assembly as Article 289.

5. The appointment of an Election Commissioner to the post of Chief Election Commissioner is seen as a renewal of tenure.

6. In 1991, 120 Lok Sabha MPs signed a notice of impeachment seeking the dismissal of T.N. Seshan, although the House was dissolved before the matter could be pressed (Ali 2001, p. 26).

7. Provision had been made for twenty-six permanent staff and twenty-four temporary, but not all posts were filled.

8. In 1966, an amendment to the Representation of the Peoples' Act was passed, creating a statutory post of District Election Officer to consolidate the local functioning of elections.

9. Resisting such conflicts was a question of 'mustering moral courage', according to the then Chief Election Commissioner, S.P. Sen Verma, in a remarkably frank discussion of the conflicting pressures facing those co-opted to undertake Election Commission work:

> In the first place, since as election officers you are officers of the commission, the Commission will stand by your side in your difficulty provided you are on the right lines. In the second place, the Commission takes special care in appointing by and large only permanent officers of Government as election officers ... I agree that it requires strong moral courage for an officer to say 'No' to his political boss even when the boss asks him to do something wrong or contrary to the law. The boss may not be able to dismiss you from service but he may harass you in many respects. He may arrange for your transfer to a so-called bad or penal station where facilities for the education of your children may not exist or he may seek to stop your promotion by various means and methods and so on and so forth. These are genuine difficulties and there is the rub as to why officials sometimes succumb to the unjust orders of their political bosses. But herein comes the question of your mustering moral courage. (Inaugural Address to the first All India Conference of Election Officers, New Delhi, 3 and 4 November 1971, quoted in Bhalla 1973, p. 27)

10. Notwithstanding its importance, Fadia manages to cover the subject in one sentence.

11. The Election Commission accepted that the registration was imperfect, due to a combination of ignorance and apathy amongst the population, lack of organization and experience of the political parties, and the inexperience and defective organization of the government machinery in some states (Election Commission 1955, p. 69). For a more objective, but not wholly critical, review of the process see Bhalla (1973, chapter 3).

12. Bhalla (1973, pp. 105–6) records the deletion of H.V. Kamath, an MP from Madhya Pradesh, from the electoral rolls; and the name of an MLA from Andhra Pradesh was removed from the register, instead of his wife's name.

13. The inquiry was held after Lok Satta found 340 'voters' registered from one house. This was in a poor area with only thatched huts as lodgings—in a 'posh area' 150 'voters' were enrolled from one house.

14. In 1995, the Supreme Court halted an Election Commission voter identification card campaign which required voters to prove their citizenship (Ali 2001, p. 66). By 2000, 374 million cards had been issued, just over half of the registered electorate (Election Commission 2000, p. 3). The Commission hoped that by 2009, coverage of the electorate would be sufficient to make possession of a voter identification card a requirement for voting, but had to recognize that this would disenfranchise a significant section of the population. Other forms of identification were accepted, in the absence of a voter identification card. National Election Survey data indicated that around 10 per cent of those who did not vote said it was because they did not have the correct identification ('No Barriers to Participation', *The Hindu*, 26 May 2009).

15. *A.C. Jose vs Sevari Pillai* (AIR 1984 SC 921).

16. The practical difficulties of finding a suitable date for elections are emphasized by the Election Commission:

> In a country as huge and diverse as India, finding a suitable period when elections can be held throughout the country is not simple. The Election Commission, which decides the schedule for elections, has to take account of the weather—during winter, constituencies may be snow-bound, and during the monsoon, access to remote areas restricted—the agricultural cycle, so that the planting or harvesting of crops is not disrupted,—exam schedules, as schools are used as polling stations and teachers employed as election officials, and religious festivals and public holidays. On top of this, there are the logistical difficulties that go with the holding of an election—mobilisation and movement of civil and para-military police forces, printing and distribution of hundreds of millions of ballot papers, sending out ballot boxes, setting up polling booths, appointing millions of officials to conduct poll and counting and oversee the elections. (Election Commission 2000, p. 3)

17. The Chief Election Commissioner T.N. Seshan complained that the decision when to hold the delayed round of polling was taken by members of the Congress party, rather than the Election Commission. 'Seshan silently endured criticism on the postponement of polls after Rajiv's assassination before finally disclosing that the dates were not his choice but he merely went along with the advice of the Government' (Fadia 1992, p. 85).

18. Under the Election Symbols (Reservation and Allotment) Order of 1968, and the ruling in *Sadiq Ali vs Election Commission of India* (AIR 1977 SC 2155), the Commission has been given jurisdiction over the allocation of party symbols when under dispute (Ali 2001, p. 56).

19. Other redistributions have been carried out on an ad hoc basis. After the two-member Constituencies Abolition Act 1961, the Election Commission was in charge of dividing the double-member constituencies, and the reorganization of states (for example, the Bombay Reorganization Act, 1960; Punjab Reorganization 1966; Goa, Daman and Diu Reorganization Act 1987) were accompanied by Delimitation Orders passed by Parliament (Butler *et al.* 1995, pp. 14–15).

20. In 1996, there were 13,952 candidates; in 1998, 4,750; and in 1999, 4,370 (Election Commission 2000: 4).

21. Details of minor disputes are in Bhalla (1973, chapter 7).

22. Congress leader Manmohan Singh quashed Election Commission proceedings against his right to stand for the Rajya Sabha from Assam on a technicality (*The Hindu*, 2 December 1999).

23. *Kanwar Lal Gupta vs Amarnath Chawla and Others* 1975(2) SCR 2599ff called Amarnath Chawla's case.

24. In 1998, an all-party parliamentary committee was established, led by Indrajit Gupta, to examine the issue of state-funding of political parties. It proposed increased support for political parties, both in terms of financial support and provision of centrally funded support for political campaigns.

25. In 1984, the Election Commission expanded the model code of conduct to restrict Central/state governments advertising in the media in such a way as to influence the elections, and prevent ministers from using official aircrafts during the campaign (Ali 2001, p. 112). In 1991, the code was extended, covering the general conduct of campaigning, conduct of meetings and processions, behaviour of parties and candidates on polling day, and regulating the use of government officials and resources.

26. Press release of the Election Commission, 22 March 2009.

27. These moves were given force by the Representation of the People (Amendment) Ordinance of 2002, which codified disclosure of a candidate's criminal record and assets and liabilities.

28. According to Swami (1995, p. 4), Seshan was selected by the Chandra Shekhar government ahead of V.S. Rama Devi after the intervention of Subramanian Swamy (then Minister of Law), who was looking for a sympathetic presence after a run-in with the previous Chief Election Commissioner R.V.S. Peri Sastri. 'He was brought in to harass us' complained BJP spokesman K.R. Malkani (quoted in *India Today*, 30 June 1991, p. 20); whilst the Janata Dal leader I.K. Gujral thought that Seshan targeted him (and countermanded his election from Patna in 1991) as an act of revenge for transferring Seshan from his post as Cabinet Secretary. The Congress leadership was challenged through Seshan's attempt to take action against members of the Rajya Sabha not resident in the states they claimed to represent (threatening Manmohan Singh) and an attempt to remove Sitaram Kesri from the Union Cabinet (Swami 1995).

29. These innovations in electoral administration are outlined by the Deputy Election Commissioner R. Balakrishnan in the press note 'Schedule for General Elections, 2009' issued by the Election Commission of India, 2 March 2009. Available from http://eci.nic.in/press/current/pn020309.pdf (last accessed July 2009).

30. Full results are available in de Souza *et al.* 2008: 253–4, Table 4.11. Thirty-five per cent of respondents had 'No Opinion'.

31. See de Souza *et al.* 2008, p. 44. Those expressing no opinion have been excluded.

REFERENCES

Ali, Rehna. 2001. *The Working of the Election Commission of India*. New Delhi: Jnanada Prakashan.

Austin, Granville. 1999. *Working a Democratic Constitution: The Indian Experience*. Oxford: Oxford University Press.

Bhalla, R.P. 1973. *Elections in India (1950–1972)*. New Delhi: S. Chand and Co.

Butler, David, Ashok Lahiri, and Prannoy Roy. 1995. *India Decides: Elections 1952–1995* (third edition). New Delhi: Books and Things.

———. 1989. *India Decides: Elections 1952–1989*. New Delhi: Living Media.

de Souza, Peter R., Suhas Palshikar, and Yogendra Yadav. 2008. *State of Democracy in South Asia: A Report*. New Delhi: Oxford University Press.

Election Commission. 2000. *Elections in India: Major Events and New Initiatives 1996–2000*. New Delhi: Election Commission of India.

———. 1978. *Report on the Sixth General Elections to the Lok Sabha and General Elections to the Kerala Legislative Assembly 1977: Volume 1*. New Delhi: Government of India Press.

Election Commission. 1966. *Report on the Third General Elections in India 1962: Volume 1.* New Delhi: Government of India Press.

———. 1959. *Report on the Second General Elections in India 1957: Volume 1.* New Delhi: Government of India Press.

———. 1955. *Report on the First General Elections in India 1951–52: Volume 1.* New Delhi: Government of India Press.

Fadia, B.L. 1992. 'Reforming the Electoral Commission', *Indian Journal of Political Science*, 53(1), pp. 78–88.

Farmer, Victoria L. 2000. 'Depicting the Nation: Media Politics in Independent India', in Francine R. Frankel, Zoya Hasan, Rajeev Bhargava, and Balveer Arora (eds), *Transforming India: Social and Political Dynamics of Democracy.* Oxford: Oxford University Press, pp. 254–87.

Godbole, Madhav. 2002. 'Report of Constitutional Review Commission: Some Reflections', *Economic and Political Weekly*, XXXVII(39), pp. 4001–8.

Jha, Nagesh. 1963. 'Delimitation of Constituencies: A Plea for Some Effective Criteria', *Indian Journal of Political Science*, vol. 24, pp. 129–47.

Katju, Manjari. 2009. 'Election Commission and Changing Contours of Politics', *Economic and Political Weekly*, XLIV(16), pp. 8–12.

Kumar, B. Venkatesh. 2001. 'Criminalisation of Politics and Election Commission', *Economic and Political Weekly*, XXXVI(24), pp. 2119–21.

Kumar, Sanjay. 2002. 'Reforming Indian Electoral Process', *Economic and Political Weekly*, XXXVII(33), pp. 3489–91.

Kumar, S. Nagesh. 2004. 'A Clean-up in Andhra Pradesh', *Frontline*, 21(3).

McMillan, Alistair. 2008. 'Delimitation in India', in Lisa Handley and Bernie Grofman (eds), *Redistricting in Comparative Perspective.* Oxford: Oxford University Press, pp. 75–96.

McMillan, Alistair. 2000. 'Delimitation, Democracy, and End of Constitutional Freeze', *Economic and Political Weekly*, XXXV(15), pp.1271–6.

Mitra, Subrata K. and V.B. Singh. 1999. *Democracy and Social Change in India: A Cross-sectional Analysis of the National Electorate.* New Delhi: Sage Publications.

Mozaffar, Shaheen and Andreas Schedler. 2002. 'The Comparative Study of Electoral Governance— Introduction', *International Political Science Review*, 23(1), pp. 5–27.

Narayan, Jayaprakash. 2001. 'Distorted Verdicts', *Seminar*, vol. 506, pp. 42–9.

Noorani, A.G. 1998. 'Creeping Arbitrariness', *The Statesman*, 24 February.

Pastor, Robert A. 1999. 'The Role of Electoral Administration in Democratic Transitions: Implications for Policy and Research', *Democratization*, 6(4), pp 1–27.

Roy, A.K. 1999. 'Role of Election Commission in Ensuring Fair Polls', *Economic and Political Weekly*, XXXIV(37), pp. 2633–4.

Rudolph, Susanne Hoeber, and Lloyd I. Rudolph. 2002. 'New Dimensions of Indian Democracy', *Journal of Democracy*, 13(1), pp. 52–66.

Shiva Rao, B. 1968. *The Framing of India's Constitution: A Study.* New Delhi: Indian Institute of Public Administration.

Sridharan, E. 2001. 'Reforming Political Finance', *Seminar*, vol. 506, pp. 29–36.

Swami, Praveen. 1995. 'Seshan Tamed', *Frontline*, 12(16).

Venkatesan, V. 2003. 'A Forceful Reiteration', *Frontline*, 20(7).

———. 2002. 'Fighting Disclosure Norms', *Frontline*, 19(15).

———. 2000. 'Setting the Agenda for Electoral Reforms', *Frontline*, 17(1).

———. 1994. 'Of Party Polls', *Frontline*.

8 The Party System*†

E. Sridharan

THE PUZZLE OF PARTY SYSTEM FRAGMENTATION

This chapter aims at providing a long-range overview of the process of fragmentation of the Indian party system at the national level over sixty-two years since Independence in 1947: from the first general elections in 1952 to the fifteenth general elections in 2009, as also the evolution of coalitions and possible trends towards reconsolidation into a less fragmented system with fewer poles.[1] It describes and analyses the process of fragmentation of the one party-dominated national party system, dominated by the encompassing centrist umbrella-type Indian National Congress (henceforth Congress) party. This process has resulted in an evolving national party system, still in flux, in which no party has achieved

a parliamentary majority in the last seven general elections (1989, 1991, 1996, 1998, 1999, 2004, and 2009), necessitating minority and/or coalition governments. The party system at the national, that is, in the Lok Sabha, level has become increasingly fragmented since 1989, even while party systems at the state level have become bipartisan or bipolar, hence *less* fragmented, in more and more states. An indicator of the fragmentation of the national party system is the Laakso–Taagepera index (N) (of the effective number of parties). The values of N by votes/seats (Table 8.1) were 4.80/4.35, 5.10/3.70, 7.11/5.83, 6.91/5.28, 6.74/5.87, 7.6/6.5, and 7.98/5.01 in 1989, 1991, 1996, 1998, 1999, 2004, and 2009 respectively, whereas in the eight general elections between 1952 and 1984 the effective number of parties by seats exceeded three only once (3.16 in 1967), and the effective number of parties by votes exceeded five only once (5.19 in 1967).[2]

This chapter is an overview of the party system and focuses on parties' electoral trajectory, and hence their position, in the evolution of the party system, rather than on their social bases or organizational dynamics.

*I thank Adnan Farooqui for research assistance in preparing most of the tables in this chapter.

†The names of all political parties appear in their abbreviated form here. For their full forms see the list of abbreviations in the preliminary pages of this volume.

Table 8.1: Effective Number of Parties in Lok Sabha Elections

S. NO.	YEAR	EFFECTIVE NUMBER OF PARTIES (VOTES)	EFFECTIVE NUMBER OF VOTES (SEATS)
1	1952	4.53	1.8
2	1957	3.98	1.76
3	1962	4.4	1.85
4	1967	5.19	3.16
5	1971	4.63	2.12
6	1977	3.4	2.63
7	1980	4.25	2.28
8	1984	3.99	1.69
9	1989	4.8	4.35
10	1991	5.1	3.7
11	1996	7.11	5.83
12	1998	6.91	5.28
13	1999	6.74	5.87
14	2004	7.6	6.5
15	2009	7.98	5.01

Source: See *Journal of the Indian School of Political Economy*, XV/1–2 (Jan.–June 2003), Statistical Supplement, Tables 1.1–1.13, 293–307. For 2004, the index was calculated by the Centre for the Study of Developing Societies, New Delhi, and for 2009 by the author.

The chapter describes the evolving fragmentation at the electoral and legislative levels in terms of the shifts in vote shares, seat shares, and the evolution of electoral alliances at both the national and state levels, since the national party system is an aggregate of state-level party systems. It also assesses competing explanations for these shifts to uncover their underlying logic.

There are, broadly speaking, two classes of explanations for the configuration of party systems in the comparative literature. One can be called the social cleavage theory of party systems, and the other the political-systemic theory of party systems, of which the most elaborate are the electoral rules theories of party systems, with theorizing based on the division of powers among various levels of government being an influential recent development.[3] The social cleavage theory postulates that the party system will reflect the principal cleavages in society, as for example between capital and labour in ethno-culturally homogeneous industrialized societies

that have parties positioned along a Left–Right spectrum. The political-systemic theory, particularly the electoral rules theory, postulates that the larger political system's and, more specifically, electoral system's rules, principally, the district magnitude (number of representatives elected from each electoral district or constituency), the structure of the ballot (choosing a party list, an individual candidate, or a mix of the two), and the decision rule or electoral formula (proportional representation, simple plurality, or first-past-the-post (FPTP), variants of each) create varying disproportionalities between votes and seats, and hence incentives for the coalescing or splitting of political forces, which will be reflected in the number, relative weight, and ideological positioning of political parties.[4] For example, a very proportional system consisting of large, multi-member constituencies conduces to a low effective threshold of representation, and hence to even small parties getting elected and playing a role in government formation in multi-party coalitions.[5] In such a system, small parties would not have much incentive to merge with larger parties at the cost of ideological compromise, whereas the opposite would hold true in a FPTP system. For explanations emphasizing the division of powers between levels of government, national, state/provincial, and local, the argument goes as follows. Other things being equal, the greater the political and economic powers of state/provincial governments in federal systems over decisions that most affect the lives of citizens, the greater a political prize the capture of power at the state/provincial level represents, and hence, the greater incentive there is for political entrepreneurs to form state-level political parties, and for voters to vote for such parties. Conversely, the more centralized the powers over decisions that most affect citizens, the more incentive there is for political entrepreneurs to coordinate to form nation-wide political parties, and for voters to vote for such parties and ignore state-level parties. Hence, a more multi-party system can be expected under the former circumstances and a less multi-party system under the latter circumstances.

I will discuss competing explanations of the evolution of the Indian party system in the later part of the chapter, some of which will fall into one or the other broad category of explanations outlined. However, before this it is logically necessary to lay out the historical background to the adoption of the FPTP system and the patterns of fragmentation in the unavoidable minimum detail.

PATTERN OF FRAGMENTATION OF PARTY SYSTEM: 1952–89

After Independence, India opted for the Anglo-Saxon type single-member constituency, simple plurality electoral system, or FPTP system.[6] The latter system was adopted in the Constituent Assembly and early parliamentary debates, not so much from a focused debate on the merits of alternative electoral systems as regards their effects on the representation of parties and social groups, but from a default assumption of this system being somehow natural, carried forward largely unconsciously from British and colonial practice since 1935. There was an awareness that this system would tend to under-represent territorially dispersed groups like the Scheduled Castes and Muslims, but that was sought to be remedied by the device of reservation for Scheduled Castes, guaranteeing representation, and promises to be fair to minorities rather than by electoral-systemic engineering. The two-member and three-member constituencies that existed in the first two elections and encompassed one-third of the seats in the first two Parliaments, were, in embryonic form, distributive vote systems, but were abolished in 1961. It was felt that a proportional representation (PR) system, where the allocation of seats to individual legislators is more difficult to understand, would not be workable in a largely illiterate country, and also that the country required stable, single-party majority governments, which would be the likely result of the FPTP system whereas PR systems would produce unstable, multi-party coalition governments.

Congress Hegemony, 1952–67

The first four general elections to the Lok Sabha, 1952, 1957, 1962, and 1967, coincided with elections to all the state assemblies. In the first three of these, the Congress party won an over two-thirds majority of seats in the Lok Sabha on the basis of only a plurality of votes of 44–8 per cent (Table 8.2). It also won a majority of the seats in nearly all state assembly elections from 1952–62, again on the basis of mostly a plurality of votes against a fragmented opposition.

The Bipolarization of State Party Systems, 1967–89

The 1967 election marks a break, with the Congress winning only 283 seats on the basis of its lowest ever vote share until then (40.8 per cent), and losing power in eight out of 16 states. The 1971 elections saw a restoration of a two-thirds Congress majority in the Lok Sabha with 43.7 per cent votes and 352 seats. However, from the vantage point of 2009, the post-1967 period represents a secular decline in Congress strength nationally, and in state after state. In the 'exceptional' post-Emergency elections of 1977, the Congress faced a temporarily united opposition consisting of the JP, formed just before the elections, and having a seat adjustment with Jagjivan Ram's Congress for Democracy, and the CPI(M), thus consisting of virtually the entire opposition except for the CPI and the DMK. The Congress was trounced, plunging to its lowest-till-then vote and seat figures of 34.5 per cent and 154 seats respectively. The JP won a majority (295 seats) on the basis of 41.3 per cent of the vote. This was a Congress-like victory in reverse, that is, a catch-all umbrella party winning a seat majority on the basis of a vote plurality, but not, however, against a fragmented opposition.

In 1980, another Congress restoration took place following the disintegration of the JP, again a near two-thirds majority of 353 seats (out of 542) on the basis of a plurality of 42.7 per cent. The 1984 elections, another 'exceptional' election following the assassination of Prime Minister Indira Gandhi, saw the highest-ever Congress vote share (48.1 per cent) and 415 seats, or a three-quarters majority. The 1989 elections marked another turning point, with the Congress crashing to 39.5 per cent and 197 seats against an opposition electoral alliance consisting of seat adjustments, of the National Front coalition (of the JD and regional and minor parties) supported by the BJP and the Left parties, which

Table 8.2: Party Seats, Seat Shares, and Vote Shares 1952–2009

	1952	1957	1962	1967	1971	1977	1980	1984	1989	1991	1996	1998	1999	2004	2009
Total Seats	489	494	494	520	518	542	529	542	529	521	543	543	543	543	543
Indian National Congress (INC), (INC) in 1980	364 (479)	371 (490)	361 (488)	283 (516)	352 (441)	154 (492)	353 (492)	415 (517)	197 (510)	232 (492)	140 (529)	141 (474)	114 (453)	145 (414)	206 (440)
	74.4%	75%	73%	54.4%	68%	28.4%	66.7%	76.6%	37.2%	45%	25.8%	26%	21%	26.7%	37.9%
	45.0%	47.8%	44.7%	40.8%	43.7%	34.5%	42.7%	48.1%	39.5%	36.5%	28.8%	25.9%	28.3%	26.4%	28.6%
BJP, BLD in 1977, BJS till 1971	3 (94)	4 (130)	14 (196)	35 (251)	22 (160)	295 (405)	–	2 (229)	86 (226)	120 (468)	161 (471)	179 (384)	182 (339)	138 (364)	116 (433)
	0.6%	0.8%	2.8%	6.7%	4.2%	54.4%		4%	16.5%	23%	29.6%	33%	34%	25.4%	21.4%
	3.1%	5.9%	6.4%	9.4%	7.4%	41.3%		7.4%	11.5%	20.1%	20.3%	25.5%	23.8%	22.2%	18.8%
JD(U) in 1999, JD 1989–98, SWA till 1971	–	–	18 (173)	44 (178)	8 (56)	–	–	–	142 (243)	59 (307)	46 (196)	6 (190)	21 (60)	8 (33)	20 (55)
			3.6%	8.5%	1.5%				27%	11.3%	8.5%	1.1%	3.8%	1.5%	3.7%
			7.9%	8.7%	3.1%				17.7%	11.8%	8.1%	3.2%	3.1%	1.9%	1.5%
CPI	16 (49)	27 (110)	29 (137)	23 (106)	23 (87)	7 (91)	11 (48)	6 (66)	12 (50)	14 (42)	12 (43)	9 (58)	4 (54)	9 (33)	4(56)
	3.3%	5.5%	5.9%	4.4%	4.4%	1.3%	1.8%	1.1%	2.3%	2.7%	2.2%	1.6%	0.7%	1.6%	0.7%
	3.3%	8.9%	9.9%	5.0%	4.7%	2.8%	2.6%	2.7%	2.6%	2.5%	2.0%	1.8%	1.5%	1.3%	01.4%
CPI(M)	–	–	–	19 (62)	25 (85)	22 (53)	36 (63)	22 (64)	33 (64)	35 (60)	32 (75)	32 (71)	33 (72)	43 (69)	16(82)
				3.7%	4.8%	4.1%	7%	4.1%	6.2%	6.7%	6%	5.9%	6.1%	7.9%	3.0%
				4.4%	5.1%	4.3%	6.1%	5.7%	6.5%	6.2%	6.1%	5.2%	5.4%	5.7%	5.3%
LKD, JPS in 1980, INCO till 1977	–	–	–	–	16 (238)	3 (19)	41 (294)	3 (174)	0 (117)	0(78)	–	–	–	–	
					3.1%	0.6%	7.7%	0.6%	27%	–					
					10.4%	1.7%	9.4%	5.6%	0.2%	0.1%					
SP in 1991, JP till 1989	–	–	–	–	–	–	31 (432)	10 (219)	0 (156)	5 (345)	17 (111)	20 (164)	26 (151)	36 (237)	23(193)
							5.9%	1.8%	–	1%	3.1%	3.7%	4.8%	6.6%	4.3%
							19.0%	6.7%	1.0%	3.4%	3.3%	5.0%	3.8%	4.3%	3.4%
BSP	–	–	–	–	–	–	–	–	–	–	11 (117)	5(249)	14 (225)	19 (435)	21(500)
											2%	0.9%	2.6%	3.5%	3.9%
											3.6%	4.7%	4.2%	5.3%	6.2%
PSP, KMPP in 1952	9 (145)	19 (189)	12 (168)	13 (109)	2 (63)	–	–	–	–	–	–	–	–	–	–
	1.8%	3.8%	2.4%	2.5%	0.4%										
	5.8%	10.4%	6.8%	3.1%	1.0%										
SSP, SOC till 1962	12 (254)	–	6 (107)	23 (122)	3 (93)										
	2.5%		1.2%	4.4%	0.6%										
	10.6%		2.7%	4.9%	2.4%										

(contd...)

(Table 8.2 contd...)

	1952	1957	1962	1967	1971	1977	1980	1984	1989	1991	1996	1998	1999	2004	2009
Others	47	31	34	45	53	52	35	79	44	55	115	141	143	140	128
	9.6%	6.3%	6.9%	8.6%	10.2%	9.6%	9.1%	14.6%	8.9%	11%	21.2%	26%	26.3%	25.8%	23.6%
	16.5%	7.6%	10.5%	10.0%	13.8%	9.9%	8.5%	10.0%	12.2%	12.1%	21.5%	26.3%	27.1%	28.6%	29.2%
Independents (IND)	38	42	20	35	14	9	9	5	12	1	9	6	6	5	9
	7.6%	8.5%	4%	6.7%	2.7%	1.7%	1.7%	0.9%	2.26%	0.2%	1.7%	1.1%	1.1%	0.9%	1.7%
	15.9%	19.4%	11.1%	13.7%	8.4%	5.5%	6.4%	8.1%	5.2%	3.9%	6.3%	2.4%	2.8%	4.3%	5.2%

Sources: Butler *et al.* (1995); Election Commission of India, Statistical Report on General Elections, vol. I (Ver. I)—National and State Abstracts, for 1996, 1998, 1999; for 2004 and 2009, Election Commission of India website: www.eci.gov.in

Notes: a. Elections were not held in 13 constituencies: 12 in Assam and 1 in Meghalaya.

b. Elections were not held in Assam (14 seats).

c. Elections were not held in Jammu and Kashmir (6 seats) and Punjab (13 seats); 3 countermanded seats results excluded.

d. Figures in parenthesis are seats contested, upper percentage is seat share, lower percentage is vote share.

resulted in a large number of one-on-one contests with the Congress.

The post-1967 period also saw a very important de-linking of parliamentary and state assembly elections after 1971, and a suspension of organizational elections within the Congress from 1972 to 1992, hand-in-hand with the centralization of power at the top of the party apparatus. It also saw the emergence of anti-Congress alliances, then of a principal opposition party to the Congress in state after state, in most states representing a consolidation of the non-Congress space at the state level. The Index of Opposition Unity (IOU) showed an upward trend in state after state over 1967–89.[7] This is particularly so if one considers opposition coalitions—and first party plus its pre-electoral allies—as a single party for the purposes of the IOU. In other words, a consolidation of the non-Congress opposition, state by state, broadly in tandem with such consolidation in state assembly elections, took place over the period, and even led to the displacement of the Congress as one of the two leading parties or coalitions. *This bipolar consolidation was the key feature and driving force of the fragmentation of the national party system.*

The following pattern of bipolarization is discernible state-wise over 1967–89 for Lok Sabha and assembly elections. In Madhya Pradesh (MP), Rajasthan, Himachal Pradesh (HP), and the Union Territory of Delhi, the movement towards a two-party system began as early as 1967 with the consolidation of the non-Congress vote behind the BJS, the ancestor of the BJP. This system has remained stable to date.

In three other states, Kerala, West Bengal, and Tripura, a bipolar, Congress versus Left, two-alliance system emerged. Here the Congress (West Bengal) or a Congress-led alliance of state-based minor parties (Kerala, Tripura) contested against a Left Front coalition of the CPI (M), CPI (since the late 1970s in Kerala), and smaller Left parties, the two coalitions alternating in power.

In five other states, Punjab, Jammu and Kashmir (J&K), Andhra Pradesh, Assam, and Goa, a Congress–regional party two-party system came into

being over 1967–89, changing in the 1990s with the rise of the BJP in all of these states, often in alliance with the regional party.

In one major state, Tamil Nadu, the process began in 1967, and led to the elimination of the Congress from the top two positions. It became an essentially bipolar contest between the two leading parties, the DMK and the AIADMK, with one of the two being allied to the Congress for parliamentary and state assembly elections. In this arrangement, which was stable from 1977 to 1996, the Congress was given the lion's share of seats in parliamentary elections in exchange for the regional ally receiving the lion's share of state assembly seats. Since 1996, the regional parties have been contesting the majority of Lok Sabha seats too, giving a few to their Congress or BJP allies.

In the Northeastern Rim states of Mizoram, Meghalaya, Nagaland, and Manipur, and in Sikkim, an unstable two-party or two-alliance contest prevailed between the Congress and a variety of regional parties.

Finally, the Congress retained preponderance until 1989 in seven major states, Uttar Pradesh (UP), Bihar, Haryana, Gujarat, Maharashtra, Karnataka, and Orissa, where no alternative party or alliance consolidated itself as a successful challenger for parliamentary elections, although a broad-front anti-Congress alliance, if put together, could have challenged the Congress, as happened in 1967 and 1977.

However, just after the 1989 elections and the state assembly elections in early 1990, the Congress remained the leading party in more states (12) in terms of Lok Sabha seats and in terms of vote share (17) than any other, and remained one of the two leading parties in more states (20) in terms of Lok Sabha seats (20) and vote share (24) than any other. In the state assemblies, it remained the leading party in more states (9) and in terms of vote share (11) than any other, and one of the two leading parties in terms of vote share in more states (24, or all, except Tamil Nadu) than any other. However, many of these were very small states, the Congress having lost UP, Bihar, Orissa, and Haryana to the JD, MP, and HP to the BJP, and Rajasthan and Gujarat to a JD–BJP coalition in both Lok Sabha and state assembly elections (except Haryana, which did not have assembly elections in 1989–90).

PATTERN OF FRAGMENTATION OF PARTY SYSTEM: 1989–2009

The 1989 election results were not just another repeat of a broad-front anti-Congressism of the JP kind, but signified a more far-reaching and seismic shift in the party system, rooted in the shifts in party organizational strength and support bases at the state level in an increasing number of states, and in India's political economy and changing patterns of social mobilization. The shifts in major party vote shares and seats over 1989 to 2009 in the Lok Sabha are shown in Table 8.2. The major trends of 1989–2004 are the relative decline of the Congress, and the rise of the BJP and regional or single state-based parties.[8] While the Congress retained a vote plurality in all seven elections over 1989–2009, it failed to convert that into a seat plurality in 1996, 1998, and 1999.

Prior to 1989, the BJP and its predecessor the BJS, the political arm of the RSS, had never exceeded 10 per cent of the vote or 35 seats nationally, except in 1977 when, as a component of the JP, it won 99 of the 295 seats won by the JP (more than the 86 seats it won in 1989). Its rise since then has been steady in terms of both vote and seat shares. It experienced a meteoric rise in seats from a derisory two in 1984 (despite 7.4 per cent votes) to 86 (out of 226 contested, mostly in de facto alliance with the JD) in 1989 owing to the combination of three effects—seat adjustments with the JD, resulting in one-to-one contests against the Congress in most of the seats it contested in UP, Delhi, Rajasthan, Gujarat, HP, and MP, an increase in contested seats and a sizeable and regionally concentrated swing in its favour.

In 1989–91, the BJP contested alone with a communally polarizing platform against the backdrop of the Babri Masjid agitation of the late 1980s, the upper-caste backlash against the National Front government's decision to implement the Mandal Commission recommendations for reservation of government jobs for backward classes defined in caste terms, and the Rath Yatra launched by L.K. Advani to 'liberate' the claimed 'Ram Janmabhoomi' inside the Babri Masjid and the communal violence that followed in its wake. Its vote share zoomed to 20.1 per cent, and it won 120 seats (of an unprecedented 468 contested), becoming the second largest party in terms of seats and votes. It swept UP and Gujarat, and turned in strong performances in its traditional strongholds of MP, HP, and Rajasthan, winning over 40 per cent votes in each. More significantly, and portending developments to come, it significantly increased its vote share in several states of the peninsula and the east.

The BJP came to form state governments on its own for the first time ever in 1990. It formed the government on its own in MP and HP, and formed coalition governments with the JD in Rajasthan and Gujarat. The only time that it had dominated state governments earlier was when it was part of the JP in 1977–9, during which period the Jana Sangh component of the JP had dominated the government and occupied the Chief Minister's post in MP, HP, and Rajasthan. Thus, the BJP had arrived as a *state-level* political force, whereas earlier it had essentially been a sub-state force, thereby contributing to national party system fragmentation.

In 1991, with the external support of the eleven-member AIADMK and some smaller allies, the Congress was able to form a minority government dependent on abstention in confidence votes by a section of the opposition. It began adding to its numbers by splitting small parties such as the TDP and Ajit Singh's faction of the Lok Dal in fractions of one-third or more (legal under the Anti-Defection law), and attained a majority on its own exactly half-way through its term (end 1993).

In 1996, its vote share declined still further to a then-historic low of 28.7 per cent, having been hit badly by the breaking away of the bulk of its Tamil Nadu unit—which formed the TMC and won 20 seats—and marginally by the breaking away of factions called the Congress (Tiwari) and the Madhya Pradesh Vikas Congress. For the first time, the

Congress was overtaken as the single largest party by the BJP, winning only 141 seats compared to the BJP's 161, although it remained the single largest party by vote share with 28.8 per cent compared to the BJP's 20.3 per cent.

In 1996, the BJP experienced the limits of contesting alone with a communally polarizing agenda. Despite being catapulted to its higher-ever seat tally of 161 seats due to its more regionally concentrated vote, making it the largest party in the Lok Sabha and capable of forming the government for twelve days, its vote share remained stagnant at 20.3 per cent, and it failed to win parliamentary support from enough other parties to form a minority or coalition government. Six states—UP, MP, Gujarat, Rajasthan, Bihar, and Maharashtra—accounted for 143 of its 161 seats, with UP and MP alone accounting for almost half.

These results can be seen as a delayed reflection of the realignment of political forces represented by the results of the elections to the assemblies of 15 states between November 1993 and March 1995, which by and large represented major gains for the BJP, some regional parties like the TDP and Shiv Sena, and state-based parties such as the SP, the SMT, and the BSP, while at best a holding operation for the Congress in some stronghold states such as HP and MP (Yadav 1996).

A United Front (UF) government consisting of 11 parties participating in government, including two parties represented only by Rajya Sabha members and three parties as formally part of the UF coalition but not participating in government, and supported from outside by the Congress, was formed in June 1996. The Congress withdrew support to Prime Minister Deve Gowda in April 1997, but continued to support the UF government after his replacement as Prime Minister by I.K. Gujral, eventually withdrawing support to the UF in November 1997, precipitating fresh elections in February–March 1998.

In 1998, the BJP shelved its overt Hindutva agenda to strike explicit or tacit alliances with a range of state-based parties, both regional and others, many of which had earlier been with the UF, a strategy that it consolidated after its victory.[9] The BJP strategy was certainly helped by the fact that the Congress had toppled the UF government, and

was the principal opponent of the constituents of the UF in several major states. Thus, in 1998, the BJP contested the elections with as many as 16 pre-election allies, including three independents, with significant seat-sharing arrangements spread over eight states. The BJP won 25.6 per cent votes and its pre- and post-election allies 15.5 per cent, totalling 37.3 per cent for pre-elections allies and 41.07 per cent, including post-election allies, and won a total of 282 seats (excluding two nominated Anglo-Indian seats). The BJP got 182 seats and its pre-election allies 72 seats with post-election allies getting another 28, bringing the allied total to 100 seats. This catapulted the BJP to power as it emerged once again as the single largest party (the Congress got only 141 seats) and led the single largest pre-election alliance.[10] A BJP-led 12-member minority coalition government consisting of 11 pre-election (including two independents and one from a one-Rajya Sabha MP party) and one post-election ally, and dependent on the support or abstention in confidence votes of eight post-election allies (including TDP, National Conference, and HLD[R]) and pre-election allies who opted out of the ministry, assumed power in March 1998 (Table 8.3).

State-wise, the BJP fared better in 1998 compared to 1996, crucially due to the support of its allies. Geographically and socially, the BJP spread its influence and consolidated itself in new areas and new social groups in the 1990s, in the south and the east, among lower castes and classes (Heath 1999). Viewed over 1989–99, this expansion has been at the expense primarily of the JD, and secondarily of the Congress, principally in UP and Bihar.

In 1999, essentially the same BJP-led pre-election coalition fought the Congress-led coalition, the latter being a more tentative coalition with state-by-state agreements but no common national platform. The UF disintegrated, being reduced to the Left Front and the rump JD(S) of Deve Gowda. The twenty-one-party BJP-led alliance was formally christened the NDA; this figure counts the SMT, Ramakrishna Hegde's Lok Shakti, and the Sharad Yadav faction of the JD as one party, the JD(U), into which they merged. The Congress alliance was much smaller, the main difference being that the BJP was now allied

Table 8.3: BJP-led Coalition in 1998

S.NO.	PARTY	SEATS WON	VOTE (IN PER CENT)
1	BJP	182	25.59
2	AITC	7	2.42
3	SHS	6	1.77
4	JNP	1	0.12
5	HVP	1	0.24
6	SAD(B)	8	0.81
7	AIADMK	18	1.83
8	PMK	4	0.42
9	MDMK	3	0.44
10	LKS	3	0.69
11	BJD	9	1.0
12	TRC	0	NA
13	SMT	12	1.77
14	Independent (Maneka Gandhi)	1	0.10
15	Independent (Satnam S. Kainth)	1	0.09
16	Independent (Buta Singh)	1	0.09
Post-election Allies			
17	TDP	12	2.77
18	JKNC	3	0.21
19	HLD(R)	4	0.53
20	AC	2	0.05
21	MSCP	1	0.05
22	SDF	1	0.03
23	Anglo Indians#	2	NA
24	BSMC	1	0.05
25	Citizen Common Front	1	0.02
26	RJP(Anand Mohan)%	1	0.07
	Total	284	41.07

Source: http://www.eci.gov.in/SR_KeyHighLights/LS_1998/Vol_I_LS_98.pdf accessed on 3 May 2008; Arora, 'Negotiating Differences: Federal Coalitions and National Cohesion', Table 5, p. 190.
Notes: #nominated members
%Anand Mohan defected from RJP to support the NDA

Table 8.4: NDA Coalition in the 1999 Election

S.NO.	PARTY	SEATS WON	VOTE (IN PER CENT)
1	BJP	182	23.75
2	TDP	29	3.65
3	JD(U)@	21	3.10
4	BJD	10	1.20
5	DMK	12	1.73
6	SHS	15	1.77
7	AITC	8	2.42
8	INLD	5	0.55
9	SAD-B	2	0.69
10	MDMK	1	0.44
11	PMK	5	0.65
12	HVC	1	0.07
13	MADMK	1	0.11
14	ABLTC	2	0.22
15	MSCP	1	0.06
16	SDF	1	0.03
17	Independent (Maneka Gandhi)	1	0.54
18	Janatantrik BSP	0	NA
19	AC	0	0.02
20	Democratic Bahujan Samaj Morcha	0	0.07
21	TRC Post Election Allies	0	0.09
22	JKNC	4	0.12
23	RLD	2	0.37
	Total	303	41.65

Source: http://www.eci.gov.in/StatisticalReports/LS_1999/Vol_I_LS_99.pdf, accessed on 2 May 2008.
Note: @Samata Party, Lok Shakti, and JD (Sharad Yadav group) agreed to formally merge to form the JD(U).

to the DMK in Tamil Nadu, while the Congress was allied to the AIADMK.

The NDA won a more decisive victory, getting 299 seats with the BJP alone getting 182 as in 1998. With post-election adherents like the National Conference and Ajit Singh's RLD, the number went up to 303 seats (see Table 8.4). The Congress got a lowest-ever 111 seats, and only 134 with allies. However, in terms of vote share, the BJP alone declined to 23.8 per cent, while the Congress rose to 28.4 per cent, remaining the single largest party. The NDA formed the government with the twenty-nine member TDP and five other smaller pre-election allies opting to support it from outside.

In 2004, the incumbent BJP-led NDA coalition contested against the newly formed Congress-led coalition, called the UPA after the election, and lost (see Table 8.5 for detailed results, alliance-wise, and Table 8.6 for shifts in alliances). The major change was that the Congress party became 'coalitionable' in a significant way for the first time, following a conscious decision to adopt a coalition strategy. The NDA consisted of 13 parties, having lost the DMK, MDMK, and PMK in Tamil Nadu, the INLD in Haryana, and Ram Vilas Paswan's newly formed LJNP in Bihar, and having added the AIADMK in Tamil Nadu, the SDF in Sikkim, the MNF in Mizoram, IFDP, and the NPF. It won 189 seats and 35.88 per cent votes, with its lead party, the BJP, winning 138 seats (down by 44) and 22.2 per cent votes (down by 1.6 per cent). The Congress-led alliance consisted of 19 parties. This meant the addition of eight new allies—including the DMK-led alliance in Tamil Nadu—since the 1999 elections, and the dropping of two old allies, the AIADMK and Ajit Singh's RLD. The Congress-led alliance won 222 seats and 36.53 per cent votes (only a whisker ahead of the NDA in vote share, but 33 seats ahead). With the external support of the Left parties (61 seats) it gained a majority in the Lok Sabha and formed a government. The UPA also enjoyed the unilateral external support

Table 8.5: Coalitions in the 2004 Election

PARTY	SEATS CONTESTED	SEATS WON	CHANGE FROM 1999	VOTE (IN PER CENT)	CHANGE FROM 1999
Congress allies	535	222	69	36.53	−0.39
Congress	414	145	31	26.44	−1.85
TRS	6	5	5	0.60	0.60
IND (Congress)	6	1	1	0.16	0.16
RJD	28	24	17	2.39	−0.38
LJNP	11	4	4	0.66	0.66
NCP	22	9	2	1.78	−0.36
JMM	7	4	4	0.41	0.20
PDP	3	1	1	0.07	0.07
MUL	2	1	−1	0.19	−0.03

(contd...)

(Table 8.5 contd...)

PARTY	SEATS CONTESTED	SEATS WON	CHANGE FROM 1999	VOTE (IN PER CENT)	CHANGE FROM 1999
KCM	1	0	0	0.05	−0.04
JDS	1	0	−1	0.05	−0.03
RPI	2	0	0	0.04	−0.09
RPI(A)	1	1	0	0.09	−0.04
PRBP	1	0	0	0.06	0.06
DMK	16	16	4	1.81	0.08
MDMK	4	4	0	0.43	−0.01
PMK	6	6	1	0.56	−0.10
PDS	2	0	0	0.02	0.02
AC	1	0	0	0.62	0.60
NDA	543	189	−89	35.88	−2.39
BJP	364	138	−44	22.16	−1.59
TDP	33	5	−24	3.04	−0.61
JD(U)	33	8	−13	1.94	−0.99
IND(BJP)	1	1	1	0.18	0.18
IFDP	1	1	1	0.07	0.07
SHS	22	12	−3	1.77	0.24
BJD	12	11	1	1.30	0.10
SAD	10	8	6	0.90	0.21
AIADMK	33	0	−10	2.19	0.27
AITC	31	2	−6	2.06	−0.51
MNF	1	1	1	0.05	0.05
SDF	1	1	0	0.04	0.01
NPF	1	1	1	0.18	0.18
Left	112	61	18	8.01	0.13
CPI	33	9	5	1.32	−0.16
CPI(M)	69	43	10	5.66	0.26
JDS(Left)	1	1	1	0.09	0.09
KEC	1	1	0	0.09	−0.01
IND(Left)	1	1	1	0.08	−0.07
RSP	4	3	0	0.43	0.01
FBL	3	3	1	0.35	0.01
BSP	435	19	5	5.33	1.16
SP +	247	39	11	4.93	0.79
SP	237	36	10	4.31	0.55
RLD	10	3	1	0.61	0.24
Others	3,563	13	−14	9.32	0.69

Table 8.6: Net Effect of Changes in Alliances in 2004

	CONGRESS ALLIANCE (UPA)		NATIONAL DEMOCRATIC ALLIANCE	
	SEATS	VOTE (%)	SEATS	VOTE (%)
New allies added in 2004	49	6.32	4	2.53
Alliances of 1999 dropped	3	2.80	31	3.96
Net Gain/Loss (+/−)	+ 46	3.52	−27	−1.43

Source: CSDS Data Tables.
Notes: New allies of the Congress are: NCP, TRS, DMK, MDMK, PMK, LJNP, PDP, and JMM.
   Old Congress allies now dropped include: RLD and AIADMK.
   New Allies of the NDA are: AIADMK, SDF, MNF, IFDP, and NPF. Old NDA allies now dropped include: DMK, MDMK, PMK, INLD, RLD, LCP, AC, NC, TRC, Democratic Bahujan Samaj Morcha, Janatantrik BSP, HVC, and LJNP.
   The LJNP was formed after the 1999 Lok Sabha Elections, and in 1999 it was a part of the JD(U).
   Arunachal Congress merged with the INC. Bahujan Samaj Morcha merged with the BSP in 2004 before the general elections.
   TRC merged with the Congress in 2002.
   HVC merged with the Congress in 2004 before the general elections.

of two other significant parties (with whose support it could potentially retain a majority even if the Left withdrew), that is, the SP (36 seats) and the BSP (19 seats).

The major difference between 2004 and earlier elections was the success of the Congress' coalitionability, which was critical to its universally unexpected victory.[11] The state-wise pattern was as follows. Coalitions (or merger, with the HVC in HP) were critical to the Congress victory in Tamil Nadu, AP, Bihar, Jharkhand, J&K, and HP. They were critical for the reduction in the Congress margin of defeat/improvement of position compared to 1999 in Maharashtra and Goa. The lack of a coalition (due to the BJP's decision to contest alone) was critical for the margin of Congress victory and BJP defeat in Assam, Haryana, and Jharkhand (where an NDA coalition of not only the BJP and JD (U), but also the JMM, was a possibility).

In 2009, the UPA coalition defeated the depleted NDA by a much greater margin with the Congress winning 206 seats on its own and 263 with its

pe-electoral allies, of which, compared to 2004, it had lost the Left as a partial seat adjustment partner in Jharkhand, Andhra Pradesh, and Tamil Nadu, as well as the JD, LJP, TRS, PMK, MDMK, and PDP, but added the AITC and the NC (Table 8.7). The NDA suffered major-ally depletion with the loss of the TDP, BJD and the split in the Shiv Sena but added the AGP, RS, and RLD. The Congress-led UPA formed a six-party government of the Congress, AITC, DMI, NCP, NC, and Muslim League but excluded some pre-electoral (JMM, Bodoland People's Front, KCM) and all post-electoral supportes who consisted of 9 parties and 3 independents totalling 59 MPs. This coalition resembled the NDA in that the legislative coalition including post-electoral allies constituted a considerable surplus majority and hence provided insurance against

Table 8.7: Coalitions in the 2009 Election

PARTY	SEATS CONTESTED	SEATS WON	VOTE SHARE (IN PER CENT)
UPA		263	36.87
Congress	440	206	28.56
AITC	5	19	.2
DMK	22	18	1.83
NCP	68	9	2.04
National Conference	3	3	0.12
JMM	42	2	0.4
Muslim League	16	2	0.21
AIMIM	1	1	0.07
Bodoland People's Front	2	1	0.16
Kerala Congress (Mani)	1	1	0.1
VCK	3	1	0.18
NDA		159	24.33
BJP	433	116	18.81
JD(U)	55	20	1.52
Shiv Sena	47	11	1.55
RLD	9	5	0.44
Shiromani Akali Dal	10	4	0.96
TRS	9	2	0.62
AGP	6	1	0.43
Third Front		80	20.92

(contd...)

(Table 8.7 contd...)

PARTY	SEATS CONTESTED	SEATS WON	VOTE SHARE (IN PER CENT)
(Left Front subtotal)		–24	–7.46
BSP	500	21	6.17
BJD	18	14	1.59
AIADMK	23	9	1.67
MDMK	4	1	0.27
JD(S)	33	3	0.82
TDP	31	6	2.51
HJC	10	1	0.2
JVM(P)	16	1	0.23
CPI(M)	82	16	5.33
CPI	56	4	1.43
AIFB	21	2	0.32
RSP	16	2	0.38
Fourth Front		27	4.7
SP	193	23	3.43
RJD	44	4	1.27
Others with seats		14	6.09
AUDF	25	1	0.52
NPF	1	1	0.2
SDF	1	1	0.04
BVA	1	1	0.05
Swabhimani Paksha	1	1	0.12
Independents	3,829	9	5.16
Others without seats		0	7.09

Source: CSDS Data Tables.
Note: The cells for Seats Contested for the alliances are left blank because none of the alliances were perfect sharing of seats; the UPA was explicitly limited to state-level alliances only, with state-level partners contesting against the Congress in other states.

defection by any ally, rendering no ally pivotal, and also from the fact that the BJP numbers, down to 116, made it like the Congress during the NDA, in being too small to form a viable alternative coalition given that several parties like the Left, SP, RJD, TDP and BSP would not be prepared to ally with it due to differences on secularism and their need for religious minority votes.

Most states remained or became bipolar in the 1989–2006 period, except notably UP. However, in a number of apparently bipolar or two-party states, *if we look at vote shares we find the presence of a significant, often growing, third party* that has a vote share in double digits, but is not yet large enough to win a significant number of seats. *It is obviously cutting into the potential vote share of one or both the two main parties or alliances in a way that makes it a threat to either or both of the two main parties as well as makes it attractive as a potential ally of either one of them in order to defeat the other.* This is the case in states like Assam, Orissa, Goa, West Bengal, Manipur, and Arunachal Pradesh.

This rising third party was the BJP in all of these states, and the BSP in Punjab, UP, and, in a small way, MP. By emerging as a significant third party in vote share at the state level and hence both threatening to cut into the votes and seat prospects of either or both the dominant parties, thereby *creating incentives for the weaker of the two leading parties, to ally with it, typically the regional party,* since both the BJP, nationally, and the regional party in the state face the Congress as their principal opponent. This was the pattern in Maharashtra, Punjab, Orissa, Goa, Bihar, and West Bengal (following the Congress split in which the AITC emerged as the major Congress faction), Haryana, Karnataka, and, since 1999, Andhra Pradesh. In some of these states, possibly Maharashtra and Orissa, the BJP can potentially go on to eat up the share of its regional alliance partner and transform the state into a Congress–BJP two-party state, as happened in Rajasthan and Gujarat over 1989–91.

Thus, a process of bipolar consolidation has been taking place in many states, but of *multiple bipolarities* (for example Congress–BJP, Congress–Left, Congress–regional party), contributing to fragmentation at the national level, and contributing directly or indirectly to the potential bipolar consolidation of a Congress-led alliance versus a BJP-led one, although both alliances are as yet unstable, marked by the exit and entry of smaller parties. Furthermore, both alliances are not perfect one-on-one seat adjustments but partial ones, in which the total seats contested by each alliance may exceed the total number of seats (Table 8.7). For example, in 2009, the Congress alliances with its partners were explicitly limited to the partner's main seat only, so that the latter were free to contest seats agains the Congress in other states and did so, contributing to a larger effective number of parties by votes in 2009 despite the effective number of parties by seats shrinking. What this reflects is the drive by several smaller parties like SP and the NCP to expand their base horizontally across states, which brings them into conflict with the Congress which needs to have as broadly multi-state a base as possible to be able to defend its status as the leading national party.

EVOLUTION OF ELECTORAL ALLIANCES AND COMPETING EXPLANATIONS FOR FRAGMENTATION (AND RECONSOLIDATION?) OF PARTY SYSTEM

There are broadly seven explanations for the fragmentation of the Congress-dominated national party system over the decades, none of which excludes the others. One of these can also potentially explain the process of reconsolidation of the party system into one with larger alliances and fewer poles. I shall outline the competing explanations in roughly chronological order of their relevance and applicability to understanding the decline of the Congress-dominated party system. I shall then outline the evolution of alliances, drawing on the patterns of fragmentation and possible reconsolidation in the earlier sections, and finally make an argument for the best explanation for the process that has been unfolding.

The first (set of) explanation(s) is that centred on the growing politicization of social cleavages along regional lines since the late 1960s, due to the increasing centralization of the Congress party and Congress governments, and the latter's insensitivity to regional concerns about language, cultural identity, political autonomy, and economic development. This is understood to have led to the rise and/or further consolidation of regional parties such as the DMK and its offshoots, Akali Dal, NC, AGP, and small parties in the Northeastern Rim states.[12]

The second explanation highlights the electoral-systemic feature of delinking between parliamentary and state assembly elections since 1971. This probably facilitated the pre-electoral alliances and post-electoral coalitions of non-Congress forces for national elections such as in 1977 and 1989, and of non-BJP forces in 1996, since doing so became easier without compromising their fundamental interests at the state level where their basic social constituencies and power bases lay. Delinking also meant smaller agendas and less crowded bargaining tables, and hence less insurmountable collective action problems, or, to put it simply, one-at-a-time battles with the Congress.[13]

The third explanation emphasizes the growth in political consciousness and assertion of newly prosperous or newly mobilized sections of the electorate, primarily intermediate and backward-caste peasants in the Green Revolution areas of north India, which acted both as a farmers' and intermediate castes' lobby from the late 1960s to the early 1990s.[14] These castes had not been part of the core base of the Congress in the northern belt, and had not been granted a position of commensurate influence in the party power structure. Fragmentation, whereby these castes or interest groups tended to vote or form new parties of the erstwhile socialist PSP/SSP/agrarian Lok Dal/JD kind, was rooted in the inability or unwillingness of the groups that controlled the Congress to accommodate them.

The fourth explanation, dovetailing with the first and the third, and complementary to them, is that of the growing centralization of, and suspension of, democracy within the Congress party since 1972, leading to the exit of both traditional voters and politicians whose voices were not being heard, particularly certain regional groups and intermediate and backward-caste farmers in the northern belt, to new or other parties. This is in line with the logic of 'disillusioned' voting, whereby voters of a party from whom they fail to get their desired policy dividends or have their voices heard turn away to rival or new parties. This explanation stresses the importance of the organization and functioning of parties as machines to retain and expand their voter base.[15]

The fifth explanation is that of the influence on incentives of a systemic feature of the polity, the division of powers in the Constitution between the Centre and the states. With the powers that are more relevant to the daily lives of people in a largely rural society, such as agriculture and land use, irrigation and water supply, electricity, police, education, health, and other social expenditures being vested in the states, there are incentives to organize to capture power at the state level.[16]

The sixth explanation is the growing politicization of communal and caste cleavages in the 1990s, leading to the collapse of a catchall party like the Congress in states like UP and Bihar where such politicization led to a collapse of the middle ground, and the gravitation of huge chunks of the electorate—SCs, Muslims, OBCs, and upper castes—to communal and caste-based parties such as the BJP, BSP, SP, and (in Bihar) RJD.[17]

The seventh explanation, which I consider the most comprehensive and powerful, is one that attaches greatest significance not to social cleavages or the dominant Congress party's structure and functioning, but to the systemic properties of the FPTP electoral system working themselves out in a federal polity.[18] This is reinforced by the second (the delinking of national and state elections since 1971) and fifth explanations (the division of powers making state-level power politically attractive). This explanation is based on the proposition known as Duverger's Law, namely, that the FPTP system (single-member district, simple plurality system) inclines towards a two-party system because of the tendency over time for third and more parties to get eliminated due to the combination of two effects—a 'mechanical effect' of over-representation or under-representation of parties, depending on whether they get more or less than a certain (varying) threshold of votes; and a 'psychological effect', whereby voters tend to not 'waste' their votes on parties which have no realistic chance, but vote 'sophisticatedly' (or strategically/tactically) for the party that they feel has the best chance of defeating their least-liked party. These two effects taken in combination will tend to aggregate votes around the leading party and its principal rival. Duverger's Law argues that the FPTP system produces an imperative of consolidation of voters (and politicians) around a principal rival party so it could have a realistic chance of winning against a dominant party, thus leading to the elimination of third parties, or at least an alliance of other parties, against a leading party.

Duverger's Law applies essentially at the constituency level.[19] It need not translate to the national level and produce a national two-party system where strong local/state parties exist as in a federal polity, particularly one like India's, where the states are linguistic and cultural entities reflecting such social cleavages. In such a system, where parties compete to form the government at both national and state levels, Duverger's Law can apply at the state level, leading to two-party or bipolar systems due to the consolidation of the state-level opposition to the principal party at the state level, whether a national or regional party, in a principal rival, while at the same time leading to a multi-party system nationally because the state-level two-party systems do not consist of the same two parties.[20] Indeed, they can consist of a variety of parties, some national, some purely state-level. The consolidation of two-party or two-alliance systems at the state level, which I have described in the foregoing sections, is the playing out of Duverger's Law in practice.

The first, third, and sixth explanations are all variants of the social cleavage theory of party systems, which postulates that parties will be formed around social cleavages and the party system will reflect this in its axes of polarization.

The second, fifth, and seventh relate to the behavioural incentives set up by the systemic features of the political system, the second and the seventh relating to the electoral system specifically, and the seventh specifying a mechanism whereby the behaviour of politicians, voters, and parties determines the change in the party system over time. The fifth explanation emphasizes the importance of the federal division of powers as an incentive structure for the formation of state parties, and for voters to vote for such parties.

The fourth explanation focuses on political parties as machines, and is intermediate between social cleavage theories and political-systemic theories.

Let us take an overview of the evolution of electoral and government coalitions and then return to the competing explanations. The evolution of alliances in the Indian party system can be summarized as follows. The first phase of broad-front anti-Congressism in the 1960s and early 1970s was characterized by *intra-state alliances* of the Samyukta Vidhayak Dal (SVD) type or the JP, where, within each state, the component parties of the alliance or the Janata Party, for example the Jana Sangh, BKD/BLD, Socialists, Swatantra, and Congress (O) had their state units, strongholds, and interests without any ideological glue. The second phase, again of broad-front anti-Congressism, was that of the JP, which unified ideologically disparate non-Congress parties in order to enable one-on-one contests aggregating votes at the constituency level so as to win, reflects the imperative of aggregation to win regardless of ideology. This also consisted of intra-state alliances of disparate parties within the overall umbrella of unification of those parties at the national level. Intra-state alliances cannot be stable unless there is both an ideological and programmatic compatibility and an intra-state territorial compatibility, in that some of the parties have pockets of strength within the state which are not contested by their allies in the state; this applies to both the classic case of Kerala (for both the Left and the Congress) and in West Bengal. This territorial alliance was also fundamentally different from that of the Congress and the AIADMK from 1977 to 1996, in that it was not based on a trade-off of state assembly seats for Lok Sabha seats between the national and regional parties.

The National Front coalition was a new departure in three senses. First, learning from the Janata experience, it did not try to unify very different parties, but put together a coalition of distinct parties based on a common manifesto. Second, it brought in the explicitly regional parties like the DMK, TDP, and AGP, and the Left parties, unlike the SVD or Janata phase experiments. Third, it also marked the beginning of *inter-state alliances* of parties or *territorially compatible alliances*, where parties do not compete on each other's turf. However, the territorially compatible loose alliance put together by the National Front–BJP–Left in 1989–90 foundered on the rock of ideological incompatibility. This indicated once again the unsustainability of a broad anti-Congress coalition, unless its ideological

extremes moderated or set aside their positions (as the Jana Sangh did in post-1967 SVD coalitions and in the post-1977 Janata phase). Another clear case of a *territorial alliance* was the post-election coalition of the UF from 1996–8; however, it had a certain secular ideological mooring, ranged as it was against a hardline, perceivedly 'anti-system' BJP.

The period since 1991 has also seen the growth and sustenance of *intra-state alliances based on ideology* (like the BJP–Shiv Sena) and based on the territorial compatibility of two kinds, different from both the Left Front kind and the Congress–AIADMK trade-off kind of 1977–96. This consists of intra-state alliances, which are the reverse of the historical Congress–AIADMK kind in which there is no trade-off of Lok Sabha for state assembly seats between the regional and the national party. On the contrary, the regional party allies with the state unit of the national party, with the former getting the lion's share of both Lok Sabha and assembly seats. Examples are the BJP–AIADMK–smaller parties in 1998 and 2004, the BJP–DMK–smaller parties in 1999, Congress–DMK in 2004 and 2009, the BJP–TDP in 1999 and 2004, the BJP–AITC in 1999 and 2004, Congress–AITC in 2009, BJP–BJD in Orissa in 1998, 1999, and 2004, BJP–HVP in 1996 and 1998 and the BJP–INLD (Chautala) in 1999, RJD–Congress in 2004, and JD(U)–BJP in 2004 and 2009.

There is also the reverse of this pattern, viz., an alliance between a minor state party and a national party, in which the latter gets the lion's share of both Lok Sabha and assembly seats, the key being territorial compatibility, in which the national party does not contest in the smaller regional party's intra-state strongholds. Examples are the BJP–LKS in Karnataka in 1998 and 1999, the BJP–Samata in Bihar over 1996–9, the BJP–HVC in HP, and the Congress–JMM–smaller parties in 2004 and over a quarter-century of the Congress-led United Democratic Front in Kerala and the Congress-led alliances in Assam since 2001. It is anybody's guess how long these non-ideological alliances will last. In some of these cases, the base of the smaller party or even the regional party which is a senior partner may be eaten up by a larger, better-organized party like the BJP, as in fact happened to the Janata Dal in Rajasthan and Gujarat from 1989 to 1991.

The clear emphasis of alliances since the 1990s has been on territorial compatibility at the expense of ideological compatibility, particularly the BJP's alliances of 1998, 1999, 2004, and 2009, and the Congress alliances of 2004 and 2009, and even the UF coalitions of 1996 and 1998. This is an improvement on the SVD and JP alliances, which were neither programmatic nor territorially compatible. However, *the most important point to be noted is that in the whole history of alliances since the 1960s, with the exception of the Left Front, limited to three states, alliances have been driven by the imperative to aggregate votes to win and not by ideology, programme, or social cleavages*, except for overarching differences between the Congress and the BJP on secularism.[21]

With this observation I return to the competing explanations for fragmentation of the party system. It is clear that the explanations deriving from the social cleavage theory of party systems, that is, the first, third, and sixth explanations, can explain fragmentation of certain kinds. The first can explain the shift away from the Congress to regional parties in certain states like Tamil Nadu, Andhra Pradesh, Assam, Punjab, J&K, and the Northeastern Rim states, including the formation of such parties as in the case of Assam. These were not simply cases where regional parties were formed due to economic incentives deriving from state-level powers. The third can explain the shift of votes away from or consolidation behind the agrarian parties of the Janata family—the BKD, Socialists, BLD, Lok Dals, JD, and so forth, again including the formation of new parties. The sixth can account for the rise of communal and caste-based parties like the BJP, Shiv Sena, BSP, and SP, including the formation of new parties. The fourth can explain the exit of former Congress voters to rival or new parties. The fifth explanation reinforces all of these in that it explains the incentives for single state-based party formation. The second explanation further reinforces these by explaining how delinked state assembly elections facilitate collective action for alliances.

However, while these explanations can account for various types of fragmentation, they cannot

explain the periodic counter-tendencies towards alliances that tend to reconsolidate the party system. It is here that I find the seventh explanation, based on Duverger's analysis of the systemic properties and imperatives of the FPTP electoral system, useful. This explanation can account for both fragmentation at the national level and tendencies towards alliances. The key point here is to remember from the account of the first two sections that *fragmentation of the party system at the national level is a product of its opposite at the state level*, that is, the concentration of vote share between two parties or alliances, but *different* pairs of parties or alliances in most states, leading to a multitude of parties at the national level, each with a limited base in one or a few states. This latter phenomenon is explained by the systemic tendencies of the FPTP system captured by Duverger's Law, which have been working themselves out at the state level since 1967. The seventh explanation also fits well with the tendencies towards broad alliances driven, as we have seen, by the imperative to consolidate votes at the constituency and state levels, rather than by ideology, programme, or social cleavages, and to consolidate seats at the parliamentary level to form governments.

I conclude that the Indian party system is evolving over successive elections, and that the various trends and counter-trends will play themselves out over the coming years and decades. The basic driving force is the FPTP system's bipolarizing tendency, tempered by the large number of politically salient cleavages resulting from social heterogeneity. Since no switch to a proportional representation system or mixed member system is on the cards, the basic tendencies can be expected to continue. It is too early to say whether the FPTP system's inexorable imperative to aggregate votes regardless of ideology will push the national party system towards loose bipolarity at the national level between two broad alliances, each territorially compatible internally, one broadly left of centre and the other broadly right of centre, or whether India's multiple social cleavages intertwined with geographical diversity and incentives for regional parties to compete not only at the state level, but also to increase their parliamentary presence, will prevail to create so diversified an ideological space that bipolar consolidation will be impossible at the national level.[22]

NOTES

1. This chapter is an updated and more developed version of Sridharan (2002a), and also draws upon, in parts, Sridharan (2004).

2. For the Laakso-Taagepera indices of the effective number of parties, at both the national and state assembly levels, see *Journal of the Indian School of Political Economy*, XV (1–2), 2003, Statistical Supplement, Tables 1.1–1.13, pp. 293–307. For 2004, the index has been calculated by the Centre for the Study of Developing Societies, New Delhi; author's computation for 2009.

3. See Lipset and Rokkan (1967), for the classic statement on the social cleavage theory of party systems, and Bartolini and Mair (1990), for a modified version which essentially argues that social cleavages do not translate automatically into party systems but offer easy mobilization opportunities. Much the same is argued by Kothari (1997: 58), when he says:

> Those who complain of 'casteism in politics' are really looking for a sort of politics which has no basis in society....Politics is a competitive enterprise...and its process is one of identifying and manipulating existing and emerging allegiances in order to mobilise and consolidate positions...

He thus makes the social cleavage theory of party systems appear somehow natural. For recent works within the electoral rules theory of party systems, see Lijphart (1994), Taagepera and Shugart (1989), Grofman and Lijphart (1986); and older classics, Duverger (1963), Rae (1967). For recent emphasis on the division of powers between various levels of government in federal systems as an explanatory variable, see Chhibber and Kollman (1998) and (2004).

4. Taagepera and Shugart (1989) emphasize ballot structure, district magnitude, and electoral formula as the basic variables. Lijphart (1994) emphasizes, in addition, a derivative variable, effective threshold of representation, and assembly size, and considers the special cases of Presidentialism and *apparentement* (linking of party lists).

5. See Lijphart (1994: 22, Table 22).

6. For a detailed analysis of the early debates on adopting an electoral system, see Sridharan (2002b: 344–69).

7. A measure of the fragmentation of the opposition space represented by the percentage share of the largest non-Congress (in today's terms, non-ruling party) vote in the total opposition vote. The higher the IOU, the less fragmented the opposition space.

8. Regional party is something of a misnomer as it implies a party strong in two or more states in a region. All the regional parties, however, are single-state-based parties, except the Janata Dal (United), which is strong in Bihar and Karnataka, and the CPI (M), strong in West Bengal, Tripura, and Kerala, if one considers them regional parties. These sets of states do not constitute recognizable regions. The JD (U) and the CPI (M) are really national parties with a limited geographical spread, the former being a rump of the once much larger Janata Dal.

9. For the BJP's use of coalitions as a strategy to expand its base across states, see Sridharan (2005).

10. For details of the alliances, pre- and post-election in 1998, see Arora (2000: 184–5, 190, 194).

11. For details of the argument and figures, see Sridharan (2004).

12. For a concise overview of regional parties in the party system up to the mid-1990s, see Manor (1995).

13. See Chhibber (1999: 105); Chhibber and Kollman (2004).

14. See Brass (1980), for Singh (1990), Frankel (1991), and (1989).

15. See Kohli (1991), for an analysis of the 'crisis of governability' centred on the centralization of the Congress party. This argument gells with Riker's ideal type of disillusioned voting, in Riker (1976). See Chibber (1999: ch. 5), for an argument emphasizing the exit of traditional supporters of the Congress, rather than the entry of new groups into politics.

16. See Chibber (1999: chs 2 and 5).

17. For a general analysis of the decline of the Congress and the emergence of a post-Congress polity, see Yadav (1999). For specifics that show the polarization of the vote by community and caste, see Heath (1999), and for the BJP vote see Heath and Yadav (1999). See Chandra (1999), for an analysis of the rise of the BSP.

For a view that Duverger's law does not apply to a significant fraction of constituencies over time, see Diwakar (2007).

18. See Sridharan (1997), for a detailed version of the argument presented in capsule below.

Dwakar's (2007) argument is still consisent with convergence towards state-level bipolar its not two party systems, in most states.

19. For a view that Duverger's law does not apply to a significant fraction of constituencies over time, see Diwakar (2007).

20. Diwakar's (2007) argument is still consistent with convergence towards state-level bipolar if not two-party systems, in most states.

21. For a detailed overview of state-level coalition politics in India, see Sridharan (1999). For a detailed state-wise analysis of the BJP's coalition strategies since 1989, see Sridharan (2005). For a detailed analysis of the Congress' coalition strategies and their criticality in the 2004 elections, see Sridharan (2004).

22. Ordeshook and Shvetsova (1994) argue that Duverger's law will work even under conditions of social (ethnic, religious, linguistic, and so on) heterogeneity, while Taagepera and Shugart (1989) tend to argue that the effective number of parties will increase with the increase in social heterogeneity.

REFERENCES

Arora, Balveer. 2000. 'Negotiating Differences: Federal Coalitions and National Cohesion', in Francine Frankel, Zoya Hasan, Rajeev Bhargava, and Balveer Arora (eds), *Transforming India: Social and Political Dynamics of Democracy*. New Delhi: Oxford University Press, pp. 176–206.

Bartolini, Stefano and Peter Mair. 1990. *Identity, Competition and Electoral Availability: The Stabilisation of European Electorates, 1885–1985*. Cambridge: Cambridge University Press.

Brass, Paul. 1980. 'The Politicization of the Peasantry in a North Indian state: I and II', *Journal of Peasant Studies*, 7(4): 395–426 and 8(1), pp. 3–36.

Butler, David, Ashok Lahiri, and Prannoy Roy. 1995. *India Decides: Elections 1952–1995*. New Delhi: Books and Things.

Chandra, Kanchan. 1999. 'Mobilizing the Excluded', *Seminar*, August, pp. 45–51.

Chhibber, Pradeep. 1999. *Democracy without Associations*. New Delhi: Vistaar Publications.

Chhibber, Pradeep K. and Ken Kollman. 2004. *The Formation of National Party Systems: Federalism and Party Competition in Canada, Great Britain, India and the United States*. Princeton: Princeton University Press.

———. 1998. 'Party Aggregation and the Number of Parties in India and the United States', *American Political Science Review*, 92(2), pp. 329–42.

Diwakar, Rekha. 2007. 'Darverger's Law and the Size of the Indian Party System', *Party Politics*, 13(5), pp. 539–61.

Duverger, Maurice. 1963. *Political Parties: Their Organisation and Activity in the Modern State*. New York: Wiley.

Frankel, Francine R. 1991. 'Middle Classes and Castes in India's Politics: Prospects for Political Accommodation', in Atul Kohli (ed.), *India's Democracy*. New Delhi: Orient Longman, pp. 225–61.

———. 1989. 'Caste, Land and Dominance in Bihar: Breakdown of the Brahmanical Social Order', in

Francine R. Frankel and M.S.A. Rao (eds), *Dominance and State Power in Modern India*, vol. I. New Delhi: Oxford University Press, pp. 96–132.

Grofman, Bernard and Arend Lijphart. 1986. *Electoral Laws and Their Political Consequences*. New York: Agathon Press.

Heath, Anthony and Yogendra Yadav. 1999. 'The United Colours of Congress: Social Profile of Congress Voters, 1996 and 1998', *Economic and Political Weekly*, XXXIV (34–5), pp. 2518–28.

Heath, Oliver. 1999. 'Anatomy of BJP's Rise to Power', *Economic and Political Weekly*, XXXIV(34–5), pp. 2511–27.

Kohli, Atul. 1991. *Democracy and Discontent*. New York: Cambridge University Press.

Kothari, Rajni. 1997. 'Caste and Modern Politics', in Sudipta Kaviraj (ed.), *Politics in India*. New Delhi: Oxford University Press.

Lijphart, Arend. 1994. *Electoral Systems and Party Systems*. New York: Oxford University Press.

Lipset, Seymour Martin and Stein Rokkan. 1967. *Party Systems and Voter Alignments*. New York: Free Press.

Manor, James. 1995. 'Regional Parties in Federal Systems', in Douglas Verney and Balveer Arora (eds), *Multiple Identities in a Single State*. New Delhi: Konark, pp. 105–35.

Ordeshook, Peter and Olga Shvetsova. 1994. 'Ethnic Heterogeneity, District Magnitude and the Number of Parties', *American Journal of Political Science*, 38(4), pp. 100–23.

Rae, Douglas. 1967. *The Political Consequences of Electoral Laws*. New Haven: Yale University Press.

Riker, William A. 1976. 'The Number of Political Parties: A Re-examination of Duverger's Law', *Comparative Politics*, 9(1), pp. 93–106.

Singh, Ranbir. 1990. 'Changing Social Bases of Congress Political Support in Haryana', in Richard Sisson and Ramashray Roy (eds), *Diversity and Dominance in Indian Politics*. vol. I. New Delhi: Sage Publications, pp. 294–311.

Sridharan, E. 2005. 'Coalition Strategies and the BJP's Expansion, 1989–2004', *Commonwealth and Comparative Politics*, 43(2), pp. 194–221.

———. 2004. 'Electoral Coalitions in 2004 General Elections: Theory and Evidence', *Economic and Political Weekly*, XXXIX(51), pp. 5418–25.

———. 2002a. 'The Fragmentation of the Indian Party System, 1952–1999: Seven Competing Explanations', in Zoya Hasan (ed.), *Parties and Party Politics in India*. New Delhi: Oxford University Press, pp. 475–503.

———. 2002b. 'The Origins of the Electoral System: Rules, Representation and Power-sharing in India's Democracy', in Zoya Hasan, E. Sridharan, and

R. Sudarshan (eds), *India's Living Constitution: Ideas, Practices, Controversies*. New Delhi: Permanent Black, pp. 344–69.

Sridharan, E. 1999. 'Principles, Power and Coalition Politics in India: Lessons from Theory, Comparison and Recent History', in D.D. Khanna and Gert W. Kueck (eds), *Principles, Power and Politics*. New Delhi: Macmillan, pp. 270–90.

———. 1997. 'Duverger's Law, its Reformulations and the Evolution of the Indian Party System', Centre for Policy Research, May 1, and IRIS India Working Paper No. 35, February, IRIS Center, University of Maryland.

Taagepera, Rein and Matthew Soberg Shugart 1989. *Seats and Votes*. New Haven: Yale University Press.

Yadav, Yogendra. 1999. 'Electoral Politics in the Time of Change: India's Third Electoral System, 1989–99', *Economic and Political Weekly*, XXIV (34–5), pp. 2393–9.

———. 1996. 'Reconfiguration in Indian Politics: State Assembly Elections 1993–1995', *Economic and Political Weekly*, XXXI (2–3), pp. 95–104.

II Social Cleavages, Identity, and Politics

9 Class and Politics

John Harriss

Why should we bother any more about class in political analysis in India? Lloyd and Susanne Rudolph argued, after all, in their work on India's political economy twenty years ago, that class politics is not a strong determinant of political action: 'class politics in India [they say] is marginal (in the sense that) India's parties do not derive their electoral support or policy agenda from distinct class constituencies or from organised representatives of workers and capital' (1987: 20). Is class not very largely a redundant category? Or, if not redundant, is it not one of limited analytical power?[1] There are several reasons why these views may be held. The concept of class is usually associated with Marx—even though he in fact wrote rather little about it—and arguments about the likely processes of class formation and class struggle deriving from his analysis of capitalism appear to have been falsified by the course of modern history. The expectations of classical sociologists with regard to the character of 'industrial society' in general have not been realized. The industrial working class has nowhere developed either the size or the coherence that Marx, in common with classical sociologists, anticipated. And though 'class politics' have had moments of great significance in Western societies, where some major parties retain at least a sense of their particular association with capital or with labour, it seems plain that politics now is rarely driven very directly by class interests. If political parties were once highly organized and linked with society through ideology and mass movements, they are now more frequently the followings of more or less charismatic leaders, or depend upon the findings of focus groups, which are fed back to potential supporters through media sound bites, for the mobilization of support.

In part, at least, it seems that these trends have come about because the actual class structure of contemporary societies is so much more complicated than the notion of a fundamental opposition between 'capital' and 'labour' suggests. Both 'capital' and 'labour' are divided into diverse fragments, and in modern societies very large numbers of people do not fit very clearly into either of these fundamental class categories. In the contemporary world, too, there is a lot of evidence showing that workplaces are much less significant arenas of politics than are living places (a point that is taken up further below). The 'middle class' is notoriously difficult to define precisely, and yet there can be no doubt that in many societies large numbers of people, quite commonly a majority, are part of the 'middle class'. To these basic difficulties with class analysis is added the further objection that it seems evident that in contemporary politics—and perhaps a fortiori in India—much more hinges upon questions of identity, of caste, religion, language, and other markers of ethnicity, than upon matters of class interest. One of the more momentous recent events in Indian political history is, for instance, the achievement in 2007 of undisputed power by the Bahujan Samaj Party in Uttar Pradesh, based upon what seems an unlikely coalition between Dalits and members of upper castes, especially Brahmins. Perceptions of identity seem, without question, to be a much more powerful force than class interests. Elsewhere in the world, too, cultural concerns apparently outweigh what analysts may define as class interests. With regard to the United States, for example, Frank (2004) takes the case of Kansas, a state once famous for radicalism that has become solidly conservative, in order to explain how and why it is that so many people in America clearly vote against their class interests. Republican political entrepreneurs have very successfully elevated 'moral' issues, over abortion rights, gay marriage, and national pride, to take precedence over possible concerns about income distribution, so that there is formed an extraordinary electoral alliance between finance capitalists and blue-collar workers. 'Culture wars' may be much more powerful drivers of politics than class.

The purpose of this chapter is not to attempt to make a case for reasserting the primacy of class in political analysis, but rather to show that the concept remains highly significant when it is deployed, as it should be, in the context of an analysis that takes account of different dimensions of social life. Certainly any social science that does not take account of class—and there is quite a lot of it about—is deceptive. The chapter proceeds by first offering a brief examination of the concept of class. It goes on to consider the class structure of Indian society and

its possible implications for politics, before taking up particular themes to show how they are illuminated by class questions: the nature and functioning of Indian democracy; the pattern of Indian development; and the understanding of contemporary politics. In each case, particularly the last, I am concerned with showing the importance of the middle class, difficulties of definition notwithstanding, for the understanding of historical trends.

THE CONCEPT OF CLASS

The concept of class, whether derived from Marx or from Weber, refers to the significance of economic endowments—whether material means of production or possession of particular skills ('human capital'), or cultural traits (sometimes referred to as 'symbolic capital'), or social connections (sometimes described as 'social capital'), which influence a person's power in the markets vis-à-vis labour or money—for the differences in the matrices of opportunities and constraints that confront all human beings as they 'make out' through their lives. Herring and Agarwala (2006) have discussed this at length. Different groups of people broadly share particular matrices according to their positions in the structures of production and distribution through which societies are reproduced; and their relationships (class is fundamentally a relational concept) are substantially determined by these differences in class positions. This is the *class structure*, or what Marx refers to as 'class-in-itself'. It is another matter as to whether the groups of people defined by the class structure actually think of themselves in these terms and are aware of their commonalities. This is the dimension of *class consciousness*, or of 'class-for-itself' as Marx defines it; and we may then examine the historical social processes of *class formation*—those that bring about collective organization amongst people who broadly share class positions—and of *class struggle*, when classes pursue their interests in opposition to those of others. A Marxian interpretation of history finds in these processes the essential dynamics of societal change over time, while in the Weberian view, class is only one dimension of power relationships (the others being those of 'status' or honour, and of 'party'), and it is envisaged that change comes about as a result of complex interactions amongst the different dimensions of power.

Another important idea is that people who share a class position have interests in common, and a great deal of the difficulty or misapprehension surrounding the idea of class follows from the notion that people can be expected to act in pursuit of class interest. Clearly, they very often do not (as in the case of the blue-collar workers of Kansas in the recent past), and then it is sometimes argued that this demonstrates 'false consciousness'. It is very questionable as to how far this is a useful idea, if at all. Rather, we must come to terms with the ways in which perceptions of interest are filtered cognitively. In this connection, it may be important to take account of the ways in which class relationships are actually experienced. In the context of rural India, it is still quite commonly the case that class relationships are experienced in terms of caste. The majority of labourers frequently come from a particular Dalit group—*paraiyars*, for instance, in northern Tamil Nadu—while property-owning rich peasants are from a particular 'dominant caste' (in this case *mudaliars*). The class relation between labour and capital in these circumstances may then have an important religious dimension, for paraiyars—historically at least and sometimes still in the present—also perform a range of religious services for members of the dominant caste (Harriss 1994). Such cultural 'embedding' of class relationships influences the way in which they are perceived; it may influence the extent to which they are regarded as legitimate, and will hence exercise a strong influence upon class consciousness and the possibilities of class struggle.[2] Specifically, caste loyalties may obstruct the formation of class consciousness, or in some circumstances enhance it, as has happened in parts of the Thanjavur district of Tamil Nadu, where there are particular concentrations of paraiyar labourers (Béteille 1974; Bouton 1985). Class analysis entails, therefore, taking account of the cultural context (the historically specific habits of thought and behaviour of a particular group of people), and the intersections (in Weber's terms) of 'class', 'status', and 'party'. From a political point of view, it has to be recognized that classes-for-themselves do not just arise but are made,

by political leaders in particular historical contexts. The cases of the two Indian states in which class-based political mobilization has occurred—West Bengal and Kerala—help to make this point. It is hard to explain in purely 'structural' terms how and why it has come about that class politics have developed in these states. If it is present in West Bengal, for instance, why is it not in Bihar?

The critical matter for politics is whether or not class consciousness is developed, amongst whom, and in what ways. Here we face difficult questions, both vis-à-vis analysis and political practice, surrounding the aggregation or the fragmentation of classes both in- and for-themselves, as well as regarding the ways in which the possibility of the development of class-for-itself is affected by culture. While in the context of a capitalist economy it makes sense, on one level certainly, to conceive of the class structure in terms of the broad opposition between 'capital' and 'labour', and to explore explanations for historical change in terms of struggle between the capitalist class and the working class, it is clearly the case that each of these class categories aggregates together groups of people who, though they may have in common such fundamentals as ownership, or not, of means of production, are in other ways very different. A big question, for instance, concerning the politics of the working class in India is whether or not those in the organized sector or in 'formal' employment recognize commonalities of interest with those in 'informal' work. Another big question concerns the relationships of different fractions of the capitalist class. With regard to India, this question has generally been framed in terms of the relationships between agricultural or landed capital and industrial capital—between 'rich farmers' and 'big business'—while in other societies, and increasingly in India, the big issue concerns the relationships between 'finance capital' and 'industrial capital'. Then there is the question of the definition of the 'middle class'—those apparently increasing numbers of people who own small capitals or whose endowments are in terms of professional skills or attributes that may be described as 'cultural capital' or perhaps 'social capital', rather than as ownership of physical or financial means of production—and of its relations with capital and with labour. Deshpande

(2003, ch. 6) discusses the definition of the middle class and its class practices in India. In the light of these general considerations, we now examine the class structure and class formation in India.

CLASS STRUCTURE AND CLASS FORMATION IN INDIA

The Working Class

The Rudolphs point out, fairly enough, that 'Organised labour as a potential actor in class politics [in India] must contend with formidable obstacles' (1987: 24). In the first place, as is by now generally understood, the overwhelming majority of those in the Indian labour force are in informal employment, unprotected by labour legislation and with very little access to social security. Barbara Harriss-White estimates that 'Approximately 83 per cent of the population work wholly in the informal sector' (2003: 5); while Rina Agarwala calculates that only 7 per cent of the labour force as a whole, or 18 per cent of the non-agricultural labour force, is in formal, protected employment (2006: 422). According to her, 45 per cent of India's non-agricultural labour force is constituted by those who are self-employed or are micro-entrepreneurs, and another 38 per cent are part of the 'informal proletariat'—casual workers and regular workers—in informal enterprises. And one of the consequences of economic liberalization in India, as elsewhere in the world, has been to encourage the informalization of labour, so that the share of organized, formal employment in the labour force as a whole has been declining. Clearly there is a great deal of variation in the conditions of life and labour of the Indian 'working class', and it cannot be expected that a common political class consciousness can be at all easily developed.[3]

The 'organized working class' potentially plays a particularly important role in politics, as it has an exceptional ability to challenge the structural power of capital. The extent of working-class organization, it has been shown (Rueschmeyer *et al.* 1990) exercises an important influence upon the prospects for social democracy, and upon the pattern and rate of economic development. Those in protected, formal-sector employment, however (the 7 per cent of the Indian labour force, according to Agarwala's calculations), may

constitute a privileged 'labour aristocracy', concerned above all with the preservation and extension of their own advantages. This charge is often laid at the door of the Indian formal working class. It is commonly held, too, that it is fragmented, and therefore weak, because of the way in which unions have been incorporated into competing political parties, with the result that workers are divided by party political allegiances.[4] It is also the case, as Chibber has shown, that the organized working class was very effectively co-opted by the Congress in the period after Independence through the formation of the Indian National Trade Union Congress (INTUC), 'which was sworn to uphold Congress policy in industrial matters (and) under the aegis of a largely friendly government and bureaucracy...grew by leaps and bounds'—in opposition to the Communist All India Trade Union Congress (AITUC). The resulting 'demobilization of labour removed from the scene the agent that could have been pivotal in giving the state more leverage against the business class' (Chibber 2003: 126). While this argument is a strong one, it does not mean that industrial peace was lasting, and Teitelbaum (2006) has recently questioned the common view that organized labour is fragmented and weak. He shows that the numbers of *functioning* unions (as opposed to those of all that have been registered) have remained fairly constant and that their average size has tended to increase, and that fragmentation at firm level is probably much less than has been commonly supposed ('On average companies tend to negotiate with one or two unions'). The level of industrial disputes has remained high, absolutely and relatively, while the continuing strength of labour is also shown by the continuing failure of the state to 'reform' protective labour legislation, and by the ways in which union resistance has slowed the pace of economic reforms. Teitelbaum concludes that, contrary to common scholarly belief, there is a 'continued prevalence of class conflict and aggressive representation of working class interests in India' (2006: 415).

The idea of the existence of a 'labour aristocracy' barricaded up in a kind of citadel of security and privilege may also be questioned. It is true that entry into the 18 per cent of 'good jobs' in organized non-agricultural employment has often been subject to 'the principle of particularism' because of the importance of personal contacts and recommendation in entry into these jobs. This has tended to build self-reinforcing networks that are likely to be restricted to people from particular caste and residential backgrounds, and may enhance consciousness of caste loyalties at the expense of the development of any sense of class identity. However, it is also true that these putative aristocrats of labour often share common places of residence with the informal proletariat, and that this tends to associate them with wider popular interests and grievances. The constraint on the formation of a radical proletariat is rather the fact that aspirations to become part of the petite bourgeoisie are often strong amongst those in formal employment. The conclusion of my own research in Coimbatore, for instance, was that

> (The city) does not have a labour aristocracy in the sense in which this term has commonly been used. But neither does it have an effectively radical proletariat, when petty bourgeois aspirations are common and the community of working people is both divided in several ways and susceptible to populist politics. (Harriss 1986: 281)

The deliberate casualization or informalization of the conditions of employment that is sought in the context of economic liberalization and is very widely attested (Castells 1996) is aimed specifically at the *dis*organization of labour, and historically it has proven difficult—with a few exceptions, such as amongst load carriers and dock workers—to organize those in informal employment whose conditions of work are characterized by irregularity and insecurity. There are now indications of change, however, as some groups of informal workers, such as construction workers and women employed in rolling bidis, have begun to become organized. Agarwala has shown that such informal working-class politics are taking on a different character, with demands being targeted at the state rather than being directed against employers, and for welfare benefits rather than for workers' rights. Some of the organizations involved set out specifically to link the issues of women's rights, rights to housing, and rights to livelihood (Harriss 2007); and the informal workers' unions 'appeal to state responsibilities to citizens, rather than to workers' rights' (Agarwala 2006: 432). They are struggling not

against informality (the historical objective of Trade Union organization), but for rights within this status. Agarwala maintains that, nonetheless, the emerging identity of informal workers 'simultaneously asserts their informality and their position within the working class' (Agarwala 2006: 437). It should not be assumed that the informal proletariat will be forever quiescent, nor that links cannot be made between 'organized' and 'unorganized' workers, as has happened in those countries in which there has been a development of what is described as 'social movement unionism' (Waterman 1991).

CAPITAL/BIG BUSINESS

While arguing that 'Organised capital, the second actor, also faces formidable ideological, sectoral and structural constraints', the Rudolphs still concede that '"Business interests" in India, while not publicly represented in competitive party politics, are better represented than those of organised labour...' (1987: 25, 31). But the argument that private capitalism in India is essentially dependent upon the state is a key element in their general case that Indian politics are 'centrist', and that class cleavages are not at all pronounced. The argument rests on the fact that the public sector has been pre-eminent in the industrial economy, and that while some firms were able to benefit from the extensive regulation of industry by the post-Independence state, the system of licences and controls still meant that business was subject to dictation by the state. Other scholars disagree, or present a more qualified view. Vivek Chibber, in particular, in a richly documented study of the relationships of state and big business (2003), has shown that contrary to the paradigmatic case of South Korea, the Indian state was not successful in disciplining big business (which is part of the reason why, as I discuss later, India's 'developmental state' was less successful in securing economic growth). Still, there is a lot of evidence suggesting that India's economic development was constrained by a political climate that was at least ambiguous with regard to private-sector development, if not actively hostile to it, and that higher rates of economic growth have followed from a shift in political attitudes and hence in the 'investment climate', starting in the 1980s (Kohli 2006). And while there undoubtedly are differences amongst big business, based on the differing needs and interests of different sectors and between the old business houses and new groups (like Reliance), partly reflected in the shifting political influence of the Federation of Indian Chambers of Commerce and Industry (FICCI) and the Associated Chambers of Commerce and Industry (ASSOCHAM) on the one hand, and the newer Confederation of Indian Industry (CII) on the other, Indian capital is not (in Kohli's view) so factionalized as to have inhibited the development of common positions and a move towards 'India Incorporated'—or, in other words, the kind of partnership between state and private capital that is characteristic of South Korea.[5]

THE MIDDLE CLASSES

There is continuity between the big bourgeoisie and the 'middle class', and an important fraction of the internally varied social group that may be described as the 'middle classes' is that of the petite bourgeoisie, the owners of small capitals, who have at times played a significant role in the politics of many countries. In India, the idea that the social groups described by Michael Kalecki as 'intermediate classes', of 'small landowners, rich and middle peasants, merchants of rural and semi-rural townships, small-scale manufacturers and retailers', might be class elements of significance for the general direction of Indian politics and political economy is one that has been revived and advanced by Barbara Harriss-White (2003).[6] She argues that these groups 'consolidate themselves above all in the informal and black economies', which account for at least 88 per cent of the Indian economy as a whole, and comments that while it has been argued that they 'show no signs of concerted class action, relying instead on particularistic tactics', it is precisely 'the mass reliance by this class coalition on such tactics (that) *is* a generalised characteristic of their politics' (ibid.: 53). Harriss-White argues that these intermediate classes, which she also refers to as 'local capital', redefine the state's official development project, and that they exercise considerable power,

not primarily through political parties but rather 'collusively, in overlapping organisations of diverse kinds: cultural, co-operative and philanthropic, as well as trade associations' (2003: 52).

These intermediate classes constitute only one fraction of the middle classes, however. 'The dominant fraction,' Fernandes and Heller suggest, 'consists of those with advanced professional credentials or accumulated cultural capital who occupy positions of recognised authority in various fields' (2006: 500). This is the fraction of the middle class that in Deshpande's 'definition to think with' (2003: 139–42) articulates the hegemony of the ruling bloc in Indian society, in the senses both of 'giving voice to' and of linking or connecting (the relations between the ruling bloc and the rest of society), and it is the class that is most dependent on cultural capital, especially including the ability to use English, and the cosmopolitan manners of the upper castes. It is people from this fraction who are described by Fernandes and Heller as 'the new middle class'. The petty bourgeoisie (or what I have referred to as the intermediate classes) is a middle category, some members of which may aspire to and try to emulate the practices of the dominant fraction. 'The third, and most numerous, are the subordinate middle class fraction of salaried workers who have some educational capital, but do not occupy positions of authority over other workers' (Fernandes and Heller 2006: 500); and in Deshpande's view, this is the 'mass fraction', engaged in the 'exemplary consumption of ideologies (that are produced by the elite fraction), thus investing them with social legitimacy' (2003: 141).

Lately, one of the more striking features of Indian politics has been the apparent withdrawal of the middle classes from party politics, as evidenced through the changing social composition of those who vote in elections (Alam 2004: ch. 2, 26–44). This does not mean, however, that they do not play a pivotal role in Indian politics, as I shall argue in the later sections of this chapter. It remains, here, to consider the classes of India's dominantly rural society.

Agrarian Classes

India is still primarily an agrarian society, which has for long exhibited distinct class differentiation. While it is a 'peasant' society in which large numbers of people hold what may be seen as an ambiguous class position, having at once some ownership rights over means of production whilst also being workers, there have also long been landless workers on the one hand, and landlords and dominant peasants who have employed their labour power on the other. A crucial question with regard to recent politics has been whether or not, or the extent to which, the process of differentiation that Lenin argued was taking place after the abolition of serfdom in late nineteenth-century Russia—towards class polarization between capitalist farmers and labour—is underway.[7] In post-Independence India, the abolition of the tax-farming superior rights-holders, the zamindars, in the first phase of land reform, which had the effect of enhancing the rights and the power of the rich peasants, the main beneficiaries of zamindari abolition, may be seen as having created conditions for the kind of process that Lenin described. Then the advent of higher-yielding varieties of wheat and rice in the later 1960s, during the so-called 'green revolution', and the fillip that this gave to modern agriculture, seemed to many observers in the 1970s to be bringing about further class differentiation in rural society (Frankel 1971). The Indian case provided the main fuel for a major debate that took place at that time between those who held that class differentiation on the lines defined by Lenin was indeed taking place, and other scholars who argued—drawing their inspiration from Lenin's Russian contemporary, the agricultural economist, A.V. Chayanov—that the peasant economy of independent small producers was still reproducing itself (Harriss 1982). Some political leaders and policymakers in India feared that the process of differentiation was leading to class polarization and agrarian conflict—as was reflected in a Home Ministry report of 1969 on 'the causes of the present agrarian unrest' (Frankel 1978/2004: 373–4). It seemed to many at the time that 'the green revolution was turning red'. Then, also, and even more so subsequently, there was widespread recognition of the political weight of the rich peasantry that benefited so much from agricultural modernization, and the influence that it exercised on India's economic development (Mitra 1977; Bardhan 1984/1998 and see below). Lloyd and Susanne Rudolph,

however, found in the evidence that they advanced to demonstrate the dominance of those they labelled 'bullock capitalists'—'yeoman farmers' owning between two and a half and fifteen acres of land— further justification for their view that Indian politics is distinctly 'centrist', because the politics of the agricultural economy remained, as they saw it, sectoral rather than class oriented (1987: ch. 13, 333–92).

The twenty-five years or so that have elapsed since the debates of the 1970s were at their height have shown that none of the models of agrarian class formation that were then being explored has proven very robust. The trends of change in rural society may be summed up in the following three (interlocking) propositions:

1. *The differentiation and polarization of peasant classes has been nearly frozen.* Though the tradition of studies of 'agrarian change' has been much less vibrant in recent years than it was in the 1970s, research shows that there has generally only been what Byres referred to as 'partial proletarianization', and that small and marginal peasant producers have continued to reproduce themselves (Byres 1981; Harriss 1994; Harriss-White and Janakarajan 2004). This commonly takes place now as a result of the role of migration (both rural–rural and rural–urban, and short term and long term), of the remittances associated with it, and of increasing employment outside agriculture. It has also been assisted by the improved availability of institutional credit (though this has latterly become more restricted again), in some cases by micro-finance schemes, and by state welfare provision (Harriss-White and Janakarajan 2004). The rural partial-proletariat and the increasing mass of rural workers (reckoned now to be almost 50 per cent of the rural population as compared with 28 per cent in 1951) constitute, as Herring and Agarwala put it, 'the truly awkward class: largely unattached to anyone's land, selling labour power as a commodity in an unpredictable market, often uprooted by pushes and pulls of market forces, and largely without representation' (2006: 344).

2. *Land is no longer the principal basis of status and power, and neither does it serve to limit the livelihood possibilities of the poor.* The latter part of this proposition is explained by the increased

importance of non-agricultural employment amongst rural people, both locally and in distant cities and rural regions to which we have just referred. It has generally been the case that where the incidence of rural poverty has declined, this has come about as a result of the tightening of labour markets. The first part of the proposition should not be overestimated, for it is certainly still the case that landownership can be the basis of considerable wealth in areas of high agriculture, like the south Indian delta regions, and that it remains an important aspect of status and power. There is a strong tendency, however, for rural power-holders to invest outside agriculture, and in education, sometimes so as to secure employment in the public sector (see, for example, Rutten 1995 on the former; and Jeffrey 1997, on the latter). In other cases, as the profitability of agriculture has declined, or, as a result of the ways in which members of landowning higher castes have sought to secure their continuing status distinction, there has been a tendency for them to move out of agriculture (Mayer 1996 and Harriss 2006a on the former and Gidwani 2000 on the latter). Alongside these developments has come about the emergence of a new generation of local leaders, as Krishna (2003) has explained with regard to rural Rajasthan, from amongst the educated but often unemployed younger men, and elsewhere from amongst the 'ruppy' class of upwardly mobile, young, and newly rich men from middle-ranking caste backgrounds (the term was suggested by Kulkarni in a newspaper article, referred to by Mayer 1996: 54). The class power of 'rich farmers' coming mainly from higher-ranking castes appears to have declined significantly since the Rudolphs dwelt upon it at length. 'Farmers' movements' that have been successful in drawing support from across rural classes, sometimes on caste lines but also by invoking the imagery of conflict between rural *Bharat* and urban India, have more strongly represented the interests of the most intensively commercialized producers. They were powerful in the 1980s and played a major political role (Nadkarni 1987; Omvedt 1993), but have become less significant since the early 1990s. Zoya Hasan has suggested, with regard to Uttar Pradesh, that this form of mobilization of class interests has been eclipsed by the politics of Hindutva

(Hasan 1998). And now, while it remains true that the class interests of rich farmers are still a significant factor in India's political economy (as is discussed below), the crisis of the agricultural economy over much of the country in the early years of the twenty-first century is one marker of the declining political weight of this class. The fact that they are so divided, notably over the reactions to the globalization of the Indian economy—which is supported by the Shetkari Sanghatana, one of the biggest farmers' organizations, and opposed by others—does not help their case. Class interests are not necessarily perceived in the same way, and the differences profoundly affect class formation and the possibilities of class struggle (Herring and Agarwala 2006; and Herring 2006).

3. '*The poor loosen the ties of dependence but exercise little leverage over the political space*'.[8] Here, the category of 'the poor' refers to numerous rural labourers and small peasant petty commodity producers. There is by now abundant evidence of what Frankel and Rao described as 'the decline of dominance'—referring to 'the exercise of authority in society by groups who achieved socio-economic superiority and claimed legitimacy for their commands in terms of superior ritual status' (1989: 2).[9] The reasons for this decline include those changes in the basis of status and power in rural society that were just described. Simultaneously, there has developed much greater assertiveness amongst people from lower castes and classes—assisted by the expansion of literacy and basic education. This has usually had a distinctive base in caste differentiation, however, as in the mobilizations of particular Other Backward Caste (OBC) groups in Bihar and Uttar Pradesh, in particular, and in those of Dalits and of tribal people. 'The poor' have loosened ties of dependence, but the class interests of rural labourers and semi-proletarians are only weakly articulated politically—except perhaps in Kerala and West Bengal, where the Communist Party of India (Marxist) (CPI[M]) is well organized.

Though class struggle did not develop in the Indian countryside in the wake of the green revolution, as was feared it would at the time—it did not, after all 'turn red'—Indian rural society is now riven by armed conflict, with (it is said) 20 per cent of districts being affected by violent agrarian insurgency that has been described by the Prime Minister as 'the single biggest internal security challenge ever faced by our country' (Herring and Agarwala 2006). This Naxalite insurgency is said by its leaders to be a 'class war', and is underlain by a range of factors that include the economic exploitation of landless workers, as well as other dimensions of subordination and oppression. Alpa Shah, however, provides a more complex view of the activities of the Maoist Communist Centre in Jharkhand, showing the continuities between the local state and the MCC:

> the MCC's initial grassroots support is a rural elite— including entrepreneurs who tried to maintain their dominance through their connection with the informal economy of the state. The primary reasons they supported the MCC were not ideological but because connection with the MCC held the promise of protection to further capture state resources. (Shah 2006: 309)

The insurgency has roots that are more tangled than the claim of 'class war' might lead one to suppose.

In the remainder of this chapter I want to show the relevance of the foregoing analysis of class structure and class formation for the understanding of key issues and the historical trends of Indian politics—for the nature of Indian democracy, the political economy of development, and for the current reshaping of Indian society and the state.

CLASS, THE STATE, AND DEMOCRACY

The balance of class forces in India in the later colonial period was not such as to be conducive to democracy, according to leading theories of democratization. As Barrington Moore reasoned in his *Social Origins of Dictatorship and Democracy*, India presents the paradox of the establishment of political democracy in the absence of an industrial revolution. Even though, by comparison with other colonial territories, India had seen a more significant development of local industrial capitalism and the leading classes associated with it—the capitalist big bourgeoisie and the industrial working class—the country was still overwhelmingly an agrarian economy and society, subject to the power of landlords and rich peasants from the dominant landholding castes.

The development of industrial capitalism is reckoned to be conducive to democracy because it weakens landlord power, with its interests in forms of control over labour that entail the lack of freedom (whether through actual bondage or looser forms of control such as are involved in what is described as 'semi-feudalism' (Bhaduri 1973; Harriss 2006b). Up to a point, at least, capitalism actually strengthens subordinate classes, as Rueschmeyer *et al.* have argued (1990), and according to their comparative analysis, historically democratization has depended above all on the development of the working class and a shift in the balance of class power in its favour. This structural explanation of the rise of democracy is in distinction to the earlier theory advanced by Lipset (1959) on the basis of a comparative cross-country analysis, which seemed to show that democratization is associated with 'modernization', brought about by economic development and widespread higher education that strengthen the 'moderate' middle class. As Rueschmeyer *et al.* argue, the middle class has historically been ambivalent with regard to democracy, fearing and seeking to curtail it when it threatens to give power to lower classes (as we perhaps see in India in the present, a point that is discussed later). But whether holding to either one of these views—the modernization/middle class theory associated first with Lipset, or Rueschmeyer *et al.*'s argument about the role of the working class—it is hard to explain the emergence of a formally democratic regime in India after Independence, given the relative weakness of both these classes in the later colonial period. The Indian case fits rather better, in fact, with what are described as 'transition' theories of democratization, which focus on the agency of political elites and conceptualize democracy as a set of government institutions and procedures that are negotiated between political leaders, especially between reformers within an authoritarian regime and moderate dissidents. This is a description that fits quite well the predominantly English-speaking, upper-caste and middle-class elites, many of them lawyers, most of them Congressmen, who participated in the Constituent Assembly that decided upon parliamentary democracy as the institutional framework for the new Indian state. Their leaders had, mostly successfully and under the influence of the Gandhian line of class conciliation, sought to control the mobilization of popular, lower-class forces (in class struggle) during the fight for Independence, nipping them off when they started to threaten the established order of property and class relations(Pandey 1982). For most of them the establishment of the authority of the Central government was of paramount importance, and alternative forms of more decentralized political organization and the possibilities of direct democracy received little attention (Austin 1966).

The fact that Indian democracy was the gift of a middle-class and upper-caste political elite which had often checked popular aspirations to political agency has had profound implications for the way in which democracy has worked in practice in a still largely agrarian society. The relations of the elite and the masses were marked by 'mutual incomprehension', in Kaviraj's words (1991). The use of English by the political elite was associated with ideas about and concepts of the consolidation of rational-legal institutions and structures, and through them of the modernization of Indian society, which the elite was not successful in communicating to society at large. There was a failure, as Kaviraj says, in developing 'a common political language', and no reshaping of common beliefs. Eventually the gap came to be filled by the rise of new political elites who were better able to communicate with the masses, but who have not shared the same vision of modernity and have not sought to build democratic political organizations through which people from subordinate classes may acquire agency. Yogendra Yadav has described as the 'second democratic upsurge' those changes of the last fifteen years or so that have brought to prominence a new generation of political leaders from lower-caste backgrounds and the intermediate classes who articulate popular aspirations, but who are themselves 'completely undemocratic in their organisational set-up as well as style of functioning' (1996: 100). The result has been that, as Khilnani puts it (1997), the meaning of democracy in India has been reduced simply to 'elections', and the rights of democratic citizenship remain restricted (Chatterjee 2004). This is to be understood as the outcome of the class structure

of the Indian state, and the particular history of the formation of Indian democracy.

CLASS AND THE POLITICS OF DEVELOPMENT

It is known that the Congress organization was increasingly dominated during the 1930s by 'prosperous proprietor castes, owning holdings between twenty-one and a hundred acres'—rich peasants and smaller landlords, therefore—actual or potential class mobilizations against them having been clamped down, as we have noted; and that 'By 1949 conservative coalitions built by the dominant landowning castes in alliance with urban businessmen had captured effective control of most District and Pradesh Congress Committees' (Frankel 1978: 74). Contemporary ethnographic research, notably like that of F.G. Bailey (1963), showed that individuals from amongst these dominant landowning castes came to function as mediators or brokers between the mass of rural people and the political system (given the state of 'mutual incomprehension' that I have referred to), and that they were able to deliver votes for particular candidates in elections by drawing on caste and factional loyalties, and on the material dependence of poor peasants and landless labourers upon them. The local power of rich peasants was enhanced in many parts of the country through the effects of the first phase of land reforms in the early 1950s with the abolition of the zamindari system in large parts of, in particular, northern India, which removed the upper layers of rights-holders and secured rich peasants rights to property; and their dominance was secured by the persistence of the hierarchical ideology of caste, through which they were able to claim 'legitimacy for their commands in terms of superior ritual status' (Frankel and Rao 1989/1990: 2).[10] Over time, as Frankel (1978) has shown in her detailed analysis of Indian politics through the 1950s and 1960s, these dominant rich peasants and their leaders became increasingly able to resist and manipulate the efforts of the Central government, in the time of the Nehruvian state, to bring about social and economic reform. One of the crucial events in the history of this period was the defeat at the Nagpur Congress of 1959 of the 'Resolution on Agricultural Organisational Pattern', which had proposed radical land redistribution and agrarian reform, as a result of the criticism mounted by Charan Singh and others who represented rich peasant interests. The ability of the Central government to implement its programmes became increasingly constrained. The Central leadership was 'locked out' by local power-holders from amongst the dominant peasant proprietors, and perforce came to depend increasingly on state-bureaucratic agency to bring about social transformation (Kaviraj 1988). In the 1970s, these rich peasant-kulaks 'marched boldly through the door of politics', as Byres memorably put it (1981), when they became more strongly represented in the Lok Sabha than ever before, in 1977, at the elections held after Indira Gandhi's Emergency. And in the 1980s the 'Farmers' Movements', of which they were the leaders, became a powerful political force.

The rich peasant/farmers thus came to constitute one of the dominant class interests in post-Independence India. Another, according to the analyses of Bardhan (1984), Frankel (1978), and, more recently, Chibber (2003), is that of the big bourgeoisie—as explained above. The 'strangulating embrace' of these two dominant classes—each of them powerful, neither able to establish control over the other—left the Indian state with a significant degree of autonomy, but little capacity to discipline or exercise authority over either of them, and it was for this reason that the Indian would-be 'developmental state' was relatively unsuccessful by comparison with those of East Asia.[11] As Bardhan (most influentially) and others have shown, the inability of the state to discipline the dominant classes led to the frittering away of public resources in a variety of subsidies and transfer of payments that crippled the state development project. For Bardhan, too, these two 'dominant proprietary classes' were joined by a third, the (middle) class of white-collar workers and public-sector professionals, who were able to secure unproductive rents through their power to make demands upon the public purse and manipulate controls and regulations. What the Rudolphs described as the 'centrism' of Indian politics and the lack of political class cleavages is to be

explained in terms of this compromise of class power in the Indian state.

The final question to be addressed is that of the ways in which the politics of class underlie the current conjuncture of Indian politics and the 'reinvention' of India through neo-liberalism in public policy, the rise of Hindu nationalism, and the re-shaping of Indian democracy that is associated with the 'second democratic upsurge'. We shall be concerned particularly with the politics of the middle class, especially its dominant fraction.

HEGEMONIC ASPIRATIONS: NEW MIDDLE CLASS POLITICS[12]

The class structure of India during the late colonial period and the circumstances of the time, we have seen, gave the elite fraction of the middle class in India a strategic role in the creation of the new Indian state. In India, as elsewhere in the world, it has been the middle class, and not the working class, that has been of pivotal importance in determining the political outcomes of capitalist development. After Independence the middle class played a vital role in the dominant class coalition, both as a manager of the ruling bloc (as Deshpande argues) and as an important actor in its own right, articulating the developmental project of the dominant classes (the big bourgeoisie and the dominant peasantry) of the Nehruvian state around secular nationalism and state-led developmentalism, and expanding its own niche (in the manner that Bardhan explains). However, it was not successful in establishing hegemony, given the 'failure to establish a common political language', of which Kaviraj speaks so eloquently, and the inherent contradictions of development planning, which led in the end to the frustration of the aspirations of many in Indian society. Gradually, therefore, new claims arose from below, which the middle-class political elite sought to meet mainly through accommodation within the pyramidal structures of patronage of the Congress party, or sometimes through exclusion. By the 1990s, however, the drift of the Congress had reached a point of crisis. The party lost power, and in the aftermath the government of V.P. Singh sought to implement the long-standing, long neglected, recommendations of the Mandal Report concerning the extension of reservations—partly, at least, it seems reasonable to assert, in order to consolidate its own support. Opposition to Mandal from many in the different fractions of the middle class brought them together in the embrace of Hindu nationalism, in opposition to the independence and assertiveness of the lower classes. At the same moment in modern Indian history, at the beginning of the 1990s, the economic conjuncture in the aftermath of the Gulf War provided an opportunity for influential policymakers from amongst the leading fraction of the middle class to bring about an important shift in policy towards economic liberalism, which has been widely supported by the 'new middle class'. As Fernandes and Heller put it, 'The political project of the new middle class represents an opportune-alliance of market-oriented commercial and professional interests eager to exploit new market opportunities and socially conservative elements protecting a range of status privileges' (2006: 504). This political project, sometimes described in terms of 'elite revolts'[13] has substantially reshaped the political economy, politics, and society of India through a distinctive combination of economic liberalism and social illiberalism. Once again, the middle classes have played a strategic role.

The 'new middle class' is defined above all by its politics and 'the everyday practices through which it reproduces its privileged position' (Fernandes and Heller 2006: 497). The unifying claims of the discourse of Hindu nationalism and the meritocratic ideas associated with economic liberalism are in fact belied by the ways in which the new middle class draws on cultural capital to create and maintain its social distinction. It is also strongly associated with what I have described as 'new politics', based in neighbourhoods rather than workplaces, and built up around local associations in civil society (Harriss 2006c). Through their activities, such associations are held by middle-class activists involved in them to be 'diverting the dirty river' of the corrupt 'old politics' of political parties and the social movements associated with them. These arguments, however, abstract civil society from the field of class relations, whereas the

reality is that civil society is distinctly stratified in class terms. On the whole, it is a sphere of middle-class activism, outside the arena of formal politics. Such activism is one of the defining features of the middle class, which—as we have noted—has steadily withdrawn from participation in electoral politics. Members of the informal working class, on the other hand, are largely excluded from active participation in civil society organizations, so that increasing opportunities for political participation in the 'new politics' of civil society organizing may be associated with increasing political inequality. 'New politics', holding out the promise of 'empowerment', constitutes the governmentality of the post-liberalization state in India, but it is exclusive with regard to the lower classes of the informal proletariat (Harriss 2007).

The big bourgeoisie, however, is actively supportive of middle-class activism, as for example in the city of Bangalore, where several big companies joined with leading civil society organizations in the Bangalore Agenda Task Force, pursuing the objective of creating a 'global city'. Big business and such leading civil society organizations are part of what Solomon Benjamin (2000) describes as the 'corporate economies' of Indian cities. These are the spaces of the industrial, bureaucratic, and IT-sector elites; they are plugged into higher level political circuits, and have direct links with state-level and national parastatal agencies (including finance corporations and development authorities). They operate through 'master planning' and mega-projects, which have made it possible for the capitalist class to achieve 'hegemony in the shaping of the urban form' (as Janaki Nair [2005] puts it), that is quite unprecedented, bypassing local municipal authorities.[14] In this way the corporate economy elites often ride roughshod over the rights or claims of the populations of the 'local economies' of the cities, where most people live and make their livings, where tenurial rights and rights of access to public services are often unclear and contested, and people relate to the state usually through the mediation of local 'big men'. There is a long history in India of efforts by the middle and upper classes to exclude poor people from their space in the city, and these have even been scaled up latterly, in efforts in all the metropolitan cities to establish modern, 'global cities', attractive to international capital.

CLASS MATTERS

The Rudolphs' argument in their important work on India's political economy, that 'India does not have class politics', only holds in the limited sense in which they use the term 'class politics'. This is in a way that obscures in particular the central, strategic role that has been played in Indian politics by the middle classes. Their argument also neglects the ways in which class relationships continue to influence the style and functioning of Indian democracy, and India's political economy. The arguments of this chapter have shown that the marginalization of class in the study of Indian politics seriously limits analysis.

NOTES

1. Articles in a special issue of *Critical Asian Studies*, edited by Ronald Herring and Rina Agarwala, including especially the editors' introduction, and a paper by Vivek Chibber, analyse in some detail why it is that the concept of class has tended to disappear from South Asian studies. See Herring and Agarwala (2006) and Chibber (2006).

2. For a comparable case from another society, see Newby (1977) about agricultural workers in England.

3. The work of the late Rajnarayan Chandavarkar on the question of the formation of working-class consciousness is outstanding (1994, 1999, and 1981, pp. 603–47). Other key sources are the works of Jan Breman (especially Berman 1996), and the collection edited by Parry *et al.* (1999).

4. The Rudolphs argued, for instance, that 'Organisational involution undermines the possibility of collective bargaining by a few powerful, representative unions and of a major voice for labour in national policy' (1987, p. 25).

5. Kohli refers, here, in part to the seminal work on Indian business organization by Stanley Kochanek (1996a, 1996b, and 1974).

6. The definitional quotation, from Aijaz Ahmed, appears on p. 43.

7. A text taken from Lenin's work and a series of classic articles concerning the differentiation of the peasantry can be found in Harriss (1982).

8. This statement is quoted from the Poverty Reduction Strategy Paper for Bangladesh, authored principally by Hussain Zillur Rahman in 2005, but it clearly applies more widely across South Asia.

9. See also Mendelsohn (1993).

10. Defining the political relations that they describe in terms of 'dominance'.

11. See Corbridge and Harriss (2000) for a comparative discussion.

12. This section heading reproduces the title of the essay by Fernandes and Heller (2006) on which I have drawn extensively.

13. See Corbridge and Harriss (2000), following observations made by Sudipta Kaviraj. The term is also used, though more cautiously, by Yogendra Yadav: 'It may be an exaggeration to say that the BJP represents the rebellion of the elite, but it is nevertheless true that its rise to political power has been accompanied by the emergence of a new social group that is defined by an overlap of social and economic privileges' (1999, cited in Fernandes and Heller [2006, p. 504]).

14. As David Harvey has said with regard to 'the Neoliberal state' in general, 'The boundary between the state and corporate power has become more and more porous. What remains of representative democracy is overwhelmed, if not totally though legal corrupted by money power' (2005, p. 78).

REFERENCES

Agarwala, R. 2006. 'From Work to Welfare: A New Class Movement in India', *Critical Asian Studies*, 38(4), pp. 419–44.

Alam, J. 2004. *Who Wants Democracy?* Hyderabad: Orient Longman.

Austin, G. 1966. *The Constitution of India: Cornerstone of a Nation*. Oxford: Oxford University Press.

Bailey, F.G. 1963. 'Politics and Society in Contemporary Orissa', in C.H. Phillips (ed.), *Politics and Society in India*. London: Allen and Unwin, pp. 97–114.

Bardhan, P.K. 1984/1998. *The Political Economy of Development in India*. Oxford: Blackwell, 2nd edn. New Delhi: Oxford University Press.

Benjamin, Solomon. 2000. 'Governance, Economic Settings and Poverty in Bangalore', *Environment and Urbanisation*, 12(1), pp. 35–51.

Béteille, A. 1974. 'Agrarian Relations in Tanjore District', in André Béteille, *Studies in Agrarian Social Structure*. New Delhi: Oxford University Press, pp. 142–70.

Bhaduri, A. 1973. 'A Study in Agricultural Backwardness Under Semi-feudalism', *Economic Journal*, 83(329), pp. 120–7.

Bouton, M. 1985. *Agrarian Radicalism in South India*. Princeton: Princeton University Press.

Breman, J. 1996. *Footloose Labour: Working in India's Informal Economy*. Cambridge: Cambridge University Press.

Byres, T. 1981. 'The New Technology, Class Formation and Class Action in the Indian Countryside', *Journal of Peasant Studies*, 8(4), pp. 405–54.

Castells, M. 1996. *The Rise of the Network Society*. Oxford: Blackwell.

Chandavarkar, R. 1999. 'Questions of Class: The General Strikes in Bombay', in J. Parry, Jan Breman, and Karin Kapadia (eds), *The Worlds of Indian Industrial Labour*. New Delhi: Sage Publications.

———. 1994. *The Origins of Industrial Capitalism in India: Business Strategies and the Working Classes in Bombay 1900–1940*. Cambridge: Cambridge University Press.

———. 1981. 'Workers' Politics and the Mill Districts of Bombay between the Wars', *Modern Asian Studies*, 15(3), pp. 603–47.

Chatterjee, P. 2004. *The Politics of the Governed*. New Delhi: Permanent Black.

Chibber, V. 2006. 'On the Decline of Class Analysis in South Asian Studies', *Critical Asian Studies*, 38(4), pp. 357–87.

———. 2003. *Locked in Place: State-Building and Late Industrialization in India*. Princeton: Princeton University Press.

Corbridge, S. and J. Harriss. 2000. *Reinventing India: Liberalization, Hindu Nationalism and Popular Democracy*. Cambridge: Polity Press.

Deshpande, S. 2003. *Contemporary India: A Sociological View*. New Delhi: Penguin Books.

Fernandes, L. and P. Heller. 2006. 'Hegemonic Aspirations: New Middle Class Politics and India's Democracy in Comparative Perspective', *Critical Asian Studies*, 38(4), pp. 495–522.

Frank, T. 2004. *What's The Matter With America? The Resistable Rise of the American Right*. London: Secker and Warburg.

Frankel, F. 1978/2004. *India's Political Economy: The Gradual Revolution*. New Delhi: Oxford University Press.

———. 1971. *India's Green Revolution: Economic Gains and Political Costs*. Princeton: Princeton University Press.

Frankel, F. and M.S.A. Rao (eds). 1989/1990. *Dominance and State Power in Modern India: Decline of a Social Order*, vols I and II. New Delhi: Oxford University Press.

Gidwani, V. 2000. 'Laboured Landscapes: Agroecological Change in Central Gujarat, India', in A. Agrawal and K. Sivaramakrishnan (eds), *Agrarian Environments: Resources, Representations and Rule in India*. Durham: Duke University Press, pp. 216–47.

Harriss, J. 2007. 'Antinomies of Empowerment: Observations on Civil Society, Politics and Urban Governance in India', *Economic and Political Weekly*, XLII(26), pp. 2717–24.

———. 2006a. 'Postscript: North Arcot Papers', in J. Harriss (ed.), *Power Matters: Essays on Politics, Institutions and Society in India*. New Delhi: Oxford University Press.

———. 2006b. 'Making Out on Limited Resources', in J. Harriss (ed.), *Power Matters*, pp. 33–69.

———. 2006c. 'Middle Class Activism and the Politics of the Informal Working Class: A Perspective on Class Relations and Civil Society in Indian Cities', *Critical Asian Studies*, 38(4), pp. 445–66.

———. 1994. 'Between Economism and Post-modernism: Reflections on "Agrarian Change" in India', in D. Booth (ed.), *Rethinking Social Development: Theory, Research and Practice*. Harlow: Longman, pp. 172–96.

———. 1986. 'The Working Poor and the Labour Aristocracy in a South Indian City: A Descriptive and Analytical Account', *Modern Asian Studies*, 20(2), pp. 231–84.

——— (ed.). 1982. *Rural Development: Theories of Peasant Economy and Agrarian Change*. London: Hutchinson.

Harriss-White, B. 2003. *India Working: Essays on Society and Economy*. Cambridge: Cambridge University Press.

Harriss-White, B. and S. Janakarajan. 2004. *Rural India Facing the Twenty First Century: Essays on Long-Term Village Change and Recent Development Policy*. London: Anthem Press.

Harvey, D. 2005. *A Brief History of Neoliberalism*. Oxford: Oxford University Press.

Hasan, Z. 1998. *Quest for Power: Oppositional Movements and Post-Congress Politics in Uttar Pradesh*. New Delhi: Oxford University Press.

Herring, R. 2006. 'Why Did "Operation Cremate Monsanto" Fail? Science and Class in India's Great Terminator-Technology Hoax', *Critical Asian Studies*, 38(4), pp. 467–94.

Herring, R. and R. Agarwala. 2006. 'Introduction— Restoring Agency to Class: Puzzles from the Subcontinent', *Critical Asian Studies*, 38(4), pp. 323–56.

Jeffrey, C. 1997. 'Richer Farmers and Agrarian Change in Meerut District', *Environment and Planning A*, 29(12), pp. 2113–27.

Kaviraj, S. 1991. 'On State, Society and Discourse in India', in J. Manor (ed.), *Rethinking Third World Politics*. Harlow: Longman, pp. 72–99.

———. 1988. 'A Critique of the Passive Revolution', *Economic and Political Weekly*, XXIII(45–47), pp. 2429–44.

Khilnani, S. 1997. *The Idea of India*. London: Hamish Hamilton.

Kochanek, S. 1996a. 'Liberalisation and Business Lobbying in India', *Journal of Commonwealth and Comparative Politics*, 34(3), pp. 155–73.

———. 1996b. 'The Transformation of Interest Politics in India', *Pacific Affairs*, 68(4), pp. 529–50.

———. 1974. *Business and Politics in India*. Berkeley: University of California Press.

Kohli, A. 2006. 'Politics of Economic Growth in India, 1980–2005', *Economic and Political Weekly*, XLI (13–14), pp. 1251–9 and 1361–70.

Krishna, A. 2003 'What is Happening to Caste? A View from Some North Indian Villages', *Journal of Asian Studies*, 62(4), pp. 1171–94.

Lipset, S.M. 1959. 'Some Social Requisites of Democracy: Economic Development and Political Legitimacy', *American Political Science Review*, 53(1), pp. 69–105.

Mayer, A. 1996. 'Caste in an Indian Village: Change and Continuity, 1954–1992', in C. Fuller (ed.), *Caste Today*. New Delhi: Oxford University Press, pp. 32–64.

Mendelsohn. 1993. 'The Transformation of Authority in Rural India', *Modern Asian Studies*, 27(4), pp. 805–42.

Mitra, A. 1977. *Terms of Trade and Class Relations*. London: Frank Cass.

Moore, B. 1966. *Social Origins of Dictatorship and Democracy: Lord and Peasant in the Making of the Modern World*. Boston: Beacon Press.

Nadkarni, M.V. 1987. *Farmers' Movements in India*. New Delhi: Allied Publishers.

Newby, H. 1977. *The Deferential Worker: A Study of Farm Workers in East Anglia*. London: Allen Lane.

Omvedt, G. 1993. *Reinventing Revolution: New Social Movements and the Socialist Tradition*. Armonk, NY: M.E. Sharpe.

Pandey, G. 1982. 'Peasant Revolt and Indian Nationalism: The Peasant Movements in Awadh, 1919–22', in R. Guha (ed.), *Subaltern Studies I: Writings on South Asian History and Society*. New Delhi: Oxford University Press.

Parry, J., J. Breman, and K. Kapadia (eds). 1999. *The Worlds of Indian Industrial Labour*. New Delhi: Sage Publications.

Rudolph, L.I. and S.H. Rudolph. 1987. *In Pursuit of Lakshmi: The Political Economy of the Indian State*. Chicago: University of Chicago Press.

Rueschemeyer, D., E. Stephens, and J. Stephens. 1990. *Capitalist Development and Democracy*. Cambridge: Polity Press.

Rutten, M. 1995. *Farms and Factories: Social Profile of Large Farmers and Rural Industrialists in West India*. New Delhi: Oxford University Press.

Shah, A. 2006. 'Markets of Protection: The "Terrorist" Maoist Movement and the State in Jharkhand, India', *Critique of Anthropology*, 26(3), pp. 297–314.

Teitelbaum, E. 2006. 'Was the Indian Labour Movement Ever Co-opted? Evaluating Standard Accounts', *Critical Asian Studies*, 38(4), pp. 389–418.

Waterman, P. 1991. 'Social Movement Unionism. A New Model for a New World'. Working Paper-General Series, No. 110. The Hague: Institure of Social Studies.

Yadav, Y. 1996. 'Reconfiguration in Indian Politics: State Assembly Elections 1993–95', *Economic and Political Weekly*, XXXI(2–3), pp. 95–104.

10 Caste and Politics

Surinder S. Jodhka

Analysing democratic political processes in terms of castes and communities has become commonplace in contemporary India. From the lay public to psephologists of the popular media and serious academic analysts, almost everyone treats caste as an important variable influencing the working of the Indian political process. Caste communities are presented as determining electoral outcomes; and they work as pressure groups and influence the governance agenda of the Indian state at the local, regional, and national levels. Caste considerations also tend to structure political parties, their leaderships, and programmes. This reality of the working of the democratic political process is, interestingly, very different from the visions of those who laid the foundations and framed the Constitution of the Indian republic.

Notwithstanding the ambivalent attitude of the early nationalist leadership on the subject of caste, and the frequent disputes that arose about its 'real' value for the social and cultural life of the Indian people during the freedom struggle,[1] the post-Independence political leadership took a clear position against giving it any legitimate place in the political organization of the new democratic nation (Kaviraj 1997; Mehta 2003: 58–9). Articulating the then 'mainstream' position on the subject among the middle-class elite of the country in his well-known book *The Discovery of India*, Pandit Jawaharlal Nehru, India's first Prime Minister, wrote in 1946:

> In the context of society today, the caste system and much that goes with it are wholly incompatible, reactionary, restrictive, and barriers to progress. There can be no equality in status and opportunity within its framework, nor can there be political democracy... . Between these two conceptions conflict is inherent and only one of them can survive. (p. 257)

The Chairman of India's Constituent Assembly and the first Law Minister of independent India, B.R. Ambedkar, was even more emphatic on this. He wrote:

> You cannot build anything on the foundations of caste. You cannot build up a nation; you cannot build up a morality. Anything you will build on the foundations of

caste will crack and will never be a whole. (Ambedkar 2002: 102)

The opening pages of the Indian Constitution, its Preamble, envisaged a nation where the values of equality, liberty, and fraternity would be supreme. Drawn mostly from the historical experience and cultural traditions of the West, these ideas reflected a vision of liberal democracy and a modern society that were to ensure a dignified existence to each and every individual, and endow them with certain fundamental rights vis-à-vis the state and fellow citizens. They contradicted very fundamentally the spirit of caste and hierarchy as principles of social organization. The Directive Principles of State Policy (Article 38) of the Indian Constitution made it clear further by explicitly stating that

> The state shall strive to promote the welfare of the people by securing and protecting as effectively as it may a social order in which justice, social, economic and political, shall inform all the institutions of national life. (as in Shah 2002: 2)

Any form of discrimination on grounds of religion, race, caste, gender, or place of birth was made punishable by law.

Following the practices in democratic regimes of the Western world, the Indian Constitution invested all legislative powers in certain institutions of governance, which were to be made up of elected representatives of the Indian people. Representatives to these bodies were to be chosen by strictly following the principle of universal adult franchise.

While caste was decried by the middle-class leaders of independent India, they did not simply take a moral position against this 'traditional' institution. The 'mainstream' Indian political leadership recognized the 'crippling' impact that the working of the system over the centuries would have had on the subordinated sections of the Indian people, and the implications of this 'ancient' system on building a true democracy and individual citizenship. It was to address these concerns that the Indian Constitution instituted certain legal and institutional measures, albeit temporarily, to enable groups and communities of people who had been historically disadvantaged in the given social system to participate in the game of democratic politics on equal terms (Galanter 1984).

There will be little dispute about the positive effects the Indian policies and programmes of affirmative action have had in enabling the historically deprived sections of Indian people to participate in the economic and political life of the nation. India has also been exceptionally successful in having been able to institutionalize a healthy system of democratic governance at different levels of its political system. However, while these achievements are certainly commendable, they have not meant an end of caste in the social or political life of the nation. In fact, many would argue that politically, caste is a much more active institution today than it ever was in the past, and this is largely thanks to the electoral processes and competitive politics. Though it may appear that the democratic and electoral experience has belied the hopes of the founders of the modern nation, the survival of caste, or its increased involvement with politics, is no reflection on the working of democracy in India, or an evidence of its failure. The available literature on electoral systems and other aspects of political life clearly points towards a process that has been described by the Indian political scientist as the deepening of democracy (see Yadav 1999; Palshikar 2004) and it is becoming more inclusive of social groups and categories of the Indian population (Jayal 2001).

How does one make sense of this apparently contradictory reality? The contemporary Indian political experience also raises questions about the manner in which the institution of 'caste' and its relationship with modernity and democracy have been imagined and theorized by sociologists and social anthropologists, an imagination that has become part and parcel of the middle-class commonsense on the subject of caste and its place in modern-day India. In other words, this 'survival' of caste clearly points to a flawed understanding of the reality of caste, and that of the sociology of democratic politics. Thus, it may be worth our while to begin this chapter with a critical overview of the popular and sociological/anthropological understandings of the caste system.

CASTE WITHOUT POLITICS: ORIENTALIST IMAGININGS AND ANTHROPOLOGY OF INDIA

As it came to be popularly understood by the early twentieth century, there was something simple and straightforward about the Indian caste system. The Orientalists and colonial administrators had worked out its ethnographic details and theories quite well. In fact, the idea of Scheduled Castes (SCs) or 'Depressed Classes' had also been worked out by the colonial rulers. According to this understanding, caste derived its legitimacy from classical Hindu scriptures. The framework of the *varna* hierarchy, as worked out so meticulously by Manu, was the beginning and the ultimate explanation of the caste system. Though the varna theory did not provide any specific position to the 'untouchables' in the Hindu rankings of social grouping, they could easily be accommodated at the bottom of the caste hierarchy, outside the varna system, by using the larger logic of the system.

More recent historical research on the subject has seriously undermined this 'commonsense' about the caste system. Not only did the colonial rulers, through a process of enumeration and ethnographic surveys, raise consciousness about caste, they also produced the conditions where 'caste became the single term capable of expressing, organizing, and above all "synthesizing" India's diverse forms of social identity, community and organization' (Dirks 2001:5). A similar point has also been made by Peter Mayer about the notion of the *jajmani* system, which, he argues, is popularly believed to be an ancient and pan-Indian reality, but in fact originated in northern India during the late nineteenth century (Mayer 1993).

The influence of *colonialism and its forms of knowledge*, to use Bernard Cohn's expression (Cohn 1996), was quite fundamental to the way sociology and social anthropology developed in India. The three central categories through which colonial rulers had tried to make sense of India were those of the village, caste, and religious communities. Notwithstanding its cultural and religious diversity, India for them was a land of Hinduism. Though Islam and Christianity were also practised by a

large number of Indians, these were essentially foreign religions. As is well known, Orientalist scholars identified some of the classical Brahmanical scriptures as canonical texts for understanding the Indian tradition and its past history. This Indological 'book-view' of India continued to be an important reference point and a source of knowledge about the 'natives' throughout the colonial period, and greatly influenced the nationalist understanding of Indian society (Cohn 1996; Dirks 2001; Das 2003; Breckenridge and van der Veer 1993).

Interestingly, the disciplines of sociology and social anthropology in India also began with empirically documenting the dynamics of village society and the caste system. Even while they advocated a shift away from the 'book-view' towards a 'field-view' of India, the categories through which India was to be imagined remained, more or less, the same. For example, the village typically became a convenient entry point for anthropologists interested in understanding the dynamics of Indian society (Jodhka 1998). Similarly, sociologists and social anthropologists universally assumed that the caste system was a peculiarly Indian reality, and an aspect of Hindu religion.

Caste was not merely an institution that characterized the structure of social stratification; it represented the core of India. It was both an institution and an ideology. Institutionally, 'caste' provided a framework for arranging and organizing social groups in terms of their statuses and positions in the social and economic system. As an ideology, caste was a system of values and ideas that legitimized and reinforced the existing structures of social inequality. It provided a worldview around which a typical Hindu organized his/her life.

Apart from being an institution that distinguished India from other societies, caste was also an epitome of the traditional society, a 'closed system', where generation after generation of individuals did similar kinds of work and lived more or less similar kinds of lives. In contrast, modern industrial societies of the West were projected as 'open systems' of social stratification, societies based on class, where individuals could choose their occupations according to their abilities and tastes. If they worked for it, in such open systems of stratification they could move up in the social hierarchy and change their class position. Such mobility at the individual level was impossible in the caste system.

Putting it in a language of social science textbooks, G.S. Ghurye (1991) identified six different features of the Hindu caste system, namely, segmental division of society; hierarchy; restrictions on feeding and social intercourse; civil and religious disabilities and privileges of different sections; lack of unrestricted choice of occupation; and restrictions on marriage.

Though seemingly simple and obvious, this list represented caste as a total and unitary system. Thus, it was possible to define caste and to identify its core features, which were presumably present everywhere in the subcontinent. Similarly, caste was also not merely about occupational specialization or division of labour. It encapsulated within it the features of a social structure and normative religious behaviour, and even provided a fairly comprehensive idea about the personal lives of individuals living in the Hindu caste society. Indian sociologists also pointed to the difference between varna and *jati*. While in the popular understanding there were only four varnas, the actual number of caste groups was quite large. According to one estimate, in each linguistic region 'there were about 200 caste groups which were further sub-divided into about 3000 smaller units each of which was endogamous and constituted the area of effective social life for the individual' (Srinivas 1962: 65).

Perhaps the most influential theoretical work on caste has been of Louis Dumont. He approached the Hindu caste system from a structuralist perspective that focused on the underlying structure of ideas of a given system, the 'essential principles', which may not be apparent or visible in its everyday practice. Caste, according to Dumont, was above all an ideology, and the core element in the ideology of caste for Dumont was hierarchy. Hierarchy was not merely another name for inequality or an extreme form of social stratification, but a totally different principle of social organization. Such a principle, Dumont suggests, was 'the opposition of the pure and the impure'. Hierarchy, defined as superiority of the pure over the impure, was the keystone in Dumont's model of the caste system (Dumont 1998: 43). An important aspect of

his theory was the specific relationship that existed between status and power in Hindu society. Unlike in the West, where power and status normally went together, in the caste system there was a divergence between the two. In caste society, status as a principle of social organization was superior to power. 'Status encompassed power.'

Such theorizations of caste have been further extended by works of scholars like Moffatt (1979) who emphasized upon the underlying ideological unity and cultural consensus across caste groups in its governing normative order. Srinivas's concept of sanskritization will also fit well in such a theory. Sanskritization was a

> ...process by which a 'low' Hindu caste, or tribal or other group, changes its customs, ritual, ideology, and way of life in the direction of a high and frequently, 'twice-born' caste. Generally such changes are followed by a claim to higher position in the caste hierarchy than that traditionally conceded to the claimant caste by the local community. (Srinivas 1972: 6)

Such theorizations of caste were extensively criticized for their ideological bias and weak empirical groundings (see Berreman 1971; Mencher 1974; Béteille 1979; Gupta 1984). However, they have continued to be popular and influential. Why does this happen? As I have argued elsewhere (Jodhka 2004) the idea of caste has been very deeply embedded in the modern Indian self-image, which is itself a mirror reflection of the Orientalist and colonial images of India. The Indian past is thus constructed as an unchanging tradition, and its future is imagined through an evolutionary schema where the Western society is presented as a model for imitation in the name of modernization.

In such an evolutionary imagining of India, caste is expected to disappear with the unfolding of the processes of industrialization, urbanization, and modernization. Politics has no place in such an understanding of caste or processes of social change. Even when mainstream anthropologists of this genre talked about social inequality and untouchability, it was rarely described as being an oppressive system, with an agency that enforced codes of behaviour and reproduced regimes of subordination and domination.

In such a framework, caste was also seen as being fundamentally different from class. While caste was traditional, class was to emerge with the process of secularization of occupations and industrialization/ urbanization. While caste was seen as a social institution, class represented an open system of economic opportunities.

CASTE, MODERNITY, AND DEMOCRATIC POLITICS IN 'DEVELOPING' INDIA

Notwithstanding their personal predispositions towards a liberal view of democratic politics and faith in evolutionist notions of social change, the inevitability of the Western style of modernization, or their preoccupation with categories inherited from colonial and Orientalist writings on India, social anthropologists recognized the tremendous resilience that the institution of caste was showing on the ground. Quite early on they had begun to report on the likely impact that caste could have on the working of 'modern' institutions, and in turn the implications of a new form of politics for the system of caste hierarchy. For example, some of them were quick to recognize the fact that instead of completely replacing the traditional 'ascriptive structures' of caste society with an open system of social stratification based on individual choice and achievement, new modes of governance and the growing use of modern technology could in some ways strengthen caste, while weakening its structural logic.

Commenting on the nature of the change being experienced in caste with the rise of non-Brahmin movements in southern provinces, G.S. Ghurye had argued as early as 1932 that the attack on hierarchy by such mobilizations did not necessarily mean the end of caste. These mobilizations generated a new kind of collective sentiment, 'the feeling of caste solidarity', which could be 'truly described as caste patriotism' (Ghurye 1932: 192).

M.N. Srinivas developed this point further in his writings during the late 1950s. Focusing specifically on the possible consequences of modern technology and representational politics, both of which were introduced by the colonial rulers in India, he argued

that far from disappearing with the process of modernization, caste was experiencing a 'horizontal consolidation'. Commenting on the impact of modern technology on caste, he wrote:

> The coming in of printing, of a regular postal service, of vernacular newspapers and books, of the telegraph, railway and bus, enabled the representatives of a caste living in different areas to meet and discuss their common problems and interests. Western education gave new political values such as liberty and equality. The educated leaders started caste journals and held caste conferences. Funds were collected to organize the caste, and to help the poorer members. Caste hostels, hospitals, co-operative societies etc., became a common feature of urban social life. In general it may be confidently said that the last hundred years have seen a great increase in caste solidarity, and the concomitant decrease of a sense of interdependence between different castes living in a region. (Srinivas 1962: 74–5)

Similarly, the introduction of certain kinds of representational politics by the British helped in this process of the horizontal consolidation of caste.

> The policy which the British adopted of giving a certain amount of power to local self governing bodies, and preferences and concessions to backward castes provided new opportunities to castes. In order to be able to take advantage of these opportunities, caste groups, as traditionally understood, entered into alliances with each other to form bigger entities. (Srinivas 1962: 5)

However, this was not a one-way process. The caste system too was undergoing a change. The horizontal solidarity of caste, which also meant a kind of 'competition' among different castes at the politico-economic plane, eventually weakened the vertical solidarity of caste (Srinivas 1962: 74; Bailey 1963). This process received a further impetus with the introduction of democratic politics after India's Independence.

Faced with the question of change in the caste order, Louis Dumont too followed Srinivas and speculated on similar lines. Castes, he argued, did not disappear with the process of economic and political change, but their logic was altered. He described this process as change from 'structure' to 'substance'. This substantialization of caste indicated:

...the transition from a fluid, structural universe in which the emphasis is on interdependence and in which there is no privileged level, no firm units, to a universe of improbable blocks, self-sufficient, essentially identical and in competition with one another, a universe in which the caste appears as a collective *individual* (in the sense we have given to this word), as a substance. (Dumont 1998: 222, emphasis in original)

These attempts at theorizing about the changing realities of caste opened up many new possibilities for looking at the dynamic relationship between caste and the democratic political process. Thus, by the 1960s, sociologists and political scientists began talking about caste and politics in a different language. Discussions shifted from a predominantly moral or normative concern with the corruption that caste had brought into the democratic political process to more empirical processes of interaction between caste and politics. The gradual institutionalization of democratic politics changed caste equations. Power shifted from one set of caste groups, the so-called ritually purer upper castes, to middle level 'dominant castes'. Democratic politics also introduced a process of differentiation in the local levels of the power structure. As Béteille reported in his study of a village in Tamil Nadu during the late 1960s:

...a vast body of new structures of power have emerged in India since Independence. Today traditional bodies such as groups of caste elders (which are functionally diffuse) have to compete increasingly with functionally specific structures of power such as parties and statutory panchayats. (Béteille 1970: 246–7)

However, this differentiation did not mean that these new structures were free of caste. Caste soon entered in their working, but the authority of these institutions had to be reproduced differently. Though traditional sources of power continued to be relevant, introduction of universal adult franchise also made the 'numbers' of caste communities in a given local setting critical. Power could be reproduced only through mobilizations, vertically as well as horizontally. This also gave birth to a new class of political entrepreneurs. Over the years, some of them have begun to work successfully without confining their political constituency to a single caste cluster, thus undermining the logic of caste politics (Krishna 2001).

Caste Associations

While sociologists and social anthropologists talked about the horizontal consolidation of castes or its substantialization into 'ethnic communities', political sociologists worked on the phenomenon and possible roles of caste associations in democratic politics. Beginning in the late nineteenth century, different parts of the subcontinent saw the emergence of 'caste associations'. While on the face of it caste associations appeared to be a typical case of Indian tradition trying to assert itself against the modernizing tendencies unleashed by colonial rule, they in fact represented a different kind of process. Lloyd and Susanne Rudolph were among the first to study the phenomenon of caste associations in democratic India. They looked at caste associations as agents of modernity in a traditional society like India. They argued that caste association was

...no longer an ascriptive association in the sense in which caste taken as jati was and is. It has taken on features of the voluntary association. Membership in caste association is *not* purely ascriptive; birth in the caste is a necessary but not a sufficient condition for membership. One must also 'join' through some conscious act involving various degrees of identification....(Rudolph and Rudolph 1999[1967]: 33, emphasis in original)

Through his study of *The Nadars of Tamilnad*, Robert Hardgrave further reinforced their thesis by arguing that the caste association of Nadars worked like a pressure group, and had played an important role in the upward social mobility of the community (Hardgrave 1969). M.N. Srinivas, too, similarly argued that caste associations came up as agents of social mobility for caste communities at the time when British rulers introduced the enumeration of castes (Srinivas 1966).

A little later, Rajni Kothari also argued more or less along similar lines while writing on caste and the democratic political process in India. In the introduction to the celebrated volume, *Caste in Indian Politics* (1970) that he edited, Kothari argued against the popular notion that democratic politics was helping traditional institutions like caste to 'resuscitate and re-establish their legitimacy'. This could lead to 'disintegrative tendencies' and could potentially 'disrupt the democratic and secular framework of Indian polity'. In reality, however,

> ...the consequences of caste-politics interactions are just the reverse of what is usually stated. It is not politics that gets caste-ridden; it is caste that gets politicised. Dialectical as might sound, it is precisely because the operation of competitive politics has drawn caste out of its apolitical context and given it a new status that the 'caste system' as hitherto known has eroded and has begun to disintegrate ... (Kothari 1970: 20–1)

Caste federations, he argued,

> once formed on the basis of caste identities go on to acquire non-caste functions, become more flexible in organization, even begin to accept members and leaders from castes other than those with which it started, stretches out to new regions, and also makes common cause with voluntary organizations, interest groups and political parties. In course of time, the federation becomes a distinctly political group'. (Kothari 1970: 21–22)

Speaking in a less enthusiastic language, Ghanshyam Shah also made a similar point. Although in the long run caste associations did promote competitive politics and participation, they also exacerbated parochialism, he argued (Shah 1975). Notwithstanding the deviation they brought into the process of democratic politics—as understood in the classical Western textbooks on democracy—caste associations did play a role in spreading the culture of democratic politics in areas that were hitherto governed exclusively by tradition. As argued by Arnold *et al.*

> The caste association was a social adapter, improvised to connect two sets of social and political forms. It helped to reconcile the values of traditional society with those of new order by continuing to use caste as the basis for social organization, but at the same time introducing new objectives—education and supra-local political power ... (1976: 372)

In their comparative study of caste associations in different parts of south India, they found that, interestingly, leaders of these associations did not come from the traditional caste authorities but from 'the most enterprising of the misfits—the western educated, the lawyer, the urban businessmen, the retired government servants. These men were few in number; but they looked back over their shoulders, hoping that the rest of their community supported them and would help the misfits to establish themselves more firmly in their non-traditional careers' (ibid.: 372).

Although caste associations have continued to be important actors in politics and the community life of Indian citizens, the interest of social science research in the subject declined during the ensuing decades. More important and interesting trends emerged in Indian politics during the 1980s and 1990s, which changed the matrix of the caste-politics relation, as I have discussed below. However, before we come to that, it may be useful to also point to some other factors or processes that impacted the caste-politics relation. Perhaps the most important of these was the process of development planning initiated by the Indian state during the post-Independence period. Though 'caste' was rarely treated as a relevant variable in the visualization, designing, or administration of various developmental schemes and programmes initiated by the Indian state during the post-Independence period, they did have far-reaching implications for social and political arrangements at the local and regional levels.

One of the most important developmental initiatives taken by the Indian state soon after Independence was the introduction of land reform legislations. These legislations were designed to weaken the hold of the non-cultivating intermediaries by transferring ownership rights to the tillers of the land. Even though land reform legislations were invariably subverted by locally dominant interests, they ended up weakening the hold of the traditionally powerful but numerically small groups of upper castes (Moore 1966; Frankel and Rao 1989/1990; Jaffrelot 2000; Stern 2001). In a village in Rajasthan, for example, though the 'abolition of *jagirs*' (intermediary rights) was far from satisfactory, it made considerable difference to the overall landownership patterns, and to the local and the regional power structures. The Rajputs, traditionally upper-caste and the erstwhile landlords, possessed far less land after the land reforms than they had done before. Most of the village land had moved into the hands of those who were the tillers of land, from 'Shudra' caste categories (Chakravarti 1975: 97–8).

Other similar initiatives of the Indian state aimed at rural social change, such as the Community Development Programme (CDP), Panchayati Raj, and the Green Revolution, directly helped the rich and powerful in the village, who mostly belonged to the locally dominant castes groups, to further consolidate their hold over local and regional politics.

THE THIRD MOMENT OF CASTE: DALIT MOVEMENTS AND AFTER

As I have tried to show above, a large majority of those who led the freedom movement and inherited power from the colonial masters came from urban, upper-caste families. The rise of middle-level castes during the 1960s also meant a change in the political landscape of India. While in some regions the Congress party was able to accommodate the growing aspirations of these middle-level caste groups (see, for example, Weiner 1967; Manor 1989; Lele 1990), it could not do so everywhere (Jaffrelot 2003). It was in this context that regional politics began to acquire increasing significance. The socialist parties also played a role in making caste an issue in their struggle against the 'hegemonic' Congress party (Vora 2004).

The general election of 1967 is believed to have been the turning point in Indian politics. For the first time during the post-Independence period, the Congress party was defeated in as many as eight states. From then on, the flavour of regional politics changed significantly. While in some cases these agrarian castes formed their own political parties, elsewhere they emerged as powerful factions within the Congress party, invariably around a caste identity. Over the years, they were able to virtually oust the ritually upper castes from the arena of state/regional politics. Scholars working on Indian politics have documented this story quite well (see, for example, Nayar 1966; Kothari 1970; Frankel and Rao 1989/1990; Brass 1990; Hasan 1998; Kohli 2001; Vora and Palshikar 2004).

However, by the 1980s India began to witness new trends in the domain of caste politics. The introduction of separate quotas for the Other Backward Classes (OBCs) by the then Prime Minister, V.P. Singh, on the recommendations of the Mandal Commission in 1990 revived the question of 'caste and politics', and gave a new political legitimacy to caste, normalizing it as a mode of doing politics. However, this resurgence of caste in its new *avatar*, as Srinivas (1996) famously put it was not merely a consequence of the act of the wily politicians who, on one fine morning, decided to implement the Mandal Commission Report on reservations for 'OBCs' in an attempt to consolidate their votes. It was also not simply a case of tradition reasserting itself due to the oft-quoted weaknesses of Indian modernity. Caste appeared in a very different mode during the 1990s. In fact, some important processes that began to unfold themselves around this time expanded the meanings of democratic politics in the country.

Castes are unequal not merely in the ritual domain. Their inequalities are far more pervasive. In most of mainland rural India where caste seemingly matters more, it is also a reality that conditions social and economic relations (Chakravarti 2001). The political economy of Indian agriculture, for example, has been closely tied to caste. Thus, apart from asking questions like 'what happens to caste when it participates in modern democratic politics' or 'what happens to democracy when caste communities act like vote-banks', one should also examine the question about whose, or which caste groups', participation in politics is being talked about.

The existing formulations on the subject of caste and democracy are mostly based on the experience of middle-level caste groups (as discussed above). It was these caste groups whom Srinivas had described as the 'dominant castes' (Srinivas 1959). Although some of them were at one time quite marginal to the local power structure, they were mostly above the line of pollution, and, more significantly, had traditionally been cultivators and landowners. When electoral politics based on the principle of universal adult franchise offered them new opportunities, they were able to politicize themselves rather easily.

Notwithstanding considerable regional differences, the first three decades after Independence saw a growing consolidation of the middle-level caste groups at the local and regional levels of Indian politics. While those at the middle levels of the traditional caste hierarchy gained from the developmental process and democratic politics, those at the bottom of the caste hierarchy continued to experience social and political exclusion. In fact, in some regions, the rise of middle-level caste groups in state politics meant a stronger master to deal with for the Dalits at the local level.

Indian society and polity witnessed several shifts during the 1980s and 1990s. These shifts have also transformed the paradigm for understanding caste–politics relationships. The growing consolidation of democratic politics at the grassroots brought about some important changes in the grammar of Indian politics. Political scientists described this as a shift from the 'politics of ideology' to the 'politics of representation' (Yadav 1999; Palshikar 2004).

This shift was clearly reflected in the nature of social and political mobilizations that appeared during the 1980s. These 'new social movements' questioned the wisdom of the developmental agenda being pursued with much enthusiasm by the postcolonial state in India. The following decade saw the beginning of liberalization policies and a gradual withdrawal of the state from the sphere of economy, and eventually a disenchantment with the Nehruvian framework of development and social change (see Jodhka 2001).

Coupled with the changes in the geopolitics of the world following the collapse of the Soviet Union, the end of the Cold War, the unleashing of new technologies of telecommunications, this period also saw the beginning of a new phase in the reach of global capital. This process of 'globalization', as it came to be known, was not confined to the economy alone. It also influenced culture and politics everywhere, and opened up new possibilities for social action and networking. It was around this time that 'new' political questions like environment, gender, and human rights came up almost simultaneously in different parts of the world. Networking across national boundaries gave them a different kind of legitimacy and strength. For example, the movement against the construction of the dam across the Narmada river invested considerable amount of energy in mobilizing internal public opinion and global funding agencies against the project. Similarly, the question of human rights violations is watched and commented upon by global agencies. The question of gender rights is articulated

more or less similarly at the global level, and women's organizations working in India actively network with their counterparts in other parts of the world.

It was in this new context that the question of caste and politics began to be articulated in the language of identity politics by Dalit groups in different parts of the country. A common identity of the SCs or ex-untouchable communities was that of 'a constructed, modern identity' (Kaviraj 1997: 9) which was mobilized by a new leadership that arose from within the Dalit groups, and used the language of equality and democratic representation.

The questions of caste oppression and untouchability were first raised from below during the freedom movement by people like Jyotirao Phule and B.R. Ambedkar. Dalit groups also launched movements for dignity and development during the first half of the twentieth century (Juergensmeyer 1982; Omvedt 1994). The British colonial rulers also introduced some special provisions for the welfare of the 'depressed classes'. Following the initiatives of colonial rulers, independent India also institutionalized some special provisions for the SCs to enable them to participate in the democratic political process, and share the benefits of development through reservations or quotas in jobs and educational institutions.

Until the 1980s, the Dalit question had remained subsumed within the nationalist agenda for development. In electoral politics, too, the SC communities were mostly aligned with the 'mainstream' political formation, the Congress party. The question of autonomous Dalit politics and identity was confined to only a few pockets, in states like Maharashtra, Karnataka, or Andhra Pradesh and was largely a concern of urbanized individuals who articulated the question of Dalit identity through literature and other cultural forms (Mendelsohn and Vicziany 2000).

However, over the years the size of the Dalit middle class grew, thanks largely to the policy of reservations in government jobs and educational institutions. As they grew in numbers, they also felt more confident in articulating their experiences of discrimination at the workplace, and the continued caste-based prejudice against their communities in the society at large. They began to form separate associations of SC employees, and mobilized themselves during events of discrimination suffered by their caste fellows (Mendelsohn and Vicziany 2000). It was around this time that Ambedkar was rediscovered as a universal icon of Dalit identity and a symbol of their aspirations (Zelliot 2001).

These new developments in the larger ideological and social environment were happening at a time when rural India was experiencing disintegration in its traditional social and power arrangements. The ritually 'pure' dominant castes who had gained from the institutionalization of democratic politics and rural development programmes initiated by the Government of India during the first three decades of Independence also began to experience internal differentiation. Those in the upper segments of the rural economy began to look towards cities for further mobility (Jodhka 2006) and those at the bottom began to question their subordination. Continued experience of participation in the democratic political process over three or four decades also gave those at the bottom a sense of self-worth.

As discussed above, even though traditionally upper castes were politically marginalized with the introduction of universal adult franchise after Independence, it did not lead to a democratization of rural society. In caste terms, rural power revolved around the landowning dominant caste and in class terms, it was the rich landowners and moneylenders who continued to control the rural economy (Thorner 1956; Jodhka 2003). Independent studies by scholars from different regions tended to suggest that panchayats too became an arena of influence and power for the already dominant groups in rural India (Frankel and Rao 1989/1990).

However, more recently studies have pointed to a process of loosening of the traditional structures of power/domination. On the basis of his work in Rajasthan, Oliver Mendelsohn, for example, argued that while Srinivas was right in talking about 'dominant caste' during 1950, such a formulation made less sense in present-day rural India. The 'low caste and even untouchable villagers were now less beholden to their economic and ritual superiors than was suggested in older accounts' (Mendelsohn 1993: 808). Similarly,

'land and authority had been de-linked in village India and this amounted to an historic, if non-revolutionary transformation' (ibid.: 807).

Writing on the basis of his field experience in Karnataka, Karanth argued that the traditional association of caste with occupation was weakening, and that jajmani ties were fast disintegrating (Karanth 1996). In an extensive survey of fifty-one villages of Punjab, I too found a similar change taking place in rural Punjab, where the older structure of jajmani or *balutedari* relations had nearly completely disintegrated (Jodhka 2002). As was also argued earlier by Karanth in the case of Karnataka, with the exception of a few occupations, no longer was there any association between caste and occupation in rural Punjab. Further, Dalits in Punjab had also begun distancing themselves from the village economy, and disliked working in farms owned by local Jats. They were also trying to construct their own cultural centres like religious shrines and community halls in order to establish their autonomy in the rural power structure. In the emerging scenario, local Dalits have begun to assert for equal rights and a share of the resources that belonged commonly to the village, and had so far been in the exclusive control of the locally dominant caste groups or individual households. This new-found sense of entitlement and assertion among Dalit communities was directly responsible for the frequent caste-related conflicts and violence being reported from rural Punjab (Jodhka and Louis 2003). A study from rural Bihar also reported a similar erosion of traditional jajmani ties. Here, too, the village community's hold over the individuals' choice of occupation was virtually absent (Sahay 2004).

It is in this changed context of a combination of factors that one has to locate the new agency among Dalits. The new class of political entrepreneurs that has emerged from amongst the ex-untouchable communities used the idea of 'Dalit identity' and mobilized the SC communities as a united block on the promise of development with dignity. Some of them, such as Kanshi Ram and Mayawati, have been quite successful in doing so (Shah 2002; Pai 2002).

However, the point that emerges from the 'third moment of caste' is that caste collectivities do not participate as equals, even in modern democratic politics. Historical experience shows that different caste groups participate in democratic politics with different sets of resources. While it has become quite difficult for locally dominant groups to prohibit the traditionally marginalized caste communities from participating in the political process, this has not meant an end of social inequalities or caste and rank. Being a Dalit, or in some cases OBC, continues to be a marker of disadvantage and social exclusion. Notwithstanding the rise of autonomous Dalit politics and their substantial empowerment in some contexts/pockets of the country, the realities of caste in terms of power and dominance have not disappeared. Even when ideologically caste has weakened considerably and older forms of untouchability are receding, atrocities committed on Dalits by the locally dominant castes have in fact increased (Béteille 2000; Shah 2000). The fact that caste violence is almost always a one-way process where Dalits end up at the receiving end also says enough about the continued inequalities of caste groups. It is in this context that any analysis of caste and politics should always begin with the question: whose caste and politics are we talking about?

CASTE AND FUTURE OF CASTE POLITICS

Social science discourse on the subject of caste and democracy has indeed been able to go beyond the rather simplistic notions of modernity and democracy that guided the visions of the nationalist leadership at the time of India's Independence from colonial rule. Looking back, we can now understand that their over-enthusiastic faith in the project of modernity and change, and the belief that 'all relations active in Indian society could be erased and entirely new ones written down through a heroic, comprehensive legislative act' (Kaviraj 2000: 98) had its origin in the then prevalent flat functionalist and evolutionary notion of democracy. As has been convincingly argued by social scientists over the last three decades or so, even the ideas of tradition and modernity are of little value when presented as dichotomous categories. They tend to de-historicize the experience of change.

Notwithstanding its pan-Indian character, caste relations had divergent structures and regional

specificities. As I have tried to show elsewhere (see Jodhka 2004), even ideologically they were not completely identical. More important for us is to recognize the fact that participation in the political process does not mean the same thing for everyone. Caste, after all, is not a monolithic unit, a single static identity. As the social scientific writings on caste and politics discussed above show, caste and democratic politics can coexist and support each other, while also changing the assumed essential logic of the two. As Sudipta Kaviraj, writing in a slightly different context, argued, 'caste groups instead of crumbling with historical embarrassment, in fact, adapted themselves surprisingly well to the demands of the parliamentary politics'. Their participation in electoral politics also transformed 'the structural properties of caste in one fundamental respect: it created a democracy of castes in place of a hierarchy' (Kaviraj 2000: 103). In competitive electoral politics, what mattered for a political party was the number of votes a given caste group had, and the extent of its spatial concentration. Thus, in the Indian case 'democratic equality', the experience of participating in electoral politics, 'has mainly been translated *as equality between caste groups*, not among caste-less individuals' (ibid.: 109, emphasis added).

While it is true that in electoral politics the number of votes a particular caste group has matters much more than its ritual status in the 'traditional' hierarchy, such arguments need to be qualified. Do caste groups vote *en bloc* for a specific party or a candidate? How are cross-caste alliances worked out, making them viable for the electoral process? How do the processes of internal differentiation within caste categories—along caste, sub-caste, and class lines—influence voting behaviour and electoral outcomes? What could be the future of caste in democratic politics?

While popular interest in elections has grown, as have the sponsorships of surveys of voting behaviour, much of this is being done by and for the popular media. Although these surveys point to a positive relationship between caste and voting behaviour[2] they also show that no caste or religious community votes for a single political formation. In terms of structural variables, class and rural–urban differences also matter. Also, much more work needs to be done on the subject to evolve methodological tools that can tell us about the complex relationship of caste with electoral politics. The electoral victory of the Bahujan Samaj Party (BSP) in Uttar Pradesh in 2007 also pointed to the role of the political leadership, and their ability to build viable cross-caste alliances.

According to some commentators, it is the leaders and media experts who present/analyse electoral politics in caste terms, and make caste appear to be the single determining sociological variable in electoral politics. While the BSP is popularly seen as a political party of the Dalits and is led by a Dalit woman, in its electoral mobilizations 'it did not pay too much attention to caste arithmetic and it did very well by imaginatively bringing a coalition of interest between different groups' (Gupta 2007: 3388).

More importantly, however, such alliances, of caste-based political parties or caste communities, inevitably also end up introducing an element of fluidity in the electoral process. Apart from creating an ambiguity regarding the political strength of a particular caste group, such alliances increase the role of individual political entrepreneurs. While in the short run such a process could give the impression of a heightened sense of caste identity, in the long run it is bound to erode the logic of caste politics. At the social and economic levels, too, caste groups are undergoing processes of internal differentiation and dispersion through migration. Such processes are bound to fragment and weaken caste identity and the sentiment of caste solidarity. In other words, the future of caste in politics is anything but bright.

NOTES

1. For a useful exposition of contestations on the subject of caste among the Indian social reformers during the colonial period, and later among the leaders of the nationalist freedom movement, see Bayly (1999).

2. See, for example, the surveys carried out by the Centre for the Study of Developing Societies, New Delhi (http://www.lokniti.org).

REFERENCES

Ambedkar, B.R. 2002. 'Caste in India', in Ghanshyam Shah (ed.), *Caste and Democratic Politics in India*. New Delhi: Permanent Black, pp. 83–107.

Arnold, David, Robin Jeffrey, and James Manor. 1976. 'Caste Associations in South India: A Comparative Analysis', *Indian Economic and Social History Review*, 12(3), pp. 353–73.

Bailey, F.G. 1963. 'Closed Social Stratification in India', *European Journal of Sociology*, 4(1), pp. 107–24.

Bayly, Susan. 1999. *Caste, Society and Politics in India*. Cambridge: Cambridge University Press.

Berreman, Gerald D. 1971. 'The Brahmanical View of Caste', *Contributions to Indian Sociology* (ns), 5(1), pp. 16–25.

Béteille, A. 2000. 'The Scheduled Castes: An Inter-regional Perspective', *Journal of Indian School of Political Economy*, XII (3–4), pp. 367–80.

———. 1979. 'Homo Hierarchicus, Homo Equalis', *Modern Asian Studies*, 13(4), pp. 529–48.

———. 1970. 'Caste and Political Group Formation in Tamilnad', in Rajni Kothari (ed.), *Caste in Indian Politics*. Hyderabad: Orient Longman, pp. 245–82.

Brass, P. 1990. *The Politics of India Since Independence*. Cambridge: Cambridge University Press.

Breckenridge, C.A. and Peter van der Veer (eds). 1993. *Orientalism and the Postcolonial Predicament: Perspectives on South Asia*. Philadelphia: University of Pennsylvania Press.

Chakravarti, A. 2001. 'Caste and Agrarian Class: A View from Bihar', *Economic and Political Weekly*, XXXVI(17), pp. 1449–62.

———. 1975. *Contradiction and Change: Emerging Patterns of Authority in a Rajasthan Village*. New Delhi: Oxford University Press.

Cohn, B. 1996. *Colonialism and its Forms of Knowledge: The British in India*. Princeton: Princeton University Press.

Das, V. (ed.). 2003. 'Introduction', *Oxford India Companion to Sociology and Social Anthropology*, vol. II. New Delhi: Oxford University Press.

Dirks, N.B. 2001. *Castes of Mind: Colonialism and the Making of Modern India*. Princeton: Princeton University Press.

Dumont, L. 1998. *Homo Hierarchicus: The Caste System and its Implications*. New Delhi: Oxford University Press.

Frankel, F. and M.S.A. Rao (eds). 1989/1990. *Dominance and State Power in Modern India: Decline of a Social Order*, vols I and II. New Delhi: Oxford University Press.

Galanter, Marc. 1984. *Competing Equalities: Law and the Backward Classes in India*. New Delhi: Oxford University Press.

Ghurye, G.S. 1991. 'Features of Caste System', in D. Gupta (ed.), *Social Stratification*. New Delhi: Oxford University Press, pp. 35–48.

Ghurye, G.S. 1932. *Caste and Race in India*. London: Kegan Paul.

Gupta, D. 2007. 'When the Caste Calculus Fails: Analysing BSP's Victory in UP', *Economic and Political Weekly*, XLII(33), pp. 3388–96.

————. 1984. 'Continuous Hierarchies and Discrete Castes', *Economic and Political Weekly*, XIX(46), pp. 1955–8.

Hardgrave, R.L. 1969. *The Nadars of Tamilnad: The Political Culture of a Community in Change*. Berkley: University of California Press.

Hasan, Z. 1998. *Quest for Power: Oppositional Movements and Post-Congress Politics in Uttar Pradesh*. New Delhi: Oxford University Press.

Jaffrelot, C. 2003. *India's Silent Revolution: The Rise of Low Castes in North Indian Politics*. New Delhi: Permanent Black.

————. 2000. 'The Rise of the Other Backward Classes in the Hindi Belt', *The Journal of Asian Studies*, 59(1), pp. 86–108.

Jayal, Niraja Gopal (ed.). 2001. *Democracy in India*. New Delhi: Oxford University Press.

Jodhka, S.S. 2006. 'Beyond "Crises": Rethinking Contemporary Punjab Agriculture', *Economic and Political Weekly*, XLI(16), pp. 1530–7.

————. 2004. 'Sikhism and the Caste Question: Dalits and their Politics in Contemporary Punjab', *Contributions to Indian Sociology* (ns), 23(1&2), pp. 165–92.

————. 2003. 'Agrarian Structures and their Transformations', in Veena Das (ed.), *Oxford India Companion to Sociology and Social Anthropology*, Vol. II. New Delhi: Oxford University Press, pp. 1213–42.

————. 2002. 'Caste and Untouchability in Rural Punjab', *Economic and Political Weekly*, XXXVII(19), pp. 1813–23.

———— (ed.). 2001. *Community and Identities: Contemporary Discourses on Culture and Politics in India*. New Delhi: Sage Publications.

————. 1998. 'From "Book-View" to "Field-View": Social Anthropological Constructions of the Indian Village', *Oxford Development Studies*, 26(3), pp. 311–31.

Jodhka, S.S. and Prakash Louis. 2003. 'Caste Tensions in Punjab: Talhan and Beyond', *Economic and Political Weekly*, XXXVIII (28), pp. 2923–6.

Juergensmeyer, M. 1982. *Religious Rebels in the Punjab: The Social Vision of Untouchables*. New Delhi: Ajanta Publications.

Karanth, G.K. 1996. 'Caste in Contemporary Rural India', in M.N. Srinivas (ed.), *Caste: Its Twentieth Century Avatar*. New Delhi: Penguin, pp. 87–109.

Kaviraj, Sudipta. 2000. 'Democracy and Social Inequality', in Francine R. Frankel, Zoya Hasan, Rajeev Bhargava and Balveer Arora (eds), *Transforming India: Social and Political Dynamics of Democracy*. New Delhi: Oxford University Press, pp. 89–119.

Kaviraj, Sudipta (ed.). 1997. *Politics in India*. New Delhi: Oxford University Press.

Kohli, A. (ed.). 2001. *The Success of India's Democracy*. Cambridge: Cambridge University Press.

Kothari, Rajni. 1970. *Caste in Indian Politics*. Hyderabad: Orient Longman.

Krishna, Anirudh. 2001. 'What is Happening to Caste? A View from Some North Indian Villages', Duke: Terry Sanford Institute of Public Policy, Working Paper SAN01–04.

Lele, J. 1990. 'Caste, Class and Dominance: Political Mobilization in Maharashtra', in F. Frankel and M.S.A. Rao (eds), *Dominance and State Power in Modern India: Decline of a Social Order*, vol. II, New Delhi: Oxford University Press, pp. 115–211.

Manor, J. 1989. 'Karnataka: Caste, Class, Dominance and Politics in a Cohesive Society', in F. Frankel and M.S.A. Rao (eds), *Dominance and State Power in Modern India: Decline of a Social Order*, vol. I, New Delhi: Oxford University Press, pp. 322–61.

Mayer, Peter. 1993. 'Inventing Village Tradition: The Late 19th Century Origins of the North Indian "Jajmani System"', *Modern Asian Studies*, 27(2), pp. 357–95.

Mehta, Pratap Bhanu. 2003. *The Burden of Democracy*. New Delhi: Penguin.

Mencher, Joan. 1974. 'The Caste System Upside Down, or the Not-So-Mysterious-East', *Current Anthropology*, 15(1), pp. 469–493.

Mendelsohn, O. 1993. 'The Transformation of Authority in Rural India', *Modern Asian Studies*, 15(4), pp. 805–42.

Mendelsohn, O. and M. Vicziany. 2000. *The Untouchables: Subordination, Poverty and the State in Modern India*. Cambridge: Cambridge University Press.

Moffatt, M. 1979. *An Untouchable Community in South India*. Princeton: Princeton University Press.

Moore, B. Jr. 1966. *Social Origins of Dictatorship and Democracy: Lord and Peasant in the Making of the Modern World*. Middlesex: Penguin Books.

Nayar, B.R. 1966. *Minority Politics in the Punjab*. New Jersey: Princeton University Press.

Nehru, Jawaharlal. 1946[1992]. *The Discovery of India*. New Delhi: Oxford University Press.

Omvedt, Gail. 1994. *Dalits and the Democratic Revolution: Dr Ambedkar and the Dalit Movement in Colonial India*. New Delhi: Sage Publications.

Pai, S. 2002. *Dalit Assertion and the Unfinished Democratic Revolution: The Bahujan Samaj Party in Uttar Pradesh*. New Delhi: Sage Publications.

Palshikar, Suhas. 2004. 'Revisiting State Level Politics', *Economic and Political Weekly*, XXXIX(14–15), pp. 1477–80.

Rudolph, Lloyd I. and Susanne H. Rudolph. 1999[1967]. *The Modernity of Tradition: Political Development in India*. Hyderabad: Orient Longman.

Sahay, Gaurang R. 2004. 'Hierarchy, Difference and the Caste System: A Study of Rural Bihar', *Contributions to Indian Sociology* (ns), 23(1 and 2), pp. 113–36.

Shah, G. (ed.). 2002. *Caste and Democratic Politics in India*. New Delhi: Permanent Black.

———. 2000. 'Hope and Despair: A Study of Untouchability and Atrocities in Gujarat', *Journal of Indian School of Political Economy*, XII (3 and 4), pp. 459–72.

———. 1975. *Caste Associations and Political Process in Gujarat: A Study of Gujarat Kshatriya Sabha*. Bombay: Popular Prakashan.

Srinivas, M.N. (ed.). 1996. *Caste: Its Twentieth-Century Avatar*. New Delhi: Viking.

———. 1966. *Social Change in Modern India*. Berkley: University of California Press.

———. 1962. *Caste in Modern India and Other Essays*, Bombay: Media Promoter and Publishers.

———. 1959. 'The Dominant Caste in Rampura', *American Anthropologist*, 61(1), pp. 1–16.

Stern, R.W. 2001. *Democracy and Dictatorship in South Asia: Dominant Classes and Political Outcomes in India, Pakistan, and Bangladesh*. Cambridge: Cambridge University Press.

Thorner, D. 1956. *The Agrarian Prospects of India*, Delhi: University of Delhi Press.

Vora, Rajendra. 2004. 'Decline of Caste Majoritarianism in Indian Politics', in Rajendra Vora and Suhas Palshikar (eds), *Indian Democracy: Meanings and Practices*. New Delhi: Sage Publications, pp. 271–98.

Vora, R. and S. Palshikar (eds). 2004. *Indian Democracy: Meanings and Practices*. New Delhi: Sage Publications.

Weiner, Myron. 2001. 'The Struggle for Equality: Caste in Indian Politics', in Atul Kohli (ed.), *The Success of India's Democracy*. Cambridge: Cambridge University Press, pp. 193–225.

———. 1967. *Party Building in a New Nation: The Indian National Congress*. Chicago: Chicago University Press.

Yadav, Y. 1999. 'Electoral Politics in the Time of Change: India's Third Electoral System, 1989–99', *Economic and Political Weekly*, XXXIV(34–35), pp. 2393–9.

Zelliot, E. 2001. *From Untouchable to Dalit: Essays on the Ambedkar Movement*, 3rd edition. New Delhi: Manohar.

11 Gender and Politics

Amrita Basu

The place of women in Indian politics reflects the opportunities and constraints that are associated with its democracy. Women have been key actors in the numerous social movements and non-governmental organizations that underlie India's vibrant civil society. India's most influential, if controversial, Prime Minister was Indira Gandhi, and her daughter-in-law, Sonia Gandhi, is the major force within the Congress party today. India's President is Pratibha Patil, and several state leaders have been women, including Mayawati, who served four times as Chief Minister of Uttar Pradesh. Over a million women are represented in the three-tiered panchayats. Moreover, with the growth of a multi-party system since the early 1990s, political parties have increasingly sought women's electoral support. And yet most women continue to lack effective political power in parties and the state. Women's access to power is still mediated by their relationship to male kin, and is often indirect and symbolic. Parties have done little to provide women access to the networks and resources that would enable them to ascend the ranks of party hierarchies.

The account that follows addresses several questions concerning the relationship between women and political parties, social movements, and states. The first set of issues concerns the determinants of party success in recruiting, retaining, and promoting women. To what extent are there systematic differences between parties of the Left, Right, and Centre, and between national and regional parties in this regard? How important are differences between parties in power and those in opposition in promoting women's participation and representation? How effective are quotas in increasing women's representation within parties?

Another important question concerns the relationship between women's electoral support for particular parties and these parties' commitments to eradicate gender inequality. Parties have increasingly directed their appeals at women by addressing their distinctive interests and identities, and by involving women in electoral campaigns. At what point, if any, do parties that receive significant women's support feel compelled to represent their interests? To what extent have women's movements pressured parties to address gender inequality and to honour their pre-election commitments?

A second set of issues concerns the relationship between women's leadership and their exercise of power. A significant number of women have occupied leadership positions in India at the state and national levels. What impact have they had on women's participation in party politics during their tenure in office? What are the systemic and structural obstacles to their effectiveness?

A third issue concerns the relationships between political parties and social movements in which women have been active. While some movements have deliberately refrained from allying with political parties, others have worked closely with them. Some movements have feared that a close relationship with political parties might lead to their co-optation and deradicalization, while others have seen parties as vital to advancing women's political interests. What are the costs and benefits of each strategy? How successfully have women's movements strengthened parties' commitments to gender equality?

Parties have also allied with ethnic/religious movements, many of which have mobilized extensively among women. The intersection of party and movement-based mobilization has acquired unprecedented significance amidst the growth of ethnic and religious politics. Examples include the Bharatiya Janata Party (BJP), Telugu Desam Party (TDP), and Dravida Munnetra Kazhagam (DMK). These parties have not only viewed women as vote banks, but also made them figureheads and spokespersons for their parties, and often very militant ones at that. They have involved women in activities that break with their traditional gender roles. And yet they have generally not offered them lasting institutional power, nor rights that would increase their autonomy from their families. What explains the ability of these movements to appeal to women while undermining their interests? What implications has this had for these parties' representation of women's interests?

WOMEN AND POLITICAL PARTIES

In keeping with their core ideological commitments, the three major political parties, that is, the Congress party, BJP, and Communist Party (Marxist) [CPM], have all approached women's issues in very different ways. As a right-of-centre confessional party, the BJP has mobilized women around Hindu nationalist themes, but has interspersed these with displays of its secular commitments. As a Left-leaning secular party, the CPM has mobilized poor women around questions of poverty and redistribution. As a centrist party with historically secular, socialist leanings, Congress has claimed women's support through its commitment to minority rights and secularism. However, these parties' ideologies have not determined their positions on gender inequality. The Congress party has sacrificed and the BJP has asserted commitments to secular law and a Uniform Civil Code (UCC), in both cases on grounds of electoral expediency. All three parties have been most successful in organizing women when they have allied with social movement organizations, whether in the form of women's movements or religious organizations.

The anti-colonial movement in India entailed extensive women's mobilization, followed by substantial institutional gains. Many scholars have commented upon women's varied and extensive roles: from participation in 'terrorist' groups to non-violent civil disobedience, and from the activism of the urban middle classes to that of the rural poor. The aftermath of Independence witnessed the drafting of a Constitution which protected women from discrimination, and directed the state to work towards gender equality. Women achieved the right to vote without much of a struggle, and became active in large numbers in public and professional arenas. Most strikingly, the number of South Asian women in leadership positions is to a significant extent the result of women's involvement in nationalist movements.

For women's rights activists, the major failure of the Congress party resulted from its ambivalent stance towards secularism. When Congress tried to pass the Hindu Code Bill providing equal rights to men and women within the family in 1944, it encountered deep-rooted opposition from conservative religious groups, which viewed secular law as undermining religious and patriarchal authority. The Bill Congress passed in the mid-1950s was deeply compromised by concessions to this opposition. Its secular commitments further

declined in the mid-1980s around the infamous
Shah Bano issue. An elderly Muslim woman sought
maintenance from her husband under the Indian Penal
Code. When a judge ruled in her favour, the orthodox
Muslim community vigorously opposed his decision,
and then Prime Minister Rajiv Gandhi placated them
by passing the so-called Muslim Women's Protection
of Rights in Divorce Act in 1986, which denied
Muslim women the right to demand maintenance
from their husbands beyond a three-month period.
To the extent that women's rights were inextricably
linked to the secular democratic framework, a growing
chasm developed between the Congress party and the
women's movement.

The undivided Communist Party, and, after its
split in 1964, the Communist Party of India (CPI)
and the CPM, had strong women's organizations
that mobilized women. However, until the early
1980s, these organizations were unequivocal in
subordinating gender to class inequality. The growth
of the autonomous women's movement, followed by
the growth of the religious right, led some Communist
activists to raise questions of gender inequality more
forcefully. The National Federation of Indian Women
(NFIW), which was affiliated with the CPI, became
more active and in 1981, the CPM formed the All
India Democratic Women's Association (AIDWA).
Unlike its predecessors, AIDWA accepted members
who were not affiliated to the CPM, collaborated
actively with autonomous women's groups, and
addressed violence against women.

Women have also played extremely important
roles in Hindu nationalism. First, they are among
the movement's most extraordinary orators. In its
most militant phase in the late 1980s and early
1990s, Vijayraje Scindia, Uma Bharati, and Sadhvi
Rithambara were at the forefront of the movement.
Indeed, according to a PUDR report, Uma
Bharati and Sadhvi Rithambara were in Ayodhya
in December 1992, goading mobs to destroy
the mosque. Their voices on cassettes that the
government banned were filled with vicious anti-
Muslim propaganda and injunctions to violence.

This association of women and violence is not
confined to the leadership level. Thousands of 'ordinary'
women have been associated with violent Hindu

nationalist campaigns. The Durga Vahini, the women's
organization affiliated with the Vishwa Hindu Parishad
(VHP), and the Rashtriya Sevika Samiti, the women's
wing of the Rashtriya Swayamsevak Sangh (RSS), train
women to use rifles and wield *lathis*. According to a
PUDR report these women's organizations have played
an important role in the many riots that have taken
place since the early 1990s. They have directed Hindu
mobs towards Muslim localities, prevented the police
from aiding Muslim families, and engaged in post-riot
looting of homes and shops. In Gujarat in 2002, Hindu
women's organizations either failed to prevent the
violence, or participated in it.

In contrast to the VHP and RSS, the BJP
has presented itself as an advocate of secularism,
democracy, and women's rights. It has taken a strong
stand in favour of the UCC, which would extend
the same rights to men and women regardless
of their religious backgrounds. It has expressed
a commitment to reservations for women in
Parliament. It has condemned sexual violence
and supported the creation of more employment
opportunities for women.

Indeed, there are striking similarities between
the 2004 election platforms (see Table 11.1) of the
BJP and the Congress party. The BJP-led National
Democratic Alliance (NDA) manifesto promised
to unveil a National Policy on Women's Economic
Empowerment, which would ensure means of
livelihood for all women and increase the incomes of
all working women. It committed itself to a national
childcare plan, workplace flexibility, greater career
opportunities, and hostels for working women in
every town, and the removal of gender disparities in
education, wages, and property rights. It promised to
promote female self-employment and entrepreneurship.
It pledged to enforce laws against female foeticide,
dowry, child marriage, trafficking, rape, and family
violence. It guaranteed introducing a Bill to reserve 33
per cent seats for women in the Parliament and state
legislatures in the first session of Parliament.

The Congress party manifesto was similar. It also
proposed 33 per cent reservations for women in the
Parliament, legislation curbing dowry, raising the
age of marriage, and improving widows' conditions.
It supported the creation of micro-credit schemes

and producer cooperatives. In addition, it devoted more attention than the BJP to decentralization through the panchayats and to complete legal equality for women. This includes giving women an equal share in matrimonial property and equal rights of ownership over assets. Although the Congress manifesto devoted more attention to women than the NDA manifesto, the BJP would have supported all of its provisions in principle.

Not all of the BJP's positions or actions on women's issues are conservative. This lack of consistency is also evident in the BJP itself. Although the BJP closely aligned itself with the VHP on the temple issue in the early 1990s, it has not articulated a position on questions that many fundamentalists consider vital in developing a coherent worldview: how to govern the economy, reform the legal system, and create a religious state.

The BJP's relatively liberal positions on women's rights are in part a product of electoral exigencies. Particularly during the early period of its ascent in the 1980s, BJP was especially keen to distinguish itself from the Congress party. Its support for the UCC in the 1990s was in part a response to Rajiv Gandhi's handling of the Shah Bano issue. It signalled that unlike Congress, which was swayed by religious fundamentalists, the BJP was committed to secularism. Expediency has also meant that the positions the BJP women's organization assumes are often inconsistent. It is difficult to identify a single one of the vital issues

before the women's movement—dowry, sati, female foeticide—on which the BJP Mahila Morcha holds a unified position. Like all political parties, it also makes certain promises that it does not keep. For example, it did not implement reservations for women, which it pledged to do at election time.

The contradictions between the BJP's various positions are best explained by its combined party and movement identities. As a political party, the BJP is guided by an electoral logic that has entailed extending its base from upper-caste, upper-class men to include women and lower-caste groups. However, through its connection with the RSS and the VHP, the BJP also seeks legitimacy on the basis of a militant movement identity. The BJP-affiliated women's organization, the Mahila Morcha, is responsible for electoral campaigns, whereas the Rashtriya Sevika Samiti, which is affiliated with the RSS, and the Durga Vahini, which is affiliated with the VHP, refrain from direct involvement in party politics. Their work entails educating girls and women in the principles of Hindu nationalism.

ELECTIONS

Women's voting rates increased from 37 per cent in 1952 to a high of 68 per cent in 1984; they fell to 47 per cent in 1991(Kumari and Kidwai 1998: 2). However, women are under-represented in Parliament (Fig. 11.1), and in higher level decision-making bodies. The representation of women in Parliament

Table 11.1: Major Party Election Results

	1991		1996		1998		1999		2004				2009	
	%	SEATS	%	SEATS	%	SEATS	%	SEATS	%	SEATS			%	SEATS
Congress	37.3	225	29	143	25.4	140	28.4	112	26.69	145[a]	UPA		48.3	262
BJP & Allies	19.9	119	24	193	36.2	250	41.3	296	35.91	189	(Only) Congress		37.9	206
Janata	10.8	55	Joined with UF		Joined with UF		1	1	Joined with Congress		NDA (Only) BJP		30 21.4	161 116
United Front	–	–	31	180	20.9	98	–	–	–	–	(Only) Janta Dal United		3.7	20
Communists[b]	–	48	Joined with UF		Joined with UF		5.4	32	7.0	53	Left Parties		4.4	24
Others							23.9	107	19.9	78	Fourth Front (Allied with UPA)		4.2	23
											Others		13.4	73

Source: *India Today*, 15 July 1991, 16 March 1998; *Economic Times* website, *economictimes.indiatimes.com*; and *The Hindu*, 20 May 2004
Notes: [a]The more relevant figures in 2004 for Congress and allies were 35.82 and 219, respectively
[b]Includes both the CPM and the CPI

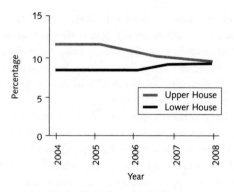

Figure 11.1: Women in Parliament

Source: Women in Parliaments World Classification. http://www.
ipu.org/wmn-e/arc/classif300908.htm.

has not increased much from the 4.4 per cent (or 22
women) in the first Parliament (1952–7) to 8.8 per
cent (48 women) in the 1998 elections, to 8.3 per cent
(45 women) in 2004.

Political parties' record in nominating women to
run for political office is very poor. As Tables 11.2 and
11.3 demonstrate, the number of women candidates
that political parties have nominated to run for office
was low throughout the 1980s and the 1990s when
the women's movement was extremely active. With the
decline of the Congress and the growth of the BJP, a
major party realignment was underway. The percentage
of women candidates from all parties was 4.5 per cent
in 1984, and increased in the intervening elections
to 7.6 per cent in 1999. The proportion of female

candidates who were elected, 8.9 per cent in 1999, was
hardly greater than that in 1984, at 8.2 per cent.

The data in Tables 11.2, 11.3, and 11.4 highlights
the extent to which women's under-representation in
political office results from party biases, for women
are much more likely to be elected than men. In 1999,
women constituted 7.6 per cent of all candidates,
and 23.3 per cent of all candidates who were elected.
Women were thus three times more likely than men
to be elected. Similarly, in the preceding elections
in 1984, 1989, 1991, 1996, and 1998, women were
two or three times as likely as men to be elected. The
relatively small number of women in political office is
thus more a reflection of biases on the part of parties
than that of the electorate. It may be that parties only
ran women in elections they considered winnable. If
they felt that the electorate was less likely to vote for
a woman, all else being equal, it made sense to run
women in seats where victory was more likely. That
61.8 per cent of women candidates were elected in
1984 fits with this explanation.

In 1999, 7.6 per cent of all candidates and 8.9
per cent of all elected candidates were women. The
second and third columns from the right make it clear
that women are somewhat more likely to be elected
than men, but this gap is decreasing over time (most
likely because parties are running women in less safe
constituencies; see Table 11.2).

Both Congress and the BJP claim to be strong
advocates of reserving a third of the seats in

Table 11.2: Proportions of Male and Female Candidates of All Political Parties

ELECTION YEAR	PERCENTAGE OF ALL CANDIDATES WHO WERE MEN (EXCLUDING ALL INDEPENDENTS)	PERCENTAGE OF ALL CANDIDATES WHO WERE WOMEN (EXCLUDING ALL INDEPENDENTS)	PERCENTAGE OF ELECTED CANDIDATES WHO WERE MEN (EXCLUDING ALL INDEPENDENTS)	PERCENTAGE OF ELECTED CANDIDATES WHO WERE WOMEN (EXCLUDING ALL INDEPENDENTS)	PERCENTAGE OF ALL CANDIDATES WHO WERE ELECTED (EXCLUDING ALL INDEPENDENTS)	PERCENTAGE OF WOMEN CANDIDATES WHO WERE ELECTED (EXCLUDING ALL INDEPENDENTS)	PERCENTAGE OF MALE CANDIDATES WHO WERE ELECTED (EXCLUDING ALL INDEPENDENTS)	PERCENTAGE OF INDEPENDENT CANDIDATES WHO WERE WOMEN
1984	95.5	4.5	91.8	8.2	33.5	61.8	32.2	2.5
1989	95.3	4.7	94.4	5.6	21.1	25.0	20.9	2.2
1991	95.1	4.9	92.1	7.9	16.9	27.2	16.4	2.8
1996	94.7	5.3	92.5	7.5	16.1	22.9	15.7	4.0
1998	93.1	6.9	92.2	7.8	18.9	21.3	18.8	4.0
1999	92.4	7.6	91.1	8.9	19.9	23.3	19.6	4.0
2004	92.2	7.8	91.6	8.4	17.6	18.9	17.5	4.9

Table 11.3: Proportion of All Candidates and Elected Candidates of All Political Parties

ELECTION YEAR	PERCENTAGE OF ALL CANDIDATES WHO WERE WOMEN	PERCENTAGE OF ALL CANDIDATES WHO WERE ELECTED	PERCENTAGE OF ALL ELECTED CANDIDATES WHO WERE WOMEN	PERCENTAGE OF ALL WOMEN CANDIDATES WHO WERE ELECTED	PERCENTAGE OF ELECTED CANDIDATES WHO WERE WOMEN (EXCLUDING ALL INDEPENDENTS)	PERCENTAGE OF ALL ELECTED CANDIDATES WHO WERE WOMEN (EXCLUDING ALL INDEPENDENTS)	PERCENTAGE OF WOMEN CANDIDATES WHO WERE ELECTED (EXCLUDING INDEPENDENTS)	PERCENTAGE OF INDEPENDENT CANDIDATES WHO WERE WOMEN
1984	3.0	9.7	8.2	25.9	4.5	8.2	61.8	2.5
1989	3.2	8.6	5.5	14.6	4.7	5.6	25.0	2.2
1991	3.6	6.2	7.9	13.7	4.9	7.9	27.2	2.8
1996	4.3	3.9	7.4	6.7	5.3	7.5	22.9	4.0
1998	5.8	11.4	7.9	15.7	6.9	7.8	21.3	4.0
1999	6.1	11.7	9.0	17.3	7.6	8.9	23.3	4.0
2004	6.5	10.0	8.2	12.6	4.4	8.3	18.9	(no data)

Table 11.4: The BJP

ELECTION YEAR	NO. OF CANDIDATES	NO. OF CANDIDATES ELECTED	NO. OF WOMEN CANDIDATES	NO. OF WOMEN CANDIDATES	PERCENTAGE OF CANDIDATES WHO WERE	PERCENTAGE OF ALL CANDIDATES WHO WERE	PERCENTAGE OF WOMEN CANDIDATES	PERCENTAGE OF ELECTED CANDIDATES	AVERAGE MARGIN OF DEFEAT FOR WOMEN CANDIDATES
1984	224	2	9	0	0.9	4.0	0.0	0.0	32.2
1989	225	85	10	5	37.8	4.4	50.0	5.9	16.6
1991	477	120	26	8	25.2	5.5	30.8	6.7	42.5
1996	471	161	27	14	34.2	5.7	51.9	8.7	14.7
1998	388	182	32	15	46.9	8.2	46.9	8.2	15.4
1999	339	182	25	15	53.7	7.4	60.0	8.2	6.0
2004	364	138	30	10	8.2	37.9	33	7.2	(no data)

Table 11.5: The Congress Party

ELECTION YEAR	NO. OF CANDIDATES	NO. OF CANDIDATES ELECTED	NO. OF WOMEN CANDIDATES	PERCENTAGE OF WOMEN CANDIDATES	PERCENTAGE OF ALL CANDIDATES WHO WERE	PERCENTAGE OF CANDIDATES WHO WERE	PERCENTAGE OF WOMEN CANDIDATES	PERCENTAGE OF ELECTED CANDIDATES	AVERAGE MARGIN DEFEAT FOR WOMEN CANDIDATE
1984	491	404	39	37	82.3	7.9	94.9	9.2	0.3
1989	510	197	56	15	38.6	11.0	26.8	7.6	13.3
1991	502	244	48	21	48.6	9.6	43.8	8.6	8.3
1996	529	140	49	16	26.5	9.3	32.7	11.4	12.5
1998	477	141	38	10	29.6	8.0	26.3	7.1	16.1
1999	453	114	51	14	25.2	11.3	27.5	12.3	13.5
2004	417	145	45	12	10.8	7.8	26.7	8.3	(no data)

Source: For 2004 data: 'Statistical Report on General Elections, 2004 to the 14th Lok Sabha', Election Commission of India, accessed online: http://eci.nic. in/statistical Report ICS 2004/vol/LS2004.pdf. Also Rana (2006).

Parliament for women. 'We want to field more women candidates but there are few of them,' BJP President Venkaiah Naidu claimed (Singh 2003). However, the data does not bear out Naidu's contention that women do not win elections. As Table 11.4 shows, the BJP's record of nominating women to run for elections has been unimpressive. Women formed only 5.7 per cent of its candidates in 1996, 8.2 per cent in 1998, and 7.4 per cent in 1999. Women, however, were much more likely than men to be elected. The percentage of women candidates who were elected was 51.9 per cent in 1996, 46.9 per cent in 1998, and 60 per cent in 1999. The most likely explanation for the greater success of BJP women is that Congress was more willing to run female candidates in contests where the party was not confident of winning.

Compared to the BJP, the Congress party (Table 11.5) has fielded more women candidates and their performance has been less impressive. The percentage of Congress candidates who were women was 7.9 per cent in 1984, and then hovered between 9–11 per cent between 1989 and 1999. The Congress party nominated more women than the BJP in every election. However, a larger proportion of women candidates were elected from the BJP than from the Congress. Between a quarter and a half of all female Congress party candidates were elected, compared to 52–60 per cent of BJP women candidates. Since the Congress nominated a larger number of female candidates than the BJP, the total number of women Members of Parliament (MPs) is not strikingly different for the BJP and the Congress. However, this figure masks the significantly different rates of electoral success among women from the two parties.

For the 2004 elections, women constituted 3541 out of 5435 contestants. Party nominations of women for political office were consistent with previous years. Women formed 8.24 per cent (39 out of 334) of BJP candidates, 10.79 (45 of 372) of Congress candidates, and 11.59 per cent (eight out of 61) of CPM candidates.

WOMEN'S MOVEMENTS

The major phases of social movement activism in the post-Independence period preceded and then followed

Indira Gandhi's declaration of a state of national Emergency (1975–7). A wide range of movements emerged, opposing deforestation, the violation of tribal land rights, the mistreatment of slum dwellers, and the oppression of the lower castes. Women and questions of gender inequality were at the forefront of these movements. During this same period, numerous urban feminist organizations were formed autonomously from political parties. They included the Samata Manch (Equality Forum), Stree Sangharsh Samiti (Women's Struggle Committee), Stree Mukti Sangathan (Women's Freedom Organization), Feminist Network Collective, Stree Shakti Sangathan (Women's Power Organization), Purogami Sangathan (Forward Stepping Organization), the Forum against Oppression of Women, Saheli, the Progressive Organization of Women, the Women's centre, Kali for Women, and Manushi. Their primary concerns included violence against women, as manifest in 'dowry deaths', the rape of women by the police and security forces, and domestic violence.

Urban feminist groups were fiercely committed to retaining their autonomy from political parties to prevent the lure of resources, influence, and power from blunting their radicalism. While largely retaining their autonomy from parties and staying out of the electoral domain, they worked closely with the courts and the bureaucracy. The grassroots movements with which women were closely associated were those of the poorest and most marginal groups (tribals, the landless poor, slum dwellers, subsistence agriculturalists), which generally had little electoral clout and no electoral aspirations. The urban feminist movement was primarily drawn to non-electoral issues like violence against women.

Correspondingly, the most important gains that women achieved were in the courts and the bureaucracy, not in the electoral arena. The government appointed women to some key posts and created the National Commission on the Status of Women to investigate women's conditions and make recommendations. Struggles that got lodged in the courts often remained there for a long time, legal battles diverted women's attention from grassroots struggles, and the focus on rights was associated with the narrow construction of women's interests and identities (Menon 2000). Nonetheless, these battles provided women with arenas within the state in which they could seek redress.

By contrast, both grassroots movements and the feminist movement put less effort into electoral politics and had less of an impact on it. Unlike a range of other social movements, the women's movement played a relatively small role in the two crucial elections that removed the Congress party from power (in 1977 and 1986). In 1977, the Gandhian Socialist leader Jayaprakash Narayan organized the movement for total democracy that ultimately brought about the downfall of the Congress and the election of the Janata party. A decade later, V.P. Singh resigned from the Congress and formed the Jan Morcha (Peoples' Front), an avowedly 'non-political' movement which brought new groups into politics and helped bring the National Front to power in 1989. It was during this period that the women's movement began to interact more closely with political parties and the state. In 1996, women's organizations met and formed the National Alliance of Women, which lobbied political parties to allocate more tickets for women to contest the parliamentary elections, and demanded that parties and the Parliament unconditionally implement 33 per cent reservation of seats for women. Its other demands included: 33–50 per cent allocation of seats at all levels in decision-making bodies, from the panchayats to the Lok Sabha, for women; the public declaration of assets of political candidates; right to recall elected members; and the right to information that affects all people.

The past two decades have witnessed a confluence of two trends: on the one hand attempts by political parties to foster closer ties to social movements and non-governmental organizations, and on the other, the attempt by some feminists to work with parties and the state. As one scholar argues, women cannot easily give up on the state because it will not give up on women (Randall 1998: 204). The attempt to achieve greater power within the state may represent both a positive response to the state's invitation and a defensive attempt to safeguard the gains women have achieved. Many activists have expressed frustration that the protest tactics they had pursued for so long had not yielded better results.

The most important instance of collaboration between women's organizations and the state has

occurred around the issue of reservations for women in local government. Women's representation on the three-tiered panchayats in the rural areas provides an important case study of both the modest gains and serious constraints that surround women's increased representation in local governing bodies. They also suggest the different costs and benefits to women of a strategy that relies on the state, as opposed to one that relies on political parties.

The enactment of the Constitutional Amendments (Seventy-third and Seventy-fourth) providing 33 per cent reservation for women to the three tiers of local self-government (*panchayati raj* system) represented a milestone in the process of decentralization. The Seventy-third Amendment Act made the *gram sabha* (village assembly), comprising all adult villagers, the focal point of village governance. The amendments contain provisions for the reservation of 33 per cent of elective seats for women in the village, block, and district councils (Seventy-third Amendment) and an equal number in the urban municipal councils (Seventy-fourth Amendment). As a result, an estimated five million women entered local politics directly or indirectly in the last ten years. India's population consists of 15 per cent Scheduled Castes (SCs) and 7.5 per cent Scheduled Tribes (STs). Consequently, 22.5 per cent of seats are reserved for them, out of which one-third are for women. The reservation of seats in each state is proportional to their population. The reservation of seats for women, SCs, and STs applies also to office bearers, so that one-third of *sarpanch*s (heads of panchayats) must be women.

As regards urban local bodies, the Seventy-fourth Amendment now provides three types of institutions of urban self-government with one-third reservation of seats for women. These are, first, *nagar* (town) panchayats for areas that have both rural and urban features. Second, for smaller urban settlements, provision is made for municipal councils, and third, for larger urban areas, municipal corporations. Municipalities with large areas contain wards (section of the village). The first elections for the three tiers of urban local bodies were held in most states in 1994–5. While women's role in the village councils has been well researched, there is a dearth of material on the female elected representatives of the local urban bodies.

The state panchayat laws do not provide for a formal involvement of political parties in elections to village panchayats, except in the three states of Kerala, Tripura, and West Bengal. It is often difficult for women to win panchayat elections without support from a political party. However, most parties are disinterested in panchayat elections at the local level. The TDP in Andhra Pradesh, BJP, and the Janata Dal (JD) prefer party involvement in elections to higher-level panchayats. The CPM is the exception to this rule, for it has been actively involved in panchayat elections at the local level in Kerala and West Bengal. The record of most political parties in supporting women candidates for panchayat elections has been poor.

Women's participation in the panchayats is constrained by a dearth of financial resources, the lack of independent staffing, and reliance on an uncooperative bureaucracy. The key functionaries, namely the secretaries, are state government employees, and they often fail to appear at panchayat meetings, so that meetings must be postponed. There are innumerable occasions when women sarpanches have to visit the panchayat samiti office to get schemes implemented and encounter condescension by the bureaucracy. Bureaucratic regulation and surveillance undermines the authority of women sarpanches.

The Constitutional Amendment Act (Article 243 G) is vague about the extent to which the state can usurp the panchayats' power. Reluctant to abdicate their power, legislators at the national and state levels have suspended the functioning of panchayats and exercised vigilant control over them. Despite the constitutional provisions mandating elections at all levels of the panchayats every five years (Article 293 B), elections to the panchayat are erratic.

A major impediment to women's effective exercise of power in the panchayats is the growing violence, harassment, and corruption that pervade the political process. Violence and killings, especially against Dalit women, have been on the rise. Sukhiya Bai, a tribal woman sarpanch from the Betul district of Madhya Pradesh, was harassed to such an extent that she committed suicide by pouring kerosene over herself on 11 February 2003 (Panchayati Raj [PR] update, March 2003). Young Suman Mahajan Karkale, a Dalit woman sarpanch from the Nanded

district of Maharashtra, was faced with character assassination and intimidation to prevent her from carrying out her functions. Despite her representation to the CEO of Nanded division, she has not received any redress (PR update, August 2002). Men from her village physically attacked S. Ponni, a female panchayat member from Kancheepuram district in Tamil Nadu because she questioned the panchayat President (Tambiah 2002).

To what extent have women panchayat members acquired a sustained commitment to political participation? A longitudinal study in two districts in Haryana and one district in Rajasthan showed that in the two elections of 1994 and 2000, the overall percentage of women who won the elections was less than 33 per cent. In the second round, only 30 per cent of the earlier number re-contested the polls in the de-reserved seats (given the rotation of constituencies). Nearly all the women said that the de-reservation of seats was a major reason for their not contesting the elections again. They feared that in unreserved seats, money, muscle power, and the vested interests of the liquor and drug mafia would all work against them. The small numbers of women who did contest elections in reserved or partially reserved seats for caste constituencies demonstrated increased confidence, and were ready to take on elections to the state legislative assemblies (Kaushik 2004).

There are no nationwide studies of the impact of the panchayat reforms on women. Most of the available data examines the local and to some extent the state level and the mixed results across states in part reflect the different cultural and political environments of these states. These studies suggest that the most promising aspect of panchayat reforms is that women have acquired resources and the development of skills, which have enabled them to excel in managing development. They have been able to articulate their priorities for basic needs and amenities such as food, drinking water, schools, healthcare centres, roads, and security. Two detailed village surveys carried out in two districts, Birbhum in West Bengal and Udaipur in Rajasthan, found that women invest more than men in projects that meet community needs, which are for water and roads in West Bengal and water in Rajasthan (Chattopadhyay and Duflo 2004). In West Bengal, the panchayats are authorized to establish informal education centres. In Rajasthan, while the panchayats can spend money on local infrastructure, they cannot run schools as in West Bengal.

In rural Punjab, over 4500 women heading 2446 panchayats have a common minimum programme: to work for the uplift of weaker sections of society, adult literacy, pensions for the aged and the poor, better education and healthcare facilities, and the development of their villages in their five-year term (*Grassroots* Sept. 2003). Another success story is the Belandur gram panchayat in Karnataka, where six out of twelve members are women. It is estimated that collections of local taxes have risen more than seven times. With the devolution of responsibility to the panchayats, the cost of the delivery of government services has gone down significantly, and a system of transparency and accountability has developed.

Women panchayat members have also taken up questions of gender inequality in many places. In UP, 100 village leaders have banned the practice of giving or demanding dowry (*Grassroots* Sept. 2003). In Akola district in Maharashtra, an all-women panchayat had the only liquor shop of the village closed down as it was resulting in the men of the village returning home drunk and beating their wives. In Himachal Pradesh in the Kherian Gram Panchayat of Kangra, a woman sarpanch put an end to the practice of female foeticide by imposing a penalty of Rs 500 on anyone guilty of the practice. Other panchayats have followed suit.

In Madhya Pradesh, the Institute of Social Sciences, New Delhi, awarded a woman sarpanch in Jamunia taluk in district Sehore the 'Outstanding Woman Panchayat Leader Award' for 2003. Her other achievements included providing women with land rights, distributing land to ninety-five couples under a housing scheme, and ensuring that the documents were in the woman's name. In Orissa, the Narayanpur gram panchayat under the leadership of its sarpanch Rajeshwari Rao passed a resolution banning child marriage. Even families who had performed child marriages before the ban was put in place were not spared—the adults responsible were required to pay a fine of Rs 1000, to be used for the children's education. Those who attend a child marriage

ceremony or support it in any way were rendered ineligible for any post in the panchayat (PR update July 2000).

If there has been resistance to women's representation in the panchayats at the local level, there has been much greater resistance to reservations for women at the national level. There has been a great deal of debate within both the women's movement and political parties about the desirability of reservations for women in the legislative assembly and Parliament. The urban feminist movement largely supports reservations, while political parties have been ambivalent. However, the former does not hold uniform positions on the form the Bill should take and the strength of feminists does not rival the influence of political parties.

Three successive governments, dating back to 1996, have supported the Eighty-first Amendment Bill guaranteeing at least 33 per cent reserved seats for women in Parliament and the legislative assembly. However, although most political parties have endorsed the Bill in their election manifestos, they have not supported its passage in Parliament. It was defeated in 1996, 1998, 1999, and 2000, when a range of parties expressed either ambivalence or opposition to it. As a compromise measure, the then Home Minister, L.K. Advani, supported the Chief Election Commissioner's proposal to require all political parties to reserve 33 per cent of seats for women contestants. Critics fear that political parties will nominate women in unwinnable constituencies. As we have seen, thus far parties' records in nominating women candidates have been poor. Women constitute only 10–12 per cent of the membership of political parties (Rai 1997: 105). The Congress-led national government has committed itself to the passage of the Bill, which was debated in the upper house of Parliament in 2008; however, many parties remain opposed to its passage.

There has been far more resistance offered to state- and national-level reservations for women by political parties than by the broad public. A survey by *India Today* indicates that 75 per cent of women and 79 per cent men favour the active participation of women in politics, and 75 per cent of both men and women favour reservations in legislative bodies (cited in Rai and Sharma 2000: 159). Interestingly, many parties have opposed the Bill on the grounds that it does not take account of caste inequality. The Janata Dal, Rashtriya Janata Dal (Lalu Prasad Yadav), Samajvadi Janata Party, and Bahujan Samaj Party have all opposed the Bill, because it makes no provision for reservations on a caste basis for Other Backward Classes (OBCs).

The women's movement largely supports the Bill. Vasanth and Kalpana Kannabiran, two prominent activists, argue that it is important to look beyond the actions of the elites who have supported the Eighty-first Amendment:

> ...at a deeper level, the reason why this negligible group is able to speak out so loud and clear is because masses of underprivileged women have a far more important political presence that over runs and refuses to be contained by the vote bank politics of mainstream parties. (Kannabiran and Kannabiran 1997: 197)

Opposition to the Eighty-first Amendment Bill from some segments of the women's movement partly reflects a distrust of political parties. One worry is that quotas could form a ceiling rather than a minimum; another is that women candidates might be pliable because of their dependence on male party leaders (Kishwar 1996: 2867–74). An even more significant worry is that reservations treat women like a homogeneous group, which increases the likelihood of the 'biwi (wife) brigade' of educated, upper-class, upper-caste women being elected, particularly because the Bill does not provide for sub-quotas of OBCs (Menon 2000; Raman 1995).

WOMEN'S LEADERSHIP

Women who have been elected to Parliament without the support of an organized constituency have been few in number, and relatively ineffective in challenging gender inequality. The representation of women in Parliament has not increased much from the 4.7 per cent (or 22 women) in the first Parliament (1952–7). The largest number ever was the 8.1 per cent (44 women) who were elected in the 1984 elections. Forty-nine women were elected to Parliament between 1991 and 1996 (5.2 per cent). Women occupied 4.1 per cent of the 22 per cent of parliamentary seats that

were reserved for SCs. Two women MPs were from the STs; most of them were upper caste. Women MPs are disproportionately educated and affluent compared to the general female population.

The power of women MPs is generally very limited. They are expected to strictly adhere to party policy with respect to women, and none of them have placed questions concerning gender inequality high on their agendas. Although they have regular contact with women's wings of political parties and with the party leadership on issues regarding the family, they do not have much to do with autonomous women's organizations.

The women's movement has even fewer links with women who command political power. Consider the roles of some women who have emerged as power brokers within Indian politics today. They include the Italian-born Sonia Gandhi, who was positioned to become Prime Minister in 2004; Jayaram Jayalalitha, who heads the regionally based AIADMK and is the former Chief Minister of the southern state of Tamil Nadu; Sheila Dikshit, Chief Minister of Delhi; Vasundhara Raje, former Chief Minister of Rajasthan; Uma Bharati, former Chief Minister of Madhya Pradesh; Mamata Banerjee, the head of the Trinamul Congress party of West Bengal; Mayawati, four times Chief Minister of UP; and Rabri Devi, the former Chief Minister of Bihar. Three of these women, Gandhi, Jayalalitha, and Mayawati, were directly responsible for the downfall of Bharatiya Janata Party governments. Following the 2003 Assembly elections, which brought five women Chief Ministers to power (Dikshit, Raje, Bharati, Jayalalitha, and Rabri Devi), women governed over half the country.

All these women, with the possible exceptions of Mayawati and Uma Bharati, rose to power as appendages to men rather than through movements or institutional channels. Rabri Devi only emerged from her role as housewife and mother of nine children when her husband was imprisoned, and she replaced him as the Chief Minister of Bihar. Sheila Dikshit rode to power on the coat-tails of her powerful father-in-law, Uma Shankar Dikshit. Vasundhara Raje Scinida is the daughter of Vijayaraje Scindia and is of royal lineage; Jayalalitha was the mistress of actor-turned-politician M.G. Ramachandran, whom she succeeded as Chief

Minister of Tamil Nadu. Sonia Gandhi is the widow of former Prime Minister Rajiv Gandhi and the daughter-in-law of former Prime Minister Indira Gandhi. Sonia Gandhi's popularity precipitated a backlash against her. The BJP engaged in a vicious smear campaign that directed attention to her foreign origins, leading Sonia Gandhi to withdraw her candidacy for prime ministership, though she remains a major force behind the scenes. These women have demonstrated extraordinary ambition and skill in acquiring the power they have achieved. Nonetheless women experience more constraints than men in gaining political power.

Thus, while India's women leaders may be important symbols of the nation, in the absence of support from organized movements they have not become powerful in their own right. In such a scenario, their connections to male family members assume paramount importance. Nor do these women share common values, ideas, or agendas. Their role in bringing down governments may be as close as they will ever come to collaborating. Their deepest commitments are to their parties and to themselves, not to the collective interests of women.

And yet, there is also enormous opportunity in a possible alliance between the women's movement, as it seeks out a national presence and a role in the state, and the small number of party women who are staking out independent positions. It is precisely such an alliance that is needed to address the problem that Gail Omvedt identifies when she describes the women's movement as anti-political (Omvedt 1993: 310).There is no question that the farmers' movement and caste-based, ethnic, and religious nationalist movements have all had a much bigger impact than the women's movement on electoral politics. The question of how to engage in elections selectively and creatively poses an important challenge for the women's movement.

As a general matter, the stronger the democratic institutions and practices, the greater the opportunities this affords individual women to achieve representation, and women's movements to work with the party system. High levels of women's activism in democratic settings is an index of the strength of both political parties and women's movements, which have often pressured political parties to increase women's representation and address gender inequality. Many feminist demands assume the existence of a democratic framework that includes an independent judiciary, an accountable state, and a representative Parliament.

Unlike most nations in South Asia, and indeed in the postcolonial world, India has enjoyed a long history of strong, legitimate institutions, numerous and varied political parties, and regular, open elections. This has enabled a strong women's movement to emerge and endure without incurring state repression. The women's movement has played a critical role in bringing questions of gender inequality before the courts, bureaucracy, and, increasingly, political parties. With the growth of a multi-party system and the rise of the BJP, the women's movement has sought alliances with Left and democratic parties. Conversely, women have also become an increasingly important constituency for political parties.

However, if, from feminists' perspective, democracy is part of the solution, it is also part of the problem. First, the alliance between certain civil society groups and political parties has also led parties to co-opt the demands of autonomous women's groups. The willingness of the BJP to take up the UCC has led the women's movement to drop the demand. Moreover, civil society not only gives rise to feminist and human rights movements, but also to chauvinist ethnic and religious nationalist movements, which have strong ties to parties. Thus democratization may paradoxically be linked to the growth of anti-democratic movements, which effectively mobilize women without advancing their interests. This is one of the critical challenges that women's movements must confront in the years to come.

REFERENCES

Chattopadhyay, Raghabendra and Esther Duflo. 2004. 'Impact of Reservation in Panchayati Raj: Evidence from a Nationwide Randomized Experiment', *Economic and Political Weekly*, XXIX(9), pp. 976–86.

Grassroots. 2003. New Delhi: Press Institute of India.

Kannabiran, Vasanth and Kalpana Kannabiran. 1997. 'From Social Action to Political Action: Women and the 81st Amendment', *Economic and Political Weekly*, XXXII(5), pp. 196–7.

Kaushik, Susheela. 2004. 'Sustainable Politics; Women in Panchayati Raj: Second Round of Elections, 2001', in

Susheela Kaushik, *Voices of Women in Panchayati Raj*, Friedrick Ebert Stiftung.

Kishwar, Madhu. 1996. 'Women and Politics: Beyond Quotas', *Economic and Political Weekly*, XXXI(3), pp. 2867–74.

Kohli, Atul. 2001. *Democracy and Discontent: India's Crisis of Governability*. Cambridge: Cambridge University Press.

Kumari, Abhilasha and Sabina Kidwai. 1998. *Crossing the Sacred Line, Women's Search for Political Power*. New Delhi: Orient Longman.

Menon, Nivedita. 2000. 'Elusive Woman: Feminism and Women's Reservation Bill', *Economic and Political Weekly*, XXXV(5–44), pp. 3835–44.

Omvedt, Gail. 1993. *Reinventing Revolution: New Social Movements and The Socialist Tradition in India*, New York: ME Sharpe.

Panchayati Raj update, 1998–2004. New Delhi: Institute of Social Sciences.

Rai, Shirin. M. 1997. 'Gender and Representation: Women MPs in the Indian Parliament', in Anne Marie Goetz (ed.), *Getting Institutions Right for Women and Development*. London: Zed Books, pp. 104–22.

Rai, Shirin M. and Kumud Sharma. 2000. 'Democratizing the Indian Parliament: The Reservations for Women Debate', in Shirin Rai (ed.), *International Perspectives on Gender and Democratization*. Basingstoke: Macmillan Press, pp. 149–65.

Raman, Vasanthi. 1995. 'Women's Reservation and Democratization: An Alternative Perspective', *Economic and Political Weekly*, XXXIV(5), pp. 3494–7.

Rana, Mahendra Singh. 2006. *India Votes: Lok Sabha and Vidhan Sabha Elections*. New Delhi: Sarid and Sons.

Randall, Vicky. 1998. 'Gender and Power: Women Engage the State', in Vicky Randall and Georgia Waylen (eds), *Gender Politics and the State*. London and New York: Routledge, pp. 85–205.

Singh, Jyotsna. 2003. 'Women on the Rise in Indian Elections', BBC News World Edition, 20 November. Available at www.onlinewomeninpolitics.org.

Tambiah, Yasmin (ed.). 2002. *Women and Governance in South Asia: Reimagining the State*. Colombo: International Center for Ethnic Studies.

12 Regionalism and Secessionism

Sanjib Baruah

Not all states are hardwired to respond to secessionist demands the same way. Were the majority of Quebecois to vote to secede from Canada, the split would probably occur peacefully. A break-up would be bitter for sure, but it is hard to imagine Canadian tanks rumbling through the streets of Montreal trying to prevent this outcome. China, on the other hand, is likely to react differently: regions aspiring to nationhood there routinely face the full might of the Chinese state. Indeed, China does not rule out the use of force even in the case of Taiwan—a separate country, though not universally recognized. From its perspective, the wishes of the people of Taiwan are quite immaterial (Bert 2004).

Secession—that is, when regions seek separate nationhood—has been aptly called a 'state-shattering form of self-determination' (Wohlforth and Felgenhauer 2002: 251). In order to explain the difference in attitudes among states towards secession, Wayne Bert points to a distinction made by Richard Rosecrance between traditional states 'anchored in the 19th century and focused on territory, sovereignty, material production, nationalist rhetoric and national defence', and virtual states that are 'based on mobile capital, labour and information, or a "negotiating entity" that depends as much on economic access abroad as on economic control at home'. However, while Canada may not be a 'traditional state', it can hardly be called a 'virtual state'. Bert brings in Kenneth Waltz's notion of the 'perilous lives' of weak states to explain Chinese attitudes (Bert 2004: 122–3, 129). However, the 'weakness' reflected in Chinese attitudes towards secession is very particular. A classification that might deal better with the difference is perhaps Robert Cooper's categories: 'postmodern' states that perceive no security threats in the traditional sense, traditional 'modern' states that 'behave as states always have, following Machiavellian principles and *raison d'état*', and the failed states in the 'pre-modern' zone (Cooper 2002: 12–15). None of these taxonomies are satisfactory. Yet the need for such distinctions suggests that a convincing explanation must take the national identities of states seriously, and that 'they cannot be stipulated deductively. They must be investigated empirically in concrete historical settings'

(Katzenstein 1996: 24). Chinese insecurity vis-à-vis claims to nationhood by regions can be understood only through a historical understanding of Chinese state identity. With the century of national humiliation being the 'master narrative of modern Chinese history', the notion of reclaiming and reunifying lost 'sacred territory' as a means to 'cleansing national humiliation' (Callahan 2004: 205, 212) is central to the identity of the Chinese state.

Indian attitudes are closer to the Chinese, and not to the Canadians. In the history of postcolonial India, a number of regional or ethnonational movements have turned into armed independentist[1] movements. Confrontations between security forces and militant regionalists have been deadly. Civilians have paid a heavy price, accounting for serious blots in India's human rights record. Yet, India has also been relatively successful in taming independentist aspirations. The best-known success story is the Dravidian movement of the 1960s. The contrast with Sri Lanka, as Linz *et al.* (2007) point out, is striking. If Tamil separatism in India became a non-issue by the 1970s, in Sri Lanka, from a non-issue it became one of the world's most violent and intractable conflicts. India's success is explained this way:

> Virtually all the strategic decisions facing multinational India, the rejection of a unitary state, the acceptance of multiple but complementary political identities, the upgrading of regional languages and the maintenance of English as a link language, the maintenance of polity-wide careers, the constitutional espousal of 'equal distance and respect' for all religions, and the creation of mutually beneficial alliances between polity-wide and regional parties, India, unlike Sri Lanka, made choices and alliances, especially in South India, that...increased the chances of peaceful democracy in a potentially conflictual setting. (Linz *et al.* 2007: 93–4)

Regional—or self-determination—movements in India are said to have followed an inverse 'U' curve. Heightened mobilization of group identities are followed by negotiations, and eventually such movements decline 'as exhaustion sets in, some leaders are repressed, others are co-opted, and a modicum of genuine power sharing and mutual accommodation between the movement and the central state authorities is reached'. Whether particular regional movements have gone through this inverse 'U' curve has been a function of the level of institutionalization of the authority of the state, and whether leaders have been secure enough to seek accommodation and compromise. The different trajectories of the Tamil, Sikh, and Kashmiri movements—the first being accommodated, and the latter two turning into violent confrontations between the state and militant regionalists—is the result of changes in the level of institutionalization of the Indian state, and the sense of security of leaders at the helm (Kohli 1997: 326–9).

Whether a government is democratic or authoritarian does not determine attitudes towards secession. Democratic India and authoritarian China both reject plebiscite as an instrument to decide the claims of regions to nationhood. Their positions vis-à-vis such claims are based on legal and historical arguments, and not on the wishes of the people living in the region. Thus, if China were to take a turn towards democracy, it is unlikely that attitudes towards its restive regions would change. If anything, politicians uncertain of popular support might be more inclined to pursue an aggressively nationalistic agenda, and view all regional claims as threats to national unity. But in the case of Canada, since its political discourse acknowledges 'the remedial theory of secession', the polity might find it easier to accept the Independence of Quebec (Bert 2004: 118–19).[2]

International factors are important in determining the success or failure of a region's claims to nationhood. Successful secessions do not occur only because regional movements, with aspirations for independence, gain strength and emerge victorious. Changes in the international environment play a decisive role. In South Asia, this became apparent in 1971 when India intervened in Bangladesh's liberation struggle and ensured its success. Changes in the international institutional environment have in recent years made available attractive alternatives to state-shattering forms of self-determination. The political space for regions in the European Union and paradiplomacy—international activities on the part of regions and stateless nations—has taken the wind out of some long-standing demands for nationhood. There are a number of regional 'embassies' in Brussels engaged in lobbying the European Commission and networking with each other. For regions such as the Basque Country, Catalonia, Scotland, or the Tyrol, this form of international recognition compensates for the relatively marginal status within the nation-states in which they are located. Even in the case of China, Hong Kong's two-systems-one-country model hardly fits the standard conception of indivisible sovereignty, and its potential success might have implications for Tibet and Taiwan as well (Pei 2002: 332). A solution to the Kashmir crisis might also ultimately lie in thinking outside the box of absolute and indivisible national sovereignty.

The rest of this chapter will have four sections. I will first present a constructivist view of regions and argue that like nations, regions are contested constructs. Second, I will look at how the postcolonial Indian state has tried to stabilize regional identities through three waves of reorganizing states. Third, I will look at the implications of the growing influence of regional parties in India's national politics. The fourth section has a few reflections on the tensions between the nation and the region in South Asia.

REGIONS AND NATIONS: CONTESTED CONSTRUCTS

Neither regions nor nations are self-evident and pre-political realities on the ground. Regionalism and aspirations of regions to independent statehood can be located in the process that some geographers describe as the territorialization of political life; it never becomes 'fully accomplished once and for all, but remains a precarious and deeply contentious outcome of historically specific state and non-state projects' (Jones and MacLeod 2004: 447). Regions are 'relatively permeable, socially constructed, politically mediated and actively performed "institutional accomplishments"' (Philo and Parr, cited in Jones and MacLeod 2004: 434). Defined in this manner, one would hardly expect a sharp dividing line between regions and nations—they are both territorializing projects, and sometimes there may exist tension between the two.

'The retrospectively constructed official nationalisms of India and Pakistan,' writes historian

Ayesha Jalal, 'have sought to ignore, if not altogether delegitimate, the multiple alternative strands of popular nationalism and communitarianism that lost out in the final battle for state power' (Jalal 2001: 741). Indeed, the foundational myths of India and Pakistan deliberately obscure the fact that these two national projects developed in explicit opposition to alternative regional imaginings. The fate of *Punjabiyat* or Punjabi regional identity under the pressures of the politics of the Partition of 1947 illustrates the tension. Western Punjab today is the core of Pakistan, providing 'a sharp counterpoint to any conception of Punjabi identity founded on regionalism' (Singh 2006: 17). Muslims constituted more than half the total population of pre-Partition Punjab, but today they rarely represent 'themselves through the idiom of *Punjabiyat*'. Instead, they identify themselves as Pakistanis and as speakers of Urdu—Pakistan's national language. Punjabi Hindus too deserted the cause of Punjabiyat (Jodhka 2006: 13). They mostly identify as Hindi speakers, and are on the forefront of Indian nationalism—both in its secular and Hindu variants. Thus in north India, religion, not language, has been the primary line of cleavage, though political elites 'seeking to advance the interests of their religious communities' have made language into a 'symbolic barrier', even when it was not really a barrier to communication (Brass 1974: 22, 27). So in a diminished post-Partition Punjab, it was left to the Sikhs to carry on the mantle of Punjabiyat. Indian attitudes towards Punjabi regionalism cannot be separated from the historically constituted identity of the postcolonial Indian state. This is even more the case with Indian attitudes towards Kashmiri regionalism.

Students of regionalism in postcolonial India cannot entirely exclude from their consideration the two Partitions in the subcontinent: the contested process of imagining and constructing two, and subsequently three, nation-states. The resistance to cross-border regions, as well as the erasure of the historical memories of some of these regions from the public discourse of the post-Partition states, and the facts of the continuous movement of people, goods, and ideas through the porous post-Partition borders, are part of the politics of regionalism in the post-Partition subcontinent. So are the regional conflicts within each post-Partition nation-state, as well as the efforts to create new intra-state regions, the phenomenon of regional parties, and tensions between the region and the nation.

The uneasy relationship between region and nation is nicely illustrated through the political history of India's largest state, Uttar Pradesh (UP). In the years immediately following the Partition and Independence, when there was considerable fear of further fragmentation, UP became a counterpoint to the idea of linguistic states, and was constructed as postcolonial India's 'heartland'. Apparently Jawaharlal Nehru believed that there was less 'provincialism' in UP than in any other part of the country. There was an effort to use the Hindi-speaking states of northern India as 'a buffer to contain the linguistic principle as the basis for statehood' (Kudaisya 2006: 22, 381). Ironically, representing itself as India's heartland has not been rewarding for UP. Due to this self-image, says Gyanesh Kudaisya, UP 'has failed to develop a regional identity of its own; its public life has been marked by a lack of cohesiveness; and the state's successive political leadership has failed to develop a regional agenda'. Kudaisya believes that it is time for UP to rethink its status as India's heartland. He favours breaking up UP into regions. The separation of Uttaranchal from UP in 2000 is, for him, a step in the right direction (ibid.: 411–14).

In discussions of Indian politics, the terms 'region' and 'regional' are sometimes used quite loosely. Thus, a regional party can be any political party with a 'regional' political presence, that is, a party that contests and wins elections in only one or two states. However, not all such parties have regional agendas. Parties like the Asom Gana Parishad (AGP) of Assam, the Akali Dal of Punjab, the National Conference of Jammu and Kashmir, the Telegu Desam of Andhra Pradesh, and the Dravida Munnetra Kazagham (DMK) and its various offshoots in Tamil Nadu have regional agendas, or at least they did during some phases of their political careers. But the small Marxist parties of West Bengal do not. The Shiv Sena in Maharashtra may have started from a regional platform. However, today, while its electoral profile may be regional, its ideology is indistinguishable from a pan-Indian party of the Hindu

right. But while it is important to find a more precise way of defining terms like 'region' and 'regional', this essay takes a constructivist view. Regions cannot be defined objectively.

It may be useful to distinguish *regional spaces* and *spaces of regionalism* (Jones and MacLeod 2004: 435). A good example of a regional space may be the category northeast India, which points to little more than directional location. Following Peter Sahlins' insight, it can be said that this official identification has not 'stuck' as vernacular practice (Sahlins 2003). Therefore northeast India is a regional space, but not a space of regionalism. When state identifications do not 'stick', insurgent spaces of regionalism can thrive in civil society (Jones and MacLeod 2004: 441–2). This has been made abundantly clear in northeast India. For the state is not the only actor in the territorialization of political life. Regional projects often originate in society and in order to 'stick', state identifications have to resonate in society. But states have an interest in stabilizing territorial identifications, and such a territorialization of political life can be the foundation for a federal polity capable of generating legitimate policy outcomes. On the other hand, state attempts at stabilizing territorial identification are always open to challenges (Sahlins 2003).

Regions are political projects and contested constructions, even when they appear to be pre-political and almost 'natural'. For instance, as a 'territory inhabited by the Telegu-speaking people Andhra has a history stretching back more than a millennium', although Andhra Pradesh, as a state of the Indian Union, goes back only to 1953, with significant new areas added in 1956 (Talbot 2001: 4). As far back as the early centuries of the second millennium, 'regional societies' in the Deccan had 'matured and became more self-confident', and regional languages such as Telegu began performing roles that were earlier reserved for Sanskrit. Thus, 'well before the modern age' language was 'important in Indian conception of culture, region, and community' (ibid.: 7–9). Many other regions in India—not always language-based—have similar long histories. Manipuris, for instance, claim that theirs is one of the oldest instances of state formation in Asia. The *Cheitharol Kumbaba*, or the royal chronicle, lists a continuous lineage of kings that supposedly goes as far back as the year AD 33.

However, antiquity does not explain why some regional identities are more resilient than others. Benedict Anderson's lament about nations celebrating 'their hoariness but not their astonishing youth' (Anderson 1986: 659) applies to regions as well. The medieval Telegu linguistic region bore 'little resemblance to the bounded enumerable community of modern Telugu speakers'. Linguistic ties of the medieval era did not have 'the focus and intensity of modern linguistic nationalisms' (Talbot 2001: 9). The connection between language and regional or national identity is quite contingent. In the Tamil case, it was the particular discursive practices around the theme of love and devotion for the Tamil language that enabled Tamil speakers to imagine themselves as 'a singular community and a potential nation unto themselves'. Thus, when the intensity of 'language devotion' led a young 'devotee' to burn himself alive in 1964, says Sumathi Ramaswamy, it was a case of ideology transforming 'its speakers, who ought to have been masters of the language, into its subjects, a critical reversal of the patrimonial imagination it inherited from European modernity' (Ramaswamy 1997: 243–4, 256).

The historical factors that animate particular regionalisms are contingent, though not the conditions that made regional and national imaginings the global norm (Anderson 1983; Gellner 1983). Once the history of 'language devotion' had engendered the Tamil regional narrative with powerful notions of community and homeland, it became possible for Tamil regionalism to take an independentist turn in the 1950s and early 1960s. But subsequently the demand for a separate Dravida Nadu became more moderate, and eventually the theme of independence disappeared altogether. Tamil speakers acquired a state of their own and regional political parties—offshoots of the Dravidian movement—have continuously formed the state government in Tamil Nadu since 1967. Hence the frequent reference to the Tamil case, as evidence of India's ability to contain regionalism (see Linz et al. 2007: 50–106; Kohli 1997).

The territorialization of political life involves state as well as non-state actors, and thus even the most

powerful of regional narratives can be contested. This would not come as a surprise to most contemporary students of identity, who subscribe to the constructivist position that identities are 'ultimately fluid, chosen, instrumentalizable, responsive to change in relevant incentive structures, and susceptible to manipulation by cultural or political entrepreneurs' (Lustick et al. 2004: 213). Nor would changes in the saliency of particular regional identities surprise those who take a more objectivist view of ethno-cultural landscapes. Rather than hierarchical or parallel, the predominant pattern of ethnic groups' relations in India has been described as one of segmentation. Within 'language, tribal, or religious groups', there are supposedly 'parallel ethnic structures' with 'internal hierarchical ethnic group relations' and 'a complete societal division of labour'. There are thus 'ethnic groups within ethnic groups' in India (Brass 1974: 11–12).[3]

As I will elaborate in the next section, the Indian Constitution makes breaking up and creating new states relatively easy. While this might have allowed the accommodation of regionalism in some cases, it also provides incentives for political projects built around alternative regional narratives. It makes exit options available to regions within regions. Thus, even in ancient Telegu country, the demand for a separate Telengana has been recently revived. Other examples of contested regional narratives include that of the Bodos in Assam. While the Bodos appear to have settled for a compromise—in the form of the Bodoland Territorial Autonomous Council—the Bodo narrative fundamentally challenges the ethnic Assamese construction of Assam (see Baruah 1999: 173–98). Meiteis and the Nagas have diametrically opposite views about Manipur's past, present, and future. Contested regional narratives are a persistent theme in the political conflicts of northeast India today.

Contested constructions of regions also produce irredentist claims. Thus, as recently as 2004, the Government of Maharashtra approached the Supreme Court of India about transferring the Marathi-speaking Belgaum area from Karnataka to Maharashtra. The dispute goes back to 1956, when boundaries drawn by the States' Reorganization Commission had left some predominantly Marathi-speaking areas in Karnataka, and some predominantly Kannada-speaking areas in what subsequently became Maharashtra. The Naga demand for Nagalim—greater Nagaland—can also be seen as the irredentist face of the contested nature of regions, though it also marks the rejection by Nagas of the unilateral determination of the boundaries of Nagaland, without taking into account the wishes of the people.

STABILIZING REGIONS AS A STATE PROJECT

During the early years after Independence—following the Partition and the merger of what were 'native states' during British colonial rule—India's provinces and their boundaries seemed incoherent. There was an unmistakably provisional quality to those borders. The provinces were classified into Parts A, B, and C states: colonial era provinces, former 'native states' or groups of 'native states', and a third mixed category of smaller territories. It was generally expected that these units would be reorganized. During India's anti-colonial resistance, the Indian National Congress had committed itself to a postcolonial political order of linguistically defined regions. As far back as 1922, it began organizing the branches of the movement not along the colonial structure of presidencies and provinces, but along language lines. In 1928 a committee headed by Motilal Nehru outlined a vision of a future polity organized into linguistic states. But after Independence, the Congress rejected linguistic reorganization despite its previous commitment to it. Under the leadership of Jawaharlal Nehru, the post-Independence Congress party was initially unwilling 'to bring these identities into the decision-making process at the center and politicise them' (Adeney 2002: 25) fearing that it might threaten the unity of the fledgling new nation. However, the Constituent Assembly had left the task of reorganizing state boundaries to future Parliaments, giving it unlimited powers to take on the task. Eventually, pushed by powerful political pressures from below, Nehru reversed his position on linguistic reorganization because of electoral considerations.

Alfred Stepan's *Arguing Comparative Politics*, puts Indian federalism in a very different context from the older literature on comparative federalism.

Distinguishing between 'holding together' and 'coming together' federations, he argues that US-style 'demos constraining' federalism is unsuitable for a 'robustly politically multinational' country like India. Requirements of supermajorities—the support of two-thirds of state legislatures for constitutional amendments—make the United States an extreme outlier on the demos-constraining end of federations, and far from the norm (Stepan 2001: 315–61). Stepan showers praise on Article 3 of the Indian Constitution, which allows Parliament to create new states and redraw state boundaries with a simple majority, barely consulting the relevant state. This is unthinkable in a 'coming together' federation, which must be 'demos constraining' in order to protect state rights. Stepan has a highly positive assessment of the way India's political classes have used the Constitution's demos-enabling feature. He marvels at the 'relatively consensual manner' in which 'most of the boundaries of the states in India were redrawn between 1956 and 1966, and later a process of creating new tribal states in the North-east was begun'. The demos-enabling features of Indian federalism, Stepan believes, explain 'the survival of India as the world's largest multi-cultural, multi-national democracy'. This feature has 'allowed the majority at the center, to respond to minority demands from states for greater linguistic and cultural autonomy'. Had India been a unitary state, 'neither the majority, nor the minorities, would have had this constitutional flexibility available to them' (ibid.: 354).

By the 1960s, it appears that a few discernible rules, albeit not formally articulated, had emerged in the Indian Central government's approach to regional demands. Such demands had to first, stop short of secession; second, groups making demands had to be linguistically or culturally defined—and not defined by religion; third, be backed by popular support; and fourth, be acceptable to linguistic minorities when it is a matter of breaking up a multilingual state (Brass 1974: 18–19). However, there were exceptions; and in any case these rules were not applied to the two later waves of reorganization. The special regional dispensation of small and financially dependent states in northeast India, for instance, was the product of a national security-driven policy process in a border region inhabited by many minority groups (Baruah 1999: 91–115). The considerations were also very different when the states of Jharkhand, Chhattisgarh, and Uttaranchal were created in 2000. While the demands were old, the interests of political parties in the highly competitive political environment of the period pushed the process. According to one scholar, the fact that no transborder regional community was invoked and that there were no perceived national security threats facilitated the process. 'Ethnic communities in the three new states,' writes Maya Chadda, 'were unconnected with foreign enemies or cross border nationalities, unlike in Punjab, Kashmir, and Assam.' To her, this latest wave of states reorganization illustrates the value of the flexibility that the Constitution gives to the Parliament. The Constitution, she points out approvingly, 'said little about the kind of federal units the Indian Union was to have, or the basis on which they would be created, i.e., geography, demography, administrative convenience, language, or culture. That decision was left entirely to the wisdom of Parliament' (Chadda 2002: 46–7).

The argument for a holding together federation being demos enabling is based on the idea of reconciling diversity with policymaking efficacy (Stepan 2001: 338–9). However, efficacy can sometimes be in conflict with legitimacy. The idea of divided sovereignty and citizens with dual allegiance—to the national and regional political communities—is central to the federal vision of a legitimate political order. Federalism, as a political principle understood as an aggregate of politically organized territories (Piccone and Ulman 1994: 5) is arguably the opposite of the nation-state. In that sense federation building, and not nation building, is the appropriate project for India (Baruah 1999: 200–13). The relative success of the first wave of states reorganization in India was because it was built on the principles of the 'security for territorially concentrated linguistic groups' and dual, but complementary, allegiances. However, later reorganizations, including 'the belated recognition of a Punjabi state', were not based on the same principles (Adeney 2003: 57–8). A Punjabi Punjab was not acknowledged till 1966,

when Haryana was separated from Punjab, because the demand came from a religiously defined—and not a language-based—group. Arguably, the decisions and non-decisions of India's central political elites, made possible by the demos-enabling features of Indian federalism, account also for some of most serious regional challenges that India has faced. The persistent political turmoil in northeast India provides another example. The national security-driven process of making and breaking states has reinforced the idea of de facto ethnic homelands, in the imaginations of both local activists and tacticians of conflict management, perpetuating a politics of violent displacement and ethnic cleansing (Baruah 2005: 183–208)

REGIONALIZATION OF NATIONAL POLITICS?

The so-called regionalization of Indian politics—which refers to the increasing role of regional parties in national politics—has often confused outside observers. The phenomenon is often miscast 'as a force tending towards the disintegration of the Indian Union'. But in India, regional parties are not even all regionalist 'in the sense of representing demands for cultural autonomy or grievances against the central state'. Many of them are no more than 'merely personality-driven offshoots of parties that were once nominally national in scope' (Jenkins 2000: 62–3).

Yet, whatever their agendas, regional parties increasingly share the same political space as polity-wide parties. They are electoral allies of polity-wide parties, and not only do they form governments at the state level, they also participate in coalition governments at the Centre. India has come a long way since the period immediately following Independence, when regionalism was viewed as a challenge to national unity. But while politics in India may have made its peace with regionalism, its implications in terms of public policy and the health of the polity are far from clear.

While many of India's current crop of regionalist politicians are not secessionist, they do not have a 'coherent view of Indian identity'. They view the economy as 'a cluster of regional units, each engaged in zero-sum relations with one another, and with the

Centre'. In matters of culture they are 'parochial—devoted to tending their own vernacular gardens' (Khilnani 2004: 26). This is hardly a satisfactory situation. Under these conditions, it is easy to see why in Indian politics the label 'regional' says so little about policy preferences. Few would argue that regional issues have moved up on the national policy agenda because of the growing influence of regional parties. Regional parties have formed state governments, while participating in coalition governments at the Centre during India's economic reforms. Yet they have rarely questioned the economic agenda of the Central government, even though many states may have faced a fiscal crisis as a result of those policies. Instead, regional parties prefer getting financial deals for their states, in exchange for political support to the government in New Delhi (Sridhar 2004). Indeed, the most significant impact of the Congress party's fall from dominance in 1989 has been not on economic policy, but on the politics of patronage. In the period of Congress dominance, voting for a regional party may have jeopardized Central government allocations for roads or schools. But voters no longer have to make this trade-off. Even by voting for 'parties espousing an aggressive regional, ethnic, or linguistic agenda' they stand 'a reasonable chance of that party gaining access to discretionary expenditures' (Rodden and Wilkinson 2004).

The logic of a 'patronage-democracy' (Chandra 2004: 258) explains this paradox. Basic public goods, such as the security of life and property, access to education and public health, and a minimum standard of living, have become market goods rather than entitlements. Elections are 'auctions for the sale of government services'. Individual politicians are more important in patronage politics than the political party or party ideology, because groups of supporters are beholden to them. A collective allocation of resources through policy might be credited to a party or its leadership, but credit for goods delivered through patronage goes to individual politicians. They use patronage to develop their power base, which in turn gives them leverage in negotiations with political parties for positions within the party and the government (ibid.). This also explains the phenomenon of dynastic politics—a son, a daughter,

or a spouse following a parent or a spouse as a Member of Parliament or a state legislature.

The dynamics of a patronage democracy are apparent during election campaigns. The allocation of tickets by political parties—especially by resourceful polity-wide parties—is the most intense part of an election campaign. Parties dispense resources to fight elections, and being a candidate of a winning party means access to governmental patronage resources, and even direct control of such resources through ministerial positions. Individual politicians may generally prefer contesting as candidates of polity-wide parties because they control more resources compared to regional parties, given their countrywide fund-raising abilities. Considerations of electability, and ties to personalistic networks that connect the party 'grassroots' to the Centre shape the selection of party candidates.

Parties realize that in order to win, they have to be tuned in to local realities, and when possible, even understand the nuances of regional issues. Under these conditions, a polity-wide party may sometimes decide not to go it alone, and instead form an electoral alliance with a regional party. In the 1990s, politicians in Assam in their political rhetoric sought to blur the distinction between polity-wide and regional parties. The AGP tried to present itself as 'a regional party with a national outlook'. But the local Congress party leader responded by saying that while the Congress may be a national party, it has 'a regional outlook' (Prabhakara 2004). While the AGP, with its roots in a social movement, was trying to improve its access to institutional channels and widen its appeal as an electoral party, the Congress was not willing to be an inert player either. It understood the challenge presented by the electoral appeal of its regional competitor, and tried to adjust its political rhetoric accordingly. Indeed, when regionalism is successfully mobilized, the logic of India's patronage democracy can even turn polity-wide and regional parties into natural allies, with little consequence for public policy.

REGION AND THE NATION

Today the Indian polity faces no clear and imminent danger from either the garden-variety regionalism that is now part of mainstream Indian politics, or from claims of regions to nationhood. But trust and understanding between citizens is a necessary condition for making policies using universalistic criteria. Trust, in this context, is the willingness to wait: certain regions or groups can be helped more than others because of the 'expectation that other policies another time will have the effect of benefiting other groups' (Barry 1999: 263). Given the agendas of India's mainstream regional parties, one can legitimately ask: with friends like these, who needs enemies? Indian attitudes towards its restive regions are those of a traditional 'modern' state outlined at the beginning of this essay. They are somewhat dissonant with India's current image as a mature democracy, a dynamic economy, and an emerging major power. A hyper-nationalist militarist reaction to regions claiming nationhood is especially incongruous when the claim involves an implicit critique of the modular nation form.

A scholar of the Punjab conflict has proposed an alternative reading of South Asian history, focusing on constitutional designs that could have averted the Partition of 1947 (Singh 2000). Such alternatives, he maintains, might have been 'more attuned with the provincial realities of sub-continental India' than what the postcolonial Indian state could offer in terms of regional autonomy (Singh 2003: 52). In a more recent essay, he acknowledges that undivided Punjab may now be a hopelessly romantic idea. Watching the changing-of-guards ceremony at the Wagah border, which divides the Indian from the Pakistani side of Punjab, left him with 'unsettling thoughts' about the transnational academic project of Punjab Studies, with which he is associated. With 'the symbolism, the aggression, and the choreographed Punjabi machismo', the daily ritual on the Wagah border, he writes, had all the hallmarks of the Balinese cockfight—the subject of a famous essay by Clifford Geertz (1973). Even considering the ritual nature of this display of a 'highly charged sense of nationhood', the ceremony at Wagah made apparent that 'however much West Punjab resembles the East, it is also now part of a distinct cultural and religious tradition with a strong sense of difference' (Singh 2006: 17).

The early 1990s saw the end of the movement for an independent Khalistan: the militant assertion

of Punjabi regionalism. It was not a political settlement that brought it to an end, but a successful counter-insurgency campaign that killed thousands of rebels—actual and suspected—and their sympathizers. Between 35,000 and 70,000 people were victims of the troubles in Punjab. Human rights groups have documented political killings, enforced disappearances, torture, arbitrary arrests, unlawful detentions, and secret cremations of victims (Kumar et al. 2003). An activist describes the condition in Punjab, after the end of the movement for Khalistan, as the peace of the graveyard (Bose 2003).

This was an extraordinarily violent response to a regional movement, which has its roots in the tensions between the region and the nation in the subcontinent's modern history, and—considering the significant support that the movement enjoyed in the Sikh diaspora—also had the mark of our post-national times.

NOTES

1. Independentist is a more neutral term than 'separatist' or 'secessionist'. The term is commonly used in Puerto Rico to refer to political groups that stand for Puerto Rican Independence.

2. Some critics, however, challenge the notion that there is a consensus in Canada about secession being 'no big deal'. The 'admirable Canadian placidity', as André Liebich puts it, was 'briefly shattered' just before Quebec's second referendum on Independence in 1995, when polls indicated that the Independence option might win (Liebich 2002, p. 9).

3. Brass here elaborates the ideas of Donald Horowitz and Myron Weiner.

REFERENCES

Adeney, Katherine. 2003. 'Multiple Identities, Dual Loyalties and the Stabilisation of Federalism in India: Observations on Maya Chadda's "Integration through Internal Reorganization: Containing Ethnic Conflict in India"', Global Review of Ethnopolitics, 2(2), pp. 57–9.
———. 2002. 'Constitutional Centring: Nation Formation and Consociational Federalism in India and Pakistan', Commonwealth and Comparative Politics, 40(3), pp. 8–33.

Anderson, Benedict. 1986. 'Narrating the Nation', *Times Literary Supplement*, 13 June.

———. 1983. *Imagined Communities*. London: Verso Press.

Barry, Brian. 1999. 'Self-Government Revisited', in Ronald Beiner (ed.), *Theorizing Nationalism*, Albany, NY: State University of New York Press, pp. 247–78.

Baruah, S. 2005. *Durable Disorder: Understanding the Politics of Northeast India*. New Delhi: Oxford University Press.

———. 1999. *India Against Itself: Politics of Nationality in Assam*. New Delhi: Oxford University Press.

Bert, Wayne. 2004. 'Retaining Separatist Territories: Comparing China and Canada', *China: An International Journal*, 2(1), pp. 108–32.

Bose, Tapan. 2003. 'Introduction', in Ram Narayan Kumar, Amrik Singh, Ashok Agarwal, and Jaskaran Kaur (eds), *Reduced to Ashes: The Insurgency and Human Rights in Punjab*. Kathmandu: South Asia Forum for Human Rights, pp. iii–viii.

Brass, Paul. 1974. *Language, Religion and Politics in North India*. Cambridge: Cambridge University Press.

Callahan, William A. 2004. 'National Insecurities: Humiliation, Salvation, and Chinese Nationalism,' *Alternatives*, 29(2), pp. 199–218.

Chadda, Maya. 2002. 'Integration through Internal Reorganization: Containing Ethnic Conflict in India', *The Global Review of Ethnopolitics*, 2(1), pp. 44–61.

Chandra, Kanchan. 2004. 'Elections as Auctions', *Seminar*, 539 (Issue on 'A Mandate for Change'), pp. 25–8.

Cooper, Robert. 2002. 'The Post-Modern State', in Mark Leonard (ed.), *Re-Ordering the World*. London: The Foreign Policy Centre, pp. 11–20.

Geertz, Clifford. 1973. 'Deep Play: Notes on the Balinese Cockfight', in Clifford Geertz (ed.), *The Interpretation of Cultures*. New York: Basic Books, pp. 412–53.

Gellner, Ernest. 1983. *Nations and Nationalism*. Ithaca, NY: Cornell University Press.

Jalal, Ayesha. 2001. 'South Asia', *Encyclopedia of Nationalism: Fundamental Themes*, vol. 1. San Diego, CA: Academic Press, pp. 737–56.

Jenkins, Rob. 2000. 'Appearances and Reality in Indian Politics: Making Sense of the 1999 General Election', *Government and Opposition*, 35(1), pp. 49–66.

Jodhka, Surinder S. 2006. 'The Problem', *Seminar*, 567 (Issue on 'Re-imagining Punjab'), pp. 12–16.

Jones, Martin and Gordon MacLeod. 2004. 'Regional Spaces, Spaces of Regionalism: Territory, Insurgent Politics, and the English Question', *Transactions of the Institute of British Geographers*, 29(4), pp. 433–52.

Katzenstein, Peter J. 1996. 'Introduction: Alternative Perspectives on National Security', in Peter J. Katzenstein (ed.), *The Culture of National Security: Norms and Identity in World Politics*. New York: Columbia University Press, pp. 1–32.

Khilnani, Sunil. 2004. 'Branding India', *Seminar*, 533 (Issue on India 2003).

Kohli, Atul. 1997. 'Can Democracies Accommodate Ethnic Nationalism? Rise and Decline of Self-Determination Movements', *Journal of Asian Studies*, 56(2), pp. 325–44.

Kudaisya, Gyanesh. 2006. *Region, Nation, 'Heartland': Uttar Pradesh in India's Body Politics*. New Delhi: Sage Publications.

Kumar, Ram Narayan, A. Singh, A. Agrawal, and J. Kaur. 2003. *Reduced to Ashes: The Insurgency and Human Rights in Punjab*, Kathmandu: South Asia Forum for Human Rights.

Liebich, André, 2002, 'Canadian, Eh?' *JEMIE* (*Journal on Ethnopolitics and Minority Issues in Europe*), 4. http://www.ecmi.de/jemie/download/Focus4–2002_Liebich.pdf (accessed 12 May 2007).

Linz, Juan J., Alfred Stepan, and Yogendra Yadav. 2007. '"Nation State" or "State Nation"? India in a Comparative Perspective', in K. Shankar Bajpai (ed.), *Democracy and Diversity: India and the American Experience*. New Delhi: Oxford University Press, pp. 50–106.

Lustick, Ian S., Dan Miodownik, and Roy J. Eidelson. 2004. 'Secessionism in Multicultural States: Does Sharing Power Prevent or Encourage It?' *American Political Science Review*, 98(2), pp. 209–29.

Pei, Minxin. 2002. 'Self-Administration and Local Autonomy: Reconciling Conflicting Interests in China', in Wolfgang Danspeckgruber (ed.), *The Self-Determination of Peoples: Community, Nation, and State in an Interdependent World*. Boulder: Lynne Rienner Publishers, pp. 315–32.

Philo, C. and H. Parr. 2000. 'Institutional Geographies: Introductory Remarks', *Geoforum*, vol. 31, pp. 513–21.

Piccone, Paul and Gary Ulmen. 1994. 'Re-Thinking Federalism', *Telos*, vol. 100, Summer, pp. 3–16.

Prabhakara, M.S. 2004. 'Northeastern Challenges', *Frontline*, 21(8), pp. 10–23.

Ramaswamy, Sumathi. 1997. *Passions of the Tongue: Language Devotion in Tamil India, 1891–1970*. Berkeley: University of California Press.

Rodden, Jonathan and Steven Wilkinson. 2004. 'The Shifting Political Economy of Redistribution in the Indian Federation', Paper presented at the annual meeting of the International Society for New Institutional Economics Tucson, Arizona, USA, 30 September–3 October.

Sahlins, Peter. 2003. 'Response Paper', American Council of Learned Societies Project on 'Official and Vernacular Identifications in the Making of the Modern World', http://www.acls.org/crn/network/meetings_nyc_sahlins.htm (last accessed 12 May 2007).

Singh, Gurharpal. 2006. 'Beyond Punjabi Romanticism', *Seminar*, vol. 567 (Issue on 'Re-Imagining Punjab'), pp. 17–20.

——. 2003. 'Critical Reflections on Celebrating Success: A Response to Maya Chadda', *Global Review of Ethnopolitics*, 2 (2), pp. 52–4.

——. 2000. *Ethnic Conflict in India: A Case-Study of Punjab*. London: Macmillan Press.

Sridhar, V. 2004. 'The Neo-liberal Consensus', *Frontline* (Chennai), 23 April.

Stepan, Alfred. 2001. *Arguing Comparative Politics*. New York: Oxford University Press.

Talbot, Cynthia. 2001. *Precolonial India in Practice: Society, Region, and Identity in Medieval Andhra*. New York: Oxford University Press.

Wohlforth, William and Tyler Felgenhauer. 2002. 'Self-Determination and the Stability of the Russian Federation', in Wolfgang Danspeckgruber (ed.), *The Self-Determination of Peoples: Community, Nation, and State in an Interdependent World*. Boulder: Lynne Rienner Publishers, pp. 227–52.

13 Politics and National Identity

Sunil Khilnani

India's modern history bears testimony to the primacy of politics. In contrast to Europe, where changes in the economy and productive processes defined the nature of modernity, in India it is the increasingly intrusive presence of the state, and the accompanying expansion of the domain of politics, that has remade society, and its terms of identity and agency. That state has, since 1947, existed in a democratic form. The relationship between India's democratic state and its unparalleled diversities has never been for Indians simply a subject of academic interest—nor are the problems posed by this relationship confined to the realm of political understanding. The success or failure of India's democracy in sustaining the country's diverse identities is an urgently practical question, involving the destinies of over a billion human beings, and depends on the exercise of political judgement. Those in India who have thought deepest about its diversities and their democratic articulation into a national identity have also been political actors— men and women who had to make judgements and to act. In considering the relationship between identity and politics in India, it is therefore important to be able to move between the perspectives of political understanding and political judgement.

Democracy, in the sense of a system based on the separation of powers, a free press and liberties of association, on universal suffrage and individual rights, and on the routine alternation of governments through open elections, is now fully consolidated in India (since Independence, the country has held fifteen national elections and many more in its regional states). In this respect, India's political system has succeeded in institutionalizing uncertainty (Przeworski 1991: 13–14). Democracy as a type of government, a political regime of laws and institutions, has achieved a real—that is to say, inherently problematic—existence. Equally significantly, however, the *idea* of democracy has penetrated the Indian political imagination: an idea which assumes the plasticity of the human world and which refuses the divine ordination of the social order, which promises to bring the alien apparatus of the state under the control of the collective will of a community.

Seen from a distance, India's democracy—intensifying as it is within a society where economic unevenness is also rising—seems to be eliciting forms of political identification and representative agencies that threaten its cohabiting diversities. The most spectacular manifestation of this has been the rise of the party of Hindu nationalism, the Bharatiya Janata Party (BJP), which hopes to endow with political significance the fact that a majority of Indians worship in the Hindu faiths, and thus to redefine the nature of India's secular state. From the opposite direction comes a proliferation of parties rooted in regional identities—vocal in their demands—that also seem a threat to the Indian Union. Yet, recent prediction-defying 2009 elections, serve to remind us that matters are more complicated.

Since the late 1980s, the rise of the BJP has been matched by two other and even more significant processes. The first is a rebalancing—driven in part by economic developments—of the relations between the national government in New Delhi, the 'Centre', and the regional states. The second is the rise of lower-caste parties. India's democracy has ensured that the relation between particular and collective belonging, the question of the form and content of the Indian nation, has stayed continuously in contention: democratic politics is, precisely, a perpetual struggle to persuade people to see themselves in certain ways, a competition over political identifications.

The character of India's unsettled democracy can be considered from at least three perspectives: the relationship between democracy and equality; between democracy and liberty; and between democracy and diversity. India's performance across these domains has been mixed, and each merits a full discussion in its own right. The focus in this essay is on democracy and diversity, and will be limited to a discussion of diversities within India (rather than the relationship between India's diversities and the world).[1] I would like to suggest that from this perspective, India's democratic frame has been relatively effective in giving space to India's diversities, and self-correcting in the moments when diversity has been devalued. I begin by outlining the two main and opposing twentieth century responses to the fact of India's diversities, responses that gave rise to rival

ideas of the Indian nation and nationalism. I turn then to the view of Indian identity associated with Jawaharlal Nehru, and briefly sketch his efforts to give form to a provisional view of Indian identity—one that relied on political skills for its sustenance, and that required regular restatement.

Finally, I take up some of the ways in which India's democratic frame has encouraged the emergence of a range of political identities—including some that wish to limit the country's diversity in the name of a more narrow national identity. But I hope to show that such movements themselves have been constrained, if also fostered, by the workings of Indian democracy.

CONSTRUCTING A NATION

The fact of India's diversities, which gave its peoples many particular attachments, has led most observers to doubt India's capacity to be a nation. This was the premise of British colonial rule in India. Colonial administrator John Strachey put the point across brusquely in 1885: 'there is not, and never was an India, nor ever any country of India', he declared, 'possessing according to European ideas, any sort of unity, physical, political, social or religious; no nation, no "people of India"'.[2] The single trait that struck outsiders as common across the subcontinent was the caste order: but this was more a principle of division rather than unity, and one that no Indian intellectual was morally inclined to justify. Tocqueville, in his notes for a planned work on India, voiced a common view when he explained that India had been repeatedly conquered because its civilizational order deprived Indians of patriotic feeling. Instead of a nation, in India 'each caste forms a separate little nation, which has its own ethos, customs, laws and government. The national spirit of the Hindus is trapped within caste. Their country is their caste' (de Tocqueville 1962).

The European belief that India was not—and could not—be a nation was predictably manifest in the taxonomic practices of the British Raj. These divided the subcontinent between the princely states and British India, enabling the British to rule the latter as a series of segmented communities, with separate electorates for each designed to defend their now frozen identities; and each was encouraged to establish its own preferential relationships with the Raj.[3] The Raj's policies helped to constitute India as a society composed of communities, which, it proclaimed, posed hazards to one another in the absence of the pacifying effects of imperial power. Equally, however, the Raj introduced Indians to the possibility of conceiving of themselves as individuals, whose rights and interests were defendable in courts of law, and who could associate to pursue common interests.[4] The result was a bifocal perspective on the idea of representation (and of what exactly required representation). Communities were seen variously as possessing indivisible identities, each of which could press the state for uniform treatment, regardless of size; or, alternatively, as numerical aggregates of individual interests, with the state giving greater due to numerically weightier groups. By the 1940s, these conceptions were to clash with horrible confusion. Jinnah and the Muslim League argued that every Hindu and Muslim should be treated in the first instance as a member of their community (rather than as individuals), and that the state should give equal regard to each community (an argument with a liberal pedigree, which could be construed as one for the protection of minorities). Congress, on the other hand, in claiming to speak for all Indians, wished to disconnect individuals from their more particular communities, and to persuade them to view themselves as members of a larger community— as Indians.

The imperially induced perturbations in conceptions of collective identity provoked Indian elites into specifying forms of political community in various, sometimes conflicting, ways: invoking religion, caste, region as well as nation—as they grasped for a stable entity that could lay claim to displacing the British. 'Indian nationalism' is in many ways a misleading shorthand term used to describe a period of intellectual and political ferment in the late nineteenth and twentieth centuries, which encompassed the different projects of anti-colonialism, patriotism, and nationalism. The possible bases for a shared community across the subcontinent were vigorously debated in regional languages (especially in Bengal and Maharashtra, two regions exposed longest to the British), and a sense of regional identity came into

being as part of the struggle to define a larger Indian community. The belief that Indian nationalism had subsequently to unite and subordinate these regional identities is thus a misreading of the relationship between nation and region in India. In fact, the senses of region and nation emerged simultaneously through parallel self-definitions. This point is essential to any understanding of the distinctive, layered character of Indianness, as also to understanding the relationship between region and nation today.[5]

By the middle decades of the twentieth century, the debate over the nature of India's identity had, in the broadest terms, taken two directions. The first accepted the diagnosis that India's internal diversities and myriad particularisms were disabling, and wished to expunge these. This view, much impressed by the prowess of European nationalisms, sought to interpret nationalism in India in terms of an overarching religious identity, which found in religion a social glue for the nation. This idea of 'communalism', as it came to be called in India, was adopted by both Muslim and Hindu nationalism. It insisted that homogeneity was the only possible basis for nationhood—as the BJP manifestos of the 1990s were to put it, 'one nation, one people, one culture'. The importance of Western ideas and models in shaping this religious nationalism is significant. V.D. Savarkar, the ideologue of Hindutva (the ideology of today's BJP), was a non-believing Brahmin from western India, an admirer and translator of Mazzini, who founded a secret society modelled on Young Italy (its members, planning to assassinate the Viceroy, learned bomb-making from a Russian revolutionary in Paris); others, like Aurobindo Ghose, educated at King's College, Cambridge, returned to rediscover and propagate his spiritual traditions, while Vivekananda, also steeped in European thought, urged upon his young followers the 'three Bs': beef, biceps, and the Bhagavad Gita.

Contrasting with this emulative view was another strand, itself rich with internal disagreement and diversity, that rejected the European (and Japanese) specifications of nationalism. Thus, Tagore, both in his well-known lectures on *Nationalism* and throughout his thought and writing, stressed the distinctiveness of India's identity as compared with other cultures: the 'idea of India', he insisted, militated 'against the intense consciousness of the idea of separateness of one's own people from others'.[6] Tagore saw India not as an exclusively Hindu civilization, but as a confluence of many cultures: strikingly, he preferred to evoke India through the imagery of rivers and oceans, rather than by the more common nationalist invocation of land. For his part, Mahatma Gandhi located India's unity in a self-produced religious morality, one that assembled eclectic elements from folk and popular devotional Bhakti traditions, as well as from Christian and Islamic scriptures. While he refused to separate religion and politics and certainly used Hindu symbols, he recoiled from the martial vision of Hindu nationalists, and instead resurrected an older, feminized patriotism that valued India's differences. Nehru too saw heterogeneity as India's strength—he had a Madisonian sense that large-scale mixture was good for liberty, for cultural and intellectual creativity, and as a way of spreading risks. But while Gandhi rejected the modern state, and Tagore too had misgivings about it, Nehru saw it as necessary if India was going to make its own way in the world.

Nehru, in command of the Indian state for the first seventeen years after Independence, is the link between the ideas of Tagore and Gandhi and their translation into state practice. He had to devise a nationalism particular to India that would also be compatible with the exigencies of the modern (and very un-Indian) state. No Indian intellectual understood more clearly the potentialities of nationalism in India. He saw at once its power to unite the country and its power to endanger it, both internally and externally. His view was based on a critical reading of the experience of other nationalisms—the spectres of Balkanization, or the self-destructive militarism of imperial Japan—as well as of India's own history, and it manifested a willingness to invent and, crucially, to temporize, when it came to defining the terms of India's identity.

Recent academic theorists have urged us to see nationalism as the global diffusion of a standardized, modular form devised in the West—whether in the Gallic version of a community of common citizenship or the *volkisch* idea of a shared ethnic or cultural origin. While certainly attracted by the political and economic example of the modern West, Nehru was far less taken by its cultural models. By 1947, he was convinced that Indian nationalism could not simply model itself on European examples.[7] Nor did he accept that all nations had to specify their identities in identical ways.

Nehru's understanding of the link between culture and power avoided the liberal presumption that individuals could transcend their cultural inheritance, and remake themselves however they—or their state—saw fit; a view that placed abstracted individual rationality before any sense of cultural identity.[8] Equally, though, he steered away from the perception of cultures as self-enclosed wholes, as hermetic communities of language or belief—a view that sustains, on the one hand, the conservative idea of the state as an instrument at the community's disposal, and on the other the more benign view of the state as a curator of cultural exhibits, responsible for preserving communities. Rather, cultures were overlapping forms of activity that had commerce with one another, mutually altering and reshaping each other: this, Nehru insisted, was one of the most vivid insights to be gleaned from a study of India's history. India was a society neither of liberal individuals nor of exclusive communities or nationalities, but of interconnected and historically accreted differences. As he put it in a remarkable metaphor, India 'was like some ancient palimpsest on which layer upon layer of thought and reverie have been inscribed, and yet no succeeding layer had completely hidden or erased what had been written previously' (Nehru 1946).

Nehru used a romanticized version of India's past to create an enabling fiction: one that might resist both the divisive effects of the colonial state and the legacy of India's deeply inegalitarian social order. But his essential point, about the nature of differences and connections in India—the image of Indian identity as layered—was not off-beam. That he was able to transform this metaphor into a policy of state is striking in at least two respects. First, in the particular political circumstances after Partition, the pressures were for other, more simple definitions. With the creation of Pakistan as the putative state of all Muslims in the subcontinent, many in India felt that the Indian state should become Pakistan's mirror: defining itself through the possession of the Hindu majority and become a Hindu state. Yet, a combination of political

skills and chance events—such as the death of
Gandhi at the hands of a Hindu extremist, and shortly
thereafter, of Sardar Patel, Nehru's main rival for power,
and himself a sympathizer with the Hindu cause—
made it possible for Nehru to temper this mirroring
ambition. And so, after 1947, the subcontinent
contained within it, in the shape of Pakistan and India,
two radically different conceptions of dealing with
diversity within the frame of the modern state, two
distinct ideas of state and national identity. That Nehru
could consolidate his alternative conception is also
striking in a second respect, because there were few
intellectual or theoretical anchors against the political
tides towards narrower and religious conceptions of
national identity. Today, the idea of 'multiculturalism'
is a familiar if vague one, ensconced within a large
academic penumbra; but during the middle decades of
the twentieth century this was a radically unusual way
to envisage the construction of a new state, particularly
one of India's size and assorted diversities.

DEFINING A NATIONAL IDENTITY FOR A DIVERSE SOCIETY

It required, then, a major act of intellectual and
political imagination on Nehru's part in order to
materialize this conception of a plural Indian identity
through a format of state arrangements that imprinted
subsequent practice. As I have suggested, Nehru
achieved it not from a position of pre-eminence, or on
the basis of a shared consensus, but through political
skill, and often from positions of vulnerability.[9] Three
aspects of this achievement are worth recalling.
First, he used the instruments of the inherited
colonial state, and transformed the state's orientation.
Unusually, perhaps even uniquely among anti-colonial
nationalist movements, the pre-Independence
Congress party lacked the capacity to impose by
force its definition of a national identity. Unlike
many other anti-colonial movements—such as in
Algeria, Indonesia, and Vietnam—the Congress had
no military arm (Subhas Bose was alienated from
the Congress party precisely for choosing to oppose
the British in this way). Consequently, it could not
turn this against its 'own' peoples in order to impose
nationhood—again, unlike these other movements. In

this respect the acquisition of the state in 1947, with
its military and bureaucratic arms, provided Congress
with the minimal preconditions for sustaining any
sense of nationhood. But now a new justification
was offered for the use of these instruments: they
were not, as the Raj had proclaimed, merely there
for keeping social order and meting out even-handed
punishments and rewards. They were a means to
impart cohesion and to draw Indians into a shared
project of development. Nehru managed at once to
pull nationalism away from a primarily culturalist
definition and towards a developmental content, and
thereby recast the purposes of the colonial state. With
the British gone, but with their state largely intact
and in the possession of Indians, the state's energies
were directed towards remedying an array of social
ills: poverty, caste injustice, and 'communalism' (the
use of religion for political ends), whose defeat Nehru
believed required the agency of a unitary and expansive
state. In retrospect, this over-reliance on the state was
to debilitate the very project of development that had
sanctioned it. Interestingly and fatefully absent from
Nehru's redescription of the state and its purposes was
the use of mass education—of the daily inculcation
of a nationalist ethic through ordinary schools, a
technique used by most nation-states.[10] In this respect,
the Nehruvian state failed both to educate and to
inculcate. But it *did* serve to hold the country together.

Second, the Constitution was to play a key
role in formatting the relation between Nehru's
conception of India's diversities and its democratic
order. The Indian Constitution is best seen not as a
strong ideological statement of a logically consistent
world view, but rather as a force field that tries to
stabilize a range of often contradictory considerations.
The basic elements of the institutional design that
set the terms for Indian identity were fourfold:
universal suffrage within a single electorate, the
allocation of powers between the Central state and
the regional governments, policies of 'reservation' or
affirmative action directed at improving the position
of historically disadvantaged caste groups, and legal
pluralism in civil law—intended to instil in religious
minorities trust in the new state.

As Nehru conceived it, and as the Constitution
articulated it, Indian national identity was neither

exhaustive nor immutable. Rather, Indianness was an assemblage of other belongings, themselves alterable within limits: attachments of language, of culture, and of religion, with these elements only weakly arranged in a lexical ordering. The mobility of such elements was recognized in several ways.

Among the provisions in the Constitution, the Central state tacitly adopted the principle that India's internal units—the regional states comprising the Union—were not based on naturally fixed identities and boundaries. These boundaries could be redrawn, and the Central state could quite easily create new units through legislating into existence more states (as it has done over the past fifty years—most recently in 2000, when three new states were created). Regional identities were thus not seen as requiring absorption within an encompassing Indian one; rather, the Constitution enabled the state to recognize new identities, to accede to the claims of various cultural groups for their own regional governments. The Constitution also accepted the principle of treating its constituent units asymmetrically. Thus it was accepted that Kashmir, India's only Muslim-majority state, would be treated differently, and it was granted more autonomy than other states of the Union; though ironically this has since been undermined by New Delhi's unwillingness and inability to allow democratic politics to consolidate there.

Further, on the issue of language, a basic marker of regional as well as national identity and a subject of considerable contention in pre-Independence debates, the Constitution achieved a deft compromise. Instead of adopting a 'national language', the decision was taken to defer this choice, and to create the category of 'official languages', those in which public business could be done. Alongside Hindi and English, India has a 'schedule' or list of around another 22 nationally recognized languages, a list that has expanded over the past five decades at virtually no political cost. (The most recent constitutional amendment to include more languages was in 2003, and more can be expected.) The status of English and Hindi has meanwhile been subject to parliamentary review every ten years, which has allowed their continued use and acceptance on pragmatic grounds without giving them a permanent and irrevocable status.

The still trickier matter of religion was also handled through improvization. With the decision to end the Raj's practice of divided electorates (where Muslims voted only for Muslims, Hindus for Hindus, and so on) and to establish universal suffrage within a single, common electorate, new protections had to be found for religious minorities in order to keep their trust in the state. In parallel to the recognition of Indians as possessing regional linguistic identities, the Constitution enabled the law to recognize Indians as attached to religious communities. Thus, the legal pluralism of colonial practice was now established as a constitutional feature: on matters of civil and customary law, citizens could choose to be governed either by their own religion or by the state's civil law. Given his views about the mutable, transactional nature of cultures, Nehru had hoped and expected that these protections would change, and that individuals and their communities would in time opt for a common civil code—and indeed these provisions too were subject to parliamentary review. In this case Nehru's optimism was perhaps misplaced. In later decades Hindu nationalists were able to use such special provisions as fodder for their attacks, while conservative Muslim clerics have found in them a means to control their flock.

The issue of caste identities, too, was handled with contingent expedience. The 'reservation' of places in educational institutions and in government employment for those groups at the very bottom of the caste order was similarly subject to parliamentary review every decade. In fact, it became a permanent fixture of India's democratic politics. The determination of groups eligible for the benefits of 'reservation' was left to the regional legislatures, giving politicians a resource to manipulate.

Thus, the fundamental markers of identity—language, caste, and religion—were granted a degree of fluidity and revisibility from the viewpoint of how the state recognized their claims. This provisionalism rendered language, caste, and religion as part of political rather than cultural categories. As such, their form and implications depended heavily on the skills of political leadership—skills that in subsequent decades were available in erratic supply, thereby placing the burden of intervening in disputes over the terms of identity on non-elected bodies and the courts.

Nehru made it a point to regularly restate the principles underlying his practice.[11] However, perhaps the most noteworthy—and third—aspect of how he handled the dilemmas of national identity was his willingness to defer certain potentially divisive matters of identity. This tactic of temporizing in response to calls for decisive definitions of a uniform Indian identity—for instance, from advocates of Hindi as the national language, or Hindu reformers who wished to abolish multiple legal codes in favour of a common one—has been seen as a potential weakness both from the perspective of Western theories of nationalism (theories that guided the thinking of Hindu nationalists), and from liberal theory. In fact, it was one of the more creative and enabling aspects of the nationalist imagination installed after 1947.[12]

CONTESTING NATIONAL IDENTITY

Nehru was able to institute a certain conception of the national community. But this specification of diversities within a democratic frame represented a contingent, historical success. The initial conception failed to foresee exactly how its provisions would subsequently come to be used. This of course is the risk of revisibility, and what triumphed was not a work of ideological purity or philosophical beauty, but a messy work in perpetual progress. Alternative versions of nationalism, which invoked narrower ideas of religion and culture, continued to be present as live political projects, and much of Nehru's prime ministerial life was spent trying to contain and limit these alternatives, whether in the form of Hindu 'communalism' or break-away claims. Indeed, within two decades of Nehru's death in 1964, India's layered, plural self-definitions faced challenges from these quarters.

By the mid-1980s, Indian intellectuals were puzzling over why, four decades after the end of colonialism, the identities of religion and caste had begun to invade national politics. This, the first serious challenge to India's plural identity, has generated an important debate about the nature of Indian

secularism.[13] But such debates were themselves symptoms of much wider changes in society, and in terms of political identity.

It is impossible to briefly recount even a conceptual narrative of Indian politics over the past quarter century, but some points must be noted. The axis of connection between state and society since 1947 had been the Congress party: it had served as a kind of translation machine, enabling communication between the elites and the masses. But Congress was entering a period of crisis, brought on partly by historical fatigue and the waning of the earlier anti-colonial aura—an inevitable generational obsolescence—and partly by the political 'awakening' of the lower castes and the poor, who from the 1980s were coming into the democratic system in increasing numbers. At previous moments of expansion in the political arena—for example in the 1920s or again in the 1950s, Congress had been able to reach out and accommodate this: either by reorganizing itself as it had done under Gandhi in the 1920s, or by reorganizing the Indian state system, as it had done under Nehru with the creation of linguistic states in the 1950s. But now, in the 1980s, Congress recoiled: unable to find innovative modes of response, it centralized and blocked internal channels of communication.

The results of this recoil were immediately felt. Regional groups and newly politicized castes were no longer able to find a voice within the party. Dissent was forced out, either onto the streets or into new political parties,[14] and demands against the Central state were now asserted more aggressively. In the 1950s, the regional call was for cultural recognition in the form of unilingual states; by the end of the 1960s, movements in western states like Maharashtra were calling for the restriction of economic opportunities to their own 'native sons'; and by the 1980s, demands had escalated to full-throated separatism in states like Punjab and Kashmir.

In reaction, the Central state now resorted to describing these regional demands as 'anti-national' and as threats to 'national integrity', in order to justify a still greater concentration of powers. This of course merely provoked still further dissent.

Moreover, a crucial change in the treatment of the terms of national identity became evident. Previously, national leaderships had never invoked religion for electoral purposes. This taboo fell in the 1980s. Thus, the insecurities of different religious minorities were played on: Hindu minorities in Kashmir and Punjab, Muslim minorities in north India, all were invited to support Congress in return for safety and favours. The implications of this deviation from the Congress principle became clear in the Congress-orchestrated anti-Sikh violence that followed Mrs Indira Gandhi's assassination in 1984. The Indian nationalism of Mahatma Gandhi and Nehru had both resisted invoking religion for political purposes, and had also avoided defining the nation in terms of a majority community—both men saw that India was a nation of incipient minorities, where every citizen might potentially define themselves as a member of some minority. However, now the appeal to a more simplified sense of democracy—as the rule of the majority, which had a permanent (because religious) identity, began to change Nehru's pluralist rendition of national identity.

This was manifest in two ways. First, the new majoritarian sense of democracy exacerbated the alienation of those in the regions. Here, one has to recall the distribution across the country of both the electorate and seats to the national Parliament. India's largest state sends 80 members to India's 543-seat Parliament; smaller states like Punjab and Kashmir send, respectively, just 13 and 6. It is possible to win national elections while simply ignoring the claims of dissident states. In a paradox of democratic procedure—one that Europeans today find themselves wrestling with—certain smaller regional states were faced with structural disenfranchisement. Second, the currency of a language of majoritarian democracy gave purchase to the rivals for Central power enabling their own claims to represent the nation. Thus, the practices of the Congress began to revive the imagination of Hindu nationalists. The BJP, a direct beneficiary, explicitly styled itself as the legitimate heir to the Congress, and indeed it shared more with the political horizons of the Congress era than with the pattern of politics that began to emerge from the mid-1990s. The

BJP did offer a bold restatement of nationalism, albeit one entirely contrary to Nehru's.

CHALLENGES TO NATIONAL IDENTITY: HINDUTVA AND REGIONALISM

The BJP is the most recent incarnation of a Hindu nationalist party, created in 1980 out of the old Bharatiya Jan Sangh (Indian People's Party), itself an upgrade of the pre-1947 Hindu Mahasabha. But the BJP is a curious political phenomenon, not quite a political party like any other. In fact, it is merely the visible peak of a much larger, largely subterranean, mass of organizations known as the Sangh Parivar, all of whom are committed to the ideology of Hindu nationalism, or *Hindutva*—organizations that range from political associations, civil society groups, religious sects, and para-criminal gangs. The organization that directly controls the BJP is the Rashtriya Swayamsevak Sangh (RSS), a hierarchical, cadre-based movement founded in the 1920s in direct emulation of Mussolini's Brown Shirts, and which espouses Hindu supremacism. It was the extremist Hindus associated with the RSS who were responsible for Mahatma Gandhi's assassination, and for many years the RSS was a banned entity. Yet today, this extraordinary manifestation of esoteric power has become an extremely powerful element in India's political life, while remaining untransparent and unaccountable to constitutional norms. The RSS leadership determines all senior and significant appointments within the BJP, and virtually all senior BJP leaders (including former Prime Minister A.B. Vajpayee and former deputy leader, L.K. Advani) have been members of the RSS.

The BJP's definition of Indian nationalism is contrary to that associated with Nehru. It subscribes to Savarkar's definition of the ideology of Hindutva (the literal translation of this neologism is 'Hindu-ness'), which excludes as non-Indian all those religions whose origins do not lie within the territorial space of India (in effect, all religions except Hinduism, Buddhism, and Sikhism), and which views adherents of the 'non-Indian' religions as suspect or secondary citizens. Hindutva celebrates a glorious ancient Hindu past; but in the hands of the BJP, Hindutva also encompasses the armoury of the modern state, and in fact its understanding of nationalism is essentially a modern one, modelled on nineteenth-century European nationalisms. It is important to recognize this modernizing ambition of the BJP. It is not proposing a return to a traditional Hindu polity: it has no pastoral image of a stateless India composed of village republics, nor does it stipulate that all Indians must be Hindus. Its dreams are powerfully statist: to eliminate any legal and political recognition of cultural and religious differences. Although it declares itself as a positive project of 'cultural nationalism' ('one nation, one people, one culture', as its manifestos declare), in fact the BJP advocates a negative programme, one that seeks to efface all the signs of non-Hinduness that are integral to India. It hopes to fulfil the project of creating a modern Indian nation-state that contains a culturally and ethnically pure community, with a single Indian citizenship, defended by a state that has both God and nuclear warheads on its side.

Originally, Hindu nationalism was an ideology of the upper, Brahminic castes, but in recent decades it expanded beyond this elitist base, gaining support among the country's middle classes and castes to whom it offered a religious argot tailored for democratic times. The re-definition of the diverse forms of Hindu religion in the narrow terms of Hindutva achieved two things for the BJP. It allowed the party to successfully exploit an idiom of cultural dispossession, which resonates deeply in Indian politics (especially among the vast numbers excluded from the privileged circle of those who have some knowledge of the English language). And it enabled the BJP to claim to express some of the aspirations of India's expanding and selectively Westernized middle classes. Rising consumerism and the extension of the market during the 1980s did not nourish an individualistic hedonism, nor did it breed liberal individuals. Rather, it was experienced as an opportunity to consume the pleasures of modernity within collective units like the family (or even caste groups): several of the great Bollywood box office hits had as their recurring theme the celebration of domestic consumption, dining, and marriage. For many Indians, modernity is being sampled through the conservative filters of religious

piety, moralism, and domestic virtue, all veins of sentiment that the BJP and the Sangh Parivar have effectively mined and recharged.

Yet the rise of the BJP is only one of several complicated ways whereby a half-century of democracy has modified the terms of national identity. Even more important has been the restitution of powers to the regional states—and linked to this, the mobilization of lower-caste parties rooted in the regions. I noted earlier that identities of region and nation had historically emerged in tandem in India, and arguably this process—after some disruption in the later decades of the twentieth century—has now resumed its deeper historical pattern. Regional and national identities are today reinforcing one another, even as each helps the other to a sharper definition.

In a counter-trend to the centralizing energies of the 1970s and 1980s, the centre of gravity of India's democracy is being re-calibrated as much by economic developments as political ones. India's regional states are very large: the population of the largest, Uttar Pradesh, is around 166 million (and over the next decade, India is projected to have four states with populations over 100 million and 10 over 50 million). However, growing demographic weight is not the sole impetus: the reinvigoration of regional politics has also been encouraged by a combination of perceived opportunities and threats. First, although the Constitution withheld important fiscal and economic powers from regional governments, in recent years real economic powers have begun to flow to them. The reasons are various, and sometimes ironic: one is that national governments in New Delhi have preferred to pass to regional governments the responsibility—and blame—for liberalizing economic reforms (Jenkins 1999). Second, regional parties have found effective ways to use the opportunities presented by a declining Congress. For instance, they have taken advantage of the fact that the powers to legislate policies of affirmative action, to 'reserve' places in education and employment, lie with regional legislatures. Thus, political parties based on caste have found in these policies a powerful tool for electoral gain. Finally, the threat that the Hindu nationalists might capture power at the national level and use it to impose a singular definition of Indian identity has also acted as a spur to developing stronger regional poles of opposition. Such developments have resulted in more intense competition for control of these governments. Indeed, since the 1990s, the crucial arena of democratic competition has shifted to the regional states, which have become the basic units of political choice for Indians.

The two national parties, the Congress and BJP, can today only patchily claim to be true national parties. In 2004, for instance, they together managed to win less than half the vote share, with the rest going to regional and lower-caste parties (a proportion that has been relatively stable over the past decade). Although the BJP has sought to position itself as the new national party, it has never won more than one-fourth of the national vote share. It has proved very difficult in India to muster numerical majorities that can win power at the national level; and it is even more difficult to transform such victories, should they occur, into sustainable state power.

The evolution of India's centre-state relations is placing significant constraints on national-level movements and political parties, limiting sweeping ambitions. Electoral outcomes at the regional level have become difficult to sum into legible national choices—on the contrary, some have argued that election outcomes are simply an aggregation of regional verdicts. In the past, people voted in regional state elections as if they were voting in national elections, but now quite different logics are at work. With the delinking since the 1970s of cycles of national and state elections—every year, elections are being held in several Indian states—the possibility of pan-Indian electoral 'waves' around a single issue has dissipated. The BJP has vainly sought to conjure such a single issue, which could work to realign choices in both state and national elections: the destruction of the Babri Mosque in 1992, and the repeated attempts to revive the Ayodhya temple issue are examples.

That the meanings of India's national politics are being determined at the regional level does not imply, however, that India is experiencing 'regionalism', in the sense of centrifugal pulls weakening the Union. The earlier phase of secessionist sentiment has largely receded (with the exception of Kashmir—though even here there are some signs of change, with the

2002 elections raising the possibility of a revival of a democratic process there). The emerging politics of the regions is not isolationist, nor does it seek to withdraw from the Centre. On the contrary, these regional parties and the proliferation and fragmentation of the party system are actually helping to hold India together.

Since 1989, India has been governed by coalitions of various sorts, grouped mainly around the Congress and the BJP: the recent 2009 elections can be seen as having consolidated a two-coalition system. These coalition governments in New Delhi have forced regional parties and elites—with invariably parochial horizons—to become involved in national issues, to learn the rudiments of the Constitution, and perforce to enter the national imagination, even as they work to extract benefits for their own kind.

Another assumption about the diffusion of power in the era of coalitions was that India's economy and politics would suffer. Yet, the last two decades have seen India's highest growth rates: and while these cannot be claimed as the causal result of coalitions, it *is* the case that coalition governments have helped to secure a wider consensus for reforms, as well as to ensure their continuity across governments. Politically, too, the emergence of coalition governments in Delhi has had integrative functions for the nation, rather than destabilizing ones. Survey evidence makes clear that most Indians now see themselves as having dual allegiances, at once to their regional state and to India; and in fact Indian Muslims identify with India to a higher degree than do their Hindu compatriots. Indian-ness continues to be consolidated as a textured, rather than flat, conception of political identity.[15]

DEMOCRACY AND NATIONAL IDENTITY

The task of accommodating India's diversities into a shared national identity through democratic means has been an intricate undertaking, generating tensions, ironies, and paradoxes. In some important respects, democracy has failed India's diversities, both across space and in time. The instances of Kashmir and Punjab—and one might add the northeastern states of Nagaland and Mizoram; and the dates 1984 (anti-Sikh violence), 1992 (the destruction of the

Babri Mosque), and above all 2002 (the anti-Muslim violence in Gujarat) are etched into this history of failures, episodes when self-proclaimed majorities tried with bloody determination to redefine India's national identity.

Yet, if one stands back for a moment from particular episodes and locations and views India's democratic experience over time and on a continental scale, the darker shadings in the picture may look somewhat different. Much of the recent discussion on democratic transitions has focused on the shift from authoritarian regimes and dictatorships to democratic ones: that is, a shift from *one* modern regime to *another* modern regime form. But India's transition to a democratic regime and its consolidation is quite different, and cannot be mapped by the terms of the 'democratic transitions' literature. In fact, what we see in India is an *historical* or *epochal* shift, from an ancient regime to a modern political form which makes it truly a transition of Tocquevillean proportions. Such shifts are wrenching, often bloody affairs: think of the violent histories (both internal and external) of America and France since the eighteenth century, as they struggled to make themselves democratic nation-states.

India *has* had its episodes of violence, beginning with the horror of Partition in 1947, and it can expect to face recurring episodes in the future. That any Indian citizen at all should be killed by fellow citizens or by the state because of who they are, because of their identity, or the beliefs they profess, is inexcusable. Yet, if one accepts the calculations of those who have tried to sum the figures, one can put at roughly 15,000 the number of deaths in communal (that is, religious) violence since 1947;[16] and even after adding casualty figures from the insurgencies in Kashmir, Punjab, and the Northeast (all of which received international support), the figures remain low—both relative to India's overall size, and also in comparison to other societies that have gone through this long transition. For the most part, India's many identities have been relatively lightly molested by the state, and by one another. What has been called the Indian model of containing diversities, the 'salad bowl' rather than the 'melting pot', a model that allows distinct ingredients to retain their individuality—has on the whole been kept to.

Paradoxically, it may well be that the very things that Strachey and Tocqueville had claimed precluded India from becoming a nation have actually provided fruitful material for this task, and this for two reasons. It has made it difficult to entrench majoritarian or dominant identities which, had it happened, may well have led excluded groups to press for exit (as happened within the supposedly homogenous state of Pakistan, with the secession in 1971 of Bangladesh). And second, it has forced India's political elites to be inventive, they could not create a sense of nationhood simply by imitating existing models. There are at least two distinct ways of dealing with diversity: one is through generalization, the project of systematic transformation or erasure of particular identities in favour of more general ones (a project common to both religious and cultural nationalists, as well as Communists, who see class as a universal category). The other, which India has followed, is through composition, the recognition of differences of different kinds, and their locations within a shared frame.[17]

In a second paradox, it is precisely the workings of India's democracy that has created identities that threaten this democracy that *have* led to majoritarian excess. The identities of religion and caste that figure in Indian politics today are the creation of democracy, and not the intrusion of the primordial: they are ways of asserting, in the language of modern representative politics, claims to recognition and fair treatment; and as such they will have to be addressed and accommodated by the resources of democratic politics itself. There are, in India's democratic experience, examples of self-correcting mechanisms which show how this might be done. Though at times purely symbolic, one should not underestimate the power of symbolism in a society where the majority are non- or semi-literate (think, for instance, of the symbolic significance of different religious and caste backgrounds of holders of high state office). However, many of these self-correcting mechanisms are not purely symbolic, and have directly practical effects: for example, the reassignment of powers to the regions in ways that have also integrated them into national power.

There is also a paradox in the fact that in India, as in many other places, democratic politics and the protection of diversities rely for their continuance on non-democratic instruments and agencies. Democracy, that is to say, and the proliferation of identities that ensue from the workings of its politics, can challenge and sometimes even subvert democracy itself; hence the recourse to agencies outside the democratic field to moderate the pressures of democratic identity assertion. One of the cornerstones of India's democracy today is a non-elected body, the Election Commission, an agency invented in India, and legislated into existence in 1950, on the eve of India declaring itself a republic. Made up of three commissioners with a status equivalent to Supreme Court judges, the Election Commission is charged with the impartial conduct of political elections. However, since its inception its responsibilities have expanded to include, for instance, the supervision of internal democracy within political parties, the maintenance of codes of secular conduct during campaigning, and even the making of essentially political decisions about when elections will be held. The Indian Election Commission has become an important defender of the principle of diversity, a model now adopted in a number of democracies (including South Africa), and it has become the country's most trusted institution: amongst Indians, 46 per cent expressed a great deal of trust in the Election Commission, as compared with only 20 per cent with a great deal of trust in elected representatives.

Nehru and his generation understood that the future of democracy in India would not be fully congruent with the will of its creators. They knew as well that they could not entirely quieten the more aggressive forms of nationalism and political identification that have indeed since emerged. But the original arrangements, designed to sustain a national identity that did not seek to efface the country's layered diversities, have on the whole and over time managed to constrain such forms to intermittent life. No democracy can hope to be self-guaranteeing; but the longer it endures, the more it is able to develop resources to endure still further in time.

NOTES

1. See Khilnani (2004).
2. Strachey (1888, pp. 5–8), delivered this judgement in a lecture in 1885, the very year the Indian National Congress was formed—a movement whose raison d'etre was to refute this view.
3. See, for example, Cohn (1987).
4. On the peculiar character of Indian civil society, see Kaviraj and Khilnani (2001, Chs 9 and 15).
5. For studies that offer excellent insight into this process, see Pollock (2003) and Bayly (1998).
6. Tagore to Charles Freer Andrews, March 1921, cited in Sen (2005). See also Berlin (1996).
7. See Nehru (1946).
8. Cf Amartya Sen for a view of reason's prior claims over identity. See Sen (1999).
9. Cf Kothari (1970), for the argument that the Nehru period rested on a consensus.
10. This failure opened opportunities for Hindu nationalists, who have understood the importance of education. See Benei (2001).
11. Nehru did this in several ways: Nehru's correspondence with his own political colleagues is a continual commentary on his practice, a statement of his principles, intentions, and revisions. See, for example, Nehru (1985–9). In his public speeches, as well in his use of public spectacles, such as the annual Republic Day parades, he sought to reiterate his conception.
12. The Constituent Assembly debates over language are very revealing on the subject of the differing ideas of national identity. See King (1997), Rai (2001), and Dasgupta (1970, Ch. 5).
13. Some of the important contributions to this debate are collected in Bhargava (1998).
14. For a study of the decline of Congress and the rise of rival parties against the background of blockages in internal party democracy, see Chandra (2003).
15. Cf also responses to the question: 'We should be loyal to our region first and then to India'. According to NES, the percentage of respondents who agree with this has declined—67.1 per cent in 1971, 52.9 per cent in 1996, 50.7 per cent in 1998.
16. See Varshney (2002), for an earlier estimate and Wilkinson (2004).
17. I owe the formulation of this distinction to Sudipta Kaviraj.

REFERENCES

Bayly, C.A. 1998. *The Origins of Nationality in South Asia: Patriotism and Ethical Government in the Making of Modern India*. New Delhi: Oxford University Press.

Benei, Veronique. 2001. 'Teaching Nationalism in Maharashtra Schools', in Veronique Benei and C.J. Fuller (eds), *The Everyday State and Society in India*. New Delhi: C Hurst & Co. Publishers.

Berlin, Isaiah. 1996. 'Rabindranath Tagore and the

Consciousness of Nationality', in Isaiah Berlin, *The Sense of Reality*. London: Chatto & Windus, pp. 249–68.

Bhargava, R. (ed.). 1998. *Secularism and its Critics*. New Delhi: Oxford University Press.

Chandra, Kanchan. 2003. *Why Ethnic Parties Succeed*. Cambridge: Cambridge University Press.

Cohn, Bernard. 1987. *An Anthropologist among the Historians*. New Delhi: Oxford University Press.

Dasgupta, Joytindra. 1970. *Language Conflict and National Development*. Berkeley: University of California Press.

de Tocqueville, Alexis. 1962. 'Ebauches d'un ouvrage sur l'Inde', in J.J. Chevalier and A. Jardin (eds), *Alexis de Tocqueville: Oeuvres Completes*. Paris: Gallimard.

Jenkins, R. 1999. *Democratic Politics and Economic Reform in India*. Cambridge: Cambridge University Press.

Kaviraj, S. and S. Khilnani (eds). 2001. *Civil Society: History and Possibilities*. Cambridge: Cambridge University Press.

Khilnani, Sunil. 2004. 'The Idea of India in the Era of Globalisation', in Kay Glans (ed.), *Visions of Global Society*. Stockholm: Axess Publishing.

King, Robert D. 1997. *Nehru and the Language Politics of India*. New Delhi: Oxford University Press.

Kothari, R. 1970. *Politics in India*. New Delhi: Orient Longman.

Nehru, Jawaharlal. 1985–9. *Letters to Chief Ministers 1947–1964*, 5 Vols. New Delhi: Nehru Memorial Fund.

———. 1946. *The Discovery of India*. Calcutta: Signet Press.

Pollock, Sheldon (ed.). 2003. *Literary Cultures in History: Reconstructions from South Asia*. Berkeley: University of California Press.

Przeworski, Adam. 1991. *Democracy and the Market*. Cambridge: Cambridge University Press.

Rai, Alok. 2001. *Hindi Nationalism*. Hyderabad: Orient Longman.

Sen, Amartya. 2005. *The Argumentative Indian: Writings on Indian History, Culture and Identity*. New York: Farrar, Straus and Giroux.

———. 1999. 'Reason before Identity', The Romanes Lecture, Oxford.

Strachey, John. 1888. *India*. London: Kegan Paul.

Varshney, Ashutosh. 2002. *Ethnic Conflict and Civic Life: Hindus and Muslims in India*. New Haven, Connecticut: Yale University Press.

Wilkinson, Steven. 2004. *Votes and Violence: Electoral Competition and Ethnic Riots in India*. Cambridge/New York: Cambridge University Press.

14 The Hindu Nationalists and Power

Christophe Jaffrelot

Sometimes, political movements try not to be involved in politics. They may adopt such an attitude for tactical reasons: they do not want to appear to be political in order to woo more followers or to escape the repression of the state, which may reject the kind of politics they embody. They may also try to avoid politics because they do not want to compromise and cause any degradation to their ideological purity—their so-called ideals being often, in fact, radical and exclusive. However, a movement promoting a project for the whole society needs to enter the political arena to get its views implemented. One way out, here, may consist in creating a party in charge of the mess that is politics. The Trade Union Congress did it with the Labour Party in Britain. Then the mother organization may have difficulties when it comes to maintaining harmonious relations with its subsidiary. Most of the time, the former disapproves of the way the latter compromises on its principles, and the party may do so well that it may try to emancipate itself.

In India, the Sangh Parivar is experiencing such a situation—to some extent. Its matrix, the Rashtriya Swayamsevak Sangh (RSS—National Volunteers Corps), has developed a strictly codified ideology of Hindu nationalism, which is political to the core—but the movement does not want to appear as political, lest this label dissuade potential followers from joining its ranks, and lead the state to repress postures that are not legitimate from the point of view of the Constitution. The RSS also looked at politics as something dirty, which might distract its activists from the long-term achievements it aimed to achieve. It has, therefore, promoted the emergence of a political party, with which relations have been rather complicated, especially when it has been in office.

THE RSS, A NATIONALIST SECT

The RSS was founded in 1925 in reaction to what was then perceived as aggressive pan-Islamism on the part of the Muslim minority. In the early 1920s, the movement in defence of the Khilafat—threatened by the dismantling of the Ottoman Empire during the post World War I peace talks—had in effect occasionally degenerated into outbreaks of violence directed against Hindus.[1] These incidents provoked a sort of majoritarian inferiority complex among some members of the Hindu intelligentsia, for which the ground had already been laid by the colonial stereotype that described Hindus as a meek, even effeminate, 'race' (Bamford 1985 [1925]).[2]

The Foot Soldiers of Hindutva

The RSS, created to overcome this feeling of vulnerability, was supposed to enable Hindus to assimilate the qualities perceived as being at the root of Muslim strength, starting with their allegedly intense sense of community. Hindu nationalism, generally speaking, relied on a strategy of stigmatization and emulation of so-called threatening others. As a result Hindu nationalists have always tried to imitate those who, according to them, were posing a threat to Hinduism—mainly the Muslims and Christians—in order to resist them more effectively. For instance, they tried to build pan-Hindu temples which could welcome all the members of the community, like the mosques. At the same time, RSS ideologues have always endeavoured to demonstrate that the Hindus met the criteria, as codified by nineteenth-century Western scholars, of a nation. This ideological construct was primarily based on an ethnic myth, according to which the Hindus descend from the first Aryans who lived on the subcontinent. One of the main instigators of Hindu nationalism, V.D. Savarkar, declared in 1923 in his treatise on 'Hinduness' (Hindutva), which directly inspired K.B. Hedgewar, founder of the RSS: 'All Hindus claim to have in their veins the blood of the mighty race incorporated with and descended from the Vedic fathers' (Savarkar 1962 [1923]: 85).

This conception owes much to the writings of nineteenth-century European Orientalists and socio-religious reform movements such as the Arya Samaj.[3] The invention of this tradition of an ethnic Golden Age going back to the Vedic era is the touchstone of Hindu nationalism. Its proponents worked out a national territory clearly delimited by the Himalayas and the sea, from the land covered in the first Aryan invasions, *Aryavarta*, which in the Vedic texts is the sacred land of sacrificial rites. Hindu nationalist ideologues also saw in this prestigious antiquity a common language, Sanskrit, which scholarly research

into Indo-European civilization helped to establish as the mother of all languages. The aim of the RSS was to restore the grandeur of the Hindus' culture, and their supremacy over a land that had been invaded by foreigners so many times.

The very structure of the RSS and its everyday activities—which, like its ideology, have changed little over time—reflect its ambition of acting as a crucible and an agent for a new Hindu nation. In its basic units, the *shakhas* (local branches), dozens of children and adolescents in uniform gather to partake in daily calisthenics and ideological instruction, where they learn of the former glory of Vedic India and the kingdoms predating the Muslim invasions, or those that offered resistance to them. Although the movement arose out of an initiative of Maharashtra Brahmins, who have continued to lead it since its founding by Hedgewar, the mission of the shakhas is to recruit members without regard for caste or class. The shakhas are in fact the framework for the psychosocial reform on which the Hindu nation is supposed to be built, as a 'brotherhood in saffron'.[4] The aim of this institution is to inculcate in the *swayamsevaks* (volunteers) a nationalist conscience and sense of solidarity among equals, which will make the RSS the spearhead of the Hindu nation in a sociological context dominated by caste, sect, and regional distinctions. The ambition of its leaders to make it the matrix of a homogenous Hindu nation from all perspectives (historical references, sociological behaviours, ideological allegiances, and so on) meant that their plan was conceived as a long-term endeavour: the aim was to cover the entire country with a network of shakhas radiating out from its place of origin in central India: Nagpur in Maharashtra.

This aim has, to a large extent, been achieved. In 2004, the movement had 33,758 shakhas and 48,329 *upshakhas* ([sub branch] simply because in some cities and towns the RSS has much more than one shakha),[5] comprising mostly young Hindus, and a constantly renewed membership. The network nevertheless remains fairly sparse in southern India, particularly in Tamil Nadu where the population, which is very attached to Dravidian culture, is not especially receptive to the RSS' Sanskritized references, and is even hostile towards its desire to make Hindi the national language. Elsewhere, this coverage provides the movement with a means to carry out in-depth actions at the local level.

The Sangh and its Parivar

The value of social work can be clearly seen in the services rendered to populations in distress: the RSS has always come to the aid of Hindu refugees, be they victims of Partition or those who, since 1990, have fled the upsurge of violence in Kashmir.[6] Its volunteers also participate regularly in rescue operations following natural disasters such as earthquakes. Their discipline and the promptness with which they set up tent camps, collect aid donations, and distribute goods of prime necessity is always noteworthy.[7] This strategy of social work, which in the eyes of RSS cadres symbolizes a form of Hindu solidarity that should be spread through the society to make it a nation, enables it to gain access to new social milieus.

The RSS's vocation of working in (and on) society acquired a new dimension when it founded a series of specialized institutions. Soon after Independence, anxious to counteract an increasingly active Communist Party, it formed union organizations on a double front: the Akhil Bharatiya Vidyarthi Parishad (ABVP), created in 1948 for the students, and the Bharatiya Mazdoor Sangh (BMS), which was founded in 1955 for the workers and now, with 1.8 million members, is the country's largest union organization.[8] Other, more sector-based organizations were also founded in the 1950s, such as the Vanavasi Kalyan Ashram (Ashram for Tribal Welfare) instituted in 1952, which mainly aimed to offset the influence of Christian missions among the tribal populations, whose conversion was perceived as a process of 'denationalization'. In 1964, this stake even justified setting up a new branch, the Vishwa Hindu Parishad (VHP), also aiming to bring together the greatest possible number of representatives of Hindu sects to form a sort of consistory. This creation again partakes of the logic of stigmatization and emulation of threatening others, since it developed in reaction to the feelings of vulnerability sparked by the proselytism of the international Christian network. RSS leaders endeavoured to transpose its structure, perceived as a model of effectiveness; in other words,

to endow Hinduism with a Church. In 1979, the 'RSS family' expanded with the addition of another new organization aimed to fight untouchability and aid the most destitute. The Seva Bharati (Indian Service, a recruitment agency for volunteer social workers) dispenses healthcare on occasion, but is mainly involved in educational work. This line of action, to some extent, overlaps that of the Sarasvati Shishu Mandir, which, since 1952, has formed a network of schools with a highly ideologized and Sanskritized curriculum. This includes schools in slums and villages where education needs are far from being met.

As early as the 1950s, therefore, the RSS had developed a network of front organizations, which came to be known as the 'Sangh Parivar', the family of the RSS. One of the first components of this nebula—which has not been mentioned yet, but which was bound to play a major role—was the Jana Sangh, a political party founded in 1951. The relationship between this party and its mother organization was to be very complicated, as one could have expected from the very conception of power evolved by the RSS.

THE RSS' CONCEPTION OF POWER: THE RAJ GURU MODEL

The key word in the RSS lexicon is probably 'renunciation'. Indeed, it has always tried to associate itself with the values of asceticism and sacrifice. A medical practitioner by training, Hedgewar refused to work as a doctor or marry so as to better devote himself to the cause of a Hindu nationalist revival. His asceticism and devotion led to his being likened to a guru in the RSS ranks. Madhav S. Golwalkar, whom he appointed to succeed himself as leader of the RSS in 1940 shortly before his death, enjoyed the same status, symbolized this time by the nickname 'Guruji', due to his spiritual quest. The members of the RSS consider these two dignitaries of the movement *jivan muktas* ('liberated while living'), and their mausoleums remain places of pilgrimage in Nagpur (Andersen and Damle 1987: 37, 80).

Beyond these tutelary figures, the entire RSS structure conforms to the same rationale. As early as 1927, Hedgewar undertook to train *pracharaks* (preachers and full-time cadres) in officers' training camps. They were to spearhead the RSS as artisans of new shakhas throughout India. They were—and still are—young militants with organizational skills, who agree to forgo founding a family and undertaking a career, even though many of them are still in university or have already graduated. Their commitment/enrolment is on a voluntary basis, and the organization takes care of their needs with the help of local patrons. This renunciation constitutes a great source of prestige among adolescents they are supposed to attract to shakhas or among associated organizations (ABVP, BMS, VHP, and so on.) they are assigned by the RSS to lead. An invocation of the values of renunciation is of course illegitimate, because these men are not working towards their own salvation; they are looked upon as *karma yogis* because they dedicate all their energy to the 'salvation' of their nation.

In its attempt to fashion Hindu society into a nation, the RSS has always claimed to care little about coming to power. Its aim was to transform society from below through the network of shakhas. Keeping such a long-term perspective in mind, Hedgewar systematically turned down requests from parties for support from the militant forces of the shakhas (Joshi 1970: 15). In his view, changes coming from state-related institutions could never be as effective as those emerging from society itself. In his manifesto, published in 1938, which was the RSS' main ideological treatise before Independence, Golwalkar dismissed as irrelevant any ambitions regarding the state (Golwalkar 1939: 59).

This disinterest in state power and enthusiasm for social work resulted from the conviction that the fundamental principle of Hindu national identity resides in society itself, apart from the state, and that the custodian of social order must be the spiritual counsellor of state power. In the brahminical interpretation of the Hindu tradition that the RSS developed, he who holds temporal power remains subject to spiritual authority, which enables him to preserve the dharma: the king is thus guided by a Brahmin, the Raj Guru. Emphasizing its respect for the spiritual values of renunciation, the RSS offers to fulfil the role of dharmic advisor to the state, as suggested by Golwalkar himself:

The political rulers were never the standard-bearers of our society. They were never taken as the props of our national life. Saints and sages, who had risen above the mundane temptations of self and power and had dedicated themselves wholly for establishing a happy, virtuous and integrated state of society were its constant torch-bearers. They represented the *dharmasalta* (*sic*) [religious authority]. The king was only an ardent follower of that higher moral authority. (Golwalkar 1966: 93)

Golwalkar elaborates further:

We aspire to become the radiating Centre of all the age-old cherished ideals of our society—just as the indescribable power which radiates through the sun. Then the political power which draws its life from that source of society, will have no other [goal than?] to reflect the same radiance. (Golwalkar 1966: 103)

These views reveal the limits of the RSS' indifference to power, but help us clarify its relationship to the state: ideally, the movement would like to be the counsellor of a like-minded government in the hands of 'its' political party. But how could the Jana Sangh seize power without diluting the ideology of the Parivar that it was part of?

IN SEARCH OF A POLITICAL STRATEGY

Despite denying any political ambition, in 1951 Golwalkar agreed to form a party under pressure from certain RSS members concerned with the movement's absence in this field.[9] In 1948, the RSS, having been banned after Gandhi's assassination by a (former) swayamsevak, realized the extent of its isolation in a political system dominated by the secular and progressive ideas propounded by Nehru, who viewed this movement as the Indian version of fascism. Golwalkar assigned a number of pracharaks to build up the new party, the Jana Sangh (People's Association), but drew a clear demarcating line between the two organizations whose hierarchies, for one, were quite distinct.[10]

The Jana Sangh: From Instrumentalism to Coalition Politics

The party was structured along the model of the 'RSS networks' of the 1950s. Its leaders, including

Deendayal Upadhyaya, who was the most influential, did not seem interested in capturing power, but contended themselves with propagating the Hindu nationalist ideology. Its ultimate objective was not the conquest of power, the state being an unimportant institution, but the reform of society. In 1962, Upadhyaya still looked upon elections as an 'opportunity to educate the people on political issues' (Upadhyaya 1962: 20). However, the Jana Sangh gradually adopted an instrumentalist strategy, manipulating identity symbols for political mobilization (Brass 1991, especially ch. 3), like the protection of the cow, the promotion of Hindi, or the defence of Ayurvedic medicine. Nevertheless, the Jana Sangh was caught in a stranglehold by the 'Congress system'[11]: on the one hand the 'Hindu traditionalists'[12] among the Congress at the local level were already active in favour of issues such as protection of the cows and the promotion of Hindi as the national language, thereby depriving the Jana Sangh of arguments; on the other hand, the highest level of the state, embodied by Nehru, and later his daughter Indira Gandhi, strictly defended secular positions and conducted campaigns against the Jana Sangh and the RSS, even banning some of its shakhas.[13]

Now, this cause of isolation could hardly be counterbalanced by the access to grassroots Hindu society, as the RSS lacked intermediaries who were powerful enough. It was true that the RSS had created a press agency and more or less official organs, but its means remained limited—especially with respect to radio broadcasting, which Indira Gandhi used in an extremely populist fashion in the 1970s. Moreover, the RSS militant network and its offshoots were only expanding slowly, and could not be entirely detailed to the task of political mobilization. The fact that it did not appeal to religious figures (sect leaders, sadhus[holy-men]), who preferred to invest their efforts in more conservative organizations such as the Ram Rajya Parishad (Council of the Kingdom of Ram) also proved detrimental.

The effects of these various constraints were clearly felt in 1966, when the Hindu nationalists launched a huge campaign to protect cows with an eye to the approaching fourth general election. The official aim was to secure a constitutional revision that would have enabled the Centre to pass a legislation in this regard, since some states had not prohibited cow slaughter. Faithful to the secular heritage handed down by her father, Indira Gandhi made no concessions, despite the scale of the demonstrations held outside Parliament and the hunger strike undertaken by several religious personalities. The movement also slackened due to a lack of coordination between the Hindu nationalists and these prestigious figures of Hinduism, whose political allegiances or independent spirit created an obstacle to planning such an agitation. Compared to the 1962 elections, the Jana Sangh only progressed by three percentage points, with 9.4 per cent of the vote in the 1967 elections, its ideological isolation limiting the scope of its alliances with other opposition parties.

In the late 1960s, it finally decided to tone down its Hindu nationalist militancy in order to be more palatable to other opposition parties loyal to the spirit of the Constitution, be they socialist or pro-farmer parties, or those born of splits with the Congress, such as the Congress (Organization). Indira Gandhi's declaration of a state of Emergency in 1975 accelerated this evolution, which led the Jana Sangh to merge within the Janata Party (People's Party), a coalition of anti-Congress forces. It supplied the group with the largest contingent of MPs, and the party won a strong majority in the 1977 elections. The rationale behind this strategy of integration obviously involved working on the political system from within. The aim was to try and produce a political culture that combined a somewhat watered-down form of Hindu nationalism with the 'Hindu traditionalism' of the former Congress members.

Hindu nationalist influence was reflected in the government through three types of agendas, revealing the penetration of the ideological categories inherited from the RSS. First of all the group of ex-Jana Sangh Members of Parliament (MPs) backed a bill to amend the Constitution that aimed to make the ban on slaughtering cows a matter of federal jurisdiction. Next, ex-Jana Sangh MPs introduced a bill aiming to control conversions which were often coupled, according to them, with bribes or other forms of pressure. This desire for 'top-down' intervention, which targeted the Christian missionaries who were particularly active in tribal areas, reflected, despite the 82.6 per cent Hindus counted in the 1981 census, the dread of a demographic decline that forms part of the RSS' majoritarian inferiority complex. Finally, the Hindu nationalists took part in a campaign to revise history textbooks, which—having been written by Communist-leaning members of the intelligentsia—did not, according to them, portray the Hindu kingdoms and their struggles against Muslim invaders in a favourable enough light.

Although limited in scope, these projects and demands reveal the Hindu nationalist conception of power. The state is called upon to intervene to make minorities respect Hindu culture and assimilate into it by swearing allegiance to its symbols of identity, and by identifying with its history. For the Muslim and Christian communities, this implies confining their own religious practices to the private sphere, and engaging in a genuine process of acculturation.

These ideological options contributed to the marginalization of former Jana Sangh members, who had to finally withdraw from the Janata Party in 1980. This break prompted the RSS to reorient its strategy along more political lines, in which the religious dimension took on a more instrumental form, as it had in 1966-7.

Even before this split, the problems encountered by Hindu nationalists in 1979 in their relations with other components of the Janata Party had prompted Deoras, who had succeeded Golwalkar in 1973, to unleash an offensive from a political perspective. During a lecture to the VHP, he declared:

> Hindus must now awaken themselves to such an extent that even from the elections point of view the politicians will have to respect the Hindu sentiments and change their policy accordingly....If others put up demands, they were accepted, but even genuine demands by Hindus are ignored. This is because Muslims and other minorities usually vote *en bloc* while Hindus are divided. Once Hindus get united, the government would start caring for them also.[14]

Since the political wing of the RSS, rechristened the Bharatiya Janata Party (BJP) after the 1980 split, persevered in a strategy of integrating legitimate politics at the price of considerably watering down its Hindu nationalism, the VHP was put in charge of organizing the campaign Doras longed for to spark a 'Hindu awakening'.

The 1980s–90s: Religious Mobilization for Electoral Purposes

The implementation of an instrumentalist strategy in the course of the 1980s generated a much greater Hindu mobilization than it had in 1966-7, both from the standpoint of scale as well as duration and electoral impact. This contrast can partly be explained by changes in the two aforementioned variables, and in the communal relations that rekindled the majoritarian inferiority complex.

The VHP chose to focus its agitation on the demand to rebuild the temple that once stood above the supposed birthplace of the god Ram in Ayodhya (a city located near Faizabad in Uttar Pradesh). The building was said to have been replaced by a mosque in the sixteenth century after the Mughal dynasty rose to power. In 1949, an idol of Ram mysteriously appeared in the mosque—placed there in all likelihood by Hindu nationalists—provoking demonstrations of fervour that prompted the authorities to place seals on this holy place. A few decades later, the choice of this issue remained a very judicious one, given the extent to which the figure of Ram is worshipped, particularly in north India. The VHP, in fact, immediately rallied several religious figures (sect leaders and sadhus), whose prestige further amplified its capacity for mobilization. The central theme of the agitation was the condition of a prisoner (an allusion to the seals), that Ram had been reduced to, represented as he was in the propaganda as being behind bars.[15]

The political nature of this agitation can be deduced from its chronology. The first phase of mobilizations took place in 1984, with elections looming in early 1985. The VHP's plans were thwarted, however, by the assassination of Indira Gandhi by her Sikh bodyguards, which brought the problem of national unity to the forefront of the electoral issues.

However, the VHP relaunched its movement, which significantly reached its peak in another election year, 1989. The BJP, finally convinced of the strategic relevance of this agitation, became an active participant. Demonstrating a remarkable capacity for planning around the religious calendar and the political agenda, in January, during the Magh Mela (fair held in the Hindu month of *Magh*, usually coinciding with the months of January–February) in Allahabad, a Hindu celebration that lent solemnity to the plan, the VHP announced that come what may, the first stone of the temple would be laid (*shilanyas*) on 9 November, the date recommended by VHP astrologers and which fell right in the middle of the election campaign. In the meantime, RSS militants, VHP sadhus, and the BJP candidates running for election canvassed thousands of towns and villages to consecrate bricks stamped with Ram's name, which were to be used to build the temple. This *Ram-shila puja* (consecration of the bricks stamped 'Ram') followed the same scenario everywhere. The bricks were carried in processions akin to those organized for religious celebrations, in which idols are carried along a precise route, and the ceremonies ended with Vedic-inspired rituals.[16] This campaign had a considerable impact until the first stone was laid on 9 November.

Due to its association with such an emotionally charged cause, BJP gained some popularity which partly translated into electoral terms: in November 1989, it won 88 seats out of 543 in the Lok Sabha as against two in 1984, and acquired an absolute or relative majority in the legislative assemblies of three states in the north (Madhya Pradesh, Himachal Pradesh, and Rajasthan).

This strategy of manipulating Hindu symbols took on a more explicitly political dimension in 1990 when BJP President L.K. Advani covered 10,000 kilometres in a car made to look like the chariot of Arjun, a central figure in the Mahabharata. This *Rath Yatra* was greeted along its path by displays of fervour that were particularly intense among women, who at times offered their *mangalsutras* (a necklace received on their wedding, usually made of precious stones and metals) as a sign of their devotion to Ram's cause. Started on 25 September 1990, the itinerary would take Advani to Ayodhya just when the VHP had decided to begin the *Kar Seva* (literally 'service-action', construction of the temple) on 30 October. However, Advani was arrested in Bihar before he could enter Uttar Pradesh. Despite these exceptional measures, nearly 50,000 people (including a number of sadhus) arrived at the mosque on the planned date and stormed it. Repressive measures reportedly claimed several dozen lives, a fact the VHP and BJP immediately exploited: the martyrs' ashes were

carried in a procession throughout India, and tens of thousands of videos showing the massacre of Ram worshippers were sold clandestinely.

The atmosphere thus created partly explains the BJP's electoral gains during the early elections held in May and June 1991: the party, which fielded 473 candidates as compared to 225 in 1989, in fact garnered 19.9 per cent of the votes cast and 119 seats in the Lok Sabha, making it the second largest national party. Its influence now extended to the south of the country, since it captured 28 per cent of the votes in Karnataka. In the north, its gains enabled it to take control of a fourth state: Uttar Pradesh.

Why Instrumentalism Works

Many Hindus proved receptive to this discourse: they were aware of the political gains the BJP was pursuing under cover of pseudo-religious rituals, but this did not dissuade them. On the contrary, their support was precisely because they subscribed to the overall party ideology, in particular its anti-Muslim bias. The religious sincerity of the Hindu nationalist movement's approach was less important than defending the community that it represented in political terms. This attitude reflects the context that prevailed in the first half of the 1980s, characterized as it was by a reactivation of the Hindu 'majoritarian inferiority complex', as well as the variables that had previously jeopardized the success of the instrumentalist strategy.

The majoritarian inferiority complex revisited

In 1981, the conversion of several hundred Dalits in Meenakshipuram (Tamil Nadu) to Islam (Mathew 1982) was criticized in the press, and not just by Hindu nationalist sections of the media,[17] as a conspiracy funded by Arab countries. At the same time, the extravagant expenditures (for building mosques, for example) and commercial investments made by Indian Muslims working in the Persian Gulf awakened latent fears in some Hindus through the reinforcement of this minority's social and religious visibility.[18] More importantly, in 1985 Rajiv Gandhi yielded to the pressure levied by certain Muslim leaders who protested against a Supreme

Court decision that in their eyes violated the *Shariat* (recognized as a source of law in the Constitution). This ruling entitled a Muslim woman (Shah Bano), who had been divorced by her husband according to customary Muslim law, to maintenance. Rajiv Gandhi, anxious not to alienate the leaders of a minority that traditionally voted for the Congress, agreed to exempt the Muslim community from the article of the Penal Code by virtue of which the Supreme Court had made its ruling. This decision, which seemed to vindicate Hindu nationalist claims that minorities were imposing their will on the government, gave rise to heated protests, even among the intelligentsia. To some degree, this was a reactivation of the majoritarian's inferiority complex that had been behind the founding of the RSS in the 1920s.

The erosion of secularism

Rajiv Gandhi's pro-Muslim stance in the Shah Bano case marks the acceleration in the erosion of the secular stance of the Congress which had begun in the early 1980s. Shortly after her return to power in 1980, Indira Gandhi had tended to exploit communal sentiments for political ends: on the one hand she granted the Muslim university of Aligarh an autonomous status as representing a minority (Graff 1990), and on the other, she made many visits to temples and, in 1983, allowed one of her lieutenants, C.M. Stephen, to state that the political culture of the Congress was 'on the same wavelength' as the Hindu culture.

This communalization of politics took a new turn under Rajiv Gandhi's government. He in fact attempted to balance the ruling made in the Shah Bano affair by deciding to remove the seals from the Ayodhya mosque (Nugent 1990). Such a concession to Hindu nationalist demands in February 1986 left them free to rekindle their agitation at a time when their capacity for mobilization had reached its limit. In 1989, the government once again allowed the shilanyas to take place on a plot of land, the property title of which was disputed in the high court. At the time, Rajiv Gandhi was obviously seeking to mobilize Hindu opinion, as evidenced in the themes of his campaign speeches.[19] In fact, this tactic helped primarily to remove any obstacle that the Congress' secular line had imposed until then on the

instrumentalist strategy of Hindu nationalists: first, the latter were left at liberty to act until the repression of October 1990, which came too late to thwart their capacity for mobilization; and second, their propaganda ended up being legitimated by the use of comparable themes within the Congress itself.

Consolidating the Hindu nationalist networks

In 1966–7, the attitude of the religious figures involved in the cow protection movement contributed to reducing its impact. Starting in 1984, the VHP was able to circumvent this obstacle, since it had now gathered together enough religious figures who could obscure the influence of critical sect leaders, legitimize the campaign in the name of the Ram temple, and mobilize the public.

Most religious figures whose prestige went beyond their sect or region continued to remain at a distance from the VHP's regular activities. One of them, the Dwarka *shankaracharya*, even tried to short-circuit the plans of the VHP with Congress support by attempting to undertake the temple construction himself. The Uttar Pradesh government prevented this, but the undertaking had in any case failed to destabilize the VHP, which now had in its ranks religious figures who understood the working of politics, and were able to adhere to a rigorous calendar of actions. Most religious leaders who joined the movement were even less disturbed by the nationalist reinterpretation of certain rituals since they shared the RSS' ideology.

Among the religious leaders involved with the Hindu nationalists were some 500 personalities forming the Parliament of Dharma, a VHP consultative institution that claimed to represent a sort of consistory of Hinduism. Since 1984, its plenary sessions had lent the VHP's programme—and particularly its constantly reiterated demand to return the Ayodhya site to the Hindus—the support of an assembly in saffron. Beyond that, many of these ascetics participated actively in the Hindu nationalist agitation, Ram shila pujas, or the Kar Seva, during which some of them were arrested for leading several thousands of demonstrators.

Besides, the campaign for the Ram temple made extensive use of audiovisual techniques: cassettes containing speeches by VHP sadhus were distributed, and over 100,000 copies of a video film showing the 'martyrdom of the temple builders' were sold in the Hindi version alone, even though it had been banned by the authorities.

The context of the 1980s, marked as it was by the resurgence of the Hindu majoritarian inferiority complex, the removal of secular hurdles, and the emergence of new intermediaries for RSS propaganda, largely explains the magnitude of the Ayodhya movement. The Sangh Parivar pursued its rise to power while surfing on this movement in the 1990s.

THE BJP IN OFFICE: THE SANGH PARIVAR UNDER TENSION

In 1996 the BJP became the largest party in the Lok Sabha, but A.B. Vajpayee was unable to form the government. He was in a position to do so in 1998, but only for a year, because of the looseness of the coalitions supporting him and his team of ministers. One year later, the BJP mooted a robust coalition, which was to rule India for five full years: for the first time, the Congress was out of power for one complete term of the Lok Sabha. However, this success created tensions within the Sangh Parivar, precisely because it was achieved thanks to the making of a coalition whose partners exerted strong constraints over the BJP.

How the BJP Kept the RSS Happy

In October 1999, L.K. Advani admitted that a new phase had begun in the career of the BJP in 1996, when Vajpayee failed to form a coalition government: 'It was felt that on an ideological basis we couldn't go further. So we embarked on the course of alliance-based coalitions'[20]—this was a nice way of establishing a direct relationship between the way the BJP had diluted its Hindu nationalism, and the making of alliances. Both phenomena had culminated, in 1998, in the formation of the National Democratic Alliance (NDA). The BJP and its alliance partners evolved a National Agenda for Government in March 1998, based on which Vajpayee formed his government.[21] The mainstays of the Sangh Parivar's programme—the Ram temple to be built at Ayodhya, the abolition of Article 370 of the Constitution, and the establishment

of a uniform civil code—were not included in this agenda because most of the BJP's allies disapproved of their Hindu nationalist connotations. In 1999, the election manifesto of the NDA promised 'a moratorium on contentious issues',[22] which continued to be the same three ones.

Why have the RSS leaders ostensibly accepted such a dilution of its ideology? It was because, first, this was not such a high price to pay for having sympathetic rulers in office, who would enhance the legitimacy of the Sangh in the public sphere—and protect the organization. Senior RSS leaders H.V. Seshadri and K.C. Sudarshan—the then joint General Secretary of the organization—were in the front row at the swearing in ceremony of the Vajpayee government in 1999, and gave their blessings to the newly appointed ministers (who sought such a gesture from them). A few months later, Sudarshan declared: 'With a government in power that is not inimical to us, we shall be able to work better'.[23]

One of the first decisions Vajpayee made after forming his government in March 1998 was to appoint six new governors, five among whom were BJP members. Among them, S.S. Bhandari, Bhai Mahavir, and Suraj Bhan were swayamsevaks from whom the RSS could expect benevolent gestures. Indeed, the way the organization could benefit from the BJP being in office was especially obvious at the state level. In Uttar Pradesh, as early as 25 July 1998, Rajendra Singh—the then RSS chief—had formally met top bureaucrats in Lucknow, and lectured them on 'nationalism and honesty'.

Besides, some of the policies implemented by the Vajpayee government met with the RSS' approval. This was most evident in the field of education, the Minister for Human Resources and Development, Murli Manohar Joshi, being notoriously close to the RSS leadership. One of the organization cadres at the movement's Delhi head office even declared: 'He is the most frequent to come here to consult RSS Organising Secretary K. Sudarshan. We know that our project of nation-building cannot be accomplished without basic education.'[24]

Though his attempt to institutionalize the recitation of the Saraswati Vandana in schools failed in 1998, immediately after the 1999 elections Joshi

appointed personalities who had been close to the
Sangh Parivar as heads of the directive body of the
Indian Council of Historical Research (ICHR)
and the Indian Council of Social Science Research
(ICSSR), B.R. Grover and M.L. Sondhi, respectively.
B.R. Grover—who retired from Jamia Millia Islamia as
Reader and became a member of the ICHR in 1998—
was one of the historians who had provided the Sangh
Parivar with archaeological 'evidence' that the Babri
Masjid had been built over a Ram temple in Ayodhya.
Sondhi, a former Indian Foreign Service (IFS) officer
who had joined politics, won a Lok Sabha seat in
Delhi on a Jana Sangh ticket in 1967. Besides, Joshi
also appointed Krishna Gopal Rastogi, a former
RSS pracharak, to the search committee for faculty
appointments at the National Council for Educational
Research and Training (NCERT). The apprehensions
that have been aroused by the placement of RSS
fellow travellers in key positions began to materialize
in February 2000 when the ICHR 'suspended' two
volumes of its series called 'Towards Freedom' by
Sumit Sarkar and K.N. Panikkar, who were known for
being highly critical of the Sangh Parivar.[25]

The RSS also appreciated the defence policy of
Vajpayee's government. In May 1998, the organization
applauded the nuclear tests at Pokharan. In his report
before the Akhil Bharatiya Pratinidhi Sabha in March
1999, H.V. Seshadri highlighted the achievement of
Vajpayee's government in the field of security issues:

> The series of 5 nuclear blasts at Pokharan on May 11th
> and 13th of last year, carried out on the strength of entirely
> indigenous input by way of materials and also of sheer
> scientific and technological excellence placing Bharat at
> the top of nuclear world on par with any of the giants in
> that field, the absolute secrecy maintained all through until
> it was broadcast on the TV by our Prime Minister, the
> political grit and courage displayed by the central leadership
> in taking that historic decision in the light of our national
> security requirements, and the way it has acted as a great
> moral booster not only to our army but to all our patriotic
> countrymen—all this has proved to be the one greatest
> moment of all-round national jubilation and celebration
> during the Golden Jubilee Year of our Independence.[26]

Seshadri also congratulated—implicitly—
L.K. Advani, the Home Minister, for his policy in
Jammu and Kashmir in the warmest terms:

> The achievement in the field of internal national security
> by way of liquidating and nabbing of thousands old
> saboteurs and insurgents in Kashmir has been unequalled
> to this day. (Singh 1994)

Bones of Contention

A few bones of contention remained, though, between
the BJP and the RSS—or, even more clearly, between
the BJP and other components of the Sangh Parivar.
In the economic domain, the Vajpayee government
gradually betrayed the ideal of Swadeshi by which the
Hindu nationalist movement used to swear. In early
1999, the Swadeshi Jagaran Manch, an RSS offshoot,
had organized a Swadeshi Mela in order to promote
the notion of 'self-reliance' (Sreedathan 1999: 10–11).
Vajpayee had inaugurated it by saying: 'We are all part
of the same family. It's good that you have come up
with ideas but if I can't execute them, I'll say sorry.'[27]
Economic nationalism was certainly not on his agenda
any more. His government introduced the Insurance
Regulatory and Development Authority (IRDA) Bill
as early as the first session of the thirteenth Lok Sabha
in December 1999 to allow the entry of private Indian
and foreign companies into the insurance business,
ending the monopoly of the public-sector Life
Insurance Corporation of India (LIC) and General
Insurance Corporation (GIC). In February 2000,
the government enhanced ceilings on foreign direct
investment by 23 to 100 per cent in eight sectors,
including drugs and pharmaceuticals, mining, and the
film industry. The then Commerce Minister, Murasoli
Maran, declared: 'We want to create an Indian fever
[among foreign investors] just as there was a China
fever not too long ago.'[28] An agreement to remove
import controls on consumer goods was also signed
with the United States, and the level of protectionism
that India had started reducing since the early 1990s
continued to diminish. The Bharatiya Mazdoor Sangh,
the Labour Union of the Sangh Parivar, protested
on behalf of its anti-globalization ideology,[29] and the
RSS itself objected to this policy. In March 2000, the
Akhil Bharatiya Pratinidhi Sabha passed a resolution
supporting an 'India-centric and need-specific' model
of development.

The BJP and other units of the Sangh Parivar were
also at cross-purposes on the Ayodhya issue. One

of the VHP's related bodies, the Ram Janmabhoomi Nyas, supervised the cutting of stones and the carving of the 212 pillars for the temple in Sirohi (Rajasthan), and in January 2000, Ashok Singhal, the VHP Working President, declared that Hindu saints would build the Ram temple at Ayodhya 'once the chiselling of stones is over'. He argued that there was no legal ban on the construction given that the property acquired by the Centre belonged to the temple diety.[30] The RSS itself reaffirmed its interest in Ayodhya during the last election campaign. In September, its supreme Chief, Rajendra Singh, emphasized that Muslims, whose rulers had allegedly 'destroyed 3,000 temples', should hand over the sites in Benares, Mathura, and Ayodhya, where mosques had been built on so-called Hindu sacred places.[31] However, the Vajpayee government resisted these pressures, arguing that Ayodhya was one of the issues that had been removed from the BJP's agenda because of the compulsions of coalition politics.

So long as the BJP remained in office, the RSS resigned itself to the dilution of the BJP's ideology, but things changed after the 2004 defeat, which was considered by most components of the Sangh Parivar other than the BJP as a rejection of the moderate line of conduct advocated by Vajpayee. Soon after the elections, the General Secretary of the VHP, Praveen Togadia, declared: 'The Bharatiya Janata Party betrayed the Hindus. The BJP left its core ideology of Hindutva and trust on the basis of which they had been voted to power.'[32] In August, the BJP held a *chintan baithak* (brainstorming session) in order to reflect upon the party's strategy. Madan Das Devi, representing the RSS, declared that the Sangh expected the BJP to return to Hindutva. However, Vajpayee stressed the need to keep the NDA intact. The ten-point 'document of conclusions' resolved to continue with the NDA experiment, but committed the party to moving closer to the RSS. A new administrative position was created within the party, that of 'regional organization secretary', to improve coordination between the Delhi headquarters and the state units. It is significant that the first six holders of this new position were all pracharaks.[33] More importantly, L.K. Advani, who had replaced V. Naidu as party President in 2004, was openly

criticized by K. Sudarshan, who had taken over from Rajendra Singh in 2000 as Sarsanghchalak. In an unprecedented move, the latter said, during the course of a TV interview, that the former—and A.B. Vajpayee—should make room for new faces. L.K. Advani objected, stating that such an attitude reflected abnormal interference on the part of RSS leaders in the working of the BJP. In his concluding statement at the National Executive meeting of the party on 18 September 2005, he declared:

> From time to time and depending on the issue at hand, the BJP leadership has had no hesitation in consulting the RSS functionaries. After such consultations, the Party takes its own independent decisions. Some of these decisions may differ—and have indeed differed—from the stated positions of the RSS and certain constituencies of the 'Sangh Parivar'.
>
> But lately an impression has gained ground that no political or organizational decision can be taken without the consent of the RSS functionaries. This perception, we hold, will do no good either to the Party or to the RSS. ... We feel that the RSS should continue to play its role to strengthen the ethical, moral and idealistic moorings of the workers as well as functionaries of the BJP, as in the past, and in the largest interest of the nation.
>
> The BJP greatly appreciates the continuing interaction we have been having with the RSS and with other organizations in the Sangh Parivar. Their views provide valuable inputs for our decision making process. *But the BJP as a political party is accountable to the people, its performance being periodically put to test in elections. So in a democratic, multi-party polity, an ideologically driven party like the BJP has to function in a manner that enables it to keep its basic ideological stances intact and at the same time expand itself to reach the large sections of the people outside the layers of all ideology.* (Jaffrelot 2007: 189–92, emphasise mine)

The last sentence of this excerpt was intended to justify what the RSS leaders called the dilution of the BJP's doctrinal purity. But this overall plea for the recognition of the party's autonomy was not appreciated by K. Sudarshan. At the end of 2005, Advani resigned from the post of party President and was succeeded by Rajnath Singh. Ironically enough, this episode recalled the expulsion of Balraj Madhok—a former Jana Sangh President, who had also objected to interference of the RSS in the working of this party—by Advani himself in 1973, after he replaced Vajpayee as party President.[34] In both cases the RSS had decided to intervene in party affairs in an even more systematic manner at the behest of an 'activist'[35] *Sarsanghchalak*: in 1973 Deoras had just taken over from Golwalkar and in 2005, Sudarshan had had the time to impose his own—similar—style. These two men showed that the RSS can be actively interested in party politics.

CONCLUSION

The Sangh Parivar is obviously facing a structural dilemma. On the one hand the RSS views politics as something vulgar, which may endanger its doctrinal purity, and the state, which has to be reformed, as an unimportant institution compared with society. On the other hand, its leaders have admitted the need to play a political role as a raj guru of some sort, through a party designed to capture power so that the Sangh Parivar could benefit from such an access to the state apparatus.

Such a stand implies a major contradiction when the party in question needs to be part of a coalition. The RSS could not be the Raj Guru of the Janata Party because in this party, the ex-Jana Sanghis had secular partners who exposed their 'dual membership', and twenty years later the BJP could not retain its initial agenda because it had to concede to other members of the NDA that did not share its ideology.

To surmount these contradictions, the RSS needs to win elections on its own. Indeed, things have been much easier at the state level when the BJP got an absolute majority, like in Gujarat. Then the xenophobic dimensions of the Hindutva movement found expression in the 2002 pogroms and the rule of law was put on trial, revealing the anti-democratic foundations of the Hindu nationalist movement.[36]

NOTES

1. Regarding this Muslim mobilization movement, see Minault (1982).

2. For an analysis of this stereotype, see Spear (1932, pp. 198–201).

3. I endeavoured to retrace this genealogy in the first chapter of *The Hindu Nationalist Movement and Indian Politics* (1999).

4. To borrow from the title of the book by Andersen and Damle (1987).

5. *The Hindu*, 13 March 2004.

6. In December 1990, the Hindu nationalists in Delhi—where 14,000 Pandit families had reportedly migrated—claimed to have set up six refugee camps, provided aid amounting to Rs 1.3 million, found work for 1400 people, and registered 800 children in school (interview with Mange Ram Garg, BJP party secretary in Delhi, in charge of the Kashmiri Migrants Cell, 8 December 1990).

7. At the time of Partition in 1947, the RSS had organized a food drive to bring meals prepared on the outskirts of Delhi to the capital, which was being flooded by refugees from western Punjab (interview with M.C. Sharma, *Oral History Transcript* [Hindi], 327, New Delhi, Nehru Memorial Library, p. 154).

8. For more details, see Jaffrelot (2006).

9. S.P. Mookerjee Papers, 168, Nehru Memorial Museum and Library, New Delhi. Regarding the origin and history of the Jana Sangh, see Graham (1990).

10. For an insider's view of the first involvement of the RSS with politics via the Jana Sangh, see Malkani (1980, pp. 113–21).

11. This concept, introduced by R. Kothari in the 1960s, refers to the Congress' capacity to dominate the Indian political space on the basis of the legitimacy it inherited from the Independence movement, by recruiting supporters among local notables and adjusting to new swings of opinion so well that government opposition at the local level sometimes seemed orchestrated by Congress members themselves (Kothari 1964).

12. By these terms, B. Graham is referring to Congress members involved in associations for the promotion of the Hindi language, defence of cows, and the revival of Ayurvedic medicine (1988, p. 174).

13. This was particularly the case in Delhi in 1970 (*The Times of India*, 26 June 1970).

14. *Hindu Vishva*, 14 (7–8), March 1979, p. 92.

15. Regarding the movement's first phase, see van der Veer (1987).

16. For a detailed report on a *Mahayajna*, see for example the one on Bhopal, *Madhya Pradesh Chronicle*, 11 November 1989, p. 9, and *Dainik Bhaskar*, 11 November 1989, p. 3.

17. *The Times of India*, 21 March 1981.

18. In Moradabad, a riot broke out in 1980 in an atmosphere made tense by a tract criticizing plans to build a Koranic school financed by money from the Gulf countries. (Saberwal and Hasan n.d.).

19. He launched his election campaign in Faizabad—a town near Ayodhya—calling for a *Ram Rajya* (Kingdom of Ram), an expression coined by Gandhi to name the ideal

state that would come about after Independence, but which acquired strong militant Hindu connotations in the context of 1989.

20. Interview with L.K. Advani, *Outlook*, 25 October 1999, p. 38.

21. For the full text, see *Organiser*, Varsha Pradipada Special, 29 March 1998, pp. 27–30.

22. *For a Proud, Prosperous India: NDA Election Manifesto, 1999 Lok Sabha Elections*, New Delhi, BJP office, 1999, p. 1.

23. Cited in *Frontline*, 24 April 1998, p. 117.

24. Cited in Bhaumik (1999, p. 23).

25. Over thirty academics, including Irfan Habib, R.S. Sharma, and Ravinder Kumar—all former chairmen of the ICHR—immediately denounced the 'grossest form of censorship' and 'plan to spread a distorted and fictitious history of the national movement' (*The Hindu*, 17 February 2000). S. Gopal, the General Editor of the 'Towards Freedom' project, also protested that the ICHR intervention amounted to 'an infringement of the academic rights and freedom of the authors ...' (*The Hindu*, 22 February 2000). According to K.N. Panikkar, the withdrawal of the two volumes was intended to prevent the exposure of the 'collaborative role' played by the Hindu Mahasabha vis-à-vis the British during the colonial period (*The Hindu*, 25 February 2000).

26. *The Organiser*, 4 April 1999, p. 12. The RSS has always favoured the development of nuclear weapons. In the early 1990s Rajendra Singh—himself a nuclear physicist—declared that 'The day Pakistan comes to know that we also have a nuclear bomb, there would an end to the possibility of a Pakistan nuclear bomb being dropped here' (Singh 1994, p. 9).

27. Cited in *India Today*, 8 February 1999, p. 33.

28. Cited in *The Hindu*, 3 February 2000. Similarly, Vajpayee's government began the process of public disinvestment from Indian Airlines in January 2000. In that case it was decided to offload 51 per cent equity. Before that, the public-sector equity of the Gas Authority of India had been sold to foreign companies.

29. In February 1999, the Twelfth National Conference of the BMS was marked by new criticisms such as: 'The succumbing by successive Indian Government to pressures of international trade regimes exerted by superpowers is a big blow to Indian sovereignty in the economic field' (*The Organiser*, 28 February 1999, p. 11).

30. Ibid., 30 January 2000.

31. *Indian Today*, 27 September 1999, p. 66.

32. *The Hindu*, 15 May 2004.

33. *The Hindu*, 7 August 2004.

34. See M.R. Varshney (1973).

35. W. Andersen and S. Damle use this word to qualify the RSS swayamsevaks interested in politics—of which

Deoras was probably the first typical example (Andersen and Damle 1987, p. 114).

36. For more details on this point, see Jaffrelot (2001, pp. 509–34).

REFERENCES

Andersen, W. and S. Damle. 1987. *The Brotherhood in Saffron: The Rashtriya Swayamsevak Sangh and Hindu Revivalism*. New Delhi: Vistaar.

Bamford, P.C. 1985 [1925]. *Histories of the Non-Cooperation and Khilafat Movements*. Delhi: Government of India Press.

Bhaumik, S.N. 1999. 'Murli's Mission', *India Today*, 6 December.

Brass, P. 1991. *Ethnicity and Nationalism*. New Delhi: Sage Publications.

Golwalkar, M.S. 1966. *Bunch of Thoughts*. Bangalore: Vikrama Prakashana.

———. 1939. *We or our Nationhood Defined*. Nagpur: Bharat Prakashan.

Graham, B. 1990. *Hindu Nationalism and Indian Politics: The Origin and Development of the Bharatiya Jana Sangh*. Cambridge: Cambridge University Press.

———. 1988. 'The Congress and Hindu Nationalism', in D.A. Low (ed.), *The Indian National Congress. Centenary Hindsights*. New Delhi: Oxford University Press.

Graff, V. 1990. 'Aligarh's Long Quest for "Minority" Status—AMU (Amendment) Act, 1981', *Economic and Political Weekly*, XXV(32), pp. 1771–81.

Jaffrelot, Christophe. 2007. *Hindu Nationalism: A Reader*. Princeton: Princeton University Press.

———. 2006. 'Work and Workers in the Ideology and Strategies of the BMS', in C. Jaffrelot (ed.), *The Sangh Parivar. A Reader*. New Delhi: Oxford University Press, pp. 355–70.

———. 2001. 'Hindu Nationalism and Democracy', in N. Jayal (ed.), in *Democracy in India*. New Delhi: Oxford University Press, pp. 509–34.

———. 1999. *The Hindu Nationalist Movement and Indian Politics*. New Delhi: Penguin.

Joshi, A. 1970. 'How Congress and Mahasabha Tried to Appropriate the RSS', *Organiser*, 15 August.

Kothari, R. 1964. 'The Congress "System" in India', *Asian Survey*, 4(12), pp. 1161–73.

Malkani, K.R. 1980. *The RSS Story*. New Delhi: Impex India.

Mathew, G. 1982. 'Politicisation of Religion: Conversions to Islam in Tamil Nadu', *Economic and Political Weekly*, XVII(25), 19 June, pp. 1027–34, and XVII(26), 26 June, pp. 1068–72.

Minault, G. 1982. *The Khilafat Movement: Religious Symbolism and Political Mobilization in India*. New York, Columbia University Press.

Nugent, N. 1990. 'Rajiv Gandhi, the Congress Party and the 1989 Parliamentary Elections', Hull Conference on the National and State Politics in Post-Election India, 10–12 May.

Saberwal, S. and M. Hasan. n.d., 'Communal Riot in Moradabad, 1980', Occasional Papers on History and Society, 19, Nehru Memorial Library, New Delhi, mimeograph.

Savarkar, V.D., 1962 [1923], *Hindutva: Who is a Hindu?* Bombay: Asia Publishing House.

Singh, R. 1994. *Ever-Vigilant We have to be*. New Delhi: Suruchi Prakashan.

Spear, P. 1932. *The Nabobs*. London: Oxford University Press.

Sreedathan, G. 1999. 'Swadeshi is the Mantra', *The Organiser*, 7 February.

Upadhyaya, D. 1962. 'Jana Sangh', *Seminar*, 29 (January).

van der Veer, Peter 1987. 'God Must be Liberated! A Hindu Liberation Movement in Ayodhya', *Modern Asian Studies*, 21(2), pp. 283–301.

Varshney, M.R. 1973. *Jana Sangh, RSS and Balraj Madhok*. Aligarh: Varshney College.

15 Minorities and Politics*

Bishnu N. Mohapatra

How does one grapple with the 'minority question' in India? Who shapes or articulates or constructs the discourses on minorities? The categories of 'majority' and 'minority' are enormously complex. What kind of categories are they? Undoubtedly, they are collective categories, more than a mere collection of individuals. Who belongs to the majority and who to the minority, is not always very clear. In the case of India, the status of a group varies as it moves from one level to the other. There are scholars who suggest that to view a society in terms of majority and minority is to view it as being composed of bounded, culturally or linguistically or racially unified communities. Over the years, anti-essentialism has become central to many works on identity politics and on multiculturalism. Against the idea that identities have fixed essences, these works have shown that identities are primarily differentiated, hybrid and multilayered. Broadly speaking, anti-essentialism as a methodological

strategy has made it possible to interrogate the claims of the leaders who present their community as a homogeneous entity. It has also helped unmask the ways in which identity politics tends to paper over contradictions inherent within a community such as class, caste, and so on. No doubt these are clear-cut advantages. But the question is how far can we push the logic of anti-essentialism? If a minority community has no coherent ontological dimension, does it mean that the community simply does not exist? Let us take a concrete example. Against the people who argue that the Muslim community has a fixed and undifferentiated essence, scholars have pointed out that it is divided within in terms of class, caste, and other affiliations. In the same way the claims of the Hindu Right that the Hindus form a homogeneous entity is found to be erroneous. From this can we conclude that the idea of a Muslim community is simply a fiction? If community as an entity cannot exist then how do the categories of majority and minority make sense? Are they fictitious too?

This essay is informed by this basic conviction that it is possible to talk of communities, collective

*Views expressed in this article are those of the author and should not be attributed to any institution.

identities without being essentialistic. One should not adopt an extreme anti-essentialism that makes collective identity and agency impossible. It is not surprising then that several marginalized groups today find such radical anti-essentialism as politically disempowering or debilitating. Some of them, feminists for instance, even take recourse to 'strategic essentialism' as a way out. It is possible to speak of minority or majority community without suggesting that it is either undifferentiated or completely hybrid.

If one were to look into history it is quite evident that majority–minority relations in India have not always been conceived within the 'rights-discourse'. Gandhi's discourse on inter-community relations, even in the tragic days of Partition, was based on fellowship and mutual identification. Talk of rights was never admitted into it for, according to him, that was simply centred on claims and counter-claims. The language of 'fellowship', 'bhaichara' (brotherhood) survives even today. The utility of this language need not be jettisoned. However, since Independence, the inter-community relations and the minority rights have been and are still framed within rights-discourse. It is presupposed within a constitutional democratic order where minority communities enjoy certain rights that are not dependent on majority community's goodwill or fellowship. In principle, a democratic state along with its institutions is portrayed as the protector of minority rights. The protection of minority rights in India, as this chapter argues, not only needs a responsive state but also a vigilant civil society.

No doubt the Indian Constitution contains several provisions that are meant to protect the distinct cultural or linguistic or religious identity of the minority communities. It also provides for the functioning and sustenance of institutions created by them. The desire of the makers of the Constitution to create a secular state was also essentially a response to India's plural social order. However, in spite of all these, nearly six decades after the Constitutional Republic was inaugurated, the minorities in India have expressed their feeling of alienation. Even the track record of the Indian state's responsibility to protect the lives of the minorities is, to put it mildly, not satisfactory. Communal violence in the past many decades in India, in which the minority groups

suffer the most, cannot be explained away in terms of the rise of general violence in the country. It is not surprising that the security concern has remained and continues to be so at the top of the agenda of the religious minorities in India. Can this be explained in terms of the gaps that exist between constitutional theory and its practice? Some people try to explain the issue by showing the growing decline of certain foundational values including secularism on the Indian polity. For others, if secularism, on which rested the notion of 'minority rights', has become a highly contested doctrine, then one should look for another foundation. The principle of 'substantive equality', as some scholars suggest, can be such an alternative foundation. We do not have to be deconstructionists or postmodernists to believe that no foundation, even a desirable principle like substantive equality, in politics can ever be fully secure. Nor can it provide the ultimate resting place for 'minority rights'. For instance, special provision for minorities can be justified on the ground that it addresses the problems of inequality in society. For some it amounts to mere appeasement of minorities and violates the principle of equality. No doubt the positions are based on two different conceptions of equality. Can these contending views be reconciled? In fact some argue that the crisis of Indian secularism lay not in the doctrine itself but in its non-negotiated character. Can one say the same thing with regard to minority rights?

During the days of the Constituent Assembly debates, the issue of minority rights for religious minorities was subjected to much discussion and controversies. By the end of the debate, except granting political safeguards to the religious minorities, other rights meant to protect their identity and prevent discrimination against them were put in place. However, the discussion on religious minorities was filled with anxieties that cannot be explained only by Partition. There was an underlying fear that according too much recognition to the religious minorities would disrupt the project of Indian nationhood. Even the well-meaning liberals belonging to the Congress shared this view. The Nehruvian vision that emerged at the end, emphasized the idea of non-discrimination and the idea of an inclusive nation. Many who believed in the liberal utopia and the rationality of modernity believed that the project of development would eventually blunt the rough edges of identity politics in India. This did not happen and the power of majoritarianism kept the idea of an exclusive nation alive. Unless the ideology of majoritarianism in its different forms is squarely tackled, the regime of minority rights in India would remain painfully fragile. To the extent that the special provisions for minorities are viewed as 'appeasement', it would undermine the basis of minority rights. A minimal consensus among different political parties on this is an absolute necessity.

CONTEXTS AND QUESTIONS

India's diversity is indeed proverbial. More than a billion people who live in the country speak about 4600 languages/dialects (including the eighteen recognized in the Eighth Schedule of the Constitution [*The Constitution of India* 1995: 326]) belonging to twelve language families and 24 scripts. The country has nearly 2800 ethnic communities and nearly 20,000 caste groups.[1] India houses all the major religions of the world. According to the 2001 Census of India (*Census of India* 2001), nearly 80.5 per cent were Hindus, and Muslims, Christians, Sikhs, Buddhists were 13.4 per cent, 2.3 per cent, 1.9 per cent, 0.8 per cent of the total population, respectively. A cross-cutting of communities across a large territory is a significant feature of India's diversity. It is also worth remembering that these religious groups are not monoliths, they are internally diverse, and there are communities who tend to think of themselves as bearers of plural religious identities (Mayaram 1997; Nandy 1999).[2] It is within these complex diversities that one has to locate the majority–minority relations in India.

The history of social pluralism and collective living in India is quite complex. Mapping this history is beyond the scope of this essay. Yet, I would like to point out few salient features of this historiography Scholars point out that in ancient India the state's engagement with social pluralism was by and large positive. The ritual/symbolic incorporation, the argument goes, was one of the important modes through which the state managed the diversities. Of course, the over-arching hierarchy was always maintained. During the Mughal period, the rulers tried to incorporate people from different religious and ethnic backgrounds into the emerging institutions of governance. It is argued that within these 'non-modern' times there was very little possibility of majority–minority conflict. The ineluctable conflict between the 'self' and the 'other' that acts as a propelling force for identity politics in our times was not conceivable in the past. The 'modern conditions' are considered responsible for the rise of the majority–minority problematic. In the case of India, like in other postcolonial societies, colonialism mediated these conditions to a large extent.

Whether or not the portrayal of a harmonious collective living in India's non-modern past fits into history is not the issue here. There is no doubt that politics of diversities underwent dramatic changes in the 'modern' period. It is also true that the new governmental practices, or to use Foucault's expression 'governmentality', beginning with the colonial period pressed for the identity concerns of the communities for new forms of mobilization. But it will be futile to suggest today that the only way to restore peace between state and minorities is to revive the traditional resources of tolerance and of ritual incorporation of differences into the formal political structure. These options are neither pragmatic nor do they fit in with the values such as 'equality' and 'rights' on which India's democracy is based. At this point, it is crucial to outline the contexts in which the problematic of minority rights or majority–minority relations in India is discussed in recent times.

Scholars of Indian democracy tend to agree that the last two decades of the twentieth century witnessed a great deal of social churning in the country. A large number of people belonging to the marginal sections of the Indian society finally 'arrived' to stake their claims and assert their rights in the polity. The high turnout of the poor and the Dalits in the last few elections is projected as one of the indicators of their growing assertion (Yadav 1997, 2000; Khilnani 1997). The growing agency of the poor and of the hitherto marginalized social groups in the country is also felt in the realm of the civil society in the form of their movements against the state and the dominant interests in the society. The demand for political equality has been intense for quite sometime now. However, the contradiction between the political and the socio-economic one, so aptly pointed out by B.R. Ambedkar (*Constitutional Assembly Debates* [*CAD*]: 979), still persists and continues to animate democratic politics in the country.

The social churning is only a part of the story. The rise of the Hindu Right during the later part of the last century is equally significant. The mobilization of Hindus around the issue of Ram Janmabhoomi (the birth place of Ram) and the eventual demolition of the Babri Masjid on 6 December 1992, in Ayodhya, shook the secular foundations of the Indian polity. Undoubtedly, with this the relationship between the religious minorities (particularly the Muslims) and the Hindu majority hit its lowest point. Once again, the wreckage of the Babri Masjid brought forth the issue of the nature of Indian polity and state and above all the 'idea of India' into the domain of fierce contestation. A variety of explanations are offered concerning this tragic event. The votaries of Hindutva interpret the event as a logical outcome of the state's policy of 'appeasement' and consider it as fallout of the postulates of Nehruvian secularism, which they claim to be inauthentic and pro-religious-minorities. The secularists tend to explain the event in terms of growing communalization of the Indian society over a period of time. Some point out the Indian state's eroding capacity to engage with the religious minorities in the country that contributed to the worsening of communal situation in the country. It is true that notwithstanding the campaign of the Bharatiya Janata Party (BJP) and other Hindu organizations such as the Rashtriya Swayamsevak Sangh (RSS), the Vishwa Hindu Parishad (VHP), the Bajarang Dal, a larger number of people disapproved the demolition of the masjid.[3]

The reactions of the Muslims were predictable. Most of them were angry and dejected. The projection of this event in the electronic media offended their religious and cultural sensibilities. The communal riots in different cities that followed the demolition, took the level of pathos and helplessness of the Muslims to a different level. The Indian Muslims found themselves, as someone evocatively pointed out, 'in a twilight terrain where hope and despair live in uneasy truce'.[4]

Despair arising out of communal violence was not something new to the Indian Muslims. According to

available data, during 1978–93, communal violence in India increased dramatically in comparison to the previous decade. After the Partition holocaust, communal violence (Varshney 2002; Nandy 1999) subsided till 1960; it rose once again, peaking in 1969 and then a substantial decline between 1971–7. The number of districts (Hasan 1988: 2469) affected by communal violence increased from 61 in 1961 to 250 in 1986–7. Even the Christian minorities have expressed a deep sense of insecurity as a result of increasing atrocities against them in recent years.[5] Several reports on communal violence over the years have very clearly established that these are not natural outcomes of diversities in Indian society. In many instances the violence is collectively engineered with the direct or indirect complicity of the state and its law-enforcing agencies. The anti-Sikh violence in Delhi and other cities in the wake of Indira Gandhi's assassination in 1984 demonstrated the point quite well. Once the feeling of insecurity increases in the minds of the minorities, then the presence of secularism as a mere policy of intent or the existence of constitutional safeguards alone are not enough. In this context, demands on the part of the minorities for the effective implementation of the available safeguards and for the protection of their lives and property are of great value. No minority rights-talk in India is or can ever be free from such existential anxieties.

A keen observer of the political scene in India would agree that discussion on minority rights in recent decades has never been conducted in isolation. It usually comes with a host of other related issues such as, gender justice, class, and so on. The Shah Bano case in 1985 and the subsequent legislation, titled the Muslim Women Act, 1986, very clearly exposed the contradiction between women's right to equality and the collective right of the Muslim community.

Against this complex backdrop, the issue of minority rights in India has to be discussed. What are the doctrinal issues involved? How did the minority discourse evolve in India? What are the epistemic and political spaces the discourse occupies and how have the political processes in the country affected it? How does one view the enabling aspects of minority rights in a society characterized by intricate diversities? I have deliberately highlighted the issue of religious minorities in this essay, for I think it is politically the most salient today. Although the problem of linguistic minorities emerges from time to time, it does not have the disruptive edge that it once had in the first two decades after Independence. We are familiar with the play of passion that occurred during the formation of the States' Reorganization Commission in the early years of Independence (formed in 1954 and submitted its report in 1956) and also during the formation of Punjab in 1966. It can also be argued that the Indian state's strategy to deal with territorially-confined linguistic minorities within the constitutional framework has been quite successful. One of the well-tested and familiar strategies of the Indian state has been to reorganize existing state boundaries. This is a means by which some minority groups can attain the status of a majority within the confines of the state. One can cite the creation of three new provinces (Jharkhand, Chhattisgarh, and Uttarakhand) as the recent examples to support the foregoing argument. Yet, it will be wrong to claim that the problems of the linguistic minorities are over in India. If one were to take a cursory glance at this issue from the vantage point of the tribals living in several provinces of the country, one would clearly see their vulnerabilities and the lack of adequate recognition towards their languages from the state and the dominant linguistic groups. However, in a comparative sense, India's agony over religion and religious identity still remains. This is the reason why a substantial part of this essay is devoted to the issue of religious minorities in India.

MINORITY RIGHTS: A CONTEXTUAL THEORIZATION

The last two decades have witnessed a remarkable upsurge of community mobilizations all around the world. The greater theoretical awareness of 'pluralities' or 'diversities' in the context of inequality and hegemony in several societies has been constitutive of a particular kind of collective mobilization that Charles Taylor evocatively called the 'politics of recognition' (Taylor 1994). There are three fundamental ways in which contemporary politics of recognition tends to draw our attention. First, it manifests as a negation. Often it interrogates the notion of a monolithic nation state and puts forward a critique against the process of homogenization in a society. It also unmasks the unequal relationship among various cultural/religious/ethnic groups. Second, the politics of recognition is not only about dignity; it is also about entitlements, substantive rights, and freedom. It is this that has brought the politics of multiculturalism directly into the domain of democracy. Finally, the recognition of ascriptive diversities has raised serious questions regarding the liberal definition of 'rights', 'community', citizenship, and so on. A detailed discussion of the 'multiculturalism' debate is not attempted here. However, I will try to bring out only the key theoretical ideas raised by this debate that has a direct bearing on our discussion on minority rights.

The presence of contesting Christian sects centuries ago raised the issue of majority and minority in the West. In order to avoid religious persecution and violence, it was necessary to articulate the idea of toleration. The pragmatic defense of the initial defense of the existence of internal minorities within a nation-state, quite paradoxically, came through the articulation of individual rights. From this arose the liberal-individualist position—a network of procedures, arrived at lawfully, society makes the varied cultural world of the people remain outside the domain of the public sphere. This stance of 'neutrality' is often defended by invoking the principle of 'equality'. It is not true that liberals usually overlook pluralism in societies. Indeed, 'the fact of pluralism' (Rawls 1993) is recognized by the liberals as an inescapable or an antecedent condition of modern societies. The insistence on neutrality and anti-perfectionism tends to keep the politics of difference at bay.

The idea of an universal citizen is often employed by the liberal individualists as a counter-idea to that of a culturally-rooted individual. During the last three centuries this idea of a 'citizen-man' has been used by the democrats to undermine the privileges of the wealthy and the aristocrats in Europe and to pull down the barriers that existed between the people and the process of democratic governance. Pushing aside the earlier conception of citizenship, such as the civic-republican ideal, based on solidarity, the liberal-individualist tradition completely severed all cultural attachments making the gap between individual freedom and community-belonging unbridgeable.

The liberal ambivalence towards cultural/ethnic diversity has been subjected to scrutiny in recent times. The argument is that the individual-rights framework, though important, is not enough for the protection of minority cultures and identities in a multicultural society. Ethno-cultural and religious minorities in several societies are demanding special forms of recognition, often in the idiom of 'group rights'. The conventional liberal suspicion towards these communitarian demands is found to be unjustified. The defenders of group rights often argue that the liberal-individualist stance neither promotes equality nor freedom; it in fact legitimizes the dominant culture and values in a society. On this view, the cultural world to which individuals belong shape their choices and make their life-plans more meaningful and purposive (Kymlicka 1995). The defenders of minority rights are often critical of the individualist bias of liberalism and see no objection in supporting special provisions for the minority groups in a society. They also believe that recognition of diversities can make a democratic state more legitimate and responsive. Finally, the relationship between individual well-being and the prosperity of the cultural group to which they belong is viewed as complementary (Kymlicka 1989; Tamir 1993; Raz 1994). One can see in these theoretical exercises attempts to reconcile the demands of unity and diversity, between the citizenship values and the import of cultural membership (Taylor 1991; Parekh 1999).

It is within these contending claims for unity and separateness that the debate on 'minority rights' is played out in the multicultural societies in the West as well as in India. In concrete terms, 'minority rights' encompasses several heterogeneous claims. Two types of claims are quite familiar. First a minority group demands rights against the larger society, to protect itself against the majoritarian tendencies of the society. In some cases a minority culture wants rights against its own members, who in the name of individual right can challenge certain collective practices. There are occasions in which a minority group wants autonomy as the best way of protecting their collective existence. In other circumstances they need special and exclusive provisions in order to survive as a community. In

exceptional circumstances they can demand the right to self-determination as the only option for protecting their culture and way of life in the world. Normatively speaking, the rights that can be morally justified as being granted to the minority groups depends upon specific circumstances and other contingent factors in a given society. It is quite possible that a minority group can start with the demand for special provisions but due to specific circumstances finds self-determination as the only option to counter the forces of majoritarianism. Yet one can see that all such demands tend to share some crucial features. They go beyond an abstract conception of citizenship of liberal democracy; and they make the recognition and protection of cultural differences central to the project of democratization.

Although the protection of minority rights takes different forms in different societies, some of the underlying normative claims can be universal. These 'universal claims' (for example, right against discrimination based on ascriptive grounds, right to form associational life that helps sustain cultural separateness and so on) do usually inform the constitutional practices in many parts of the world. Several international instruments such as the Universal Declaration of Human Rights (1948), the International Covenants on Civil and Political Rights (1966), and the Declaration on the Rights of Persons Belonging to National or Ethnic, Religious and Linguistic Minorities (1992), articulate the minority rights in universal terms with the underlying belief that these instruments provide the broad guidelines for nation-states to frame policies towards their minorities. Article One of the Declaration of 1992 says that the 'states shall protect the existence and the national or ethnic, cultural, religious and linguistic identity of minorities within their respective territories and shall encourage conditions for the promotion of that identity' (Massey 1999: 121; Vijapur 1999). It further says that the 'states shall adopt appropriate legislative and other measures to achieve those ends' (Massey 1999: 121). The international instruments by and large take the existence of nation-states for granted and tend to locate the issue of minority rights within the broader problematic of inviolable-territoriality and unitary state-sovereignty. For instance, take Article 8 (Clause-4) of the Declaration, which says, 'Nothing in the present Declaration may be construed as permitting any activity contrary to the purposes and principles of the United Nations, including sovereign equality, territorial integrity and political independence of states' (Massey 1999: 124). Whether or not these international instruments are effective is not the issue here. The point is how much of these universal declarations, though useful, offer an adequate framework for understanding the minority rights issue in a postcolonial society like India. This is where the need for a contextual theorization is intensely felt. In fact, in recent years research on multicultural politics, minority rights and such other issues has taken a turn in this direction.[6] A contextual understanding of minority rights encourages us to examine the ways in which certain values are moulded and mobilized within a given society and the manner in which universal principles are subjected to the logic of space and time. It also prompts us to focus our attention on the interaction between general ideas and the ways they operate on the ground. I also strongly believe that a contextual reading of minority rights in India is bound to be historical. But before I turn to history, one more thing has to be sorted out. It is the question of the definition of 'minority'.

Like most terms in social science, 'minority' is not an easy term to define. Let me cite an oft-quoted definition given by Capotorti: 'a group numerically inferior to the rest of the population of the state, in a non-dominant position, whose members—being nationals of the state—possess ethnic, religious or linguistic characteristics differing from those of the rest of the population and show, if only implicitly, a sense of solidarity, directed towards preserving their culture, tradition, religion or language'.[7] Minimally, a weak numerical position as well as socio-economic status remains central to the definition of a minority. But it is difficult to ascertain the levels of the weakness in numbers and a group's status to fit into this definition. For instance, if the Muslims belong to a minority group at the all-India level, it is not so when we consider the province or local level as the relevant unit. For instance, the Muslims are not a minority in Jammu and Kashmir. Jains, numerically speaking, are one of India's religious minorities. But they have never claimed nor have they been accorded the status

of a minority in the country. Two conclusions follow from this. First, although an important dimension, numerical weakness alone does not define a minority. Second, minority status is essentially fluid and it varies across level and time.

In any given context, a minority identity of a group is not solely dependent upon certain objective factors such as population, economic well-being and so on. It is now widely recognized by scholars that the group should also possess a subjective awareness of its distinct status in relation to others. The nature of interaction between the objective and subjective dimensions, to a large extent depends upon historical specificities. Besides these two dimensions, state plays a crucial role in the construction of minority identity. The role of the state and politics should be at the centre of one's understanding of minority rights/ identity in postcolonial societies, especially in India.

COLONIAL STATECRAFT AND COMMUNITARIAN MOBILIZATIONS

There is no doubt that colonial state for its own survival exploited the existing ascriptive divisions and through this process reified their existence in the Indian society. For instance, the granting of separate electorates to the Muslims in 1909, on the plea of a handful of elite Muslim leaders, is a clear example of colonial state's policy of counterpoise.[8] But to suggest that it is the colonial state alone that created the divisions among ascriptive communities would be an exaggeration. However, there are other ways in which the role of the colonial state and its varied practices towards the inter-community relations can be understood. The argument here is that colonialism did not inaugurate the communal differences/conflict (Bayly 1985) in India but through its interventions changed their trajectories and political possibilities. Colonial governance proceeded slowly and haltingly in India. In order to simplify what the colonial administrators saw in India (which was full of complexities, dense pluralities), it had to be put in their familiar grids of mapping, measuring, and counting. Sudipta Kaviraj (1992) argues that the strategies of enumeration initiated by the colonial state robbed the communities (caste, religious and others) of their fuzziness. The enumerated character of communities, he further argues, opened up new possibilities for political mobilization. Enumeration through census[9] not only offered legitimacy to the colonial epistemology that viewed Indian society as a congeries of communities, it also became an integral part of its 'governmentality'. We do not know how people in India undertook inter-community comparison in the past, particularly in the pre-enumeration period. Armed with numbers and other relevant information, in the early part of the twentieth century, people compared the status of their groups with others. For instance, caste groups in the Madras Presidency reflected quite purposefully on their relative position vis-à-vis other caste groups. In the Bengal Presidency, the linguistic groups such as Oriyas and Biharis always compared their educational, and employment status with their rival Bengalis. In the United Provinces, the Muslims also felt relatively deprived in comparison to their Hindu counterparts. With the introduction of the constitutional reforms, the relative deprivation argument was often used by the communities to ask for special representation to protect their interests. The process of enumeration, coupled with the introduction of constitutional reforms, opened up a space for the articulation of majority–minority discourse in India during the early part of the twentieth century.

As early as 1880s, Syed Ahmad Khan raised the fear of Hindu majoritarianism in the context of the colonial state's policy of introducing native representation at the local level. As time passed, the demands for special protection for the Muslims in the legislatures and various services of the colonial state, gave rise to a 'vocabulary of minorityism' (Hasan 2001) that survived even into the postcolonial period.

The provision of separate electorate, granted in 1909 for the 'minorities' was based on the belief that without special protection, the 'Hindu majority' will dominate these small groups. When the expansion of the electorate after the 1935 Act came into effect, the collective consciousness of the minority groups got inevitably sharpened. Research on provincial politics in the 1930s and 1940s quite clearly suggests that in provinces having a sizeable population of Muslims, the electoral competition gave rise to inter-community

antagonism (Page 1982). The rise of collective demands from various religious and caste groups in the early part of the twentieth century fitted quite well with the British perception of the Indian society as a country of discrete religious, caste and other groups. It is within this context that 'minority rights' as special provisions for minority groups emerged.

It was natural that the Indian National Congress had to react to these constitutional provisions. To begin with, the attitude of the Congress towards the issue of separate electorate was clearly ambivalent. This measure, as the Congress nationalists perceived it, was against the spirit of an undifferentiated Indian nationalism. The temporary acceptance of the 'separate electorate' by the Congress was dictated by sheer political pragmatism rather than any principled commitment to political safeguards for the minorities. This is not to say that there was no principled discussion on 'minority safeguards' within the Congress. In the Congress resolution of 28 December 1927, assurance was given 'to the two great communities that their legitimate interests will be safeguarded in the legislatures and such representation of the communities should be secured for the present, and if desired, by the reservation of seats in joint electorates on the basis of population in every province and in the Central Legislature'.[10] It further resolved that 'in the future constitution, liberty of conscience shall be guaranteed and no legislature, Central or Provincial, shall have power to make any laws interfering with liberty of conscience' (Ansari 1996, Vol. II: 96). The Nehru Report of 1928 further elaborated the spirit of the Congress resolution accepted a year ago. Under the chairmanship of Motilal Nehru, the committee visualized independent India to be a secular state without a state religion. According to the report, 'if the fullest religious liberty is given, and cultural autonomy provided for, the communal problem is in effect solved, although people may not realize it' (ibid.: 101). It strongly rejected the provision of separate electorate for the minorities. It was considered detrimental to the growth of a national spirit and any 'communal representation as a necessary evil' (ibid.: 112). Reservation of seats for the Muslims in Punjab and Bengal was rejected. Wherever the Muslims were in a minority and demanded special representation, the committee recommended reservation of seats for a period of ten years in strict proportion to their population. In the North Western Frontier Province, similar concessions were recommended for the non-Muslim minorities. In order to protect the educational and cultural interests of the minorities, a proposal for establishing communal councils was also turned down on the ground that it would 'keep the communalism' alive.

The discourse on minority rights during the 1920s and 1930s was premised upon the existence of a single-state system. The term minority made sense within the imaginary of a territorial state. The division of people in terms of majority and minority still encompassed a broader conception of political community. The idea of conferring 'universal rights' to citizens irrespective of their ascriptive status was widely shared by the Indian leaders during the 1930s and 1940s. Once again, this idea was very much based on the concept of a unified political society. To be a part of a minority (whether religious or linguistic or caste-based) was not to seek a separate state but to seek special collective rights within an evolving conception of constitutional democracy. Even as late as the 1940s, the Muslim League's demand was not for carving out a separate state but for special protection of the Muslims' interests and constitutional protection of their collective identity. Due to a host of complex reasons, things changed, and the status of being a 'minority' became, in the eyes of the Muslim League and other separatist forces, synonymous with being 'inferior', disadvantaged and permanently crippled. Within the changed milieu, it was not surprising that in the famous Lahore address Jinnah very clearly announced that 'Musalmans are not a minority. Musalmans are a nation according to any definition of a nation, and they must have their homeland, their territory and their state' (Hasan 2001: 57). Demand for a separate state for the Muslims, in a sense, was a setback to the 'minority discourse' in the colonial India. However, it is also true that, in spite of or perhaps because of the setback, the interest in resolving the 'minority rights' issue within the framework of a constitutional democracy never diminished.

MINORITY–MAJORITY CONUNDRUM: THE POST-COLONIAL PREDICAMENT

In a constitutional democracy, minority rights are best understood when they are seen along with a broader regime of rights.

Part-III of the Constitution of independent India provides a set of 'fundamental rights' for all its citizens. It too contains rights that are meant to be enjoyed only by specific groups. Take for instance, the Right to Equality (Articles 14–18), Right to Freedom (Articles 19–22), Right to Freedom of Religion (Articles 25–28) which are the fundamental rights meant for all the citizens of the country. Their justiciability makes sure that any infringement with these rights can be contested in the judiciary of the country and the state has to provide adequate constitutional grounds for its suppression. Some of the key rights in the Fundamental Rights Chapter of the Indian Constitution embody the principle of non-discrimination. The Article 15 (1) reads thus: 'The State shall not discriminate against any citizen on grounds only of religion, race, caste, sex, place of birth or any of them' (*The Constitution of India*, as modified up to the 1 January, 1995: 7). The next provision elaborates the general principle further:

> No citizen shall on the grounds only of religion, race, caste, sex, place of birth or any of them, be subject to any disability, liability, restriction or condition with regard to a) access to shops, public restaurants, hotels, and places of public entertainment; or b) the use of wells, tanks bathing ghats, roads and places of public resort maintained wholly or partly out of state funds or dedicated to the use of the general public. (ibid.)

The principle of non-discrimination is also reflected in Article 16 which suggests that 'no citizen shall, on grounds only of religion, race, caste, sex, descent, place of birth, residence or any of them be ineligible for, or discriminated against in respect of, any employment or office under the state' (ibid.). Another area to which the Indian Constitution has extended the principle of non-discrimination is that of education. Clause 2 of Article 29 provides that, 'no citizen shall be denied admission into any educational institution maintained by the state or receiving aid out of state funds on grounds only of religion, race, caste, language or any of them' (*The Constitution of India* 1995: 14).

Non-discrimination and the equal treatment of citizens by the state are inevitably related. These two principles together have laid down the foundation of equal citizenship in India. However, the Constitution provides exceptions to the principles of non-discrimination and equality. For instance, it can make special provisions for the welfare of women and children. The state through special provisions can also legislate to improve the conditions of citizens belonging to socially and educationally backward classes or to the Scheduled Castes and Tribes. The adoption of universal suffrage by rejecting the communal electorate (Article 325) also reflects the constitutional commitment to the principle of equal citizenship. It is true that the individual remains at the core of the equal citizenship principle, enshrined in the constitution. However, one can see clearly in Articles 15 and 16, a productive combination of rights meant to be enjoyed by individuals as citizens and obligation of the state towards the citizens belonging to specific communities. The awareness of individual and community in their relationship remains central to the Indian constitutional discourse since 1950. Even though, the right to equality, as a fundamental right of the Constitution, applies to all the citizens of the country, it has special significance for minorities particularly for the disadvantaged ones. In a strict sense, these rights are not minority rights; but their significance for the minority community is relatively more significant.

The principle of non-discrimination, though important, is not enough. Similarly, the presence of universal rights alone is not sufficient to address the claims of the minorities. Article 29 (1) of the Constitution says: 'Any section of the citizens residing in the territory of India or any part thereof having a distinct language, script or culture of its own shall have the right to conserve the same' (*The Constitution of India* 1995). Language is fundamentally social and a right to conserve one's own language is inescapably a collective right. This, the Supreme Court declared, includes even the citizens' 'right to agitate for its protection'.[11] According to this judgment, this right is more or less 'absolute', 'unqualified' and 'positive' (Wadhwa 1975: 98). According to Article 30 (1), 'all minorities, whether based on religion or language, shall have the right to establish and administer

educational institutions of their choice' (*The Constitution of India* 1995: 14). It further provides in Article 30 (2) that: 'the State shall not, in granting aid to educational institutions, discriminate, against any educational institution on the ground that it is under the management of a minority, whether based on religion, or language' (ibid.: 15). The first part of the article protects the right of the minorities to have their own educational institutions. The second involves a limited obligation on the part of the state towards these institutions. It only instructs the state not to discriminate these institutions while providing financial assistance for promoting education. One of the objectives of this article is clearly to do with the protection of the distinctive identities of the linguistic and religious minorities of the country. In a famous judgment connected with Article 30, the Supreme Court declared that,

> [T]he minorities, quite understandably, regard it as essential that the education of their children should be in accordance with the teachings of their religion and they hold, quite honestly, that such an education cannot be obtained in ordinary schools designed for all the members of the public, but can only be versed in the trends of their religion and in the tradition of their culture.[12]

The special rights for minorities, Justice Khanna observed in another case,

> were designed not to create inequality. Their real effect is to bring about equality by ensuring the preservation of the minority institutions and by guaranteeing to the minorities autonomy in the matter of administration of these institutions. The differential treatment for minorities by giving them special rights is intended to bring about an equilibrium, so that the ideal of equality may not be reduced to a mere abstract idea, but should become a living reality and result in true, genuine equality, an equality not merely in theory, but in fact...it is only the minorities who need protection, and article 30 beside some other articles is intended to afford and guarantee that protection.[13]

The relationship between the state and the minority educational institutions has raised a lot of issues concerning the state of minority rights in India. It has been made clear through judicial pronouncements that the state can lay down some restrictions in the matters dealing with syllabi for examinations, conditions of employment of teachers, and health and hygiene of students, but it cannot force a minority educational institution to teach in a particular language.[14] The state can also prescribe reasonable conditions while giving grant-in-aid to the educational institutions administered by a minority community. The nature of state intervention in the minority-governed educational institutions in the country still remains a sensitive issue. In this, the role of the Supreme Court has been of great significance.

Besides the above-mentioned articles, the Constitution of India also contains special provisions for the education of the linguistic minorities. The issue of linguistic minorities is indeed quite old. The early stirrings of the linguistic groups in India can be traced to the early part of the twentieth century. Within the larger provinces of the British empire several language groups perceived themselves as minorities, and demand for reorganization of provinces on linguistic lines were often raised by them. Because major language groups lived in distinct territories, it was easy for them to put forward their collective claims before the colonial state. As early as the 1920s, the National Congress recognized the identity-claims of the language groups. The recognition of their distinctness and the redrawing of the provincial boundaries were the main strategies through which linguistic minorities were made into majorities within the provincial arenas. In spite of the Congress' early promise, reorganization of provinces was not an easy affair in the post-independent India. Even the reorganization of provinces did not resolve the problem of linguistic minorities in the country.

Article 347 of the Constitution states:

[On] a demand being made in that behalf the President may, if he is satisfied that a substantial proportion of the population of a State desire the use of any language spoken by them to be recognized by that State, direct that such language shall also be officially recognized throughout that State or any part thereof for such purpose as he may specify. (*The Constitution of India* 1995: 212)

A sizeable and vocal linguistic minority can take advantage of this provision in order to get their language recognized by the state. The Constitution allows persons to submit their petitions for the redress of grievances to the state in any language (Article 350), and provides for education in their mother-tongue to the children of linguistic minorities (Article 350A). In the wake of the States' Reorganization Commission's recommendations, a special officer for linguistic minorities was created (Article 350B), whose function was to look into the implementation, or lack of it, of the safeguards for the linguistic minorities in the provinces. The unresolved problems of linguistic minorities in India have created tensions among groups in the provinces.

MINORITIES AND BACKWARDNESS

The discussion on economic and educational backwardness of the minority groups in general and the Muslims in particular in India has a long history. During the colonial period, the claims of the minority groups for special provisions and safeguards were inextricably linked to their economic and educational backwardness. As pointed out earlier, the theme of backwardness is still one of the crucial components of minority-rights discourse in the post-colonial period. In the past, so also today, Muslim groups often use the theme of economic and educational backwardness to show their relative status vis-à-vis other communities in the country. The Gopal Singh Committee Report drew attention, among other things, to the educational backwardness of Muslims. It too highlighted Muslim under representation in government employment (*Dr. Gopal Singh Panel Report on Minorities*, 14 June 1983). More than half of the Muslim urban population live below poverty line, compared to about 35 per cent of the Hindus. In urban areas majority of Muslims are self-employed (53.4 per cent) in comparison to 36 per cent amongst the Hindus. The self-employed category for the Muslims included by and large low-status occupations such as cobbler, rickshaw-puller, small artisan, and so on (Razzack and Gumber 2000: 11). According to a recent report, 43 per cent Muslims and 27 per cent Christians live below poverty line in comparison to 39 per cent of Hindus in India (Shariff 1999: 44).

How does educational and economic backwardness feature in the minority-rights discourse in the post-colonial India? There is no doubt that considerable regional and class variations exist as far as Muslims' economic status is concerned. For instance, a large number of Muslims in UP and Bihar, in comparison to other states, are poor. The situation of Muslims in Kerala, for instance, is not the same as that of Rajasthan. Even within one province, the economic condition of Muslim wage-labourers is not the same as that of the professional class. Yet, the theme of backwardness is incorporated in the minority-rights discourse as a generalized state of affairs, as a marker of the community as a whole, and its collective predicament. The backwardness of the minority communities in general and of Muslims in particular, in the above discourse, does not stand alone as an empirical idea. It usually gets fitted or has been made to fit with the story of discrimination and neglect of minorities by the Indian state. At the level of political common sense, this empirical description is incorporated into the normative notions of 'peripherality' and injustice.

In the contemporary minority discourse, welfare concerns and identity issues are often blended together. Although analytically separate, in reality, they stand imbricated with one another. The issue concerning Urdu language clearly demonstrates the point we are making. The decline of Urdu in north India has had a negative impact on Muslims' ability to get employment. The demand of Muslims to give Urdu a proper status in select provinces was and is still directly related to real economic benefits. This is also related to identity concerns of the community. The neglect of Urdu then becomes a sign of the community's powerlessness, and a reflection of majority community's politics of 'mis-recognition'. In a sense, the concern for Urdu language embodies simultaneously the issue of economic welfare as well as of identity for the Muslims. Likewise, the demand for the protection of educational institutions managed by Muslims and Christians clearly involves the simultaneous presence of economic and identity concerns.

Since the process of 'mandalization' unfolded in the 1990s, the framing up of welfare issues within the minority discourse has undergone some significant changes. A detailed discussion on this process and its impact on Indian society are beyond the scope of this paper. Still, it is essential to outline some of its significant features for the argument that follows. V.P.

Singh's decision to implement the recommendations of the Mandal Commission quickened the process, particularly in north India, of making a political block composed of Other Backward Classes (OBCs). The already existing contradiction between this block and the upper caste became sharper. The reservation of jobs for the OBCs, no doubt, was the immediate issue against which violent protests broke out in many places in the country. However, its impact on provincial and national politics was quite significant. The growing assertion of Hindutva forces and the decline of the Congress helped create the formation of a new space for political mobilization comprised of deprived communities such as Dalits, OBCs and so on. This new context too created new political possibilities for Muslim groups in India. The OBCs among the Muslims, like their counterparts among the Hindus, got the benefit of reservation in government jobs. In the realm of electoral politics, political parties tried to forge a coalition among different deprived groups such as Dalits, OBCs, and Muslims, and so on. The process still continues today.

With such sectional mobilizations, it was difficult to sustain the concept of an undifferentiated, deprived Muslim community fighting for its due share in the polity. The element of caste within the Muslim communities was always there. But in the post-Mandal times, it acquired a new salience and the lower-caste identities among them began making their presence felt much more sharply. Its impact on Muslim communities cannot be discussed in abstract. At one level, this heightened sense of caste was also symptomatic of their subaltern status within their community. Only on the basis of micro-studies that we can meaningfully talk about the ways in which 'subalternization' of politics has impacted on the collectivistic concerns of the religious minorities in the country. Yet, a few general points can be made in this regard. The articulations of Dalit-Christian and lower-caste Muslims surely have opened up new possibilities in the realms of inter-community relationship and electoral politics. As discussed above, the fact of economic and educational backwardness of Muslims was invariably used as a cementing force for the symbolic construction of the community. However, with the growing awareness of caste-identity, the theme of backwardness is now used by the low-caste groups within the Muslim community to undermine their old leadership, and to forge new linkages with similar groups belonging to other religions. The debate on reservation of jobs for Muslims in recent years brings this dimension to the fore (Wright 1997).

To address various minority concerns, a Commission was formed in 1978. Until 1992, when the National Commission for Minorities received statutory status, the Commission had functioned under the guidance of four chairpersons. Very early on, the need for providing a constitutional basis to the Commission was voiced in the Parliament (*Lok Sabha Debates*, 22 February, 1978, 28 March 1978, 5 and 11 April 1978, 10 May 1978, 26 July 1978 and 2 August 1978). Members had also expressed their fear that without effective power, the Commission's role in safeguarding the interests of the minorities would be limited. An attempt was made with the help of the Forty-sixth Amendment Bill in 1978 to give it a constitutional status, but without any success. A year later, another attempt (Fifty-first Amendment Bill) also met with the same fate. In 1990, there was yet another proposal to set up two National Commissions (one for the Scheduled Castes and Tribes and the other for the minorities) by suitably amending the Constitution. Finally, the National Commission for the Scheduled Castes and Tribes was given the constitutional status and the Minorities Commission was left out. In 1988, the linguistic minorities were put outside the ambit of the Minorities Commission.

On 4 May 1992, the Welfare Minister, Sitaram Kesari, introduced the National Commission for Minorities Bill in the Lok Sabha. On 11 May, a serious debate ensued between the supporters and the opponents of the Bill on the floor of the Lok Sabha that lasted for nearly five hours on that day and continued even to the next day. The defenders of the Bill offered broadly two reasons for conferring the minority commission with a statutory status. The first was an argument for greater efficacy. They argued that armed with statutory power, the Minorities Commission would be an effective instrument of protection of minority rights. The implication was that in its first incarnation, it was a mere advisory institution without much power at its command. The

second was that the Bill, as Sitaram Kesri pointed out, would 'instill confidence in the minorities' (*Lok Sabha Debates*, 11 May 1992: 91). This in turn would increase the legitimacy of the argument.

The supporters of the Bill, mostly belonging to the Congress and other non-BJP parties, grounded their arguments on the principle of secularism. Their starting assumption was that the Indian constitution embodied several provisions exclusively for the minorities. The existence as well as the protection of minority rights remained central to their understanding of secularism. In their arguments, a minority community appears as one that is vulnerable, at least potentially threatened and inadequately represented in various spheres of society. It was also assumed in their discourse that without an effective watchdog it would be impossible to check the acts of discrimination against the minorities. The notion of minority rights, which ran through the arguments of the defenders of the Bill, was broad and contained both the positive as well as its negative elements. They highlighted the ways in which minorities suffer from discrimination and indignities in the society.

On the other hand, the opponents of the Bill, mostly belonging to the BJP, described it as 'divisive' and 'retrograde'. Some even described the introduction of the Bill as a ploy by the Congress to win Muslim votes. In the Lok Sabha, L.K. Advani spearheaded the BJP's opposition to the Bill. In a long speech on 11 May 1992, he argued that the Bill would create separateness and division in the country. He even went further and suggested that it was against the spirit of the Constitution as conceived by its founding fathers. To him, even enacting a commission for the minorities would be an unjustified concession to them. The lack of precise definition of 'minority' also came in for a lot of criticism from the opponents of the Bill. Advani feared that the power given to the Central government by the Bill to decide who is a minority could be used for partisan ends. He also argued that contrary to the objectives of the Bill, the Muslims would be the prime beneficiaries of the Commission. This fitted quite well with the 'appeasement of Muslim thesis' propagated by the Hindutva forces in general and his party in particular. It was also pointed out that a National Integration-cum-Human Rights Commission could act as a proper watchdog for minority rights. The terms of the debate, as far as the opponents of the Bill were concerned, were not something new. In fact, the suspicion of the Hindu Right towards any special provision for minorities had had a long history. However, in this context the old argument took on a new meaning. The position of the Congress and others, from the point of view of the Hindu Right, appeared as an abandonment of the principle of neutrality of the state towards different religious groups in the country.

For the defenders of the Bill, the forces of majoritarianism could only be countered by instituting proper safeguards. Attempts were also made on the floor of the House to ground the proposed National Commission on a shared but minimal understanding of rights of minorities at all levels of the society. The argument is that once a minority is defined in relation to the jurisdiction of a particular law, one group may be a majority within the sphere of a state but can very well be a minority within a district within that particular state. Similarly, a religious group may be in a majority if one takes the national level into account but a minority within the context of a province or other such levels. The minority problem, as P.M. Sayeed remarked in the House, 'is not therefore just a Muslim problem. It is a political problem and a national problem' (Lok Sabha Debates, 11 May 1992: 200). By keeping this in view, some even argued for creating parity between National Minorities Commission and the National Commission for Scheduled Caste and Tribes. Participating in the debate, Syed Shahabuddin emphasized the need for bringing the minority rights discourse within the ambit of continuous deliberation of the House. He said:

> Let me caution you, the minorities sometimes, all over the world, tend to exaggerate their woes; their troubles; their sufferings and their grievances. There has to be balance and that balance can only be reached between the claims which are legitimate and the act of omission and commission on the part of the Government which deprived them in actual practice with the enjoyment of those rights, the balance can only be reached if there is a free and [f]air discussion in the national spirit on the floor of this august House. Therefore, I hope at least that will become a routine. It had become a post office. I hope you shall put some life into it. (Lok Sabha Debate, 11 May 1992: 201–2)

The Bill was finally passed on 17 May 1992 and came to effect a year later. It provided for a seven-member Commission and the its functions remained by and large the same as provided in the Government order of 1978 and as amended in 1988. The new Commission, while discharging its duty of protecting minority rights, was empowered to exercise the power of a civil court trying a suit. The point of discussing the debate is to demonstrate the contestatory terrain of minority rights in India. Any special provision for the religious minorities immediately becomes a matter of contention. Those who opposed it, accuse the supporters of political manipulation as well as appeasement of minorities. A minimal consensus on this is yet to be achieved by the contending political parties in India. This is one of the reasons why the theme of minority rights, in terms of offering special provisions, creates so much controversy both in legislatures as well as in civil society.

The functioning of the National Commission for Minorities is a case in point. The Annual Reports clearly reveal that there is no doubt that during 1978–92 the Minorities Commission received a large number of complaints concerning the discrimination of minorities from different parts of the country. During the first two years of its existence, it received 441 complaints both from individuals and organizations.[15] In the year 1989–90, the Commission had received 381 representations, of which 243 came from individuals belonging to minority communities and 138 from several minority organizations (The Twelfth Annual Report of The Minorities Commission (1-4-1989 to 31-3-1990), chapter VII: 90). Right from its inception in 1992, one of the important functions of the National Minorities Commission has been to act as a storehouse of grievances pertaining to the minorities in the country. After checking the nature of grievances, the Commission usually takes up the case and advises the concerned authorities for its redressal. From time to time, the Commission sends its committee to look into the incidents of communal violence and recommends the concerned government as to how to combat such incidents in future.

There are three areas in which the advisory role of the Commission is clearly evident. The first area deals with the security concern of the minorities in different parts of the country. The second theme on which it spends a lot of its institutional energy are the incidents of discrimination (related to both individuals and groups) faced by the minorities. Many a time minority communities draw the Commission's attention to the interference of government with their educational institutions. The third area in which the Commission takes a lot of interest regarding the economic and educational backwardness of the minority groups in the country. It generates and compiles data on the theme, produces reports, and from time to time, makes the state and Central governments aware of their duties towards the welfare of the minorities. It is possible to argue that the National Commission has succeeded in raising the problems of the minorities and aggregating them for the purpose of policy-making. At this point it is worth remembering that aggregating the problems of minorities is one thing and to persuade the state to devise and implement the solutions is quite another. In the latter respect, the role of the Commission has been quite limited. Since 1992, not a single Annual Report, submitted by the Commission to the Central government, has been discussed in the Parliament. Often the concerned authorities did not take the Commission's recommendations seriously. According to one of its former Chairpersons, even his letters of recommendations to the Central as well as state governments were often not even acknowledged (Mahmood 2001). From the vantage point of efficacy, it is obvious that the National Minorities Commission has not done that well. As an institution it has not taken roots. However, from the minority rights point of view, it is clear that through its practices, the Commission has helped vitalize a discourse that tries to blend the security concerns of the minorities with that of their dignity that links their economic well-being with their collective identity. It has also highlighted the point that the protection of minority rights needs a responsive democratic state.

POSTSCRIPT

The contemporary discourse on minorities contains two important issues. The first issue is articulated in the demands for physical security and non-discrimination. The second one highlights the economic status of the minority groups in the country. The economic and educational backwardness of the minorities remain important. Whether it is the plight of the 'Dalit Christians' or of the plebeian Muslims, the issue of deprivation is put upfront. The issue of honour and dignity, an overarching theme in recent decades, is often seen in connection with these two issues. I have argued that the identity question and the concerns for economic prosperity, although analytically separable, remain overlapping within the minority-rights discourse.

Significant developments concerning religious minorities in India have occurred during the last three or four years. The constitution of a high level committee by the Prime Minister in 2005 and the submission of its report (popularly known as *Sachar Committee report*—going by the committee's chairperson Justice Rajinder Sachar) in 2006; the creation of a separate Ministry of Minority Affairs [Annual Report 2007–2008, Ministry of Minority Affairs, Government of India] at the Centre by the United Progressive Alliance Government in 2006; and finally the gruesome violence against Christian minorities in Kandhmal of Orissa in 2007–8 together demonstrate how the problems of the developmental deficit and the physical insecurities of minority groups continue to shape and animate minority rights discourse in India. Both these concerns, it seems, may not be connected in older ways, but their mutual impingement continues to remain salient in India.

No doubt attempts were and continue to be made by the Central government and certain 'liberal' forces to 'developmentalize' the minority question and take it out of the nationalism–communalism problematique of the past. I think the *Sachar Committee report* can be read as an effort in guiding the minority question in this direction. Notwithstanding the empirical richness of the report, the revelation of Muslims' socio-economic and educational backwardness was not something new. Years ago, the Gopal Singh report had conveyed a similar conclusion. However, in a changed national scenario, findings of backwardness resonated in new ways among Muslim communities seized by majoritarian stereotypes and an intense psychosis caused by violence and discrimination. In some curious ways, the *Sachar Committee report* also contained possibilities of transforming the fact of developmental deficits into a larger democratic story. It was not surprising that young Muslims in different parts of the country raised the question as to why even after fifty-six years of constitutional democracy in India equal citizenship in terms of certain basic human development is denied to so many of them. The report, quite predictably, did not answer this fundamental question, but it created new occasions for re-interpreting old questions and revisiting past understandings.

Some argue that a focus on developmental deficits, rather than on identity-related questions, would create new contexts for civic-political rather than ethnic mobilization among the Muslim communities in India. No doubt in the past, excessive emphasis on identity issues, though legitimate, did not push their democratic agency very far. The majoritarian forces saw the interest articulation of religious minorities as a religious group through a lens of exclusivist nationalism. Even some well-meaning liberals fear that mobilization of secular interest through a religious grid may undermine the future of Indian democracy. Though analytically distinct, in some situations the opposition between 'identity' concerns and 'secular' interest cannot be sustained. But the tension between the two will remain for the foreseeable future.

The primary concern of the Ministry of Minority Affairs is to devise policies for and monitor existing programmes meant for minorities. Providing scholarship to students, making credit available to potential entrepreneurs, persuading institutions to create more spaces for deserving individuals, overseeing the functions of institutions such as National Commission for Minorities, and making efforts for a fair distribution of governmental resources are some of the key strategies through which the Ministry addresses the developmental deficits of the minority communities. In some sense, the government of India is devising new modes of governing its minority groups. Whether or not these modes will affirm and strengthen the democratic agency of the minority groups is an open question. As I finish this essay, a bill for the prevention of communal violence is being discussed by the Indian Parliament.

The recent communal conflagration and violence in Kandhmal in Orissa, once again, highlighted the need for ensuring greater commitment and responsibility of the state to protect the lives of its citizens belonging to minority groups. I think 'right to life', in an evocative sense, brings both the developmental and identity concerns of minority communities to a new blend. With greater mobilization of minority communities, the struggle for equal citizenship has entered a new phase in India. But without the establishment of adequate institutions, the protection of minority rights can never be strengthened.

NOTES

1. Quoted in Nandy (1998). See also Singh (1994).

2. The Anthropological Survey of India's *People of India* suggests that nearly 15 per cent of communities in India occupy a zone of intermediate identities. It is also pointed out that 64.2 per cent of all communities of India are bilingual. Quoted in Mayaram (1998).

3. Opinion polls suggested that only 22.7 per cent of the Indian electorate found the demolition justified. Against this, 38.1 per cent termed it as unjustified. See Mitra and Singh (1999: 145–6).

4. Statement of Mohd. Zeyalul Haque quoted by Hasan (1996, p. 177).

5. *Lok Sabha Debates* on Atrocities on Linguistic and Religious minorities in the country on 17 and 18 August 2000. Mostly the discussion veered around the attacks on the Christians and the churches in several parts of India.

6. For instance works of Will Kymlicka, Michael Walzer, Rajeev Bhargava, Niraja Jayal, Joseph Carens, Jeff Spinner, just to cite a few, provide some of the best examples in this tradition.

7. Quoted in Rothermund (2000, p. 324).

8. For an early academic articulation of the counterpoise argument see Krishna (1939).

9. For an interesting and incisive discussion on the impact of census on social categories see Cohn (1987, Chapter 10).

10. Resolution passed on 28 December 1927 by the Indian National Congress at its 42nd session held in Madras quoted in Ansari (1996, Vol. II, p. 95). The 'two great communities' mentioned in the Resolution referred to the Muslims and the Depressed Classes.

11. The judgment of the Supreme Court in the case *Jagat Singh vs Pratap Singh*, quoted in Wadhwa (1975, p. 98).

12. The Case of Kerala Education Bill 1957, quoted in Massey (1999, p. 42).

13. *The Ahmedabad St. Xavier's College Society vs State of Gujarat*, quoted in Massey (1999, p. 43).

14. The judgment of Justice M. Hidayatullah in *State of Kerala vs Rev. Mother Provincial*, quoted in Massey (1999: 45). Also see the judgment in *DAV College vs State of Punjab* quoted in Mahajan (1998, p. 99, footnote-14).

15. The division of the complaints, minority community wise, was the following: Muslims-294, Christians-48, Sikhs-23, Buddhists-15, Parsis-3, Linguistic Minorities-58. *Third Annual Report of the Minorities Commission* (for the year ending 31st December, 1980), Annexure X.

REFERENCES

Documents and Primary Sources

Annual Report 2007–8, Ministry of Minorities Affairs, Government of India.
Annual Reports of the Minorities Commission, 1978–1991.
Census of India, 1991, 2001.
Commissioner of Linguistic Minorities Reports (Relevant years).
The Constitution of India (as modified up to 1 January 1995 edition)
Constitutional Proposals of The Sapru Committee, 1945.
Constitutional Assembly Debates (CAD), Vols I-XII.
Dr. Gopal Singh Panel Report on Minorities, 14 June 1983.
Jawaharlal Nehru: Letters to Chief Ministers (1947–1964), Vols 1–5.
Laws of State Minorities Commissions and Boards (National Commission for Minorities Publication), 1998.
Lok Sabha Debates (Relevant years).
Minorities India (Newsletter of National Commission for Minorities), 1997–1998.
People of India: An Introduction, (ed. K.S. Singh), Anthropological Survey of India, 1992.
Readings on Minorities: Perspectives and Documents (2 vols) Ed. Iqbal A. Ansari. Delhi, Institute of Objective Studies, 1996.
Social Economic and Educational Status of the Muslim Community of India: A Report, Prime Minister's High Level Committee, Cabinet Secretariat, Government of India, November 2006.
The National Commission for Minorities Act 1992.
India Human Development Report, Abusaleh Shariff (National Council of Applied Economic Research), 1999.

Books and Articles

Ahmad, Imtiaz, Partha S. Ghosh, and Helmut Reifeld (eds). 2000. *Pluralism and Equality: Values in Indian Society and Politics*. New Delhi: Sage.
Alam, Javed. 2008. 'The Contemporary Muslim Situation in India: A Long-Term View', *Economic and Political Weekly*, XLIII(2), pp. 45–53.
———. 2000. 'A Minority Moves into Another Millennium', in Romila Thapar (ed.), *India's Another Millennium*. Delhi: Viking, pp. 137–51.

Baird, Robert D. 1978. 'Religion and the Legitimation of Nehru's Concept of the Secular State', in B.L. Smith (ed.), *Religion and The Legitimation of Power in South Asia*. Leiden: E.J. Brill, pp. 73–87.
Bajpai, Rochana. 2000. 'Constituent Assembly Debates and Minority Rights', *Economic and Political Weekly*, XXXV (21–22), pp. 1837–45.
Basu, Amrita and Atul Kohli (eds). 1998. *Community Conflicts and the State in India*. New Delhi: Oxford University Press.
Baumeister, Andrea. 2000. *Liberalism and the 'Politics of Difference'*. Edinburgh: Edinburgh University Press.
Bayly, C.A. 1985. 'The Pre-history of "Communalism"? Religious Conflict in India 1700–1800', *Modern Asian Studies*, 19(2), 1985, pp. 177–203.
Beaglehole, J.H. (1967), 'The Indian Christians: A Study of a Minority', *Modern Asian Studies*, vol. 1, no. 1, pp. 59–80.
Bhargava, Rajeev. 1999. 'Should We Abandon the Majority-Minority Framework?', in D.L. Seth and Gurpreet Mahajan (eds), *Minority Identity and the Nation-State*. Delhi: Oxford University Press, pp. 169–205.
——— (ed.). 1998. *Secularism and its Critics*. New Delhi: Oxford University Press.
Bhargava, Rajeev, Amiya Kumar Bagchi, and R. Sudarshan (eds). 1999. *Multiculturalism, Liberalism and Democracy*. New Delhi: Oxford University Press.
Bilgrami, Akeel. 1992. 'What is a Muslim? Fundamental Commitment and Cultural Identity', *Economic Political Weekly*, XXVII(20–21), pp. 1071–78.
Bose, Sugata and Ayesha Jalal (eds). 1999. *Nationalism, Democracy and Development: State and Politics in India*. New Delhi: Oxford University Press.
Brass, Paul. 1991. *Ethnicity and Nationalism: Theory and Comparison*. New Delhi: Sage.
Carens, Joseph H. 2000. *Culture, Citizenship, and Community: A Contextual Exploration of Justice as Evenhandedness*. Oxford: Oxford University Press.
Chandhoke, Neera. 1999. *Beyond Secularism: The Rights of Religious Minorities*. New Delhi: Oxford University Press.
Chatterji, Joya. 1998. 'The Bengali Muslim: A Contradiction in Terms? An Overview of the Debate on Bengali Muslim Identity', in Mushirul Hasan (ed.), *Islam, Communities and the Nation*. Delhi: Manohar, pp. 265–82.
Chatterjee, Partha. 1995. *The Nation and Its Fragments*. New Delhi: Oxford University Press.
Cohn, Bernard. 1987. *An Anthropologist among the Historians and other Essays*. New Delhi: Oxford University Press.
Das, Veena. 1995. *Critical Events: An Anthropological Perspective on Contemporary India*. New Delhi: Oxford University Press.
——— (ed.). 1992. *Mirrors of Violence: Communities, Riots and Survivors in South Asia*. New Delhi: Oxford University Press.

Engineer, Asghar Ali. 1991. *Communal Riots in Post-Independent India* (second edn.). Hyderabad: Sangam Books.

Fernandes, Walter. 1999. 'Attacks on Minorities and a National Debate on Conversions', *Economic Political Weekly*, XXXIV(3–4), pp. 81–4.

Frankel, Francine R., Zoya Hasan, Rajeev Bhargava, Balveer Arora (eds). 2000. *Transforming India: Social and Political Dynamics of Democracy*. New Delhi: Oxford University Press.

Galanter, Marc. 1984. *Competing Equalities: Law and the Backward Classes in India*. New Delhi: Oxford University Press.

Gopal, S. 1988. 'Nehru and Minorities', *Economic and Political Weekly*, Special Number, XXIII(45–47), pp. 2463–66.

Gupta, Raghuraj. 1985. 'Changing Role and Status of the Muslim Minority in India: A Point of View', *Journal of Muslim Minority Affairs*, 5(1), pp. 181–202.

Hansen, Thomas Blom. 2000. 'Predicaments of Secularism: Muslim Identities and Politics in Mumbai', *Journal of the Royal Anthropological Institute*, 6(2), pp. 255–72.

———. 2000. 'Governance and Myths of State in Mumbai' in C.J. Fuller and Veronique Benei (eds), *The Everyday State and Society in Modern India*. New Delhi: Social Science Press, pp. 31–67.

———. 1999. *The Saffron Wave: Democracy and Hindu Nationalism in Modern India*. New Delhi: Oxford University Press.

Hardgrave Jr., Robert L. 1993. 'India: The Dilemmas of Diversity', *Journal of Democracy*, 4(4), pp. 54–68.

Hasan, Mushirul (ed.). 2001. *India's Partition: Process, Strategy and Mobilization*. New Delhi: Oxford University Press.

———. 1997. *Legacy of a Divided Nation: India's Muslims since Independence*. New Delhi: Oxford University Press.

———. 1996. 'Minority Identity and its Discontents: Ayodhya and its Aftermath', in Praful Bidwai, Harbans Mukhia, and Achin Vanaik (eds), *Religion, Religiosity and Communalism*. Delhi: Manohar, pp. 167–203.

———. 1988. 'In Search of Integration and Identity: Indian Muslims Since Independence', *Economic and Political Weekly*, Special Number, XXIII(45–47), pp. 2467–78.

———. 1979. *Nationalism and Communal Politics in India*. Delhi: Manohar.

Hasan, Zoya. 1998. *Quest for Power: Oppositional Movements in Uttar Pradesh*. New Delhi: Oxford University Press.

Jayal, Niraja Gopal. 1999. *Democracy and the State: Welfare, Secularism and Development in Contemporary India*. New Delhi: Oxford University Press.

Kabir, Humayun. 1968. *Minorities in a Democracy*. Calcutta: Firma K.L. Mukhopadhyay.

Kaviraj, Sudipta. 1992. 'The Imaginary Institution of India', in Partha Chatterjee and Gyanendra Pandey (eds), *Subaltern Studies*, vol. VII. New Delhi: Oxford University Press, pp. 1–39.

Khalidi, Omar. 1993. 'Muslims in Indian Political Process: Group Goals and Alternative Strategies', *Economic and Political Weekly*, XXVIII(1–2), pp. 43–54.

Khilnani, Sunil. 1997. *The Idea of India*. London: Hamish Hamilton.

Kothari, Rajni. 1988. *State Against Democracy: In Search for Humane Governance*. Delhi: Ajanta Publications.

Krishna, K.B. 1939. *The Problem of Minorities or Communal Representation in India*. London: George Allen and Unwin Ltd.

Krishna, Sankaran. 2000. *Postcolonial Insecurities: India, Sri Lanka, and the Question of Nationhood*. New Delhi: Oxford University Press.

Kymlicka, Will. 1995. *Multicultural Citizenship: A Liberal Theory of Minority Rights*. Oxford: Clarendon Press.

——— (ed.). 1995. *The Rights of Minority Culture*. Oxford: Oxford University Press.

———. 1989. *Liberalism, Community and Culture*. Oxford: Oxford University Press.

Kymlicka, Will and Wayne Norman (eds). 2000. *Citizenship in Diverse Societies*. Oxford: Oxford University Press.

Larson, Gerald, James. 1997. *India's Agony over Religion*. New Delhi: Oxford University Press.

Lijphart, Arend. 1996. 'The Puzzle of Indian Democracy: A Consociational Interpretation', *American Political Science Review*, 90(2), pp. 258–68.

Madan, T.N. 1993. 'Whither Indian Secularism?', *Modern Asian Studies*, 27(3), pp. 667–98.

Mahajan, Gurupreet. 1998. *Identities and Rights: Aspects of Liberal Democracy in India*. New Delhi: Oxford University Press.

Mahmood, Tahir. 2001. *Minorities Commission: Minor Role in Major Affairs*. Delhi: Pharos Media & Publishing (P) Ltd.

———. 1997. *Minorities Commissions: Raison d'etre, Role and Responsibilities*. National Commission for Minorities Publication.

Massey, James. 1999. *Minorities in a Democracy: The Indian Experience*. Delhi: Manohar.

Mayaram, Shail. 1998. 'Rethinking Meo Identity: Cultural Faultline, Syncretism, Hybridity or Liminality', in Mushirul Hasan (ed.), *Islam: Communities and the Nation*. Delhi: Manohar, pp. 283–306.

———. 1997. *Resisting Regimes: Myth and Memory in a Muslim Community*. New Delhi: Oxford University Press.

Metcalf, Barbara D. 1995. 'Too Little and Too Much: Reflections on Muslims in the History of India', *The Journal of Asian Studies*, 54(4), pp. 951–67.

Misra, Salil. 2001. *A Narrative of Communal Politics: Uttar Pradesh, 1937–39*. New Delhi: Sage Publications.

Mitra, Subrata K. and V.B. Singh. 1999. *Democracy and Social Change in India*. New Delhi: Sage Publications.

Nandy, Ashis, Sikha Trivedy, Shail Mayaram, and Achyut Yagnik. 1995. *Creating a Nationality: The Ramjanmabhumi Movement and the Fear of the Self*. New Delhi: Oxford University Press.

Mohapatra, Bishnu N. 2001. 'Democracy and the Claims of Diversity: Interrogating the Indian Experience', Paper presented at the Conference on Dialogue on Democracy and Pluralism in South Asia, Delhi, March.

Nandy, Ashis. 1999. 'Coping with the Politics of Faiths and Cultures: Between Secular State and Ecumenical Traditions in India', in J. Pfaff-Czarnecka, Darini Rajasingham-Senanayake, Ashis Nandy, and Edmund Terence Gomez (eds), *Ethnic Futures: The State and Identity Politics in Asia.* New Delhi: Sage Publications, pp. 135–66.

———. 1998. 'Pluralism as the Politics of Cultural Diversity in India', in Rukmini Sekhar (ed.), *Making a Difference.* New Delhi: SPIC MACAY Publication, pp. 53–72.

———. 1988. 'The Politics of Secularism and the Recovery of Religious Tolerance', *Alternatives,* 13(3), pp. 177–94.

Page, David. 1982. *Prelude to Partition: The Indian Muslims and the Imperial State System of Control 1920–1932.* Delhi: Oxford University Press.

Parekh, Bhikhu. 1999. 'Balancing Unity and Diversity in Multicultural Societies', in Dan Avor and Avner de-Shalit (eds), *Liberalism and its Practice.* London: Routledge, pp. 85–101.

Pettit, Philip. 2000. 'Minority Claims under Two Conceptions of Democracy', in Duncan Ivison, Paul Patton and Will Sanders (eds), *Political Theory and the Rights of Indigenous Peoples.* Cambridge: Cambridge University Press, pp. 199–215.

Rawls, John. 1993. *Political Liberalism.* New York: Columbia University Press.

Raz, Joseph. 1994. *Ethics in Public Domain.* Oxford: Clarendon Press.

Razzack, Azra and Anil Gumber. 2000. *Differentials in Human Development: A Case for Empowerment of Muslims in India.* New Delhi: National Council of Applied Economic Research Publication.

Rothermund, Dietmar. 2000. 'Individual and Group Rights in Western Europe and India', in Imtiaz Ahmad, Partha S. Ghosh, and Helmut Reifeld (eds), *Pluralism and Equality: Values in Indian Society and Politics.* New Delhi: Sage Publications, pp. 320–46.

Seth, D.L. and Gurpreet Mahajan (eds). 1999. *Minority Identities and the Nation-State.* New Delhi: Oxford University Press.

Shaikh, Farzana. 2001. 'Muslims and Political Representation in Colonial India', in Mushirul Hasan (ed.), *India's Partition: Process, Strategy and Mobilization.* New Delhi: Oxford University Press, pp. 81–100.

Shakir, Moin. 1980. 'Electoral Participation of Minorities and Indian Political System', *Economic Political Weekly,* Annual Number, XV(5, 6, and 7), pp. 221–6.

Shariff, Abusaleh. 1999. *India Human Development Report.* New Delhi: Oxford University Press.

Singh, K.S. 1994. *People of India,* The Anthropological Survey of India, vol. 1 & vol. VIII(1996). New Delhi: Oxford University Press

Smith, Donald, Eugene. 1963. *India as a Secular State.* New Jersey: Princeton University Press.

Tamir, Yael. 1993. *Liberal Nationalism.* New Jersey: Princeton University Press.

Taylor, Charles. 1994. 'The Politics of Recognition', in David T. Goldberg (ed.), *Multiculturalism: A Critical Reader.* Oxford: Blackwell.

———. 1991. 'Shared and Divergent Values', in Ronald L. Watts and Douglas M. Brown (eds), *Options for a New Canada.* Toronto: Toronto University Press.

Tully, James. 1995. *Strange Multiplicity: Constitutionalism in an Age of Diversity.* Cambridge: Cambridge University Press.

Upadhyaya, Prakash Chandra. 1992. 'The Politics of Indian Secularism', *Modern Asian Studies,* 26(4), pp. 815–83.

Varshney, Ashutosh. 2002. *Ethnic Conflict and Civic Life: Hindu as Muslims in India.* New Haven and London: Yale University Press.

———. 1993. 'Contested Meanings: Hindu Nationalism, India's National Identity, and the Politics of Anxiety', *Daedalus,* Vol. 122, Summer, pp. 227–61.

Vijapur, Abdulrahim P. 1999. 'Minorities and Human Rights: A Comparative Perspective of International and Domestic Law', in D.L. Seth and Gurpreet Mahajan (eds), *Minority Identities and the Nation-State.* New Delhi: Oxford University Press, pp. 242–72.

Wadhwa, Kamlesh Kumar. 1975. *Minority Safeguards in India.* New Delhi: Thompson Press (India) Ltd.

Weiner, Myron. 1997. 'India's Minorities: Who are They? What do They Want?', in Partha Chatterjee (ed.), *State and Politics in India.* New Delhi: Oxford University Press, pp. 459–95.

Wright Jr., Theodore. 1966. 'The Effectiveness of Muslim Representation in India', in Donald E. Smith (ed.), *South Asian Politics and Religion.* New Jersey: Princeton University Press.

———. 1997. 'A New Demand for Muslim Reservations in India', *Asian Survey,* xxxvii(9), pp. 852–58.

Yadav, Yogendra. 2000. 'Understanding the Second Democratic Upsurge: Trends of Bahujan participation in electoral politics in the 1990s', in Francine R. Frankel, Zoya Hasan, Rajeev Bhargava, Balveer Arora (eds), *Transforming India: Social and Political Dynamics of Democracy.* New Delhi: Oxford University Press, pp. 120–45.

———. 1997. 'Reconfiguration in Indian Politics: State Assembly Elections 1993–1995', in Partha Chatterjee (ed.), *State and Politics in India.* New Delhi: Oxford University Press, pp. 177–207.

III Political Processes

16 Political Parties

Zoya Hasan

Democratization in former colonial states has been inconsistent and erratic. India has been an exception. It has maintained and consolidated a democratic system, despite the fact that the preconditions often associated with democracy, ranging from industrialization and mass literacy to a minimum standard of living, were absent in the 1950s when India first became a democratic, secular republic (Kohli 1988; Jayal 2001; Frankel *et al.* 2000). Yet, democracy has not only endured, it has developed into a vibrant system. The democratic process has deepened, drawing historically disadvantaged groups into the political system. Political parties have undoubtedly played a decisive role in this process. It is hard to conceive of India's democratic system and its success without the crucial role played by political parties.

Political parties were significant institutions even before Independence. After Independence, they assumed a new importance. On the one hand, they provide the linkage between institutions and constituencies within the polity, and on the other, they provide the crucial connection between the political process and policymakers, and bring to the forefront issues affecting the interests of social groups and the public at large. Yet, there is a great deal of dissatisfaction with parties. Parties and politicians are accused of weakening the democratic fibre of the country: by practising corrupt politics, by eschewing a long-term perspective on social welfare, and by maximizing their personal gains and influence at the expense of larger national interests. However, without political parties the democratic system would not have worked. Parties remain the principal force around which contestation and mobilization are organized, working to structure political alternatives and formulating policies and translating them into effective choices for the people. Parties are, in short, the agencies and mechanisms through which power is organized and exercised in a democracy.

The most striking feature of India's party politics is that it does not fit neatly into any of the theories of liberal democratic politics or the conventional categories of party systems known in the West. Political parties in India do not correspond to

European or American party processes. At the same time, India's traditional social divisions have not translated easily into the party political system. Congress dominance, for instance, was not based on a particular caste, religion, or class; in fact, no party based exclusively on a single social cleavage such as majority–minority or caste can hope to sustain its dominance throughout the country. Political parties display numerous contradictory features, which reveal the blending of different forms of modern organization and participatory politics with indigenous practices and institutions. Parties are indeed complex, and an important reason for this complexity is the social heterogeneity that has made it impossible for a single set of parties to emerge across the country, as has happened in more homogeneous societies. Thus, there exist many types of parties. Among them should be noted the continued presence of one of the oldest parties in the world, the Congress (established in 1885); the emergence of the right-wing Bharatiya Janata Party (BJP); and the world's longest surviving democratically elected Communist party government at the state level in West Bengal.

Major changes have taken place in Indian party politics since Independence (Manor 1990: 62–98). From 1989 the leadership, organization, electoral strategies, and support base of political parties have undergone significant changes. To understand the significance and implications of these developments, it is useful to distinguish broadly two important phases in its development. One-party dominance, moderate levels of political participation, and elite consensus characterized the first phase. This has given way to a second phase of greater democratization and the opening up of the political system to non-elite participants. Major changes in party politics include the replacement of the Congress system with multi-party competition; an intensification of political competition; and fragmentation of the party system and coalition politics. Particularly marked is the decline of one-party dominance, the rise of the BJP as the single largest party in Parliament, and the advent of coalition politics. Since the last six parliamentary elections have not produced a single-party majority, they have necessitated a coalition government.

Equally significant is the democratic upsurge among the hitherto underprivileged and the influence of subaltern sections on the structure of electoral choices and outcomes. A significant aspect of the political process is that on the one hand, parties are the key to democratization, leading to a deepening of democracy; and on the other, they lack strong organizational structure or internal democracy and mobilize support along ethnic lines.

Through a combination of these processes—the creation of new parties and groups and their pursuit of sectional strategies—parties have increasingly fragmented over the years (Sridharan 2000: 475–503). Frequent party splits, mergers, and counter-splits led to a significant increase in the number of parties.

Political parties are registered with the Election Commission of India (ECI) under the law. The registered parties are granted recognition at the state and national levels by the ECI on the basis of their poll performance at general elections according to criteria prescribed by it. There are three types of parties according to the criteria laid down by the ECI: national parties, multi-state parties, and state parties.[1]

NATIONAL PARTIES AND PARTY DOMINANCE

The Congress party has been the most important political institution in India's modern political history. Led by the Cambridge-educated Jawaharlal Nehru, Congress reaped the rewards of its role during the anti-colonial movement against the British. It won nearly three-fourths of the seats in Parliament in the national elections in 1952, 1957, and 1962. The Congress ruled every state until 1967. However, an important feature of Congress dominance was the large degree of autonomy that provincial units were able to assert in relation to the central party leadership—a far cry from the situation that obtained after Indira Gandhi. Their recommendations for candidates for parliamentary or assembly seats or Chief Minister were almost always accepted by the central leadership. Although led by upper-caste/class leadership, there were Muslims, Scheduled Castes (SCs), Scheduled Tribes (STs), and various regional and linguistic groups represented in its higher echelons. It enjoyed enormous prestige with the rural and urban masses. Its hegemony was based on a concrete set of achievements: an independent model of industrial growth; considerable reduction in large-scale feudal landholdings, which benefited the upper peasantry; growth in infrastructure; expansion in educational facilities and technical personnel. A noteworthy feature of this project was a national definition of the polity with an emphasis on the state's responsibility towards society. It did deliver some tangible benefits to the broad mass of the population through various development projects, the initiation and construction of the public sector, and the provision of public services such as health, education, and transport.

This political system worked until the split in the Congress in 1969. The split transformed the Congress party from a loose coalition of ideologically diverse groups, which stretched from the Right to the Left to a populist party, in which the supremacy of the parliamentary wing over the organizational was once and for all established. Political rule was entirely dominated by central command and control, and in party affairs, by the high command. From this period onwards, it evolved into an electoralist catch-all party. The breakdown of the Congress system was starkly evident after Indira Gandhi's disastrous Emergency experiment, which resulted in a sharp and substantial drop in the vote base. After the defeat of the Congress in the 1977 election and the formation of the first non-Congress government at the Centre led by the Janata Party, a conglomeration of four parties (Jana Sangh, Bharatiya Lok Dal, Congress [O], and the Socialist Party), the backward castes emerged as a major force in national politics. However, once again the disenchantment with the Janata Party's uninspiring leadership and its internecine squabbling brought the Congress back to power in 1980. In the 1984 election, held after Indira Gandhi's assassination, the Congress polled the highest vote and seat tally ever as a sympathy vote swept the country and brought her son Rajiv to power. But the underlying trends signified the collapse of one-party dominance and the end of the Congress epoch in Indian politics (Hewitt 1989: 151–71).

With the decline of Congress dominance, the second phase of party politics began taking shape. New opposition parties and ideologies began to take centrestage from the late 1980s. This period saw the emergence of the BJP as a major force in Indian politics. It soon overshadowed the Congress as the largest party in the 1996, 1998, and 1999 elections. At no point before 1989 had the BJP received even one-tenth of the national vote. It emerged for the first time as the single largest party in 1996; its vote share increased to 20.3 per cent. The BJP-led government under A.B. Vajpayee lasted only 13 days. Subsequently, the United Front government, consisting of the Janata Dal, some Left parties, and some state parties, formed a government for the first time in 1996, with Deve Gowda as the Prime Minister. In 1998, the BJP-led alliance secured 253 of the 543 seats and in 1999, the National Democratic Alliance (NDA), a coalition of 24 parties led by the BJP, won 304 seats.

Among political parties, the BJP is atypical. It is not a denominational party, but it promotes Hindu interests. The BJP can be better defined as an ethnic party, the promoter of a Hindu ethnicity and nationalism defined along religious lines, which is something much narrower than a broad, encompassing, multi-ethnic Indian nationalism. Its aim is to create a unified Hindu nation through the politics of polarization. It was founded on the ideology of Hindutva, which encourages Hinduness. It is the political outgrowth of an extremist right-wing ideological movement. It has enduring ties with its parent organization, the Rashtriya Swayamsevak Sangh (RSS), and its various fronts like the Vishwa Hindu Parishad (VHP) and the Bajrang Dal, sharing features of the fascist type of organizations minus the cult of the supreme leader. Many of its party cadres come from the RSS, and its affiliation to the RSS–VHP network has proved decisive in its recent growth.

During the six years of BJP-led NDA rule at the Centre (1998–2004), the party struggled to achieve what Christophe Jaffrelot called a 'division of labour', with Vajpayee, perceived as more moderate, on one side, and the RSS and other elements of the Sangh which continued to pursue a Hindu nationalist agenda on the other (1996: 449). The BJP came to power denouncing Nehruvian secularism, advocating militant Hindu nationalism, and encouraging anti-Muslim rhetoric and action (Heath 1999: 232–56). Arguably, the anti-Muslim sentiment was deflected on to the international scene, where a range of issues identified

Muslims as a threat surrounding India, whether in Kashmir, Bangladesh (infiltration across the border), or the Middle East, where the BJP government dramatically reversed the policy of supporting Palestine to forge a new relationship with Israel. After September 2001, the 'fight against terrorism' became the centrepiece of the BJP's domestic and foreign policy. In some of these actions, the BJP had the support of groups that went far beyond its own traditional social base. The NDA lost control of the government in the elections of April–May 2004, and was defeated by the United Progressive Alliance (UPA), led by the Congress. The Congress emerged as the single largest party with 145 seats, and the UPA secured 220 seats.

The BJP's vote share dipped from 22.2 per cent in 2004 to 18.8 per cent in 2009. Their number of seats dropped to 116 in 2009 from 138 in 2004 (*The Hindu*, 26 May 2009). In 1999 when the NDA was at its peak, the vote share of the alliance was 41.1 per cent which came down to 24.1 per cent in 2009. Marking a major retreat for the BJP, it implied a shrinking of its social base of support, a decline in its voter base in its strongholds and failure to make inroads into other states. It also revealed its difficulties in holding on to allies or adding new ones to compensate for those who left the alliance. Big allies like the Telugu Desam Party (TDP), Trinamool Congress, and Biju Janata Dal had moved out of the NDA for fear of losing minority support. Its capacity to represent and accommodate diverse interests severely dented, the BJP was increasingly less attractive to existing and potential allies.

The balance between the BJP and the Congress shifted decisively to the advantage of the Congress in 2009. In this election, voters delivered a significant verdict with the Congress and its alliance winning 262 just 10 short of the majority mark. The Congress won 206 seats, crossing the threshold of 200 seats for the first time since 1991. The party has made major gains in Andhra Pradesh, Uttar Pradesh, Kerala, and Rajasthan.

REGIONAL PARTIES AND COALITION POLITICS[2]

The 1980s, a period of great turbulence in Indian politics, marked the appearance of several new

political parties. As the Congress went into a long decline and the Janata Party unravelled, several regional parties emerged in various states and enlarged their support (Verney 2002: 134–58). In the process, national parties were marginalized, or became adjuncts to the state parties in major states of the country. Many of these state-based parties are not confined to one state, but exist in several states, whether recognized or not. Parties such as the Samajwadi Party (SP), Rashtriya Janata Dal (RJD), Janata Dal (Secular), Janata Dal (United) have units, and have fielded candidates in many states. National parties such as the CPI[M], Communist Party of India (CPI), Bahujan Samaj Party (BSP), and the Nationalist Congress Party could also be described as multi-state parties because their presence and representation in the Lok Sabha is limited to a few states.

Regional parties with an explicitly regional-ethnic character include the TDP in Andhra Pradesh, the Dravida Munnetra Kazagham (DMK), and the All India Anna Dravida Munnetra Kazhagam (AIDMK) in Tamil Nadu, Asom Gana Parishad (AGP) in Assam, and the Akali Dal in Punjab. For example, the Akali Dal represents only the Sikhs and the AGP represents caste Hindu Assamese. While the SP and the BSP in Uttar Pradesh (UP) are essentially ethnic in character and represent the backward and lower castes, they also share the characteristics of an electoralist party, promoting the interests of distinct social constituencies (Arora 2000).

The story of UP is a telling illustration of the fragmentation of the party system, and with it the nature and dynamics of catch-all parties in particular. For many decades after Independence, UP was the fulcrum of politics and remained central to the formation of any government in New Delhi. The party which won UP invariably formed the government at the Centre. But more important than the number of parliamentary seats was the strategy of building inclusive social coalitions which would include the majority of the electorate. The withering away of the Congress umbrella and its social coalition of Brahmins, Dalits, and Muslims gave rise to new alliances represented by caste- and community-based parties. This led to the institutionalization of caste-based fragmentation and the exponential growth of the BSP and SP in UP at the expense of the Congress (Pai 1998; 2002). The BSP emphasized its distinct character as a Dalit-based party, and attempted to mobilize the underprivileged using caste as a tool to break the existing system, so as to distinguish itself from the Congress and the BJP and create an alternative space as a Dalit party. Subsequent years witnessed a shift in its strategy as the party attempted to gain the support of Brahmins by providing them with tickets, further weakening the influence of national parties. Its social engineering collapsed in the 2009 elections with both Brahmins and Muslims returning to the original Congress 'coalition of extremes'.

On the other hand, the contrasting trajectory of the Left parties that have been elected to power in Kerala, West Bengal, and Tripura stresses the centrality of broad-based mobilization in determining the salience of social cleavages on patterns of voting and party strategies. The most important of these is the CPI(M), which has run the state government in West Bengal for nearly three decades, and has deep pockets of influence and support in Kerala and Tripura as well, where too it has regularly won elections. The Left parties were able to establish a strong presence in these three states by focusing on distributive policies and radical reforms, rather than the politicization of caste differences and subordination (Rodrigues 2006: 199–252).

The vote share of Left parties has varied from 7 in 1957 to below 8 per cent in 2009. The 2004 parliamentary election represented a high point for the Left, as it surpassed its own previous record of 56 seats in 1991. The Left bloc had 61 MPs, and the overall vote share for the Left was 8.3 per cent, compared to less than 8 per cent in 2009. However, the elections of 2009 delivered a severe blow to the Left parties. The CPI(M) suffered its worst defeat since its inception after the split in the united CPI in 1964. Its seat share plummeted to 24, its vote share declined from 5.7 in 2004 to 5.3 per cent in 2009. Between the CPI(M) and CPI, the strength of the CPI has declined to just 4 and that of the CPI(M) to 16. Most of the Left MPs are drawn from West Bengal and Kerala. This underlines the limits of the Left's

electoral support, which has been unable to grow beyond West Bengal, Kerala and Tripura, despite their resolve and attempts to do so. Their vote share has fluctuated in their strongholds at the same time as it has not registered an increase in the other states such as Andhra Pradesh, Bihar, Punjab, Maharashtra, and Tamil Nadu where they have had some presence.

In the 1990s (Arora 2000), political power shifted from the grand encompassing parties which had dominated politics for close to three decades to regional parties and multi-party coalitions. Until the late 1980s, it was taken for granted that national parties would govern India. Regional and state-based parties did, of course, contest elections, but their role was insignificant. In 1952, about 50 parties contested elections, while the number had gone up to 342 in 2009 (Chandra 2009). Since the fragmentation of the party system that set in after the decline of one-party dominance and the coming to power of a non-Congress coalition government more and more parties have been formed with the largest number in last elections—over a hundred new parties formed between 2004 to 2009 (ibid).

While there has been no actual decline in the number of national parties from 1957, the number of Indians who vote for them has come down. Until 1996 the total number of seats won by regional parties did not change much. Their numbers varied between a low of 31 (1957) and a high of 75 (1984). The major change occurred in 1996 when the number of seats won by them went up to 127, in 1999 it climbed up to 158 and in 2004 to 159 and 28.1 per cent of the vote. This increase has taken place at the expense of national parties, especially the BJP and the Congress, which had just over 320 seats between them in 2009. The combined votes of the Congress and the BJP in the 2004 and 2009 elections was under 50 per cent. The vote share of regional parties remained the same—roughly 29 per cent in the last three elections. This means more than half the voters continued to vote for parties other than the two big parties. Even though the balance appeared to have shifted in favour of a national party reflected in the resurgence of the Congress, regional parties remain significant because states continue to be the principal arena of politics and hence state-specific parties are still relevant (Lok

Niti team, *The Hindu*, 2009). Indeed, a striking feature of this election was the strong showing of regional parties, such as the Janata Dal (United) in Bihar, Biju Janata Dal in Orissa, Trinamool Congress in West Bengal, and DMK in Tamil Nadu.

Six elections between 1991 and 2009 did not produce an absolute majority for a single party or coalition, and, as a consequence, minority and/or coalition governments. However, the 2009 elections resulted in a near majority for the Congress-led UPA which won 262 seats. In the first five national elections from 1952 to 1971, India had a one party dominant system in which the Congress party received a plurality of votes averaging more than 40 per cent, while the second largest party could win only 10 per cent of the vote. In the 1989, 1991, 1996, 1998, and 1999 elections, the Congress majority was well short of the vote share needed for a seat majority. These elections saw the vote share of the second party or alliances go up, thereby making the system more pluralistic and competitive.

More than eighteen state parties have held power both at the Central and state levels, while many more have shared power at the state level. Both regional and state-based parties are contenders for power in all the states except Gujarat, Rajasthan, Madhya Pradesh, and Himachal Pradesh. Taken as a whole, all these changes have substantially altered India's party system, and the transformation has been far-reaching. Three major trends post-1989, the decline of the Congress, the rise of the BJP, and that of regional and state-based parties have led to the formation of minority and coalition governments. After a considerable change in parties and the party system, two coalition blocs have emerged. Both the NDA, led by the BJP, and the UPA, led by the Congress, were propped up by a host of state-based and regional parties eager to share the spoils of office. Some major state parties are not part of the two coalition blocs, and from time to time they attempt to revive a Third Front, opposed to both the Congress and the BJP.

The succession of coalition governments since the 1990s, while reflecting the expanding process of democratization, is based on spatial, not ideological, compatibility. This was the case with the BJP's alliances in 1998, 1999, and 2004, as well the Congress-led UPA in 2004. Thus, in 2004, the strategic alliance of the Congress and the Left, forged in the six years of the Vajpayee period, formed the lynchpin of the new dispensation built around a strong opposition to communal politics; at the same time, there was a range of issues, especially in economic and foreign policies, where their policies and perceptions differed, resulting in the withdrawal of support by the Left parties in August 2008 on the issue of the controversial Indo-US nuclear deal and the growing strategic partnership between the two countries.

PRAGMATISM OF INDIAN PARTIES

One remarkable feature of political parties in India since the 1990s has been their tendency to move away from ideological frameworks. It is important to note that until this period, there were different types of parties in India. There were parties that represented the interests of the established order, and parties that sought basic social and economic transformations and engaged in struggles on behalf of the interests of the oppressed and those marginalized in society. However, this has changed as most political parties are more like each other on many issues and are devoted to parliamentary politics, including the Left parties. The ideological differences between parties are minimal, and hence they are likely to adopt the same mix of policies when in power. By and large, Indian parties are more pragmatic than ideological, which makes party boundaries highly flexible and permeable. The majority of leaders and legislators could be in one party or the other because their presence in the party is often influenced by their success in obtaining the party ticket. Parties seem to have no distinct ideology that would distinguish one party from another in the course of election campaigns, for instance, although what they do when they are in power embodies or expresses interests of various kinds (Sarangi 1984: 189–207). The idealism that exemplified the first few decades after Independence has been replaced with a purposefulness characterized by self-interest, flexibility, and dissimulation. The nationalist fervour in the aftermath of Independence has given way to the politics of unbridled power, involving all the features of bargaining, negotiation, and compromise. Intra-party debates on secularism versus religion or market versus the state in the Congress, or globalization versus *swadeshi* in the BJP are fairly infrequent. Even secularism, which has been a defining difference between parties, is confined to the Congress, the BJP, and the Left parties. None of the state or regional parties has displayed any real ideological reluctance in allying with communal parties such as the BJP, if their interests so require, despite the party's open association with the demolition of the Babri mosque in Ayodhya in 1992, the pogrom in Gujarat in 2002, and its active association with numerous anti-Muslim campaigns.

The explanation for these changes is traceable to the radical transformations taking place in both state and society, and the way in which individuals and groups perceive their roles as constitutive elements of a political community (Nayyar 2001: 361–96). During the earlier decades, each political party tried to locate itself in an ideological continuum and in relation to the state. The economic policy paradigm shift that took place in 1991 entailed shifting priorities away from distributive justice to high growth as a state goal, the demotion of planning and the planning commission, public-sector industries, and the encouragement of private investment to achieve this goal. These changes were quite significant as they involved a shift from a multi-class state committed to pro-poor measures to a narrow conception of the state that is more closely aligned with business, capital, and the middle classes, and openly committed to a capitalist path of development. The new phase is characterized by an intensification of conflict in the economy and polity, and a clear tension between the economics of markets and political democracy. The result of this shift was a widening gap between these classes and the bulk of people, who have not gained significantly from the economic reforms of the past two decades or so.

The growing disjunction between policies and the support base of parties is an obvious consequence of these processes. The Congress has had to reconcile the contradiction between economic reforms, which benefit the elite and upper-middle classes, and its mass support among the poor, who have been the

losers in this process. This discrepancy results from the effect of two factors: the change in India's social structure—from an elite–mass structure to one with a substantial middle class sandwiched between these two poles—and the parties' need to continue to cater to a range of groups. Earlier, party leaders used to argue that they represented the interests of the people. Now, since the parties tend to represent sectional interests, they seem to claim that they themselves are 'the people'. On the one hand, this represents a step in the inclusion of marginalized groups. On the other, the parties and their leaders can afford to be undemocratic and authoritarian, because their own interests are submerged in that of the group (Hasan 2006).

This shift towards pragmatism is a strong tendency in the development of parties globally. Both the Democratic Party in the United States and the Labour Party in Britain, as well as other many parties of the Left have embraced the free market policies first made acceptable by Bill Clinton, and subsequently by Tony Blair. Indian parties are not immune to this trend. Quite a few major parties have moved ideologically in a rightward direction, even as they remain politically opposed to the right-wing BJP. Except for the CPI and CPI(M), no other political party uses the term socialism or anti-imperialism; these terms have virtually disappeared from the political discourse. Almost all the political parties today, despite each one's familiar slogan to defend the interests of the poor, the disadvantaged, and the marginalized, increasingly think and act in similar ways. In spite of some differences between parties, there is a fair degree of consensus on economic and foreign policies. No matter which party comes to power the Central and state governments are unwilling to roll back neo-liberal economic policies, which virtually all political parties support, many of which have been pushed through without much opposition or dissent.

Ideological depolarization has other implications as well. Every party becomes a pragmatic party from the electoral point of view. When ideological polarization becomes irrelevant, mobilization of support using other social cleavages, which are electorally salient, tends to rise. Therefore, it is not surprising that we find today many political parties openly allying with specific caste or religious groups and trying to promote regional and local interests. In short, political parties have undergone a gradual transformation from policy-oriented parties to 'office-seeking' parties.

Although, in general, parties do profess to stick to their party ideology—or at least are known by certain ideological labels—in their actual support they seem to be more pragmatic, inasmuch as they are not reluctant to give up their ideological stance or put it on the backburner if that helps gain them a share of political power. Such a trend has been witnessed among both the national and the state-level parties, which are less inhibited when it comes to sharing power or coalescing in government formation with groups who, till the other day, were their bitter political opponents. Second, the resulting coalitions and alliances are neither ideological nor have any common objective to cement them together; they are merely short-term tactical arrangements established by ambitious politicians and are rooted in the exchange of mutual benefits and compulsions of power. The mobilization of the electorate is done through a strategy of support to regional-cum-segmental or ethnic issues, without extending overriding support to either national or primarily local issues.

ORGANIZATION AND FUNCTIONING OF PARTIES

In terms of party structure, political parties are varied in organization, functioning, leadership, and decision-making, and do not fit into one model. The working of parties varies enormously depending upon the way they have evolved, their status as the ruling or opposition party, their support bases, leadership styles and traditions, and their geographical location and spread (Suri 2005). The organization and support structure of most parties reflect the diversity and heterogeneity of society and the groups they claim to represent. While parties have been instrumental in democratizing state and society, they have tended to become internally less democratic.

Very few parties have properly institutionalized the norms of recruitment and membership. Almost no party maintains a proper register of

membership, or a record of decision-making or policies adopted. Most parties are mass parties, and very few restrict their membership. Even the BJP does not restrict its membership to the majority community, notwithstanding the primacy it may give to the advocacy of their interests. The self-reported membership of parties in India is fairly high, higher than the global average, and much higher than most countries in Europe and North America (*State of Democracy in South Asia: A Report* 2008: 86). In fact, evidence shows that party membership has actually increased in the last decade (Ibid.). However, these impressive figures are not based on verifiable membership, as most parties do not maintain membership registers. Self-reported membership can be seen as a form of party identification, but even then it is an impressive phenomenon.

Although a fundamental distinction can be made between mass and cadre parties, most parties in India are mass parties; that is to say, such a party attempts to base itself on an appeal to the masses. It attempts to organize not only those who are influential or those who represent special interests, but also any citizen who is willing to join a party. But all mass parties tend to be highly centralized. Only the CPI(M) and the BJP can be loosely described as cadre parties dominated by groups of activists. Even these two parties, however, no longer fit the description of cadre parties.

The CPI(M) is organized on the principles of democratic centralism, but in reality the centralization of power tends to be high. Although one leader can dictate the 'line' to the party, some leaders do exercise more authority and influence than others within the core leadership. In view of the changes in all types of parties and the unavoidable trend towards transformation into mass parties, the classification of parties as cadre and mass parties is not particularly relevant (*State of Democracy in South Asia* 2008).

Most other parties seem to be similar in their style of functioning, too. Nearly all of them are based on loyalty to leaders rather than loyalty to values or institutions. Nearly all of them lack internal party democracy; they are, in varying degrees, centralized (Manor 1981: 25–40). The Election Commission is supposed to ensure inner party democracy by insisting on organizational elections at periodic intervals. However, very few parties hold regular elections, and when elections are held they are notional, as invariably the party President nominates the office bearers. As many as 18 recognized regional political parties had not responded to the Election Commission's reminders to hold organizational elections in 1997 (Gill 1997). Only the seven recognized national political parties bothered to reply to the Chief Election Commissioner's reminders, indicating their commitment to hold organizational elections which has remained a commitment and nothing more than that. In the BSP, no internal elections are held, and all office bearers are nominated by the party President. The Left parties hold elections regularly, but these are largely non-competitive.

However, the national parties have been equally reluctant to hold elections. In the Congress party, elections have invariably been announced and postponed on several occasions. Prime Minister P.V. Narasimha Rao actually held an organizational election in 1994, but such was the turmoil during and the fallout after that election, that he nullified it and once again resorted to nomination for the highest positions in the party organization. Elections had been repeatedly promised since the Congress President, Sonia Gandhi, reconstituted the party's top decision-making body in 2004, and renamed it the Congress Steering Committee. But elections were not held, and the party posts were filled by nomination. Until the late 1960s, the Congress had a strongly rooted organizational network, which was the envy of other political parties. It was not a 'cadre-based' organization, but had plenty of substance as an institution. In most parts of the country, thanks to its robust organization, its influence penetrated downward quite effectively, at least to the sub-district level and sometimes further. It was also a formidable instrument for the performance of several other key tasks—three of which were especially important. It could gather and transmit upward accurate information (political intelligence) from lower levels in the system. It could represent the views of important social groups. The Congress leadership has not been able to reverse the process of centralization. This is the root cause of the

deinstitutionalization of the Congress and the decline of political parties. Rahul Gandhi who took over as a general secretary of the party in 2007 has since then shown a keen interest in restoring internal democracy in the Congress, beginning with the Youth Congress. He admitted 'democracy' in political parties 'is non-existent in India. You cannot enter politics unless you are well connected'. Rahul Gandhi has pushed for holding of organizational elections within the Congress claiming that 'just because I'm the outcome of that system doesn't mean I can't change that system' (*The Times of India* 5 May 2009).

The BJP is also not an institutionalized party; it has not had a contest for the post of the party President since its inception in 1980. Elections have taken place at the state level, but this practice has been jettisoned in the past few years in favour of an 'election by consensus'. The BJP's predecessor, the Jana Sangh, also avoided a contest for party posts. The party goes through the formality of elections in accordance with the party constitution, but the name of the President is usually decided by the RSS. The party President nominates the entire team of office bearers. The BJP has always had to struggle to establish its primacy as a political party by reworking its relationship with the RSS.

Parties in India still refuse to lay down settled and predictable procedures for almost everything they do, from the selection of candidates to the framing of an agenda. On issues that are of crucial importance to most parties, the top echelons appear to play a decisive role. At the same time, with issues of a local character, parties have some scope for negotiation, discussion, and consultation. The local leaders cannot hope to influence crucial decisions of parties such as nomination of candidates, but in the bigger parties there is often some room to accommodate the insights and sentiments of local leaders. It is mainly the Left parties, such as the CPI(M) and the CPI, which have stronger institutional structures and norms.

The structure of decision-making in most parties is highly centralized. One major issue of concern is the widespread prevalence of the 'high command' culture (a synonym for the party President), with the high command taking all the important decisions. The Congress led the way, but most other parties have been quick to follow the model. The Congress high command structure has become so deeply entrenched that all parties have simply accepted it. Among the contemporary parties, the BSP epitomizes the high command culture to the utmost. Its President, Mayawati, heads the party, and there are no other leaders; the rest are all workers and 'cadres'. Indeed, one of the most enduring images associated with the BSP is that of Mayawati presiding over party meetings: she occupies the lone ornamental chair placed on the stage, while other party members, including senior members, sit on the floor (Ramaseshan 2007: 60–1).

A remarkable feature of Indian politics lies in the advent of parties centred around one person, be it a politician or movie stars turned leaders. There is a proliferation of parties that promote family rule and personality cults around the family name, caste, or charisma. Parties have become a preserve of families and are subservient to one supreme leader. The leader can wilfully impose her/his offspring or relatives on the party. Twenty-seven MPs in the Fifteenth Lok Sabha and a large number of cabinet ministers in the second UPA government belonged to prominent political families—an indication that politics has indeed become a family business. Major and mini dynasties control national and regional parties.

Family rule or dynasty is a striking feature of the Congress, but it is only fair to add that neither family rule nor the dynastic pattern is the monopoly of the Congress. Quite a few political families have sprung up in the recent past, and more are mushrooming all the time. In other words, what began in the Congress now extends to the bulk of party politics. From the Karunanidhi clan in Tamil Nadu to the Abdullah and Mufti families in Kashmir, the Thackerays and Pawars in Maharashtra, Sangmas in Meghalaya, Patnaiks in Orissa, and the Mulayam Singh Yadav clan in Uttar Pradesh, parties have become a family business propped up by an unremitting focus on these leaders. The most striking change has occurred in the cadre-based DMK which has yielded itself to dynastic pressures and gradually turned into a family enterprise. Family control or dynastic rule is not as pervasive in ideology-based parties as it is in others.

One consequence of family dominated politics is that parties have become a closed shop with entry restricted only to those who have the right credentials of birth (Sanghvi 2009). As the political class becomes a self-perpetuating dynastic elite Indian politics is rendered less representative. Such politics of inheritance has undermined internal democracy and obstructed institutionalization of parties because it can constrain the individual discretion and personal power of charismatic leaders (Chandra 2005: 87–125).[3] In the absence of clear democratic procedures, parties will continue to be plagued by the factionalism that has been so detrimental to both their own interests and the stabilization of party structures (Chandra 2004). All in all, the internal structures of parties, and the lack of intra-party democracy in particular have impeded the growth of strong and vigorous parties.

A larger consequence of the decline of ideology and the rise of one-leader or one-family centred parties is the reduction of party organizations into election winning machines, which depend for their success on the charisma of the leader and their capacity to raise massive funds. An important aspect of the struggle for power is the financing of election campaigns. This has assumed tremendous importance because winning and losing elections has become the only role a party envisages for itself. The party and the leader's ability to win a majority in the national or state elections is the sole basis for judging the success or failure of a party and its top leader. Since most parties function as vote-gathering machines, there is a distinct unwillingness to enlist public support through political campaigns and movements between elections, build cadres, or mobilize people around new political initiatives. The privileging of elections at the expense of other aspects of the democratic process implies that parties are inattentive to the need for constant organizational renewal, or to the requirements of popular mobilization. Leaders are valued for their capacity to attract crowds, strike deals and alliances, and raise resources as elections become more and more expensive in India.

Electioneering is labour-intensive and expensive in India's sprawling urban and rural constituencies. Parties and candidates need large sums of money for advertising, polling, consulting, travel, vehicles and fuel, and the printing of campaign materials that are to reach voters in constituencies. Historically, parties have been dependent for finance on big businesses and wealthy individuals, especially parties of the Right and the Centre (Sridharan 2006: 311–40). During the 1950s and 1960s, the business community contributed the bulk of the funds (Venkatesan 1999). There are laws to limit campaign finances and restrict the expenditure of parties in elections, but they are largely inoperative because it is easy to circumvent them. Since the 1980s, there has been a closer and more open link between big businesses and the corporate sector and parties after the lifting of the ban on company donations in 1984 (Sridharan 1999: 229–54). The objectives of corporate funding of parties underwent a significant change in the wake of liberalization and the perceived irreversibility of the economic reform process. Nowadays, organized industry and business houses fund parties and dominate policy making for individual benefits.

The growing nexus between politics and the corporate sector and the dependence of parties on the corporate sector for funds is a not a new feature of party politics, but has become more manifest. This is also because the unrealistic ceiling on election funding has made the process of election and party financing less than transparent. The Election and Other Related Laws (Amendment) Act 2003 was one measure that promised major changes in the financing of political parties and their candidates for elections. However, these provisions have failed to ensure transparency in party finances—both how money is raised and spent. Consequently, there is a growing dominance of special interests in the polity, leaving parties politically vulnerable to these leading interests. This limits the ability of parties to boldly articulate the concerns of the marginalized and poor people. Political finance reform is necessary for the stability of democracy itself, because election funds raised through corrupt means increase cynicism about parties and politicians (Suri 2005: 1–62).

CRITICAL ISSUES CONFRONTING PARTIES

Political parties in India have played an important role in democratic consolidation. They have done so through a politics of accommodation and consensus that binds the political class together despite their different party affiliations (Arora 2007). They have facilitated the inclusion of varied groups in the political system, by giving voice to historically excluded groups, and helping them to gain access to the political system. At the same time, it is increasingly difficult to reconcile the absence of intra-party democracy within parties with the robustness and resilience of the democratic polity (ibid.).

There is considerable dissatisfaction with parties and politicians as vehicles of representation and governance. Paradoxically, voters feel that parties are essential for the functioning of democracy, but do not seem to trust them to make democracy work (*State of Democracy in South Asia: A Report*). The biggest institutional weakness of parties is that they are leader-centric and lack internal democracy, as leaders are unwilling or unable to institutionalize party elections or procedures for the selection of candidates, and increase the participation of members in party functioning (Suri 2005). The absence of internal democracy, dynastic rule, elite capture, and the inability of parties to offer real choices to the people are among the major issues confronting India's parties.

By a long way the most disturbing trends are noticeable in political parties which function as family fiefdoms and without a trace of internal democracy. Most political parties lack the political capacity to take the lead in formulating and debating policies which reflect people's aspirations and needs. Although parties and party leaders do profess to stand for ideology, in reality they are flexible and not at all reluctant to give up their ideological stance or put it on the back burner if that helps them to gain a share of political power or to obtain a ticket for contesting an election. Although the divergence between election rhetoric and the actual implementation of government policy remains large particularly with regard to policies that have distributive and welfare outcomes, the UPA government has attempted to shift away from technocratic strategies of governance to a political approach which focused on inclusive growth through social and welfare measures. At one level, the Congress has stuck to the neo-liberal path of market-oriented reforms, which was aimed at generating economic growth but at another level to contain the ill-effects of the market economy, it came out with legislations like the National Rural Employment Guarantee Act, and a host of other social welfare schemes which held out promise of relief, particularly for the rural poor.

Though encountering serious problems with regard to the healthy functioning of parties, the fact remains that there is no alternative to political activity based on party competition. Parties cannot be dispensed with as long as we have a democratic parliamentary system of government. India's democratic stability, which defies conventional theories of democracy, underscores the positive relationship between parties and democracy. In India, the legitimacy of party-based governments has never been questioned. Even frequent elections for Parliament, state assemblies, and panchayats have not alienated the electorate; in fact, they seem to give the mass of voters a sense of popular control over government. The significant changes in the social composition of India's ruling elite since Independence, both in politics and in the bureaucracy are largely due to parties opening their doors to new recruits from marginalized groups, which ultimately make their way into the government. This is obvious from the significant increase in the number of lower-caste legislators and senior civil servants in influential government positions (Suri 2005). This trend signals a social revolution that is giving voice to previously marginalized groups (Jaffrelot 2002). Despite the erosion of party organizations and the degeneration of politicians, which so preoccupies intellectuals, the media, and the middle classes, the Indian voter, going by the over 60 per cent turnout in national elections and an even higher turnout in state assembly elections, appears satisfied with the choices that political parties offer.

None of this minimizes the seriousness of the problems facing political parties and the political system they run. The most serious problem is the failure of parties to keep their promises to the electorate—promises to implement economic development alongside the reduction of social inequalities. India cannot build a truly inclusive polity without an inclusive economy. Parties need to think why, six decades after Independence, more than a quarter of our population still lives below the official poverty line, and millions are deprived of the basic necessities of life or face daily preventable problems such as malnutrition and endemic hunger, or lack of purchasing power. Parties must ask why faster and more effective political intervention to relieve the suffering of millions of the poorest and disadvantaged is not forthcoming. These are the difficult questions confronting our political parties. This is the great unfinished agenda of the nation-building project that parties have yet to implement.

NOTES

1. If a political party is treated as a recognized one in four or more states, it shall be known as a national party throughout India, but only so long as that political party continues to fulfil thereafter the conditions for recognition in four or more states on the results of any subsequent general election, either to the Lok Sabha or to the legislative assembly of any state. If a political party is treated as recognized in less than four states, it should be known as a state party in the state or states in which it is so recognized, but only so long as that political party continues to fulfil thereafter the conditions for recognition on the results of any subsequent general election to the Lok Sabha, or, as the case may be, to the legislative assembly of the state, in the said state or states.

2. All election statistics are available on the Election Commission of India's website. www.eci.gov.in

3. Kanchan Chandra, for instance, argues that the lack of democracy within the Congress in Uttar Pradesh, compared to Karnataka during the 1970s, prevented it from incorporating newly mobilized backward-caste groups.

REFERENCES

Arora, Balveer. 2007. 'Can Democracy Flourish with Undemocratic Parties', *The Tribune*, Chandigarh, 15 August.

———. 2000. 'Coalitions and National Cohesion', in Francine Frankel, Zoya Hasan, Rajeev Bhargava, and Balveer Arora (eds), *Transforming India: Social and Political Dynamics of Democracy*. New Delhi: Oxford University Press.

Centre for the Study of Developing Societies (Delhi). 2009. *How India Voted*, 27 May.

Chandra, Kanchan. 2009. 'A Rope of Many Strands: Why a Fragmented Party System Stabilizes India's Democracy', *The Indian Express*, 28 May.

———. 2005. 'Elite Incorporation in Multi-ethnic Societies', in Ashutosh Varshney (ed.), *India and the Politics of Developing Societies: Essays in Memory of Myron Weiner*. New Delhi: Oxford University Press, pp. 87–125.

Chandra, Kanchan. 2004. *Why Ethnic Parties Succeed: Patronage and Ethnic Head Counts in India.* Cambridge: Cambridge University Press.

Frankel, Francine, Zoya Hasan, Rajeev Bhargava, and Balveer Arora (eds). 2000. *Transforming India: Social and Political Dynamics of Democracy.* New Delhi: Oxford University Press.

Gill, M.S. 1997. 'CEC', *The Indian Express,* 1 May.

Hasan, Zoya. 2006. 'Bridging a Growing Divide? The Indian National Congress and Indian Democracy', *Contemporary South Asia,* 15(5), pp. 473–88.

Heath, Oliver. 1999. 'Anatomy of BJP's Rise to Power: Social, Regional and Political Expansion in the 1990s', *Economic and Political Weekly,* XXXIV(34–5), pp. 2511–17.

Hewitt, Vernon. 1989. 'The Congress System is Dead: Long live the Party System and Democratic India', *Journal of Commonwealth and Comparative Politics,* 27(2), pp. 157–71.

Jaffrelot, Christophe. 2002. *India's Silent Revolution.* New Delhi: Permanent Black.

———. 1996. *The Hindu Nationalist Movement and Indian Politics.* London: Hurst & Co.

Jayal, Niraja Gopal (ed.). 2001. *Democracy in India.* New Delhi: Oxford University Press.

Kohli, Atul (ed.). 1988. *India's Democracy: An Analysis of Changing State-Society Relations.* Princeton: Princeton University Press.

Manor, James. 1995. 'Regional Parties in Federal Systems: India in Comparative Perspective', in Balveer Arora and Douglas Verney (eds), *Multiple Identities in a Single State: Indian Federalism in Comparative Perspective.* New Delhi: Konark Publishers, pp. 107–35.

———. 1990. 'Parties and the Party System', in Atul Kohli (ed.), *India's Democracy: An Analysis of Changing State Society Relations.* Princeton: Princeton University Press.

———. 1981. 'Party Decay and Political Crisis in India', *Washington Quarterly,* 4(3), pp. 25–40.

Nayyar, Deepak. 2001. 'Democracy and Development', in Niraja G. Jayal (ed.), *Democracy in India.* New Delhi: Oxford University Press.

Pai, Sudha. 2002. *Dalit Assertion and the Unfinished Revolution: The Bahujan Samaj Party in Uttar Pradesh.* New Delhi: Sage Publications.

Pai, Sudha. 1998. 'The BSP in Uttar Pradesh', *Seminar,* November, 471.

Ramaseshan, Radhika. 2007. 'Fault Lines in the Indian Party System', in Arvind Sivaramakrishnan (ed.), *Short on Democracy: Issues Facing Indian Political Parties.* Delhi: Imprint One, pp. 56–70.

Rodrigues, Valerian. 2006. 'The Communist Parties in India', in E. Sridharan and Peter Ronald deSouza (eds), *India's Political Parties.* New Delhi: Sage Publications, pp. 199–252.

Sanghvi, Vir. 2009. 'Politics of Inheritance'. *Hindustan Times.* 30 May.

Sarangi, Prakash. 1984. 'Party and Party System: A Conceptual Analysis', *Political Science Review,* 23 (3&4), pp. 189–207.

Sridharan, E. 2006. 'Parties, the Party System and Collective Action for State Funding of Elections: A Comparative Perspective on Possible Options', in E. Sridharan and Peter deSouza (eds), *India's Political Parties.* New Delhi: Sage Publications.

———. 2000. 'Fragmentation of the Party System', in Zoya Hasan (ed.), *Parties and Party Politics in India.* New Delhi: Oxford University Press.

———. 1999. 'Toward State Funding of Elections in India: A Comparative Perspective on Possible Options', *Journal of Policy Reform,* 3 (3), pp. 229–54.

Srinivasraju, Sugata and Pushpa Iyengar. 2009. 'Where the Family Heirs' Loom', *Outlook,* 8 June.

State of Democracy in South Asia: A Report. 2008. New Delhi: Oxford University Press.

Suri, K.C. 2005. 'Parties Under Pressure', http://www.democracy-asia.org/qa/india/KC%20Suri.pdf.

Venkatesan, V. 1999. 'Party Finance: Chequered Relations', *Frontline,* 16 (16).

Verney, Douglas. 2002. 'How has the Proliferation of Parties Affected the Indian Federation? A Comparative Approach', in Zoya Hasan, E. Sridharan and R. Sudarshan (eds), *India's Living Constitution: Ideas, Practices, Controversies.* New Delhi: Permanent Black, pp. 134–58.

Yadav, Yogendra and Oliver Heath. 2000. 'The United Colours of the Congress', in Zoya Hasan (ed.), *Parties and Party Politics in India.* New Delhi: Oxford University Press.

17 Politics and Culture

Stuart Corbridge

Shortly after the September 2001 attacks on the World Trade Center in New York City, the United States government of George W. Bush declared that Afghanistan would be the first front in a global war on terror that was expected to last not for years, but for decades or possibly generations. A second front was opened in Iraq in 2003, alongside circuits of extraordinary rendition and other spaces of the exception.[1] Bush, Dick Cheney, and Donald Rumsfeld declared that the war on terror(ism) was also a war for freedom, and would win the support of all freedom loving peoples.

Interestingly, in the years after 2003–4, when support for Bush and the USA ebbed sharply around the world, publicly expressed support for the US in India remained constant, and, at times, increased slightly. Part of the reason for this is that the US war on terror coincided in India with a marked warming of relations with the US, as well as with a restructuring of the Indian economy. This unleashed a middle-class consumer boom and an extraordinary fêting of American entrepreneurs, including Bill Gates and Warren Buffett. It is worth noting, even so, that bullish attitudes towards the US in India have also been bolstered by a community of non-resident Indians (NRIs) in the USA, which has on occasions edged close to the Israeli lobby in a thinly veiled bid for joint action against the 'Muslim threat'. It has also coincided with a sharp rise in the use of the word 'terrorist' to define threats to state power in India, whether by Naxalities, sundry Islamic groups (including student movements), or individuals at the wrong end of police firings/encounters.

Another way of putting this is to say that a new front is being opened up in a long-standing war of politics on culture—allowing for very restrictive definitions of both terms. For more than two centuries now Western countries have been inclined to define non-Western Others in terms of their 'cultures' (Said 1993). Very often, these were feminized and made to bear the scars of unreason and non-seriality (Anderson 1998): that is, limited group identities formed along the lines of ethnicity or religion. In colonial times, Western rule was partly justified with reference to the assumed limitations of these non-Protestant cultures. Politics, or the politics of the West's view of itself, denoted Reason. Especially from the middle part of the nineteenth century, politics in Western Europe was linked discursively to the formation of forms of bureaucratic rule which promoted the governmentalization of the state and of politics. European cultures were civil and civilizing. Europeans were increasingly learning to rule themselves in the names of reason and (belatedly) freedom; albeit powers of freedom that recognized some well-defined and restrictive norms of behaviour, as well as the responsibilities for governing oneself, one's family, and one's community and workplace that freedom brought with it (Rose 1999). Politics, defined here as 'powers of self-policing and the rational allocation of resources', in turn became a matter of tweaking the machine, or, to alter the metaphor, of steering the boat of enlightened accumulation. In the second half of the twentieth century these political settlements were made flesh in the corporatisms of Western Europe and the pluralism of the US. In both cases, enlightened elites presumed to govern their political landscapes in the name of a broader national interest.

In the colonies these seemingly benign forms of rule were undercut from the start by the disciplinary and sovereign powers of the imperial state, and by racialized assumptions about the unfitness of colonial subjects to rule themselves. After Independence in 1947, the Nehruvian state in India sought to invent new citizens and a new civil society. Indians were given the right to vote, and the state promised to provide education and healthcare to help them function as responsible and thoughtful citizens. New temples of the future were placed before the population by a modernizing elite. Nehru famously asked labourers close to the Bhakra Nangal dam on the Sutlej river in northwest India, 'where can be a greater and holier place than this...[a] place where man works for the good of mankind?' (Nehru 1980: 214). Industrialization and secularism would quickly manufacture new Indians, and politics in India would just as quickly adapt itself to the Anglo-Saxon norm. It would dispense with culture, or unreason—with casteism, sub-nationalism, and limited ethnicities, and above all, with communalism. A sense of generalized morality would replace older ('earlier') limited or group moralities.

Except, of course, it did not. Nor did the West ever achieve this exalted state. Somewhere between the years of bureaucratic rule that Max Weber looked forward to in the 1910s, and the classic years of US-sponsored modernization theory in the 1950s (a particularly crude version of long-standing convergence models), came two World Wars, the coupling of immigration policies in the US to frankly eugenicist claims about the biological worth of different ethnic groups, the rise of fascism, and, most gruesomely, the Nazi concentration camps (themselves blamed by some on the death of God in hyper-reasoning Germany). Politics 'at home', never mind politics 'abroad'—in Ethiopia, India, or the Philippines—was ever marked by cultural considerations, if by culture we refer here to broadly shared sets of socially produced and (yet) biologically inscribed meanings. More recently, too, after twenty or thirty years when politics in the US or the UK was seemingly based around resource allocation issues (and even class), a notable shift has taken place towards political issues that are by any standards inseparable from cultural claims or concerns: abortion rights, stem-cell research, evolution, sexuality and lifestyle choices, and multiculturalism.

In India, the fading of the Nehruvian dream in the 1970s and 1980s also led to new forms of politics and new interpretations of their meanings. Central to this have been the continuing rise of caste-based politics, or the ethnicization of caste, and the politics of Hindu nationalism. Both have raised profound questions about the idea of India: about its political culture(s). In the rest of this essay I consider how a group of public intellectuals in India—led by, but not restricted to, Partha Chatterjee, Sudipta Kaviraj, Ashis Nandy, and Vandana Shiva—have seized on the evident contradictions of the Nehru years, *and most notably the attempt to silence non-elite cultural politics in the name of the non-cultural nature of elite politics*, to point the way to new understandings of some key events and terms in the contemporary Indian political landscape: nationalism, secularism and toleration, civil and political societies, modernity and tradition. At stake in this work are the forms of rule and freedom proposed by different readings of the politics–culture coupling.

POLITICS, CULTURE, AND EVENTS

British India was governed in large part through
the machineries of what Nicholas Dirks (2001)
has called 'the ethnographic state'. The Raj made
copious reference to its civilizing missions and its
commitments to prepare Indians to govern their own
country as reasoning individuals. Particularly from
the time of the Census of India in 1872, however,
and the more extensive Census of 1881, prospectively
individual men and women in India were required
to present themselves to the authorities as Hindus,
Muslims, or Sikhs, and as Brahmins, Yadavs, or
Chamars (Untouchables). In this fashion, Dirks
reports, caste identities were solidified and became
the precipitate of imperial (divide and) rule. Britain's
attempt to govern India through separate electorates,
and even by reference to affirmative action for the
Depressed Classes/Scheduled Castes (SCs), ensured
that the modernity it spoke of would be an ever-
receding horizon, the promise that could not be kept
(after Dirks 2001: 10). In some quarters, too, the
typical Indian pre- or proto-individual/citizen was
fixed, as by Max Weber, as 'a Hindu who lived in
dread of the magical evil of innovation'. India, or at
least its dominant religious culture, was defined by its
timelessness and other-worldliness. Its temporal and
spatial coordinates, as Louis Dumont (1970) would
later describe them, were rooted in the dominance of
spiritual authority over kingly power (the Brahmin
over the Kshatriya). Indians were wed to an ideology
of rigorous hierarchy that was not only at odds with
growing ideas of *homo equalis* in the West, but which
also undercut the possibilities of forms of nationalism
that would bind together the radically separate groups
that were made to coexist in the subcontinent.

This is not to suggest that all British writers or
officials thought in these terms. Some efforts were
made to irrigate India's fields and to improve the
country's means of communication. The imperial
power even found it understandable, if at times
distasteful, that reasoning men (and some women)
would join together, in 1885, as the Indian National
Congress to discuss India's future in reasonable
terms. Nevertheless, when the British were removed
from India in 1947, not least at the direction of a

man, Mohandas Karamchand Gandhi, described by
Churchill as a 'half naked fakir'—as the embodiment
of a weaker culture, not a rational politics—it was
widely recognized that the economy of India was in
dire straits (average per capita incomes had barely
risen in the countryside since 1900), and that Britain's
chief legacy to independent India was the bloodshed
of a Partition that it had authorized and in large
measure provoked. The assassination of Gandhi by
Nathuram Godse on 30 January 1948 was a horrible
blow for Nehru, but it also provided him with a
political opportunity (as did the unexpected death
of Sardar Patel in 1950). After briefly proscribing the
Rashtriya Swayamsevak Sangh (RSS), to which Godse
had once belonged, Nehru moved—in the 1950s—to
reinvent India as a fast industrializing economy and a
secular polity. Planning, noted Ronald Inden (1995),
not inaccurately, became the new 'godhead' of the
postcolonial state.

One common interpretation of the Nehru
years (1947–64), or those of the Second and Third
Five-Year Plans (the so-called Nehru–Mahalanobis
years, 1956–66), is that this was a period when
the state was in 'command' over society. Lloyd and
Susanne Hoeber Rudolph took this line in their
account of *The Political Economy of the Indian State*
(1987), and a similar thesis of rising/falling state
autonomy underpinned Pranab Bardhan's lectures
on *The Political Economy of Development in India*
(1984). Atul Kohli (1990), too, traced many of the
problems that accumulated in India in the 1970s and
1980s—slower growth, more social conflict—to the
deinstitutionalization of the Congress party under
Nehru's daughter, Indira Gandhi. A political party
that once had been reasoning and inclusive had
been turned by Mrs Gandhi into a cynical assembly
of men and women who were inclined to do her
bidding. 'India is Indira, Indira is India', as the awful
accompanying slogan had it.

There is something to be said for this story of
rise and fall, even if the old binaries of late-1980s
scholarship—command versus demand politics;
strong Congress, weak Congress; good father, bad
daughter—have been superseded by a third period
of the 'reinvention' of India after the critical years of
1990 (Mandal) to 1992 (Ayodhya, following the push

to economic liberalization in 1991). While the Nehru years never did approximate a full-blown version of what James Scott (1998) calls 'high modernism', there were clear and varyingly successful efforts made in this period to erase 'backward' cultural practices by means of modern politics. The Constitution of India, which was as much Ambedkar's work as Nehru's, provided one key template for the production of modern Indians through its justiciable and largely individualized Fundamental Rights. Government legislation in favour of universal primary education and against untouchability offered further signs of the state's intention to produce reasoning men and women who would not be held back by culture as custom. Put another way, while the postcolonial state accepted the diagnosis of the colonial state that 'culture' in India embodied unreason and backwardness, the Nehruvian state, unlike the British Raj, moved sharply to maintain that culture could be smashed by state-directed economic modernization.

The politics of agrarian reform in the 1950s should be seen in part through this lens. It aimed to create a class of smallholding and largely self-provisioning peasant households that would no longer be weighed down by the 'depressor' of landlordism, absentee or otherwise (Harriss 1993). Even the provisions for compensatory discrimination that were specified on a group basis in 1950 (for Scheduled Tribes[STs] now as well as SCs) were presented as time-bound instruments that would dissolve the necessity for their reproduction ten years hence. The Scheduled Communities were to be uplifted out of their existence by 1960, at which time, presumably, the expectation was that they would shed the skins of their old cultures (for which, read states of oppression and ignorance) and take their place as deliberative voters in the modern Indian polity. The Nehru–Mahalanobis plans, and the provision for Hindi to become the national language in 1965, also took shape with reference to the optimistic time horizons that characterized the mid-century years in the 'Third World', as in North America and Western Europe.

However, this is also a very partial reading of the Nehru years. And if it can be linked to an account of Nehru as a master politician—a man who led India through the minefield of states' reorganization in the 1950s while refusing to open a door to secessionism (Brass 1990; King 1997)— it can also be read as evidence of the unrealistic cultural perceptions built into the Nehruvian model for the transformation of India.

Take the question of affirmative action for Adivasis (tribals). Nehru coupled his support for the 1950 legislation (and again in 1960) with a number of declarations about the particular 'genius' of this population group. The commitment to erasure which was being proposed for SCs (because based on exploitation) was tempered in the case of the STs by a form of paternalism born of well-intentioned exoticism. Culture and politics blurred here in a way that defied exemplary modernism, although it must be recalled that it was often Adivasi land that was taken by the state to pave the way for India's industrial futures. By the same token, the commitments which the successive governments of Pandit Nehru made to agrarian reform and a common language were undercut in practice by the existence of competing sovereignties in the countryside, where leading Congress officials were often rich farmers, and in the south, where anti-Hindi riots rocked Madras in 1965.

Bhim Rao Ambedkar caught part of the flavour of these years in a famous statement he made to the Constituent Assembly: 'On the 26th January 1950 we are going to enter a life of contradictions. In politics we will have equality, and in social and economic life we will have inequality' (Constituent Assembly Debates). But what Ambdekar was picking up here was the stalled nature of the modernist project in India. He wanted more action on the part of India's politicians to 'restore non-Brahmans to their rightful place in the public sphere, as persons with administrative talents' (Corbridge and Harriss 2000/2003: 212). Specifically, he called for concerted legal action against untouchability (ahead of the Untouchability Offences Act of 1955), and for land reforms that would specifically and overwhelmingly benefit the SCs, which never happened. Critically, Ambedkar argued that, 'Untouchability is not a religious system but an economic system which is worse than slavery ... [it] is a gold mine to the Hindus' (1945: 196–7).

Believing, then, with Nehru, that religion was largely a smokescreen for economic exploitation—that it was a cultural code with mainly external reference points—Ambedkar looked to a rational state to smash the false idols of culturally inspired oppression. What he was less able to articulate—notwithstanding his late conversion to Buddhism in 1956, one year before his death—was the productive power of cultural and religious resources. When Ambedkar and Nehru looked upon Gandhi, they saw the 'father of the nation', of course, but also a man who projected into public space a body and a world view that was saturated in the troubling cultures of religion, unreason, and indigeneity. Whereas Gandhi advertised his Indianness through his 'half nakedness' and his constant invocations to the virtues of spinning, for Nehru the first duty of the independent state was 'to feed the starving people and clothe the naked masses' (speech to the Constituent Assembly, 22 January 1947; see also Trivedi 2007). More recently, this stark opposition between the naked and the clothed, or tradition and modernity, has been convincingly unpacked by social scientists, who have been able to step outside the circles of reasoning that informed the world views of Nehru and Ambedkar. In part, they have been encouraged to do so by events. Most of the convergence theories that seemed plausible in the 1950s and 1960s—the proposed triumph of politics over culture—no longer seemed tenable by the 1970s or 1980s. The Iranian revolution of 1978–9, and the rise of politicized Islam through the 1980s and 1990s, should have given the lie to claims that globalization would lead to a 'flat world' or the 'end of history'. Meanwhile, in India, the seemingly inexorable rise to power of the Bharatiya Janata Party (BJP), and the broader Sangh Parivar, in the 1980s and 1990s came to haunt those accounts of India's painful economic and political transitions that were overly focused on the travails of the Congress party or the fiscal crisis of the Indian state. The big political events of the 1980s and 1990s—the storming of the Golden Temple and the assassination of Indira Gandhi, the Shah Bano divorce and maintenance case, the demolition of the Babri Masjid—dramatized what some called the rise of religious politics in post-1980 India, and what others referred to as its return or

liberation (after a period of collective amnesia that followed Partition and the assassination of Mahatma Gandhi). Either way, the convenient idea that India's present history could be described in terms of the upward march of Reason and Westernization now had to be dropped. The central questions of politics and culture had to be rethought and made considerably more complicated, not to say more hybrid.

POLITICS, CULTURE, AND THEORY
Passive Revolutions and Political Society

Culture and politics were not entirely separated in academic accounts of India's political economy in the 1970s and 1980s. The early work of Partha Chatterjee and Sudipta Kaviraj is distinguished by its borrowings from the Italian Marxist, Antonio Gramsci. Gramsci had revolutionized Marxist thought in the inter-war years by focusing on the ways in which the bourgeoisie was able to consolidate its rule by proposing its own cultural and political values as those of Italian society more generally. Gramsci's concept of cultural hegemony represented a challenge to conventional Marxist–Leninist views about false consciousness and the inevitability of the revolution (or proletarian truth claims). It also pointed to the need for cultural–political work in opposition to the state and the capitalist class. Tactics and ideological work assumed an importance in post-Gramscian work, which they had not previously achieved in the Marxist tradition.

Partha Chatterjee (1997 [1977]) picked up on some of these themes in his analysis of the Emergency in India, and in the positioning there of Indira Gandhi as a sort of a *Bharat Mata* (Mother of India) like figure. But what Chatterjee and Kaviraj would take rather more from Gramsci was his idea of a 'passive revolution' (Gramsci 1971; and see Kaviraj 1988). One of the consistent refrains of critics like Chatterjee and Kaviraj, and also of Ashis Nandy and Vandana Shiva, is that the Nehruvian project for the modernization of India was not only at odds with indigenous values (variously specified by these and other authors, as of course by Gandhi), but that it had to be imposed top-down, in technocratic fashion, and with substantial violence. Instead, then, of local manufacturing centres scaling up in India to slowly forge a major industrial platform, the mid-century optimism—or belligerence—of modernization theory insisted that 'heavy industries' should be planted in Indian soil by executive direction from New Delhi, ideally with some measure of foreign aid.

For many commentators, here was Nehru's genius. By combining non-alignment with import-substitution industrialization, Nehru received financial and technical support both from the US, West Germany, and the UK, *and* from Czechoslovakia and the Soviet Union. From the same perspective, it was later argued that Nehru and his successors, Lal Bahadur Shastri and Indira Gandhi, sidestepped the prospect of prolonged agrarian conflict by pushing the Green Revolution in the 1960s and 1970s. This was another example of a Gramscian passive revolution: the state playing the role that a limited bourgeoisie could not in producing (agrarian) capitalism 'top-down', with (passive) technocratic considerations substituting for (active) politics and class conflict. For Chatterjee and Kaviraj, in contrast, this is where the roots of Indira's Bonapartism were first planted and watered—in the formation of an overly developed state within a context in which formal democracy preceded industrialization, and could be held (as in 1975–7) to be a block on the latter (too much trade unionism, high real wages, strikes, and so on). More significantly, in terms of their later and more sustained arguments, India's passive revolution was destined not only to be mired in violence (Nandy's point also, and related to the land seizures and forcible evictions that accompanied rapid industrialization), but also to be rooted in shallow, and at times inhospitable, soil.

Here is the gist of the argument. Whereas Nandy and Vandana Shiva (1991) are inclined to see state-led industrialization as inherently violent, and at odds with Gandhi's account of what is authentically Indian, Chatterjee and Kaviraj emphasize a domestic clash of cultures within India. We see this early on in Chatterjee's accounts of the nationalist movements in British India (Chatterjee 1986, 1993). These were never singular, nor did they amount to a simple demand to step into the shoes of the British. As Chatterjee points out, the figurative power of Gandhi, and of swadeshi, was bound up with their refusal to define the future modern as a process of mimicry.

The power of the British was contested in terms of the technologies of rule provided by the Raj—the law courts and the ballot box, limited as it was—but also in opposition to British demands for the Indian 'child' to become the European 'adult'. Gandhi's insistence on India's right to be different—its civilizational values, its family structures—paved the way for a critique of Empire and imperial reason that was (more) powerful precisely because the inner spiritual domain had remained largely off limits to the British, especially after 1857–8. It was here, Chatterjee argues, that 'nationalism launches its most powerful, creative, and historically significant project: to fashion a "modern" national culture that is nevertheless not Western' (1993: 6).

However, this project was never secure, as indeed most political projects are never quite secure. Nehru may have ditched his Western clothes for recognizably 'Indian' threads, but his politics in the 1950s and 1960s exemplified a commitment to modernity that many in the West would have recognized very well. Unsurprisingly, then, the more consistent argument of Chatterjee and Kaviraj over the past two decades is that the postcolonial state and the passive revolution in India were each undermined by their moorings in feet of vernacular clay (Kaviraj 1984: 227). As Chatterjee puts it, the 'hegemonic movement of nationalism was not to promote but rather, in quite a fundamental sense, to resist the sway of ... modern institutions' ... 'the new subjectivity that was constructed here was premised ... on particularity and difference' (1993: 75).

Taking the argument further, the suggestion is that Indian citizens, post-1947, are not citizens in the Western sense. Not only have they not yet learned how to participate in elections as rights-bearing individuals, they also have not been (and for the most part are still not) denizens of the cosy environs of civil society, where civility, respect for others, and for the rule of law define the nature of daily exchanges. Rather, as Chatterjee argues in *The Politics of the Governed* (2009), most people in India, as in 'most of the world', inhabit the rough-and-tumble worlds of political society. Here, people get by in the face of formal legal structures that work only for a minority, and with the help of various protector figures (political bosses, *dadas*, *dalaals*, gangsters) upon whom they necessarily depend for access to basic livelihood needs.

This contention resonates with a broader body of work on politics and culture in the global south. There is, first, a certain pessimism in Chatterjee's analysis, although that word conjures up a normative world that Chatterjee largely refuses. When it comes to the economy in India, however, there is little in his formidable corpus that suggests optimism about the country's performance. The role played by the state or private capital in pulling substantial numbers of people out of poverty is largely unaddressed. Chatterjee rather stresses the impossibility of development, and what he calls the 'unscrupulously charitable theoretical gestures' (2004: 39) of the neoliberal development establishment, with its specious faith in civil society, untutored participation, free markets, and individual empowerment. Roberto da Matta notes that a popular saying in Brazil holds that, 'To our enemies, the law, to our friends everything!' (1991: 168). This seems to be Chatterjee's take on India. Civility, abstract reason, and the rule of law define the cultures of those English educated urban elites who inhabit India's small 'walled up ... enclaves of civic freedom' (2004: 4). For the vast majority of people who live in political society, however, what is needed is the support and protection of 'friends'. The last thing that a poor person needs is to be handed over to the police. Much like Jean-Philippe Platteau (1994), too, and further back Max Weber (1930), Chatterjee, with Kaviraj, seems to subscribe to an oil and water perspective on the distinctiveness of political traditions. Platteau (1994) argues that World Bank schemes for promoting development in Africa are based on forms of political presentism which assume what they need to demonstrate and produce: capable modern subjects who have regard for distant strangers. In his view, such generalized moralities, and the trust in the written contract law they support, take generations to build up. Most Africans live in worlds of limited morality, where trust is reposed in kith and kin.

As for Africa, so for India. One implication of Chatterjee's oeuvre is that the 'inner worlds' of most Indians dance to a different beat from those heard by India's metropolitan elites. The country's feet of vernacular clay are washed by local dialects and languages, and by cultural norms that continue to be strongly informed by religiosity and caste. Culture matters, hugely. The mobilization of India's vernacular cultures allows ordinary people to speak their own truths back to the top-down, modernizing power of the state. More importantly, perhaps, the fact that 'the state' in India has to recruit its lower-level personnel from within these vernacular life worlds means that the government and its projects are weakened, or even sabotaged, from within. It is not that the state in India lacks territorial reach. Rather, the Centre doesn't hold because the cultural assumptions of government personnel in the country's 'commanding heights' are generally not shared by those in the states, and far less those in the state's field offices or trenches (to follow a mapping proposed by Joel Migdal [2001]).

Chatterjee's move here is an important one, and its purchase is troublingly on display in Iraq, where the arrogance of American assumptions about building a 'desert USA' are now shown up as so much neoconservative bluster. But it is also a controversial move, for like most binary oppositions the juxtaposition of elite/vernacular, or civil society/ political society, elides the possibility of translation. Chatterjee's unusual definition of civil society—a zone of formal freedoms, the law and individual rights, rather than an area of associational life between the family and the state—leaves his work poorly placed to comment on political movements among the poor which contest government corruption in the name of legal rights and with the active support of some elite Indians. An obvious example is the Mazdoor Kisan Shakti Sanghatan in Rajasthan and the broader right to information movement. Chatterjee's continuing insistence on the political importance, if not always priority, of the inner domain (of spirituality, or even the Indianness of Indian cultures) also pushes his work on secularism and toleration in a direction that some scholars find disconcerting, not least in the wake of the rise in the 1980s and 1990s of militant Hinduism.

Hindutva and (Pseudo-)Secularism

What we should properly call the rebirth of Hindu nationalism in the 1980s has raised issues of extraordinary importance for the study of politics and culture in India. Why does religion offer such a powerful account of the 'imagined nation'? How far and why was the Sangh Parivar successful in the 1980s in re-centring Hinduism around the hyper-masculine figure of Ram and away from the androgynous or even feminized accounts of Hinduism that have appealed to many Westerners (the Beatles at Rishikesh ...), and which Godse read into Gandhi (whom he accused very directly of 'emasculating' eternal India—Akhand Bharat—when he assented to Partition)? To what degree were ordinary Indian women and men made aware of Ayodhya by the astonishing *yatras* (pilgrimages/processions) that the BJP and Vishwa Hindu Parishad (VHP) used to mark out India's sacred geography in the 1980s and 1990s (including the brilliantly coordinated *Ekatmatayajna* of 1983)? And how far by television, with Doordarshan's screening of a serialized version of the Ramayana in the late 1980s (Rajagopal 2001)?

The Sangh Parivar's attention to detail in its projects of landscape-making is remarkable. Its cartographies of loathing and desire have sought to fix the geography of eternal India around sacred mountain ranges, rivers, temples, and towns, all the while affirming the country's 'essential' Hindu-ness—what Savarkar, the éminence grise behind militant Hinduism, called *Hindutva*, or Hindu culture. The story of Ayodhya, and the destruction of the Babri Masjid in December 1992, is well known. Much less well-advertised have been the attempts by the Sangh Parivar in Gujarat to rebuild certain villages which were destroyed in the earthquake that caused mass destruction in January 2001 as synechdocal representations of Hindustan. The previously mixed-religion, mixed-caste village which the VHP wrongly supposed to be sited closest to the epicentre of the earthquake was rebuilt in double-quick time by the Parivar as a village only for high-caste Hindus. Much of the funding came from VHP temple associations in Connecticut, Ohio, and New Jersey. Another village, now called Indraprastha, was self-consciously rebuilt by Sahib Singh Verma, a staunch BJP man and former Chief Minister of Delhi, as a model village, with each community located hierarchically in its place, and all focused on a library of nationalist and Vedic literature at its centre (Simpson and Corbridge 2006).

The Sangh Parivar, however, necessarily trades in absences as well as presences. This is apparent in Kachchh in terms of its opposition to forms of memorialization that don't share its nationalist visions. More broadly, it is evident in the way it seeks to distribute a historical geography of belonging, or of freedoms and unfreedoms. Peter Van der Veer has suggested that 'Nationalism is a selective, homogenizing discourse that tends to demarcate social boundaries sharply and to narrow the diversity and ambiguity of everyday life' (1994: 105), although this is arguably less true of civic than of religious nationalisms. In the case of Hindu nationalism, the principal aim of Savarkar's followers and descendents has to been to 'nationalise Hinduism and Hinduise the nation' (Basu *et al.* 1993: 39–40). That is to say, full citizenship rights in a god-given India should only be invested in those who 'regard this land ... from the Indus to the seas as his fatherland as well as his Holyland' (Savarkar 1949: 110–13). For Savarkar, this included Hindus, Sikhs, Buddhists, and Jains. Muslims, Christians, and Jews might aim to be Muslim–Hindus, Christian–Hindus, or Jewish–Hindus, but this hyphenated condition was clearly intended as a mark of exclusion, not of inclusion. The first two of these religions marked out a geography of conquest and imperialism, from which the so-called 'Indian religions', led by suitably masculine and even avenging Hindus, had to recover forcibly.

This act of recovery has also had regard to the alleged perils of another form of nation-building in India, that of secularism—and this provides a point of return to the work of Chatterjee and Nandy. Particularly in the build up to the celebration of fifty years of Independence in India, the charge was floated by various RSS ideologues that Nehru was a 'guilty man'. He was painted as someone responsible for leading India down the road of slow, public-sector economic growth (the Parivar ever anxious to appeal to its urban, middle-class supporters), and for promoting an ideology of 'pseudo-secularism' that at best appeased and at worst outright favoured India's Muslim minority population.

The basis of this charge turns on a particular inflexion of the politics/culture couplet. India's secular ambitions, according to the Parivar, placed a form of high politics at odds with various cultural truths (that is, an essentialized and biologized account of the cultural politics of the Hindu 'race'). Chatterjee and Nandy, needless to add, have always been opposed to this construction. But they too, along with T.N. Madan most notably, have proposed with some regularity that the postcolonial state's ideology of secularism has more in common with militant Hinduism than most 'progressive thinkers' like to admit. Specifically, they are both 'fearful of diversities, intolerant of dissent ... and panicky about any self-assertion or search for autonomy by ethnic groups' (Nandy et al. 1995: 19; Madan 1987).

The particular form in which this broad argument is fleshed out varies among Nandy, Madan, and Chatterjee. Briefly, Nandy (1990) starts from the Gandhian premise that the nation-state is an originary source of violence. It deploys the truth claims of Reason and Modernity to ride roughshod over the life-worlds and cultural systems of ordinary Indians, some of whom then turn to 'a false religion—religious fundamentalism—in a tragic effort to take charge of the state in the name of a political project that outdoes the violence of its secular counterpart' (Corbridge and Harriss 2000/2003: 195). In opposition to both these controlling ideologies, Nandy commends a return to South Asia's true 'religions of faith'; religions which he maintains are inherently open, heterodox, and tolerant. Madan (1987), for his part, is less willing than Nandy to dismiss the strengths of secularism within a Western setting, where it has contributed to an expansion of human freedoms. But he is careful to maintain that what works in the West doesn't always work in the non-West. For Madan, secularism in India is an alien import. It is at odds with the self-understandings of ordinary Indian men and women. Madan recognizes that secularism in India (equal respect for and distance from all religions on the part of the state) is different from a process of secularization (the desacralization of public, and even private, life). He nonetheless rejects the former because it will attract the attention of politicians anxious to meddle in what must remain pure worlds of faith.

Chatterjee's objection to secularism in India is more philosophical. He notes that the state in postcolonial India has both failed to keep out of religion, and/or to keep an equal distance from competing faiths. The Nehruvian state compelled Hindu temples to open themselves to 'Untouchable' (or SC) worshippers. Nehru's grandson, Rajiv Gandhi, later courted the Muslim vote by upholding Muslim Personal Law in the Shah Bano divorce case—a decision that was a gift to the Sangh Parivar. Chatterjee, for his part, advances the view that each religious group should police itself, according to precepts that its members would contest but also find fair. Chatterjee is not minded to see religion as a threat to a tolerant, secular state. He proposes that true tolerance can grow out of faith-based religions, and that a robust definition of tolerance in a multicultural society must begin from a politics of difference that allows minority groups to say 'we will not give reasons for not being like you' (1997: 258).

Caste, Ethnicity, and Region

Once again, this is a radical move by Chatterjee, and it is a considerable remove from Amartya Sen's (1996) claim that the removal of secular protections in contemporary India would make tense community (read, Hindu–Muslim) relations more 'wintry' than they already are. It proposes yet another coupling of politics and culture, one that is localized and communitarian. Central government—the high polity—is asked not to police or adjudicate community relations, or to stand above and outside them. Rather, it is invited to respect the political settlements that will arise locally according to different, if also partially overlapping, cultural understandings and codes.

As several critics have pointed out, however, Chatterjee's appeal to tolerance, much like Nandy's appeal to faith or Vandana Shiva's (1989) suggestion that women are naturally the best guardians of India's threatened environments, assumes a good deal about the unity of the communities they propose to entrust with various powers of policing. These appeals also make some robust assumptions about the terrain upon which these policing strategies take place. Aihwa Ong (2007), in her recent discussion of gender and citizenship in Malaysia, notes the limitations imposed upon the Sisters in Islam by the requirement that they contest the power of conservative, male Islam from within forms of Quranic textualizm. The Sisters' main demand has been for education, and thus the right to read and interpret the Quran for themselves. Meanwhile, the state in Malaysia, imbued with an ideology of developmentalism, and mindful of the need to bring women into the world of paid, formal-sector work, has provided important citizenship spaces for women beyond those which one part of the Muslim community has proposed to police.

A similar argument might be made with regard to temple entry issues in India, or the Shah Bano case. What evidence is there to suggest that, in the absence of state policies to promote more secular concepts of citizenship, the ambitions of SC men and women to attend for worship would always be respected and allowed? Or that a woman could demand maintenance from her husband under the provisions of a Uniform Civil Code (UCC) (here, Section 125 of the Code of Criminal Prodedure)? In addition, it might reasonably be asked whether arguments for community self-rule are sufficiently attentive to the likely effects of such self-rule on other communities. We know rather little about how different Muslim communities read the politics of the Sangh Parivar, and respond to it (Kakar 1996). It seems likely, however, that some among these communities are now drawing on transnational resources—financial, ideological, and other—to construct political spaces in which to contest the claims both of Hindutva and secularism. Some of these spaces then get pulled into the so-called war on terrorism by governments that are troubled by the rise of what they call 'political Islam'.

This observation in turn suggests a second: namely, that arguments rooted around the tolerance of 'religion as faith' have been inattentive to the base politics of politicized Hinduism. The suggestion here is that Hindu nationalism was made to be resurgent in the 1980s and 1990s by upper-caste Hindu communities, who felt threatened by various political movements 'from below'. From this perspective, the rise of militant Hinduism should be seen as an 'elite revolt' against an earlier, and in some respects very successful, pattern of mobilization by subaltern groups against the injustices of caste hierarchy and oppression (Corbridge and Harriss 2000/2003). Elements of this were apparent in the late nineteenth century when

Jotirao Phule's critique of 'Brahmanical tyranny and conspiracy' helped push some high-caste Hindus to mobilize around a politics of cow protection. Charges of functionalism notwithstanding, the need for a Muslim 'Other' can be said to have become equally urgent for India's Forward Castes in the 1980s. By then, a long history of non-Brahmanism in the south, especially in the Madras Presidency and Tamil Nadu, was being mirrored in Gujarat, Bihar, and Uttar Pradesh (UP). It had also led on to the decision of Prime Minister V.P. Singh, in 1990, to enact some of the key provisions of the Second Backward Classes Commission (the so-called Mandal Commission Report, which had been shelved in New Delhi for ten years). The extension of a system of reserved jobs to the community of Other Backward Classes (OBCs) was a major challenge to the economic and political interests of India's high-caste elites (Jaffrelot 2005).

The rise to power in the 1990s of politicians like Kanshi Ram and Mayawati in UP, and Lalu Prasad Yadav in Bihar, seemed to give the lie to the idea that there could be a single—never mind self-policing—Hindu community in India. The refusal of these politicians to accept traditional Brahmanical interpretations of 'the caste system' (all three words were rendered problematic) often went hand in glove with forms of political action that resisted the modernizing ambitions of Nehru and his acolytes. Gone, it seemed, were earlier ideas of the 'national interest' and the 'politics of reason'. Mayawati concentrated on bringing her SC supporters into the UP government services, and in adorning public squares with statues of Ambedkar. Meanwhile, Lalu Yadav focused on the politics of *izzat* (honour or dignity). His Janata Dal (later Rashtriya Janata Dal) set out to challenge the demeaning language often used by Bihar's Forward Castes (especially Brahmins, Bhumihars, and Rajputs) when dealing with the state's Backward Classes. Politics became more sectional, less interested in positive sum games. According to many Delhi-based commentators, the most likely outcome of this new politics would be the looting of state resources by Lalu's supporters, and the condemnation of Bihar to still more years of slow economic growth. They saw Lalu as a buffoon, or a threat to democracy.

This is not the place to comment on these predictions, although it is worth noting how Lalu Yadav reinvented himself as a 'respectable' politician when he was sworn in as the Union Railway Minister in 2004 (*Financial Times*, 24 September 2006). Rather, the point to make here is that the rise and reworking of caste-based politics, in addition to cutting into the terrain of the Hindu nationalists, is presenting new questions and opportunities for students of politics and culture in India. Intriguingly, for those who can't see past the occasional absurdities of a Lalu or a Mayawati, their rise to power has encouraged the growth of a rational choice perspective on Indian politics.

This has been a long time coming. Most studies of politics in India before the late 1990s were based in Marxism, narrative history, comparative political economy, public administration, or the pluralism of Myron Weiner and his followers. This began to change with the publication of important books and articles on the politics of Hindu–Muslim violence in India, notably the work of Ashutosh Varshney (2001) and Steven Wilkinson (2006), and from a different perspective, Paul Brass (2005). This work pointed out that incidents of communal violence across India are distributed very unevenly. Certain cities are much more dangerous than other cities of a comparable size or location: Mumbai and Ahmedabad, say, as compared to Calcutta and Surat. And the countryside remains largely pacific. Why? What underlying factors account for these irregular patterns? (Possible answers: lack of bridging social capital across the Hindu–Muslim divide; levels of electoral competition; Muslim populations of a certain size relative to the majority population; policing strategies; competition for jobs; and the like.).

Without a doubt, however, the most rigorous application of rational choice methodologies to Indian politics is to be found in Kanchan Chandra's, *Why Ethnic Parties Succeed: Patronage and Ethnic Head Counts in India* (2004). The world that Chandra describes is far removed from a world of ideological politics, or abstract Nehruvian principles. Rather, it is her argument, on the basis of an ethnographic study of UP politics between 1996 and 1998, that voters who are interested in either material advancement

and/or self-assertion do their level best to vote for the party or candidate they expect to win. In UP, these are ethnically based parties. This is a term which Chandra uses to include horizontally organized caste-based parties (such as the Bahujan Samaj Party), but which can also include a broader regional party mobilizing on the basis of ascriptive/exclusive identities. By the same token, politicians gravitate to those parties which provide 'competitive rules for intra party advancement', or which give 'a comparative advantage in the representation of elites from its target ethnic category' (2004: 2).

As Chandra points out, the implications of her argument for the survival of democracy in India are not at first glance encouraging. '[A] politics of ethnic head counting appears to subvert democratic competition by producing predetermined results based on ethnic demography' (2004). She goes on to argue, however, that what appear to be fairly fixed ethnic identities are more plastic than at first seems likely. Different communities struggle at different times to be scheduled as OBCs, for example, and this creates an opportunity for political entrepreneurs to recast local political landscapes. Another example might come from Bihar, where Lalu Yadav ruled in the 1990s on the basis of Yadav–Kurmi–Muslim votes in a first past the post electoral system. By the early 2000s, Lalu Yadav's command of the Yadav and Kurmi votes had been substantially challenged. Rival political entrepreneurs from within the 'creamy layers' of the OBCs now began to mine votes from within the SC communities, particularly the Paswans. Ethnic targeting deepened Bihar's democracy.

Chandra also points out that national politics in India has so far resisted the 'ethnic turn', at least to some degree, presumably because voters can still be persuaded that it makes sense, financially or otherwise, to vote for the Congress and the BJP. Nevertheless, even at the level of the Central government, it is notable that no party has been able to rule on its own since the collapse of Rajiv Gandhi's government in 1989. Coalition governments have become the norm, all of them with a high complement of caste or regionally-based political parties. And this in turn has promoted fresh work on the languages of politics and on its performativity, two topics that are often sidelined in a rational choice perspective. How do voters read a politician like Jayalalitha in Tamil Nadu? How does she present herself to the electorate? How does she deal with her Brahmanism in a political milieu dominated by non-Brahmanism? How is the issue of 'corruption'—which seemingly swirls about her—decoded and understood? Or what of Lalu Yadav, especially when he served as the de jure or de facto Chief Minister of Bihar? Might he be seen as a modern-day Shudra king, the sort of figure who appears at Holi to upset the established order (Corbridge *et al.* 2005: 236)? Might his rough prose and flamboyant political performances signify something more than just crassness or egocentrism? It is just these sorts of questions, I would suggest, questions around the (heavily gendered) cultures of political performance, that the rise of caste-based politics is helping to promote. They sit alongside more traditional concerns for political ideology and the distribution of resources, and those emanating from a rational choice perspective.

SUMMING UP

Recent academic work on politics and culture in India—as elsewhere—has firmly turned its back on the old master narratives of modernization theory, or on those clichéd versions of globalization theory that presume to tell us about the inexorable rise of the middle classes. Happily, ideas about the inevitable triumph of politics over culture, or of modernity over tradition, were critiqued almost from the time they were announced—whether by Samuel Huntington (1971) from the Right or various neo-Marxists on the Left, or, in the Indian context, by anthropologists led by M.N. Srinivas (1966) or the American political scientists, Lloyd and Susanne Rudolph (1967).

A more profitable way to address the enormous and baggy topic of 'politics and culture' is to think through the technologies of power and rule that are proposed by their coming together in different combinations. What versions of freedom are proposed, and for whom, by constructions of culture

that are rooted in race or blood, or in other more or less fixed forms of identity? What versions of freedom are proposed, and for whom, by secularists, feminists, proponents of religious faith, caste associations, neoliberals, and others? How and where are these proposals made and contested: through the ballot box, in the law courts, through direct action, through the media? And at which spatial scales? How are these proposals articulated and objected to: through what languages, calculative practices, forms of performance, and so on? This is by no means a finished list of questions, but it does point in the direction of some of the most important work now being produced under the banner of 'politics and culture'. Instead of looking for a distinctively Indian notion of culture, or a distinctive culture of Indian politics, the most significant work on politics and culture in India will expose the interests and assumptions that lie beneath (or behind) forms of discourse which trade heavily in binaries or stereotypes. This is the key political task we confront when writing about politics and culture.

NOTE

1. To borrow from Agamben (1998) and pointing back to Guantanamo Bay in Cuba/USA.

REFERENCES

Agamben, G. 1998. *Homo Sacer: Sovereign Power and Bare Life*. Stanford: Stanford University Press.

Ambedkar, B.R. 1945. 'What Congress and Gandhi have done to the Untouchables', in Vasant Moon (ed.) *Dr Babasaheb Ambedkar: Writings and Speeches, Volume 1*. Bombay: Government of Maharashtra.

Anderson, B. 1998. *The Spectre of Comparisons: Nationalisms, Southeast Asia and the World*. London: Verso.

Bardhan, P. 1984. *The Political Economy of Development in India*. Oxford: Oxford University Press.

Basu, T., P. Datta, T. Sarkar, S. Sarkar, and S. Sen. 1993. *Khaki Shorts, Saffron Flags*. New Delhi: Orient Longman.

Brass, P. 1990. *The Politics of India Since Independence*. Cambridge: Cambridge University Press.

———. 2005. *The Production of Hindu-Muslim Violence in Contemporary India*. Seattle: University of Washington Press.

Chandra, K. 2004. *Why Ethnic Parties Succeed: Patronage and Ethnic Head Counts in India*. Cambridge: Cambridge University Press.

Chatterjee, P. 2004. *The Politics of the Governed: Reflections on Popular Politics in Most of the World*. New York: Columbia University Press.

———. 1997. *A Possible World: Essays in Political Criticism* [including, from 1977, the essay 'Nineteen Seventy Seven']. New Delhi: Oxford University Press.

———. 1993. *The Nation and Its Fragments: Colonial and Postcolonial Histories*. Princeton: Princeton University Press.

———. 1986. *Nationalist Thought and the Colonial World*. London: Zed.

Corbridge, S. and Harriss, J. 2000/2003. *Reinventing India: Liberalization, Hindu Nationalism and Popular Democracy*. Cambridge: Polity Press and New Delhi: Oxford University Press.

Corbridge, S., G. Williams, M. Srivastava, and R. Véron. 2005. *Seeing the State: Governance and Governmentality in India*. Cambridge: Cambridge University Press.

da Matta, R. 1991. *Carnivals, Rogues and Heroes: An Interpretation of the Brazilian Dilemma*. South Bend, Indiana: University of Notre Dame Press.

Dirks, N. 2001. *Castes of Mind*. Princeton: Princeton University Press.

Dumont, L. 1970. *Homo Hierarchicus*. London: Paladin.

Gramsci, A. 1971. *Selections from the Prison Notebooks*. New York: International Publishers.

Harriss, J. 1993. 'Does the "Depressor" Still Work? Agrarian Structure and Development in India: A Review of Evidence and Argument', *Journal of Peasant Studies*, Vol. 19(2), pp. 189–227.

Huntington, S. 1971. 'The Change to Change: Modernization, Development and Politics', *Comparative Politics*, 3(3), pp. 283–322.

Inden, R. 1995. 'Embodying God: From Imperial Progresses to National Progress in India', *Economy and Society*, 24(2), pp. 245–78.

Jaffrelot, C. (ed.). 2005. *The Sangh Parivar: A Reader*. New Delhi: Oxford University Press.

Kakar, S. 1996. *The Colors of Violence: Cultural Identities, Religion, and Conflict*. Chicago: University of Chicago Press.

Kaviraj, S. 1994. 'On the Construction of Colonial Power: Structure, Discourse, Hegemony', in D. Engels and S. Marks (eds) *Contesting Colonial Hegemony: State and Society in Africa*. London: Curzon Press, pp. 112–27.

———. 1988. 'A Critique of the Passive Revolution', *Economic and Political Weekly*, XXIII(45–7), pp. 2429–44.

———. 1984. 'On the Crisis of Political Institutions in India', *Contributions to Indian Sociology*, 18(2), pp. 223–43.

King, R. 1997. *Nehru and the Language Politics of India*. New Delhi: Oxford University Press.

Kohli, A. 1990. *Democracy and Discontent: India's Growing Crisis of Governability*. Cambridge: Cambridge University Press.

Madan, T.N. 1987. 'Secularism in its Place', *Journal of Asian Studies*, 46(4), pp. 747–59

Migdal, J. 2001. *State in Society: Studying How States and Societies Constitute and Transform One Another*. Cambridge: Cambridge University Press.

Nandy, A. 2003. *The Romance of the State and the Fate of Dissent in the Tropics*. New Delhi: Oxford University Press.

———. 1990. 'The Politics of Secularism and the Recovery of Religious Tolerance', in V. Das (ed.), *Mirrors of Violence*. New Delhi: Oxford University Press, pp. 69–93.

Nandy, A., S. Trivedy, S. Mayaram, and A. Yagnik. 1995. *Creating a Nationality: The Ramjanmabhumi Movement and Fear of the Self*. New Delhi: Oxford University Press.

Nehru, J. 1980. *An Anthology* [edited by S. Gopal]. New Delhi: Oxford University Press.

Ong, A. 2007. *Neoliberalism as Exception: Mutations in Citizenship and Sovereignty*. Durham, NC: Duke University Press.

Platteau, J.P. 1994. 'Behind the Market Stage where Real Societies Exist', parts I and II, *Journal of Development Studies*, 30 (3), pp. 533–77 and 753–817.

Rajagopal, A. 2001. *Politics After Television: Hindu Nationalism and the Reshaping of the Public in India*. Cambridge: Cambridge University Press.

Rose, N. 1999. *Powers of Freedom*. Cambridge: Cambridge University Press.

Rudolph, L. and S.H. Rudolph. 1987. *In Pursuit of Lakshmi: The Political Economy of the Indian State*. Chicago: The University of Chicago Press.

———. 1967. *The Modernity of Tradition*. Chicago: The University of Chicago Press.

Said, E. 1993. *Culture and Imperialism*. New York: Knopf.

Savarkar, V. 1949. *Hindu Rashtra Darshan: A Collection of Presidential Speeches Delivered from the Hindu Mahasabha Platform, 1938–1941*. Bombay: Khare.

Scott, J.C. 1998. *Seeing Like a State: How Certain Schemes to Improve the Human Condition Have Failed*. New Haven: Yale University Press.

Sen, Amartya. 1996. 'Secularism and its Discontents', in K. Basu and S. Subrahmanyam (eds), *Unravelling the Nation: Sectarian Conflict and India's Secular Identity*. New Delhi: Penguin, pp. 11–43.

Shiva, V. 1991. *The Violence of the Green Revolution*. London: Zed.

Shiva, V. 1989. *Staying Alive: Women, Ecology and Survival in India*. New Delhi: Kali for Women.

Simpson, E. and S. Corbridge. 2006. 'The Geography of Things that May become Memories: The 2001 Earthquake in Kachchh-Gujarat and the Politics of Rehabilitation in the Prememorial Era', *Annals of the Association of American Geographers*, Vol. 96, pp. 566–85

Srinivas, M.N. 1996. *Social Change in Modern India*. Berkeley: University of California Press.

Trivedi, L. 2007. *Clothing Gandhi's Nation: Homespun and Modern India*. Bloomington: Indiana University Press.

van der Veer, Peter. 1994. *Religious Nationalisms: Hindus and Muslims in India*. Berkeley: University of California Press.

Varshney, A. 2001. *Ethnic Conflict and Civic Life: Hindus and Muslims in India*. New Haven: Yale University Press.

Weber, M. 1930 [1905]. *The Protestant Ethic and the Spirit of Capitalism*. London: Unwin.

Wilkinson, S. 2006. *Votes and Violence: Electoral Competition and Ethnic Riots in India*. Cambridge: Cambridge University Press.

18 Political Mobilization

Arun R. Swamy

> Against the British in India it was essential for the Indian National Congress to win mass approbation. It did not need, however, to effect mass mobilization. It needed mass support, but it did not need to evoke a mass upheaval.
>
> D.A. Low (1988: 54)

The year 2005 arguably marked a century of modern political mobilization in India. Although the Indian National Congress was founded in 1885, the early Congress was, notoriously, an organization of the professional elite. Other, more popular forms of mobilization that may have existed in the late nineteenth century were focused on the provincial arena. However, after 1905 it is possible to think of an all-India political space, interacting with these regional spaces and often shaping them, with contending parties seeking to set a 'national' agenda, drawing new regional allies into the 'national' arena to do so. The Swadeshi movement, launched to oppose the Partition of Bengal, was the first effort at popular political mobilization to be undertaken across several provinces. The subsequent division between the so-called Moderates and Extremists, which led to the Congress split in 1907, can be interpreted as an effort by 'out-groups' in the national arena to win broader support by incorporating new elements into the political equation.

My purpose here, though, is not to settle upon a date, but to use that date to draw attention to an aspect of political mobilization that does not often receive attention. This is the strategic aspect, whereby contending parties in one conflict seek to prevail by enlisting new allies by drawing in previously indifferent parties, or changing the terms of conflict by reframing the issues. In India, repeatedly over the century since 1905, the 'national' political arena has been enlarged as some actors in it seek to turn a losing situation around by courting new allies, 'mobilizing new sources of support', as one might say. Similarly, Indian politics is replete with examples of the strategic redrawing of conflict boundaries as issues get reframed.

Identifying 'political mobilization' with this strategic manipulation of the lines of conflict is a little unorthodox. The word 'mobilization' suggests the setting in 'motion' of previously inert entities. In purely top-down views of mobilization, this is achieved by elites—broadly understood to include political elites—who stir up the rabble or capture alienated individuals for their own purposes. In bottom-up views, mobilization is self-generated, as like-minded individuals band together around natural sources of solidarity. In either view, as Low suggests in the epigram above, 'mobilization' carries the imminent threat of 'upheaval'.

In the view I present, elites do not *necessarily* cause political action to occur, but they do help to define which potential lines of division are more salient than others. They do so by providing the means for the expression of grievance, shaping the manner in which interests and grievances are expressed, and defining the context in which mobilization occurs, through the introduction of policies and institutions that create new opportunities or grievances.

This strategic *channelling* of political activity is especially important in understanding electoral behaviour, which raises the question of whether electoral participation counts as 'political mobilization'. Unlike Low, I do assume that winning 'mass support' for a party at election time is among the most important forms that political mobilization can take. This is especially true for India, where continued electoral politics remain the central arena for political mobilization, even to the extent that non-electoral forms of mobilization typically aim to influence or enter electoral politics. In short, while I agree with the substance of Low's characterization of the 1930s Congress strategy, I suggest that activities that obtain 'mass approbation' without effecting 'mass upheaval' do indeed constitute political mobilization. Indeed, any analysis of *political mobilization in India* needs to first explain how the electoral arena became and remained the central locus of mobilization efforts. This is the main focus of this chapter.

The chapter argues that while the fundamental driver of Indian politics, over the last century, has been the successive emergence of new groups and interests available for political mobilization, the nature and outcome of this mobilization has been shaped by the interplay between two strategies of alliance-building. The first, the *anti-hegemonic alliance*, unites intermediate powers against one that exercises or seeks to exercise hegemony. The *sandwich alliance*,

by contrast, unites the extremes of a power hierarchy against those in the middle.

I proceed by first undertaking a broad survey of approaches to the study of political mobilization, in order to situate the present chapter's argument in the larger field of political science and other approaches to the study of Indian politics. I then examine two successive half-centuries of political mobilization in India to identify the principal cleavages that emerged in those periods, and the role of alliance-building strategies in shaping their mobilization.

APPROACHES TO STUDYING POLITICAL MOBILIZATION IN INDIA

The study of political mobilization is such a vast topic that only the most cursory of reviews can be attempted here. The brief survey of approaches in comparative politics undertaken below, highlights two kinds of analyses, which have been largely missing from the study of Indian politics. One is the study of how political strategies influence whether a potential cleavage becomes an active source of conflict. The other is the systematic comparison of the way cleavage structures emerge across Indian states. Each is discussed in turn after the general overview.

Political Mobilization and Comparative Politics

For the sake of efficiency, I suggest, adapting from Harold Lasswell's famous definition of politics, that the study of political mobilization can be divided into four questions: *who* is mobilized, for *what* purpose, *when*, and *how*. Many approaches to the analysis of political mobilization centre around one or two of these questions. Different scholars also vary according to whether they adopt a broadly structural or *macro* analytic approach or a *micro* analytic one that focuses on explaining the actions of elites or even individuals. Additionally, answers to each question can range from broadly *structural* or macro-analytic approaches, to those that focus more on elite activity or individual motives and strategies.[1]

The question of *who* is being mobilized is typically answered in one of two ways. Structurally inclined analysts focus on identifying some collectivity—

economic classes, cultural communities, or other kinds of social groups—on whose behalf a demand is made. There can often be many possible answers, and accordingly analysts will differ over which collectivity is being mobilized. To cite one famous Indian example, the Chipko movement against logging, undertaken by hill women in what is now Uttaranchal state, was variously viewed as a peasant movement to preserve access to forest resources, an environmental movement to prevent deforestation, a women's struggle against the impact of logging on domestic labour, or even a regional movement against plains domination.

Microanalytic approaches avoid this kind of ambiguity by adopting a narrower approach to the 'who' question by asking which individuals are actually participating in collective political action. Here, the answers are often tied to 'how' mobilization is effected, since quite different kinds of people participate in electoral politics than, say, in direct action or revolutionary activity. A weakness of this approach is that scholars often focus excessively on the self-interest of politically active individuals. At the same time, this kind of focus often shows that politically active individuals are better educated or better-off than the group they seek to represent, forcing analysts to inquire whether the issues activists focus on are salient for the larger constituency.[2] As we will see, this question is very relevant for the present essay.

For obvious reasons, the second question analysts ask about political mobilization—'what' interests and grievances motivate political action—is central to understanding its *consequences*. Macroanalytic approaches to this question tend to examine how a set of policy issues, such as the role of agriculture in the economy or the cultural policy of the state, create more persistent divisions or 'cleavages' in society. Often scholars working in this vein treat the 'who' and 'what' questions together through a systematic analysis of the social divisions or 'cleavage structures' arising out of fundamental policy conflicts in a given society or set of societies. In the best-known effort along these lines, Lipset and Rokkan (1967) argued that the party systems of Western Europe were shaped by the varying intensities of four basic cleavages—centre vs periphery, secular vs religious, rural vs. urban, and owner vs. worker—and that these

in turn stemmed from conflicts generated by the two major transformations of the modern era, the National Revolution and the Industrial Revolution.

The strength of Rokkanian[3] analysis is that it draws our attention to the relationship between political activity (mobilization) and political outcome (policies, or regime types); it identifies stable *patterns* of mobilization; and allows for comparison among cases. However, macroanalytic approaches to cleavage structures share two weaknesses that are closely related. First, they do not always tell us why a particular cleavage—such as the Hindu–Muslim cleavage in India—is salient at some times and not at others in the same place. Second, their broad brush analysis of important policy conflicts frequently overlooks important differences in policy details that can have a powerful impact on political conflict. As we will see, a narrower focus on elite strategies and on the nuances of policies can often provide a better explanation for the emergence or decline of importance cleavages than do broader structural approaches.

The third important question, then, centres on the timing of mobilization. Scholars adopting a structural approach usually assume that deeper socio-economic forces determine the moment when a particular issue enters the policy agenda or a particular group enters formal politics. Some do argue that various responses by leaders to this initial mobilization are possible and these in turn explain the subsequent patterns in the country's politics. This effort to explain stable parameters in a country's politics as the legacy of a particular historical moment—or 'critical juncture'—is central to the Rokkanian analysis of cleavage structures.

The identification of critical junctures does allow some scope for the study of political strategy and can illuminate many deeper tendencies in a country's politics, but these efforts often underestimate the variability of political conflict in the short run. As I have already suggested, if we are interested in why certain conflicts occur at one point in time and not another—that is, explaining the timing of mobilization rather than taking it as a given and examining its consequences—we need to pay attention to the mobilizational or policy choices made by political elites in all periods not just major socio-economic transitions.

The last observation brings us to the fourth issue that scholars studying political mobilization might address—the *process* by which a group comes to be mobilized around a particular set of interests. Efforts to explain why mobilization occurred through revolutionary activity, social movements, or other methods lend themselves well to structural approaches, as the explanation often lies in social structure. For example, Bouton (1985) explained why agrarian radicalism occurred in some parts of south India and not in others by pointing to the high degree of polarization of both caste and class hierarchies in the places where it did occur— Kerala and Thanjavur district in Tamil Nadu. This kind of explanation does not help us understand timing, though.

Social movement theories, which fall in the middle of the micro–macro spectrum do address questions of timing by focusing, for example, on the availability of organizational vehicles or resources for particular kinds of mobilization, or the opportunities for political mobilization provided by a country's institutional structure or policy matrix ('Oppurtunity Structure'). However, resource mobilization theory frequently ignores the *content* of mobilization—that is, the specific issues around which mobilization occurs—while opportunity structure theory does not address the process by which opportunity structures are translated into mobilization.

A different approach to the 'how' question involves studying the process by which a particular grievance is politicized. Collective action frame theory a newer approach to studying social movements, does this through a focus on the symbolic resources used to motivate members. This is also where addressing dividends the role of policy or political entrepreneurship in highlighting or shaping cleavages is likely to pay. Unfortunately, though, there has been little systematic attention paid in political science—whether among India specialists or more generally—to the consequences of different types of political strategies. This is because political strategies appear to many scholars to be ad hoc, invented for particular situations, offering little possibility for comparative study.[4] However, the two strategies that this essay focuses on, the anti-hegemonic and the

sandwich alliances, are generic forms that can be adapted to many contexts, allowing for comparison.

Anti-hegemonic and Sandwich Alliances

Anti-hegemonic and sandwich alliances are general categories that include the styles of populist mobilization that I have earlier termed empowerment and protection populism, respectively (Swamy 1996; 1998). These terms drew attention to rhetorical styles that united upwardly mobile social groups against established elites, or appealed to vulnerable and marginalized groups respectively. By contrast, the terms 'anti-hegemonic strategy' and 'sandwich tactic' emphasize the more generic modes of alliance-building that frequently result in these distinctive modes of populism. They allow us to incorporate into a single framework calculated tactical alliances and diffuse populist appeals, and to compare alliances that operate on a spatial or temporal plane with those whose building blocks are strata in a social hierarchy. Indeed, both alliance patterns have their correlates in international relations and these analogies provide important clues to their functioning.

The common feature to those two alliance types is that the elements of each coalition are drawn to it not so much by shared substantive concerns (at least not of a permanent variety) as by their shared relationship to a third party. That is, they are united by a shared foe rather than by shared interests. Consequently, in a dynamic social situation such as that characterizing a developing country, the relative situation of particular groups can change rapidly, and with it, so will their interests and the alliance they are drawn to.

In the most general terms, an *anti-hegemonic alliance* is one that unites powerful actors against a greater power that exerts or seeks to exert hegemony over them. The analogy here is with international alliances among powerful states that feel threatened by a rising superpower. In domestic politics, a very close analogue is provided by conflicts over the centralization of power between national governments on one hand, and advocates of states' rights on the other. In disputes over socio-economic policy, anti-hegemonic alliances tend to favour policies that broaden the elite, adopting redistributive policies that identify broad groups of beneficiaries over the most needy, or promote upward mobility among disadvantaged sectors.

From the perspective of their social composition, anti-hegemonic alliances in domestic politics unite out-groups or counter-elites across diverse social domains against a core elite. These counter-elites might be the elite segments of upwardly mobile social strata, or the established elites of relatively peripheral regions who find common cause in opposing the core group. In India, anti-hegemonic alliance-building strategies can be detected among the Extremists within the Congress in the early twentieth century, among representatives of minority groups *outside* Congress in the 1930s, among the various 'national' opposition parties in the 1960s, and among regional parties in the 1990s. Notably, the last three alliances were directed against the Congress, and only the last was successful.[5]

The *sandwich alliance*, by contrast, unites the extremes of a power hierarchy against powerful mid-level actors. In international relations, sandwich alliances occur when superpowers champion small states against 'regional bullies', or wealthy countries respond to challenges from newly industrializing countries by championing the interests of very poor countries. In domestic politics, there is a 'sandwich' corollary to the conflict between central authority and states' rights mentioned above in centralization is frequently supported by local minorities, who feel threatened by the power that local elites or majorities enjoy in a decentralized polity.

As sandwich alliances are commonly put together by defensive elites against counter-elites, their policies often do demonstrate an ad hoc *tactical* character rather than a consistent strategic vision. It is therefore easier to specify which of the two policies prefer a sandwich alliance than to spell out a consistent policy agenda.[6] In social and economic policy, their redistributive proposals are often reactive rather than proactive, and may take their specific form from the proposals of the anti-hegemonic alliances that they are seeking to defeat. Subject to this qualification, sandwich alliances are likely to favour means tested distributive measure that target benefits more narrowly to the most needy over broad entitlements; the provision of social insurance over structural measures that redistribute social and economic

power; direct spending on public goods such as primary education over statutory measures aimed at guaranteeing upward mobility; and anti-inflationary macroeconomic policies, as inflation is more likely to hurt the poor.

What is consistent about sandwich alliances is the way they construct their policies to unite the ends of a power hierarchy against the middle. As I have previously shown (Swamy 1998, 2003) 'sandwich' responses commonly fall into two categories—proposals to target benefits demanded by counter-elites more narrowly than they would like, and proposals to substitute alternate policies that are more likely to appeal the least privileged groups. The targeting approach seeks to create fissures between weak and strong elements of the anti-hegemonic alliance while the substitution approach outflanks it by appealing to vulnerable groups directly. As with the anti-hegemonic alliances, this approach can, and has to be, adapted to incorporate new interests as older ones become more ambitious and join the anti-hegemonic alliance. In India, sandwich alliances were attempted by British authorities against the Congress; by the Congress in turn against the elites of minority groups in the 1930s; and by the Congress against alliances of regional, farmers', and backward-caste parties from the 1960s to the 1980s.

The advantage of focusing on alliance-building strategies rather than on concrete alliances of specific groups is that the former approach can accomodate the shifting position of social groups over time. For example, it is difficult to apply a structural approach, which tends to attribute relatively fixed interests to particular classes, to the political behaviour of property-owning peasant castes in India over the last seventy years. When they were first enfranchised by the Government of India Act of 1935, 'middle peasants' effectively occupied the lowest socio-economic rung among the *politically relevant* segments of society. By the 1960s, they were clearly in the middle sectors of society, and by the 1990s, arguably at the top. This matches their position in different alliances, as these groups formed the bottom of the Congress sandwich alliance in the 1930s, led the anti-hegemonic challenge to Congress in the 1960s, and moved towards the Bharatiya Janata Party (BJP) in the 1990s.

As this example makes clear, I do not suggest that alliance strategies can reshape society as they choose. An effective analysis of alliance-building strategies requires an understanding of the coalitional possibilities offered by the available and emerging cleavage structures.

Cleavage Structures in Indian Political Mobilization

As suggested above, a second type of research that would benefit the study of political mobilization in India is the systematic comparative analysis of cleavage structures. This is not to suggest that students of Indian politics should seek to replicate the particular cleavages that Lipset and Rokkan (1967) discovered for Western Europe, but rather that they should identify relevant cleavages for India that vary in intensity across Indian states.

One potential application of this approach would be the study of how peasant and 'backward' castes have been formed across states. Two important sets of edited volumes in the 1980s—Omvedt (1982) and Frankel and Rao (1989/1990)—attempted something along these lines. However, these volumes did not systematically explore the links between variations in cleavage structures across states and party politics. In particular, the Frankel and Rao volumes did not examine why the 'backward caste' cluster was stronger in some states than in others. A second, obvious area where cleavage structures vary across states and require explanation has to do with religious cleavages. There has been almost no systematic work done on this.

At the same time, though, as we have already noted, the study of cleavage structures cannot explain why particular cleavages become salient at a particular point in time. Especially in Indian politics, characterized as it is by a large variety of cross-cutting cleavages, the study of political mobilization necessarily involves understanding the strategic uses of cleavage structures and not merely their existence, and an understanding of policy details is often crucial to this.

The example of Other Backward Class (OBC) reservations illustrates this well. While it is clear that the OBC/middle peasant coalition—which

many scholars in the 1980s foresaw and which the Janata Dal tried to give expression to—has now fractured in a number of ways, it is not clear that this outcome was inevitable. This fracture happened because the effects of reservations for the OBCs on the principal cultivator castes varied tremendously across states. Supreme Court rulings limiting all categories of reservations to 50 per cent of the available seats led the 1979 Mandal Commission to adopt a methodology for identifying backward castes that effectively sought to ensure that the sum of all reserved categories did not exceed fifty per cent of the state's population. As we will discuss in greater detail below, this, combined with pre-existing variations across states in the status of peasant groups,[7] ensured that the principal peasant groups would be included in the OBC category in some states, but not others. V.P. Singh's decision in 1990 to implement the Mandal Commission's recommendations nationally then divided the 'backward' from the 'forward' segments of the middle-peasant/backward-caste coalition pitting peasant castes from different regions against each other in a way that state-specific reservations had not. Subsequently, 'forward' peasant castes gravitated towards the BJP, and the 'all-or-nothing' character of reservations created further opportunities for the BJP to woo 'more backward' segments of the OBC cluster away from Yadav-dominated OBC parties in Uttar Pradesh (UP) and Bihar.

This vignette suggests that what is required for understanding political mobilization is not just an identification of cleavages, but a dynamic focus on their emergence over time, and the role of strategy in shaping this emergence. In what follows, I will tell the story of Indian political mobilization principally from the perspective of the national arena, incorporating discussions of rural class cleavages, urban class cleavages, rural/urban cleavages, centre-periphery cleavages between the Union and states as well as within states, and caste, linguistic, and religious cleavages as they seem relevant. The role of policies and political entrepreneurship in creating or superseding cleavages, and bringing together or breaking apart various kinds of social coalitions will be evident throughout.

CLEAVAGE, ALLIANCE TYPE, AND INDIAN POLITICAL MOBILIZATION

Most accounts of Indian politics point to the accommodative character of the Indian National Congress as the central explanation of Indian democracy.[8] Between 1930 and 1965, the Congress was said to have met challenges from newly politicized groups by *expanding* its social base to incorporate them, and, in Weiner's (1967) characterization, using its local organization to mediate among them. Mirroring Weiner's view on the ideological plane, Kothari's (1989) conceptualization of India as a 'dominant-party system' pictured the Congress as a 'party of consensus' that mediated between the views of various smaller 'parties of pressure'. Taken together, these descriptions constituted the 'Congress system'. For most scholars, the emergence of serious electoral challenges to the Congress in the 1960s was followed by the 'erosion' of the Congress organization under Indira Gandhi and the 'deinstitutionalization' of Indian politics in general, leading in turn to increasing fiscal indiscipline and social violence.[9]

Not all scholars applauded the accommodative tendencies of Indian politics, or of the Congress. Indeed, many ascribed India's slow rate of economic growth in the first three decades following Independence to the accommodation of rival interests in policymaking.[10] However, even these scholars had few kind words for the character of Indian politics following the 1969 Congress split, after accommodative politics was generally viewed as having come to an end. Rather, the view that a shift to 'populist' appeals by all parties was undermining development was widely shared among scholars who held very different views about the direction that development should take.

In retrospect, what is remarkable about this analysis is its static and undifferentiated approach towards the relationship between social cleavages and institutions. For example, many scholars blamed Indira Gandhi for destroying the Congress party's ability to mediate between rival social groups in the manner described by Weiner, but ignored the fact that the type of institution represented by Nehru's Congress—which, at the local levels, was a classic

patronage machine—can only exist when the general level of social mobilization is low, or when the resources available for patronage are high. The sharp reversals suffered by the Congress in the 1967 elections suggest that the Congress 'system' was in any event on its last legs. What has been remarkable about Indian democracy since then is the survival of the electoral principle through several decades of increasingly *competitive* mobilization of new political interests.

In the sections that follow, I examine the last century of political mobilization in three sections covering periods of roughly equal length. The first describes the role of sandwich tactics in the transformation of the Congress into an electoral party in the late 1930s. The second examines the emergence of cleavages that defined opposition to the Congress in the 1950s and 1960s, and provided the basis for anti-hegemonic alliances among them. The third examines alliance-building within the context of competitive electoral politics.

From Agitation to Elections, 1905–39

Early political conflict among Indian social groups occurred along lines of cleavage that divided the urban middle class. The first groups to be mobilized into modern politics were the urban professional classes. However, unlike Europe, where the line of conflict lay between the landed upper classes and the new urban elite, in India, the grievances of the urban professional groups were directed primarily at the colonial government. However, efforts to maintain a united front against the British were always confronted with the problem of social cleavages among Indian groups. In the late nineteenth century, these consisted of distinct, if overlapping, lines of conflict that divided various segments of the new middle classes from their mostly Brahmin, metropolitan (based in Bombay, Calcutta, and Madras), and upper professional core.

Lower middle-class (clerical) groups, middle-class representatives of smaller urban centres and peripheral regions, and members of relatively disadvantaged castes and communities were all variously attracted to more militant and nativist forms of political expression. Thus, Tilak (of Poona), Lajpat Rai (of Punjab), and many other noted Extremist leaders shared this peripherality vis-à-vis mainstream metropolitan Congress politics, though none came from a disadvantaged background in any other sense. In a similar vein, the Cambridge School historians (Baker and Washbrook 1975) detected in the politics of the nineteenth-century Madras Presidency and the twentieth-century Madras Congress an ongoing cleavage between, on the one hand, the Mylapore Brahmin clique that dominated provincial patronage structures from Madras, and, on the other, both Brahmin notables from lesser towns and non-Brahmin notables generally. The non-Mylapore luminaries included Gandhians in Congress (such as the Brahmin C. Rajagopalachari of Salem) and many who joined the anti-Brahmin Justice Party.

These conflicts entered the all-India arena through the divide between the so-called Moderates and Extremists. Ostensibly divided by tactical considerations—the Moderates preferring a constitutional approach to winning concessions from the British, the Extremists opting for a path of direct action—the split also reflected a centre–periphery conflict. While Moderates were associated with the schism between the established, anglicized, and avowedly Liberal professional elite of the major presidency towns, Extremists were typically drawn from a counter-elite that represented, variously, lesser towns in the major presidencies, and espoused a nativist style of politics in which swadeshi (of indigenous origin) and swaraj (self-government) were entwined. Notably, economic nationalism frequently formed an integral part of this kind of approach, as the Swadeshi movement of 1905–8, with its boycott of British goods, had its roots in earlier efforts to promote indigenous economic enterprise by such figures as Lala Lajpat Rai.

Other social groups, especially rural ones, were not brought into play in a significant way until the 1920s and 1930s, with the possible exception of cow agitation movements in north India. Again, they were initially brought into political action around conflicts with British social groups and policy. Business groups were enlisted to the cause through a platform of economic nationalism, which appealed to India's budding manufacturing industry at a time of global depression. Gandhi's earlier and famous championing

of sharecroppers in Champaran, Bihar, in 1918 fit this pattern, in that the sharecroppers' landlords were British indigo planters. More importantly, the 1930s Civil Disobedience movement's focus on revenue reduction for tax-paying peasants famously ignored the concerns of class contradiction among Indian agrarian classes.

As is generally acknowledged, it was the need to undermine the claims of minority representatives, from the Muslim League to the Justice Party in Madras and the Depressed Classes (that is, Dalits) under the leadership of Ambedkar, which led the Congress leadership to turn more seriously to the question of how to mobilize the masses. British authorities' decision to give minority representatives equal weight in the Round Table Conferences of the early 1930s represented in the clearest fashion the 'sandwich' logic of British responses to Congress since Curzon. 'The people of India,' Curzon had once declared, 'are the voiceless millions ... [whom] the plans and policies of the Congress party would leave ... untouched.'[11] In the late 1920s and early 1930s, British authorities replicated this argument by claiming that Congress spoke only for the Hindu upper castes (of northern India), and that British presence was required to protect India's many minorities from their dominance.

As early as the Nehru Report of 1928, Congress leaders sought to turn the tables on the British strategy by claiming that the British were advocates of communal representation who spoke only for 'a handful of upper class people' among the minorities, while the real interests of the poor among these groups lay in economic questions.[12] Notably, the Nehru Report was the first to call for universal suffrage in an Independent India, and the failure of the Round Table Conferences was followed by the 1931 Karachi Resolutions, when the Congress first committed itself to basic social and economic reforms. The Congress election manifesto of 1936 made explicit the connection between this new emphasis on the social and economic concerns of the masses, and the need to undermine the claims of leaders like Jinnah to speak for their constituencies.

As Low (1988, 1999: 239–67) has shown in detail, it was Congress support for the anti-revenue agitations by peasants, along with various other direct relief and social welfare works undertaken by local Congress committees that actually helped them win the support of poorer Indians. Ironically, the revenue boycott agitations were frequently quite local, and, as recent scholarship by the Subaltern Studies School has demonstrated, frequently quite independent of the Congress, which championed but did not initiate most revenue agitations. Nonetheless, that the Congress' record of championing 'bread and butter' issues actually mattered to rural voters became evident when the Government of India Act of 1935 gave the vote to most tax-paying peasants. Their overwhelming support for the Indian National Congress in Hindu-majority provinces ratified the Congress' claim to speak for the mass of Indians over such sectional parties as the Justice Party of Madras or even the Muslim League, which lost to local agrarian parties in the Muslim majority provinces of Punjab and Bengal. Equally importantly, Congress did not win the support of the peasantry by emphasizing structural contradictions between them and other social classes. Although the abolition of zamindari did enter the Congress agenda in the 1936 elections, class-based appeals proposed by socialists were explicitly ruled out, as Low (1988) has shown.

The Emergence of Opposition, 1940–75

In the immediate wake of Independence, the principal cleavages were centre–periphery ones—cultural and territorial—generated by the requirements of settling on the role of minority regions and cultures in a new nation. The pre-eminence of the Hindu-Muslim cleavage faded somewhat with the creation of Pakistan, at least until the 1980s, but the issues of how to draw state boundaries, the status of Hindi as an official language, and legislation promoting social reform among Hindus were all contentious.

The most immediately visible reactions to these conflicts came with the growth of regional parties and movements, especially in the south. The Telugu-speaking region witnessed widespread rioting in support of the demand that all Telugu-speaking areas should be consolidated into one state. Meanwhile, the Tamil-speaking portion of erstwhile Madras Presidency witnessed the birth of an avowedly separatist party,

the Dravida Munnetra Kazhagam (DMK), which was especially opposed to granting special status to Hindi.[13] The Telugu state agitation led eventually to the redrawing of state boundaries along linguistic lines throughout the country. This act went a long way in defusing the potential for linguistic separatism, but created new cleavages within linguistic states between more and less economically advanced regions. These became salient in the 1990s when the BJP made inroads into the relatively disadvantaged regions of Maharashtra, Andhra Pradesh, and Karnataka.

Conversely, the perception that the government was giving minority groups too many concessions created a constituency for a more aggressively assimilationist nationalism. Hindu nationalists professed such an ideology but their principal organization, the Rashtriya Swayamsevak Sangh (RSS), had been content to operate outside the electoral arena, while individual Hindu nationalists like Shyama Prasad Mookherjee, President of the Hindu Mahasabha, operated within the government. However, the RSS was banned briefly after the assassination of Mahatma Gandhi, and came to support the idea of electoral participation by its cadres. Accordingly, the Bharatiya Jana Sangh, or Jan Sangh, as it was popularly known, came into being around this time, to represent not so much a Hindu–Muslim cleavage, but also, uneasily, a Hindi versus linguistic minority cleavage, and, most uneasily, a Hindu versus secular state cleavage (Graham 1990).

Cleavages stemming from social inequalities—of both caste and class—were, of course, also important. The (undivided) Communist Party of India (CPI) emerged as an important force in West Bengal, Kerala, Tamil Nadu, and Andhra Pradesh primarily by emphasizing agrarian class cleavages. Moreover, the Socialist Party, which broke off from the Congress in 1952, emerged as the largest opposition party in the first general election held that year. However, the success of Left parties proved to be their own undoing as they strengthened Nehru's hand within the Congress, facilitating a leftward shift between 1952 and 1957 on the part of the Congress itself. Many socialists rejoined the Congress or allied with it in the Praja Socialist Party (PSP), while the CPI split in 1964 over whether to oppose the Congress.

The economic policies of the Nehru period opened up new lines of cleavage, beginning around 1956–7. While land reform legislation aimed primarily at non-cultivating landlords might have been presumed to solidify the Congress' support among the peasantry, and the government's policy of protecting the domestic market from trade should have won over big business, various other economic policy initiatives had the effect of alienating big businesses and the middle peasantry, opening up a cleavage between the state on one hand and property-owning classes on the other. Among these policy initiatives was Nehru's unsuccessful attempt to promote cooperative farming, which alarmed leaders of the richer peasant groups like Charan Singh of UP. Even more important was the launch of the famous Mahalanobis model of development in the Second Five-Year Plan, beginning in 1957. With its bias in favour of capital-intensive industry and, more strongly, in favour of intermediate and capital goods over consumer goods, a bias enforced through stringent licensing requirements for private-sector investment, the new development model inadvertently created a sizable constituency for a party that represented private property generally. The Swatantra Party was formed in 1957 as a direct result of these policies, bringing under one roof representatives of big business, traditional aristocrats, and some cultivator groups, notably in Andhra Pradesh (Erdman 1967).

Another conflict stemmed from the government's decision to alter the Hindu personal law through the various bills that came to be known as the Hindu Reform Code. Among other provisions, the Code introduced divorce, female inheritance, and abolished polygamy. Opposition to these provisions probably received added impetus from additional legal measures aimed at abolishing all caste disabilities related to access to temples, and mandating preferential policies (reservations) in public employment and education for former outcaste groups, although these measures had their origins in the British period. Both the Jana Sangh and the Swatantra Party capitalized on these sentiments, albeit on grounds consistent with their broader ideological stances, the Jana Sangh decrying the policy as discriminatory as it reformed only the

Hindu Code, and the Swatantra condemning the further intrusion of the state into private matters.

The principal socialist faction that remained opposed to the Congress, Ram Manohar Lohia's Samyukta Socialist Party (SSP), came to emphasize social inequalities other than class, in ways that ironically brought it closer to conservative parties. Representing the aspirations of the upwardly mobile lower peasantry of eastern UP and Bihar, the SSP sought the replacement of English with Hindi, which drew it closer to the Jana Sangh, and opposed the heavy industry emphasis of the Mahalanobis development model on the grounds that it depressed employment creation, which aligned it with the Swatantra Party. Other planks on the SSP platform, notably land reform and the extension of job and educational reservations to the OBCs, did come in conflict with the agenda of the two conservative parties, but were not relevant until Socialists were in governing coalitions with these parties.[14]

The emergence of the various cleavages outlined above became the basis for Selig Harrison's (1960) famous prediction that India was entering its 'most dangerous decades'. The implication behind Harrison's assessment, however, was that these cleavages would lead to the rise of anti-system movements that would threaten the continuance of democracy in, or even the unity of, India. While most of these violent challenges did transpire, the primary arena for expressing all of these grievances remained the electoral one. This essay suggests two reasons for this. First, the formation of anti-hegemonic alliances gave many parties rooted in the above cleavages a stake in the system as they were able to use the opportunity to challenge Congress hegemony in elections winning power in many states. Second, Congress maintained its dominance in Indian politics through the use of sandwich tactics.

The formation of anti-hegemonic alliances in the 1960s must be traced back to the conflicts over economic and cultural policy initiatives undertaken in the 1950s. In particular, Nehruvian socialism, as exemplified by the Second Five-Year Plan and the social reforms ushered in by the Hindu Reform Code, created diverse sources of disaffection with the centralization of authority in Delhi. The resulting points of convergence among these three opposition streams made it possible by the mid-1960s for these very different parties to consider electoral alliances between themselves, and with other regional parties like the DMK to prevent the Congress from benefiting from the split in the opposition vote. The primary motivation for these alliances was clearly tactical. The 'first-past-the-post'[15] voting system that India had adopted from Britain allowed the Congress, with only about 43 per cent of the national popular vote in most elections, to win large majorities in both national and state legislatures. Nonetheless, a shared aversion to Congress 'centralism' provided a useful point of departure for the strategy that Lohia termed Non-Congressism in 1967, more so after the Congress split in 1969 led to most of the local Congress organization, much of which had been in the hands of dominant cultivator groups, joining the opposition.

To what extent did these tactical shifts represent new types of political mobilization? It could be argued that tactical alliances among various opposition parties do not mobilize new voters or form new cleavages. Or, in the terms made famous by such analysts as Prannoy Roy and Ashok Lahiri, their effect is to reduce the 'split' factor in election outcomes, not produce a 'swing'. However, this criticism would be overstated. The 1967 election, which saw the Congress returning with a greatly reduced majority at the Centre and losing control of many states, did see important shifts among voters and increases in turnout.

The broader claim here is that from 1967 onwards, national politics in India witnessed the coalescence of an anti-hegemonic alliance, in which middle peasants from different regions provided the core constituency, and which was united by opposition to the Congress' centralizing tendency. Central to this was the gradual exit from the Congress of powerful middle peasant-dominated state factions, beginning with Charan Singh of UP, whose leadership of the Jat peasantry of western UP gave him a power base until his death in the 1980s. Charan Singh himself was well educated, with degrees in law and economics and, as Terence Byres (1993) has shown, actively engaged in intellectual activity on behalf of the upper peasantry. He articulated an economic model that placed surplus producing peasants at its centre. After leaving the Congress in 1967, Charan

Singh repeatedly sought to create a broad coalition of the rich and poor peasantry of UP and to foster opposition unity in doing so, eventually merging his Bharatiya Kranti Dal (BKD) with the SSP and the Swatantra Party to form the Bharatiya Lok Dal (BLD) in the 1970s. Equally important was the Congress split of 1969, which saw the exit of middle peasant-dominated factions from many states.

It is important to realize, however, that a major impetus for anti-Congress sentiment in the 1960s came from food shortages during the drought years of 1965 and 1966. These could be directly attributed to the neglect of agriculture under the Mahalanobis Plan. Changing the policy mix towards agriculture in order to achieve self-sufficiency in food was an early priority of Mrs Gandhi's government which took the decision, even before the Congress split government—to invest in new technologies, notable among which were the promotion and adoption of chemical fertilizers, pump irrigation, and high-yield variety (HYV) hybrid seeds in wheat and rice cultivation. The policy proved extremely successful in improving foodgrain production by the 1970s.

Under Indira Gandhi the Congress also responded innovatively to the opposition challenge by further mobilizing the very poor. Mrs Gandhi's famous *Garibi Hatao* campaign in 1971 successfully outflanked the opposition through an appeal to the very poor. In a classic instance of what I have termed 'sandwich tactics', she made an appeal over the heads of the various voices in the periphery, and sought to incorporate still more disadvantaged groups within the Congress coalition. During this period the Congress undertook a wave of nationalizations, including, most notably, that of the largest private-sector banks, and initiated a number of pilot poverty alleviation schemes aimed at delivering subsidized credit to small farmers. However, a macroeconomic crisis triggered by the global oil shock of 1973 and the costs of the war with Pakistan in 1971 largely undermined the prospect of significant progress on the poverty alleviation front. Meanwhile, the rising inflation led to increasing middle-class unrest and street protest.

Compared to the 1950s, the 1960s had already witnessed a dramatic increase in non-electoral political mobilization, often violent in nature. This occurred across all cleavages. In 1965 the Central government's decision to implement the constitutional provision to declare Hindi the sole official language was repealed when student-led demonstrations in Madras (now Tamil Nadu) turned violent after the police fired on one group of students. Still more violent political movements came into being in the late 1960s, especially around agrarian class cleavages. Fissures in the Communist movement led to a violent rural uprising centred in West Bengal, which came to be known as the Naxalite revolt after the village of Naxalbari, where it began. The Naxalite movement held out the prospect of violent revolution in India for the first time, and remains a vehicle for violent agrarian radicalism today. While it was again led primarily by middle-class students, it was crushed through ruthless police action taken by the Congress government in West Bengal.

Middle-class students were again at the centre of the most dramatic and successful political movements of the 1970s, those demanding the dismissal of Congress state governments in Gujarat and Bihar in 1974 and 1975. The Nav Nirman agitation in Gujarat, which began as a violent protest against rising mess prices in one college campus in early 1974, snowballed into a state-wide agitation against state government corruption and rising food prices. It eventually attracted the support of leading political figures including veteran Gandhian and former Socialist leader Jayaprakash Narayan (JP) from Bihar, and Indira Gandhi's former rival in the Congress, Morarji Desai. The national Congress leadership was eventually forced to sack the Chief Minister, Chimanbhai Patel, dissolve the assembly, and call fresh elections in 1975, in which a united opposition won against a divided Congress when Chimanbhai Patel launched his own party. The Bihar movement, inspired by the Gujarat example, was also begun by students and also called for the resignation of the Chief Minister, but was led by JP, who declared its goal to be the complete transformation of the social order in the countryside. Unlike the Gujarat experience, though, the Bihar agitation met with a consistently repressive response from Mrs Gandhi, and eventually transformed itself into an all-India front to remove her from power.

Militant labour mobilization also started to become prominent during this period, and affected both the private and public sectors. The high point, of course, was the nation-wide railway strike in 1974, which Indira Gandhi eventually ended by arresting all the principal union leaders including George Fernandes, and as many as 20,000 striking workers. The subsequent assassination of Union Railways Minister Lalit Narain Mishra in early 1975 contributed to what Kohli (1990) termed the 'crisis of governability'.

The climax of this confrontation came in mid-1975, when Mrs Gandhi's election to Parliament in 1971 was overturned by a court decision on the grounds that she had used government machinery for campaign purposes. It is worth remembering that the charges themselves were relatively minor, and that the judge had himself stayed the execution of his order pending a ruling by the Supreme Court. Nonetheless, the JP-led opposition movement demanded that she resign immediately, threatening civil disobedience until she did so. Indira Gandhi, of course, eventually responded by declaring a state of Emergency and arresting the leaders of the movement, including JP and Morarji Desai, as well as her principal opponents in her own party, such as Chandra Shekhar. Not until the Emergency was lifted and elections held in January 1977 did political mobilization of any sort resume.

It is important to recognize that most of the non-electoral types of mobilization were led by disgruntled sections of the middle class, and represented their concerns. The depth of their support was always in question. Thus, the most telling feature of the national phase of the JP movement was the fact that it was Mrs Gandhi, the incumbent Prime Minister, who challenged him to test his support at election time, rather than the reverse. Her confidence in her capability to win an election was demonstrated again in her otherwise inexplicable decision to hold elections in 1977. Conversely, the opposition's lack of confidence on this score was reflected in their insistence that the Prime Minister resign before her appeal to the Supreme Court could be heard. Underlying the views of both parties was the awareness that the very poor might still support the Congress.

Competitive Mobilization, 1977

The sixth general election held in 1977 after the eighteen-month Emergency is a watershed in post-

Independence Indian history. Within days of being released from prison, the leaders of three major non-Communist opposition parties and two dissident factions of Mrs Gandhi's Congress (R) merged to form the Janata Party, which swept the elections in north India and came to power with a majority of two-thirds in the Lok Sabha.[16]

Following the 1977 election, Indian politics changed in three significant and related ways. First, and most obviously, even after the Congress returned to power in 1980, electoral politics was always predicated on the possibility that the incumbent party could lose. This did not mean, however, that agitational politics ceased to be important. Quite the contrary; the second major change was in the ways that movement and protest politics became almost institutionalized, forming part of a continuum of interest representation, with movements frequently transforming themselves into parties. This, in turn, reflected the broadening social profile of active political mobilization, most obviously represented by the coming of age of two important social groups, the middle peasantry and the backward classes or OBCs.

The emergence of the middle peasantry as an important 'demand group', as they were termed by Rudolph and Rudolph, was directly related to the Green Revolution strategy of the 1960s. The decision to subsidize the spread of chemical fertilizers, HYV seeds, and irrigation in areas where farmers seemed willing to adopt them had resulted in improved yields, and created a new class of small and medium farmers who produced for the market. With Charan Singh's BLD now a principal constituent of the Janata Party, farmers' interests were placed at the forefront of the Janata Party's agenda. The avowed aim of the Janata Party was to introduce a more Gandhian model of economic development that put the countryside first, and for Charan Singh in particular, this meant not only reducing the share of investment going to industry, but also opening up opportunities for new agrarian classes to invest in small-scale industry. Thus, the influence of the middle peasantry was seen not only in policies concerning the farm sector, but also in industrial policy, and particularly in the expansion of the policy of reserving certain lines of manufacture for the small industry sector (Tyabji 1989). In short,

the interests of the upper peasantry did not lie simply in preserving their status, but lay also in the opportunities to transform themselves into something other than farmers.

A similar logic can be found in the other major social group that came into its own in the Janata period. This was the OBCs, whose cause had been championed by the Lohia socialists, who eventually merged into the BKD, as well as by the DMK in Tamil Nadu. The OBCs are, of course, a highly elastic social category, whose existence stems from a constitutional provision that permits states to identify disadvantaged groups 'other' than the constitutionally protected categories of Scheduled Castes (SCs) and Scheduled Tribes (STs), and to provide for educational and employment preferences for such groups. This open-ended provision meant that both the questions of *who* was backward and the question of what preferences they would receive became the subject of state politics. In the event, the only states that made serious use of these provisions were the southern states of Karnataka and Tamil Nadu, both of which had a history of reservations for OBCs even before Independence. The Janata government appointed the Mandal Commission to carry out a nation-wide survey of castes and communities and recommend a single nation-wide list of OBCs. This single act not only defined a new social coalition, but also created a rift in another.

Beginning with the merger of the Lohiaite socialists with Charan Singh's farmer party, there has been an effort in India to create a grand coalition of the middle and poorer peasants classified as OBCs. This social cluster was even celebrated in the 1980s by numerous authors as an emerging hegemonic social coalition that would transform Indian politics by moving social power decisively downwards. However, there were significant contradictions between the interests of the middle peasantry and the OBCs. Much of the middle peasantry came from land-controlling 'dominant' peasant communities in northwest or peninsular India—Jats, Patidars, Marathas, Kammas, Reddis, Lingayatas, and Vokkaligas—whose members were not easily classified as 'backward'.[17]

The Mandal Commission carried out its task through state-by state surveys that attempted to identify which castes existed—itself not a simple act, as the unit 'caste' could be taken to mean small local *jatis*(castes) or large clusters of jatis—and then determine whether these 'castes' were relatively 'backward' according to a long list of criteria, which included comparing the caste's average measures of economic well-being to the state average. When the Commission was done, the list varied tremendously across states. It included the bulk of the cultivating peasantry in some regions, notably eastern UP and Bihar, but excluded the Jats of Haryana, Rajasthan, and western UP, the Patidars of Gujarat, Maratha/Kunbis of Maharashtra, Reddis and Kammas in Andhra Pradesh, and Vokkaligas and Lingayats in Karnataka. This did reflect a certain social reality—not only did 'backward' peasant castes like Yadavs come from poorer regions, but their relative social status in those regions was often lower. Partly due to ecological reasons and partly due to historical ones—British land revenue settlements in the peninsula and northwest tended to be with the village-level cultivator, and in the east and northeast with revenue farmers—regions where peasants were described as 'backward' typically had a more hierarchical social structure. Paradoxically, the middle peasant/OBC coalition was rescued temporarily by the collapse of the Janata government in 1979 and the return of Mrs Gandhi's Congress (I) to power in 1980. The Congress (I) indefinitely shelved the implementation of the Mandal Commission Report. Not until the Janata Dal government of 1989/90 was the Mandal Commission Report brought back to the political agenda.

Between 1980 and 1990, both middle peasant and backward-caste issues were active sources of mobilization, but on a state-by-state basis and not necessarily in tandem. Beginning with the Tamil Nadu Agriculturalist Association's (TNAA) agitation over the cost of power to pumpsets in 1978, farmer's organizations became prominent in a number of regions, where they used direct action tactics that included blocking roads and occasionally engaging in violence against government property in order to focus attention on the basic economic issues of procurement price and input cost.[18] They succeeded in gradually increasing the effective subsidy to agriculture, but did not succeed in enabling the shift in sectoral priorities called for by the more ambitious farmers' representatives or in institutionalizing farmer power in

decision-making, in part because they were divided by both economic and cultural considerations.[19] However, appeals to farmer interests were successful in Haryana, where, in 1987, Devi Lal led the Lok Dal, once the party of Charan Singh, to victory.

Similarly, while the Congress government at the Centre shelved the Mandal Commission Report, individual state Congress governments introduced backward-class reservations. However, in accordance with the logic of the sandwich alliance, they did so in states where dominant peasant castes had been excluded from the OBC label, such as Karnataka and Gujarat, but not in UP and Bihar where the large Yadav caste cluster was identified as OBC. In Gujarat, where violent middle-class riots against the reservations policy eventually forced the resignation of Chief Minister Madhavsinh Solanki and the withdrawal of reservations, Congress had built its famous 'KHAM' coalition—composed of 'Kshatriyas' (principally composed of an upwardly mobile OBC group), Harijans (Dalits), Adivasis, and Muslims—which pointedly excluded Patidars, the peasant proprietor caste who had come to dominate the state's professional and political life, and which was not included in the OBC category. Conversely, in Karnataka, where the backward caste lists drawn up by the Congress government of Devraj Urs had excluded the two dominant peasant castes, the subsequent Janata Party government of Ramakrishna Hegde in Karnataka found itself in a continuous tussle over the efforts of these castes, which formed the backbone of the state Janata Party, to be included in the backward caste lists.

During the election of 1989, opposition forces sought again to unite middle-class peasants and OBCs into a single anti-hegemonic alliance. This was done in three stages: first, the various agrarian and socialist factions of the erstwhile Janata Party merged into the Janata Dal (JD) under the leadership of Congress rebel leader V.P. Singh; second, they formed an alliance called the National Front with like-minded regional parties; and third, the National Front agreed on seat adjustments with both the BJP and the Communist Party of India—Marxist (CPI[M]) in order to minimize the division of the Congress vote. At least in the Hindi states, the

JD's 1989 election campaign wove a single populist tapestry out of promises to farmers to write off their debts and increase investment in agriculture, promises of reservations for the backward classes, and charges of corruption against Rajiv Gandhi. However, once in power, as a minority government existing on 'outside support' from the Left and the Right, the JD government found it difficult to hold its various constituencies together, leave alone satisfy outside supporters. At that time V.P. Singh's unilateral decision to implement the Mandal Commission recommendations brought about the demise of not only his government and his party, but also the middle peasant/OBC coalition.[20] After 1990, the available evidence suggests that the support of middle peasant groups swung decisively towards the BJP in many states including Gujarat and northern Karnataka or towards regional parties allied with it.

The BJP itself, of course, was the other pole of all-India political mobilization in the 1980s. Formed after the Janata experiment had broken down, it drew members of both the erstwhile Jana Sangh and Swatantra parties into a new right-wing party that initially sought to break its association with the militant Hindu nationalism of the Jana Sangh. However, the party's disastrous performance in the 1984 elections, when it won only two seats, led to a new strategy, which Jaffrelot (1996) has termed 'ethnonationalist mobilization'. The centrepiece of this strategy was of course the movement to replace the Babri mosque in Ayodhya with a temple dedicated to Ram. Launched in 1987, the movement may well have benefited from the broadcast of Hindu epics by the Rajiv Gandhi government (Rajagopal 2001), and it is credited with creating a mass base for the BJP, which won 86 seats in the 1989 elections. Yet, the BJP's vote share was not much higher than the range of the erstwhile Jana Sangh. This does not suggest that the initial Babri Masjid movement had greatly widened the BJP's base prior to 1989. Rather, it was only after the BJP revived the movement in 1990, immediately after V.P. Singh's ill-fated decision to implement Mandal, that we see a major shift in votes for the BJP, much of it at the expense of the JD, in states like Gujarat, Rajasthan, and UP, where the Dal had received the support of dominant peasant castes.[21]

The two agitations, over the Mandal recommendations and the Babri Masjid/Ram Mandir controversy, merged, as many scholars (for example, Parikh 1998) have pointed out and so did the underlying cleavages they represented. The Mandir agitation was viewed by many as a way to undermine OBC reservations and was supported by groups opposed to reservations; conversely, the two JD chief ministers of UP and Bihar, both OBCs from the Yadav caste cluster, became the champions of minority rights and secularism, taking police action against the provocative march led by BJP president Advani to Ayodhya. Thereafter, politics in many states began to lean towards an upper caste versus lower caste pattern, with dominant peasant castes giving the former a mass base they had never had.

Other cleavages, too, opened up in the 1980s and 1990s. There were dramatic increases in separatist and other ethnic violence in Punjab, Assam, and Kashmir (in addition to the long-standing separatist war in Nagaland). These conflicts demonstrated the limits and possible pitfalls of electoral mobilization.[22] However, in Punjab and Assam the incorporation of separatist sentiments through regional parties was an important part of the solution to these conflicts, and in Kashmir, too, if a solution is to be found, it will have to involve the revitalization of electoral processes.

The 1990s also saw the emergence of more militant forms of mobilization among the Dalits or SCs. This was most notable in north India with the rise of the Bahujan Samaj Party (BSP), which completed the decimation of the Congress in UP by mobilizing their Dalit voters away from them. However, and importantly, although the BSP's rhetoric emphasizes a cleavage between Dalits and the upper castes, it is with the OBCs that the BSP has found it most difficult to work carrying on a feud with the OBC-dominated Samajwadi Party as late as the 2009 elections. In UP, this initially enabled the BJP to create its own sandwich alliance by allying with the BSP.

The BJP's expansion in the 1990s was due to sandwich tactics used in other, less obvious ways. The two most important were first, the effort to split the OBC category in UP and Bihar by courting the less prosperous castes among the OBC groups, who had come to resent Yadav dominance in the OBC coalition. Second, the BJP very adroitly challenged centre-periphery cleavages in a number of states by supporting the creation of new states in the disaffected regions of existing ones. In particular, the BJP's support for the formation of the state of Jharkhand in Bihar represented an effort to undercut the seemingly impregnable electoral fortress of Lalu Prasad Yadav's Rashtriya Janata Dal (RJD).

In the final analysis, however, the most successful use of sandwich tactics continue to be practiced by the Congress, which survived as a viable contender for power between 1996 and 2004 by emphasizing issues of poverty and championing the rights of religious minorities. Even when the party appeared to have been virtually wiped out in the two largest states, UP and Bihar, it retained a base in much of the country, primarily among the poor, allowing it to remain the largest party in terms of votes.

The use of sandwich tactics also explains the Congress party's return to power in 2004 at the head of the United Progressive Alliance (UPA) and, even more, its stunning victory in 2009, when it became the first full-term government to be re-elected in twenty-five years and the first party in eighteen years to cross 200 seats, increased its vote share and revived in UP winning a quarter of the seats while contesting without allies there. These victories make clear that the party's ability to retain a substantial base during the 1990s, especially among the poor, received far less notice at the time than it deserved. There is certainly no space to provide an explanation here, but a hypothesis consistent with the argument of this chapter can be offered. A good part of the explanation, I surmise, lies in the large poverty alleviation programmes initiated by the Congress government in the 1980s and 1990s.

As I have already indicated, sandwich alliances have relative policy preferences not absolute ones, so no exhaustive list of policies that supported Congress' pro-poor image can be given. Some important measures, though, can be mentioned. All had a social insurance thrust rather than seeking to alter the structural condition of poverty. First, the Integrated Rural Development Programme (IRDP) launched by Charan Singh was transformed by Mrs Gandhi from a plan to give local governments development funds to a micro-loan programme, which was widely criticized

for creating no enduring assets and for not reaching the poorest members of rural society. However, it did distribute substantial funds to the nearly poor. Second, and more importantly, rural employment schemes modelled on the successful employment guarantee scheme (EGS) of Maharashtra were launched in the 1980s, and gradually, in the 1990s, displaced the IRDP as the principal source of Central government social welfare funds. Finally, school lunch programmes, used successfully by the AIADMK in Tamil Nadu, became popular in several Congress states, notably Madhya Pradesh, and a part of the Congress national manifestos from the 1990s on.

Finally, of course, the National Rural Employment Guarantee Act (NREGA) of 2005, which guarantees a hundred days of work a year on public work projects to every poor rural household, was the centerpiece of the 2004–9 UPA government's social programmes. The history of Congress-initiated rural social insurance programmes reminds us that the NREGA was a logical extension of twenty-five years of Congress policy, not merely a policy grafted on by the UPA's allies in the Left front, as some have suggested.

The 2009 elections have provided important pieces of evidence in support of the main argument of this chapter. To reprise, the argument is that Indian political mobilization revolves around two strategies of alliance building—anti-hegemonial alliances and sandwich alliances; that the advantage has historically been with sandwich alliances owing to the internal contradictions within anti-hegemonial alliances; and that the Congress party's long survival is due to its repeated reinvention of the sandwich alliance in different periods. While the rise of the BJP in the 1990s made this interpretation seem dated, four outcomes of the 2009 elections provide support to it.

First, and most importantly, the early evidence from exit polls and election reports suggests strongly that the NREGA was a major, and perhaps the most important reason for the Congress' victory in 2009, providing strong evidence for the continued relevance of sandwich alliances in Indian politics.

A second notable outcome is the success of the Janata Dal (United), or JD(U), in Bihar, where the RJD's longstanding coalition of OBCs and Dalits collapsed this time around. Analyses of Bihar politics suggest two reasons for this—Chief Minister Nitish Kumar's successful record on development in such areas as building infrastructure, and his ability to woo the less privileged segments among both OBCs and Dalits (Sharma 2009). Nitish Kumar, in other words, built a sandwich alliance of his own.

Third is the marked decline in the overall in the BJP's national vote share, which went down from 22 per cent in 2004 to 18 per cent in 2009, despite the BJP contesting many more seats, which reflected the loss of key allies in West Bengal, Orissa, and Andhra Pradesh. By contrast the Congress remains steady at about 26 per cent to 28 per cent over the last three elections, with relatively few allies. This suggests strongly that the idea that a bipolar contest between the Congress and the BJP was emerging was overstated.[23]

Finally, however, the various constituents of the erstwhile JD, formed, as an anti-hegemonial alliance in the 1980s, remain viable. In the 2009 elections former JD parties won sixty-nine seats.[24] Moreover, for the first time in a decade, most are relatively free of strong commitments to either of the major parties. The electoral situation does not rule out, and the framework developed here would suggest, a recoalescing of the JD and National Front as an alternate pole in Indian politics.

CONCLUSION

This brief survey of a century of political mobilization in India has obviously left out many examples, especially at the regional and local levels. Neither has it been exhaustive in surveying the types of mobilization that occur in India. The short shrift given to popular movements and other kinds of direct action by subaltern groups is greatly regretted.

What I have focused on, however, is the type of mobilization that sustains or challenges the overarching democratic regime. The strategies and processes that create, break down, and recreate social coalitions in the party system are central to this. Fortunately, it is one of the attributes of Indian democracy that there is a fair amount of exchange between the party system of mobilization and extra-party mobilizations, and I have attempted to focus on these interactions.

The central thesis of the essay is that two broad recurring patterns of alliance building have played a major role in the formation and mobilization of social cleavages. The anti-hegemonic coalition and the sandwich tactic are recurring devices for coalition-building that have been used with different kinds of substantive social cleavages and have parallels elsewhere. Recognizing them will help to establish a basis for more fruitful comparisons to political mobilization in other countries.

Secondly, I have tried to indicate that formal politics matter. Government policies and elected politicians help to shape cleavages around which political mobilization occurs. This is evident in the centrality of government policy to opposition mobilization in the 1960s and the dramatic effect that the Mandal Report had on cleavage patterns in the late 1980s.

Finally, I have indicated a need for a systematic comparative study of the cleavage structures of Indian states. Such a study would help us to not only understand past patterns of mobilization, but also perhaps to anticipate future ones.

NOTES

1. In comparative politics, 'structural' explanations focus on broad socio-economic parameters, in particular the distribution of power among classes. I use the term 'macro-analytic'—adapted from Skocpol and Somers' (1980: 174–97) 'macro-causal' category—to refer to explanations that focus on the general attributes of a polity—both structural and institutional ones—as opposed to the 'micro-analytic' examination of the interplay of actors and groups within it. While micro-analytic explanations today are usually identified with rational choice theory, any focus on political process would fit this description. The historical institutionalist school (Steinmo et al. 1992) straddles the two varieties. The study of political strategy clearly falls into the micro-analytic camp.

2. This is most commonly found to be true for nationalist, ethnic, or other kinds of cultural movements. See, for example, the work of Deutsch (1953, 1961), Gellner (1983), and Brass (1974, 1991).

3. As Lipset and Rokkan's (1967) theory is largely derived from the prior work of Stein Rokkan, originally

published in Norwegian, I will refer to this approach as 'Rokkanian'.

4. Ironically, this tends to be true even of game theory, which takes strategy as the object of its inquiry, as these approaches tend to be highly deterministic, treating the choice of strategy as a necessary consequence of the strategic situation or 'game' that actors face.

5. Arguably, the formation of the Indian National Congress was itself an instance of an anti-hegemonic alliance against the British. One might also add an alliance of middle peasant and backward caste-based parties in the 1980s, though this is in some ways a transition between the 1960s and 1990s variants.

6. Borrowing from rational choice theory, we can think of redistributive policies in a sandwich alliance as 'side-payments' elites make to marginalized groups to avoid more costly payments to counter-elites.

7. I sketched out some explanatory factors, including variations in patterns of cultivation and the different types of revenue systems by the British, in Swamy (1997) and the appendix to Swamy (1996).

8. See, especially, Weiner (1967, 1989), Rudolph and Rudolph (1987), and Varshney (1998).

9. See Rudolph and Rudolph (1987) and Kohli (1990). Kohli saw the sharpening of electoral competition as driving a politics of 'competitive populism', while Rudolph and Rudolph, who popularized the term 'deins titutionalization', blamed Indira Gandhi for turning to a plebiscitary style of politics.

10. To cite the two most famous examples, Bardhan (1984) argued that investment was constrained by the rent-seeking activities of 'rich farmers', business, and a white-collar middle class, while Frankel (1978) suggested that the democratic compromise prevented land reform.

11. Cited in Brown (1985).

12. Cited in Coupland (1944).

13. The DMK was, of course, descended from the *Dravida Kazhagam*, which had sought an independent Dravidian state, and from the Justice Party, which founded the Non-Brahmin Movement. However, it was the DMK that became, effectively, a Tamil separatist party. See Barnett (1976) for a detailed account.

14. See the various essays in Brass (1984a).

15. Also known as the single-member plurality (SMP) method, this allows for one representative per district or constituency to be elected on the basis of a plurality, thereby making it possible for the largest party in a multi-party system to win most or even, in theory, all the seats even with a minority of the votes. Single-member plurality is also used in Canada and, in conjunction with a presidential system of government, in the United States.

16. The three opposition parties were the Jana Sangh,

the Congress (O), and the Bharatiya Lok Dal, itself formed by earlier mergers among Charan Singh's BKD, the SSP, and the Swatantra and other parties. Of the two dissident Congress (R) factions, one was the Congress for Democracy led by Dalit leader Jagjivan Ram, who had defected as soon as the Emergency was lifted. The other group, comprising of former socialist 'young Turks' like Chandra Shekhar, had been imprisoned during the Emergency and had no name.

17. There were probably differences of interest between the richer and poorer farmers of, for example, western UP and eastern UP respectively, but these did not take on a zero-sum game. In principle, all could benefit from higher prices or cheaper credit to the farm sector.

18. For a review of these issues, see Varshney (1994).

19. The most important organizations are the Bharatiya Kisan Union (BKU) in the Punjab/Haryana/western UP Jat belt, Sharad Joshi's Shetkari Sanghatana in Maharashtra, and the Karnataka Raitha Sangha.

20. V.P. Singh was most probably motivated by his rivalry for leadership of the JD with Devi Lal of Haryana, who had claimed Charan Singh's mantle as leader of the Jat caste cluster and the prosperous farmer interest in northern India. Devi Lal himself faced a challenge from Charan Singh's son, Ajit Singh.

21. I made this argument in Swamy (2004). It should be cautioned that since the BJP and the JD had a tactical alliance over much of India in 1989, we cannot easily determine which party benefited more from the votes of the other. However, the virtual disappearance of the JD from Gujarat and Rajasthan, where it had shared power on an equal basis with the BJP, strongly indicates that this was the case.

22. In at least two—Assam and Kashmir—and possibly all three, electoral reverses suffered by the regionally dominant ethnic group were important in the motivation for separatism.

23. Vote figures from Election Commission of India.

24. This is the total for the Samajwadi Party (23), ID(D) (20), BJD (14), RLD (5) RJD (4), and JD(S) (3).

REFERENCES

Baker, C.J. and D.A. Washbrook. 1975. *South India: Political Institutions and Political Change, 1880–1940*. Delhi: Macmillan.

Bardhan, Pranab. 1984. *The Political Economy of Development in India*. New York: Oxford University Press.

Barnett, Marguerite Ross. 1976. *The Politics of Cultural Nationalism in South India*. Princeton: Princeton University Press.

Brass, Paul R. 1991. *Ethnicity and Nationalism: Theory and Comparison*. New Delhi: Sage Publications.

———. 1984a. *Caste, Faction and Party in Indian Politics, Vol. 1: Faction and Party*. New Delhi: Chanakya Publications.

———. 1984b. 'Division in the Congress and the Rise of Agrarian Interests and Issues in Uttar Pradesh Politics', in John R. Wood (ed.), *State Politics in Contemporary India: Crisis or Continuity*. Boulder and London: Westview Press, pp. 21–52.

———. 1974. *Language, Religion and Politics in North India*. Cambridge: Cambridge University Press.

Brown, Judith. 1985. *Modern India: The Origins of an Asian Democracy*. Oxford University Press.

Bouton, Marshall M. 1985. *Agrarian Radicalism in South India*. Princeton: Princeton University Press.

Byres, Terence. 1993. 'Charan Singh, 1902-87: An Assessment', in David Arnold and Peter Robb (eds), *Institutions and Ideologies: A SOAS South Asia Reader*. London: Curzon Press Ltd., pp. 265–301.

Collier, Ruth Berins and David Collier. 1991. *Shaping the Political Arena: Critical Junctures, the Labor Movement and Regime Dynamics in Latin America*. Princeton: Princeton University Press.

Coupland, Reginald. 1944. *The Indian Problem: Report on the Constitutional Problem in India*. New York, London: Oxford University Press.

Deutsch, Karl W. 1961. 'Social Mobilization and Political Development', *American Political Science Review*, Vol. 55 (September), pp. 634–47.

———. 1953. *Nationalism and Social Communication*. Cambridge, MA: MIT Press.

Erdman, Howard. 1967. *The Swatantra Party and Indian Conservatism*. Cambridge, UK: Cambridge University Press.

Frankel, Francine. 1978. *India's Political Economy, 1947-77: The Gradual Revolution*. Princeton: Princeton University Press.

Frankel, Francine and M.S.A. Rao. 1989/1990. *Dominance and State Power in Modern India: Decline of a Social Order*, Vols 1 and 2. New Delhi: Oxford University Press.

Galanter, Marc. 1984. *Competing Equalities: Law and the Backward Classes in India*. Berkeley: University of California Press.

Gellner, Ernest. 1983. *Nations and Nationalism*. Ithaca: Cornell University Press.

Graham, B.D. 1990. *Hindu Nationalism and Indian Politics: The Origins and Development of the Bharatiya Jana Sangh*. Cambridge: Cambridge University Press.

Harrison, Selig. 1960. *India: The Most Dangerous Decades*. Princeton: Princeton University Press.

Jaffrelot, Christophe. 1996. *The Hindu Nationalist Movement and Indian Politics*. New Delhi: Penguin Books India Ltd.

Kohli, Atul. 1990. *Democracy and Discontent: India's Growing Crisis of Ungovernability*. Cambridge: Cambridge University Press.

Kothari, Rajni. 1989 [1964]. 'The Congress 'System' in India', in Rajni Kothari (ed.), *Politics and the People: In Search of a Humane India*, Vol. 1. New Delhi: Ajanta Publications.

Lipset, Seymour Martin and Stein Rokkan (eds). 1967. *Party Systems and Voter Alignments*. New York: Free Press.

Low, D.A. 1999. *Britain and Indian Nationalism: The Imprint of Ambiguity, 1929-1942*. Cambridge: Cambridge University Press.

———. 1988. 'Congress and "Mass Contacts", 1936-1937: Ideology, Interests and Conflict Over the Basis of Party Representation', in Richard Sisson and Stanley Wolpert (eds), *Congress and Indian Nationalism: The Pre-Independence Phase*. Berkeley: University of California Press, pp. 134–58.

Omvedt, Gail (ed.). 1982. *Land, Caste and Politics in Indian States*. New Delhi: Authors Guild.

Parikh, Sunita. 1998. 'Religion, Reservations and Riots: The Politics of Ethnic Violence in India', in Amrita Basu and Atul Kholi (eds), *Community Conflicts and the State in India*. New Delhi: Oxford University Press, 33–57.

Rajagopal, Arvind. 2001. *Politics after Television: Hindu Nationalism and the Reshaping of the Public in India*. Cambridge: Cambridge University Press.

Rudolph, Lloyd I. and Susanne Hoeber Rudolph. 1987. *In Pursuit of Lakshmi: The Political Economy of the Indian State*. Chicago: The University of Chicago Press.

Sarkar, Sumit. 1989. *Modern India: 1885-1947*. New York: St. Martin's Press.

Sharma, Supriya. 2009. 'Bihar Transformed.' NDTV News Blogs: A Fine Balance, 22 May 2009. Available at http://www.ndtv.com/news/blogs/a_fine_balance/bihar_transformed.php.

Skocpol, Theda and Margaret Somers. 1980. 'The Uses of Comparative History in Macrosocial Inquiry', *Comparative Studies in Society and History*, 22(2), pp. 174–97.

Steinmo, Sven, Kathleen Thelen, and Frank Lonstroth (eds). 1992. *Structuring Politics: Historical Institutionalism in Comparative Analysis*. Cambridge, UK: Cambridge University Press.

Swamy, Arun R. 2004. 'Ideology, Organization and Electoral Strategy of Hindu Nationalism: What's Religion Got to Do With It?', in Satu Limaye, Mohan Malik, and Robert Wirsing (eds), *Religious Radicalism in South*

Asia. Honolulu: Asia Pacific Center for South Asian
Studies.

Swamy, Arun R. 2003. 'Consolidating Democracy by
Containing Distribution: "Sandwich Tactics" in Indian
Party Competition, 1931–96', *India Review*, 2 (2), pp.
1–36.

———. 1998. 'Parties, Political Identities and the Absence
of Mass Political Violence in South India', in Amrita
Basu and Atul Kohli (eds), *Community Conflicts
and the State in India*. New Delhi: Oxford University
Press.

———. 1997. 'National Politics, Regional Politics and Party
Systems' in C. Steven LaRue (ed.), *India Handbook:
Prospects onto the 21st Century*. Chicago: Fitzroy
Dearborn Publishers.

———. 1996. 'The Nation, The People and The Poor:
Sandwich Tactics in Party Strategies and Policy
Models, India 1931–1996', Berkeley. Unpublished
PhD dissertation, University of California, Berkeley.

Tyabji, Nasir. 1989. *The Small Industries Policy in India*.
Calcutta: Oxford University Press.

Varshney, Ashutosh. 1998. 'Why Democracy Survives',
Journal of Democracy, 9(3), pp. 36–50.

———. 1994. *Democracy, Development and the Countryside:
Urban-Rural Struggles in India*. Cambridge, UK:
Cambridge University Press.

Weiner, Myron E. 1989. 'The Indian Paradox', in Myron
E. Weiner (ed.). *The Indian Paradox: Essays in Indian
Politics*. New Delhi: Sage Publications.

———. 1967. *Party-Building in a New Nation: The Indian
National Congress*. Chicago: University of Chicago
Press.

Zaidi, A.M. (ed.). 1986. *Promises to Keep: A Study of the
Election Manifestoes of the Indian National Congress,
1937–1985*. New Delhi: Indian Institute of Applied
Political Research.

19 Political Leadership

Ramachandra Guha

Among the major democracies of the world, India stands out for the sheer size of its electorate. Many of its states are larger than a large European country. At the same time, India stands out also for the social and cultural diversity within this electorate, with voters speaking many different languages, following many different faiths, and divided into thousands of different endogamous groups. Due to its size, it is likely that India has produced many more political leaders than other countries—leaders who have won and lost elections, run and mis-run governments, and exercised the political imagination of their constituents in myriad other ways. As a result of its diversity, it is also likely that the political leaders in India reflect, represent, and act upon a far greater variety of social and economic issues than elsewhere.

In the first weeks of 1952, India held its first general elections. This was an exercise that attracted great interest within and outside the country. Never before had elections been held in a nation where so many of its citizens could not read and write. Some observers were cynical; thus, a British official in the service of the government of free India wrote to his father that 'a future and more enlightened age will view with astonishment the absurd farce of recording the votes of millions of illiterate people'.[1] Others were more hopeful; thus, an American political scientist covering the polls remarked that 'the leading Indian parties and party workers are surpassed by those of no other country in electioneering skill, dramatic presentation of issues, political oratory, or mastery of political psychology' (Park 1952).

In that first election, voters had their choice of parties from across the political spectrum. On the Left, there was the Communist Party of India (CPI), whose cadres had recently come overground after a failed insurrection; on the Right, there was the newly formed Jana Sangh, whose professed policy was to defend and advance the Hindu interest. In the middle was the Congress party, the great legatee of the freedom struggle. But no longer was the Congress as unified as it had once been; in fact, in the lead-up to the elections, some of its most important leaders had left to start parties of their own, such as the Kisan Mazdoor Praja Party (KMPP) and the Socialist Party.

Also contesting the elections were several regional parties, and a party calling itself the Scheduled Caste Federation (SCF).

Each of these parties had gifted and charismatic leaders, each skilled in 'the dramatic presentation of issues' and 'political oratory', and perhaps also in 'mastery of political psychology'. They included the Communist A.K. Gopalan and the Socialist Jayaprakash Narayan, S.P. Mookerjee of the Jana Sangh, B.R. Ambedkar of the SCF, and J.B. Kripalani of the KMPP. The Congress had its own array of stalwarts, spread across the states—they included Gobind Ballabh Pant in Uttar Pradesh, B.C. Roy in Bengal, K. Kamaraj in Madras, S. Nijalingappa in Mysore, and Morarji Desai in Bombay. Towering above his party men, and above all the others, was the Congress President and Indian Prime Minister, Jawaharlal Nehru.

Since those epochal polls of 1952, India has witnessed fourteen further general elections, as well as countless elections to state assemblies. These elections, and the governments they have given rise to, have produced a variety of leaders, professing a variety of ideologies and using a variety of political methods with varying degrees of effectiveness. Because of its size, India has probably produced *more* political leaders than other democracies; because of its diversity, it has almost certainly produced more *interesting* ones.

For all this, the academic literature on political leadership in India is scarce. There was a promising beginning, when a conference was organized in 1956 at the University of California under the title 'Leadership and Political Institutions in India'. The proceedings were later published; the articles included explorations of the traditional Hindu ideas of leadership; appreciations of the great nationalist leaders Subhas Chandra Bose, Jawaharlal Nehru, and Vallabhbhai Patel; analyses of the major political parties then active in India; and ethnographic accounts of leaders and factions within castes and villages (Park and Tinker 1959).

Unfortunately, this volume of the 1950s remains the sole published contribution to the subject. In subsequent decades, political scientists have written with insight and depth about the functioning of parties and the process of voting in India, but less

so about Indian political leaders. If we except those two long-serving Prime Ministers, Jawaharlal Nehru and Indira Gandhi, there have been few biographies of our major politicians. Major politicians of major states have been relegated to the status of 'provincial' leaders, even when their province consists of forty or fifty million people. There are no serious studies, for example, of the life and work of Sheikh Abdullah of Kashmir, or E.M.S. Namboodiripad of Kerala, or Master Tara Singh of Punjab, or C.N. Annadurai of Tamil Nadu—each of whom had a defining influence on the history and politics of his state.

In the absence of biographies to build upon, scholars have shied away from analytical exercises as well. What have been the major forms of political leadership in independent India? What have been the styles of rhetoric and forms of social mobilization associated with each of these forms? How do these change in and out of office? How do different kinds of leaders and leadership strategies interact with one another? These and related questions are scarcely touched upon in the literature.

This chapter draws upon research conducted over a number of years on the social and political history of independent India. The object of that exercise was empirical rather than analytical—its object being to narrate a history (in fact, multiple histories) rather than frame or design concepts (Guha 2007).[2] Drawing on that research, this chapter offers a preliminary typology of the forms of political leadership in independent India. It takes as its point of departure an earlier—but apparently failed—attempt to open up the field. This was an essay by W.H. Morris-Jones, which distinguished between three political idioms in India, which he called the 'modern', the 'traditional', and the 'saintly', respectively.

In Morris-Jones's definition, 'the modern language of politics is the language of the Indian Constitution and the Courts; of parliamentary debate; of the higher administration...' It 'is a language of ... programmes and plans'. On the other hand, the traditional idiom of politics 'knows little or nothing of the problems of anything as big as India and its vocabulary scarcely includes policies and Plans'. Its concerns are local and sectarian: thus, 'caste (or subcaste or "community") is the core of traditional politics'. Finally, there was the saintly idiom, illustrated at the time Morris-Jones was writing by the work of Acharya Vinoba Bhave, 'the "Saint on the March" who tours India on foot preaching the path of self-sacrifice and love and polity without power' (Morris-Jones 1963).

Morris-Jones's framework, suitably modified and elaborated, is still useful in understanding the styles of political leadership that have been on display in independent India. The paradigmatic 'modern' leader, of course, was India's first Prime Minister, Jawaharlal Nehru. He thought and acted as if he spoke for India as a whole; not merely or even principally for any section of it. The claim was widely accepted, and endorsed by the three successive victories enjoyed by his Congress party in general elections.

If one tries to read Nehru's political philosophy in Western terms, then the label that probably fits best—or least badly—is 'social democratic'. He was simultaneously a believer in free elections and a free press, and in the state occupying the 'commanding heights' of the economy. His political vision was probably universal and certainly national; and his political practice, in the sense Morris-Jones uses the term, was unquestionably 'modern'. That is, he paid respect to the ideals of the Constitution, to the autonomy of the courts, and to the procedures of parliamentary debate. There was a telling incident early in the procedures of the Constituent Assembly, when a Congress parliamentarian entered the well and started shouting at the President of the Assembly. It was Nehru who got up and persuaded the errant member to return to his seat and maintain the discipline of the House. Afterwards, Nehru told him that 'this is not a public meeting in Jhansi that you should address "Bhaio aur Behno" [brothers and sisters] and start lecturing at the top of your voice'.[3]

Nehru also thought in terms of 'programmes and plans'; the Planning Commission was never more important than in his day. All in all, he was a political leader whose style can perhaps be described as 'national-*constitutionalist*'. On the other hand, the style of India's other long-serving Prime Minister, Indira Gandhi, is more accurately described as 'national-populist'. Like Nehru, she took as their theatre of operation the country as a whole—notably, she also led the Congress party to victory in three general

elections. However, she paid far less respect to the formal institutions of a constitutional democracy. Rather than plans and programmes being discussed and debated in Parliament, they were designed and implemented from the Prime Minister's Office. When the Courts and the Constitution raised impediments, the Courts were re-staffed and the Constitution amended. These changes were justified by the claim that the political leader in question had the support of the people. Hence my preferred term of description for this style of political leadership: 'national-*populist*'.

Where Nehru and Indira claimed to act for India as a whole, other political leaders have had a more restricted sphere of operation. Some of the most interesting leaders have operated at the level of the state or province. They have based their politics on the claim that they, and the party they led, most fully represented the interests of the people of their state.

Consider thus the careers of Sheikh Abdullah, from the state of Jammu and Kashmir in the far north; and of C.N. Annadurai, from the state of Tamil Nadu (previously Madras) in the deep south. Both led political parties—the National Conference in the first case, the Dravida Munnetra Kazhagam in the latter— that professed to represent the interests of a specific, vulnerable, linguistic group against a powerful and unfeeling Centre. Both were brilliantly gifted orators, with an ability to hold an audience spellbound, and to leave them with words and phrases that circulated for weeks afterwards. Both spent long periods as rebels (Abdullah was in jail for eleven years), but both also had spells as rulers, as elected Chief Ministers of their states. Both toyed with the idea of independence, yet both eventually abandoned secessionism for a place within the Indian Constitution.

A near-contemporary of Abdullah and Annadurai was the Sikh leader, Master Tara Singh. Unlike them, he never fought elections to the state assembly. He was simultaneously a mentor of a political party, the Akali Dal, and the leader of an influential and wealthy religious body, the Shiromani Gurdwara Parbandhak Committee. Like Abdullah and Annadurai, he inveighed against the domination of New Delhi and the Congress party. His main demand was for a separate state of Punjabi speakers, a demand fulfilled only after his death.

The movements led by Abdullah and Annadurai were based on the identities of language and region; that led by Tara Singh on the identities of language, region, and religion. Contemporaneous with these movements was the struggle for Jharkhand, which was based on the claims of territory and ethnicity. This aimed to create a separate state within the Indian Union to protect the interests of the tribals of central India in general, and the tribals of the Chotanagpur Plateau in particular. The initiator of the Jharkhand movement was Jaipal Singh, another gifted orator who was deeply revered by his followers, who bestowed upon him the title of 'Marang Gomke' (Great Leader). Jaipal formed a Jharkhand Party, which fought both assembly and parliamentary elections. However, it was only in 1998, long after his death, that a Jharkhand state was created out of the tribal districts of Bihar.

In later years, among the more important regional leaders in India have been the film stars-turned-politicians N.T. Rama Rao (NTR) of Andhra Pradesh and M.G. Ramachandran (MGR) of Tamil Nadu. Linguistic nationalism was perhaps at its most intense in south India. It found its fullest expression in the field of films. Among largely illiterate populations, cinema quickly became the chief form of popular entertainment. The leading film stars emerged as the symbols and embodiments of the people's tongue. Their success on the silver screen prepared NTR and MGR for their second, and equally successful, career in the sphere of politics, where, like the Sheikh and Anna before them, they were able to persuade the electorate that they best embodied the interests of the state against the Centre.

It is tempting also to see E.M.S. Namboodiripad and Jyoti Basu as essentially 'regional' leaders. The ideology they professed faith in, Communism, was in theory not confined to the region, nor indeed to the country even. It stood, indeed, for a *world* proletarian revolution, to be brought about by armed struggle. In practice, however, the bullet was abandoned in favour of the ballot box, through which success was found, episodically, in three states of the Indian Union, Kerala, West Bengal, and Tripura.

For long stretches of time, Communism in Kerala was identified with E.M.S. Namboodripad,

and Communism in West Bengal with Jyoti Basu. In power and out of power, they spoke out against the domination of the Congress party and of the Central government. Jyoti Basu's government, it was said, began every discussion on federalism with the words, 'Centre *kom diyé ché*' (the Centre has given us less than our rightful share).

In these respects, the rhetoric of Namboodiripad and Basu was akin to that used by other regional leaders. However, within their states they followed a more actively redistributive agenda, favouring the interests of the landless against the propertied classes. On the other hand, the policies of the more conventional kind of regional leader (such as MGR and NTR) were based on subsidies and hand-outs. Perhaps we may define these styles of political leadership as 'Communist-regional' and 'populist-regional' respectively.

The most influential and pervasive forms of Indian regionalism have been based on language. This is a traditional or ascriptive identity, into which one is born. Another traditional identity with a powerful political resonance is, of course, religion. As we have seen, the politics of the Akali Dal has been based on the claims of language *and* religion. Before Independence, a powerful political party based exclusively on the claims of faith was the Muslim League, whose leader, Muhammad Ali Jinnah, presented himself as the 'sole spokesman' of the Muslims of the subcontinent (Jalal 1985).

After Independence, the most successful party based on religion has been the Bharatiya Janata Party (or BJP), which was known in an earlier incarnation as the Jana Sangh. Working with its affiliated organizations, the Rashtriya Swayamsewak Sangh (RSS), the Vishwa Hindu Parishad, and the Bajrang Dal, this has sought to construct a unified 'Hindu' community, and then present itself as the most authentic and reliable defender of its interests.

For the first four decades of Indian Independence, this construction had limited success. However, the Ayodhya campaign of the 1980s and 1990s brought much electoral benefit to the BJP. In the 1989 general elections, the party won 11.5 per cent of the votes; in the 1998 elections it won 25.6 per cent. As the largest single party in Parliament, it headed a coalition that ran the Union government for the next six years at a stretch.

In the period of its greatest influence, *c.* 1989–2004, the two most influential BJP leaders were L.K. Advani and Atal Bihari Vajpayee. The former was the 'hard' face of the Hindutva ideology, projected when the party needed to assert a militant and unforgiving image, hard on India's 'evil' neighbour Pakistan and harder still on its 'unreliable' minorities. The latter was the 'soft' or benign face, projected when political compulsions called for dialogue with Pakistan or for tolerance towards the minorities.

More recently, a BJP leader has combined two varieties of 'traditional' politics—the one based on the identity of region or language, and the other based on the identity of religion. This is the Gujarat Chief Minister, Narendra Modi. His policies and practices sometimes seek to pose Hindus against Muslims, and at other times Gujarat against the rest of India.

Language and religion are important markers of identity; so too is caste. In recent years, in fact, caste has probably played as crucial a role in political mobilization as those other forms of group attachment. As the joke goes: 'Elsewhere, you cast your vote; in India, you vote your caste'.

Here, it is necessary to distinguish between two meanings of caste: *jati*, the endogamous group one is born into; and *varna*, the place that group occupies in the system of social stratification mandated by Hindu scripture. There are four varnas, with the former 'untouchables' constituting a fifth (and lowest) strata. Into these varnas fit the 3000 and more jatis, each challenging those in the same region that are ranked above it, and being in turn challenged by those below.

In the sphere of democratic politics, those belonging to the three top strata constitute the 'forward' castes, and those belonging to the fourth and fifth stratas the 'backward' castes. Although no precise figures are available, those in the fourth strata (known generally as the Other Backward Classes or OBCs) are probably little more than 50 per cent of the Hindu population, and those in the fifth strata (known as Scheduled Castes [SCs] or Dalits) a little less than 20 per cent.

Despite their numerical preponderance, the OBCs and Dalits had historically been denied political,

administrative, economic, and social power. The Congress, which ran the government at the Centre from 1947 to 1977 and was also in office in many states, was dominated by the forward castes. Its main leaders, with rare exceptions, were Brahmins, Kayasths, and Kshatriyas. Again, the Jana Sangh was once known, not without reason, as a 'Brahmin-Bania' party. The CPI claimed to fight for the downtrodden, yet (as its critics never failed to point out) its most influential leaders were often Brahmins.

In the 1950s, B.R. Ambedkar tried to build a political platform for the Dalits; in the 1960s, the socialist theoretician Rammanohar Lohia attempted to do the same for the OBCs. Their successes were limited; however, in the 1980s and 1990s their ideas were revived and amplified by a new generation of caste-based parties. The Bahujan Samaj Party founded by Kanshi Ram (and later led by Mayawati) has provided a powerful vehicle for the political aspirations of the Dalits. Likewise, Mulayam Singh Yadav's Samajwadi Party and Lalu Prasad Yadav's Rashtriya Janata Dal have projected themselves as parties that represented the interests of backward castes against the forwards. All these parties enjoyed spells—sometimes lengthy ones—in the government.

These three varieties of politics—based on language or region, religion, and caste, respectively—have a great deal in common. They all seek to define a political community on a basis of a single, primordial, identity. They all claim that their party alone represents the interests of the community so defined. Sometimes the interests are defensive: the resisting of other political communities that seek to swamp it. At other times the interests are offensive: the claiming by the community of a dominant position for itself.

Political leadership, in this context, is likewise both defensive as well as offensive. As an opposition leader, C.N. Annadurai sought to fight for his Tamil people against the encroachments of the Centre; as the Chief Minister, he sought instead to consolidate Tamil pride. Likewise, Mayawati progressed from attacking the upper castes when out of power to affirming the importance of the Dalits when in power, as for example, by constructing dozens of statues of their revered leader B.R. Ambedkar. Hindutva politicians have also alternated between postures that appear defensive and even at times paranoid (as in the talk of ever increasing Muslim birth rates), and policies that aggressively portray their party as willing to take on the world (as in the atomic tests of 1998).

These three varieties of politics are also akin in the forms of patronage they practice when in office. When, in 1967, the Jana Sangh joined a coalition government in Madhya Pradesh, they asked for the education portfolio, so that 'they could build up a permanent following through the primary schools'. They eventually got Home, where they maintained the communal peace by keeping their followers in check, yet took great care 'to see that no key post in any department went to a Muslim' (Noronha 1976: Ch. 8). Likewise, Dalit officials appear to get many of the key administrative posts in Uttar Pradesh when Mayawati is in power, to be replaced by Yadav officials if Mulayam comes to replace her as Chief Minister.

The modern idiom of politics was based on a wider vision, one that went beyond the sectarian demands of caste, language, and religion. I use the past tense advisedly, for with the fragmentation of the polity, the Government of India is increasingly influenced by the claims of parties based on these identities. Wider visions, whether 'national-constitutionalist' or 'national-populist', have lost their significance and importance. In contrast, sectarian identities have grown in political influence.

The rise of smaller parties which effectively articulate a sectarian identity has led to a deepening of the democratic process. Groups that were previously excluded from decision-making have thrown up chief ministers and even Prime Ministers. Writing in the 1970s, the journalist and old India hand, James Cameron, pointed out that the prominent women in Indian public life all came from upper-class, English-speaking backgrounds. 'There is not and never has been a working-class woman with a function in Indian politics,' remarked Cameron, 'and it is hard to say when there ever will be' (Cameron 1974: 122). Within two decades there was an answer, or perhaps one should say a refutation, when a lady born in a Dalit home became chief minister of India's most populous state.

However, this deepening of democracy has come at a cost, namely that there is now no political leader who can really think of or act for the country as a whole. When a single party was dominant at the Centre, it was possible to design long-range policies; now, when the government is constituted by a coalition of a dozen or more parties, each representing a specific sectarian interest—these based variously on caste, language, region, or religion—its policies are determinedly short-term, aimed at placating or satisfying one or the other of those interests. It is possible that the wide-ranging policies of economic and social development that Jawaharlal Nehru crafted in the 1950s—among them the boost to heavy industrialization, the reform of archaic personal laws, and an independent foreign policy—would not have been feasible in the fragmented and divided polity of today. Even programmes focused on specific sectors, such as the thrust to agricultural development that Lal Bahadur Shastri and Indira Gandhi provided in the 1960s, would now be difficult to bring to fruition. In the past, in allotting portfolios to ministers, their relevant experience and abilities were taken into account. Now, the distribution of ministries is dictated more by the compulsions of having to please alliance partners, who demand portfolios seen either as prestigious or profitable. And in the execution of their duties, cabinet ministers are prone to think more of the interests of their caste, community, party, or state, rather than of India as a whole.

The pattern is reproduced in the states, where ministerial assignments are likewise made not on the basis of aptitude or ability, but according to caste and religious quotas. In Karnataka, Lingayat, and Vokkaliga claims are balanced against one another and against those of the Dalits and the Muslims; in Kerala, Nairs, Ezhavas, Christians, and Muslims all demand representation in proportion to their share of the population. Here, too, while in office, ministers are expected to attend first of all to the interests of their community. In both the Centre and the states, *policy* has therefore become hostage to *patronage*; this is a consequence of the growing assertion of the traditional idiom over the modern. This assertion has led to a significant change in the style and substance of political leadership in India. Arguably, Indira Gandhi was the last genuinely *national* leader in India; after her death, no leader has had a comparable countrywide appeal, cutting across the divides of caste and religion and language.

What, then, of the third idiom of Indian politics, the saintly? W.H. Morris-Jones thought that this operated at the margins of formal politics. His exemplar here was Vinoba Bhave, who never joined a party or campaigned during an election. However, even as he wrote, the saintly idiom was radically reshaping party and electoral politics in one state of the Union, Kerala. Here, the CPI had come to power in the assembly elections of 1957. However, its social and educational policies were controversial and became the target of protest. The opposition to the CPI government was initiated by the Congress—who were not reconciled to their loss of office in the state—yet it was transformed into a widespread popular movement under the leadership of a social worker named Mannath Padmanabhan. An austere, dhoti-clad man, Mannath was greatly respected because of his work in running the schools and colleges of the Nair Service Society. Now, at the age of eighty, he assumed the leadership of a campaign aimed, as he put it, to dispatch 'these Communists, bag and baggage, not merely from Kerala, but from India and driv[e] them to their fatherland—Russia'.[4]

The people of Kerala followed Mannath in part for the same reasons that the people of India had once followed Mahatma Gandhi; namely that his personal integrity was unimpeachable, and that he had never sought or held political office. Under his leadership the movement's message was carried into schools and colleges, churches and temples, into the homes of fisherfolk, peasants, merchants, and workers. The protests spilled out into the street, forcing the government to crack down, the beatings and arrests in turn giving the Centre in New Delhi (where the Congress was in control) an excuse to dismiss the state government and impose President's Rule. In the mid-term elections held in 1960, the Congress was returned to power.

Fifteen years after Mannath Padmanabhan helped transform the political landscape of his state, another 'saint' abandoned social work to help transform the political landscape of his country. This was Jayaprakash Narayan. An authentic hero of the freedom struggle, 'JP' left the Congress after Independence to help start the Socialist Party. Then he left party politics altogether to join Vinoba Bhave in his 'Sarvodaya' movement. He worked on Bhave's land redistribution schemes, but also involved himself in matters of wider import. Through the 1960s, for example, JP worked tirelessly to help reconcile the rebellious Nagas to the Union of India, and to compel New Delhi to grant genuine autonomy to the people of Jammu and Kashmir.

Jayaprakash Narayan commanded respect because of his social work, and also because it was believed that Jawaharlal Nehru had pleaded with him to rejoin politics and become his successor as Prime Minister. That he had turned down high office added greatly to the aura around him. Ever since he had left the Socialists in 1957 he had stayed scrupulously clear of party politics. However, in the spring of 1974, the students of Bihar launched a struggle against corruption in the state administration. The police came down hard; many protestors were badly injured, and several died. Now the students asked JP to join and lead the movement. He agreed, on two conditions—that it be non-violent, and that it not restrict itself to Bihar.

In August 1974, Narayan toured the Bihar countryside, to a rapturous reception. After his tour, he called for a conference of all opposition parties to 'channel the enthusiasm among the people into the nation-wide people's movement'. The Bihar struggle, wrote JP, had 'acquired an all-India importance and the country's fate has come to be bound up with its success and failure'. He appealed to Trade Unions, peasant organizations, and professional bodies to come aboard to help him 'fight corruption and misgovernment and blackmarketing, profiteering and hoarding, to fight for the overhaul of the educational system, and for a real people's democracy' (Bhattacharjea 2004; *Everyman's Weekly* 1974).

The appeal was successful, and through the winter of 1974–5 the opposition to the Central government grew. Notably, this opposition was conducted—as in Kerala in 1958–9—not in the legislature, but in the streets. As the protests intensified, the Allahabad High Court passed a judgement against Prime Minister

Indira Gandhi, who responded by declaring a state of Emergency and jailing her political opponents, Jayaprakash Narayan among them. Strikingly, while the Emergency was at its height, the Prime Minister sought, and obtained, a certificate of approval from Vinoba Bhave, seeking thus to neutralize the moral halo of the saint on the other side.

In 1977 the Emergency was lifted, and fresh elections called. Four Opposition groupings combined to form the Janata Party; with Jayaprakash Narayan as its main campaigner, it won the elections. In this respect, too, JP was Mannath Padmanabhan writ large: like him, he claimed he had no political ambitions of his own; like him, he yet led a movement that successfully brought down an elected government and helped replace it with one that he could bless.

Our three idioms of politics may be differentiated in terms of styles of rhetoric. The modern idiom is often expressed through a rhetoric of *hope*—the offer of a better and fuller life, whether expressed in material terms or otherwise. The traditional idiom, on the other hand, privileges a rhetoric of *fear*—warning the members of a caste, or religion, or region, that they would be swamped by their enemies if they do not bind together. Finally, the saintly idiom expresses itself through a rhetoric of *sacrifice*—the need to give up on worldly ambitions to bring down an immoral regime.

Thus far, I have analysed political leadership in independent India in terms of sociology and ideology—namely the social bases of a leader's support, and the ideas and policies used to legitimize his or her leadership. But the attractions of the leader are often so great, and the devotion of his (or her) flock often so complete, that sociology and ideology are inadequate in understanding them. One must take recourse, therefore, to the Weberian category of 'charisma', where charismatic leaders are the 'bearers of specific gifts of body and mind that were considered "supernatural" (in the sense that not everybody could have access to them)' (Weber *et al.* 1978: 1111–12).

In his pomp, which ran roughly from 1947 to 1957, Jawaharlal Nehru was certainly considered by many (perhaps most) Indians to possess gifts of body and mind that few others had access to. The reverence he commanded was extreme. Thus, when he travelled through India while campaigning in the 1952 general elections,

> almost at every place, city, town, village or wayside halt, people had waited overnight to welcome the nation's leader. Schools and shops closed: milkmaids and cowherds had taken a holiday; the kisan and his helpmate took a temporary respite from their dawn-to-dusk programme of hard work in field and home. In Nehru's name, stocks of soda and lemonade sold out; even water became scarce ... Special trains were run from out-of-the-way places to carry people to Nehru's meetings, enthusiasts travelling not only on foot-boards but also on top of carriages. Scores of people fainted in milling crowds. (Anonymous 1952: 23)

Some of Nehru's charisma was inherited, based on the fact that Gandhi, the Father of the Nation, had nominated him as his political heir; some of it based on his own personal attributes (real or imagined). Likewise, in her pomp—which ran for a much shorter period, say from 1969 to 1973—Indira Gandhi also commanded love and veneration from all social classes and all parts of the nation. Her charisma was also in part inherited (from her father), and in part her own. It was at its height during the elections of 1971, fought and won by Mrs Gandhi on the slogan *Garibi Hatao!* (let's end poverty). In asking for votes, she exploited her 'charming personality', her 'father's historical role', and, above all, that stirring slogan, Garibi Hatao. The message strung a strong chord, for, as one somewhat cynical journalist wrote:

> The man lying in a gutter prizes nothing more than the notion pumped into him that he is superior to the sanitary inspector. That the rich had been humbled looked like the assurance that the poor would be honoured. The instant 'poverty-removal' slogan was an economic absurdity. Psychologically and politically, for that reason, it was however a decisive asset in a community at war with reason and rationality.[5]

The charisma enjoyed by regional and caste leaders is less 'supernatural'. Here, the leader is not bestowed gifts beyond the reach of the ordinary man or woman; rather, he or she is seen as most consistently embodying the aspirations of that ordinary man (or woman). It was said of Master Tara Singh, for example, that he was viewed by many

Sikhs as 'the only consistent and long-suffering upholder of the Panth as a separate political entity, as the one Sikh leader who relentlessly pursued the goal of political power territorially organized for the Sikh community, and as a selfless leader without personal ambition' (Nayar 1960: 143). Many Tamils saw Annadurai in the same way. Backward caste leaders have likewise presented themselves as consistent and long-suffering upholders of the interests of their community.

When it comes to charisma, the great low-caste leader, B.R. Ambedkar, stands in a class of his own. For the charisma he enjoys has grown exponentially since his death. While he lived, Ambedkar was admired for the acuity of his mind and his commitment to social reform. But his political base was limited; he could not even win a reserved seat to the Lok Sabha. Only his fellow Mahars followed him without question, other Dalit sections instead choosing to cast their lot with Gandhi and the Congress. On the other hand, Ambedkar is now venerated in Dalit homes and hamlets all across India. One anthropologist writes that 'across Tamil Nadu, statues, portraits, posters and nameplates bearing the image of Dr Ambedkar proliferate. Halls, schools, and colleges named after him abound and even his ideological opponents feel obliged to reproduce his picture and lay claim to his legacy' (Gorringe 2005: 112). Pretty much the same is true of most other states of the Union. Wherever Dalits live or work, photographs of Ambedkar are ubiquitous: finely framed and lovingly garlanded, placed in prominent positions in hamlets, homes, shops, and offices. Meanwhile, due to pressure from Dalit groups, statues of Ambedkar are put up at public places in towns and cities—at major road intersections, outside railway stations, in parks.

Fifty years after his death, B.R. Ambedkar is worshipped in parts of India which he never visited and where he was completely unknown in his own lifetime. Wherever there are Dalits—which means, pretty much, almost every district in India—Ambedkar is remembered and, more importantly, revered.[6]

One danger of charismatic authority is that it may, if unchecked, lead to the assertion of dictatorial tendencies. As a consequence of her victory in the 1971 elections, wrote Khushwant Singh, 'Indira Gandhi has successfully magnified her figure as the one and only leader of national dimensions'. Then he added, ominously:

> However, if power is voluntarily surrendered by a predominant section of the people to one person and at the same time opposition is reduced to insignificance, the temptation to ride roughshod over legitimate criticism can become irresistible. The danger of Indira Gandhi being given unbridled power shall always be present. (Singh 1971)

In fact, even before the elections Mrs Gandhi had been charged with fostering a cult of personality. As her critic, S. Nijalingappa, pointed out, the history of the twentieth century

> is replete with instances of the tragedy that overtakes democracy when a leader who has risen to power on the crest of a popular wave or with the support of a democratic organisation becomes a victim of political narcissism and is egged on by a coterie of unscrupulous sycophants who use corruption and terror to silence opposition and attempt to make public opinion an echo of authority.[7]

Long before Khushwant Singh and Nijalingappa, B.R. Ambedkar had also warned against the unthinking submission to charismatic authority. Speaking in the Constituent Assembly of India, Ambedkar quoted John Stuart Mill, who cautioned citizens not 'to lay their liberties at the feet of even a great man, or to trust him with powers which enable him to subvert their institutions'. This warning was even more pertinent here than in England, for, as Ambedkar argued,

> in India, Bhakti or what may be called the path of devotion or hero-worship, plays a part in its politics unequalled in magnitude by the part it plays in the politics of any other country in the world. Bhakti in religion may be the road to the salvation of a soul. But in politics, Bhakti or hero-worship is a sure road to degradation and to eventual dictatorship. (*Constituent Assembly of India, Debates* 1988: 979)

These were prescient anticipations of the Emergency of 1975–7, when Indira Gandhi chose to suspend all democratic rights and silence all Opposition. Her ability to do so had been greatly strengthened by her earlier transformation of the Congress into an extension of her will. Once the party was run autocratically, and once it had been given a mandate by the people, it was easy then to equate the interests of the individual with the interests of the nation as a whole. (As a Congressman of the time famously put it: 'Indira is India, and India is Indira'.) Jawaharlal Nehru, on the other hand, could not always get his way even within the Congress party. It must also be said that, unlike Mrs Gandhi, Nehru was conscious of the need to suppress the authoritarian instincts within him, and aware also that political popularity was 'often the handmaiden of undesirable persons; it was certainly not an invariable sign of virtue and intelligence' (Nehru 1936 [1949]: 204; Fischer 1959).

The conversion of charisma into authoritarianism, carried out at an all-India level by Indira Gandhi, has been manifested by other Indian political leaders working in their own, more restricted, spheres. Sheikh Abdullah, Bal Thackeray, Lalu Prasad Yadav, Mayawati, Mulayam Singh Yadav, and J. Jayalalithaa have all been the object of great adoration on the part of their followers; they have then used this personal charisma to gain total control over the apparatus of their respective parties. Further, they have encouraged their followers to threaten and intimidate independent journalists, judges, officials, and professionals. Finally, rather than allow their successor to be chosen by a process of democratic election, they have anointed a close kin as their successor. (The exceptions here are Jayalalithaa and Mayawati, who are both unmarried.)

This survey of political leadership in independent India has focused on the domain of party politics. However, some of the most interesting (and effective) political leaders have refused to engage with parties and elections altogether. Consider thus the careers and influence of the Naga separatist, Angami Zapu Phizo, and the Sikh separatist, Jarnail Singh Bhindranwale. Both were imbued by their followers—these mostly young men—with a quasi-saintly image; both inspired their followers to lay down their lives for the cause. Both qualified, in Weberian terms, as 'charismatic'. Also very influential in his day was the RSS leader M.S. Golwalkar, whose following also consisted chiefly of young men, devoted to the ideal of the Hindu *rashtra* in part because their chief mentor was

a austere, ascetic individual who shunned material reward or political power. While Golwalkar did not himself ever speak at election rallies or formally identify himself with a particular political party, the RSS did actively help the Jana Sangh during Assembly and Lok Sabha elections. On the other hand, the followers of Phizo and Bhindranwale rejected constitutional politics altogether.

Nor has this survey considered individuals active in civil society and social movements. One such figure, endowed with a certain degree of charisma, is the social worker and environmentalist, Medha Patkar. Originally the leader of a movement to stop a dam on the Narmada river, she has emerged as the spokesperson for displaced people everywhere. Her commitment to Gandhian non-violence and her eschewing of party politics have enhanced the respect and credibility she commands.

As a preliminary attempt to open up a field that requires more intensive and more skilled tilling, this essay had a limited purpose—namely to point to the sheer variety of political leadership in independent India. For the history of Indian democracy has been peopled with colourful characters. They have claimed sometimes to represent a specific caste cluster or religious group, at other times a specific province or linguistic group, at yet other times the nation as a whole. They have used different idioms—the modern, the traditional, the saintly—and different strategies of political action, some centred on the street, others in the legislature. Their methods and policies have sometimes worked to deepen democracy in India, but at other times to undermine it.

NOTES

1. Penderel Moon to his father, 29 January 1952, letter in Mss. Eur. F. 230/26, Oriental and India Office Collections, British Library, London.

2. The empirical evidence in this essay draws from that larger work.

3. *Hindustan Times*, 11 December 1946.

4. Cf profiles of Mannath in *The Illustrated Weekly of India*, 28 June 1959, and in *The Current*, 16 September 1959.

5. See reports in *Thought*, issues of 20 March and 20 May 1972.

6. The posthumous political importance of Ambedkar awaits a serious scholarly analysis. For clues to how important he is to the Dalit consciousness today, see, among other works, Prasad (2004); Franco *et al.* (2004).

7. S. Nijalingappa to Indira Gandhi, 11 November 1969, in Zaidi (1972), p. 231.

REFERENCES

Anonymous. 1952. *The Pilgrimage and After: The Story of How the Congress Fought and Won the General Elections.* New Delhi: All India Congress Committee.

Bhattacharjea, Ajit. 2004. *Unfinished Revolution: A Political Biography of Jayaprakash Narayan.* New Delhi: Rupa and Co.

Cameron, James. 1974. *An Indian Summer.* London: McGraw-Hill.

Constituent Assembly of India, Debates. 1988. rpt, New Delhi: Lok Sabha Secretariat.

Fischer, Margaret W. 1959. 'Nehru: The Hero as Responsible Leader', in Richard L. Park and Irene Tinker (eds), *Leadership and Political Institutions in India.* Princeton: Princeton University Press.

Franco, Fernando, Jyotsna Macwan, and Suguna Ramanathan. 2004. *Journeys to Freedom: Dalit Narratives.* Kolkata: Samya.

Gorringe, Hugo. 2005. *Untouchable Citizens: Dalit Movements and Democratisation in Tamil Nadu.* New Delhi: Sage Publications.

Guha, Ramachandra. 2007. *India After Gandhi: The History of the World's Largest Democracy.* London: Macmillan.

Jalal, Ayesha. 1985. *The Sole Spokesman: Jinnah, the Muslim League, and the Demand for Pakistan.* Cambridge: Cambridge University Press.

Morris-Jones, W.H. 1963. 'India's Political Idioms', in C.H. Philips (ed.), *Politics and Society in India.* London: George Allen and Unwin.

Nayar, Baldev Raj. 1960. *Minority Politics in the Punjab.* Princeton: Princeton University Press.

Nehru, Jawaharlal. 1949[1936]. *An Autobiography, with Musings on Recent Events in India.* Rpt, London: The Bodley Head.

Noronha, R.P. 1976. *A Tale Told by an Idiot.* New Delhi: Vikas Publishing House.

Park, Richard L. 1952. 'India's General Elections', *Far Eastern Survey,* 9 January.

Park, Richard L. and Irene Tinker (eds). 1959. *Leadership and Political Institutions in India.* Princeton: Princeton University Press.

Prasad, Chandra Bhan. 2004. *Dalit Diary: 1999–2003.* Chennai: Navayana Publishing.

Singh, Khushwant. 1971. 'Indira Gandhi', *Illustrated Weekly of India,* 14 March.

Weber, Max, Guenther Roth and Claus Wittich, and Ephriam Fischoff (eds). 1978. *Economy and Society: An Outline of Interpretive Sociology.* Berkeley: University of California Press.

Zaidi, A. Moin. 1972. *The Great Upheaval, 1969–1972.* New Delhi: Orientalia India.

20 Local Politics

Anirudh Krishna

OF DISTANCE AND MEDIATION

For most Indians, the state is distant in both physical and cognitive terms. A British colonial administrator, writing at the dawn of the twentieth century, described the situation at that time.

> In England, justice goes to the people; in India, the people come to justice.... An aggrieved person might have to travel any distance up to fifty miles over a road-less country....A police matter, again, involved a journey to the station, perhaps ten miles off. Trials...involved much hanging about, many journeys to and fro, and a constant spending of money...[the villager] had to find his way to this strange tribunal in an unknown land as best he could, in charge of the police, whose tender mercies he dreaded, or alone. (Carstairs 1912: 12–13)

The situation of the villager in relation to the formal institutions of the state has changed significantly since that time, but aspects of distance and dread continue to inflect these interactions. A passage from Shukla's (1968) semi-fictionalized account provides a flavour of these interactions in post-Independence north India:

> Langar...filed a case in the civil court. He needed a copy of an old judgment for the case. For that you have to first make an application to the Tehsil Office. There was something missing from his application, so it was rejected. Then he made a second application...[but] the copy clerk asked for a five-rupee bribe...[and an] argument started... Langar knew that the copy clerk would find some excuse to reject his application. An application, poor thing, has a life like an ant's. You need no great strength to kill it... Too few stamps, the file number incorrect, one column incomplete.... That's why Langar is now completely prepared...and from dawn to dusk spends his day making rounds of the tehsil. He is scared that some news of the application will appear.... He doesn't want to miss it and have the application rejected. It's already happened once.... It's when a man's fortune is bad that he is fated to see the inside of a court or police station. (Shukla 1968 [1992]: 33–5)

Langar, like most other rural Indians of that time, was illiterate, and thus ill-equipped to negotiate his way through the state bureaucracy. The labyrinth of laws and procedures that encumbers ordinary people's everyday encounters with the Indian state is hard to penetrate even for much better-educated Indians.

Significant changes have occurred over the past fifty years, and educational achievement has risen enormously, particularly over the last twenty-five years, as discussed below. Even today, however, 'the state can and often does appear to people in India as a sovereign entity set apart from society.... A local administrative office, a government school, a police station: to enter any of these is to cross the internal boundary into the domain of the state' (Fuller and Harriss 2000: 23).

Since government organizations appear distant and forbidding, intermediaries are usually involved when individuals need to make contact with the state. Some 'expeditor is usually involved who may not be a man with any official power, but he is always someone who is familiar with the intricacies of administration' (Weiner 1963: 123).

These two themes—a distant state and mediated interactions—provide important insights into the nature of politics at the grassroots level in India. People functioning as intermediaries with the state acquire influence and amass political capital. By helping individuals lodge applications and receive programme assistance from government departments, and by helping groups and communities acquire roads, schools, and other development benefits, intermediaries acquire influence which they convert into political support. One's standing in politics at the local level is a function quite largely of what one does as an intermediary. Individuals rise to positions of influence and importance when they help, through intermediation, to bridge the distance to the state.

In most parts of India this distance is bridged usually in ad hoc, opportunistic, and personalized ways, but these ways have been changing in some fundamental respects, bringing into play an entirely new class of mediators. The nature of intermediaries who help bridge the distance to the state—as well as the form of the distance itself—has changed as a consequence of influences exerted from above and from below. As distance has reduced—from above, through decentralization and strengthening panchayats, and from below, through reduced timidity and increased assertiveness—the nature and content of local politics has changed.

These changes have tended, in most part, to strengthen the practice of democracy in India; more people are more actively and routinely involved in local politics. Occupying both formal and informal positions of political power in Indian villages, a new group of leaders has arisen, which is challenging old practices and relationships. This new set of intermediaries is influencing, mostly for the better, who gets what from the state at the local level. Previously oppressed and marginalized people are more prominently represented in these leadership positions.

Unfortunately, institutions at the local level continue being disarticulated and weak. 'In contemporary India,' states Yadav, 'the chain that links peoples' needs to their felt desire to their articulated demand to its aggregation and finally to its translation into public policy is impossibly long and notoriously weak' (1999: 2399).

Government and party bureaucracies reach down in hierarchal form from the national to the district level, but they are thin on the ground at levels below the district (Kohli 1990; Kothari 1988; Krishna 2002). Non-governmental organizations (NGOs) are rising in national prominence, but at local levels they are still very thinly represented, and other formal civil society groups remain mostly an urban presence in India (Chhibber 1999). Panchayats represent perhaps the best hope of establishing formal institutionalized state presence at the grassroots, but up to a few years ago these bodies had continued to function mainly as implementing agencies of the Central government, and not as bodies representing to the state the voice and aspirations of ordinary people (Jain 1993; Mayaram 1998; Mooij 2005). Unless these bodies are strengthened and more firmly incorporated within the fabric of the state, and unless other state and societal institutions are extended to cover the last mile, the distance experienced by ordinary Indians will not diminish in the visible future. Politics at the local level will continue to remain an expression of how ordinary people are assisted by particular individuals to travel the uncovered distance from the state.

Changes occurring over the previous quarter-century have helped transform, mostly in positive ways, the manner in which this distance is usually traversed. A new set of intermediaries has arisen, and is democratizing participation and influence in local politics. In order to understand their rise to influence, one must take account of a broader set of changes.

THE HISTORICAL ACCOUNT

Historically, caste and patron–client links have formed the building blocks of political organization in India (Migdal 1988; Weiner 1989). Caste associations have been the pre-eminent mode of interest formation and interest articulation for ordinary villagers (Bailey 1957; Morris-Jones 1967; Panini 1997). High caste was associated with greater wealth and larger political clout, and these privileges were backed by an influential ideology that allotted occupation and status in the village according to the caste into which a person was born (Dumont 1970). Village chiefs belonging to the highest landowning castes administered justice in the village on behalf of the state.

> The lowest level of the political system, namely, the village, enjoyed a considerable measure of autonomy as well as discreteness from the higher levels...[the state was] willing to let villagers govern themselves in day-to-day matters, and wherever a dominant caste existed, its council, on which the leading landowners were represented, exercised power in local matters'. (Srinivas 1987: 30, 34)

Richer and higher-caste persons exercised administrative control on behalf of the ruler, and other people's relations with the state were mediated exclusively and monopolistically by these individuals (Bailey 1957; Carter 1974; Cohn 1969; Frykenberg 1969; Gupta 1998; Spear 1973).

This distance between the state and ordinary people reinforced and preserved caste hierarchies, with upper-caste landowners acting as intermediaries and local representatives of the state. 'Everyday caste practice disciplined social conduct without frequent direct recourse to the power of the state' (Kaviraj 2000: 141). All persons took up the occupations allotted to their own caste group. In southern Rajasthan, for instance, Balais flayed dead cattle, turned their skins to leather, and made shoes that the upper castes could wear (lower castes, including Balais themselves, were denied the right to wear shoes in public); Nais worked as barbers, and their women helped as midwives;

Kumhars made earthen pots for storing grain and water; Dholis beat the drum on festive occasions and funerals; Suthars were the carpenters of the village community; and so on. In the relatively autarchic economy of the village, fifty or a hundred years ago, all necessary tasks were divided up among castes within the village—or, alternatively, people were divided into castes in order that particular tasks could be performed (Pinhey 1909 [1996]).

Possibilities for change were circumscribed by this ossification of social and economic status and guarded by political roles reinforced from above. The system was regulated and enforced by the upper-caste groups. The state relied upon these people not only for gathering the revenue and keeping the peace (of a certain kind), but also for procuring other services and placing other demands upon villagers (Lupton 1908). Duties and rights in village society were allocated according to caste, and the lowest castes were often required to perform forced labour, or begaar (Chaubisa 1988).

Even after Independence and the advent of democracy, this inglorious tradition—of banking upon the strong to gain the allegiance, or at least the compliance, of the weak—was found useful and continued by political parties. 'Congress's inheritance of the British unitary centre and the chastening effects of Partition facilitated accommodations with regional and sub-regional power brokers' (Jalal 1995: 249). The modus operandi of the Congress party, imitated less successfully by other parties, consisted of enlisting the largest landlords of the area, and using their inherited influence to garner votes among the lower classes (Chakravarty 1975; Frankel and Rao 1989; Hasan 1989; Migdal 1988; Kothari 1988). These landlords' influence was bolstered by providing them with exclusive access to agencies of the state, and by letting development benefits from the state pass as patronage through their hands.

Political parties, which should have provided linkages between citizens and public officials, were mostly poorly organized in the countryside (Kohli 1987; Weiner 1967). Building party organizations is a long and tedious affair, requiring toil without reward for several years, and leaders of major political parties were only too glad to take the easy way out. Party leaders struck deals with village strongmen, mostly upper-caste landowning elites, who could deliver blocks of votes by dint of their traditional domination over other villagers. In exchange for bringing in the vote, these village strongmen were provided with privileged access to state officials (Hasan 1989; Krishna 2003; Migdal 1988; Singh 1988). When ordinary villagers needed to make contact with government officials, they would go with a note from the local strongman, so few villagers dared to cross their strongman or vote against his preferred candidates.

It was a convenient and mutually advantageous bargain. The ruling party got its votes with relatively little effort; so investment in organization building could be deferred or avoided altogether. This led to the village strongmen increasing their hold over other villagers. By delivering the vote, they preserved their dominant positions. Their utility to parties for electoral purposes allowed large landowners to successfully avoid or evade the most stringent provisions of the land reform laws that were implemented in the 1950s and 1960s. Parties and state governments connived with landlords to water down the implementation of these laws (Ladejinsky 1972). As a result, 'the power and influence of the landlords was curtailed though not undermined' (Hasan 1989: 58). Technological changes tended in many instances to further reinforce the dependence of poorer villagers on the richer for loans, employment, and links with the state (Harriss 1982).

Some analysts have remarked upon the continuing importance of caste and patron–client linkages for political mobilization in rural India (Béteille 1996; Karanth 1997; Kothari 1988), and to some extent these influences continue to hold sway. Many villagers who grew up in earlier times still follow the lead of their erstwhile feudal lords. 'How do you vote in elections?' I asked Gangaram Prajapat, sixty-five years old and of the potter caste. 'As Thakur Sahib tells us,' he responded promptly and quite unselfconsciously, referring to the upper-caste landlord of his village.[1]

However, other, especially younger, villagers hew to very different versions of influence and loyalty. The nature of caste has changed considerably. The links between caste and occupation and caste and wealth are no longer as close as they used to be (Mayer 1997;

Parry 1999; Sheth 1999). Different forms of political association have arisen and gained ground, and the salience of older patronage-based associations has waned considerably in comparison.

The relation of caste to political organization is mediated by the nature of state policies. Varying stimuli introduced by the state have resulted in reconfiguring caste and political association.[2] As the nature and rules of the political game have changed once again over the past twenty-five years, caste and other forms of social aggregation have changed further in response.

Individuals who perform mediation functions vis-à-vis the state are considerably different than before. Ability, rather than caste, is the new currency of political exchange. Rising rural education has had a great deal to do with these changes, for it is the more educated individuals who can more capably bridge the distance with the state, bringing home to their villages diverse development benefits in the form of employment-generating projects, infrastructure, and loans.

THE UPSURGE IN RURAL LITERACY

Rural literacy in India has grown from 12 per cent in 1951 to 59 per cent in 2001. Growth of this magnitude over so much time—an increment of much less than 1 per cent per year—does not by itself portend revolutionary changes. But a more telling account of change becomes obvious when one considers that this change is not equally distributed over all age groups. Rapid growth in educational achievement has been witnessed only in the past twenty-five years, and the impacts of growing education on local politics have only recently begun to be felt.

To illustrate the changes that have occurred, Tables 20.1 and 20.2 provide results from the original surveys conducted in the second half of 2005 within twenty villages each in Rajasthan and Karnataka. Every individual resident in these villages was surveyed by teams of experienced investigators. A diverse mix of villages was selected from two districts of Karnataka (Dharwar and Mysore) and two districts of Rajasthan (Ajmer and Udaipur), including some villages that are located quite close to major roads and market centres, and others that are more remotely situated. Schools

Table 20.1: Percentage of Villagers with Five or
More Years of School Education
(all residents of 20 villages of Rajasthan)

CASTE GROUP	AGE GROUP (YEARS)				
	11–20	21–30	31–40	41–60	61+
Upper (n=4,467)	89	76	57	41	27
OBC (n=14,222)	64	43	26	14	7
SC (n=2,569)	64	40	23	12	4
ST (n=4,067)	32	16	9	2	2
Muslims (n=819)	57	45	29	21	11
AVERAGE (n=26,124)	64	45	29	18	11

Source: Original data collected in 2005
Note: n = number of observations (that is, the number of individuals)

had been opened in some villages more than fifty years ago, whereas other villages have received public schools no more than twenty years ago. Different caste and economic groups are also represented within this mix of villages.

Regardless of the nature of village or caste group, however, rapid generational change in educational achievement is readily apparent. Let us first consider these figures for the villages studied in Rajasthan, a state usually regarded as being backward in terms of education. All individuals who have five or more years of formal education are considered in the following analysis to be functionally literate.[3]

Consider how functional literacy increases regularly as one moves from the right to the left in Table 20.1. Among people in these twenty villages aged 61 years and older, no more than 11 per cent are functionally literate, and among Scheduled Castes (SCs) and Scheduled Tribes (STs), this percentage is virtually insignificant, at 4 per cent and 2 per cent, respectively.

Now consider villagers aged between 11 and 20. On an average, 64 per cent are functionally literate. Scheduled Castes and Other Backward Classes (OBCs) are still lagging behind the upper castes, but the inter-generational increase has been fastest in their cases. Recorded at just 4 per cent among SCs who are 61 years and older, functional literacy is at 64 per cent

for the generation that is between the ages of 11 and 20—and it is expanding further among villagers of a still younger age group.

The *majority* of young villagers of the SC and OBC caste groups are functionally literate, a remarkable improvement as compared to the situation over 20 years ago. Scheduled Tribes still lag behind: less than one-third are functionally literate in the age group of 11 to 20. Even in their case, however, the increase has been considerable over the previous ten-year cohort. Whereas only 16 per cent of STs in the age-group of 21–30 are functionally literate, *twice* as many STs in the age-group of 11–20 have acquired functional literacy.

An increasing realization that it is necessary to be functionally competent in a world where knowledge of numbers and letters matters ever more is prompting parents to invest increasingly in their children's education. Indeed, children's education comes immediately after basic food in the order of households' spending priorities, as colleagues and I ascertained in 108 village communities of Andhra Pradesh, Gujarat, and Rajasthan (Krishna 2004, 2006b; Krishna *et al.* 2005).

To be sure, educational achievement is still higher among men compared to women—a gender gap persists—but the magnitude of this gap has also been reduced over time. While 46 per cent of men and only 9 per cent of women aged 31 to 40 years are functionally literate in these twenty Rajasthan villages (resulting in a gender gap of 37 per cent), 46 per cent of women aged 11 to 20 years and 77 per cent of men of the same age group are functionally literate. The gender gap has narrowed to 23 per cent, and it is being reduced further as more and more children of both sexes are being sent to school by their parents. In the age group of 7 to 12 years, 68 per cent of girls and 88 per cent of boys have at least one year of school education.

Parents in Rajasthan and elsewhere are increasingly attaching great importance to education, and progressively more children are enrolling in—and continuing to attend—schools (Dubey 2001; PROBE 1999). This trend of increasing educational achievement started earlier, and it has proceeded further in some southern states, of which Kerala is

Table 20.2: Percentage of Villagers with Five or
More Years of School Education
(all residents of 20 villages of Karnataka)

CASTE GROUP	AGE GROUP (YEARS)				
	11–20	21–30	31–40	41–60	61+
OBC (n=15,376)	86	59	37	30	19
SC (n=5,032)	85	50	24	16	6
ST (n=2,010)	71	32	16	13	11
Muslims (n=635)	82	65	36	21	21
AVERAGE (n=23,067)	85	55	32	25	15

Source: Original data collected in 2005.
Note: n = number of observations (that is, the number of individuals)

the best-known example (Drèze and Sen 1995; Heller 2000). Karnataka has also made early strides, as the figures in Table 20.2 show.[4] Once again, a regular progression is observed from right to left in terms of educational achievement.[5]

Eighty-five per cent of these Karnataka villagers aged between 11 to 20 years are functionally literate, compared to 55 per cent in the age group of 21–30. Every ten-year cohort has consistently registered an increase in educational achievement—and the most notable increases have been registered by the last two cohorts. Within the space of twenty years, *functional literacy has leapt from 32 per cent to 85 per cent* in these Karnataka villages, and this increase has been shared almost evenly across all the caste groups.

The gender gap in educational achievement has also narrowed over the same period of time. Whereas 43 per cent of men and 22 per cent of women aged 31–40 years are functionally literate, resulting in a gender gap of 21 per cent, 87 per cent of men and 83 per cent of women in the age group of 11–20 are functionally literate in these villages; the gender gap has virtually disappeared.

It is not just in Rajasthan and Karnataka that such trends and effects have been experienced. From rural Gujarat, Breman reports that 'households have reduced their agrarian capital...to enable the younger generation—the boys at first but later also the girls— to go to secondary schools and eventually to colleges

to prepare themselves for a life outside agriculture and away from the village' (1993: 317).

Similar accounts available from other Indian states, including some usually considered to be lagging behind in terms of social change indicators, suggest that the upsurge in rural education is broadly based across the country. In Uttar Pradesh,

> school attendance among 5–14 year old children rose faster within Dalit communities than within the general population between 1987–88 and 1993–94.... Education has given Chamar young men a sense of individual dignity and confidence in the face of upper castes...while school participation rates are lower for girls than boys, the number of girls going to school or college is increasing at all levels. (Jeffrey et al. 2004: 967–9)

Based on his village study in north Bihar, Chaudhary concludes similarly that

> the traditional bases of power have lost their ground... modern bases of power, such as numerical strength, educational [achievement], contact with extension agencies...are dispersed in terms of castes...Yadavas and Kurmis are persuading their children to get college education.... The numbers of Harijan children in schools are also increasing. (1987: 113–14)

Analyses show how education and information are critical for political activity. Regardless of caste and wealth, villagers who are more educated participate more actively in diverse political activities (Krishna 2006a). Political efficacy and individual capacity are crucially affected by educational attainment (Drèze and Sen 1997; Sen 1999).

The recent upsurge of educational achievement in rural areas has resulted in fundamentally altering political attitudes and behaviours at the local level. 'Centuries of unequal struggle against his environment have taught him to endure,' claimed Jawaharlal Nehru, depicting a typical rural Indian of that time, 'and even in poverty and submission he has a certain calm dignity, a feeling of submission to an all-powerful fate' (1946: 357). Submission and fatalism are hardly in evidence any more, especially among younger villagers.

> The odds that a *dalit* [Scheduled or Backward caste] will vote are much higher today than that of an upper caste. This has been accompanied by a significant rise

in their sense of efficacy and their involvement in more active forms of political participation.... The textbook rule about political participation is that the higher you are in the social hierarchy, the greater the chance of your participating in political activity. Contemporary India is perhaps the only exception to this rule. (Yadav 1999: 2397)

As younger villagers of both genders and all caste groups gain rapidly in functional literacy (with STs of Rajasthan lagging behind by one or two 10-year cohorts), important effects are being felt on patterns of leadership in Indian villages. The Langars of the past, who had felt traumatized by the prospect of seeing the inside of a court or police station, are being replaced by more competent and assertive younger villagers.

A new group of intermediaries is arising, with increasing representation from backward castes and SCs. Twenty or thirty years ago when people, presently older than 61 years, were occupying leadership positions, less than 2 per cent of STs in these Rajasthan villages, and less than 4 per cent of SCs were functionally literate. SCs and STs—but also OBCs in Rajasthan—had leaders who were not equipped to negotiate the written-down world of state bureaucracies and governmental procedures. Their transactions with the world outside the village had to be conducted necessarily through intermediaries from other groups. The situation of SCs in Karnataka villages was not dissimilar: only 6 per cent had acquired functional literacy, and their ability to interact directly with state officials was also limited. While raising demands for development projects and other benefits from the state, members of these groups were forced to act via external intermediaries.

The recent upsurge in rural education has resulted in generating the supply of new leadership and new intermediaries, who are more competent in dealing directly with the state on behalf of their social groups. SCs, OBCs, and STs of Karnataka, and to a lesser extent the STs of Rajasthan, are prominent among this new set of local leaders.

High caste has relatively little to do any more with who helps ordinary villagers in their interactions with the state. The nature of local politics has changed as a result.

THE CHANGING NATURE OF MEDIATION

'When poorer people meet local state officials, they do so with reference to their non-state networks.... The state is met through the persons who bring [social and organizational] practices to life, as well as through a broader range of caste leaders, brokers (*dalaals*), and political fixers (*pyraveerkars*)' (Corbridge *et al.* 2005: 108).

While the need for intermediaries continues to remain important, the nature and social origin of intermediaries has undergone a fundamental change. Villagers, particularly young villagers, have become increasingly assertive in demanding services and economic benefits from political parties. Political activity based on caste affiliation and caste rank is becoming less common, and social and political relationships are being transformed as education and information spread across the countryside.

A new type of political entrepreneur has emerged. I first came upon these new village leaders—or *naye neta,* as they are commonly known in this area—when I was carrying out field research in southern Rajasthan in the late 1990s. I have since found similar new leaders in action in every other Indian state that I have visited at the grassroots, including Andhra Pradesh, Karnataka, Gujarat, and Madhya Pradesh.

Chunnilal Garasiya, Congress party leader and state minister in Rajasthan, has on numerous occasions profiled these naya netas as follows:

> They are usually between twenty-five and forty years of age...[and] educated to about middle school [level]. They read newspapers, have low-level contacts in numerous government offices, and are experienced [in dealing] with the government bureaucracy and with banks, insurance companies, and such like....Their caste does not matter. These new leaders can be of any caste, but they must have knowledge, perseverance and ability. (personal interview)

These new political entrepreneurs have gained considerable influence over the past twenty years. Compared to any other type of leader, more villagers by far consult the naya neta for diverse tasks involving party politics, market transactions, and interacting with government officials, as we will see below.

Three sets of factors have contributed to these developments. The vast expansion in rural education has helped produce a supply of younger villagers, especially men, who can liaise effectively with government officials and party organizers.

At the same time, the demand for these types of intermediary services has also increased enormously, especially over the past twenty years. state expenditures in rural areas have increased exponentially over the last two decades; a plethora of new development programmes and agencies have been introduced. Villagers as well as government officials are keen to find intermediaries who can help transact on their behalf the growing business in development programmes and benefits.

New leaders, who are more able to gain these benefits and services from the state, have arisen, and villagers look to these persons for assistance, regardless of caste or economic background. 'The criterion for voting was earlier *jati* (caste), now it is *vikaas* [development]. Development work done in a village has the most effect on voting,' a long-time observer of local politics pointed out to me.

Party organizers provide another source of demand for the new entrepreneurs' services. Weak grassroots organizations have led political parties in India to rely for support on pre-existing social organizations. Where they previously relied on caste- or patronage-based voting, they are now finding it useful to forge links at the village level with the rising group of young and educated leaders. Intensified competition has provided each party with an incentive to reach out to new leaders with influence among the villagers. The old caste-based leadership is no longer the only or even the primary contact that party organizers seek when they go into villages looking for votes.

The emergence of these new non-caste-based political entrepreneurs is neither an entirely new phenomenon, nor is it confined to Rajasthan and Madhya Pradesh, the two states where I first saw these new leaders in action. Bailey (1960) had anticipated that new forms of leadership would come up when villages experienced further external influences. 'Power within the village community is achieved not only in the relationships which exist

inside that community,' he observed. 'There is now an additional resource in the hands of the ambitious man: the relationship which he can establish with the Administrators. He can use this relationship to achieve his ends within the village.' (Bailey 1960: 114–15) As governmental and, of late, market activity have expanded within rural areas, leadership based on such outside connections has gained importance, and it is overshadowing, in many instances, other forms of leadership that derive from ethnic or religious groupings within the village.

Such new forms of intermediation had started becoming evident in the late 1970s and early 1980s, as reported by Reddy and Hargopal (1985) for Andhra Pradesh and by Mitra (1992) for Orissa and Gujarat. Manor (2000) indicates how such roles are also quite widespread in other states, including Madhya Pradesh, Uttar Pradesh, and Karnataka.

When they need to make contact, for instance with banks and insurance companies, with the police or the *tahsil* (administrative division), with district-level party officials, or with any of a huge number of extension agencies and government departments that implement development projects and oversee employment-generating works, most villagers seek assistance from the new village leaders. In a survey that I conducted along with my colleagues in 1998, more than 2,000 residents selected by random sampling among sixty-nine villages of Rajasthan and Madhya Pradesh were asked which type of leader they would consult if they needed to make contact with a specified list of government departments and market-based organizations. They were asked to select between five different leader types— including party politicians, old patrons, panchayat representatives, caste leaders, and the new village leaders. Table 20.3 presents these results. In 2004, we repeated the same exercise in 36 villages of Andhra Pradesh. Table 20.4 presents these later results. In each of these different situations involving mediation with different government or market organizations, as the data in Tables 20.3 and 21.4 show, more than 60 per cent of villagers in Rajasthan and over 50 per cent in Andhra Pradesh selected the new leaders as their first choice among different intermediaries. Caste leaders and traditional patrons fall far behind

Table 20.3: Mediation by Different Types of Local Leaders in Rajasthan and Madhya Pradesh

PERCENTAGE OF VILLAGERS WHO PREFER EACH TYPE OF LEADER FOR MEDIATION WITH:	TYPES OF LEADERS (IN PER CENT)				
	POLITICAL PARTY OFFICIALS	TRADITIONAL PATRONS	ELECTED PANCHAYAT OFFICIALS	CASTE LEADERS	NAYA NETAS
(a) Dealing with the police or the tahsil	6	4	5	20	62
(b) Getting a bank loan or an insurance policy	5	15	7	8	63
(c) Learning about agricultural technology	6	3	17	11	61
(d) Replacing a non-performing school teacher	4	1	18	11	64
(e) Getting wage employment	4	3	11	8	70

Source: Krishna (2002)
Note: Based on interviews with a random sample of 2,400 individuals in sixty-nine villages

Table 20.4: Mediation by Different Types of Local Leaders in Andhra Pradesh

PERCENTAGE OF VILLAGERS WHO PREFER EACH TYPE OF LEADER FOR MEDIATION WITH:	TYPES OF LEADERS (IN PER CENT)				
	POLITICAL PARTY OFFICIALS	TRADITIONAL PATRONS	ELECTED PANCHAYAT OFFICIALS	CASTE LEADERS	NAYA NETAS
(a) Dealing with the police	16	2	17	10	52
(b) Getting a bank loan	7	3	24	4	59
(c) Treatment in a government hospital	11	2	18	3	62
(d) Admission to high school or college teacher	6	4	22	9	54

Source: Original data collected in 2003
Note: Based on interviews with a random sample of 1,751 individuals in thirty-six villages

in terms of assisting with villagers' critical demands from the state.

The naya netas have become the crucial mediators between ordinary rural Indians and the state. Their higher levels of education give younger villagers a distinct advantage in these dealings. Despite being a necessary condition for exercising the new leadership, however, education is hardly sufficient for this purpose.

A great deal of hard work is also required—to scurry around from office to office; to fill out forms and lobby government officials; to supervise construction labour on behalf of officials; to fill out forms and keep accounts; to arrange elaborate 'site visits' when officials or politicians come to the village.... To do all this and also attend to villagers' everyday concerns—taking a sick person to hospital, often in the middle of the night, and keeping up one's contacts among doctors and hospital officials; to have someone's government pension approved and paid out in time (and know the associated rules and the people in charge in the tehsil and block offices); to get someone a loan from a bank.... To badger, pester, entreat, implore, threaten, cajole, and bribe, if necessary—and to do these things every day and also be accessible at night—does not add up to a comfortable life.

People born to comfort and privilege find it hard to tread these paths; the new leadership is drawn disproportionately from educated youngsters belonging to the middle and lower segments of the caste hierarchy. Backward castes constitute 41 per cent of the population, but they provide 49 per cent of the new leaders in the sixty-nine Rajasthan villages that I studied (Krishna 2003). Scheduled Castes—previously marginal to village politics—now contribute more than their share of new leaders; they constitute 22 per cent of these villages' population, but 26 per cent of new leaders hail from these castes (ibid.). Proportionately fewer new leaders are drawn from the upper-caste groups.

The great demand for their services among fellow villagers gives the new leaders positions of influence within the village. Unlike the old village patrons, however, the new leaders cannot easily use their special connections with the state to benefit at the expense of other villagers. The spread of education and information among other, especially younger, villagers has given rise to a more widespread capacity for independent action.

Leaders, young or old, can no longer easily deceive a significant percentage of villagers. 'The [former] rural elites are losing some of their powers,' observed Robinson:

> the vote banks are collapsing....The critical factor is that some members of the central, state, and district bureaucracies, and increasing numbers of the poor have both begun to realize that their 'interpreters' have been carefully and systematically distorting their messages in both directions. (Robinson 1988: 10)

Leadership exercised in the spirit of service is more likely to create a fund of obligations. New leaders with political ambitions or aspirations to higher social status are careful not to overcharge villagers for the services they provide. Not all new leaders behave in such laudable ways, but there is a significant percentage—more than half, as far as I could make out—who are in it for the long haul, and who invest in institution-building at the grassroots. Instead of dividing villagers by caste or religion, these new leaders build wide-ranging social networks that bring together villagers of different castes. The larger and more cohesive this network, the more successfully a new leader can negotiate with officials, attracting greater development benefits to his village. Larger networks promise greater collective benefits, and greater benefits help new leaders consolidate their position in the village.

Non-caste-based political entrepreneurs in these villages are more successful than others in delivering economic benefits and providing avenues for greater political participation. For the most part, villagers associate with these new political entrepreneurs, regardless of caste or religion.

This emergent new pattern of political exchange differs in significant respects from the standard model of clientelism. Successful clientelistic parties usually build 'political machines that reach from the summits of national politics down to the municipal level' (Kitschelt 2000: 849). Resources for patronage are generated and made available to lower levels by people at the top, and each successive link downward has power only to the extent that it receives patronage resources from above. Control within this hierarchical chain of favours and fealty is maintained by a credible threat to withhold resources from the top.

The contemporary Indian situation differs from this model in two important respects. First, the interactions that new village leaders have with politicians at higher levels are hardly those of a client locked in a hierarchical relation with a patron. Naya netas are not bound to any particular political party. Rather, they look around for whichever politician can provide them credibly with the most resources to finance development works in their village, and they switch allegiance easily from one set of politicians to another. Parties chase after naya netas as much as—or more than—naya netas chase after parties. Consequently, the top half of the clientelistic pyramid is inverted to some extent.

The bottom half of the pyramid is also different in present-day India. Naya netas perform diverse services on behalf of ordinary villagers, and they expect to be repaid for these services at election time, quite as the model of clientelism indicates. However, naya netas have hardly any means available to monitor precisely how different villagers cast their votes on election day. They cannot, therefore, hold villagers to account in this respect (any more than caste leaders could do in their day). One naya neta informed me that 'it is a matter of keeping faith. People can obviously vote as they wish. But most people remember well who has helped them in times of need. And it is only a rare person who is faithless.'[6]

Faith must be kept on both sides, however. Individual villagers are not bound to follow any particular naya neta, and new leaders who are effective and honest in their dealings attract a sizeable following among their fellow villagers. But villagers are watchful and wary. Alternative naya netas are available in most villages, and any hint of cheating or diminished effectiveness can result in a transfer of allegiance by a majority of villagers.[7]

Rather than being pyramid-shaped, the structure of political exchange in this context is more akin to an hourglass. The man in the middle constitutes a critical central point, with chains of influence radiating both upward and downward.

LOCALIZATION AND FRAGMENTATION

Analyses of national-level survey data also indicate a declining association between caste and political activity. Interpreting a range of recent national surveys, Oldenburg (1999) observes that:

> Citizens now do not vote according to the orders of caste leader, political patron, or even husband; nor are their votes typically 'bought' in any direct way. There is a genuinely secret ballot....Women in 1998, when asked who they consulted before voting, overwhelmingly said, 'no one' (65 percent); another 17 percent consulted their husbands; and 11 percent other members of the family... only 16 percent of the men admitted to being guided by someone else...[and of those] who sought advice, only seven percent sought it from caste and community leaders...that is, less than <u>two</u> percent of the electorate got direct advice on how to vote from caste and community leaders....In 1971, 51 percent of the respondents agreed that it was 'important to vote the way your caste/ community does' (30 percent disagreed), but in 1996 the percentages were reversed: 51 percent disagreed with that statement (29 percent agreed)....In 1998, 'caste and community' was seen as an issue by only 5.5 percent of the respondents...members of particular castes (and especially members of the large caste groupings such as 'Dalit' or 'Other Backward Classes') can be found voting for every party....It is less and less true that knowing the caste of a voter lets you reliably predict the party he or she will vote for.

Some other analyses show that in some areas caste is being reconstructed by ambitious political entrepreneurs, who build constituencies for themselves by promising economic gains and political efficacy to others of the same caste. Caste-based associations have been erected and strengthened to deliver these types of benefits in some parts of India, and people in these regions have mobilized for

political action together with others of the same caste group (Chandra 2000; Jaffrelot 2003).

In other parts of India, however, caste has lost ground as a unit of political activity. Reporting on panchayat elections in the state of Uttar Pradesh held in summer 2000, for example, Pal (2000: 3289), observes that 'the caste factor, which has been considered the bedrock of Indian politics, was pushed to a secondary position....In fact, caste character has, to some extent, been [replaced by] group character, comprising different castes and communities having almost similar socio-economic status in rural society and economy' (Pal 2000: 3289).

Development is the primary concern of villagers today, and leaders who help uphold their development-related aspirations are valued and supported by ordinary villagers far more than leaders of other stripes. Different forms of political associations have been created in different places to answer to citizens' economic and political needs. New and emergent forms of political organization are gaining ground in different parts. Explanations for local politics couched in terms of caste or patronage can no longer be assumed; they need to be established.

The locus of public decision-making has changed, becoming more localized than before. The new village leaders represent villagers' collective and individual demands to the state. But they also mediate in the reverse direction, performing important agency functions on behalf of government officials and party politicians. Government officials need to assemble large numbers of villagers to participate in departmental programmes—otherwise they are unable to achieve their targets of work. Politicians need to pull villagers together for purposes of voting or participating in rallies organized by their party. Since they lack any independent means of contacting individual villagers—and because villagers will hardly turn out at the behest of someone they do not know and cannot trust—officials and politicians both look to individuals in the village who are well known and frequently contacted by villagers in need.

Parties are not distinguishable from each other in terms of ideology or programmes,[8] and they do not usually have any permanent organization at the local level, so all parties are driven to seek alliance with men of influence in the village. 'Despite the apparent centralization of decision-making power in New Delhi, it is the national leadership that is more dependent on effective local leadership than vice versa' (Brass 1997: 321). Where they previously contacted traditional patrons in the village—landed, upper-caste, and older males—officials and politicians are increasingly striking bargains with other villagers whose influence in the village has become relatively stronger, especially over the past few decades.

Instead of reaching out for relatively large territories controlled by regional *satraps* or high-caste patrons, parties are increasingly forced to compete at the localized level of an individual village. Their electoral fate depends in large part on how many villages they can attract into their fold—and each village must be competed for separately and individually.

The rapid increase in the discretionary development funds made available to individual Members of Parliament (MPs) and Members of Legislative Assemblies (MLAs) bears testimony to the fact that politicians are not unaware of these developments. Large and increasing budgetary allocations are provided to each parliamentary (and legislative) constituency under these schemes, which are used at the discretion of the area MP (or MLA) to finance construction and employment-generating projects in particular communities. In the fiscal year 1998–9, a sum of Rs 10 million was allocated for this purpose to every MP. By 1999–2000, the allocation was doubled, and each MP was provided with Rs 20 million. At the state level, MLAs have voted similar schemes into existence, and the amount allocated increased in Rajasthan from Rs 500,000 in 1998–9 to Rs 2.5 million in 1999–2000, an increase of *five times* over the previous fiscal year.[9]

Members of Parliament and MLAs utilize these subventions to make political bargains with influential villagers, and naya netas play a prominent part in these transactions. Anita Kunwar Sisodiya, of Dhoodalka village in Mandsaur district, Madhya Pradesh, one of the few female naya netas whom I met, considers that her education and knowledge of the rules has enabled her to garner

a disproportionately large amount of development funds for her village. Since she has been able to unite her village in collective action, overriding caste divisions, she has been able to bargain more effectively with politicians and government officials.

Political competition has fragmented in this manner. Hopefully, this 'fragmentation of political power [will] present a unique opportunity to decentralize some of the institutions of public integrity and restore their proper functioning' (Mehta 1997: 58).

Institution-building at levels below the district remains an unfinished task of democracy and state-building. As the state is distant, it is approached with hesitation and through intermediaries.

A new set of younger, more educated, and non-caste-based political entrepreneurs are democratizing politics at the village level, and are helping make established socio-economic and political structures more accountable to the ordinary villager. Villagers' engagements with the state and with markets are becoming more widespread than ever before. In my view, this rise of a new group of mediators represents a welcome new development.

However, the emergence of these new leaders does not represent a sustainable solution to the problem of institutional distance. Parties continue to be weakly organized, and villagers still cannot resort to party or any other institutionalized channels. When they need to communicate upward, with government officials or party functionaries, villagers still need to seek assistance from particular individuals. The nature of these individuals has changed, no doubt. Upper-caste and landed individuals have been replaced to a significant extent. Traditional bonds of servitude and loyalty have given way to newer and more equal relationships. But there are still no institutionalized places that villagers can access easily, where their demands and grievances can be attended to—directly, reliably, and conveniently.

Until such institutions are built—until the state is extended downwards to cover the last mile—mediation will continue to be the currency of local politics in rural India. Keeping track of the changing nature of mediation will help keep current our understanding of power and influence in the countryside.[10]

NOTES

1. Interviewed in Kundai village, Udaipur district, 15 June 1998.

2. 'Caste itself as we know it is not a residual survival of ancient India but a specifically colonial form of (that is, substitute for) civil society that both justified and maintained an Orientalist vision,' states Dirks (2001, p. 60).

'Under colonial rule, caste...could take on a new and different form...it was appropriated and reconstructed by British rule. And even after decolonization, academic preoccupations have continued to be fascinated with the same chimeric forms that so preoccupied the British, even as they have mistaken the effects of British rule for the traditional predicates of it.'

'Traditional India was not a rigid society,' asserts Bayly (1988: 156–8), 'It was British rule which made it so.... Hierarchy [within] Hindu society which was theoretical rather than actual over much of India as late as 1750 was firmly ensconced a century later.... The British indirectly stimulated these changes.'

3. I have found, as have others (PROBE 1999), that individuals with just two or three years of formal education are often unable to write clearly or work with numbers, so I opted to work with five or more years of education as a working definition of functional literacy, not finding any better or generally accepted definition in the literatures that I consulted.

4. I should like to thank Kripa Ananthpur, who helped arrange for these village surveys in Karnataka.

5. The numbers of villagers within the 'General' or 'Upper' caste group is so inconsiderable in these twenty villages of Dharwar and Mysore districts that it is not possible to conduct any meaningful analysis, especially after disaggregating by age group; thus, this category is not shown in Table 20.2.

6. Interview with Mothulal Vaishnava, *naya neta* of Kailashpuri village, Udaipur district, 22 May 2002.

7. Such large-scale transfers of allegiance are not unknown. Villagers cast their lot with some naya neta depending upon how well he serves their needs, that is, how honestly, dedicatedly, effectively, and efficiently he conducts transactions on their behalf. Reputation plays an important role in determining how much villagers respect some new leader. Most new leaders, particularly politically ambitious ones, are keen to present an image of selfless duty to villagers. The truth may, however, be quite different from the image.

8. Summarizing the results of the 1999 national elections, the *Economist* (9 October 1999) stated that 'no party, bar those on the left, offered voters a clear-cut ideology or philosophy of government'. A comparison of election manifestos of the two major parties revealed hardly any difference—and a great deal in common—in terms of what they held out by way of promises for rural development programmes (Krishna 2002, pp. 229, ff. 24).

9. Annual development expenditures of the Central government and the state government of Rajasthan.

10. The literature on local politics in urban areas is not nearly equally extensive, and this necessarily brief review has focused upon rural areas, where 70 per cent of Indians continue to reside, and for which scholarly analyses are available for a wider area and covering a longer period of time. For some interesting insights related to local politics in urban areas, see Manor (1993); Satterthwaite (2006); Varshney (2001); and Wilkinson (2004).

REFERENCES

Bailey, Frederick G. 1960. *Tribe, Caste and Nation: A Study of Political Activity and Political Change in Highland Orissa*. Manchester: Manchester University Press.

———. 1957. *Caste and the Economic Frontier: A Village in Highland Orissa*. Manchester: Manchester University Press.

Bayly, C.A. 1988. *Indian Society and the Making of the British Empire*. Cambridge, UK: Cambridge University Press.

Béteille, Andre. 1996. *Caste, Class and Power: Changing Patterns of Stratification in a Tanjore Village*. New Delhi: Oxford University Press.

Brass, Paul. 1997. *Theft of an Idol: Text and Context in the Representation of Political Violence*. Princeton, NJ: Princeton University Press.

Breman, Jan. 1993. *Beyond Patronage and Exploitation: Changing Agrarian Relations in South Gujarat*. New Delhi: Oxford University Press.

Carstairs, R. 1912. *The Little World of an Indian District Officer*. London: Macmillan.

Carter, Anthony T. 1974. *Elite Politics in India: Political Stratification and Political Alliances in Western Maharashtra*. Cambridge: Cambridge University Press.

Chakravarty, Anand. 1975. *Contradiction and Change: Emerging Patterns of Authority in a Rajasthani Village*. New Delhi: Oxford University Press.

Chandra, Kanchan. 2000. 'The Transformation of Ethnic Politics in India: The Decline of the Congress and the Rise of the Bahujan Samaj Party in Hoshiarpur', *Journal of Asian Studies*, 59 (1), pp. 26–61.

Chaubisa, M.L. 1988. *Caste, Tribe and Exploitation: Exploration of Inequality at Village Level*. Udaipur: Himanshu Publications.

Chaudhary, S.N. 1987. *Dynamics of Rural Power Structure: Case Study of an Indian Village*. New Delhi: Amar Prakashan.

Chhibber, Pradeep. 1999. *Democracy Without Associations: Transformation of the Party System and Social Cleavage in India*. New Delhi: Vistaar Publications.

Cohn, Bernard S. 1969. 'Structural Change in Indian Rural Society', in Robert. E. Frykenberg (ed.), *Land Control and Social Structure in Indian History*. Madison: University of Wisconsin Press, pp. 53–122.

Corbridge, S., G. Williams, M. Srivastava, and R. Veron. 2005. *Seeing the State: Governance and Governmentality in India*. New York: Cambridge University Press.

Dirks, Nicholas B. 2001. *Castes of Mind: Colonialism and the Making of Modern India*. Princeton, NJ: Princeton University Press.

Dubey, Surendra N. 2001. *Education Scenario in India, 2001*. New Delhi: Authors Press.

Dumont, Louis. 1970. *Homo Hierarchicus: An Essay on the Caste System*. Chicago: University of Chicago Press.

Drèze, Jean and Amartya Sen. 1997. *Indian Development: Selected Regional Perspectives*. New Delhi: Oxford University Press.

———. 1995. *India: Economic Development and Social Opportunity*. New Delhi: Oxford University Press.

Frankel, F. and M.S.A. Rao (eds). 1989. *Dominance and State Power in India*. New Delhi: Oxford University Press.

Frykenberg, Robert E. 1969. *Land Control and Social Structure in Indian History*. Madison: University of Wisconsin Press.

Fuller, Christopher J. and John Harriss. 2000. 'For an Anthropology of the Modern Indian State', in C.J. Fuller and V. Benei (eds), *The Everyday State and Society in Modern India*. New Delhi: Social Science Press, pp. 1–30.

Gupta, Akhil. 1998. *Postcolonial Developments: Agriculture in the Making of Modern India*. Durham, NC: Duke University Press.

Harriss, John. 1982. *Capitalism and Peasant Farming: Agrarian Structure and Ideology in Northern Tamil Nadu*. New Delhi: Oxford University Press.

Hasan, Zoya. 1989. *Dominance and Mobilization: Rural Politics in Western Uttar Pradesh, 1930-1980*. New Delhi: Sage Publications.

Heller, Patrick. 2000. 'Degrees of Democracy: Some Comparative Lessons from India', *World Politics*, 52(4), pp. 484–519.

Jain, S.P. 1993. 'Reorganizing Grassroots Institutions for Sustainable Development', *Indian Journal of Public Administration*, 39(3), pp. 396–405.

Jalal, Ayesha. 1995. *Democracy and Authoritarianism in South Asia: A Comparative and Historical Perspective*. Cambridge, UK: Cambridge University Press.

Jaffrelot, Christophe. 2003. *India's Silent Revolution: The Rise of the Low Castes in North Indian Politics*. New Delhi: Permanent Black.

Jeffrey, Craig, Roger Jeffery, and Patricia Jeffery. 2004. 'Degrees without Freedom: The Impact of Formal Education on Dalit Young Men in North India', *Development and Change*, 35(5), pp. 963–86.

Karanth, G.K. 1997. 'Caste in Contemporary Rural India', in M.N. Srinivas (ed.), *Caste: Its Twentieth Century Avatar*. New Delhi: Penguin Books, pp. 87–109.

Kaviraj, Sudipta. 2000. 'Modernity and Politics in India', *Daedalus*, 129(1), pp. 137–62.

Kitschelt, Herbert. 2000. 'Linkages Between Citizens and Politicians in Democratic Polities', *Comparative Political Studies*, 33(67), pp. 845–79.

Kohli, Atul. 1990. *Democracy and Discontent: India's Growing Crisis of Governability*. Cambridge, UK: Cambridge University Press.

———. 1987. *The State and Poverty in India: The Politics of Reform*. Cambridge, UK: Cambridge University Press.

Kothari, Rajni. 1988. *State Against Democracy: In Search of Humane Governance*. New Delhi: Ajanta Publishers.

Krishna, Anirudh. 2006a. 'Poverty and Democratic Participation Reconsidered', *Comparative Politics*, 38 (4), pp. 439–58.

———. 2006b. 'Pathways Out of and Into Poverty in 36 Villages of Andhra Pradesh, India', *World Development*, 34(2), pp. 271–88.

———. 2004. 'Escaping Poverty and Becoming Poor: Who Gains, Who Loses, and Why? People's Assessments of Stability and Change in 35 North Indian Villages', *World Development*, 32(1), pp. 121–36.

———. 2003. 'What is Happening to Caste? A View from Some North Indian Villages', *Journal of Asian Studies*, 62(4), pp. 1171–93.

———. 2002. *Active Social Capital: Tracing the Roots of Development and Democracy*. New York: Columbia University Press.

Krishna, Anirudh, M. Kapila, M. Porwal, and V. Singh. 2005. 'Why Growth is not Enough: Household Poverty Dynamics in Northeast Gujarat, India', *Journal of Development Studies*, 41(7), pp. 1163–92.

Ladejinsky, Wolf. 1972. 'Land Ceilings and Land Reforms', *Economic and Political Weekly*, VII(7), p. 403.

Lupton, W.J.E. 1908. *Report on the Question of the Assessment of Land and Water Revenue in Ajmer-Merwara with Proposed Revenue Rates for District Ajmer*. Ajmer: Scottish Mission Industries Co. Ltd.

Manor, James. 2000. 'Small-Time Political Fixers in India's States', *Asian Survey*, 40(5), pp. 816–35.

———. 1993. *Power, Poverty and Poison: Disaster and Response in an Indian City*. New Delhi: Sage Publications.

Mayaram, Shail. 1998. 'Panchayats and Women: A Study of the Processes Initiated Before and After the 73rd Amendment in Rajasthan', Mimeo, Jaipur: Institute of Development Studies.

Mayer, Adrian. 1997. 'Caste in an Indian Village: Change and Continuity 1954-1992', in C.J. Fuller (ed.), *Caste Today*. New Delhi: Oxford University Press.

Mehta, Pratap B. 1997. 'India: Fragmentation amid Consensus', *Journal of Democracy*, 8(1), pp. 56–69.

Migdal, Joel S. 1988. *Strong Societies and Weak States*. Princeton: Princeton University Press.

Mitra, Subrata K. 1992. *Power, Protest and Participation: Local Elites and the Politics of Development in India*. London and New York: Routledge.

Morris-Jones, W.H. 1967. *The Government and Politics of India*. New York: Anchor Books.

Mooij, Jos (ed.). 2005. *The Politics of Economic Reform in India*, New Delhi: Sage Publications.

Nehru, Jawaharlal. 1946. *The Discovery of India*. Calcutta: Signet Press.

Oldenberg, Philip. 1999. 'The Thirteenth Election of India's Lok Sabha (House of the People)', Available at http://www.asiasoc.org/publications/indian_elections.13.a.html.

Pal, Mahi. 2000. 'Uttar Pradesh Panchayat Elections: From Politics to Tactics', *Economic and Political Weekly*, XXXV(37), pp. 3289–91.

Panini, M.N. 1997. 'The Political Economy of Caste', in M.N. Srinivas (ed.), *Caste: Its Twentieth Century Avatar*. New Delhi: Penguin Books, pp. 28–68.

Parry, Jonathan. 1999. 'Two Cheers for Reservation: The Satnamis and the Steel Plant', in Ramachandra Guha and Jonathan P. Parry (eds), *Institutions and Inequalities: Essays in Honour of Andre Béteille*. New Delhi: Oxford University Press.

Pinhey, A.F., Lt. Col. 1996 [1909]. *History of Mewar*. Jodhpur: Books Treasure.

PROBE. 1999. *Public Report on Basic Education in India*. New Delhi: Oxford University Press.

Reddy, G. Ram and G. Haragopal. 1985. 'The Pyraveerkar: The "Fixer" in Rural India', *Asian Survey*, 25(11), pp. 1147–62.

Robinson, Marguerite S. 1988. *Local Politics: The Law of Fishes. Development through Political Change in Medak District, Andhra Pradesh (South India)*. New Delhi: Oxford University Press.

Satterthwaite, David. 2006. 'The Role of Federations Formed by the Urban Poor in Communal Asset Accumulation', Paper presented at the Brookings Institution/Ford Foundation Workshop on Asset-Based Approaches to Poverty Reduction in a Globalized Context, Washington DC, 27–8 June.

Sen, Amartya. 1999. *Development as Freedom*. New York: Alfred Knopf.

Shukla, Srilal. 1992 [1968]. *Raag Darbari: A Novel*. New Delhi: Penguin Books.

Sheth, D.L. 1999. 'Secularization of Caste and Making of New Middle Class', *Economic and Political Weekly*, XXXIV(34–35), pp. 2502–10.

Singh, Rajendra. 1988. *Land, Power and People: Rural Elite in Transition, 1801–1970*. New Delhi and London: Sage Publications.

Spear, T.G.P. 1973. *Twilight of the Mughals: Studies in Late Mughal Delhi*. Karachi: Oxford University Press.

Srinivas, M.N. (ed.). 1987. *Caste: Its Twentieth Century Avatar*. New Delhi: Penguin Books.

Varshney, Ashutosh. 2001. 'Ethnic Conflict and Civil Society: India and Beyond', *World Politics*, 53(3), pp. 362–98.

Weiner, Myron. 1989. *The Indian Paradox: Essays in Indian Politics*. New Delhi and London: Sage Publications.

———. 1967. *Party-Building in a New Nation: The Indian National Congress*. Chicago: Chicago University Press.

———. 1963. *Political Change in South Asia*. Calcutta: K.L. Mukhopadhyay.

Wilkinson, Steven. 2004. *Votes and Violence: Electoral Competition and Ethnic Riots in India*. New York: Cambridge University Press.

Yadav, Yogendra. 1999. 'Politics', in Marshall Bouton and Philip Oldenburg (eds), *India Briefing: A Transformative Fifty Years*. New York: Asia Society, pp. 3–38.

IV Ideological Contestations in Indian Politics

21 Nationalism

Sudipta Kaviraj

In approaching the history of Indian nationalism, we face and have to find a way around a familiar problem—the partially helpful, partly obstructive presence of Western political theory. What pass as theories of nationalism in social science, produce as much confusion as help in understanding *our* nationalism. This is because of two different reasons. First, the discussion in Western social science itself is unclear; while a number of people advance what they regard as 'theories' of nationalism, different authors mean different things by theory. It is not always clear if authors are advancing *explanatory* theories—which would seek to explain why nationalism arises and where, or historical *observation* detecting patterns in what might appear disconnected phenomena. It appears that most authors are doing the latter, optimistically hoping that this would produce the first kind of theory. Second, although driven by the grand ambition of producing a general theory, many of the 'theorists' show inadequate historical understanding of anti-colonial nationalisms—the serious differences between European and anti-

colonial forms of nationalist ideology. Often these theories are tinged with a residual regret that subject peoples ungratefully overthrew European dominion, disregarding the fact that European rule brought them railways and telegraph, and often, democracy, though ground for this last belief is rather shaky. In many colonial settings, European powers reluctantly introduced limited representative institutions, but these cannot be confused with democracy. Therefore, while it is essential to think theoretically about Indian nationalism, we get limited assistance from the Western social science.

A somewhat different way of drawing upon the Western theoretical literature is not to take their global claims literally, but to follow individual suggestions regarding 'causal factors' that social scientists have found explanatorily significant. In recent literature, two suggestions have been particularly influential, though they tend to pull in somewhat different directions. The first was Ernest Gellner's startling inversion of the common sense historical sequence between the state and the nation (Gellner 1983), and Benedict Anderson's conception of the nation as an 'imagined community' (Anderson 1983). Read straightforwardly, Gellner's thesis appears inapplicable to an explanation of the origins of Indian nationalism. Its reversal of prior common sense was of course startling and persuasive. The cases of nationalist success in Germany and Italy probably excessively influenced the imagination of social science—after all, these were the two most recent cases of success of nationalism in Europe, and in both pre-existing nations secured the states that were their collective objects of desire. It was common in social science thinking to assume that the imagination of nations always precedes the creation of states that these nations demand. Against this standard view, Gellner suggested that the more historically salient process was the reverse one. In the most important European cases, entrenchment of stable state boundaries created the prior condition of establishing a stable, continuing relationship between the state and a given body of subjects. Fixing of territorial boundaries coincided with and causally encouraged the development of early capitalist industrial economies. It is the demand of industrial capitalist economies for mobility and substitutability of trained manpower that led to the growth of modern standardized education systems in these societies. For Gellner, it is a uniform process of cultural production of modern individuals devised by pre-existent modern states which create the cultural sentiments of modern nationalism. Since, for Gellner's story, early development of capitalist industries is a temporal *pre-condition* for the emergence of nationalism, his theory cannot explain the *origins* of Indian nationalist sentiments, which occurred in a country that saw very sparse industrial development till the mid-twentieth century. Clearly, his insight can throw light on the evolution of a particular form of nationalism *after* Independence from the British rule, but not its origins in the nineteenth century.

Recently, Benedict Anderson's suggestions in *Imagined Communities* have had the deepest influence in the analytics of modern nationalism. Because of Anderson's familiarity with Southeast Asian history, his reflections were less restricted by the primacy of European experience; his work has a weaker causal orientation, is less interested in setting down *conditions* under which nationalism emerged. Anderson also

offers a startling thesis—rather like Durkheim's suggestion about modern individualistic 'religion'—that as a sense of membership towards religious communities decline, and modern social conditions force individuals to exist in abstract relationships outside of face-to-face pre-modern communities, nationalism produces a new kind of 'imagined' community which replicates the intensity of religious emotions of communal belonging. Anderson's thesis views the contribution of what he calls 'print-capitalism' to this process as crucial. It is true that the idea of print-capitalism suits the facts of early modern European history better than the colonial world, but if the attachment of capitalism is taken away, the hypothesis acquires much greater plausibility in colonial conditions. Print was less decisively linked to a form of capitalism in India, but in its more artisanal form, it certainly played a decisive role in the growth of nationalist discourse.

Critics like Chatterjee have seriously contested Anderson's vaguer claim about the 'modular' influence of European nationalism (Chatterjee 1993). How persuasive it is depends crucially on how the notion of 'modularity' is read. A strong notion of the modular will imply that colonial nationalisms were essentially imitated from the historically prior precedents from successful European nation-states. True, colonial intellectuals, not surprisingly, selected those instances from the complex history of European nationalism which particularly suited their purpose. A Gellnerian narrative was in any case unavailable to them; but, even if it had been, it would not have commanded great persuasive power. The idea that states eventually produced nations, rather than the other way around, would have been discouraging for their political projects. Under the circumstances, it is hardly surprising that Indian nationalists endlessly read and commented on the two great narratives of European nationalism—Italy and Germany—where clearly a sense of national identity acquired immense power and drove a political movement of unification in a state. In retrospect, two rather distinct reasons seem to have drawn Indian nationalists to the cases of Italy and Germany. The first was that these were the most recent cases of successful national movements and fresh in political memory. But the second reason was perhaps more deeply significant—the process of a pre-existing nation achieving control of their state paralleled the historical aspirations of the colonial societies accurately. In any case, a more convincing story of Indian nationalism has to be told in exclusive Indian terms, by attending to the historically specific circumstances in which nationalism emerged as a collective mentality in India.

HISTORICAL PRECONDITIONS FOR INDIAN IDENTITY

There is an Indian version of the debate about the modernity of nationalism. Historians and sociologists agree that the political sentiment of unification and aspiration towards a common political entity was a predominantly modern phenomenon. Even those who reject this view and insist on pre-existing formations of collective mentality usually concede that pre-modern collective self-recognitions were primarily cultural, rather than political, in the modern sense. It is entirely reasonable to assert that for many centuries, people living in the subcontinent recognized a common repertoire of mythical and literary narratives, religious doctrines, and a loose, but commonly intelligible set of symbolic ideas and icons. It is pointed out, for instance, that among Hindus, the two epics and some literary-religious narratives around Rama or Krishna or the human figure of the Buddha were commonly recognized as sacred. Clear evidence exists of a public sphere of Sanskrit literary craft to which both northern and southern creative writers and artists belonged and in which they discussed a commonly held canon of literary excellence. Authors like Appaya Dikshita vied with the creations of Kalidasa, and composed a *Hamsasandesa* to compete with the *Meghaduta*. Masters of various fields of Sanskrit knowledge moved to the northern city of Varanasi from all parts of the subcontinent. Most remarkably, during the period of Mughal rule, this public sphere seems to have developed interesting ways of interconnecting the spheres of Sanskrit and Persianate learning and literature.[1]

A significant cultural process began from the end of the first millennium through the development of vibrant vernacular literary and political cultures,

starting with the relatively early instance of Tamil to the later emergence of vernacular literatures of great vitality in all regions of the subcontinent. Again, a remarkable feature of this development of vernacular literary spheres was that intellectual bilingualism continued until the eighteenth century. Sanskrit and Persian continued to act as linguistic vehicles for serious cognitive practices while maintaining their interaction with growing vernacular production. What was remarkable and distinctive about medieval Indian history was the simultaneous existence of two types of connections and exchange—a *lateral* exchange between the two cosmopolitan cultures of Sanskrit and Persian, and a vertical exchange between the vernaculars and these two cosmopolitan languages. Complex historical processes of this kind gave rise to an equally complicated structure of 'common culture' in pre-modern India. Some of the peculiar features of modern Indian political culture derive, in my view, from this 'deep structure' in history. The success of Indian nationalism and the state it fashioned after Independence is at least partly because it adapted to this historical structure, instead of trying to dismantle it by the unprecedented power of the modern state.

Following some early nationalist writings, we can distinguish between two forms of cultural commonness—of first and second degree, based on the distinction between use and intelligibility of language. It is a common fact that individuals' use of language is narrower than their linguistic understanding.[2] An individual fluently using a particular language can also understand another, though he might not be able to use it with much fluency. This is the common pattern of Indian bilingualism—individuals normally use one particular language, but can understand or partially use others. Common use of Tamil, for instance, would give a certain kind of cultural commonness to a group of people; but many of them would find English or Hindi intelligible. The circle of use and the circle of intelligibility are likely to be different for most ordinary Indians. Linguistically and culturally, ordinary Indians would be exposed to the constant social operation of both the vertical and the lateral connections between first degree and second degree common cultures. Intellectual elites of course, often operated in a vernacular and a cosmopolitan language. To take an example from Vaisnava religion, spread of Vaisnava ideas and ideals to regional communities always required the vehicle of a vernacular devotional literature in Tamil or Bengali; but the meta-local aspiration of the Vaisnava religious imagination required the articulation of at least some of their more intricate theological ideas in Sanskrit. Vaisnava culture in medieval India exhibited an early form of 'federal' structure. This is equally true of many other Hindu and Islamic religious sects which practised bilingualism between a vernacular and a cosmopolitan language. Similarly, religious travel like pilgrimages or requirements of trade encouraged common people to understand neighbouring languages or dialects to supplement the vertical diglossia of intellectual elites by a lateral version of their own. However, the central operative point about pre-modern culture is not the bare fact and extent of linguistic diglossia, but what this implied. This meant that common individuals were practised in the notion of first and second degree commonness. Bengali Vaisnavas would of course treat Gaudiya Vaisnava worshippers as a group with a common culture; but a slightly diluted version of cultural commonness would also include for them those who believed in somewhat different versions of the Vaisnava faith in other regions. This long historical capacity to produce a first and second degree commonness was adapted to modern political construction by Indian nationalism in the twentieth century.

THE NATIONALIST HISTORY OF NATIONALISM

Nationalist narratives are not disinterested, positivist accounts of past events: what is crucial to them is a particular way of including the present—the history of themselves, of those writing the history—into this history. The political interest of Indian nationalism lay in highlighting selected aspects of past history, but when it came to narrativizing the present, these histories emphasized what was common to all strands of the nationalistic thought, so that the entire history of modern India could be viewed as a seamless process of preparation for Independence. It was in the

interest of Indian nationalism, therefore, to produce a *teleological* history of itself—a story that showed a single Indian nationalism running from Ram Mohan Roy to Jawaharlal Nehru (Kaviraj 1994). The standard narrative acknowledged some internal progress—in refinement of ideas, greater clarity of purpose, and intensity of political effort—as the movement became more 'mature'.

The Indian National Congress (INC) came to undisputed power after the British left, and it sought to give itself an appropriately grand and uncontested history. In fact, during the actual nationalist struggle for Independence, although the Congress was always an ideologically ecumenical and sociologically complex political association of nationalists of various stripes, it contained significant differences. At the time of the nationalist movement, these political rivalries were intense and bitter. After Independence, however, these conflicts suddenly became historically irrelevant, and the Congress, in writing official histories of Indian nationalism, extended to these dissentient trends a retrospective narrative generosity. Official histories of Indian nationalism accordingly restated the benign view of a teleological progress towards eventual freedom, and offered to these trends the honour deserved by intense but misguided nationalists.

Analytically, this history is seriously flawed because it does not make distinctions in some cases, and in others makes misleading ones. I propose to disaggregate the history of Indian nationalism in two primary ways. First, the teleological narrative obscures rather than reveals the significant differences between the successive stages of growth of a nationalist imaginary. As we shall see, using a definition of nationalism drawn from its most developed stage, it masks the differences in content between this stage and the ideas of earlier periods. Against this general and casual definition of nationalism, it is possible to discern at least three quite separate stages in intellectual culture from the late eighteenth century, which are nationalist in fairly different senses. Apart from this disaggregation, which is primarily temporal, I shall suggest a second disaggregation of Indian nationalism in its third, most developed phase. Once ideologically developed nationalism emerged, it soon developed differential emphases, quite different grounds of justification of its ideas and political claims, and seriously divergent visions of the social future after Independence. As the departure of the British came palpably closer, these differences about the social constitution of the nation, the fundamental principles of the future state, became more intensely inflamed. A decisive victory of the Nehruvian elements within the Congress in the 1950s appeared to equate Indian nationalism with the secular, pluralist, modernist vision of what the nation should be. But it did not mean that radically different versions of the nationalist idea—religious, exclusivist, aggressive—entirely disappeared. When the Congress version of state nationalism faded and became seriously undermined in the 1980s, Hindu nationalism made a strong reappearance in the political life, and sought to impose its own anti-pluralist version of history into the institutions and discourses of the state. In some ways, the rise of Hindu nationalist politics in the 1980s was not because nationalism had declined, but because it was complex. Exhaustion of one of its strands led to a revival of another. The reasons for the rise of Hindu nationalism should be sought not outside, but in the complex history of pre-Independence nationalist politics.

EARLY REGIONAL PATRIOTISM

An interesting question arises about the time from which the history of nationalism should begin. The outbreak of violence in 1857–8 was undoubtedly one of the most widespread and politically serious challenges to British colonial power. Should it, as some nationalists contend, be regarded as the 'first war of national Independence'? This is a significant question because the answer to this puzzle turns on a convincing definition of nationalism. Is opposition to colonial rule the fundamental criterion for deciding what qualifies as nationalism? If it is, then the war against British rule in northern India in 1857 would qualify as the start of Indian nationalist politics; and ironically, the early years of the INC—which was a wholly loyalist political organization at its origins—will not, overturning some of the certainties of conventional nationalist historiography. At the same

time, it is entirely unclear that a successful uprising against the British in 1858 would have resulted in anything like a single nation-state in the whole of the colonial territory. The general consensus that does not regard the events of 1857–8 as the inaugural chapter of the history of nationalism, evidently, implicitly relies on a modernist definition of the nationalist political imaginary.

Two distinct ideas come together to form the recognizably modern ideas of nationalism. The first is a growing sense, caused by diverse historical circumstances, of specialness amongst groups of people (Greenfeld 1992). The second is a politicization of this idea, and an extension to the belief that these special people could not remain politically colonized by alien rulers. It appears from the Indian case that the two ideas are distinct and exclusive of each other; the first can exist without the second. At least there is a long historical gap between the emergence of the first idea and its slow conversion to the second. On the first issue, if a pre-existing *ethnie* is a requirement for the emergence of modern nationalism, the Indian case provides intriguingly indecisive evidence. What is undeniably true is that there existed stable pre-modern identifications of territories over which regional kingdoms were formed. From the second millennium, many of these territorial unities also saw the development of regional cultures based on new vernacular literatures. Areas that coincide with modern Orissa, Bihar, Bengal, Assam, or Andhra had territorial names with venerable genealogies, often stretching to ancient epics like the Mahabharata. If modern nationalist aspirations followed the patterns of pre-existing ethnie, nationalist movements and states should have emerged in each of these territories—which were united by a long line of criteria from Stalin's famous definition—long history, common culture, long spells of political unity, common language, often, because of their more modest size, common religious heritages (Stalin 1935). Ironically, the first signs of emergence of a sense of specialness among people did in fact appear in these linguistically bounded regions.

Entrenchment of British rule in eastern India led to critically significant cultural consequences. Modern education, coveted by a section of the indigenous people rather than imposed by the rulers, led to the rapid growth of new elites of an entirely untraditional character. Pre-eminence in traditional society was based on control over land, military, or administrative titles derived from the successor states to the Mughal Empire, or in case of Brahmins, religious prestige. Some segments of the traditional elites used their skills of high literacy—in esoteric languages like Sanskrit and Persian—to acquire English and move into the two new types of employment opened by colonial rule. Service of the colonial state and the acquisition of professional skills based on modern forms of knowledge provided new avenues to social power. Ram Mohan Roy still lived in a world divided between a fatally declining post-Mughal aristocracy and emerging modern elite. He is rightly regarded as the first modern intellectual in Indian history—a role he could play, paradoxically, on condition that he also acted as the last medieval one. But this world was quite transient; he could dispute the Hindu Sastras against conservative pandits, conduct debates on rationalist religion with Christian missionaries, and compose his first treatise in favour of monotheism in erudite theological Persian. Three decades later, this transient world of composite elements, drawn from three high cultures, had been decisively replaced by a new modern one entirely dominated by modern Western cognitive systems and intellectual discourse carried out in English. But the decisive end to the competition between traditional and modern forms of knowledge was marked by the origin of a new kind of contest between English, the new high language of Indian society and aspiring modern vernaculars.

The rise of this new, modern culture introduced two great divides, transforming the cognitive and intellectual map of the Indian society. It created an increasingly fraught division between those who adopted the new culture and started enjoying its forms of power, and those who continued to adhere to older forms. More significant, for a time, was a new kind of divide between those regions which came to be dominated by modernist elites and others still untouched by the modern cultural processes like Western education. The modern elite in Bengal established its undisputed social dominance inside its own geographic region, and, as British colonial power expanded towards the north-west, they supplied the critically significant professional manpower in collaborative administrative positions and modern professions. After the British power was established in southern India, the predominantly Tamil elite performed exactly comparable functions. Modern research by historians has revealed the surprising consequences of this cultural change. Initially the modernist elite, and subsequently literate Bengalis, were impressed by their own cultural resemblance to the British, and the immense gulf in language, idiom, cognitive orientation, and cultural taste from their illiterate fellow subjects; very sharply from people of neighbouring regions—like Bihar, Orissa, or Assam—whom they began to regard as culturally backward, ignorant, and incapable of attainment of high rationalism. Consequently, a sense of special destiny, similar to Greenfeld's description of the whole of the English people becoming elite (Greenfeld 1992), spread rapidly among the Bengali upper class, producing an intense sense of modern patriotism based primarily in a separate, and in this case, narrow but significant high modernist literary culture. A further consequence of this separation of high Bengali culture was, however, a deep sense of divide between Bengalis and other 'backward' Indians. Instead of moving early modern Bengali intellectuals towards conception of an Indian nation, it fostered a deep sense of regional patriotism for Bengal as a land, and for the Bengali language, and its new high literature. Since it was clearly the providential establishment of British rule which made all this possible, this intensified the political loyalty of the early Bengali elite towards the empire. Bengali poets in the early stages of this cultural transformation found no inconsistency in singing the praises of Bengal and Britannia at the same time. For the historical analysis of Indian nationalism, this period is significant because it demonstrates the relatively sudden but rapid growth of intense regional patriotism, but it leads neither to disaffection towards the empire nor to fellowship with other inhabitants of the country. Under a thin disguise of worshipping Bengal, the Bengali elite worshipped themselves in splendid isolation from all other Indians, in cosy proximity to their British benefactors. It is ironic, to say the least, to regard this stage as an unproblematic early stage of development of eventual *Indian* nationalism, for it clearly lacked two necessary conditions. Rather than being critical it was deeply loyal to the British rule; and second, its sense of patriotism and territorial identity was strictly confined to Bengal and its Bengali-speaking inhabitants, to the detriment of other Indians. Yet, it already contained some seeds of eventually different ideas. Ram Mohan Roy famously hoped in a letter that the British would not leave India for at least the next 200 years; yet his correspondence showed he was sensitive to the indignity of alien rule (Robertson 1999); and the self-regard of the Bengali elite could easily develop into greater aspirations in collaboration, and eventually towards the very plausible conclusion that a group of people who were so utterly indistinguishable from the British in their intellectual attainments could certainly practise representative government without foreign assistance. The pattern of ideas that I designate as regional patriotism, which seems to confirm arguments by both Anthony Smith (1991) and Leah Greenfeld, was thus a *structure* of ideas quite different from later, more mature forms of nationalism; yet it could be genetically linked to later developments in entirely different directions.

EMERGENCE OF ANTI-COLONIAL PATRIOTISM

Interesting temporal dislocations appear in the process through which this combination of patriotism and colonial loyalty gets transformed. Early manifestations of anti-colonial discontent appear, not entirely surprisingly, in literature. By the 1860s, Bengali creative writers started evincing a sharper discontent against British rule—entirely distinct from the traditionalist ideological imagination of the rebellion of 1857–8, during which the modernist elites of the whole of colonial India saw their destiny firmly connected to the British. Colonial ideology, promising economic prosperity and enlightened modern government, began to be compared with the historical reality of the British rule. Absorption of the ideas of political economy instigated an entirely novel discontent about slow economic growth, colonial exploitation, and particularly, de-industrialization. In

a parallel move, intellectuals who adopted new liberal ideas about political life developed a discontent about the lack of representation in government and began to detect indignity in unrepresentative foreign government. And most significantly, those who adopted ideas of political equality from the European Enlightenment found the racial basis of colonial rule repugnant in principle. Colonial education, meant to produce Indians with a European imagination, had in fact produced those results, but with additional unintended consequences in the long term. Ideas of liberal political equality, if taken seriously, were bound to undermine the placid justification of colonial rule.

Signs of such disaffection with colonial rule began to appear in Bengali literature in the 1860s, though not in political discourse. British rule was broadly liberal, but the administration kept watch over direct expression of political ideas, and tended to punish criticism by an expansive definition of 'sedition'—pushing the expression of criticism from journalism and political discourse into the partial secrecy and expressive ambiguity of literary writing. Literature used elaborate conventions of artistic speech, much harder to understand for administrators who did not know the vernacular. In any case, there was always the perpetually effective excuse of fictionality of expressive literature, making charges of seditious incitement hard to prove in law courts. Bankim Chandra Chattopadhyay appears as a crucial figure of expressive transition for several reasons. His serious expositions of political and moral principles of liberalism, in his early writings, showed an exemplary clarity of thought and expression, and a lucid grasp of its anti-colonial implications. As his thinking became more seriously anti-colonial, he used his masterly control over literary satire to write the first expressions of a sharp, deeply insightful anti-colonial criticism. His subsequent artistic work in immensely popular historical novels continued this effective subterfuge of literary fiction for expressions of intense anti-colonial feeling in imaginary theatres where unjust power was defied by heroic protagonists of defiance. Above all, Bankim Chandra's work was pioneering because he broke with conventional thinking on two crucial issues. First, he showed with great force and consistency that intellectually serious adoption of Enlightenment principles by Indians made it impossible to remain loyal to the colonial government; rather, it produced a moral obligation to defy colonial power—overturning decisively the previous connection between rationalist education and political loyalty. Eventually, this alteration in ideas led to the most significant sociological shift for the bases of political power—in time, it turned the class that was most loyal to the British colonial rule before 1850s into its bitterest political enemy, fatally disrupting the chain of native collaboration with imperial power. Equally significant was Bankim's suggestion, through his historical novels, that the indignity of subjection was shared commonly by all Indians, not restricted to Bengalis, and therefore, educated Bengalis should learn to regard illiterate Indians of other regions as essential parts of their nation rather than poor and backward 'others' sidelined by modern history. This was a historic act of re-drawing the imaginative boundary between the self and the other, between Bengalis and Indians, and performed a foundational role in the origins of 'Indian' nationalism.[3]

Bankim's thinking was unambiguously clear in rejecting loyalist collaboration and suggesting opposition to colonial rule. The second suggestion emerging from his immensely influential fictional art was much less straightforward. Clearly, 'we' should oppose the British, and eventually act for an end to subjection: but the boundaries and contents of his all-important 'we' were seriously underdetermined. His historical fiction turned the attention of the new Bengali intelligentsia towards the histories of defiance against unjust rule in India's past, rather than Bengal's. From his historical novels—which are imaginary extensions of real histories—there emerged a clear line of implication that the boundary of the Bengali self should be merged in something larger. But the designation of this larger self remained troubled and ambiguous. Constant stress on historical cases of subjection tended to view pre-modern Islamic empires in the same light as modern colonialism, interpreting Islamic rule as a prior case of foreign conquest, an anachronistic extension of modern imperialism backwards into the past. At times, in Bankim's imaginative world, the collective subject against

British rule—the 'we'—appeared to be Bengali, at other times, Hindu, at still others, Indian. In a sense, the three potential identities that are seen at play in Bankim's imaginative world—communities produced by the vernacular regional culture, by religious community, and by a territorial pluralist internally complex nation—remained the fundamental, irreducible real sources of political affiliation.

EMERGENCE OF POLITICAL NATIONALISM

Historically, slow dissatisfaction with British government assumed two primary forms; for British policies affected two fundamental classes in Indian society in quite different ways. As the modernist elite formed, expanded, and spread to different regions, they started feeling mildly discontented. Admitted freely into the colonial administration, initially they could not progress beyond a level. And what rankled most were the legal devices by which British interests sought to dominate business enterprise. Frustrated in what they regarded as their legitimate ambitions, sections of the modernist elite began to ponder the restrictions colonial institutions placed on the supposedly universal principles of liberal society. Disappointment of the modern elite was comparatively mild though, and they perceived the dependence of their own eminence on British power too vividly to try to endanger or challenge it. British land revenue policies affected the lives of the poor peasantry in a different way—often driving them to a point of desperation. From the period of high empire, these two lines of dissatisfaction found expression in two utterly different forms of political activity. Modern elites began to take advantage of the freedom of expression and association provided by British law to form associations that became increasingly political, leading to the establishment of the entirely loyal INC in 1895. Peasant discontent against land revenue demands from zamindars and the state found expression in repeated uprisings.[4] But these two types of politics were utterly unconnected. The elites despised the poor peasants and feared the political disorder of the rebellions. The peasants viewed the new elites as mere instruments of the colonial state, indifferent to others' fates. Sociologically, elite discent was spread across the whole country in thin layers, particularly in urban metropolitan areas. Rebellions by the peasantry were always intense local affairs which created utter disorder on a local scale. Both were relatively easy for the colonial state to control—elite discontent by a combination of disregard and occasional concessions, and peasant revolts by decisive use of military force. Both were early expressions of nationalism, of divergent character, but, unconnected to each other, they presented no threat to British rule. To present a serious political challenge to British authority in India, a movement was required which could combine the popular support of peasant movements with the country-wide scale of middle-class politics.

Sociologically, that was precisely the combination achieved by Gandhi's mobilizations in the early 1920s. The non-cooperation movement, for the first time, combined elite support with intense petty bourgeois mobilization and linked these two with successful appeal to masses of the peasantry. Mass nationalist agitations from now on combined three dissimilar kinds of resources—they could draw upon the financial and strategic power of modern elites and business, the intellectual resources of a rebellious petty bourgeoisie, and the immense power of numbers of the Indian peasantry. In sociological terms, for the first time, these movements could be called the mobilization of an entire nation. In the 1920s, India seemed to have developed a form of pluralistic nationalism that had found an answer to the question of how to integrate inside it the quite divergent aspirations of identities based on regional vernacular cultures and religious communities.

Gandhi was indispensable to Indian nationalism in a second way as well. Colonial education produced another fatal disruption in Indian cognitive culture. Societies are bound together usually by a Gramscian 'common sense'—a generally accepted and intelligible common grid of descriptive and evaluative concepts through which average members of a society cognitively approach and act upon their social world. Despite social inequalities of status, income, and education, this 'common sense' imparts an indispensable cognitive and practical cohesion to a society—a fundamental Durkheimian

idea. Education and cognitive change, a critically significant process in the making of the modern elite, decisively disrupted this unity of a social 'common sense'. Accepting rationalist cognitive procedures, modernist elites began to conceive of the sphere of politics primarily as a field of disenchanted and amoral instrumentalist power. Other segments of the Indian society, untrained in and mistrustful of modern education, regarded political life in primarily religious-ethical terms. Gandhi, for the first time, was able to fashion an idiom of political argument which could appeal to and therefore connect these two spheres of entirely divergent forms of 'common sense'. Gandhian nationalism effected not merely a sociological, but also a cognitive and imaginative connection between elite and mass conceptions of political order (Chatterjee 1986; Nandy 1983).

INTERNAL COMPLEXITIES OF INDIAN NATIONALISM

By the second decade of the twentieth century, the idea of a nation became a dominant force in Indian politics; no political group could function without defining its own relation to or place within the increasingly complex field of the nationalist imaginary. Two types of complexities were particularly significant, and Indian nationalist politics under the Congress devised highly specific and interesting solutions to the problems these complexities posed. First, the identity of 'being an Indian' was temporally a modern invention, made possible, as the British tirelessly stressed, by the common frame of British political rule; politically, at least, it did not have much historical depth. Ironically, this did not mean that there were no historically deep identities in India—two types of identity were clearly of venerable ancestry which had obviously continued over a long past history. The first kind of identity was based on territorial regions, held together by durable political structures of regional kingdoms, and subsequently fortified by the rise of vernacular linguistic cultures. Second, identities based on religious communities were also of long standing. Communities of religious sects flourished among Hindus, and from the tenth century, Islamic communities developed in various regions and produced flourishing cultures, often supported by political dominion. Early Christian communities existed in south India, and small religious groups of Jains and other faiths were spread across the subcontinent. What is crucial in this picture of religious diversity is the fact that none of these communities became entirely coincident and dependent on political power—making the identity of the ruler and his subjects entirely fixed and convergent, as happened in the Westphalian settlement in Europe. Linguistic cultures based on vernaculars were the most stable constituents of cultural identity, but these did not find an easy translation into political power. With the standardizing techniques of modern printing and the emergence of a normative high language, linguistic regional identities became reinforced, producing an intense form of early regional patriotism. One of the most interesting and unusual historical developments regarding identity was that as an *Indian* nationalism gradually began to emerge, it resolved its potential contradiction with regional linguistic identities by conceiving of the national identity as a *second-order* one which did not cancel, but rather subsumed cultural communities of linguistic regions. Individuals could feel simultaneous, but distinct patriotic affects for both their region and their 'nation'. The long-term logic of subsumption that had characterized Indian political life for centuries was simply translated into a modern form by pluralist nationalists. The political imagination behind the Indian state was thus an ingenious hybrid of the ideas of empire-state and nation-state; in fact the nation-state absorbed with clever adaptation the complex and flexible arrangement of power that characterized pre-modern empires (Dasgupta 1970).

An identical solution, based on similar principles, was advanced for the relation between religious and national identities. By working for a pluralist 'secular' state, which would not give priority to any community, and a liberal legal structure that was to act 'blind' to faith differences among individuals, nationalists hoped to calm the anxieties of various religious communities. But unlike the settlement of the relation between the regional and national identities, that between the national and religious identities remained deeply contentious. Abstractly,

the idea that all communities were to be treated with dignity was generally acceptable—but precisely because of the subtle ambiguity in what it practically implied. What did this imply in institutional terms? Some sections of the modern elite interpreted this to mean the establishment of a democratic constitution with guarantees of religious freedom for individuals and protection for minority groups. British colonial discourse, apart from direct policies of 'divide and rule' also introduced a deeply unsettling element into Indian political discourse by asserting that although in Europe *majority* was a *deliberative* concept, in the Indian context, majority and minority referred not to results of deliberative processes of voting, but to *identity* communities—an idea that British political elites also applied to Ireland. Sections of the Muslim elite translated their demands into an 'equal treatment' of communities—which meant more than proportional weight to Muslim constituencies. Establishment of a liberal democratic government, they argued, would lead to a subjection of the Muslim minority to a Hindu majority rule. Equal treatment must mean either a veto for the Muslims, or a loose confederation of provinces which would leave the Muslim-majority areas large powers of self-government, effectively turning them into majorities in those regions, or, as it turned out eventually, a separate state. This was a paradoxical solution, as this meant that every minority must try to set up a state in which it forms a majority—a solution that created serious problems for the state of Pakistan subsequently. There were similar views among Hindu nationalists who saw the two religious communities as politically irreconcilable, and translated democracy into a simple majority principle. These groups called for the new national state to be a Hindu state. In fact, this revealed how the luminously clear notion of equal treatment of people ran into serious difficulties regarding its institutional translation.

Equal treatment of religious communities could also be read in a wholly different way, as suggested by Gandhi. For Gandhi, it was impossible to build the state in India without reference to religious groups, but he also thought that since Indian society contained several religious communities, the state should give *equal respect* to all because their fundamental principles were remarkably similar. After Independence, political pragmatism added another idea to the Gandhian one—that the state should maintain *equal distance* from all religious communities (Bhargava 1998, 2007). The nationalist movement included others—like Nehru and the Communists—who believed that the modern state should be atheistically secular, and religious considerations simply should not intrude into the organization of collective political life. Interestingly, the Gandhian and Nehruvian positions had fundamental disagreements on philosophical first principles, but concurred in practice—from a deeply religious, and an equally deeply sceptical starting point, the two views recommended practical, political conduct of tolerance between communities based on ideas of pluralism. After Partition, this interesting practical consensus formed the basis of state secularism in India.

INTERNAL DIVERSITY

The question of 'communalism' touched on fundamental issues of nationalist construction. Was the 'nation' modern or ancient? Was the state to be based on a particular identity? What kind of identity was it to be based on? On long-term identities like religion or region, or an entirely new identity of a politically conceived Indianness? What chances of success could a historically recent identity have? All the significant questions central to academic historical sociology were, in fact, crucial for the construction of the Indian nation-state. An example can demonstrate the internal diversity of the large field of ideas collectively designated as Indian nationalism. It was more like a field of thought, rather than a doctrine.

Schematically, four kinds of ideological positions emerged on the question of religious identity and its relation to the state. Implicitly starting from the Orientalist view that there was an essential difference between European and Indian society, which was incapable of individuation, one opinion held that a nation-state needed to be founded on a vivid sense of common identity. In India, this identity could be provided only by religious communities which constituted the horizons of people's culture and social life. Religious communities were in that sense putative nations, which had lived quite separately

in history and in uneasy proximity during colonial rule. A nation-state in the Indian subcontinent was to be based, therefore, on religious communities. By its nature, this opinion would have split into movements for two states. Even if Hindu nationalists might have allowed inclusion of non-Hindus into the state, if the state was based on religious identity that would have meant offering them an inferior form of citizenship, which they were bound to reject. Muslim separatism equally accepted the colonial premise that in non-European conditions, the distinction between majorities and minorities was not one produced transiently by the deliberative process of elective decisions, but by the solid permanent divisions of identity. Ideals of ordinary democracy could not be applied to societies outside Europe; this implied that democracy had no solution to questions of identity diversity. If democracy was not a safeguard for identity minorities, it followed that every group must seek to establish a state in which it would form a majority. In essence, a belief that the nation-state required a prior basis in identity and that identity in India was predominantly religious must result in the demand for at least two nation-states.[5]

Curiously, a startlingly different interpretation of the relation between the claims of religion and the principles of state construction came from Gandhi. Gandhi began from the undeniable sociological fact that Indian society was deeply religious, and it followed that religious individuals would want not merely their personal lives but also the important questions of public life to be governed by religious principles—which they assumed were given by God, not by fallible human reason. Two ideas appeared to Gandhi to be obvious in the Indian context. First, the central principles of all religions were similar, at least non-contradictory—an optimistic interpretation of the facts of religious life. Second, on a personal level, if an individual's religion was highly significant for him, it must be apparent that to others, their religion would be equally important. This fundamental conception of reciprocity, read into traditional religion, then produced the effortless corollary that religious individuals must understand and respect others' need to practise their own religious lives unhindered. These two ideas were sociologically confirmed by the actual practice of religious syncretism in the Indian subcontinent. Gandhi's approach obviated the considerations of identity—majorities and turned the social fact of religious diversity into the fundamental argument for a pluralist nation-state.

By contrast, leftists like Nehru and the Communists constructed an argument for pluralism from very different theoretical grounds. Even Nehru, despite his admiring collaboration with Gandhi, rejected Gandhi's conception of how religion worked in the world as excessively optimistic and romantic, and believed that a condition for a pluralistic nation-state was that its public institutions should be secular, that is, free from religious influence, and religion should become a matter of individual conscience and private observance. Recently, theorists have pointed out that the actual practice of secularism in India was quite different from the ideas of more radical, modernist secularism supported by the radical Left. In fact, after the 1940s a subtle differentiation of positions took place—with Communists maintaining a hard atheistic stance, and Nehru moving away to a more moderate conception of secularism modifying his initial hostility to religious belief. In any case, the secularism of Indian state institutions practised the principles of equal respect for and equal distance from all religious groups—ironically, a view philosophically closer to ideas coming from Gandhi and Tagore rather than the radical Left. Although Nehru was in uncontested control of the institutions of the state for nearly two decades, and his personal intellectual sympathies would have been towards a more modernist secularism, the requirements of political realism made the practice of state secularism less uncompromising than his intellectual principles (Bhargava 1998).

DIVERSITY OF NATIONALISM AND CONSTRUCTION OF THE STATE

It follows from this picture of Indian nationalism, that any attempt at deriving policies or even fundamental principles from this body of thought involved serious internal contestation. Different visions of state building could, and did, speak in the name of Indian nationalism claiming its immense emotional authority.

Clearly, there was no single road from nationalist thinking to the detailed institutional architecture of the nation-state. It is interesting to attend to the politics of this crucial translation—how, from the diverse, and intensely contested mass of ideas, the outlines of a state structure emerged through constitutional discussions in the late 1940s. As long as the assumption of political power was far away, Indian nationalism could accommodate the luxuriant diversity of political and social perspectives, and accommodation of diversity added to its political strength because quite diverse ideological groups could coalesce into an effective coalition against British rule. After Independence, this diversity of political tendencies had to be persuaded to take some practical decisions about institutional form.

For nearly three years, the Constituent Assembly engaged in detailed discussions about the principles on which the institutions of independent India would be founded. The two central issues of identity—the relation between the nation and religious communities, and between the nation and regional cultures—had to be resolved before political institutions could be given a decisive form (Austin 1966). Partition formed the background to the debates in the Constituent Assembly—first, the constitutional concession for a separate state of Pakistan, followed by the hideous communal rioting during transfer of populations. Indian Constitution makers faced a clear and decisive choice between two ways of viewing the nation-state's relation to religious identity—India could be conceived constitutionally either as a Hindu state, or a pluralist nation founded on secular principles. The Constituent Assembly, despite resentment from Hindu nationalist groups, decided in favour of a state of religious pluralism. Significantly, the Indian constitutional settlement avoided the excessively modernist solutions tried by the Soviet Union or Ataturk's Turkey in which the secularism of the state pits it in a relation of constant hostility to popular religious practice. It admitted a more realistic, practical solution in which the state distanced itself from all religions, and simply committed to treating them with equal respect in this sense. In effect, the Indian solution was to deny the comprehensive and exclusive demand of the *national* identity, to the exclusion of all others. A complex national identity was not in competition with other identities, but subsumed the rest. The principle was to deny an exclusive claim of any single identity, but to acknowledge that in the modern world, individuals would require several kinds and levels of identity which could exist in a pluralist combination.[6]

Eventually, a very similar solution was found institutionally for the fraught relation between regional and national identity. The national identity of an Indian did not collide with her identity as an inhabitant of a region; indeed, in the 1950s, to be 'an Indian', an individual had to be something else as well—a Tamil, or a Bengali, or a Marathi. This solution was translated into the constitutional devices of Indian federalism—particularly after the states' reorganization on the basis of linguistic identity in 1956. At the time of Independence, the federal structure was simply based on the administrative consequences of British rule. The states' reorganization process of 1956 was a fundamental concession to the idea of a complex, pluralistic identity as a basis of the nation-state.

BANAL NATIONALISM

Historically, Indian nationalism went through three clear phases—an enthusiastic phase during the nationalist movement for Independence, followed by a period of institution construction, but afterwards it faced the danger of sinking into banality by constant reiteration. Institutions of the Indian state came to reflect most closely the pluralist, secularist, complex version of nationalist imaginary that Nehru and the modernist elites of India preferred over alternative versions favoured by the Hindu nationalists, or even by Gandhi. State nationalism stressed India's cultural, linguistic, religious pluralism, and declared its commitment to respect them, and to treat them as sources of the nation's strength rather than weakness. This form of nationalism began to permeate Indian social life through the agencies of the state and civil society. Two vehicles of nationalism were particularly influential because of their reach and popularity—the schools system, primarily supported by state finance, accepted its curricular recommendations; and Hindi popular films which trawled the regional literatures

to offer stories of social reform. By the 1960s, Indian nationalism came to be equated in public culture and intellectual discussions with this specific 'Nehruvian' interpretation of its central principles. But in the decades after Independence, nationalism as a political ideology—and more significantly as a political *imaginary*—underwent another crucial transformation. During the movement for Independence, nationalism—of all varieties—claimed enthusiastic support from its adherents as an emancipatory idea, opposed to the oppressive powers of the colonial state. With Independence, it went through a crucial re-positioning in the political universe; it became closely linked to the self-interpretation of the nation-state. Through the endless rituals of institutional repetition, which were meant to make it unforgettable, it suffered the subtle decrepitude of the over-familiar. Because it was constantly presented, people did not have to think about it anymore. The dull repetitiousness of state-controlled media, the spontaneous invocations by high and popular culture, the endless evocation of the deeds of the nationalist leaders in political arenas and everyday social spaces began to make people forget, instead of remember, what Indian nationalism was in its days of opposition. It began by the 1970s falling into a state of banality.

From the 1970s there was a reverse process as well. Banality and boredom were caused by the fact that practically no one challenged the central tenets of state nationalism—they came to acquire the ironic respect reserved for clichés. But the close association of the state to this form of nationalism began to bring in opposite results. All the state's actions claimed nationalism for its ideological justification, and since its actions had differentially beneficial results for social groups, inevitably, after a few decades, groups which were marginal or hostile to the state began to ask whose state it was, and began to question its customary claim to act in universal interest. Long spells of uncontested Congress government associated that form of nationalism too closely with the Congress, as it assumed the right to decide what could be regarded as falling within 'national' interest. Congress nationalism, soiled by its ineptitude in governance, accusations of corruption, and general inertia, came to be seriously challenged by three different claims of identity. From the 1970s, political groups based on lower-caste identities have asserted that the constitutional promises of reform were ineffectual, and no serious change has taken place in the caste-based inequalities of income and opportunities—for these groups, the nation-state has acted entirely in favour of the upper-caste groups. A decade later, Hindu nationalist groups mounted a second serious challenge to pluralist nationalism, claiming that for electoral advantage the Congress promoted the interest of religious minorities at the expense of the Hindu community.[7] Regional identities did not offer a general challenge to the idea of an Indian nation-state after 1956, but in particular regions, like Kashmir, Punjab, Assam, and the Northeast, serious dissatisfaction with the Indian nation-state has festered for a long time. Significant political groups in these regions have disputed the right of the state to speak on behalf of the entire nation, and of the Indian nation's right to unproblematically subsume them. In recent years, the militancy of regionalism in Punjab and Assam has declined, but Kashmir remains an intractable problem. Due to a process of long-term degradation of democracy, it has slowly turned into a case of convex perceptions of injustice based on regional, religious, and economic issues. With its connection with the political ambitions of Pakistan—to justify and complete the two-nation idea that formed its basis, and more recently, entanglements with the larger instability of the Islamic world of the Middle East—its solution or chances of accommodation with conventional Indian nationalism appear remote.

But the recent resurgence of new forms of Indian nationalism—through a serious challenge from a modernist Hindu nationalism and the response in the form of a renewed justification for Nehruvian pluralism from the Congress—seems to point to an interesting sociological reality. Six decades of significant economic change, driven by the forces of a capitalist economy and a powerful interventionist state, have produced a relatively large, economically powerful, and politically assertive modern professional class which supports the idea of a modern nation-state in India—against forces advocating primacy of regional identities or separatist politics. Despite their conflict in other ways, both the state and the market operate on a *national* scale, and the social classes associated with them support the idea of a strong national state as a precondition for further economic growth. If the state is able to force an equitable distribution of the gains of this economic resurgence, it will gather greater legitimacy among the common people. But this constitutes a firm sociological basis for the idea of Indian nationalism.

NATIONALISM AND GLOBALIZATION

Clearly, in the last few decades, the world has entered a new phase of accelerated economic integration generally designated as globalization. Two primary forces—both economic—have driven this process. First, after the collapse of communism and the slow liberalization of mixed economies in many parts of the world, the entire world has come to be encompassed by varying forms of the capitalist economy, with unprecedented density and speed of trade. Unexpectedly, economies like China, still politically controlled by a Communist regime, but functioning as a massive manufacturing powerhouse for the world capitalist economy, have emerged as the primary beneficiaries of economic globalization. A second aspect of economic globalization is a gradual perception of indivisibility of global 'common goods' like the environment. Both capitalist trade interconnections and perception of common indivisible interests have raised demands for collective controls over these processes. Some utopian theorists of globalization see in this the historic demise of the nation-state. In actual fact, the decline of the powers of the nation-state are extremely uneven across the world—what is happening is that the state is undergoing a serious historical transformation, and the functions that were bundled together in the familiar structure of the nation-state during the last three centuries are becoming unpacked, and redistributed between various levels of political authority—sub-national, regional, and international. Although most countries are subjected to similar economic pressures from global capitalism, the political transformation of the nation-state is very uneven and following divergent paths. In Europe, regionalism is generally endorsed by democratic nation-states, but that kind of 'decline' is very different from other cases, where the minimal authority of the state has failed. In a third kind of case, as in Iraq or former Yugoslavia, a state formerly held together by coercive means, has unravelled as a consequence of democratization. If it is acknowledged that capitalist globalization affects all states, but not in the same fashion, or with the same consequences, it appears that the Indian case is not like any of these three other types. It is not similar to Europe, as South Asian Association of Regional Cooperation (SAARC) is an insubstantial regional entity. India is not in any sense a 'failed state'; and it is not in serious danger of disintegration. On the contrary, the cases of India and China show an opposite process. The state has played a crucial role in controlling the consequences of globalization, and assisted the economies in re-positioning themselves to benefit from increased trade flows. It is plausible that the Indian nation-state might have to accept more stringent international obligations on questions relating to the environment and trade, but these hardly threaten the state with imminent decline of its powers. Rather, the recent dramatic growth of the Indian economy has set off a scramble among political parties to claim credit for this change, and a general infusion of a sense of nationalism among political and business leaders. There has not been a similar resurgence of intellectual formulations of nationalism, but there are significant trends in political discourse and academic writing which collectively represent an attempt to reconfigure the central ideas of Indian nationalism in a new age. On one side, Hindu nationalist politics suggests a revision in the direction of a modernist but distinctly less pluralist conception of the nation, but its attractiveness seems to be in decline. On the other, there is a widespread collective effort to restate the principles of Nehruvian pluralist nationalism in the historically altered context, seeking to readjust state institutions to meet demands of inclusion from marginalized and disadvantaged political groups. It appears that Indian nationalism is at the threshold of a new stage, rather than the end of its story.

NOTES

1. For a long-term historical view of culture and power in the world of Sanskrit, see Pollock (2006).

2. Bhudev Mukhopadhyay, a Bengali thinker in the nineteenth century, makes that argument in Mukhopadhyay (1983).

3. For Bankimchandra's ideas on the development of Indian nationalism, see Chatterjee (1986), Raychaudhuri (1988), and Kaviraj (1995).

4. The classic study of peasant uprisings in colonial India is Guha (1983).

5. For a detailed historical account of the emergence of Hindu nationalism, see Jaffrelot (1996).

6. For analyses of different aspects of Indian secularism and divergent assessments, see Bhargava (1998).

7. For details of the rise of Hindu nationalism in recent decades, see Jaffrelot (1996).

REFERENCES

Anderson, Benedict. 1983. *Imagined Communities*. London: Verso Books.

Austin, Granville. 1966. *India's Constitution: Cornerstone of a Nation*, Oxford: Clarendon Press.

Bhargava, Rajeev. 2007. 'The Distinctiveness of Indian Secularism', in T.N. Srinivasan (ed.), *The Future of Secularism*, New Delhi: Oxford University Press.

_____ (ed.). 1998. *Secularism and Its Critics*. New Delhi: Oxford University Press.

Chatterjee, Partha. 1993. *The Nation and Its Fragments*. Princeton: Princeton University Press.

_____. 1986. *Nationalist Thought and the Colonial World*. London: Zed Books.

Chatterjee, Partha and Gyan Pandey (eds). 1992. *Subaltern Studies*, VII, New Delhi: Oxford University Press.

Dasgupta, J. 1970. *Language Conflict and National Development*. Berkeley: University of California Press.

Gellner, Ernest. 1983. *Nations and Nationalism*. Oxford: Blackwell Publishing.

Greenfeld, Liah. 1992. *Nationalism: Five Roads to Modernity*. Cambridge, MA: Harvard University Press.

Guha, Ranajit. 1983. *Elementary Aspects of Peasant Insurgency in Colonial India*. New Delhi: Oxford University Press.

Jaffrelot, Christophe. 1996. *The Hindu Nationalist Movement in India*. New York: Columbia University Press.

Kaviraj, Sudipta. 1995. *The Unhappy Consciousness*. New Delhi: Oxford University Press.

_____. 1994. 'The Imaginary Institution of India', in Partha Chatterjee and Gyan Pandey (eds), *Subaltern Studies*, VII. New Delhi: Oxford University Press.

Mukhopadhyay, Bhudev. 1983. *Samajik Prabandha* [Essays on Society]. Kolkata: Pascim Banga Pustak Parsad.

Nandy, Ashis. 1983. *The Intimate Enemy*. New Delhi: Oxford University Press.

Pollock, Sheldon. 2006. *Language of the Gods in the World of Men*. Berkeley: University of California Press.

Raychaudhuri, Tapan. 1988. *Europe Reconsidered*. New Delhi: Oxford University Press.

Robertson, Bruce Carlisle. 1999. *The Essential Writings of Ram Mohan Roy*. New Delhi: Oxford University Press.

Smith, Anthony. 1991. *National Identity*. London: Penguin Books.

Srinivasan, T.N. (ed.). 2007. *The Future of Secularism*. New Delhi: Oxford University Press.

Stalin, Joseph. 1935. *Marxism and the National and Colonial Question*. London: Lawrence and Wishart.

22 Secularism

Neera Chandhoke

WHAT IS SECULARISM ABOUT?

Despite the fact that the decade of the 1980s witnessed the onset of a richly textured and nuanced debate on secularism, till date neither scholars nor political practitioners seem to be quite sure what secularism is about. Is it about erecting a 'wall of separation' between the state and religion and thereby devaluing religion? Is it about the state treating all religions as equal and thus validating religious identities? Is it about building minority rights into the concept and practice of secularism? And if so, do minority rights *not* contravene both meanings of secularism—that of state indifference/neutrality towards religion and formal equality of all religions? Above all, two troubled and troublesome questions stalk the conceptual debate on secularism: One, considering the pervasiveness of religious sensibilities in India, is secularism appropriate for the country? Two, has secularism, as practised in the country, proved capable of warding off the communalization of Indian society and polity?[1] Does it have the capacity to do so? Given the centrality of these questions to

political and social life, it is not surprising that the secularism debate has been dogged by sharp and often acerbic polemics. That this polarization has occurred among like-minded scholars is surprising. But that these polemics hamper the conceptual and political understanding of secularism is perhaps not entirely unexpected. The pervasive uncertainty that dogs secularism, however, breeds several unfortunate consequences. For, as Madan points out, though the ambiguity of secularism was at one point considered its strength, its vagueness is now a poor foundation for clear-headed public policies (2003: 65).

Much of the ambiguity that attends these debates can be traced to the fact that scholars tend to employ two different interpretations of secularism as a hinge for their respective critiques/defence of the concept. These two meanings are that of secularism as the separation of state and religion, and secularism as equality of all religions. The first interpretation holds that (a) the state shall not concern itself with religious beliefs, practices, and institutions; (b) that the state shall not be associated with a particular religion; (c) that the state shall permit freedom of conscience, belief, and religion for all its citizens; and (d) that the state shall not discriminate between citizens on the basis of their religious beliefs. This understanding of secularism comes to us from the history of Western Europe, during the course of which the domain of state policy and that of religion was separated. In particular it has come to us from the US, in the formulation of President Thomas Jefferson that a 'wall of separation' exists between the state and religion. Jefferson in effect referred to the First Amendment to the Constitution of the US. The Establishment Clause in the First Amendment prohibits the establishment of a national religion by the Congress, and prohibits preference for one religion over another. In the famous *Board of Education of Kiryas Joel Village School District vs Grumet*, Justice Souter interpreted the clause to mean that the government should not prefer one religion to another, or religion to irreligion. The second part of the clause, known as the 'Free Exercise Clause', states that the Congress cannot prohibit the free exercise of religion. The freedom to believe is part of the general grant of freedom to expression, assembly, and association. The second interpretation of secularism, as detailed below, was generated in and through the Indian historical experience; that the state shall treat all religious groups equally.

SECULARIZATION AND SECULARISM

Much of the confusion is caused by the fact that the concept of secularism tends to elide into that of secularization. Secularism, it is often presumed, follows or accompanies the secularization of society, or that secularization is an *essential prerequisite* for secularism as state policy. Thereupon a number of scholars have argued that secularism is simply inappropriate for a deeply religious country like India. Yet secularism and secularization are to some extent independent of each other, and one need not necessarily follow the other. Kemal Attaturk did, after all, establish a secular state in religious Turkey. And the leaders of the freedom struggle in India sought a way out of religious conflict in and through the adoption of the principle of secularism. In other words, the extent of religious belief or unbelief does not necessarily correlate positively with the extent of

state separation from or control over religion (Keddie 2003: 16).

It is, by now, generally agreed that the assumed binary distinction between secularized and religious societies is an optic illusion, and that the distinction is a matter of degree. Secularization does not necessarily imply that people have become areligious or anti-religious, or that religion has disappeared from both the public domain and the domain of personal belief. What it does imply is that religion is just *one*, and not necessarily the most important, way in which people understand themselves and their relationships. Religion may continue to matter, but the way in which it matters has changed from earlier times, when religiosity provided *the* overarching guide to everyday life. For with the coming of the age of reason and the age of science, individuals no longer needed to refer to a body of sacred beliefs, which were by reason of sacredness considered outside the purview of rational investigation, to live their lives. They had other intellectual resources to help them do so, in the form of knowledge provided by science and knowledge provided by reasoned and rational thinking. Therefore, since religion had lost its capacity to provide a comprehensive worldview, it was demoted.

The secularization of society is of some interest to sociologists, but it also holds important implications for politics and state policy. First, on the assumption that rational individuals are able to either *balance* religious and non-religious considerations, or *subordinate* the former to the latter, the state can leave religious beliefs and institutions well nigh alone. It does not need to keep them under check. Second, the state no longer requires the sanction of religion to legitimize its power or translate power into authority. Correspondingly, since the public domain has been cleared of religion, the state can subordinate religious projects to secular ones, and ignore the salience of religion in people's lives *as long as these beliefs do not contravene the core secular values of that society*. Secularism in a secularized society is, in other words, premised upon the separation of the public and private spheres of individual and collective existence. Therefore, it is relatively easy to essay a wall of separation between the state and religion, or assert the dominance of the secular over the sacred in public life.

HISTORICAL EVOLUTION OF
SECULARISM IN INDIA

In India, however, matters are different. Few would contest that religious sensibilities dominate individual and collective lives to some extent. And few would contest that since the early decades of the twentieth century, the politicization of religious identities has inexorably propelled religion into the public sphere.[2] By the 1920s, at the very time when Mahatma Gandhi set out to forge a major mass movement that could take on colonialism, the politicization of religious identities, whether in the form of the Muslim League or that of the Hindu Mahasabha, could have hampered the project of building a pan-Indian freedom struggle. Mahatma Gandhi looked for a principle that could bind people who subscribed to different faiths together, and which could weld them into a mass movement. This principle he found in the doctrine of *sarva dharma sambhava*, which can be read as 'equality of all religions' or 'all religions should be treated equally'. Given Mahatma Gandhi's religiosity, the notion of sarva dharma sambhava was not only a pragmatic principle designed to bring people together, it was also a normative principle that recognized the value of religion in people's lives. On the other hand, for Pandit Nehru, profoundly uneasy as he was with the kind of political passions that religious identities had the power to evoke, secularism meant something else altogether. Nehru's preferred notion of secularism was that of *dharma nirpekshata*, or that the state would not be moved by religious considerations in enacting policy. It is therefore not surprising that public debate on the issue has been polarized between those who subscribe to the Nehruvian meaning of secularism, and those who subscribe to the meaning that Gandhi gave to the concept.

However, that Pandit Nehru continued to believe that the state could abstract the domain of policymaking from that of religion is debatable. For, the recurrent communal riots which culminated in the frenzy of the Partition proved that religious prejudices, more than religious sensibilities, had become a constituent feature of Indian politics. To ignore this would have been bad historical understanding as well as bad politics. In the process

of coming to terms with this unpalatable reality of Indian politics, Pandit Nehru's understanding of secularism came much closer to the notion of sarva dharma sambhava. Nehru, who by that time had become India's first Prime Minister, made this clear on various occasions. First, secularism did not mean 'a state where religion as such is discouraged. It means freedom of religion and conscience, including freedom for those who may have no religion' (Gopal 1980: 327). Second, for Nehru, the word secular was not opposed to religion.

> It is perhaps not very easy even to find a good word for 'secular'. Some people think that it means something opposed to religion. That obviously is not correct. What it means is that it is a state which honours all faiths equally and gives them equal opportunities; that, as a state, it does not allow itself to be attached to one faith or religion, which then becomes the state religion. (ibid.: 330)

For Nehru, the concept of the secular state thus carried three meanings: (a) freedom of religion or irreligion for all, (b) the state will honour all faiths equally, and (c) that the state shall not be attached to one faith or religion, which by that act becomes the state religion. The creed of secularism therefore discouraged fears that one group had the right to stamp the body politic with its ethos, *even* if it is in a majority. Conversely, a religious group would not be disprivileged in any way *even* though it happened to be in a minority (Chandhoke 1999: 49). In effect, the meaning that secularism acquired in the Indian context added one more dimension to the generic concept of secularism: not only the recognition of faith, but the *equal* treatment of all faiths.

This understanding has been reinforced in various ways. Crossman and Kapur suggest that the notion that secularism means equal respect for all religions has come to dominate legal and political thought: 'Following from the dominant understanding of secularism as sarva dharma sambhava, the constitutional discourse does not insist on a wall of separation between religion and politics' (1999: 58). The former Chief Justice of India P.B Gajendragadkar, for instance, interpreted secularism as (a) the state does not owe loyalty to one religion; (b) it is not irreligious or anti-religious; (c) it gives equal freedom to all religions; and (d) that the religion of the citizen has nothing to do in the matter of socio-economic problems (ibid.: 58, n.12). Jacobsohn, who has carried out a close reading of the various arguments offered by the Supreme Court during the Bommai case in 1994, isolated the dominant theme in these arguments as

> equal treatment of religions, often referred to in Indian tradition as *sarva dharma sambhava*....In the same vein Justice Sawant emphasised that 'The state is enjoined to accord equal treatment to all religions and religious sects and denominations. It is a theme that was echoed by Justice Reddy, who literally underlines the point by declaring '*Secularism is...more than a passive attitude of religious tolerance. It is a positive concept of equal treatment of all religions*'. (2003: 146–7, italics in the original)

Accordingly, the judges ruled that the destruction of the Babri mosque by a mob, which had been encouraged in this task by government and party officials, was a clear violation of the equal treatment principle. Secularism, ruled Justice Sawant, was a part of the basic structure and the soul of the Constitution, and could not be infringed in any way. For these reasons the court upheld the dismissal of four state governments ruled by the Bharatiya Janata Party (BJP), and the imposition of President's rule in these states.

Though on other occasions the decisions of the Court have proved controversial—such as the famous 1996 'Hindutva' judgement, where Justice Verma endorsed Hindutva as representing 'a way of life' in the subcontinent and therefore as not violative of secularism—on balance the Court has upheld the understanding of secularism as equal treatment of all religions. The matter, however, has not been settled, and as we shall see, interpretations of secularism continue to swerve between the notion of secularism as the separation of state and religion, and the notion that secularism implies equal respect for all religions. But before we map the debate oriented around these different interpretations, it is necessary to recollect that the entire discussion of secularism has taken place against a particular background: that of the communalization of society. Communal riots have not only violated the fundamental right to life, to dignity, and to property in a major way, they have endangered the basic right of citizens to live with dignity and

to freely practice their religion vide Article 25 of the Constitution.

THE CRISIS OF SECULARISM: INTELLECTUAL RESPONSES

Regrettably, the communalization of society has been paralleled by the communalization of the polity. Though the role of individual administrators and police officials in the communal riots that have scarred the body politic since the late 1960s has been well-documented, in 1984 the *state* came to be seen as complicit in the genocidal attacks on the Sikh minority. In 1992, not only was the Central government inactive when mobs demolished the Babri mosque, both the Central and state governments failed to prevent massive riots, which, following the demolition, targeted members of both the communities.

In 2002 in Gujarat, about 2000 Muslims were killed in a massive pogrom against the minority. The pogrom followed the death of a number of Hindus when a train compartment in which they were travelling was set on fire by a crowd of Muslims at Godhra station. The Amnesty International Report 2008 states that five years after the violence in Gujarat, in which thousands of Muslims were attacked and 2000 killed, justice continues to elude the victims. Most victims and survivors indicated in the media that members of the ruling party, the BJP, were implicated in the violence, but no substantive inquiry has been carried out (Amnesty International 2008).

The inability of the state to prevent communal riots, and the role of state officials in fomenting communalism, has necessarily caused a great deal of consternation and apprehension. Has secularism been able to achieve the desired objectives of safeguarding the life, property, and dignity of citizens? Has secularism been able to ensure equality to all religious groups or help in establishing inter-religious harmony? Given the communalization of Indian society and of the polity, it is not surprising that scholars wonder whether secularism is appropriate for the country at all. Others rush to defend secularism as the only option for a society that has repeatedly been bitterly divided over religion. In effect, the academic community has been deeply, and more often than not caustically, divided on the issue.

For instance, in a piece provocatively titled 'An Anti-Secularist Manifesto', which was originally written in the 1980s, Ashis Nandy argued that since the modern state seeks to dominate individual and collective lives, it not only banishes rival ideologies such as religion to the periphery, it hierarchizes the two domains by typing religious affiliations as inferior ways of being. This impoverishes understanding within the modern public sphere as well as inhibits dialogue between the two spheres, which might otherwise have proved enriching for both. Second, because religious identities have been exiled to the metaphorical closet, they come to be frozen in time. This in turn inhibits a dialogue within and between religions. But since religious identities constitute an endearing feature of humanity, Nandy seems to say, they must perforce make their appearance in the public sphere. This is made possible through the democratization of the polity. The problem is that religious identities, which are regarded as *de trop* by formal politics, make their appearance either in the form of religious instrumentalism, or religious fundamentalism. In sum, whereas secularism provides us with an impoverished public sphere devoid of any substantive system of meaning, the entry of religious identities into the public sphere impoverishes religion, because religion is subordinated to political pursuits. Societies are consequently left with few substantive resources which can enrich individual or collective lives, which can negotiate relationships between religious communities, and which can control pure politics. For, over time, whereas the ills of religion have found political expression, the strengths of religion are not available for checking corruption and violence in public life. In the end we are left with a denuded and impecunious version of religion that serves narrow and partisan ends.

Nandy finds an alternative to the twin ills of secular public spaces filled with crippled and truncated personalities who are forced to deny their faith and turn themselves against their inner natures, and religious zealots using religion for their own narrow partisan ends. This alternative is the recovery of the tradition of tolerance, which exists in and through unarticulated but lived faiths. 'Faith,' writes Nandy, 'is more lived out than articulated and tolerance or forgiveness is given expression in the actualities of living, not in ideological or even theological propositions' (2002: 47). But for this we have to discover the original meaning of faith, and liberate it from the second meaning that modernity has imposed upon religion—that of ideology.

It is clear that Nandy hinges his critique of secularism on the notion of the separation of religion and politics, although he accepts that secularism holds another meaning for India: the idea of equality of all religions (2002: 34–5). However, for some inexplicable reason he puts aside the second conception of secularism as an 'avoidable Indianism', and uses secularism in its 'proper English sense' (ibid.: 35). In short, Nandy, who is a critic of modernity, would rather apply universalistic and transhistorical categories to attack the Western, deracinated, and alien concept of secularism that he considers forms the linchpin of state practices in India, than look at the specific connotations that secularism has acquired in and for the country.

T.N. Madan is often lumped together with Nandy as anti-secularist. And his critics quote one of his aphorisms as evidence of the fact—'I believe that in the prevailing circumstances secularism in South Asia as a generally shared credo of life is impossible, as a basis for state action impracticable, and as a blueprint for the foreseeable future impotent' (1998: 298). Madan cites three reasons for this belief: one, that the majority of people living in the region are active adherents of some religious faith; second, Buddhism and Islam have been declared state religions; and third, secularism is incapable of countering religious fundamentalism. Yet there are major differences between Nandy and Madan's position, notably that Madan does not give notice to secularism as Nandy does. In a postscript added ten years after the publication of the 1987 piece, Madan, addressing his critics, insists that he had not dismissed secularism. What he had done was caution against the 'easy confidence of secularists regarding [the] unproblematic adaption of secularism' (1998: 318).

The four core arguments of Madan are as follows: it **was** possible to privatize religion in the West **because** developments internal to Christianity—such as **the** Reformation—facilitated the process. In South Asia, however, major religious traditions do not assume any radical antinomy between the sacred and the secular. Second, for the inhabitants of the region, religion as the doctrine of overarching ends is more important than any other social or cultural factor. This is because religion establishes the place of individuals in society, and because it gives meaning to their lives. It is both moral arrogance and political folly to impose the ideology of secularization on believers. On the contrary, these beliefs must be taken seriously, and the religious should be given the same place in society as the non-religious. Third, the denial of the legitimacy of religion in social and political life serves to provoke fanaticism or fundamentalism on the part of religious zealots. Fourth, traditions of religious pluralism can help us carry forward inter-religious harmony. For this, suggests Madan, we should see how Gandhi employed the resources of religious tolerance to promote inter-religious understanding. The Gandhian worldview also aids us in placing spiritually justified limitations on religious institutions and symbols in certain areas of collective life. In sum, the only way that secularism may succeed is if we take both religion and secularism seriously, and not reject the former as superstition and reduce the latter to a mask for communalism or mere expediency.

The critiques of secularism have not gone unchallenged. Akheel Bilgrami accused Nandy of practising both nostalgia and skewed historiography (1998: 384); and Vanaik (1997: chapter 4) suggested that both Nandy and Madan support a form of religious communitarianism, which celebrates the traditional idea of the embedded self rather than the modern idea of the free, equal, individuated self. By upholding the religious community as a vital political unit, Vanaik alleges, anti-secularists regress from the progressive, political trajectory of modernity. The critics of secularism may be anti-communal, accepts Vanaik, but they land up sharing a discursive terrain with religious communalism. In their different ways and through different political projects, they legitimize the politics of religious identities.

The exaggerated nature of these and other criticisms of what is considered an anti-secularist position are perhaps understandable when we recollect the highly charged political atmosphere in which the debate on secularism was conducted in the 1980s and the 1990s. In these two decades, the religious Right appeared on the political scene to mobilize civil society in the cause of Hindutva, a mobilization that resulted on the one hand in the destruction of the Babri mosque, and on the other in the ascent of the BJP to power in the Central government in 1986. However, the polarized debate served to obscure what was significant in Nandy and Madan's argument. Both theorists sought to grapple with the uncomfortable fact that religious identities in India have lasted longer than might once have been hoped, and that the politicization of religious identities has led to incivility, violence, riots, and murderous assaults. Can secularism help us to ward off the communalization of society and the polity?

In answering this question, both Nandy and Madan raised two sets of distinctions to the forefront of the debate: that between secularism and secularization, and that between the state and civil society. If India's civil society is deeply religious, then this poses a problem for secularism as a state project. Therefore, both theorists sought the answer to communalism in the practices of civil society; particularly that of tolerance. Though Nandy dismissed secularism altogether, Madan suggested that state practices of secularism have to be based on the recognition of religious practices. This has to be buttressed by discovering and strengthening the internal resources of religious pluralism and tolerance. Tolerance is too important to be left only to the state. But in the end, both theorists ground their understanding of tolerance in largely undefined and unarticulated lived practices. That these practices may have changed or degenerated in the context of competitive electoral politics, and an equally competitive market economy, is something that they would rather not take into account.

Other arguments that hinge on the mismatch between secularism and non-secularization of the Indian polity recognize the salience of religious identities, but go in different directions. Vanaik proposes that traditional beliefs and practices are responsible for undermining the secular state, because they have blocked the project of the rationalization and democratization of society. Far from endorsing religious beliefs, Vanaik argues that the root cause of religious communalism is religion itself. The struggle against religion should not be limited to setting up a state equally tolerant of all religions, but extend to the secularization and diminution of religion in civil society. Secularism in India must mean three things: the right to freedom of worship, the primacy of citizenship, and the non-affiliation of the state to any religion and impartiality (1997: 171).

On the other hand, Bilgrami not only recognizes the political presence of religious communities in India, but he would rather that these communities had a large role to play in designing the secular principle. Secularism, suggests Bilgrami, has run into trouble because it stands in a conceptual and political space that lies outside the sphere of substantive political commitments. In other words, Nehruvian secularism did not emerge as the product of a dialogue between religious communities. Instead, it was adopted from an Archimedean point. And it is precisely this feature that makes it unsustainable. Had secularism been grounded in debate and the understanding of different communities, it would have proved more compelling, for then all groups would have had reason to subscribe to the notion of secularism (1998).

SECULARISM AND EQUALITY: INTELLECTUAL RESPONSES

Scholars may have arrived at some consensus that India's civil society is constituted in major part by the presence of religious communities. Some of these scholars may also agree that the Indian version of secularism is grounded in the principle of equality of all religions, and not in that of the separation of the state and religion. For instance, Jacobsohn suggests that whereas

> in the United States it is at least possible to envision a clear separation of Church and state, in which religion and politics are maintained as distinct areas of human striving, and where the neutrality of equal treatment is broadened to require a hands-off policy for governing the

relations between secular and religious institutions...such an arrangement is inconceivable in India, where, upon initial analysis, religious and secular life are so pervasively entangled that a posture of official indifference cannot be justified either politically or constitutionally. (2003: 10)

However, this consensus does not close the debate on secularism because another question arises to complicate matters. What does it mean to treat religious groups equally? Does the state stay away from religious beliefs and practices equally? Or does it intervene in the internal affairs of religious groups for whatever reason, equally? Does not the equal treatment of religious groups reproduce the empirical fact that one of these religious groups is numerically dominant and culturally hegemonic, and that minority groups are at risk because they are vulnerable to assimilation on the one hand and cultural domination of the majority on the other? Does equality, in other words, imply that special protection should be granted to the culture and religion of minority groups to protect them against advertent or inadvertent assimilation? What exactly does equality imply?

These questions, which are absolutely central to our understanding of what secularism means in and for India, are further complicated by the realization that the principle of equality of all religions does not stand by itself either in the Constitution, or in and through political practices. No concept or practice is autonomous of others, but the stance the state adopts towards the plurality of religious groups is peculiarly and perhaps intrinsically bound up with another project that the Indian state had adopted at Independence—that of social reform. For Jacobsohn, secularism as a basic feature of the Constitution has to be understood within the broader framework of the document's commitment to social reform; or that meaningful social reform required attention to the critical role of religion in Indian life (2003: Ch. 4). Article 25 of the Fundamental Rights chapter of the Constitution makes this quite explicit: *subject* to public order, morality, and health...all persons are equally entitled to freedom of conscience and the right to freely profess, practice, and propagate religion. The second section of Article 25 states that nothing in this Article shall affect the operation of any existing law or prevent the state from making any law regulating or restricting any economic, financial, political, or other secular activity that may be associated with religious practice, or in providing for social welfare and reform, or the throwing open of Hindu religious institutions of a public character to all classes and sections of Hindus. This must be the only case where the right to religion has been prefaced by numerous ifs and buts.

The question that is relevant for this argument is, however, another one—is the Indian state entitled to intervene equally in all religions in the pursuit of social reform? This is the logical inference of the doctrine of equal treatment of all religions. However, any answer offered in response to this question cannot but be complicated, for it is heavily dependent on the answer we give to the questions raised in the paragraph above—*what exactly does equality of treatment mean?*

To negotiate this particular issue, we need to once again briefly revisit the history of the freedom movement. In the 1920s, the political project of fashioning secularism was accompanied by an overlapping project, that of commitment to the rights of minorities to their own culture and religion. This commitment formed part of the Nehru Constitutional Draft of 1928, the Karachi Resolution of 1931, and later documents issued by the Indian National Congress. Admittedly the commitment to minority rights, like the commitment to secularism, initially stemmed from pragmatic considerations—to stave off the demand for separate electorates based on religion in post-Independent India. But in time minority rights, like secularism, became a credo of faith for those Congress leaders who sought to conceptualize a society in which all religious communities would be able to live without the constant danger of being swamped by the majority.

In one way the Partition of India signified the failure of the secular/minority rights project. The Congress leaders failed to convince the leadership of the Muslim League that the members of the Muslim community would be armed with equal citizenship rights as well as constitutional protection to their own religion in post-Independence India. But in another and a more significant sense, the secular project can be considered a success. For, despite the fact that the Constituent Assembly met amidst wide-scale

rioting, atrocities heaped by one religious community on another, massacres, and looting of property, and despite the fact that the country had been partitioned in the name of religion, the makers of the Constitution stood firm in their commitment to secularism as the unstated but explicit principle underlying the Constitution. It was not even considered necessary to mention secularism in the Constitution. It was only in 1976 that the Emergency regime of Prime Minister Indira Gandhi inserted the word secular along with the word socialist into the Preamble of the Constitution.

More significantly, the framers of the Constitution held fast to their commitment to the rights of minorities to their own culture and religion. In the Constituent Assembly, the suggestion that religious minorities should be represented through separate electorates was dropped after Partition, because Partition was seen as a consequence of the introduction of separate electorates by the colonial power. But the right of minorities to their own culture and the right to run their own religious institutions was granted vide Article 29, and more importantly by Article 30, of the Fundamental Rights chapter. These Articles have to be read along with Article 25, which provides for freedom of conscience and the right to freely profess, practise, and propagate religion. In sum, whereas Article 25 grants individual rights, Articles 29 and 30 recognize groups as bearers of rights.

The grant of minority rights was accompanied by a special concession made to the minorities; they could retain their own personal laws. It is instructive to recollect that whereas the colonial government codified criminal and procedural law in India, it held back from codifying personal laws of Hindus and Muslims. Personal laws relate to marriage, dowry, dissolution of marriage, parentage and legitimacy, guardianship, adoption, gifts, wills, inheritance, and succession (Larson 2001: 4). They are, therefore, crucial for gender justice. The reasons why the minorities were allowed to do so are intricate, and outside the purview of this chapter (Jayal 1999: Chapter 3). In short, the acceptance that the Muslim and Christian minority could be governed by their personal laws in matters of adoption, marriage, divorce, and inheritance had to do with the political need to secure minority identities. Whether this was a wise move or not has been a matter for some debate, because it brought into question both the role of the Indian state in providing a secular public sphere, and its self-arrogated role as social reformer (ibid.: 103). Moreover, though Article 44 of the Directive Principles of state Policy stated that the government should enact a Uniform Civil Code (UCC) in due course, the time has still not come for the realization of this particular idea. The problem is that immediately after Independence, the government set out to reform the personal laws of the Hindu community through a series of legislations known collectively as the Hindu Code Bill. And through the Constitution and a series of parallel legislations, the government set out in a determined fashion to reform the Hindu caste system. In other words, government intervention in the affairs of religious groups proved to be *selective*. Whereas the Hindu community was socially reformed through legislation from above, the personal laws of the minorities were left alone.

The first substantive debate on secularism emerged in the aftermath of precisely this development. D.E. Smith (1963) suggested that the liberal democratic theory of secularism carries three connotations: (a) liberty and freedom of religion, (b) citizenship and the right to equality, non-discrimination, and neutrality, and (c) the separation of state and religion. In India, argued Smith, the first two principles have been incorporated into the Constitution both as the basis for secularism, and as important constitutional values in their own right. However, the right of the state to intervene in the affairs of religion have deeply compromised these two principles. The core of the problem of Indian secularism, argued Smith, lies in the non-separation of state and religion. Therefore, he concluded that India has *some*, but not all, the features of a secular state. On the other hand, V.P. Luthera (1964) argued that since the wall of separation between religion and the state does not exist in India, the country is not and cannot be secular.

In time, this academic debate was paralleled by an overlapping debate in political circles. The Hindu right, capitalizing upon the selectiveness with which Congress governments have intervened in religious affairs, accused the government of practising pseudo-secularism. It is not that the Hindu right dismisses secularism. The argument goes deeper; if secularism means equality of all religions, then minority rights and retention of personal laws violate the basic precepts of secularism. It may appear ironic that the religious right, devoted as it is to the establishment of a majoritarian state, has no problem with secularism as the doctrine of strict equality between religious groups, till we recollect that the doctrine of formal equality is profoundly indifferent to background inequalities. And the Hindu right prefers to ignore inequalities. For instance Arun Shourie, who has emerged as *the* ideologue for the Sangh Parivar, has argued that first, the individual and not religion or caste or region should be considered the unit for state policy, and second, that nothing should be conceded to a religious group that has not been conceded to other groups (1997). This, according to Shourie and other proponents of Hindutva, constitutes genuine secularism, and it is this form of secularism that is subscribed to by the BJP, as against the pseudo-secularism defended by liberals and the Left.

SECULARISM, UNEVEN STATE INTERVENTION, AND MINORITY RIGHTS: INTELLECTUAL RESPONSES

Matters came to a head in the mid-1980s with the Shah Bano case. The case was not the first of its kind in independent India. Nor was the Supreme Court judgement the first time the judiciary had ruled on the issue of maintenance of divorced Muslim women. But in the 1980s the decision of the Court, and the subsequent passage of the Muslim Women's Bill by Parliament, aroused a storm of protest from the Muslim community, particularly from the patriarchal sections. The scale of the protest can only be understood as a response to the massive mobilization of the Hindu rights in the mid-1980s. But whatever the reason, the unprecedented protest of the Muslim community had important political implications.

To return to the argument, the case at hand was fairly straightforward. Shah Bano, an elderly woman who had been divorced by her husband, appealed to the high court of Madhya Pradesh that her former husband should pay her maintenance under Section 125 of the Criminal Procedure Code (CrPC).

According to this section, the former husband of a divorced woman has to pay her maintenance if she is destitute, and if she possesses no means for her own survival for as long as she lives or until she remarries. The high court ruled in favour of Shah Bano. However, Shah Bano's husband, Ahmed Khan, moved the Supreme Court as an appellant on the ground that he was not obliged to pay his former wife maintenance beyond the traditional three-month period of *iddat* under Section 127 (3) of the CrPC. This section rules that if, under the personal law of certain communities, certain sums were payable to women in the form of *mehr* or dower agreed upon at the time of marriage, then this, along with maintenance for the period of iddat, released the husband from further obligation. The Supreme Court, in effect, had to pronounce on the relation between Sections 125 and 127 (3) of the CrPC on the one hand, and the relationship between the CrPC and personal laws on the other. On 23 April 1985, a Supreme Court Bench under Chief Justice Chandrachud confirmed the judgement of the MP high court, and stated that Article 125 of the CrPC overrides all personal laws, and that it is uniformly applicable to all women. The Court thus subordinated not only Section 127, 3(b) of the CrPC to Section 125, but also personal laws to the civil code. The Bench also called upon the Government of India to enact a UCC under Article 44 of the Constitution.

As expected, the leaders of the Muslim community and in particular the ulama opposed the judgement on the ground that it constituted a disregard for the personal laws of the Muslim community, which are based on the *Shariat*. They argued that since the Shariat is divinely sanctioned, it can neither be tampered with nor interpreted by the Court. The controversy snowballed into a major political problem as thousands of Muslims took to the streets to demonstrate against the judgement. Ultimately Prime Minister Rajiv Gandhi's government, then in power at the Centre, bowed before the uproar. In February 1986, the government introduced a Bill in Parliament that sought to exempt Muslim women from the protection provided by Article 125 of the CrPC. The Muslim Women

(Protection of Rights on Divorce) Bill in essence abrogated the limited right to maintenance under Section 125, because it stipulated that the husband, at the time of divorce, should pay the amount of the mehr/dower, the properties given to his former wife by her relatives, friends, husband, and his relatives, make a one-time fair and reasonable provision for her as provided for in the Koran, and provide two years' maintenance for her children as well as three months' payment. The woman could ask a magistrate to direct her husband to give her these properties. In case the woman was unable to maintain herself, the magistrate could order her relatives to maintain her if they were to inherit her property. Alternately the state wakf board would support her. If the woman and her husband so decided, they could apply to be governed by Sections 125–128 of CrPC. That is, if the man consented, the exemption from Article 125 could be overruled. The Bill was passed in Lok Sabha on 6 May and in Rajya Sabha on 8 May 1986.

The passage of the Bill aroused massive demonstrations as liberal, Left, and feminist sections, who considered the Bill regressive and violative of gender justice, mobilized against it. Oddly enough, the protestors shared a common ground with the Sangh Parivar, which attacked the Bill on the same basis. In fact, the Sangh Parivar argued even more vociferously than the feminists about the need to subordinate the personal laws of the minority to a UCC in order to secure basic rights for all women. Although it became increasingly clear that right-wing forces were less interested in gender justice than they were in subordinating minority identities to majoritarianism, the argument was persuasive for many right-thinking Indians. Those who defended the rights of the minorities to their own cultures and community identity were frankly on a weak wicket. How could the government, or the defenders of secularism, justify the retention of personal laws of the minorities when these violated the basic precepts of gender justice? Second, why did the state not interfere in personal laws in the cause of social reform when it had done so in the case of the Hindu majority?

In the process, defenders of secularism were laden with two more theoretical tasks: one, to justify selective state intervention in religion and square this with secularism, and two, fit minority rights into the secular project. This was absolutely essential to counter the onslaught of the religious right, which grounded its arguments in the basic precepts of classical liberalism-non-discrimination, rights, and individualism. Four different kinds of arguments were offered to negotiate the challenge both to minority identities and to the rights of the members within the minority.

Writing against the background of the demolition of the Babri mosque and the subsequent communal riots in 1994, Partha Chatterjee raised the crucial question troubling defenders of secularism: is secularism adequate to counter the political challenge of Hindu majoritarianism? The Hindu Right, pointed out Chatterjee, was simply not threatened by secularism because it was perfectly at ease with the institutional procedures of the Western/modern state (1998: 345–6). There is a further problem with secularism, he suggested. If we accept that secularism means a strict separation of religion and politics, this particular meaning can prove fairly compatible with the persecution of and discrimination against minorities. But if secularism means equidistance from all religious groups, then the political biography of the Indian state belies the norm. The state *has*, after all, intervened selectively in different religious communities. The dilemma is the following: if the state adopts secularism as separation, then minorities cannot be protected; however, if it interprets secularism as equidistance, its own practices violate the norm.

A better way to protect minorities, suggested Chatterjee, is through the establishment of the norm of toleration. But rather than look to the practices of everyday life to discover toleration, he grounded the concept in the liberal precepts of autonomy and respect for persons, and extended the principle to cover group rights. He negotiated the problem that group rights pose to liberal democratic theory in the following way: provided a group gives reasons for what it does to its own members, it can refuse to give reasons for doing what it does in the public domain, or, that internal accountability or democracy validates the rights of the community over its own members. Chatterjee in effect moves away from the normative

principles of secularism to another normative principle, that of democratic accountability within groups, in order to build in minority rights into the principle of toleration.

Bhargava came to an understanding of why secularism necessarily involves differential treatment for different groups from another theoretical direction. He begins his argument by distinguishing between three kinds of secularism. The first kind, hyper-substantive secularism, seeks to bring about a separation between religion and the state in the name of a package of ultimate substantive values, for example autonomy, development, or reason. The second kind of secularism, ultra-procedural secularism, separates religion from the state in the name of purely impersonal, value-free, rational procedures and rules, such as bureaucratic and technocratic rationality. The third kind, and one that Bhargava clearly prefers over the other two, is contextual secularism. Contextual secularism implies principled or non-sectarian distance, or non-absolutist separation between the state and religion. In other words, this avatar of secularism combines substantive values and procedures, without any commitment to the priority of either. Bhargava argues that contextual secularism, which is enshrined in the Constitution, enjoins the state to exclude religion for some purposes, as for instance in the decision to exclude separate religious electorates, and to include it for others, as, for example, in accepting personal laws. But contextual secularism is always guided by non-sectarian principles, which are consistent with a set of values constitutive of a life of equal dignity for all (1998: 515). Admittedly, in recent times sectarian considerations have become important, as Bhargava accepts, and religion has entered politics where it should not have been allowed to do so, and excluded when much could have been achieved by inclusion. Yet contextual secularism is the only appropriate form of secularism in India.

Further elaborating the concept, Bhargava maintains that contextual secularism has within it room for ultimate ideals; it is neither obsessively opposed to them nor hysterical about their internal conflicts. But when such conflicts introduce a surfeit of passion and frenzy into political life, threatening thereby the structure of the ordinary but dignified life of all citizens, then the state relies on minimalist procedures to control, and sometimes remove from political life, all controversial ultimate ideals (1998: 515). That is, though the state may not be able to relate to every religion in exactly the same way, it must ensure that the inclusion or exclusion of religion in politics is guided by non-sectarian principles, which are consistent with a set of values constitutive of a life of equal dignity for all. In sum, secularism for Bhargava is (a) fully compatible with the defence of differentiated citizenship rights; and (b) the secularity of the state does not necessitate strict intervention, non-interference, or equidistance, but any or all of these as the case may be.

Amartya Sen defends secularism as part of a more comprehensive idea, that of India as an integrally plural country made up of different religious beliefs, language groups, and divergent social practices. Secularism, he suggests, is part of a bigger project of recognizing this heterogeneity. Engaging with six strands of critiques against secularism, Sen argues that any re-examination of the difficult question relating to the principle of symmetrical treatment of different religious communities must arise within a commitment to secularism. 'Secularism is basically a demand for symmetric political treatment of different religious communities....Balanced political treatment can be achieved...in rather disparate ways' (1998: 484). Although Sen accepts that this interpretation raises many questions that need to be explored, this by itself, he insists, does not contradict the overarching argument for secularism.

Chandhoke (1999) suggested that secularism cannot be abstracted from the wider conceptual context of which it forms one part. It can only be understood as an intrinsic component of the historical, constitutional, and political practices of democracy, freedom, equality, justice, and rights. Why should we subscribe to the notion that each individual/group is free to practice his/her/its own religion, and that this right is equally held by all, *unless* we subscribe to the generic right to freedom and equality? And why should a society subscribe to the right to freedom and equality unless it subscribes to the value of democracy? Secularism, in other words,

is not an autonomous concept. Therefore, in order to unravel the meaning of secularism, we should first try to unravel the implications of the attendant concepts that give it [secularism] meaning—equality, freedom, and democracy.

In other words, we should shift the debate away from secularism per se to the antecedent moral principles from which secularism derives its specific meaning. The antecedent moral principle that informs the practice of secularism as equality among religions is that of equality. However, if we begin to look closely at equality, we find that it is by no means a self-evident concept. Whereas in a purely formal sense equality means that each should be treated equally, this interpretation ignores the fact that the constituency for equality is supremely unequal. If we apply formal equality in an unequal society, we land up reproducing inequality, which is something the egalitarians have been warning against. Equally procedural equality can facilitate the subordination of minorities to majorities.

There is only one way out of reproducing inequality through equal treatment, and that is to treat different groups differently, or according to their specific circumstances. In this sense, equality of religion would mean protecting those groups whose identities and religious beliefs are under constant threat of being subordinated to the majority. Of course, this would mean that we add to the original egalitarian agenda, which is closely involved with the notion of redistribution, the idea of recognition. It also means that we think out in detail the relationship between group rights and individual rights. Individuals need access to their cultures/religious affiliations because this gives them their basic system of meaning. However, groups and their rights are important only insofar as they are important for individuals. Therefore, individual rights cannot be subordinated to group rights.

THE ROAD AHEAD

Debates on secularism in India have alerted us to the fact that we cannot abstract the practice of secularism from the historical context in which it is embedded, and evaluate it against an ideal that has been formulated in other societies and contexts.

This does not mean that the practice of secularism in India should have nothing to do with secularism as an idea. If secularism is the conceptual and the practical opposite of the theocratic state, then it carries certain connotations: (a) freedom of religion for all (Article 25), and (b) non-discrimination and equality of treatment (Article 14). Given these core features, secularism in India appears fairly close to the ideal, at least in the way it has been embodied in the Constitution. In fact, we do not even have to use the term secular to practice secular politics; all that we need to do is to faithfully follow the provisions of the Constitution (Chandhoke 2004). For, if the principle of equality is followed rigorously, the state cannot possibly align with one religion to the detriment of others.

However, there is one region where committed secularists need to work harder in order to prevent the hijacking of the concept by the Hindu Right. The Hindu Right is fairly comfortable with the idea of formal equality as coded in the concept of sarva dharma sambhava. What it is not comfortable with is the idea of substantive equality, which dictates that the vulnerable need special protection. But this meaning of secularism as substantive equality is only available to us when we relocate the concept of secularism to the constitutive context of equality, democracy, rights, and freedom. Secularism cannot be understood in abstraction from democracy and its attendant principles because it derives its essential meaning from these antecedent moral concepts.

Locating secularism in the principle of democracy and equality has one further advantage: it will ensure that both inter-group as well as intra-group relations are regulated by the norms of equality. We can defend minority rights in order to protect minorities from assimilationist agendas. However, as Jacobsohn suggests, while the opponents of the cultural assimilationist quest for unity have frequently found themselves defending their occasional support of the claims of minority communities, this has exposed them to charges of hypocrisy and pseudo-secularism. Moreover, though the defence of minority rights has been principled and free from crass political considerations, it has not sustained a compelling argument that rivals in rhetorical power the case for

Indian unity made from the other side (2003: 284–5). This is because defenders of minority rights always lay themselves open to the charge of violating the rights of the individual within the group. Therefore, the relationship between group rights and individual rights is something that still needs to be worked out in full. The quest for a substantive conception of secularism constitutes a research agenda in itself.

NOTES

1. See the collection of essays in Needham and Sunder Rajan (2007) on these two sets of concerns.

2. See Tejani (2008) for an account of the historical and intellectual history of secularism in the country.

REFERENCES

Amnesty International. 2008. *The State of the World's Human Rights*, section on India. Available at http://thereport. amnesty.org/regions/asia_pacific/india. Last accessed on 25 February 2009.

Bhargava, Rajeev. 1998. 'What is Secularism For?', in R. Bhargava (ed.), *Secularism and its Critics*. New Delhi: Oxford University Press, pp. 486–542.

Bilgrami, Akheel. 1998. 'Secularism, Nationalism, and Modernity', in R. Bhargava (ed.), *Secularism and its Critics*. New Delhi: Oxford University Press, pp. 345–79.

Chandhoke, Neera. 2004. 'Re-presenting the Secular Agenda for India', in Mushirul Hasan, (ed.), *Will Secular India Survive?* New Delhi: ImprintOne, pp. 50–71.

———. 1999. *Beyond Secularism: The Rights of Religious Minorities*. New Delhi: Oxford University Press.

Chatterjee, Partha. 1998. 'Secularism and Tolerance', in R. Bhargava (ed.), *Secularism and its Critics*. New Delhi: Oxford University Press, pp. 380–417.

Crossman, Brenda and Ratna Kapur. 1999. *Secularism's Last Sigh?* New Delhi: Oxford University Press.

Gopal, S. (ed.). 1980. *Jawaharlal Nehru: An Anthology*. New Delhi: Oxford University Press.

Jacobsohn, Gary Jeffrey. 2003. *The Wheel of Law: India's Secularism in Comparative Constitutional Context*. New Delhi: Oxford University Press.

Jayal, Niraja Gopal. 1999. *Democracy and the State: Welfare, Secularism and Development in Contemporary India*. New Delhi: Oxford University Press.

Keddie, Nikki R. 2003. 'Secularism and its discontents', *Daedalus*, Summer, pp. 15–30.

Larson Gerald, James. 2001. 'Introduction: The Secular State in a Religious Society', in James G. Larson (ed.),

Religion and Personal Law in Secular India: A Call to Judgment, Bloomington: Indiana University Press, pp. 1–14.

Luthera, V.P. 1964. *The Concept of the Secular State and India*. New Delhi: Oxford University Press.

Madan, T.N. 2003. 'The case of India', *Daedalus*, Summer, pp. 62–66.

———. 1998. 'Secularism in its Place', in R. Bhargava, (ed.) *Secularism and its Critics*. New Delhi: Oxford University Press, pp. 297–320.

Nandy, Ashis. 2002. 'An Anti-Secularist Manifesto', in Ashis Nandy (ed.), *The Romance of the State and the Fate of Dissent in the Tropics*. New Delhi: Oxford University Press, pp. 34–60.

Needham, Anuradha, Dingwaney and Rajeshwari Sundar Rajan. 2007 (ed.). *The Crisis of Secularism in India*. Durham, Duke University Press.

Sen, Amartya. 1998. 'Secularism and Its Discontents', in R. Bhargava (ed.), *Secularism and its Critics*. New Delhi: Oxford University Press, pp. 454–87.

Shourie, Arun. 1997. *A Secular Agenda*. New Delhi: Harper Collins.

Smith, Donald Eugene. 1963. *India as a Secular State*. Princeton: Princeton University Press.

Tejani, Shabnum. 2008. *Indian Secularism: A Social and Intellectual History*. New Delhi, Permanent Black.

Vanaik, Achin. 1997. *Communalism Contested: Religion, Modernity and Secularisation*. New Delhi: Vistaar.

23 Representation[*]

Yogendra Yadav

Thinking about political representation in contemporary India requires simultaneous engagement with two levels of meaning embedded in this rich concept (Pitkin 1967; Dovi 2008). Political representation invites us to think, first of all, about the relationship between people or the citizens and their formal political representatives, between those who get represented and those who represent. But any sustained reflection on this relationship draws us into thinking about the setting, the mechanism, and the substance of representation—where, how, and what is being represented. An understanding of political representation in a narrow sense usually presupposes a larger understanding of the working of representative democracy. In the context of contemporary India, however, the relationship between these two levels is more intimate and constitutive:

mechanisms of formal political representation have become a hinge that connect two largely disjointed arenas in the working of democracy in India. That is why the paradox of political representation in the narrow sense of the term has come to reflect a larger paradox of Indian democracy.

The paradox of political representation understood narrowly involves a tension between the profile, policies, and politics of those who represent and the desires and demands of those who get represented. On the one hand, the practice of representative democracy for over half a century has led to a widening of the pool from which political representatives are recruited, accompanied by a reduction in the mismatch between the social profile of the representatives and those who are represented. This deepening of 'descriptive representation' co-exists, on the other hand, with a thinning of 'substantive representation'. Progress on 'Who is the representative?' has been accompanied by a step back in 'what does the representative do?' and eventually 'what gets represented?'

This paradox is of course linked to the larger paradox of Indian democracy which takes many

*I am grateful to the editors of this volume for their suggestions, feedback, and, above all, for their perseverance and extraordinary patience. I have drawn upon some of my earlier writings (Yadav 2008, 2001). Suhas Palshikar and Alistair McMillan would discover that the essay also draws upon many of the ongoing conversations with them.

forms. It manifests itself in the form of the contrary pulls of the institutional design and workings of representative democracy. The institutional designs for authenticating claims to representation, accountability devices for popular control over elected representatives, and the mechanisms for linking the policy agenda of representative institutions with the needs and interests of the represented have not kept pace with the radical upheaval brought about by the democratic upsurge from below (SDSA Team 2008). Sometimes the paradox appears in the form of a split: the domain of the formal institutions of parliamentary democracy does not quite reflect the dynamism of 'popular politics' (Chatterjee 2004). For historians of contemporary politics, the paradox takes the form of two contrary narratives, both of which appear simultaneously plausible: the story of the decline and demise of democracy and that of the deepening and strengthening of democracy (Khilnani 1997; Mehta 2003). From a different vantage point, this appears as a paradox of the promise and outcome of democracy: the radical promise of democracy continues to be subscribed to precisely by those who appear to have got little substantive outcomes from the working of this democracy (Bardhan 2005). Or it can be seen as the paradox of democratic politics: political understanding and practices are thinning precisely when politics matters more and involves more people than before (Yadav and Palshikar 2009b).

This chapter does not aim to disentangle, far less resolve, this multilayered paradox. Rather, it seeks to spell out the background conditions that make this paradox analytically instructive and politically engaging. Accordingly, the first section takes a look at how the question of political representation has been approached in three cognitive fields to show how the limitations of each of these has stunted our collective ability to think about this question in a meaningful and integral manner. The second section offers an analytical account of the historical context of the inauguration of the institutions of modern representative democracy. This context enables us to appreciate why representative democracy has had deeper anchors in India than in many other post-colonial societies while providing a clue to why it has taken the shape that it has in India. The third

section spells out the specifically Indian features of the working of modern representative democracy. The focus here is on how the institution of election has come to play a pivotal role in Indian politics. This enables us, in the fourth section, to bring out the consequences of the working of this kind of representative democracy for some of the key aspects of political representation in the narrow sense of the term, especially for regions, communities, identities, and issues like poverty. The deficits identified in this section lead to some concluding remarks on the theme of reforming the system of political representation.

APPROACH

Since a paradox lies in the eyes of the beholder, there is reason to suspect that a good deal of the contrariness that we noticed above might be a function of the received frames with which we study political representation in India. Much of what we take as 'normal' in democracy and politics is of limited provenance (Kaviraj 2003; Chatterjee 2004; Chakraborty 2000). Therefore, we need to examine carefully if at least some layers of the paradox of political representation may arise from misplaced expectations. This requires us to pay some attention to three sites that have generated professional frames for understanding political representation: the interpretative dispute about assessing democracy in India, the dominant common sense on democracy, and democratization and the academic scholarship on 'election studies'.

The interpretative dispute that lies at the heart of the democratic enterprise in today's India concerns the present and the future course of Indian democracy (Khilnani 1997; Kohli 2001; Mehta 2003). On the one hand there is the story of 'the decline and fall' of Indian democracy. On this reading, democracy made a decent beginning in India, especially in the first two decades after Independence, but suffered a steady decline since then and a particularly steep erosion in the last two decades. Democracy faces difficult, if not bleak, prospects in view of governmental instability, proliferation of parties, regionalization of politics and the rise in caste-based mobilization, communalism, corruption, and criminalization in the political arena.

This reading often leads to a call for wide-ranging and urgent reforms, usually a series of reforms in the legal-constitutional design of democratic politics, to cleanse politics of its current ills (Kashyap *et al.* 2000).

Over the last few years, many voices have questioned this reading from different vantage points. Commentators have drawn attention to the elitist (upper-class, upper caste) bias in this reading and argued that the story could look very different from a subaltern, especially Dalit, vantage point (Jaffrelot 2003). Much of the fresh empirical findings about political behaviour and attitudes of a cross-section of the citizens have served to cast doubts on this dominant wisdom: they have shown that while the citizens are quite critical of political actors and organizations, they do not share the sense of doom about democracy; that there has been something of a participatory upsurge notwithstanding claims of popular apathy (SDSA Team 2008; Yadav 2000). Some recent attempts to place Indian democracy in a comparative international perspective have had the effect of showing Indian democracy in a much better light than Indian political scientists have been accustomed to. Comparison with other democracies in the world has shown that unlike many other parts of the world, democracy has become here the 'only game in town' and that support for democracy and the Indian nation-state is of a level higher than was normally supposed (Linz *et al.* 2006). These counter-readings have not produced a common alternative story of Indian democracy. They offer a variety of diagnoses of the current situation and varying prescriptions of what is to be done.

This larger interpretative dispute finds an echo in a split response to the state of political representation in the narrow sense of the term. One set of observers notes, quite accurately, the broadening of the base of political representatives, thanks to the inauguration of the constitutionally protected third tier of democracy. This expansion coincides with and reinforces a noticeable shift in the social profile of the elected representatives in the upper tiers as well (Jaffrelot and Kumar 2009). This transformation can appear as nothing short of a social revolution through the ballot. Another set of observers of Indian democracy focus, quite appropriately, if narrowly, on the representation, or rather the lack of it, of popular issues and concerns in the political and policy agenda. If the exercise of legislative and executive power for redistribution of resources in keeping with the priorities of the citizens is one measure of the working of the representational mechanism, Indian democracy's record would appear pretty dismal (Roy 2009; Jalal 1995). More often than not, a steep rise in the political representation of the 'backward' castes has been characterized by a period of governmental mess and non-performance. No wonder, this perspective draws attention to the severe deficits of representation. Add to this some ideological purism and an upper caste vantage point, and the deficit appears as nothing short of the failure or a crisis of representative democracy.

This interpretative dispute has deep theoretical underpinnings. An understanding of political representation in the Indian context not only makes strenuous demands on the empirical skills of packing millions of isolated bytes of information into a coherent story, it also presupposes a certain assurance about answering some foundational questions. These foundational questions have to do with the yardstick implicit in any attempt to measure the success or otherwise of the democratic enterprise. Thus discussions on representation often proceed as if we know what democracy is, that we agree upon what it means to advance or regress on the path of democracy (democratization is the name for this presumably much traversed and well mapped path these days), that we can measure the deficits of Indian democracy from the vantage point of an ideal that is within cognitive even if not practical reach, which then allows us to spell out a 'roadmap' for democracy reform. The debates on this question take place as if it is a matter of differences about drawing the correct trend line, as if the coordinates are given and shared. A more distant view of debates on political representation invites us to entertain a suspicion that the dispute is as much about which axes to use in order to create a graph as it is about how to use the available information to plot India in the given space. In this view, the challenge of understanding political representation in contemporary India is as much a theoretical puzzle as it is an empirical task; it is deeply implicated in the larger dispute about the relevance of democratic theory received from the Western academia.

The trouble with the dominant and received democratic theory is that it is rather narrow, if not downright parochial (Keane 2009; Dunn 2005). Based on the historical experience of democracy in a very small though privileged part of the globe, and increasingly distanced from the rich tradition of reflections on democracy even within the Western tradition, this theory threatens to marginalize different experiences and conceptions of democracy in different parts of the world. This imagination privileges form over substance and draws our attention selectively to a few elements in the democratic practice in India. Based on a formal 'check-list model' of democracy that focuses on standard institutional requirements to qualify as democracy, this approach treats democracy as if it were a piece of hardware. You can pick it and install it anywhere you want. The dominance of this approach has marginalized another possible way of looking at democracy, one that treats democracy like software, a language, which must make sense to the users if they have to do things with it. It must be adapted to suit the users' needs, their tastes, and their capacities. On this reading, popular common sense is not external to democracy; it is not one of the 'factors' that aid or inhibit democracy: it constitutes the heart of the democratic enterprise (Taylor 2007).

The academic discipline of 'election studies' has served to reinforce the biases of democratic theory. Although the system of competitive elections is expanding to most of the world, election studies continue to interpret and evaluate electoral politics all over the globe in the light of the narrow historical experience of Western Europe and North America. This tendency often goes unnoticed, for the game of electoral politics appears similar all over the world (Klingemann 2009). Since the end-product of this game is recorded in a format that is universally recognized and lends itself to easy surface comparison, it is all too easy to believe that we are looking at the same game in all these cases. The familiar format or register distracts our attention from a more fundamental disjunction: the historical conditions in which the game is played are radically different. When placed in a new context, the same and familiar set of institutional rules lead to a radically different choice-set, resulting in different meanings of the vote and very different outcomes.

This influence of 'election studies' has meant that thinking about political representation tends to focus far too much on the 'formal sector' of politics (national political parties, manifestos, electoral outcomes) to the neglect of the substance of politics, the meaning of the vote, shaping of the agenda and party political platforms, the back calculus of politics and the role of money and crime in shaping and restricting political choices. This utterly messy aspect of politics is of course well known, but is not considered worthy of theoretical attention. It is noted as an embarrassment rather than a structural attribute. The critics see this as a negation of 'free and fair' elections, rather than a constitutive element of elections in the Indian setting.

The existing body of knowledge on elections and voting behaviour (Narain et al. 1978; Hebsur 1992) leads us to view the dynamics of political representation in India as a series of absences or 'lacks', if not maladies. There is a lack of stable and enduring alignment of voters with political parties (low level of party identification, high aggregate and individual volatility, absence of safe seats). This is related to a lack of pure interest-based political identification and organizations. The choice of representatives is marked by ascriptive identities, ethnicities, politics of caste–community-based vote banks, group identification of interests and political preferences rather than individual voting. Lack of an informed citizenry and low levels of knowledge and awareness of the electorate make matters worse. This leads to lack of issue orientation and ideology as reflected in clientelistic as opposed to programmatic political orientations, pragmatic preferences instead of ideological considerations, exaggerated role for charismatic personalities and the electoral game turning into an auction. Finally, this faulty mechanism results in the lack of policy outcomes as a result of electoral choices. Elections result in routine anti-incumbency that does not yield much. Those who get represented wield little control over those who represent them.

This dominant approach has suppressed an alternative reading of the apparently unique features of Indian elections. Instead of viewing these as deformities or lacks, the challenge is to capture the specificity of this encounter between the modern structure of formal political choice and the historically constituted public sphere with its own definition of politics and its patterns of organization of political interest. This opens the way to reinterpret what is often seen as electoral 'volatility', party 'fragmentation', 'casteism' in politics or the 'absence of ideology', and the widespread 'clientelism' in Indian elections. Such an interpretation would aim to provide a dynamic analytical narrative of the working of representative democracy in India, which recognizes the historical and structural influences that shape and constrain institutional development and engagement, and relates them to a changing socio-economic environment that generates fluid patterns of political identity and association. The present essay takes this approach to understanding political representation in India.

CONTEXT

Modern representative democracy made a deceptively easy entry in India. Within two decades of the inauguration of democratic elections based on universal adult franchise, the phenomenon of elections had ceased to surprise the students and observers of Indian politics. Like tea, cinema, or cricket, there is something about elections that makes it appear like an age-old Indian passion. Like the ever present piece of furniture in the household, elections only serve to remind everyone of the mundane and the quotidian routine of politics. It is therefore worth remembering that historically this apparently natural, taken for granted, world of elections is a recent import and quite an extraordinary development in the Indian society.

The modern practice of elections requires at least four sets of beliefs that had no currency in pre-modern times. It requires a specific kind of public arena, a set of actors with a given role definition, a purpose which orients the entire activity, and some agreed rules of the game. The encounter with modern politics under conditions of colonialism laid the foundations of a new kind of public sphere in India, making it possible for the multitude of people living in this land to think of themselves as Indians (Kaviraj 2003). The successful national movement ensured the passage from subjecthood to citizenship, thus creating the collective agency that participates in the election ritual. The creation of a republic in 1950 institutionalized the idea of popular sovereignty

which in operational terms was translated in the form of universal adult franchise granted by the Indian Constitution. The Constitution also met the final condition of specifying the procedures and protocols of representation including the rules of deciding the winner in the electoral race and implicitly accepting the existence of organized political interests in the form of political parties. Thus, modern political representation came to India at the founding moment of the Indian nation-state along with the package of liberal democracy accepted at that time. Setting up of a democratic state completed the process of the reconstitution of the public sphere in modern India that began with the colonial encounter. The democratic constitution formalized the sphere of modern politics, comprising institutions and practices of dealing with power that could not be traced back to operations of power in the pre-colonial past, as the prime mover in society. If the creation of a nation-state formalized the capacity of political power to act freely of external powers, the democratic state invested modern politics with a capacity to act autonomous of the logic of economy or that of the principal social divisions (Kothari 1972). While there was some discussion about the nature of electoral rules to be adopted, there is no evidence to suggest that anyone in the Constituent Assembly seriously contemplated a non-competitive or non-representative form of democracy.

This is perhaps why representative democracy took roots in India but not everywhere else it was tried. A look at the experience of elections in other post-colonial societies of Asia and Africa helps to illustrate the alternative paths electoral democracy could have taken (Weiner and Özbudun 1987). In many of these countries, free and fair elections in a minimal sense still remain a distant aspiration. Even when elections are held in a more or less free and fair manner, party competition at the time of elections merely reflects the pre-existing ethnic divisions in the society. One round of clean elections is not followed by another and elections fail to evoke popular interest and respect. In contrast, elections evoke deep public interest and passion and have come to be the hub of public activity, almost a public festival, in contemporary India. The system of elections has come to be a regular institution that commands a fair degree of public acceptance.

If elections in India did not take the familiar and tragic path in most former colonies, these also did not take the coveted path of Western democracies. The designers of Indian democracy had expected that the institution of regular and fair system of elections would be accompanied by many features that they had seen in European democracies: the consolidation of political competition along the lines of a two-party system, electoral choices being made by individual voters along ideological lines, elections becoming an occasion for effective accountability of the rulers to the ruled and thus producing policy outcomes that work to the advantage of common citizens. More than half a century of representative democracy has not fulfilled this expectation (Yadav 1999). We are beginning to be conscious that this expectation was not realistic in the first place. Elections in India did not and could not have produced the same outcomes as these did in the first world. This difference is not the result of any essential cultural difference or Indian exceptionalism; it is simply the outcome of the historically unique circumstances in which the game of universal adult franchise was instituted in India. The challenge therefore is to capture the specificity of this encounter between the modern structure of formal political choice and the historically constituted public sphere with its own definition of politics and its patterns of organization of political interest.

ATTRIBUTES

One of the first attributes of the Indian elections that strikes any observer is the role elections play in Indian politics, as reflected in their public visibility. Banners, posters, and hoardings fill the streets; massive processions and rallies are a norm; the media is full of election news and every street corner is buzzing with political gossip. Though on a steady decline of late, this kind of visibility of Indian elections symbolizes the pivotal role elections have come to occupy in Indian politics. If a tension between the pre-existing social form and the borrowed legal-political structure provides the basic frame for understanding Indian democracy, the story of Indian politics is a story of the attempt by millions of ordinary people to write their own political agenda in an alien script. An encounter

such as this requires, if it is to lead to meaningful outcomes, bridges or hinges which connect the two different worlds. The institution of elections came to perform this crucial role in India. It became the hinge that connected the existing social dynamics to the new political structures of liberal democracy allowing for reciprocal influence. Elections are often the site for a fusion of popular beliefs and political practices with high institutions of governance. Thus election is an occasion for the transfer of energy and resources from the 'unorganized' to the 'organized' sector of democracy. This is the moment when the legal–constitutional order of liberal democracy makes a contact with the messy social and political reality of India. The chasm that separates the two worlds and the absence or non-functioning of the other possible bridges has resulted in the unusual salience of the institution of elections. This unique role is what accounts for the continued dynamism of the electoral process in India, while a number of other imported institutions and processes are floundering.

Specifically, Indian elections are not merely about the voters choosing their representatives, indicating their preferences about public policies or selecting their governments. In the absence of well functioning local bodies or accountable local officials, elections to Parliament and state assemblies also perform a routine municipal function of attending to local grievances and connecting the people to the administration. Notwithstanding a robust media that routinely uses public opinion polls, elections are still the principal occasion for dissemination of political ideas and information and also the only reliable method to gauge public opinion on the big issues facing the country. Elections are also an occasion for settling, unsettling, or resettling local equations of social dominance and the arena of struggles for social identity and dignity. Elections force political parties to take into account ideas, interests, and entities that do not lend themselves to easy aggregation through the instrumentalities of the 'organized' sector. Thus elections often appear as the only bridge between the people and power, as the only reality check in the political system. This accounts for the festival-like character of the Indian elections and the fierceness with which elections are contested here. At the same time this also means that elections are overloaded and the necessity of multiple processing leads to under-emphasis on the representational functions of elections.

The second set of electoral attributes relate to the 'electoral system' in the narrow sense of the term. Of course, the pivotal nature of elections is not written into the legal-constitutional design of Indian polity, nor is it directly a function of the electoral system chosen by the constitution-makers. The Indian Constitution prescribed the first-past-the-post (FPTP) or the simple plurality method of election by all adults living in electoral constituencies, all of which now elect a single member (initially there were some triple and a large number of double-member constituencies). This electoral system was chosen for its simplicity and familiarity. The danger of under-representation of social minorities was sought to be avoided by a system of 'reserved seats', constituencies where all the candidates had to be from a designated community, for Scheduled Castes (SCs) and Scheduled Tribes (STs) in proportion to their share in population (McMillan 2005). The possibility of under-representation of religious minorities, which became a reality in the case of the Muslims, was shelved in the aftermath of Partition (Ansari 2006). The choice of an electoral system may have added to the salience of elections indirectly: locality-based elections made for an easy transition to representative democracy and did facilitate the role elections have come to play in local politics.

In practice, the FPTP system did not produce the expected consequences, at least not at the national level. It did not produce anything like a two-party system; an extended period of one-party dominance has given way to a multi-party system with one of the highest effective number of political parties among the electoral democracies of the world (see chapter by Sridharan in this volume). Accordingly, stable majority governments have given way to a routine of coalition governments, much like in a system of proportional representation. In part, at least, this was a function of the scale of the Indian polity. With the intensification of electoral competition, the nation is no longer the effective unit of political choice; state level politics is the real arena for political choices and partisanship (Yadav and Palshikar 2009a). The

national level election is in many ways an aggregation of the verdict that is delivered at the state level.

Thus some of the effects of the working of FPTP are visible at the state level: there is a tendency towards a bipolar competition and stable majorities in most of the states. In the Indian context, the FPTP produced a different, unexpected, and under-analysed effect. The requirement of plurality in a single-member constituency coupled with the demographic mosaic forced political parties to forge social coalitions at the local level. Since no single caste or community tends to be in a majority in any of the state assembly or parliamentary constituencies, winning elections requires gaining support from more than one caste or community group. This unintended consequence has performed a significant integrative role in Indian polity and constitutes the principal defence of the FPTP system. Thus Indian elections are about a familiar game acquiring a character of its own and becoming virtually a new game.

Perhaps what contributed most to making this game different was a new condition that no one ever thought through. The design of representative democracy in India simply lifted a system of representation that was meant for much smaller political communities and applied it to a continental polity. This resulted in a manifold increase in the scale of representation and led to a qualitative difference in the nature of the relationship between the representative and the represented. An Indian member of Lok Sabha typically represents a population over 21 lakh and an MLA in one of the major states represents anything between 2 and 5 lakh. A comparison with the scale in Britain (less than a lakh for each member in the House of Commons), which served as the model, brings out the sharp contrast. The mega-scale of the system of representation had many consequences for the nature of political representation: the minimum requirements of resources and information needed for this kind of election result in a very high entry barrier for a new entrant to the system. This is related to the relatively fluid relationship between voters and parties that characterize Indian elections. Compared to some of the European polities, Indian elections witness a low level of voters' identification with political parties. Given the very high degree of aggregate and individual volatility that is routinely witnessed in Indian elections, concepts like alignment, realignment, or dealignment do not have much applicability in the Indian context. This is not to say that the changes are patternless, but that the lie of the land is very different in the Indian case (Yadav 1996a).

The hinge-like character of elections is reflected in the set of attributes of electoral participation in India that defies global commonsense in three respects. One, in an era characterized by global concern over declining electoral turnout, India is something of an outlier. After rising for the first two post-Independence decades, electoral turnout at the national level has remained fairly steady, but has registered a rise in the state assembly elections. Two, as one goes down the tiers of democratic competition, turnout and political participation increases in India, rather than going down as it does in most established democracies. Panchayat elections tend to witness the highest turnout, followed by state assembly elections, and a much lower turnout for the national elections. Three, India also defies the established common sense about a positive correlation between socio-economic status and electoral turnout. Dalits and Adivasis (tribals) at the bottom or the margins of the Hindu social hierarchy have caught up with caste Hindus in their participation levels; a Dalit has a greater likelihood of casting a vote than a Brahmin. Since the Emergency, rural India tends to record higher turnout than towns and cities. Within urban India, slums and working class areas witness a higher turnout in elections than the 'middle class' localities. The huge gap that existed earlier between male and female turnout has been nearly closed now. Religious and ethnic minorities do not generally record lower turnouts. Although this pattern of turnout in election does not hold for all forms of electoral participation and that in turn is not replicated in political participation, yet there is no doubt that India has witnessed something of a 'democratic upsurge' from below and the social base of popular participation in turnout, electoral activities, and politics is much wider compared to what it was earlier (Yadav 2000; Palshikar and Kumar 2004; Yadav and Palshikar 2009b).

This distinctiveness in the level and patterns of electoral participation is in turn related to popular attitudes towards representative democracy in general and elections in particular. If the subalterns are using the vote as a weapon of the weak, it reflects a certain degree of approval of the system of representative democracy. Clearly the weak do not view elections merely in instrumental terms; they associate something special, perhaps even sacred (Banerjee 2007), with the occasion of elections and value the ritual of equal citizenship. Even though a significant proportion of the electors do not vote, the non-voters are not necessarily alienated from the system. Voters and non-voters, all reject unequivocally the idea that elections should be dispensed with and record a surprisingly high degree of support for democracy (SDSA Team 2008). Subaltern participation in politics has its flip side. When the weak use the vote as their weapon, they often do so in order to assert their group identity, to the detriment of considerations such as policy, representative and government. Besides an act of participation is often simultaneously an act of co-option or a gesture of granting legitimacy to a system that often brings little to the people.

The linkage between the inherited social cleavages and new political divisions provide a crucial mechanism to understand the hinge-like function of the Indian elections. This linkage is often seen as a peculiar Indian pathology of 'casteism in politics' or the operation of 'vote banks' in elections. Viewed in a more comparative light, the connection between caste and politics appears to be the Indian version of the more general phenomenon of the operation of social cleavages in voting behaviour almost all over the world. If caste appears to be omnipresent and omnipotent in Indian elections, it is partly due to two types of double-counts: several forms of social divisions (*jati*, *varna*, religious sect, occupational divisions, religious communities, migrant or linguistic groups, or even class) tend to get classified under the label of 'caste' and multiple forms of possible linkages of the caste of the voters and their political preference (caste of the candidate, and the party leader, and the caste or caste-group represented by the party) pass for 'caste-based voting'. In part this is also due to glossing over crucial analytical distinction between pattern and trend: while caste blocs often determine the initial level of support for a party, they do not explain changes across elections. Besides, the relationship between caste and politics does not necessarily mean that caste determines politics; very often it is the other way round (Kothari 1970). In fact if there is something distinctive about Indian elections, it is not the existence and role of the institution of caste in elections but the capacity of electoral politics to forge social identities. The systemic imperative to forge local social coalitions for obtaining electoral plurality has led to the coalescing of several adjacent jatis into a single caste for purposes of politics, not to mention the more explicit political coalition of caste groups (Sheth 1999).

The excessive and obsessive attention paid to the role of caste in Indian elections has often resulted in a neglect of other kinds of social cleavages. What is true of caste is also true of ethnicity: electoral politics shapes these communities as much as it is shaped by the pre-existing ethnic groups. Gender difference has marked political opinions, attitudes, and behaviour for as long as there is evidence to trace it (Deshpande 2004, 2009). Notwithstanding popular impressions, a substantial proportion of women do not vote the way the men in their family do. Gender gap in voting has not followed a simple trajectory but it is clear that this gap is big enough to make a difference, sometimes a decisive difference to who forms the government. Class, understood not so much as a meta-historic agent of transformation but as an empirical phenomenon of either income-based strata or occupational division, is an important variable in voting behaviour and often overshadows caste or community in urban India (for example, for Delhi see Kumar 2004). In rural India too, class divisions provide a powerful clue to mapping the differences within caste and community groups. In the operation of these multiple and cross-cutting cleavages, India is not very different from the rest of the world. One of the distinguishing attributes in this respect is the near absence of generational cleavage in political behaviour or even opinions in India. There are, no doubt, some age-cohort differences depending upon the political context when a person was socialized into politics, but there is virtually no life-cycle difference between different generations. Despite much hype in this regard, the Indian youth does not vote or think very differently from her elders (Yadav and Palshikar 2009b).

Finally, the hinge-like character of Indian elections means that elections are the site for an encounter between two very different kinds of belief systems, the high ideology of modern politics on the one hand and somewhat inchoate and home-grown belief systems on the other. Since the outcome is anything but neat, and there is little patience with the intricacies of the emerging hybrid language of politics, this gives rise to an impression that Indian elections are 'devoid of ideology'. Often the operation of patronage, interests or social identity in Indian elections, as everywhere else, is seen as an evidence for the irrelevance of the ideological dimension in India. An alternative reading would suggest that Indian elections are as much about ideology as they are anywhere else, but this element cannot be captured by a single and familiar spectrum like Left–Right dimension. Electoral politics is the site for a new hybrid language of politics, distinctly modern and specifically Indian, which does not fit easily into the received frames of political theory.

CONSEQUENCES

Establishment of a system of quite fair and largely free elections, at least in the more obvious sense of the term, is something India can legitimately take pride in. Compared to the rest of the world, including most electoral democracies in post-colonial settings, Indian elections are characterized by a very low degree of electoral disputes and frauds. There has been more than one instance where credible allegations regarding widespread fraud would lead one to doubt whether the party that won the election was indeed voted by the people: West Bengal in 1972, Assam in 1983, Punjab in 1992, several elections in Nagaland and Jammu and Kashmir including the most notorious election of 1987. This is an embarrassing but finite list and would still pass as an exception to the general rule of free and fair elections. The increasing independence of the Election Commission (see chapter by McMillan in this volume), the demise of one-party dominance, and the rise of media power has ensured that the trend is towards a sharp reduction in the more obvious instances of malpractices and fraud—all this is good news. If we proceed beyond this and ask what this system of elections has achieved for the ordinary citizen, the answers are harder to get and less encouraging.

Are Indian elections an effective instrument of meaningful political change? Indian elections have, in a sense, over-corrected for the first stage of one-party dominance where each successive election used to bring the same party back to power. The period since the demise of the Congress system has witnessed a very high rate of regime alteration. At times the casualty rate of the incumbent state government was as high as three-fourths (Yadav and Palshikar 2009a). This was linked to a very high level of aggregate volatility or a high degree of shift in the vote share for all the parties as well as a high level of individual volatility or the proportion of voters who changed parties across two elections (Heath 2005). This was widely perceived to be an anti-incumbency reflex of the Indian voter. However, volatility need not be seen as synonymous with instability, or as an outcome of an anti-incumbency itch, or as a sign of a system which has not yet settled down, almost threateningly so. Volatility is best interpreted as the voters' search for better governance or responsiveness, a sign of social churning, and a routine oscillation that takes place in the absence of social transformation. Viewed in this frame, the real difficulty with Indian elections is not that they lead to excessive change but that they offer little meaningful choice that can be the basis of political change. While the number of political parties has multiplied manifold, this has not led to any expansion in the choices available to the voters. Faced with this deadlock, the impulse for change degenerates into routine oscillation (Yadav and Palshikar 2003).

Do elections offer an opportunity to reorganize political power or for shifting the locus of power? At least in one respect the participatory upsurge has resulted in very real changes in the locus of political power. Whereas the Constitution of India provided for a weak federal system, and the post-Independence period was characterized by a clear centralization of political power, a process of 'electoral federalism' has seen the diffusion of some central power and a stronger role for state governments. As competitive politics has taken a decisive 'regional' turn, the state has become the effective level of political choice in a Lok Sabha

election. In the 1970s and 1980s the voters voted in the state assembly elections as if they were choosing their Prime Minister; since the 1990s they vote in Lok Sabha elections as if they are choosing their chief minister. This has reduced the ability of national parties and governments at the Centre to present or claim a general mandate, and has given greater power to politicians and governments at the state level.

This has been accompanied by a serious and substantial dilution of state representation in the upper house of the Parliament. As political parties freely shuffle nominations to Rajya Sabha with little regard to domicile and little fear of loss of credibility, the constitutional design of the upper chamber as representing the interests of the states stands subverted. The Supreme Court's decision upholding the legal dilution of residential requirement in Rajya Sabha was a fatal setback in this respect. This paradoxical development has produced a consequence that no one designed or anticipated: as Lok Sabha, rather than Rajya Sabha, becomes the principal arena for the representation of states, the onus of maintaining the federal balance has also been shifted to Lok Sabha (Yadav 2007; McMillan 2001). This has served to legitimize an ill-conceived freeze in the Lok Sabha on the number of seats for each state which violates the basic principle of one-person-one-vote, besides working to the disadvantage of some of the already disadvantaged units of the Indian Union. A similar encounter between the political process and the institutional frame can be seen at the third tier of democracy. The passage of the Seventy-third and Seventy-fourth Amendments to the Constitution and the extension of constitutionally secured representative politics to the third tier set in motion a political process that appears to be gaining momentum. At the same time the state governments appear determined not to grant any real powers or resources to the new tier of political representation. Instead of redistributing resources and redirecting developmental policies at the local level, the principal function that the third tier performs now is to supply cadre and lower level functionaries to political parties in desperate need of an organization. Often it is much worse: the political energy released by this process leads to an intense, violent but vacuous quest for local political dominance.

How have the democratic upsurge, electoral volatility, and the shift in the locus of political power affected the pattern of social dominance? Since participation in elections is seen to be an affirmation of citizenship, the very act of participation confers dignity on the hitherto excluded segments of society. This opens up the potential for the mobilization of group interests, and at the extreme the potential for the stoking of inter-group violence. But a substantive question here would be about whether elections offer an opportunity for changing and challenging the entrenched elites. If so, the potential for disturbing hierarchical structures can in itself be seen as an outcome of electoral politics. This brings us face to face with simultaneous advance and retreat in the political representation of the lower social order. There is no doubt that the post-Mandal era in our polity has led to some improvement in the presence of landowning or otherwise numerically large Other Backward Classes (OBC) communities in the Hindi heartland states. Even though the quantum of change is much smaller than is popularly believed and the legislatures continue to massively over-represent the forward castes, there is a qualitative change in the political dynamics as the momentum has shifted away from the hitherto dominant communities (Jayal 2006).

Yet this advancement comes with built-in stagnation and retreat. The rise in the political representation of some backward communities has not led to a corresponding rise in the representation of many other communities that would be a part of the 'lower social order'. There is little awareness about or willingness to engage with the severe under-representation of the 'lower' OBCs or the Most Backward Castes cutting across the north–south divide. Similarly there is little attention to an equally severe under-representation of the 'Maha Dalits', the Dalit communities at the bottom of the SCs. The *Sachar Committee Report* has served to bring some attention to the gross under-representation of the Muslims in the Parliament and state assemblies, but the issue is yet to acquire the national salience necessary for any remedial action (Prime Minister's High Level Committee 2006). There is little improvement in the political representation of marginalized social groups like women and the poor that do not possess a self-conscious political identity. The Women's Reservations Bill has brought some attention to the fact that women's presence in legislatures has actually witnessed a marginal decline since Independence (Dhanda 2008). There is no such data to track the presence of the 'poor' in our legislatures. But if the episodic analysis of the disclosures of property filed by candidates at the time of their nominations is anything to go by, our legislatures are dominated by the super-rich (Association for Democratic Reforms).

Finally, do elections provide a forum for citizens' control over public policy? In a limited and direct sense they do: a whole host of populist schemes announced during every election testify to the need to respond to public demand. As the survival rate of governments has become respectable, this had led to a serious competition among state governments to respond to people's needs such as electricity, water, and roads, things which the state has the capacity to deliver in a direct and visible manner. At the same time, electoral politics is still characterized by a lack of delivery, accountability, and responsiveness. Short-term interests are the only ones which can be realized, as survival becomes the only government imperative. There is a strong tendency towards populism, rather than substantive politics so as to deliver long-term benefits in areas such as health and education.

This is related to the paradox of co-existence of democracy and poverty in contemporary India. The majority rules in democracies and we should be surprised if those who (can) rule do not use this power to improve their conditions of life. The paradox is even deeper in India than in many other societies. Some of the standard reasons why democracies do not care about poverty do not hold true in India (Bardhan 2005; Varshney 2004). One, the institutional design of Indian democracy (parliamentary system, asymmetrical federalism, flexible constitutional amendment) does not place significant obstacles to the democratic popular will. Two, the party system is highly competitive with very high electoral volatility. Three, as noted above, the poor have not opted out of democratic politics, at least not from routine participation in electoral politics. Four, unlike some other poor democracies, India is not a failed state and its failure to address poverty cannot be put down to a more generalized incapability. All this makes it even more intriguing that representative democracy should not (be able to) do very much about poverty.

Before closing the discussion on the outcomes of the system of representative politics, it may be relevant to note one irony in the recent emphasis on the social profile of political representatives. The discussion on quality of representation is being reduced to the social identity of the representative precisely at a time when the political representative is increasingly marginal to the most vital decisions concerning legislation and governance. The passage of the amended anti-defection law has left only one answer to the classical question of whom does the elected representative represent: they cannot but represent their political party. The rise of political families or the party supremo with a coterie within each political party complicates much of the routine discussion about the nature of political representation. True, the political families come from a more diverse social background than before. But it would be facile to assume that these families represent the interest of the communities they come from. The rule of political families or the supremo from agrarian communities has proved to be more conducive for the capture of state power by organized industrial and business interests than was the case before. In any case, the issue of political representation itself is declining in salience due to a shift in the locus of decision-making from the legislature and executive to independent bodies and the judiciary. Simultaneously, the media has emerged as the key and not-so-neutral mediator in how any political issue is represented to the public and thus sets limits to the political agenda. It is not a coincidence that the judiciary and the media have remained nearly untouched even by the limited presence of the lower social order as in the legislatures and are thus immune to the pressures of the democratic upsurge.

REFORMS

One way to summarize the argument offered so far is to spell out the implications of this reading of political representation for the issue of reforms in representative democracy, an issue that has occupied extraordinary public attention in India in the last two decades. If nothing else, this issue illustrates how a distorted reading of representative democracy can induce distortions in the practice of representative democracy. Over the last two decades, a good deal of well-intentioned, though diffused, enthusiasm for reforming democracy has turned into a conservative platform for refashioning the political structures to suit the interest of a small, hitherto entrenched but now threatened class. The resultant agenda of political reforms amounts to nothing short of undoing the results of the democratic upsurge of the last two decades (Yadav 1996b, 2001).

If the argument offered above has any merit, the agenda of political reform in India has to be different from the challenge in the advanced industrial democracies, for our problem is not demobilization and slowing down of democracy. At the same time, unlike other new democracies of the Third World, India does not face the challenge of democratic transition or consolidation. The real failure of the current phase of Indian democracy is not the failure to hold free and fair elections, nor the inability of the people to affect change in governments through the exercise of their free vote, but the growing distortion in the mechanism of political representation, the growing distance between the electors and the elected, and the inability of the mechanism of competitive politics to serve as a means of exercising effective policy options. Clearly, the institutional frame of representative democracy has failed to translate popular participation and enthusiasm into a set of desirable consequences.

This is not merely a universal deficit in the promise of democracy. We are looking at a range of failures that are rooted more specifically in our experience. Some of them were written into the logic of democracy in a society like India. The fundamental contradiction—pointed out by Dr Ambedkar—that of instituting equal citizenship in a highly unequal society lies at the root of many of the failures. Social inequality was further accentuated by unequal access to the means of forming and disseminating public opinion. Another contradiction was built into the act of importing political institutions, especially those that required autonomy in a cultural setting where attitudinal prerequisites were missing. There was the structural problem of constituting a polity to coincide with the boundaries of a civilization when much of the meaningful political action and mobilization could take place in micro-settings. Some other failures of the democratic experiments are not structural, but specific to the history of democracy over the last 50 years. The weak policy orientation of Dalit-Bahujan politics, a lack of emphasis on institution building, the decision not to change the character of the bureaucracy and the retreat of the state in the face of the forces of globalization were in no way necessary to the design of Indian democracy. But these have contributed substantially to the democratic deficit facing us today. The litmus test for any agenda for reforming the system of political representation is its ability to deepen the ongoing process of democratization for the social groups and communities that have historically been denied access to political power.

This is not the place to begin offering such an agenda. It may be relevant though to note that such an agenda would require getting rid of some of the reigning superstitions of our times: the idea that there is a universally valid institutional design of liberal democracy; the suggestion that a set of best political practices can and should be replicated all over the world; the theory that the idea of democracy can be reduced to a standard 'checklist'. Once it is recognized that there is no universally applicable and valid package of political reforms or a model of democracy, it follows that a reasonable starting point for thinking about political reforms is here and now. We can thus take the next step of working towards an agenda that is anchored in time and space, is consequence sensitive, takes the logic of politics as integral to thinking about institutional design, and is conscious of the differential consequences for different social groups.

REFERENCES

Ansari, Iqbal A. 2006. *Political Representation of Muslims of India: 1952–2004*. Delhi: Manak.

Banerjee, Mukulika 2007. 'Sacred Elections', *Economic and Political Weekly*, XL(17), pp. 1556–62.

Bardhan, Pranab. 2005. 'Democracy and Poverty: The Peculiar Case of India', in *Scarcity, Conflicts and Cooperation: Essays in Political and Institutional Economics of Development*, Cambridge, US: MIT Press.

Chakraborty, Dipesh. 2000. *Provincializing Europe: Postcolonial Thought and Historical Difference*. Princeton, NJ: Princeton University Press.

Chatterjee, Partha. 2004. *The Politics of the Governed: Reflections on Popular Politics in Most of the World*. New Delhi: Permanent Black.

Deshpande, Rajeshwari. 2009. 'How did Women Vote in Lok Sabha Elections 2009?' *Economic and Political Weekly*, XLIV(39), pp. 83–7.

———. 2004. How Gendered Was Women's Participation in Election 2004?', *Economic and Political Weekly*, LI(18), pp. 5431–6.

Dhanda, Meena (ed.). 2008. *Reservations for Women*, Delhi: Women Unlimited.

Dovi, Suzanne. 2008. 'Political Representation', *The Stanford Encyclopedia of Philosophy (Winter 2008 Edition)*, Edward N. Zalta (ed.), URL = <http://plato.stanford.edu/archives/win2008/entries/political-representation/>.

Dunn, John. 2005. *Democracy: A History*. New York: Atlantic Books.

Heath, O. 2005. 'Party Systems, Political Cleavages and Electoral Volatility in India: State-wise analysis 1998–1999', *Electoral Studies*, 24(2), pp. 177–99.

Hebsur, R.K. 1992. Studies on Indian Politics: Research Designs and Stragegies, A Trend report sponsored by and submitted to Indian Council of Social Science Research. Unpublished.

Jaffrelot, Christophe. 2003. *India's Silent Revolution: The Rise of the Lower Castes in North India*. London: Hurst & Co.

Jaffrelot, Christophe and Sanjay Kumar (eds), 2009. *Rise of the Plebeians: The Changing Face of the Indian Legislative Assembly*, London: Routledge.

Jalal, Ayesha. 1995. *Democracy and Authoritarianism in South Asia: A Comparative and Historical Perspective*. Cambridge: Cambridge University Press.

Jayal, Niraja Gopal. 2006. *Representing India: Ethnic Diversity and the Governance of Public Institutions*. London: Palgrave Mcmillan.

Kashyap, Subhash C., D.D. Khanna, and Gert W. Kueck (eds). 2000. *Reviewing the Constitution?* Delhi: Shipra Publications.

Kaviraj, Sudipta 2003. 'A State of Contradictions: The Post-colonial State in India', in Quentin Skinner and Bo Stråth (eds). *States and Citizens: History, Theory, Prospects*. Cambridge: Cambridge University Press, pp. 145–67.

Keane, John. 2009. *The Life and Death of Democracy*. London: W.W. Norton & Company.

Khilnani, Sunil. 1997. *The Idea of India*. New York: Farrar Straus Giroux.

Klingemann, Hans-Dieter. 2009. *The Comparative Study of Electoral Systems*. Oxford: Oxford University Press.

Kohli, Atul (ed.). 2001. *The Success of India's Democracy*. Cambridge: Cambridge University Press.

Kothari, Rajni (ed.). 1970. *Caste in Indian Politics*. New Delhi: Orient Longman.

Kumar, Sanjay. 2004. 'A Tale of Three Cities', *Seminar*, 534.

Linz, Juan J., Alfred Stepan, and Yogendra Yadav. 2006. '"Nation State" or "State Nation"? India in Comparative Perspective', in Shankar Bajpai (ed.), *Democracy and Diversity: India and the American Experience*. New Delhi and Oxford: Oxford University Press, pp. 50–106.

McMillan, Alistair. 2005. *Standing at the Margins: Representation and Electoral Reservation in India*. New Delhi: Oxford University Press.

————. 2001. 'Population Change and the Democratic Structure', *Seminar*, 506, October.

Mehta, Pratap Bhanu. 2003. *The Burden of Democracy: Interrogating India*. New Delhi: Penguin Books.

Narain, Iqbal *et al.* 1978. *Election Studies in India: An Evaluation*. Mumbai: Allied Publishers.

Palshikar, Suhas and Sanjay Kumar. 2004. Participatory Norm: How Broad-based is it?', *Economic and Political Weekly*, XXXIX(51), pp. 5412–17.

Pitkin, Hanna Fenichel. 1967. *The Concept of Representation*. Berkeley: University of California.

Prime Minister's High Level Committee [Sachar Committee] 2006. *Social, Economic and Educational Status of Muslim Community of India*. New Delhi: Cabinet Secretariat, Government of India.

Roy, Arundhati. 2009. *Listening to Grasshoppers: Field Notes on Democracy*. London: Hamish Hamilton.

SDSA Team. 2008. *State of Democracy in South Asia: A Report*. New Delhi: Oxford University Press.

Sheth, D.L. 1999. 'Secularisation of Caste and Making of the New Middle Class', *Economic and Political Weekly*, XXXIV(34 and 35), pp. 2502–10.

Taylor, Charles. 2007. 'Cultures of Democracy and Citizen Efficacy', *Public Culture*, February.

Varshney, Ashutosh. 2004. 'Why Haven't Poor Democracies Eliminated Poverty?', in Ashutosh Varshney (ed.),

India and the Politics of Developing Countries: Essays in Memory of Myron Weiner. New Delhi: Sage.

Weiner, Myron and Ergun Özbudun (eds). 1987. *Competitive Elections in Developing Countries*. Durham, NC: Duke University Press.

Yadav, Yogendra. 2008. 'The Paradox of Political Representation', *Seminar*, vol. 586, October.

————. 2007. 'Epilogue: What does Fieldwork do in the Field of Elections?', in A.M. Shah (ed.), *The Grassroots of Democracy: Field Studies of Indian Elections*, New Delhi: Permanent Black, pp. 345–68.

————. 2001. 'A Radical Agenda for Political Reforms', *Seminar*, 506, October.

————. 2000. 'Understanding the Second Democratic Upsurge: Trends of Bahujan Participation in Electoral Politics in the 1990s', in Francine R. Frankel, Zoya Hasan, Rajeev Bhargava, and Balveer Arora (eds), *Transforming India: Social and Political Dynamics of Democracy*. New Delhi: Oxford University Press, pp. 120–45.

————. 1999. 'Electoral Politics in the Time of Change: India's Third Electoral System, 1989–99', *Economic and Political Weekly*, XXXIV(34 and 35), pp. 2393–9.

————. 1996a. 'Reconfigurations in Indian Politics: State Assembly Elections, 1993–95', *Economic and Political Weekly*, XXXI(2 and 3), pp. 95–104.

————. 1996b. 'Electoral Reforms: Beyond Middle Class Fantasies', *Seminar*, vol. 440, April.

Yadav, Yogendra and Suhas Palshikar. 2009a. 'Revisiting "Third Electoral System": Mapping Electoral Trends in India, 2004–2009', in Sandeep Shastri, K.C. Suri, and Yogendra Yadav (eds), *Electoral Political in Indian States*. New Delhi: Oxford University Press, pp. 1–45.

————. 2009b. 'Between *Fortuna* and *Virtu*: Explaining Congress' Ambiguous Victory in 2009', *Economic and Political Weekly*, XLIV(39), 26 September, pp. 33–46.

————. 2003. 'From Hegemony to Convergence: Party System and Electoral Politics in the Indian States, 1952–2002', *Journal of Indian Institute of Political Economy*, XV(1 and 2), January–June, pp. 5–44.

24 Social Justice*

Gopal Guru

State and social justice are exclusively related to each other in the Indian context. The nature of the state assigns this exclusivity to the relationship between the two terms. To put it differently, in the laissez faire state it is the market paradigm that seeks to define the parameters of justice. In such a society, the state could play a secondary role in defining and monitoring justice. But in welfare capitalism the state acquires relatively more autonomy than just monitoring justice. It not only monitors but also conceptualizes—through an enlightened bureaucracy—and decides the social justice agenda for the marginalized. Theoretically speaking, the marginalized are supposed to set the social justice agenda and through different levels of intervention activate the state in favour of this agenda. But in actual practice, it is the state that not only gains complete control of social justice agenda but it does so by reducing the marginalized to passive recipient of social justice. Thus it is the historical inability of

*I would like to thank Pratap Bhanu Mehta for pushing me into deeper theoretical discussion. However, the deficiencies, if any, are entirely mine.

the market to dictate the social justice agenda to the state plus the dissociation of the marginalized from that it invests the state with an exclusive hold over the social justice agenda. However, this is not to suggest that there is no social justice discourse that can exist outside the sphere of the state. As mentioned above, social justice could exist in market-driven societies or communitarian or tribal societies which may not have a formal presence of the state. In such contexts, unlike welfare states where the state administers social justice through constitutional as well as institutional arrangements, it is the element of morality that has a bearing on the justice question.

In contemporary India, the state has acquired a huge role in determining social justice both as a concept as well as policy. The state continues to enjoy pre-eminence in terms of creating a new vocabulary of social justice. This is because social justice theory in India is a relatively recent phenomenon, although its possibilities were always present in the history of philosophical thinking that prompted some social groups to politically organize themselves to seek the social good. In the Indian context, there are basically two different traditions, orthodox and heterodox,[1] which offer definite philosophical cues about social justice. Of the two, the heterodox tradition seems more radical and vocal than the orthodox. As historical evidence that is available throughout the Indian history, both in oral and written form, clearly suggests that the heterodox tradition sought to challenge the orthodox tradition of justice, right through the medieval to the modern period.[2] However, it has to be noted here that the orthodox tradition is not culturally specific and can include protagonists of justice even from the lower castes. Thus, this tradition includes Eknatha, a Brahmin saint from Paithan in Maharashtra, as well as Chokhamela, a Mahar saint from Mangalvedha near Pandharpur, also in Maharashtra. Both these saints held a conservative view of social justice that sought to accommodate the Untouchables into the system without interrogating the caste system as such on the other hand, the heterodox tradition tried to define social justice through a radical interrogation of the caste system and caste-related social hierarchies that sustain the Brahminical notion of justice. In the modern period, social justice became the major concern of modern social and political thought particularly in the feminist and Shudra–Atishudra tradition (Guru 2007: 221–38). These traditions made social justice a major plank for social mobilization partly because it had a twin adversary to confront—colonial power and local social power. This intellectual and political engagement with the colonial and local configurations of power is evident, for example, in the thought and work of Jotirao Phule and B.R. Ambedkar. Such an engagement is pervasive in this tradition partly because both Phule and Ambedkar realized that annihilation of the structures of caste injustice, would be a lifelong struggle. For the others, particularly the upper layers of the Hindu social order, the concern with social justice does figure but in conformity with the colonial configuration of power alone. Hence, this tradition seeks a nationalist resolution of injustice. This is prominent in Bankim's writings, for example. Thus, after Independence, social justice remains more a concern for the Atishudra–Shudra tradition. The Atishudras and Adivasis remain the major constituency for social justice primarily because these social categories exist on the margin

of both material (positional) and cultural (dignity/recognition) resources. The heterodox tradition involving the theory and practice of social justice form a part of India's intellectual heritage represented by Phule and Ambedkar. As against this tradition, India also has an orthodox tradition.

In the historical context, particularly in the pre-modern period (before the arrival of colonial modernity), the orthodox tradition of social justice always existed as a governing or disciplining, rather than enabling, principle as it sought to regiment people both in terms of time and space (caste and patriarchy). This principle was fundamentally arbitrary in nature as it lacked universal application. More importantly, the arbitrariness that defined this principle gave enormous power to the twice-born who could then exercise their choice to walk in and out of the time–space dimension of social interaction. For example, the Untouchables were prohibited from appearing in public spaces during the mornings and evenings when the twice-born transacted their daily business because even their shadow was considered ritually polluting for the twice-born. However, this also meant that the twice-born restricted their own freedom to move in the public space in continuous time and thus cannot be said to have exercised this 'choice' positively. These self-imposed restrictions entailed the upper castes following a fragmentary time and space regime. Unlike the upper castes, the Untouchables did not have the choice to develop, to use a Foucauldian term, 'technology of the self'. The upper castes conferred certain negative rights on Untouchables such as the right to carcasses and its raw hide, right to leftover food, right to ride a buffalo, and right to cast-off clothes of the lord. It is in this sense that social justice, based on an arbitrary construction of caste distinction, was defined negatively. Social transgressions or crossing of social boundaries were considered as violation of justice. This was the dominant form of social justice that had hegemonic influence over the entire social organization. In the pre-modern past, administration of social justice was ensured by the presence of social structures like caste panchayats. By and large, caste panchayats which were active among the lower castes, imposed much stricter restrictions on their members who were supposed to remain within the limits of the social codes of their particular castes. Any attempt to transgress these boundaries by way of inter-caste marriage or inter-caste dining was considered a serious violation of one's own dharma. These self-imposed restrictions made the job of both the state as well as the social authority of upper castes a lot easier. Since the Untouchables were not considered assets but were used as *begar* by the political authority of the time,[3] they escaped the larger gaze of the political authority. During this period, caste as the basis of justice was active in holding society together. This integration was ensured through the strict observance of rules of purity and pollution. Caste panchayats monitored these Untouchability practices. Thus, every caste and sub-caste had its own panchayat, which had functional autonomy but only within this ideology that had a strong Brahmainical core. But by and large, caste panchayats were governed by the centralized Brahminical ideology of purity–pollution.

During the colonial period, the locus of defining and practising social justice shifted from the Dharma Shastras and caste panchayats to colonial political institutions. The colonial response to the question of social justice was strategic rather than consistent. For example, the British tried their best to uphold the principle of procedural justice in favour of Untouchables (Nikumbe 2006) against all the social-political pressure. At the same time they also sought to rigidify caste divisions particularly after the 1857 rebellion, on the one hand, and social struggle driven by modern notions of social justice, on the other. Some argue that colonialism ended up making the traditional order more rigid. The modern notion of social justice was based on the universal principles of egalitarianism. The aspiration for egalitarianism found its articulation in the demand for equal worth. The modern notion of justice was defined not in terms of relative worth but comparative worth (Ambedkar 1990: 7).

At this point of time it is important to provide some explanation so as to justify the use of comparative worth as the constitutive category of social justice. For the lower-caste struggle for justice the notion of comparative worth is preferable to relative worth for the following reasons. First, relative worth is grounded in the principle of mutual respect. In this framework of

mutual respect, everbody has worth in his or her own way. To put it in simply, every labour/work including scavenging has worth.[4] Thus, the relative dimension assumes a moral arrangement of differential worth that everybody has to acknowledge. Thus the notion of relative worth keeps the hierarchical arrangement of worth intact. People tend to enjoy their relative worth without asking for parity in worth. Hence, the notion of relative worth lacks politics. In fact it avoids confrontation with other/superior notions of worth. The notion of comparative worth is deeply political in the sense that it attacks the notion of relative worth on the ground that it fails to undermine the hierarchical arrangement of worth. For example, Dalits object to Gandhi's exclusive use of the term Harijan on the grounds that the upper castes attach value to this term as long as it does not include them and is confined to the Untouchables only.

The notion of comparative worth is also empowering for another reason. It helps question the arbitrary ways that the upper castes adopt for the distribution of worth. For example, orthodox Hindus assign more worth to animals than human beings. It is this power to distribute worth in the most arbitrary ways that the Mahad Chavdar tank (in Ratnagiri district of Maharashtra) struggle led by Ambedkar sought to challenge. Using the principle of comparative worth, he asked the caste Hindus, 'You allow the cows, dogs, donkey and cats to drink water from the tank but do not allow human beings to even draw water from the same source' (Ambedkar 1990: 7). He uses the principle of comparative worth both for pointing out the moral inconsistency within the Hindu social order as well as for creating a spirit of critical inquiry that is necessary to reject the idea of absolute worth. It could be argued that as far as Dalits are concerned, since they are struggling to get recognition of equal worth, their struggle would naturally rule out any moral aspiration for absolute worth. Those who pursue absolute worth necessarily arrogate to themselves all possible worth and do not have the moral capacity to share it with others. In short, such people want to enjoy a monopoly of worth. *The idea of justice was novel in this respect. Conceptions of justice were now articulated through struggle. The idea of struggle was premised on the possibility that society could in fact be reshaped by the agency of marginalized groups. This possibility is more recent than we often acknowledge, and was made available only with the onset of colonial modernity.* The idea of social justice, which motivated the emancipator struggle in the past, was subsequently codified into the Indian Constitution, which in turn delegated to the Indian state the responsibility to look after the distributive aspect of social justice. In the context of the centrality of state, particularly in the post-Independence period, social struggle, as we shall discuss in some detail in the following sections, came to play only a subsidiary role in defining social justice. In fact the object of such struggles is to use state power in favour of the social constituency that it represents. Social struggles become the springboard that could be used either on the margins of state power (Dalit leaders either in the Congress party or its allies, or taking it over altogether (Bahujan Samaj Party [BSP] in Uttar Pradesh a limited sense of the term). As the historical experience shows, the mediation between the logic of liberal power and the social struggle leads to the conversion of social justice as motivational principle of resistance to pacificatory (policy) source of individual accomodation. At certain historical junctures, state power and social struggle seem complementary to each other. I further argue in the following section that the state became an important source of the imagination as well as administration of social justice. On the other hand, social struggle and its protagonists, who were at the forefront of this struggle for social justice, by and large chose to monitor and mediate between the social constituency of justice and the state. I will explain in the following sections why the 'struggle' or 'contest' notion of social justice, came to be replaced by the 'sponsored' notion of justice which, as mentioned above, underlined the centrality of the state—both in matters of expanding the vocabulary of social justice and also concretizing it in terms of policy. The centrality of the state in social justice discourse as modern vocabulary raises some essential questions.

First, what makes justice social? Does it become social just because it emanates from the emancipatory struggle launched by different social groups from time to time? Second, why does social struggle lose control over its own capacity to sustain a creative imagination and radical orientation of social justice? To put it

differently, why does it concede so much intellectual and political space to the state in terms of defining the social justice agenda? Why do social groups allow the state to preside over the social justice agenda? Third, as a corollary to the second, to what extent has the state in India consolidated the dividends accruing from this moral investment? That is to say, to what extent has it contributed to the innovation and enrichment of the vocabulary of social justice and the corresponding expansion of spheres of opportunity that are so necessary for translating people's aspirations into reality? What are the implications of the 'state sponsored' model for the very concept of social justice? Conversely, it would be quite interesting to know what implications the sponsored notion of justice has for the solidarity of different social groups. And finally, it is necessary to explore what implications the 'contest' or struggle notion of social justice has for institutional well-being.

Let me therefore begin by addressing one of the lead questions, why is justice social? I would like to argue that although there are different notions of justice (Heller 1987; Walzer 1983; Young 1990), in the Indian context it acquires a specific social dimension from both the 'contest' as well as 'sponsored' standpoints. As will be clear from the following discussion, these standpoints are social for opposite reasons. The struggle concept of social justice is basically contestary in nature because, first, it belongs to the realm of the oppositional imagination which involves subaltern contestations of dominant or elite notions of justice and seeks to convert them in favour of an egalitarian social order. Second, the contest notion of justice is primarily social because all contestations involve social groups with competing claims for refashioning and reordering their life vision through re-description and redistribution of moral and material resources. Such claims in turn are supported and sustained by the language of rights regarding, for example, fair distribution of primary goods such as self-respect and material resources. The articulation of this language could be found in the peasant and Dalit struggles for the redistribution of surplus land and a different identity name respectively.

This notion of justice is social not only because it *seeks to interrogate* the system of hierarchical social relations, but more fundamentally it seeks to alter these social relations along egalitarian lines. Babasaheb Ambedkar was influenced not just by the need to achieve individual freedom but more importantly by the need to promote associational social life as something to be intersubjectively realized through *maitree* (friendship) (Ambedkar 1957). Ambedkar visualized maitree, accordingly orienting social relationships both in intra- as well as inter-caste terms. In fact for him inter-caste maitree was much more important. In this sense it is human values that play an important role in defining social justice. Third, justice acquires its social character in as much as it motivates struggling social groups to forge a solidarity, *which is so important for the very realization of social justice.* Thus, social justice becomes a *socially unifying principle that can be deployed for the contestation of dominant structures.* The contest or struggle concept of justice underlies a shared vision of social goods, solidarity being one such social good. The united Dalit struggle led by Ambedkar and later on by the Dalit Panthers against caste, class, and gender oppression sufficiently reflects this solidarity aspect.[5] Justice also acquires a social character fundamentally because it seeks to reorient social relationships along lines of mutual recognition, dignity, and self-respect.

The social dimension of the concept of justice is constitutive of self-respect as a social good that keeps motivating the struggle of some social groups. For example, agricultural labourers' demand that they be paid wages on time and also on site, articulates this desire for self-respect. To put it differently, this demand involves the counter assertion that the labourers will not collect their wages from the landlord's *haveli* (manson), which is not just intimidating but humiliating as well.[6] The rural poor's struggle for dignity is also evident in the slogan that was raised during the struggle in 1972 against drought conditions, '*Bhik Nako, kam day*' (give us work and not free dole).[7] In this regard it is interesting to note that the rich farmer movement led by Sharad Joshi in the mid-1990s, was also built around the theme of dignity. This was evident in their refusal to accept agricultural subsidy from the state and their subsequent demand to participate in the global market.[8] However, the caste movement and the rich farmers' movement

differ from each other in terms of their conception of dignity. In caste movements, the organized articulation of dignity is based on a narrow social base. However, dignity as a core value does not remain fettered to this narrow base; in fact it promises to shed off its narrow confines and grow into universalism. The caste movement locates the question of dignity in the moral relationship between one person and the other. It seeks to alter the system that underlies and renews structures of indignity. Dignity as pursued by the caste movement lies outside the utilitarian framework. The farmers' movement on the other hand defines dignity basically in terms of maximizing its material prospects. The rich peasantry feels the loss of self-esteem as its capacity to participate in the international market is undermined by the state. To this extent it could be argued that globalization provides an opportunity to redeem dignity at least for some. Second, and most important, the farmers' notion of dignity is limiting in nature as it is self-propelling and self-seeking. The notion of diginity as visualized by the caste movement relates to the 'other' who is the source of indignity. These movements consciously choose to work with the other and try and generate among such people the ethical capacity for equal recognition. Ambedkar's and Phule's movements were aimed at addressing the other as well as the self. Both these examples express the dignity concern through the language of rights. However, there is a difference between the two situations as far as the usage of this language is concerned. In the case of the labourers, the relevance of the state provides the conditions within which this language becomes active, while in the case of the rich farmers' struggle for dignity, it is the irrelevance of the state that makes the language active. Thus, the collective nature of the struggle for dignity assigns a social dimension to the concept of social justice.

Finally, the principle of co-responsibility also assigns a definite social character to the concept of justice. The principle of co-responsibility, which has a bearing on the conceptualization of social justice, is rooted in the historical explanation of social relations. Social relations that are historically evolved contain within them certain wrongs that are socially perpetuated and culturally handed down from one generation to another. These wrongs always implicate some social group or the other—in the Indian case it is women and Untouchables. The principle of co-responsibility makes it morally imperative on the part of members of the dominant sections to own up to the problematic past which has been created, perpetuated, and handed down to them by their ancestors. Gandhi's notion of social justice is deeply influenced by the principle of co-responsibility. As we shall see in greater detail in the following sections, the policy of compensatory discrimination as adopted by the Indian state with regard to Dalits and Adivasis has its justification in the principle of co-responsibility. This principle also makes justice social to the extent that it compels those who are at the receiving end of continuous success to acknowledge the contribution that others have made in the success of the former. To put it differently, it would be ethically unfair to claim the copyright or individualize one's success as purely personal. It is always the result of social contributions made by others. The principle of co-responsibility makes the notion of compensation socially consensual. Compensation is constitutive of the collective acknowledgement of historical as well as contemporary wrongs committed either by institutions or individuals. As we shall see in greater detail in the following section, compensation as an operative principle of justice becomes the central concern of state-sponsored social justice. Compensation, as I will argue later, has become the dominant expression of the social justice concern in post-Independence India. It has become almost the final vocabulary that tends to overwhelm the discourse on social justice in post-Independence India. This is so because it has been singularly sponsored and regulated by the state in India. The contest notion of justice, on the other hand, vests intellectual autonomy and political initiative with the struggling social groups, which play an important role in creating the conceptual space for social justice.

The 'sponsored notion of justice' acquires social meaning interestingly for opposing rather than identical reasons. As I have already mentioned, the contest notion of social justice is based on social and political solidarity among the deprived sections of the society.[9] The state-driven or-sponsored notion of social justice in its operative form characterized

by what is called the policy regime, acquires social meaning in as much as it continuously seeks to disaggregate social groups into fractions and minuscule percentages. It also has an element of cunning internal to it in the sense that it offers an opportunity to the state to achieve a fragmentary impact on the solidarity of the disadvantaged. This fragmentary impact on solidarity is evident from the claims that in the recent times are being put forward by different caste groups for quotas within quotas.

Historically, caste identity has been the axis of discrimination and subordination for certain groups. In order to address subordination and bring about justice the state has to 'recognize' caste. It does so by enacting policies that offer opportunities and compensatory benefits along caste lines. The fact that the state uses these categories in turn reinforces the incentives in society to use them, and therefore 'solidifies' caste identity. But there are two further disjunctures. First, the benefits within any given state category (Scheduled Caste [SC], Scheduled Tribe [ST], Other Backward Classes [OBCs]) are not evenly distributed—and so there is a demand for further sub-classification of state categories. Second, while there was consensus in society that Dalits should be beneficiaries of state affirmative action, other groups also mobilize their numerical power in a democracy to seek the same benefits. So the narrative of subordination and discrimination gets broadened to include OBCs and minorities. The aspirations of social groups now are determined by the logic of democracy and state power, rather than the logic of justice.

The state-sponsored notion of social justice is also social but in a limited sense of the term, to the extent that it is defined by the state, in terms of the social identity or sociologically defined location of a person. The unit of distribution of different goods is an individual (even in the Indian context) who is socially situated (caste, gender, tribe, OBC, and now religious minorities) rather than constituted by universal criteria. Hence social justice in India is defined in terms of caste, geographical isolation (Adivasis), gender, and now religion. The sponsored notion of justice is primarily based on such considerations. At this point, we need to address the question, is it the cunning of the state that uses social justice to deliberately devise a fragmentary agenda, or is fragmentation something which is internal to the inconsistencies that are inherent in the social struggle of the marginal? To what extent can these internal inconsistencies explain the conditions within which the marginalized social groups withdraw from the conceptual domain of social justice thus conceding so much intellectual ground to the state? These interrelated questions could be addressed in terms of the following factors.

First, taking a cue from the well-known social contractarian position, let me argue that different social groups which are motivated by the politics of presence, recognition, and distribution do not find themselves in a position to reconcile, on their own, due to mutually conflicting interests. Both the rich and the poor realize that social Darwinism is detrimental to them. For producers and consumers or the rich it is the fear of property being confiscated, while for the poor it is the fear of death and physical insecurity, that makes the intervention of the state immanent. The producers seek recognition from enlightened consumers who can better appreciate the quality of products. But Indian capitalism, for historical reasons, is incapable of creating a class of enlightened consumers on its own. Hence the corporate class requires the state to create this class which responds to this design as it is also subjectively committed to fulfil its ever-growing middle-class aspirations and Dalits/Adivasis and OBCs are no exception to this. In a limited sense the state is required to produce this class through mediation between growing aspirations and distribution. While the terms for market-based recognition are designed within a particular frame of freedom, governed by rational choice, it is the state which plays a dominant role in deciding the terms of distribution. Since the state plays this dominant role, it often leads to subordination of the group that is seeking distribution and recognition. Here a distinction between recognition and subordination is in order. For an accurate understanding of recognition and its relationship with subordination it is necessary to disaggregate the term recognition. One could argue that recognition has two dimensions—radical and regressive. Radical recognition is defined in terms

of an unconditional acknowledgement of the worth of a person by civil society and public institutions. However, such recognition becomes difficult in a democracy which is based on the notion of exception. Those who are the beneficiaries of exception exist only by courtesy of those who have exceptional power to exceptionalize others. The politics of presence, which basically emanates from the idea of exception, gets linked to the idea of maladjustment. Thus, exception, maladjustment, and maldistribution in the structures of power hierarchy, even in a democracy, constitute subordination. It is in this sense that recognition defined in terms such as 'each according to his/her social origin' becomes regressive. The struggle to exist at the level of subordination has serious political implications. Those who chose their subordination through exception prefer to exist within the network of 'patronage democracy', without, however, challenging the ruling ideology. However, the terms of recognition may not be same as the terms of subordination. This inability to produce consensus therefore makes third-party (state) intervention immanent. Third-party intervention becomes attractive even for the protagonists of social justice (Scheduled Caste/ Scheduled Tribe political aspirants) who, through democratic process, are reduced to junior partners in chalking out the social justice agenda. Since the protagonists form part of the sponsored notion of social justice, this association eliminates the grounds on which the state could be condemned for its 'cunningness'. It is more the moral inconsistency of the protagonists rather than the cunning of the sense that can explain why the former concede more intellectual space to the state in terms of setting and shaping the social justice agenda. Second, and perhaps interestingly, the sponsored political mobility of the protagonists is analogous to the sponsored notion of social justice. These Dalit and Adivasi legislators, who invariably depend for their electoral victory on party support are forced to abide by whatever vision of social justice the party in power tends to hold for the former (Guru 1985). Thus, it is complete political dependence on the dominant party that can explain the secondary if not subservient role that the protagonists tend to play in matters of social justice. This dependence, as we will see in the last section of this chapter, compels these legislators to participate in the process which converts social justice as a substantive principle of permanent settlement into social justice as symbolic adjustment. Policies can be theoretically expansive and rhetorically quite promising but in actual practice they could be quite constraining or limiting. Policies tend to have a limiting impact, in the sense that the social demand for inclusion into opportunity structures grows in excess of the actual policy frame. These protagonists fail to look beyond this limiting policy frame partly because their political survival is ironically tied up with their allegiance with polices even if the latter are limiting in nature.

Third, as I have argued in the above section, the contest notion of social justice creates an agency among the marginalized. The political response of agency to its discrimination and deprivation has some bearing on the conceptualization of a substantive notion of justice. Thus oppositional imagination and politics assign normative weightage to the concept of social justice. However, the logic of co-optation of this agency within the state dissolves the former into a pragmatic agent of social justice, which is then found mediating between the state and the beneficiaries of different welfare policies that the state uses more for pacificatory than emancipatory purposes. In addition, this conversion of agency into agents leaves huge scope for the state to legislate on the question of social justice. Hence those who struggle as agency for assigning transcendental meaning to social justice ultimately become pragmatic agents who then lobby for policy rather than the principle of social justice.[10] The struggle for principle takes place in the streets while the lobbying for policy takes place in the corridors of power, both institutional and non-institutional. Thus, social justice as a struggle concept undergoes a kind of metamorphosis and becomes policy in the process of its concretization.

In addition to these two factors there are two more factors that can explain the overwhelming presence of the state in the discourse on social justice. First, the tactical withdrawal of the Indian corporate class from social responsibility thereby pushing the social justice agenda onto the plate of the state. The corporate class in India seems to have shown some inclination towards social justice by way of paying

taxes to the state. However, this class did not create more opportunity space in the form of private sector reservations so as to accommodate the social justice concern. Hence the social pressure on the corporate class to further open up, moving away from just paying taxes and diversifying its opportunity structures. The corporate class seems to be enjoying negative protection from the state, that too without paying too heavy a price for this protection. Considering the favours that it has received from the state, one cannot expect the corporate class to dictate to the Indian state in social justice matters. It therefore feels compelled to allow the state to enjoy relatively more autonomy in this sphere but at the same time is trying hard to resist any attempt by the state to bring the social justice agenda into its territory by way of reservations in the private sector (Mehta 2006). As mentioned above, there is not much of an intellectual discourse on social justice in India and this allows the state to design its own agenda on social justice. However, the state does on occasion seek validation through intellectuals whose views agree with its agenda discourse as there it is confined to reservations unlike in the US where there is a constitutional tradition around which the discourse is built (Rawls 2000: 74).

Before concluding this point, let me add that socialist and Left parties in India too have been ineffective in articulating a conception of justice. It is this intellectual lacuna that assigns a prominent role to the state in producing the vocabulary of social justice, and shaping its policy in the light of this vocabulary. Let us explore the vocabulary of social justice that the state in India has developed, and the policies that it has followed during the last few decades. It would be quite interesting to note here that the state seems to have taken initiatives in adopting a capacious vocabulary of social justice as if it were driven by its intuition rather than mass agitation. I would like to argue that it is not surprising to see the state adopting certain forms of institutional expansion (institution of several commissions and committees), in the absence of any massive social struggle. New social movements which are isolated and local in nature, raising issues of self-respect and dignity, cannot be said to have launched a protracted and nationwide struggle for social justice. In fact, these movements define justice less in terms of the material distribution of resources through compensatory policies, and more in terms of recognition of their cultural difference (White 1998: 123). There is a difference between social struggle and struggle for formal political power. Ideally any genuine social struggle defines itself in terms of generating an oppositional imagination and political activism against the totality of social dominance. Those who are involved in such struggles continue to remain in opposition, because they fear that if they become powerful they are likely to reproduce the repressive, coercive mechanism, against which they fought in the first instance. This is a difficult challenge which not every leader who begins with a radical social struggle agenda can sustain. As mentioned above, this challenge gets diluted into the individual aspiration of Dalit and bahujan leaders who loose their intellectual and moral capacity to push the principle of social justice to its logical end.

To return to the vocabulary of social justice developed by the state in India, the constitution of different commissions and committees including the Sachar committee, I would argue, is one such move that has come up even in the absence of any visible struggle. I would further like to argue that the state adopts social justice policy not because it is inherently benign and finds the need for such a vocabulary morally compelling. As is often the case in all societies, it is the anxiety of the state that leads to such proactive initiatives. This anxiety has to be understood in terms of the possible perhaps massive interruption of social forces. That is to say, those who are at the losing end in the 'development process', cannot be expected to remain acquiescent in their continuous marginalization. Such social groups from the margin always carry the possibility of producing a crisis for the state. The state has to become proactive in order to eliminate the possibility of accumulation of social crises that can become quite subversive if left unattended. In its move to interrupt the accumulation of crises, it either adopts a new vocabulary or makes the existing one more expansive in nature. This could be termed 'bailing out' the state in anticipation. The state in India seems to have adopted compensation

as the dominant mode of responding to the justice concern and in turn bailing itself out from the awkward situation that it always finds itself in.

COMPENSATION AS THE FINAL VOCABULARY

The idea of compensation has a normative as well as instrumental aspect to it. At the normative level, it underlies the principle of co-responsibility which the state shares both directly and indirectly for social harm which is historically perpetuated and contemporarily reproduced by the dominant social forces. Owning responsibility definitely points to sensitivity—though post-facto—on the part of the state. However, delivering social justice through compensation is also short-sighted. *First,* compensation could become ethically seductive to the extent that it interrupts if not aborts the process that can lead to justice as outcome by inducing the victim to settle not for a final outcome but for immediate relief (Guru 2008).

Second, compensation coupled with pragmatism also leads to moral loss at another level. The victim once compensated in kind, tends to forgo the moral claim to criticize either the government or the tormentor, and justice as a transcendental good gets regressively converted into an instrumental good. *Third,* the idea of compensation is also seductive for another reason. Pursuit for justice as outcome involves invoking a set of procedures and procedures in turn often demand that the victim reveals delicate details to the public. In order to avoid this public gaze the victim prefers to settle for compensation. Thus, compensation tends to convert moral loss into a quantifiable gain and quantifiable gain into moral loss. Compensation creates an irreducible tension between procedural (fair outcome) and moral conceptions of justice. *Fourth,* as a corollary to the third, compensation is morally offensive. A victim feels tormented because of the difficult choice that is before him—between pure justice or practical justice or true justice or actual justice. Fifth, as mentioned above, the pragmatism of victims tends to encourage the state to deploy the idea of compensation much more regularly and widely. Ironically, the state finds a purpose in compensation. Government in fact is happy to suggest 'one-time compensation' as the solution for long-time or structural forms of injustice. But for some, compensation cannot be the sole criterion for justice. It is difficult to compensate for a moral injury—a scar on the heart and mind. For such a quality of victimhood, the value of dignity is non-negotiable and cannot be sacrificed in a pragmatic trade-off. It is, on the contrary, ontologically related to the moral being and hence cannot be compensated through pragmatism. Such class of victims thus suggest, 'It may be in your interest(state) to treat compensation as the final vocabulary, but how can it be in our interest to treat it as the final solution?' In fact, such responses suggest that distributive justice through compensation provides only a provisional solution, hence making contestation almost endemic to compensation.

Although legal and political institutions do not offer a satisfactory delivery of justice yet it is difficult to practise justice-related policies and programmes without them. They are crucial for the administration of social justice. These institutions work on the assumption that historically accumulated forms of discrimination need to be redressed through continuous compensation rather than contingent or ad hoc intervention on the part of the state. Social justice by quota, by and large, involves procedural aspects of justice and the differentiation of institutions and 'role rotation' within these institutions. To this extent social justice has a deep middle-class orientation. Since everyone puts a lot more premium on jobs in the institutional sector, social justice issues become highly competitive and contestatory. Accommodation by quota at different levels of public institutions, however, has led some scholars to argue that this accommodation would adversely affect institutional well-being (Béteille 1991: 591–608).

Second, social justice as defined in terms of quotas has led to the articulation of social conflict, which could be interpreted as creative as well as destructive. At the vertical level, it seeks to create tension between the upper caste, and OBCs, SCs, and the minorities. At the horizontal level, it leads to the fierce and active social conflict among various sub-castes of the SCs. This happens because of the corresponding tension between the state act of making social justice socially expansive and at the same time failing to provide the necessary opportunity structures that give concrete expression to this expansion. Since this point warrants greater elaboration, for want of space I address the tension as seen by some scholars between institutional well-being and social justice-related policies like reservations (Béteille 1991).

In recent years, some leading Indian scholars have argued that social justice driven by a mere claim to occupy institutions through quotas may adversely affect institutional well-being (Béteille 1991). The demand to insulate certain 'key' institutions from reservations or quotas essentially suggests this fear of mediocrity. This line of argument thus puts modernity before democracy and, further to this, it suggests that participation in the institutional life of a democracy needs to be preceded by good training, merit, and efficiency. Further to this, this critique of the quota system also advises those who are seeking participation in democratic institutions the need to develop the moral stamina to endure training in institutional functioning based on rational procedures and protocols; and cultivate the cultural habits that are necessary for learning the use of political means in a modernist way. This commitment, articulated through a de-personalized bureaucracy, according to these scholars, could then guarantee institutional well-being. These scholars suggest that compensatory discrimination can put this institutional well-being in jeopardy, particularly when it is taken as matter of right. The language of rights, according to this view, is vacuous if not supported by modernist concerns (merit, efficiency, and excellence). According to them affirmative action or equal opportunity can uphold the standards of merit and efficiency, which constitute modernity. According to this perspective, modernity is privileged over democracy. These scholars thus look at the relationship between democracy and modernity in a sequential manner, putting modernity before democracy (Bardhan 2001: 236).

I would in fact argue for reversing the sequential order, thus putting democracy before modernity. This I believe is the most constructive approach to the progressive understanding of social justice. I would further like to argue that the discourse on social justice can make sense only when it operates in the conundrum of democracy. That is to say, for concretizing social justice democracy has to be treated as the initial condition, modernity as the interim, and democracy again as the ultimate condition. At this point, I would like to raise two pressing questions. First, why does democracy become an unavoidable stage in the discourse on social justice? Second, should these social groups—the beneficiaries of quotas—care more for social justice as a matter of right than anything else including modernity? Let me ask a related question here what happens if they put democracy before modern institutions?

In response to the first question, it needs to be argued that in the specific social context of India, the primacy of democracy over modernity becomes necessary to free the excluded social sections from the arbitrariness (in the form of the caste ideology) that has been the basis of the orthodox conception of social justice. This element of arbitrariness lingers on in Indian society, leading to an unequal and differential response to modernity. In a caste-ridden society like India, the primacy of modernity over democracy, which for some historical reasons favours the upper castes, is bound to maintain the relative gap between the upper castes and those who have not even arrived at modernity. That is to say, historically the upper castes find themselves closer to modernity than the lower castes who are not even on the margins of modernity (Seal 1968: 114). Social justice concerns would therefore demand their participation and hence democracy as the pre or initial condition for their arrival at modernity. It is necessary to provide them a democratic passage. To put it differently, in a society that is already imbalanced in terms of the distribution of social and material resources, the primacy of modernity over democracy would not only maintain but widen the relative gap between those who are the favourites of history and those who are still largely outside the frame of modernity. Democracy becomes an attractive option to narrow this gap, if not eliminate it completely. Second, democracy offers scope for the realization of social justice. Democracy, though a single process, is built up around several interconnected points. Social justice is one of the important points. If social justice means dignified accommodation into opportunity structures,

the demand for accommodation needs to be put forward by those who see a definite promise in social justice. In order to make this demand, these deprived sections need to be free and conscious about their rights. It is democracy that offers this freedom. Thus treating democracy as precondition for both imagining and actualizing social justice seems reasonable and defensible, on the grounds that it offers an opportunity which can subsequently be converted into an asset, that is, modernity. Democracy thus reduces the waiting time, so to say. It, at the same time, puts a huge moral pressure on those from the margins of modernity to convert the opportunity into an asset. In order to achieve this conversion, the excluded need to take institutional mechanisms seriously. To put it differently, democracy is a necessary but not sufficient condition for the sustenance and enrichment of social justice. Both democracy and social justice require solid institutional back-up. Institutional back-up, in turn, requires modernity for effective intervention in the social justice agenda. Thus, modernity becomes an important condition for the legitimation of the concept of social justice. The absence or lack of modernity concern among the beneficiaries of social justice offers a chance to its opponents to rubbish social justice.

As mentioned earlier, social justice as an ideal does not become applicable on its own. It requires an institutional context for its expansion and realization. Institutions thus are expected to function in accordance with modern criteria—depersonalization, merit, efficiency, and skill. Modernity becomes absolutely essential, if these institutions are to serve the ideal of social justice. Therefore I would like to suggest that once marginalized people get a democratic push into opportunity structures, the logic of modernity has to be intensified among them, thus not allowing compensatory discrimination to overwhelm institutional well-being. Interestingly, Ambedkar himself realized the need to look at these two essential orders not in isolation but in conjunction.

He treated democracy as the sphere of opportunity or the initial condition and modernity as the interim condition. He sought to intensify the modern spirit first among the Dalits with the purpose of infusing confidence among them. For this intensification of modernity among Dalits, Ambedkar created several educational institutions. He took care to organize these educational institutions on the basis of modern criteria and applied them in appointments to these institutions as well. He went beyond his immediate social constituency and selected professionally competent personnel belonging to different caste, religious and regional backgrounds. Thus, in Ambedkar's notion of social justice one finds a creative combination of democracy and modernity. Ambedkar looked at democracy as an initial condition or the sphere which could be used for converting opportunity (quota) into an asset. For him this conversion could be achieved only through modernity. Ambedkar tends to treat democracy as an initial condition of social justice both as consciousness and also as material possibility. He does not take the position that social backwardness or historical discrimination is the final condition within which a claim to social justice can be established without further moral justification. For Ambedkar, moral justification needs to be internal to social justice implicating the most marginalized sections in society. Moral justification is internal to the Bahujan or heterodox concept of social justice, as the most marginalized cannot afford to either rubbish or trivialize such institutions. Further, claims for social justice on the basis of social disabilities meet just the partial condition when understood from the point of view of the subaltern universe of justice. For him the final condition of a just and decent society lies in neo-Buddhism. At the interim stage, he finds modernity slipping through his fingers; he feels disenchanted with modernity and hence suggests conversion to Buddhism.

Modernity as an interim condition needs to create differentiated opportunity structures that are necessary for the realization of social justice (Rawls 2000). It is through these opportunity structures and their radical rotation (Walzer 1983: 134) that it becomes possible to assign new secular roles well outside the traditional system of rigid hierarchy. Thus, rotation of roles as an expression of social justice can be rendered possible only through adequate expansion of the institutional structure. Radical reshuffling of roles was also aimed at creating a generic identity among those who were otherwise tied to traditional occupations that were considered as defiling and degrading. Thus, radical rotation had the double

purpose of first delinking a particular person from the derogatory meaning that emanated from traditional occupations and second, assigning a new modern meaning to a person or social group.

In the context of the idea of radical rotation, it is necessary to create a wide network of institutions. With all its limitations, the Indian state did produce different institutional structures that, at least theoretically, were supposed to facilitate radical rotation and some degree of role reversal in modern institutions of state. This radical rotation is noticeable. Lower castes have gone up and upper castes have been pushed to the bottom. The social transition articulated through the process of rotation and mediated through institutional differentiation, however, seems to be inadequate as it generates scope for simple equality and not so much for complex equality (Walzer 1983: 134). As Walzer observes, in simple equality, people from different social destinations entered new institutions and began participating in them. But it is also true that these institutions could not acquire the capacity to promote overlapping social goods. That is to say, some of these institutions become more attractive than others. Thus, upper-caste bureaucrats compete to join certain institutions and show persistent hesitation or avoid joining certain other institutions (Guru 2008). For example, the state in India has created public institutions based on particularistic social grounds—caste, gender, religion, geographical isolations, and ethnic backgrounds.[11] In fact, the state in India seems to be following David Hume, who said, 'Giving every one what is of most use to him' (Barry 2005: 171). The institutional structures created by the state are betraying their modernist promise in as much as they are pushing some of the lower caste into the same occupations that in the past sought to perpetuate the sense of stigma against these castes.[12]

STATE AND SOCIAL JUSTICE: A CRITICAL APPRECIATION

In the final section I would like to discuss the limits of both the sponsored and contested notions of justice. Let me begin by making the observation that the state in India has a progressive as well as a regressive side to it. That is to say, it has acquired enormous authority through its control over the official discourse of social justice. Of course the state would not like to call it authority but responsibility for achieving the welfare of the marginalized. And the state further claims that it has achieved this not through soliciting help from intellectuals but mostly from experts whom it recruited through various civil service examinations. However, despite state claims, quotas as compensation help the beneficiaries only symbolically, while they offers massive political advantages to the state. It creates friction among groups who, instead of questioning the incapacity of the state in providing equal opportunity, hold the 'more privileged' social groups (in fact these are some individuals from these groups) accountable for the unequal advantage emanating from the quota system. Second, the state also believes that compared to the landless, the waiting-to-be middle class Dalits are less like to become critically dangerous. Hence, the state and its institutional arms suggest rather over-enthusiatically that there is nothing wrong with the expansive and extensive concept of social justice. What is needed, the government seems to be suggesting, is to bring new social groups and new opportunity structures (the corporate sector and even non-governmental organizations [NGOs]) under the social justice regime. These new groups include women, religious minorities, and certain OBCs to name a few. It is interesting to note that certain upper castes are also making claims for inclusion in the quota system. Thus, social justice has posed both political and intellectual challenges having implications for subaltern solidarity and the efficacy of institutions.

Second, the sponsored notion of justice has the following problems. Social justice as a necessary and achievable ideal empowers the state to convert it into policy and codify it into rules. This conversion of social justice into policy and then into rule by implication assigns the state the authority to implement social justice. The state as authority renders the language of rights ineffective. The state seeks legitimacy for its authority through the consent of those who are the beneficiaries of different social justice policies. Ironically, these beneficiaries themselves demand regular state intervention for the stricter monitoring of policies. State policing and disciplining, thus, become necessary in a context

where the beneficiaries of policy witness large-scale malpractices in its administration. The state's authoritative measures to bring the beneficiaries under its 'benign' surveillance, look deeply problematic as such efforts, howsoever benevolent they may be, ultimately undermine the dignity of the beneficiaries (Guru 2008). Perhaps it is for this reason that both Foucault and Walzer were skeptical of state intervention in the spheres of social justice. Looking at Walzer's critique of the state or political power, David Miller writes, 'The reason is that he [Walzer] is distrustful of political power, afraid that to allow the state to operate inside the spheres of justice would be to open the door to the simplest and worst form of tyranny; the coercive assignment of social good' (Miller 1995: 14). While this is not the place to examine the full implications of Walzer's position for the social groups who require state intervention as a minimum guarantee from the local community, on which Walzer seems to put premium, I must quickly add that it will not be totally in the interest of Dalits, Adivasis, and women to put everything into the basket of the community, which appears to be locally just to Walzer (Barry 2005: 75). They, as suggested by Ambedkar[13] and in contemporary times by Barry (ibid.), among others, would want to dismantle the local as a heap of junk. They, like Ambedkar, would throw in their lot with the state.

Third, the disaggregation principle is available both to the state for rectification of social imbalance and to marginalized groups as a device to give vent to intra-group tensions. As has been understood, we require a political system in which the state is able to continually hold in check those social and occupational groups which, by virtue of their skill or education or personal attributes, might otherwise stake a claim to a disproportionate share of society's rewards (for example Malas from Andhra Pradesh, Mahars from Maharashtra, or Chamars from UP). In the contemporary period, certain sub-castes of the SC cluster are already making demands for further disaggregation of quota in proportion to the percentage of their population. For example, the government of Andhra Pradesh led by Chandra Babu Naidu[14] and more recently, the Tamil Nadu government led by M. Karunanidhi have introduced this internal classification. However, social justice which is ideally aimed at generating the animating passions of egalitarian politics, in effect leads to the disturbing expressions of envy and resentment, and it is also true that such passion festers in every subordinate group (Mala/Madiga) and creates a deep sense of mutual enmity. For a reasoned perspective, one therefore needs to adopt a more analytical and normative approach to social conflicts (both vertical and horizontal) that are endemic to the very concept of social justice. Positions that are less informed by the double perspective—analytical and normative—which is so necessary to minimize, if not completely eliminate, the role of emotions and passions seem to rein in the social justice discourse in India. Positions that are devoid of analytical rigour invariably lead to untenable conclusions. These are some of the limitations that are associated with the sponsored notion of social justice. This is not to suggest that the contest notion of social justice is free from limitations. Let me point to at least a couple of limits of this particular notion of justice.

First, as mentioned earlier, principles and policies that have a bearing on social justice, have a differential impact on the beneficiaries of social justice. Policies rather than principles are more seductive as they lead to the unscrupulous pursuit of self-interest. To this extent, they have a regressive impact on the very essence of social justice. Policies as an effective source of seduction can lead to a conceptual shift. To put it differently, those who latch on to social justice cease to take an interest in social justice more as a pragmatic solution to the immediate problems rather than as a transcendental principle. The logic of parliamentary politics plays an important role in causing the conceptual shift. Such logic converts the substantive conception of social justice into symbolic satisfaction. Dalit political parties and their agents are primarily responsible for this atrophy. Let me offer two examples that can explain this conceptual shift. In 1959 and 1964, the Republican Party of India (RPI) led a massive countrywide Dalit struggle for land. But this demand was subsequently given up in favour of cultural gain. The RPI got Ambedkar's life-size statue installed in the premises of the parliament and reservation for Neo-Buddhists. In more recent times,

the shift from the substantive to symbolic is evident in 'Dalit–Sarvajan' politics in UP. I would like to argue that the concept of social justice remains sacrosanct as long as it resides in the sphere of collective social struggle. Outside, it is rendered murky by those who are motivated more by pragmatism than transcendental concerns. It undergoes a peculiar kind of metamorphosis the moment it enters the state arena. Within the liberal framework, social justice poses a paradox for the marginalized: social justice as principle is vacuous without policies and policies are seductive without principle.

Second, the state notion of justice also has a problem in as much as it leads to the ownership claim of socially discriminated groups over the pragmatic rather than substantive conception of social justice. In the process the state acquires genealogical power to give a caste to the concept of social justice. Once ownership is established, these social groups struggle to protect it. They fight not for upholding social justice as universal principle but tend to use its policy aspect in order to consolidate their narrow ends. Thus social justice as principle is robbed of its universal character.

Third, as a corollary to the first, it can be provocatively argued that social justice policies are like the tenders that political parties use in the competition for capturing office. And to that extent social justice policies are informed more by calculation (Tamil Nadu and Andhra) and less by serious reasoning and analysis. Social justice as an administrative, rather than conceptual, category is sustained by the feedback from party workers and party- and community-related bureaucrats. Social justice policy is hardly informed by debate and discourse that, as mentioned before, is anyway sparse in India. It is very seldom that political parties choose to deliberate seriously or systematically on social justice. Also, one does not find these parties providing a set of reasons through theoretical or philosophical engagements. This anti-intellectual stance gels very well with the politics of social justice and the policy regime. But this pragmatic take on social justice tends to reify the very concept of social justice into self-serving rhetoric and this in effect denies social justice an authentic grounding in complex social reality. To put it differently, in the political practice of the marginalized, social justice gets abbreviated into slogans which in turn get written on the wall. These slogans however, remain as a stale summary of the larger philosophical content of social justice.

Finally, a couple of points of criticism in regard to the positions on the critical relationship between social justice and institutional well-being. As mentioned earlier, the language of rights which defines and sustains the concept of social justice would tend to destroy the institutional fabric if it failed to enrich its content with the mediation of modernity. To put it differently, insistence on the right to enter institutions without acquiring the necessary calibre and culture would certainly be detrimental to institutions. What is assumed in such a standpoint is that the social justice constituency is likely to press for entry into institutions without the necessary calibre. Hence, it could be suggested, without claiming that scholars of this view are suggesting, that the very idea of quota-based social justice be altogether abandoned or at best retained in the form of affirmative action. At worst, it should be re-apportioned to some sector so as to limit its 'damaging' impact. In fact, the state has already adopted this option by keeping some institutions away from reservation. As a result, social justice overflows in certain institutions like the social justice ministry and related welfare departments. What is objectionable about this old hierarchy in new institutions is that it fails to create an overlapping sense of social good, which makes all the institutions equally weighty and worthy of respect. The question therefore is, have we generated this overlapping sense of good in India? The answer is, no. Some bureaucrats do not want a posting in the social welfare ministry or are sent to it as punishment. One could therefore argue that our notion of institutional well-being needs to be expanded from mere institutional well-being to overall well-being.

It is also necessary to offer some response to those scholars who, for perhaps the right reasons, are concerned about institutional well-being and hence warn against efforts that treat social justice as a matter of right at the cost of institutional well-being. As mentioned above, such warnings are motivated by the fear of mediocrity, which is considered by some as detrimental to institutional well-being. This line of thinking, which may look attractive to many, however, has its own problems. First, it seeks to reverse the value order thus treating modernity as an end and democracy as an obstacle to achieving this end. One needs to reverse this order and make democracy an initial and enabling condition as well as the desirable end. Modernity has to be treated not as an end in itself but an interim condition that would enrich the democratic content of both institutions and those who occupy these institutions. After all, modernity is a condition that entails a set of procedures that are necessary for the fair, and hence democratic, redistribution of both material and moral resources. Second, the argument that privileges modernity over democracy is also problematic as it assumes that institutions are always and already in good shape and occupied by persons who have the required human and moral resources to protect their well-being. The question that can be raised here is: does cultural and moral capital constitute a one-time given asset? Conversely those, at least some of them, who have come to occupy these institutions through the social justice route, are forced to remain extra-rational because it is not given. Second, and for quite contrary reasons, the fear of mediocrity is misplaced. Let me explain this by citing a case of Dalit legislators. Those who occupy these institutions, particularly the political ones, are worthy of condemnation for the opposite reason that they do not use these institutions in favour of the downtrodden even within the prescribed framework (Guru 1985). The Dalit presence in institutional/parliamentary politics is characterized mostly by their being marginal both in time and space. They are hardly known by their intellectual presence. However, this is not to suggest that their remaining at the margins is something which is pathological in nature. In fact, it needs to be understood as a structural constraint within which these beneficiaries of reservation have to work. But, this produces a dilemma for the liberals. Should they tolerate the politics of silence or should they talk about it? If they remain silent, it increases the 'responsibility of the state to take over many things including social justice that have a bearing on the life conditions of the marginalized.

Institutional well-being is certainly important. It is also true that social justice should not override institutional interests and vice versa. However, this position favouring institutions looks tenable only in the context where the institutions function on the basis of fair and rational procedures. These institutions are therefore devoid of partisan human interest. Or to put it differently, these institutions as modern structures are detoxified of some pre-modern particular social tendencies. Modern structures are depersonalized so to say. They are empty, to be taken over by any person from any social background. These are not already occupied but filled by personnel through universally agreed-upon criteria and set procedures. Thus the question of institutional well-being is contingent on the question of their being completely empty of prejudices. To this extent, institutional well-being becomes defensible and not otherwise. It is in this context the question needs to be raised: are public institutions in India fully committed to the principles of rationality and impartiality. Is institutional impartiality in congruence with the realization of the ideal of social justice? The experience with institutional procedures in the Indian context makes the argument for institutional well-being contingent on the quality of modern bureaucrats embodying a secular social consciousness. In India, the state seems to have failed to detoxify these institutions as their procedures still contain the pre-modern elements that are present in some of the personnel. This is evident from the state's own policy of appointing an observer from the quota constituency on selection committees that are held in public institutions. If the procedures are perfect, then why do you require the observer?

As mentioned earlier, institutions in themselves are filled with such elements. In fact, the modern institutions are empty of predatory power. Their modern character hinges on those who occupy them subsequently. The character of a person becomes absolutely important. Character depends on virtue, which in turn is defined in terms of three things— distribution, methods, and outcome (William 2006: 206). Taking a cue from Bernad William, one could argue that if virtue as a moral/ethical resource is

equally present among persons then perhaps one may not require an observer from a particular caste sitting on the selection committee. It is in this sense that virtue becomes justice and justice becomes virtue.

NOTES

1. Ravidas, Chokamela, Tukaram, the non-Brahmin saints of Medieval period, sought to radically question the caste hierarchy while the upper castes like Eknath and Anukampa affected only a mild critique of caste system. Similarly in Buddhist tradition, the notion of egalitarian is stronger than any other tradition that were contemporary to Buddha.

2. The saint and/Warkari tradition as represented, for example, by Karma Mela (an untouchable saint) and Tukaram (from Maratha caste) from Medieval Maharashtra clearly bring out the contestation between these two traditions.

3. This is disputed by Ram Narayan Rawat. Rawat made a presentation on 'Writing New History: The Chamars of UP' at the Centre for Political Studies, Jawaharlal Nehru University, New Delhi, 25 March 2009.

4. This is an important dimension of the Gandhian framework of social justice.

5. Dalit Panther from Maharashtra, DSS from Karnataka, Dalit, OBC, Muslim Maha Sangha led by Shabbir Ansari, Dalit Christian Liberation Movement led by the late Arvind Nirmal. Dalit, Muslim, OBC solidarity on the issue of Mandal Commission—these struggles belong to the larger tradition of Ambedkar and Lohia.

6. Roma Chatterji, a social activist working among the Kol tribals of Bundelkhand, in Uttar Pradesh.

7. This was the slogan, the Dalit and Left parties gave during the 1972, serious statewide drought situation that existed.

8. Sharad Joshi's Shetkari Sanghatana, made this demand in the 1990s.

9. In this regard it is important to keep in mind the first Mandal agitation phase (from 1989 to 1994). This phase represented the broader unity among Dalit Muslims, OBCs, and *adivasis*, which came to gather in support of *Mandal Report*.

10. Prominent examples of these agents could be found in Dalit political parties and also in the premises of social justice ministry and social welfare departments.

11. Mahatma Phule Mandal, Sathe mandal, Naik Mandal in Maharashtra.

12. The states of Maharashtra and Tamil Nadu have supported such caste-based occupations.

13. Ambedkar considers the local community as the den of ignorance and communalism.

14. Sub-categorization in Andhra Pradesh was turned down by a Supreme Court Order. Chandra Babu Naidu, the ex-Chief Minister of Andhra Pradesh introduced the ABCD division within already existing quota of 16 per cent.

REFERENCES

Ambedkar, B.R. 1990. *Ambedkaranche Bahishkrut Bharatatil Agralekh*. Mumbai: Government of Maharashtra.

——. 1957. *Buddha and His Dhamma*. Mumbai: People's Education Society.

Bardhan, Pranab. 2001. 'Sharing the Spoils: Group Equity Development and Democracy', in Atul Kohli (ed.), *The Success of India Democracy*. Cambridge: Cambridge University Press, pp. 226–41.

Barry, Baran. 2005. *Why Social Justice Matters*. Cambridge: Polity Press.

Berbad, Willaim. 2006. *The Sense of the Past: Essays in History and Philosophy*. Princeton and Oxford: Princeton University Press.

Béteille, Andre. 1991. 'Distributive Justice and Institutional Well-Being', *Economic and Political Weekly*, March, pp. 591–600.

Burnyeat, Myles (ed.). 2006. *The Sense of the Past: Essays in the History of Philosophy*. Princeton: Princeton University Press.

Guru, Gopal. 2008. 'Democracy in Search of Dignity', in Ujjwal Singh (ed.), *Human Rights and Peace in India*. New Delhi: Sage, pp. 74–89.

——. 2007. 'Twentieth Century Discourse on Social Justice: A View from the Quarantine India', in Sabyasachi Bhattacharya (ed.), *Development of Modern Indian Political Thought and the Social Sciences*. New Delhi: Oxford University Press, pp. 221–38.

Guru, Gopal. 1985. 'Party Politics in a Reserved Constituency: A Study of Parliamentry Segment in Maharashtra', unpublished PhD Thesis, New Delhi: JNU.

Habermas, Jurgen. 1988. *Reason, Justice and Modernity*. Cambridge: Cambridge University Press.

Heller, Agnes. 1987. *Beyond Justice*. New York: Basil Blackwell.

Marion Young, Iris. 1990. *Justice and the Politics of Differences*. Princeton: Princeton University Press.

Mehta, Pratap Bhanu. 2006. 'Affirmation and Reservation', *Economic and Political Weekly*, XXIV(7), pp. 2951–4.

Miller, David. 1995. 'Introduction', in David Miller and Michael Walzer (ed.). *Pluralism, Justice and Equality*, New York: Oxford University Press, p. 14.

Nikumbe, C.H. 2006. *Aaddhya Ashprush Uddharak: Gopal Baba Walangkar* (Marathi). Pune: Sugawa Publications.

Rawls, John. 2000. *Theory of Justice*. Delhi: Universal Law Publishing Co.

Seal, Anil. 1968. *Emergence of Indian Nationalism: Collaboration and Competition*. Cambridge: Cambridge University Press.

Walzer, Michael. 1983. *The Spheres of Justice*. Oxford: Martin Robertson.

White, Stephen K. 1988. *The Recent Work of Jurgen Habermas: Reason, Justice and Modernity*. Cambridge: Cambridge University Press.

V Social Movements and Civil Society

25 Social Movements

Amita Baviskar

'A million mutinies' is how V.S. Naipaul characterized India in 1990. Yet, despite the salience and significance of social movements on the Indian political landscape, they remained relatively under-researched until the last thirty years. In retrospect, it seems remarkable that major collective campaigns in the early decades of independent India, such as the anti-Brahmin movement and the Telengana struggle for land rights in the 1940s, the agitations for the formation of linguistic states and the Bhoodan movement in the 1950s, did not figure in contemporaneous scholarship. The overwhelming emphasis of political scientists at that time seems to have been on formal political institutions, especially electoral representation, federalism, and international policy. The study of politics was largely equated with governance and the exercise of state power. Historians of modern India also concentrated on the institutional processes leading to Independence, the positions adopted by political parties and their leaders. The collective mobilization upon which this edifice depended, the multiple scales of social action that were bundled together into an account of 'the nationalist movement', did not receive much attention until the late 1970s. The same preoccupation with institutions and institutional processes pervaded much of the sociological analysis of the period. Sociological inquiry was preoccupied with understanding the impact of diffuse social processes such as modernization and sanskritization on caste and agrarian relations. For all these disciplines, it was only in the 1980s that the study of social movements acquired a critical mass and momentum, enabling it to become a full-fledged field of inquiry with its own conceptual corpus, theories, and debates.

This essay reviews the scholarship on social movements in India by situating it within two dynamic fields: the history of social movements since Independence, and the wider intellectual landscape within which ideas of collective action, protest, and resistance have travelled. It does not attempt to provide an exhaustive survey of the literature, which can be found in Shah (1990) and Singh (2001). For the purpose of this essay, a social movement is defined as *sustained collective action* over time. Such action is often directed against the state and takes the form of demanding changes in state policy or practice. Collective action must be marked by some degree of *organization*. Spontaneous, disorganized protest cannot be called a social movement. This organization may include a leadership and a structure that defines how members relate to each other, make decisions, and carry them out. Those participating in a social movement have *shared objectives and ideologies*. A social movement has a general orientation to bring about (or prevent) change. These defining features are not constant, and may change over the course of a social movement's life.

EARLY STUDIES ON SOCIAL MOVEMENTS

The works of M.S.A. Rao (1978–9) and Ghanshyam Shah (1977, 1979) were the first systematic attempts to study contemporary social movements. The two volumes edited by Rao compiled accounts of collective action by different groups: the first volume on peasants and backward classes, and the second on sects, tribal groups, and women. Along with this documentation, Rao presented a typology of social movements, a classificatory exercise that, like others of that time, sought to analyse collective action in terms of its effects on social structure.[1] Movements were classified according to their orientation to change (whether radical or limited), and the focus of change (whether all of society or specific social groups). This four-fold schema yielded the following categories of movements: revolutionary (radical movements that sought to transform all society, such as the Naxalite struggle); reformist (movements for limited change for all society, such as the backward classes movement); redemptive (radical change for specific social groups, such as millenarian movements); and alternative (limited change for a specific social group, such as a sectarian movement). Shah (1977) categorized social movements as revolt, rebellion, reform, and revolution, in terms of their objectives or the nature of change in the political system they sought to achieve. Later, both Rao (1979) and Shah (2002) were to distance themselves from these structural–functionalist frameworks of analysis, with their homeostatic view of society as existing in a state

of equilibrium disturbed by social movements. More dynamic conceptions of social relations, where social movements were one of several interrelated modes of political action, came to the fore in the 1980s.

While these early studies of social movements were influenced by American social science theories of the 1950s and 1960s, they also engaged critically with their propositions. For instance, Ghanshyam Shah's comparative analysis of the students' movement in Gujarat and Bihar (1977, 1979) rebutted Ted Gurr's notion of social movements as catalysed by 'relative deprivation' (Gurr 1970). However, the dominant model of social movements in the United States at that time—McCarthy and Zald's (1977) 'resource mobilization theory' with its entrepreneurial view of success as contingent upon a movement's ability to harness resources of various kind, and its more political version as exemplified in the work of Piven and Cloward (1977), Charles Tilly (1978), and Doug McAdam (1982)—seems to not have had much impact on the study of social movements in India.

SOCIAL MOVEMENT THEORY AND THE CHALLENGE OF 'NEW SOCIAL MOVEMENTS'

Ghanshyam Shah's work on student movements also incorporated a line of analysis that was to characterize many subsequent studies of social movements, viz., how the class background of the actors shaped the movement's goals and strategies. The debate on class and collective action has a long lineage within Marxist scholarship, and many of the essays in M.S.A. Rao's edited volumes grappled with the Marxist assertion that organized movements of workers and peasants would shoulder the historical burden of bringing about radical social transformation. This perspective was also reflected in the analyses of agrarian movements by A.R. Desai (1979, 1986), Arvind N. Das (1982), and D.N. Dhanagare (1983). However, events around the world jolted Marxist verities and sparked off a new wave of theorizing on social movements, which was to continue into the 1990s. The emergence of a spectrum of interconnected, multi-stranded social movements in North America and Europe confounded leftist political theory with its emphasis on class struggle

(Zinn 1980). The movement for civil rights for African–Americans and its more militant siblings such as Black Power and the Black Panthers; the students' movements against imperialism centred around the Vietnam War; the peace movement for nuclear disarmament and the environmental movement against air and water pollution; the women's movements that ranged from the quest for equal opportunity to radical feminism, all sharply challenged the notion that class conflict was the central social contradiction around which social transformation would be organized. The ideological diversity of these movements and the varied social locations of their members defied conventional Marxist explanations, leading scholars such as André Gorz to bid 'farewell to the working class' (1982). While social theorists such as Rudolf Bahro (1982) sought to incorporate the new surge of movements within a reworked framework of socialist politics, others such as Jurgen Habermas (1981) and Alain Touraine (1985) argued that the 'new social movements' demonstrated that class had become redundant as an organizing form of social identity and action. New social movements were the products of a post-industrial social formation where the welfare state had made classic forms of exploitation and deprivation obsolete, but where modern society created new forms of alienation. These movements reflected and responded to this discontent: they were communitarian in that they sought to reclaim a 'lifeworld' disenchanted by modernity, and universalist in that their politics exceeded class struggle and the '*problems of distribution*' [and addressed] the very '*grammar of forms of life*' (Habermas 1981: 33, emphasis in original). This meta-critique demanded a new conceptual apparatus.

SOCIAL MOVEMENTS OF THE 1970s

Similar questions about the role of class politics in social movements; the relationship of social movements to the rest of the polity, especially the state; and issues of ideology arose in India in the 1970s and 1980s, when the country experienced a surge of political activism not witnessed since the days of the Quit India movement. The background for this activism was an economic crisis perceived to have been exacerbated by the failure of the ruling Congress party to check price rise and corruption.[2] Widespread unrest provided the political context for social movements of various kinds. The students' movement in Bihar was guided by the Sarvodaya leader Jayaprakash Narayan, whose call for *sampoorna kranti* (total revolution) galvanized thousands to participate in street demonstrations, often confronting the police and paramilitary forces.[3] In Gujarat, where the movement was loosely linked to Sarvodaya, its goal was described as *navnirman* (reconstruction). While Sarvodaya and Navnirman were informed by a mix of Gandhian and socialist principles, this period was also marked by the emergence of the Naxalite movement for revolutionary change, driven by Maoist ideology and concentrated in and around West Bengal (Mohanty 1977; Banerjee 1980; Ray 1988). Breaking sharply with the ideologies of the organized Communist Parties of India, the leaders of the Naxalite movement, Charu Mazumdar and Kanu Sanyal, advocated the violent overthrow of the state and propertied classes by peasants and other exploited classes. While the movement was brutally suppressed by the West Bengal government and became less powerful within that state, Naxalite groups went on to increase in number, expanding their area of influence in east and central India, particularly the states of Bihar, Andhra Pradesh, Chhattisgarh, Jharkhand, and Maharashtra.

If the Naxalite movement reinvigorated the question of class struggle by highlighting the continuing conflict between landlords and peasants, the rise of the Dalit Panthers in Maharashtra and Tamil Nadu (Zelliot 1992; Nagaraj 1993; Omvedt 1995; Guru and Chakravarty 2005) over the same period provided a different critique of the prevailing power structure by arguing that class relations in India were subsumed within the cultural framework of caste. The Dalit movements highlighted how caste ideology continued to form the basis for social exclusion and discrimination; their attempts to challenge dominant caste practices met with violent reprisals. The first generation of Dalits to have had some access to formal education (albeit limited to a small section of men), enabling them to reflect critically on their experience of caste by engaging with the writings of B.R. Ambedkar and others, also produced a body of autobiographical writing that offered social critique through the medium of literature, giving voice to questions of cultural identity and social oppression. At the same time that the Dalit movement was provoking an examination of how class and caste related to each other, the women's movement was making the relationship between class and gender a more central issue in political debate. As preparation for the United Nations Decade for Women (1976–85), the Indian government commissioned a report on the status of women in India (CSWI 1974), which drew upon research and activism all over the country. Through campaigns against dowry, discriminatory personal laws, women's rights to landed property, among other issues, women's groups in urban and rural India focused on patriarchal domination in the lives of Indian women, with Marxist feminists emphasizing the intersection of patriarchy and class-based exploitation (Omvedt 1980; Basu 1992; Kumar 1993; Ray 1999).

This period also saw the crystallization of an environmental movement around the Chipko struggle against deforestation and commercial forestry in the Himalaya, and the Kerala Sastra Sahitya Parishad-led campaign to stop the building of a dam in Silent Valley (CSE 1982; Guha 1989a).[4] In its own way, the environmental movement also raised the question of inequities in the distribution of natural resources and class conflict, especially as refracted through state policies that favoured the industrial elite. However, both the Chipko and Silent Valley campaigns also challenged the prevailing model of development in terms of its environmental impact on biodiversity and the physical landscape. While these movements initiated a debate on environment and development, a more wide-ranging critique of development on the grounds of both ecology and social justice, including a conception of the cultural rights of subaltern groups, came to be explicitly formulated only in the latter half of the 1980s with the Narmada Bachao Andolan (Movement to Save River Narmada) (Baviskar 1995). However, the basic contours of this political critique can also be found in older struggles for tribal identity and autonomy, such as the Jharkhand movement (Sengupta 1982; Singh 1982, 1983a, 1983b; Devalle 1992; Munda and Bosu Mullick 2003).

The catalyst for the social movements of the late 1970s was the state of Emergency imposed by Prime Minister Indira Gandhi in 1975. This period, when civil and political rights were suspended, the media censored, and political activists jailed, was itself precipitated by the conspicuous threat posed to the ruling Congress party by the students' movement of the early 1970s, and collective action by organized workers such as the railways Trade Union. The lifting of the Emergency in 1977 and the electoral defeat of the Congress unleashed a political upsurge in which social movements came into greater prominence. Of these, the movement that most directly responded to the experience of Emergency was the one to safeguard democratic rights and civil liberties, broadly defined as the human rights movement (Gudavarthy 2008; Singh 2005). All the major social movements of this period showed a strong degree of cross-fertilization. As personnel and ideas were exchanged between movements, political ideologies and strategies were contested, and collaboratively produced and refined.

ANALYSING THE MOVEMENTS OF THE 1970s

The most influential scholarly perspective on the movements of the 1970s and early 1980s is the work of Rajni Kothari (1988). Kothari described these movements as 'non-party political formations', a new organizational form that allowed them to avoid the corruption and compulsions of electoral politics. According to Kothari, after the Emergency and the subsequent fiasco of the Janata regime that replaced the Congress at the Centre, people's faith in electoral democracy had been shaken. The Emergency had proved that the state's commitment to safeguard the democratic rights of citizens was not guaranteed. A vigil upon state action could be maintained only by civil society, mobilized through non-party political formations. Kothari's analysis resonated with observations about 'new social movements' in Europe: that their sphere of action 'is largely a space of non-institutional politics which is not provided for in the doctrines and practices of liberal democracy and the welfare state' (Offe 1985: 826).[5] While Kothari's claim that social movements ranged themselves against the state in defence of democracy would certainly hold true for the human rights movement, other movements had a more complex relationship with the state. Conservationist groups within the environmental movement, for instance, while criticizing ecologically destructive state projects and policies, also successfully deployed their access to Prime Minister Indira Gandhi and other top leadership to achieve their objectives (Rangarajan 1996; Mishra 1996). The women's movement fit Kothari's conception even less; it succeeded in getting the state to enact progressive legislation even before there was widespread demand for or social acceptance of it (Menon 1999). There were thus multiple positions within and across social movements that defied clear characterization with respect to their relationship to the state.

Like their counterparts in Europe and North America, many scholars of the Marxist persuasion who studied social movements in India persisted in trying to fit the surge of collective action in the 1970s and 1980s into the framework of class conflict. For some, class remained the only 'true' line of social cleavage; the chatter around 'new social movements' was a sign that academia had lost its political moorings (Brass 1991). For others who examined social movements more closely, matters were not so easily resolved (Guha 1989b). In her earlier work, Gail Omvedt had noted that rural movement activists were uncomfortable with scholarly efforts to place them in theoretical pigeonholes, and were wary of being labelled 'feminist' or 'environmentalist' (Omvedt 1987). Yet her Marxist training led her to adopt the same reductionist stance and insist that the apparently 'new green movements in India [were] survival movements of the rural poor' (ibid.: 36), thereby asserting the primacy of class above other axes of social identity such as gender, caste, and tribe. Later, as her involvement with the Dalit movement deepened, Omvedt was to move away from an orthodox Marxist line. In *Reinventing Revolution* (1993), which remains the most detailed examination of social movements in India, Omvedt argues for a more nuanced analysis of the connections between class, caste, gender, and environment.

In the studies of social movements published in the early 1990s, a new methodological tendency came into prominence, viz., the use of ethnographic techniques such as participant observation. Research conducted in this manner yielded a new perspective on social movements, enriching and complicating the more structuralist enquiries of the past that sought to classify collective action in terms of its relationship to a static social system, or to the project of revolution (Hobsbawm 1965). Elements of this perspective can be discerned in Ramachandra Guha's classic monograph *The Unquiet Woods* (1989a), a history of peasant resistance in the Himalaya leading up to the Chipko movement. Guha's fieldwork gave him a vantage point for distinguishing not only between different ideological strands within the Chipko movement, but also between the 'public' face of Chipko as an environmental movement and its 'private' face as an enduring peasant movement against the state.[6] The delineation of diverse layers of political consciousness within what is apparently a unified social movement by observing its internal dynamics was both a methodological and a conceptual choice. Influenced by Ranajit Guha's path-breaking work *Elementary Aspects of Peasant Insurgency* (1982), itself inspired by Antonio Gramsci's writings on hegemony and consciousness (Gramsci 1971), the field of subaltern studies defined itself by reading colonial and nationalist history against the grain, to analyse the insurgent consciousness of subalterns in all their complexity. David Hardiman (1987) used the subaltern approach to incisively dissect how, in western India, Adivasi religious beliefs became entangled with prohibitionist politics and the larger nationalist movement led by M.K. Gandhi.[7] Understanding collective action in terms other than the grand narratives of nationalist or class struggle is a move that illuminates the meaning and experience of resistance in the context of domination, enabling an appreciation of the contradictions that are an intrinsic part of subaltern consciousness and collective action (Guha 1982; Amin 1995). The subaltern impress is evident in Ramachandra Guha's research on Chipko, as is the influence of social historians such as E.P. Thompson (1966) who popularized the study of 'history from below' and political scientists such as James Scott (1976, 1985, 1990) who brilliantly illuminated collective resistance by demonstrating its lurking presence even in 'unheroic' times.[8]

The highlight of sociological research on collective action that uses ethnographic methods has been its ability to go beyond and beneath social movements' presentation of themselves. They have probed the internal organization of social movements in terms of the power relations between activists and other members, and analysed how varying, and at times contradictory, ideologies and understandings are reconciled or encompassed to create an apparently unified movement (Basu 1992; Baviskar 1995, 2001; Gupta 1997; Ray 1999; Rangan 2000; Chakrabarti 2007). This has been a controversial approach. Some scholars have argued that revealing the internal dynamics of progressive movements, warts and all, renders them more vulnerable to being discredited by their adversaries (Brosius 1999). Scholarly research must be self-reflexive and recognize the larger field of power/knowledge within which both academic practices and social movements are situated. When conducted with critical empathy, ethnographic research is able to show that political interests and identities are not pre-given, but are forged through the experience of mobilization and struggle. Such scholarly writing now exists alongside sophisticated accounts of social movements written by activists and supporters (Sangvai 2000), and plays an interlocutory role by clarifying and refining a movement's discursive and other strategies.[9]

GLOBALIZATION AND OTHER SOCIAL DYNAMICS: ISSUES FOR FURTHER RESEARCH

Since the 1990s, many social movements in India have become embedded in global networks and alliances, in part as a consequence of the transnational projects and discourses with which they now have to contend. The links forged by Dalit groups with the movement against racism, the participation of sections of the environmental movement in the transnational opposition to neoliberalism as embodied in the World Trade Organization and multilateral financial institutions, and the increasing ties between the movements for Adivasi rights and the international campaigns on indigenous peoples are some instances of a growing trend. How articulation

within transnational networks changes the dynamics and discourses of a social movement has, however, not been adequately examined (Keck 1998; Khagram et al. 2002; Khagram 2004). The Indian literature offers only stray insights into the effects of international links on a movement's self-representations (Baviskar 2005; Ghosh 2006).[10] In addition, the changed equations in situations where rural-based movements build alliances with metropolitan groups and the media have also been relatively neglected as an issue for study, even though they have become increasingly significant in shaping a movement's success (Sethi 2001).

Another key feature of social movement politics from the 1990s is the institutionalization of campaigns and the growing presence of non-governmental organizations (NGOs), whose work intermeshes with grassroots mobilization. Such NGOs may provide support in various forms, including funding, networking, advocacy, documentation, and publicity. NGOs that frame their work as 'rights-based mobilization', as opposed to 'service delivery', not only participate in existing social movements, but also initiate campaigns that take on many aspects of social movement mass mobilization. For instance, the Wada Na Todo Abhiyan (Campaign for Government Accountability to End Poverty) claims to bring together more than 3000 NGOs to ensure that the state adheres to the Millennium Development Goals of ending poverty and social exclusion for all citizens by 2015.[11] The Campaign emerged from the World Social Forum 2003, itself a hybrid product of social movements and rights-based NGOs, supported by the United Nations, bilateral funding agencies, and private foundations. It remains to be examined how the presence of NGOs in the field of social movement mobilization changes its dynamics. If the hallmark of the previous generation of social movement activists was their 'grassroots' political experience, from which they derived their credibility, NGO activists tend to draw their strength from more diffuse networks, formal academic qualifications in the social sciences, as well as professional employment in the development sector. These transformations in the web of significant relationships and the concomitant shifts in the construction of authenticity and accountability require further study. For instance, when NGO movement leaders can secure financial support outside their membership base and the rank and file no longer need to provide the material resources to sustain the campaign, it has implications for the decision-making process, and for the extent of individual and collective commitment that the campaign calls for. These and other changes, for instance in the relationship between movement leadership and its members, remain relatively unexamined.

The major social movements of the 1990s in India, revolving around 'market [liberalization], mandir/masjid and Mandal' (Deshpande 2003), have yet to fully find their chroniclers and interpreters (Ludden 1996; Hansen 1999). To this triad may be added the Marxist–Leninist revolutionary movement, which has greatly expanded its geographical range in the subcontinent (Banerjee 1980, 1984; Duyker 1987; Mukherjee 2007; Ray 1988; Singh 2006). Also under-studied are the relations between social movements and political parties, between, say, the Ram Janmabhoomi movement and the Bharatiya Janata Party, or between the Dalit movement and the Bahujan Samaj Party (Pai 2002). It is also notable that, far from keeping a distance from electoral politics, in line with Kothari's characterization of non-party political formations, several contemporary social movements and campaigns, such as that for the Right to Information, directly engage with political parties and parliamentary democracy in order to achieve their goals. The complementarities between movement dynamics and more institutional political forms require further exploration. An extreme instance of this is when state actors begin to mimic and adopt social movements' repertoire of mobilization techniques (Heller 2005; Baviskar 2007), thereby dissolving the distance between the state and social movements that had appeared to be a given in studies of collective action. These and other issues that shed light on the place of social movements in contemporary political life await further analysis.

NOTES

1. See also essays by Mukherji (1977) and Oommen (1977).

2. The fact that the world economy was in recession because of 'oil shock' due to the unexpected raising of petroleum prices by Organization of Petroleum Exporting Countries (OPEC) in 1973 had a bearing upon the state of India's economy, as did the 1971 war with Pakistan, which led to the creation of Bangladesh.

3. For an account of the Sarvodaya movement through the biographies of its leaders, including Vinoba Bhave and Jayaprakash Narayan, see Ostergaard and Currell (1971).

4. CSE (1982); Guha (1989a). Besides his pioneering study on the Chipko movement, Ramachandra Guha has published a number of essays that, taken together, provide an insightful account of the personalities and ideologies of the environmental movement in India, and its prehistory. See Guha (1988), (1992), and (2000).

5. Similar themes around the relationship of social movements to the state and electoral democracy were also addressed by Mohanty and Mukherji (1998). On the impact of social movements on state policies regarding poverty and inequality, see Ray and Katzenstein (2005).

6. For a different perspective on Chipko as a social movement, disputing Guha's analysis for neglecting the regional dimensions of discontent in the Himalaya, see Rangan (2000). An older reading, presenting Chipko as an ecofeminist movement, can be found in Vandana Shiva's 1988 book *Staying Alive*. Sinha *et al.* (1997) criticize Guha's work as a 'neo-traditionalist' romanticization of peasant politics.

7. See also Sundar (2007) for a similar perspective, vividly presented, on Adivasi resistance in Bastar, central India.

8. This brief sketch of how historians have studied social movements cannot do justice to the rich conceptual and empirical debates that have taken place among subalternists and their critics. Since the focus of this chapter is post-Independence India, I have not attempted to present a fuller account of these debates, but have only highlighted the areas where subaltern scholarship has been influential in shaping the study of contemporary social movements. Readers interested in a review of subaltern studies may consult Chaturvedi (2000).

9. For instance, Gail Omvedt's characterization of the Sardar Sarovar dam issue as a symmetrical conflict between two groups of landed peasants (those who were threatened with submergence and those who stood to gain from irrigation) challenged the dominant social movement claim that the gains from the dam were minuscule, illegitimate, and would worsen social inequalities. Omvedt's intervention forced the anti-dam movement and its supporters to engage more closely with the alternatives to large dams, which would address the issue of water scarcity for drought-prone regions.

10. An exemplary account of such articulation is found in Conklin and Graham's study (1995) of the indigenous movement in Amazonia.

11. See http://www.wadanatodo.net/default.asp. Last accessed on 13 March 2009.

REFERENCES

Amin, Shahid. 1995. *Event, Memory, Metaphor: Chauri Chaura 1922–1992*. Berkeley: University of California Press.

Bahro, Rudolf. 1982. *Socialism and Survival*. London: Heretic Books.

Banerjee, Sumanta. 1984. *India's Simmering Revolution: The Naxalite Uprising*. London: Zed Books.

———. 1980. *In the Wake of Naxalbari: A History of the Naxalite Movement in India*. Calcutta: Subarnarekha.

Basu, Amrita. 1992. *Two Faces of Protest: Contrasting Modes of Women's Activism in India*. New Delhi: Oxford University Press.

Baviskar, Amita. 2007. 'The Dream Machine: The Model Development Project and the Remaking of the State', in Amita Baviskar (ed.), *Waterscapes: The Cultural Politics of a Natural Resource* New Delhi: Permanent Black, pp. 281–313.

———. 2005. 'Red in Tooth and Claw?: Searching for Class in Struggles over Nature', in Raka Ray and Mary Fainsod Katzenstein (eds), *Social Movements in India: Poverty, Power, and Politics*. Lanham, MD: Rowman and Littlefield, pp. 161–78.

———. 2001, 'Written on the Body, Written on the Land: Violence and Environmental Struggles in Central India', in Nancy Peluso and Michael Watts (eds), *Violent Environments*. Ithaca: Cornell University Press, pp. 354–79.

———. 1997. 'Tribal Politics and Discourses of Environmentalism', *Contributions to Indian Sociology*, 31(2), pp. 195–223.

———. 1995. *In the Belly of the River: Tribal Conflicts over Development in the Narmada Valley*. New Delhi: Oxford University Press.

Brass, Tom. 1991. 'Moral Economists, Subalterns, New Social Movements, and the (Re-) Emergence of a (Post-) Modernised (Middle) Peasant', *Journal of Peasant Studies*, 18(2), pp. 173–205.

Brosius, J. Peter. 1999. 'Analyses and Interventions: Anthropological Engagements with Environmentalism', *Current Anthropology*, 40(3), pp. 277–88.

Chakrabarti, Anindita. 2007. 'A Sociological Study of the Svadhyaya Movement', PhD dissertation, University of Delhi.

Chatterjee, Partha. 1993. *The Nation and its Fragments: Colonial and Postcolonial Histories*. Princeton, NJ: Princeton University Press.

Chaturvedi, Vinayak (ed.). 2000. *Mapping Subaltern Studies and the Postcolonial*. London: Verso.

Conklin, Beth and Laura Graham. 1995. 'The Shifting Middle-Ground: Amazonian Indians and Eco-Politics', *American Anthropologist*, 97(4), pp. 695–710.

CSE (Centre for Science and Environment). 1982. *The State of India's Environment: A Citizens' Report*. New Delhi: CSE.

CSWI (Committee for the Status of Women in India). 1974. *Towards Equality: Report of the Committee for the Status of Women in India*. New Delhi: Department of Social Welfare, Ministry of Education and Social Welfare, Government of India.

Das, Arvind N. (ed.). 1982. *Agrarian Movements in India: Studies on 20th Century Bihar*. London: Frank Cass.

Desai, A.R. (ed.). 1986. *Agrarian Struggles in India after Independence*. New Delhi: Oxford University Press.

——— (ed.). 1979. *Peasant Struggles in India*. Bombay: Oxford University Press.

Deshpande, Satish. 2003. *Contemporary India: A Sociological View*. New Delhi: Viking.

Devalle, Susana B.C. 1992. *Discourses of Ethnicity: Culture and Protest in Jharkhand*. New Delhi: Sage Publications.

Dhanagare, D.N. 1983. *Peasant Movements in India, 1920–1950*. New Delhi: Oxford University Press.

Duyker, Edward. 1987. *Tribal Guerillas: The Santals of West Bengal and the Naxalite Movement*. New Delhi: Oxford University Press.

Ghosh, Kaushik. 2006. 'Between Global Flows and Local Dams: Indigenousness, Locality, and the Transnational Sphere in Jharkhand, India', *Cultural Anthropology*, 21(4), pp. 501–34.

Gorz, André. 1982. *Farewell to the Working Class*. Boston: South End Press.

Gramsci, Antonio. 1971. *Selections from the Prison Notebooks*. New York: International Publishers.

Gudavarthy, Ajay. 2008. 'Human Rights Movements in India: State, Civil Society and Beyond', *Contributions to Indian Sociology*, 42(1), pp. 29–57.

Guha, Ramachandra. 2000. *Environmentalism: A Global History*. New York: Longman.

———. 1992. 'Prehistory of Indian Environmentalism: Intellectual Traditions', *Economic and Political Weekly*, 27(1–2), pp. 57–64.

———. 1989a. *The Unquiet Woods: Ecological Change and Peasant Resistance in the Himalaya*. New Delhi: Oxford University Press.

———. 1989b. 'The Problem', *Seminar*, Issue on 'New Social Movements', Vol. 355, pp. 13–15.

———. 1988. 'Ideological Trends in Indian Environmentalism', *Economic and Political Weekly*, 23(49), pp. 2578–81.

Guha, Ranajit 1983. *Elementary Aspects of Peasant Insurgency in Colonial India*. New Delhi: Oxford University Press.

——— (ed.). 1982. *Subaltern Studies*, Vol. 1. New Delhi: Oxford University Press.

Gupta, Dipankar. 1997. *Rivalry and Brotherhood: Politics in the Life of Farmers in Northern India*. New Delhi: Oxford University Press.

Gurr, T.R. 1970. *Why Men Rebel*. Princeton, NJ: Princeton University Press.

Guru, Gopal and Anuradha Chakravarty. 2005. 'Who are the Country's Poor?: Social Movement Politics and Dalit Poverty', in Raka Ray and Mary Fainsod Katzenstein (eds), *Social Movements in India: Poverty, Power, and Politics*. Lanham, MD: Rowman and Littlefield, pp. 133–60.

Habermas, Jurgen. 1981. 'New Social Movements', *Telos*, vol. 49, pp. 33–7.

Hansen, Thomas Blom. 1999. *The Saffron Wave: Democracy and Hindu Nationalism in Modern India*. Princeton, NJ: Princeton University Press.

Hardiman, David. 1987. *The Coming of the Devi: Adivasi Assertion in Western India*. New Delhi: Oxford University Press.

Heller, Patrick. 2005. 'Reinventing Public Power in the Age of Globalization: Decentralization and the Transformation of Movement Politics in Kerala', in Raka Ray and Mary Fainsod Katzenstein (eds), *Social Movements in India: Poverty, Power, and Politics*. Lanham, MD: Rowman and Littlefield, pp. 77–106.

Hobsbawm, Eric J. 1965. *Primitive Rebels: Studies in Archaic Forms of Social Movements in the 19th and 20th Centuries*. New York: Norton.

Keck, Margaret E. 1998. *Activists beyond Borders: Advocacy Networks in International Politics*. Ithaca, NY: Cornell University Press.

Khagram, Sanjeev. 2004. *Dams and Development: Transnational Struggles for Water and Power*. Ithaca, NY: Cornell University Press.

Khagram, Sanjeev, James V. Ryker, and Kathryn Sikkink (eds). 2002. *Restructuring World Politics: Transnational Social Movements, Networks, and Norms*. Minneapolis: University of Minnesota Press.

Kothari, Rajni. 1988. *State against Democracy: In Search of Humane Governance*. New Delhi: Ajanta Publishers.

Kumar, Radha. 1993. *A History of Doing: An Illustrated Account of Movements for Women's Rights and Feminism in India, 1800–1990*. New Delhi: Kali for Women.

Ludden, David (ed.). 1996. *Making India Hindu: Religion, Community and the Politics of Democracy in India*. New Delhi: Oxford University Press.

McAdam, Doug. 1982. *Political Process and the Development of Black Insurgency, 1930–1970*. Chicago: The University of Chicago Press.

McCarthy, John D. and Mayer N. Zald. 1977. 'Resource Mobilization and Social Movements: A Partial Theory', *American Journal of Sociology*, 82(6), pp. 1212–41.

Menon, Nivedita (ed.). 1999. *Gender and Politics in India*, New Delhi: Oxford University Press.

Mishra, Bijoy Kumar. 1996. 'Reframing Protest: The Politics of Livelihood and Ecology in Two Environmental Movements in India', PhD dissertation, Cornell University.

Mohanty, Manoranjan. 1977. *Revolutionary Violence: A Study of the Maoist Movement in India*. New Delhi: Sterling Publishers.

Mohanty, Manoranjan and Partha Nath Mukherji (eds). 1998. *People's Rights: Social Movements and the State in the Third World*. New Delhi: Sage Publications.

Mukherjee, Arun. 2007. *Maoist 'Spring Thunder': The Naxalite Movement, 1967–1972*. Kolkata: K.P. Bagchi.

Mukherji, Partha. 1977. 'Social Movement and Social Change: Towards a Conceptual Clarification and Theoretical Framework', *Sociological Bulletin*, 26(1), pp. 38–59.

Munda, Ram Dayal and S. Bosu Mullick. 2003. *The Jharkhand Movement: Indigenous Peoples' Struggle for Autonomy in India*. Copenhagen: International Working Group on Indigenous Affairs.

Nagaraj, D.R. 1993. *The Flaming Feet: A Study of the Dalit Movement in India*. Bangalore: South Forum Press and ICRA.

Naipaul, V.S. 1991. *India: A Million Mutinies Now*. New York: Viking.

Offe, Claus. 1985. 'New Social Movements: Challenging the Boundaries of Institutional Politics', *Social Research*, 52 (4), pp. 817–68.

Omvedt, Gail. 1995. *Dalit Visions: The Anti-Caste Movement and the Construction of an Indian Identity*. New Delhi: Orient Longman.

———. 1993. *Reinventing Revolution: New Social Movements and the Socialist Tradition in India*. New York: M.E. Sharpe.

———. 1987. 'India's Green Movements', *Race and Class*, 28(4), pp. 29–38.

———. 1980. *We will Smash this Prison!: Indian Women in Struggle*. London: Zed Press.

Oommen, T.K. 1977. 'Sociological Issues in the Analysis of Social Movements in Independent India', *Sociological Bulletin*, 26(1), pp. 14–37.

Ostergaard, Geoffrey and Melville Currell. 1971. *The Gentle Anarchists: A Study of the Leaders of the Sarvodaya Movement for Non-violent Revolution in India*. Oxford: Clarendon Press.

Pai, Sudha. 2002. *Dalit Assertion and the Unfinished Democratic Revolution: The Bahujan Samaj Party in Uttar Pradesh*. New Delhi: Sage Publications.

Piven, Frances Fox and Richard A. Cloward. 1977. *Poor People's Movements: Why They Succeed, How They Fail*. New York: Pantheon Books.

Rangan, Haripriya. 2000. *Of Myths and Movements: Rewriting Chipko into Himalayan History*. New Delhi: Oxford University Press.

Rangarajan, Mahesh. 1996. 'The Politics of Ecology: The Debate on Wildlife and People in India, 1970–95', *Economic and Political Weekly*, XXXI(35–7), pp. 2391–409.

Rao, M.S.A. 1979. *Social Movements and Social Transformation: A Study of Two Backward Classes Movements in India*. New Delhi: Macmillan.

———— (ed.). 1978–9. *Social Movements in India* (two volumes), New Delhi: Manohar.

Ray, Rabindra. 1988. *The Naxalites and their Ideology*. New Delhi: Oxford University Press.

Ray, Raka. 1999. *Fields of Protest: Women's Movements in India*. Minneapolis: University of Minnesota Press.

Ray, Raka and Mary Fainsod Katzenstein (eds). 2005. *Social Movements in India: Poverty, Power, and Politics*. Lanham, MD: Rowman and Littlefield.

Sangvai, Sanjay. 2000. *The River and Life: People's Struggle in the Narmada Valley*. Mumbai: Earthcare Books.

Scott, James. 1990. *Domination and the Arts of Resistance: Hidden Transcripts*. New Haven, CT: Yale University Press.

———— . 1985. *Weapons of the Weak: Everyday Forms of Peasant Resistance*. New Haven, CT: Yale University Press.

———— . 1976. *The Moral Economy of the Peasant: Rebellion and Subsistence in Southeast Asia*. New Haven, CT: Yale University Press.

Sengupta, Nirmal (ed.). 1982. *Fourth World Dynamics: Jharkhand*. New Delhi: Authors Guild Publications.

Sethi, Harsh. 2001. 'Movements and Mediators', *Economic and Political Weekly*, XXXVI(4), pp. 268–70.

Shah, Ghanshyam (ed.). 2002. *Social Movements and the State*, Readings in Indian Government and Politics. New Delhi: Sage Publications.

———— . 1990. *Social Movements in India: A Review of the Literature*. New Delhi: Sage Publications.

———— . 1979. 'Direct Action in India: A Study of Gujarat and Bihar Agitations', *Contributions to Asian Studies*, Vol. 14, pp. 47–66.

Shah, Ghanshyam. 1977. *Protest Movements in Two Indian States*. New Delhi: Ajanta Publishers.

Shiva, Vandana. 1988. *Staying Alive: Women, Ecology and Survival in India*. New Delhi: Kali for Women.

Singh, K. Suresh (ed.). 1983a. *Tribal Movements in India*, Vol. II, New Delhi: Manohar Publications.

———— . 1983b. *Birsa Munda and his Movement 1874–1901: A Study of a Millenarian Movement in Chotanagpur*. Calcutta: Oxford University Press.

———— (ed.). 1982. *Tribal Movements in India*, Vol. I, New Delhi: Manohar Publications.

Singh, Prakash. 2006. *The Naxalite Movement in India*. New Delhi: Rupa.

Singh, Rajendra. 2001. *Social Movements, Old and New: A Post-Modernist Critique*. New Delhi: Sage Publications.

Singh, Ujjwal Kumar. 2005. 'Democratising State and Society: Role of Civil Liberties and Democratic Rights Movements in India', *Contemporary India*, 4(1–2), pp. 31–56.

Sinha, Subir, Shubhra Gururani, and Brian Greenberg. 1997. 'The "New Traditionalist" Discourse of Indian Environmentalism', *Journal of Peasant Studies*, 24(3), pp. 65–99.

Sundar, Nandini. 2007. *Subalterns and Sovereigns: An Anthropological History of Bastar, 1854–2006*, 2nd edn, New Delhi: Oxford University Press.

Thompson, E.P. 1966. *The Making of the English Working Class*. New York: Vintage Books.

Tilly, Charles. 1978. *From Mobilization to Revolution*. Reading, MA: Addison-Wesley.

Touraine, Alain. 1985. 'An Introduction to the Study of Social Movements', *Social Research*, 52(4), pp. 749–87.

Zelliot, Eleanor. 1992. *From Untouchable to Dalit: Essays on the Ambedkar Movement*. New Delhi: Manohar Publications.

Zinn, Howard. 1980. *A People's History of the United States*. New York: Harper & Row.

26 Farmers' Movements

Sudha Pai

As a primarily agricultural society, India has experienced a wide variety of movements connected with land. This chapter examines mobilization by different strata of peasants/farmers, either to change the agrarian structure that they felt was exploitative, or to seek redress of specific grievances from either landlords or the state, without seeking to overthrow the system. The farmers' movements form part of the wide variety of social movements witnessed in post-Independence India. However, unlike the women's movement or environmental movements, which also address civil society, farmers' movements have been directed at the state. The centrality of the state in a developing country characterized by agricultural backwardness means that farmers' movements are largely a response to change in agricultural policy. A second determining factor has been a growing capitalist tendency and class differentiation in the agrarian sector, which has helped shape agrarian mobilization. These features have determined the trajectory that farmers' movements have taken in the country.

In order to examine the vast range of movements witnessed in the post-Independence period, this chapter constructs a typology, and significant movements falling within each category are discussed. This enables a broad overview of the wide variety of agrarian movements experienced in the country, and an analysis of the features of specific movements. Such an exercise cannot be undertaken in isolation and is related to developments taking place in Indian politics. Our typology of agrarian movements is based upon a fivefold criteria:[1] (a) the pattern of landownership, which determines the mode of production, class structure, and prevailing agrarian relations; (b) state policies, as major shifts in the agrarian economy have occurred due to the introduction of new policies. Also, most movements are either against particular state policies or make demands that the state cannot ignore; (c) technology-based change, which is a powerful and independent force; although much scholarship shows that there is no automatic connection between improved technology and political consciousness and action. The impact varies over time, by region, crop, and the organization of the productive process; (d) the pattern of mobilization which is based on class, and at times caste; (e) leadership, together with strategies, issues, and demands. Such a categorization is both historical and analytical, that is, it takes into consideration both developments taking place over time in the agricultural economy and the emergence of new agrarian structures and relationships, leading to fresh concerns which form the base of movements of various types.

Based on these criteria, agrarian movements in post-Independence India fall into three categories:

1. Anti-feudal movements against exploitation by landlords or against the state, demanding re-distribution of land, higher wages for labour, lower rents to small peasants, and an end to other exploitative practices. In the immediate post-Independence period, discontent arising out of the failure of the state to fulfil its promise of land reform resulted in a number of 'land grab' movements led by peasant leaders, who in many cases belonged to Socialist and Communist parties/organizations. While agitations against landlords continue in the form of Naxalite movements, the issue of land redistribution lost importance with the shift from an institutional to a technological agrarian policy in the mid-1960s.

2. Movements by rich peasants/capitalist farmers following the Green Revolution in the 1960s, and the resulting commercialization of agriculture and class differentiation. Led by rich farmer organizations, these movements acted as pressure groups upon the state, and demanded policies beneficial to them. A section of the bigger farmers who benefited from the Green Revolution became the new power holders in the countryside. The state, and not the landlord, was viewed as the 'enemy', and larger issues such as urban versus rural interests and terms of trade with industry have been central to these movements. Employing strategies different from the first category, they have in some cases mobilized the smaller peasantry, but have little to offer to small tenants and landless labour. Based primarily upon economic interests, some employed a caste-class strategy, reflecting the specificities of the Indian context.

3. Since the early 1990s, due to a general crisis in Indian agriculture that resulted in a slowdown in the rate of agricultural growth, and the structural adjustment programme (SAP) leading to the globalization of the Indian economy and resultant changes in the policy regime, farmers' movements have entered a new phase. There have been few large, organized rich farmers' movements as in the 1980s. Rather, movements are smaller, largely against state governments that have introduced market-oriented policies, and no longer attract the small/marginal farmer as issues have undergone considerable change. However, in recent months, with the deepening of economic reforms, movements attracting smaller farmers have emerged against the acquisition of agricultural land by state governments for the industrial/mining projects of private national and international companies.

THE 'PEASANTRY' AND PEASANT MOVEMENTS

A systematic study of the 'peasantry' began in Central and Eastern Europe due to an interest in the different path of modernization adopted by peasant societies in this region, as compared to Western Europe. After World War II, scholars began to investigate the nature of the 'peasantry' that emerged from colonialism (Shanin 1971; Redfield 1955; Chesneaux 1973; Wolf 1971; Fanon 1971; Moore Jr. 1966).

As part of this trend in India, three main approaches can be identified in the immediate post-Independence period: Marxist, nationalist, and subaltern, which dealt with both the nature of the peasantry and the potential for movements. Desai (1979) and Dhanagare (1983) broadly employing the Marxist approach, questioned the notion of the Indian peasant in the works of Barrington Moore (1966) and Theodore Shanin (1971) as 'passive', and non-existent within a subsistence economy. Such an approach failed to take into consideration the fact that in the former colonies, commercialization of agriculture had started a process of differentiation, which created landlords, rich, middle, and poor peasants, and led to agrarian struggles (Desai 1979: xxii–iii). Moreover, though Marx and Engels found the peasantry to be internally split, unorganized, and politically impotent unless mobilized by the working class, the peasant revolutions that shook the Third World countries were launched and often led by peasants themselves (Dhanagare 1983: 3). Dhanagare argued that peasant movements in India needed to be studied along two axes: the class character of the actors involved, and the historical factors which contribute to the progressive development of the political consciousness of the peasantry (ibid.). His framework laid the basis for a number of studies of peasant movements in the colonial and postcolonial world.

The Naxalite movement of the late 1960s demonstrated that the poor and landless could be as assertive as the rich peasantry, and redirected attention towards peasant insurgency in the colonial period. It prompted the Subaltern approach to write a 'history' from below of the poorer peasantry, the reproduction of the small peasant economy, and the sources of revolt. It challenged attempts to explain all peasant resistance in terms of 'essential' class interests or 'moral economy'. Chatterjee held that in India, peasants have conceptualized relationships of power and the ensuing conflicts in terms of the 'idea' of community, or as a collective 'form of consciousness' arising out of the existing bonds of caste and community (Chatterjee 1982: 12, 1988: 34–5). Some underlined the role of 'peasant consciousness' in revolts in the colonial period (Guha 1983). While others argued that the assertive 'rich peasant', *as a class* mobilizing the poorer peasantry was a creation of the post-Independence technological shift in agriculture (Hardiman 1981: 246–50). This approach spawned many works on peasant revolts in colonial and postcolonial India (Gough 1974).

The nationalist viewpoint, like in many other countries emerging from colonialism, focused on the issue of land reform. The revival of theoretical interest in the 'institutional question'[2] among scholars in development economics led it to be viewed as a fundamental condition for agricultural development (Myrdal 1968). Literature that scientifically examined the issue of land reform for developing countries also emerged (Warriner 1969). These ideas were supported by many academic writings from within the country

(Dantwala 1961; Khusro 1973; Singh 1961; Thorner 1956; Joshi 1975).

At the same time, agrarian upheavals in many parts of the country led by the Communists, such as the Telengana revolt (Rao 1978) on the eve of the transfer of power, made land reforms an issue of urgent action by the government. The *Congress Agrarian Reforms Committee 1949* provided a programme of land reform within the parliamentary-democratic framework, that is, peasant farming after land reform, assisted by cooperative organization (Frankel 1978). It was based on the argument that the major 'depressor' or obstacle to rapid agricultural development was the outmoded agrarian structure, the removal of which would also enable rapid industrialization (Thorner 1956). This viewpoint underlay the entire programme of land reform 'from above' undertaken by the government.

A more radical strategy of 'land to the tiller' was provided in *On the Agrarian Question in India* (1948) by the ideologues of the Communist party. It argued that the main reason behind agricultural backwardness was the continuation of 'semi-feudal' relations on land, which were squeezing the peasantry. Critiquing the land reform programme of the Congress government, they argued that what was needed was land to the tiller, no compensation to landlords, strict imposition of ceilings, rapid extension of the banking system to rural areas, elimination of usury, and the introduction of state trading in agricultural commodities to guarantee a fair minimum price to the peasantry (Kotovsky 1964; Sen 1962: vii).

The failure of land reform created considerable discontent among the poorer peasantry and landless labour and, according to some, turned the vast majority of the peasantry into an agrarian proletariat (Desai 1986: xviii). Left parties took advantage of this to mobilize 'land grab' movements in West Bengal, Kerala, Andhra Pradesh, Karnataka, and Uttar Pradesh (UP) in the 1960s and 1970s (*Statesman*, New Delhi, 10 May 1970). The Socialists, Communists, the Praja Socialist Party (PSP), and the Bharatiya Khet Mazdoor Sangh in districts of eastern Uttar Pradesh jointly led land grab movements in districts with high population density and smallholdings, such as Ballia, Azamgarh, Jaunpur, and Ghazipur (Saxena 1987). In Karnataka, the

Socialist party and the Pranthiya Raita Sangha under the Communist party led agitations in North and South Kanara districts between 1950 and 1972 against the prevailing rent system, debts and non-implementation of the Tenancy Act, non-distribution of wasteland among the poor peasants/agricultural labourers, and landlord atrocities (Assadi 1997: 30). Similar agitations took place in Tamil Nadu and Andhra Pradesh (Béteille 1971; Bouton 1989; Mencher 1978). While the amount of land gained by peasants was negligible, it created political consciousness among them and put pressure on the government, contributing to legislation such as the Ceilings Act 1974.

These anti-feudal movements were described as providing a model of agrarian transformation for India that relied not on a 'single revolutionary leap', but on the 'dynamic interdependence' of parliamentary and extra-parliamentary action following each other in quick succession. The latter created possibilities for further legislative action, and the limitations of the former could release forces for further extra-parliamentary action (Joshi 1975). However, by the late 1970s, issues of land distribution and equity were overshadowed by capitalist developments in the agricultural sector.

RICH PEASANTS/CAPITALIST FARMERS' MOVEMENTS

The 1960s witnessed the emergence of movements led by a rich peasant/capitalist class, following the introduction of a new agricultural policy popularly described as the Green Revolution.[3] Signalling a shift from an 'institutional' (based on land reform) to a 'technological' (based on bio-chemical and mechanical innovations)[4] agrarian strategy on the part of the state to meet the acutely growing demand for foodgrains, it marked the end of equity concerns of land re-distribution. Greater class differentiation and inequality was in fact in-built, as it was a 'selective approach' in which the existing resources earlier distributed thinly over large areas were now concentrated in selected districts that had assured water and good communication, and were in the hands of 'progressive' farmers who owned at least five acres (Dasgupta 1980; Frankel 1971). In contrast to

the Nehruvian policy of transferring food at cheap prices to urban areas through state trading, in the mid-1960s the Congress party decided to follow a different path to industrialization: make agriculture productive (through investment in technology), but transfer resources through taxation or terms of trade.

A number of changes are indicative of class differentiation and the rise of a rich peasant/capitalist class distinct from the middle and smaller peasantry: the use of fertilizers doubled from 16.1 kilograms to 32 kilograms between 1971–2 and 1981–2; the area under irrigation rose, much of this due to use of pumpsets, which increased to four million in 1979–80; and the manufacture of tractors, which was 880 in 1960–1, rose to 81,500 by 1981–2 (Nadkarni 1987: 48–50).

While some scholars use the terms *rich peasant* and *capitalist farmer*[5] interchangeably, others have argued that they are distinct. Rich peasants had the ability to use the bio-chemical inputs (seeds and fertilizers) of the new technology, while capitalist farmers could use both bio-chemical and mechanical innovations (tractor, harvester, and the like) as they had larger holdings (Byres 1986). While rich peasants were largely found in some districts in states such as UP, capitalist farmers were characteristic of the more prosperous Punjab districts (Randhawa 1974). However, they agreed that what marked them out was the fact that they were a *surplus-producing class*. The question of whether the 'middle peasant' had adopted the new technology also occupied much space. Omvedt (1982) held that about 15 per cent of all rural families could be classed as 'rich farmers' by the 1980s. This category comprised the traditional feudal castes of Brahmins and Rajputs; however, increasingly, the middle *kisan* (farmer) castes were dominant in the more capitalist regions—the Patidars, Marathas, Jats, Vokkaligas, Lingayyats, Kammas, and Reddys. Lenneberg (1988: 452) argued that the 'middle peasant'[6] had also taken to cash cropping, and not merely the rich farmer. The Rudolphs preferred the term 'Bullock capitalists' to describe the 'mix' of capitalist, pre-industrial, and non-capitalist features that characterized the prosperous 'middle peasant'.[7] Finally, some raised the larger issue that the distinction between peasants and farmers was no longer valid.[8]

More significant was the debate on the prevailing *mode of production*[9] in agriculture, and the *extent of capitalist farming*. Pointing to the large-scale continuance of traditional forms of exploitation such as informal bondage, indebtedness, and leasing-out to 'semi-serfs', which gave the landlord social and economic dominance, Amit Bhaduri (1973) and Pradhan H. Prasad (1985) argued that semi-feudalism remained the dominant tendency and the *basic constraint* to faster growth in agriculture. Others such as Rudra *et al.* (1969) held, using five variables as indicators,[10] that capitalism was 'barely visible', and was gradually emerging and semi-capitalism still remained the main tendency. Disagreeing, Thorner (1967) observed 'capitalist stirrings', and found merchants, former moneylenders, and advocates investing in a gradually expanding 'advanced (agricultural) sector'. Similarly, Utsa Patnaik (1971, 1986) arguing that the tests employed by Rudra were valid only in a situation where capitalism was already dominant, in a study of 66 big farmers in five states in 1969,[11] concluded that 'a class of big farmers was emerging and this was a phenomenon common for every region'. Much depended on the region selected by scholars; the debate demonstrated that generalization about capitalist tendencies at the national level was not of much use; there were enormous regional differences due to historical and socio-economic reasons (Raj *et al.* 1985; Das and Nilakant 1985; Rudra 1982).

The new strategy produced spectacular gains. In 1967–8, high output yielding varieties (HYVs) of wheat recorded a high of 16.6 million tonnes, one-third more than the previous peak output of 12.3 million tonnes achieved in 1964–5 under a good monsoon. In 1968–9, despite a drought, the output rose even higher (Frankel 1971). However, the benefits of the Green Revolution were not evenly distributed, and increased existing class and regional inequalities. In terms of regions, eastern India (Bengal, Bihar, Orissa, and Assam) and north-western India (Punjab and western UP) came to constitute 'polar opposites', with the latter advancing far ahead of the former (Patnaik 1980: 1). The reasons lay in the wide variations in historically given economic and tenurial conditions, the lack of proper implementation of land reform policies, and patterns of investment prior to

the initiation of the new technology (ibid.: 2–3). Big farmers with over 20 acres, who gained the most, were able to shift to double-cropping, large-scale mechanized farming, and private tubewells; those with over 10 acres were able to buy land, improve land under cultivation, and buy modern farm equipment; and farmers with 5–10 acres experienced some improvement in their net income, enabling them to improve their living standards. The bottom 20 per cent of all farmers, that is, those with less than 10 acres for want of sufficient capital—particularly in the eastern states—did not benefit as much (Frankel 1971: 192).

The increasing class differentiation made bigger landowners conscious of their interests, leading to rich farmers' movements in the 1970s. There is a positive correlation between the high productivity districts and these movements: Punjab, Haryana, western UP, Gujarat, irrigated districts of Maharashtra and Karnataka, coastal Andhra Pradesh, and parts of Tamil Nadu. The leadership was provided by rich farmers' organizations such as the Bharatiya Kisan Union (BKU) in western UP, Punjab, and Haryana; and the Karnataka Rajya Ryot Sangha (KRRS) in Karnataka and the Shetkari Sangathan (SS) in Maharashtra. Unlike earlier movements, they were directed against the state and not the landlord. As big farmers began to produce for the market, the nature of demands changed: higher prices for agricultural produce and lower prices for technological inputs such as seeds, fertilizers, electricity, and water charges, and easier terms for loans (Byres 1988: 139).[12] Hence, they were not ideology-based, but issue-based, to safeguard and promote the interests of their adherents over a protracted period and across many crises (Gupta 1997: 1). Moreover, farmers expected help from the state, as within a decade of its introduction, the Green Revolution reached a 'plateau' and yields and profits did not continue to rise as expected (Dasgupta 1980).[13]

These issues played a central role in the emergence of rich farmers' organizations, a list of which is provided in Appendix 26A.2. The immediate factor leading to the formation (out of the merger of many smaller movements) of many big farmers' organizations, such as the Khetibari Zamindara Union in Punjab in 1972 (Singh 1990: 23–4), BKU in UP in October 1986, or the KRRS in the early 1980s (Assadi 1997: 56) was due to strong protests/movements against the lowering of the procurement price of foodgrains, hiking of electricity and water rates, the demand for higher prices for cash crops, and the like. These farmers' organizations preferred to remain non-political,[14] and were described as a form of 'rural unionism', which brought supra-local politics to the countryside (Gupta 1997: 18); or as agrarian lobbies or pressure groups to voice their demands (Sahasrabudhey 1986:30). Some scholars described them as 'New Farmers' Movements' (Brass 1995) part of the New Social Movements of the 1980s, as they had distinct characteristics: the peasantry was no longer characterized by pre-political backwardness or social insularity; nor was it simple and passive; it stressed the primacy of remunerative prices and was non-political; and class antagonism was replaced by class collaboration (Omvedt 1998).

Consequently, the 1980s witnessed a number of well-organized, geographically separate, agitations/protests on issues of state policy, rather than full-fledged 'movements'. Common methods were the *gherao* of officials, roadblocks, large rallies of farmers at the Boat Club at Delhi, and so on. The imposition, for example, of market cess on agricultural products and the upward revision of electricity tariffs by the Punjab government in 1982 initiated a series of agitations (Singh 1987). In Maharashtra, the price of onions, sugarcane, and tobacco sparked off agitations in 1980 and 1987 (Lenneberg 1988: 32). One of the largest demonstrations by the BKU was in March 1987 against the increase in electricity rates (Gupta 1997: 32). As agrarian issues occupied a central place in politics in the 1970s and 1980s, in many cases the Central and state governments concerned had to concede the demands of the farmers.[15]

However, farmers' organizations did raise larger ideological issues such as 'Bharat versus India', or the existence of an 'urban bias'[16] on the part of the Indian state. The BKU in the Punjab grew out of a sense of 'being exploited by the urban elite'. It held that government policies favoured the industrial-business combine and that the terms of trade were pitched against agriculture,[17] and demanded the removal of 'discrimination' against the rural areas through the provision of educational facilities and

economic development (Singh 1990: 25–7). The KRRS criticized the emphasis on industrialism that perpetuated agrarian backwardness, and led agitations using Gandhian methods of non-cooperation such as 'Swaraj' or 'Villagization' to highlight the neglect of the countryside (Assadi 1997). The Shetkari Sangathan (SS) articulated the grievances of an increasingly literate, politically aware, and mobile rich and middle peasantry, whose vision was an improved village life (Lenneberg 1988: 461).

The question as to whether these agitations were *class-driven* or *multi-class based* has been much discussed. They attempted the horizontal mobilization of the bigger, middle, and even smaller farmers by claiming to speak on behalf of the entire rural community. The term kisan in the north and *raithapi* (peasant) and *krishika* (farmer) in the south was used to avoid the question of the internal exploitation between different categories of the peasantry. Arguing that small farmers can support the price agitations on non-economic grounds, Varshney held that rather than having a narrow class base in the surplus-producing rich peasantry, they gained the support of *all sections* of the landed peasantry, even that of the small farmers, and, to a lesser extent, the marginal farmers, as seen from their support for higher output and lower input prices (Varshney 1995: 116, 137–8). Some scholars argued that farmers' agitations were more successful in precisely those regions where the smaller farmers had been drawn into the support base of the organization, as in Maharashtra, where commercial crops like onion and tobacco were grown not only by big farmers, but small peasants too, who were fairly enthusiastic supporters of the SS (Nadkarni 1987). Based on her analysis of the SS, Lenneberg also argued that most studies seemed to assume that the middle peasant is being squeezed out of existence due to capitalist development. However, this significant intermediate group with rising aspirations grew cash crops on a part of its holdings, was numerically important, and politically assertive (Lenneberg 1988: 461). Others point out that a movement need not be exclusively about the interests of a class to be so described; capitalist farmers tried to protect their class interests while including some concessions for the smaller peasantry, thereby gaining their support (Das 2001:

106). The KRRS practised the 'politics of cooption' by bringing in the problems of smaller farmers to gain their support (Assadi 2002: 353). They glossed over differences, arguing, 'we cannot divide ourselves into landlord and landless farmers and agitate separately for the agitation will have no strength nor will carry any weight' (Natraj 1980: 1967–8).

However, most studies hold the position that the farmers' movements had little to offer to small peasants, and even less to landless labourers. The notion of a united front was put forward to strengthen the movement, but in fact it was also a way to neutralize the threat from below.[18] Omvedt held that the farmers' movement was 'basically of the rural rich', and 'led by the rural rich peasants' in contradiction to the interests of the middle and the poor peasantry (Omvedt 1980: 2042). Similarly, Patnaik and Hasan argued that the farmers' movements represented the interests of the new rural capitalist producers *clearly and consistently*, as poor peasants and labourers, being substantial purchasers of foodgrains, stood to lose from farmers' agitations, and were therefore outside their support base (Patnaik and Hasan 1995: 287). But it must be conceded that in contrast to the other organizations, Sharad Joshi's SS often revealed sensitivity to problems faced by the landless labourers in Maharashtra (Gupta 1997: 11).

Along with the spread of the Green Revolution, a specific caste–class combination and clan-based leadership also contributed to the successful mobilization of the small and medium peasantry in parts of north India, particularly UP. Charan Singh mobilized a substantial section of the cultivating middle/backward castes—Jats, Gujjars, Tyagis, and so on—both as 'kisans' and 'backward castes' (Pai 1993:50). The Bharatiya Kranti Dal (BKD) formed by him in 1967 in UP represented the rich peasants and big landowners and, in caste terms, the Jats and other backward castes. In fact, the mobilization of the prosperous peasantry as a class was reinforced by their simultaneous mobilization as a status order, that of the backward castes (Rudolph and Rudolph 1984: 322). The BKU in west UP also used the *Bhaichara* system and *Khap* or traditional caste-panchayat, which contributed to the successful mobilization of the smaller peasantry.

In the late 1980s, attempts were made by farmers' organizations to form an apex organization, the BKU, and enter into electoral politics, but both proved unsuccessful. The initiative for the former came from farmers' leaders based in the states of Tamil Nadu (C. Narayanswamy Naidu), Karnataka (Nanjundaswamy), and Maharashtra (Sharad Joshi). An inter-state coordination committee under the leadership of Joshi was formed, but disagreements arose on the question of leadership. Two political parties, the Indian Toilers party in Tamil Nadu and the Kannada Desa in Karnataka, were formed; the BKU supported candidates of the Akali Dal, while Tikait supported leaders such as Devi Lal and Chandra Shekhar, but all these attempts failed (Assadi 1997: 116). These initiatives came too late; by the end of the decade, agrarian issues had lost political importance.

GLOBALIZATION AND FARMERS' MOVEMENTS

During the 1990s, a number of significant developments in the Indian economy have impacted upon the agricultural sector, and farmers' movements have undergone a change. The adoption of the SAP in 1991, leading to the globalization of the economy, has resulted in major policy shifts, with serious implications for agriculture: freeing of controls, removal of subsidies and price support, a move towards dependence on market forces, and the opening of the economy, leading to the freer import/export of agricultural commodities (Bhalla 1994); and in the external arena, the establishment of a multilateral trading system in agriculture, following the Dunkel text (Nayyar and Sen 1994). Many state governments have also introduced a range of market-oriented policies, the most important being the reversal of land reform/ protection policies. While no new agricultural policy was announced in 1991, these changes were reflected in the National Agricultural Policy announced by the Bharatiya Janata Party-led National Democratic Alliance coalition government on 28 July 2000, the main goal of which was *to make agriculture an industry*.[19] Second, as Tables 26A.1.1 and 26A.1.2 on ownership and operational holdings (Appendix 26A.1) show, there has been an increasing fragmentation of holdings: marginal holdings have doubled, medium holdings have dropped, and large holdings have drastically declined. This trend, together with the steep rise in the price of inputs, has made agriculture less attractive to big farmers, and impoverished small ones. Third, the agricultural sector has experienced several unfavourable trends: a marked slowing down in the rate of agricultural growth, widening of disparities between the agricultural and non-agricultural sectors,[20] and a decline in the prices of several commodities, together with a steep worsening of the economic status of farmer households.[21] Equally worrying has been the slowing of growth rates in states with high irrigation, which had shown dynamism during the Green Revolution (Vaidyanathan 2006a) and the urgent need for strategies for dry land agriculture and watershed management (Shah and Vijayshankar 2002).

Against this backdrop, farmers' suicides in many states have generated controversial debate. Some scholars argue that farmers' suicides are a product of 'a crisis rooted in economic reforms (Patnaik 2004) that is, in the shift in agricultural policies due to the SAP (Venkateshwarlu 2006; Rao 2004; Sainath 2004, 2005, 2006; Chandrakant 2004). Between 1996 and 1998, it is held, suicides were by farmers growing particular crops such as cotton, and in backward regions such as, for example, Telengana; however, beginning in 2003, they have risen in numbers and spread to farmers growing a wide variety of crops, and even to the prosperous coastal region of Andhra Pradesh. The overwhelming proportion of deaths is still among small/marginal farmers who need loans to buy the more expensive seeds, fertilizers, and water (Rao 2004). The suicides, therefore, are *not a localized sociological phenomenon*, are visible in areas where commercial agriculture has spread, and have taken place at a particular juncture of 'Development' on a large scale (Vidyasagar and Chandra 2004: 1).

In contrast, other scholars have argued that the available evidence does not corroborate apprehensions that liberalization has adversely affected the domestic price of farm products generally, or shifted the terms of trade against agriculture. While there has been a removal of quantitative restrictions on imports of crop/livestock products, the overall increase in the volume of foreign trade is still too small relative to the country's agricultural production to significantly impact domestic production and pattern of resource use (Vaidyanathan 2006b: 4010). Moreover, Vaidyanathan holds that the inference that suicides are due to high indebtedness in the new open economy is unwarranted, the reasons being more complex. The National Sample Survey (NSS) estimates (June 2002) show that the quantum of debt owed by an average rural household is less than 3 per cent of the total value of its assets held. The debt-to-assets ratio ranges from 0.2 per cent to a maximum of 7 per cent (ibid.: 4009). Farmers are driven to the extreme step not only because of high and imprudent borrowing, leading to a debt trap, but also because of the 'failure of expectations' of high yields and good prices after high investments (ibid.) and because it enormously 'widened the gap between aspirations and achievements' (Mohanty and Shroff 2004). Thus, Vaidyanathan argues that suicides are the result of a 'more general crisis facing Indian agriculture', which needs to be corrected with better-targeted and planned public investment (ibid.).[22] In sum, the 'institutional barrier'—comprising governance, the quality of public systems, and economic policies—has become the most serious impediment to agricultural growth (Vaidyanathan 2006a).

Some studies, while not denying the agricultural crisis, point out that states such as Andhra Pradesh, Karnataka, and Punjab, where big farmers had already taken to capitalist agriculture, were quick to introduce/encourage the new agricultural policies. However, they failed to provide/regulate the basic requirements for export-oriented capitalist agriculture, either through state mechanisms or the private sector, leading to severe stress on the local resource base. This has resulted in declining capital formation, public investment, share of agriculture in the Gross Domestic Product, adverse terms of trade, falling return-cost ratios, and so on.[23] In practically every state there has been the failure of *delivery systems* (Saxena 2004) namely, provision of water, seeds, fertilizers, and credit at affordable prices to small farmers. Thus, it is a combination of external market pressure and lack of internal support structures during a period of transition from a command to a market system that has driven large numbers of farmers to take the extreme step (Pai n.d.).

There have been few large-scale, organized rich farmers' movements during the 1990s, as in the 1980s. With the changed economic environment, farmers' movements display different features. An important reason is the increasing *class fragmentation* within the farming community. A small elite class of prosperous farmers, which is attracted to the new policies and supportive of the same, has arisen in some states. Beginning with Karnataka in 1995 (Menon 1995) many state governments amended their Land Reform Acts, removing restrictions on the sale/purchase of agricultural land and encouraging private 'agribusiness' companies, which produce cash crops for the domestic and international markets (Panini 1999) The new policy regime created a class of prosperous farmers, in parts of Karnataka, who prefer to buy food and produce cash crops such as flowers, grapes, mulberry plants, and the like, for the domestic/international market as they fetch higher prices; enter into contracts with private agribusiness companies, which guarantee assured returns; go in for multiple cropping, which is made possible and grown in polyhouses, where they are less dependent on the agricultural cycle or the weather (ibid.: 2168). These farmers are able to afford better houses, transport, and English education for their children, and now have few interests in common with smaller farmers unable to use these opportunities due to lack of funds and knowledge (ibid.). Consequently, a division has emerged between big/small farmers over the impact of globalization on agriculture, and joint movements as in the past are no longer possible. Panini points to a split in the KRRS in the late 1990s and a decline in the force of ideology to mobilize bigger farmers in Karnataka, who, having benefited from agribusiness, are no longer enthusiastic supporters of campaigns against multinational agribusiness firms as they were in the past, as seen in their opposition to some recent movements (ibid.). Similarly, in Maharashtra, the SS, a market-oriented farmers' movement under Sharad Joshi,[24] supported globalization, as it would 'end the license raj, bureaucratization and Nehruvian Command Economy', introduce 'competitive capitalism' in agriculture and remove poverty (Joshi 1994:10).

Second, big farmers' movements have become smaller and are mainly in states/regions where capitalist agriculture has spread. This is because agriculture is a state subject, and with the end of centralized planning, many state governments have been active in adopting new market-oriented policies. These movements are no longer able to mobilize smaller farmers, as their interests/needs are now different. While they still raise 'traditional' issues such as the availability/price of inputs and the price of output, increasingly the stress has been on issues associated with the global international trading system, patents, biotechnology, and the like. The KRRS in the early 1990s was one of the first to lead a number of movements against the new economic policies, arguing that it was part of a larger strategy for 'trapping India in the vicious circle of exploitation and converting her into a neo-colony' (Assadi 2003:530). The KRRS identified four issues associated with global capital that would adversely affect Indian agriculture: pressure to withdraw agricultural subsidies; introduction of seed-manufacturing multinational companies (MNCs) that will destroy the autonomy of farmers; introduction of a patents regime through which MNCs would appropriate the knowledge system; and biotechnology or genetically-modified food, which has the potential to destroy biodiversity and create monopolies. Based on these issues, it opposed the opening up of agricultural land to investment by private industry/agro-industry, held seminars, adopted resolutions, organized seed satyagrahas, and attacked MNCs such as KFC, Cargil, and Monsanto (Assadi 1997: 365; Panini 1999: 2169).

In more recent years, such movements have been witnessed in a number of states/regions with better off farmers. The BKU of Punjab staged a protest in New Delhi in October 2004 against the falling price of cotton crops due to the 'state government's reluctance to buy it' (*The Times of India*, New Delhi, 27 October 2004). In Rajasthan, the Kisan Mazdoor Vyapari Sangh, active in the Sriganganagar region, has agitated over the last year against rising power tariffs and water, forcing the state government to concede some of its demands (Bunsha 2006; *The Times of India* 14 November 2006). In Gujarat, the Bharatiya Kisan Sangh (BKS) led protests and hunger strikes in June 2003 against the rise in power tariffs as part of power reforms (*The Hindu* New Delhi, 16 March 2004).

The various state-level organizations, however, have held national conventions to jointly discuss problems and strategies against government policies. A number of organizations joined the 'Seize Delhi' agitation led by the KRRS, demanding the total rejection of the Dunkel Draft in 1992: the BKU of UP and Punjab, the Rajasthan Kisan Sanghathan, Rajasthan, the Kisan Mazdoor Vyapari Sangh, Kisan Mazdoor Sanghathan of West Bengal, and Samata Sanghathan of Orissa, among others (Assadi 1997: 363). The KRRS and other organizations also joined protests held by international collectives such as People's Global Action and Via Campensa, held at Seattle, Prague, Washington, and Geneva. One of the largest rallies was held jointly with the BKU, led by Mahendra Singh Tikait, Vandana Shiva, Medha Patkar, and other farmers' organizations in November 1995 (Menon 1995). The thirty-first All India Kisan Sabha Conference (with 1.88 crore members), held at Nasik in Maharashtra in February 2006, had delegates from all parts of the country, and was one of the largest gatherings in recent years to discuss ways to confront the growing agrarian crisis in the country, and prevent the mass suicides of peasant occurring in several states (Bunsha 2006: 125). Putting forward an agenda for action, it demanded greater public investment in irrigation and fertilizers, and farmer-friendly policies to help them handle the pressures exerted by the world economy (ibid.).

Suicides by farmers have also generated protests. More than 1000 farmers from Andhra Pradesh held a protest demonstration in New Delhi on 4 June 1998, organized by the Rytanga Atmahatyala Nivarna Aikya Porata Vedika (Platform for United Struggle to Prevent the Suicide of Farmers) of the state. They submitted a memorandum to the Speaker of the Lok Sabha, which held that the deaths were the result of the new economic and agricultural policies being pursued by the Central government for the last seven years (*Deccan Herald*, Hyderabad, 5 June 1998). However, no large-scale movements have taken place in recent years, despite the rising suicides. Rather, the issue has been taken up by voluntary organizations and non-governmental organizations (NGOs), who

are putting pressure on the government for both short-term ameliorative measures to help farmers, and longer-term corrective policies.

In contrast to the above, more recently, movements that have attracted many smaller farmers and, in some cases tribals, have arisen against the acquisition of land by state governments for industrial/mining projects to be undertaken by large, private national and international companies. These can be described as movements in reaction to the deepening of economic reforms, and while such protests are not new, they represent a direct clash between the interests of local farmers and domestic/global capital supported by the government. A good example is that of Orissa, where state-wide protests erupted in October 2006, beginning with the police firing at Kalinga Nagar against tribals protesting against land acquisition on 2 January 2006 (Das 2006). The Orissa government has signed about forty-two memorandums of understanding and over 100,000 acres are needed to house private industries, in addition to the land the companies would get on lease for thermal power plants, mining iron ore, bauxite, coal, and other minerals. The government failed to persuade the tribals of Kalinga Nagar who have continued to block the Daitari-Paradip national highway since 2 January 2006; nor has it been able to acquire land elsewhere (ibid.) The attempt to establish SEZs (Special Economic Zones) by big private Indian companies such as Reliance has also generated protests[25] leading the Central government to promise that no hasty action would be taken without the consent of the local farming and other communities involved. Thus, in recent months we have been witnessing the beginning of movements by small farmers against the impact of increasing globalization of the economy, and the failure of the state to protect their livelihoods.

FUTURE DIRECTIONS: RISING CAPITALIST TENDENCIES

Agrarian mobilization has been shaped by two developments in post-Independence India: the centrality of the state in directing agrarian policies and a capitalist tendency in agriculture. Agrarian policies have undergone a number of changes, and farmers' movements have primarily been a response to the policies enunciated by the state. The growth of capitalism in agriculture can be traced to shifts in state policy—from an institutional strategy based upon distributive justice and concerns of equity, to a technological strategy aimed at rapid agricultural growth and, finally, a freeing of controls under globalization—which have promoted the interests of the bigger and more prosperous rich peasants/capitalist farmers. Out of the interplay of these interrelated developments, three distinct phases can be identified in the farmers' movements in India: anti-feudal movements demanding land in the immediate post-Independence period; rich farmers' movements in the 1970s and 1980s; and fewer movements in the 1990s, despite globalization and a deepening crisis in agriculture.

Farmers' movements must be understood as part of the larger changes taking place within the Indian polity and economy. There were anti-feudal movements in many parts of the country led by Left parties/organizations, demanding land and focusing on associated issues such as wages and rents in the immediate post-Independence period. However, successful large-scale horizontal mobilization by big farmers' organizations against the state was witnessed mainly in the 1970s and the 1980s. A number of factors made these movements possible. A central feature has been a growing capitalist tendency in the post-Independence period, despite the attempt through planning to create a socialistic economy. The early shift from an institutional to a technological strategy led to a move towards capitalist agriculture and increased class differentiation, leading to the emergence of the rich peasant/capitalist farmer in many regions, who held both economic power and political influence. These developments enabled the emergence of rich farmers' movements led by large 'autonomous' farmers' organizations. Described by some scholars as New Social Movements, certain specific features characterized these movements: led by rich farmers, they were able to mobilize sections of medium and small farmers through caste and clan-based mobilization, through the use of inclusive categories such as kisan/*raiyat*, or by pointing to the rural–urban divide; they did not aspire to capture power, but brought pressure on the state to introduce policies favourable to them; and due to common demands, state organizations were able to jointly organize national level movements. More importantly, they took place during a period when Indian agriculture was performing well, and the terms of trade were favourable. Equally significant is that during this period, agrarian issues were important, and a rich farmers' lobby was present in many state legislatures, enabling it to levy pressure on the government to fulfil the demands of farmers.

In contrast, the 1990s have witnessed many changes: a SAP, resulting in globalization of the economy; a general crisis in agriculture, reflected in slower growth and a marked worsening of the economic conditions of farmers' households, accompanied by increasing class differentiation and capitalist agriculture. During the 1990s, state governments adopted new market-oriented agricultural policies such as a reversal of land reform laws, freeing of controls on land, encouragement to private investment, and agribusiness companies. These developments have affected the farming community. The lack of farmers' movements during the phase of globalization and increasing problems, particularly for smaller farmers, remain a controversial subject. While some scholars hold that the impact of globalization on Indian agriculture is still low, others point to the fragmentation of the farmers' movements in the 1990s along *ideological and class lines*. Market-oriented big farmers' organizations such as the SS and sections of the KRRS have supported the new agrarian policies. A small but powerful elite section of big capitalist farmers in prosperous states such as Andhra Pradesh, Karnataka, and Maharashtra find the new agricultural market-oriented policies attractive, and are supportive of them. This class has moved rapidly towards agro-industry, partnerships with MNCs, and export-oriented agriculture, and has become part of the class base of the state, which ensures that their interests are looked after, while others such as the BKU and BKS have strenuously opposed the new policies and led movements against them. They are unhappy that state governments, during a period of globalization, have withdrawn their responsibility towards rural development, land reform, and market regulation. The poor peasantry and the landless are the worse hit due to the downturn in agriculture, and have been unable to organize themselves against the new policies. However, with the deepening of economic reform and greater integration with global capital, movements by smaller farmers/tribals in some parts of the country against the state have begun, and are bound to intensify in the coming years unless corrective measures are taken by the Indian state.

NOTES

1. In constructing this typology, I have drawn upon Rudolph and Rudolph (1984).

2. The institutional question argued that redistribution of excess land from unproductive big landlords to a medium self-owning peasantry would increase productivity. See Myrdal, Vol. II, (1968).

3. The term Green Revolution refers to a new technology introduced with the help of the United States in order to increase foodgrain production. It is a technological package consisting of new high-yielding seeds, chemical fertilizers in place of the organic ones used earlier, assured and controlled irrigation that often needed pumpsets, and pesticides to control weeds and pests. See Dasgupta (1980).

4. In the 1960s, many economists argued that for an agricultural revolution to take place, technological investment in agriculture was necessary. See Schultz (1964).

5. Four major classes with regional variations could be identified by the end of the 1960s: capitalist farmers owning more than 10 acres, who used hired labour, often rented out land, and extracted surplus in the form of rent; rich farmers owning roughly 4–10 acres, self-cultivating and often leasing-in land to increase their holdings; middle farmers owning between 2 and 4 acres, who are part-owners, part-tenants, and depend on family labour; small and marginal farmers who operate 1–2 acres, most of whom are tenants and supplement their income with agricultural and landless labour. See Pai (1993: p. 16).

6. By middle peasant, Lenneberg meant the middling group of small and medium holders who participated actively in the market in an attempt to maximize their economic returns by growing cash crops on a part of their land. They did not disappear with the Green Revolution, but managed to survive and represent a typically Indian middle peasant class that she feels scholars have neglected (Lenneberg 1988, p. 459).

7. The Rudolphs describe the bullock capitalists as owning between 2.5 to 15 acres, and as self-employed and self-funded farmers using the biological inputs but not the agricultural machinery, with holdings large enough for a pair of bullocks to plough, but not enough to make use of tenants or agricultural labour (Rudolph and Rudolph 1987).

8. Varshney argues that the peasant defined as those producing for home consumption and the farmer for the market, is legitimate for historical cases drawn from Europe. However, in developing countries with scientific advances, the so-called peasantry has used the new technology in a rational manner, thereby aiding rather than impeding the process of modernization. Varshney (1995: 2, n. 3). Similarly, Gupta examining the BKU in UP, pointed to the need to 'reintegrate' the terms 'peasant' and 'farmer'. The old 'peasant mentality' arising out of isolated rural communities—he argued—has vanished, replaced by farmers who are proficient in the use of new technology and produce for the market despite retaining in many ways a peasant outlook. He describes the Jats as the 'farmer-peasant' of west UP (Gupta 1997: 25–7).

9. The mode of production debate stems from the indices Marx used to identify capitalist development, in this case agriculture. Writing on primitive accumulation in agriculture, he points out that it means accumulation prior to the full-fledged onset of capitalism. The transition to capitalism was marked by the separation of direct producers from the means of production and the formation of a class of free labour, and tendencies towards concentration of considerable 'masses of capital' and 'labour power' in the hands of the producers of commodities. The study of the transition to capitalism thus entails a discussion of this historical process, and the extent to which it has been established. It is an analysis of this process in Indian agriculture following the introduction of the Green Revolution that sparked off this debate.

10. These were (a) cash outlays on wages per acre; (b) the percentage of total produce marketed; (c) value of modern capital equipment used per acre; (d) cash profits per acre; and (e) value of output per acre. Further, Rudra argued that there had to be valuable association of these with each other. He found that while some were associated, others were not, and so held that capitalism was barely visible in the countryside.

11. In contrast to Rudra, Patnaik, using the same indices, relied on the higher average value of each: cash wages, ratio of sales to output, value of output per acre, capital equipment, etc. Her argument was that this was better to capture the emerging capitalist tendencies, whereas Rudra's method had failed to do so as it was better suited to a system where capitalism had already emerged. See Patnaik (1971).

12. In the early 1980s, the BKU in UP and Punjab, the KRRS, and the SS presented many Memorandums to

the respective state governments along these lines. Assadi (1997); Kehar Singh (1990); Lenneberg (1988).

13. The oil shock led to a rise in the price of fertilizers, pumpsets cost more as electricity rates were raised, the new seeds were not easily available, and prices rose. The technology was not neutral to scale and as the cost of inputs rose sharply, the second generation of big farmers who had adopted the new technology did not gain as much (Rao 1975).

14. Yet, political factors played a role. The formation of the Punjabi Suba and the greater importance this gave to the Akali Dal, whose base lies in the Jat Sikh peasantry, gave an impetus to the formation of the BKU (Singh 1990: 36–7). Similarly, the BKU received a boost in 1979 when a large rally was held to celebrate the birthday of Charan Singh, then the Prime Minister of India.

15. See B.M. (1978) and (1980).

16. On theories of urban bias, see Lipton (1978).

17. A study in 1982 based in Punjab argued that while the average cost of production of wheat in the state increased by 116.8 per cent between 1967–8 and 1977–8, the procurement price rose only by 54.9 per cent (Singh 1990: 33).

18. Charan Singh, one of the most significant leaders of the farmers, resolutely opposed any further distribution of land, and held that surplus should be absorbed in small-scale industry, leaving a stable peasantry in the countryside (Pai 1993).

19. While it promised 'growth with equity', its key aspects were the need to 'accelerate the growth of agro business' and provide growth that, while catering to the domestic market, 'maximizes benefits from exports of agricultural products in the face of the challenges arising from economic liberalization and globalizations'. In short, the role of the state is not of a protector/provider as in the past, but that of a facilitator for promoting faster agricultural growth. The full text is available on the website of the Union Ministry of Agriculture. http://agricoop. nic.in/agpolicy02.htm part of the website of the Union Ministry of Agriculture and Cooperation, accessed on 24 February 2009.

20. On this, see Vaidyanathan (2006b).

21. The Situation Assessment Survey of the farming community commissioned by the Ministry of Agriculture and carried out by the National Sample Survey Organization in 2003 (January–December) brings out the pathetic condition of India's farmers in income, expenditure, and indebtedness. See Narayanamoorthy (2006).

22. A similar view is put forward by Rao and Gopalappa (2004, pp. 5591–8).

23. In the case of Andhra Pradesh, the Ramachenna Reddy Commission 2005, set up to enquire into the farmers' suicides, in its Report highlighted that the Telugu Desam Party (TDP) government had neglected the agricultural sector, and recommended strengthening of the system of agricultural credit, quality inputs, and credit for small farmers. See Kumar (2005).

24. See interview of Sharad Joshi in *Business India*, 22 September 1997.

25. See, 'PMK to launch "save cultivable lands campaign"', *The Hindu*, New Delhi, 28 October 2006.

REFERENCES

Assadi, Muzaffar H. 2003. 'Interfacing Globalisation, Social Movements and the Indian State: Myths, Discourses and Challenges', *MICA Communications Review*, 1(2), pp. 49–58.

———. 2002. 'Resistance to Economic Reforms: Agrarian Social Movement and Alternative Vision from the Experience of Karnataka', *Indian Journal of Political Science*, 63(4), pp. 351–69.

———. 1997. *Peasant Movement in Karnataka 1980–94*. New Delhi: Shipra Publications.

B.M., 1980, 'Appeasing Rich Farmer Lobby', *Economic and Political Weekly*, XV(9), pp. 459–61.

———. 1978. 'Rich Farmers' Lobby in Full Cry', *Economic and Political Weekly*, XIII(48), pp. 1966–7.

Béteille, Andre. 1971. *Caste Class and Power, Changing Patterns of Stratification in a Tanjore Village*. Berkeley: University of California Press.

Bhaduri, Amit. 1973. 'Agricultural Backwardness Under Semi-Feudalism', *Economic Journal*, 83(329), pp. 120–37.

Bhalla G.S. (ed.). 1994. *Economic Liberalisation and Indian Agriculture*. New Delhi: Institute for Studies in Industrial Development and Food and Agriculture Organization of the United Nations.

Bouton, Marshall. 1989. *The Sources of Agrarian Radicalism: A Study of Thanjavur District, South India*. New Jersey: Princeton University Press.

Brass, Tom. 1995. *New Farmers' Movement in India*. UK: Taylor and Francis.

Bunsha, Dionne. 2006. 'Confronting Agrarian Crisis', *Frontline*, February, pp. 125–7.

Byres, T.J. 1988. 'Charan Singh (1902–87): An Assessment', *Journal of Peasant Studies*, 15(2), pp. 139–89.

———. 1986. 'The Agrarian Question, Forms of Capitalist Agrarian Transition and the State: An Essay With Reference to Asia', *Social Scientist*, 14(162–3), pp. 3–67.

Chandrakant, W. 2004. 'Ryots Reeling Under Market Forces', *The Hindu*, New Delhi, 12 June.

Chatterjee, Partha. 1988. 'For an Indian History of Peasant Struggles', *Social Scientist*, 16(11), pp. 3–17.

Chatterjee, Partha. 1982. 'Agrarian Relations and Communalism in Bengal 1926–1935', in R. Guha (ed.), *Subaltern Studies*, Vol. 1. New Delhi: Oxford University Press.

Chesneaux, Jean. 1973. *Peasant Revolts in China 1840–1949*. London: Thomas and Hudson.

Communist Party of India. 1948. *On the Agrarian Question in India*. Bombay: People's Publishing House.

Dantwala, M.L. 1961. 'Agrarian Structure and Economic Development', *Indian Journal of Agricultural Economics*, XVI (1), pp. 10–25.

Das, Arvind N. and V. Nilkant (eds). 1985. *Agrarian Relations in India*. New Delhi: Manohar Publications.

Das, Prafull. 2006. 'Churning in Orissa', *The Hindu*, New Delhi, 13 January.

Das, Raju. 2001. 'The Political Economy of India: A Review Essay', *New Political Economy*, 6(1), pp. 103–17.

Dasgupta, Biplab. 1980. *Agrarian Change and the New Technology in India*. New Delhi: MacMillan Co. of India.

Desai, A.R. (ed.). 1986. *Agrarian Struggles in India After Independence*. New Delhi: Oxford University Press.

———. 1979. *Peasant Struggles in India*. New Delhi: Oxford University Press.

Deshpande, R.S., D. Rajasekhar, Pradeep Apte, and Dhanamanjari Sathe (eds). 2004. *State of the Indian Farmer A Millenium Study*, Vol. 23, 'NGOs and Farmers', New Delhi: Academic Foundation for Department of Agriculture and Cooperation, Ministry of Agriculture, Government of India.

Dhanagare, D.N. 1983. *Peasant Movements in India*. New Delhi: Oxford University Press.

Fanon, Frantz. 1971. *The Wretched of the Earth* (translated from the French by Constance Farrington). London: Macgibbon and Kee.

Frankel, Francine. 1978. *The Political Economy of India*. Princeton, New Jersey: Princeton University Press.

———. 1971. *India's Green Revolution Economic Gains and Political Costs*. Bombay: Oxford University Press.

Gough, Kathleen. 1974. 'Indian Peasant Uprisings', *Economic and Political Weekly*, IX(32), pp. 1391–1412.

Guha, Ranajit. 1983. *Elementary Aspects of Peasant Insurgency in Colonial India*. New Delhi: Oxford University Press.

Gupta, Dipankar. 1997. *Rivalry and Brotherhood Politics in the Life of Farmers in North India*. New Delhi: Oxford University Press.

Hardiman, David. 1981. *Peasant Nationalist of Gujarat: Kheda District 1917–1934*. New Delhi: Oxford University Press.

Jha, Praveen K. (ed.). 2002. *Land Reforms in India Issues of Equity in Rural Madhya Pradesh*, Vol. 7, New Delhi: Sage Publications.

Joshi, P.C. 1975. *Land Reforms in India Trends and Perspectives*. New Delhi: Allied Publishers.

Joshi, Sharad. 1994. *Selections from Sharad Joshi's Writings on Agriculture and Economic Freedom*. Pune: Shetkari Sangathana.

Khusro, A.M. 1973. *The Economics of Land Reform and Farm Size in India*. New Delhi: Macmillan.

Kotovsky, Grigory. 1964. *Agrarian Relations in India*. New Delhi: People's Publishing House.

Krishnaswamy, Chetan. 1995. 'Towards Reform Agriculture Policy Tabled', *Frontline*, pp. 41–2.

Kumar, Ravinder. 1968. 'The Rise of the Rich Peasant in Western India', in D.A. Low (ed.), *Soundings in Modern South Asian History*. London: Weidenfeld and Nicholson.

Kumar, Nagesh. 2005. 'Focus on the Farm Sector', *The Hindu*, New Delhi, 22 December.

Lenneberg, Cornelia. 1988. 'Sharad Joshi and the Farmers: The Middle Peasant Lives', *Pacific Affairs*, 61(3), pp. 446–64.

Lipton, Michael. 1978. *Why Poor People Stay Poor: Urban Bias in World Development*. Cambridge, MA: Harvard University Press.

Mencher, Joan. 1978. *Agriculture and Social Structure in Tamil Nadu*. New Delhi: Allied Publishers.

Menon, Parvati. 1995. 'Acting for Change Amendments to the Karnataka Land Reforms Act', *Frontline*, pp. 39–41.

Mohanty, B.B. and Sangeeta Shroff. 2004. 'Farmers' Suicides in Maharashtra', *Economic and Political Weekly*, XXXIX(52), pp. 5599–606.

Moore, Jr., Barrington. 1966. *Social Origins of Dictatorship and Democracy-Lord and Peasant in the Making of the Modern World*. Harmondsworth: Beacon Press.

Myrdal, Gunnar. 1968. *Asian Drama, An Inquiry into the Poverty of Nations*, Vol. II, Harmondsworth: Penguin Books.

Nadkarni, M.V. 1987. *Farmers Movements in India*. New Delhi: Allied Publishers.

Narayanamoorthy, A. 2006. 'State of India's Farmers', *Economic and Political Weekly*, XLI(31), pp. 471–3.

Natraj, Lalitha. 1980. 'Farmers' Agitation', *Economic and Political Weekly*, 15(47), pp. 1967–8.

Nayyar, Deepak and Abhijit Sen. 1994. 'International Trade and Agricultural Sector in India', in G.S. Bhalla (ed.), *Economic Liberalisation and Indian Agriculture*. New Delhi: Institute for Studies in Industrial Development, pp. 61–107.

Omvedt, Gail. 1998. 'Peasants, Dalits and Women: Democracy and India's New Social Movements', in M. Mohanty, P.N. Mukherji, and Olle Tornquist (eds), *People's Rights Social Movements and the State in the Third World*. New Delhi: Sage Publications, pp. 223–42.

Omvedt, Gail. 1982. *Land Caste and Politics in the Indian States*. New Delhi: University of Delhi.

———. 1980. 'Cane Farmers' Movement', *Economic and Political Weekly*, XV(48), pp. 2041–2.

Pai, Sudha. n.d. 'Globalization, Agricultural Policy and Farmers' Suicides: A Case Study of Andhra Pradesh', unpublished paper.

———. 1993. *Uttar Pradesh: Agrarian Change and Electoral Politics*. New Delhi: Shipra Publications.

Panini, M.N. 1999. 'Trends in Cultural Globalisation From Agriculture to Agribusiness in Karnataka', *Economic and Political Weekly*, XXXIV(3), pp. 2168–73.

Patnaik, Utsa and Zoya Hasan. 1995. 'Aspects of Farmers Movements in Uttar Pradesh in the Context of Uneven Capitalist Development in Agriculture', in T.V. Satyamurthy (ed.), *Industry and Agriculture in India Since Independence Vol. 2 Structures of Power, Movements of Resistance in the Series Social Change and Political Discourse in India*. New Delhi: Oxford University Press, pp. 274–300.

Patnaik, Utsa. 2004. 'A Crisis Rooted in Economic Reform', *Frontline*, 21(5), pp. 5–16.

———. 1980. 'Some Suggested Areas of Research To the Study of India's Agricultural Development', Unpublished Paper, Centre for Economic Studies and Planning, School of Social Sciences, JNU, New Delhi.

———. 1971. 'Capitalist Development in Agriculture: A Note', *Economic and Political Weekly*, VI(39), pp. A123–30, Review of Agriculture.

Prasad, Pradhan H. 1985. 'Semi-Feudalism the Basic Constraint of Indian Agriculture', in Arvind N. Das and V. Nilakant (eds), *Agrarian Relations in India*. New Delhi: Manohar Publications.

Raj, K.N., Amartya Sen, and C.H. Hanumantha Rao (eds). 1985. *Studies on Indian Agriculture*. New Delhi: Oxford University Press

Randhawa, M.S. 1974. *Green Revolution in Punjab*. New Delhi: Vikas Publishers.

Rao, V.M. and D.V. Gopalappa. 2004. 'Agricultural Growth and Farmer Distress Tentative Perspectives from Karnataka', *Economic and Political Weekly*, XXXIX(52), pp. 5591–8.

Rao, C. Hanumanth. 2004. 'Saving small farmers', *The Hindu*, New Delhi, 11 June.

———. 1975. *Technological Change and Distribution of Gains in Agriculture*. New Delhi: Macmillan.

Rao, K. Ranga. 1978. 'Peasant Movement in Telengana', in M.S.A. Rao (ed.), *Social Movements in India: Studies in Peasant and Backward Class Movements*, Vol. I. New Delhi: Manohar.

Redfield, Robert. 1955. *Little Community: Viewpoints for the Study of a Human Whole*. Chicago: The University of Chicago Press.

Rudolph, Lloyd I. and Susanne H. Rudolph. 1987. *In Pursuit of Lakshmi: The Political Economy of the Indian State*. Chicago: The University of Chicago Press.

———. 1984. 'Determinants and Varieties of Agrarian Mobilisation', in Meghnad Desai, Susanne H. Rudolph, and Ashok Rudra (eds), *Agrarian Power and Agricultural Productivity in South Asia*. New Delhi: Oxford University Press, pp. 281–344.

Rudra, Ashok. 1982. *Indian Agricultural Economy*. New Delhi: Allied Publishers.

Rudra, Ashok, A. Majid, and B.D. Talib. 1969. 'Big Farmers of Punjab', *Economic and Political Weekly*, IV(52), pp. A213–21 (Review of Agriculture).

Sahasrabudhey, Sunil. 1986. *The Peasant Movements*. New Delhi; Ashish Publications.

Sainath, P. 2006. 'Vidharbha: The "forced privatization" of cotton', *The Hindu*, New Delhi, 17 October.

———. 2005. 'Seeds of doubt in Maharashtra', *The Hindu*, New Delhi, 20 September.

———. 2004. 'How the better half dies', Parts I, II, *The Hindu*, New Delhi, 1 and 2 August.

Saxena, Naresh. 2004. 'Improving Programme Delivery', *Seminar*, 541, pp. 49–54.

Saxena, Kiran. 1987. 'Agrarian Situation in UP: A study of Land Grab Movement—1970', *Indian Journal of Politics*, XXI(3 and 4), pp. 47–63.

Schultz, Theodore. 1964. *Transforming Traditional Agriculture*. Chicago: Chicago University Press.

Sen, Bhowani. 1962. *Evolution of Agrarian Relations in India*. New Delhi: People's Publishing House.

Shah, Mihir and P.S. Vijay Shankar. 2002. 'Land Reforms in Madhya Pradesh: Redefining the Agenda' in Praveen Jha (ed.), *Land Reforms in India Issues of Equity in Rural Madhya Pradesh*, Vol. 7, Sage Series on Land Reforms in India. New Delhi: Sage, pp. 371–413.

Shanin, Theodore (ed.). 1971. *Peasants and Peasant Societies*. Modern Sociology Readings, Harmondsworth: Penguin.

Singh, Hardeep. 1987. 'Emergence and Growth of BKU', MPhil dissertation, Jawaharlal Nehru University, New Delhi.

Singh, Baljit. 1961. *Next Step in Village India: A Study of Land Reform and Group Dynamics*. New Delhi: Asia Publishing House.

Singh, Kehar. 1990. *Farmers' Movements and Pressure Group Politics*. New Delhi: Deep and Deep Publications.

Thorner, Daniel. 1967. 'India's New Farms', *The Statesman*, New Delhi 1–4 November.

———. 1956. *Agrarian Prospect in India*. New Delhi: Delhi University Press.

Vaidyanathan, A. 2006a. 'Agrarian Crisis: Nature, causes and remedies', *The Hindu*, New Delhi, 8 November.

———. 2006b. 'Farmers' Suicides and the Agrarian Crisis', *Economic and Political Weekly*, XLI(38), pp. 4009–13.

Varshney, Ashutosh. 1995. *Democracy, Development and the Countryside*. Cambridge: Cambridge University Press.

Venkateshwarlu, K. 2006. 'Seeds of discontent', *Frontline*, January, pp. 128–9.

Vidyasagar, R. and K. Suman Chandra. 2004. 'Farmers' Suicides in Andhra Pradesh and Karnataka', Research Report Series-64, National Institute of Rural Development, (NIRD), Hyderabad.

Warriner, Doreen. 1969. *Land Reform in Principle and Practice*. London: Oxford University Press.

Wolf, Eric R. 1971. *Peasant Wars in the Twentieth Century*. London: Faber and Faber.

Appendix 26A.1: Ownership and Operational Holdings of Farmers in India

Table 26A.1.1: Size-Distribution on Ownership Holding—All India

SIZE CLASS (ACRES)	PERCENTAGE OWNERSHIP HOLDINGS					PERCENTAGE AREA OWNED				
	53–5	61–2	71–2	82–3	92	53–4	61–2	71–2	82–3	92
Landless (00.01)	23.1	11.7	9.6	11.3	11.3	0.00	0.00	0.00	0.00	0.00
Marginal (.01–2.49)	38.2	48.4	53.0	55.3	60.6	6.2	7.6	9.8	12.2	16.9
Small (2.5–4.99)	13.5	15.1	15.5	14.7	13.4	10.1	12.4	14.7	16.5	18.6
Semi-medium (5.00–9.99)	12.5	12.9	12.0	10.8	9.3	18.4	20.5	21.9	23.4	24.6
Medium (10.0–24.99)	9.2	9.9	7.8	6.5	4.5	29.1	31.2	30.7	29.8	26.1
Large (25 and Above)	3.6	2.9	2.1	1.4	0.9	36.1	28.2	22.9	18.1	13.8
All	100	100	100	100	100	100	100	100	100	100

Source: NSS Data on Landholding, 8th Round, No. 36, 1954–5; 17th Round, No. 144, 1961–2; 26th Round, No. 215, 1971–2; 37th Round, Nos 330 and 331, 1982; 48th Round, No. 388, 1992

Table 26A.1.2: Percentage Distribution of Operated Area Operational Holdings—India (Rural)

	PERCENTAGE DISTRIBUTION OF OPERATED HOLDINGS				PERCENTAGE DISTRIBUTION OF OPERATED AREA			
	60–61 (17TH)	81–82 (37TH)	91–92 (48TH)	02–03 (59TH)	60–61 (17TH)	81–82 (37TH)	91–92 (48TH)	02–03 (59TH)
Marginal	39.1	56.0	62.8	69.7	6.9	11.5	15.6	22.6
Small	22.6	19.3	17.8	16.3	12.3	16.6	18.7	20.9
Semi-medium	19.8	14.2	12.0	9.0	20.7	23.6	24.1	22.5
Medium	14.0	8.6	6.1	4.2	31.2	30.1	26.4	22.2
Large	4.5	1.9	1.3	0.8	29.0	18.2	15.2	11.8
All size	100	100	100	100	100	100	100	100

Source: Estimates of 17th, 26th, and 37th Rounds, Nos 144, 215; 59th Round, No. 492

Appendix 26A.2: List of Some Important Farmers' Organizations

1. Karnataka Rajya Raiyat Sangha (Karnataka)
2. Shetkari Sanghatana (Maharashtra)
3. Bharatiya Kisan Union (Uttar Pradesh)
4. Bharatiya Kisan Union (Punjab)
5. Bharatiya Kisan Sangh (Gujarat)
6. Tamilaga Vyavasavayigal Sangham (Tamil Nadu)
7. Kisan Mazdoor Vyapari Sangh (Rajasthan)
8. Kisan Sanghathan (Rajasthan)
9. Kisan Mazdoor Vyapari Sangh (Rajasthan)
10. Kisan Mazdoor Sanghathan (West Bengal)
11. Samata Sanghathan (Orissa)
12. All India Kisan Sabha (National Level Organization)

(*Source*: Deshpande *et al.* 2004, pp. 180–6)

27 The Women's Movement

Anupama Roy

The women's movement in India, like most social movements, is made up of strands that differ on the relative primacy of issues, strategies of mobilization, and forms of collective action. While specific issues have taken precedence at different historical moments, more often than not, there has been a broad consensus within the movement over what constitutes 'transformatory change' for women. It is generally agreed, for example, that collective action around issues concerning women has to be directed against various layers of domination, namely, caste, class, culture, and ideology, and consist of non-institutionalized political action as well as action for change through and within institutions. Again, while power is sought to be dismantled at the level of both society and the state, the issue of autonomy has figured in the movement in significant ways, shaping specific perspectives on feminist politics, determining the relationship among women's organizations, and their alliances with other movements and groups.

It has become more or less customary to see the women's movement in terms of a chronological evolution, referring to it metaphorically as two or three successive historical waves. While the metaphor of the wave indeed invokes a powerful imagery, it captures the trajectory and constituent elements of the movement rather inadequately. Unlike an enormous wave that advances, engulfs, erodes, and retreats, recoups and advances again, the women's movement may be seen as undulating wave motions continually interlocking, reforming, regrouping, and reconfiguring. While inappropriate as an illustration of the movement's progression, the analogy of the wave is nonetheless significant for indicating the oppositional politics that the movement represents. In this chapter, therefore, while tracing the trajectory of the women's movement in India, I shall focus on the specific issues and concerns around which the movement has wound itself, and the manner in which they have propelled the movement forward. I will look, in particular, at the ways in which specific issues have emerged and sustained in the movement; the contests over new issues; the changes in the form, content, and course of the movement; the solidarities that have been sought at its different layers, and the factors that enable alliances between the women's and other democratic movements.

ORGANIZING FOR POLITICAL SUBJECTIVITY: FROM EDUCATION TO FRANCHISE

The origin of the women's movement in India is more often than not traced to organized struggles by women in the nineteenth century around issues of social reform. The nature and content of the debates and organizational activities around *stree-swadhinata* (women's self-determination) were determined largely by the colonial condition, especially at a time when the colonial government, faced with a struggle for national self-determination, was experiencing a growing crisis of legitimacy. The various strands in the debate framing the 'women's question', reflected, therefore, the multifarious relations of domination and subordination, the nature of colonial authority, and the complex socio-political forces and ideological formulations that structured narratives of 'womanhood'.

The foundation for stree-swadhinata and equality was laid down through reforms in education and the removal of practices like child-marriage, sati, purdah or seclusion, and resistance to widow remarriage. These reforms, however, worked within the limits of the reigning patriarchal ideology, where women were seen as passive recipients of the measures of improvement worked out by male reformers on their behalf.

The period of social reforms was followed by the nationalist period, which is generally seen as one in which the 'activist' woman made her appearance in various forms, as Gandhi's *satyagrahi* (practitioners of *satyagraha* [soul-force/struggle] for truth), as the 'dictator' leading the satyagraha, as the nurse who tended the satyagrahis injured by police batons, and as the passive resister who voluntarily and wilfully broke laws to suffer imprisonment. The visibility of women in the public sphere in this period was, however, surrounded by a discourse of 'true womanhood' and 'women's proper place', which, in the course of legitimizing and facilitating women's participation, ensnared them within an essentialist construction of femininity. Thus, while it may not be denied that in the early twentieth century, especially the period of Gandhian mass movements in the 1920s and 1930s,

women participated voluntarily and in large numbers in the struggle for national liberation, the ideology of 'domesticity' referring to the specificity of the realm of the domestic as a sphere of female activities, distinct from the public (male) sphere relatively inferior and yet complementary to it, also became entrenched. The nationalist movement opened up possibilities for women's public participation by foregrounding their sacrosanct 'femininity' as an embodiment of the spiritual essence of India. On the other hand, by positing India as sovereign in spirit, and by identifying the material-public-political world as the domain in which the struggle for equality and self-determination was to be waged, the national movement simultaneously edged out the issue of women's emancipation from the political domain onto the cultural/spiritual, making it non-negotiable with the colonial state (Chatterjee 1994: 131–3). Thus, while the nationalist discourse widened the scope of women's public participation, unlike the period of social reforms, it maintained a public silence on women's issues. Like the reformists, however, the nationalists glossed over the possibility of any radical re-structuring of power relations within the family.

The nationalist silence on the women's question was ruptured by women's organized struggle for equal political rights vis-à-vis voting and sitting in legislatures, and for reforms in personal laws. From 1917 to 1942, the period immediately before the country plunged into the Quit India movement, women activists petitioned provincial legislators, colonial officials, and the committees set up periodically by the colonial government to deliberate on matters of political reforms. They also addressed their demands to leading political parties, including the Indian National Congress and the Muslim League. It is important to note that only a small minority of men could vote on the basis of a qualifying property criterion, and women had no voting rights at all. It is significant that while the removal of sex discrimination formed the basis of women's demand for voting rights, women's organizations which took up the issue with the colonial government placed it within the larger agenda of 'universal franchise'. The prioritization of 'universal franchise', rather than an emphasis on women's suffrage, placed women's demands in consonance with the nationalist demand for 'national' citizenship and self-determination. A careful distancing from the adoption of a critical stance towards 'their' men, while appealing to the colonizer, was a constant characteristic of women's campaigns. Yet women's activism in this phase also took shape in relationship with suffragist feminisms in other countries, in particular Irish and British suffragists some of whom were also campaigning in India. It is interesting to see how this association vacillated between moments of solidarity in a universal sisterhood, and moments when this sisterhood was fractured by the nationalist anxieties of Indian feminists. Frequently, therefore, the latter resisted their Western sisters' condemnation of Indian social structures as oppressive, and the figuration of Indian women as 'gendered subjects of an irrational patriarchal system'.[1]

The first all-India women's organization came into existence in 1926, with the setting up of the National Council for Women in India (NCWI). The NCWI aimed at securing women's rights through social reforms and women's and children's welfare. The All India Women's Conference (AIWC) was set up in 1927 in Poona. Its members were primarily women from the upper and upper-middle classes and princely families, women members of the Indian National Congress party, the Communist Party, professional women like doctors and educationists, and social workers. The AIWC took up the question of women's education, and it was at its initiative that the Lady Irwin College for women was set up in Delhi in 1932. It also organized a large number of literacy schools and handicraft centres, which helped women from poor families learn basic skills in order to earn and be relatively independent economically. A significant concern for women's groups in this period, in particular the AIWC, was the campaign against child marriage. As a result of these struggles the Sarada Act was passed in 1929, fixing the age of marriage at fourteen for girls and eighteen for boys. In the 1930s, the AIWC directed its energies towards fighting for women's equal rights in inheritance and marriage, and reforms in the personal laws of different communities. The idea that there should be a Uniform Civil Code (UCC) for the whole of India was proposed at this point, and was bitterly opposed by orthodox sections in all the communities. Under pressure

from progressive nationalists and the women's movement, particularly the AIWC, and other regional organizations of women like the Mahila Atmaraksha Samiti in Bengal, Andhra Mahila Sangham in Andhra, and Women's Self Defence League in Punjab—all of which were led by Communist women—the B.N. Rau Committee was set up to suggest changes and unify the laws governing the Hindu community. The Hindu Code Bill was eventually passed after Independence in 1956.

There were, however, other forms of organized struggle in which women participated in substantial numbers. In the early 1930s, for example, a number of women—Kalpana Dutt, Priti Lata Waddedar, Bina Das, Suniti Das, and Suniti Ghosh—were involved in revolutionary armed struggle against the colonial state. Several women were also involved in Trade Unions, particularly in Bombay, Madras, Kanpur, and Coimbatore, which were important centres of textile industry in the 1920s. Considering that they were fewer in numbers in comparison to the total labour force, their active participation was a significant development. Women, moreover, played an active role in the struggle of peasants against landlords. Their participation in the Telangana struggle against the Nizam of Hyderabad in 1947 and the Tebhaga struggle in north Bengal in 1946–7 is especially noteworthy.

DISMANTLING THE NATIONALIST CONSENSUS: RALLYING AROUND DEVELOPMENT

The women's question after Independence was reframed in a context of widespread discontent with the development policies of the government. Development planning in India in the years after Independence continued to show a disregard for women's productive functions, placing women in atavistic roles as symbols of cohesion and continuity amidst the turbulent flux of modernity.[2] The sexual difference inherent in 'welfare' measures envisioned for women did not dismantle structural inequalities and sexual hierarchies within public institutions and society. Significantly, this period, which is often erroneously seen as one in which women's activism was at a decline, saw the emergence of the National

Federation of Indian Women in India (NFIW). Among the largest women's organizations in India today, NFIW was founded in 1954 as the women's wing of the Communist Party of India (CPI), with Aruna Asaf Ali among its prominent leaders.

Towards Equality, the report of the Committee on the Status of Women in India (CSWI), set up in 1971 to study the impact of development and nation-building on women, drew attention to the hierarchized and unequal status of women after three decades of planned development. Shattering the complacency which had accompanied the nationalist resolution of the women's question, *Towards Equality* drew on massive data to reveal the substantial erosion of women's political, social, and economic status after Independence, in particular the increasing marginalization of rural and poor women. The report was perhaps the first to identify a trend towards the declining child sex ratio and the 'missing women', an issue that has assumed enormous significance for the women's movement in recent years. The report was also instrumental in generating a renewed national debate on the women's question, particularly in the politics of development, and stimulated an academic concern over women's issues, which cumulated and led on to what may be seen as the emergence and subsequent consolidation of women's studies as a discipline in India (Mazumdar and Agnihotri 1999). The report of the CSWI, its major recommendations, and the documents that were produced by various working groups set up under the pressure of the revelations made in the report formed the initial thrust of demands set out by a network of national women's organizations, which came into existence informally in 1980, 'demanding explicit provisions for the imperative development needs of women in the Sixth Five-Year Plan' (Agnihotri and Mazumdar 2005: 68).

Women's activism in the 1970s and 1980s was one among several democratic rights struggles in the period, all of which stressed the need to redefine development. Large-scale unemployment, poverty, and marginalization of the people had generated student uprisings, worker's agitations, and peasant, tribal, anti-caste, and consumer action movements. These movements spanned the political spectrum from Gandhian-socialists who espoused non-violent

protest based on explicitly moral values over specific working or living conditions, to the far left, including the Maoists, who took recourse to violence to express discontentment with government policies (Kumar 1989: 20). Poor peasants and landless labourers, who faced increasing unemployment, stagnation of wages, and caste oppression, were drawn into regional struggles organized by the Left parties. Rural struggles became increasingly militant among groups united by economic and cultural oppression, including the Dalits and *adivasi*s. With increasing expropriation of their agricultural lands and access to forest resources, many became industrial and agricultural wage labourers. The adivasi women, traditionally less restricted than caste Hindu and Muslim women initiated strong struggles, particularly in the Shahada movement in Maharashtra, against men's consumption of alcohol and against domestic violence. Middle-class women in urban Bihar and Gujarat, including students, housewives, and office workers, participated in a large-scale movement against political corruption and the rising prices of food and fuel. The movement of the middle class became associated with the *nav-nirman* or total revolution movement led by Jayaprakash Narayan, a Gandhian leader. In Maharashtra, an anti-price rise movement was organized by a temporary coalition of women belonging to the CPI, the Communist Party of India (Marxist) (CPI[M]), and the social democratic Socialist Party. All these struggles precipitated the declaration of Emergency in 1975, under which non-parliamentary groups on both the Left and right of the political spectrum were banned, large numbers of political activists were imprisoned, and fundamental rights stood suspended (Gothoskar *et al.* 1982: 92–3).

The emergence of the Self-Employed Women's Association (SEWA) in 1972 is often cited as an important development of the decade. Women also participated actively in the peasant struggles in Bihar and the Chipko movement, which challenged developmental policies. It is interesting however, that while participation in these movements sharpened women's critique of development, a feminist analysis of development, which could lead to more focused demands, including women's land rights, failed to emerge.

THE QUEST FOR AUTONOMY AND THE EMERGENCE OF THE 'NEW' WOMEN'S MOVEMENT

Following the state of national Emergency (1975–7), a vibrant civil rights movement emerged in India. A number of civil liberties and democratic rights groups came up at the national and state levels, which, while working within constitutional-legal frameworks, focused on the extra-legal and socio-economic contexts of violations of people's rights by the state and its agencies. By this time, two different and opposing perspectives on women's struggles against oppression had developed—one which saw women's issues as woven within an integrated framework of democratic struggles and proposed that women's struggles against oppression should be part of mass organizations, whether Trade Unions, revolutionary organizations, or political parties; and another, which preferred to see women's groups focus on the specific nature of women's oppression, *autonomous* of mass organizations. While the first—the affiliated women's groups—considered the mass base of political parties a source of strength and held that party organizations provided the space from where feminist demands could be raised, the autonomous groups found organizational compulsions constraining on both the manner in which women's issues were framed, and the relative primacy that was accorded to them. The energies spent in negotiating the space for the articulation of women's issues within party organizations, they felt, would lead to smaller gains compared to those achieved by an independent women's movement, which, through its vigorous presence, would compel political organizations to take note of it and, once entrenched, it would multiply and unfold in multifarious ways.

Significantly, the drive towards autonomy became a central motif of the women's movement in the 1970s and 1980s, giving it the label of the 'autonomous women's movement'. The label manifested the desire to disengage the 'women's question' from the dominant theoretical framework of the Left and democratic rights movements, which focused solely on class and the repressive state, respectively. It expressed the concerns of the women's movement woven focally around women's interests, gender-centred issues, and the control of female sexuality, all of which were critical aspects of institutionalized male domination, as understood within the conceptual framework of patriarchy (Chakravarty 2005: 43). Most women's groups were, however, sufficiently open to allow both views to coexist and developed links with the Left, the working class, tribal and anti-caste organizations, campaigned around specific issues, and debated and disseminated theories of women's oppression. In the early years, however, campaigns were relatively sporadic and minor compared to the pace of theoretical activity. Most of the groups remained fairly loose until the beginning of the 1980s and few had names, so much so that at the first socialist-feminist conference in Bombay in 1978, their identification was primarily regional—as the 'Bombay group' or the 'Delhi group' (Kumar 1989: 21–2).

With the 1980s, however, both mass-based and affiliated women's organizations as well as the autonomous women's groups invigorated the struggle for women's rights. Delhi housed the headquarters of most national-level women's organizations, including the AIWC, Young Women's Christian Association (YWCA), All Indian Democratic Women's Association (AIDWA), NFIW, and Mahila Dakshita Samiti (MDS). Bombay became the centre for protests against rape and violence with the setting up of the Forum Against Rape, in 1981,[3] which later emerged as a sustained network of autonomous women's groups in the form of the Forum Against Oppression of Women (FAOW) (Mazumdar and Agnihotri 1999). A number of autonomous women's groups like Manushi (1979), Saheli (1981), Jagori (1984), the feminist press—Kali for Women (1984)—were set up all over the country. Drawing their members from the urban, middle-class, educated, and professional women, these groups set up documentation and resource centres, and organized and coalesced activities including agitation against specific issues of violence against women, and provided legal and humanitarian aid. While the affiliated groups prioritized the alleviation of poverty, promoting literacy, and availability of jobs as the primary needs of women, the autonomous groups raised issues of violence against women in all its manifestations— rape (including custodial rape), dowry deaths,[4] amniocentesis and selective abortion of the female foetus, women's health, the use of contraceptives and reproductive choice, sexual division of labour and patriarchy as it manifested itself in several forms, in particular in the family, the power relations that inform it, and the legal and institutional practices that sustain women's subordinate familial roles.

Irrespective of women's activism within or autonomous of political organizations, political parties have been desultory in prioritizing, promoting, or giving importance to women's concerns. This is most evident from women's insignificant presence in the organizational structures of political parties, the insubstantial numbers given party candidatures in elections, and their extremely meagre representation in Parliament. Yet, despite the dispute among women's groups over the definition, form, and content of struggles around women's issues, it would be a mistake to assume that affiliated women's movements would invariably function within the dominant party paradigms, or that with their mass base, they would be more effective in their campaigns on women's issues than the autonomous women's groups, which have a much smaller membership. The manner in which women's issues are articulated and the degree of success they have achieved in specific campaigns, has in practice depended on the nature of the political field in which a particular organization is situated.[5]

TALKING DIFFERENTLY: ADDRESSING IDENTITY AND EQUALITY

In the 1980s, in a political context where the 'politics of presence' and the corresponding question of identity became increasingly important, there was a reconfiguration of the framework of universalism within which women's groups had hitherto functioned, irrespective of their perspectives on affiliation and autonomy. The recognition that 'difference', of class, caste, religion, sexuality, etc., formed significant axes around which the diversity of women's experience occurred, gave critical reflexivity to the women's movement, deepening its quest for substantive equality. On the other hand, it also opened up areas of tension, especially in the movement's position on gender justice and reform of religious-personal laws, where acceptance of a differentiated universalism involved strategic withdrawal from the position of universalism.

The emergence of Dalit feminist voices from the mid-1980s drew attention to caste identities, which had hitherto been assumed as transcendable for the larger sisterhood among women. Young Dalit feminists in Mumbai formed the Mahila Sansad, and by the mid-1990s, Samvadini—Dalit Stree Sahitya Manch, a forum of the Dalit feminist literary movement, had emerged. By the 1990s, there were several independent and autonomous assertions by Dalit women, including the formation of the National Federation of Dalit Women and the All India Dalit Women's Forum. In December 1996, the Vikas Vanchit Dalit Mahila Parishad organized at Chandrapur put forth a proposal to commemorate 25 December, the day on which, in 1927, B.R. Ambedkar had symbolically burnt the *Manusmriti* at Mahad, as the Bharatiya Streemukti Divas or the Indian Women's Liberation Day.[6] In 1997 the Christi Mahila Sangharsh Sangathana, an organization of Dalit Christian women, was established (Rege 1998: 2006).

The assertion of autonomous Dalit women's organizations at both the regional and national levels threw up several crucial theoretical and political challenges, questioning both the Brahminism of the women's movement and the patriarchal practices of Dalit politics. The debates around Dalit women's assertion of identity underscored the importance of reframing feminist activism, and redefining gender so as to bring into its fold the multiple sites of oppression, and dismantle the brahmanical frameworks of unencumbered, universalist, and transcendental feminism. The Dalit Bahujan feminist politics and writings, which were made visible in the 'new' discourses on caste and gender in the political contexts of the 1980s and 1990s, pushed feminist politics into rethinking 'difference' and recovering its understanding of sites on which the relational identities of caste and gender had been stated politically (Rege 2006). The space for debates on difference within the women's movement has continued to open up as the Indian lesbian, gay, bisexual, and transgender (LGBT) movement sought to place diversity of sexualities and genders on its agenda, demanding that this diversity be respected and discrimination against LGBT people stopped. It is not surprising, therefore, that the central concern of the Seventh National Conference of the Autonomous Women's Movement in Kolkata in September 2006, was affirming diversity without divisiveness.

The struggle to differentiate the feminist universal through the insertion of the multiple experiences of oppression, prepared the ground for a broader platform of action. On the other hand, in the political contexts obtaining in the late 1980s and 1990s, the women's movement had to grapple with issues of religious identity, which complicated the way in which women's groups had hitherto seen the relationship between women's rights and rights of communities to preserve their religious and cultural identities. The constitutional guarantee of the 'cultural and educational rights' of religious and cultural communities and minority groups (Articles 25–30 in the chapter on Fundamental Rights in the Constitution of India) forms the basis of the rights of religious communities to administer themselves in civil matters by their own personal laws. This cluster of rights has constituted a field of tension for both the women's movement, the right-wing Hindu organizations, and Hindu nationalist parties. The latter have seen special provisions for religious minorities as disabling and weakening the process of national integration, and have pushed for a UCC, which, incidentally, the Constitution of India also enumerates as a Directive Principle for future Indian governments to act upon. The Hindu nationalist demand for a UCC has been couched in the aspiration for a common national identity which transcends and disregards particular religious identities. The women's movement's adherence to the demand for a UCC, first articulated in the colonial context, was, however, based on the understanding that the right of the community to autonomously manage its affairs through its personal laws was oppressive for women, and inimical to their rights to equality. Personal laws, they argued, limited the choices available to women with regard to economic freedom, and inhibited

their equality by allotting them a subservient and dependent position in matters of family, inheritance, and financial autonomy.

A series of events in the 1980s and 1990s, however, saw a communalization of the demand for a UCC by right-wing Hindu groups, and a subsequent retraction of the demand for a UCC by women's groups, who shifted to a position where they could reconcile gender justice with the right to equality of religious communities. In 1985, the Supreme Court of India decided the landmark case of Shah Bano, a Muslim woman divorcee, for maintenance. While delivering a judgement in her favour, the Supreme Court simultaneously suggested that a UCC be put in place by the government.[7] The judgement triggered off protests among sections of Muslims, who called for upholding the sanctity of the *Shariat* (Islamic legal code). Subsequently, the then government brought a highly retrograde legislation, the Muslim Women's (Protection of Rights on Divorce) Bill 1986, which freed Muslim men from the obligation placed on them by Section 125 of the Criminal Procedure Code (CrPC) vis-à-vis abandoned or divorced wives.[8] The Shah Bano case, 1985, and the Muslim Women's Bill, 1986, became rallying issues for a diverse range of organizations, for the protectors of the *Shariat* and the autonomy of the Muslim community; for diverse strands of the women's movement; for democratic rights groups, who opposed the communalization of women's issues and appealed for a gender-just UCC; for Hindu communalists, for whom the Supreme Court judgement vindicated their claims that the Muslim community was 'barbaric' and 'anti-national'; and for their Muslim counterparts, for whom the reversal of the Supreme Court judgement became the ultimate source of redemption of their dignity as Muslims.

The debates and demonstrations following the incident of Sati in September 1987 in Deorala, a village in Rajasthan, reflected the manner in which the rights of Hindu women were similarly imbricated with questions of religious identity, community autonomy, and eventually 'a politics of power'. In both cases, what was at stake was women's economic freedom, their right to property, and the very bases on which the structures of domination within communities were organized. Wives and widows claiming their right to property threatened to destabilize more than just economic structures. They aimed to transform radically the multifarious whorls of domination that informed their lives as women. Yet, in both cases the (male) religious leaders and fundamentalists were able to raise the 'community in danger' alarm, and reaffirm their claims to representing the community. In both cases the government sacrificed women's rights in order to strike a balance with the two communities, aiming eventually at strengthening its electoral prospects with both (Kumar 1993: 177).

With the rise and consolidation of the Hindu right around the issue of the Ram temple in Ayodhya, which witnessed in its course communal riots and the demolition of the Babri Mosque at the temple site, government inactivity during the entire sequence of events, and the relative invisibility of (Hindu) public opposition to these, the Muslim community closed its ranks, preferring reforms from within the community.[9] The period also saw a vehement and vociferous rise in upper-caste opposition to caste-based reservations in jobs. The Hindu right-wing in particular kept up a tirade against the state for promoting caste and community-based privileges, and for 'pampering' religious minorities and Scheduled Castes and Tribes (SC/ST), raising vigorously the demand for a UCC. In this context, women's groups rethought their long-standing demand for a UCC. Apprehensive that in the changed political circumstances it had come to embody a universalism dominated by an ideology of exclusion through the denial and elimination of the religious-cultural identity of religious minorities, women's groups unanimously gave up the demand for a UCC.

There is a fundamental difference, however, in the grounds on which the different strands in the women's movement have sought to reconcile the goal of gender justice with the democratic ideal of diversity and pluralism. While the AIDWA, a mass-based women's organization affiliated to the CPI(M), has taken the position that gender justice need not necessarily be linked to an umbrella legislation and that such a legislation might actually prove counter-productive preferring reforms in personal laws, other women's groups have been more inclined to see personal laws as 'conceptually flawed' (Raman 1999: 4). Broadly, the latter have couched their demands in terms of an 'exit' option for individual members, reforms from within the community, critical relations between the community and its members, and an alternate set of rational codes, which could provide recourse to members who exercise the choice to 'exit'. Women's groups have broadly drawn consensus on three possible ways in which this could happen: (a) support for and initiation of attempts to bring about reform within personal laws; (b) bringing about legislation in areas not covered either by secular or personal laws—such as domestic violence and right to the matrimonial home—thus avoiding a direct confrontation with communities and the wider communal politics; (c) working or setting up a comprehensive gender-just framework of rights covering areas covered not only by personal laws, but also by the 'public' domain of work (crèches, equal wages, maternity benefits, and so forth), which should be available to all citizens. They have proposed that wherever these laws do not conflict with personal laws, they should be automatically applicable, and where they do conflict, it should be up to individual citizens to make the choice (Menon 1998: PE-3).

Significantly, Muslim women and Muslim women's groups are increasingly pressing for equality through reforms in personal laws. Groups like Majlis, and Awaz-e-Niswaan, women's research and action groups, and Muslim women's rights networks like Confederation of Voluntary Associations (COVA) have tried to impress at various public fora that the vast majority of Muslim women want a change in the laws that violate the rights given to them by the Quran, and work for gender-just interpretations of Quranic verses. More importantly, Muslim women themselves have taken the initiative to reflect on the Quran and Prophetic traditions, rather than depend on the maulanas for reforms. They have, moreover, sought to highlight the socio-economic status of Muslim women and their plight during and after riots, rather than focusing only on the establishment of Shariat courts. At a public hearing organized by the Institute of Islamic Studies and Centre for the Study of Society and Secularism in Mumbai in 1998, for example, a resolution was passed expressing the resolve of Muslim women to start a dialogue with the Muslim Personal Law Board (MPLB) for reforms in personal law. The women's groups have subsequently challenged the Muslim Personal Law Board for its lack of courage in taking strong decisions, particularly with regard to the practice of triple *talaq* (divorce). In 2001, the MPLB organized a meeting with women's organizations in which Muslim women's organizations demanded that triple talaq be reformed according to the guidelines given in the Quran. The women's organizations also rejected the model *nikahanama* proposed in 2004 by the MPLB, which retained the triple talaq and framed the *Iqrarnama* (marriage agreement) in a way that closed the options for women to approach secular courts. A Muslim Women Personal Law Board was set up in 2005 in order to read, understand, and interpret the laws from a gender perspective through consensus or *ijtihad* (Hussain 2006).

At a time when the women's movement was addressing the dilemmas posed by a hegemonic Hindu identity and issues of difference which arose within the movement by recognizing that the category 'woman' was layered and traversed by multiple experiences of oppression, it had to contend with parallel activism by upper-caste Hindu women. The agitations by upper-caste Hindu men and women against caste-based reservations in government jobs (the anti-Mandal stir) saw a resurgence of women in the public sphere, women who staked their claim to equality through the elimination of competing claims by Dalit women (Tharu and Niranjana 1996: 239–45). Similarly, women of the Rashtriya Sevika Samiti, in an ironic inversion of the traditional invisibility of middle class, upper-caste women, played an active role in communal riots in the wake of the Ram Janmabhoomi movement (Sarkar 1996: 131). Quite like the anti-Mandal movement, this right-wing women's movement too contributed towards women's political self-activization and self-actualization insofar as these women stepped out of their iconic images— the endlessly raped or threatened Hindu woman—

around which anti-Muslim tirades were woven, to a new, empowering self-image of the *karsevika* rescuing the birthplace of Rama (ibid.).[10]

RECONFIGURING AUTONOMY AND COUNTERING HEGEMONIES: THE QUEST FOR ALLIANCES AND FEMINIST SOLIDARITY

The late 1980s, moving on to the 1990s, as seen in the preceding section, were informed by ideological churnings and debates within the women's movement, manifesting both the rifts and the convergences among women's organizations. The late 1990s and the period thereafter saw in particular a rallying of forces among women's groups on the issue of reservation for women in elected bodies. The struggle to enhance women's representation in elected bodies, which had first emerged in the 1920s and 1930s, was revisited in the 1970s by the CSWI while examining the political status of women. The *Towards Equality* report, the name by which the report of the CSWI is popularly known, drew attention to the deeply entrenched discriminatory structures that inhibited women's representation in political bodies. The Committe could not, however, agree on the principle of reservation for women in Parliament, and eventually rejected it. Three members of the Committee—Lotika Sarkar, Neera Dogra, and Vina Mazumdar—dissented, arguing that the Committee was being unwise in ignoring the need for institutionalized measures to eliminate—or at least weaken—institutionalized inequalities, which twenty-five years of universal franchise had failed to dislodge. The Committee, however, unanimously recommended one-third reservation for women in elected bodies at the panchayat level. A demand for increased representation of women was made again in the late 1980s, but the women's movement's critique of the government's National Perspective Plan for Women, yet again emphasized reservation up to one-third in grassroots bodies for local self-government—to throw up 'new leadership from below'—and rejected reservation in state assemblies and Parliament. The National Perspective Plan for women, issued by the government in 1988 under pressure from the women's movement, recommended 30 per cent reservation of seats for women at the panchayat and *zila parishad* levels. In 1993, the Seventy-third and Seventy-fourth Constitutional Amendment Acts provided constitutional recognition and status to local elected bodies in villages (the panchayats) and cities (the municipalities), respectively. Apart from putting in place institutions of local governance and decentralizing power structures, the amendments also sought to deepen democracy by ensuring that hitherto excluded social groups like women, SC, and ST were adequately represented in these bodies. The amendments provided, therefore, reservations for all these social groups, with the condition that no less than a third of the seats (including those reserved for women belonging to the SC and the ST communities) be reserved for women. While reservations for women in panchayati raj institutions have set in motion a process of political and economic self-determination for women at local levels, embodying what is called empowerment for women, the representation of women in the Lok Sabha has remained remarkably low, ranging from an average of 5 per cent till the 1990s, when it increased to an average of 8 per cent, to 8.8 per cent in 1999, coming down to 8.26 per cent in 2004 and climbing to 10.8 per cent in 2009.

By the time of the general elections of 1996, women's organizations put forward a joint demand to all political parties for reservation of seats for women in state assemblies and Parliament. The major parties supported the demand, although they themselves gave less than 15 per cent of their total tickets to women. The Women's Reservation Bill, which was first tabled in Parliament in 1996, has been mired in controversies and opposed by parties representing the interests of backward castes and classes, who fear that reservation for women would eventually lead to the erosion of their gains by middle and upper class and upper caste women. Notwithstanding differences in opinion, enhancing women's representation in Parliament and other political/elected bodies through reservation has continued to be a significant element on the women's movement's agenda.[11] While women's groups have held differing positions, and organizations like the Shetkari Mahila Aghadi, a peasant women's

organization opposing reservations, is apprehensive of the way in which the debate 'seemed to have set (mainly upper caste) feminists against (mainly male) OBC leaders' (Omvedt 2000), women's groups have steadfastly resisted caste-based 'quota within quota', on the ground that it signifies the introduction of a principle which does not apply equally to the 'men's seats'. The resistance, however, manifests an attempt to put forward 'women' as a unified political subject and the networks of support generated for the campaign reflect a broad political and social base.

It is interesting how networks and 'radical alliances', which have become critical both for waging successful campaigns and for claiming representativeness and legitimacy for such campaigns, lead us to the second issue that has yet again become crucial for the women's movement in contemporary times—the question of autonomy. Historically, networks have emerged organically from women's groups as large organizations, such as AIDWA, MDS, All India Coordination Committee for Working Women, and the Joint Women's Programme (JWP), with branches in different parts of the country. Women's groups have also come together for joint action despite differences in ideology and organizational perspective on specific issues. The emergence of the two informal national fora—Forum for Women and Politics (FWP) and the Forum of National Women's Organization (FNWO)—in the 1990s reflects this trend. The FNWO comprises AIDWA, AIWC, Centre for Women's Development Studies (CWDS), MDS, NFIW, and YWCA. Each of these organizations has promoted lateral networks, making efforts to bring their members together through regular visits, workshops, conventions, and campaigns. The FWP, on the other hand, comprises of autonomous women's groups such as Jagori, Saheli, JWP, Ankur, Action India, Sabla Sangh, Shaktishalini, Kali for Women, and Purogami Mahila Sangathan (Ramaswamy 1997: 191–2).

By the 1990s, however, in the context of the liberalization of the economy and the abdication of 'social' responsibilities by the state to non-governmental organizations (NGOs), there has been a proliferation of autonomous organizations running on funds from government and international bodies.

Growth of networks for campaigns on specific issues has been facilitated by funding agencies through NGOs with specialized, narrowly defined agendas. Thus, periodically, several networks seem to come alive as they coalesce, react to specific issues, and subsequently relapse into inaction till another issue propels them into action (Chakravarty 2005). The manner in which this NGO-facilitated activism has claimed the political space has led to a filtering out of women's issues from the public domain into a depoliticized and domesticated domain of negotiations and welfare. Against this background, the idea of democratization through empowerment envisaged by the women's movement's critique of the development process in the 1980s, has undergone change. Referring to the process as it was expected to unfold at the grassroots, empowerment was construed as a range of activities from individual self-assertion to collective resistance, a process aimed at changing the nature and direction of systemic forces that marginalize women and other disadvantaged sections (Sharma 1991–2: 21). In the context of the new economic policies unleashed since the 1990s, empowerment has become a prerequisite for productive investment serving the 'present global drive of western capitalism' (Mohanty 1995). Under these circumstances of the NGO-ization of the women's movement (Menon 2000: 3839), women's groups have been pushed into rethinking autonomy in their search for radical political alliances and solidarity.

The questions of autonomy in the autonomous women's movement, as discussed earlier, had been framed by issues pertaining to a way of acting without the restrictions imposed by structures, institutions, ideologies of domination, and as an organizational principle undergirding the ways in which women's groups established themselves as distinct from women's wings of political parties (Chakravarty 2005). These frameworks of autonomy, it has now increasingly been felt, are no longer significant or relevant for the viability of the women's movements as a truly autonomous force. The Seventh National Conference of Autonomous Women's Movements in Kolkata highlighted this change in the notion of autonomy, and feminist solidarities in a neo-liberal context. The changed perspective on autonomy has been compelled by a critical examination of the global economic and political developments that have created new hierarchies in a rapidly changing world, a growing disgruntlement with transient issue-based campaigns and coalitions of NGOs, and the need to plan and execute enduring interventions with transformative goals.[12]

CONCLUSION

Over the years, the women's movement in India has grappled with issues that have required the delineation of a unified feminist political subject and a feminist politics, while simultaneously taking into account the different and layered lived experiences of women. Within the movement itself, the need to evolve a specifically feminist understanding and critique of women's oppression has jostled with perspectives that see women's issues as inextricably embedded in broader issues of democratic change, or those that see the struggle against women's oppression as one which has to be fought in diverse, and sometimes disparate, locations of domination. The women's movement, therefore, exhibits both ideological diversity and a continual effort to build radical alliances within and outside the movement in a concerted struggle for liberatory change. Successive churnings within the movement have alerted it to the political and ideological dangers of putting forward 'women' as a unified category. A unified, collective body of women—as agents and subjects of liberatory change—proves elusive as it attempts to homogenize distinct entities, ironically within an abstracted category of universal woman. Within a plural society and the differential life experiences of women, spaces for women's politics emerge in dispersed locations and in response to diverse forms of oppression such as caste, class, religion, race, and the like. The struggles of women in their own local conditions demarcate in precise terms the domain in which they could usher in change and over which they could exercise control. At the same time, however, as common and integral components of various movements—peasant, tribal, Dalit, and environmental—women also become conduits for building alliances among movements.

The retraction from articulating the abstract hegemonic woman as the universal feminist subject marked the opening up of spaces for recognizing the differences of caste, class, and community among women. It also provides the basis for a feminist understanding of lived experiences of women at the intersections along these axes, and the idea of a feminist politics that involves the logic of encompassment whereby differences are seen to follow a dialectical hierarchy. While leading to an absolute and universal value of emancipation, difference is retained as a higher value, propelling the movement forward. It is this logic of encompassment that may be seen as embodied in the different strands along which the women's movement has emerged, and the issues that have taken priority at specific moments. Also, it is in the nature of encompassment that the women's movement has not unfolded as a discrete movement, but exists in an interlocking relationship of radical alliances with other social movements and socially progressive forces at the grassroots, where, too, women constitute a significant group. Such a relationship not only helps sharpen feminist politics, it dispels allegations of non-representativeness of the movement, and opens up grounds for a common struggle against domination.

NOTES

1. Kamala Visweswaran calls these moments the thematic and problematic of Indian feminism with western, referring to the times when Indian feminists concurred or disagreed with their western counterparts, respectively (1990, p. 32).

2. Among the first public expositions of this position was the report of the National Planning Committee set up in 1937, when the Congress assumed responsibility of government in several provinces. While elaborating its proposal to enhance 'every aspect of women's life and work' to realize 'an equal status and opportunity for women', the report staked claims to equality on the basis of the 'special' contribution women made to the nation and community as 'reproducers' and 'sustainers', 'as the guardians and trustees of future generations'. Even when it asked for 'economic liberty' and the 'right to mould her social and economic life in any way she chooses', which involved the 'reorganisation' of the 'functions which nature and society [have] imposed on her', the Committee declared that it did not intend to enter into a confrontation with 'traditions' which, in the past, had contributed to the happiness and progress of the individual: '... We do not wish to turn women into a cheap imitation of man or to render her useless for the great tasks of motherhood and nation-building' (WRPE 1947, pp. 32–3).

3. The issue of rape formed the core of a widespread campaign by women during 1979–80, which was brought to a head by the Mathura rape case in which the Supreme Court acquitted the policemen involved in the rape of a minor tribal girl. The campaign led to some significant changes in the Evidence Act, the CrPC, and the Indian Penal Code, including the introduction of the category of custodial rape. Women's groups remain dissatisfied with the definition of rape, which does not extend to include marital rape, and is based on assumptions of consent in marriage, the consideration of the 'character' of the victim in rape cases, the notion of 'temptation'—rape as a crime of passion. This is compounded by the inefficiency and unwillingness of the police to gather evidence in rape cases.

4. An outcome of women's struggles has been the amendment in the criminal law—Section 498A of CrPC, which encompassed for the first time a definition of cruelty that included mental cruelty.

5. Ray (2000) has shown how in what she describes as the hegemonic political field of Kolkata emanating from the predominance of a powerful and monolithic Left culture and the organizational machinery of the ruling Communist Party, the Paschim Banga Ganatantrik Mahila Samiti (PBGMS)—the women's organization affiliated to the CPI(M) and the state branch of the All India Democratic Women's Association (AIDWA)—while itself a subordinate actor in the politics of the state, was the dominant women's group. Sachetana, an autonomous women's group of academics and development workers formed in 1981—the same year as PBGMS—remained ideologically constrained and dependent on the PBGMS. On the other hand, Mumbai's political field, characterized by a heterogeneous political culture, allowed women's organizations to coexist in their separate spaces with numerous other social movements. In such a field the FAOW, an autonomous women's group could become a dominant women's group, despite its lack of mass base and affiliation to state power, because of its ability to coalesce the feminist discourse in Mumbai. Moreover, the Janwadi Mahila Sangathan (JMS), a sister organization in Mumbai of the PBGMS, while subordinate to the FAOW, in comparison to the PBGMS in Kolkata, could garner more ideological space on gender issues.

6. In Mumbai, on 25 December 2003, the Dalit Bahujan Mahila Vicharmanch publicly set aflame the Manusmriti at the historic Chaityabhoomi. Despite their

varying ideological positions many of these organizations have formed stable alliances on several issues such as that of commemorating 25 December as Bharatiya Stree Mukti Divas and reservation for OBC women (quota within quotas) in the Eighty-first Amendment Bill.

7. On 23 April 1985, the Supreme Court of India in the *Mohammed Ahmed Khan vs Shah Bano Begum* case gave divorced Muslim women the right to life-long maintenance under Article 125 of the Indian Criminal Procedure Code. Mohammed Khan, Shah Bano's ex-husband, had contested her claims for maintenance, insisting that he had, according to Muslim personal law, supported her for three months after their divorce. The Supreme Court stressed that there was no conflict between its verdict and the provisions of Muslim personal law, which, in its view, also entitled women to alimony if they were unable to maintain themselves. The Court further advised that the Muslim community take 'a lead in the matter of reform of their personal law', and that a UCC be formulated to 'help the cause of national integration'. The decision sparked off a nation-wide controversy on the question of religious personal law, and the desirability or otherwise of a UCC. See Mani (1989, p. 119). For details of the Supreme Court decision and the circumstances in which the Muslim Women's Bill was enacted, as well as the agitations which accompanied the two, see Kumar (1993, pp. 160–71).

8. The Muslim Women's (Protection of Rights on Divorce) Bill 1986, excluded Muslim women from the purview of Section 125, stating that the obligation of their husband to maintain them ended with the three-month *iddat* period, after which their families would have to support them, and failing that, the local *waqf* board.

9. Many Muslims who had earlier supported change in personal laws now began upholding those laws. The Committee for the Protection of the Rights of Muslim Women, which was formed to oppose the Bill, limited its members to Muslims.

10. Paola Bacchetta calls the Sevikas' activism a 'specifically feminine Hindu nationalist discourse', seeing the Sevikas not as women in complete complicity with men in the 'awakening of Hindutva', but as ideologues with a differential imaginary of the Hindu nation. However, even as she identifies the ways in which the Rashtriya Sevika Samiti is able to carve out a relatively autonomous discourse, Bacchetta is careful to point out that the domain of autonomy does not hold a potential for transformative or emancipatory politics for women (Bacchetta 2004).

11. For the intricacies of the debates surrounding the issue in the women's movement, see John (2000) and Menon (2000).

12. This, however, may not detract attention from the fact that the period has seen a concerted effort for equality for women in law. Successful campaigns for amendments in existing Hindu Succession Act, and the adoption in 2005 of a Domestic Violence Bill, bear evidence of effective networking by women's groups.

REFERENCES

Agnihotri, Indu and Vina Mazumdar. 2005. 'Changing Terms of Political Discourse: Women's Movement in India, 1970-1990s', in Mala Khullar (ed.), *Writing the Women's Movement: A Reader*. New Delhi: Zubaan, pp. 48–79.

Bacchetta, Paola. 2004. *Gender in the Hindu Nation: RSS Women as Ideologues*. New Delhi: Women Unlimited.

Chakravarty, Uma. 2005. 'How Autonomous in the Autonomous Women's Movement', *Samyukta: A Journal of Women's Studies*, V(2), pp. 40–60.

Chatterjee, Partha. 1994. *The Nation and its Fragments: Colonial and Postcolonial Histories*. New Delhi: Oxford University Press.

Gothoskar, Sujata, Vithubhai Patel, Vibhuti Patel, and Carol Wolkowitz. 1982. 'Documents from the Indian Women's Movement', *Feminist Review*, No. 12, pp. 92–103.

Hussain, Sabiha. 2006. 'Local Customary Justice: Muslim Women and Shariat Law', Paper presented at the Workshop on 'Women's Movement's Engagement With the Law', organized by the Centre For Women's Development Studies, New Delhi, 20–21 March.

John, Mary E. 2000. 'Alternate Modernities? Reservations and Women's Movement in 20th Century India', *Economic and Political Weekly*, XXXV(43 and 44), pp. 3822–9.

Kumar, Radha. 1993. *History of Doing*. New Delhi: Kali for Women.

———. 1989. 'Contemporary Indian Feminism', *Feminist Review*, No. 33, pp. 20–9.

Mani, Lata. 1989. 'Contentious Traditions: The Debate on Sati in Colonial India', in Kumkum Sangari and Sudesh Vaid (eds), *Recasting Women: Essays in Colonial History*. New Delhi: Kali for Women, pp. 88–126.

Mazumdar, Vina and Indu Agnihotri. 1999. 'The Women's Movement in India: Emergence of a New Perspective', in Bharati Ray and Aparna Basu (eds), *From Independence towards Freedom: Indian Women since 1947*. New Delhi: Oxford University Press, pp. 221–38.

Menon, Nivedita. 2000. 'Elusive "Woman": Feminism and Women's Reservation Bill', *Economic and Political Weekly*, XXXV(43 and 44), pp. 3835–44.

———. 1998. 'Women and Citizenship', in Partha Chatterjee (ed.), *Wages of Freedom*. New Delhi: Oxford University Press, pp. 241–66.

Mohanty, Manoranjan. 1995. 'On the Concept of Empowerment', *Economic and Political Weekly*, XXX(24), pp. 1434–6.

Omvedt, Gail. 2000. 'Women and PR', *The Hindu*, 12 September.

Raman, Vasanthi. 1999. 'The Women's Question in Contemporary Indian Politics', Paper presented at a workshop on 'In Search of Democratic Spaces', organized by Lokayan, Delhi, in collaboration with the Society for International Development, Rome, New Delhi, March.

Ramaswamy, Uma. 1997. 'Organising with a Gender Perspective', in Ruddar Datt (ed.), *Organising the Unorganised Workers*. New Delhi: Vikas, pp. 161–209.

Ray, Raka. 2000. *Fields of Protest: Women's Movement in India*. New Delhi: Kali for Women.

Rege, Sharmila. 2006. *Writing Caste/Writing Gender: Reading Dalit Women's Testimonies*. New Delhi: Zubaan.
———. 1998. 'Dalit Women Talk Differently: A Critique of Difference and Towards a Dalit Feminist Standpoint', *Economic and Political Weekly*, XXXIII(44): WS 39–WS 48.

Sarkar, Tanika. 1996. 'Hindu Women: Politicisation Through Communalisation', in Kumar Rupesinghe and Khawar Mumtaz (eds), *Internal Conflict in South Asia*. London: Sage Publications, pp. 131–43.

Sharma, Kumud. 1991–2. 'Grassroots Organisations and Women's Empowerment: Some Issues in the Contemporary debate', *Samya Shakti*, Vol. 6, New Delhi: CWDS, pp. 28–44.

Tharu, Susie and Tejaswini Niranjana. 1996. 'Problems of a Contemporary Theory of Gender', in Shahid Amin and Dipesh Chakrabarty (eds), *Subaltern Studies IX*. New Delhi: Oxford University Press, pp. 232–60.

Visweswaran, Kamala. 1990. 'Family Subjects: An Ethnography of the "Women's Question" in Indian Nationalism', PhD dissertation, Stanford University.

WRPE. 1947. *Report of the Sub-Committee on Women's Role in Planned Economy*. Bombay: Vora and Company (National Planning Committee Series).

28 Non-governmental Organizations

Rob Jenkins

Analysing the relationship between non-governmental organizations (NGOs) and Indian politics is a fraught task. Considerable terminological confusion afflicts the sizeable literature on India's NGOs. There is also a long history to be considered: India's 'modern' voluntary sector, broadly conceived, goes back to at least the late nineteenth century. Disagreements over its relationship to political activity were present from the start. Just to complicate matters, discussions of NGOs are often subsumed within the larger discourse of 'civil society'.

Since the idea of civil society is so ubiquitous, it is as good a place as any to begin the discussion of the role of NGOs in Indian politics. What civil society is and is not, whether it is culture-bound, how it arises, whether it can be promoted, what purposes it serves, whether a transnational variety is emerging—none of these questions have generated anything remotely resembling consensus. The conceptions of Locke, Marx, Gramsci, and others jostle for pre-eminence. Political theorists question the liberal assumptions often smuggled into contemporary definitions of civil society.

Development agencies debate the practical utility of the idea of civil society. Members of civil society themselves cannot agree on where its boundaries lie, and therefore, who is included within its ranks.

Amidst the conceptual ambiguity, Kaviraj has traced a common thread running through almost all the accounts of civil society: their definitions are 'based on dichotomies or contrasts'. Civil society is variously 'defined through its opposition to "natural society" or "state of nature" in early modern contract theory...; against the state in the entire liberal tradition, and contrasted to community (*Gemeinschaft*) in a theoretical tradition of modern sociology'. Civil society thus 'appears to be an idea strangely incapable of standing freely on its own' (Kaviraj 2001: 288).

NGOs—like civil society generally—are frequently located conceptually within more than just one dichotomy. In the usage that predominates in India's contemporary political discourse, an NGO is not just a non-state actor; depending on who is doing the defining, there are any number of things that NGOs are not. They are not political parties; they are not social movements; they are not Labour Unions;

they are not even, according to some critics, agents of popular struggle at all. Indeed, apart from its status as an entity distinct from the government, existing within a realm of associational freedom, the Indian NGO's defining characteristic is its *constitutional inability to engage in politics*—except, it would seem, as an unwitting tool of larger forces (Ndegwa 1996). Or so the NGOs' myriad detractors would have us believe.

This essay explores two paradoxical implications of this widespread, though of course not universal, characterization. The first is that despite their ostensible location in the non-political domain of civil society, NGOs have over the past forty years ended up playing a central, if indirect, role in India's politics. They have increasingly served as a crucial reference point, a kind of photographic negative against which other actors—party leaders, movement figures, union representatives—have sought, by contrast, to define themselves and imagine their own distinctiveness. This has invested NGOs and their actions with far more political significance than might otherwise have been the case.

The second paradox is that the more vigorously these other political actors have sought to differentiate themselves from the NGO sector, the less tangible have become the boundaries separating them from their NGO colleagues. By articulating their critique of India's NGOs through a series of stark, value-laden dichotomies, their detractors have provided a powerful incentive for NGOs to reinvent themselves. The result has been experimental cross-breeds with other species of civic association, creating new organizational hybrids. This, combined with profound institutional change in the structure of the Indian political system, has over the past two decades led to a more direct role for NGOs in India's politics.

TERMINOLOGICAL CONFUSION

What is an NGO? This question has been answered in a variety of ways in India. Internationally recognized definitions are often a starting point, but rarely a final destination. Most international institutions recognize that the term NGO encompasses a wide variety of organizational forms. A key World Bank operational document—1995's *Working with NGOs*—defined

NGOs as 'private organizations that pursue activities to relieve suffering, promote the interests of the poor, protect the environment, provide basic social services or undertake community development'(World Bank 1995: 7). This is broadly consistent with popular usage. NGOs are generally associated with charitable activities that promote the public good rather than, as with business associations or Labour Unions, advancing private interests.

Most definitions for NGOs include a list of the organizational forms they can take, based on the terms used by associations to describe themselves. These include 'community-based organizations', 'grassroots organizations', 'self-help groups', 'credit societies', and so forth. There is much disagreement as to whether each subcategory qualifies as an NGO—are credit societies about the public interest?—or whether a group's self-description is sufficient to determine its classification. Some groups that call themselves grassroots organizations may in fact have very little demonstrable following among ordinary people, raising the question of whether it is feasible to set objective criteria for defining any organization that describes itself with as vague a prefix as 'mass-based', 'grassroots', or 'people's'.

Efforts to stipulate meaningful criteria to distinguish NGOs from other forms of civil society, or to distinguish one type of NGO from another, quickly run into trouble. In one of the most systematic (and in many ways admirable) accounts of India's NGO sector, Sen distinguishes NGOs from community-based organizations (CBOs) and what he calls grassroots organizations (GROs), stating that CBOs and GROs are membership-based, whereas NGOs are not (Sen 1999). He then qualifies this statement in recognition of the fact that regulations governing various NGOs as legal entities (societies, charitable trusts, non-profit corporations) often require officials of such organizations to be members.

Sen draws on the international literature (Farrington *et al.* 1993; Korten 1990) to arrive at a definition flexible enough to accommodate the Indian context:

> In India, NGOs can be defined as organizations that are generally formed by professionals or quasi professionals from the middle or lower middle class,

either to serve or work with the poor, or to channel financial support to community-based or grassroots organizations. (Sen 1999: 332)

Community-based organizations, on the other hand, are composed of 'the poor' or 'the low-income community'—a valiant attempt at conveying the general usage in the development field, but one that inevitably sidesteps uncomfortable questions, such as what middle-class neighbourhood associations should be called. Moreover, many NGOs contest the idea that they were 'formed by' middle-class people. In the end, despite differentiating NGOs from CBOs and GROs, Sen cannot avoid, for practical reasons, including the latter two within 'the universe' of NGOs either.

Partly because defining an NGO is so tricky, data on the size of the NGO sector is similarly variable. One longstanding NGO network, the Society for Participatory Research in Asia (PRIA), estimated the number of NGOs in India in 2001 at 1.5 million. One PRIA survey found that almost three-quarters of NGOs have one or fewer paid staff, and that nearly 90 per cent of NGOs have fewer than five members of staff.[1] Raina, however, cites a figure of 200,000 Indian NGOs (Raina 2004). Statistics compiled by the Home Ministry indicate that in 2000–1 nearly 20,000 organizations were registered under the Foreign Contribution Regulation Act 1976, though only 13,800 submitted their accounts to the government as required. The total foreign funds received by these groups increased by more than 25 per cent between 1998–9 and 2000–1, from Rs 34 billion to Rs 45 billion.[2]

While it is difficult to arrive at a consistent and theoretically satisfying set of criteria that would allow us to impose precise boundaries around the NGO sector of civil society, a rough-and-ready practical definition exists, and is in widespread use. In common parlance throughout India's 'activist' community (which I take to include all people working for social change, regardless of the types of organizations with which they are affiliated, so long as they are not state employees), *public-interest groups that are not 'people's movements' are regarded as NGOs.*

The distinction is often contested, not least by avowedly 'movement' groups eager to avoid the 'NGO' label, which confers an establishment status with which many activists do not wish to be associated. Using the term NGO to refer to a group that describes itself as a people's organization is usually a not-so-subtle form of denigration. The 'movement' descriptor is prized as a symbol of political legitimacy, not in the sense of representing widespread mainstream acceptance, but in terms of a group's commitment to a radical form of political engagement, the precise content of which inevitably varies from one context to the next. The NGO label connotes an *a*political (or worse, *non*-political, or even *de*politici*zing*) form of social action.

The origins of what might thus be called 'movement populism'—the idea that more formal organizational forms are alienated from ordinary people's concerns and perpetuate elite biases—lay in the widespread discrediting of NGOs that has taken place in India since the early 1980s. However, before outlining the basis for these critiques of India's NGOs, we must return to the age of NGO innocence. Given the extent of their recent demonization, it is not surprising that NGOs once enjoyed a golden era, before their fall from grace.

NGOs AND NARRATIVES OF INDIAN DEMOCRACY

NGOs have figured prominently in many well-rehearsed narratives about the trajectory of India's democracy. These frequently involve a fall-from-grace element. Sheth and Sethi's account of the 'historical context' of the 'NGO sector' nicely encapsulates the dominant themes:

> the conversion of voluntarism into primarily a favoured instrumentality for developmental intervention has changed what was once an organic part of civil society into merely a sector—an appendage of the developmental apparatus of the state. Further, this process of instrumental appropriation has resulted in these agencies of self-activity losing both their autonomy and political-transformative edge. (Sheth and Sethi 1991)

How India's progressive intelligentsia has viewed the country's NGOs—particularly their potential contribution to an alternative form of politics—has varied considerably over the past forty years. It is because there is such variety among NGOs, and considerable diversity even among the broadly Left-leaning intelligentsia, that there are no unambiguous patterns. But broadly speaking, during much of the 1970s, intellectuals invested great hope in the country's NGOs as a force for the reinvigoration of democracy. The prevailing tendency at the time was not to distinguish too minutely between organizational forms or to split hairs over the descriptive terms applied to individual groups, both of which were later to become standard practice. Analysts seeking to understand the significance of these new 'social action groups' for Indian democracy quickly embraced the term devised to encompass such diversity: 'non-party political formations'(Kothari 1984).

The emergence in the early 1970s of a tangible sense of optimism about the NGOs' potential to play a major role in democracy's reinvigoration coincided with other important political trends. The most notable was the creeping authoritarianism of Prime Minister Indira Gandhi. She had abolished Congress's intra-party elections, following her triumphs against, first, the Congress old guard that had sought to tame her, and second, the Pakistani army during the 1971 war that created an independent Bangladesh. The movement that opposed Mrs Gandhi's increasingly personalized form of rule, her anti-Union policies, and her attacks on judicial independence—among other things—included within its ranks a large number of NGOs. Several of these traced their lineages back to Mahatma Gandhi, and adopted a Gandhian vocabulary and repertoire of tactics. Many people who would later form the mainstay of India's social activist community entered this porous field in response to a major drought in eastern Indian in the mid-1960s, at which time they emerged as articulate spokespersons for an alternative form of political engagement, even as they organized and delivered vital relief services.

The civic flowering that ensued was celebrated as a democratic rebirth. It was also widely explained as a response to the failure of India's formal political process, still dominated by elite groups, to address the pressing concerns of poor and marginalized people. The mushrooming of India's NGOs was seen as substituting for the failure of India's other democratic institutions—particularly its parties—to provide

avenues of political engagement. 'Environmental action groups' such as the Dasholi Gram Swaraj Sangh, which kick-started the Chipko Andolan in the early 1970s, were supposed to help pick up some of the institutional slack. Rajni Kothari was among the earliest and most eloquent spokespersons for this view, but an entire generation of intellectuals and activists invested enormous hope in the capacity of non-party political formations to transform the nature of politics, and to extend democracy to constituencies that had not been active participants (Sethi 1984; Sheth 1984). This was a theme that continued long after the love affair with the voluntary sector fizzled.

However, it was not just the 'weakness' of party organizations against which Sethi (1993) and other writers were reacting, but their 'strength' as well. For much of the post-Independence period, party-affiliated civic groups have dominated the political space that should have served as the natural home for alternative politics. The front organizations connected to every political party—women's wings, student federations, Trade Unions, farmers' associations—usually lacked autonomy (Rudolph and Rudolph 1987). As India's voluntary sector came of age in the early 1970s, it faced the task of transcending the partisan divisions that ran throughout civil society.

The high point of the NGOs' political role, the moment that appeared most strongly to redeem their promise, was the internal Emergency imposed by Mrs Gandhi from 1975 to 1977. NGOs were a crucial part of the nationwide protest agitations that led her to declare the Emergency (Brass 1990). During the Emergency itself, NGO leaders were imprisoned, along with more traditional (that is, partisan) political figures. The Foreign Contribution Regulation Act (FCRA) 1976, enacted at the height of Mrs Gandhi's paranoia about external subversion—the 'foreign hand'—allowed her government to deny access to foreign funding to NGOs considered likely to threaten 'the sovereignty and integrity of India, the public interest, freedom or fairness of election to any legislature, friendly relations with any foreign state, harmony between religious, racial, linguistic or regional groups, castes or communities'. This wide, though by now restated, remit continues to provide ample opportunity for government intimidation of

NGOs, and of course scope for considerable rent-seeking. NGOs also contributed to the political mobilization that helped to bring the Emergency to an end, and many were outright supporters of, or even incorporated within, opposition parties that brought about Mrs Gandhi's defeat in the 1977 general election that followed.

As the rickety Janata coalition government assumed power in 1977, there was more than a hint of Gandhian *schadenfreude* in the air: dispersed voluntary groups were cast as having rescued democracy from the havoc wrought by Nehru's legacy—not just his daughter's personalistic rule, but the entire top-down, state-centric approach to social and economic change. It was during the Janata government that a range of rural development programmes and participatory techniques pioneered by NGOs were incorporated within state policy (Franda 1983). Revisionists seek to discount the importance of NGOs in the events surrounding the Emergency, preferring to attribute the key role to movements rather than to NGOs. This, however, is to impose an anachronistic distinction that possessed none of the connotations that arose subsequently.

By the time Indira Gandhi began her second stint in office in 1980, her approach to the voluntary sector had become considerably more complex. On the one hand, she associated this constituency with those who had brought about her political downfall. Her government appointed the infamous Kudal Commission, which investigated a large number of NGOs—particularly Gandhian organizations—and exerted a chilling effect on many others. On the other hand, Mrs Gandhi had become severely disillusioned with the state's potential for effecting social change (Kohli 1990). It was under Indira Gandhi that India's movement towards a liberalized economy began, though this trend would assume more concrete form under her son Rajiv, and especially under Prime Minister Narasimha Rao from 1991.[3] Mrs Gandhi, and Rajiv even more so, embraced the idea of an NGO-led 'third sector' as a complement to government agencies and private business.

Once NGOs had received even lukewarm endorsement by the Congress establishment, it was perhaps inevitable that a major split within the larger

voluntary sector should occur. This is not to imply that conflicts were not already rife. But whereas previously the divisions were between various Gandhian sects, particularly between those that had grown close to the state and those that had remained relatively aloof, and between Gandhian and non-Gandhian organizations, the kind of overarching master cleavage alluded to earlier, between the political and non-political, had yet to assume its later, epic proportions. Ironically, it was not just from the right—for this is what Mrs Gandhi had come to represent—but from the left as well that the NGOs would be hit.

THE BACKLASH AGAINST NGOs

As the 1980s progressed, complaints about the NGO sector began to accumulate, the voices of dissent coming increasingly from within the broadly defined field of civic activism. NGOs were seen to have lost their radical edge. When exactly the rot set in, what the nature of the ills were, and why it all went wrong varies according to which critics one reads.[4] But a common theme is that the NGO field ossified. Existing organizations became bureaucratized, either directly subverted by establishment interests or undermined by the loss of vigour among activists grown older and more risk-averse. In addition, both new and existing organizations became magnets for youthful new arrivals, for whom activism was, in the words of their critics, just a career path. Slowly but surely, according to this widely repeated view, NGOs were stripped of their ability to mobilize people to take political stands on controversial issues.

There is undoubted truth in this general plot line, and its basic ingredients do not vary hugely from the narratives of organizational decline recounted by 1960s radicals in Europe or North America. Organizations such as the Association of Voluntary Agencies for Rural Development (AVARD), and the myriad groups of which it is composed, are sometimes cited in this connection. In later versions of this story, so too are organizations such as the Social Work and Research Centre (SWRC) in Tilonia, Rajasthan. Ironically, it was the SWRC's Bunker Roy who was among those who had sought in the mid-1980s to do something about the declining reputation of the

NGO field, which had suffered from the entry of less altruistic operators (Roy 1988). For his pains, Roy was rewarded with the charge of cosying up to powerful political patrons and seeking to control the NGO sector (Tandon 1986).

Arguably, what caused the dispersed grumbling about the role of NGOs to solidify into a lasting critique, which continues to resonate with many people a quarter century later, was a 1984 broadside issued by Prakash Karat of the Communist Party of India-Marxist (CPI[M]). Karat's article, 'Action Groups/Voluntary Organizations: A Factor in Imperialist Strategy', was published in the CPI(M) journal *The Marxist*, and subsequently appeared in book form (Karat 1988). Karat claimed the existence of 'a sophisticated and comprehensive strategy worked out in imperialist quarters to harness the forces of voluntary agencies/action groups to their strategic design to penetrate Indian society and influence its course of development'. The 'left forces' were advised 'to take serious note of this arm of imperialist penetration'. This would require, among other things, 'an ideological offensive to rebut the philosophy propagated by these groups', not least because 'it tends to attract petty bourgeois youth imbued with idealism'(Karat 1988: 2–3).

Since Karat's seminal contribution is often cited, although without much attention to its detailed content, it is worth noting a few salient features of his analysis. First, while Karat's focus was on the foreign funding of NGOs, his sights were just as firmly trained on those whose ideological support for the voluntary sector lent it what he considered spurious legitimacy. Second, because he stressed this ideological dimension, Karat's targets were not just development agencies, but academics as well, and because academics were represented as an intrinsic component of 'imperialism', a notion he invested with a definite agency of its own, Karat condemned not just foreign scholars, but by extension certain Indian academics too. Third, unlike subsequent critics of the NGO phenomenon, Karat did not distinguish much between different types of NGOs, except insofar as their sources of funding were concerned. In fact, his distaste for the entire 'social action' phenomenon, which he blamed for what he saw as widespread

political *in*action, was never far from the surface. In Karat's black-and-white world, 'the whole voluntary agencies/action groups network is maintained and nurtured' by external funds (Karat 1988: 34).

Upon closer examination, it is clear that Karat's eagerness to attribute the rise of the NGO sector to imperialist forces stems mainly from political self-interest: Karat's narrative of foreign subversion (the mirror image of Mrs Gandhi's 'foreign hand') casts both Karat himself and the Left in general as victims. International funding agencies were using NGOs 'as a vehicle to counter and disrupt the potential of the Left movement' (ibid.: 2), which apparently the imperialists recognized as the staunchest protectors of India's sovereignty. In other words, the main target of this ideological manifestation of imperialist aggression was none other than Karat's own CPI(M).

The excesses of Karat's theory—not the legitimate concern that foreign funding may undermine the responsiveness of grassroots organizations to local articulations of need—served to absolve the Left parties of their manifest failure to mobilize the great mass of marginalized Indians into a sustained political force in most parts of the country. Karat was arguing, in effect, that Kothari and others had it wrong: people were not turning to non-party formations because India's party system offered them no meaningful choice. The problem, as India's industrialists would claim a decade later when faced with foreign competition, was the lack of a level playing field. The NGO sector, which was poaching on the Communists' political turf, had access to cheap sources of finance whereas Left parties did not. Karat's proposal was to strengthen the FCRA such that '[a]ll voluntary organizations which claim to organise people for whatever form of political activity should be included in the list of organisations (just as political parties) which are prohibited from receiving foreign funds' (Karat 1988: 64).

The self-serving nature of Karat's plea has not prevented it from becoming the prevailing discourse among social activists since the late 1980s. Karat's dictum—that 'those organisations receiving foreign funds are automatically suspect' and 'must be screened to clear their bonafides'(ibid.)—was incorporated not only into the official state oversight process (the

Home Ministry's implementation of the amended FCRA), it also increasingly manifested itself in the informal ideological litmus test applied by social activists themselves. In such a context, it is not surprising that civic groups would take elaborate measures to avoid *direct* contact with foreign funders, giving rise to an intermediary resource-channelling sub-sector, which—in a self-fulfilling prophecy—would come to be widely seen as synonymous with the entire NGO sector. This marks the origin of the contemporary meaning of NGO, both in Sen's value-neutral definition, which stresses the 'channeling of funding' to grassroots and community groups, and in its pejorative sense—the NGO label deployed as a term of abuse by one civic group against another.

Karat's call to mount 'a sustained ideological campaign against the eclectic and pseudo-radical postures of action groups' (Karat 1988: 65) was taken up with gusto, resolving itself along the now-familiar movement-NGO dichotomy. Thus, movements worked at the grassroots, while NGOs were office-based. Movements were radical, NGOs reformist. Movements sought people's empowerment; NGOs made the poor dependent on charity.[5] Movements were political, NGOs depoliticizing.

In an article published in 2002, environmental activist Dunu Roy, too, cites 1984 as a watershed in the evolution of India's environmental movement, reminding his readers that it was in that year that Karat published his influential tract. Roy recalls that environmental NGOs were among those criticized by Karat and other Left-party-affiliated intellectuals. Their crime, as Roy summarized the charges levelled against him and his colleagues, was 'being part of an imperialist design of pitting environmental concerns against working class interests'(Roy 2002). Roy argues that this provoked 'a schism between political and apolitical environmentalists'. Here, the divide was not between those affiliated with parties and those in the 'non-party' arena, but between 'action groups' that challenged the state's orthodoxy and 'NGOs' incapable of transcending the conceptual boundaries of the existing paradigm. This pattern of activist one-upmanship has persisted, the use of the NGO sobriquet serving as a marker of the critic's distinctive political position.

The NGOs' critics often plead that they are voices in the wilderness, waging a lonely struggle against an orthodoxy that lauds the beneficial effects of NGOs. As Sangeeta Kamat puts it in her book, *Development Hegemony: NGOs and the State in India*, 'what is clear is that the supporters of voluntary organizations far outstrip their detractors and critics'(Kamat 2002: 21). Convinced that NGOs remain an object of popular and official veneration, *despite more than twenty years of constant vilification at the hands of the state and of other non-party groups*, a wide range of observers continue to fulminate against a position that no one—or at least no one worth arguing with—really propounds. Even Chandhoke, one of the most level-headed analysts in this crowded field, whose book on civil society is filled with lucid observations, warns of trouble ahead 'if we begin to think that civil society is mainly inhabited and represented by non-governmental organizations [NGOs], or indeed that NGOs are synonymous with civil society'(2003: 70–1). It is not clear who *does* think in these terms, but we are assured that 'it is this very notion that forms the stuff of current orthodoxy' (Chandhoke 2003: 71). Perhaps in the 1970s or early 1980s such warnings offered a useful corrective to lazy civic utopianism. But by the early 1990s, and certainly by the twenty-first century, when Kamat's and Chandhoke's books were published, the orthodoxy had moved very much in the opposite direction.

Kamat's catch phrase, 'the NGO-ization of politics', which casts NGOs as agents of depoliticization, captures the current conventional wisdom—that NGOs are the non-political face of civil society, and that their expansion threatens to depoliticize the movement sector. The movement-versus-NGO duality, cast in explicitly zero-sum terms, is now a mainstay of the international development discourse (Petras and Veltmeyer 2001). One of the objectives of the World Bank's Comprehensive Development Framework of the late 1990s—a key element in what has become the Aid Effectiveness Agenda[6]—was to funnel less aid through NGOs, and to focus on building viable state institutions rather than bypassing those that do not work. Misgivings about the NGO sector in the international development community were a major feature of the literature even in the early 1990s (Hulme and Edwards 1995; Smillie 1995).

By 2000, what one British magazine called the 'Backlash Against NGOs' (Bond 2000) was already an established talking point among Western publics. NGOs operating transnationally had become a particular target of criticism.[7] Described as 'interest groups accountable only to themselves', NGOs have been confronted with the question: are 'the champions of the oppressed ... in danger of mirroring the sins of the oppressor?' (ibid.)

STRUGGLE POLITICS, CONSTRUCTIVE WORK, AND THE WRONG KIND OF RIGHTS

Kamat has, however, articulated the NGO-movement dichotomy slightly differently—as a contrast between groups pursuing 'struggle-based politics' and those engaged in 'constructive development'. Influenced by post-modernism, Kamat portrayed the latter group as having bought into the modernist myth of progress, while stumbling headlong into liberalism's political trap of expecting constructive work amidst the poor to give way over time to more radicalized forms of mobilization. This critique is consistent with a long radical tradition which sees running health clinics, schools, livelihood programmes, and so forth as politically disempowering. Mumbai Resistance, a group formed to protest the hijacking by 'NGO celebrities' of the 2004 World Social Forum held in Mumbai, argued that by working to ameliorate suffering, 'NGOs come to the rescue' of the state—declaring it, in effect, 'absolved of all responsibilities'.[8] Moreover, 'the NGOs give employment ... to certain local persons' who 'might be vocal and restive persons, potential opponents of the authorities'.[9] Chandhoke agrees that NGOs undermine radical movements by drawing away from the path of militant resistance that segment of the non-conformist youth that might have been expected to embrace it. And by 'bailing out' government agencies through service-delivery work, NGOs have 'rescued and perhaps legitimized the non-performing state ... [and] neutralized political dissent ...'(Chandhoke 2003: 76).

Kamat's stark struggle-politics-versus-constructive-development dichotomy has two shortcomings. First, it violates one of the key methodological tenets of the post-structuralist school in which she roots her analysis: she frames her analysis in terms of a strict binary opposition, thus committing the mortal sins of 'reifying' social relations and 'essentializing' political identities. Second, Kamat gives short shrift to the tradition in India of combining radical social action with hands-on development. As Mahajan reminds us:

> Gandhiji's first 'satyagraha' in support of the indigo labourers in Chamaparan, while primarily a political struggle, also had elements of voluntary action or 'constructive work' (as Gandhiji called voluntary action), such as training villagers in hygiene, educating children, building roads and digging wells. After this, Gandhiji made constructive work an integral part of his political strategy, where periods of intense struggle for Independence were interspersed with long periods of voluntary action for the alleviation of suffering and social and economic upliftment of the poor. (Mahajan 1997)

Not only do many organizations engage in both struggle-oriented and constructive work, the tendency to see development activities as inherently status-quoist ignores the fact that groups often engage in constructive work precisely in order to challenge the hegemonic 'truths' propagated by official state ideologies. For instance, for some years beginning in the 1990s, the Rajasthan-based Mazdoor Kisan Shakti Sangathan (MKSS) operated a small number of 'fair price' (or 'ration') shops, which sell subsidized commodities such as foodgrains and kerosene. Launching any kind of business initiative was a source of much debate within the MKSS. Some saw it as a costly diversion of scarce energies; others perceived a risk that the group's opponents would portray the MKSS as committed to profiting from, rather than fighting for, the rural poor. The main motivation for running the ration shops was to counter the neoliberal orthodoxy that food subsidy bureaucracies—in India's case the Public Distribution System (PDS)—inevitably produce unacceptable levels of corruption, including diversion of foodgrains to the non-needy. The idea that the PDS was inherently pernicious, that no amount of reform could improve poor people's access to food, was considered a dangerous myth, propagated chiefly by the World Bank. By operating shops in a transparent fashion, the MKSS hoped to demonstrate that it was possible to treat customers fairly and provide a livelihood for the shop's proprietors without resorting to corruption (Jenkins and Goetz 2004).

Clearly, NGOs are in a no-win position when it comes to carving out a more political role. As we have seen, for Mrs Gandhi and the Left parties, NGOs were destabilizing the state; whereas for non-partisan intellectuals—whether liberal or post-modern—they were propping it up. While NGOs have long been branded apolitical, adopting a more confrontational posture has done little to enhance their status among movement populists. One critic complained that whereas 'NGOs earlier restricted themselves to "developmental" activities, they have expanded since the 1980s to "activism" or "advocacy"—funded *political* activity'.[10] The fear is that through 'platforms such as the World Social Forum ... NGOs are being provided an opportunity to legitimise themselves as a political force and expand their influence among sections to which they earlier had little access'.[11]

Where politics is concerned, NGOs are damned if they do and damned if they don't. NGOs that attempt to graduate from a 'welfarist' approach to one based on 'empowerment' are dismissed as dabbling in matters for which they are not qualified (Sen 1999: 333). Human rights NGOs are a particular sore spot. NGOs 'may even have performed a disservice to the idea of human rights', argues Chandhoke, 'because rights have not emerged through the struggles of people, but from the baskets of funding agencies' (2003: 87). The rights discourse has been articulated by elites through 'layers of mediation ... provided by NGOs who are conversant with modes of information gathering'; that NGO workers, in other words, have been, moulded into glorified bureaucrats rather than fighters for the poor (ibid.: 88).

Even when seeking to organize people to demand rights, as opposed to sounding off about rights in international meetings, NGOs are frequently dismissed as driven by a neoliberal project to create individual economic actors rather than politically mobilized collectivities. Kamat claims that when NGOs pursue

a rights agenda, 'their concern is often limited to oppression caused by feudal social relations, and does not refer to capitalist social relations' (Chandhoke 2003: 22). However, almost no evidence is provided to support this claim. Indeed, even foreign-funded NGOs have lent their support to campaigns to curb abuses perpetrated by Western multinationals operating in India and other developing countries.[12]

The no-win situation faced by NGOs is also apparent when they seek to link rights claims to issues of identity. One line of attack claims that '[t]he foreign-funded NGO sector has, with remarkable uniformity, propagated certain political concepts', most notably 'the primacy of "identity" — gender, ethnicity, caste, nationality — over class'.[13] Another, however, argues the opposite—that their disembedded approaches to rights 'ensure that NGOs will ignore issues of ... caste, gender, and environmental justice in their own work'(Kamat 1996). Worst of all, the rights-based work of 'movements' is undermined by '"advocacy NGOs", which ... redirect struggles of the people for basic change from the path of confrontation to that of negotiation, preserving the existing political frame'. The problem, put baldly, is that 'NGOs bureaucratise people's movements'.[14] Though desperately seeking to shed their mainstream essence, NGOs appear doomed to remain intellectually and politically out of their depth.

BLURRING BOUNDARIES AND BRIDGING DIFFERENCES

Despite the persistence of conflicts (and the habit of binary thinking) among activists, some of the old barriers are eroding. Chandhoke argues that 'when they have tied up with oppositional social movements', occasionally 'NGOs have been able to transform political agendas' (2003: 71). The struggle against the Narmada Dam was, for a time, an example of this kind of coming together. Wagle notes that ARCH-Vahini, a Gujarat-based 'voluntary agency ... active in the areas of rural health and development', was said to have 'played an important part in the initial period of the struggle'(Wagle 1997: 437, 457). When ARCH-Vahini and other groups began to question the strategy of the leadersip of the Narmada Bachao Andolan (NBA) however, they were dismissed as insufficiently aware of popular feeling in the area, embodying an 'NGO mindset' (ibid.: 438).

India's hosting of the 2004 World Social Forum (WSF) in Mumbai, for example, revealed a more constructive relationship among different sectors of civil society. Much of the early planning phases suggested that WSF 2004 would provide an occasion for another round of internecine warfare among the various NGO factions, between NGOs and movement groups, among party-affiliated groups, and between party and non-party organizations.[15] There were also groups that chose not to participate, organizing an alternative event under the banner of 'Mumbai Resistance'. Still, WSF 2004 generated considerable common ground, according to Raina, even amidst 'the divisive world of Indian social movements and NGOs' (Raina 2004: 12).[16] Raina noted that approximately 200 organizations (NGOs, movement groups, and others) formed a WSF 2004 steering committee that accommodated a wide variety of organizations and embraced the full spectrum of ideological tendencies.

That even the previously highly doctrinaire CPI(M) has been increasingly willing to join hands with NGOs is one indication of a new spirit of coalition-building. Critics charge the CPI(M) with compromising its earlier principled stand. One report complained that '[i]n a number of forums, CPI(M) members and NGOs now cooperate and share costs—for example, at the People's Health Conference held in Kolkata in 2002, the Asian Social Forum held in Hyderabad in January 2003, or the World Social Forum ... in Mumbai in January 2004'.[17] Another group, the aforementioned Mumbai Resistance collective, was incensed by the 'revisionist' position adopted by Thomas Isaac, then a member of Kerala's Planning Board, during a previous CPI(M)-led government. Isaac's ideological transgression had been to distinguish between *types* of NGOs. Granting the central tenet of Karat's critique—that 'there is a larger imperialist strategy to utilize the so-called voluntary sector to influence civil society in Third World countries'—Isaac argued that

> there are also NGOs and a large number of similar civil society organisations and formations that are essential

ingredients of any social structure. Therefore, while being vigilant about the imperialist designs, we have to distinguish between civil society organisations that are pro-imperialist and pro-globalisation and those that are not....[18]

This was outright heresy for many movement leaders weaned on anti-NGO rhetoric. Critics saw the CPI(M) compromise on NGOs as consistent with the party's compromises on privatization, foreign investment, and other issues, demonstrated by the actions of economically liberalizing CPI(M) state governments in West Bengal and Kerala.

NGOs are, in fact, often eager to support movements. This occurs informally—the provision of meeting space, office help, vehicles—and sometimes in more systematic ways. Local people often fail to distinguish in practice between certain NGOs and their associated movement groups. These can be seen as dual-purpose associations. In Rajasthan, the movement-oriented MKSS is closely linked to the SWRC, clearly an NGO. The movement-like activities of social activist Anna Hazare in Maharashtra are difficult to disentangle from the Hind Swaraj Trust, an NGO that he also helps to run (Jenkins 2004). In Mumbai, the Rationing Kruti Samiti, a formidable movement for accountability in the PDS during the 1990s, was closely interwoven with the activities of an NGO called Apnalaya, but remained organizationally separate. In the northern districts of Karnataka, a similar division of labour characterized the relationship between the India Development Service, which pursues fairly conventional NGO activities, and the Samaj Parivarthan Samudhay, which assumed a militant campaigning role against government and corporate abuses.

Another well-known example is the Shramajeevi Sanghatana, an activist group that spawned an NGO-front organization, the Vidhayak Sansad. These two groups provided the empirical material for Kamat's analysis of 'NGO-ization'. Though she anonymizes the organizations in her text, it is evident that these are the groups discussed.[19] In Kamat's account, it was the establishment of the Vidhayak Sansad that de-radicalized the Shramajeevi Sanghatana. She frames her story as a cautionary tale of inadvertent NGO contagion. It was the Sanghatana's engagement with the Central government agency created to assist and regulate NGOs, Council for Advancement of People's Action and Rural Technology (CAPART) that brought about the movement's tragic demise. To continue working with CAPART, the Sanghatana had to float a conventional NGO—Vidhayak Sansad—to oversee the health, education, and livelihood programmes essential for rehabilitating people freed from bonded labour, the Sanghatanas main field of work. Ultimately, the Sanghatana allegedly began to internalize the norms associated with the NGO's mainstream conception of progress. This manifested itself as what Kamat considered shockingly liberal notions, such as the rule of law and the promotion of science and technology as means of improving people's living conditions.

Kamat cites the case of the Bhoomi Sena (Land Army), 'one of the earliest militant tribal organizations in Maharashtra', as another example of the negative effects wrought by the dual-purpose organizing strategy. A Bhoomi Sena stalwart recounted to Kamat the story of one Sena organizer who

> thought he could take the [foreign donor] money for the activists, and he floated a rural development agency, and told activists you can work for Bhoomi Sena but you can be part of this agency and it will help you take care of your family, so you can dedicate yourself to Bhoomi Sena. Many of our activists became more involved with that work, and this broke the Bhoomi Sena ... (Kamat 2002: 24)

Kamat portrays this case as paradigmatic of how movements get 'hijacked', a term drawn from Rajni Kothari, one of India's most well-known political scientists, whose disillusionment with 'non-party political formations' could be seen in his writings of the late 1980s and early 1990s (1989: 235–50; 1993: 119–39). Chandhoke also uses the term 'hijacked' on a number of occasions (2003: 24, 82). And yet, it is worth asking whether the Bhoomi Sena leader's account of that organization's decline might not be self-serving. The narrative bears a striking resemblance to Prakash Karat's analysis of the forces arrayed against the Left parties. In both cases, NGOs were seized upon as useful scapegoats. The Bhoomi Sena's failure to sustain itself as an effective movement, to build a more durable cadre in support of the cause, can be blamed on well-meaning but

misguided activists who failed to recognize the danger of NGO contagion. The movement's leadership itself can be left blameless.

The existence of dual-purpose vehicles is just one manifestation of a gradual blurring of the lines between the movement and NGO categories, which have long stood in mute opposition to one another at the conceptual level, while carrying on a voluble conversation in practice. In any case, the NGO-movement divide always reflected rhetorical positioning more than substantive differences. The trend since the mid-1990s has been towards the creation of hybrid organizational forms, in which the tactics and structural features of both movement-style groups and NGOs have been incorporated pragmatically.

The Bharat Gyan Vigyan Samithi (BGVS), founded in late 1989 to promote literacy, is a good example of organizational cross-breeding.[20] It is a classic NGO in many respects, undertaking programmes, channelling funds to CBOs, and focusing on conventional good works. That, however, is just part of the organization's identity. Formed in association with a government initiative—the Total Literacy Mission—the BGVS nevertheless sees itself, with some justification, as a 'broad democratic movement'—one 'in which even the state participates'. The BGVS particularly aims to encourage women's 'participation in a process of social mobilization'.[21]

Although engaged in constructive development work, the BGVS clearly sees itself as part of struggle-oriented politics. Its approach has stressed the need to 'link literacy with many basic livelihood problems and even with questions of exploitation, oppression, and discrimination against women'. The organization describes itself as a 'movement', and its activities as 'campaigns'—for instance, the Total Literacy Campaign.

In a reversal of the logic underlying the Shramajeevi Sanghatana and Bhoomi Sena examples, where movements gave birth to NGOs—allegedly with disastrous results—the BGVS has worked in the opposite direction. It is an NGO that sees itself as capable of spawning movements. Movements thus created can, in turn, catalyse the formation of additional NGOs. By tapping into local women's movements of various kinds—such as the anti-liquor campaigns in Andhra Pradesh in the 1990s—BGVS programmes have, in the words of the BGVS own documentation, assisted 'the conversion of the literacy movement into a women's employment generation programme'. Nor does the BGVS appear to recognize boundaries between mobilizational and electoral politics, with some local groups working 'to enhance women's participation in panchayats and the use of the panchayati raj structures to effect changes to further benefit women'.

The BGVS is perhaps best viewed as a civic group attempting to harness the comparative advantage of different organizational forms and mobilizational tactics. Indeed, the group's use of the term 'movement' is better understood if we see it as 'mobilizing people in large numbers and building up a momentum for change'. In its 'Samata campaign', the BGVS 'aim was to consciously develop and transform the literacy campaign into a cultural and economic movement for women'. The guiding principle behind new initiatives was retaining the 'basic people's movement character of the campaigns'.

ENGAGING WITH PARTIES AND ELECTORAL POLITICS

The blurring of the boundaries between NGOs and movement groups, and, as we have seen, between NGOs and the state, is just one of many factors that have allowed NGOs to enter, gradually and often indirectly, into the domain of electoral politics. Thanks to India's constitutionally mandated system of democratic decentralization—which created new tiers of elected local government, including one for every village—there is now an almost 'natural' point of entry for NGOs into a sphere once reserved for political parties. And because electoral contestation now takes place regularly—unlike in the 1970s and 1980s, for instance, when elections were sometimes held at the whim of ruling parties at the state and local levels—parties themselves have a much greater incentive to court NGOs, particularly those with strong grassroots networks.

A good example of an *indirect* means through which NGOs impinge upon electoral politics is to be found in Krishna's study of what he calls '*naya netas*' (new politicians)(Krishna 2002)—members of non-

elite castes who have emerged as important 'political fixers'.[22] Krishna found that people increasingly turn to naya netas, rather than established figures from dominant landowning castes, to assist in brokering transactions with officials at the block or district headquarters. However, naya netas have also been instrumental as 'political entrepreneurs' who, on behalf of a village or hamlet, negotiate with party leaders at election time for the price to be paid for the locality's votes. This works best in places that have high stocks of social capital for naya netas to 'activate', in the form of en bloc voting.

Interestingly, in some cases it is through NGO-led projects that naya netas obtain the skills and contacts necessary to ply both their retail trade (assisting people with their work at government offices) and their wholesale trade (bargaining with parties in exchange for local support). NGOs draw on many more local people for their operations than is reflected in the data on the number they formally employ. For many rural development NGOs, just to take one category, outreach to remote locations (where dialects may be spoken) requires a large number of field operatives who are not employees, but are paid on a casual basis as and when projects arise. The biggest NGOs involve thousands of young people as outreach workers, survey enumerators, health education assistants, and so forth. This exposes them to the world of officialdom and often involves training in technical skills, such as the management of minor irrigation works. The NGO-implemented government programmes are a training ground for naya netas, often bringing them into contact with party leaders.

It is not surprising to find that among the NGOs that have become increasingly close to political parties as a result of the new incentives thrown up by democratic decentralization are those that have effectively straddled the NGO-movement divide. One example is the Kerala Sasthra Sahithya Parishad (KSSP). While many of its leading lights have enjoyed a long association with the CPI(M), the KSSP has also managed to maintain a reputation for defending its organizational autonomy. This independent streak was demonstrated most visibly in the late 1970s during the campaign spearheaded by the KSSP against the planned Silent Valley power plant, a project backed by the state's CPI(M)-led coalition government.

When, in the 1990s, another CPI(M)-led government in Kerala initiated India's most far-reaching democratic decentralization programme, the KSSP was closely involved in designing the mechanisms through which popular participation could be engendered, all the way down to the neighbourhood level. It also played a major role in the massive training programmes aimed at assisting local communities in formulating comprehensive development plans.[23] In the decade prior to the launching of the new decentralization initiative in 1996, much discussion within the CPI(M) had centred on the loss of enthusiasm among local cadres. By using decentralization as a means to re-establish links with the KSSP, the CPI(M) hoped not only to benefit from the expertise of the KSSP, but also to rekindle interest among people disillusioned by the ceaseless factionalization of the state CPI(M), which seemed to some like a carbon copy of the Congress.[24] Kerala's CPI(M) embraced the movement mode of political organizing, naming its radical decentralization initiative 'The People's Plan Campaign'.

Another organization that at one time edged close to party politics was the Ekta Parishad (EP), or 'United Forum'—a group based mainly in Madhya Pradesh (MP). The EP, like the BGVS, defies classification. It calls itself 'a mass movement based on Gandhian principles', but is in essence a coalition of NGOs whose common agenda is to place livelihood resources in the hands of ordinary people. It 'patterns itself after a Trade Union'—though the workers involved are in the informal sector: agricultural labourers, small-scale peasant proprietors, forest dwellers, and so forth. It calls itself a 'non-party political entity', specifically citing Rajni Kothari, though it distances itself less from party activity than other such organizations, stating openly that it 'has at different times provided backing to candidates who support the land issue and pro-poor policies'. The EP's literature even recounts the familiar explanation for its existence: 'there is a vacuum left by political parties and people are looking for other channels for representation'.[25] Its leader wants to broaden the 'public space' within which people can demand rights.

Party competition is seen as constraining that space, because party discipline requires adherence to a full party programme, limiting the range of independent positions that party members may take.

The EP 'mobilizes people ... on the issue of proper and just utilization of livelihood resources'. It pursues *morcha*s (which it translates as 'campaigns') and more sporadic activities, such as *padyatras* (long-distance protest marches) and rallies. Its focus has been on pressuring the state government to implement laws that prevent the alienation of tribal land. The EP counts among its successes the creation of a state-wide task force on land alienation and restitution, the distribution of over 150,000 plots of land, and having pressured the state to withdraw spurious criminal cases against tribal people. It claims a membership of 150,000 dues-paying members, but says its wider following constitutes a 'formation' of more than 500,000.

The EP sees struggle (*sangharsh*) as peacefully coexisting alongside 'the promotion of constructive work'. It has assisted organizations to establish 'grain banks' designed to help Adivasis (tribals) to evade the grasp of moneylenders. This kind of constructive work, because it attacks feudal relations rather than capitalist modes of production, would likely not qualify under Kamat's demanding definition of what constitutes radical political engagement.

The EP has nevertheless found itself further enmeshed within the electoral sphere. During the decade (1993–2003) in which Congress Chief Minister Digvijay Singh was in power in MP, EP became associated with the Congress, and with Singh in particular. Singh was also said to have drawn on the local popularity of NGO workers affiliated with the EP, assisting them to win seats on village councils in exchange for their support for Congress candidates.

Like many other movement groups and NGOs, EP activists were not above bolstering their claims of influence by recounting the interest taken in their work by some political figure or other, or inflating their claims to legitimacy by referring to the group's strength in a given locality or among a particular constituency. 'Ekta Parishad is a force to be reckoned with' in the Chambal region—according to Ekta Parishad anyway—'so much so that during the general elections ... Chief Minister himself comes down to

Mahatma Gandhi Sewa Ashram at Joura to negotiate and canvas support with Ekta Parishad members' (Ramagundam 2001: 29).

The EP's strategy of hitching its fortunes to Digvijay Singh's Congress party was considered a mistake by many of MP's activists. By siding openly with Congress during the 2003 assembly elections and appearing on public platforms with the Chief Minister, the EP sacrificed much of its credibility among activists, and earned the hostility of the Bharatiya Janata Party (BJP) which ousted Singh from power.[26]

Movements have wrestled, individually and in federations such as the National Alliance of People's Movements, with the question of how best to approach the electoral sphere. Should they endorse individual candidates? Or should leading members of the organizations concerned extend support to specific candidates, without invoking the movement's name or membership? The NBA's Medha Patkar has at times taken the latter option. But when Patkar voiced her individual support for a Congress candidate (former state Home Minister R.R. Patil) in the Maharashtra state assembly elections in 2004, it was inevitable that this would be portrayed as NBA backing for the Congress party as a whole.[27] Whether such support is in exchange for promises of action on the movement's demands is impossible to say, but as Raina has argued, 'the degree of mobilisation under the NBA banner has been difficult to ignore for most of the mainstream parties, and individuals from these parties have covertly and overtly supported the movement from time to time ...'. (Raina 2004: 15–16).

The MKSS, which as we have seen is part of a movement-NGO duo, has increasingly entered the electoral arena. A few MKSS workers contested the inaugural panchayat elections in 1995, but with only the half-hearted blessing of the organization. One who was elected was subsequently found to have engaged in corruption, a major embarrassment for an organization dedicated to rooting out fraud. The group's response in the next round of panchayat elections in 2000 was not to back away from electoral politics, but to insist that anyone associated with the MKSS wanting to contest panchayat elections subscribe to a list of principles, including, most notably, a commitment to thoroughly implement the social audit provisions contained

within Rajasthan's newly amended local government legislation—provisions which the MKSS had been instrumental in having passed. Among the MKSS's winning candidates was a sarpanch who proceeded to both strengthen the MKSS in the area and demonstrate the possibility of implementing development programmes without rampant corruption. In the 2005 panchayat polls, MKSS supported twelve candidates contesting for the post of sarpanch. Only two were elected, but the MKSS had not selected candidates on the basis of their 'capacity to win'. Rather, the overriding criterion was their 'commitment to follow the norms evolved collectively by the MKSS in discussions held over the last year'. The objective was 'to influence the mainstream political process in the area so that issues of importance to the MKSS became part of the debate'.[28]

The ability of NGOs to engage in electoral politics is limited by their legal status as charitable entities. Some NGOs, such as the Lok Shikshan Sansthan, a Chittorgarh-based 'autonomous organization' that promotes Adivasi rights, explicitly build into their founding documents' provisions that *prohibit* members from contesting elections.[29] Whether this is driven by legal requirements or strategic calculations is difficult to know. Other cases are less clear-cut. At least one women's Self-help Group (SHG), established through a rural credit programme in Maharashtra, voiced an intention to use the SHG as a platform for contesting the next panchayat elections. This was despite a resolution taken by the coordinating body for the SHGs that forbade their use for political purposes. How precisely it could prevent leading SHG members from exploiting their prestige to further their political careers remained unclear.[30]

Many NGOs, such as the Karnataka-based SEARCH, train some of the hundreds of thousands of people elected to panchayati raj institutions. Because one-third of panchayat seats are reserved for women, some NGOs specialize in training women representatives or women's groups seeking to engage with the participatory structures—beneficiary groups, vigilance committees—established under local government regulations. Not surprisingly, NGOs engaged in providing information, guidance, and support to elected representatives or aspirants for local-government office can begin to resemble political parties in certain respects. NGOs that implement watershed development and other such grassroots projects become intimately involved in the workings of village panchayats.

One NGO that has openly declared its ambition to facilitate the entry of its members into elected office is the Young India Project (YIP). The YIP has helped organize many Unions of agricultural labourers and other marginalized groups in rural Andhra Pradesh. The membership of these unions, which coordinate their activities with the YIP, was reported in 2000 as 173,000. The unions work to obtain benefits from anti-poverty schemes, and to insist on the distribution of surplus lands. The unions also support the election of their own members to panchayati raj institutions, with the support of YIP. In the 1995 panchayati raj elections in the state, members of these unions were said to have contested approximately 7000 village panchayat seats, allegedly winning 6100 (Mediratta and Smith 2001; Suvarchala 1999; Bedi 1999).

India is not the only country where democratic decentralization has provided an opportunity for NGOs and movement groups to enter into the electoral domain. As in India, this has been especially evident among groups that straddle the NGO-movement divide. Clarke tells us that Chilean NGOs 'played an important role in helping Popular Economic Organisations (*Organizaciones Econimicas Populares*) and Self-Help Organisations (*Organizaciones de Auto-Ayuda*) to contest the 1992 local elections and to subsequently participate in local government structures'. NGOs in the Philippines 'sit alongside political parties in local government structures created under the 1991 Local Government Code and have actively participated in election campaigns, including the 1992 Presidential and the 1995 local and Congressional elections' (Clarke 1996).

CONCLUSION

Clarke's review of the relationship between NGOs and politics in the developing world observes that the NGO sector is often a political microcosm, reflecting larger ideological struggles. The field of 'NGO action ... in parts of Asia and Latin America, and to a lesser

extent in Africa,' he argues, is 'an arena within which battles from society at large are internalised' (Clarke 1996). India's experience exemplifies this trend.

The organizational forms assumed by India's civic groups are far too varied and complex to be reduced to simple dichotomies, and yet the competition for legitimacy, and the profound desire of activists to demonstrate their closeness to ordinary people, their autonomy from the state, their financial independence, their ideological purity—in short, their distinctiveness—has reinforced a fundamental divide between 'political movements' and 'apolitical' (or depoliticizing) NGOs.

This is in one sense a reflection of how crowded the market for social and political entrepreneurs is in India. But it is also a hangover from the myth (as opposed to the more complex reality) of Gandhi's mode of political action—an unattainable ideal in which personal sacrifice gives rise to an organic flowering of mass collective action. This is what Morris-Jones called the 'saintly idiom' in Indian politics. It provides a constant 'reference point', 'an ideal of disinterested selflessness by contrast with which almost all normal conduct can seem very shabby' (Morris-Jones 1963: 133–54).

However, could it not be the case that groups which zealously defend their 'movement' credentials—their non-NGO status—doth protest too much? Could it be that their critical stance towards NGOs reveals their own political insecurities? It is reasonable enough to interrogate NGOs about the nature of their accountability, the biases smuggled into their programmes, the distortionary impact of their role on the larger civil society. All too often, however, these searching questions are absent when critics turn their attention to the other half of this alleged dichotomy—people's movements, which are regarded as somehow organically accountable. But how true is this in practice? What exactly are the mechanisms of accountability through which social movements are answerable and sanctionable by larger publics? How democratic are people's movements? Movement leaders often possess social and political clout, which either preceded their participation in the movement, or else resulted from it. Their political contacts, media profile, or specialist knowledge of law or administration makes them difficult to overrule. Dissidents from within movement groups are in some cases branded as lackeys of NGOs.[31]

One hypothesis at least worth considering is that the persistence of the movement-NGO dichotomy as a point of social and organizational differentiation reflects the desperation of social activists to shore up their legitimacy in the face of profound new challenges. Many activists are acutely aware that not only has the initial wave of 'social action group' dynamism ebbed, but, indeed, that one of the main justifications for the existence of such a diversified social-movement landscape—that parties were no longer capable of inducting new social groups into the formal political process—was seriously undercut by the electoral successes since the early 1990s of parties based on lower-caste identity.

Other shifts in the political terrain have disrupted established fault-lines as well. In the development discourse, the *post*-Washington Consensus on economic policy has supplanted the earlier certainties of neoliberal prescription. Once easily adopted positions against neoliberalism must now yield to more difficult judgements on the role of the state. Whether to engage with, or remain aloof from, the domain of parties and electoral politics is among these hard choices. Arguably, activists in India are increasingly in tune with the sentiments expressed by one observer of the Philippines case: 'NGOs cannot simply avoid politics or leave it in the hands of traditional politicians' (Abad 1993). The stakes are too high. The idea of civic groups transforming themselves into party-like organizations is not without precedent in India. After all, the Bahujan Samaj Party (BSP), the most successful of India's Dalit-assertion parties, originated as a civil society formation—a Trade Union once dismissed by its critics as an NGO.

NOTES

1. http://www.indianngos.com/ngosection/overview.htm.

2. *The Economic Times*, 4 September 2003.

3. For a contrary view on reform's trajectory, see Rodrik and Subramanian (2004).

4. Different emphases can be found in, for example, Jain (1986); Sethi (1987); and Tandon (1987).

5. Foreigners often agree. One French academic who founded an NGO in India observed: 'Very often, NGOs think that they are doing good work but they actually are creating new forms of dependence. I have seen some poor people totally dependent on NGOs'. See 'Interview with Dr Guy Sorman', TERI Silver Jubilee Interview Series, http://www.teriin.org/25years/intervw/sorman.htm.

6. For a description of the new aid agenda, see Booth (2003).

7. The conservative Washington-based American Enterprise Institute has established NGO watch, which focuses on groups that 'have strayed beyond their original mandates and have assumed quasi-governmental roles'. See http://www.ngowatch.org/info.htm.

8. 'Economics and Politics of the World Social Forum', *Aspects of Indian Economy*, 35 (September), 2003, http://www.rupe-india.org/35/wsfmumbai.html.

9. Ibid.

10. 'Economics and Politics of the World Social Forum', *infra* (emphasis in original).

11. Ibid.

12. The campaign against a Coca-Cola bottling plant in Kerala was taken up by the UK-based development NGO Christian Aid, among other organizations. See http://www.christian-aid.org.uk/campaign/letters/0401_mylama.htm.

13. 'Economics and Politics of the World Social Forum', *infra*.

14. Ibid.

15. In March 2002 and February 2003, the author discussed with members of the coordination committee, the Byzantine arrangements for ensuring that all major groups would be accommodated.

16. Raina (2004) notes particularly the 'divisions even among the movements sharing the same ideology', not to mention 'the historical differences between the left, the Gandhians, the dalits, the Socialists, the environmentalists, as well as the new and the traditional among the women, worker and peasant movements' (p. 13).

17. 'World Social Forum Controlled by Euro-American Bourgeoisie', Report of the Independent Media Centre (USA), January 2004.

18. 'People's Plan is Different from World Bank Programme', *Frontline*, 2–15 August 2003.

19. Confusingly, Kamat gives Shramajeevi Sanghatana the fictitious name of a real organization—the Shramik Sanghatana, another Maharashtra-based activist group.

20. Much of the following is drawn from the organization's website (http://www.bgvs.org/html/literacy_campaign.htm), as well as from discussions with activists associated with the BGVS.

21. Report of the Committee of the National Literacy Mission, 14 December 1990.

22. This is the term used in Manor (2003, pp. 816–35).

23. At least one KSSP critique from within the CPI(M) echoed the fall-from-grace narrative outlined earlier. A party vice-President claimed in 2003 that though the KSSP had been born as a popular democratic organization in the 1960s, it had lost its democratic character in the 1970s and had [by the end of the century] degenerated to the level of being yet another of the 70,000-odd non-governmental organizations (NGOs) ... whose main job is to campaign for the development strategy of the G-8 nations (see 'KSSP Draws Flak in DYFI Organ', *The Hindu*, 25 November 2003).

24. Author's interview with a member of the KSSP's executive committee, Trichur, 11 January 1999.

25. All quotes come from www.ektaparishad.org, but further background material is drawn from Ramagundam (2001).

26. Personal communications from two Bhopal-based activists, 3 and 26 February 2005.

27. See 'Quietly Efficient', *Frontline*, 6–19 November 2004.

28. MKSS email circular, 14 February 2005. For further details, see Kerbart and Sivakumar (2005).

29. http://studentorgs.utexas.edu/aidaustin/OFI2004/ofi_lss/presentations/LSS_answers.pdf

30. International Fund for Agricultural Development, (2000, p. 35).

31. Challenges to NGOs as agents of accountability-seeking are treated in greater detail in Goetz and Jenkins (2005).

REFERENCES

Abad, Florencio. 1993. 'People's Participation in Governance: Limits and Possibilities—The Philippine Case', in E. Garcia, J. Macuja and B. Tolosa (eds), *Participation in Government: The People's Right*. Quezon: Ateneo de Manila University Press, p. 159.

Bedi, Narinder. 1999. 'Development of Power', in D. Rajashekhar (ed.), *Decentralised Government and NGOs: Issues, Strategies and Ways Forward*. New Delhi: Concept Publishing Company, pp. 130–42.

Bond, Michael. 2000. 'The Backlash Against NGOs', *Prospect*, April.

Booth, David (ed.). 2003. *Fighting Poverty in Africa: Are PRSPs Making a Difference?* London: Overseas Development Institute.

Brass, Paul R. 1990. *The New Cambridge History of India: The Politics of India since Independence*. Cambridge: Cambridge University Press.

Chandhoke, Neera. 2003. *The Conceits of Civil Society*. Oxford: Oxford University Press.

Clarke, Gerald. 1996. 'Non-Governmental Organizations and Politics', Papers in International Development, No. 20, Swansea, UK: University of Swansea.

'Economics and Politics of the World Social Forum', *Aspects of Indian Economy*, No. 35 (Mumbai, September 2003), http://www.rupe-india.org/35/wsfmumbai.html

Farrington, J., Anthony Bebbington, Kate Wellard, and David J. Lewis (eds). 1993. *Reluctant Partners? Non-Governmental Organizations, the State and Sustainable Agricultural Development*. London: Routledge.

Franda, Marcus. 1983. *Voluntary Associations and Local Development: The Janata Phase*. New Delhi: Young Asia Publishers.

Goetz, Anne Marie and Rob Jenkins. 2005. *Reinventing Accountability: Making Democracy Work for Human Development*. London: Palgrave/Macmillan.

Hulme, David and Michael Edwards (eds). 1995. *Non-Governmental Organisations: Performance and Accountability—Beyond the Magic Bullet*. London: Earthscan.

'Interview with Dr Guy Sorman', *TERI Silver Jubilee Interview Series*, http://www.teriin.org/25years/intervw/sorman.htm.

Jain, L.C. 1986. 'Debates in the Voluntary Sector: Some Reflections', *Social Action*, 36(4), pp. 404–16.

Jenkins, Rob. 2004. 'In Varying States of Decay: Anti-Corruption Politics in Maharashtra and Rajasthan', in Rob Jenkins (ed.), *Regional Reflections: Comparing Politics across India's States*. New Delhi: Oxford University Press.

Jenkins, Rob and Anne Marie Goetz. 2004. 'Civil Society Engagement and India's Public Distribution System: Lessons from the Rationing Kruti Samiti in Mumbai', Consultation Paper for the World Bank, *World Development Report 2004: Making Services Work for Poor People*, Washington DC.

Kamat, Sangeeta. 2002. *Development Hegemony: NGOs and the State in India*. New Delhi: Oxford University Press.

———. 1996. 'The Structural Adjustment of Grassroots Politics', *Sanskriti*, 7(1).

Karat, Prakash. 1988. *Foreign Funding and the Philosophy of Voluntary Organizations: A Factor in Imperialist Strategy*. New Delhi: National Book Centre.

———. 1984. 'Action Groups/Voluntary Organizations: A Factor in Imperialist Strategy', *The Marxist*, 2(2), pp. 51–63.

Kaviraj, Sudipta. 2001. 'In Search of Civil Society', in Sudipta Kaviraj and Sunil Khilnani (eds), *Civil Society: History and Possibilities*. Cambridge: Cambridge University Press, pp. 287–323.

Kerbart, Eric and Sowmya Sivakumar. 2005. 'Panchayat Elections in Rajasthan: A View from the Field', *Economic and Political Weekly*, XL(8), pp. 723–4.

Kohli, Atul. 1990. *Democracy and Discontent: India's Growing Crisis of Governability*. Princeton: Princeton University Press.

Korten, David. 1990. *Getting to the Twenty-First Century: Voluntary Action and the Global Agenda*. West Hartford, CT: Kumarian Press.

Kothari, Rajni. 1993. 'The Yawning Vacuum: A World without Alternatives', *Alternatives*, 18(2), pp. 119–39.

———. 1989. 'End of an Era', in Rajni Kothari (ed.), *Politics and the People: In Search of Humane India*. Delhi: Ajanta Publications, pp. 235–50

———. 1984. 'Non-party Political Process', *Economic and Political Weekly*, XIX(5), pp. 216–24.

Krishna, Anirudh. 2002. *Active Social Capital: Tracing the Roots of Development and Democracy*. New York: Columbia University Press.

Mahajan, Vijay. 1997. 'Voluntary Action in India: A Retrospective Overview and Speculations for the 21st Century', mimeo, New Delhi.

Manor, James. 2003. 'Small-time Political Fixers in India's States: "Towel over Armpit"', *Asian Survey*, 40(5), pp. 816–35.

Mediratta, Kavitha and Clay Smith. 2001. 'Advancing Community Organizing Practice: Lessons from Grassroots Organizations in India', COMM-ORG Working Paper, University of Toledo, August 2001.

Morris-Jones, W.H. 1963. 'India's Political Idioms', in C.H. Philips (ed.), *Politics and Society in India*. London: George Allen and Unwin, pp. 133–54.

Ndegwa, Stephen N. 1996. *The Two Faces of Civil Society: NGOs and Politics in Africa*. West Hartford, CT: Kumarian Press.

'People's Plan is Different from World Bank Programme', *Frontline*, 2–15 August 2003.

Petras, James and Henry Veltmeyer. 2001. *Globalization Unmasked: Imperialism in the 21st Century*. London: Zed Books.

'Quietly Efficient', *Frontline*, 6–19 November 2004.

Raina, Vinod. 2004. 'Social Movements in India', in Francois Polet (ed.), *Globalizing Resistance: The State of the Struggle*. London: Pluto Press.

Ramagundam, Rahul. 2001. *Defeated Innocence: Adivasi Assertion, Land Rights and the Ekta Parishad Movement*. New Delhi: Grassroots India Publishers.

Report of the Committee of the National Literacy Mission, 14 December 1990.

Rodrik, Dani and Arvind Subramanian. 2004. 'From "Hindu Growth" to Productivity Surge: The Mystery of the Indian Growth Transition', KSG Working

Paper No. RWP04–13, John F. Kennedy School of Government, Harvard University, March.

Roy, Bunker. 1988. 'Voluntary Agencies: Twenty Years from Now', *Mainstream*, 26, pp. 17–19.

Roy, Dunu. 2002. 'Environmentalism and Political Economy', *Seminar*, 516.

Rudolph, Lloyd I. and Susanne Hoeber Rudolph. 1987. *In Pursuit of Lakshmi: The Political Economy of the Indian State*. Chicago: The University of Chicago Press.

Sen, Siddhartha. 1999. 'Some Aspects of State-NGO Relationships in India in the Post-Independence Era', *Development and Change*, Vol. 30, pp. 332–3, 327–55.

Sethi, Harsh. 1993. 'Action Groups in the New Politics', in P. Wignaraja (ed.), *New Social Movements in the South*. London: Zed Books.

———. 1987. 'Trends Within', *Seminar*, no. 348, pp. 21–4.

———. 1984. 'Groups in a New Politics of Transformation', *Economic and Political Weekly*, XIX(7), pp. 305–16.

Sheth, D.L. 1984. 'Grassroots Initiatives in India', *Economic and Political Weekly*, XIX(6), pp. 259–65.

Sheth, D.L. and Harsh Sethi. 1991. 'The NGO Sector in India: Historical Context and Current Discourse', *Voluntars*, 2(2), pp. 49–68.

Smillie, Ian. 1995. *The Alms Bazaar: Altruism Under Fire—Non-Profit Organisations and International Development*. London: Intermediate Technology Publications.

Suvarchala, G. 1999. 'Empowerment of Gram Panchayat Members: Experiences of Young India Project, Penukonda, Andhra Pradesh' in D. Rajasekhar (ed.), *Decentralized Government and NGOs: Issues, Strategies and Ways Forward*. New Delhi: Concept Publishing, pp. 97–118.

Tandon, Rajesh. 1987. *The State and Voluntary Agencies in India*. New Delhi: PRIA.

———. 1986. 'Regulating NGOs: New Moves', *Lokayan Bulletin*, 4(3), pp. 37–42.

The Economic Times, 4 September 2003.

Wagle, Subodh. 1997. 'The Political Dynamics of Grassroots Environment-Development Struggles: The Case-Study of the Struggle against the Narmada Dam', *Journal of the Indian School of Political Economy*, 9(3), pp. 409–62.

World Bank. 1995. (Operations Policy Department), Working with NGOs: *A Practical Guide to Operational Collaboration between the World Bank and Non-Governmental Organziations*. Washington DC: The World Bank, p. 7.

VI Politics and Policy

29 The Political Economy of the State

Devesh Kapur

While the characterization of India as a land of paradoxes may be a cliché, it does not make it any less true. The same could be said about the Indian state, whose performance varies greatly, successfully managing many difficult tasks while performing poorly on seemingly basic ones. The Indian state can organize elections for an astounding 700 million voters with less controversy than the United States; it can conduct censuses for a billion people reasonably well; it periodically organizes a temporary city for millions of people during the Kumbh Mela without mishaps; it runs an efficient space programme; and has managed to keep one of the world's largest armed forces away from politics.

Yet the same state does an abysmal job of providing decent primary education and health to its citizens, despite intense political competition, low incumbency, and strong electoral participation of the very large number of poor and less educated voters. Its record of providing basic social services has been and continues to be weak, and in areas like adult literacy, vaccination coverage, and malnutrition, India's performance lags behind many poor countries 'not widely regarded as emerging superpowers' (Pritchett 2009). This is certainly not because of lack of intent. In terms of rhetoric and government policy and practice, few countries have had as much of an official commitment to improve the well-being of its people and in particular to reduce poverty through specific targeted programmes as India. While the Indian state is certainly not a 'failing state', its dismal performance in a host of basic public services has led one observer to memorably describe it as a 'flailing state' (ibid.).

The role of the Indian state in economic development, the reasons thereof, and its manifold consequences have been extensively documented (Chakravorty 1988; Jalan 1991; Bhagwati 1993; Drèze and Sen 2002; Panagariya 2008). Much of the literature (especially prior to the 1990s) on India's political economy focused on its economic *policies*, their rationale, and their consequences. This literature also examines the various attempts at liberalization and reforms—the failed attempts in reforming industrial and trade policy in the 1960s, the result of ham-handed arm-twisting by the United States and the Bretton Woods institutions, and weak political leadership in India (Lewis 1995); the upsurge in the state's involvement in the economy in the 1970s, driven less by strong ideological commitments than the single-minded pursuit of power; and why renewed attempts by the Indian state to launch reforms in the 1980s floundered as much by passive resistance of the bureaucratic establishment as by more active mobilization of adversely affected interest groups (Waterbury 1993).

A range of explanations have been advanced in explaining the failures of the Indian state. Economists unsurprisingly, put the onus on poorly conceived policies, in particular the command and control aspects of India's trade and industrial policies that created powerful incentives for rent-seeking behaviour (Bhagwati and Desai 1970; Bhagwati and Srinivasan 1975). Others such as Lipton (1977) argued that these polices persisted because of an 'urban-bias' in Indian policymaking although this was a time when rural lobbies were just beginning to exercise influence on the Indian state. Kohli (1987) emphasized the importance of purely political variables, namely regime type and the leadership's ideology, in this regard. While the analytical emphasis on policies was well deserved, it tended to neglect the more prosaic weaknesses of the Indian state on the implementation side. More broadly, it had been apparent to observers quite early on that the Indian state's ability to follow through and enforce its obligations was always severely limited relative to the rhetoric. Myrdal's (1968) characterization of certain states as 'soft states', as those in which 'governments require extraordinarily little of their citizens' and 'obligations that do exist are enforced inadequately if at all', was based on his analysis of India.

These different perspectives and views, notwithstanding, there is some agreement (even if perhaps not exactly a consensus), that the performance of the Indian state has been better at the macro-level than at the micro-level, and indeed institutional performance has (for the most part) also been better at the federal level than at the state and local level. Why has this been the case?

THE MACRO-STATE: POLICIES AND INSTITUTIONS

The Indian state's record in macroeconomic management has been relatively good, whether compared to other developing countries or in contrast to its feeble performance in microeconomic policies and ground level implementation. Thus for much of the period prior to the 1991 economic reforms, Joshi and Little (1994) concluded that India's record was the most 'conservative' (amongst 17 countries studied) with respect to inflation, monetary policy, and external debt. India's much better inflation record (at least until the 1990s) owes much to the political aversion to inflation institutionalized by democracy, given the negative impact on the large number of poor voters (largely because the poor do not have access to financial instruments to protect themselves against inflation) and the relatively lower levels of income inequality in India.[1] Thus, instead of an independent central bank and monetary targeting to anchor inflationary expectations, democratic politics has been the best political anchor to rein in inflation.

An important exception to India's good macroeconomic record has been its large fiscal deficits, especially in recent decades. The effects of populist monetary or fiscal consequences tend to converge over time since expansionary fiscal policies eventually have monetary consequences through higher interest rates and/or to the extent that the deficits get monetized, through inflation or (if financed externally) a debt problem. It is this interconnectedness between microeconomic inefficiencies and macroeconomic problems that fed the growing fiscal crisis in India by the late 1980s and which soon spilled over to the balance of payments. The political explanation for India's large fiscal deficits is distributional conflicts—the growing limitations in the state's capacity to mediate and moderate the many demands being placed on it. In the 1980s, efforts to rein in an increasingly profligate fiscal policy were stymied more by a powerful agrarian 'demand polity' that grew out of efforts to revitalize Indian agriculture (especially from the late 1960s onwards) than by the state's role in industrialization, which had a larger element (at least till the early 1980s) of a 'command polity' with an emphasis on public investment (Rudolph and Rudolph 1987). Subsequently, it remained high in the 1990s because of an inability to raise taxes and growing current expenditures, whether on public sector wages or the myriad of subsidies.

Bardhan (1984, 1998) attempted to reconcile some of these views in pointing to the deadlocked contradiction of the heterogeneous dominant classes' interests, namely the rich industrialists, the farmers, and the public sector bureaucracy, as the reason for India's stagnation which had gradually frittered away Nehru's 'command' economy.

> The Indian public economy has thus become an elaborate network of patronage and subsidies. The heterogeneous proprietary classes fight and bargain for their share in the spoils of the system and often strike compromises in the form of 'log-rolling' in the usual fashion of pressure group. (Bardhan 1984)

With no group hegemonic, as each group sought to grab more public resources, fiscal deficits grew, public investment declined, pulling down the growth rate. However, the class balance and heterogeneity may have indirectly contributed to the maintenance of democratic processes. The fact that there was a diversity of elements in the ruling coalition, with each pulling in different directions contributed to economic stagnation. But it contributed to political democracy because no single class or group could dominate Indian politics. The necessity of producing compromises amongst this heterogeneous ruling coalition helped produced a centrist oriented polity (Rudolph and Rudolph 1987).

However, even as Bardhan saw a deadlock among the proprietary classes, major changes were afoot. A decade later, Bardhan tried to explain the political economy of the reforms that began in 1991 as the result of 'an increase in the diversity, fluidity, and fragmentation in the coalition of dominant interest groups' (Bardhan 1998). But how and why did that happen? An important reason why most observers of the Indian political economy failed to see the impending changes in economic policies, was the tendency to see the Congress party and the upper castes as hegemonic. Underlying shifts in political power, towards states and away from a

weakening Centre on the one hand and in favour of lower castes on the other, meant that erstwhile elites who had controlled the state apparatus were now more favourably inclined towards markets to secure their economic options. At the same time, the empowerment of lower castes increased the political pressures to enhance group privileges.

During its first three decades, corruption at the apex of the Indian state was relatively less, compared to recent years. The state was also more stable as a single political party dominated. Nonetheless, economic growth in the latter period doubled, while per capita growth nearly tripled. What explains India's growth acceleration, in particular the changing role of the state?

There is little dispute that India's economic policies changed sharply after 1991. There is also no dispute that India's growth rate accelerated a decade prior to that pivotal year, from around 1980. However, there is much less agreement on the causes of growth and even less understanding on what political factors underlay these changes. According to Panagariya (2004), two key factors accounted for much of the spurt in the growth rate during the 1980s:

> First, liberalization played a significant role. On the external front, policy measures such as import liberalization, export incentives, and a more realistic real exchange rate contributed to productive efficiency. On the internal front, freeing up of several sectors from investment licensing reinforced import liberalization and allowed faster industrial growth. Second, both external and internal borrowings allowed the government to maintain high levels of public expenditure and thus boost growth through demand.

This view was challenged by Rodrik and Subramanian (2005) who, while accepting that some 'liberalization' occurred during the 1980s, argue that reforms in the 1980s were less pro-liberalization than pro-business, in that they helped boost profits of existing business without threatening them with real competition. The shift in policy, they maintain, was mainly 'attitudinal', having to do with the government's attitude towards business and the private sector, rather than as policy reforms, whether external or internal liberalization. Were the attitudinal changes a necessary precursor to the later policy changes, and if so, why did they occur? Yet another explanation comes from Virmani (2004). Although concurring with Rodrik and Subramanian that the reforms were 'incremental' rather than 'revolutionary', he argues that two other factors were important—the 'output gap' and 'credibility' of reforms. Since the mid-1960s, the Indian economy had underperformed, increasing the gap between the potential and the actual Gross Domestic Product (GDP). The policy changes during the 1980s provided an opportunity to catch-up and in particular make better use of under-utilized capital. In addition, politically credible signals of the intent to reform failed policies gave greater confidence to the private sector to invest.

The fact that economic growth between the 1980s and 1990s differed little, led a number of analysts to question the impact of the reforms.[2] However, as more years have gone by, three facts stand out. First, if the post-reform period is extended into the first decade of the new millennium (which recorded the fastest growth rates ever), the post-reform growth story is perceptibly better. Second, there has been a fundamental structural transformation in the degree of India's engagement with the global economy. Trade to GDP ratios almost tripled since the commencement of economic liberalization (Table 29.1), non-debt foreign capital inflows increased hugely and India accumulated substantial foreign exchange reserves

as an insurance against external shocks. The deeper integration with the global economy also led to the growth of a sizeable pro-globalization domestic business lobby (in contrast to the earlier protectionist 'Bombay Club'). Third, growth in the latter period has been more sustainable. While growth in the former period was grounded by a major macroeconomic crisis, India's economy and growth has been more resilient subsequently and withstood the two major international crises after 1991—the 1997–8 Asian financial crises and the global economic crisis of 2008–9—and the numerous domestic political crisis from the 1992 razing of the Babri Masjid to the Gujarat riots of 2002.

Discussions of the Indian state's economic management often ignore its stewardship of an important economic policy instrument, namely the exchange rate.[3] Post-Independence, India's exchange rate regime operated in practice as a fixed nominal exchange rate. By the end of the 1950s and in the first half of the 1960s, mounting inflation led to an appreciation of the Real Effective Exchange Rate (REER) and despite severe trade and capital controls and foreign aid, India's Balance of Payments (BOP) problems mounted. In June 1966, under pressure from the United States and the Bretton Woods institutions, India undertook a large nominal devaluation (36.5

Table 29.1: India: Macro-indicators

	GROSS DOMESTIC SAVINGS (% OF GDP)	GROSS DOMESTIC CAPITAL FORMATION (% OF GDP)	TRADE/GDP (%)	EXPORTS/ EXTERNAL DEBT	TAX/GDP	DIRECT/ INDIRECT TAXES	CENTRAL TAX REVENUES/ STATE TAX REVENUES[a]	PUBLIC SECTOR EMPLOYMENT (IN MILLION)
1950–1			12.2	18.9	6.2	0.58	1.32	
1960–1	11.2	14.0	10.2	0.64	7.7	0.42	1.18	7.1
1970–1	14.2	15.1	7.0	0.22	10.3	0.21	1.06	11.1
1980–1	18.5	19.9	13.5	0.498	13.65	0.197	0.898	15.5
1990–1	22.8	26.0	14.6	0.49	15.4	0.16	0.964	19.1
2000–1	23.7	24.3	22.5	1.07	14.5	0.31	0.81	19.1
2007–8	37.7	39.1	40.6[b]	2.96[b]	18.9	0.52	0.94	18.2[c]

Source: RBI, *Handbook of Statistics of Indian Economy, 2008–9*; GOI, *Indian Public Finance Statistics 2008–09*, August 2009; Panagariya (2008), Table 2.2
Notes: [a]Central Tax Revenues are net of transfers to states and state tax revenues are the sum of own taxes and transfers from the central tax pool.
[b] Data for 2008–9;
[c] Data for 2005–6.

per cent) but due to a complex tax regime and high inflation, the REER depreciation was only about 7 per cent (Joshi and Little 1994). The devaluation of 1966 is widely regarded as having been a political disaster and severely shaped India's macro policies and political economy over the next two decades.

After the breakdown of the Bretton Woods regime in 1971, the rupee was pegged to the pound sterling until 1975, which led to an automatic depreciation of the rupee by 20 per cent (due to the weakness of the sterling) without drawing political attention. Thereafter, the rupee was pegged to a basket of currencies in the mid-1970s and a de facto crawling band around the US dollar by the end of the decade. By the mid-1980s, exchange rate policy became much more active leading to depreciation in the nominal rate of 47 per cent and the REER of 35 per cent (Joshi and Little 1994). In July 1991, amidst the BOP crisis, the rupee was devalued by 9 and 11 per cent in two stages. It switched to a floating exchange rate regime in 1993 after a transitional phase of dual exchange rates for two years. The liberalization of the trade and payments system culminated in August 1994 with India finally accepting the International Monetary Fund (IMF) Article VIII, and thus the rupee officially became convertible on the current account. In 2000, India replaced its severe Foreign Exchange Regulation Act (FERA, passed in 1973), by the Foreign Exchange Management Act (FEMA) moving from a system of administrative controls to a regulatory framework. The post-float period was marked by a consensus to maintain moderate external imbalances, and as a result, the Reserve Bank frequently intervened to maintain exchange rate stability.

An important explanation for the improved management of India's exchange rate, and more broadly the stability and growth of its financial sector, has been the role of the Reserve Bank and the Ministry of Finance (along with other institutions like the Securities and Exchange Board of India (SEBI) that were set up by them in the 1990s). Post-Independence, as with many public institutions, the Reserve Bank of India's (RBI) autonomy eroded over the decades and affected its ability to manage the exchange rate. While in general this function is shared between the central bank and the executive, the ill-defined

provisions of the RBI and the Banking Compliance Acts and the ideological climate in this period, undermined the RBI's role. However, more than the specific provisions of the RBI Act, it was the economic model that undermined the RBI's role in exchange rate management. Since 1951, but particularly from 1956 (when the Second Five-Year Plan was launched), macroeconomic policy in India was yoked to planning, leaving the RBI little role to play (Khatkhate 2004). Adherence to the fixed exchange rate was necessary (from the narrow perspective of the planned model) because any change in its level would have upset the careful balance that was part of a plan's design.

However, as we saw earlier, following the breakdown of Bretton Woods, monetary policy and especially exchange rate policy, became gradually depoliticized even as fiscal policies became more politicized. An observer trying to understand the political economy of exchange rate management in India is faced with two puzzles:

1. why did India not adopt an undervalued exchange rate as an explicit instrument to promote its hallowed goal of import substitution industrialization?; and

2. why have India's exchange rate and financial sector policies been reasonably sound despite the limited independence of the central bank?

Exchange rate policies affect different parts of the economy in very different ways. Consequently, they can become a major target of political conflict. Pre-Independence, Indian industrialists consistently argued for monetary and exchange rate policies that would afford them some degree of protection and sought to project their interests as no mere capitalist interest, but as a general national interest. For long, Indian economic thinking had been characterized by 'export pessimism' and the inflationary consequences of devaluation stemming from a belief that India's import basket was relatively inelastic. As a result there was a strong opposition to devaluation. And until the 1990s, the small size of the export sector meant that there were no strong lobbies in favour of maintaining a competitive exchange rate regime. By the end of the decade, the growing importance of trade in the Indian economy, and the particular economic and political importance of the Information Technology (IT) sector, meant that pressures grew from the private sector to maintain a 'competitive' exchange rate. India's greater integration with the world economy became pronounced in the first decade of the new millennium. Merchandise trade as a percentage of GDP increased from less than 15 per cent of the GDP in 1990–1 to nearly 41 per cent in 2008–9 (Table 29.1). If services trade is included, the ratio was 54.2 per cent in 2008–9 compared to just 30.9 per cent in 2003–4. Between 2003–4 and 2008–9, India's total merchandise exports grew from nearly $45 billion to $163 billion and imports from $51 billion to $252 billion, while its economic growth averaged 7.25 per cent. Foreign Direct Investment (FDI) inflows grew markedly and as a result the external sector emerged as a major factor shaping the actions of the Indian state.

If the Indian state's handling of exchange rate policies has been reasonably adept, this is also true (albeit to a lesser extent) on one side of the fiscal ledger, namely tax revenues. As a fraction of the GDP, tax revenues increased slowly but steadily from 1950 to 1990 and then declined somewhat in the 1990s, before again increasing after 2000 to nearly 19 per cent of the GDP in 2007–8 (Table 29.1). The increase in the first four decades was mainly due to increases in indirect taxes (such as excise and trade taxes), which have more distortionary effects. India's complex fiscal federalism, with assignments of tax powers and tax sharing arrangements at different levels of the government, have influenced the incentives for

revenue mobilization and made it difficult to enact and implement comprehensive tax reforms. Selectivity and discretion, both in designing the structure and in implementing the tax system, contributed to erosion of the tax base and created powerful special interest groups (Rao and Singh 2006). Nonetheless, there has been a sharp reduction in the rates and dispersion of trade taxes and a shift to direct taxes driven in part by the introduction of the Value Added Tax (VAT) in 2005. The likelihood of integrating the tax on goods and the tax on services into a common Goods and Service Tax (GST) by 2010 will be a landmark in India's tax reforms. That this will have been achieved without external pressure or significant political acrimony, and in a reasonable period of time (compared to other major policy changes), is a testimony to the founder fathers' vision of creating a constitutional body (the Finance Commission) which has anchored India's fiscal federalism as well as the political skills of the Indian state.

THE MICRO-STATE: POLICIES AND INSTITUTIONS

Independent India's commitment to democratic politics meant that its polity had to grapple with the harsh reality of India's poverty—the sheer number of the poor (who were also now voters), the intensity of poverty and destitution, and a deeply stratified and hierarchical society. Addressing the

Table 29.2: India: Micro-indicators of Development

	PER CAPITA GNP AT FACTOR COST (CONSTANT 1999–2000 PRICES, IN RS)	POVERTY (HEAD COUNT RATIO)[a]	LITERACY RATE (% OF POP.)	LIFE EXPECTANCY (YEARS)	INFANT MORTALITY	CRUDE BIRTH RATE	CRUDE DEATH RATE	SEX RATIO (FEMALES PER 1000 MALES)
1951	6237	45.3 (Round 3)	18.3	32	146	39.9	27.4	946
1961	7566	45.3 (Round 16)	28.3	41	129	41.7	22.8	941
1971	8692	52.9 (Round 25)	34.5	46	134	41.2	19	930
1981	9454	43.0 (Round 38)	43.6	52	104	37.2	15	934
1991	12726	35.5 (Round 46)	52.2	58	80	32.5	11.4	927
2001	18074	27.5	64.8	62	68	24.8	8.9	933
2008	27371	(2004–05)	68	68	53	23.1	7.4	

Source: RBI, Handbook of Statistics of Indian Economy, 2008–9; Datt (1998). Table 1.
Note: [a]The numbers in parentheses represent rounds of the National Sample Survey (NSS).

needs of vulnerable and marginalized groups in the society has preoccupied the energies of intellectuals and policymakers and has been a focus of political rhetoric in India to a degree that is uncommon among developing countries. Levels, changes, and measurement of poverty have been a major preoccupation of (often contentious) Indian policy debates,[4] and the Indian state has deployed a large number of programmes with different instruments and objectives. The salient features of changes in poverty and human development in India are provided in Table 29.2. While clearly there have been improvements in all aspects (except in the gender ratio), the changes have been modest, both relative to other comparable countries and especially given India's rapid growth in recent years (Ravallion 2009).

The puzzle is not that India's policy has been preoccupied with addressing poverty—but that its repeated efforts in this direction have yielded such meagre results. Like Sisyphus, the Indian state appears condemned to incessantly launch poverty programmes and then with little to show for its efforts begin the process all over again. What features of the Indian state explain the continual failure and why does India persist with these programmes instead of reaching the poor through other programmes such as direct cash transfers?[5]

India's Poverty Programmes

Specific purpose transfer schemes—designed to address issues of categorical equity—have been a key part of India's anti-poverty arsenal since their inception. Central Sector Schemes (CSS) route funding directly to the local level, bypassing the states; hence their growth (CSS funding is currently comparable to Central Plan Assistance) can be viewed as a compensatory mechanism for the Central government to exercise influence within states, after instruments such as industrial licensing were abolished. Price supports and food subsidy are the most expensive of the government schemes. Between 2003–4 and 2007–8, explicit subsidies of the Central government averaged 1.6 per cent of the GDP; just two items, food and fertilizers, accounted for nearly four-fifths of all subsidies.[6] These subsidies accrue largely to surplus grain producers (confined mainly

to the north-western states of Punjab, Haryana, and western Uttar Pradesh, and the southern state of Andhra Pradesh where the procurement takes place and where consequently the support is more effective), and the parastatal agency (the Food Corporation of India) in charge of the logistics of grain procurement, storage, and distribution. A part eventually reaches the below poverty line (BPL) households through the public distribution system (PDS), whose targeting performance has been severely wanting. The Government of India's (GOI) own internal evaluation has found that about 58 per cent of the subsidized foodgrain issued from the Central Pool does not reach the BPL families because of identification errors, non-transparent operation, and corrupt practices in the implementation of the PDS. Over 36 per cent of the budgetary subsidies on food are siphoned off the supply chain and another 21 per cent reach households above the poverty line (Planning Commission 2005).

The CSS initially focused on area development (backward areas, arid areas, hilly regions), wage employment, and promoting self-employment (by transferring a productive asset). The first area development programme—the Community Development (CD) Programme—began in the early 1950s (with support from the Ford Foundation) and sought to involve the entire rural community in rural development. However, while the initial pilots were promising, as the programme expanded it gave 'birth to a large, slow-moving bureaucracy which, since the programme cut across various ministerial lines of authority, became involved in turf wars with other bureaucracies'.[7] A review by the Indian government in 1957 (headed by Balwant Mehta) was even more critical of the enormous administrative burden put on ill-trained and ill-equipped local bureaucracy.

Over the years, other types of schemes came into being, that is new forms of transfers, such as old-age pensions and housing and basic services like education and health. These investments have led to some convergence in physical investment for a set of public goods across Indian villages perhaps because construction works provide lucrative opportunities (Banerjee and Somanathan 2007). But similar institutional impediments have bedevilled the actual services provided by these facilities.

Innumerable reports and analyses on India's poverty programmes agree on four broad conclusions. First, a large fraction of the resources in these programmes are spent on the administrative costs of the programmes or are siphoned off with their intended beneficiaries receiving only modest amounts. Second, the corruption stems from the discretionary power of public functionaries to where and what types of works to take up, who should be entrusted with their construction, the identification of individuals entitled to specific subsidies, and the actual disbursement of the entitlements. Third, these facts are well known to the state functionaries who are supposed to implement and monitor these programmes. And fourth, all this persists because there is little accountability in the system. If anything, the accountability is perverse in that punishment is more likely to be meted out to someone who does *not* participate in the hierarchical systems of corruption, than someone who does.

Building on Michael Kalecki's classic formulation of developing countries as 'intermediate regimes', K.N. Raj (1973) argued that the ruling coalitions in India are too heterogeneous to form a coherent class and 'intermediate regimes' can do little by way of redistribution.[8] On the other hand, they have a strong propensity to secure and retain their support base by yielding to pressures for lower taxes and/or higher subsidies. Increasing political assertiveness by socially marginalized groups who have been politically empowered both by the emergence of regional and identity based political parties as well as greater representation in public offices at all levels, has forced the Indian state to manage these pressures through a range of instruments that seek to give something to each pressure group, ranging from agricultural subsidies to subsidized supply of food and other essentials through the PDS and efforts to extend the scope and duration of affirmative action programmes. And last but not the least, a significant commitment to anti-poverty programmes.

So why do new poverty programmes come up awaiting the same fate? One reason for the initiation of the new (anti-poverty programmes) may be due to the incentives of newly incumbent politicians at the beginning of their electoral political cycle.

As Mani and Mukand (2007) argue, a 'visibility effect' distorts governmental resource allocation and explains why politicians neglect provision of essential public goods, despite their considerable benefits. Greater democratization widens the gap in resource allocation between more visible (such as specific poverty projects) versus less visible (such as malnutrition prevention) public goods. However, while this explains the specific instruments to address poverty in India, it does not explain why these projects continue—the politician is more interested in 'ribbon cutting' for a new project than what happens to it later. To understand 'project persistence' beyond public choice explanations of bureaucracies seeking to maximize their budgets, one must turn to the insight of Coate and Morris (1999) who argued that any policy intervention creates new special interests that gradually develop a vested interest in the perpetuation of that policy. That 'policy persistence' is reflected in the persistence of anti-poverty programmes in India, rather than forceful steps to improve general government performance at the local level, underpinned by interest groups not only in the state but civil society as well.

In the classic principal-agent framework, voters delegate to their elected representatives, who in turn delegate to specific administrative systems and bureaucratic structures certain tasks. If those tasks are not performed, voters should hold politicians accountable and anticipating that, the latter have an incentive to make the bureaucracy accountable. The incumbency disadvantage in India may suggest that voters do hold politicians accountable and that attempts at patronage go only so far if one is going to lose in any case (although it could be argued that with increasing competition this could still be an equilibrium outcome).[9] Why then do India's poverty projects continue to perform poorly?

Institutions and Incentives

Several studies indicate that the institutional effects of colonialism—especially land-tenure institutions—continue to cast a long shadow on contemporary economic outcomes in India (Banerjee *et al.* 2005; Iyer forthcoming). While these studies help explain the regional variance in economic performance in

India, they are less helpful in understanding how these historic variables have shaped political cleavages and thereby the complex interaction between structural factors stemming from institutional legacies and the nature of competitive electoral politics. Indeed, the conclusion a reader may draw from these studies is history as destiny (or perhaps in this case karma) with little room for human agency and variables such as leadership or ideology.

Human agency has been very much manifest in the design and implementation of India's poverty programmes. Historically, India has exhibited a large reliance on targeted transfer payments and subsidies, and significant underprovision of social services such as education, though this may now be changing. Why has this been the case? Keefer and Khemani (2004) offer, and reject, three explanations. First, the poor (such as poor farmers) might prefer targeted transfers rather than public services such as education because they have high discount rates (the benefits of transfers are immediate while the returns from education emerge after a period of time). Second, the poor might be coerced or manipulated by organized elite interest groups, such as large farmers, to vote for particular policies favoured by these groups even if they are detrimental to their interests. Third, Indian public expenditures might simply exhibit the influence of organized special interests, common even in industrialized democracies. The failure of democratically elected governments to provide adequate services to the poor cannot just be explained by lack of participation of the poor in the political process. Using individual-level data of who votes in India, Ravishankar (2007) demonstrates that socio-economic status is uncorrelated with the decision to vote. Moreover, the propensity to vote varies little by an individual's caste or religion. Furthermore, contrary to the dominant view originating from the social capital literature that greater heterogeneity leads to less participation, at the constituency-level, ethnic heterogeneity, especially caste-based fractionalization, leads to greater political participation. Hence, rather than electoral participation per se, the nature of that participation—which in India's case, is clientelist—must play an important role.

Clientelism can be viewed as the natural outcome of political competition when the credibility of

political competitors is limited. In these cases, political promises are credible only to 'clients'. Political clientelism is a particularistic approach to politics based on 'materialistic inducements targeted to individuals and small groups of people whom politicians know to be highly responsive to such side-payments and willing to surrender their vote for the right price' (Kitschelt and Wilkinson 2007: 9–10). Clientelistic policies tend to take informal means to the pursuit of particularistic goods as opposed to the provision of public goods through institutional means, creating an opaque system where the relationship between patron and client is unequal, though not all-powerful (Helmke and Levitsky 2006: 10–11).

For Keefer and Khemani (2004), the explanations lie in the nature and degree of social polarization, incomplete information of voters, and lack of credibility of political promises to provide broad public goods (as opposed to private transfers and subsidies). Electoral competition therefore revolves around distributing public resources as club goods (goods with excludability characteristics) rather than providing pure public goods such as basic services with broad access. When a political challenger cannot convince voters that s/he will provide better public services if elected but can convince them that s/he will provide greater private transfers then the incumbent's spending policies will be skewed towards private transfers rather than broad public goods. The differential credibility of promises related to public goods versus private transfers can be attributed to three factors—one, the history of past electoral competition and the types of political reputations to which this leads; two, the extent of social fragmentation of voters; and three, limited information among voters about the quality of public services. Limited political credibility may also be behind the political appeal of affirmative action ('reservations') because narrow appeals to ethnic constituencies are the only credible promises that politicians can make in ethnically fragmented societies. The problem of course is that such reservations may further worsen overall public service performance by strengthening clientelist relations and reducing the incentives of political competitors to invest in broad policy reputations across the electorate. In the Indian case, it would seem that the most negative impact of clientelism is not on jobs or even policies, but on implementation (Chandra 2007), where it can subvert well-designed poverty programmes.

The 'messiness' of the Indian state at the local level, and its far removal from the Weberian ideal has been a particular refrain of anthropologists and geographers studying the Indian state. While Gupta (1995) finds that the conceptual distinctions between civil society and the state blur at the local level, for Chatterjee (2004) 'political society'—a transient mediating space between the state and civil society—is the arena where strategies of negotiation and survival of subaltern groups lay waste to the stratagems of the state and civil society groups. Nonetheless, as Corbridge et al. (2005) argue, based on their work on poverty programmes in eastern India, while 'the state' in India is indeed best understood as a complicated tangle of networks and relationships, despite all its messiness, both theoretical and practical, it is becoming more responsive to the poor to some (even if small) degree.

One question that is becoming increasingly important is the relative roles of the state and the markets in redistribution. Thus, in West Bengal where the achievement of the Left Front government in land redistribution is often cited, Bardhan and Mookherjee (forthcoming) find that most changes in land distribution have occurred through market sales and/ or household subdivision—almost four to six times as large as the redistribution achieved by the state mandated *patta* programme. The land area distributed was substantially less (about a third) than the total amount of land vested, leading the authors to speculate that much of the remainder may have been used for private purposes by local officials. And in rural Uttar Pradesh, Kapur et al. (2009), find major improvements in the consumption of status goods among Dalits and caste-relationships, following the introduction of market reforms in 1991. While multiple causal factors—the direct and indirect effects of economic growth (the latter manifest in significant circulatory migration), the ascendancy of a Dalit political party as well as lagged effects of prior public investments— make precise attribution difficult; it points to the role of markets even for socially marginalized groups.

Another area that has received attention is the effect of political reservations on the provision of pro-poor public goods. While Chattopadhyay and Duflo (2004) find positive effects of women reservations on the provision of local benefits, more recent studies challenge their findings. Ban and Rao (2008) do not find any difference in the performance of female leaders from male leaders, although institutional factors matter more for women than for men, with women performing better than men in situations in which they have more political experience and live in villages less dominated by upper castes. Bardhan et al. (2008) find that the benefits from women reservations are not even targeted to female headed households, nor on the provision of the benefits preferred by women (drinking water and roads). Indeed they find that women reservations worsened targeting to SC/ST and landless households, in particular in villages with greater land inequality and poverty among SC/ST groups. However, reservations seem to have more positive effects in the case of SC/ST reservations (Pande 2003). SC/ST *pradhans* allocate more benefits to their own village when the share of SC/ST households is high (Besley et al. 2004; Bardhan et al. 2008). The ambiguity of these results and their sensitivity to spatial and temporal coverage reveal both the analytical potential, and the fundamental limits of using 'natural experiments' to understand political economy at the national level.[10]

The Demand Side Puzzle

While there are good political economy explanations regarding weaknesses on the supply side, the absence of pressure from the demand side is more puzzling. Why is greater demand for effective services not more strongly articulated through the political system, which is necessary to bring accountability into the government delivery system? Why is there much greater demand for places of worship than schools or toilets? And why is there such swift (and often violent) public mobilization if a place of worship is disrespected but virtually none, when school teachers and doctors don't show up?

Several factors may account for weaknesses on the demand side. On the one hand, identity politics that thrives on social cleavages also makes it more difficult to organize collective action on behalf of the poor more generally. On the other, it has been argued that much of identity politics is about the politics of dignity and, as when that cognitive battle is gradually won the focus will turn on more pressing day-to-day concerns leading to greater pressure on governments to perform. While there is some evidence on the latter from the south, public institutions are not simply off and on switches that can be turned on when there is greater demand for better quality services. It may also be the case that poverty programmes and basic public services are more of an issue for 'mass politics' rather than 'elite politics' (a distinction first elaborated by Varshney 1998), and the lack of voice of India's middle classes, who in effect have been exiting from many public services, has made the state less responsive.

Organizational Capabilities

From the first evaluation of the CD programme in 1957, a common feature of India's anti-poverty programmes is that they all falter on the unforgiving, tedious terrain of implementation. One key reason for this is purely administrative, but no less important because of that. While each centrally sponsored scheme has the resources of a particular central ministry to call upon to aid in its design, stipulate conditionalities for disbursement, and so on, the delivery is necessarily by the local administration (the district administration and, now increasingly, the Panchayati Raj Institutions [PRIs]). Few states have the administrative capacity to access grants from 200 plus schemes, spend money as per each of its conditions, maintain separate accounts, and submit individual reports. This administrative capacity is even more limited in those states where the need is the most. Monitoring is rendered difficult not just because of limitations in the monitors themselves, but the sheer number and dispersion of the schemes across communities and locations.

The continued entry of programmes with little exit inevitably leads to a crowding-out effect. No matter how wide the entry of the policy funnel in terms of numbers and scale of poverty programmes, the absence of exit of the earlier programmes means that since they all have to pass through the narrow end of the funnel, namely local public administration, this inevitably results in programmes of the most

recent political incumbents getting priority with older programmes atrophying away. Two trends since the late 1980s have worsened the problem—anti-incumbency leading to more frequent turnover of governments and coalition governments. Both increase the proliferation of anti-poverty programmes as new incumbents seek to distance themselves from older political symbols and coalition partners seek to leave their own mark on their ministries.

The literature has focused primarily on incentives and accountability of public employees, but largely ignored the bread and butter issues of public administration namely, that an adequate number of employees with the appropriate skills is a sine qua non for effective governance. Contrary to public perception, a wide range of government functions in India are significantly understaffed, be it the police, judiciary, or public health departments. The Indian state is over bureaucratized but understaffed.

Despite much ado about India being a 'patronage democracy', large amounts of budgeted expenditures are unspent and hundreds of thousands of government jobs are unfilled. Indeed in recent years, even as academic writing on the clientelist and patronage underpinnings of Indian politics has increased, public sector employment has declined. Total employment in the public sector (including Central government, state government, local government, and quasi-government bodies such as state-owned firms) increased rapidly in the 1970s and 1980s from 11.1 million in 1971 to 15.5 million in 1981 and 19.1 million in 1991. It barely changed in the 1990s (it reached 19.14 million in 2001), before declining to 18.2 million in 2006 (Table 29.1).[11] As a fraction of the labour force the decline is marked.

Perhaps even more important, large numbers of public employees lack the necessary skills for the task they are assigned to. However, there is no systematic data on this vital issue. In the early decade after Independence, public recruitment was necessarily through State Public Service Commissions, based on time-tested cadre and recruitment rules. There were some operational problems with this procedure (long lead times, expanding size of governments, new cadres, and so on). In addition, there were also changes in the design of state institutions. As new entities such as PRIs, Urban Local Bodies (ULBs), and other organizational forms acquired political salience, there was greater demand for flexibility and autonomy in recruitment. New forms of recruitment thus came into being for a variety of reasons. These cover certain categories of services, primarily the ones provided by local governments. There is good reason to believe that government employees recruited by these methods are not adequately skilled commensurate with their responsibilities, which may explain the poor quality of local public service delivery.

Decentralization

If *local* public administration is critical to the successful implementation of any poverty programme, it raises the obvious question whether its quality is endogenous to India's political economy. And in particular, is its weakness the result of the lack of decentralization. Decentralization involves the delegation of authority over the delivery of an anti-poverty programme to local governments rather than to bureaucrats appointed by a Central government who are ill-equipped to monitor and control discretionary behaviour at the local level. Experiments with such patterns of decentralization have recently become widespread throughout developing countries, motivated primarily to reduce corruption and targeting inefficiencies in the delivery system.

Furthermore, political agents at the local level may have greater credibility both because of spatial proximity to the community and reputation developed through social interaction over an extended period of time. However, if resources continue to be concentrated in higher tiers of the government, voters may be apathetic to local elections and have little or no information about the resource availability and capability of local governments. In such circumstances, clientelist promises to a few voters may be easier to make and fulfil due to closer social relations between the elected representatives and their clients. While it has long been recognized that decentralizing power to local governments is essential given India's sheer size, its politicians have long resisted the transfer of resources and authority for local development to elected district and local panchayats, even to the

limited extent mandated by the Seventy-third and Seventy-fourth Constitutional Amendments.

During the 1970s and 1980s, the major concern was the growing centralization of power and resources at the Centre, undermining India's federalism. However, it is evident that there has been a fundamental transformation in Centre–state relations especially since the 'third transformation' in Indian politics circa 1989–90 resulting in the power of states increasing relative to the Centre (Yadav 1999). This transformation is in turn the result of the changes of the party system in India and the rise of regional parties and the decline of national parties. The transformation in Centre–state relations is however, in stark contrast to the continued centralization of power at the state level, with little devolution of power to the local governments notwithstanding the Seventh-third and Seventy-fourth Amendments. The transformation of the party system in India has centralized power at tier two of the government, namely at the state level. Regional parties have little incentive to decentralize power. Controlling resources at the local level is vital for patronage and electoral payoffs, not only at the state level but also at the national level since unlike the past, state level parties can leverage their influence at the national level as coalition partners. The locus of rents has also moved to those areas where state governments are constitutionally empowered, especially the allocation of land, mining, and the social sectors. When voters are in rural areas and the wealth is in urban areas, it is inevitable that those who are elected with support from rural voters will want to control the rents that accrue from urban areas, specially land, housing, and urban infrastructure. This means that there is no incentive for local governments to engage in experimentation and innovation. This equilibrium is unlikely to change unless there is a statutory delegation of more fiscal powers and a greater statutory share of state level fiscal resources.

This has had several effects. One, no matter what the design and resources of any poverty programme, with resources coming from the Centre, since they all have to be implemented by local public administration under the control of state governments, the latter have huge incentives to control local public administration and thereby these resources. This also explains the acquiescence of state level politicians in the progressive centralization of the financing of social programmes. Second, the more the resources available in these programmes, the less the incentives to concentrate state level efforts on the broad public goods with the greatest effects on the poor, especially primary health and primary education, despite the fact that these two areas are constitutionally the responsibility of state governments. And third, since state governments are part of coalition governments at the Centre, the price extracted is a ministerial berth and each ministry will have its version of poverty programmes; thus both proliferation of poverty programmes and lack of exit are virtually guaranteed. The mismatch between the incentives of the implementation agents on the one hand and design and funding of these programmes on the other ensure that implementation is the Achilles heel of India's poverty programmes. To add to this, many states with strong regional parties like Tamil Nadu and Andhra Pradesh would prefer to see less transparent devolution and more centrally sponsored schemes, since these favour states that have good absorption capacity in terms of execution capability and preparation of state level schemes for central funding.

Informational Transparency

A common argument is that information dissemination about the quality of public services can assist in building political credibility and in mobilizing voters around the issue of basic services. Thus, it has been argued that Indian states with greater media presence have more responsive governments (Besley and Burgess 2002). Greater transparency, for instance through the Right to Information (RTI) Act, can reveal the difference between expenditures undertaken in the name of the poor and actual benefits the poor received from such expenditure. This could foster demands for greater accountability from the delivery system.

While these are valid arguments, their limits should also be recognized. First, as Anand *et al.* (2006) show, inequality in access to media (and therefore information) in India has several implications for the substantive aspects of democracy and development in India. Second, while it has become common to argue that increased information would improve oversight and accountability, this is to some degree an article of faith. After all, there is no shortage of elected officials in India whose record on corruption and even violent crime is shamelessly transparent, but with little apparent negative consequences. And third, the media's role as a guardian of the public interest raises the question—who guards the guardians? Reports of politicians having substantive ownership stakes in the media and parts of the media taking money for planting (or not planting) stories, raise troubling questions on the role of civil society itself, whose own actions may be less heroic and more compromised than is generally acknowledged.

EMERGING RESEARCH

On the first anniversary of the terrorist attacks on Mumbai in 2008, an op-ed reflecting on the performance of the Indian state noted that while India 'had police officers who were willing to die doing their duty; but not state officials who could buy bulletproof vests that were not sub-standard', leading the author to wonder, 'how can a people who have much to be proud of, be endowed with a state that has much to be embarrassed about?' (Mehta 2009).

That the Indian state has presided over many positive changes can hardly be doubted. Rapid growth has sharply increased the economy's capacity to absorb shocks without significant disruptions. That this has happened even as the economy has become far more globally integrated over the years indicates that globalization and stability can very well go hand in hand. At the macro-level, there appears to be a decoupling between the economy and politics, indicating perhaps that economic activity and performance have simply become less dependent on political outcomes and stability. Major economic policy changes have occurred and virtually none reversed despite political parties of all possible stripes in power, resulting in policy stability. More rapid economic growth and a rapidly expanding private sector, is increasing options even in basic public services (education, health, water) and whittling away the state's monopoly power.[12] A new breed of local political entrepreneurs (naya netas), empowered by the panchayat system appears to be emerging (Krishna 2007).

At the time of writing, a new massive poverty programme, the National Rural Employment Guarantee Scheme (NREGS), seemed to be performing better, the result of strong in-built provisions of decentralization and transparency with beneficiaries and works selected by the Gram Sabha. The requirement of involving civil society has led to faster real time feedback. Complementary institutional changes such as the RTI Act and representation of women have also helped. The Central government, recognizing this, has begun to include the increase in capacity of local governance as a design component of new CSS, such as the Jawaharlal Nehru National Urban Renewal Mission and the National Rural Health Mission.

Yet, there are clear troubling portents as well. The state's inability to provide basic services has led to reduced life-chances for its many poor citizens and increased inequality as they pay for much-needed services from the private sector providers, it has also created space for uncivil private actors, ranging from radical religious groups to radical left movements, with the Maoist movement the most evident. This issue as well as several others—growing resource conflicts over land and water; political communication and the role of the media; migration and urban politics; and how the ease of making money in political office and the lack of accountability might be leading to the emergence of crony capitalism[13]—are all likely candidates for future research on the political economy of the Indian state.

NOTES

1. For instance, Desai *et al.* (2005) argue that democracy lowers inflation in low-inequality countries but not so in high-inequality countries.

2. Variations in the period, covered in different studies, lead to differing growth rates when comparing pre-reform and post-reform, or 1980s and 1990s.

3. The discussion on India's exchange rate policies is drawn from Kapur and Patel (2003).

4. Deaton and Kozel (2005) provide an excellent discussion of the issues.

5. This discussion draws on Kapur and Mukhopadhay (2007).

6. This data is from Table 7.2, 'India Public Finance Statistics 2008–09', Ministry of Finance, GOI, September 2009. The fertilizer subsidy goes mainly to producers, in an ill-designed cost-plus scheme that has allowed inefficiency in the industry to persist for many years.

7. Based on Ford Foundation documents available at—http://www.fordfound.org/elibrary/documents/0136/018.cfm

8. A broadly similar argument has been made by Bardhan (2005).

9. Ravishankar (2007) examines the 'anti-incumbency factor' in Indian elections and shows that incumbent members of the Parliament from both national and state ruling parties are less likely to win than incumbents from opposition parties. Additionally, these aforementioned explanations assume that unlike most Western democracies, Indian voters care only about pocketbook voting (where they look at their own personal finances) and not sociotropic economic voting (wherein voters care about macroeconomic outcomes). Using micro-data from multiple post-poll surveys, Ravishankar (2007) shows that for Indian voters, pocketbook voting is as common as sociotropic voting. Indian voters are certainly affected by clientelist ties, but within limits; they care equally about broad economic outcomes.

10. For a thoughtful treatment of this issue, see Deaton (2009).

11. *Source*: 'Employment Statistics in India', *Economic and Political Weekly*, 3 May 2003 for 1971–2001, and *Economic Survey*, Government of India, 2008, for 2005. About 70 per cent of the public sector employment is in state government and quasi-government bodies with central and local governments accounting for the remainder.

12. Wilkinson (2007) argues that this is especially the case after 2000.

13. The average assets of MPs elected to the 15th Lok Sabha in 2009 compared to their counterparts elected to the 14th Lok Sabha in 2004 tripled (from Rs 1.86 crore to Rs 5.33 crore) in five years while the number of MPs with assets worth over Rs one crore doubled from 156 in 2004 to 315 in 2009. And the assets of the 304 MPs of the last Lok Sabha, who also contested the polls in 2009, increased from Rs 1.92 crore in 2004 to Rs 4.8 crore. *Source: Association for Democratic Reforms (ADR). The data is based on the basis of mandatory affidavits filed by the MPs during elections.*

REFERENCES

Anand, Bharat, Dmitri Byzalov, and Devesh Kapur. 2006. 'The Dimensions and Implications of Media Inequality in India'. Paper prepared for the annual meeting of the

American Political Science Association, Philadelphia, Pennsylvania. 20 August–3 September 2006.

Ban, Radu and Vijayendra Rao. 2008. 'Tokenism or Agency? Impact of Women's Reservations on Village Democracies in South India', *Economic Development and Cultural Change*, 56, pp. 501–30.

Banerjee, Abhijit and Rohini Somanathan. 2007. 'The Political Economy of Public Goods: Some Evidence from India', *Journal of Development Economics*, 82(2), pp. 287–314.

Banerjee, Abhijit, Lakshmi Iyer, and Rohini Somanathan. 2005. 'History, Social Divisions, and Public Goods in Rural India', *Journal of the European Economic Association*, 3(2–3), pp. 639–47.

Bardhan, Pranab and Dilip Mookherjee. Forthcoming. 'Determinants of Redistributive Politics: An Empirical Analysis of Land Reforms in West Bengal, India', *American Economic Review*.

Bardhan, Pranab, Dilip Mookherjee, and Monica L. Parra Torrado. 2008. 'Impact of Political Reservations in West Bengal Local Governments on Public Service Provision', mimeo.

Bardhan, Pranab. 2005. 'Democracy and Distributive Politics in India', Working Paper, Berkeley: University of California.

———. 1998. *The Political Economy of Development in India*. New Delhi: Oxford University Press.

———. 1984. *The Political Economy of Development in India*. Oxford: Basil Blackwell.

Besley, Timothy and Robin Burgess. 2002. 'The Political Economy of Government Responsiveness: Theory and Evidence from India', *Quarterly Journal of Economics*, 117(4), pp. 1415–51.

Besley, T., R. Pande, L. Rahman, and V. Rao. 2004. 'The Politics of Public Good Provision: Evidence from Indian Local Governments', *Journal of the European Economic Association*, 2(2–3), pp. 416–26.

Bhagwati, Jagdish. 1993. *India in Transition: Freeing the Economy*. New York: Oxford University Press.

Bhagwati, Jagdish and Padma Desai. 1970. *India: Planning for Industrialization: Industrialization and Trade Policies Since 1951*. London: Oxford University Press.

Bhagwati, Jagdish and T.N. Srinivasan. 1975. *Foreign Trade Regimes and Economic Development: India*. New York: Columbia University Press.

Chakravarty, Sukhamoy. 1988. *Development Planning: The Indian Experience*. New Delhi: Oxford University Press.

Chandra, Kanchan. 2007. 'Counting Heads: A Theory of Voter and Elite Behaviour in Patronage Democracies', in Herbert Kitschelt and Steven Wilkinson (eds), *Patrons, Clients and Policies: Patterns of Democratic Accountability and Political Competition*. Cambridge: Cambridge University Press, pp. 84–109.

Chatterjee, Partha. 2004. *The Politics of the Governed: Considerations on Political Society in Most of the World*. New York: Columbia University Press.

Chattopadhyay, R. and E. Duflo. 2004. 'Women as Policy Makers: Evidence from a Randomized Policy Experiment in India', *Econometrica*, 72(5), pp. 1409–43.

Coate, Stephen and Stephen Morris. 1999. 'Policy Persistence', *American Economic Review*, 89(5), pp. 1327–36.

Corbridge, Stuart, Glyn Williams, Manoj Srivastava, and René Véron. 2005. *Seeing the State: Governance and Governmentality in India*. Cambridge, UK: Cambridge University Press.

Datt, Gaurav. 1998. 'Poverty in India and Indian States: An Update', Food Consumption and Nutrition Division Discussion Paper No. 47, International Food Policy Research Institute.

Datt, Gaurav and Martin Ravallion. 1998. 'Why Have Some Indian States Done Better than Others at Reducing Rural Poverty?', *Economica*, 65(257), pp. 17–38.

Deaton, Angus. 2009. 'Instruments of Development: Randomization in the Tropics, and the Search for the Elusive Keys to Economic Development', The Keynes Lecture. Available at http://www.princeton.edu/~deaton/downloads/Instruments%20of%20development%20v1d_mar09_all.pdf

Deaton, Angus and Valerie Kozel. 2005. 'Data and Dogma: The Great Indian Poverty Debate', *World Bank Research Observer*, 20(2), pp. 177–99.

Desai, Raj M., Anders Olofsgård, and Tarik M. Yousef. 2005. 'Inflation and Inequality: Does Political Structure Matter?', *Economics Letters*, 87(1), pp. 41–6.

Drèze, Jean and Amartya Sen (2002). *India: Development and Participation*. New York: Oxford University Press.

Gupta, Akhil. 1995. 'The Discourse of Corruption, the Culture of Politics and the Imagined State', *American Ethnologist*, 22(2), pp. 375–402.

Helmke, Gretchen and Steven Levitsky. 2006. 'Introduction', in Gretchen Helmke and Steven Levitsky (eds), *Informal Institutions and Democracy: Lessons from Latin America*. Baltimore: The Johns Hopkins University Press, pp. 1–30.

Iyer, Laxmi. Forthcoming. 'Direct Versus Indirect Colonial Rule in India: Long-term Consequences', *The Review of Economics and Statistics*.

Jalan, Bimal. 1991. *India's Economic Crisis: The Way Ahead*. New Delhi: Oxford University Press.

Joshi, Vijay and I.M.D. Little. 1994. *India Macroeconomics and Political Economy, 1964–91*. Washington DC: World Bank.

Kapur, Devesh, Chandra Bhan Prasad, D. Shyam Babu, and Lant Pritchett. 2009. 'Compared to What? (and by Whom?). Markets as a Solvent of Social Institutions', mimeo.

Kapur, Devesh and Partha Mukhopadhyay. 2007. 'Sisyphean State? Why Poverty Programs in India Fail and Yet Persist'. Paper presented at the 2007 Annual Meeting of the American Political Science Association. 30 August–2 September 2007.

Kapur, Devesh and Pratap B. Mehta (eds). 2005. *India's Public Institutions: Performance and Design*. New Delhi: Oxford University Press.

Kapur, Devesh and Urjit Patel. 2003. 'Large Foreign Currency Reserves: Insurance for Domestic Weaknesses and External Uncertainties?', *Economic and Political Weekly*, XXXVIII(11), pp. 1047–53.

Keefer, Philip and Stuti Khemani. 2004. 'Why do the Poor Receive Poor Services?', *Economic and Political Weekly*, XXIX(9), pp. 935–43.

Khatkhate, Deena. 2004. 'Reserve Bank of India: A Study in the Separation and Attrition of Powers', in Devesh Kapur and Pratap B. Mehta (eds), *India's Public Institutions: Performance and Design*. New Delhi: Oxford University Press, pp. 320–52.

Kitschelt, Herbert and Steven Wilkinson (eds). 2007. *Patrons, Clients and Policies: Patterns of Democratic Accountability and Political Competition*. Cambridge: Cambridge University Press.

Kohli, Atul. 1987. *The State and Poverty in India: The Politics of Reform*. Cambridge: Cambridge University Press.

Krishna, Anirudh. 2007. 'Politics in the Middle: Mediating Relationships between the Citizens and the State in Rural North India', in Herbert Kitschelt and Steven I. Wilkinson (eds), *Patrons, Clients and Policies*, pp. 141–58.

Lewis, John P. 1995. *India's Political Economy New Delhi: Governance and Reform*. New Delhi: Oxford University Press.

Lipton, Michael. 1977. *Why Poor People Stay Poor: Urban Bias in World Development*. London: Temple Smith.

Mani, Anandi and Sharun Mukand. 2007. 'Democracy and Visibility', *Journal of Development Economics*, 83(2), pp. 506–29.

Mehta, Pratap Bhanu. 2009. 'The Measure of Our Strength', *Indian Express*, 26 November.

Myrdal, Gunnar. 1968. *Asian Drama: An Inquiry into the Poverty of Nations*. Harmondsworth: Penguin.

Panagariya, Arvind. 2008. *India: The Emerging Giant*. New York: Oxford University Press.

———. 2004. 'India in the 1980s and 1990s: A Triumph of Reforms', Working Paper, IMF.

Pande, Rohini. 2003. 'Can Mandated Political Representation Increase Policy Influence for Disadvantaged Minorities?

Theory and Evidence from India', *American Economic Review*, 93(4), pp. 1132–51.

Planning Commission. 2005. 'Performance Evaluation of Targeted Public Distribution System'. Programme Evaluation Organization, Planning Commission, Government of India, New Delhi.

Pritchett, Lant. 2009. 'A Review of Edward Luce's In Spite of the Gods: The Strange Rise of Modern India', *Journal of Economic Literature*, 47(3), pp. 771–80.

Raj, K.N. 1973. 'The Politics and Economics of Intermediate Regimes', *Economic and Political Weekly*, VIII(27), pp. 1189–98.

Rao, Govinda M. and Nirvikar Singh. 2006. 'The Political Economy of India's Fiscal Federal System and its Reform', *Publius*, 37(1), pp. 26–44.

Ravallion, Martin. 2009. 'A Comparative Perspective on Poverty Reduction in Brazil, China and India', World Bank Policy Research Working Paper No. 5080.

Ravishankar, Nirmala. 2007. 'Voting for Change: Turnout and Vote Choice in Indian Elections'. PhD Thesis. Massachusetts: Harvard University.

Rodrik Dani and Arvind Subramanian. 2005. 'From "Hindu Growth" to Productivity Surge: The Mystery of the Indian Growth Transition', *IMF Staff Papers*, 52(2), pp. 193–228.

Rudolph, Lloyd I. and Susanne Hoeber Rudolph. 1987. *In Pursuit of Lakshmi: The Political Economy of the Indian State*. Chicago: The University of Chicago Press.

Varshney, Ashutosh. 1998. 'Mass Politics or Elite Politics? India's Economic Reforms in Comparative Perspective', *Journal of Policy Reform*, 2(4), pp. 301–35.

Virmani, Arvind. 2004. 'India's Economic Growth: From Socialist Rate of Growth to Bharatiya Rate of Growth', Indian Council for Research on International Economic Relations, Working Paper No. 122.

Waterbury, John. 1993. *Exposed to Innumerable Delusions: Public Enterprise and State Power in Egypt, India, Mexico, and Turkey*. Cambridge: Cambridge University Press.

Wilkinson, Steven. 2007. 'Changing Patterns of Party-Voter Linkages in India', in Herbert Kitschelt and Steven I. Wilkinson (eds), *Patrons, Clients and Policies: Patterns of Democratic Accountability and Political Competition*. Cambridge: Cambridge University Press, pp. 114–20.

Yadav, Yogendra. 1999. 'Electoral Politics in the Time of Change: India's Third Electoral System, 1989–99', *Economic and Political Weekly*, XXXIV(34–5), pp. 2393–9.

30 Business and Politics

Aseema Sinha

We know from James Scott's work (1985) a fair amount about the 'Weapons of the Weak' adopted by peasants. But, how does business—a 'strong' section of society—respond to and live under interventionist states? For much of India's existence, and for that matter many dirigiste societies, the Leviathan has ruled. India initiated deregulation policies in 1985, yet the state's regulations continue to affect private business activity in India. What are the 'weapons of the strong' in such state-centric conditions? Do these responses contribute to development-enhancing policies, or to particularistic collusion between business and state actors? The relationship between business and the state in India warrants far more scholarly attention than has been undertaken to date.

In February 2000, a photograph of the then Prime Minister (PM), Atal Behari Vajpayee and then Finance Minister, Yashwant Sinha, flanked by many pre-eminent CEOs appeared in the national dailies.[1] As part of the pre-budget consultations, Vajpayee had addressed FICCI, a national business association.

Currently, business delegations travel with the Finance Minister and the PM on international trips frequently. Such public camaraderie would have been impossible even a decade or two back, when PMs refused to address business associations. Rajiv Gandhi was the first PM to address a business association meeting in 1985. How has the nature of the relationship between the business sector and the government changed after liberalization (1985/1991)? How did distrust and distance give way to regular consultation and interaction? For observers of India, this transformation in the business–politics relationship is quite surprising. For years the Indian state over-regulated, imposing entry, exit, and everyday restrictions on the private sector. The relationship between business associations and the government was distant, and any regular interactions between collective organizations representing business and the state were few and far between. Pranab Bardhan describes the pre-existing relationship well:

> But the public-private ties are quite different in India from tightly integrated working relationship of the East Asian government with private business, none of the well-

developed networks of MITI in Japan or IDB in Taiwan, which allow industry experts within the state apparatus continuously involved in information dissemination and consensus building, coaxing, arm twisting, with representatives of private capital. Not merely is the cultural distance between the gentlemen administrator and the private capitalist rather large in India (although narrowing in recent years with a diversification in the social background of the recruits in civil service), what is more important is that in the Indian context of contending heterogeneous classes, such a close liaison and harmonizing of interests of the state with private business would have raised an outcry of foul play and strong political resentment among the interest groups, the electoral repercussions of which Indian politicians can afford to ignore much less than say the LDP politicians in Japan. (Bardhan 1993)

This chapter maps the ongoing changes in the business–politics relationship in India in an attempt to capture the nature of historical patterns and changing trends and transformations. This question has two distinct dimensions: changes within the private sector and from the perspective of the government. First, how does the private sector, a powerful social actor in its own right, respond to a strong state in post-reform India? Second, what contributes to the increased policy responsiveness to business on the part of the government? Initially, I discuss some of the theoretical expectations and puzzles that emerge from a comparative study of business in India. I go on to map the business–politics relationship during the era of the developmental state. The second section highlights the major transformation in the economic basis of capitalism in India, which provides the preconditions for the changes witnessed more recently. The third section focuses on certain key aspects of the business–politics relationship in post-reform India, such as the changing role of business associations, the global activities of Indian business, and the entry of business into the national Parliament.

THEORETICAL DEBATES AND EMPIRICAL PUZZLES

Two dominant approaches to business–government relationships can be found in the literature. One approach, focusing on the nature of state intervention

in economic life, is insufficiently attuned to how state regulations impact business and capital, and what capital needs from the state. The second approach attends more closely to specific market processes (sectoral or business-wide), yet oversimplifies its subject matter by assuming that business actors respond to the state in homogenous ways.

Theories of State

The theory of the developmental state suggests that the state 'guided markets' (Wade 1990) and ensured long-term and collaborative interactions with business actors (Evans 1995). Most of these studies suffer from a statist bias, and fail to incorporate a sufficient understanding of how business actors and associations affect the design and policies of the developmental state.[2] A complete theory of the developmental state requires an analysis of what capital needs from the state; this becomes even more crucial after liberalization, when the boundaries of state action are being redrawn. Other theories of the state posit that state regulation invites rent-seeking or collusion (Krueger 1974; Srinivasan 1985) but these a priori expectations have never been confronted with direct empirical evidence about business behaviour. Similarly, most analysts of structural adjustment reforms assume that business actors welcome economic reforms. However, that is a gross simplification. The diversity of business responses within India—between the import versus export industry-based industrialists, between large and small firms, and between the national versus regional business groups[3]—shows that liberalization policies do not affect business groups in a uniform manner. Thus, we need an ethnographic analysis of how deregulation affects business, and their responses to deregulation.

Studies of Business Influence[4]

Studies focusing on specific business influences on the government are of two types. One model suggests that business may impose a structural constraint on macroeconomic policy by its threat of exit (Lindblom 1984; Winters 1996). However, this approach views business as a collective entity, assuming that all investors have a common set of interests vis-à-vis the state. Similarly, most analysts assume that business actors welcome economic reforms. The conflict between the Bombay Club[5] and the export-oriented capitalists in India, to name one such division within the Indian business classes, suggests that business groups have divergent interests on many issues related to economic reforms. India's experience foregrounds the diversity and competition between and among business groups, and even within business houses. These differences may arise from the regional location, sectoral presence, or pre-existing ties with the government. A study of competition between and among business is as important as the posited unity of class action. A rich body of research has analysed the sectoral origins of business power over government (Gourevtich 1986; Rogowski 1989) while analyses of the regional organization of business are rarer. Yet, sectoral studies of business influence fail to highlight the precise mechanisms through which sectoral interests are translated into policy outcomes. Thus, we need an analysis of the institutions and organizations through which business interests are communicated to the government, and the manner in which they shape public policy. Thus, both sectoral and structural (business-as-capital) approaches fail to pay attention to how institutions (pre-budget meetings between the government and business leaders), networks (ethnic links of entrepreneurs with regional states and parties), and organizations (business associations) mediate business–state relations.

India-specific Studies

Studies on Indian business are relatively few, and a large proportion of them deal with the colonial and nationalist periods (Ray 1979, 1994; Tripathi 1984, 1981, 1991; Berna 1960; Tomlinson 1981). One recent study by Vivek Chibber, argues that the business classes defeated Nehruvian plans for a strong developmental state in the 1940s and the 1950s (Chibber 2003). George Rosen's early study (1966) is an explicit treatment of post-Independence political and economic interactions, but focuses on policies and classes and not on institutional mediations between economic groups and the state. Stanley Kochanek's study of business and politics in India stands out as particularly useful as he analysed the business associations explicitly (Kochanek 1974).

He documented a major insight, which has stood the test of time: the licence-quota-permit raj [or rule] engendered particularistic one-to-one relationships between Indian business and the state, despite the overall aura of hostility (Kochanek 1987; Herring 1999; Kohli 1989; Rudolph and Rudolph 1987). Yet, it is clear that the relationship between business and politics has undergone a substantial change in the 1980s and the 1990s. Kochanek's brief analysis of the Confederation of Indian Industry (CII) is the only partial study of the recent business–politics relationship (Kochanek 1995–6). Yet, we do not know if corrupt and firm-level dealings been replaced by class-wide and positive-sum relationships between business and state actors.

ECONOMIC CHANGE, BUSINESS, AND THE DEVELOPMENTAL STATE

Economic changes in different sectors of the Indian economy, technological changes, the import-substitution strategy, all have transformed the economic potential, role, and activities of business in India. Statist developmentalism played an indispensable role in that transformation from the 1950s to the 1980s. During the 1970s and 1980s, crucial structural changes had begun in the economic basis; these were to leverage India's business strengths in the 1990s. The economic power of India's entrepreneurial classes has grown manifold, both at the national and regional levels, and had diversified as well.

Despite the conventional view that states harmed private activity, the reality is that the state-led developmental state in India (1947–90) facilitated the rise of nascent and new businesses, provided credit and budgetary support in the form of concession finance to both the private and public sectors, and defended the interests of national business against outside capital. More indirectly, public-sector effort provided the background for private capital to thrive and develop by laying the massive infrastructure of a modern industrialized economy. Even more interestingly, and counter-intuitively, restrictive regulations on prices and the poor quality of infrastructure forced Indian companies to evolve cost-saving techniques and innovate. This is most true in the case of the pharmaceuticals sector in India, where punitive price and cost regulations ensured that Indian companies learnt how to produce medicines at cheap rates.[6] No less than Ratan Tata, one of India's leading business leaders, recently admitted that it was the ability to innovate around obstacles of red tape, bumpy roads, and poor infrastructure that give Indian companies an edge. Ratan Tata said: 'Being in this market, contrary to what everyone believes you always need to be more competitive than what you have to be outside, because the buying power in this country is so low. So, you are always thinking of how to address that segment of the market.'[7]

India grew slowly from 1945 to the 1980s. Behind this slow growth lay an expansion and diversification of investment and economic activities. In the 1980s, India's economy grew more rapidly than ever before—at times approaching 6 per cent a year—and in new patterns. At the state level, growth rates had accelerated in the late 1970s, with some states growing much more rapidly than others; this also underlay the rising growth rates after 1980 (Sinha 2005a). Despite the fact that India's growth has been in the service and manufacturing sector, one of the most striking structural changes in the past 60 years has been in agriculture. Food production rose even as the share of the annual gross domestic product (GDP) for which agriculture accounted dropped from 42 per cent in 1980 to 24 per cent in 2004. Over the same period, the net agricultural production doubled, going from 96 million metric tonnes in the 1980s to 180 million metric tonnes in 2000 (GoI 2007). Figures such as these bespeak the success of the Green Revolution. The key was a more intensive application of capital and technology to farming. Yet, this application did not proceed evenly throughout the country. Some parts of the country began growing enough not only to feed themselves, but also to sell, thereby funding investments beyond farming. In some states—Punjab, parts of Uttar Pradesh, and Tamil Nadu—technical improvements in agriculture affected other sectors of the economy as prospering farms required more inputs, more processing infrastructure, and more construction. Rising incomes stimulated a demand for goods and services, fuelling industrialization

in Gujarat, Tamil Nadu, Andhra Pradesh, Punjab, Haryana, and parts of West Bengal. Farmers invested in real estate, small-scale industry, and transport. Growth among these smaller cities broadened the base of economic transformation in India by creating more scope for the burgeoning agricultural sector to promote industry.

In the industrial and urban sectors of the economy, while growth was slow and stagnant from the 1940s and in the 1980s, diversification and depth became possible. India was able to produce everything, from nuclear reactors to bread, generating and unleashing different types of entrepreneurial energies across diverse areas and regions. After 1992/1993, subsequent to the economic reforms of 1991, a sharp rise in the rate of economic growth was reported. The growth rate of the GDP is estimated at between 7.5 and 8.5 per cent in 2003–4, 2004–5, and 2005–6. Industrial growth has been moderate but stable, at around 6 per cent per annum (GoI 2007). The nature of India's growth pattern underwent significant structural changes: the service sector grew much faster and fuelled a large proportion of India's rising growth rate. Thus, the most striking aspect of India's growth acceleration has been its composition. The services sector grew by 43.7 per cent (in current rupees) and 34.4 per cent (in current dollars) in the last two decades, and constitutes more than 50 per cent of the economy (GDP)(Kapur 2002: 92). Thus, many of the new business groups in India were in the service sector in the form of technocratic capitalists, those who were educated in the public sector,[8] and then branched out to form their own companies in Information Technology (IT), pharmaceuticals, hotels, and other commercial ventures in the new economy. Baru notes that 'nearly a quarter of the top one hundred private companies in India today are owned by first generation businessmen' (Baru 2000: 214). Significant churning and change within the business class, with old business houses becoming less important and new ones joining the field, is one of the striking features of the evolving business-politics landscape. Such new groups include Reliance, Ruias (Essar), Mallya (UB group), Abhay Oswal, Mithals, Nagarjuna, as well as the new pharmaceutical companies, Ranbaxy, Sun Pharma, Dr Reddy's Laboratories, and in other sectors TVS

Sundaram, Hero Honda, Onida, Videocon, among others (Baru 2000:5). Agrarian capitalists and their linkage with regional industry is another area where transformation in the nature of capitalism in India is most evident, and deserves more analysis.

REGIONALIZATION, REGIONAL CAPITALISM, AND BUSINESS

The formation of business and commercial classes in many states and a regional bourgeoisie, apart from national capitalist classes, were the impetus for industrialization at the regional or sub-national level, in interaction with the sub-national state (Sinha 2005a; Baru 1997, 2000; Upadhya 1988,1997). Sinha argues that regional states in India exploited the structure of the licence-raj [rule] to satisfy regional investment hunger and pursued regional developmental strategies. In many cases, regional states acted entrepreneurially, circumventing Central constraints in an attempt to maximize regional capitalism and development (Sinha 2005a: 91, passim). Baru, in a similar vein, notes:

> The process of agrarian change in many parts of the country has laid the foundations for capitalist development in the non-farm sector. This process has allowed a new generation of agrarian capitalists or other middle class professionals to make the transition to capitalist entrepreneurs ... the latter seek political and material support from state governments and regional political parties. It is not surprising that regional parties... have been most active in states where regional business groups have been more dynamic and assertive. (Baru 2000: 226)

The prominent regional parties with linkages to business groups are in Maharashtra (Shiv Sena), Punjab (Akali Dal), Andhra Pradesh (TDP), and even in West Bengal CPI(M),[9] and Tamil Nadu (DMK). These classes, in active collaboration with regional parties and states, fuelled the creation of sub-national developmental states (Sinha 2005a), as well as creating a demand for the reform of the national regulatory regime, and challenging the power and authority of many national business groups (Baru 2000: 224–5). Thus, the business class in India became regionalized

as well as embedded within regional states and parties. The expansion of economic activity, India's size, India's federal political institutions, and diversity of capitalist development dating back to colonial times has created a large, diversified, and complex class. 'Business' is, thus, not a homogenous category in India.

BUSINESS: A HOMOGENOUS CATEGORY?

At the national level, business is arrayed along different dimensions: organized versus unorganized sector (a legal category); foreign versus domestic business groups (ownership); large versus small-scale sector (size); and import versus export (markets) business firms (Tyabji 1981). In the pre-reform period (1947–85), national-level associations represented the foreign versus domestic business classes. The Federation of Indian Chambers of Commerce and Industry (hereafter FICCI) was home to domestic business groups, while the Associated Chambers of Commerce and Industry (hereafter ASSOCHAM) represented the foreign and multinational groups.[10] Sectoral differences within the business community may be as salient. A rich body of research analyses the sectoral—such as automobiles, IT, pharmaceuticals, steel, and the like—origins of business power over government (Gourevitch 1986; Rogowski 1989). Sectoral studies on India, such as that of Sridharan on electronics (1996), Heeks on software (1996), and Pingle on the automobile, steel, and computer industries (1999), highlight the differences across sectors. This diversification seems to challenge the idea that business could constitute a single capitalist class in India; fragmentation, competition, and conflict mark the actions of the business class even after globalization and an increased role of business in policymaking. This is most evident in the competition between the national business associations—FICCI, CII, and ASSOCHAM.

INTER-BUSINESS COMPETITION IN INDIA[11]

In the late 1980s and early 1990s, the business system entered a competitive and transitional phase accompanied by internal churning within the existing and predominant business association (FICCI), and the revitalization of another business association (ASSOCHAM). This provided the initial window of opportunity for a new organization to enter the associational marketplace by providing many developmental services to both the government and the industry (CII). The Mumbai business houses—some of which are prominent members of the industrial elite in India—had left FICCI after an internal fight over bogus membership and the control of decision-making within FICCI. They joined ASSOCHAM, in the process revitalizing it with resources, talent, and new ideas. At this time, ASSOCHAM was privy to a significant influx of money and talent into the organization.[12] Thus, when the Confederation of Engineering Industry (CEI) thought of catering to the needs of the wider industry, it first thought of a merger with ASSOCHAM.[13] This would have made the unified body a very powerful organization. ASSOCHAM's President at that time expressed the desire and need to unite business voices in India. This, he felt, would increase the power of the business sector over the government. He pointed out:

> Countries which have made the most progress in the postwar era like Japan, Germany and France, have fundamentally one chamber, which is very powerful and is consulted in policymaking. The Japanese PM sometimes even comes to meet the head of Keidanren, the apex body of the captains of industry. The German and Paris chambers of commerce are almost a part of the respective governments and the status of the British Confederation of Industry is well known. (Roy 1991)

Simultaneously, the competition between the two main national organizations had heated up. Federation of Indian Chambers of Commerce and Industry's sponsorship of the joint business councils, involving cooperation and networking with business actors from other countries as well as government officials, was a source of envy for members of other associations. Members of the CEI felt that their exclusion from these councils, and their monopolization by FICCI, was unfair.[14] Competition was also evident through the movement of members from one organization to another. After 1987, ASSOCHAM saw the entry

of many new members, other chambers, and big corporate houses. From 1987 to 1991, the direct membership doubled to 500, and the indirect membership increased eightfold to 52,000. In 1991, nine more big companies became 'patron members' of the association.[15] These included a wide array of industrial companies, which added to the prestige and reputation of the organization. After this induction, ASSOCHAM enjoyed the patronage of such companies as Tata Sons, Bajaj Auto, Mahindra and Mahindra, Chowgule and Co., Hindustan Unilever, India Tobacco Company (ITC), Phillips Carbon Black (RPG), Shaw Wallace and Company, Premier Automobiles, The Mafatlal Spinning and Company, The MRF, Modi Xerox, DLF Universal, Indian Aluminum, and the Amalgamation Ltd (Simpson group). Many of these companies had left the FICCI and joined ASSOCHAM, thus levying competitive pressure on FICCI.[16] It could be argued that through this transformation, CEI wanted to replace FICCI as the single most powerful industry association in the country (Raman 1991; Ghosh 1992; Roy 1992).

In response to the business model presented by CII, FICCI sought to organize itself and deal with the rise of CII, a powerful competitor (Sharif 1994; Guha 1994).[17] Many of the reforms initiated by FICCI—the campaign to expand membership and subscription, organizational changes, and changing purposes to deal with international competition—were in direct response to CII's perceived strengths.[18] The FICCI decided to go into the business of trade shows and exhibitions, a domain in which CII had already carved a name for itself, and also began publishing a journal called *Quality Trends*, following in the footsteps of CII's quality movement.[19] In an effort to strengthen its secretariat, a five-member core team was set up to oversee a radical restructuring of the administrative structures and procedures. FICCI decided to appoint an economic expert as CEO, who would also function as secretary-general. It was at this time that Amit Mitra was chosen to be the Secretary-general.[20] Clearly, public relations and handling public events was prioritized, given the positive publicity being received by CII. A new division titled 'Protocol' was set up to handle visits of foreign delegations, besides looking after the other major functions of the chamber. 'We want to give better hospitality and have proper management of important events', said A.K. Rungta, senior Vice-President, FICCI.[21] In 1998, a corporatist drive was launched to make FICCI a more efficient organization. The leadership of FICCI also began to track news stories on the two organizations, and undertake a comparative evaluation of the media coverage of the two associations.[22] As with the CII, which seeks to make each of its divisions self-earning and profit-oriented, it was decided that FICCI would run on a profit basis.[23] In the mid to late 1990s, FICCI launched a new membership initiative with a view to shake off its 'old economy image'. In 2000, around 220 members from the so-called technology, media, and telecom (TMT) sectors joined the association, including such companies as Infosys, S. Kumars, Aptec, Sony Entertainment, Hughes Network systems, and Silverline Tech. Faced with competition, FICCI realized that 'unless we have a good membership base we will lose our voice as an apex industry chamber and also lack financial muscle'.[24] Reciprocally, a resurgent FICCI has begun to put competitive pressure on CII: Tarun Das recently said, 'Yes we are very different from FICCI but their presence has kept us on our toes, we have to constantly innovate'.[25] Thus, competition within the business system shaped the transformation of existing organizations (in this case FICCI and ASSOCHAM) into developmental associations.

Yet, this competition prevented united collective action on the part of all three associations, or any moves towards merger or unity. India, despite globalization and the transformation into developmental associations, continues to be a 'state dominated pluralist system', in which numerous groups vie for the state's attention and business is fragmented. Despite many attempts to unite business action, merger moves between CII, FICCI, and ASSOCHAM, or even joint efforts or campaigns between the associations could not succeed.[26]

The first such merger was mooted in June–July 1990, but came to naught.[27] In July 1992, an apex committee constituted by the Presidents of the three chambers—FICCI, CII, and ASSOCHAM—was proposed. It was considered necessary to coordinate among the three chambers given the economic liberalization, which had changed the role of the chambers from 'representation' to that of 'partners of economic growth'. The main task of the committee was to have joint meetings with the PM, government leaders, and foreign dignitaries.[28] This body failed to take shape at that time as leading industrialists in FICCI felt that such a body would affect its functioning.[29] Again, in 1995, another joint body was mooted to coordinate strategy vis-à-vis external actors. The initiative for a unified front was first mooted by L.M. Thapar and S.K. Birla in early 1995 (members of FICCI). CII President Rajive Kaul also favoured the idea of working together with both FICCI and ASSOCHAM on issues relating to external relations. This effort followed a realization by top industrialists that 'they are wasting their time, energy and money in separately hosting visiting foreign businessmen under the aegis of ASSOCHAM, CII or FICCI when the issues for discussion are common. So why not constitute a coordinated body which gives equal representation to the three apex chambers (Dobhal 1995)? However, this body was never instituted, and the three chambers today continue to invite foreign dignitaries separately.[30] In 1993, attempts to form an India International Business Council (IIBC) by R.P Goenka, with the support of the foreign ministry of the Government of India and the inclusion of all three chambers came to naught, as it increased in-fighting rather than any collective or cooperative action.[31] Again in 2000 there was some effort to present a joint set of recommendations on the annual budget, but the three chambers could not agree to do so. The FICCI proposed the joint proposal idea, but CII and ASSOCHAM preferred to go it alone and give their separate suggestions to the Finance Minister.[32] Thus, competitive politics between the three chambers has continued to be a pervasive feature of the interest representation map in India. On one hand, the lack of business unity affects the nature of business coherence and the strength with which the business community can negotiate with the government. On the other hand, this competition stimulates the adoption of developmental features by both the CII and FICCI.

ECONOMIC AND POLICY CHANGES IN THE 1990s

Beginning in 1985 and more systematically in 1991, India liberalized its economy. Important domestic regulatory changes were accompanied and followed by a change in India's global strategy. Trade, technology, and foreign direct investment (FDI) were all encouraged. This policy change had a clear impact on India's economy. Net FDI inflows as a percentage of gross capital formation increased from 0.23 per cent in 1980 to 2.6 per cent in 2002, while the total trade in goods and services as a percentage of GDP increased from around 16 per cent to around 31 per cent. After 1992/1993, subsequent to the economic reforms of 1991, a sharp rise in the rate of economic growth was reported. The growth rate of the GDP was estimated at between 7.5 and 8.5 per cent in 2003–4, 2004–5, and 2005–6 (GoI 2007). Liberalization of the economic policy also affected the nature of India's growth pattern and facilitated a structural change in the economy: the service sector grew much faster and fuelled a large proportion of India's rising growth rate. How are these economic and policy changes reflected in the institutional relations between the class actors—capitalist class—and the state, the carriers of these transformations?

TRENDS AND DEVELOPMENTS IN THE 1990s

A number of developments in the business and politics relationship need to be taken note of. First, and most significantly, business and the state came closer, and evolved a mutually beneficial relationship at both formal and informal levels.[33] The earlier hands-off relationship stands radically transformed. Interestingly, globalization and global competition catalysed this coming together of business and state in diverse ways. Second, business associations became much more developmental and functional and revived themselves. At the centre of this development lay the rise and transformation of the CII, but the other major associations—FICCI and ASSOCHAM—also changed and transformed themselves. However, this was accompanied by an increase, and not a decrease, in the number of associations and their activities. Increased competition and fragmentation in business collective action coexists with an increase in their power and functional role in a liberalizing economy. Interestingly, this period also saw intense competition and conflict amongst the big business houses, represented by the Tatas, Reliance, and the like. Big business did not seek to exercise power as a collectivity, despite the establishment of many forums where they came together to address and shape public policy. Third, many businessmen and houses began to participate in direct politics and seek representation in the mainstream of the political system. Thus, many businessmen stood for elections, made their relationship with parties public (like Anil Ambani, for instance), and joined the Rajya Sabha in greater numbers. Let me elaborate on each in turn.

Globalization Brings the National State and Indian Business Closer[34]

Globalization in the 1990s and beyond has bound the state and business in a curious relationship of mutual dependence in India. Counter-intuitively to our expectations, this relationship of mutual dependence was activated in the 1990s in and around negotiations concerning the multilateral regime in trade. As Indian companies and business actors began confronting and engaging with global forces, they realized the functional need for a strong state to defend them, and ensure that the terms on which they competed globally would favour them. Reciprocally, the state found itself out of its depth in global negotiations, in terms of the complex information and implementation costs, which led it to seek a closer interaction with business partners. Also, state actors sought to legitimize their international negotiations through increased interactions with industry leaders. These challenges and impetus transformed the institutional basis of state–business interactions— both formal and informal—as well as the texture of the relationship in significant ways. Globalization also made foreign capital and Indian capital in foreign markets more central to policy debate and the policy formulation process. Thus, globalization provided the stimulus and the site for changing state–business relations in India.

The Beginning of Business's Role in Policymaking, 1999–2007

One of the most radical changes in the trade policy process in India after 1999–2000 has been in the manner in which the government seeks policy inputs from industry firms and industry associations, both during the formulation and implementation stages of policymaking. In fact, the incorporation of business in trade policymaking is one of the only instances of the serious integration of business opinion and input in policy formulation in India; in other policy domains business input is sought, but rarely as intensively as on issues of international trade. This significant change was a product of compliance pressures and dilemmas created as a result of changes in the international trade regime under the aegis of the World Trade Organization (WTO).

As late as 27 May 1997, the former Commerce Secretary and India's chief negotiator at the Uruguay Round, A.V. Ganesan, said that apart from some sections of the Indian bureaucracy and politicians, there seemed to be very little awareness of the 'dramatic changes' brought about by the WTO rounds.[35] He failed to note that one of the reasons (though not the only one) for this state of affairs was that the Government of India neither consulted nor shared any information about General Agreement on Tariffs and Trade (GATT)or the WTO with any industry business group during the Uruguay round; the policymaking process regarding international negotiations was closed and insular with no interaction with any outside actor. S. Venkitaramanan, a senior government official, similarly noted in 1997:

> GOI should engage the trade and business community in an intensive dialogue in order to arrive at agreed methods for handling the impending confrontations with WTO. On and off consultations will not do. We should not face WTO without a proper defense strategy. Such a strategy cannot be devised in isolation at New Delhi or Geneva. It has to involve and talk to those who are affected. (Venkitaramanan 1997)

Another senior government official said:

> the Government should be more open with industry and make public details of all trade-related agreements it entered into with the rest of the world .... The agreements are not supposed to be a secret. If 135 other nations know about it, why [should] not the domestic industry should be told about it.[36]

The insularity of the state apparatus was mirrored in the attitude of business persons and business associations, who did not know or care about the ongoing WTO negotiations till as late as 1999–2000. Indian industry had come to maturity under a closed economy environment concerned more with lobbying for changes and exceptions in the domestic policy environment than with international trade regimes. Its interest in multilateral trade negotiations was non-existent.[37] During the Uruguay round (1986–94), the Indian industry was more concerned with domestic liberalization than with the losses and gains India sustained at the multilateral level. Businessmen, and even business associations, did not care to educate themselves about how the WTO would affect them. They hardly carried out any research or careful study of the WTO and GATT. As an illustration, the CII, the so-called professional association, thought that the WTO was not at all important in the mid and late 1990s.[38] In the early 1990s the three all-industry associations issued 'statements' in favour of a globally consistent IPR regime without any analysis, but because the government asked them to issue statements in support of the government's policy at that time.[39] As noted by G.V. Ramakrishna, 'The fault also lies with industry. There has been a complete lack of initiative on its part. It has never bothered to find out what was happening at the [WTO-related] meetings abroad.'[40] A CII report acknowledged that Indian industry (during the Uruguay round) was 'not so much concerned with what was happening in the Uruguay round. It was not even fully aware of the items of agenda that were being negotiated.'[41] Rahul Bajaj, a businessman of national repute, said in 2001:

> India was a party to the Uruguay negotiations from the beginning and it was given an opportunity to participate in these rounds ... it is unfortunate that neither the Indian government nor the Indian business took these

discussions very seriously. We did not adequately prepare for these negotiations and we faltered at every point. (Bajaj 2001)

In 1999, CII thought about setting up an office in Geneva at the site of the WTO, but nothing came of that proposal till 2004 when Arun Shourie urged CII to set up an office. This time, a small office was indeed set up, but again closed by 2006 for financial reasons (Rao 1999).[42] Around 1997–8, at a seminar organized by the government to discuss the impending ministerial meeting in Singapore, N. Shankar, a prominent business person, appealed to the government: 'Please educate us about how we may prepare for the WTO'. The government official replied: 'You are too late; The WTO is a done deal now; the negotiations on IPR, on MFA and some other aspects are over; its over and done with and it may be too late to learn about how to cope with it!'[43] Even in globally oriented industries like software, awareness about General Agreement on Trade in Services (GATS), the services negotiation, was minimal. The National Association of Software and Services Companies (NASSCOM) began to be active on (GATS)-related issues in as late as 2002. A senior member of NASSCOM admitted, 'Industry's time horizon is shorter run and can't understand all these rules and offers; the software majors were quite unaware of what was going on in the services negotiations.'[44]

In 1998–9, the government made the first overtures to involve business groups in the process of trade policymaking; till then, business associations were requested to comment on WTO agreements, but not involve themselves in the formulation of policy or discussions associated with negotiations.[45] In April 1999 the government began organizing workshops on WTO-related issues, where

> the government called for comprehensive industry involvement in the process of preparation for India's mandate in the World Trade Organization ministerial meet in November. Special secretary, ministry of commerce, N.N. Khanna, asked for detailed, specific but WTO-compatible demands from the industry that could be included as part of India's mandate for the WTO negotiations.[46]

The government delegation to Seattle's ministerial meeting, for the first time, included two members each from CII, FICCI, and ASSOCHAM.[47] Three members of CII—Omkar Goswami (Economic Advisor to CII), Gopal Krishnan (Tata Group), and T.R. Bhowmick (Economists, Research Group)—were in Seattle, two of them part of the official government delegation.[48] Seattle, although a failure, brought home to the Indian government the need for much wider consultations, as well as the need to involve industry as a 'stakeholder'. After Seattle's debacle, the government constituted an expert and business group under the recently reconstituted 'Prime Minister's Council on Trade and Industry' to come up with a 'strategy paper' on WTO: 'The Group was asked to consider and recommend a strategy for a Reconvened WTO Ministerial Conference' (Srinivasan and Bajaj 2000). This group was led by two industry stalwarts, one from CII (Rahul Bajaj) and the other from FICCI (N. Srinivasan), and invited a number of experts, government officials, WTO negotiators, and sector-specific representatives to discuss and debate the ongoing WTO negotiations and evolve India's negotiating position.[49] For about three months in 2000, the group met one to two days a week at FICCI's office to discuss both general and sectoral issues, and came up with a report and set of recommendations.[50] One of the recommendations was:

> [T]the urgent need to strengthen the domestic machinery both at the policymaking level and at the level of regulation and infrastructural support, particularly with respect to the multilateral trade regime. While there has been a considerable increase in the quality and frequency of interaction between government, business and other stakeholders in society in shaping our economic policy in general and trade policy in particular, this interaction must deepen and widen and be sustained on an on-going basis. (Srinivasan and Bajaj 2000: 41)

Thus, by the late 1990s, there had been a sea change in the nature and extent of consultations conducted with private business. By 2003, the government was consulting regularly with business groups, and the three national associations—FICCI, CII, and ASSOCHAM—had become part of official advisory bodies on trade, and were involved both formally and informally in the trade-making process. Since 1998, business actors and associations have been part of the official delegates to ministerial meets. Thus, the policy process associated with global trade has been radically transformed, and involves business inputs at the policymaking stage.

Global Role and Activities of Indian Business

The collective action of business in a closed economy like India (India remained quite closed till 1991) is unlikely to be affected by international factors. Yet, the closed nature of the Indian political economy from the 1950s to the early 1990s led a sectoral business association like CEI (so named at that time) to specialize in parallel international activities, starting in the mid-1980s. At that time, FICCI dominated official international activities through its control and monopoly of the Joint Business Councils. Joint Business Councils consisted of businessmen from India and different nations, as well as government officials of the relevant countries. In 1990, around thirty to forty joint business councils with different countries were sponsored by FICCI. Rivalry over the Joint Business Councils has always marked the conflict between FICCI and ASSOCHAM in the 1980s and 1990s.[51] The CEI found itself completely excluded from these business councils, leading it to initiate independent and parallel links with international business actors.

The CEI (then known as AIEI) also began specializing in organizing trade fairs and exhibitions in the mid to late 1970s; in 1976 it organized its first trade fair. The fairs provided an important service to its membership base: marketing and exporting skills. These skills, while not completely necessary in a closed economy like India, allowed companies to become more competitive, and establish global technological and marketing connections. Second, this allowed CEI to open a parallel line to international firms and other international actors such as the World Economic Forum (WEF), and business associations such as the Confederation of British Industry or United States Chamber of Commerce. The engineering fair, titled Indian Engineering Trade Fair, and the Auto Export Fair became a staple of CII's activities. Initially, the

engineering and auto fairs were held every four years, but they became so popular that they began to be held every two years.[52]

Further, CII established international offices in collaboration with the national or sectoral business association of the relevant country. The first international office was in Saudi Arabia. Since CEI modelled itself after the Confederation of British industries, the United Kingdom has continued to be an important office. In 1988, CEI had four international offices. As globalization and competition with FICCI accelerated, CII continued to set up international offices in many countries.[53] The period between 1994 and 1996 saw a massive spurt as six new offices were set up. By 2001, CII had eleven offices with an annual expenditure of Rs 28.52 million. In 2004 it had fourteen offices, and a new office had been set up in Geneva to monitor the activities of the WTO, an interesting development (see Figure 30.1).

Moreover, the linkage of CII with the WEF established in the mid-1980s was to pay rich dividends after globalization when the state, business, and provincial-level actors all sought the network opportunities that such a forum provided. It

Table 30.1: Expansion of International Activities of CII

	NUMBER OF INTERNATIONAL OFFICES	TOTAL EXPENDITURE ON INTERNATIONAL OFFICES (IN RS MILLION)
1990	3	3.33
1991	3	4.19
1992	3	2.36
1993	2	2.91
1994	3	4.20
1996	10	22.18
1997	12	27.86
1998	13	36.19
1999	12	32.30
2000	8	29.90
2001	11	28.52
2004	15	Not Available

Source: *Annual Report* of CII (Various Years).
Note: Data for 1995 was not found as the relevant Annual Report was not available.

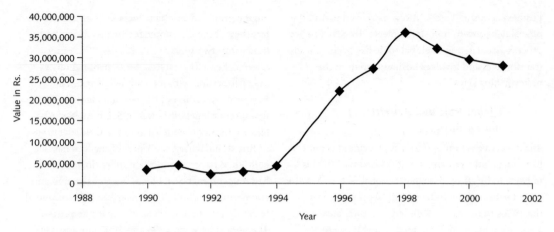

Figure 30.1: CII's Expenditure on International Offices

Source: *Annual Report* of CII (Various Years)

was PM Rajiv Gandhi and industrialist Rahul Bajaj[54] who facilitated the initial links between CEI and WEF.[55] In 1982 Rajiv Gandhi visited Switzerland and suggested that WEF hold a summit in India, where he would ensure that his mother, Mrs Indira Gandhi, the PM, would address the summit. WEF needed a business association linkage in India; this was facilitated by Rahul Bajaj, who took Rajiv Gandhi's idea to Tarun Das.[56] The CEI/AIEI was cash-rich and excluded from the domestic political and business process. They saw in this linkage a crucial opportunity. In 1984 WEF held its first summit in India. As it happened, Rajiv Gandhi inaugurated it, after his mother's assassination in 1984. Since then, WEF and CII's linkage has become a crucial high profile event (Vidyasagar 2004). Thus, openings in the domestic political environment and alliance with a reformist PM coincided with the international activities of the CII.

In the 2000s, Indian business became quite active in international fora. Mergers, acquisitions, court cases, and capturing markets in the Western world became important strategies. In February 2005, the TATA group set up an office in Washington, DC to deal with the complex regulatory environment in the United States as Ratan Tata unveiled a more aggressive global strategy of acquisitions. Ranbaxy has had an office in the US since the 1990s, and has also acquired companies.

Table 30.2: Global Acquisitions and Mergers of Prominent Indian Business

NAME OF BUSINESS	DATE OF MERGER/ ACQUISITION	COMPANY ACQUIRED/ MERGED WITH
TATA	Feb. 2000	Tetley Group
	Sep. 2002	Regent Hotel (renamed Taj Lands End)
	Jul. 2003	Gemplex
	Nov. 2004	Tyco Global Network
	Feb. 2005	Hispano Carrocera
	Mar. 2005	Indo Maroc Phosphore S.A. (IMACID)
	Jul. 2005	The Pierre
	Jul. 2005	Indigene Pharmaceuticals Inc
	Jul. 2005	Teleglobe International
	Aug. 2005	INCAT International
	Sep. 2005	Wündsch Weidinger
	Oct. 2005	Pearl Group
	Oct. 2005	Financial Network Services
	Oct. 2005	Good Earth Corporation and FMali Herb Inc
	Nov. 2005	Comicrom
	Dec. 2005	Starwood Group (W Hotel)
	Dec. 2005	Brunner Mond
	Jan. 2006	Tertia Edusoft
	Jan. 2006	GmbhTertia Edusoft AG
	May-2006	JEMCA
	Jun. 2006	Eight 'O Clock Coffee Company
	Oct. 2006	Energy Brands Inc
	Dec. 2006	Corus
Total		23

NAME OF BUSINESS	DATE OF MERGER/ ACQUISITION	COMPANY ACQUIRED/ MERGED WITH
Reliance	Oct. 2003	FLAG Telecom
	Jun. 2004	Trevira
Total		2
Mittal		
	1989	The Iron & Steel Company of Trinidad & Tobago
	1992	Sibalsa
	1994	Sidbec-Dosco
	1995	Hamburger Stahlwerke
	1998	Inland Steel Company
	1999	Unimetal Group
	2001	Alfasid
	2001	Sidex
	2003	Nova Hut
	2004	Polskie Huty Stali
	2004	Skopje
	2004	BH Steel
	Oct. 2004	International Steel Group
	Jun. 2006	Kryvorizhstal
	Jun. 2006	Arcelor
	Dec. 2006	Sicartsa from Grupo Villacero
Total		16
Ranbaxy		
	1995	Ohm Lab
	2000	Bayer's genetic business
	2005	genetic product portfolio from EFARMES
	Mar. 2006	Terapia
	Mar. 2006	generic business of Allen SpA, a division of GlaxoSmithKline (GSK)
	Mar. 2006	Ethimed NV
Total		6

Source: Author's database collected from the websites of companies and newspapers

The Emergence and Transformation of Collective Business Action in India

In India, in 1992, an engineering association called the Confederation of Engineering Industry transformed itself into an all-industry association, and changed its name to the Confederation of Indian Industry (CII).[57] At that time, FICCI and ASSOCHAM, two national associations, dominated India's business scene. While many regional and sectoral business associations represented the diversity of business in India, delayed international opening and democratic continuity cemented a well-connected, protectionist elite—the FICCI was especially powerful, with strong connections to the ruling Congress party and the bureaucratic apparatus (Kochanek 1974, 1996, 1987, 1995–6). Nevertheless, another association rose to challenge its dominance in the early 1990s. Within a decade, the CII rose to become a nationally recognized association, representing diverse sectors of Indian industry. In response, FICCI, until then the dominant business association, revived itself, and became increasingly developmental in nature.[58] Thus, currently India has two dominant developmentally oriented associations— the CII and FICCI—which compete with each other, but also pursue many developmental activities at both the Central and provincial levels.[59] This transformation in business collective action in the early 1990s coincided with a comprehensive liberalization programme, wherein the role for collective action seemed accentuated. What governance role could a business association perform in the face of the apparent withdrawal of the state from regulatory activity? Liberalization seemed to reduce the role of political lobbying, yet an organization that developed new tools of political access and influence rose to prominence.

Political Representation and Business[60]

In 2004, Anil Ambani, then co-owner of the powerful Reliance empire, filed nomination papers for the Rajya Sabha in Uttar Pradesh with the tacit support of the Samajwadi Party.[61] Simultaneously, he committed a massive Rs 10,000 crore investment in Uttar Pradesh to build a 3500 MW power plant that would feed most of north India and generate at least 50,000 jobs. He also became an honorary member of the Uttar Pradesh Development Council (UPDC) headed by Amar Singh. Such explicit partisan linkage seemed to go against the dictum that most businessmen financed and supported all parties in an attempt to maximize their returns and minimize their political risks. Yet, it highlighted a new phenomenon, the entry of business actors into direct politics, and their open and public courtship of political parties, and national and sub-national institutions of power after a long hiatus.[62] While this led to a more careful scrutiny of the political role and power of business, it also created new challenges and dilemmas of the conflict of interest and the role of money power in politics and elections. Businessmen entered the national legislative institutions in large numbers, both in the Rajya Sabha and the Lok Sabha.[63] In the current Rajya Sabha, thirty-eight members out of 239 define their occupations as either 'industrialist', or 'trader', which is 15 per cent of the Upper House. One hundred and nineteen out of 529 Lok Sabha members are businessmen, industrialists, or traders, that is, 22.3 per cent of its total membership.[64] As evident from Table 30.3, the proportion of business representation has seen a significant increase in the Rajya Sabha, while remaining stable, albeit pretty high, in the Lok Sabha. Interestingly, despite the greater public debate

Table 30.3: Business Representation in Parliament, 1991–2007

PARLIAMENT TERM	NO. OF BUSINESS MEMBERS (IN %)	NO. OF NON-BUSINESS MEMBERS (IN %)	NO. OF NON AVAILABLE (IN %)	TOTAL
LOK SABHA				
14th LS, 2004–9	119 22.33	393 73.73	21 3.94	533 100.00
LS 13th 10.10.1999–6.2.2004	99 17.43	449 79.05	20 3.52	568 100.00
LS 12th 10.3.1998–26.4.1999	78 14.80	441 83.68	8 1.52	527 100.00
LS 11th 15.5.1996–4.12.1997	109 20.19	421 77.96	10 1.85	540 100.00
LS 10th 20.6.1991–10.5.1996	82 15.07	440 80.88	22 4.04	544 100.00
RAJYA SABHA				
TERM	NO. OF BUSINESS (IN %)	NO. OF OTHER (IN %)	NO. OF NA (IN %)	TOTAL
Current	38 15.90	192 80.33	9 3.77	239 100.00
RS1998	31 12.60	211 85.77	3 1.22	246 99.59
RS1994	8 9.88	69 85.19	4 4.94	81 100.00

Source: Author's calculations from the Parliament website.

about the entry of prominent businessmen to the Rajya Sabha, what may be more striking is how the occupational base of the typical Lok Sabha has changed over the past few years.[65] In contrast to earlier Lok Sabhas, where agriculturalists, Trade Union members, and lawyers dominated, businessmen and traders now occupy quite a significant presence in the lower house. Interestingly, many members categorize themselves as both agriculturalists (farmers) and industrialists or businessmen, highlighting how agrarian surplus is moving into industry, a point noted above.

CONCLUSION

A systematic study of the changing business and politics relationship in India is overdue; the last full-length study was completed in 1974. This chapter could only hint briefly at the patterns and transformations currently underway in the business and politics relationship in India. A more thorough examination is still awaited. Such an ethnographic and institutional study of Indian business will be very valuable in understanding the changing nature of capitalism in India, and its impact on the dominant institutions of a representative democracy and the changing economic configurations of power.

Here, I briefly note a trend. Massive changes in India's agricultural sector in the near future will transform the nature of agrarian capitalism once again in the next ten years. Many Indian and multinational companies are moving into agriculture, retail, and the food processing industry. Companies such as ITC, Pepsi India, Monsanto, Tata Rallis, Bharti, Reliance, Mahindra Shubh Labh, and Hindustan Unilever among others, as well as biotech companies, are moving into new areas and into areas at the junction of industry and agriculture. Sunil Mittal, Chairman of Bharti Enterprises, sums up the private sector's optimism: 'the greatest area of development is going to be in the area of agriculture', which like telecom is a business which can transform India, and more importantly, transform rural India'.[66] This movement is likely to have a significant impact on 30 per cent of India's population, which continues to live in rural areas. Its exact contours need more analysis and assessment for understanding the nature of capitalism in India.

NOTES

1. These included: G.P. Goenka (FICCI chief), Sudhir Jalan (former FCCI President) and FICCI's vice President, A.C. Muthia.

2. These problems with the developmental state literature are exemplified by its classics: Johnson (1982) and Woo-Cumings (1999).

3. Regional business groups are those whose core business interests are confined to his/her state of origin.

4. Two very good edited collections on Asia and developing countries exist; neither has a chapter on India. See Maxfield and Schneider (1997) and Macintyre (1984).

5. A group of CEOs organized themselves in 1996–8 protesting against the lowering of tariffs and import quotas and seeking protection against international openness. Rahul Bajaj (Bajaj Scooters) and A.P. Godrej (Godrej group) form part of this informal group that existed for a few years and then dissipated.

6. I elaborate this argument in an ongoing journal article, 'When Controls and External Pressure lead to Innovation: Contrasts between Pharmaceutical and Software Growth Patterns in India'.

7. 'Unleashed: Why Indian Companies are Setting their Sights on Western Rivals', *The Financial Times*, 7 February 2007, p. 9.

8. There are many examples of this career path among the new industry houses; one of the most prominent is Anji Reddy, who was a scientist in the Indian Drugs and Pharmaceutical Ltd., a public-sector company, which he quit to set up his own company (Dr Reddy's Laboratories or DRL).

9. Most entrepreneurs support the CPI(M) in West Bengal.

10. The distinction—tie-wallahs and dhoti-walls— outlined by Kochanek is relevant here.

11. This section is drawn from Sinha (2005b).

12. See 'Significant Increase in ASSOCHAM Membership', *The Patriot*, 9 July 1990; 'Big Rise in ASSOCHAM Membership', *Hindustan Times*, 9 July 1990; 'Sharp Rise in Assocham Membership', *Business Standard*, 9 July 1990. The annual revenue of ASSOCHAM increased from 25 lakh to 1 crore as a result of the increase in membership. Also see 'Assocham to Enlarge Membership', *The Telegraph*, 26 November 1990; 'Assocham Membership Doubles', *The Financial Express*, 27 November 1990; 'Assocham to Have Enlarged Panel', *Business and Political Observer*, 27 November 1990; 'Membership of ASSOCHAM Crosses 50,000', *The Times of India*, 16 May 1991.

13. 'CEI May Merge with Assocham, Change Name', *The Economic Times*, 15 May 1991; Roy (1991); 'Merger of Assocham and CEI Welcomed', *The Independent*, 18 May 1991; 'CEI Changing Name to take on FICCI, Assocham', *Business and Political Observer*, 7 November 1991.

14. Interview with CII official, New Delhi, 23 August 2003.

15. 'Nine more Companies Join ASSOCHAM', *The Statesman*, 18 February 1991; '9 Big Companies Join Assocham', *Hindustan Times*, 18 February 1991.

16. See 'More Companies Join ASSOCHAM', *Times of India*, 18 February 1991; 'New Assocham Patron Members', *The Independent*, 18 February 1991; 'ASSOCHAM Gains 9 More Members', *Indian Express*, 18 February 1991.

17. In 1994, the newly appointed Secretary-General of FICCI, Dr Amit Mitra, said, 'I am glad that Tarun Das has worked wonders with the Confederation of Indian Industry. It has helped wake FICCI up.'

18. 'FICCI Wakes up to New Challenges', *Business Standard*, 5 January 1992.

19. 'Chambers Vie with Each Other for Supremacy', *Indian Express*, 28 May 1992.

20. Interviews; also see 'FICCI Posed for a Major Restructuring Exercise', *Indian Express*, 12 May 1994; 'FICCI Confirms Mitra as Secretary-General', *The Economic Times*, 11 June 1994; 'Interview with A.K. Rungta: FICCI to Stress Promotional Work', *The Hindu*, 12 June 1994.

21. Ibid. Also see 'FICCI Stops Buckling under New Initiative in US', *The Economic Times*, 18 May 1994; 'Showdown in FICCI, Secretary-General May be Replaced', *The Economic Times*, 11 May 1994.

22. I thank John Echeverri-Gent for providing me with some information on this issue.

23. 'FICCI Acquires New Economy Flavor', *The Times of India*, 16 January 2001.

24. Alok Mittal, advisor, FICCI. See 'FICCI Acquires New Economy Flavor', *The Times of India*, 16 January 2001.

25. Interview with author, 2–3 June 2005, Stanford University.

26. One exception was during the visit of the then Prime Minister, P.V. Narasimha Rao, to the US in May 1994, when all three chambers decided to present a 'united front'. See 'Chambers to Put up United Front in US', *Business Standard*, 14 May 1994.

27. 'FICCI Chief against Trade Bodies Merger', *The Financial Express*, 2 July 1990.

28. 'FICCI, ASSOCHAM, CII Plan Joint Panel', *Indian Express*, 27 July 1992.

29. 'Apex Body of Chambers Hanging Fire', *The Telegraph*, 28 September 1992; 'FICCI Stymies Apex Panel of Chambers', *Business Standard*, 28 September 1992.

30. See 'Divided Chambers', *The Business and Political Observer*, 20 January 1997.

31. 'New Body Leaves Chambers Unhappy', *Times of India*, 10 October 1993.

32. 'Apex Chambers Divided on Growth Rate Proposals to FM: FICCI for Joint statement, CII and ASSOCHAM Want to Go Separately', *Business Standard*, 10 October 2000.

Also see 'Unholy Chamber Wars over JBC: Assocham versus FICCI', *M.P Chronicle* (Bhopal), 4 August 2000.

33. Some important works that look at the role of business and liberalization include: Kochanek (1996), Nayar (2001), Pedersen (2000), and Kohli (1989).

34. This section is drawn from Sinha (forthcoming).

35. 'Call for Awareness Programme on WTO', *The Hindu* (Madras edition), 28 May 1997.

36. 'Declare all Trade pacts: Ramakrishna', [The Chairman of the Disinvestment Commission], *The Observer*, 24 July 1997.

37. An interview with a member of a business association, who had long-standing interactions with many business leaders, confirmed this (January 2002, New Delhi).

38. Confidential interview with a CII official, New Delhi, 17 January 2003.

39. One exception to this lack of knowledge was some companies in the pharmaceutical sector, most notably Parvinder Singh from Ranbaxy, who were the few members of the Indian business class to perceive the 'writing on the wall' regarding the upcoming patent regime.

40. 'Declare all Trade Pacts: Ramakrihsna', *The Observer*, 24 July 1997.

41. 'WTO: the Reality of the New Trading Order: Proceedings and WTO 2000 Series of Workshops: 30th March–12 July 1999', Research Department, CII.

42. Rao (1999), notes that the CII thought of setting up a WTO-related office in 1999.

43. Confidential Interview, New Delhi, January 2002. The person was at this seminar and heard the exchange first-hand.

44. Interview with a high-level official of NASSCOM, 8 April, Washington DC.

45. In the early 1990s, the CII and FICCI issued statements supporting the Dunkel draft. These statements were requested by the government. Confidential interviews revealed that at that time, a careful analysis of the Dunkel draft on Indian industry had not been done.

46. 'Government calls for industry involvement in WTO talks', 29 April 1999, at http://www.rediff.com/business/1999/apr/29cii.htm.

47. The CII's then President, Shekhar Datta, was in Singapore in April 1996 for the World Trade Congress meetings; this two-day meeting was a forerunner to the ministerial meetings in December 1996. India was represented by its Commerce Secretary, Tejender Khanna, and Shekhar Datta; 'India Should Push for Global Trade pact to avoid Bias', *The Observer*, New Delhi, 25 April 1996.

48. Interview with CII official, 1 January 2002.

49. A notable feature of the deliberations was the joint collaboration between the CII and FICCI, two competitor business associations, which have a running feud and have on most occasions failed to undertake joint programmes.

50. Interviews with a participant of the group.

51. 'Assocham to strengthen Overseas Links', *Business Standard*, 2 July 2000; 'Apex Chambers Agree to Restructure JBC's Secretariat', *The Observer*, New Delhi, 15 July 1995; 'Unholy Chamber Wars over JBC', *M.P Chronicle*, Bhopal, 4 August 2000.

52. The Engineering Trade Fair was held in 1993, 1997, 1999, and 2001. The Auto Expo was held in 1993, 1996, 1998, and 2000.

53. One of its most active international offices is in Singapore. Shomikho Raha explores this aspect in his ongoing doctoral thesis, 'Changing Reason of State in India: Domestic Structural influence in selected cases of the Ganga water-sharing dispute, nuclear policy and industry partnership with Singapore', Trinity College, Cambridge University.

54. Rahul Bajaj is CEO of Bajaj Auto, India's premier scooter company.

55. World Economic Forum officials confirm this. Collette Mathur, the director of WEF, outlined the emergence of WEF-CII connections in a recent speech. See Skaria (2004).

56. Interview with a CII official, New Delhi, 11 March 2004.

57. The CII's historical antecedents lie in the engineering industry. In 1974, the Association of Indian Engineering Industry (AIEI) was formed as a result of a merger of two engineering associations. In 1986 AIEI was re-christened as the Confederation of Engineering Industry (CEI) as it began to invite other associations to join it. In 1992, it expanded its scope to become an all-industry association, and renamed itself the Confederation of Indian Industry (CII).

58. Following Doner and Schneider (2000), I define developmental associations as associations that improve the functioning of markets and states. For example, a developmental association may work towards the provision of better infrastructure by the state, or help firms to improve their quality performance or secure export markets through trade fairs, market surveys, etc.

59. While ASSOCHAM, a smaller organization, is less powerful and visible, it also performs many developmental activities.

60. Ideally, this section should analyse the role of campaign finance or that of money in elections. I am unable to analyse that, given constraints of space and the problematic nature of the data on that issue.

61. See the story, http://www.the-week.com/24jul25/currentevents_article10.htm. Last Accessed on 28 March 2008. Interestingly, in March 2006, Anil Ambani resigned from the Rajya Sabha after the split with his brother, Mukesh Ambani. The fight between Anil and Mukesh broke out at the end of 2004. It is believed that his close association with the

Samajwadi party affected the way the Congress government and party reacted to his conflict with his brother. Mukesh is supposed to be close to the Congress party.

62. During India's national movement, similar involvement of businessmen with the Indian National Congress was widespread.

63. Other prominent members from the business community to have joined the Parliament include Vijay Mallya of the UB Group (Janata Party), Naveen Jindal of Jindal Steel (Congress), Rajkumar Dhoot of Videocon (linkage with Shiv Sena), Hotelier Late Lalit Suri, a trader-cum-industrialist, and B.J. Panda (Biju Janata Dal).

64. Drawn from the author's constructed database of 'Occupational Background of the Indian Parliament'.

65. I am in the process of constructing a more systematic database concerning the occupational background of Rajya Sabha and Lok Sabha members over time.

66. Cited in Center for the Advanced Study of India (CASI), 2006.

REFERENCES

Bajaj, Rahul. 2001. 'Foreword', in B.R. Sabade, *WTO: A Threat or An Opportunity*. Pune: Centre for Business and Industry.

Bardhan, Pranab. 1993. 'The Intermediate Regime: Any Sign of Graduation', in Pranab Bardhan, Mrinal Datta-Chaudhuri, and T.N. Krishnan (eds), *Development and Change*. New Delhi: Oxford University Press.

Baru, Sanjaya. 2000. 'Economic Policy and the Development of Capitalism in India: the Role of Regional Capitalists and Political Parties', in Zoya Hasan, Rajeev Bhargava, Balveer Arora, and Francine Frankel (eds), *Transforming India: Social and Political Dynamics of Democracy*. New Delhi: Oxford University Press.

———. 1997. 'Indian Enterprise', *Seminar*, 449 (January).

———. 1996. 'New Business Groups and Liberalization in India', paper presented at Seminar, Cornell University.

Berna, James J. 1960. *Industrial Entrepreneurship in Madras State*. New York: Asia Publishing House.

Center for the Advanced Study of India (CASI). 2006. 'India's Second green Revolution? The Sociopolitical Implications of Corporate-led Agricultural growth', *CASI Newsletter*, Fall.

Chibber, Vivek. 2003. *Locked in Place: State Building and Late Industrialization in India*. Princeton and Oxford: Princeton University Press.

CII. *Annual Report*. Various years. New Delhi: CII.

Dobhal, Koteshwar P. 1995. 'Move to Unite Apex Trade Bodies Gets a New Thrust', *The Observer (ND)*, 22 August.

Doner, Richard and Ben Schneider. 2000. 'Business Associations and Economic Development Why Some Associations Contribute More than Others', *Business and Politics*, 2(3), pp. 261–88.

Evans, Peter. 1995. *Embedded Autonomy*. Princeton: Princeton University Press.

Ghosh, Indranil. 1992. 'Renaming CEI Raises Many an Eyebrow', *The Financial Express*, 4 January.

Gourevitch, Peter. 1986. *Politics in Hard Times: Comparative Responses to International Economic Crises*. Ithaca: Cornell University Press.

Governmemt of India (GoI). 2007. *Economic Survey*. Government of India Press.

Guha, Nandini. 1994. 'He is Bent on Making FICCI Fighting Fit', *Financial Express*, 16 June.

Heeks, Richard. 1996. *India's Software Industry*. New Delhi: Sage Publications.

Herring, Ronald. 1999. 'Embedded Particularism: India's Failed Developmental State', in Meredith Woo-Cumings (ed.), *The Developmental State*. Ithaca: Cornell University Press, pp. 306–34.

Johnson, Chalmers. 1982. *MITI and the Japanese Miracle: The Growth of Industrial Policy, 1925–1975*. Stanford, California: Stanford University Press.

Kapur, Devesh. 2002. 'The Causes and Consequences of India's IT Boom', *India Review*, 1(2), pp. 91–110.

Kochanek, Stanley A. 1996. 'Liberalization and Business Lobbying in India', *Journal of Commonwealth and Comparative Politics*, 34(3), pp. 155–73.

———. 1995–6. 'The Transformation of Interest Politics in India', *Pacific Affairs*, 68(4), pp. 529–50.

———. 1987. 'Briefcase Politics in India: the Congress Party and the Business Elite', *Asian Survey*, 27(12), pp. 1278–301.

———. 1974. *Business and Politics in India*. Berkeley: University of California Press.

Kohli, Atul. 1989. 'The Politics of Economic Liberalization in India', *World Development*, 17(3), pp. 305–28.

Krueger, Anne O. 1974. 'The Political Economy of the Rent Seeking Society', *American Economic Review*, 64(3), pp. 291–303.

Lindblom, Charles. 1984. 'The Market as Prison', in Thomas Ferguson and Joel Rogers (eds), *Political Economy: Readings in the Politics and Economics of American Public Policy*. New York: M.E. Sharpe.

Macintyre, Andrew (ed.). 1984. *Business and Government in Industrializing Asia*, Ithaca: Cornell University Press.

Maxfield, S. and B. Ross Schneider (eds). 1997. *Business and State in Developing Countries*. Ithaca: Cornell University Press.

Nayar, Baldev Raj. 2001. *Globalization and Nationalism: The Changing Balance of India's Economic Policy, 1950-2000*. New Delhi: Sage Publications.

Pedersen, Jorgen Dige. 2000. 'Explaining Economic Liberalization in India: State and Society Perspectives', *World Development*, 28(2), pp. 265–82.

Pingle, Vibha. 1999. *Rethinking the Developmental State: India's Industry in Comparative Perspective*. New York: Palgrave.

Raman, A. Thothathru. 1991. 'CEI Changing Name to Take on FICCI, Assocham', *Business and Political Observer*, 7 November.

Rao, N. Vasuki. 1999. 'India Enlists Industry to Boost WTO role', *Journal of Commerce, Inc.*, 20 May.

Ray, Rajat K. (ed.). 1994. *Entrepreneurship and Industry in India 1800-1947*. New Delhi: Oxford University Press.

———. 1979. *Industrialization in India: Growth and Conflict in the Private Corporate Sector, 1914-1947*. New Delhi: Oxford University Press.

Rosen, George. 1966. *Democracy and Economic Change in India*. Berkeley and Los Angeles: University of California Press.

Rogowski, Ronald. 1989. *Commerce and Coalitions: How Trade Affects Domestic Political Alignments*. New Jersey, Princeton: Princeton University Press.

Roy, S. 1992. 'Muscling into the Top', *Business Standard*, 12 January.

———. 1991. 'CEI, ASSOCHAM Merger Move: Industry Eager to Speak with One Voice', *The Economic Times*, 16 May.

Rudolph, Lloyd I. and Susanne H. Rudolph. 1987. *In Pursuit of Lakshmi: The Political Economy of the Indian State*, Chicago and London: The University of Chicago Press.

Scott, James. 1985. *Weapons of the Weak: Everyday Forms of Peasant Resistance*. New Haven, Connecticut: Yale University Press.

Sharif, Arif. 1994. 'FICCI's Mitra Mantra', *The Economic Times*, 5 June.

Sinha, Aseema. forthcoming. *When David Meets Goliath: How Global Trade Rules Shape Domestic Politics in India*.

———. 2005a. *The Regional Roots of Developmental Politics in India: A Divided Leviathan*. Indiana: Indiana University Press.

———. 2005b. 'Understanding the Rise and Transformation of Business Collective Action in India', *Business and Politics*, 7(2).

Skaria, George. 2004. 'Celebrating India's Participation: Rahul Bajaj gets special mention in Schwab, Collette's speech', *The Financial Express*, 22 January, http://www.financialexpress.com/fe_full_story.php?content_id=50980 last accessed on 15 December 2004.

Sridharan, Eswaran. 1996. *The Political Economy of Industrial Promotion: Indian, Brazilian, and Korean Electronics in Comparative Perspective 1969-1994*. Westport, Connecticut: Praeger.

Srinivasan, T.N. 1985. 'Neoclassical Political Economy, the State and Economic Development', *Asian Development Review*, 3(2), pp. 38–58.

Srinivasan, N. and Rahul Bajaj. 2000. 'Strategy for a reconvened WTO Ministerial Meeting: Report and Recommendations', Prime Minister's Council on Trade and Industry.

Tomlinson, Brian R. 1981. 'Colonial Firms and the Decline of Colonialism in Eastern India', *Modern Asian Studies*, 15(3), pp. 455–86.

Tripathi, Dwijendra (ed.). 1991. *Business and Politics in India: a Historical Perspective*. New Delhi: Manohar.

———. 1984. *Business Communities of India: A Historical Perspective*. New Delhi: Manohar.

———. 1981. *The Dynamics of Tradition: Kasturbhai Lalbhai and his Entrepreneurship*. New Delhi: Manohar.

Tyabji, Nasir. 1981. 'Stratification of Indian Business', in Amiya Kumar Bagchi and Nirmala Banerjee (eds), *Change and Choice in Indian Industry*. Calcutta: K.P. Bagchi & Co.

Upadhya, Carol. 1997. 'Culture, Class and Entrepreneurship: A Case Study of Coastal Andhra Pradesh, India', in Mario Rutten and Carol Upadhya (eds), *Small Business Entrepreneurs in Asia and Europe: Towards a Comparative Perspective*. New Delhi: Sage Publications.

———. 1988. 'The Farmer-Capitalists of Coastal Andhra Pradesh', *Economic and Political Weekly*, XXIII (27–8), pp. 1376–93.

Venkitaramanan, S. 1997. 'WTO and Its Implications', *The Economic Times*, 25 November.

Vidyasagar, N. 2004. 'Get, Set, Grow', *Times of India*, 11 February, http://www.ibef.org/artdisplay.aspx?cat_id=105&art_id=1420, last accessed on 26 January 2005.

Wade, Robert. 1990. *Governing the Market: Economic Theory and the Role of Government in East Asia*. Princeton: Princeton University Press.

Winters, Jeffrey. 1996. *Power in Motion: Capital Mobility and the Indonesian State*. Ithaca, NY: Cornell University Press.

Woo-Cumings, Meredith (ed.). 1999. *The Developmental State*. Ithaca, NY: Cornell University Press.

31 Government Accountability

Dilip Mookherjee

DEFINITION

In *Democracy, Accountability, and Representation*, Przeworski *et al.* (1999) define government accountability as follows: 'Governments are "accountable" if citizens can discern representative from unrepresentative governments and can sanction them appropriately, retaining in office those who perform well and ousting from office those who do not' (ibid.: 10). This definition implicitly equates government accountability with an aspect of democracy: the ability of citizens to remove non-functioning governments. Even in non-democracies, accountability may exist if officials respond to pressure exerted directly or indirectly by citizen groups. It is therefore necessary to expand the definition of accountability as 'the ability of citizens to put effective pressure on officials who deviate from the expressed wishes of a majority among them'.

Alternatively, accountability can be defined in terms of outcomes rather than processes of government. A lack of accountability may be said to occur if government policies or their implementation exhibit systematic bias in favour of some groups at the expense of others, which cannot be justified by their demographic size, intensity of need, or special constitutional status accorded on historical grounds. Such biases can take many forms: favouritism towards the wealthy vis-à-vis the poor, discrimination in favour of upper-caste groups, corruption which benefits government officials at the expense of taxpayers or public service recipients. It also includes the criterion of responsiveness to changes in circumstances that alter citizen needs and abilities: if a particular region is afflicted with a natural disaster, its citizens deserve special forms of government support to help them cope with the crisis. In other words, accountability refers to the extent to which actual policies and their implementation coincide with a normative ideal in terms of what they ought to be.

In this broad sense, accountability amounts to evaluating the nature of governance itself, in outcome-oriented terms. One can broaden this definition even further if one views the representation of different citizen groups within government in proportion to their demographic weight or special needs as a desirable end in its own right. Alternatively, one may view such representation as a means to the end of securing improvements in accountability, as defined more narrowly above. Accordingly, I shall refer to the narrower definition in the subsequent discussion.

DETERMINANTS

What are the mechanisms that promote accountability? Alternatively, how do lapses arise? The fundamental sources of a lack of accountability arise from the problem of agency inherent in government: the delegation of authority over policy decisions and their implementation by citizens to a set of officials who may pursue agendas that may not coincide with the public good. The extent to which a government is accountable depends therefore on (a) the personal objectives of government officials; (b) perceptions of citizens or other watchdog agencies concerning their performance; and (c) mechanisms by which citizens or watchdog agencies can exert pressure or sanction or remove governments they perceive as not accountable, combined with the willingness of citizens to do so.

The first factor refers to the extent to which the intrinsic motivation of government officials internalizes the normative ideals or shared consensus of the public good, rather than the pursuit of self-interest: it can be viewed as a dimension of public *morality*. The second factor pertains to public *awareness*: the quality of information available to the public or watchdog agencies (such as the media, judiciary, non-governmental organizations [NGOs], or other civil society organizations), which enables them to evaluate the performance of government accurately. This includes both institutions of oversight, as well as the ability and willingness of citizens and watchdog agencies to process the available information and form reasonable judgements. The third factor concerns *sanctioning/pressure mechanisms* by which citizens or watchdog agencies can remove or exert pressure on governments they perceive as not responsive to their interests. These include formal institutions of government, such as elections, or separation of powers between executive, legislative, and judiciary branches with formal processes of oversight. They also include more informal mechanisms of pressure, such as social movements, public discussions, political meetings,

lobbying, bribing, campaign finance contributions, acts of civil disobedience, or violence. Both the presence of such institutions of oversight and pressure, as well as the willingness of citizens and watchdog agencies to engage in them, affect the actual extent to which governments are accountable.

It is clear from the above discussion that government accountability in a given society will ultimately depend on political institutions, as well as a number of key socio-economic characteristics that affect political awareness and political participation.

Key *political institutions* include (a) elections and their conduct; (b) rules defining the Constitution and term of government; (c) political parties and political competition; (d) laws concerning financing of election campaigns, and lobbying; (e) mandated representation on the basis of gender or caste; and (f) separation of powers within government between the executive, legislative, and judiciary branches; independence of media and regulatory institutions from executive or legislative branches.

Another important determinant of government accountability concerns *bureaucratic institutions*, which affect the extent to which bureaucrats appointed by the government to implement its policies act in the public interest. Bureaucrats are devolved substantial powers over citizens, businesses, and other social groups by politicians: they maintain law and order, collect taxes, and administer government programmes. Even if political institutions created a high level of accountability of elected political officials to the general public, poor bureaucratic institutions may prevent the former from imposing effective checks and balances on bureaucrats, creating problems of bureaucratic corruption. The quality of public administration thus depends intrinsically on myriad details of bureaucratic institutions, such as systems of pay, monitoring and sanctioning, recruitment, task assignments, planning and information systems, and oversight by legislative and judiciary branches.[1]

Traditional, top-down development strategies followed by India and many other developing countries since the 1950s have accorded bureaucrats appointed by Central and state governments the major role in administering government programmes. This has been widely perceived to have progressively resulted in low levels of accountability of government, with poorly informed decisions concerning public projects, high levels of bureaucratic corruption taking the form of diversion of public funds, distorted allocation to benefit local elites, and low rates of attendance of teachers and doctors in government schools and hospitals. Accordingly, attempts have been made to remedy these problems by reducing the extent of centralization of government functions: the Seventy-third and Seventy-fourth Constitutional Amendments passed in the early 1990s now mandate *Panchayati Raj*: the creation of three tiers of local governments (panchayats), and devolution of a number of functions to these local governments. Such a strategy of *government decentralization* represents an important reform aimed at enhancing government accountability.

It should be noted that government decentralization may or may not be accompanied by a reduction of authority of Central or state government ministers, who may still retain discretionary authority over the allocation of resources across regions and localities. The real (intended) shift of authority concerns intraregional allocations and their implementation, from state-appointed bureaucrats to elected local governments. Panchayat officials instead of state bureaucrats are supposed to decide which local projects will be constructed, how they will be maintained, and how their benefits will be allocated within the local community. Panchayati Raj therefore attempts to reduce the discretionary authority of state-appointed bureaucrats, and expand that of elected local governments. The hope is that the closer proximity of decision-makers to local areas will result in superior information concerning local needs and conditions. Moreover, electoral discipline and village meetings (*gram sabhas* and *gram sansads*) will bring superior sanctioning and pressure mechanisms to bear on decision-makers.

Nevertheless, there are many concerns that Panchayati Raj may worsen accountability on a number of dimensions. First, it is possible that local governments will be more vulnerable to 'capture' by wealthy, educated, and upper-caste elites, than are state governments. This may happen if institutions of democracy function less well at the local level than at the state level, owing perhaps to weaker oversight

mechanisms, media attention, or lower levels of political participation or citizen awareness in local governance.[2] Second, the actual implementation of Panchayati Raj may differ from what is mandated. Implementation of the provisions of the Seventy-third and Seventy-fourth Constitutional Amendments has been devolved to various state governments; it has varied considerably across different states in terms of the de facto devolution of power and funds to local governments (Chaudhuri 2006). Some states, such as Karnataka and Kerala, have devolved significant funds to local governments on a formula-basis, thus limiting the discretionary authority of Central or state governments over the distribution of funds across regions. West Bengal has started a system of elected local governments at three tiers since 1978, and has transferred to them substantial authority over the administration of centrally sponsored development schemes. The capacity of local governments to supplement grants with local taxes and user fees also varies considerably. Accordingly, in many states (such as Uttar Pradesh and Bihar) panchayats have been devolved very limited funds, functions, and capacities, while others (such as Kerala, Karnataka, or West Bengal) have witnessed substantial devolutions.

A related set of institutional reforms aimed at limiting problems of bureaucratic inefficiency and corruption falls under the category of *civic decentralization* and *competition*. These seek to limit the monopoly power of bureaucrats by expanding the range of alternatives and information available to citizens. The public sector may be opened to competition from private providers. Instead of providing services directly, the government may offer vouchers, cash, or in-kind aid to households on a means-tested basis, which subsequently selects between public and private providers. The government may be required to disseminate information about citizen entitlements, and provide avenues for citizens to file complaints about poor service conditions. These correspond to what Hirschman (1970) referred to as *exit* and *voice*—as disciplining devices on poorly performing public institutions. Especially in schools, the voice option can include citizen and NGO participation in school management. These reforms reduce the vertical hierarchical character of traditional top-down state bureaucracies by empowering citizens in a variety of ways. They represent an alternative form of decentralization, which does not change the traditional character of government, but instead provides citizens with greater exit and voice options. They include legal reforms, such as the Right to Information Act, as well as those that allow greater space for civil society organizations to emerge as an alternative provider of public services, and as a protagonist in public interest litigations (PILs).

Finally, an important determinant of government accountability is the *pattern of political participation and awareness* of different citizen groups.[3] These in turn may depend on education, socio-economic characteristics (such as caste, gender, or wealth), and on 'social capital', defined broadly to include both the presence of active civil society organizations and norms concerning political behaviour. Apart from average levels of awareness and participation, their distribution across different citizen groups is a key determinant of accountability. If citizens of a particular group (defined by region, caste, or class) are less aware or less willing to engage in sanctioning or pressurizing government, the latter is less likely to be responsive to their interests. If more educated, upper-caste, or wealthy citizens exhibit substantially greater political awareness or participation, it would be natural to expect governments to be less accountable to the interests of the less educated, lower castes, or the poor.

RECENT EMPIRICAL RESEARCH FINDINGS

In recent years, there has been a growing body of research in the political economy of government accountability, which attempts to provide empirical assessments of various determinants and institutional reforms. These are based on detailed survey-based micro-evidence that carefully measures the delivery and functioning of government programmes, and relates these to policy reforms or variations in household and community characteristics across time and regions. In what follows, some of these research findings in the Indian context are described. Some words of caution are in order here: this is not a comprehensive survey. Moreover, many of these studies pertain to specific regions of India, so their validity in a broader all-India context must await further research.

Besley and Burgess (2002) study the role of the media. They provide evidence for the role of local newspapers in increasing the responsiveness of Indian state governments to natural disasters, using a panel study of major Indian states. In states with a wider readership of local newspapers, responses of state governments and relief efforts during disasters were significantly higher.

Bardhan and Mookherjee (2003, 2004) examine the relative importance of political ideology and political competition in the implementation of land reform in West Bengal between 1978 and 1998. Using a sample of eighty-nine villages, they find no evidence of the role of political ideology, and some evidence that political competition mattered. Specifically, they find that land reform implementation was not related positively to the relative dominance of Left Front parties in local government, either across villages, or within villages over time. If anything, the increased dominance of the Left Front after securing a majority, was associated with lower land reform implementation.

Foster and Rosenzweig (2001) examine the impact of political decentralization on pro-poor accountability, on the basis of an all-India panel dataset of 250 villages. They find that increased local democracy between the early 1980s and late 1990s (measured by whether local governments were selected via local elections) led to increased responsiveness on the part of local government spending to the needs of the poor, measured by the allocation of local infrastructure spending between roads (favoured by the landless poor) and irrigation (favoured by landowners).

The relation between socio-economic attributes and political participation or awareness is investigated by Krishna (2006) in the context of Madhya Pradesh and Rajasthan, and by Bardhan et al. (2007) in the context of West Bengal. Both studies find that education and gender are the two key determining factors, while wealth and caste do *not* matter significantly. These results suggest an important role for educational policy in improving government accountability. The importance of literacy is also indicated in a study by Besley *et al.* (2004) which finds that south Indian villages with higher literacy rates were more likely to hold village meetings that discussed resource allocation issues within the village, and the actions of local governments. Villages that held meetings targeted public benefits more closely in favour of landless and illiterate individuals by an order of 8–10 percentage points.

The studies of Krishna and Bardhan cited above suggest that socio-economic inequality does not matter significantly in the accountability of local governments. In the West Bengal context, Bardhan and Mookherjee (2004, 2006) and Bardhan *et al.* (2007) find corroborating evidence which showed that development programmes administered by panchayats that involved the allocation of private benefits (such as IRDP credit or agricultural minikits) were well-targeted to the poor, and were not significantly affected by the local distribution of land. On the other hand, they find some evidence of discrimination against Scheduled Castes (SCs) and Tribes (STs), both in the allocation of development resources across villages, and within villages with high land inequality.

Land inequality may also affect fiscal corruption: in the West Bengal panchayats studied in Bardhan and Mookherjee (2004), increased inequality in local land distribution between 1978 and 1998 was associated with significant increases in the fraction of local government expenditures allocated to government consumption (salaries and administrative expenses of government officials). At the same time, local revenues collected by the local government decreased, despite the nominal progressivity of local taxes with respect to landholdings. These results suggest that rising land inequality allowed greater collusion between big landowners, who were allowed to evade taxes, and local government officials, who consumed a larger share of the (shrinking) revenues collected.

Concern with reducing discrimination on the basis of gender and caste have motivated mandates to represent women and SCs and STs in legislatures and panchayats. The effects of these reservations on the targeting of benefits to women and low-caste groups have been studied by a number of authors, with varying conclusions. Pande (2003)

and Chattopadhyay and Duflo (2004) find evidence that mandated reservations improved allocation to targeted groups in state legislatures across India, and in panchayats in Birbhum district of West Bengal, respectively. Besley *et al.* (2004) find favourable effects of low-caste reservations of *pradhan* positions in south Indian panchayats on targeting in favour of low-caste households, but no favourable effects of reservations for women. Bardhan *et al.* (2005) find no favourable targeting impacts of either kind of reservation in a sample of West Bengal panchayats.

These studies clearly scratch the tip of the iceberg, investigating the role of specific determinants and policy reforms in specific regions of India. Their limited scope is dictated by the difficulty of creating reliable data-bases at the micro level that are amenable to careful statistical analysis, and that enable inferences to be made concerning accountability. Clearly, such research efforts have to multiply considerably in the future if we are to learn more about government accountability in India and what can be done to improve it.

NOTES

1. See Dasgupta and Mookherjee (1998) and Mookherjee (2004) for a detailed discussion of these in the context of the Indian tax administration.

2. See Bardhan and Mookherjee (2000) for an analysis of factors that affect the relative accountability of governments at local and national or state levels, and the argument that this is likely to be highly context-dependent.

3. For an analytical model that illustrates these effects, see Grossman and Helpman (1996) and Bardhan and Mookherjee (2000).

REFERENCES

Bardhan, P. and D. Mookherjee. 2006. 'Pro-Poor Targeting and Accountability of Local Governments in West Bengal', *Journal of Development Economics*, 79(2), pp. 303–27.

———. 2004. 'Poverty Alleviation Efforts of West Bengal Panchayats', *Economic and Political Weekly*, XXXIX(9), pp. 965–74.

———. 2003. 'Political Economy of Land Reforms in West Bengal 1978–98', Working Paper, Institute for Economic Development, Boston University.

———. 2003. 'Capture and Governance at Local and National Levels', *American Economic Review*, 90(2), pp. 135–9.

Bardhan P., D. Mookherjee, and M.P. Torrado. 2005. 'Impact of Reservation of Panchayat Pradhans on Targeting in West Bengal', in A. Dhar (ed.), *Some Contemporary Issues in Development and Growth Economics*. Kolkata: Allied Publishers.

Bardhan P., S. Mitra, D. Mookherjee, and A. Sarkar. 2007. 'Local Democracy in Rural West Bengal: Political Participation and Targeting of Public Services', mimeo, Department of Economics, Boston University.

Besley, T. and R. Burgess. 2002. 'The Political Economy of Government Responsiveness: Theory and Evidence from India', *Quarterly Journal of Economics*, 117(4), pp. 1415–51.

Besley, T., R. Pande, and V. Rao. 2004. 'Participatory Democracy in Action: Survey Evidence From South India', Working Paper, World Bank.

Besley, T., R. Pande, L. Rahman, and V. Rao. 2004. 'The Politics of Public Good Provision: Evidence From Indian Local Governments', Working Paper, World Bank.

Chattopadhyay, R. and E. Duflo. 2004. 'Impact of Reservation in Panchayati Raj: Evidence from a Nationwide Randomised Experiment', *Economic and Political Weekly*, XXXIX(9), pp. 979–86.

Chaudhuri, S. 2006. 'What Difference Does a Constitutional Amendment Make? The 1994 Panchayati Raj Act and the Attempt to Revitalize Rural Local Government in India', in P. Bardhan and D. Mookherjee (eds), *Decentralization and Local Governments in Developing Countries: A Comparative Perspective*. Cambridge, US: MIT Press, pp. 153–201.

Dasgupta, Arindam and Dilip Mookherjee. 1998. *Incentive and Institutional Reform in Tax Enforcement: An Analysis of Developing Country Experience*, New Delhi: Oxford University Press.

Foster, A. and M. Rosenzweig. 2001. 'Democratization, Decentralization and the Distribution of Local Public Goods in a Poor Rural Economy', mimeo, Brown University.

Grossman, G. and E. Helpman. 1996. 'Electoral Competition and Special Interest Politics', *Review of Economic Studies*, 63, pp. 265–86.

Hirschman, A. 1970. *Exit, Voice and Loyalty*. Cambridge, MA: Harvard University Press.

Krishna, A., 2006. 'Poverty and Democratic Participation Reconsidered: Evidence from the Local Level in India', *Comparative Politics*, 38(4), pp. 439–59.

Mookherjee, D. 2004. *The Crisis in Government Accountability: Governance Reforms and India's Economic Performance*. New Delhi: Oxford University Press.

Pande, R. 2003. 'Can Mandated Political Representation Increase Policy Influence for Disadvantaged Minorities?' *American Economic Review*, 93(4), pp. 1132–51.

Przeworski, A., S.C. Stokes, and B. Manin (eds). 1999. *Democracy, Accountability, and Representation*. Cambridge, U.K., and New York: Cambridge University Press.

32 The Political Economy of Reforms*

Rahul Mukherji

This essay traces the process of economic reforms that led to the boom in India's corporate sector, competitiveness, and economic growth beyond 1991. The process that led to India's transition from import substituting industrialization (ISI) towards trade-led growth (TLG) provides valuable insights into the politics of economic transition. High tariffs, an overvalued exchange rate, import controls, and industrial licensing characterized ISI in India, which lasted for over four decades since 1947.[1]

There were a number of reasons to be sceptical about the future of economic reform in India. The trade and investment reforms of 1991 occurred in a thriving democracy at a time when the ruling Congress party held an insecure majority. Second, the size of the Indian economy had made it easy for the government to pursue ISI, compared with countries characterized by small internal markets (Haggard 1990: 26–30). India's democracy and its size made it a particularly interesting economic transition.[2]

Democracies find it difficult to switch quickly to a trade-friendly policy change. These policies hurt small but powerful interests, such as the politician and the bureaucrat who thrive on government controls, industrialists used to the comfort of the home economy, subsidized rich farmers, and managers and workers in inefficient firms.[3] Authoritarian regimes, on the other hand, in Taiwan and Korea have successfully initiated economic transitions. They managed labour and business consistent with the demands of TLG. They allocated credit for export promotion, increased taxes, pursued a tight money policy, and successfully reduced the risks for the exporter by providing vital information and finance. President Soeharto of Indonesia was able to redefine the state's relations with labour and business by destroying old institutions and

*The author benefited from presenting earlier versions of this chapter at the Department of Political Science, Columbia University, and at a conference of the Network on South Asian Politics and Political Economy (NETSAPPE) at the University of Michigan, Ann Arbor. Discussions with David Baldwin, Jack Snyder, Jagdish Bhagwati, Helen Milner, Sumit Ganguly, Premachandra Athukorala, Pratap Mehta, Ashutosh Varshney, Rob Jenkins, Atul Sarma, Aseema Sinha, Kanti Bajpai, and Gyanesh Kudaisya have helped. The shortcomings rest with the author.

creating new ones.[4] Allende's Chile, Rawling's Ghana, and Ozal's Turkey had military governments. In the newly democratized Bolivia, Paz Estenssoro enjoyed a great deal of autonomy (Nelson 1993: 433–42). China engaged with the global economy, promoted competition, and grew at a breathtaking pace, while curbing the civil rights of its citizens.[5]

The trajectory of India's economic transition was different from the economic reforms under authoritarian regimes. Prime Minister Rajiv Gandhi's reform efforts, initiated in the 1980s, enjoyed limited success in relation to the big bang reforms of 1991.[6] The balance of payments crisis of 1991 was necessary for, but not sufficient to explain, the changes that occurred thereafter. India had faced a balance of payments crisis in 1966 but had sustained ISI with renewed vigour from 1969 (Mukherji 2000: 375–92; Frankel 2005: Chs 10–12). It is remarkable that a Congress party-led coalition government of Prime Minister P.V. Narasimha Rao could initiate far-reaching reforms after 1991.

Critical to an understanding of economic reforms is the manner in which the weight of policy ideas shifted to favour private initiative and trade promotion during the 1980s. Moreover, *synergistic issue-linkage* between the International Monetary Fund (IMF), the executive, and Indian industry at the time of the foreign exchange crisis of 1991 was critical for pursuing reforms. This was a situation where the Indian executive attempted to gain domestic approval for industrial, trade, and investment liberalization by linking it to the perceived benefits of an international agreement with the IMF (Putnam 1988: 446–8; Moravcsik 1993: 25–6). The import substituting (IS) industry in India would have opposed lower tariffs and a liberal foreign investment regime. It acquiesced to liberalization because the IMF was the only source of foreign exchange for the import of raw materials and intermediate goods needed to produce goods for the domestic economy, at the time of the balance of payments crisis.

This chapter traces the path that ISI traversed in India (George and McKeown 1985: 21–58; Pierson 2004: Ch. 2). It locates a mechanism that began with ISI but changed to TLG.[7] The process highlights ISI's propensity to sow the seeds of its own destruction by generating unsustainable fiscal deficits. These deficits contributed substantially to India's balance of payments crisis. The Gulf War-driven exogenous shock (1990) was less of a burden on India's balance of payments than the two oil shocks (of 1973 and 1980). This external shock helped to convert a deteriorating internal fiscal situation into a severe balance of payments crisis. Changes in executive orientation due to an unsustainable fiscal deficit during the 1980s convinced the executive to change the course of the economic policy in 1991.

FROM IMPORT SUBSTITUTING INDUSTRIALIZATION (ISI) TO TRADE-LED GROWTH (TLG)

A path from ISI to TLG is outlined in this section. This path suggests a causal mechanism that could be fruitful for understanding economic transitions in any plural polity.[8]

Two Consequences of ISI
ISI, Democracy, and Social Mobilization

Industrialization can create political awareness among people and encourage them to participate in political activities. That industrialization and economic development facilitates political protest is borne out by the democratization taking place from southern Europe to East Asia (Inglehart 1997: 8). Even Germany, which up to World War II was considered the exception to this rule, seems to have witnessed considerable social and political mobilization after the rapid economic development in the late 1800s and the early 1900s (Berman 2001: 431–62). ISI was a strategy of economic development that generated rising economic aspirations, which found a fertile ground in India's political democracy.

ISI is a modernization strategy adopted by late industrializers, based on rapid heavy industrialization in the context of a closed economy. India's Second Five-Year Plan (1956–61) was an attempt at planned industrialization using internal economies of scale rather than trade. Its architect, P.C. Mahalanobis, pointed to a remarkable resemblance between the

Indian plan and the Soviet experiment of the late 1920s. It emphasized rapid industrialization, economic independence, and socialism, reflecting Prime Minister Nehru's vision of a modern India.[9]

Industrialization results in rapid urbanization. Rapid industrialization also rests on a literate and educated workforce with access to the print and electronic media. ISI is therefore the breeding ground for urbanization, literacy, and mass communications— the basic ingredients of a strategy of modernization.

Modernization can generate social mobilization. Urbanization, literacy, and mass communications, especially in the context of political democracy, are likely to expand political consciousness and participation (Huntington 1968: 5). Literacy and the growing spread of mass communications produce a heightened feeling of relative deprivation. Urbanization leads to erosion of traditional loyalty to the joint family and the village. Breaking old commitments to the larger family and the village community, and greater respect for individualism generates new time for new purposes, and produces new aspirations. Patron-client relations in the village are increasingly replaced either by class or sector-based or communal group demands (Huntington 1968: 39–49; Huntington and Nelson 1976: Ch. 3).

The newly mobilized people increasingly participate in politics. New groups seize opportunities and old groups feel threatened. Autonomous political participation based on voluntary action, such as the casting of a vote, takes over from old forms of coerced participation. Interest groups such as professional and cultural organizations begin to enjoy an independent voice. Political participation of mobilized people includes voting, lobbying, organizational activity, and various forms of political protests, including political violence (Huntington and Nelson 1976: Fn. 19, Ch. 1 and Ch. 3).

The practice of ISI-driven modernization in India resulted in an increase in education, urbanization, and mass communications. The literacy rate more than doubled from 23.8 per cent in 1960 to 52.21 per cent in 1990 (GoI 1999: vi). The urban population as a proportion of the total population grew steadily from 20 per cent in 1970 to 26 per

cent in 1990.[10] In 1983, only 25 per cent of India's population was within the television transmission range. With the rapid growth of the electronic media, the same figure grew from 50 per cent in 1985 to 75 per cent in 1990. Driven by a rise in literacy and political awareness, vernacular newspapers became widespread in rural and urban locations (Farmer 2000: 266; Ninan 2007: Ch. 2).

As access to literacy, urbanization, and mass communications improved, political participation and protest also witnessed a significant increase. Cases of student indiscipline increased from ninety-three in 1958 to 2665 in 1968 and to 9174 in 1978. Faced with student mobilization, Prime Minister Indira Gandhi had to declare a national Emergency in 1975. The period, 1975–9, recorded a decline in college enrolment, which could have been the result of policies undertaken to curb political unrest (Rudolph and Rudolph 1987: 227, 295).

Participation in riots per million people was stable up to 1963, but showed a steady increase thereafter. Riots as a proportion of the total cognizable offences grew steadily between 1967 and 1971. The authoritarian regime of Prime Minister Indira Gandhi brought down the incidence of rioting in 1975. When democracy returned in 1977, it was life as usual once again (Nayar 1975: 22–6; Rudolph and Rudolph 1987: 227). Communal riots in India appear to be a modern urban phenomenon, concentrated within cities and in industrial areas.[11]

Voter turnout increased rapidly at the end of the Second Five-Year Plan. It increased from 48 per cent in 1957 to 58 per cent in 1962, but stabilized in the range of 58 and 62 per cent thereafter (in 1996 the figure jumped to 67 per cent). There has been a rise in the turnout for elections to the state legislatures since 1989. Turnout at the local-level panchayat elections has also increased (Yadav 2000: 122–3).

Democratic politics in India became increasingly competitive as a result of social mobilization. From 1947 to 1967, the Congress party was congruous with the Indian political system. Major contests on Indian political issues occurred within rather than outside it (Kothari 1964: 1161–73; Morris-Jones 1968: 196–232). The election in 1967 changed this pattern. Between 1967 and 1969, the Congress lost power in eight states. What had been polarity within the Congress took the shape of polarity between the Congress and a united opposition. This bi-polarity began to spread to other states. A variety of contests such as Congress versus the Left, Congress versus the regional party or parties, and Congress versus the right-wing Jan Sangh (which later became the Bharatiya Janata Party or BJP) began to surface.[12] The Congress party under Indira Gandhi, unable to respond to an increasingly mobilized opposition, invoked a 'national Emergency' between 1975 and 1977. The electorate supported the movement against authoritarian rule and dislodged the Congress party from power in 1977.[13] This was the first successful united opposition against the Congress party at the national level.

The Janata Dal victory in 1989 was the result of a horizontal cooperation among disadvantaged and backward castes, rather than a vertical mobilization by the higher castes. The coalition of Muslims, backward castes like Ahirs, Jats, Gujars, and Yadavs—comprising the better-off among the backward and middle castes—and the Rajputs put up a formidable opposition to the Congress party. In an earlier era, such cooperation between the Rajputs (the ruling caste) and backward castes was unthinkable. The Bahujan Samaj Party—the first party to be led by a member of a Scheduled Caste—also facilitated the Janata Dal victory in 1989 (Frankel 1997: 375–82).[14] India had entered an era of coalition politics where the BJP and the Congress needed the support of significant regional parties to remain in power.

In sum, India's modernization promoted literacy, mass communications, and urbanization in the context of political democracy. This mobilized the people to participate in political protest and voting. The relative decline of the Congress party since the mid-1980s and the rise of regional, backward-caste, and minority group-based parties has been due largely to the Congress' institutional incapacity to articulate and respond to the demands of an increasingly mobilized society.

ISI and Low Productivity

ISI also generated classic conditions of low productivity in India. The infant industry protection

inspired by ISI had a deleterious impact on efficiency.[15] It was not easy to locate an infant industry, and neither was it easy to determine the optimal amount of protection needed to propel an infant industry into a mature one (Todaro 1981: 453–4). Third, ISI depended on government decisions with respect to protection and subsidy. With few clear guidelines about the optimal amount of protection, ISI generated rent-seeking behaviour that prolonged the period of protection, with negative consequences for efficiency (Krueger 1974).[16]

The ISI strategy had a negative impact on the productivity of Indian industry. The public sector accounted for 27 per cent of the gross domestic product (GDP). Its turnover investment ratio was seventy-nine in 1971, went up to two in 1981, and then declined to one in 1991. Any figure below three is considered very low. Twenty-seven out of the 129 public-sector undertakings utilized less than 50 per cent of their capacity in 1977–8 (Sarma 1995). Isher Ahluwalia's study on the productivity of the Indian manufacturing industry noted the dismal performance in total factor productivity growth in the 1970s and a positive turnaround in the 1980s, due largely to some deregulation in the economy. The capital labour ratio in the manufacturing sector of a labour-abundant economy was increasing, leading to inappropriate factor use over time (Ahluwalia 1991: Ch. 7).[17]

Timmer and Szirmai (1999) have noted that while Taiwan and South Korea were catching up with the US's level of productivity between 1963 and 1993, India did not catch up at all. The South Korean gross value added per worker as a per cent of the US gross value added per worker grew from 7.5 per cent in 1963 to 48.5 per cent in 1993. The same figures for Taiwan were 11.8 per cent and 31.3 per cent respectively. For India, the figures were 7.5 per cent and 10.1 per cent, respectively. India, Taiwan, and Korea were at the same level of productivity relative to the US level in 1963, but India lagged far behind Taiwan and Korea in the race for 'catch-up' in 1993.[18]

India's international competitiveness declined. India's share in the manufacturing exports of all developing countries came down from 22.1 per cent in 1962 to 3.4 per cent in 1990. Its share in the manufacturing exports of the world came down from 84 per cent in 1962 to 54 per cent in 1990.[19]

Social Mobilization, Low Productivity, and the Fiscal Crisis

India's ISI contributed to both the low levels of productivity and the political demands for better living and working conditions. The same people who had not expressed dissatisfaction with their abject poverty became more vocal about their economic demands. The politics of 'command' characterized by state autonomy transformed itself into the politics of 'demand' led by pressure groups (Rudolph and Rudolph 1987: 211–392; 1997: 177–86). Two things could happen under these circumstances. First, the feeling of relative deprivation could lead to political violence and the declining legitimacy of the government, provided there were few opportunities for socio-economic mobility and political participation (Gurr 1970; Davies 1970).[20] Or the government could subsidize various sectors by providing seeds, fertilizers, irrigation, housing sites, land, and concessional finance (Mitra 1991).[21] If the government spent most of its resources in a way that did not earn adequate returns on investment, this would inevitably lead to a fiscal crisis.

As Indian farmers constituted a substantial vote bank, it compelled the government to subsidize their economic activities. They could not be taxed. The fertilizer subsidy could not be reduced. The agriculture sector consumed approximately 25 per cent of the electricity, but accounted for the bulk of the losses of the state electricity boards. Out of the total power-sector losses of Rs 43.5 billion, Rs 41 billion was estimated to be due to the farm sector. Revenues as a proportion of recurrent expenditure fell from 22 per cent in 1980 to 7.5 per cent in 1989 (Chakravarty 1987: 126–7; Varshney 1995: 169–72). In 1988, the National Front government of Prime Minister V.P. Singh wrote off the debts of small farmers at a time when it had foreign exchange reserves worth $ 3.7 billion, just enough to cover two months of imports (Joshi and Little 1994: 65).

The political clout of the industrial sector, an important reason behind the degree of protection, accorded to various industrial sectors. The greater the clout of organized labour and industry, the greater the degree of protection granted to that sector (Gang and Pandey 1996). The government subsidized bankrupt industrial units on uneconomic grounds. In a study of twenty-three such industrial units, it was found that in seventeen cases, the Board of Industrial and Financial Reconstruction (BIFR) sanctioned excessive write-offs through subsidized credit (Anant and Goswamy 1995: 273–4).

Government expenditure of a non-economic kind rose due to the demands of the farmers, organized labour, and industrialists. The total non-developmental expenditure was raised from 6.5 per cent of the gross national product (GNP) in 1960 to 15 per cent in 1989. The percentage of subsidies in the expenditures of Central and state governments rose from 3.2 per cent in 1960 to 12.1 per cent in 1989 (Bardhan 1992: 324–5). The increasing demands of politically mobilized people ensured that the growth rate in government expenditure, which was 6.9 per cent between 1979 and 1983, rose to 9.5 per cent between 1983 and 1987. Rising government expenditure at a time of low productivity generated an unsustainable fiscal situation (Mundle and Rao 1992: 230–1).

The gross fiscal deficit is total government expenditure, minus government revenue plus capital grants. It measures the overall borrowing need to finance India's government expenditure. The fiscal deficit never crossed the 6.4 per cent of GDP mark till 1983. Thereafter, between 1983 and 1990, it fluctuated between 7.5 per cent of GDP to 9 per cent of GDP (GoI 1995: 16).

The twin ISI-driven dynamics of low productivity and social mobilization played an important role in generating the fiscal crisis of the Indian government (Krueger 1997: 16–17).[22] The ISI-driven modernization had generated new financial demands on the Indian government. At the same time, ISI was not a strategy that generated high productivity. Financial demands on the government at a time when Indian productivity was abysmally low created the classic condition of an unsustainable fiscal situation.

The Fiscal Crisis and Ideational Change in India

How did the ISI 'policy paradigm' change in India? First, dissatisfaction with a policy paradigm is necessary. A 'policy paradigm', implying a variety of policy-relevant theoretical ideas that share certain basic assumptions about development, generates certain behavioural expectations. When these expectations are not met, disenchantment with the paradigm begins to occur. 'Paradigm shifts', described by Thomas Kuhn, need not occur merely as a result of disenchantment with a policy paradigm. A policy paradigm could generate long periods of continuity despite disenchantment with anomalies (Kuhn 1970: Chs 4–6).[23]

It is not easy to bring about a change in policy paradigms. Thus, building on anomalies, long periods of continuity may be punctuated by the disjunctive experience of a 'paradigm shift'. According to this view, continuity is the norm, but change is sporadic and rapid (Krasner 1984: 240–4; see Kuhn 1970: Chs 9–10). It could be accompanied by major exogenous events such as depressions, wars, or a sudden change in the terms of trade (Hirschman 1989 and Bierstaker 1992). On such occasions, disenchantment with policies generated by the previous paradigm needs the support of a committed leadership with the power to implement new policies (Hall 1993: 286–7). The pro-trade technocratic orientation in India became influential in the 1980s as a result of the failures of IS policies and the international demonstration effect of the alternative paradigm. However, policy change in the direction of using trade for development had to wait till the foreign exchange crisis of 1991.

Policy puzzles persisted due to the malfunctioning of the ISI-driven policy paradigm in India. Infant industries did not mature into competitive ones. Income distribution remained highly skewed, leading to rising aspirations among the less privileged but newly mobilized people. And an increased demand for resources coupled with low productivity led to an unsustainable fiscal crisis. It, therefore, became difficult for policymakers to marry economics with politics. Moreover, developments in East Asia, China, and the Soviet Union validated the view that trade was essential for economic growth.[24]

Prime Minister Indira Gandhi began considering TLG strategies from the mid-1970s after a period of intensive autarkic industrialization between 1969 and 1974. A cabinet committee dedicated to export

promotion was set up in 1975. The commitment to reform was sustained when the Janata Party came to power between 1977 and 1979.[25] The government set up powerful committees to review the shortcomings of the old policies. Committees on trade (Chair: Abid Hussain, 1984), government controls (Chair: Dagli, 1979; Chair: Narasimhan, 1985), the public sector (Chair: Arjun Sengupta, 1985), and administrative reforms (L.K. Jha, 1981) were set up to provide a critical analysis of the past for purposes of future policy. These reports stressed that India's development needed imports and reduced government intervention. Moreover, India's growing imports had to be premised on increasing its capacity to export (Shastri 1995: 165–71; Gandhi 1985: 236; Dhar 1988: 13–14).

Prime Minister Rajiv Gandhi initiated pro-trade policy changes, which met with severe political opposition.[26] Montek Ahluwalia, a technocrat with World Bank experience, was brought in as Special Secretary in the Prime Minister's Office. In June 1990, Ahluwalia circulated a controversial paper advocating tariff reductions; freer entry of foreign investment; an increase in administered prices; an increase in the permissible asset limit under the Monopolies and Restrictive Trade Practices Act (MRTP); and labour laws to promote efficiency (Shastri 1995: 223–6). The agenda for reform was therefore clear to the executive before the foreign exchange shortfall in 1991.

The pro-trade momentum gained strength during the foreign exchange crisis of 1991. Prime Minister P.V. Narasimha Rao appointed the distinguished economist and policymaker Manmohan Singh as India's Finance Minister. In a rare tribute, the Economics Laureate Amartya Sen has praised Manmohan Singh's doctoral dissertation of the early 1960s, where Singh had argued in favour of exports for India's development.[27] The importance of trade and global economic integration were not lost on Manmohan Singh in 1991.[28]

The Fiscal Crisis and the Balance of Payments Crisis of 1991

Social mobilization and populist policies that drove the fiscal crisis were the key reasons why a relatively minor exogenous shock during the Gulf War precipitated a foreign exchange crisis in 1991. Creditor pessimism, driven largely by bad fiscal management and political uncertainty, had led to a disastrous depletion of foreign exchange reserves in 1991.

The fiscal deficit rose between 1985 and 1990. The gap between revenue and current expenditure, which was 1.5 per cent of the GDP between 1975 and 1980, rose to 3 per cent of the GDP between 1985 and 1990. Over the same period, interest payments grew by 1.8 per cent of GDP, subsidies increased by 1.7 per cent (of GDP), and defence expenditure rose by 0.8 per cent (of GDP). Interest payments and subsidies registered the highest rise, reflecting commercial borrowings and public demand management. [29]

Trade Deficit = Savings Investment Gap + Budget Deficit – (1)[30]

Equation 1 identifies the two major components of the trade deficit. The trade deficit is significantly affected by the savings investment gap and the budget deficit. In India, both the savings investment gap and the budget deficit did not augur well for the trade deficit. First, the budget deficit or the fiscal deficit during 1985–6 and 1989–90 at 10 per cent of GDP was much higher than in any period after 1950 (Joshi and Little 1994: 226).

Second, the savings investment gap was much greater in 1991 compared with the period of the two oil shocks. In 1989–90, the gap was 2.4 per cent of GDP, compared with 0.6 per cent of GDP in 1972–3 and 0.5 per cent of GDP in 1979–80. In 1989–90, public deficit (savings–investment) was 9 per cent of GDP, corporate deficit was 1.8 per cent of GDP, and household savings were 8.4 per cent of GDP (Joshi and Little 1994: Ch. 12). The household savings surplus was therefore not enough to cover corporate and public investments.

Table 32.1 describes the components of India's deteriorating balance in the current account. The customs trade deficit due to import liberalization was reduced. The trade aspect of the balance that deteriorated involved the Reserve Bank of India's purchases of public equipment for military hardware and government purchases. Transfer receipts fell as a proportion of GDP. There was a worsening of net factor income from abroad because of increased interest payments on commercial borrowing. The

Table 32.1: Components of the Balance of Payments on the Current Account, 1982–3 to 1989–90

(figures should be read as per cent of GDP)

	AVERAGE 1982/83– 1984/85	AVERAGE 1985/86– 1989/90	CHANGE
Trade balance (customs)	-2.7	-2.3	0.4
Trade balance (RBI)	-3.0	-3.2	-0.2
Net non-factor services	0.5	0.3	-0.2
Resource balance	-2.4	-2.8	-0.4
Net factor income	-0.5	-1.0	-0.5
Net int. payments	-0.8	-1.2	-0.4
Net current transfers	1.3	1.0	-0.3
Current a/c balance	-0.8	-1.7	-0.9

Source: Joshi and Little (1994: 185).

deficit in the category of net factor income from abroad rose from $1.5 billion in 1984–5 to $3 billion in 1989–90. As a result, the current account deficit, which was $3 billion (1.7 per cent of GDP) in the first half of the 1980s, deteriorated to about $7 billion (3 per cent of GDP) in the latter half.

The budget and savings deficits were the prime motors behind the deteriorating current account imbalance. The first and second oil shocks had affected the current account adversely to the tune of about 1.1 per cent of GDP and 1.5 per cent of GDP, respectively. The impact of the oil price rise in 1990 on the current account balance was not more severe (1 per cent of GDP) than the oil shocks (Joshi and Little 1994: 114, 149, 189). Yet India was less capable of dealing with the exogenous shock of 1991 on its own, largely due to the combination of a large fiscal deficit and the savings investment gap.

The adverse credit rating by Moody's in October 1990 pointed to a rise in the debt-service ratio, high dependence on commercial borrowings, increase in the debt-export ratio, the effect of the Gulf War, the budget deficit and public debt, and recession in the OECD countries. This led to a shutting down of all credit windows. Political uncertainty and mismanagement led to a further downgrading of India's credit rating in March 1991 (Bhaduri and Nayyar 1996: 27; Joshi and Little 1994: 67). Frantic moves to gain access to foreign exchange ensued, and efforts to secure foreign exchange by mortgaging gold failed. Non-resident Indians withdrew their investments parked in India. In January and June 1991, India was on the verge of a liquidity crisis with not enough foreign exchange to cover a fortnight of imports (Joshi and Little 1994: 67; Bhaduri and Nayyar 1996: 29).

The Pro-Trade Executive, Balance of Payments Crisis, and Liberalization

I have explained how the fiscal crisis transformed the Indian executive orientation. Changed executive orientation during the Rajiv Gandhi era was inadequate to generate a distinctively pro-trade policy with greater freedoms for the private sector. The executive team of P.V. Narasimha Rao and Manmohan Singh was well positioned to exploit the balance of payments crisis and the consequent dependence on the IMF so as to win the approval of Indian industry.

The Balance of Payments Crisis and Synergy

The simultaneous occurrence of a foreign exchange crisis and pro-trade executive orientation provided a compelling reason for trade and investment liberalization in India's plural polity. *An agreement between the executive and the IMF at the time of a foreign exchange crisis opened up the possibility of synergistic issue linkage in a two-level game between the International Monetary Fund, the executive, and Indian industry* (Putnam 1988: 446–8).The interests of Indian industry did not change, but their preferences changed as a result of the IMF's lender of the last resort function.

An IMF agreement with a debtor country created a temporary interest in favour of freer trade. ISI is an import-dependent industrialization strategy. Although the dominant industrial sector in India had an interest in perpetuating the closed economy after more than four decades of ISI, it acquiesced in a trade and investment promoting agreement with the IMF in the short term, because there was no one else willing to finance the imports of IS industrialists during a balance of payments crisis. Thus, the interests of industry in the IS sectors may not change, but its preferences may change temporarily in favour of

opening trade and investment due to the dire need for an agreement with the IMF.

The foreign exchange crisis of 1991 created a short-term euphoria in favour of trade and investment liberalization within the business community. The Federation of Indian Chambers of Commerce and Industry (FICCI), representing domestic capital, the Associated Chambers of Commerce and Industry (ASSOCHAM), with ties to foreign capital, and the Confederation of Indian Industry (CII), representing manufacturing industry, all supported the trade and investment liberalization from 1991 to 1993. The CII, which had positioned itself as the most influential industry organization, prepared a theme paper outlining the contours of a free economy in April 1991 (Dash 1999: 902–3 and ASSOCHAM 1995: 213–53). The CII owed its rise to Rajiv Gandhi's wooing segments of the modern Indian manufacturing industry to work closely with the government on trade and industrial policy (Sinha 2005: 1–35). It held numerous meetings with Trade Union leaders, journalists, and politicians (Dash 1999: 902; CII 1994).

The euphoria accompanying Indian industry's favouring trade and investment reform was short-lived after 1993, which was when the opposition to investment liberalization within Indian industry gained momentum. The informal Bombay Club of prominent industrialists articulated a coherent anti-multinational corporation (MNC) position.[31]

While Trade Unions did not oppose reduced tariffs or foreign investment, they successfully opposed the exit policy, which was designed to create a dent in job security in the unionized sector. The New Industrial Policy (July 1991) had established the National Renewal Fund (NRF) to restructure industries in order to promote efficiency (Venkata Ratnam 1992: 378 and Subrahmanya 1996: 59–63).[32] Widespread opposition to industrial restructuring produced a nation-wide strike on 29 November 1991 (Pandhe 1991: 1–4). The workers' strike of 16 June 1992 affected even defence installations, the Post and Telegraph Department, Income Tax and Audit, port and dockworkers, and the oil sector (Pandhe 1992: 4–8; Sen 1997: Chs 23–4.).

The IMF Agreement of 1991 won the temporary acquiescence of Indian industry for trade and investment liberalization because industry needed foreign exchange for ISI-related imports. Trade Unions opposed the exit policy, but not tariff liberalization or foreign investment. The pro-trade Indian executive team of Prime Minister Rao and Finance Minister Singh used the period between 1991 and 1993 to liberalize trade and private investment, which would be tough to reverse under normal circumstances.

The Role of the Pro-Trade Executive in Exploiting Synergy

A pro-trade and private sector-oriented executive could exploit the foreign exchange crisis to liberalize the economy up to a point from which retreat to economic nationalism would not be easy. Prime Minister Rao and Finance Minister Manmohan Singh constituted the executive team in India's Westminster-style parliamentary system. First, the crisis unified the legislature behind the executive on economic reforms, despite the rumblings of protest within the Indian Parliament.[33] Second, an executive favouring trade and private investment shared similar views about the IMF's economic agenda to a greater extent. This increased the positive sum elements in the negotiations. The larger the negotiating 'win-set' between the two, the greater the chances of an agreement with the IMF (Moravcsik 1993: 28; Evans 1993: 402–3).

The executive team of Rao and Singh were convinced liberalizers. Rao realized that the crisis was an opportunity to provide a new definition to India's development policy.[34] And the importance of trade for India's development had not been lost on Singh since the days of his DPhil thesis at Oxford. This ensured broad areas of agreement with the IMF. In his first budget speech (24 July 1991), Singh clearly stated the Indian economic problem:

> The origins of the problem are directly traceable to large and persistent macroeconomic imbalances and low productivity of investment, in particular the poor rates of return on past investments.... The increasing difference between the income and expenditure of the Government has led to a widening of the gap between the income and expenditure of the economy as a whole. This is reflected in growing current account deficits in the balance of payments. (GoI 1997: 5)

The reform team worked efficiently. Rao could carry the Congress party with him on reforms, and would leave the economic judgement to Singh (*Business India* 1997: 68, 1998: 57–8). Singh's conviction helped him to defend the economic stabilization and structural adjustment that India had undertaken after consultations with the IMF. When accused of having shared the Union Budget of 1992 with the World Bank without a proper parliamentary debate, Singh successfully defended the need to share vital information with creditors, which had been discussed in Parliament (*Lok Sabha Debates* 1992: 572–3). The IMF approved of the Government of India initiatives in a report in 1995, in which it praised India's initiatives towards economic stabilization and structural adjustment in the aftermath of the balance of payments crisis (Chopra *et al.* 1995: 1–3).

India's Economic Reforms

India's trade reforms involved a gradual reduction in trade protection with substantially increased incentives for export promotion. India's average weighted nominal tariff came down from 81.4 per cent in 1991–2 to 32.9 per cent in 1995–6. Even though this was a significant reduction, the overall protection did not come down significantly because of the substantial devaluation of the Indian Rupee. Tariff liberalization coupled with devaluation made export promotion easier than import substitution. Trade promotion was further aided by the convertibility of the Rupee in the current account in 1994. These trade policy measures gave a great boost to India's IT exports. They wiped out the import-substituting intermediate goods industry in India. In 1996, India became Sri Lanka's largest trading partner after a period of sixty years, beating Japan to the second place (Tendulkar and Bhavani 2007: 116–25).[35]

Investment policy favoured the Indian corporate sector over foreign corporations. The abolition of industrial licensing enabled Indian industrialists to make investment decisions without seeking the government's permission. The Tata group, which was not allowed to manufacture a car till 1991, could now compete with multinationals with its popular Indica brand. Tata Motors had purchased brands like Jaguar and Rover to access the international market, and was at an advanced stage in the production of the world's cheapest car—the Nano. Foreign direct investment was promoted to a lesser extent than Indian investment, even though the Foreign Exchange Regulation Act was substantially liberalized after 1991. More foreign capital arrived through the portfolio route into Indian stock markets for the benefit of Indian companies than through the direct investment of foreign companies.[36] China's globalization depended on foreign companies to a greater extent; however, India's globalization produced world-class Indian companies.[37]

Infrastructure sectors such as telecommunications, stock markets, and banks attained a high level of efficiency. The fiscal crisis inspired the Prime Minister's Office (PMO) and the Ministry of Finance (MoF) to strengthen regulations favouring the private sector in these areas. They served the middle class, the rich, and Indian industry rather well. The rural poor's access to these services was far less satisfactory. Infrastructure areas such as power, ports, and roads continued to be in poor shape, even though there had been some progress made since 1991. Success and failure in infrastructure delivery were largely the handiwork of home-grown attempts to deal with inefficiencies within the system.[38]

India's economic globalization, driven by private initiative and orientation towards competition, has catapulted it to a high growth trajectory. India's trade to GDP ratio, which stayed constant between 1980 and 1990, grew quite rapidly beyond 1991 (Nayar 2006b: 16–17). The economy, which grew at a rate just over 5 per cent between 1975 and 1990, was growing at a rate higher than 6 per cent between 1994 and 2004. The growth rate further accelerated to over 8.5 per cent beyond 2003, making India the second fastest growing economy in the world. The agriculture sector, which employed over 60 per cent of the population, was growing almost at the rate of the population growth at a time when services and industry were growing quite rapidly (Chand et al. 2007: 2528–33). The challenge for economic reforms is inclusive growth, which will promote labour-

intensive manufacturing and spur higher growth rates in Indian agriculture.

CONCLUSION: THE SIGNIFICANCE OF INDIA'S PATH

The process of trade and investment liberalization in India suggests the importance of history and process in a political explanation (Pierson 2004: 54–78; Bates et al. 1998: 3–18). The assertion that the simultaneous presence of a pro-reform executive and a balance of payments crisis could lead to trade and investment liberalization points to two important questions. First, why did the Indian executive favour trade and private investment in 1991? Second, was the balance of payments crisis of 1991 merely the result of an exogenous shock?

Trade and private investment orientation were born from the inability of import-substituting economic policy to deal with a growing fiscal deficit, which landed India in a balance of payments crisis at the time of the Gulf War. The literature on path dependence asserts that the logic of increasing returns to a particular regulatory regime can lock an inefficient trajectory because any mode of organization involves high start-up costs, learning and network externalities, and adaptive expectations (Pierson 2004: 54–78). ISI involved huge doses of public and private investment to set up a large government sector, and subsidize domestic industry. Thereafter, rent-seeking opportunities for the industrialist, the politician, and the bureaucrat, and job security of the worker created vested interests that perpetuated the system. Consistent with the conventional wisdom on path dependence, every investment that reinforced ISI made it difficult to initiate a regulatory regime that would promote India's exports.

India's transition also suggests a mechanism for change, because inherent in any self-perpetuating regulatory regime are the sources of change.[39] For example, the problem facing India's ISI lay in the un-sustainability of budget deficits in the context of low levels of productivity and dependence on foreign finance. The budget deficit was a process-driven variable, which played an important role in generating key policy change variables, the pro-reform executive orientation, and the balance of payments crisis (Elster 1999: Ch. 1).[40]

This mechanism for understanding policy change has implications for the debate on the salience of domestic and international political economy in explaining economic policy change in India. The preferences of the Indian executive were independent of the constraints posed by the global economy. However, international constraints played a role in translating the executive's preferences into policy outcomes (Frieden 1999). The executive may have had a pro-reform bent; however, this could produce either trade protection or liberalization, depending on the severity of the foreign exchange crisis. Second, the strategic situation between domestic actors was important. Had Indian industry continued to oppose liberalization in the absence of an agreement with the IMF, the pro-reform executive would have achieved very little (Milner 1998: 772–86). This could be one reason why Rajiv Gandhi's economic policies could not promote India's trade in the absence of a balance of payments crisis. Crises may be critical for economic reforms in democracies where economic policy change is generally a more gradual and consensual process.

The Indian transition holds lessons for the design of IMF conditionality. If IMF conditionalities are viewed by the debtor country as being too intrusive, trade-led development requiring structural adjustment may not be forthcoming. India went for funds twice in 1966 and 1980, but the results of 1991 were far more impressive than those of previous years.[41] What the IMF wanted India to do in 1991 was largely a part of the Indian technocratic consensus by 1990. An effort on the IMF's part to promote home-grown programmes based on country ownership of those programmes was likely to increase the former's ability to enable a country to move towards trade-led development.[42]

NOTES

1. Trade-led growth strategies, on the other hand, characterize a situation where the effective exchange rate for exports is not significantly different from the effective exchange rate for imports; see Bhagwati (1986).

2. On the definition and significance of a tough case, which is very similar to a 'crucial experiment' in the philosophy of science, see Stinchcombe (1968, pp. 25–8) and Eckstein (1975, pp. 119–20).

3. On the problems of adjustment to TLG in a democracy, see Przeworski (1991, Ch. 4); Pereira et al. (1993, pp. 1–11), and Haggard (1990, Ch. 10). On the interests of rent-seeking groups in perpetuating ISI, see Krueger (1974). On why small interests groups might organize effectively against large ones, see Olson (1971, Ch. 1).

4. For the role of the authoritarian state in facilitating economic reforms in Taiwan, see Amsden (1985) and Haggard (1990, Ch. 4). For the relationship between authoritarianism and economic transition in Korea, see Haggard (1990, Ch. 3), and Haggard and Moon (1983). For East Asia as a whole, see Wade (1990).

5. On China's transition, see Qian (2003, pp. 297–331), Naughton (1995), and Yang (1996, pp. 424–52). On China and India, see Gilley (2005, pp. 22–51).

6. On Rajiv Gandhi's halting reforms, see Kohli (1990, Ch. 11), Bhagwati (1993, pp. 73–4), and Varshney (2007, pp. 150–4).

7. For an understanding of mechanisms, see Elster (1999, Ch. 1).

8. For path dependence, see George and Mckeown (1985, p. 36). For a discussion on mechanisms, see Elster (1999, Ch. 1).

9. For the role of the state in late industrialization, see Gerschenkron (1962). For India's ISI, see Chakravarty (1987, Ch. 2). For an argument that ISI in India was a strategy of modernization, see Nayar (1974, pp. 361–3) and Nayar (1972). If India had gone the Gandhian way, emphasizing small and cottage industries, such a strategy may have been a departure from modernization.

10. Data accessed electronically from World Development Indicators (The World Bank 2007).

11. On the relationship between modernization and communal violence in India, see Kakar (1995, Ch. 6). On the rural–urban divide in communal riots, see Nandy (1999, pp. 136–8). On the relatively low incidence of communal violence in rural India, see Varshney (2001, p. 371).

12. Kothari updated his analysis for the period up to 1967 in Kothari (1970, Ch. 2). For recent analyses summarizing the trends in party competition, see Sridharan (2002, pp. 481–5) and Gowda and Sridharan (2007, pp. 3–25).

13. For a description of the mobilizations that inspired Indira Gandhi to impose a 'national Emergency' see Frankel (2005, Ch. 10) and Rudolph and Rudolph (1997, p. 183).

14. For an analysis of the entry of new groups into political competition in five districts of India, see Kohli

(1990, Chs 3–7) and Kohli (1994, pp. 93–4). On more recent accounts of the rise of marginalized groups in politics, see Jaffrelot (2007, pp. 66–85), Pai (2007, pp. 221–40), and Vivek Kumar (2007, pp. 241–70).

15. For a review of the literature supporting ISI, see Krueger (1993, pp. 44–5).

16. For a review of the literature on rent-seeking, see Krueger (1997, p. 22).

17. Although there is some controversy about the total factor productivity growth (includes labour and capital's contribution to productivity) in the 1980s, Ahluwalia's is the majority view. I am indebted to Biswanath Goldar for his insights.

18. For the India and East Asia comparison, see Timmer and Szirmai (1999, pp. 61–5). For the argument that there is no need to shift factors such as labour and capital to more productive uses for increasing the level of productivity, see Timmer and Szirmai (2000, pp. 371–92).

19. See Kathuria (1995, p. 154). India's trade to GDP ratio stagnated between 1980 and 1990. Also see Nayar (2006b, pp. 16–17).

20. On mobilization, see Huntington (1968, pp. 53–5) and Huntington and Nelson (1976, Chs 1 and 3).

21. On the impact of social mobilization on the Indian exchequer, see Bardhan (1984, Ch. 5).

22. I associate low productivity rather than slow economic growth with the fiscal crisis because a fiscal crisis may be associated with a high growth but inflation-generating expansionary policy.

23. For the relationship between 'policy paradigm' and economic policy change, see Hall (1993, pp. 277–87).

24. For the East Asian and Chinese transitions, see Haggard (1990, Chs 3–4), Amsden (1985, pp. 78–106), Naughton (1995), Yang (1996, pp. 424–52), and Qian (2003, pp. 297–333). On the impact of China's globalization on India see Alamgir (2007, pp. 254–66). For the fall of the Soviet system, see Goldman (1991) and Kennedy (1988, pp. 631–64). Also see Krueger (1998, p. 203).

25. Personal interview with Arjun K. Sengupta New Delhi, 20 August 1997. Sengupta was an advisor to Prime Minister Indira Gandhi in the early 1980s. Also see Sengupta (2001, pp. 44–65), Nayar (2006a, p. 1886), Nayar (2006b, pp. 10–13), and Kohli (2006, pp. 1254–8).

26. On the promise of Rajiv Gandhi's reforms in 1984 and 1985, see Rubin (1985, pp. 942–57). On his failure to adequately deal with politics, see Kohli (1990, Ch. 11), Bhagwati (1993, pp. 73–4), and Varshney (2007, pp. 150–4).

27. For the published version of Singh's doctoral dissertation, see Singh (1964). Also see Sen (1998).

28. For concluding that Singh was in favour of trade and private investment in 1991, I rely on the following sources:

Personal interviews with Jagdish Bhagwati, Arthur Lehman Professor of Economics, Columbia University, New York, 14 November 1997; Manmohan Singh, Member of Parliament, Ministry of Parliamentary Affairs, New Delhi, 8 August 1997; and Montek Singh Ahluwalia, Member: Planning Commission, New Delhi 25 April 2001. See also, Byres (1998, pp. 87–8) and Bhaduri and Nayyar (1996, p. 50).

29. Joshi and Little (1994, p. 226). I have relied on these figures because the Joshi and Little's figures have stood the test of time, as an authoritative account of the Indian crises. See also, Jalan (1991, pp. 1–4, 100–17).

30. For a commentary on this equation see, Krugman (1994, p. 50).

31. Interview with D.H. Pai Panandiker, New Delhi, 1 September 1997. Panandiker was Secretary General of the FICCI up to 1992. See also, Das (1997, pp. 104–13). Tarun Das was the Secretary General of CII in 1991. The Sri Ram Memorial Lecture was delivered at the PHD Chambers of Commerce in New Delhi on 21 August 1997. Kochanek (2007, pp. 425–7).

32. On India's labour laws, see Zagha (1999, pp. 161–6).

33. On the special advantages of the executive for crafting a unified government, see Milner (1997, pp. 103–6, 109–12). For divided government, see Ch. 4. On how unified government was achieved in India despite much opposition in 1966, see Mukherji (2000, pp. 383–885).

34. Personal interview with P.V. Narasimha Rao in New Delhi on 2 February 2001.

35. For an overview of economic reforms see Ahluwalia (2007, pp. 87–113). On the rise of India–Sri Lanka trade, see Kelegama (1999, pp. 95–103).

36. On the liberalization of domestic and foreign investment, see Tendulkar and Bhavani (2007, pp. 106–25).

37. On the differences between India's and China's globalization, see Khanna (2007); Gilley (2005, pp. 19–51).

38. On the regulation of infrastructure, see Mukherji (2007, pp. 300–27), Mukherji (2009), Panagariya (2008, Ch. 17–20), and Bhattacharya and Patel (2005, pp. 406–56).

39. For an account of change within the rational choice framework, see Grief and Laitin (2004, pp. 633–52).

40. Readers may think that I am contradicting myself by saying that ISI perpetuates itself but may sow the seeds of its own destruction. The literature describing the complexity of causal mechanisms shows that the same cause may have two different kinds of impact on the effect. What is therefore critical is the net impact on the effect.

41. On India's response to the crisis in 1966, see Mukherji (2000, pp. 375–92). On India's response to the IMF program between 1981 and 1984 see, Choudhry et al., (2004, pp. 59–81).

42. On the design of IMF programs emphasizing country ownership of programmes, see Khan and Sharma (2001). See also Stiglitz (2002).

REFERENCES

Ahluwalia, Isher J. 1991. *Productivity and Growth in Indian Manufacturing*. New Delhi: Oxford University Press.

Ahluwalia, Montek S. 2007. 'Economic Reforms in India Since 1991: Has Gradualism Worked?' in Rahul Mukherji (ed.), *India's Economic Transition*. New Delhi: Oxford University Press, pp. 87–113.

Alamgir, Jalal. 2007. 'Nationalist Globalism', in Baldev R. Nayar (ed.), *Globalization and Politics in India*. New Delhi: Oxford University Press, pp. 245–66.

Amsden, Alice. 1985. 'The State and Taiwan's Economic Development', in Peter Evans, Dietrich Reuschemeyer, and Theda Skocpol (eds), *Bringing the State Back In*. New York: Cambridge University Press, pp. 78–106..

Anant, T.C.A. and Omkar Goswamy. 1995. 'Getting Everything Wrong', in Dilip Mookherjee (ed.), *Indian Industry*. New Delhi: Oxford University Press, pp. 236–88.

ASSOCHAM (Associated Chambers of Commerce and Industry). 1995. *The ASSOCHAM Story*. New Delhi: ASSOCHAM.

Bardhan, Pranab. 1992. 'A Political Economy Perspective on Development', in Bimal Jalan (ed.), *The Indian Economy*. New Delhi: Viking Penguin, pp. 321–37.

———. 1984. *The Political Economy of Development in India*. Oxford: Basil Blackwell.

Bates, Robert H., Avner Greif, Margaret Levi, Jean-Laurent Rosenthal, and Barry R. Weingast. 1998. *Analytic Narratives*. Princeton, New Jersey: Princeton University Press.

Berman, Sheri. 2001. 'Modernization in Historical Perspective'. *World Politics*, 53(3), pp. 431–62.

Bhaduri, Amit and Deepak Nayyar. 1996. *The Intelligent Person's Guide to Liberalization*. New Delhi: Penguin Books.

Bhagwati, Jagdish N. 1993. *India in Transition*. Oxford: Clarendon Press.

———. 1986. 'Rethinking Trade Strategy', in John P. Lewis and Velleriana Kallab (eds), *Development Strategies Reconsidered*. New Jersey: Transaction Books.

Bhattacharya, Saugata and Urjit Patel. 2005. 'New Regulatory Institutions in India', in Devesh Kapur and Pratap B. Mehta (eds), *Public Institutions in India*. New Delhi: Oxford University Press, pp. 91–104.

Byres, T.J. 1998. 'The Creation of 'The Tribe of Pundits Called Economists', in T.J. Byres (ed.), *The Indian Economy*. New Delhi: Oxford University Press, pp. 20–73.

Chand, Ramesh, S.S. Raju, and L.M. Pandey. 2007. 'Growth Crisis in Indian Agriculture', *Economic and Political Weekly*, XLII(26), pp. 2528–33.

Chopra, Ajay, Charles Collyns, Richard Hemming, and Karen Parker. 1995. 'India: Economic Growth and Reform', Occasional Paper 134, IMF, Washington, DC

Chakravarty, Sukhamoy. 1987. *Development Planning*. Oxford: Clarendon Press.

Choudhry, Praveen K., Vjiay L. Kelkar, and Vikash Yadav. 2004. 'The Evolution of Homegrown Conditionality in India-IMF Relations', *Journal of Development Studies*, 40(6), pp. 59–81.

CII (Confederation of Indian Industry). 1994. *Report on Competitive Advantage of India*. New Delhi: CII.

Das, Tarun. 1997. 'India: A New Economic Direction', *World Affairs*, 1(2).

Dash, Kishore C. 1999. 'India's International Monetary Fund Loans', *Asian Survey*, 39(6), pp. 884–907.

Davies, James C. 1970. *When Men Revolt and Why*. New York: Free Press.

Dhar, P.N. 1988. 'The Indian Economy', in Robert E.B. Lucas and Gustave F. Papanek (eds), *The Indian Economy*. New Delhi: Oxford University Press, pp. 3–22.

Evans, Peter B. 1993. 'Building an Integrative Approach', in Peter B. Evans, Harold K. Jacobson, and Robert D. Putnam (eds), *Double-Edged Diplomacy*. Berkeley: University of California Press, pp. 397–430.

Eckstein, Harry. 1975. 'Case Study and Theory in Political Science', in Fred I. Greenstein and Nelson Polsby (eds), *Handbook of Political Science*, Vol. 7, *Strategies of Inquiry*. Reading, Mass.: Addison Wesley, pp. 79–137.

Elster, Jon. 1999. *Alchemies of the Mind*. Cambridge: Cambridge University Press.

Farmer, Victoria L. 2000. 'Depicting the Nation', in Francine R. Frankel, Zoya Hasan, Rajeev Bhargava, and Balveer Arora (eds), *Transforming India*. New Delhi: Oxford University Press, pp. 254–87.

Frankel, Francine. 2005. *India's Political Economy, 1947–1977*. New Delhi: Oxford University Press, pp. 370–80.

———. 1997. 'Decline of a Social Order', in Sudipta Kaviraj (ed.), *Politics in India*. New Delhi: Oxford University Press.

Frieden, Jeffry. 1999. 'Actors and Preferences in International Relations', in David A. Lake and Robert Powell (eds), *Strategic Choice and International Relations*. Princeton, New Jersey: Princeton University Press, pp. 39–76.

Gandhi, Indira. 1985. *Selected Speeches and Writings—Volume 4, 1980–1981*. New Delhi: Government of India—Publications Division of the Ministry of Information and Broadcasting.

Gang, Ira and Mihir Pandey. 1996. *Trade Protection in India*. New Brunswick, New Jersey: Department of Economics, Rutgers University.

George, Alexander L. and Timothy J. McKeown. 1985. 'Case Studies and Theories of Organizational Decision Making', in Robert F. Coulam and Richard A. Smith (eds), *Advances in Information Processing in Organizations*, Vol. 2. Greenwich, Connecticut: JAI Press, pp. 21–58.

Gerschenkron, Alexander. 1962. *Economic Backwardness in Historical Perspective*. Cambridge, Massachusetts: Harvard University Press.

Gilley, Bruce. 2005. 'Two Passages to Modernity', in Edward Friedman and Bruce Gilley (eds), *Asian Giants*. New York: Palgrave Macmillan, pp. 19–54.

Goldman, Marshall I. 1991. *What Went Wrong with Perestroika*. New York: Norton.

Gowda, M.V.R. and E. Sridharan. 2007. 'Parties and the Party System', in Sumit Ganguly, Larry Diamond, and Marc F. Plattner (eds), *The State of India's Democracy*. Baltimore: Johns Hopkins University Press, pp. 3–25.

GoI (Government of India). 1999. *Selected Educational Statistics 1997–98*. New Delhi: Ministry of Human Resource Development.

——. 1997. *Budget Speeches of Union Finance Ministers*. New Delhi: Department of Economic Affairs.

——. 1995. *Economic Survey 1994/95*. New Delhi: Ministry of Finance.

Grief, Avner and David Laitin. 2004. 'A Theory of Endogenous Institutional Change', *American Political Science Review*, 98(4), pp. 633–52.

Gurr, Ted R. 1970. *Why Men Rebel*. Princeton, New Jersey: Princeton University Press.

Haggard, Stephan and Chung-in Moon. 1983. 'The South Korean State in the International Economy', in John G. Ruggie (ed.), *The Antinomies of Interdependence*. New York: Columbia University Press, pp. 131–89.

Haggard, Stephan. 1990. *Pathways from the Periphery*. Ithaca: Cornell University Press.

Hall, Peter. 1993. 'Policy Paradigms, Social Learning, and the State', *Comparative Politics*, 25(3), pp. 275–96.

Hirschman, Albert O. 1989. 'How the Keynesian Revolution was Exported From the United States', in Peter Hall (ed.), *The Political Power of Economic Ideas*. Princeton, New Jersey: Princeton University Press, pp. 347–59.

Huntington, Samuel P. 1968. *Political Order in Changing Societies*. New Haven, Connecticut: Yale University Press.

Huntington, Samuel P. and Joan M. Nelson. 1976. *No Easy Choice*. Cambridge, Mass.: Harvard University Press.

Inglehart, Ronald. 1997. *Modernization and Postmodernization: Cultural, Economic and Political Change in Forty-Three Societies*. Princeton, NJ: Princeton University Press.

Jaffrelot, Christophe. 2007. 'Caste and the Rise of Marginalized Groups', in Sumit Ganguly, Larry Diamond, and Marc F. Plattner (eds), *The State of India's Democracy*. Baltimore: The Johns Hopkins University Press, pp. 67–85.

Jalan, Bimal. 1991. *India's Economic Crisis*. New Delhi: Oxford University Press.

Joshi, Vijay and I.M.D. Little. 1994. *India: Macroeconomics and Political Economy 1964–1991*. New Delhi: Oxford University Press.

Kakar, Sudhir. 1995. *The Colours of Violence*. New Delhi: Penguin Books.

Kathuria, Sanjay. 1995. 'Competitiveness in Indian Industry', in Dilip Mookherjee (ed.), *Indian Industry*. New Delhi: Oxford University Press, pp. 148–90.

Kelegama, Saman. 1999. 'The Indo-Sri Lanka Trade and Bilateral Free Trade Agreement', *Asia Pacific Development Journal*, 6(2), pp. 87–106.

Kennedy, Paul. 1988. *The Rise and Decline of the Great Powers*. London: Fontana Press.

Khan, Mohsin S. and Sunil Sharma. 2001. 'IMF Conditionality and Country Ownership of Programs', IMF Working Paper 01/142, IMF, Washington, DC.

Khanna, Tarun. 2007. *Billions of Entrepreneurs: How China and India are Reshaping Their Futures—And Yours*. Cambridge, Massachusetts: Harvard University Press.

Kochanek, Stanley. 2007. 'The Transformation of Interest Politics in India', in Rahul Mukherji (ed.), *India's Economic Transition: The Politics of Reforms*. New Delhi: Oxford University Press, pp. 412–31.

Kohli, Atul. 2006. 'Politics of Economic Growth in India', *Economic and Political Weekly*, XLI(3), pp. 1251–9.

——. 1994. 'Centralization and Powerlessness', in Joel S. Migdal, Atul Kohli, and Vivienne Shue (eds), *State Power and Social Forces*. Cambridge: Cambridge University Press, pp. 89–107.

——. 1990. *Democracy and Discontent*. New York: Cambridge University Press.

Kothari, Rajni, 1970, *Politics in India*. Boston: Little Brown.

——. 1964. 'The Congress System in India', *Asian Survey*, 4(12), pp. 1161–73.

Krasner, Stephen D. 1984. 'Approaches to the State', *Comparative Politics*, 16(2), pp. 223–46.

Krueger, Anne O. 1998. 'Contrasts to Transitions to Market-Oriented Economies: India and Korea', in Yujiro Hayami and Masahiko Aoki (eds), *The Institutional Foundations of East Asian Economic Development*. London: Macmillan, pp. 179–207.

——. 1997. 'Trade Policy and Economic Development', NBER Working Paper 5896, Cambridge, Massachusetts.

Krueger, Anne O. 1993. *Political Economy of Policy Reform in Developing Countries*. Cambridge, Massachusetts: MIT Press.

———. 1974. 'The Political Economy of the Rent-Seeking Society', *American Economic Review*, 64(3), pp. 291–303.

Krugman, Paul. 1994. *The Age of Diminished Expectations*. Cambridge, Massachusetts: MIT Press.

Kuhn, Thomas. 1970. *The Structure of Scientific Revolutions*. Chicago: The University of Chicago Press.

Kumar, Vivek. 2007. 'Bahujan Samaj Party: Some Issues of Democracy and Governance', in Sudha Pai (ed.), *Political Process in Uttar Pradesh*. New Delhi: Pearson Longman, pp. 221–40.

Milner, Helen V. 1998. 'Rationalizing Politics', *International Organization*, 52(4), pp. 759–86.

———. 1997. *Interests, Institutions and Information*. Princeton, New Jersey: Princeton University Press.

Mitra, Subrata K. 1991. 'Room to Maneuver in the Middle', *World Politics*, 43(3), pp. 390–413.

Morris-Jones, W.H. 1968. *Politics Mainly Indian*. Madras: Orient Longman.

Mukherji, Rahul. 2009. ' Interests, Wireless Technology, and Institutional Change: From Government Monopoly to Regulated Competition in Indian Telecommunications', *The Journal of Asian Studies*, 68(2), pp. 491–517.

———. 2007. 'Managing Competition', in Rahul Mukherji (ed.), *India's Economic Transition: The Politics of Reforms*. New Delhi: Oxford University Press, pp. 300–27.

———. 2000. 'India's Aborted Liberalization—1966', *Pacific Affairs*, 73(3), pp. 375–92.

Mundle, Sudipto and M. Govinda Rao. 1992. 'Issues in Fiscal Policy', in Bimal Jalan (ed.), *The Indian Economy*. New Delhi: Viking Penguin, pp. 227–50.

Moravcsik, Andrew. 1993. 'Introduction', in Peter Evans, Harold Jacobson, and Robert Putnam (eds), *Double Edged Diplomacy*. Berkeley: University of California Press, pp. 3–44.

Nandy, Ashis. 1999. 'Coping with the Politics of Faiths and Cultures', in Joanna Pfaff-Czarnecka, Darini R. Senanayake, Ashis Nandy, and Edmund T. Gomez (eds), *Ethnic Futures*. New Delhi: Sage Publications, pp. 135–66.

Naughton, Barry. 1995. *Growing Out of the Plan*. Cambridge: Cambridge University Press.

Nayar, Baldev R. 2006a. 'When did the Hindu Rate of Growth End?' *Economic and Political Weekly*, pp. 1885–90.

———. 2006b. *India's Globalization*, XLI(19), Policy Studies 22, Washington: East-West Centre.

———. 1975. *Violence and Crime in India*. New Delhi: Macmillan.

Nayar, Baldev R. 1974. 'Political Mainsprings of Economic Planning in the New Nations', *Comparative Politics*, 6(3), pp. 341–66.

———. 1972. *The Modernization Imperative and Indian Planning*. New Delhi: Vikas.

Ninan, Sevanti. 2007. *Headlines from the Heartland*. New Delhi: Sage Publications.

Nelson, Joan M. 1993. 'The Politics of Economic Transformation', *World Politics*, 45(2), pp. 433–63.

Olson, Mancur. 1971. *The Logic of Collective Action*. Cambridge, Mass.: Harvard University Press.

Pai, Sudha. 2007. 'From Dalit to Savarna: The Search for a New Social Constitutency by the Bahujan Samaj Party', in Sudha Pai (ed.), *Political Process in Uttar Pradesh*. New Delhi: Pearson Longman, pp. 221–40.

Panagariya, Arvind. 2008. *India: The Emerging Giant*. New York: Oxford University Press.

Pandhe, M.K. 1992. 'Magnificent Response to General Strike', in *The Working Class*. New Delhi: Centre for Indian Trade Unions.

———. 1991. 'Magnificent Response to Nationwide Industrial Strike', *The Working Class*. New Delhi: Centre for Indian Trade Unions.

Pierson, Paul. 2004. *Politics in Time: History, Institutions and Social Analysis*. Princeton, NJ: Princeton University Press.

Przeworski, Adam. 1991. *Democracy and the Market*. Cambridge and New York: Cambridge University Press.

Putnam, Robert D. 1988. 'Diplomacy and Domestic Politics', *International Organization*, 42(3), pp. 427–60.

Qian, Yingyi. 2003. 'How Reform Worked in China', in Dani Rodrik (ed.), *In Search of Prosperity*. Princeton, NJ: Princeton University Press, pp. 297–333.

Rubin, Barnett R. 1985. 'Economic Liberalization and the Indian State', *Third World Quarterly*, 7(4), pp. 942–57.

Rudolph, Lloyd I. and Susanne H. Rudolph. 1997. 'Regime Types and Economic Performance', in Sudipta Kaviraj (ed.), *Politics in India*. New Delhi: Oxford University Press, pp. 177–86.

———. 1987. *In Pursuit of Lakshmi*. Chicago: University of Chicago Press.

Sarma, Atul. 1995. 'Performance of Public Enterprises in India', in Dilip Mookherjee (ed.), *Indian Industry*. New Delhi: Oxford University Press, pp. 289–321.

Sen, Amartya. 1998. 'Theory and Practice of Development', in Isher J. Ahluwalia and I.M.D. Little (eds), *India's Economic Reforms and Development*. New Delhi: Oxford University Press, pp. 73–84.

Sen, Sukomal. 1997. *Working Class of India*. Calcutta: K.P. Bagchi and Co.

Sengupta, Arjun K. 2001. *Reforms, Equity and the IMF*. New Delhi: Har Anand.

Shastri, Vanita. 1995. 'The Political Economy of Policy Formation in India', PhD thesis, Cornell University, Ithaca.

Singh, Manmohan. 1964. *India's Export Trends*. London: Oxford University Press.

Sinha, Aseema. 2005. 'Understanding the Rise and Transformation of Business Collective Action in India', *Business and Politics*, 7(2), pp. 1–35.

Sridharan, E. 2002. 'The Fragmentation of the Indian Party System, 1952–1999: Seven Competing Explanations', in Zoya Hasan (ed.), *Parties and Politics in India*. New Delhi: Oxford University Press, pp. 475–503.

Stiglitz, Joseph. 2002. *Globalization and Its Discontents*. London: Allen Lane.

Stinchcombe, Arthur L. 1968. *Constructing Social Theories*. Chicago: University of Chicago Press.

Stopler, Wolfgang and Paul A. Samuelson. 1941. 'Protection and Real Wages', *Review of Economic Studies*, 9(1), pp. 58–73.

Subrahmanya, R.K.A. 1996. *Some Aspects of Structural Adjustment in India*. New Delhi: Friedrich Ebert Stiftung.

Tendulkar, Suresh D. and T.A. Bhavani. 2007. *Understanding Reforms: Post 1991 India*. New Delhi: Oxford University Press.

Timmer, Marcel P. and Adam Szirmai. 2000. 'Productivity Growth in Asian Manufacturing: The Structural Bonus Hypothesis Examined', *Structural Change and Economic Dynamics*, 11(4), pp. 371–92.

Timmer, Marcel P. and Adam Szirmai. 1999. 'Comparative Productivity Performance in Manufacturing in South and East Asia', *Oxford Development Studies*, 27(1), pp. 57–79.

Todaro, Michael P. 1981. *Economic Development in the Third World*. New York: Longman.

Varshney, Ashutosh. 2007. 'Mass Politics or Elite Politics', in Rahul Mukherji (eds), *India's Economic Transition*. New Delhi: Oxford University Press, pp. 146–69.

———. 2001. 'Ethnic Conflict and Civil Society', *World Politics*, 53(3), pp. 362–98.

———. 1995. *Democracy, Development and the Countryside*. Cambridge: Cambridge University Press.

Venkata Ratnam, C.S. 1992. 'Exit Policy', *Indian Journal of Industrial Relations*, 27(4), pp. 370–82.

Wade, Robert. 1990. *Governing the Market*, Princeton, NJ: Princeton University Press.

Yang, Dali L. 1996. 'Governing China's Transition to the Market', *World Politics*, 48(3), pp. 424–52.

Yadav, Yogendra. 2000. 'Understanding the Second Democratic Upsurge', in Francine R. Frankel, Zoya Hasan, Rajeev Bhargava, and Balveer Arora (eds), *Transforming India*. New Delhi: Oxford University Press, pp. 120–45.

Zagha, Roberto. 1999. 'Labor in India's Economic Reforms', in Jeffrey D. Sachs, Ashutosh Varshney, and Nirupam Bajpai (eds), *India in the Era of Economic Reforms*. New Delhi: Oxford University Press, pp. 160–85.

33 Politics and Redistribution

Atul Kohli

Over time, the state in India has shifted from a reluctant pro-capitalist state with a socialist ideology to an enthusiastic pro-capitalist state with a neo-liberal ideology. This shift has significant implications for the politics of redistribution in India. On the one hand the state's warm embrace of capital has been accompanied by higher rates of economic growth. Since levels of inequality in India are not enormously skewed, in comparison to, for example Latin America, the recent growth acceleration is bound to reduce poverty. On the other hand, however, the state–capital alliance for growth is leading to widening inequalities along a variety of dimensions: city versus the countryside; across regions; and along class lines. Not only does rapid economic growth then not benefit as many of the poor as it could if inequalities were stable, but the balance of class power within India is also shifting decisively towards business and other property-owning classes.

The prospect of making India's growth process more inclusive is not encouraging. If rapid growth continues, some of this will necessarily 'trickle down'

and help the poor. Beyond that, however, the scope for hastening this trickle via deliberate redistribution is limited. This is in part because deliberate redistribution is difficult anywhere, in part because the Indian state's capacity to implement pro-poor, redistributive policies has always been limited, but mainly because of the emerging ruling alliance in India, which at its core is an alliance of state and capital for growth. What might add some redistributive thrust to this growth-focused, elitist alliance is the fact that India is a vibrant democracy, with the poor and the near-poor constituting a majority. The excluded majorities are likely to continue to press their own case. A highly elitist apex and a mobilized fringe then define the political context in which India's current drama of redistributive politics is unfolding.

SOME CAVEATS

At the beginning, two caveats are in order. First, when discussing politics and redistribution I focus mainly on the state's capacity to reduce inequalities and poverty, while paying some attention to the way inequality and poverty influence politics. Poverty and inequality are, of course, distinguishable; as in contemporary India, inequalities may be widening, but poverty conditions are improving. However, one should not push this distinction too far. Setting aside the case of economic growth enveloping more and more people—often a fairly slow process—most deliberate efforts at poverty alleviation involve some deliberate redistribution and, more importantly from a political standpoint, are perceived as such. For example, strategies of poverty alleviation may focus on one or more of the following: asset redistribution, welfare provision, creation of human capital, or altering the pattern of economic growth. Since some of these strategies result in clear winners and losers, and others starkly pose the issue of who will pay, strategies of poverty alleviation readily come to be viewed as redistributive policies.

And second, while the discussion here is focused on India, it is important to keep some cross-national comparisons in mind. As far as deliberate redistribution and poverty alleviation are concerned, the Indian state's capacity has been fairly dismal. The attempts to redistribute land to the landless, to provide education and health to the poor, and to create employment via public works type of programmes have all been largely ineffective. The underlying causes include the absence of a real commitment among state elites and the poor quality of peripheral bureaucracy, but most of all the presence of powerful vested interests who have often opposed or subverted such efforts. When viewed comparatively, however, most developing country states, especially those in Latin America and sub-Saharan Africa, have been even more ineffective than India in checking growing inequalities or providing for their poor. While some East Asian cases as that of South Korea, or possibly China, indeed provide examples of 'growth with distribution', it is important that their pathways be understood correctly.

Land redistribution has been an integral component of the relatively egalitarian pathways followed by countries like China or South Korea. Early land reforms in these cases not only flattened the class profile in the countryside, but also raised peasant incomes, thus contributing to higher wages for the urban working class by reducing the size of the 'surplus poor'. Revolutionary Communists and occupying US forces helped implement land redistribution in China and South Korea respectively; these political preconditions are not likely to be replicated in India. Much is also made in the development literature of the role of labour-intensive, export-oriented industrialization in helping reconcile growth with redistribution in these cases. This is fine as it goes, but the fact is that countries like South Korea pursued both labour-intensive and capital-intensive industrialization; even in South Korea, the latter was accompanied by growing income disparities. And, of course, growing inequalities in China's recent growth upsurge are quite well known.

The quality of human capital in countries like China and South Korea is clearly superior to that in India. In this instance, there is much room for improvement in India. Once again, however, how China and South Korea got to where they are needs to be kept in mind. The efforts to improve education and health conditions in China were very much part of the revolutionary transformation of China, a process not likely to be repeated in countries like India. Even in a non-revolutionary South Korea, certain unique factors contributed to the benign outcome. First, the colonial legacy in the field of primary education was relatively favourable. Second, following land redistribution, landlords often invested the compensation they received for their lands into a system of private education, hoping that their progeny would thus find alternative routes for upward mobility. And finally, of course, public investment in education has been consistently significant, though even here one should not underestimate the role played by a growth-oriented authoritarian state, which expected primary education to lead to a productive but propagandized working class.

What one might legitimately expect from the Indian state in terms of deliberate redistribution thus needs to be tempered by a correct understanding of what others in the developing world have or have not achieved. Relatively egalitarian initial conditions and a more labour-intensive product mix have been important components in reconciling growth with distribution; both factors are largely missing in India, especially the first. Investments in education and health have been the other components in creating a more level social field in select East Asian cases. These too were facilitated in part by unique social and political conditions. While East Asian countries might provide a useful model of sorts, India, with a highly stratified society and a narrow ruling coalition, is not likely to fully replicate East Asia.

POLITICS AND REDISTRIBUTION, OVER TIME

The social origins of India's post-Independence state and its redistributive efforts have been well studied.[1] Political power in post-Independence India rested mainly in the Congress party. Led by Nehru, the early Congress party was nationalist and socialist in its ideology. While seeking to represent the interests of the 'nation' as a whole, the Congress came to be influenced disproportionately by 'proprietary classes'(Bardhan 1984). For example, business groups played a significant role in early economic policymaking (Chibber 2004), and the Congress built its political support in the countryside via upper-caste, landowning groups, thus incorporating landed interests into the heart of the body politic (Frankel 2005). Professional urban classes and well-heeled bureaucrats also exerted considerable influence on the state. And yet, the Congress was never a party of the Indian elite alone. Gandhi mobilized segments of the Indian peasantry into the nationalist movement. Nehru's socialist commitments further broadened Congress' social base, at least promising progress to India's downtrodden.

Unfortunately, Nehru and his policies failed to make any significant dent in India's poverty. The simple but powerful fact is that the overall growth rate of the economy was relatively sluggish during these years; the population grew at a significant rate; and the number of the poor in India grew steadily. Beneath this nearly banal sounding—but tragic—reality of India's slow suffering lay numerous policy choices and poorly implemented policies.

Nehru's emphasis on heavy industry meant the neglect of agriculture, a set of policy decisions with serious negative consequences for India's poor, the majority of whom lived in the countryside. It is no exaggeration to suggest in retrospect that there was no systematic policy to promote agricultural growth in Nehru's India. Much reliance was placed instead on re-educating the peasantry (via Community Development Programmes), and on altering the incentives of the land tiller via land reforms. The former was probably mistaken even in conception and given the poor quality of peripheral bureaucracy, was certainly implemented very poorly (Myrdal 1968).

India achieved some success in eliminating the largest zamindars, but much less in ensuring that land was redistributed to the rural landless. The abolition of zamindari was thus mainly a political phenomena (as distinct from a class phenomena), in the sense that many zamindars were allies of the British, lost power as the nationalists gained, and posed an obstacle to the Congress rulers' efforts to build political support in the periphery. Congress rulers thus pushed hard and succeeded in reducing the size of zamindari land holdings. Those who gained were generally the 'lower gentry', rather than the land tillers. In contrast to zamindari abolition, the several subsequent rounds of land reforms (redistributing land above a certain 'ceiling', or ensuring the rights of tenants) were mostly a failure (Herring 1983; Appu 1996). There was some variation on this score across Indian states, a subject that is discussed further below. On the whole, however, land reforms failed, mainly because state authorities in India proved either unwilling or incapable of confronting powerful class interests in the countryside (Myrdal 1968). Significant factors contributing to the state's limited capacities on this score included the Congress party's incorporation of landed interests as pillars of party support in the countryside, a federal structure in which land redistribution was the responsibility of state governments, in which the power of landed classes was especially significant; a less-than-professional lower-level bureaucracy that was readily co-opted by the rural powerful; a legal system that was biased in favour of property owners; and a relatively low level of mobilization and organization among the potential beneficiaries.

Beyond the neglect of agriculture and the failure of land reforms, other notable Nehruvian policies with adverse consequences for the poor included a capital-intensive pattern of industrialization and the neglect of primary education. The focus on heavy industry reflected both Nehru's vision of how to build a strong and sovereign India (Nayar 1989), and the prevailing economic logic of the time, which stated that since one cannot eat steel, such a focus will enhance savings and facilitate rapid industrialization (Chakravarty 1988). Whatever the underlying motives, the consequences were clear: India's industrial growth did not create enough new jobs to make a dent in the growing number of the poor. Similarly, a focus on primary education might not only have served important economic goals by raising the quality of human capital, but would also have been an important developmental end in itself (Sen 1999). Nehru's focus instead on creating 'pockets of excellence', for example by creating the Indian Institutes of Technology, remains to this day a much debated set of policies. Why India's primary education has continued to lag dramatically also remains something of an enigma. Myron Weiner's provocative argument (1991) that the neglect reflected the exclusionary mindset of India's upper-caste elites probably has some merit. However, even with a shift in national priorities on primary education (which is currently underway), the fact is that numerous problems of implementation at the level of state governments and below remain; this issue, too, is discussed further below.

By the 1970s, a new political generation had come into being, the legacy of nationalism was in decline, and along with it grew a sense in India that politics was less about the pursuit of ideals and more about mundane realities of who gets what, when and how. The Congress party was thus in danger of losing its hegemonic hold under the strain of a variety of distributive conflicts. By accentuating populism, Indira Gandhi recreated a new type of Congress hegemony in which power became even more personal, the Congress party was further deinstitutionalized, leaders below the apex came to be appointed from the top, often rewarded for little more than loyalty to Indira Gandhi, and even the well-established civil service and the armed forces felt the strain of growing politicization (Rudolph and Rudolph 1987; Kohli 1991). While politics has always been in command of economic policymaking

in India, the Indira Gandhi years were especially notable for the politicization of the economy, first in a distributive direction in the 1970s, and then in a more pro-business direction during and following the Emergency in the 1980s.

The Nehruvian model of economic development was accentuated in a populist direction by Indira Gandhi: banks were nationalized, Maharajas were stripped of their remaining privileges, anti-monopoly laws were strengthened, new taxes were imposed on the rich, access to credit was broadened, stricter land reform legislation was passed, and public works programmes that could supplement the income of the poor were brought into being. The early 1970s was thus a moment in India with real social democratic possibilities. Unfortunately, the experiment was mostly a failure because Indira Gandhi's personal power led more to centralization and powerlessness and less to the creation of a well-organized social democratic power bloc that might be capable of confronting dominant class interests (Kohli 1994).

The failures on the redistribution front were especially glaring because of the gap between promises and outcomes. The main achievement was probably to limit the growth of inequalities, although, as critics will rightly add, this was more a matter of sharing poverty than wealth. Some of the monies invested into such poverty alleviation schemes as employment generation programmes probably also did reach the poor, especially in states with committed leaders and better bureaucracies. By contrast, public education and primary health were ignored. The failure to acquire and redistribute above ceiling land and improve the lot of tenants was the most notable failure (Appu 1996). All the rhetoric and some real legislation aside, the pursuit of land redistribution was left mainly in the hands of state governments. A few state governments made good use of the new, permissive political space, but these were seldom states with Congress governments. In the modal Congress-run state, the political structures consisted of two main hierarchies: a top-down, loyalty- and patronage-based chain that was the Congress party, without a well-organized social base; and a bureaucratic hierarchy, in which the quality of bureaucracy declined as one went down the hierarchy. Where these political hierarchies stopped in the countryside began real social power, that is, the power of landowning elites. Neither the local-level party nor the bureaucratic elite were in a position to confront the landed elite; on the contrary, at times the party and the landed elite were the same people, and nearly always the local bureaucrats were deeply entrenched in local power structures. When, on occasion, some redistributive success seemed close at hand, tenants were either evicted by force, or landownership cases ended up in courts, where they probably still languish.

Starting around 1980, the Indian political system began moving in a new direction, especially in terms of developmental priorities and, related to that, in terms of the underlying state-class alliances. After returning to power in 1980, Indira Gandhi increasingly prioritized economic growth, and put the rhetoric of socialism on the back-burner. This complex political shift reflected several underlying political realities, which have been analysed in detail elsewhere (Kohli 2006a, 2006b): a growing realization that redistributive possibilities were increasingly limited; the negative impact that radical rhetoric had had on the state's relations with the corporate sector, as well as on the corporate sector's willingness to invest; and, of course, the relatively low economic growth, especially industrial growth, during the 1970s. Looking for higher rates of economic growth, Indira Gandhi in the early 1980s sought to reorder the state's class underpinnings, tilting it towards capital and against labour. Thus began a steady process which, over the next quarter of a century, propelled the power of capital in the Indian polity to near hegemonic proportions.

Indira Gandhi and her son Rajiv Gandhi moved the Indian state away from its socialist ambitions to a growth-promoting state that worked with the corporate sector. State elites increasingly downplayed the rhetoric of socialism. A major fatality of this ideological shift was that land redistribution and tenancy reforms lost lustre as policy options. While these policies had never succeeded much in India, even their desirability became questionable. Also, very few new efforts emerged to improve primary education or public health. The pattern of economic growth favoured big business houses. However, both Indira and Rajiv Gandhi kept up public investments. As a result, public investments in agriculture put a brake on the growing rural-urban divide, and by the same token, continuing public investments helped India's poor states from falling further behind in their relative rates of economic growth.

The state–business alliance for growth has pretty much continued to characterize India's model of development since about 1980, with another important liberalizing shift in 1991, when integration with the global economy also picked up speed. Unlike in some other parts of the world, India's leaders did not push for *en masse* privatization of the public sector, state shrinkage, or rapid opening to global investment. What they did instead was to slowly but surely reduce tariffs, liberalize foreign investment laws, and cut back on public investments. The more economic growth was led by private investors, the more the benefits accrued to owners of capital and their agents. A small but significant urban middle class has also been growing in the shadow of this growth upsurge. All this is not surprising.

What the Indian state has also done is to throw its weight behind the winners of the new economy, without compensating those who are being left behind. It is this activist role of the state that has further contributed to growing inequalities. The Indian state has thus continued to support Indian capital in various ways so as to enable it to compete with global competition. A variety of 'public–private partnerships' are also beginning to absorb public initiative and resources. By contrast, investments in agriculture have not kept pace, and the poorer states of India have been left to their own resources. Since new private capital has not rushed into these areas, inequalities in India continue to grow, and the county's poor do not benefit as much from growth as they might have under a modified policy regime.

POLITICS AND REDISTRIBUTION ACROSS INDIAN STATES

Contrasting developments across Indian states places redistributive politics in India in sharper relief. Over the years, the states in which poverty has come down the most include Kerala, West Bengal, Punjab, Andhra

Pradesh, and Tamil Nadu. By contrast, poverty has come down the least in Assam, Jammu and Kashmir, Bihar, Madhya Pradesh, and Rajasthan (Besley *et. al.* 2007; Datt and Ravallion 2002). While rates of economic growth are a significant predictor of these trends, an interesting fact is that for a unit of economic growth in various Indian states, poverty came down much more rapidly in some states than in others. Thus, for example, one unit of growth in Kerala or West Bengal has been four times more 'efficient' in reducing poverty (as indicated by what economists call the growth elasticity of poverty) than, say, in Bihar or Madhya Pradesh (Besley *et. al.* 2007: Table 3.1). More concretely, this means that it will take four times the growth rate of Kerala and West Bengal to reduce the same amount of poverty in Bihar and Madhya Pradesh. How does one best understand such different capacities across Indian states to reduce poverty?

The two states in which poverty has come down the most—Kerala and West Bengal—are states with long experience of Left governments. All the southern states—Kerala, Andhra Pradesh, Tamil Nadu, and Karnataka—are among the top half of the states in which poverty has come down the most. In contrast, India's BIMARU states—Bihar, Madhya Pradesh, Rajasthan, and Uttar Pradesh—are among the bottom half of the states in which poverty has come down the least. Leaving proximate determinants of such patterns aside (for example, irrigation infrastructure, growth of farm yields, access to credit), the deeper explanation of such a pattern probably lies in the nature of social and political power in these states, and, related to that, to the different policies whose results have accumulated over decades. Put as a hypothesis, it may be suggested that poverty has been reduced the most in states where effective governmental power rests on a broad political base; in such cases, rulers have minimized the hold of upper classes on the state, successfully organized the middle and lower strata into an effective power bloc, and then used this power to channel resources to the poor.

This simple hypothesis can be used to explain the varying capacities across Indian states to reduce poverty. First, let us consider the two cases of India's left-leaning states, Kerala and West Bengal. There is more of a consensus around the case of Kerala

than around West Bengal. Poverty in Kerala has been reduced sharply, and its human development indicators are far superior to that of the rest of India (Drèze and Sen 2002). And this was accomplished even though the economic growth rates in Kerala have been close to the all-India average. Underlying these redistributive achievements are complex historical roots, including the political mobilization of lower castes and classes well before Independence.[2] This broadened political base then facilitated the rise of a well-organized Communist party to power. A more pro-poor regime interacted with a more efficacious citizenry, creating what Drèze and Sen (2002) rightly called a 'virtuous' cycle. This created both a supply of and demand for a variety of successful pro-poor public policies, including land reforms, higher investments in and better implementation of education and health policies, and greater gender equality. The fact is that, when compared to other Indian states, cultivated land in Kerala is distributed most evenly, and the wages of landless labourers are the highest in India.

While the case of West Bengal is more mixed (Kohli 1987; Mallick 1994; Harriss 1993; Corbridge *et al.* 2003), the main dynamics of poverty alleviation again seem to lie in the fact that a well-organized regime with a broad political base has been relatively effective in pursuing tenancy reform, helping to push up minimum wages—though only somewhat—and implementing centrally sponsored anti-poverty programmes more effectively than other states. Land inequality in the countryside in West Bengal is also among the lowest in India by now, although the wages of agricultural labourers are only marginally above the all-India average. There is also some evidence that tenancy reforms—via enhanced security and bargaining power—have helped agricultural productivity, thus making growth in West Bengal more inclusive (Banerjee 2002).

If India's 'social democratic' states have effectively leveraged superior party organization and a broad political base to pursue modest redistributive reforms, how does one interpret the fact that all of India's southern states are above average in their poverty alleviation capacities? India's southern states share two sets of distinguishing political traits, one well-researched and the other much in need of research.

The well-established fact is that the narrow domination of Brahmins had been more effectively challenged in all the southern states relatively early in the twentieth century (Frankel and Rao 1990). Since Independence, the political base of power in these states has generally been middle castes and classes, and in some instances even lower classes. This is quite distinct from the Hindi-heartland states, where Brahmanical domination was challenged only relatively recently. The other fact is that the quality of state-level bureaucracy in the south has generally been superior. While this 'fact' needs to be documented by further scholarly research, over years of fieldwork I was repeatedly struck by a sharper sense of professionalism among state-level bureaucrats, especially in Tamil Nadu, more akin to the Indian Administrative Service (IAS) than to prevailing practices in the Hindi-heartland.

How might prolonged rule by governments with broader political bases and more effective bureaucracies influence poverty alleviation? Leaving Kerala aside, land redistribution has not been very effective in the southern states. The main policy instruments of poverty alleviation have instead been somewhat different. Over the last several decades, the southern states have invested more heavily in education and health than the Hindi-heartland states (Singh forthcoming). Another study notes that on the whole, southern states have benefited more from the subsidized public distribution of wheat and rice (Harriss 2003): the credit must go to populist leaders and a superior bureaucracy. With a more effective bureaucracy, other poverty alleviation programmes (such as a variety of employment generation programmes) have also been better implemented.

The contrast with the BIMARU states of northern India is striking. Of course, these states experienced low growth rates. However, the contrasts in the social and political structures are also notable. Well into the late twentieth century, the main mode of politics in these states was Congress party rule, which rested on a narrow political base of upper castes and classes.[3] With patron–client ties as the key defining unit of political society, factional bickering among patrons was the core trait of state politics. This personalistic bickering detracted from any constructive use of state power, whether in promoting growth or distribution. With long traditions of zamindari or *taluqadari* rule (forms of indirect rule), the quality of state-level bureaucracy that these regions inherited was also generally low. Virulent patronage politics politicized the bureaucracy in post-Independence years, further diluting the states' developmental capacity. For some three to four decades following Independence, then, a narrow political base, personalistic factionalism, and a less-than-professional state-level bureaucracy characterized the nature of state power in this region of India.

Land reforms were very poorly implemented in the Hindi-heartland states. With upper-caste landowners wielding considerable power—both in the state and in society—and with a readily corruptible bureaucracy, this failure was not surprising. A variety of other state interventions that might have helped the poor were also ineffective.

In recent decades, the political base of state power in all these states has broadened, although the social power of upper-caste landowners remains significant. Over time, this broadening of state power may lead to some greater benefits for the poor, as has recently been evident in Rajasthan and Madhya Pradesh. Meanwhile, factional bickering and a politicized bureaucracy have nearly been institutionalized in the Hindi-heartland areas, leading to policy ineffectiveness. Decades of malign neglect and policy ineffectiveness have thus cumulatively created the largest concentration of poor within India.

POLITICS AND REDISTRIBUTION: THE LOCAL LEVEL

India's local governments have generally been quite ineffective in pursuing either redistributive policies or poverty alleviation programmes. Of course, there has been some variation on this score, with some pockets of success, especially in states that have prioritized the welfare of the poor. On the whole, however, panchayats have not functioned very well because of the complicity of corrupt local politicians and bureaucrats on the one hand, and the powerful among the upper castes and classes in the village society on the other. A variety of distributive programmes sponsored in Delhi, or in state capitals, has thus failed to reach the intended beneficiaries. Future efforts to pursue such minimal poverty alleviation programmes as public works employment generation or delivery of public health and education in the countryside will require more effective panchayats.

Panchayats have a long and chequered history in India (Mullen 2007; Kumar 2006; Ghosh and Kumar 2003). As the lowest rung of the Indian state, our interest in panchayats here is limited to their evolving role in the politics of redistribution: why did panchayats play a fairly limited redistributive role in the past; how does one best understand their limited success in some regions and in some time periods; and what is their likely role now that local elections have been constitutionally mandated (in 1992–3)?

Most of India's poor live in villages. If government-sponsored programmes are to help the poor, they must somehow reach the poor. That local governments should implement such programmes and policies is clearly one viable option. Following Independence, for several decades local governments in much of India were mainly administrative organizations, in which lower-level bureaucrats sought to implement policies made at higher levels. Until 1992, when they became the law, regularly elected panchayat governments were rare in India: Maharashtra and Gujarat have conducted regular elections since the 1960s and West Bengal since the 1970s. Off and on, Karnataka flirted with elected local governments. For the most part, however, state governments found local elected governments a constraint on their ability to create patronage chains, and thus avoided them. The fact that it was political compulsion that led a few states to violate this norm—that is, to actually institutionalize locally elected governments—only underlines the general point (Ghosh and Kumar 2003).

In much of India, government-sponsored programmes in villages were implemented by lower-level bureaucrats, say, the Block Development Officer, who worked closely with local politicians, for instance, the member of the legislative assembly, and a variety of local 'big' men. The story of how these local elites appropriated much of the little that was intended for the poor is well known. The main point that is usefully reiterated is that, for some three decades following Independence, most of India's rural poor were deeply embedded in a variety of patron–client relations dominated by propertied upper castes. This was not a fertile soil for social democratic interventions. Even if the commitment of the state elite to help the poor was genuine—which it often was not—prior preconditions for success were either mobilization of the poor, or forceful public intervention via well-organized parties and a responsive professional bureaucracy. For the most part, these conditions were absent in India. As a result, panchayats either did not function, or functioned mainly as agents perpetuating the status quo.

What about the few instances in which elected panchayats actually came into being well before the constitutional amendment of 1992? Maharashtra and Gujarat have long had elected panchayats. However, local governments in these states were really not redistributive, either in intent or in outcome. Both of these are India's economically advanced states, and in both the growing economic pie enabled the accommodation of intermediate groups. The regional dominant castes—Marathas in Maharashtra and the Patels in Gujarat—were the main beneficiaries of the well-functioning panchayats during the 1960s. With her populist rhetoric and intent, Indira Gandhi during the 1970s weakened panchayats in western India, channelling resources via the bureaucracy instead (Ghosh and Kumar 2003). For the most part, the lower-level bureaucrats during the Indira phase were captured by local power structures and proved relatively inept as agents of redistributive development; a partial exception was Maharashtra's well-known employment guarantee scheme, although this functioned as a result of several unique conditions and, even then, it is doubtful whether the beneficiaries were the poorest of the poor (Bagchee 2005).

Prior to 1992, the only state in which local governments effectively supported some redistribution and implementation of anti-poverty measures was West Bengal. The ruling Communists in the state chose to penetrate the countryside by facilitating the election of 'red panchayats', and then by channelling resources to these bodies. Since the landed elite were effectively isolated at the lower rungs of the state, the panchayats were used to implement tenancy reforms and to pursue effectively the centrally sponsored schemes for the poor (Kohli 1987). The success was notable, but partial. The power of Bengali Communists in the countryside often rested on small landowners and tenant farmers, rather than on the landless. This limited their redistributive intent; for example, they seldom pushed hard for higher wages for agricultural labourers, gains that would have undermined the income of their key supporters. Over time, moreover, new stakeholders developed—school teachers, party functionaries, a variety of white-collar employees, small landholders, and tenant farmers, whose security depended on the regime; all became part of West Bengal's 'new class' (Ghatak and Ghatak 2002). While the power pyramid in the state was definitely truncated, quite a few poor were still left out of the power structure. For now, even in a Communist-run state, these poor must depend on a buoyant agrarian economy to improve their life chances.

Ever since the Seventy-third Constitutional Amendment that mandated elections for local governments, the issue that has again arisen is, can the dynamics of electoral politics be translated into gains for the poor? The few available studies on the subject are not overly encouraging. For example, there was much excitement among decentralization enthusiasts about Digvijay Singh's experiment in Madhya Pradesh (MP). One recent study of the experiment concluded, however, that local governments in MP continued to exclude the lower strata, and that the level of interest in panchayats as agents of development was pretty low (Alsop 2000). Another study found that the limited dynamism in MP depended nearly on a single leader and a few 'mission' oriented participants—traits that are not likely to be institutionalized—and that the 'success' of most programmes was 'not too high' (Kumar 2006: 85). In the case of Karnataka, at least one scholar found that the refurbished panchayats are working well for the poor, even better than in West Bengal (Mullen 2007). Her underlying reasoning is that electoral competitiveness in Karnataka inclines political leaders to seek the support of the poor by channelling real gains to them; conversely, the near hegemonic hold of the Communists in West Bengal has made them at least complacent, if not corrupt.

If borne out by further evidence, such findings are encouraging, because electoral competition is more likely to increase than decrease in the future.

The results of other studies are distinctly less encouraging. Gaiha *et al.* (1998) analysed the effectiveness of panchayats in implementing the Jawahar Rozgar Yojana (a public works scheme intended to create employment for the rural poor in the lean season). Using state-wise data across India, they found that the majority of the beneficiaries of this scheme were not the really poor. While the design of the scheme was in part to blame (wages were often set higher than the prevailing local wages, attracting those less-than-destitute), captured and unaccountable panchayats were also to blame, especially in a state like Uttar Pradesh. Another study analysed the role of panchayats in the post-1992 period in the provision of primary education and health in select states (Kumar 2006: Ch. 6). The results are definitely mixed. Even the 'red panchayats' of West Bengal have only recently made some efforts to improve literacy and health. Moreover, the 'model' that seems to attract politicians in both Madhya Pradesh and West Bengal—states in which there is some enthusiasm for panchayats—is the one that creates alternate pathways for the really poor, opening up the possibility of a two-track system, one for the better-off and the other for the downtrodden.

As one looks ahead, the types of redistributive programmes that will be pursued in India are likely to be less-than-radical. Neither asset redistribution nor a basic shift in the growth model towards greater labour intensity is on the cards. As discussed above, past failures and the emerging pattern of state–class alliance at the apex preclude these options. What is more likely is that greater investments may be made to improve education and health, and to help the poorest of the poor by creating a public works type of employment-generating programmes such as the National Rural Employment Guarantee Scheme (NREGS). Some of these programmes are already on the books. They are mainly a product of political pressures, some from those representing the interests of the poor, and others who believe that investment in 'human capital' is deemed to be supportive of growth.

The real issue with these limited programmes is whether they can be implemented properly. It is in this context that the role of panchayats becomes important. On the whole, the past performance of panchayats as agents of redistributive development has been discouraging. The factors that help explain poor performance in the past include the power of those with local influence, political and bureaucratic corruption, and low levels of mobilization among the really poor; none of these underlying variables is likely to change dramatically in the near future, though the poor may well push for policies that benefit them and their progeny.

CONCLUSION

While the rhetoric of redistribution and social justice is deeply embedded in Indian politics, concrete redistributive achievements have been limited. These limitations are rooted in part in the nature of the society, but also in patterns of politics. The caste and class structure of Indian society, and the changing balance of class forces, especially the growing power of big capital, places definite limits on the redistributive possibilities in India. However, politics also matters: the ideology and organization of rulers, quality of bureaucracy, mobilization of the lower strata, and, of course, pressures of democratic politics, all have some bearing on the extent of redistribution and poverty alleviation. The concluding issue can thus be phrased as a speculative question: can democratic forces in India moderate the emerging class and other inequities?

While my answer above has tended towards the negative, the evidence is also mixed, replete with tensions; the most significant tensions are worth underlying at the end. First, notice that whereas India's main model of development is being driven by a close alliance of state and capital, in order to win elections all national parties need to make promises to the poor. Second, below the near-hegemony evident at the national Centre, politics in state after state across India is moving in nearly opposite directions; even in Uttar Pradesh, a party of the lowest castes and classes was just installed in power. And finally, whereas in the past members of the upper castes and classes readily controlled local governments, by now the process is

a lot more complex, forcing the political and social elites to channel some resources to those below them to secure their political support. The narrow ruling alliance of a technocratic elite and business groups in India will thus continue to be under democratic, and possibly not-so-democratic, pressure from the excluded masses.

NOTES

1. An incomplete list of some of the contributions might include Frankel (2005), Chibber (2004), Potter (1996), Nayar (1989), Kohli (1987), Bardhan (1984), and Herring (1983).

2. See, for example, Patrick Heller's chapter on Kerala in Sandbrook et al. (2007). Also see Heller (1999).

3. The fact that the lowest castes also voted for the Congress in these states, say until the end of the 1960s, did not make the Congress a broad-based party. Members of the lowest castes often depended on members of upper castes, and were entangled in a variety of patronage relationships. In spite of an apparently broad social base, the Congress's effective political base in these states was thus quite narrow.

REFERENCES

Alsop, Ruth J. 2000. 'Inclusion and Local Elected Governments: The Panchayat Raj System in India', The World Bank (South Asia—Social Development Unit).

Appu, P.S. 1996. *Land Reforms in India*. New Delhi: Vikas Publishing.

Bagchee, Aruna. 2005. 'Political and Administrative Realities of Employment Guarantee Scheme', *Economic and Political Weekly*, XL(42), pp. 4531–7.

Banerjee, Abhijit. 2002. 'Empowerment and Efficiency: Tenancy Reform in West Bengal', *Journal of Political Economy*, 110(2), pp. 239–79.

Bardhan, Pranab. 1984. *The Political Economy of Development in India*. Oxford: Basil Blackwell.

Besley, Timothy, Robin Burgess, and Berta Esteve-Volart. 2007. 'The Policy Origins of Poverty and Growth in India', in Timothy Besley and Louise J. Cord (eds), *Delivering on the Promise of Pro-poor Growth*. Washington DC: Palgrave Macmillan and the World Bank, pp. 49–78.

Chakravarty, Sukhomoy. 1988. *Development Planning: The Indian Experience*. New Delhi: Oxford University Press.

Chibber, Vivek. 2004. *Locked in Place: State Building and Late Industrialization in India*. Princeton, NJ: Princeton University Press.

Corbridge, Stuart, Glyn Williams, Manoj Srivastava, and
Rene Veron. 2003. 'Making Social Science Matter—I',
Economic and Political Weekly, XXXVIII(24),
pp. 1237–47.

Datt, Gaurav and Martin Ravallion. 2002. 'Is India's
Economic Growth Leaving the Poor Behind',
Policy Research Working Paper 2846, World Bank,
Development Research Group, Poverty Team.

———. 1998. 'Why Have Some Indian States Done Better
Than Others at Reducing Rural Poverty?' *Economica*,
65(257), pp. 17–38.

Drèze, Jean and Amartya Sen. 2002. *India: Development and
Participation*. New Delhi: Oxford University Press.

Frankel, Francine. 2005. *India's Political Economy, 1947–
2004: The Gradual Revolution*. Princeton, NJ: Princeton
University Press.

Frankel, Francine and M.S.A. Rao. 1990. *Dominance and
State Power in Modern India*, 2 Vols. New Delhi:
Oxford University Press.

Gaiha, Raghav, P. D. Kaushik, and Vani Kulkarni. 1998.
'Jawhar Rozgar Yojana, Panchayats, and the Rural Poor
in India', *Asian Survey*, 38(10), pp. 928–49.

Ghatak, Maitreesh and Maitreya Ghatak. 2002. 'Recent
Reforms in the Panchayat System in West Bengal',
Economic and Political Weekly, XXXVII(1), pp. 45–57.

Ghosh, Buddhadeb and Girish Kumar. 2003. *State Politics
and Panchayats in India*. New Delhi: Manohar.

Harriss, John. 2003. 'Do Political Regimes Matter: Poverty
Reduction and Regime Difference Across India', in
Peter P. Houtzager and Mick Moore (eds), *Changing
Paths: International Development and the New Politics of
Inclusion*. Ann Arbor: University of Michigan Press,
pp. 204–31.

———. 1993. 'What is Happening in Rural West Bengal',
Economic and Political Weekly, XVIII(24), pp.
1237–47.

Heller, Patrick. 1999. *The Labor of Development: Workers
and the Transformation of Capitalism in Kerala, India*.
Ithaca: Cornell University Press.

Herring, Ronald. 1983. *Land to the Tiller: The Political
Economy of Agrarian Reform in South Asia*. New Haven:
Yale University Press.

Kohli, Atul. 2006a. 'Politics of Economic Growth in India,
1980–2005, Part I: The 1980s', *Economic and Political
Weekly*, XLI(13), pp. 1251–650.

Kohli, Atul. 2006b. 'Politics of Economic Growth in India,
1980–2005, Part II: The 1990s and Beyond', *Economic
and Political Weekly*, XLI(14), pp. 1361–70.

———. 1994. 'Centralization and Powerlessness: India's
Democracy in a Comparative Perspective', in Joel
S. Migdal, Atul Kohli, and Vivienne Shue (eds),
State Power and Social Forces. New York: Cambridge
University Press, pp. 89–107.

———. 1991. *Democracy and Discontent: India's Growing
Crisis of Governability*. New York: Cambridge
University Press.

———. 1987. *The State and Poverty in India*. Cambridge:
Cambridge University Press.

Kumar, Girish. 2006. *Local Democracy in India*. New Delhi:
Sage Publications.

Myrdal, Gunnar. 1968. *Asian Drama: An Inquiry into the
Poverty of Nations*. New York: Pantheon.

Mallick, Ross. 1994. *Development Policy of a Communist
Government since 1977*. Cambridge: Cambridge
University Press.

Mullen, Rani. 2007. 'Does Local Governance Matter? The
Relationship between Village Government and Social
Welfare in Indian States', unpublished PhD thesis,
Princeton University, Princeton.

Nayar, Baldev Raj. 1989. *India's Mixed Economy: The Role
of Ideology and Interest in Its Development*. New Delhi:
Popular Prakashan.

Potter, David. 1996. *India's Political Administrators: From
ICS to IAS*. New Delhi: Oxford University Press.

Rudolph, Lloyd and Susanne Rudolph. 1987. *In Pursuit
of Lakshmi: The Political Economy of the Indian State*.
Chicago: The University of Chicago Press.

Sandbrook, Richard, Marc Edelman, Patrick Heller, Judith
Teichman. 2007. *Social Democracy in the Global
Periphery: Origins, Challenges, Prospects*. New York:
Cambridge University Press.

Sen, Amartya K. 1999. *Development as Freedom*. New York:
Knopf.

Singh, Prerna. Forthcoming. 'World's Apart: A Comparative
Analysis of Social Development in India', PhD Thesis
in preparation, Princeton University, USA.

Weiner, Myron. 1991. *The Child and the State in India*.
Princeton, NJ: Princeton University Press.

34 Employment Guarantee and the Right to Work*

Jean Drèze

In a conversation with Mulk Raj Anand, way back in May 1950, B.R. Ambedkar described capitalism as a 'dictatorship of the private employer'. I often remembered this expression during the Rozgar Adhikar Yatra (journey for the right to work), we travelled through some of India's poorest districts—Badwani, Banswara, Gaya, Nandurbar, Palamau, Puruliya, Sonebhadra, Surguja, among others. Everywhere we went, the rural economy looked like a graveyard and unemployment was people's main concern. This concern was poignantly expressed at public hearings held on the way. One labourer, for instance, said: 'The dream I have for my son is that he should get at least 15 days of casual labour every month'. His dream was not that his son would earn the minimum wage, or become a skilled labourer—he just wanted fifteen days of casual work every month. With agricultural wages as low as twenty-five or thirty rupees a day in

*This chapter is a revised version of the author's Kapil Dev Singh Memorial Lecture, delivered in Patna on 20 December 2007. It also draws on earlier articles published in *Frontline* and *The Hindu*.

many of these districts, it is not difficult to imagine the living conditions of a family that survives on fifteen days' earnings.

EMPLOYMENT AS A CONSTITUTIONAL RIGHT

In the same conversation, Mulk Raj Anand asked Ambedkar why the right to work had not been made a fundamental right in the Indian Constitution. Dr Ambedkar laconically replied, 'I was only one of the members of the drafting Committee'. The right to work ended up in the Directive Principles of the Constitution, along with other economic and social rights, such as the right to education and the right to health.

The Directive Principles of State Policy were expected to be fought for, politically. Article 37 of the Constitution explicitly states that they 'shall not be enforced by any court'. However, this does not preclude enacting laws based on these Directive Principles. In fact, the same Article goes on to say that these Principles are 'fundamental in the governance of the country', and that it is the duty of the state to 'apply these principles in making laws'.

Recent Supreme Court orders on mid-day meals in primary schools illustrate the possibility of building legal safeguards for economic and social rights. Today, every Indian child attending primary school is entitled to a cooked mid-day meal, as a matter of right. This is a legal entitlement, enforceable in court. Without these orders, it is unlikely that mid-day meals would have been extended to more than 100 million children within a few years. The proposed Right to Education Act is another example of the possibility of framing laws that give concrete expression to the Directive Principles of State Policy.

Similarly, the National Rural Employment Guarantee Act 2005 (NREGA) can be seen as a step towards legal enforcement of the right to work. It is a limited step, especially since the employment guarantee is limited to '100 days per household per year'. Nevertheless, the Act has much value as a tool for empowerment of rural labourers.

In particular, the Act can help to break the 'dictatorship of the private employer'. Today, rural labourers have no bargaining power. The fear of unemployment divides them and puts them at the mercy of private contractors and other exploiters. If rural labourers can get employment on public works at the minimum wage, as a matter of right, they will be able to demand minimum wages from private employers as well. Guaranteed employment on public works will also empower them to resist exploitative work conditions in the private sector. Further, the Employment Guarantee Act is a unique opportunity for them to organize and fight for related rights, such as the right to social security.

The Employment Guarantee Act can also help to empower women, by giving them independent income-earning opportunities. This point emerges in several studies of Maharashtra's Employment Guarantee Scheme (EGS). For instance, in her interviews with women working under EGS in the 1980s, Devaki Jain found that 'having once tasted the value of bringing home a money wage from their own labour, they had developed a sense of confidence and also release from the authority of the family and had

started to gain the confidence to take up other types of work in the area' (Jain 2005). Similarly, in a recent assessment of the EGS, Aruna Bagchee (2005) argues that the payment of equal wages to men and women is one reason 'why the EGS was so popular among women labourers'. In areas where rural women are traditionally homebound, such as Uttar Pradesh and Bihar, the Employment Guarantee Act has an even more significant role to play as a means of empowering rural women and curbing gender discrimination.

The enactment of the NREGA is a victory of sorts for Indian democracy. It shows that the underprivileged majority is not completely marginalized in this elitist political system. With adequate political organization, their demands sometimes prevail over privileged interests.

However, the real challenge is not the enactment of the NREGA but its implementation on the ground. In India, as elsewhere, the history of social legislation shows that it often takes a long time for people to be able to claim their rights, even after laws have been passed. Some laws, such as the Minimum Wages Act 1948, have remained on paper for decades without making much impact, except in states like Kerala where labourers are vocal and organized. Similarly, NREGA is unlikely to succeed without sustained political commitment and public pressure.

A BRIEF HISTORY OF NREGA

The draft NREGA entered national policy debates in India a few years ago, like a wet dog at a glamorous party. The enactment of a national Employment Guarantee Act was a long-standing demand of the labour movement, but it had never made much headway. In mid-2004, a series of unlikely events catapulted it to the top of the political agenda, at a time when privileged interests (notably those of the corporate sector and the so-called 'middle class') had an unprecedented hold on economic policy. Within a year, employment on demand became a legal entitlement.

It may be worth recalling some of the major steps that led to this breakthrough.[1] Though there is no obvious 'starting point', an important prelude was the campaign for an Employment Guarantee Act in Rajasthan, as an extension of the employment-based drought relief programmes launched in 2001 and 2003. This was also an opportunity to create interest in a national Employment Guarantee Act among leaders of various political parties.

In early 2004, the promise of a national Employment Guarantee Act was included in the electoral manifesto of the Congress party. This promise seemed to be neither here nor there, as most people (including Congress leaders themselves) were quite sure that Congress would lose the next elections. As it turned out, however, the Congress came to power in May 2004 as the leading partner in the United Progressive Alliance (UPA) government. This alliance had the support of the 'Left parties', who were strong advocates of the Employment Guarantee Act. The Employment Guarantee Act became one of the main planks of the National Common Minimum Programme (NCMP), the official roadmap of the UPA government. In fact, it was the first item in the NCMP's list of policy commitments.

In pursuance of this commitment, the National Advisory Council (NAC) drafted a NREGA in August 2004. The 'NAC draft', which was actually based on an earlier draft prepared by concerned citizens, set the framework for all subsequent discussions on the Act.[2] However, this draft went through numerous changes and revisions before it metamorphosed into the NREG Act 2005. On 21 December 2004, the government tabled a severely diluted version of the NAC draft in Parliament. This draft (the 'National Rural Employment Guarantee Bill 2004') was so weak that it defeated the purpose of a legally enforceable employment guarantee. For instance, the Bill left it to the Central government to decide where and when the work guarantee came into force. In other words, the government was offering an employment guarantee, but without any guarantee that the guarantee would come into effect! After being tabled in Parliament, the National Rural Employment Guarantee Bill 2004 was referred to the Parliamentary Standing Committee on Rural Development.

The National Rural Employment Guarantee Bill 2004 clearly fell short of the promise made in the NCMP. The response was a broad-based campaign to 'repair' the Bill and reinstate the crucial safeguards—irreversible guarantee, universal coverage,

time-bound extension to the whole of rural India, assured minimum wages, full transparency, among others. The NAC, the Left parties, and a wide range of organizations committed to the right to work, played an active role in this campaign. This led to a series of amendments in the Bill, in July and August 2005, largely based on the recommendations of the Standing Committee, which endorsed most of the campaign's demands. The most contentious issues were settled in August 2005, in a frantic round of bargaining between the constituent parties and supporters of the UPA government, with the Left parties extracting some major last-minute concessions. Finally, the NREGA was passed in the Lok Sabha on 23 August 2005.

Interestingly, the Act was passed unanimously. Video archives give an interesting glimpse of this moving event. The Minister of Rural Development, Dr Raghuvansh Prasad Singh, made a spirited speech in Hindi, ending with 'rozgar guarantee zindabad' (long live employment guarantee) and a roaring applause. The Speaker of the House then proceeded to conduct the 'voice vote' on NREGA. When the time came for the opponents to say 'nay', there was pin-drop silence.

This political unanimity, however, was somewhat deceptive. While it would have been very difficult for any Member of Parliament to oppose the Act in public, there was a great deal of 'behind the scenes' opposition to the Act in the corridors of power, notably from the Finance Ministry. Further, this opposition was organically linked to a powerful 'anti-NREGA' lobby; very vocal in the corporate-sponsored media and related forums. The fact that this small lobby nearly succeeded in derailing the Act (and did succeed in diluting it in some important respects), in spite of its tremendous popular appeal, is a telling symptom of the elitist nature of Indian democracy. In the end, the opposition was dispersed, and the interests of the working class prevailed. But it was a narrow victory, and the possibility of a backlash against the Act (or, more likely, its quiet sabotage) should not be dismissed.

ASPECTS OF THE NREGA DEBATE

The NREGA gives a legal guarantee of employment in rural areas to anyone who is willing to do casual manual labour at the statutory minimum wage. Any adult who applies for work under the Act is entitled to being employed on local public works within fifteen days. Failing that, an unemployment allowance (one fourth of the minimum wage for the first thirty days, and one half thereafter) has to be paid. Guaranteed employment is subject to an initial limit of 100 days per household per year, which may be raised or removed over time.[3]

The need for an Employment Guarantee Act has been questioned. Why is it not enough to initiate massive employment schemes? The main answer is that an Act places an enforceable obligation on the state, and gives bargaining power to the labourers. It creates accountability. By contrast, a scheme leaves labourers at the mercy of government officials.

There is another major difference between a scheme and an Act. Schemes come and go, but laws are more durable. A scheme can be trimmed or even cancelled by a bureaucrat, whereas changing a law requires an amendment in the Parliament. Under the Act, labourers have durable legal entitlements. Over time, they are likely to become aware of their rights and learn how to defend them.

Opposition to the Act often arises from a failure to appreciate its far-reaching economic, social, and political significance. To start with, the Act can go a long way towards protecting rural households from poverty and hunger. A hundred days of employment at the statutory minimum wage is not the end of poverty by any means, but for people who live on the brink of starvation, it makes a big difference.[4] Second, NREGA can help to slow down distress migration to urban areas—if work is available in the village, many rural families will stop heading to the cities during the slack season. Third, as mentioned earlier, guaranteed employment contributes to the empowerment of women. A large proportion of NREGA workers are women, and guaranteed employment gives them some economic independence.[5] Fourth, the Act is an opportunity to create useful assets in rural areas. In particular, there is a massive potential for labour-intensive public works in the field of environmental protection—watershed development, land regeneration, prevention of soil erosion, restoration of tanks, protection of forests, and related activities.

Fifth, the Act can help activate and revitalize the institutions of local governance, including *Gram Panchayats* (village councils) and *Gram Sabhas* (village assemblies).[6] It will give them a new purpose, backed with substantial financial resources.

Last but not the least, the Act is a means of strengthening the bargaining power of unorganized workers. This, in turn, could help them to struggle for other important entitlements, such as minimum wages and social security. The process of mobilizing for effective implementation of the Act also has much value in itself, as an opportunity for unorganized workers to organize.

Having said this, the financial implications of the Employment Guarantee Act caused much concern (in some quarters) at the time of its enactment. In a note on this issue prepared by the NAC in 2004, the cost of the Act was anticipated to rise from 0.5 per cent of gross domestic product (GDP) in 2005–6 to 1 per cent of GDP in 2008–9 (NAC 2004). This was based on the assumption that the Act would be gradually extended to the whole of India within four years, starting with 150 of the poorest districts in 2005–6.[7] In the same note, the NAC argued that this was quite affordable, considering that there was much scope for increasing India's tax-GDP ratio—one of the lowest in the world at that time. As it turns out, this view has been borne out by recent experience—India's tax-GDP ratio has risen steadily in recent years, and this, along with rapid economic growth, has made it relatively easy to finance the Employment Guarantee Act as well as a range of other 'flagship programmes' of the UPA Government. In 2008–9, Central government expenditure on NREGA was around Rs 30,000 crore, or close to 0.6 per cent of GDP. This is less than the NAC estimate, but NREGA expenditure is likely to rise further in the near future—possibly quite close to the anticipated 1 per cent of GDP. Meanwhile, the initial fears about the affordability of NREGA have largely subsided.

There is an interesting parallel here with mid-day meals in primary schools. When the Supreme Court directed state governments to start providing cooked meals to school children, in late 2001, the states pleaded bankruptcy—and their plea had a ring of truth at that time. The honourable judges, however, were in no mood to surrender and told them firmly to 'cut the flab somewhere else' [*sic*]. Within a few years, public expenditure on mid-day meals rose to more than Rs 5,000 crores. With a little help from adequate funding, the mid-day meal scheme became one of the best social programmes of the Indian government. Today, it has very few opponents.

Similarly, in the case of NREGA, money followed the law and not the other way round. Whether NREGA will achieve the same degree of success and acceptability as mid-day meals remains to be seen. But the financial hurdles at least have been largely overcome, and the programme has a chance.

To the fiscal conservative, concerned with curbing public expenditure come what may, all this is perhaps a nightmare. But for those who believe that there is a case for much higher public expenditure on well-devised social programmes in India, there is an interesting lesson here about the possibility of using the law to gain a financial foothold for these programmes. The proposed Right to Education Act, if passed, could play a similar role in the field of elementary education.

EMPLOYMENT GUARANTEE ON THE GROUND

The NREGA came into force on 2 February 2006 in 200 districts, and was extended to the whole country on 1 April 2008.[8] The lively, and often acrimonious, debate that led to the enactment of the NREGA continued thereafter in a different form. On one side, opponents of the Act (handsomely represented in the corporate-sponsored media) have continued their barrage of criticism.[9] 'Expensive gravy train', 'costly joke', 'corruption guarantee scheme', 'wonky idea', 'Sonia's pet project', and 'gargantuan guzzler of taxpayers' money' is just a small sample of the colourful terms they have used to describe NREGA. On the other side, the government and its supporters have been churning out a steady stream of upbeat reports. For instance, according to a recent note from the Press Information Bureau (released on 28 December 2007), NREGA is nothing short of a 'tremendous success'.

Thankfully, there have also been informative assessments of the NREGA, on the sidelines of this propaganda war.[10] Findings of a number of field surveys are already available, and much has also been learnt from 'social audits' of NREGA across the country, notably in Dungarpur (Rajasthan), Ananthapur (Andhra Pradesh), Hardoi (Uttar Pradesh), Ranchi (Jharkhand), and Villupuram (Tamil Nadu).[11] These reports suggest that, *where work is available*, NREGA is a new lifeline for the rural poor and is also quietly sowing the seeds of significant economic, social, and political change in rural areas.

To illustrate the point, Table 34.1 presents summary findings of a recent field survey of NREGA in six states of the Hindi-speaking region (Bihar, Chhattisgarh, Jharkhand, Madhya Pradesh, Rajasthan, and Uttar Pradesh).[12] The survey covered 100 randomly selected worksites spread over ten districts in these states, and a sample of about 1,000 workers currently employed at these worksites.

The Table illustrates a number of interesting points that are also corroborated in other studies. First, NREGA is reaching the poorest of the poor, and is of particular significance for marginalized communities such as the Scheduled Castes (SCs) and Scheduled Tribes (STs). These account for 73 per cent of NREGA workers in this sample, with a similar figure (about 60 per cent) for the national average based on official data (Drèze and Oldiges 2009).

Second, NREGA is also of special significance for women, particularly in areas such as the 'Hindi heartland' (the location of this survey), where women have very limited opportunities for remunerated employment.[13] Only 30 per cent of women workers in the sample had earned any cash income, other than NREGA wages, during the three months preceding the survey. Further, most of them collected their own wages, and kept them too, confirming that NREGA is a genuine source of independent income for women, and not just an opportunity for other household members (for example, their husbands) to extract work and wages from them.

Third, NREGA workers have a positive view of the programme. A large majority (71 per cent) consider that NREGA is 'very important' for them,

Table 34.1: Perceptions of NREGA among Rural Workers

Socio-economic background of NREGA workers:	
Proportion (%) belonging to SC/ST households	73
Proportion (%) who live in a *kaccha* house	81
Proportion (%) who have no electricity at home	72
Average number of days of NREGA employment obtained by the respondent's household in the preceding twelve months	43
Proportion (%) of workers who felt that NREGA is 'very important' for them	71
Proportion (%) of workers who reported that NREGA had helped them to:	
avoid hunger	69
avoid distress migration	57
cope with illness in the family	47
avoid demeaning or hazardous work	35
Proportion (%) of workers who felt that NREGA has led to the creation of useful assets in the village	83
Proportion (%) of workers who had any complaint of 'harassment' at the worksite	11
Proportion (%) of female respondents who:	
had earned any cash income other than NREGA wages during the preceding three months	30
collect their own (NREGA) wages	79
keep their own wages	68
Proportion (%) of workers who want at least 100 days of NREGA employment over the year	98

Source: Field survey of NREGA conducted by the G.B. Pant Social Science Institute (GBPSSI), Allahabad University, in May–June 2008. The figures are based on responses from a random sample of nearly 1,000 workers, spread over ten districts located in the major states of the Hindi-speaking region (Bihar, Chhattisgarh, Jharkhand, Madhya Pradesh, Rajasthan, and Uttar Pradesh). For further details, see Drèze and Khera (2009).

and there is also much evidence—from this and other studies—that the programme is helping them to avoid hunger, distress migration, demeaning work, and other hardships associated with unemployment. Another telling sign of their interest in NREGA is the fact that almost all the respondents wanted at least 100 days of NREGA employment over the year—the current 'ceiling' under the Act.

Fourth, the respondents also had a positive view of the productive value of NREGA works—an overwhelming majority (83 per cent) felt that the programme had led to the creation of useful assets in the village. It may be argued that this assessment is biased, in so far as NREGA workers are unlikely to disparage their own work. As it happens, however, the field investigators had similar views on this matter—at most of the sample worksites, the survey teams considered that the work being done was 'very useful' (70 per cent) or 'quite useful' (22 per cent). Tentative

as they may be, these observations make interesting reading in contrast with the widely-held (but rather unsubstantiated) belief that NREGA works amount to little more than 'playing with mud', as one grumpy commentator recently put it.

Fifth, the transition to a rights-based framework appears to be leading (slowly but surely) to a major decline in the exploitation of labour at public works. As Table 34.1 indicates, there were few complaints of 'harassment' at NREGA worksites. From this and other studies, there is also much evidence of sustained progress towards assured payment of minimum wages and timely payment of wages. This is in sharp contrast with the situation that used to prevail before NREGA, when rural public works were under the control of highly exploitative contractors.[14]

Last but not the least, NREGA has shown its potential as an organizational tool for rural workers. This feature, not evident from Table 34.1, came into

sharp focus in Pati Block of Badwani District, where
NREGA had been actively used as a means of public
mobilization by Jagrut Adivasi Dalit Sangathan
(JADS), a local organization of rural workers.[15] In
this Block, NREGA workers had been able to secure
as many as eighty-five days of employment during
the preceding twelve months, on average (compared
with forty-three days in the sample as a whole).
The impact of the Sangathan's organizational work
was also evident from high awareness levels among
NREGA workers and their confidence in the power
of collective action (Nayak 2008). Many of them
had learnt to make written applications for work,
insist on the payment of minimum wages, participate
in vigilance committees, and even demand the
unemployment allowance.[16]

Thus, in spite of all its shortcomings (also well
documented), NREGA has already led to some major
achievements. All these achievements, however, are
conditional on work being available (Table 34.1
is based on a random sample of persons *currently
employed at NREGA worksites*). This is a major
qualification. Indeed, the basic principle of 'work on
demand' is yet to be put into practice, and meanwhile,
employment generation continues to happen on a
top–down basis. As a result, the scale of employment
generation has varied a great deal, depending on
the political interests of different state governments
in NREGA. The top performer in this respect is
Rajasthan, where NREGA generated as many as
seventy-seven days of employment *per rural household*
during the first year of implementation (2006–7), in
the six districts where the Act applied at that time.
This is an unprecedented achievement in the history
of social security in India, or for that matter anywhere
in the developing world. However, the general
experience is that employment generation has lagged
far behind the demand for work. In the 200 districts
where the Act was in force in 2006–7, NREGA
generated only seventeen days of employment per
rural household on average, with much lower figures
in many states, for example, less than ten days in
Bihar, Gujarat, Haryana, Kerala, Maharashtra, Punjab,
Tamil Nadu, and West Bengal.[17]

Even these figures are likely to be on the high
side, based as they are on official statistics, inclusive

of 'leakages'.[18] There is, indeed, considerable evidence
that the scale and impact of NREGA have been
severely diminished (and even, in some states,
comprehensively undermined) by major leakages. This
problem is not specific to NREGA, but the fact that
embezzled funds, in this case, are snatched away from
people who live on the margin of subsistence, makes it
particularly critical. Also, the Act (and its Operational
Guidelines) includes a range of 'transparency
safeguards' that were aimed at preventing fraud,
so that this has become something of a test case
of the possibility of eradicating corruption from
development programmes.[19] Positive experiences in
several states, notably Rajasthan and Andhra Pradesh,
suggest that strict enforcement of these safeguards
can go a long way in preventing corruption. However,
this requires a clear political choice to side with the
workers in this matter, and not with the nexus of
corrupt bureaucrats, politicians, and contractors who
benefit from the embezzlement of NREGA funds. In
this unequal battle, vested interests still have an upper
hand in many states.[20]

Further, there is still a very long way to go in
protecting the basic entitlements of rural workers
under NREGA—work on demand, minimum wages,
payment of wages within fifteen days, basic worksite
facilities, and unemployment allowance, among
others. While these entitlements have become legal
rights under the law, the current grievance redressal
provisions under NREGA are very weak, making it
possible for government officials and Gram Panchayat
functionaries to get away with gross violations of
the Act on a routine basis. Effective implementation
of NREGA requires much higher awareness levels
among rural workers, more active organizational
work, and—last but not least—stronger grievance
redressal procedures.

This is a long haul, and the last few years are best
seen as a learning phase in the difficult transition
from top-down employment schemes to a rights-
based approach. Whether this learning process will,
ultimately, enable the vision of the Act to be realized,
remains to be seen. Meanwhile, NREGA has at least
led to a major refocusing of administrative energies,
financial resources, and political attention towards the
concerns of rural workers. In this and other respects, it

is a small but significant step towards the realization of the right to work.

NOTES

1. For more detailed accounts of the genesis of NREGA, see McAuslan (2006) and Lakin and Ravishankar (2006).

2. Both the NAC draft and the 'citizens' draft' are available at www.righttofoodindia.org, along with extensive documentation on the debate that led to the enactment of the NREGA. Note that the NCMP policy commitment related not only to rural areas but also to 'urban poor and lower middle-class household[s]'. The extension of the Act to urban areas, however, is yet to be seriously considered.

3. For a reader-friendly introduction to the Act, see Dey *et al.* (2006). For the full text of the Act and related documents, see www.nrega.nic.in.

4. In a note on the financial implications of NREGA, the NAC pointed out that a net income transfer equivalent to 100 days' earnings at the statutory minimum wage would enable a large majority of poor rural households to cross the 'poverty line'. This should not be taken literally, since there are also second-round effects to consider, both negative (for example, foregone earnings in other activities) and positive (for example, multiplier effects). But it does give a useful indication of the potential impact of NREGA on rural poverty.

5. According to the official data, the proportion of women among NREGA labourers is close to 50 per cent, and rising over time (Drèze and Oldiges 2009).

6. At least 50 per cent of NREGA funds are supposed to be spent by the Gram Panchayats.

7. In fact, the Act came into force in February 2006 in 200 districts, and was extended (in two steps) to the whole country by 1 April 2008.

8. In between, the Act was extended from 200 to 330 districts (on 1 April 2007). The districts in the initial list of 200 were supposed to be the poorest in the country, based on an index of 'backwardness' devised by the Planning Commission.

9. For a few examples, see Acharya (2004, 2005), Jain (2007), Dasgupta (2008), and Ghose (2008). Interestingly, opposition to NREGA in the corporate-sponsored media swiftly vanished, and even metamorphosed into guarded support, in late 2008, when the world-wide financial crisis led to a broad-based call for higher government expenditure as a means of 'pump-priming' the economy.

10. See, for example, Shah (2007), Centre for Science and Environment (CSE) (2008), Khera (2008), Narayanan (2008), National Federation of Indian Women (NFIW) (2008), Ambasta *et al.* (2008), and the series of survey reports in GBPSSI (2008); also National Council of Applied Economic Research (NCAER) (2009) and earlier studies cited there.

11. Accounts of some of these social audits are posted at www.righttofoodindia.org.

12. For a more detailed account of the findings, see Drèze and Khera (2009).

13. On this, see also Bhatty (2006, 2008), Jandu (2008), Narayanan (2008), Ghosh (2009), and Khera and Nayak (2009).

14. For further discussion, see Drèze (2007).

15. For insightful accounts of this experience, see Khera (2008) and Nayak (2008).

16. After a long struggle, JADS secured the first-ever payment of the unemployment allowance under the NREGA, in October 2006, for more than 1,500 workers.

17. See Drèze and Oldiges (2009) for further discussion.

18. Note, however, that the figures of Rajasthan at least have some credibility. Indeed, recent social audits (in Dungarpur, Jhalawar, and Sirohi, among other locations) suggest that there is relatively little embezzlement of NREGA funds in Rajasthan, at least in the labour component of the programme.

19. These transparency safeguards include availability of the 'muster rolls' at the worksite, regular maintenance of 'job cards', formation of 'vigilance committees', social audits by the Gram Sabhas, pro-active disclosure of essential records, and separation of payment agencies from implementing agencies. For further details, see GoI (2008).

20. Recent events in Jharkhand, including a spate of NREGA-related murders and suicides, illustrate the intensity of these tensions, and the sinister nature of the nexus of corruption and violence that surrounds NREGA in some states. For further discussion, see Drèze (2008).

REFERENCES

Acharya, Shankar. 2005. 'Populism Rides Again', *Business Standard*, 27 December.

———. 2004. 'Bad Ideas Are Winning', *Business Standard*, 28 December.

Ambasta, P., P.S. Vijay Shankar, and M. Shah. 2008. 'Two Years of NREGA: The Road Ahead', *Economic and Political Weekly*, XLIII(8), pp. 41–50.

Bagchee, Aruna. 2005. 'Political and Administrative Realities of the EGS', *Economic and Political Weekly*, XL(42), pp. 4531–8.

Bhatia, B. and J. P. Drèze. 2006. 'Employment Guarantee in Jharkhand: Ground Realities', *Economic and Political Weekly*, XLI(29), pp. 3198–202.

Bhatty, Kiran. 2006. 'Employment Guarantee and Child Rights', *Economic and Political Weekly*, XLI(20), pp. 1965–6.

Bhatty, Kiran. 2008. 'Falling through the Cracks', *The Hindu*, 16 March.

CSE (Centre for Science and Environment). 2008. *NREGA: Opportunities and Challenges*. New Delhi: Centre for Science and Environment.

Dasgupta, Swapan. 2008. 'Flawed Job Scheme', *The Times of India*, 10 February.

Dey, N., J.P. Drèze, and R. Khera. 2006. *Employment Guarantee Act: A Primer*. New Delhi: National Book Trust.

Drèze, Jean. 2007. 'Dismantling the Contractor Raj', *The Hindu*, 20 November.

———. 2008. 'NREGA: Ship without Rudder?', *The Hindu*, 19 July.

Drèze, J.P. and R. Khera. 2009. 'The Battle for Employment Guarantee', *Frontline*, 16 January, pp. 4–26.

Drèze, J.P. and C. Oldiges. 2009. 'Work in Progress', *Frontline*, 14 February.

GBPSSI (G.B. Pant Social Science Institute). 2008. *Studies on Employment Guarantee*. Allahabad: GBPSSI.

Ghose, Sagarika. 2008. 'The Idiocy of Urban Thinking', *Hindustan Times*, 14 February.

Ghosh, Jayati. 2009. 'Equity and Inclusion through Public Expenditure: The Potential of the NREGS', paper presented at an international conference on NREGA convened by the Ministry of Rural Development, New Delhi; available at www.macroscan.com

GoI (Government of India). 2008. *NREGA Operational Guidelines*, third edition. New Delhi: Ministry of Rural Development.

Jain, Devaki. 2005. 'Guaranteeing Employment: Immeasurable Benefits for Women', mimeo, Bangalore.

Jain, Sunil. 2007. 'Wages of Meddling?', *Business Standard*, 12 March.

Jandu, Navjyoti. 2008. 'Employment Guarantee and Women's Empowerment in Rural India', mimeo, New Delhi: National Federation of Indian Women.

Khera, Reetika. 2008. 'Empowerment Guarantee Act', *Economic and Political Weekly*, XLIII(35), pp. 8–10.

Khera, R. and N. Nayak, 2009. 'Women Workers and Perceptions of the National Rural Employment Guarantee Act in India', mimeo, New Delhi: Centre for Development Economics at the Delhi School of Economics.

Lakin, J. and N. Ravishankar. 2006. 'Working for Votes: The Politics of Employment Guarantee in India', mimeo, Massachusetts: Department of Government, Harvard University.

McAuslan, Ian, 2006. 'The Politics of Pro-poor Policy Change in India: The National Rural Employment Guarantee Act', mimeo, United Kingdom: Institute of Development Studies, University of Sussex.

Narayanan, Sudha. 2008. 'Employment Guarantee, Women's Work and Child Care', *Economic and Political Weekly*, XLIII(9):10–12.

NAC (National Advisory Council). 2004. 'Financial Implications of an Employment Guarantee Act', available at www.nac.nic.in

NCAER (National Council of Applied Economic Research). 2009. *NCAER-PIF Study on Evaluating Performance of National Rural Employment Guarantee Act*. New Delhi: NCAER.

NFIW (National Federation of Indian Women). 2008. *Socio-Economic Empowerment of Women under NREGA*, report prepared for the Ministry of Rural Development.

Nayak, Nandini. 2008. 'Songs of Hope', *The Hindu*, 14 September.

Shah, Mihir. 2007. 'Employment Guarantee, Civil Society and Indian Democracy', *Economic and Political Weekly*, XLII(45 and 46), pp. 43–51.

VII India and the World

35 India and the World

Kanti Bajpai

India, like every other country, must navigate the waters of international politics. How do Indians view their country's relationship with the often challenging and turbulent world beyond its frontiers? Put differently, what is India's grand strategy? If grand strategy refers to a country's deployment of military, diplomatic, economic, technological, and cultural instruments in the service of security, what then is India's grand strategic plan in relation to its greatest external challenges—Pakistan, China, and the United States?

It is a commonplace of the discourse on Indian security that India does not have a strategic culture and that Indians have historically not thought consistently and rigorously about strategy. At the very least, Indians have not recorded their strategic thinking in written texts, the only exception being the ancient classic, *The Arthashastra* (Rangarajan 1987). That India does not have a tradition of strategic thinking is not altogether incorrect. On the other hand, since the country's Independence in 1947, it has had to deal with a number of security challenges, and the volume of writings on these issues is enormous.

Newspaper and magazine commentary is probably the largest single source on Indian thinking. In addition, the strategic community has produced a corpus of scholarly writings on security. A number of journals publish regularly on security matters. Finally, there are the texts of Indian Prime Ministers and other leaders, who have over the years written and spoken publicly on security policy.

Indian strategic culture, which was dominated by the worldview of its first Prime Minister, Jawaharlal Nehru, has been in ferment since the end of the Cold War. At least three different streams of thinking are vying for dominance. These three schools may be called *Nehruvianism*, *neo-liberalism*, and *hyperrealism*. To call them 'schools' is to overstate the case. Those who hold to the views associated with the three perspectives do not call themselves by the names used here, although the usage of the term Nehruvian is common enough in Indian discourse. Yet, the consistency of views across a number of influential commentators and the style of thought associated with many others who write and think about strategic affairs suggests that there are distinct, coherent, and persistent approaches to the problem of security that warrant the description of 'schools'.

A strategic culture can be understood in terms of an identifiable set of basic assumptions about the nature of international relations, the role of war, the nature of adversaries and threats, and the utility of force. We can refer to these assumptions as constituting the *central strategic paradigms* of the three schools of thought. In addition, the three perspectives can be described by their *grand strategic prescriptions* on the means that should be used to make India secure (Johnston 1995). Nehruvians, neo-liberals, and hyperrealists do share some basic assumptions, but in the end their central strategic paradigms and their strategic prescriptions differ significantly. The debate between the three schools is, therefore, quite real.

CENTRAL STRATEGIC PARADIGMS

A core strategic paradigm provides answers to the following questions:
(a) The role of war in international relations
(b) The nature of the adversaries and the threats they pose
(c) The utility of force
How do Nehruvians, neo-liberals, and hyperrealists assess the role of war, the nature of the adversary, and the utility of force? To answer this question, we need, as a beginning, to comprehend the way the three schools conceive of international relations.

The Nature of International Relations

Before we proceed to reconstruct Nehruvian, neo-liberal, and hyperrealist approaches to international relations in terms of their differences, it is important to note their areas of agreement. For while they disagree in key respects, they also proceed from a core set of common assumptions and arguments.

First of all, the three paradigms accept that at the heart of international relations is the notion of the sovereign state that recognizes no higher authority. In such a system, each state is responsible fundamentally for its own security and well-being. Above all, states strive to protect their territory and autonomy. Second, all three paradigms recognize that interests, power, and violence are staples of international relations.

States cannot avoid the responsibility of pursuing the national interest, however that is defined. Nor can they be indifferent to the cultivation of power—their own and that of other states. States must in some measure accrue power in a competitive system. Finally, conflict and war are a constant shadow over inter-state relations. While the three paradigms differ on the causes of conflict and war and on the ability of states to control and transcend these forces, all three accept that disputes and large-scale organized violence are a regular feature of international relations. Third, all three paradigms accept that power comprises both military and economic capabilities, at a minimum. States need both. While they differ on the optimum mix and use of these capabilities, proponents of the three views are in agreement that military and economic strength are vital for security. Beyond this common base, the three paradigms differ.

Fundamental to Nehruvianism is the argument that states and people can come to understand each other better, and thereby make and sustain peace. Nehruvians accept that in the international system, without a supranational authority, the threat of war to settle disputes and rivalries is in some measure inescapable. States must look after themselves in such a world, in which violence is a regrettable last resort (Krishna 1984). However, Nehruvians believe that this state of 'anarchy' can be mitigated, if not eventually supervened. International laws and institutions, military restraint, negotiations and compromise, cooperation, free intercourse between societies, and regard for the well-being of people everywhere and not just one's own citizens, all these can overcome the rigours of the international system.[1] Furthermore, to make preparations for war and a balance of power, the central objectives of security and foreign policy are, for Nehruvians, both ruinous and futile: ruinous because arms spending can only impoverish societies materially and create the very conditions that sustain violence and war; futile because, ultimately, balances of power are fragile, and do not prevent large-scale violence (as the two World Wars so catastrophically demonstrated).[2]

Neo-liberals also accept the general characterization of international relations as a state of war. That coercion plays an important role in such a world is not denied by neo-liberals. The lure of mutual gain in any interaction is also, however, a powerful conditioning factor amongst states, particularly as they become more interdependent. Neo-liberals often express their distinct view of international relations by comparing the role of military and economic power. According to them, states pursue not just military power, but also economic well-being. They do so in part because economic strength is ultimately the basis for military power. Economic strength can, in addition, substitute for military power: military domination is one way of achieving one's ends; economic domination is another. Economic power can even be more effective than military power. Thus, in situations of 'complex interdependence', force is unusable or ineffective.[3]

Most importantly, though, neo-liberals believe that economic well-being is vital for national security in a broader sense. An economically deprived people cannot be a satisfied people, and a dissatisfied people cannot be secure (Baru 2006). The key question then is: where does economic strength and well-being come from? In the neo-liberal view, it can only come from free market policies. Free market policies at home imply, in addition, free trade abroad. Free trade is a relationship of mutual gain, even if the gain is asymmetric, and is therefore a factor in the relations between states. Indeed, where Nehruvians see communication and contact as the key to the transformation of international relations, neo-liberals believe that trade and economic interactions can achieve this.[4]

Hyperrealists harbour the most pessimistic view of international relations.[5] Where Nehruvians and neo-liberals believe that international relations can be transformed—either by means of communication and contact or by free market economic reforms and the logic of comparative advantage—hyperrealists see an endless cycle of repetition in inter-state interactions. The governing metaphor of hyperrealists is threat and counter-threat (Karnad 1994a). In the absence of a supranational authority that can tell them how to behave and that is capable of enforcing those commands, states are doomed to the balance of power, deterrence, and war. Conflict and rivalry between states cannot be transformed into peace and friendship (except temporarily as an alliance against a common foe); they can only be managed by the threat and use of violence (Chellany 1999a: xviii).

From this, hyperrealists conclude that the surest way to achieve peace and stability is through the accumulation of military power and the willingness to use force (Chellany 1999b: 528). Hyperrealists reject the Nehruvian and neo-liberal concern over runaway military spending and preparedness, arguing that there is no very good evidence that defence derogates from development (ibid.: 531). Indeed, defence spending may, in the Keynesian sense at least, boost economic growth and development. Hyperrealists, like neo-liberals, are also sceptical about the role of institutions, laws, treaties, and agreements. For hyperrealists, what counts in international relations is power in the service of national interest; all the rest is illusion. The neo-liberal faith in the power of economics is equally one that hyperrealists do not share. Hyperrealists invert the relationship between military and economic power. Historically, they argue, military power is more important than, and probably prior to, economic power. A state that can build its military power will safeguard its international interests, and will build an economy and society that is strong.[6]

The Role of War, the Nature of the Adversary and Threats, and the Utility of Force

Given the Nehruvian, neo-liberal, and hyperreal approaches to international relations, how do they regard the role of war, the nature of the adversary and threats, and the utility of force?

For Nehruvians, war is a choice that states can and will make. While Nehruvians accept that the international system is anarchic and that states pursue their interests with vigour, violence is not inevitable.[7] Wars, as Nehru affirmed, are made in the minds of men, and therefore it is in the minds of men that war must be eradicated. War is not a natural, inherent activity. It can therefore be avoided and limited even when it occurs. The state of war—the fear, expectation, and preparation for war—can be overcome through wise, cooperative policies amongst states (Nehru 1961/1963).[8]

The adversary, in the Nehruvian view, is therefore not a permanent one. War arises from misperceptions and ideological systems that colour the attitudes of states and societies and spread fear and hatred. The adversary either does not comprehend India, or is misled about Indian goals and methods. Its leadership may be at fault. Ordinary citizens may support their governments out of ignorance or illusion created by government propaganda. The adversary, therefore, can be made into a friend through communication and contact with India and Indians, at both the official and non-official levels (Dubey 1999).

It is this—communication and contact between governments and peoples—rather than force that will end conflict and make India more secure. International organizations and inter-state negotiations are ways of institutionalizing communication and contact. The threat or use of force, particularly in a coercive, offensive way, is counterproductive, and will generally be reciprocated by the adversary, leaving the basic quarrel unchanged. Both parties can only be weakened and harmed by a relationship built on force. All issues are negotiable in the end. India must marshal enough force to defend itself, but it should not have so much that it makes others fearful. Certainly, force must be absolutely the last resort, even if it is used coercively (Nehru 1961/1963: 35, 45–6).

Neo-liberals, too, admit that war is a possibility between sovereign states. However, it is not the only inherent condition in the international system. Given that societies have different comparative advantages and that there is a global division of labour, states cannot escape the logic of interdependence (Baru 2006). Interdependence makes for more pragmatic policies internationally. In their external relations, states worry not just about war, but also about trade, investment, and technology (Baru 1998a: 67, 1998b: 90–1).

In the neo-liberal imaginary, therefore, adversarial relations are produced by two factors. First, like Nehruvians, neo-liberals hold misunderstanding and miscalculation as being responsible for enmity. If governments and peoples were more clear-headed and did their cost-benefit calculations correctly, they would probably see that rivalry and violence is irrational, and that the benefits of economic relations untrammelled by quarrels over territory are far greater than anything that may be gained from conflict. Second, military enmity is fundamentally an old-fashioned condition,

which cannot be sustained as economic globalization goes forward. India itself is guilty of viewing its relations with various countries in the old geo-political way because it has not understood the logic and power of globalization (Baru 1998a: 66–70; 1998b: 14–17, 2006; Subrahmanyam 1999).

Force is therefore an instrument of declining utility. For neo-liberals, force is an outmoded and blunt instrument unsuited to the new world order. states must have enough force to defend themselves, but it is economic power and the capacity to innovate in a global economy that eventually makes societies secure. Force in the service of expansionism is irrelevant. Territorial conquest and control, in a world where capital, information, and even skills flow across national boundaries, is anachronistic. States must be attentive to defence needs, but on the whole India's economic growth and modernization, and its integration into a globalized world economy form its greatest source of strength (Raja Mohan 2001b).[9] India would do better to use its increasing economic power as a way to influence others than to use force in such a role (Baru 1998a: 67).[10]

Hyperrealists offer quite different perspectives on war, adversaries, and force. War is a constant possibility in an anarchical system, and, while it can be destructive and painful, it is also the basis for a state's autonomy and security. War is not therefore an aberration, but a natural tendency of international relations. Preparing for war is not warmongering; it is responsible and wise statecraft. War comes when rival states calculate that the other side is either getting too powerful or is weakening.[11]

In the hyperrealist view, the international system is a lonely place. States have no permanent friends. Anyone can be an adversary. The adversary, as much as India, must prepare for war in the service of its interests and survival. Other things being equal, neighbouring states are more likely to be adversaries: conflicts over territory, status, and power are ever-present possibilities in intimate relationships. No amount of communication and contact or economic interaction will transform the relationship, because it is zero-sum. Only a balance of power can regulate relations with nearby or distant rivals (Chellaney 1999b: 558).

Force, in the hyperreal view, is an indispensable instrument in international relations. It is the only means by which states can truly achieve their ends against rivals. States must accept that violence may be necessary in the national interest. Force may be deployed purely defensively, but the best defence is often offence. It may even save lives on both sides. Control over territory is not old-fashioned, but rather militarily imperative, especially in conflicts with neighbours. In the end, force may have to be used to destroy the adversary's military formations and to control or wrest contested territory. No political or military leadership can responsibly avoid planning for the coercive use of force. Only 'idealists' of various stripes—Nehruvians or neo-liberals—could fool themselves into thinking that a more aggressive posture is always bad (Chellaney 1999b: 536).[12]

Nuclear Weapons

The greatest instruments of force are nuclear weapons. Since 1998, when India tested five nuclear devices, the Indian government has announced that it will build a nuclear weapons arsenal for the purposes of national security. How do the three schools regard nuclear weapons?

Nehruvians, neo-liberals, and hyperrealists differ on the broad outlines of India's nuclear policy, as well as the nature of the deterrent. They differ, first, on three basic issues: the utility of nuclear weapons; India's relationship with the non-proliferation regime; and the feasibility and desirability of disarmament. They also differ on the nature of the deterrent: Nehruvians and neo-liberals are nuclear moderates, while hyperrealists are nuclear maximalists.

Nehruvians hold that nuclear weapons are necessary for India's security as long as they cannot be abolished. Nuclear weapons are an abomination, but if others have them, particularly India's rivals, then India must also have them for deterrence (Ghose 1999: 94) Nuclear weapons are also necessary in a diplomatic sense. In a world of great and growing inequalities, nuclear weapons are not just a military, but also a political equalizer. India's capacity to resist great power pressures will in particular be enhanced by nuclear weapons.

With respect to the non-proliferation regime, and in particular the Comprehensive Test Ban Treaty (CTBT) and a putative fissile material cut-off treaty (FMCT), Nehruvians argue that India should not sign either accord, even if joining the non-proliferation regime does not adversely affect the Indian deterrent. For Nehruvians, the non-proliferation regime is a leading part of the 'new world order' that is fundamentally unequal and hegemonistic, and that must therefore be resisted (Ghose 1999: 86; Dubey 2002).

Finally, Nehruvians insist that nuclear disarmament is both desirable and feasible. It is desirable because nuclear weapons could some day be used, which would be catastrophic not just for the countries involved, but also for the rest of the international community (Mattoo 1999: 109).[13] In addition, disarmament is desirable because nuclear weapons are ethically repugnant, if not illegal, under international law (ibid.: 110).[14] Finally, disarmament is desirable because nuclear weapons in the hands of a few are discriminatory, and discrimination fosters instability and violence (Ghose 1999: 93).

According to Nehruvians, a multilateral, verifiable abolition of nuclear weapons, as proposed by India, is not only desirable, but is also feasible. Thus, they argue that if the international community could abolish biological and chemical weapons, then it can rid itself of nuclear weapons as well.[15] Abolition requires in the first place that the present nuclear weapons states (NWSs) commit themselves to its achievement in a time-bound and phased manner. Once they do so and take real steps to eliminate nuclear weapons, Nehruvians propose that India should join the process of abolition.

Neo-liberals are pragmatists in nuclear affairs (Raja Mohan 1999a: 20, 23; Subrahmanyam 1998a). Like the Nehruvians, they also believe that nuclear weapons are vital for India's security in a world which shows no signs of moving towards abolition, and which is inhabited by regional nuclear powers—China and Pakistan—that threaten India's security. Neo-liberals, like Nehruvians and hyperrealists, note that the NWSs continue to reaffirm the fundamental importance of nuclear weapons in their security postures (Subrahmanyam 1998b: 2007; Raja Mohan 1999a: 21–2).

Where neo-liberals part company with Nehruvians and hyperrealists is with respect to the non-proliferation regime. According to neo-liberals, New Delhi should, in the wake of the May 1998 tests, pragmatically reconsider its opposition to key elements of that regime. India's scientists have certified the tests as being sufficient for the construction of a credible deterrent, and a test ban could be in India's interest (Subrahmanyam 1998c: 58). Neo-liberals would cut a deal with the international community. The deal would have India join the CTBT, a possible FMCT, and the other non-proliferation regimes (such as the Missile Technology Control Regime or MTCR and Nuclear Suppliers Group). In return, it would get de facto, if not de jure, recognition of its new nuclear status, and, most importantly, the ban on dual-use and advanced conventional weapons technologies would be lifted (Raja Mohan 1999a: 6, 12–13).

While neo-liberals urge India to strike a nuclear deal with the nuclear powers, they exclude from this compact the traditional Indian idea of phased disarmament. They insist that India should be 'realistic' rather than 'normative' and 'moralistic' about nuclear weapons. Thus, C. Raja Mohan argues that India should set aside its traditional posture of 'disarmament' and focus instead on 'arms control' (1999a: 23).He even argues that India should positively oppose abolition, on two grounds. First, the incipient 'revolution in military affairs' (RMA) will give the US and its Western allies an insurmountable lead in conventional weaponry, and this can only be 'balanced' by nuclear weapons (Raja Mohan 1999a: 22).Second, the terms of global power more broadly are shifting against India, and only nuclear weapons will serve to keep India in the great game of global politics. Thus, even if the US and other NWSs agree to abolish nuclear weapons, India should keep them, at least until it can catch up in the conventional military and global power race (ibid.).

It is worth noting that not all neo-liberals are so sceptical about disarmament. Some strongly support the traditional Indian agenda on disarmament, and are closer to the Nehruvians in this regard (Subrahmanyam 1998c: 58). This softer, pro-disarmament variant of nuclear pragmatism has a substantial following and should not be discounted. Indian elite opinion has traditionally supported both nuclearization and an active stance on disarmament (Cortright and Mattoo 1996: 109–44). Having said that, it is not clear whether support for a disarmament agenda is a 'tactical' one intended to counter international criticism of India's nuclearization; whether it is an article of faith which Indians find difficult to discard; or whether it is seen as a genuine, realizable, and practical policy option. On the whole, it is much more an article of faith for Nehruvians and much more tactical for neo-liberals.

For hyperrealists, nuclear weapons are principally for deterrence. Some hyperrealists also believe that India must be prepared to fight and not just deter nuclear war (Karnad 1998: 40; Nair 1998: 90–1).[16] Nuclear weapons have a political role as well. Where Nehruvians see nuclearization as part of a strategy of resistance to a hegemonic world order, and where neo-liberals see it as a way of striking a bargain with the great powers, hyperrealists perceive the acquisition of nuclear weapons as fundamental to India's status as a great power. Without nuclear weapons, India cannot be counted as a separate pole in the international system, around which other states could cluster for protection and leadership.

Hyperrealists, like Nehruvians, urge that India should refuse to join the non-proliferation regime, so that the CTBT and a future FMCT do not constrain the achievement of a credible nuclear force (Karnad 1998: 112).[17] India needs to continue testing in order to produce a full array of nuclear weapons, increase the reliability of warhead design, and miniaturize the device. It also needs to produce more fissile material in order to test and build a sufficiently large arsenal (Karnad 2000: 45).

Finally, for hyperrealists, nuclear disarmament is both undesirable and infeasible, on strategic and technical grounds, respectively (Karnad 1998: 114). The abolition of nuclear weapons would once again create the conditions for a great power conflict, and could lead to a world war. In addition, hyperrealists argue that nuclear disarmament is unattainable: 'There is no empirical record that suggests that disarmament ever succeeded any time in history .... There is no record. It hasn't succeeded ....

[Therefore] what is the historical empirical basis on which disarmament is still conceived of as a foreign policy goal for India.'[18] States are loath to give up any weapon system until a more fearsome instrument comes along. They must also worry that others will cheat, and that those who disarm could become vulnerable to a 'break out'.

On the nature of the deterrent, Nehruvians and neo-liberals stand for a moderate posture, whereas hyperrealists are maximalists. Nuclear moderates and maximalists differ on six issues: the nature of the nuclear threat; force size and force structure; negative security assurances; nuclear readiness; command and control; and the logic of deterrence. These are summarized in Table 35.1.

Nuclear moderates see Pakistan and/or China as nuclear threats: some moderates rank Pakistan as the more serious nuclear threat, others rank China ahead, and some regard them as more or less coeval threats. Deterring either or both Pakistan and China is in their view achievable with no more than sixty to 140 simple, low-yield nuclear weapons. Tactical nuclear weapons, in the sense of battlefield devices, are unnecessary when a purely defensive deterrence is the objective. To enhance the survivability of India's nuclear force, a triad of ground, air, and sea-launched nuclear

capabilities is vital. Negative security assurances are both credible and viable if India maintains a de-mated/de-alerted nuclear posture, that is, if the warheads and delivery vehicles are kept separate and under different jurisdictions (for example between scientists and armed forces), and retaliation is assured, but at a time of India's choosing rather than instantaneous. With a small arsenal and a de-mated/de-alert posture, command and control can be a relatively simple, modest, and affordable undertaking. Nuclear moderation is possible, finally, because what suffices for deterrence is not the certainty of retaliation, but rather the mere possibility of a second strike.[19]

Maximalists estimate the nuclear threats to India to be more challenging, arguing that even the US constitutes a concern and that India must therefore, over the long term, constitute a 'tous azimuth' (all horizons) capability. Deterrence in such an environment requires a much larger arsenal—at least as large as that of the second-tier nuclear states, especially China—and a more sophisticated array of devices, including thermonuclear and tactical, with a triad to increase survivability. Negative security assurances, according to maximalists, are neither viable nor credible. No operational deployment of nuclear weapons can guarantee that a state will not

Table 35.1: Attitudes Towards Nuclear Weapons

	NUCLEAR MODERATES (NEHRUVIANS AND NEO-LIBERALS)	NUCLEAR MAXIMALISTS (HYPERREALISTS)
Nature of Nuclear Threat	Pakistan, China, or both	Pakistan, China, and the US: 'tous azimuth'
Force Size and Force Structure	• 60–140 'Hiroshima' type • No tactical weapons • Triad	• 300 warheads minimum, including thermonuclear • Tactical weapons • Triad
Negative Security Assurances	• No First Use is credible and operationally viable • Categorical non-use against non-nuclear states	• No First Use is not credible or viable • Non-use against non-nuclear states is not sacrosanct
Nuclear Readiness	• De-mated, de-alerted nuclear posture is stable • Retaliation can be delayed	• Full deployment of nuclear weapons; de-mated/de-alert is vulnerable • Retaliation should be prompt
Command and Control	Small, modest C3I— consistent with a small, restrained nuclear programme	Extensive, 'classical' C3I— even small, restrained programmes need complex command and control
Logic of Deterrence	Uncertainty of retaliation deters	Certainty of retaliation deters

use nuclear weapons first. De-mating and de-alerting and a slow-to-respond posture are inconsistent with deterrence stability, which requires the opponent to be sure that retaliation will be swift and deadly. Command and control must be extensive and sophisticated so as to ensure the safety and reliability of the arsenal against unauthorized or accidental use and during a nuclear war, which may involve a 'salvo' of exchanges. Underlying the contentions of the maximalists is their view that what deters is not the mere possibility of retaliation, but rather as close to the absolute certainty of retaliation as it is possible to engineer.[20]

In sum, Nehruvians, neo-liberals, and hyperrealists agree that India needs nuclear weapons for deterrence, but they disagree on the non-proliferation regime and on disarmament: only the neo-liberals would sign the CTBT and an eventual FMCT; and only Nehruvians regard the elimination of nuclear weapons as both desirable and feasible. In addition, Nehruvians and neo-liberals favour a moderate nuclear posture, whereas hyperrealists argue for a more maximalist position.

GRAND STRATEGY: THE REGION AND THE GREAT POWERS

Grand strategic thought focuses on the issue of means rather than ends. How do the three schools of thought deal with the operational challenges of regional security and relations with the great powers? The strategic paradigms have indicated the general predispositions of different streams of Indian thinking. What prescriptions do they offer more specifically on India's dealings with Pakistan, China, and the US?

Pakistan

Nehruvians believe that India and its various neighbours, including Pakistan, can and will live in peace. With the smaller states, there is little or no prospect of violence. With Pakistan, on the other hand, there is a long history of violence. Nehruvians see Pakistan as an aggressive state, as do the neo-liberals and hyperrealists. In the Nehruvian view, Pakistan is an artificial state, created on the basis of the erroneous 'two-nation theory' (Khan 1993: 23; Dhar 2001). A state based on Islamic precepts and on its difference with India cannot hold together.

Compounding the problem is the absence of democracy. Feudal overlords and the military together control the country. They perpetuate their domination by casting India in the role of a mortal threat (Kotru 2001; Nakra 2001). Having demonized India, Pakistan must constantly enlist powerful protectors against its bigger neighbour. During the Cold War, this meant allying with the US and China. Pakistan's alliances with Washington and Beijing gave Islamabad an inflated sense of its military and diplomatic strength. Backed by American and Chinese power, Pakistan became obdurate and aggressive.[21]

In the Nehruvian view, India's policy towards Pakistan must take account of these complexities. While relations with Pakistan are daunting, they are not hopeless. Given the intricacies of the relationship, India's moves must be geared to patient, long-run diplomacy rather than dramatic breakthroughs. The Nehruvian diagnosis rests on the view that enmity and hostility towards India comes from misunderstanding and delusion. The original Partition ideology—the two-nation theory—is a mass delusion that was propagated by Jinnah and the Muslim League (Dhar 2001). The enemy image of India sustained and elaborated by the feudals and the military is also false. The primary aim of Indian policy is of course to defend the country from military aggression and subversion. In the longer term, though, it is to undermine the two-nation theory and break down the image of India as a hostile state. Communication and contact between India and Pakistan are the only ways of doing this (Bidwai 1999: 110–11; Dixit 2001a; Parthasarathy 2001).

Various lines of policy follow. First of all, an adequate defence against aggression is vital. India cannot afford to be surprised and overcome militarily. The accent in the Nehruvian programme, though, is on the word 'adequate'. Nehruvians, we should remember, are sceptical of the use of force and of a balance-of-power politics. India, they believe, should be able to defend itself against its enemies, but should not dispose of so much force that it frightens others.[22] In addition, Nehruvians believe in the efficacy of international institutions and rules in preventing and limiting violence among states: there are alternatives to responding to violence *with* violence.

Thus, a second important line of policy is to use international law and institutions as well as bilateral treaties and agreements to tie Pakistan down. Not surprisingly, it was Jawaharlal Nehru and India that took the Kashmir issue to the UN in 1948. It is also India that has repeatedly sought to codify relations with Pakistan in treaties and agreements—most importantly, the Simla Accord, and most recently, the Lahore Declaration. While Nehruvians no longer have much faith in the UN in the matter of Kashmir and more generally in dealing with Pakistan, they insist that bilateral agreements have an important place in resolving conflict. The Simla and other agreements, including the various cooperative and confidence-building accords, must be the touchstone of India's Pakistan policy (Dixit 2001b).

A third line of Nehruvian policy is to wean Pakistan away from its external backers and supporters and to discourage those powers from interfering in the region. Weaning Pakistan away from its external dependencies will require it to shed its hostile image of India and restructure its domestic politics. Discouraging external powers from meddling in regional affairs can be achieved by pursuing a policy of non-alignment. By adopting a principled stand on great power behaviour and by refusing to permanently ally with one power or the other, India can persuade those powers to leave it and the region alone.

Finally, the core of the Nehruvian approach is to change Pakistani attitudes towards India. The only way of accomplishing this, in the end, is through communication and contact with both the Pakistani government and the people. No matter what the provocation by Pakistan, Nehruvians argue, New Delhi must hold firmly to a policy of engagement and negotiation. Summitry is one way of keeping a conversation going with official Pakistan. Trade and the benefits from it can be instrumental in showing Pakistanis that diplomatic normalization with India is profitable. People-to-people interactions (sports, culture, intellectual exchanges) can serve to demystify India in the Pakistani imagination. In sum, only a multifaceted relationship with Pakistan can bring about lasting accommodation and a robust peace.

When neo-liberals think about India–Pakistan relations, therefore, they approach the issue differently from Nehruvians. Where Nehruvians emphasize a multifaceted process of communication and contact, neo-liberals look essentially to strike bargains to the advantage of both sides. In this view, Pakistan is a threat to India's security, but can be brought around to a more pacific and accommodative view of the relationship if New Delhi uses an approach built on the promise of mutual gain, particularly economic gain (Dattar 2001). Neo-liberals argue that ultimately Pakistan's leaders and people are not above the logic of costs and benefits. Whatever their sense of national identity and their fear of India, Pakistanis will eventually measure their policies towards their neighbour in terms of the advantages and disadvantages of alternative courses of action. In the end, economic well-being is paramount for any society, and Pakistan will come around to the view that it must cut a deal with India in order to give its people a better life (Raja Mohan 2001a).

Neo-liberals do not reject the entire Nehruvian programme. The Nehruvian insistence on an adequate but not threatening defence posture and a multifaceted relationship with Pakistan is congenial to neo-liberals, who place great emphasis on economic well-being via free market policies. An overly ambitious defence posture, in their view, will channel government and private expenditures into non-productive areas and cramp economic growth (Abraham 2001; Subrahmanyam 2001). In this respect, they do not differ greatly with the Nehruvians. Neo-liberals also support the Nehruvian view of working towards a broad relationship with Pakistan and Pakistanis. The core of the neo-liberal approach is based on the primacy of economics, and therefore anything that goes beyond the traditional focus on military and diplomatic interactions is helpful. However, neo-liberals differ from Nehruvians in two key respects.

First of all, neo-liberals are not great believers in the effectiveness of international institutions and laws as well as bilateral treaties and agreements.[23] The Nehruvian 'obsession' with institutions, laws, treaties, and agreements (for example in the UN, especially in the early years), and the various bilateral accords with Pakistan are, in their view, a negotiatory dead end. The Nehruvian way constitutes a formalistic, old-fashioned approach to diplomacy and statecraft, and has been the bane of India's foreign policy. The UN resolutions are ineffective, even against the humblest states. And the bilateral accords with Pakistan are mere paper commitments, which Islamabad can ignore, even tear up at will. New Delhi should be prepared to scrap any or all of these accords if and when it is necessary to do so; the Nehruvian insistence on sticking by them in rote fashion is unimaginative and unhelpful. Neo-liberals do not necessarily reject these accords, but they want India to adopt a more flexible, non-dogmatic approach.[24]

The second difference with the Nehruvians is on the regional role of the great powers—the US, Russia, China, Japan, and the Europeans. Neo-liberals argue that keeping the great powers out of the region is futile and, worse still, positively harmful to the Indian cause. Great powers are by definition hard to keep out of strategic arenas, and in the case of the US, it is virtually impossible to do so. More importantly, great power involvement could be to India's advantage (Gupta 2000). After the Cold War, the great powers perceive India and Pakistan quite differently. An India that is booming economically in the wake of economic reforms, that is a non-expansionist power and that is a stable multi-ethnic democracy is an asset. Pakistan, with its economic problems, its revisionist agenda in South Asia and its support of revolutionary Islamic groups, and its chaotic, Islamic polity is, by contrast, a potential failed state (Subrahmanyam 2001). In this new geopolitical situation, India should cultivate the great powers and encourage them to lean on Pakistan as a way of bringing Islamabad around to a deal. From the neo-liberal perspective, what India therefore needs is omni-alignment, not non-alignment: an engagement and rapprochement with all the great powers, even China, in the service of a regional order that suits New Delhi's interests, and that is not inimical to great power preferences (Raja Mohan 1998a).

For neo-liberals, then, Pakistan policy must be geared towards bringing Islamabad to the negotiating table. Whereas Nehruvians want to fundamentally change Pakistani thinking, neo-liberals are more 'pragmatic' and 'worldly', insisting that an economic logic will eventually engineer accommodation. Economic development in Pakistan will do more to transform elite and popular attitudes than anything India can do by way of political, social, and cultural engagement. The task of getting Pakistan to come to the table will, in addition, require India to become an economic powerhouse. The example of India's economic growth, the gap in capabilities that will open up as a result, and the potential opportunities for Pakistanis in an accelerating Indian economy will give New Delhi the power to make Pakistan an offer it cannot refuse. When the economic foundation for a new relationship is built, as it increasingly has been over the past decade of reforms, flexibility in India's diplomatic stance will be crucial in encouraging Pakistan to reciprocate with its own brand of new thinking. Finally, the pressures exerted by the great powers on India's behalf will put Pakistan in a mood to negotiate seriously.

The hyperrealist prescription for dealing with Pakistan is not to worry overly about the intensity of communication and contact with that country, or to rely on the imperatives of economic change, or even to turn to others for help. Instead, hyperrealists argue, India must focus on the 'fundamentals' and on policies that have stood the test of time in the international system. Ultimately, the only language that Pakistan understands and heeds, like any other country, is the language of power and violence. The core of India's policy, therefore, is to build its military strength.[25] Given that India is eight times Pakistan's size, it should be in a position to overawe Pakistan militarily. From a position of dominance, New Delhi should dictate terms to Pakistan. With military strength will come an array of options that can be used to raise the costs of Pakistan's intervention in Kashmir. These options should be exercised, sooner rather than later. Taking the fight to Pakistan rather than reacting to Pakistani provocations is the essence of a workable, effective policy (Chellaney 1999b: 541).

What does it mean to take the fight to Pakistan? Hyperrealists argue that India should repay Pakistan in the same coin not only militarily, but also, in addition, politically and economically. Militarily, India should make Pakistan pay a much higher cost for the conflict in Kashmir. At the very least, Indian forces should be more aggressive in counter-insurgency operations, as they were in Punjab. Beyond this, Indian forces could begin to test the Line of Control or even the international boundary. Artillery fire, air strikes, and 'hot pursuit' attacks into Pakistan-held Kashmir would serve notice that India was no longer willing to fight a purely defensive internal war. Finally, at the limit, India should be prepared to attack across the international boundary to threaten Pakistan's heartland. The fact that India and Pakistan are nuclear powers does not bother some hyperrealists, who would seriously contemplate the possibility of 'limited war under nuclear conditions', arguing that India's nuclear superiority will give it 'escalation dominance', that is, the ability to control the pace and direction of military action. Politically, hyperrealists argue, there is no reason why India cannot do what the Pakistanis are doing in Kashmir. New Delhi could begin to fund and arm various dissident groups in Pakistan, including separatists or ethnic rebels in Baluchistan and Sindh, as well as unhappy religious groups in Punjab. India could increasingly play host to prominent dissident leaders as well, especially Sindhis, but also those from the Pakistani side of Kashmir (Chellaney 1999b). Finally, India could resort to economic warfare to raise the costs of conflict. New Delhi could meddle with Pakistan's currency and stock market. It could increase its own defence spending, compelling Pakistan to raise its expenditures, and driving its economy into a fiscal meltdown. As the US drove the Soviet Union out of business, so India could spend Pakistan into oblivion.

Therefore, hyperrealists in effect imply that the collapse or destruction of Pakistan is the only truly viable solution. Pakistan is an implacable foe, and with every setback or defeat it will only rebuild itself for the next round of conflict. After 1971, that should have been clear to India. Pakistanis see compromise and negotiation, restraint and cooperation as signs of weakness and incoherence in India. Unless Pakistan is reduced to a state of permanent chaos or debility, it will, Phoenix-like, rise from the ashes to challenge India again and again.

Nehruvians, neo-liberals, and hypernationalists have quite different prescriptions for how to deal with Pakistan. Nehruvians trust to patient, long-term diplomacy that builds on existing treaties and obligations, defensive defence, society-to-society contact and communication, and non-alignment.

Neo-liberals prefer a pragmatic, flexible approach to Pakistan, a reliance on economic contacts and India's growing economic strength to bring Pakistanis around, a restrained military posture, and alignment with the great powers (especially the US) rather than non-alignment. Hyperrealists want India to rely on power and force rather than treaties and economic links to take the fight to Pakistan, to subvert it from within, and eventually bring about its collapse.

China

The Nehruvian belief that states and peoples can eventually be brought around to make peace with each other extends to its relations with China. Notwithstanding the war of 1962 with China, Nehruvians do not see China as an imperial power trying to intimidate its neighbours. Rather, China is a backward country trying to improve the lives of its huge population, much like India. It is also trying to overcome the trauma of a semi-colonial occupation in the nineteenth century. Its Communist regime is repressive, but has also played a progressive role for its people. The Communists liberated and united China and incurred the wrath of the Western powers, and much of the ire against China in the international system continues to be Western-inspired. China's desire to reintegrate Hong Kong, Macao, and Taiwan is justified because these areas belonged to China historically. China's claim to Tibet is more controversial, but there is little that can be done about the Tibetan situation except hope that eventually China will realize the folly of forcible occupation. While Chinese Communism is distasteful, to mount a crusade against it internationally is counterproductive. Communication and dialogue with China and giving China its due in the international order will modify Chinese policies more than confrontation will.

India's own difficulties with China, from the Nehruvian perspective, arose from Beijing's obduracy and its involvement in the Cold War, and New Delhi's own mistakes. While China was ultimately responsible for the war of 1962, its aggressiveness was momentary and limited. In the Nehruvian view, China and India have historically never been enemies (Bhattacharjee 1999; Ranganathan and Khanna 2000). They represent two ancient civilizations with a fair degree of contact

with each other over two millennia, and no record of
hostilities. In the modern period, they generally have
been friends and are, even now, central to the prospects
of peace and security in Asia (Dixit 1999). India was
supportive of China's national liberation struggle, and
after 1949 of its membership in international society.
The war was an aberration, and was due to a series of
misunderstandings. A settlement over the border issue
and long-term peace and friendship with China are
made easier by these facts.

Nehruvians broadly endorse the kinds of policies
that the Indian government has pursued with China
since 1962 in bringing Beijing around to a settlement.
An adequate defence against China is vital. New
Delhi must be able to defend its borders, and cannot
be caught napping if India–China relations should
suddenly decay, as they did in 1961–2. However,
India's posture along the border should not be
provocative (Ranganathan 1998). Beyond this, India
has to pursue a steady, patient course of diplomacy
with China. Nehruvians have been supportive of
the general thrust of India's diplomacy with China
over the past decade. Before 1988, India insisted
that there could be no real improvement in relations
until the Chinese reverted to the military situation
before 1962, and handed back any territories taken
from 1949 onwards. New Delhi insisted that a border
settlement be based on an acknowledged principle of
demarcation, rather than mere give-and-take. Since
1988, when Rajiv Gandhi became the first Indian
Prime Minister to visit China after the 1962 war, India
has changed its approach. The basic shift has been
to broaden the relationship and refuse to hold other
areas of interaction hostage to a settlement of the
border. Thus, in the 1990s, India signed a number of
confidence-building agreements with China. Over a
decade, the Presidents, Prime Ministers, and foreign
ministers of the two countries met over a dozen
times, more than at any time since 1949. Before 1998,
Indian and Chinese military leaders were meeting
more frequently as well. In 2000, India and China
began an official security dialogue that went beyond
border issues. Finally, India–China trade blossomed,
from a mere $200 million to well over $2 billion
in the course of a decade. India has also agreed to
develop closer social links between the two societies

in terms of cultural, scientific, and sporting exchanges
(Dutt 1998).

Beyond this bilateral engagement, Nehruvians
believe that India and China have a broad geopolitical
interest in common, namely to ensure that Asia
does not become either an arena of conflict between
Asian countries themselves, or an object of Western
influence once again (Bhattacharjee 1999; Dixit
1998). India and China, as rising powers, could come
into conflict as they grow in capabilities and influence.
A number of other Asian conflicts and rivalries exist.
The Western states, and particularly the US, without
the Soviet Union to hold them in check, could begin
to interfere in the affairs of Asia, and exert pressures
on Asian countries in the name of humanitarian
concerns such as human rights. Nehruvians therefore
see a future concert with China and other Asian
powers, including Russia, as a long-term goal. India,
China, and the major Asian powers should come
together to build confidence and cooperation amongst
themselves—to avoid mutual conflict and to keep the
US and other Westerners at bay (Dutt 1999).

Neo-liberals view China differently. India–China
relations in the ancient or even more recent past are
largely irrelevant. It is the present and future of India
and China that must be determinative. In a globalized
world, where the barriers to trade, investment, and
technology have loosened as never before, the past
holds few lessons. Older quarrels, such as over the
border, are vestiges and anachronisms that have
little bearing on contemporary choices, which must
be concerned with how states can manage the
opportunities and threats of globalization above all
(Swaran Singh 1998: 38). Solving the border quarrel
is a relatively insignificant issue, though it will not be
easy to dispose of. Looking at China through the lens
of the border dispute is the wrong way to assess the
relationship. It is China's economic revolution and the
effects of economic change on its foreign and security
policies that are crucial. China is rapidly becoming a
great power. Its economic power is giving it enormous
leverage, even with rivals such as the US. In its pursuit
of great power status via rapid economic change, it is,
in addition, committed to pragmatic policies—with
Taiwan, Japan, and its other neighbours, including
India, as well as the US. For India, this has at least

two implications. First, the primary goal of grand strategy in a globalizing world is economic strength. Economic strength is good in itself in terms of better living standards and a more resilient society, but it is also a source of influence in international affairs. India must emulate China to be secure against its neighbour in the decades to come, and, more importantly, to manage its relations with other great powers as Beijing does (Raja Mohan 2000a). Second, with its eye on economic progress, China is likely to be a restrained power interested in managing and resolving conflict.[26]

Neo-liberals support the Nehruvians on an adequate rather than extravagant defence, and on a multifaceted engagement with China. From the point of view of neo-liberals, though, it is economics that should lead the way. China is interested in economic advancement through trade, investment, and technology transfers, as is India. Trade with China could be much larger than it is at present. India and China could, in addition, invest in each other's economies. There are areas of technology where they could cooperate, especially information technology (Darshan 2000a). Neo-liberals argue that India will benefit from an economic relationship with China, and in addition will gain diplomatic leverage: New Delhi should aim to 'do a China' on China. With a steadily deepening economic engagement, differences over the border and Beijing's relationship with Islamabad will be easier to resolve, on terms that suit India. The problem, in the neo-liberal view, is India, not China. India has not learned to be coldly calculative, to place economics Centre-stage in its external relations, to shed its prejudices about market-driven economics and globalization, to marginalize old-fashioned disputes over territory, and to forsake old methods, policies, and agreements. Neo-liberals are impatient with both Nehruvians and hyperrealists who they see as being old-fashioned about economics, security, and the conduct of diplomacy.

Thus, in the neo-liberal view, the Nehruvian interest in a concert with China and Russia and other Asian powers is unrealistic, even counterproductive (Raja Mohan 2000c; 1999b). Older security problems and rivalries will gradually dissipate as economics comes Centre-stage. A concert of Asians to regulate intra-Asian conflicts is an idea whose time has

probably come and gone. An economic league in Asia would be more to the point. As for even a loose alliance against the US and the West, this is highly improbable. China, Russia, and India individually have much greater stakes in a relationship with the US and the West than with each other, for the most part. In any case, India, as a secular, modern democracy, has much more in common with Western countries than with China, or even the new Russia. Flirting with China and Russia is tactically understandable: it is a signal to the US not to take India for granted. But an Asian concert of powers that excludes the US in particular is virtually impossible.

While Nehruvians think that India and China can be friends and allies and while neo-liberals argue that India and China can cut a strategic deal if they develop their economic relations, hyperrealists see China as the greatest military threat to India, far more so than Pakistan (Chellaney 1999c; Karnad 1994a; Puri 2000). The Nehruvians, in the hyperrealist view, failed in the 1950s and 1960s to comprehend Chinese goals and methods, and to prepare to meet force with force. They are no wiser about China forty years later: communication and contacts with China will do little to change the basic expansionist and aggressive tenets of the authoritarian Chinese leadership; and it is absurd to think that the two countries can combine to manage Asian security (Nanda 1999). The neo-liberals are also misguided about China. Their faith in the power of economics is exaggerated. For China, pragmatism in foreign and security policy and economic modernization is merely tactical, and will be dispensed with when Beijing feels strong enough to use unilateral means. India must therefore prepare itself militarily to deal with China. Nuclear deterrence is vital if India is to be secure against China (Singh 1998: 14). In addition, India's conventional military power must be augmented to defend Indian territory against the largest army in the world.

Beyond military preparedness on India's part, New Delhi must knit together an alliance of Asian countries that will contain China. It must do to China what China has done to India, namely encirclement.[27] In the 1950s, China took over Tibet. In the 1960s and 1970s it carefully cultivated Pakistan, diplomatically and militarily. Whenever possible, it has sought to increase its influence in South Asia amongst the smaller states, especially Bangladesh and Nepal. In the 1990s, it began to penetrate Burma. Hyperrealists argue that it is time for India to break out of this encirclement with its own counter-encirclement of China. New Delhi must put together an alliance in Southeast and East Asia all along the Chinese periphery. This would involve strengthening relations with Taiwan, Japan, South Korea, and the ASEAN states, including Vietnam and Burma, all of whom in the end must fear China more than anyone else (Chellaney 2000a; Dutt 2000). Hyperrealists favour an Indian naval presence in the South China Sea, as much as the Chinese navy is a presence in the Indian Ocean. Some hyperrealists would go so far as to insist that India reopen the Tibet question and help counter China's rule (Karnad 1994a; Chellaney 2000b; Malik 2000). A counter-encirclement will assume even greater importance as the US's position in Asia diminishes. Hyperrealists argue that the US will eventually have to pull out of Asia, leaving the field open to China. At that point, Asians will have to face up to the responsibilities of containing China by themselves.

In sum, as with Pakistan, hyperrealists envisage India taking the fight to China. They see India as being too complacent about China, and merely reactive to Chinese diplomatic and strategic moves. The Chinese, in their view, only respect power. India's own military strength, as well as an alliance system in Asia, will in aggregate be powerful enough to replace the US as the main check on Chinese ambitions. Hyperrealists see India as a potential pole of attraction in the international system, particularly so in Asia. India should be the linchpin of a system of alliances, from Israel at one end to Taiwan at the other, which combats both Islamic fundamentalism and Chinese expansionism.

Nehruvians, neo-liberals, and hyperrealists have quite different perspectives on China. China at one level is like Pakistan—a neighbour with whom India has a territorial dispute and with whom hostilities are possible. At another level, with its astonishing economic growth and size, China represents a rising power, a great power in the making, at the very least. Nehruvians in the end believe that India can create the conditions for peace and cooperation with the giant to

the north, much as it can with Pakistan. Neo-liberals argue that economics can lead the way even with China, and that a pragmatic approach to the border can bring about a stable relationship. Hyperrealists see a rising China as aggressive and expansionist, and therefore argue that only Indian military power and a containment of China by a ring of Asian powers will hold Beijing in check.

The United States

For most countries in the world, dealing with the great powers, whether nearby or distant, is a special challenge of grand strategy. Nehruvians, neo-liberals, and hyperrealists differ as much on this issue as on relations with Pakistan and China. All three groups recognize that the only great power of any significance for India is the US, and that the US is not a military threat in any foreseeable future. However, it is a diplomatic threat. Often, US policies hurt Indian interests collaterally rather than intentionally. US regional and global policies run counter to Indian preferences in various ways, and managing both the intended and unintended effects of US policies pose a special challenge, given the US's superiority over all other powers.

The Nehruvian prescription for dealing with great powers is non-alignment. Non-alignment is not neutrality, and it is not amoralism. It is a policy built around three elements: first, a refusal to be permanently attached to any great power and to judge international issues in the light of India's interests and general principles of international security; second, the fashioning of a coalition of Third World countries against great power dominance; and third, mediating between rival great powers and the fostering of international institutions and law so that the international system as a whole is made safer, and weak Third World powers in particular are afforded more protection. In short, autonomy, balancing, mediation, and institutionalism are at the heart of the Nehruvian system for managing relations with the great powers. These points deserve some elaboration.

First of all, according to Nehruvians, non-alignment served to keep India outside the East–West fray for the most part. India was able to avoid being entangled in other people's quarrels, and preserve its freedom to choose one side or the other or not to choose sides as it saw fit. Non-alignment served India's domestic stability as well. If India had chosen one particular side in the Cold War, this may have encouraged the other side to meddle in its domestic politics to punish it for its partisanship. Also, given the ideological divide between the Left and Right within India, alignment with either superpower would have been disruptive.

Second, non-alignment helped to construct a Third World coalition. Nehru himself scorned the 'trade unionism' of the Third World, but Nehruvians generally saw non-alignment as a form of collective resistance against imperial powers. Over the years, the non-aligned countries adopted a perceptible tilt towards the weaker superpower, the Soviet Union. In classical balance of power fashion, NAM drifted towards the weaker of the two superpowers to gain leverage with the more dominant superpower.

Third, in the Nehruvian view, non-alignment is more than a rejection of alliance politics and resistance to the great powers. It is an insistence that the smaller powers can help to mediate the differences between the great powers, and that international institutions, organizations, and law matter and are particularly important for the protection of weaker powers. For Nehruvians, this is a vital and ultimately the most positive aspect of non-alignment. Non-aligned states, free from the constraints of alliance responsibilities, enjoy a vantage point from which they can not only judge the actions of the great powers, but also from which they can help bridge differences. New Delhi might be in a position to offer information, ideas, and interpretations of events that would bring the rivals closer together. The mediatory function of non-alignment, Nehruvians argue, is vital for international peace and stability, and especially for the security of the smaller countries because in any global confrontation, their survival, independence, and development will be at risk (Bidwai 1998: 97).

Finally, Nehruvians argue that international institutions can play a role in checking the great powers. International organizations, international law, and international norms and conventions are ways of tethering the great powers. By promoting procedures, rules, and debate in international relations, the smaller powers might be able to slow down the great powers or, better still, get them to reconsider their goals and policies. The great powers may manipulate international procedures, rules, and debate to their advantage, but this is not certain. In any case, an international system with procedures, rules, and forums for debate must be better than one without.

Nehruvians argue that non-alignment in this larger sense is relevant in the post-Cold War world. With the US rampant, preserving India's autonomy is an even more challenging task. Non-alignment and NAM continue to be a refuge for countries that do not want to bandwagon with Washington (Rajan 1991: 24; Goyal 1991: 23). So, too, balancing against US power is a vital interest. Strictly speaking, balancing against the US is impossible. However, a coalition of developing states could resist US pressures on selected issues. The possibility of Indian leadership of a resistive coalition could well enlarge India's bargaining power with Washington. Nehruvians in the post-Cold War period also regard an India-China-Russia combine as a response to US hegemony. In the longer term, a concert of Asian powers could hold the US at bay (Dutt 1999). Since Nehruvians worry about the polarizing effects of a balance of power politics, they also support the view that India should continue to act as a mediator with the US. Thus, some Nehruvians propose that India can represent non-aligned interests to the US and act as a moderate go-between (Bidwai 1998: 97). Finally, in the post-Cold War period, a non-aligned posture that attempts to rally weaker countries in international institutions and around the flag of international rules and norms can in some measure hope to subvert the US's hold on power. Since the US is using international institutions, laws, and conventions for its own purposes, Indian diplomacy must be geared towards both sustaining international organization and preventing its manipulation by the US and its allies.

It is on the issue of how India should deal with the great powers that neo-liberalism defines its differences with both the Nehruvians and hyperrealists most clearly. For the neo-liberals, relations with the great powers represent opportunities as much as threats. India will be a full-fledged great power, in the neo-liberal view. This is more or less inevitable. While

Nehruvians do not disagree with the neo-liberals on India's destiny as a great power, for them India's great power aspirations must be built on autarky, that is, on self-reliance. Neo-liberals argue by contrast that in the contemporary world, this is not possible. India can only become a great power by raising its economic growth rates, and this is feasible if India works not against, but rather with, the great powers as a way of increasing trade, technology transfers, and investment (Gonsalves 2001).

Non-alignment, and everything it represents, therefore seems dreadfully old-fashioned to neo-liberals. In the neo-liberal view, the great powers are no longer in fundamental conflict (Raja Mohan 1999b: 31). With the end of the Cold War, there is no Manichean conflict animating international relations. One side won the Cold War, namely the United States and the Western nations, and the other side lost. The victors are not in conflict: the United States and its Western partners and Japan remain allies. Those who lost the Cold War, moreover, have accepted the fundamental tenets of the victors. There are, therefore, no rival alliance blocs vying for India's or anyone else's membership. Choosing between two great blocs and two ideological systems is no longer a factor (Malhotra 1995: 13; Mansingh 1999: 8; Raja Mohan 1999b: 31). Given that there are no great powers locked in conflict, the mediatory role of non-aligned states is also no longer a factor of any significance.

Most importantly, for neo-liberals, the idea of resisting the great powers is anachronistic. For one thing, there is only one truly great power, the United States, and its power is so overwhelming that to conceive of resistance in any real sense is impractical. Since the United States leads a coalition of great powers, its preponderance is only magnified. Besides, resistance to the great powers implies that these powers are attempting to force countries to do something that they do not wish to do. Neo-liberals argue that this is not the case. A liberal global economic order and even global non-proliferation, the two areas where the great powers do twist arms, are in the interest of most states. Even India, with some qualifications, gains from both. It is in India's interest to promote an open trading and financial

system worldwide. It is also in India's interest to curb the spread of weapons of mass destruction (WMDs). While neo-liberals want India to be a nuclear weapons power, albeit a restrained one, they also want India to join the non-proliferation order as a way of curbing the spread of WMDs (Raja Mohan 1999d: 38–9; 1998b: 44).

Neo-liberals argue that after the Cold War, the US, by and large, is no longer interested in the vast majority of smaller powers. The problem for most of the smaller powers is not therefore pressures applied against them by the big powers, but rather their own economic backwardness, malgovernance, regional hostilities, and vulnerability to fundamentalism and various non-traditional security threats (small arms, drugs, criminal mafias). The US in particular is a potential resource in dealing with these challenges. For countries like India, the real problem posed by Washington is therefore not so much its desire to dominate as its unwillingness to help the weaker states deal with these challenges. From this vantage point, resistance to the US is tantamount to cutting off one's nose to spite one's face. The challenge before the weaker powers, including India, is not how to resist the US, but rather how to cut a deal with it pragmatically and with dignity (Raja Mohan 1999c: 31, 37; Malhotra 1995: 13).

Whereas the Nehruvians want to stay aloof from great power entanglements, mediate between the great powers, and resist the domination of these powers, and neo-liberals want to cut a deal with the great powers, hyperrealists, by contrast, want India to break into the club of the great powers, to bust into the inner circle of the international order. Their view of India's relations with the great powers does not completely reject the Nehruvian and neo-liberal approaches. It does not reject the Nehruvian non-aligned view of India's role vis-à-vis the great powers; nor does it turn its back on cutting deals with other great powers, as advocated by the neo-liberals. These are acceptable lines of policy when India is weak, but they should not become the ends of policy per se. The hyperrealist view is that India has all the appurtenances of a great power, and can, through an act of will, transform its potential into actuality. Ultimately, India must sit at the high table of international affairs as a complete and assertive equal, whether the other great powers like it or not. Sitting at the table, India will help shape the world order, commensurate with its preferences.

Hyperrealists regard the international system as an anarchical arena, where power is the ultimate arbiter. In such a system, the only way of restraining the great powers is to make India strong enough to defend its interests. Hyperrealists argue that neither Nehruvians nor neo-liberals understand the necessities of power. Nehruvians are idealistic in their view that non-alignment is a means of achieving autonomy. Non-alignment is the refuge of weak powers. It works as long as it suits the great powers. In the end, India itself, during the Cold War, was forced to play a balance of power game in order to safeguard its interests. As for the rest of the Nehruvian policy—of mediation and resistance to the great powers—this also holds little appeal. Mediation does nothing for India, and a policy of resistance built on a coalition of weak non-aligned powers is futile. Nor do hyperrealists set much store by international organizations, law, and regimes in restraining the great powers, arguing, like all realists, that these are creatures of states and exist at the pleasure of the greatest powers (Chellaney 1999b: 558). Thus, procedures, rules, and debates are likely to be used by the strong against the weak, and not the other way around.

In the hyperrealist view, neo-liberals are just as guilty of woolly thinking. The neo-liberal argument that economics is the key to power in the post-Cold War international system is, in the hyperrealist view, based on a very limited, if not altogether false, reading of international history. The post-Cold War period is not different from any other period of history: military power remains the sine qua non of international security and status just as it always has. Hyperrealists maintain that the neo-liberal belief in 'economics over politics' is profoundly mistaken. If anything, politics comes before economics. In international relations, this means that military power comes before economic power. States that are front-rank military powers become front-rank economic powers, not the other way around (Chellaney 1999b: 529–31; Karnad 1994a: 3). A state that resolves to turn itself

into a major military power will solve the economic and technological problems that confront it. A state that goes around the world trying to beg and borrow economically and technologically cannot gird itself up for the challenges of social transformation, and is therefore doomed to remain a secondary power.

Relations with the US must therefore be conducted in quite a different way. New Delhi must be assertive in its relations with Washington. This means, amongst other things, being clear and firm about vital Indian interests (Karnad 1999: 40). On these, India must refuse to compromise. Thus, the nuclear programme is non-negotiable with the US. The US decision-makers must be told that India is a great-power-in-the-making, and that nuclear weapons are essential in solidifying India's status and security. Thus, US intervention in regional affairs is also tolerable as long as it is supportive of Indian goals, but on the whole Washington is not welcome in South Asia, particularly not as a mediator on Kashmir (Ramesh 1999: 3538).[28] Beyond assertiveness, India should signal its desire for a partnership with the US. When the US begins to withdraw from Asia, it will be in its interest to see India become a confident and versatile military power. An India–US alliance is possible, particularly against the common enemy, China (Chellaney 2001). India and the US also have a common interest in combating Islamic fundamentalism and terrorism (Karnad 1994b: 56–8). In the long term, however, given the logic of international politics, the US will resist India's rise to power as it will China's. Indians must be prepared to tough it out against US intimidation. The only way of dealing with the US is for India to build its military power. India must eventually be in a position to deter the US from intervening militarily in and around India's sphere of influence in South Asia, the Indian Ocean, the Gulf, nearby Southeast Asia, and of course in Indian domestic politics. While India can take the fight to Pakistan and China, it will not be in a position to do so against the US in any foreseeable future. India must therefore rely primarily on dissuasive power vis-à-vis the US.

To summarize: every country in the world has to worry about how to deal with the United States. Nehruvians, neo-liberals, and hyperrealists propose three quite different ways of dealing with the US. Nehruvians see it as an imperial power that cannot countenance any rivals, and that wants to preserve its pre-eminence at the expense of powers like India. The only way to deal with the US is to resist American policies and power by building a coalition of Third World states and others who worry about Washington's dominance. Out of resistance may come the 'conversion' of the US to points of view that are more favourable to India, and eventually to cooperation. Neo-liberals take the opposite view. For them, the US is the dominant power, one that can be supportive of Indian goals, and there is little option but to bandwagon with Washington. Hyperrealists differ from both Nehruvians and neo-liberals in arguing that the only way of dealing with the US is to build India into a military power of the first rank.

CONCLUSION

Nehruvians, neo-liberals, and hyperrealists dominate the grand strategic debate in India. The three schools are not new. From 1947 onwards, if not before, there were thinkers who were Nehruvian, neo-liberal, and hyperrealist in their approaches. For instance, the Congress party and the political Left were Nehruvians. The old Swatantra Party was close to the neo-liberals of today. The Jan Sangh had a hyperrealist bent. There are commentators in the press and academia, as well as policymakers in virtually every institution in India—political parties, the bureaucracy, the military—who can be identified with the three schools. Put differently, there are Nehruvians, neo-liberals, and hyperrealists cutting across the various segments and institutions of Indian life. All three are to be found in the press, academia, and India's governmental institutions.

The roots of the three schools of strategic thinking lie in three distinct political ideologies. To put the matter squarely, Nehruvians are Left liberals, neo-liberals are classical liberals or libertarians, and hyperrealists are conservatives. If so, the frequently heard call for Indians to be 'non-partisan' and 'non-political' with respect to international relations and security has its limits: it is not easy to cast aside deeply held beliefs about political life.

While there are areas of agreement between the three schools, there are enduring differences. This is not necessarily a weakness. Indeed, the existence of differences can be a strength. Grand strategic ideas in contention can help sharpen the thinking of each school. Contention can serve to check the extremists in each school. The expression of difference and the rise to dominance of one school or another, with shifts in the political mood of the country, can be a vital corrective, and prevent orthodoxy from installing itself. In grand strategy, as in so many other spheres of public life, difference can be vitalizing.

NOTES

1. Many of these themes are evident in Nehru's speeches. See, for instance, Nehru's thoughts on the importance of the Commonwealth and the United Nations in Nehru (1961, pp. 132–81).

2. On the fragility of the balance of power approach, see Nehru (1946/1981, pp. 536–48).

3. See Raja Mohan (2001), on how China, in contrast to India, has used trade and economic relations more generally to 'leverage' relations with the US. Also, see Baru (1998, pp. 66–7), on the influence of economics in statecraft.

4. On the importance of economics and the market in strategy, see Gupta (2001a and b); Raja Mohan (2001b); and Ramesh (1999).

5. I use the term hyperrealist to signify that the proponents of these views value force and unilateral methods much more than a prudential realism would allow.

6. For this kind of view of military and economic power, see Karnad (1994a, p. 2), and Chellaney (1999b, pp. 529–34).

7. See Krishna (1984, pp. 270–1), on Nehru's use of the term 'anarchy' in the context of international relations. On the pursuit of national interest and the necessity of defence, see Nehru (1963 [1961]: 45–6).

8. This was the historic 6 March 1946 radio broadcast by Nehru on the occasion of the institution of an Interim Government leading up to Indian Independence.

9. He makes the point that integrating with the global economy not only brings prosperity, but also status and influence, a point that India should learn from China.

10. Here he notes that '... economic policy can itself be an instrument of foreign policy if it enables a country to win friends and influence people'.

11. On the importance of national power or strength, see Chellaney (1999a, p. xviii).

12. See Chellaney on why India needs to adopt a more 'punitive', less 'reactive' posture vis-à-vis Pakistan.

13. Like the neo-liberals, Mattoo supports the signing of the CTBT and FMCT. However, unlike them, he does not reject the possibility of disarmament.

14. Mattoo notes approvingly the International Court of Justice's Advisory Opinion 'that the threat or use of nuclear weapons would generally be contrary to the rules of international law applicable in armed conflict, and particularly the principles and rules of humanitarian law'. He refers to the ICJ judgement in making his case for disarmament.

15. This was argued by Arundhati Ghose during the discussions at the seminar organized by the India Habitat Centre, 19 September 1999. See *Post-Pokhran II: The National Way Ahead*, p. 120.

16. Bharat Karnad does appear to support the development and deployment of battlefield nuclear weapons, consistent with a kind of war-fighting posture. Brig. Vijai K. Nair, on the other hand, opposes war-fighting and tactical nuclear weapons.

17. For a more extended discussion on this point, see Karnad (1998), pp. 115–20.

18. Karnad made these remarks at the seminar held at the India Habitat Centre, New Delhi, 19 September 1999. See 'Discussion—Session I', in *Post-Pokhran II: The National Way Ahead*, p. 118.

19. This characterization of the moderate posture relies on Bajpai (2000).

20. Ibid.

21. See the statement of Arundhati Ghose, quoted in Ram and Muralidharan (1998, p. 31).

22. Nehruvians in effect support what is called 'defensive' or 'non-offensive' defence. On these notions, see Gates (1991) and Moeller (1992).

23. In this respect, Indian neo-liberals are not the same as Western academic neo-liberal institutionalists, who set great store by the possibility of rules, norms, and institutions.

24. C. Raja Mohan made this point at a panel discussion on India's relations with Nepal at the India Habitat Centre, New Delhi, 22 November 2001.

25. For a general argument on the need to build military strength, see Chellaney (1999a, pp. 527–95); and Karnad (1994a, pp. 1–15).

26. See Raja Mohan (2000b) on Chinese pragmatism as a function of its modernization drive. Raja Mohan approvingly quotes Deng Xiaoping's maxim, 'Maintain a low profile, keep a cool head, and never take the lead'.

27. Chellaney, 'The Dragon Dance', http://www.hindustantimes.com/nonfram/230102/detide01.asp.

28. Ramesh urges the US to encourage India and Pakistan to move forward in resuming a dialogue, but even as pragmatic a neo-liberal as Ramesh does not canvas the possibility of US mediation on Kashmir.

REFERENCES

Abraham, Amrita. 2001. 'Mission Possible', *Indian Express*, 28 June.

Anonymous. 'IT May Bridge Gap in Sino-Indian ties', *News Time*, 23 July.

Bajpai, Kanti. 2000. 'India's Nuclear Posture After Pokhran II', *International Studies*, 37 (4), pp. 284–99.

Baru, Sanjaya. 2006. 'National Security in an Open Economy', in Sanjaya Baru (ed.), *Strategic Consequences of India's Economic Performance*. New Delhi: Academic Foundation, pp. 89–90.

———. 1998a. 'Economic Diplomacy', *Seminar*, Vol. 461, pp. 66–9.

———. 1998b. 'The Economic Dimensions of India's Foreign Policy', *World Affairs*, 2 (2), pp. 90–1.

Bhattacharjee, Jay. 1999. 'Hindi-Chini Saath-Saath: Can We Pull It Off?', *The Pioneer*, 17 September.

Bidwai, Praful. 1999. 'Lessons from Pakistan', *Frontline*, 19 November, pp. 110–11.

———. 1998. 'An Unequal Deal', *Frontline*, 11 September.

Chellaney, Brahma. 2002. 'The Dragon Dance', http://www.hindustantimes.com/nonfram/230102/detide01.asp. (no longer available).

———. 2001. 'Beating About the Bush', *The Hindu*, 8 March.

———. 2000a. 'Two-Timing China', *Hindustan Times*, 14 January.

———. 2000b. 'No Syrupy Sentiment, Please', *Hindustan Times*, 17 May.

———. 1999a. 'Preface', in Brahma Chellaney (ed.), *Securing India's Future in the New Millennium*. New Delhi: Orient Longman and the Centre for Policy Research.

———. 1999b. 'Challenges to India's National Security', in Brahma Chellaney (ed.), *Securing India's Future in the New Millennium*. New Delhi: Orient Longman and the Centre for Policy Research.

———. 1999c. 'Fall of Vajpayee', *Hindustan Times*, 21 April.

Cortright, David and Amitabh Mattoo (eds). 1996. *India and the Bomb: Public Opinion and Nuclear Choices*. Notre Dame: Notre Dame University Press.

Darshan, Rajneesh. 2000a. 'No Need to get Carried Away', *The Pioneer*, 22 June.

Dattar, Ashok. 2001. 'Will We Agree to Disagree One More Time?', *Indian Express*, 13 July.

Dhar, P.N. 2001. 'Let Us Not Bury the Future in Our Past', *The Telegraph*, 13 July.

Dixit, J.N. 2001a. 'No Euphoria Please', *Hindustan Times*, 11 July.

———. 2001b. 'Bring Back Shimla Spirit', *Indian Express*, 22 June.

———. 1999. 'Chinese Checkers', *Telegraph*, 4 May.

———. 1998. 'Signs of Revival', *Indian Express*, 28 May.

Dubey, Muchkund. 2002. 'The World Nuclear Order and India', *The Hindu*, 27 May.

———. 1999. 'India's Foreign Policy: Aims and Strategies', in Nancy Jetly (ed.), *India's Foreign Policy: Challenges and Prospects*. New Delhi: Vikas.

Dutt, J.K. 2000. 'China Muscle Building on Sea', *The Statesman*, 20 January.

Dutt, V.P. 1999. 'India, China Russia Syndrome: Is it Illusion or Reality?' *Tribune*, 17 April.

———. 1998. 'India-China: Promise and Limitation', in Lalit Mansingh, M. Venkatraman, Dilip Lahiri, J.N. Dixit, Bhabani Sen Gupta, and J.S. Pande (eds), *India's Foreign Policy: Agenda for the 21st Century*, Vol. 2. New Delhi: Konark Publishers and Foreign Service Institute.

Gates, David. 1991. *Non-Offensive Defence: An Alternative Strategy for NATO?* New York: St Martin's Press.

Ghose, Arundhati. 1999. 'Post-Pokhran II: Arms Control and Disarmament Aspects', in *Post-Pokhran II: The National Way Ahead*. New Delhi: India Habitat Centre.

Gonsalves, Eric. 2001. 'India and the Bush Administration', *The Hindu*, 16 February.

Goyal, D.R. 1991. 'Gulf War: NAM's Poor Response', *World Focus*, 12(8), p. 23.

Gupta, Shekhar. 2001a. 'The Real Battle Will be for the Market', *Indian Express*, 13 January, http://www.indian-express.com/ie/daily/20010003/shekhar.htm.

———. 2001b. Editorial, 'Business, Not Politics', *Indian Express*, 11 January 2001, http://www.expressindia.com/ie/daily/20000915/shekhar2.htm

———. 2000. 'Don't Fear the K-Word', *Indian Express*, 18 March.

Johnston, Alastair Iain. 1995. *Cultural Realism: Strategic Culture and Grand Strategy in Chinese History*. Princeton, NJ: Princeton University Press.

Karnad, Bharat. 2000. 'A Sucker's Payoff', *Seminar*, No. 485, January.

———. 1999. 'Policy on CTBT', *World Focus*, 20(10–11–12).

———. 1998. 'A Thermonuclear Deterrent', in Amitabh Mattoo (ed.), *India's Nuclear Deterrent After Pokhran II*. New Delhi: Har-Anand.

———. 1994a. 'Introduction', in Bharat Karnad (ed.), *Future Imperilled: India's Security in the 1990s and Beyond*. New Delhi: Viking.

———. 1994b. 'India's Weak Geopolitics and What To Do About It', in Bharat Karnad (ed.), *Future Imperilled: India's Security in the 1990s and Beyond*. New Delhi: Viking.

Khan, Rasheeduddin. 1993. 'Fundamentalism/Communalism in South Asia', *World Focus*, 14(11–12).

Kotru. M.L. 2001. 'Indo-Pak Dialogue', *News Time*, 23 June.

Krishna, Gopal. 1984. 'India and International Order: Retreat from Idealism', in Hedley Bull and Adam Watson (eds), *The Expansion of International Society*. Oxford: Clarendon Press.

Malhotra, Inder. 1995. 'Indo-US Relations', *World Focus*, 16(8).

Malik, J. Mohan. 2000. 'Indian Sun Should Follow the Chinese Sun', *The Pioneer*, 24 August.

Mansingh, Surjit. 1999. 'Need for Broad-Based Relationship', *World Focus*, 20(2).

Mattoo, Amitabh. 1999. 'Post-Pokhran II: Arms Control and Disarmament Issues', in *Post-Pokhran II: The National Way Ahead*. New Delhi: India Habitat Centre.

Moeller, Bjorn. 1992. *Common Security and Non-Offensive Defense: A Neorealist Perspective*. Boulder: Lynne Rienner.

Nair, Brig. Vijai K. 1998. 'The Structure of an Indian Nuclear Deterrent', in Amitabh Mattoo (ed.), *India's Nuclear Deterrent After Pokhran II*. New Delhi: Har-Anand, pp. 90–1.

Nakra, Brig. J.C. 2001. 'Indo-Pak Relations and the J-K Problem', *National Herald*, 22 June.

Nanda, S.R. 1999. 'Beyond Borders', *The Pioneer*, 20 April.

Nehru, Jawaharlal. 1946/1981. *The Discovery of India*. New Delhi: The Jawaharlal Nehru Memorial Fund and Oxford University Press

———. 1961/1963. *India's Foreign Policy: Selected Speeches, September 1946–April 1961*, New Delhi: The Publications Division, Ministry of Information and Broadcasting, Government of India.

Parthasarathy, Malini. 2001. 'Agra, Just a Beginning', *The Hindu*, 12 July.

Puri, Rakshat. 2000. 'Stooping Not to Conquer', *News Time*, 5 February.

Raja Mohan, C. 2001a. 'Pakistan as a Bridge State?' *The Hindu*, 21 June.

———. 2001b. 'Trade as Strategy: Chinese Lessons', *The Hindu*, 16 August.

———. 2000a. 'US Shadow Over Sino-Indian talks', *The Hindu*, 30 May.

———. 2000b. 'Modesty and Grand Strategy', *The Hindu*, 28 September.

———. 2000c. 'The Asian Balance of Power', *Seminar*, No. 487, http://www.india-seminar.com/2000/487/487%20raja%20mohan.htm.

———. 1999a. 'Post-Pokhran II: Nuclear Defiance and Reconciliation', in *Post-Pokhran II: The National Way Ahead*. New Delhi: India Habitat Centre.

———. 1999b. 'Agni and Sino-Indian Ties', *The Hindu*, 16 April.

———. 1999c. 'The US and the Kargil War', *World Focus*, 20(6–7).

Raja Mohan, C. 1999d. 'Nuclear Diplomacy: The Art of the Deal', *World Focus*, 20(10–11–12).

———. 1998a. 'Nuclear Balance in Asia', *The Hindu*, 11 June.

———. 1998b. 'The Nuclear Commandments', *World Focus*, 19(10–11–12).

Rajan, M.S. 1991. 'India and the NAM', *World Focus*, 12(11–12), p. 24.

Ram, N. and Sukumar Muralidharan. 1998. 'India Must Say "No" to CTBT and FMCT', *Frontline*, 3 July.

Ramesh, Jairam. 1999. 'Yankee Go Home, But Take Me With You': Yet Another Perspective on Indo-American Relations', *Economic and Political Weekly*, XXXIV(50), pp. 3532–44.

Ranganathan, C.V. 1998. 'India-China Relations: Retrospect and Prospects', in Lalit Mansingh, M. Venkatraman, Dilip Lahiri, J.N. Dixit, Bhabani Sen Gupta, and J.S. Pande (eds), *India's Foreign Policy: Agenda for the 21st Century*, Vol. 2. New Delhi: Konark Publishers and Foreign Service Institute.

Ranganathan, C.V. and Vinod C. Khanna. 2000. 'India-China Relations-II', *National Herald*, 28 April.

Rangarajan, L.N. (ed. and trans.) 1987. Kautilya, *The Arthashastra*. New Delhi: Penguin Books.

Singh, Jasjit. 1998. 'The Challenges of Strategic Defence', *Frontline*, 24 April.

Singh, Swaran. 1998. 'Sino-Indian Relations: Scope for Expanding Ties', *World Focus*, 19(10–11–12).

Subrahmanyam, K. 2001. 'Invitation to Peace: Pakistan, Not Kashmir is the Issue', *Times of India*, 18 June.

———. 1999. 'Asia's Security Concerns in the 21st Century', in Jasjit Singh (ed.), *Asian Security Concerns in the 21st Century*. New Delhi: Knowledge World.

———. 1998a. 'Nature of CTBT in Pragmatist's View', *Economic Times*, 20 July.

———. 1998b. 'Nuclear India in Global Politics', *Strategic Digest*, 28(12).

———. 1998c. 'Nuclear Tests: What Next?' *IIC Quarterly*, Summer/Monsoon.

36 Indian Defence Policy

Sumit Ganguly

Despite persistent rural and urban poverty today, India is a major Asian military power with global aspirations. It is a self-declared nuclear weapons state; it possesses a modest but growing nuclear arsenal, a million man army, a substantial and modern air force, and a two-carrier navy.[1] The Indian military has successfully prosecuted four wars against Pakistan (1947–8, 1965, 1971, and 1999) and is no longer likely to countenance a military calamity as it did with China in 1962.[2] It has also successfully helped suppress a series of domestic insurgencies and is currently involved in at least one major operation against insurgents in the state of Jammu and Kashmir.[3] Despite the end of the Cold War, many of India's security problems have not diminished. From the standpoint of Indian defence planners, the country faces two major external threats and a number of continuing internal challenges. The external threats emanate from Pakistan in the immediate term, and from China over the longer horizon. The internal challenges involve secessionist movements, class-based uprisings, and the lurking possibility of mass-scale communal violence.

Although many of the Cold War-era threats remain extant, the end of the Cold War and the dissolution of the Soviet Union has led to important changes in India's foreign policy orientation, and thereby some commensurate changes in the defence policy. Despite India's continued reliance on Russia, the principal successor state to the Soviet Union, for weapons purchases, India is now increasingly seeking to diversify its sources of supply. More than a decade after the end of the Cold War, Indian defence planners have started to shed their anachronistic Cold War-era apprehensions. Accordingly, in June 2005, India and the United States signed a ten-year defence pact. The signing of the defence pact was the culmination of a series of expanded, military-to-military contacts, joint military exercises, and high-level exchanges that had commenced in the waning days of the Cold War (Ganguly 2003).

This chapter will trace the origins of India's defence policies from the immediate post-Independence era, assess and discuss the significance of key turning points, evaluate its present status, and discuss some possible future trends. Four key propositions will emerge from this analysis. First, with marked exceptions, India's defence policies have been mostly reactive. Second, the pattern of civilian supremacy established in the early years of the state has endured despite myriad challenges. Third, as India emerges as a significant Asian military power, its defence policy is now likely to show signs of greater autonomy and innovation. Finally, the country's ability to innovate and pursue a clear-cut strategic vision will, in considerable measure, depend upon its ability to improve institutional cooperation and coordination between the uniformed services and their civilian counterparts in the Ministry of Defence.

NATIONALIST AND IMPERIAL INHERITANCES

Two key factors influenced the making of India's defence policy in the aftermath of its Independence from British colonial rule in 1947. The first stemmed from the Gandhian heritage. Gandhi's role in India's freedom struggle was simply inestimable. Consequently, his aversion to the use of force had profoundly influenced his successors, most notably, Jawaharlal Nehru. Not surprisingly, Nehru had sought to construct a world order that would rely on multilateral institutions and hobble the resort to force in international affairs. Simultaneously, Nehru was acutely concerned about the diversion of scarce resources away from economic development towards defence.[4]

A second inheritance, also from the colonial era, had a profound impact on Indian defence policymaking. This inheritance was paradoxical. On the one hand, India inherited colonial notions about the scope and extent of its borders. On the other, its leaders had been kept out of the counsels of defence policymaking during the long span of colonial rule. While Indian leaders firmly subscribed to the colonially inherited borders, they lacked an adequate understanding of defence and security issues. As a former Defence Secretary, S.S. Khera, wrote:

> For over a century before Independence, the subject of defence, the organization and control of the whole

apparatus of defense in India, was outside the influence and to a large extent outside the view, of any Indian legislature. Defence was a 'reserved' subject. Even through the various stages of political reform in India, with the creation of legislatures representative of Indian opinion, defence expenditure remained outside the vote of the Indian legislature.[5]

This paradox would have important, and, indeed, tragic consequences for Indian policymaking in the post-Independence era. The consequences were especially adverse as they concerned the defence of the Himalayan frontier against a recalcitrant China.[6]

Nehru and his colleagues were firmly committed to the defence of India's colonially inherited borders. However, Nehru, because of a profound aversion to the use of force along with his commitment to India's economic development, chose to dramatically limit defence expenditures in the post-Independence era.[7] To this end, Nehru invited a noted British physicist, Lord P.M.S. Blackett, to draw up plans for India's defence needs. Lord Blackett kept Nehru's priorities in mind and delivered his report. Even though the government accepted his recommendations, they were never implemented fully (Barua 2005).

Nehru also played a critical role in shaping the pattern of India's civil-military relations from the very outset (Cohen 1970). He had been a key member of the defence team that had led to the acquittal of the officers and men of the Japanese-inspired Indian National Army (INA), who were tried at the Red Fort for their defection from the British Indian Army on the Burma front. These individuals had chosen to join the Indian nationalist Subhas Chandra Bose's INA, and had fought alongside the Japanese in the Burma theatre.[8]

India's ability to defend its territorial claims in the former princely state of Jammu and Kashmir during the 1947–8 war with Pakistan further reinforced the belief that it possessed sufficient military wherewithal to defend its borders. Interestingly enough, Nehru made it plain that the defence of the Himalayan borders would involve multilateral diplomacy, rather than reliance on India's limited military prowess. Nehru's influence on defence policymaking was so overwhelming that even the Chief of Staff of the Indian Army agreed with this assessment (Khera 1968:

158). Nehru's Defence Minister, V.K. Krishna Menon, had also persuaded himself that the principal threat to India's security stemmed from Pakistan and that China, a Communist state, would not attack India. In an attempt to cut defence expenditures, in 1950 the Indian Army was trimmed by 50,000 men to about 500,000 (Barua 2005). As subsequent events during the Sino-Indian border war of 1962 would show, these beliefs and the strategic choices based upon them proved to be fundamentally flawed, as Indian forces were easily routed. Furthermore, the global community, with the exception of the United States and, to a lesser degree, the United Kingdom, failed to come to India's assistance in the face of Chinese aggression.

THE TRAUMA OF 1962

In 1962 India fought a disastrous border war with China. The origins of this dispute have been discussed at length elsewhere.[9] Suffice to say that Indian defence planners had grossly mis-estimated Chinese capabilities, Indian intelligence about Chinese intentions had been fundamentally flawed, and rampant political interference had utterly compromised the Indian military strategy designed to cope with a Chinese attack. Faced with Chinese intransigence along the Himalayan border, India had embarked upon a dubious military strategy known as the 'forward policy'. This had involved sending in small, lightly armed military units ('penny packets') into the Chinese-claimed territories designed to demonstrate India's control thereof. These troops lacked both firepower and logistical support. When the Chinese attacked in force, the vast majority of the Indian defences, especially in the eastern sector, collapsed. China imposed a humiliating ceasefire on India after successfully occupying what India deemed to be some 14,000 square miles of its territory. The Indian exercise had been a classic case of 'compellence failure'—the inability to match resolve with capabilities.[10]

Indeed, it was not until after the military debacle with China in 1962 that the Indian defence policy underwent a fundamental reorientation. In the wake of the disastrous defeat at the hands of the Chinese People's Liberation Army (PLA), Indian defence planners undertook a major reassessment of

India's defence needs. They came to the inexorable realization that India could ill-afford to rely on diplomatic platitudes and professions of goodwill to protect its vital national security interests. Nehru and his successor, Prime Minister Lal Bahadur Shastri, proved unwilling to formally jettison the doctrine of non-alignment, which had been a cornerstone of India's foreign policy. Accordingly, India did not seek a formal military relationship with the United States or the Soviet Union.[11] Instead, it sought and received modest military assistance from the United States, and attempted to build up its defence industrial base. To this end, the armed forces embarked on an ambitious military modernization plan that sought to create a 45 squadron air force armed with supersonic aircraft, a million man army with 10 new mountain divisions trained and equipped for mountain warfare, and a more powerful navy with greater reach.[12] However, it was not until after the 1971 war, when the Indian Navy demonstrated its prowess and utility, that civilian decision-makers granted it sufficient leeway and the necessary resources for substantial expansion.

THE LONG ROAD TO RECOVERY

Long before India could recover from the military calamity of 1962, it became embroiled in a second war with Pakistan in 1965. Pakistan's military dictatorship of Mohammed Ayub Khan initiated this war based upon an illusory belief that it enjoyed widespread support amongst the Muslim population of the disputed state of Jammu and Kashmir.[13] Pakistani decision-makers had further inferred that the Indian leadership lacked political resolve, since an earlier Pakistani incursion in the trackless wastes of the Rann of Kutch in the Indian state of Gujarat in 1964 had not encountered stiff Indian military resistance.[14] Furthermore, India had agreed to refer the case to the International Court of Justice for adjudication.

Within a week of the Pakistani incursions in Kashmir in September 1965, India opened a second front in the Punjab, and even crossed the international border. This form of horizontal escalation enabled India to relieve pressure in Kashmir. The war lasted a few weeks and was brought to a close with a United Nations-sponsored ceasefire. Since the United States evinced little interest in resolving the dispute, the Soviets swiftly stepped into the breach. Accordingly, they mediated a post-war settlement in the Central Asian city of Tashkent in 1966. Under the terms of the Tashkent Accord, the two sides agreed to return to the status quo ante, and to also abjure from the use of force to settle the Kashmir dispute. Despite significant objections from the Indian military, the political leadership under Prime Minister Shastri chose to return the strategic Haji Pir Pass that had been captured in the war.

Even though the 1965 war had not produced a clear-cut victor, the Indian armed forces had acquitted themselves admirably. Nevertheless, the memories of the 1962 military debacle rankled, and Indian fears of further Chinese malfeasance remained. Indeed, following the initial Chinese nuclear test of 1964, a firestorm of controversy broke out in India about the advisability of India acquiring its own nuclear deterrent. In the end, India chose not to embark on a crash nuclear weapons programme. Instead, it set in motion a modest effort to acquire a nuclear weapons option. To this end, in 1966 the government sanctioned the Subterranean Nuclear Explosions Project (SNEP) (Mirchandani 1968).

THE 1971 WAR AND THE CREATION OF BANGLADESH

India's defence modernization efforts proceeded apace after the 1965 war. They were, in some measure, hobbled because of adverse domestic economic conditions during the last years of the 1960s. Also, during this period, because of an American arms embargo on the subcontinent, India increasingly turned to the Soviet Union for weaponry (Barua 2005: 198).

The third Indo-Pakistani conflict did not take place over Kashmir. Instead, it stemmed from the dynamics of Pakistan's internal politics. The precise circumstances that contributed to this crisis have been discussed at length elsewhere.[15] The crisis that ultimately culminated in war had both long-term and more proximate causes. The underlying causes of this crisis could be traced to the structural imbalances that had long characterized the two wings of Pakistan.[16] The bulk of foreign assistance was disbursed in West Pakistan, most industrial investment was located in the western wing, and East Pakistanis were very poorly represented in the civil service and the military. Furthermore, East Pakistanis had long resented the imposition of Urdu as the national language of Pakistan.

The more immediate precipitants of the crisis were the results of Pakistan's first free and fair election, in which the Awami League, an East Pakistan-based political party, won an overwhelming victory in December 1970 in East Pakistan. Matters quickly deadlocked over the question of power-sharing between the two wings as both the military establishment and Zulfiquar Ali Bhutto's Pakistan People's Party (PPP), which had swept the polls in West Pakistan, proved utterly intransigent. By early March, Awami League supporters had become increasingly restive and on 25 March, the Pakistani Army embarked on a major military crackdown in East Pakistan. The military crackdown resulted in the deaths of several hundred thousand Bengalis, and the flight of about 10 million individuals into the border states of India, most notably Tripura and West Bengal.

The Indian government, under Indira Gandhi's leadership, swiftly decided that it would have to resort to war to ensure a return of the refugees to East Pakistan. To this end, her government drew up extensive politico-military plans for a sharp, swift thrust into East Pakistan. Much of this task was entrusted to General S.H.F.J. Manekshaw, the Chief of Army Staff. Manekshaw, who was given a free hand with military planning, decided that it was best to wait until he had succeeded in moving sufficient numbers of troops and armour from other fronts, and until winter had closed the Himalayan passes before embarking on a major military offensive. His decision to wait until winter made eminent strategic sense. With the Himalayan passes snowbound, the People's Republic of China (PRC), Pakistan's principal regional ally, would not be able to open a second front.

External concern and support for India's plight proved to be meagre. The American position was downright unhelpful. The Nixon administration was acutely beholden to the Yahya Khan regime in Pakistan for having served as a conduit for the opening to the People's Republic of China, and was consequently quite unsympathetic to India's concerns.[17] To neutralize what she and her advisers perceived to be an emerging US–Pakistan–China nexus, Mrs Gandhi signed a treaty of 'peace, friendship, and cooperation' with the Soviet Union in August 1971.[18] With political initiatives to resolve the crisis exhausted, with India's Himalayan flank militarily secured, and with Soviet diplomatic support guaranteed, India responded with considerable vigour to a Pakistani attack on its western borders on 2 December 1971. Within three weeks Indian troops had successfully marched into Dhaka, the capital of East Pakistan. The untrammelled Indian military victory contributed to the break-up of Pakistan, and led to the creation of the new state of Bangladesh.

India's military victory in this war put to rest any lingering doubts about its pre-eminent politico-military status in South Asia. It also allayed the military's misgivings about its performance during the 1962 Sino-Indian border war. From 1972 to 1979, the region enjoyed a period of unprecedented peace as the military balance tilted dramatically in India's favour. In large part this was possible because the United States lost interest in Pakistan, and terminated its military relationship with the country. Simultaneously, India solidified its arms transfer relationship with the Soviet Union and distanced itself from the United States.[19] Also, in 1974, for a variety of complex reasons, both domestic and external, India chose to detonate its first nuclear weapon. Faced with widespread international disapprobation and substantial sanctions, it chose not to conduct any further tests (Ganguly 1983).

ENTER THE BEAR: THE SOVIET INVASION OF AFGHANISTAN AND ITS CONSEQUENCES

The Soviet invasion of Afghanistan in December 1979 had grave and far-reaching consequences for the security of the subcontinent. The United States, under the Carter administration, had treated Pakistan as a virtual pariah state, thanks to its unbridled pursuit of nuclear weapons, its abysmal human rights record, and its military regime. Faced with the Soviet occupation of Afghanistan, the administration did an about face. It set aside its reservations about Pakistan's domestic arrangements and offered it a modest amount of military assistance in return for access to Pakistani territory to support the Afghan resistance.[20] President Zia-ul-Haq, the military dictator of Pakistan, dexterously dismissed this offer, characterizing it as 'peanuts', and chose to await the arrival of the Reagan administration. At a regional level, he also rebuffed an offer from the Indira Gandhi regime to seek a regional solution to the emergent problem.[21] His patience was suitably rewarded. The conservative Reagan administration granted Pakistan an initial tranche of military and economic assistance to the amount of $3.2 billion for five years. Included in this package were some 40 F-16 aircraft, one of the most sophisticated in the US arsenal.

India's reaction to this renewed US–Pakistan military nexus was understandably hostile. In an attempt to redress what it perceived as an emerging strategic imbalance, India promptly turned to the Soviet Union for substantial military assistance. The Soviets, pleased with India's lack of public condemnation of their invasion of Afghanistan, proved more than willing to meet its military requests. During much of the decade of the 1980s, India remained preoccupied with Pakistan's military build-up as General Zia systematically exploited the American relationship to his advantage.

THE PUNJAB INSURGENCY AND THE BRASSTACKS EPISODE

Despite the Soviet presence along its western borders, General Zia and the Pakistani military establishment could not resist the temptation to exacerbate an ethno-religious insurgency that had erupted in the Indian state of Punjab. The roots of this insurgency were indigenous, and could be traced to the exigencies of Indian domestic politics.[22] The porous border made India's efforts to contain Pakistani support exceedingly difficult, and by the mid-1980s the insurgency had gained considerable force. At this time, the Indian Army was under the leadership of General Krishnaswami Sundarji, a charismatic and dashing military officer who was keen to develop the mobility and firepower of the Indian armed forces.[23]

To this end, he had fashioned a military exercise designed to accomplish two related but different purposes. At one level, the goal of this military exercise was to test the efficacy of certain new military concepts, equipment, and an indigenously developed command and control system. At another, it was also designed to send a message to Pakistan that despite India's difficulties in the Punjab, the army was still in a position to inflict considerable pain, should the occasion arise, on the Pakistani state. The size, scope, and location of the exercise, which was held along an east-west axis, caused much misgiving in Pakistan. When the Pakistanis sought some reassurance from their Indian counterparts, they received rather prevaricative answers.

In an attempt to pre-empt what they feared might be the prelude to a possible Indian offensive, the Pakistani military chose to extend their normal winter military exercises. They also moved some key military formations near a strategic salient in the Punjab. These movements, some of which the Indian military was able to monitor, caused considerable alarm in New Delhi. In an attempt to prevent inadvertent escalation, the Rajiv Gandhi regime sought and was able to obtain American and Soviet intercession. A possible conflict was thereby avoided as both sides agreed to return their forces to their normal peacetime deployments.

Nuclear weapons may have played a role in containing this crisis. By this time, Indian intelligence had ascertained that Pakistan was well on its way towards the acquisition of a nuclear weapons capability. More to the point, as the crisis drew to a close, A.Q. Khan, a key individual in the development of Pakistan's nuclear weapons programme, gave an interview to the veteran Indian journalist, Kuldip Nayar. In that interview, he made clear that Pakistan had crossed certain important thresholds in its pursuit of nuclear weapons. Indian decision-makers saw the Khan interview as a veiled nuclear threat.[24]

THE SRI LANKAN MISADVENTURE

About the same time, India's highly activist posture in the region also led to more troubles for its armed forces. Among other matters, the Indian armed forces were called upon to carry out a peacekeeping operation in Sri Lanka. The reasons for India's intervention in Sri Lanka between 1987 and 1990 and its tragic aftermath have

been analysed at considerable length elsewhere (Muni 1993). This episode was not one of the more successful ventures of the Indian Army (Sardeshpande 1992). In all fairness, however, the mission that was entrusted to the army metamorphosed over time. Initially, the army had been tasked to enforce the Indo-Sri Lankan Accord, which sought to bring an end to the fratricidal Sri Lankan ethnic civil war. However, as one of the principal parties to the accord, the Liberation Tigers of Tamil Eelam (LTTE), reneged on the terms of the accord, the army quickly became embroiled in the Sri Lankan civil war (deVotta 2004). In the end, a new Sri Lankan regime sought a withdrawal of the Indian Peace Keeping Force, and India complied with the request. One of the key lessons for the army from this involvement in Sri Lanka was the signal importance of having clear-cut missions. It was the fitful evolution of the army's mission, from peacekeeping to peace enforcement, that led to its being bloodied without accomplishing either effectively.

KASHMIR REDUX

The Kashmir issue had mostly been dormant after the Simla Accord of 1972. Apart from periodic and predictable Pakistani denunciations of Indian perfidy, the issue had lost salience in both regional and international politics. In December 1989, thanks to a particular conjunction of internal social changes coupled with political malfeasance on the part of various regimes in New Delhi, an indigenous insurgency erupted in the state. Ironically, the Indian state had promoted these social transformations in an attempt to win over the loyalties of the population in its only Muslim-majority state. Simultaneously, a range of regimes in New Delhi had both engaged in political chicanery and had tolerated a large degree of local skulduggery to keep potentially secessionist forces at bay.[25] Once the insurgency broke out, various Pakistani regimes, both civilian and military, quickly entered the political fray. They provided extensive logistical, military, and political support for the insurgents.[26] More to the point, they helped undermine the nominally secular but pro-independence Jammu and Kashmir Liberation Front, and chose instead to support more pro-Pakistani as well as ruthless insurgent organizations such as the Hizb-ul-Mujahideen, the Jaish-e-Mohammed, and the Lashkar-i-Taiba.

The Indian state responded to this insurgency in a time-honoured fashion. It initially resorted to extraordinary repression, mostly ignored external calls for restraint, and then created space for more moderate political elements to participate in an open and fair political process. This endeavour took the better part of the 1990s, but did restore a degree of order, if not law, to the state. The Indian military was at the forefront of these counter-insurgency operations. Not surprisingly, given its extensive experience in prior counter-insurgency operations, it acquitted itself well, despite suffering significant casualties. Any further movement of the Kashmir dispute depends on New Delhi's ability to convince other moderate elements to enter the political process, to persuade Pakistani authorities to end their support for the insurgents, and on the Army's continuing vigilance.

BROADENING HORIZONS: THE INDO-ISRAELI RELATIONSHIP

The Cold War's end had a profound impact on Indian foreign and security policy. Most importantly, the Soviet dissolution had meant the end of the Indo-Soviet security relationship, as the principal successor state, Russia, was both unable and unwilling to play a similar role. Consequently, India's policymakers were forced to abandon some of the key lodestars of its foreign and security policies. To that end, India's leadership started to abandon its visceral and reflexive anti-Americanism, and sought to improve relations with the United States.[27] It also pursued better relations with states that it had shunned as squalid American stooges during much of the Cold War.[28] As part of this general transformation of India's foreign and security policies, the country chose to reassess and alter its fraught relationship with Israel.

Apart from the general reorientation of its policies at the end of the Cold War, India's interest in forging a better relationship with Israel stemmed from two specific concerns. At one level, India's policymakers saw improvements in the Indo-Israeli relationship as a possible bridge to a better relationship with the United States, given the existence of close US-Israeli ties. At another level, India also wanted to diversify its sources of weaponry, and Israel was more than willing to oblige (Withington 2001). Since India's decision to grant Israel full diplomatic status in 1992, the relationship has made considerable progress on a variety of fronts, extending well beyond defence cooperation. However, the bilateral security relationship, which covers the gamut from weapons sales to counter-terrorism cooperation, forms the kernel of the Indo-Israeli nexus.[29]

CROSSING THE NUCLEAR RUBICON

In May 1998, India chose to conduct a series of five nuclear tests, thereby ending its long-standing policy of nuclear ambiguity. Contrary to much overblown rhetoric, the tests had little or nothing to do with the jingoistic Bharatiya Janata Party (BJP)-led regime. Instead, they represented the logical culmination of a series of long-standing decisions, coupled with more immediate pressures from the global non-proliferation regime.[30] Within weeks of India's tests, Pakistan carried out its own series of tests. Both countries faced considerable international disapprobation and a raft of economic and military sanctions. Additionally, the United States, which had spearheaded the sanctions regime in pursuit of its global non-proliferation goals, started an important dialogue primarily with India to persuade it to abjure its nuclear weapons programme. Despite unrelenting efforts on the part of the US Deputy Secretary of State, Strobe Talbott, the eventual results proved meagre. His Indian counterparts proved willing to tighten their export control regime, but agreed to do little else (Talbott 2004).

THE KARGIL WAR

The overt Pakistani acquisition of nuclear weapons had greatly emboldened Pakistan's decision-makers. They had become convinced that their possession of nuclear weapons had now neutralized India's conventional superiority. Quite correctly, they had assumed that India would be unwilling to expand the scope of a future conflict for fear of escalation to the nuclear level.[31] This realization led them to embark on a 'limited probe' in Kargil district in the state of

Jammu and Kashmir across the Line of Control in April–May 1999.[32] These incursions caught the Indian military authorities unprepared. The reasons for their intelligence failure were complex.

In the aftermath of the Indian and Pakistani nuclear tests, in an effort to allay international concerns, Prime Minister Vajpayee had undertaken an effort to improve relations with Pakistan. To this end, in February 1999, he had travelled from the city of Amritsar to Lahore in Pakistan to initiate a new bus service. In Lahore, the two sides had agreed to a series of nuclear confidence-building measures. In the aftermath of the Lahore summit, Indian policy-makers had assumed that relations with Pakistan, though far from ideal, were nevertheless on the mend. Accordingly, they had reduced the normal levels of surveillance and monitoring along the Line of Control in Kashmir. Pakistani decision-makers, however, exploited this gap in Indian intelligence gathering to undertake a military probe.

Despite the initial failure to anticipate and stem a Pakistani incursion across the Line of Control, India's armed forces acted with considerable alacrity once the scope and extent of the incursions became evident in early May 1999. By early July, in a series of successful joint operations, the army, in concert with the air force, managed to evict the bulk of the intruders. Faced with imminent defeat, Prime Minister Nawaz Sharif went to Washington, DC, to plead his case to President Clinton. In a significant shift in American policy, which had frequently equivocated on questions of responsibility in terms of the onset of various Indo-Pakistani crises, the United States forthrightly blamed Pakistan for the incursions. Sharif, unable to avoid the responsibility for the crisis, used his trip to Washington, DC, as a face-saving manoeuvre. He argued that his forces had to stand down because of American pressure.[33]

OPERATION PARAKRAM AND BEYOND

In the first decade of the new millennium, India's troubles with Pakistan continued. On 13 December 2001, members of two Pakistan-based insurgent groups, the Jaish-e-Mohammed and the Lashkar-i-Taiba, attacked the Indian Parliament. In the ensuing gun battle all six of the insurgents were killed.

Indian authorities asserted that on the basis of their intelligence intercepts, they had ascertained that the six individuals were of Pakistani origin. Accordingly, they sought Pakistani compliance to a number of demands, including the return of several suspected terrorists and a dismantling of terrorist training camps within Pakistan. These demands were soon backed up with a display of significant Indian military might along Pakistan's borders. Faced with Indian military pressures Pakistan responded with equal vigour, bolstering its military capabilities along the international border. Over the next several months, the two sides remained locked into a spiral of hostility as other terrorist attacks also took place on Indian soil. Fearing an escalation of tensions, the United States sought to contain a possible escalatory spiral in the region through the dispatch of high-level emissaries to both capitals. In the early fall of 2002, India finally concluded its military mobilization, 'Operation Parakram', in the aftermath of various Pakistani assurances that support for the insurgents would cease.[34]

Indian defence planners have drawn several important lessons from this particular military operation and its aftermath. They are now seeking to find ways to conduct war against Pakistan despite its nuclear-armed status. Senior military officers concluded that the army had lacked the requisite resources to mobilize swiftly in the wake of the terrorist attacks on the Indian Parliament, which led to a loss of initiative. Accordingly, the army is now in the process of developing a new battle doctrine, which emphasizes rapid action capabilities and focuses on taking the war into enemy territory.

THE CHALLENGES AHEAD

How is Indian defence policy likely to evolve? Are changes in regime likely to contribute to significant discontinuities in policy orientation? What are the principal challenges confronting India's policymakers? How are they likely to deal with these emergent issues? As this account has sought to demonstrate, changes in Indian defence policymaking has rarely involved radical departures and disjunctures. Instead, apart from the dramatic shift that occurred in the wake of the 1962 border war, most changes have been slow, limited, and incremental. Consequently, it is most unlikely that this trend is likely to change in the foreseeable future. For example, despite India's acquisition of nuclear weapons and the creation of a Nuclear Command Authority, the overall pattern and functioning of India's civil-military relations has not undergone any dramatic changes.

Even changes of regime have not produced dramatic alterations in defence allocations, threat perceptions, and political alignments. The changes have been both nuanced and cosmetic. The defeat of the BJP-led regime in the national elections of 2004 did not lead to any dramatic departures in policy orientation. On the contrary, the new Congress-led regime evinced a remarkable continuity in its policies. Relations and defence ties with the United States, which had been strengthened during the BJP era, were continued under the new government. India's wariness about China did not dissipate, but minor, incremental efforts to reduce border tensions continued apace. Concerns about Pakistan's abetting of terror, both within and beyond Kashmir, remained undiminished, and in fact were underscored in the aftermath of a series of well-orchestrated bomb blasts in Bombay (Mumbai) in July 2006 and another significant terrorist attack on two prominent hotels, a well-known café, a Jewish cultural centre, and a major railway terminus in late November 2008. This dramatic and brazen attack, which left 179 dead was yet again, attributed to Laskhar-i-Taiba (Lamont and Leahy 2008; Perlez 2008; Ganguly 2008).

India also has to cope with a series of internal conflicts in Assam, Nagaland, and Kashmir, all of which remain subject to external manipulation. During the Maoist revolutionary period of the 1960s and beyond, China was deeply involved in fostering and sustaining the insurgencies in India's northeast. However, it ended its support in the late 1970s as it sought rapprochement with India.[35] Given the continued political volatility of this region, Indian defence planners have little or no choice but to remain alert to the renewed possibilities of Chinese malfeasance.[36] Consequently, its defence planners will pursue a strategy that remains open to the possibility of recrudescent conflict, despite the improvements in Sino-Indian relations in the first decade of the twenty-first century.

Finally, Indian defence policy faces the very substantial challenge of integrating its nuclear forces into its overall military strategy. Currently, India is developing missile capabilities, which can target most parts of Pakistan and significant parts of southern China. These capabilities will no doubt be integrated with India's nuclear arsenal. However, the precise role that India's nuclear arsenal will play in India's defence policies remains unclear. The tenor of most authoritative Indian writing on the subject suggests that in all likelihood, India will opt for a modest nuclear force with limited capabilities, but one that emphasizes survivability over war fighting.[37]

The most important challenge, that of developing a long-term strategic vision, one that is not subject to the vagaries of regime changes, minor, adverse developments within the country's immediate neighbourhood, and periodic military crises, remains. India's defence policymaking apparatus has yet to develop the requisite institutional mechanisms, the necessary routinized procedures, and the proper planning capabilities to develop such long-term strategic plans. Fashioning such a strategy will require far better coordination amongst existing bureaucratic and institutional entities, involving the uniformed services, the civilians with the Ministry of Defence, and the diplomatic corps in the Ministry of External Affairs. Unlike other major powers, who have a vast cadre of trained civilian professionals in their defence ministries, India relies disproportionately upon the services of Indian Administrative Service officers, who are deputed for varying periods to the Ministry of Defence. Consequently, it has, for the most part, been unable to develop a professional cadre of personnel who are knowledgeable about questions of defence budgeting, acquisitions, capabilities, and policymaking. The absence of such a skilled body of personnel has ill-served Indian defence policymaking, and has rendered many decisions subject to political whims and financial constraints. If India hopes to forge a strategic vision that not only seeks to cope with extant and emergent threats but one that can also promote its long-term security concerns, its present institutional structures will require a substantial overhaul. Whether or not the country can indeed forge such institutional capabilities in the foreseeable future remains an open question.

NOTES

1. For the fullest discussion of India's nuclear arsenal, see Tellis (2000).

2. For a comparative and comprehensive account of all four Indo-Pakistani conflicts, see Ganguly (2001).

3. For a discussion of the Kashmir insurgency, see Ganguly (1997).

4. For a careful discussion of Nehru's views, see Khera (1968).

5. Ibid., p. 3.

6. For a thoughtful analysis of the Sino-Indian border war, see Hoffman (1990).

7. On this subject see Thomas (1996).

8. On this matter, see Ganguly (1991).

9. The best overall treatment is Garver (2001).

10. For a discussion of the concept of 'compellence failure', see Schelling (1968).

11. In any case, it is far from clear that the United States would have been willing to enter into such a relationship because of the singular importance that it attached to Pakistan at the time. On the US-Pakistani military relationship, see Haqqani (2005).

12. On this point, see Thomas (1996).

13. One of the best treatments of this remains Brines (1968).

14. For details pertaining to the flawed Pakistani assumptions, see Ganguly (1989).

15. The best treatment remains Jackson (1975); for details pertaining to the conduct of the war, see Sisson and Rose (1990).

16. On this subject, see Jahan (1972) and Zaheer (1994).

17. Additionally, both Nixon and Kissinger had a profound personal dislike of Mrs Gandhi. For details, see Smith (2005).

18. For a discussion of the politics surrounding the signing of the treaty, see Horn (1982).

19. For a discussion of this period in India's foreign and security policies, see Mansingh (1984).

20. For the American decision to assist Pakistan and some of the long-term consequences that ensued from that decision, see Coll (2004).

21. For India's attempt to reassure Pakistan in early 1980, see Sen Gupta (1982).

22. For a discussion on the roots of the Punjab insurgency, see Tully and Jacob (1985).

23. For a detailed discussion and analysis of the Brasstacks crisis, see Bajpai et al. (1997).

24. For a more detailed discussion of the Khan episode, see Ganguly and Hagerty (2005).

25. The origins of the insurgency have been traced in Ganguly (1996).

26. Even pro-Pakistani writers concede that Pakistan has been actively aiding the insurgents. See Schofield (1996).

27. On the transformation of Indo-US relations, see Blank (2005) and Ganguly et al. (eds) (2006).

28. On this subject, see Ganguly (2003/2004).

29. See the discussion in Kumaraswamy (2002).

30. For the compelling security-related motivations underlying the Indian nuclear tests, see Ganguly (1999); for arguments that seek to pin the nuclear tests on India's unrequited quest for global prestige and status, see Perkovich (1999).

31. For a expansion of this argument, see Kapur (2003).

32. For a discussion of the concept of a 'limited probe', see George and Smoke (1974).

33. The American role is nicely captured in Talbott (2004).

34. For a critical assessment of Operation Parakram, see Sood and Sawhney (2003).

35. On this subject, see Garver (2001).

36. On the continuing political instability in the region, see Baruah (2005).

37. See the essays in Mattoo (1999).

REFERENCES

Bajpai, Kanti P., P.R. Chari, Pervaiz Iqbal Cheema, Stephen P. Cohen, and Sumit Ganguly. 1997. *Brasstacks and Beyond: Perception and the Management of Crisis in South Asia*. New Delhi: Manohar.

Barua, Pradeep P. 2005. *The State at War in South Asia*. Lincoln: University of Nebraska.

Baruah, Sanjib. 2005. *Durable Disorder: Understanding the Politics of Northeast India*. New Delhi: Oxford University Press.

Blank, Stephen J. 2005. *Natural Allies: Regional Security in South Asia and Prospects for Indo-American Strategic Cooperation*. Carlisle Barracks: Strategic Studies Institute, U.S. Army War College.

Brines, Russell. 1968. *The Indo-Pakistani Conflict*. New York: Pall Mall.

Cohen, Stephen P. 1970. *The Indian Army: Its Contribution to the Development of a Nation*. Berkeley: University of California Press.

Coll, Steve. 2004. *Ghost Wars: The Secret History of the CIA, Afghanistan and Bin Laden from the Soviet Invasion to September 10*. New York: Penguin Books.

deVotta, Neil. 2004. *Blowback: Linguistic Nationalism, Institutional Decay, and Ethnic Conflict in Sri Lanka*. Stanford: Stanford University Press.

Ganguly, Sumit. 2008. 'Pakistan Won't Cooperate with India', *The Wall Street Journal*, 4 December.

_____. 2003/2004. 'India's Foreign Policy Grows Up', *World Policy Journal*, XX(4), pp. 41–7.

_____. 2003. 'The Start of A Beautiful Friendship? India

and the United States', *World Policy Journal*, XX(1), pp. 25–30.

Ganguly, Sumit. 2001. *Conflict Unending: India-Pakistan Tensions Since 1947*. New Delhi: Oxford University Press.

———. 1999. 'India's Pathway to Pokhran II: The Prospects and Sources of New Delhi's Nuclear weapons Program', *International Security*, 23(4), pp. 148–77.

———. 1997. *The Conflict in Kashmir: Portents of War, Hopes of Peace*. Cambridge: Cambridge University Press.

———. 1996. 'Explaining the Kashmir Insurgency: Political Mobilization and Institutional Decay', *International Security*, 21(2), pp. 76–107.

———. 1991. 'From The Defense of the Nation to Aid to the Civil: The Army in Contemporary India', in Charles H. Kennedy and David Loouscher (eds), *Civil Military Interaction in Asia and Africa*. Leiden: E.J. Brill, pp. 11–26.

———. 1989. 'Deterrence Failure Revisited: The Indo-Pakistani War of 1965', *Journal of Strategic Studies*, December, pp. 73–93.

———. 1983. 'Why India Joined the Nuclear Club', *Bulletin of the Atomic Scientists*, 39(4), pp. 30–3.

Ganguly, Sumit and Devin Hagerty. 2005. *Fearful Symmetry: India and Pakistan in the Shadow of Nuclear Weapons*. New Delhi: Oxford University Press.

Ganguly, Sumit, Andrew Scobell, and Brian Shoup (eds). 2006. *U.S.-India Strategic Cooperation Into the Twenty-First Century: More than Words*. London: Routledge.

Garver, John. 2001. *Protracted Contest: Sino-Indian Rivalry in the Twentieth Century*. Seattle: University of Washington Press.

George, Alexander and Richard Smoke. 1974. *Deterrence in American Foreign Policy*. New York: Columbia University Press.

Haqqani, Husain. 2005. *Pakistan: Between Mosque and Military*. Washington, DC: Carnegie Endowment for International Peace.

Hoffman, Steven. 1990. *India and the China Crisis*. Berkeley: University of California Press.

Horn, Robert C. 1982. *Soviet-Indian Relations: Issues and Influence*. New York: Praeger.

Jackson, Robert. 1975. *South Asian Crisis: India-Pakistan-Bangladesh*. London: Chatto and Windus.

Jahan, Raonaq. 1972. *Pakistan: Failure in National Integration*. New York: Columbia University Press.

Kapur, S. Paul. 2003. 'Nuclear Proliferation, the Kargil Conflict and South Asian Security', *Security Studies*, 13(1), pp. 79–105.

Khera, S.S. 1968. *India's Defense Problem*. New Delhi: Orient Longman.

Kumaraswamy, P.R. 2002. 'India and Israel: Emerging Partnership', *Journal of Strategic Studies*, 25(4), pp. 192–206.

Lamont, James and Joe Leahy. 2008. 'Mumbai Hostage Buildings Taken', *Financial Times*, 29–30 November.

Mansingh, Surjit. 1984. *India's Quest for Power: Indira Gandhi's Foreign Policy, 1966-1982*. New Delhi: Sage Publications.

Mattoo, Amitabh (ed.). 1999. *India's Nuclear Deterrent: Pokhran II and Beyond*. New Delhi: Har-Anand.

Mirchandani, G.G. 1968. *India's Nuclear Dilemma*. New Delhi: Popular Book Services.

Muni, S.D. 1993. *Pangs of Proximity: India and Sri Lanka's Ethnic Crisis*. New Delhi: Sage Publications.

Perkovich, George. 1999. *India's Nuclear Bomb: The Impact on Global Proliferation*. Berkeley: University of California Press.

Perlez, Jane. 2008. 'New Risk in Danger Zone', *The New York Times*. 28 November.

Sardeshpande, Lt Gen. S.C. 1992. *Assignment Jaffna: IPKF in Sri Lanka*. New Delhi: Lancers.

Schelling, Thomas. 1968. *Arms and Influence*. New Haven: Yale University Press.

Schofield, Victoria. 1996. *Kashmir in the Crossfire*. London: I.B. Tauris.

Sen Gupta, Bhabani. 1982. *The Afghan Syndrome: How to Live with Soviet Power*. New Delhi: Vikas.

Sisson, Richard and Leo E. Rose. 1990. *War and Secession: Pakistan, India, and the Creation of Bangladesh*. Berkeley: University of California Press.

Smith, Louis J. (ed.). 2005. *The Foreign Relations of the United States, Crisis in South Asia, 1971*. Washington, DC: US Government Printing Office.

Sood, Lt. Gen. (retd.) V.K. and Pravin Sawhney. 2003. *Operation Parakram: The War Unfinished*. New Delhi: Sage Publications.

Talbott, Strobe. 2004. *Engaging India: Diplomacy, Democracy and the Bomb*. Washington, DC: The Brookings Institution.

Tellis, Ashley J. 2000. *India's Emerging Nuclear Posture: Between Recessed Deterrence and Ready Arsenal*. Santa Monica: The Rand Corporation.

Thomas, Raju G.C. 1996. *Democracy, Security, and Development in India*. New York: St. Martin's Press.

Tully, Mark and Satish Jacob. 1985. *Amritsar: Mrs. Gandhi's Last Battle*. London: Jonathan Cape.

Withington, Thomas. 2001. 'Israel and India partner up', *Bulletin of the Atomic Scientists*, 57(1), pp. 18–19.

Zaheer, Hasan. 1994. *The Separation of East Pakistan: The Rise and Realization of Bengali Muslim Nationalism*. Karachi: Oxford University Press.

VIII Ways of Looking at Indian Politics

37 An Intellectual History of the Study of Indian Politics

Susanne Hoeber Rudolph and
Lloyd I. Rudolph

We write about the study of Indian politics as members of a transnational community of scholars. We also write as insiders and outsiders, insiders because for over five decades, from locations in Chicago and Jaipur, we have studied Indian politics; and outsiders because in what follows we seek to be reflexive political scientists of India. According to T.N. Madan, we seek 'to render the familiar unfamiliar', that is, to gain the distance and self-consciousness that makes for a modicum of objectivity.[1]

We have not aspired to be comprehensive. What follows is selective, our 'take'[2] on what students of Indian politics have thought and written over the past sixty years or so. We have been primarily diachronic in our analysis, leaving synchronic assessments to the contributors of the seven analytic sections of this volume. This is an intellectual history of concepts and narratives about Indian politics by persons who are for the most part political scientists, but are not exclusively so.

Studying political science as a form of knowledge and as an academic discipline is like studying state formation. Both are processes. As such, they are directed and constrained by their respective historical contexts and by regnant world views. Like modern States, academic disciplines do not have a universal or self-evident character. Both States and disciplines are constructed out of historical circumstances and conceptual contestations. The stories of the formation of political science in France, Britain, Germany, and the United States are different from each other, and vary in turn from the story of the formation of political science in India.

THE SHAPING OF THE DISCIPLINE IN INDIA

Taking the long view, we see how political science in India was shaped by the global and the local. Before Independence in 1947, the most important global influence on the formation of political science was the effects of British colonial rule, and the most important local influence the nationalist response to colonial rule. The earliest colonial influence was the East India Company's training centre for incipient 'writers' and 'clerks' at Haileybury College. From 1809 they were educated in subjects that pre-figured the multifaceted discipline of political science, such as history and political economy, the laws of England, and Indian religion, history, and languages. In the early decades of the College, they were taught by men whose ideas came to influence political science, such as Thomas Malthus and David Ricardo.

The formation of political science was also influenced by the victory of the 'Anglicist' faction led by Thomas Babbington Macaulay, over the William Jones-inspired 'Orientalist' faction in Governor General William Bentinck's Committee on Public Instruction. Macaulay and the 'anglicists' were convinced of the superiority of the English language and European civilization over Indian languages and civilization. A critical turning point came in 1835, when Macaulay convinced a majority of the Company's Council to adopt his Minute on Education. Doing so reversed a half century of support for an Orientalist policy of encouraging Indian learning and languages, and replaced it with a policy that gave primacy to education in English about Western knowledge. As Macaulay famously put it at the time: '...all the books written in the Sanskrit language [are]...less valuable than what may be found in... abridgements used at preparatory schools in England.' Macaulay's goal was to form 'a class of persons, Indian in blood and colour, but English in taste, in opinions, in morals, and in intellect'.[3] The effect of implementing Macaulay's Minute was to privilege the Western knowledge of politics over the Indian.

In the colonial era, the lineages of the kind of knowledge that found its way into the twentieth-century discipline of political science could also be found in the emergence of Western-style institutions of higher education. The first colleges were founded in the early years of the nineteenth century in Bengal and Bombay presidencies. Hindu College (later Presidency College) was established in Calcutta in 1817 as a seminary to impart education in English literature, modern science, and philosophy.[4] In Bombay, Elphinstone College began as an English school, set up in 1824 by the Bombay Native Education Society, and in 1834 became a College with professorships in English literature and in the arts, science, and literature of Europe. The first Indian universities in the Bengal, Madras, and Bombay Presidencies were created in 1857 as examining and regulating bodies to control the quality of collegiate education. They were not communities of scholars, postgraduate departments, or research institutions. Like the University of London on which they were modelled, they were designed to establish and regulate minimum standards in existing institutions.

Postgraduate departments and the advancement of disciplinary learning developed only in the twentieth century. The Education Act of 1904 empowered universities to set up postgraduate teaching departments; however, these powers were not used until 1916, when Sir Ashutosh Mukherji took the lead at the University of Calcutta by creating postgraduate teaching departments and research programmes.[5] Political science was not among them. It was not until after the Second World War, in 1948, that political science was removed from the shadow of economics to a separate department, and given the authority to create syllabi, teach, and examine undergraduates. From 1920 till 1948, political science had been part of economics. Students pursuing their Masters' degree in economics could opt for four political science papers in addition to four core papers in economics, and in this manner specialize in political science. Between 1948 and 1960, there were no undergraduate courses in political science. In order to study political science, students had to try for economics honours at the undergraduate level, and opt for a Masters' in political science. In 1960, a separate undergraduate honours course was established in political science.[6]

The story was different at the University of Bombay. When it took up research and teaching at the postgraduate level soon after the close of the First World War, one of the first units to be established was a School of Sociology and Civics and Politics. In 1919 the polymath, Patrick Geddes, was appointed to a newly created chair in Sociology and Civics and Politics. One of his first doctorate students was the sociologist and cultural anthropologist, G.S. Ghurye. When Geddes returned to his multifaceted career in Scotland, England, and France, Ghurye became chairman of the department.[7]

We mention Geddes and Ghurye because they are the beginning of a social science lineage that helped to shape the study of political science in India. Ghurye became M.N. Srinivas' teacher in the department that Geddes had established. Srinivas' most important conceptual innovation, 'sanskritization', a process of social mobility in India's hierarchal caste system in which lower castes culturally emulate high-caste Brahminical culture, helped to launch the analytic study of caste in political science. Even more than the analytic study of the relationship of religion and language to politics (Brass 1974; Jafferlot 1996), the analytic study of the relation of caste to politics distinguishes the study of political science in India from its study in other nations.[8]

Before the Second World War and Indian Independence, ideas about the study of politics and political institutions had been shaped by the character of a British colonial state, interested in both control and reform. After the Second World War and Indian Independence, the universe of salient influences broadened to include ideas and best practices on a global scale. Not least among them was the idea that politics could be studied as a discipline with its own distinctive theories, methodologies, and practices. Political science as both a discipline and a profession began to enter the academy and public consciousness as Indians began to create new universities and colleges, and to study for advanced degrees and discover intellectual universes outside the British Isles.

There is a saying to the effect that there can be no such thing as Burmese physics. The laws of gravity and thermo dynamics are said to be universal; they are not limited by time and place; they are the same everywhere and always. But what can be said of Indian political science? Is political science like physics, the same everywhere and always? We can speak of Indian music, Indian poetry, even Indian philosophy as distinctive. For us, political science can be inflected by place and time. In this sense, it is possible to speak of an Indian political science, just as it is possible to speak of an American, British, French, and Japanese political science without abandoning the common ground of a shared discipline.

Political science in India has been marked by a variety of distinctive influences, for example, its colonial origins, the nationalist struggle against British colonial rule, the trauma of Partition, Gandhi's thoughts and practice, Nehru's high modernist commitment to science and socialism, the effects of cultural pluralism, and the caste system. After a beginning in the shadow of British models in the 1950s, in the 1960s and 1970s Indian political science not only began to be institutionalized as a discipline, but also began looking at home and abroad for models. Scholarship and teaching on political thought, for example, began to include the works of Bal Gangadhar Tilak, Sri Aurobindo, and M.N. Roy, along with ancient and modern Western classics, Plato and Aristotle and Hobbes, Locke and John Stuart Mill.[9] Scholarship and teaching on Indian and comparative politics became more behavioural as US-style empirical questions and methodologies and structural-functional analysis began to displace the British-style study of institutions. Beginning in the 1980s with the emergence of postcolonial, subaltern, and diasporic studies, and increasingly in the 1990s and beyond, Indian framing of questions and modes of inquiry began to influence international scholarship, a theme to which we will return when we address developments in those sub-fields.

DEFINING POLITICAL SCIENCE

We have written about the intellectual and institutional lineages of political science under British rule. We did so because those lineages might have foreshadowed the formation of an organized and institutionalized discipline of political science in post-Independence Indian academic life. That they didn't do so in the immediate aftermath of Independence can be attributed to a variety of factors. An important one is the legacy of a British-style academic culture, which valued the classical scholarship and literary culture suitable for the education of gentlemen, and disapproved of German and American-style disciplinary and technical knowledge located in specialized postgraduate departments and professional schools.[10] Reinforcing the resistance to the academic institutionalization and professionalization of specialized disciplinary knowledge was the legacy of the colonial era's Indian

Educational Service (IES), whose professors staffed India's premier colleges. Indian Educational Service officers were rewarded for administration but not for scholarly publication, an incentive that could have fostered disciplinary professionalism.[11]

We have been unable to locate an 'official' or authoritative history of political science as an organized discipline in India. The record indicates the existence of several associations and their associated journals, as well as discontinuity. An Indian Political Science Association may have been established as early as 1939.[12] In a professional association one would expect professional distinction to confer office. In the Indian Political Science Association individuals struggle for power and control for the status professional office might confer locally, and for benefits—travel and office space at the home institution. Voting is often loaded by association officers enrolling local school teachers and graduate students. We have not been able to locate a study comparable to Bernard Crick's 1967 *The American Science of Politics*.[13]

With no broadly recognized political science establishment in the form of an apex organization, or its related journals, it becomes difficult to discuss the intellectual and professional history of the discipline in India. We are left with a number of questions: who can be said to practise and define political science? Who sets standards? Who speaks to what is 'cutting edge', 'orthodox', and 'heterodox'? Can we infer answers to such questions by examining what is taught and what is examined in degree programmes, teaching syllabi, and examination questions? How about the standing and influence of political science publications? Are there journals whose imprimatur counts for professional standing? To what extent should the definition and quality of Indian political science rely on the views of Indian political scientists and attentive intellectuals, and to what extent should its definition and quality rely on the views of non-Indian political scientists and intellectuals?

In characterizing the work of Indian scholars and intellectuals on politics, we find David Riesman's metaphor of an academic procession helpful (Riesman 1958). Those at the head of the procession and those at its tail are usually unaware of each other's concerns, standards, and conditions of work. There are large

differentials with respect to professional standards, levels of compensation, quality of students, teaching loads, conditions of work, and academic freedom. At the tail end of the academic procession, one sees the quotidian activities of thousands of teachers in *mofussil* and private colleges, presenting texts imposed on them from syllabi drawn up by distant university committees. Their job is to prepare students for externally set and graded examinations. They teach what they are told to teach, and have neither the opportunity nor the inclination to conduct research or write for the profession or the wider public. In the absence of a political science establishment and certifying academic journals, it is harder to say who is at the head of the procession and who at its rear, but it is by no means impossible.

It seems clear that holding office in one of the several political science associations is not a marker of academic distinction, nor does it place incumbents at the head of the procession.[14] And those at the head of the procession rarely see any reason to participate in political science association programmes and activities. According to a 2005 editorial on the IPSA website, 'There is a large group of University Professors and Readers in general and Central University Teachers in particular who do not find these conferences worth visiting unless they are invited to preside'.[15] Political science is not alone in the weakness of its standard-setting institutions. As Partha Chattterjee noted in a study conducted at the instance of the Social Science Research Council, situated at New York,

> Unfortunately, the various professional associations, such as the Indian Economic Association, the Indian History Congress, the Indian Sociological Congress, the Indian Political Science Association, etc. have never considered themselves as professional regulatory bodies in the same way that the Indian Medical Council, for instance, thinks of itself. It is doubtful that they can take the lead in developing such professional norms of accountability. (2002: 3612)

Fourteen years after Independence, the American sociologist and intellectual, Edward Shils, brought out an ethnography on India's intellectuals that inter alia provides a valuable account of India's academic processions. He called his essay *The Intellectual Between Tradition and Modernity: The Indian Situation* (Shils 1961). In the course of giving Indian intellectuals an unsolicited report card, Shils inter alia located India's political scientists in the academic procession (ibid.: 13).[16] 'Political philosophy and analysis are largely at a standstill in India. Since Gandhi there has been no new element introduced' (Shils 1961: 23).

As Shils read the scene in the late 1950s, India's academic political scientists were overshadowed vocationally by its public intellectuals in government and politics. 'In its own way,' he tells us, 'India almost appears to be the realm of the Philosopher-King. There is perhaps no other country where intellectuals exercise such weighty influence on the public life of their country and where they are entrusted with so many responsibilities, which by and large they execute with so much proficiency' (ibid.: 97). India's higher civil service, the Indian Civil Service (ICS), and its post-Independence successor, the Indian Administrative Service (IAS), 'attracted the best of modern Indian intellect' and they were 'the most cultivated, studious, and best read of the Indian intellectual classes' (ibid.: 92).[17] Indian political scientists, however, were not to be found among 'the large corps of outstanding intellectuals who play a major part, as advisors and consultants, in the formation of policy'. Nor were they evident in Commissions of Enquiry, the institutions that made educational and cultural policy, such as the University Grants Commission (UGC) (the Indian Council for Social Science Research [ICSSR], in which political scientists were to play a prominent role, was not established until 1969), or in the 'diplomatic field', where the recruits were 'outstanding graduates of Indian [and foreign] universities', many with strong scholarly or literary interests.[18]

Political scientists were also overshadowed in the analysis and interpretation of 'politics itself, the very centre of the public sphere.... At the centre of this centre stands...' the heroic, intellectual figure of Jawaharlal Nehru. 'Few men,' Shils continues, '... occupy comparable positions in any countries.... During the struggle for Independence he was the main bearer of the ideas of the European Left of the 1930s

in India.... It was he who stood up for modern, that is, socialistic, liberal ideas against the interests of the businessmen and the ideas of the Gandhians within the Congress....' Finally, he is 'the author of numerous bulky books...which reveal a reflective, cultivated, modern intellectual...'.[19] It is Nehru's presence on the public stage and his several books that make it difficult for academic political scientists to make their mark in the early years of independent India.

However, Nehru was not alone in occupying the space that political scientists might have filled. Nehru may have been the tallest among the politicians who engaged in the political analysis and wrote the political theory that is the stock in trade of political scientists, but he was not alone. The opposition parties, according to Shils, often featured such persons. Acharya Narendra Dev, Acharya J.B. Kripalani, Ashoka Mehta, and Jayaprakash Narayan of the Praja Socialist Party; Hirendra Nath Mukerjee of the Communist Party (to which he might have added E.M.S. Namboodiripad); and C. Rajagopalachari and M.R. Masani of the recently founded (1959) Swatantra Party. Shils failed to note B.R. Ambedkar, the Scheduled Caste leader, Gandhi adversary, and Law Minister, who oversaw the making of the Indian Constitution, and Ram Manohar Lohia, who created a separate school of socialist thought and action.

In short, the study of politics in independent India began under difficult circumstances. There was little in the colonial legacy to support political science professionalism. Early efforts to organize the profession failed to attract leading scholars, and were harmed by regional and personal rivalries. And, perhaps most importantly, the analytic, theoretical, and policy space which university political scientists might have occupied was filled by talented and articulate members of a charismatic higher civil service and a heroic political class.

Nehru's establishment of a Planning Commission in March 1950 and the expectations associated with planned development further inhibited the formation of political science as an academic discipline. It is not surprising that academic political science did not begin to find its footing or make its mark until roughly the close of the Second Five-Year Plan in 1961. Political scientists were not among the social scientists called upon to formulate, implement, or evaluate the early Five-year Plans. They were not equipped to play the dominant game in town, economic planning. The practice of political science and its sub-fields tended to marginalize political economy. A UGC survey of the state of political science in 1982, including detailed reviews of university syllabi at the BA and MA levels, show virtually no courses on political economy (Narain and Mathur 1982).[20] Political science's institutional isolation from policymaking and party activity help to account for the relatively static quality of the field, and its failure to spark innovation. The fact that the Congress party under Nehru's leadership made a planned economy the centrepiece of Indian politics and policy was hardly debated. There were questions about how it could best be done, but not about whether it should be done. India's bureaucratic culture is not attuned to the utility of outside research. As Myron Weiner noted in a Ford Foundation-funded review of Indian social science research: 'Sometimes a few individuals in the government are open-minded and responsive to research, but the bureaucratic system as a whole is not. It is not responsive to innovation. So how can it be responsive to research' (Weiner 1979: 1622)?[21]

Public administration as a field lived a life somewhat separate from political science, and was closer and more relevant to the planning process. Nehru was receptive to critiques of the inherited bureaucratic structure, and invited Paul Appleby, the Syracuse University professor, to assess the adequacy of India's bureaucratic structure (Appleby 1953). The Institute of Public Administration was called on for review and assessment.[22] P.N. Masaldan was one of the weightier figures to contribute via his two volumes on planning in Uttar Pradesh (1965, 1967). M.V. Mathur, founder of the Department of Public Administration at the University of Rajasthan, participated in numerous national expert policy bodies.[23] However, these activities were the exception, not the rule.

The economists had it better. Economics as a *discipline* was regarded as knowledge worth having by Nehruvians in the government and out committed to occupying the commanding heights of the Indian economy. After the Planning Commission took centre-stage in 1951, economists were in demand.

They were sufficiently in demand for them to breach the well-fortified barriers to lateral entry into the ICS/IAS establishment. From inside and outside the Planning Commission, they produced a stream of policy-relevant books and articles. There were differences and divisions, most evident in the formulation of the Second Five-Year Plan, but by and large economists, both foreign and domestic, helped to shape and participate in what might be called the Delhi consensus.

Recognition for economics came early in post-Independence Indian academia. In the academic year 1948–9, under the leadership of the inimitable but 'authoritarian' V.K.R.V. Rao, the Delhi School of Economics (D. School) began to take shape.[24] Unlike the London School of Economics and Political Science (LSE) on which it was modelled, the D. School did without 'and Political Science' in its name and curriculum. India at the time had no equivalent of Harold Laski, the scholar, public intellectual, Labour Party leader, and professor of Political Science at the LSE.[25]

The 'D. School' ignored political science and privileged economics, a circumstance that provided fertile ground for the growth of economic talent. K.N. Raj, for many years a professor there, reports that Prime Minister Nehru took 'a very close interest in the School from around 1956', and told him to 'ask him [Nehru] for any help I needed and that, in any case, I should see him once a year and report on the progress the school was making' (Raj 1995). By the 1970s, it had become sufficiently 'world class' for members of its faculty to be offered positions in leading institutions abroad. For understandable reasons of positions available and research support its economic department could not hold the talent it had spawned, and was gutted by the workings of an international labour market. Many of its faculty members joined universities in the UK, the USA, or the Planning Commission.[26] Among those who took job abroads were Amartya Sen (LSE, Oxford, Harvard, and the winner of the Nobel Prize in Economics in 1998), Jagdish Bhagwati (Columbia University), Tapan Raychaudhury (Oxford University), T.N. Srinivasan (Yale University), and Pranab Bardhan (University of California, Berkeley). Other 'stars' stayed at home, like K.N. Raj, Sukhamoy Chakravarty, Dharma Kumar, and Raj Krishna. Some joined international institutions such as the World Bank, not least among them Manmohan Singh, former Finance Minister, who in 2004 became the Prime Minister of India.

In the discipline of sociology, the D. School, and after 1958, the Institute of Economic Growth, featured faculty who contributed to sociological and anthropological knowledge internationally, such as M.N. Srinivas, Andre Béteille, and T.N. Madan. It was another decade before Indian political scientists began to achieve the kind of national standing and international prominence that Indian economists and sociologists were accorded in the 1970s.

In the immediate aftermath of Independence, political science as an organized discipline lacked the kind of institutional support and high-level patronage that economics enjoyed. After the establishment of the Institute of Economic Growth in 1958, sociology/cultural anthropology and geography were better positioned as disciplines than was political science. Calcutta University and the University of Bombay established Political Science Departments in 1948,[27] but it was not until 1963, when Rajni Kothari was able to launch the Centre for the Study of Developing Societies (CSDS), that political science as an organized discipline came into its own. However, this hiatus in institutional formation did not mean that scholarship on politics was not being produced and published. It is to that era, an era preoccupied with the problems of state formation that we now turn.

THE EARLY DOMINANCE OF INSTITUTIONALISM

Political science in independent India began under the shadow of Partition, and the challenge posed by the convening in 1947 of a Constituent Assembly.[28] The challenge posed by writing a constitution for an independent India was unambiguous, positive, and accepted by all. Partition was another matter. It was not until generations later, in the 1980s and, more so, in the 1990s, that scholars began to address the causes and consequences of Partition.[29] The writing of a constitution led political scientists to address questions of state formation—not only the structure and powers of a Union government, but also the structure and powers of states and local governments in a federal system, a Supreme Court and a related judiciary, the rights of citizens, and other key questions of governance.

Much of the first generation of post-Independence writing embodied an institutionalist approach, which reflected both domestic and international influences. According to a recent account of institutionalism by David Apter, institutionalism 'was more or less the exclusive approach in comparative politics, up to and considerably after World War II'. It combined elements of political philosophy, natural and positive law, and history. Apter went on to say that institutionalism emphasized 'law and the Constitution, [and] how government and the state, sovereignty, jurisdictions, legal and legislative instruments evolved in their different forms', and paid particular attention to '...varying distributions of power and how they manifested themselves in relations between nation and state, Central and local government, administration and bureaucracy, and legal and constitutional practices and principles'.[30]

In India, the institutionalism prevalent at Independence was shaped by a number of factors: the immediate interest in governmental structures and norms stimulated by the challenge of the Constitution-making moment; the 'path dependence' of sixty-five years of liberal constitutional reform;[31] and the more distant influence of an Anglo-American political science which, in the war years and up through the 1950s, was heavily institutionalist.[32]

Given the presenting problem of liberal reform in the inter-war period, and, as Independence became imminent, of creating a postcolonial state from the legacies of a colonial state, it is not surprising that great attention was paid to the outstanding institutional studies of the colonial era. Foremost among them were works by two English scholars, Oxford professor Reginald Coupland's 1944 *Report on the Constitutional Problem in India*, and Arthur Berriedale Keith's 1936 *Constitutional History of India*.[33] They were driven more by pragmatic imperatives of constitutional reform than abstract theory. Coupland wrote,

'An attempt will be made to state the hard facts that must be faced and to suggest some possible ways of dealing with them if a system of government is now to be devised, both for the Provinces and India as a whole, in which the twin principles of freedom and unity are balanced and combined. (1944: 1)

Coupland and Keith represent the end of an era in political writing.[34]

Both works record what the authors considered the legislative empowerment of colonial society by the British state. That empowerment proceeded gradually as successive Indian Councils Acts in 1909 (the Morley–Minto reforms) and 1919 (the Montagu–Chelmsford reforms), followed by the Government of India Act, 1935, expanded the scope of representative government with a view to realizing responsible government. The British thought they were 'granting' Indian legislative sovereignty; Indian nationalists led by Gandhi and Nehru thought they were extracting it. At Independence and for some time thereafter, Jawaharlal Nehru's *Glimpses of World History, An Autobiography*, and *The Discovery of India* shaped the mentality of not only India's political classes, but also the knowledge of students and scholars of politics. His daughter, Indira Gandhi, returning from the political wilderness to power in 1980, made clear in a Foreward to a new edition of *The Discovery of India* that she understood how much her father's books shaped political thought in post-Independence India:

> My father's three books, *Glimpses of World History, An Autobiography,* and *The Discovery of India*—have been my companion through life.... Indeed *Glimpses* was written for me. It remains the best introduction to the story of man for young and growing people in India and all over the world. The *Autobiography* has been acclaimed as not merely the quest of one individual for freedom, but as an insight into the making of the mind of new India.... The *Discovery* delves deep into the sources of India's personality. Together these books have moulded a whole generation of Indians and inspired persons from many other countries.[35]

What was true for Nehru's books was less true for Gandhi's. Many Indian teachers of political science, like Indian intellectuals, generally shared Nehru's estimate of Gandhi's 1909 book, *Hind Swaraj*—that it was at best inconsequential, and at worst misguided,

if not foolish. His *Satyagraha in South Africa* (1928) remained unknown to the academic world and the reading public. Although they might have heard of Gandhi's *The Story of My Experiments With Truth* (1927, Vol. I; 1929, Vol. II), not many university students or educated Indians read it. It was Nehru's, and not Gandhi's, master narrative of the nationalist era, India's place in the world, and its future that shaped the mentality of several generations of political scientists.[36] It would be another generation before prominent Indian academics and intellectuals, such as Ashis Nandy, Partha Chatterjee, Thomas Pantham, Bhikhu Parekh, Faisal Devji, Margaret Chatterjee, Akeel Bilgrami, Vinit Hakar, and Anthony Parel, would recognize Gandhi as an original thinker.

Soon after Independence, and particularly as scholarship and teaching about the government and politics of India found a place in the UK and US as well as in Indian colleges and universities, W.H. Morris-Jones—for some years—took over Keith and Coupland's role as a leading scholar of institutional political science. Morris-Jones had first encountered India in 1942 during the Second World War as a young officer in the Indian Army. His first lessons in Indian politics arose from an assignment to be the '...military's ambassador to the editors of the subcontinent's great nationalist newspapers...he spent most of his time listening and learning about Indian politics. The editors turned out to be, as he put it, "good teachers, knowledgeable and patient, discerning and tolerant"' (Manor 2000).

When he returned soon after the end of the war, he became one of the first English political scientists to experience an India that was free, and in command of its own fate. When his *Parliament in India* appeared in 1957 (Morris-Jones 1957), it provided a link between pre- and post-Independence institutional political science. Where other British institutionalists such as Sir Ivor Jennings tended to view Indian versions of parliamentary government as failing to measure up to British standards (Jennings 1953), Morris-Jones appreciated the ways in which Indians shaped the practices of the 'mother of Parliaments' to suit their own needs and circumstances. Differences were interpreted as creative adaptations, rather than failures to live up to British standards.

Morris-Jones' *The Government and Politics of India* first appeared in 1964, and was republished a number of times in the US and the UK. It helped in the transition from the colonial era's legalistic version of institutional political science to the more conceptually sophisticated and methodologically varied version of institutionalism found in post-war textbooks. Morris-Jones' book introduced a generation of English, American, and Indian scholars and students to the processes and institutions of Indian governance while paying heed to cultural explanations.[37] By 1970, Morris-Jones was being challenged by an Indian and an American textbook, Rajni Kothari's *Politics in India*[38] and Robert L. Hardgrave's *India: Government and Politics of a Developing Nation*.[39] Kothari's book was influenced by the functionalism he had acquired at Stanford in 1964 under the tutelage of Gabriel Almond, in Kothari's words, 'a leading figure in American political science'.[40] The Hardgrave volume which, by 1999, had gone into its sixth edition, was written to reflect 'a particular theoretical perspective', that is, Samuel Huntington's then fashionable pessimistic version of political development. According to Hardgrave, India (in 1986) 'dramatizes...the crisis imposed by the limited capacity of institutions to respond to expanding participation and rapidly increasing demands'.[41] Finally, Rudolph and Rudolph (1987), can be counted among the books that address the Indian political system with, inter alia, an institutional perspective.[42] At the same time, our book introduces and uses a theory of political economy, the command and the demand polity, that guides the questions we ask and how we answer them.[43]

We earlier observed that the institutional approach to political science in the colonial and early Independence eras was shaped by interest in the constitution-writing process, and the writing and interpreting of India's constitution. Before leaving our account of institutionalist scholarship and turning to the scholarship of the behavioural turn and beyond, we want to examine an important continuation of the institutional mode of analysis, that is, the contribution of scholars of constitutional law, and the role of the Supreme Court in India's political system. We start with scholarship on the writing of India's constitution by a constituent assembly that sat from 9 December 1946 till 26 November 1949, when the Constitution it had devised was adopted.[44] Crucial to understanding the source of many of the ideas and practices found in the Constitution is a book by the constituent assembly's constitutional advisor, Benegal Rau, *India's Constitution in the Making*.[45] The first major text examining the operation of the constitutional government in India was M.V. Pylee's 1960 work, *Constitutional Government in India*.[46] It was followed in 1967 by H.M. Seervai's 'magisterial' *Constitutional Law of India*.[47] Granville Austin's (1966) *The Indian Constitution: Cornerstone of a nation* provided a comprehensive and insightful analysis and interpretation of the constituent assembly debates, and the operation of the Constitution the constituent assembly had created.[48]

Thirty-four years later, in 2000, Austin published another authoritative work on how, over five turbulent decades, Supreme Court interpretations of the Constitution continued to shape the Indian political system. In 1977, the future Supreme Court senior advocate and activist lawyer on behalf of affirmative action, human rights, and public interest law, Rajeev Dhavan, launched what proved to be a series of books critically evaluating the work of the Supreme Court. Dhavan (1977) provided a sophisticated inner and outer critique of the Supreme Court's jurisprudence.[49]

With the publication in 1980 of Upendra Baxi's *The Supreme Court and Politics*, constitutional scholarship took a turn from analysis focusing on legal concepts and terms towards analysis that viewed the Supreme Court and its decisions in a political context (Baxi 1980). Baxi's subsequent work joined an appreciation for epistemological questions and policy activism with keen legal analysis (Baxi 2002).[50] His 2002 essay, 'The (Im)possibility of Constitutional Justice', views the political significance of India's constitutional law in the context of a postmodern epistemological turn:

> This essay provides a *suffering* exploration of what Jean Francois Lyotard describes as the different, the clashes of phrase regimes that must forever remain incommensurable. The fairy tales and horror stories pose numerous challenges to any 'master' narrative of Indian constitutionalism. Each destroys hegemonic narrative monopolies. Both profile a distinctive dynamic of the (im)possibility of constitutional justice.[51]

Like Baxi, Bhanu Pratap Mehta places India's constitutional law in a political context. He says of his essay on the Supreme Court's watershed decision enunciating the doctrine of 'basic structure' in the 1973 *Kesavananda Bharati vs State of Kerala*[52] case that the essay '...is very much a political theorist's analysis of the large issues at stake and not a lawyer's brief...'. Mehta argues in support of judicial review in the context of a 'democratic conception of constitutionalism' that makes 'certain constitutional principles...immune from the whims of even special majorities'. At the same time, he argues that the court '...has...used the basic structure doctrine as much to expand the scope of judicial power, as it has to delineate the core values of the Constitution.'[53]

With the rise of public interest litigation (PIL) in the 1980s, legal scholarship added a new dimension. A new category of lawyer/social scientist/activist infiltrated the narrow technicism of much of Indian legal writing. Upendra Baxi, Rajeev Dhavan, and Marc Galanter for a time shifted their attention from the macro-drama at the national level of conflict between the Supreme Court and Parliament to the myriad petty, oppressive agents of the state: police rape, police blindings, NGO-state collusion and corruption, jail inhumanity, violators of environmental and other social legislation. Justices such as Krishna Iyer and P.N. Bhagwati, who had taken a permissive view in the name of social justice of a strong, even authoritarian, state, led the movement against the state's agents at the micro level. The 'epistolary jurisdiction' by which Justices Iyer and Bhagwati recognized even postcards from jail inmates as writ petitions focused attention on state impropriety and lawlessness.[54]

We conclude this section on the institutional mode of political analysis by examining the contribution of legal scholarship to the analysis and interpretation of the caste revolution in Indian society. Pre-eminent in this context is the work of Marc Galanter. After many seminal articles, he published his big book, *Competing Equalities: Law and the Backward Classes in India*, in 1984. It brought together ideas and research that went back to 1962 (Galanter 1984).[55] Although a lawyer and a professor in a law school, Galanter's work has been influenced by and has in turn influenced political scientists since

it first appeared in the early 1960s. Galanter tells us that, since the kind of law he studies is 'an intriguing instance of using law to reshape recalcitrant social patterns', if he were to start working on his subject now (early 1980s) rather than in the early 1960s, 'I would undoubtedly pay more attention to politics and administration and somewhat less to the courts' (Galanter 1984).

THE BEHAVIOURAL TURN AS REVOLT AGAINST COLONIAL INSTITUTIONALISM

It is hard to date the behavioural turn or to capture fully why it was taken. One plausible reason for the turn in India was a desire to shed the colonial legacy, which, in political science, was the institutional and legal scholarship that characterized academic work under the British *raj*. Of course, institutional political science continues to this day; there is continuity as well as change. That is why we speak of a 'turn' rather than a 'revolution'. What is more, enthusiasm for the behavioural turn proved fragile and temporary. Its Indian status bears no comparison with the hegemonic quality of behaviouralism in the USA.

Another reason for the behavioural turn was the enhanced prestige that Jawaharlal Nehru, India's Prime Minister for the first fourteen years of Independence, brought to science as a way of thinking and acting. For him, science was an antidote to tradition and religion.[56]

In the 1960s and 1970s, in the era of enthusiastic modernism, of Five-Year Plans and scientific development, and in the penumbra of Nehru's effort to place science at the centre of India's intellectual life, political scientists began to take seriously political science's claim to 'science'. They began to deprecate institutional, legalist, and normative approaches to the study of political science. It should be concerned with causality and laws, not interpretation and meaning, work with survey instruments and population samples, not case studies, and favour synchronic over diachronic analysis.

Bernard Crick, in his 1959 study *The American Science of Politics: Its Origins and Conditions*, examines the prehistory of the behavioural methodology that eventually migrated to India. Crick found that there was a '...special plausibility to American students of politics of the view that politics can be understood [and perhaps practised] by "the method of the natural sciences"'. Crick traced this view to the 'Chicago School' (Crick 1967[1959]). In 1924 Charles Merriam, Chairman of the University of Chicago Department of Political Science, and his departmental colleague, Harold D. Gosnell, published *Non-Voting: Causes and Methods of Control*, a path-breaking behavioural study that sought to explain, via statistical correlations based on data derived from random sampling and innovative survey methods, why half the eligible voters failed to turn out in the 1923 mayoral election in Chicago (Merriam and Gosnell 1924).[57]

In the mid-1950s and 1960s, well after the hiatus of the Second World War, behaviouralism advanced from its beachhead on the shores of the social sciences, and mounted an assault meant to conquer the whole of political science's territory. Timothy Kaufman-Osborn explains behaviouralism's failure in this project through the rise of subfields. He argues that the four subfield model (American politics, political theory, comparative politics, and international relations) consolidated in the early 1970s thwarted 'the behavioral revolution's effort to transform the discipline of political science into a methodologically unified enterprise'.[58] The transformation was also thwarted, Kaufman-Osborn says, by 'the exhaustion of political energies that coincided roughly with the end of the war in Vietnam' (Kaufman-Osborn 2006: 46).[59]

In the US, two articles in the December 1969 *American Political Science Review*, one of which was David Easton's presidential address, 'The New Revolution in Political Science', and the other by Sheldon Wolin, a leading theorist, titled 'Political Theory as a Vocation', called for an end to the behavioural revolution. Easton did so in the name of *relevance* and *action*, both words he italicized. The highest priority of the putative 'post-behavioral revolution', he said, was to have 'substance...precede technique'. In 1969, substance meant addressing the problems of race, poverty, and peace. Behavioural political science, he argued, had concealed an ideology of 'empirical conservatism', and had 'lost touch with reality' (Easton 1969: 1051–2). Wolin called for an end to the 'behavioral revolution' in order

to stop the discipline from being taken over by its methodologists. He called for meaning over method, the what over the how (Wolin 1969: 1068).

At one level, the behavioural turn had been welcomed in the US and in India for similar reasons, its empiricism. Kaufman-Osborn explains how behaviouralism came to displace 'the classical curriculum', the study of politics through canonical texts (Kaufman-Osborn 2006: 50–5). Behaviouralism encouraged political scientists to put aside their texts, leave their studies and libraries, and get into the 'field' to do hands-on research among voters and politicians. In the US, it was primarily in the cities, in India primarily in the villages. In Kothari's words, 'We knew very little [in the 1960s] about what ordinary people thought about with respect to socio-political, cultural and psychological subjects' (Kothari 2002: 216).

In the US, empiricism in the form of the 'behavioural revolution' was experienced as a force, liberating political science from the texts of the 'classical curriculum', the context-less study of formal institutions, and an unreflexive normativity. In India, it was experienced as a triple liberation, not only from the 'classical curriculum' and institutional formalism, but also from the culturally alien literature of the Macaulay legacy in Indian higher education. And, unlike in the US where behavioural political science was challenged in 1969 for not addressing real world problems, in India behavioural political science *was* addressing an important real world problem. Could democracy in the form of universal suffrage and competitive elections succeed in a country that lacked what Seymour Martin Lipset in 1959 called the 'requisites of democracy', chief among which was a numerous, educated, prosperous middle class?[60]

Behaviouralism not only opened an avenue for 'science' in India's political science world, it also contributed towards liberating India's intellectual life from its Brahmanical legacy. Behaviouralism had a counter-hierarchical thrust. Arriving on the scene at a historical moment, when India was becoming a constitutional democracy and introducing universal suffrage, behavioural political science proved attractive because its democratic characteristics subverted an elitist culture of knowledge. Behavioural political science sought and found knowledge about the many, not the few; about the sovereign people, not about sacred texts. It dignified knowledge about persons from all walks of life and stations in society, and rewarded the labour of those who went into the field to acquire that knowledge. As Gopal Guru writes in 'How Egalitarian Are the Social Sciences in India',

> As 50 years 'experience shows, social science practice has harbored a cultural hierarchy dividing it into the vast, inferior mass of academics who pursue empirical social science and the privileged few who are considered the theoretical pundits with reflective capacity which makes them intellectually superior to the former. To use a more familiar analogy, Indian social science presents a pernicious divide between theoretical brahmins and empirical shudras.[61]

In the year 1969 David Easton and Sheldon Wolin told American political scientists and the larger intellectual community that a 'revolution' had put an end to the rule of behavioural political science. In India, 1969 marked the establishment of behavioural political science in the ICSSR. The difference suggests that the specificity of historical settings differentially impacts the trajectory of disciplinary development. The council was to be an 'autonomous organization under the government of India mandated to help fund social science research'.[62] Throughout the 1970s and into the 1980s, a wave of social science research centres sprang up in various parts of the subcontinent:[63] the Madras Institute for Development Studies (MIDS), 1970; Centre for Social Studies, Surat, 1969; Centre for Development Studies, Trivandrum, 1970; Institute for Social and Economic Change, Bangalore, 1972; Centre for Studies in Social Sciences, Calcutta, 1973; G.B. Pant Social Science Institute, Allahabad, 1980; Institute of Development Studies, Jaipur, 1981; to name only a few. By 2003 there were twenty-seven ICSSR-funded centres. Economists like V.K.R.V. Rao and D.R. Gadgil were prominent in the founding of the ICSSR. Indeed, most of the centres were dominated by economists, an indicator of the relative weakness in India of political science as both a discipline and a profession.[64] The early vigour and growth of the ICSSR was related to the Five-Year Plans. 'A major

boost was provided to social science research by the new efforts of the Indian state at economic planning'. By 1982, Iqbal Narain and P.C. Mathur could write in a University Grants Commission-sponsored review volume, *Political Science in India: State of the Discipline and Agenda for the Future*, that political philosophy and political theory, which had been the prestige fields in the 1950s and 1960s, were being 'swamped under the mounting rush of applications for empirical research-projects' (Narain and Mathur 1982: 26). The decline in the quality and funding of social science research since the 1980s, including the decline in the quality of ICSSR staff and funding, appear to be related in turn to the fading away of a planning community, in search of good social in science (Chatterjee 2002: 3605).[65]

KOTHARI AND THE BUILDING OF THE CSDS

The career of Rajni Kothari helps narrate the story of how political science in India acquired a measure of national and international visibility. Much of his story is told through a kind of personal ethnography on which we draw, his 2002 book, *Memoirs: Uneasy is the Life of the Mind*. It details Kothari's role as an institution-builder and a conceptual and methodological pioneer. For our purposes, the story starts with a double recognition, one by Sachin Chaudhury, the fabled founding editor of *The Economic Weekly*, the other by Richard Park, perhaps the first American political scientist of India and himself something of an institution-builder. After obtaining a BSc. (Econ) at the LSE, Kothari returned from England in the mid-1950s and in 1958 took up a post as lecturer in the political science and economics departments at the University of Baroda. He reports a 'breakthrough' as a result of 'chance encounters' during his 'first field investigation' at the All India Congress Committee session at Bhavnagar in Gujarat. He gained access to 'some rather well-known individuals...and entered into extensive discussions with all types of Congressmen from different regions...discovering widespread existence of factions and groups...the play of power conflicts...and how all this was shaping the running of government at various levels' (Kothari

2002: 30). 'Spurred by the "field work" at Bhavnagar', Kothari wrote a series of six articles in 1961 under the title 'Form and Substance in Indian Politics'. 'Young though I was', Sachin Chaudhury 'reposed full trust in me' by publishing the first article in a series, counting on Kothari to deliver the rest in successive weeks. 'In a matter of a few years', Kothari writes, 'I was able to launch, along with some others, what many of [my] reviewers have dubbed as a "new political science"' (Kothari 2002: 30–1).

Kothari's second recognition happened soon thereafter when his 'Form and Substance' series, which, he tells us, 'created quite an impact', caught the attention of Richard Park, resident head of the Asia Foundation in India. Kothari quotes Park as describing the series as 'a breath of fresh air in understanding Indian politics'. Park provided Kothari with 'a small sum of money', enough it seems to transform 'a large empty hall into a workspace for half a dozen people'.[66] This space, the then unused Indian Adult Education Association located at I.P. Extension in New Delhi, became the centre that Kothari had been thinking about, a place deliberately set up to be free of official pressures and academic bureaucracy.

It was under these circumstances that in 1963 Kothari launched the CSDS. Park's 'small grant' ran for only three years. There was no assurance of continuity, much less of security or big salaries. 'The kinds of people who joined', Kothari writes, 'were least concerned about salaries and perks and security'. They joined, he says, because they felt excited about 'the prospect that lay ahead'.

The CSDS soon became the premier institution in India for social science research. It did so because Kothari attracted talented risk-takers to the centre, encouraged them to identify and pursue unconventional research subjects, and quickly built a high-morale community of scholars and intellectuals.[67]

Early in his career, Kothari became a bridge between American and Indian political science. He spent four months at Stanford University in 1964 at the instance of Gabriel Almond, the dominant figure in his day in comparative politics; then spent a year at the Center for the Study of Behavioral Sciences at Palo Alto, and encountered the Survey Research Center at Michigan, the Mecca of survey research

and electoral studies both then and now. Kothari arranged for the extended collaboration of the CSDS with Philip Jacob of the University of Pennsylvania on a cross-national study of values in politics, and with Samuel Eldersveld, of the University of Michigan's Survey Research Center, to study Kerala's 1965 state assembly election and India's 1967 national election.[68] The two projects that Kothari brought home from his Stanford visit provided a 'comfortable financial base' for the CSDS, including the means to train the teams that Kothari's centre was then building (Kothari 2002: 215–16).[69]

Kothari was not the first Indian political scientist to study electoral behaviour in India,[70] but his energetic early involvement helped establish election studies as one of the hallmarks of Indian political science.

Kothari teamed up with Myron Weiner to produce *Indian Voting Behavior: Studies of the 1962 [third] General Elections* (1965), a study that preceded Kothari and Eldersveld's studies of the 1965 assembly election in Kerala, and the 1967 [fourth] general election. The fourth general election was also carefully analysed and interpreted in the essays in a volume edited by leading members of the political science department at the University of Rajasthan, S.P. Varma, Iqbal Narain, and C.P. Bhambhri[71] (Varma *et al.* 1968–70). As India's elections, both state and national, proceeded from the first parliamentary election in 1952 though the fourteenth in 2004, Indian political scientists, particularly those associated with the CSDS, enhanced the quality of their analysis and their interpretation of electoral behaviour.[72]

MODERNIZATION THEORY TRAVELS TO INDIA

In addition to helping to transfer behavioural political science from the US to India, Rajni Kothari also helped to introduce the modernization theory and its correlate, structural functionalism, to India. Both had emanated from the work of Talcott Parsons, the Harvard sociologist who, with Edward Shils, in 1951 published the essay 'Toward a General Theory of Action', in a book of the same name.[73] They laid out the four functions of 'the social system' and the five 'pattern variables' that defined modernization.[74] The basics of structural functionalism and modernization theory soon spread to political science in the US via the writings of David Easton (1953) and Gabriel Almond. In 1960, Almond made the extraordinary claim that 'the concept of the political system... separates out analytically the structures which perform political functions in all societies regardless of scale, degree of differentiation and culture', and wrote about the 'the universality of political structure' and 'the universality of the political functions' (Almond 1960: 5, 11, 12).[75] In his 1959 Foreword to the Almond and Coleman edited volume, *The Politics of Developing Areas*, Frederick Dunn, Director of Princeton University's Center for International Studies, held that Almond had made possible 'for the first time, a comparative method of analysis for political systems of all kinds', not least the political systems of those areas of the world in which dramatic social changes are taking place—Asia, Africa, and Latin America' (Almond and Coleman 1960). Almond was instrumental in convincing the US Social Science Research Council to sponsor and fund the Committee on Comparative Politics that for more than a decade stood astride the research paradigm and funding for the study of comparative politics in the US, and cast a shadow over political science in India.[76]

As we have already noted, Rajni Kothari, along with Bashiruddin Ahmed, spent the academic year 1968–9 on the Stanford University campus at the Centre for Advanced Studies in the Behavioral Sciences. Gabriel Almond was their sponsor and mentor. At the centre, Kothari worked on what would become *Politics in India*, in his view his 'most systematic and comprehensive piece of work', a work 'preposterously known as "classics" which stands apart from all the other works that I have done' (Kothari 2002: 69).[77] Published in the US in 1970 in Gabriel Almond's Little Brown series in comparative politics (and in India by Orient Longman), to our knowledge it was the first work of an Indian political scientist to be given such international recognition. *Politics in India* not only improved Kothari's standing as a political scientist in India, but also advertised and legitimized the modernization theory and structural functional approach of the Almond-led Committee on Comparative Politics.

Modernization theory and structural functionalism performed an 'imperializing' role in India and other 'third world' countries. In the face of deep-seated cultural differences and different historical sequencing, they held that the features that had characterized Euro-American developmental history would have to be replicated if third world countries were to become 'developed', modern, and democratic. Modernization theory imagined only one historical path, that already trod by the West, and one goal, the modernity already achieved by the West.[78] 'New nations' had to discard their pasts and become like 'us' if they wished to develop politically.

COLD WAR IMPACT ON INDIAN POLITICAL SCIENCE

In the mid and late 1960s, as the Vietnam War cast an increasingly long shadow over Indo-US geopolitical relations, relations between these two countries began to turn sour. Despite being threatened by President Lyndon Johnson's 'short tether' supply of much needed food aid, India under Indira Gandhi refused to back Johnson's war in Vietnam. More generally, India persisted with its non-aligned stance in the context of the pervasive Soviet/US Cold War rivalry (Bjorkman 2007).

Indo-US tensions spilled over into academic exchanges and relationships when, in 1967, press reports revealed that the Central Intelligence Agency (CIA) had been covertly funding student, research, labour, and cultural organizations in India.[79] American scholars were increasingly accused of having CIA connections. The crisis affected political science directly when it was learned that the India branch of the Asia Foundation, which had been headed for some years by Richard Park, a respected political scientist who had been among the first Americans to write on Indian politics in the post-war period, was being covertly funded by the CIA.[80] The discovery, layered on top of mounting Indo-American geopolitical and ideological differences, generated deep suspicions of American funding agencies, and compromised the standing of those Indian political scientists whom Park had helped. Chief among them was Rajni Kothari, whom Park had 'recognized', befriended, and introduced to Gabriel Almond.

The atmosphere was made much worse in 1971 when the Nixon administration 'tilted' towards Pakistan against India during the crisis leading up to the Bangladesh war. In December 1971, in the midst of India's war with Pakistan over the formation of Bangladesh, the US threatened India with force when it sent the aircraft carrier *Enterprise* and its battle group to the Bay of Bengal. Together, these events dimmed Indian political scientists' interest in American-style political science. 'I had allowed myself,' Kothari wrote retrospectively, 'to be influenced by more contemporary and relatively conventional thinking, most of it emanating from the US and other Western countries' (Kothari 2002: 218). And Iqbal Narain and P.C. Mathur, looking back from 1984, noted that 'more and more teachers are turning away from [US style] "behavioral" political science on non-academic and quasi-political grounds' (Narain and Mathur 1982: 36).

Indira Gandhi's declaration of the Emergency on 25 June 1975[81] also had consequences for political science in India. Most political scientists of India, both American and Indian, had in the 1950s and 1960s been swept up in the Nehruvian vision of what a developmental state might do to transform India's economy and society. With that developmental enthusiasm had come a general view of the state as a benign vehicle of socio-economic change. Much of the political science written in that era had adopted Nehru's premise about the value and importance of the developmental state.[82] By the mid-1970s, Nehru had been dead for ten years, the funds for planned investment were running thin, and the Planning Commission had lost its mystique as the means to occupy and populate the commanding heights of the economy. When Indira Gandhi arrested opposition leaders and critics, clamped down on the press, and suspended civil liberties, many academics, not least political scientists, pulled their punches or fell silent. In north Indian states in particular, the Indian equivalent of *Gauleiters* and emissaries from New Delhi watched for dissenters and subversives.[83] Soon after Indira Gandhi proclaimed the Emergency Rajni Kothari, at the time a supporter of Jayaprakash

Narayan, leader of a movement seeking to drive Mrs Gandhi from power, was said to have been warned of his impending arrest and left the country.

The Emergency marked a watershed for many other political scientists in India. It delivered a blow to the mystique of the developmental state, whose Nehruvian glamour had in any case dimmed. The emphasis shifted from 'science' to normativity. Doing political science in the form of electoral studies and analyses of state-led development was perceived as the study of what is, not what ought to be. Public interest litigation brought to public attention the brutality of the police, censorship of the press, the ineffectiveness of administration, and the suffering of the ordinary citizen. The state was no longer seen as a vehicle of positive transformation. Self-help, the non-governmental organizations of civil society, and social movements became the focus of scholarly attention. Voluntary organizations drawing on Gandhian models proliferated.

The CSDS struck out in new directions as Kothari promoted Lokayan. This structure of coordination and support for the voluntary sector was a hybrid one, with one foot in research and one in action. The titles of his books suggest the new aspiration: *Footsteps into the Future: Diagnosis of the Present World and a Design for the Future*, 1975; *Democratic Politics and Social Change in India: Crisis and Opportunities,1976; State against Democracy: In Search of Humane Governance*, 1988; *Towards a Liberating Peace*, 1988.[84] These works expressed the new spirit of the times, but did not provide the elan of scholarly innovation and distinctiveness that had characterized Kothari's and the centre's early work.

The post-Emergency world of the 1980s and 1990s saw the burgeoning of a distinctive Indian version of political science, an epistemologically plural political science increasingly concerned with identity politics, civil society, and local government, topics that found a growing constituency among political scientists outside as well as inside India.

IDENTITY POLITICS

By identity politics, we have in mind what Charles Taylor has called the politics of recognition (1994), the politics associated with who and what people are, with respect and disrespect, esteem and disesteem, and the allocation of material benefits in terms of status categories. Its provenance and lineage in scholarship about India pre-date the Emergency and the political science of the 1980s and 1990s. It begins in India with the recognition of caste as a vehicle for social change via political participation and representation. E.M.S. Namboodripad's personal experience in Malabar (now part of Kerala) led him famously to say that 'caste was the vanguard of class' (Namboodiripad 1962).[85] He was referring to how, in early twentieth century Malabar, oppression inter alia by upper-caste Namboodiri Brahmins of lower-caste Iravas and the resultant formation of an Irava caste association, the Shree Narayana Dharma Paripalna Yogam (SNDP),[86] opened the way to class politics. However, the recognition of what may be the most distinctive feature of Indian politics, its caste dimension, did not enter the mainstream in India until 1970, when Rajni Kothari published what he refers to as his 'other known work', *Caste in Indian Politics*.[87] This work acknowledged and took into account earlier articles on caste in politics that we had published in 1960 and 1965, 'The Political Role of India's Caste Associations',[88] and 'The Modernity of Tradition: The Democratic Incarnation of Caste in India'. As Kothari put it in the Introduction to *Caste in Indian Politics*,

> There are...slowly coming into the picture, political scientists who...have given up the traditional political scientist's aversion to caste, and have also mercifully given up the erstwhile dichotomy between voluntary and political forms as belonging to the 'modern' secular order and caste forms as belonging the 'traditional' order....
> (Kothari 1970b: 6)[89]

As caste politics developed in India, as new identity categories and social mobility ambitions have broken through the relative acceptance of hierarchy, caste politics and its study have proliferated and differentiated. The early optimism that caste would— and did—enhance participation and representative government has been overshadowed by the fact that caste politics has become parochial, self-serving and divisive. In the process, caste politics' capacity to promote equality and public goods has diminished.[90]

The rise of Dalit politics in the 1990s and in the first decade of the millennium gave caste politics new lease on life and revitalized its study. Dalit politics renewed the dismantling of hierarchy and the pursuit of equality and respect. What followed was a marked rise in academic interest in Dalit Studies among professors, public intellectuals and post-graduate students.[91]

Identity politics in India of course extends beyond the rise and influence of caste on politics. Language, religion, 'ethnicity', and gender are important components too. In the first decades of Independence, no issue seemed more threatening and divisive than the demand for linguistic states. Selig Harrison's *India: The Most Dangerous Decades* (1960) offered the stark alternatives of balkanization or authoritarian rule. Like Nehru and many other politicians and scholars, Harrison feared linguistic nationalism and its drive for the creation of linguistic states. Observers forgot that Gandhi in 1920 had re-organized the Congress on linguistic lines by creating twenty Pradesh Congress Committees based on language.[92] Gandhi saw sharing sovereignty on the basis of language as legitimizing and stabilizing the political order. Observers also forgot the (Motilal) Nehru Report on constitutional advance of 1928, which spoke of 'the linguistic redistribution of provinces as a clear political objective'.[93] Similarly, the States Reorganization Commission report of 1956 spoke of recognizing the federal realities of Indian civilization, in which 'linguistic homogeneity...reflects the social and cultural pattern of living obtaining in well defined regions of the country'. The creation of eight linguistic states in 1956, followed by the formation of Maharashtra and Gujarat in 1960 and Punjab and Haryana in 1966, proved in the longer run to promote legitimacy and stability.

Paul Brass's 1974 book, *Language, Religion and Politics in North India*, provides a good transition from language to religion. Having himself witnessed successful re-organizations of states based on language, Brass was in a position to oppose a 'constructivist' reading of political identity to the previously dominant 'primordial' reading.[94] He argued that the alleged 'givens' of group identity do not predetermine the outcomes of communal movements. Instead, they may be altered by them. Political elites draw on a culturally available pool of symbols, metaphors, and narratives, and then shape and arrange them to meet the needs of their strategic objectives. From this constructivist, strategic perspective, political parties and social movements do not simply reflect or transmit the communal demands of identity politics. Instead, they can and do shape group consciousness by interpreting signs and signifiers of group identity in ways meant to ensure political success. In this light, the great trauma of Partition seems less the inevitable result of the clash of primordial forces, as Tory imperialists such as Winston Churchill would have us believe, than of the largely unintended consequences of calculated acts by political elites.

Strangely, political scientists have done little writing on the causes, consequences, or meaning of Partition. This stands in contrast to one of Partition's indirect consequences, Hindu-Muslim violence. Only recently have political scientists of India tackled this subject directly. In three successive years, 2002, 2003, and 2004, political scientists attempted to explain why it happened and what might be done to alleviate, if not prevent, it. In 2002, Ashutosh Varshney published *Ethnic Conflict and Civic Life: Hindus and Muslims in India*; in 2003 Paul Brass published *The Production of Hindu-Muslim Violence*; and in 2004 Steven Wilkinson published *Votes and Violence: Electoral Competition and Ethnic Riots in India*. All three count and analyse episodes of ethnic violence at the micro-level of the city rather than the macro-level of the nation, Varshney with three sets of paired cities, Brass with one city, Aligarh, and Wilkinson working with cities/constituencies. Varshney's explanation for violence and/or accommodation between the communities is civil society-centric; Brass features a mechanism, the 'institutionalized riot system', while Wilkinson finds that a state government's action can be decisive in preventing violence.

Varshney argues that the nature of civic life makes all the difference. Inter-ethnic networks can be 'agents of peace' because they can build bridges of communication and trust that make it possible to manage tensions, whereas in communities organized along intra-ethnic lines, interconnections with other communities that might support communication and build trust are weak. Wilkinson, working with 'electoral incentives', argues that ethnic riots at the constituency level are often planned and triggered by politicians to win elections. However, electoral incentives operate at the state level too. Here, because in many states multi-polar electoral competition can make Muslim votes decisive for electoral success, state-level coalition governments have electoral incentives to offer protection to Muslim voters. Brass' longitudinal analysis of a single city, Aligarh, generally agreed to be a riot-prone city, reveals a mechanism, the 'institutionalized riot system', that entails a three-part process in which 'networks of specialists' playing a variety of roles instigate and perpetuate communal animosities, enact riots, and interpret riots after they occur. Brass recognizes that Aligarh is not India, but hypothesizes that the existence of institutionalized riot systems in the towns and cities of north India and beyond can help to explain the persistence of communal violence there, and more broadly in India. It is unfortunate that the creators of these three plausible explanations for ethnic violence in India seem more concerned with establishing the hegemony of their respective creations than with examining their complementarity.

PARTHA CHATTERJEE AND THE POSTCOLONIAL, SUBALTERN STUDIES

Another distinctive contribution to political science by scholars of Indian politics has been the introduction of postcolonial and subaltern questions, concepts, and modes of analysis. Postcolonial and subaltern analysis in political science is exemplified in the work of a leading practitioner of these modes of inquiry, Partha Chatterjee, one of the few members of the Subaltern Studies collective who holds a PhD in political science. Along with many of his colleagues of the subaltern collective,[95] he has influenced not only scholarship on Indian politics, but also the agenda of the social sciences and history.[96]

The first volume of *Subaltern Studies* appeared in 1982. It was introduced and edited by the initiator and leading theorist of the subaltern studies school, Ranajit Guha.[97] Like the *Annales* school of historiography formed after the Second World War by Marc Bloch, Ferdinand Braudel, Lucien Lefebvre, and others, the Subaltern Studies 'collective', of which

Partha Chatterjee along with Sudipta Kaviraj were the credentialled political scientists,[98] influenced scholarship on the state,[99] colonialism, nationalism, and civil society. Perhaps Chatterjee's most striking concept, and the one that incorporates much of what he has to say about the postcolonial state, nationalism, and modernity, is 'a derivative discourse', the subtitle of his first book, *Nationalist Thought and the Colonial World*, published in 1986.

Chatterjee's concept of 'derivative discourse' resembles Ashis Nandy's concept of the 'intimate enemy' (Nandy 1983)[100] and Homi Bhabha's concept of 'mimicry' (Bhabha 1994: 85–92) in attributing the postcolonial authenticity malaise of India's intellectuals and political classes to 'colonial modernity'. Chatterjee mentions with approval Gandhi's 1909 warning in *Hind Swaraj* that most Indian nationalists want English rule without the Englishman, 'the tiger's nature but not the tiger' (Gandhi 1997: Ch. 4, p. 28).

The early Chatterjee follows Guha in accepting his assumption that Hegel was right about states making history, and his claim that India had no pre-colonial history because it had no pre-colonial state.[101] In Guha's reading, India acquired a history and a historiography as a result of the British-created colonial state. The minds of Indian nationalists of all stripes were occupied by the colonial modernity that the colonial state generated. After Independence the postcolonial state mimicked the colonial state. The result was the 'derivative discourse' of Indian nationalism, historiography, and governance.

Chatterjee tells us in 1999 in the 'Preface to the Omnibus Edition' that

> the principal object of study in all three books is the actual existing nation-state...called India.... That was the starting point of *Nationalist Thought and the Colonial World* [1986]: to write the ideological history of the Indian nation-state from its conception to its fruition.... *The Nation and Its Fragments* [1993] abandoned the linear narrative for a series of interventions in different disciplinary fields. But they all converged from different directions upon the same object—the Indian nation-state as it had developed after four decades of its post colonial career. The linear narrative was restored in *A Possible India* [1997] but this time it was written alongside the events described, as in a diary, rather

than after the fact, so that the end of the story was not already known before its telling. (Chatterjee 1999: v–vi)

The source of Chatterjee's state-driven postcolonial derivative discourse trope was a Gramscian-inspired Ranajt Guha phrase, 'dominance without hegemony', which Guha used as the title of his 1997 book (Guha 1997). According to Guha and Chatterjee, the postcolonial modern state in India resembled its predecessor, the British colonial 'occupying' state. Unlike the British state of the metropole that ruled India, whose claim to dominance was hegemonic, that is, based more on persuasion than on coercion, both the colonial and postcolonial states had to rely on coercion to maintain their authority. Both lacked the 'active consent' of salient sectors of civil society. The British raj competed with the nationalist elite, who aspired to speak for the people of India constituted as a nation. Both the colonial and postcolonial state tried, but, according to Guha and Chatterjee, failed to persuade and speak for subaltern classes, particularly the 'peasants'.[102]

According to Guha and the early Chatterjee, after Independence the nationalist political elite in particular and the Indian bourgeoisie in general failed to create an alternative hegemony and historiography, which would enable them to rule without relying heavily on coercion. As the early Chatterjee tells it, peasant uprisings under the leadership of Maoist and other Communist-led movements in the 1960s were 'beaten back' by the postcolonial Indian state. By 1975–7, Indira Gandhi's Emergency regime had revealed the 'authoritarian core' of the Indian state.

By the 1980s, when Marxism more generally began to fade among Indian intellectuals the later Chatterjee begins to emerge. He undertakes to see and analyse a different historical and social landscape. The hold of the Marxist master narrative that coloured his perceptions and interpretations seems to make room for the autonomy of the local and a variety of interpretive paradigms. 'From the *Fragments* book onwards,' [1993], Chatterjee tells us, 'I have been more concerned with looking at practices rather than the big frame.'[103] We are told, for example, that 'different sections' of the Indian peasantry learned to use the processes of electoral democracy to pressurize elite representatives in ways that were not clear to subaltern scholars in the 1970s. As a result, Chatterjee and other subaltern scholars spoke of early and late Subaltern Studies, whose perception of the 1970s authoritarian Indian state changed 'quite drastically through the 1980s, a change that only began to be registered through the 1990s'. The effectiveness of new social movements using new forms of mobilization, 'the power of the vote' and 'liberal rights', 'the emergence of new caste movements', and 'movements of relatively marginalized groups' 'changed our understanding of what the Indian state was like'.

The derivative discourse and historiography entailed by Chatterjee's commitment to 'dominance without hegemony', even his estimate of the effect of 'colonial modernity' on the search for an authentic Indian identity, began to recede from the foreground of his thought and interpretations. 'In the last 10–15 years' (from the mid-1980s), he tells us he has seen the emergence of 'a new ethnography of politics in India', which includes 'the caste movement' and 'extremely vocal, quite [well] organized...relatively marginalized groups...which employ a combination of legal constitutional methods as well as some extra-legal strategies.... These movements...represent an assertion of...democratic rights...'. According to Chatterjee, these developments have 'changed the picture' from the 1970s, when they were 'not the case' because 'the processes of governance have changed quite fundamentally'.

What Chatterjee does not articulate but what seems to be implied by his change of paradigm is the recognition that the much maligned monster[104] of 'colonial modernity' was not the unmitigated disaster that he, Ranajit Guha, Ashis Nandy, and Homi Bhabha have interpreted it to be. What seems increasingly apparent in our postmodern era[105] that celebrates diasporic and global hybridity is that the much deplored effects of derivative discourse, the intimate enemy and mimicry on Indian identity, may have been signs of a colonial hybridity,[106] which equipped Indians to value and manage a parliamentary democracy and a government of laws, lead in the formation of contemporary English literature, excel in cricket, and even contribute to political science.

Our examination of the intellectual history of the study of Indian politics has followed the shifting methodological scene, from the classicism of the colonial era and the institutionalism of the early Independence era to the behavioural turn and its backlash, to identity politics and postcolonial studies. The review reveals positive and negative findings. With some notable exceptions of institutions mostly located in Delhi, academic political science is in a perilous condition. University-based research is rare. Political science in the academy reflects the disarray of higher education more generally. There are few mechanisms for establishing and monitoring professional standards. The political science association and professional journals fail to command the participation of the best scholars. Even so, those engaged in the study of politics in India have innovated in the fields of identity politics and postcolonial studies, contributed sophisticated methodologies for survey, research and electoral studies: including creating a national infrastructure for implementing such studies and have strengthened India's public sphere by their contributions as public intellectuals.

NOTES

1. Madan argued that an anthropologist *can* go home again, that is, study his own community, if he can 'render the familiar unfamiliar'. See Madan (1975, pp. 131–56) and (1994, pp. 159–60). See also Srinivas (1996), where he argues that a scholar's own life 'can be looked upon as a field, with the anthropologist [and, by extension, other reflexive political scientists] being both the observer and the observed, ending for once the duality which inheres in all traditional fieldwork' (p. 657).

2. We are 'telling what we know', rather than telling 'the truth, the whole truth and nothing but the truth' about the study of Indian politics. For an elaboration of these phrases and making a place for subjective knowledge, see Rudolph and Rudolph (2003).

3. In 1835, Bentinck's Council agreed to allocate its educational funds to teaching Western learning to young Indians in the English language. Macaulay's minute, adopted on 7 March 1835, stated that in higher education, the Company's goal should be the promotion of European science and literature among the natives of India. All funds appropriated for purposes of education were to be employed on English education alone. Macaulay's project of Anglicized uniformity was deepened in 1857 when Sir

Charles Wood's 1854 Education Dispatch, recommending inter alia the establishment of English-medium universities in the three presidencies—Bengal, Madras, and Bombay—was acted upon.

The Macaulay quotes can be found in Mansingh (2003, p. 236).

4. Hindu College's foundation committee was headed by the Westernized intellectual and pioneering social reformer Ram Mohan Roy. For an account of Presidency College, the 1855 successor to Hindu College, see Gilbert (1972a).

5. For an extended comparative account of the growth of higher education in India, see Rudolph and Rudolph(1977, pp. 13–24).

Sir Ashutosh was vice-chancellor of Calcutta University from 1906 to 1914, and again from 1921 to 1923. He effected most of the postgraduate reforms, however, from his position on the senate in the intervening years. For more on the growth of higher education and academic professionalism in the Calcutta University's Presidency College see Gilbert, 'Autonomy and Consensus'.

6. We are grateful to Professor Rakhahari Chatterji for providing these particulars in a personal communication.

7. For a discussion on the particulars of how this intellectual lineage evolved, including its connection to the evolution of anthropology in Britain at Cambridge and at Oxford, see Srinivas (1998).

8. For an early account of the relation between caste and politics in Indian political science, see Rudolph and Rudolph (1960, pp. 5–22). That analysis was followed Lloyd I. Rudolph (1965 and 1967).

When we went to India in 1956, it was in part to study the connection that Tocqueville had established in *Democracy in America* between associational life and democracy. In sociology/cultural anthropology, among the first to study the relationship of caste to social change and politics were Gould (1963) and Béteille(1965).

9. An early and frequent contributor to syncretic collections of political thought was Angadipuram Appadorai. See Appadorai (1973), (1971a), (1992), and (1971b).

10. As we remarked in 'Introduction to Part IV, Professional Constraints on Politicization of Education', in our *Education and Politics in India*:

> It is significant for the role of professionalization in Indian university education that the nation's modern educational transplant came from Britain rather than from...Germany. English universities avoided the impact of professionalization, both in the sense of training for the learned crafts [law and medicine] and in the sense of research and *Wissenschaft*, longer than did those on the continent (p. 314).

11. For a discussion on the effect on academic professionalism of the Indian Educational Service, see Gilbert (1972b).

12. In March 2007, the website of an Indian Political Science Association states that its General Secretary and Treasurer, Professor C.P. Barthwal, is located in the Department of Public Administration at the University of Lucknow. The site goes on to say that the association '...is the highest and largest association of the teachers and scholars of Political Science in India. The new IPSA executive was recently elected at the 52nd All India Annual conference of IPSA at the C.C.S. University, Meerut, during 10–12 October 2003'. Subtracting fifty-two from 2003, we surmise that the association opened its doors in 1951.

Another website announces that the 53rd All India Conference of the Indian Political Science Association will be held 27–29 December 2006 in Jaipur, with Professor Madhukar Shyam Chaturvedi, Department of Political Science, University of Rajasthan, serving as the Organizing Secretary. This raises the possibility that the IPSA meets every three years, rather than annually. It may also indicate that the association has lately had trouble mounting an annual meeting.

Complicating the picture is information from the University of Chicago's catalogue records. They show that an Indian Political Science Association began publishing *The Indian Journal of Political Science* in 1939. The *IJPS*'s headquarters were initially in Lucknow, but they seem to have shifted over the years. The library's holdings currently run through Vols 64–5 of 2003–4. Further complicating the picture is the University of Chicago's library holding of *The Indian Political Science Review*, published by the Department of Political Science, University of Delhi. It began publication in 1966/1967. The library's holdings end in 1985, with Vol. 19.

We learn from Professor Rakhahari Chatterji, former Chair of the Political Science Department, Calcutta University, that Dr B.C. Roy, then West Bengal's Chief Minister, inaugurated a West Bengal Political Science Association in 1960. Initially, and for many years, Chatterji reports, Nirmal Bose, later and for some time Education Minister of the Left Front governments, was a leading member. After some years it 'became inactive', but was re-organized in 1980. From 1988, under the leadership of Professor Mohit Bhattacharya, it became active once again. It publishes an annual journal. Recent keynote speakers have included Barun De, Rakhahari Chatterji, Thomas Pantham, and Yogendra Yadav.

Chatterji reports that Nirmal Bose was active for decades in the Indian Political Science Association, which publishes *The Indian Journal of Political Science*. After Bose's death a few years ago, 'Bengali teachers in Political Science have by and large ceased to take an interest in the IPSA, which has come under the control of the South'. In the late 1970s, 'young Turks' from Calcutta, such as Partha Chatterjee and Sudipta Kaviraj, tried to gain control of this IPSA. 'Having failed to do so, they lost interest in it'.

Personal email communication from Rakhahari Chatterji, 31 December 2005.

P.C. MAthur has provided helpful comments on the north Indian affairs of the IJPA. Personal communication, 12 August 2008.

13. Crick (1967). Crick tells us that his study 'is a critical history of an idea in a particular country, not of a discipline or profession.... It was...like waking up on the other side of the mirror to see the whole school more as an expression of American political thought than of science' (pp. v, vi). Nor have we found anything comparable to Kaufman-Osborn (2006). Kaufman-Osborn tells us that

> American students of political science have repeatedly bemoaned its failure to achieve the status of a coherent intellectual discipline. This essay suggests that claims regarding the disarray of political science are, at the very least, exaggerated. For several key purposes, the profession ascribes near totemic status to four specific subfields, political theory, American politics, comparative politics, and international relations.... Subfields are vehicles of power in so far as they participate in the allocation of rewards within the discipline and, more fundamentally, insofar as they participate in structuring our understanding of the nature of politics itself. (p. 41)

14. As we noted above, efforts in the 1970s by nationally and internationally reputed political scientists to lead the Indian Political Science Association failed to bear fruit. Interviews with political scientists suggest that in addition to Partha Chatterjee and Sudipto Kaviraj, Aswini Ray, Shibani Chaube, and Rashid Uddin Khan pursued unsuccessful attempts to assume high office in the IPSA. Professor C.T. Perumal of Madras University is said to have accounted for a long period of south Indian control. Personal communications from P.C. Mathur, Rakhahari Chatterji, and Gurpreet Mahajan.

15. Editorial Notes, *Indian Journal of Political Science*, www.ijps.net/editorial.html. Last accessed 10 June 2006.

16. Inter alia, Shils did not see (perhaps it is better to say that he did not anticipate) the argument made in Chakrabarty (2000) that India's intellectual and cultural hybridity had made the European West an integral part of itself. And his condescending attitude towards Gandhi and Gandhian intellectuality blocked him from seeing the argument that has been advanced in Rudolph and Rudolph (2006), which stated that Gandhi's 1909 *Hind Swaraj* launched an opening salvo in the critique of modernity, and the formulation of a postmodern alternative to it.

17. Two recent studies of the ICS do much to sustain Shils' judgement, a judgement that runs counter to the scholarship that followed the publication in 1978 of Edward Said's seminal *Orientalism*, which 'took it for granted that colonial rule was always evil and colonialist motives were

invariably bad'. The quote is from Gilmour (2005: xvii). Dewey (1993), mounts an inner critique,

> I admire my exemplars. Frank Lugard Brayne [1882–1952] was a natural leader...he made rural reconstruction part of routine district administration.... Sir Malcolm Darling [1880–1969] was a genuine scholar. He had a burning desire to understand the problems of the peasantry....His books are the best studies of the Indian villager ever written. They propel him into the class of men, less numerous than the men of action, who make permanent additions to our knowledge. (p. viii)

18. Shils lists a good many examples, each with their respective academic credentials, most from overseas, especially Britain. Those mentioned included P.C. Mahalanobis, chief advisor to the Planning Commission; Tarlok Singh, Secretary of the Planning Commission; J.J. Anjaria and I.G. Patel, Economic Advisors to the Ministry of Finance; D.S. Kothari, Scientific Advisor to the Ministry of Defence; Homi J. Bhabha, head of the Atomic Energy Commission; and M.S. Thacker, Head of the Council of Scientific and Industrial Research. Shils (1961, pp. 93–4).

19. Ibid., p. 95.

20. A number of political economy texts have been produced by English and American political scientists: Frankel (1971) and (1978); Jenkins (1999); Nayar (1990) and Rudolph and Rudolph (1987). See also Kapur et al. 1997.

21. According to Weiner,

> Experience is seen as preferable to social science research. The secretary of a state government department involved in slum clearance and improvement prgramme and in the construction of low income housing justified the lack of research in his department: 'We know these slum dwellers well so there is no need for research. We only need to develop programs for them'. (p. 1622)

22. This was one of Appleby's proposals. Chakrabarty (2007: 209).

23. For example, he co-authored *India, Expert Committee on Assessment and Evaluation; Intensive agricultural district programme, 1968–69 to 70–71; Fifth report of the Expert Committee on Assessment and Evaluation of Intensive Agricultural Programmes,* New Delhi: Directorate of Economics and Statistics, Ministry of Agriculture and Irrigation, 1975.

24. P.N. Dhar, who was the first to be recruited by Rao, tells the story in some detail in Dhar (1995). Dhar reports that in early 1957, over Rao's objections, 'the School returned to its original status of a university department, or, more accurately, a cluster of departments under the

nominal umbrella title of the Delhi School of Economics' (p. 21). When, later that year, Rao became Vice-Chancellor of Delhi University, he saw to the creation in 1958 of an independent unit, the Institute of Economic Growth, where once again political science was ignored. It was not until 1963, when the Centre for the Study of Developing Societies (CSDS) was created, and 1969, when the Indian Council for Social Science Research was founded, that political science came into its own. These events will be dealt with below.

25. For a rounded, in-depth account of Harold Laski's intellectual and public life, see Kramnick and Sheerman (1993). Laski succeeded Graham Wallas as professor of political science at the London School Economics in 1926, and was serving as chairman of the Labour Party at the time of his death in 1950.

26. For most of the persons involved, see the late Dharma Kumar's Introduction and the essays by P.N. Dhar and K.N. Raj in Kumar and Mookherjee (1995).

27. The Political Science Department of the University of Lucknow claims on its website that 'the department has the distinction of being the first independent Department of Political Science in India'. http//www.lkouniv.ac.in/dept_poli_sci.htm. Last accessed on 19 April 2009. The site does not mention a date of founding. The University of Dhaka's website states that its political science department was established in 1937. http//www.fss.univdhaka.edu/teachers/political-science/index.htm. Last accessed on 9 April 2009. It is not clear whether the Lucknow department's claim considers the University of Dhaka to have been in India or in Bangladesh at the time of its founding. If the Lucknow department placed the Dhaka department in India, the former would precede Dhaka's, that is, be established before 1938.

28. The official beginning of the Constituent Assembly was in December 1946. Its members had been indirectly elected earlier in 1946 from the provinces of British India and the princely states. The Constitution it wrote over the subsequent three years came into effect on 26 January 1950. Its members served as Independent India's legislature, and formed its government until the first parliamentary election in 1952. Members of the Constituent Assembly affiliated with the Muslim League refused to participate after Jawaharlal Nehru, speaking for a Congress that held a majority of the seats, refused to bind Congress, and thus the Constituent Assembly, in advance to the provisions of a constitutional framework negotiated in 1946 by the Cabinet Mission. The Commission, composed of Lord Pethwick-Lawrence, Sir Stafford Cripps, and Lord A.V. Alexander, had been sent by Britain's post-war Labour government headed by Clement Atlee.

29. An early entry was the historian Ayesha Jalal's (1985) The Sole Spokesman. She dealt with the causes of Partition. So did Hasan (1993), and Mahajan (2000) in her excellent account, Independence and Partition.

A remarkable and under-appreciated study of the process of state formation in India, which takes account of its dismantling through the Partition, is Misra (1990).

The controversy over how Congress' and, specifically, Jawaharlal Nehru's, role in Uttar Pradesh before and after the 1937 provincial election may have contributed to the Partition of India as depicted in the 1959 and 1988 editions of Maulana Azad's India Wins Freedom is best dealt with in Rajmohan Gandhi (1989).

Of late, Gyanendra Pandey, a historian, has focused attention on the consequences of Partition. See Pandey (2001).

Lloyd Rudolph (a political scientist) has written about the causes of Partition in Rudolp and Rudolph (2006).

30. David Apter's account of institutionalism can be found in a sub-section of his essay, 'Comparative Politics, Old and New', in Goodin and Klingemann (1996, 1998). The quotation is on pp. 174–5.

31. For evidence of liberal constitutional reform since the first local government act of 1882 instituted by Lord Ripon, see Coupland (1944).

32. Leading exemplars of institutionalism in the World War II era include Friedrich (1950). It was first published in 1937 by Harper and Brothers. A second edition appeared in 1941, a third in 1946 and a much revised post-war edition was published by Ginn and Company, Boston, in 1950. Herman Finer's revised one-volume edition of Theory and Practice of Modern Government was published in 1949 by, Henry Holt and Company, New York. Ernest Barker's remarkable examination of institutions in France, Great Britain, and Prussia//Germany, The Development of Public Services in Europe, 1660–1930, was first published in 1944 by Oxford University Press in London and New York.

33. Keith's study took account of the last great act of constitutional reform before Independence, The Government of India Act of 1935.

34. Coupland and Keith were decathelon athletes, intellectually speaking, in the breadth of their knowledge and disciplinary skills. Disciplinarily, Keith was the more versatile of the two. He produced seventy-four books in the course of his lifetime, of which the 1144-page digest of the law of England was one, and the 575-page history of Sanskrit literature and the 555-page discourse on the Rigveda Brahmanas were others. Coupland's scholarship was wide-ranging, covering a variety of Commonwealth countries, East Africa, Zambezi, Quebec, the American colonies, and covering a variety of topics, such as Livingston, Slavery, and others. Keith exemplified the combination of classicism and contemporary political writing that characterized his generation of English scholars of politics. Both wrote in a normative historical

mode that was about to be challenged in England and America, as in India.

35. Indira Gandhi's Foreword to the Jawaharlal Nehru Memorial Fund edition of Nehru (1981 [1946], p. 7).

36. Ramachandra Guha remarks, 'While Mahatma Gandhi was alive, not many intellectuals would identify themselves as "Gandhian"...they were not inclined to take his ideas seriously, viewing them as impractical and idealist' ('Past and Present', *Hindu* Magazine, 2 December 2006).

37. Earlier, in 1961, Norman D. Palmer who taught in the same era as Morris-Jones, and was one of the first representatives of the emerging US interest in Indian politics had brought out what may have been the first post-Independence textbook on Indian politics, *The Indian Political System*. Palmer's systems approach followed David Easton, who in 1953 had published *The Political System*, influenced in turn Talcott Parsons. Palmer was closely followed by Park (1967) and preceded by the more specialized Kogekar and Park (1956). The first book published in America after Independence about Indian politics was probably Park and Tinker (1959).

Over the years, since the appearance of early post-Independence institutional scholarship, fine institutional studies too numerous to name have been published. A sampling would include Bjorkman and Chaturvedi's (1994) work on *panchayati raj*; George Mathew's work, of which the most accessible may be his synoptic essay in Kuldeep Mathur (ed.) (1996); Arora and Varney (1995); Austin (1966, 2000); James Manor's books and articles on executive institutions, leadership, parties and the party system, and state and local government, an example of which is his essay in Chatterjee (ed.) (1997); Atul Kohli's general monographs (1990) and edited books, and work on the challenges facing the developmental, secular, and welfare state in India, of which Jayal (1999), is an outstanding example.

38. Kothari (1970a). It is to be noted that Kothari's book may have been the first by an Indian political scientist to be published by a major commercial publisher in the US. It appeared in 'The Little Brown series in comparative politics', as well as in India, published by Orient Longman in 1970.

39. Hardgrave (1970). in the preface to the fourth edition (1986), we learn that 'the first three editions of this book were written by Robert L. Hardgrave, Jr., but in approaching the fourth edition—fifteen years after the book first appeared—he felt that an additional perspective would give the book a new vitality. To that end he invited Stanley A. Kochanek to join him as co-author for this revision' (p. viii). Subsequently Kochanek co-authored the fifth edition (1993) and the sixth (1999). Kochanek expects to bring out a seventh edition on his own (personal communication).

40. The quote is from Kothari (2002: 66). As Kothari tells it, during the four months he spent at Stanford, he wrote 'a series of papers which were to...end up five to six years later in *Politics in India* which is still today [2002] considered the standard advanced text in political science, both in India and abroad' (pp. 66–7).

41. Hardgrave and Kochanek, *India*, fourth edition, pp. v and vi. After stating that their book 'reflects a particular theoretical perspective', the authors back away from such a claim, saying, 'it is not essentially theoretical in either content or purpose'. But they then go on to introduce the 'pattern of interacting elements' (political culture; elites and groups; structures of decision-making; and political performances) found in Huntington and Dominguez (1975: 1–114).

42. *In Pursuit of Lakshmi's* credentials for addressing, analysing, and explaining institutions can be found in the three chapters in Part I, 'State', where institutions such as the legislature, the executive, the bureaucracy, the courts, federalism, the police, the electoral process, and the military are discussed, and the three chapters in Part II, 'Politics', where changes over time in parties and the party system, and elections and electoral behaviour are discussed.

43. See Part 3, 'Economy', Ch. 7, 'Demand and Command Polity', ibid., pp. 211–19.

44. The Constitution came into effect on 26 January 1950, a day celebrated as Republic Day.

45. Rau (1963) (B. Shiva Rao [ed.], Foreword by Rajendra Prasad). A retired Indian Civil Service officer, learned jurist, and intimate of Jawaharlal Nehru, Rau's research as Constitutional Advisor took him inter alia to Ireland and the US.

46. Pylee brought out subsequent editions in 1965 and 1967, and another book analysing the Constitution in 1962 with a new edition in 1967, and subsequent editions through 1991. Pylee (1962).

47. Seervai (1967). A posthumous edition was published in 1996 and again in 1999 by the Universal Law Publishing Company. A reviewer wrote that 'ever since its publication it has been held as a classic' (*PUCL Bulletin*, September 2001). The phrase 'magisterial' was used by Pratap Bhanu Mehta in his essay in Hasan *et al.* (2002, p. 209, n. 3). Noorani (1970), and its subsequent editions is another important study of the Supreme Court in Indian politics.

We would be remiss if we didn't mention the contributions of the late Durga Das Basu to the study of the constitutional law of India. Two of his books, the 1000-page long, humorously titled *Shorter Constitution of India*, and the considerably shorter *Introduction to the Constitution of India* have gone through many editions. At Independence, D.D. Basu's formidable *Shorter Constitution* was already in its third edition. In 2003, retired Chief Justice Chandrachud took over the editorship of what was by then the thirteenth edition. Basu (1999).

48. Perhaps the first person to examine the debates and decisions of the constituent assembly with a view to the light they throw on the presenting problems of Indian politics was Ralph Retzlaff, whose Berkeley PhD Thesis and a subsequent article examined 'The problem of communal minorities in the drafting of the Indian Constitution', in Spann (1963).

49. A year earlier, Dhavan published the first of a series of critical accounts of constitutionally challenging policy issues: (1976); (1978); Dhavan and Davies (eds) (1978); (1979); (1986); (1987).

50. Baxi's most recent policy and activist is the Future of Human Rights (2006). He has written on the Bhopal Case (1986), the Environmental Protection Act (1987), Law and Poverty (1988), Corruption (1989), Minorities (1994), the Criminal Justice System (2003), and the Juvenile Justice System (2004).

51. Baxi (2002, p. 55). He outlines 'the modes of the ongoing "critique" of the Indian Constitution', 'The Left "Critique"'; 'The Gandhian Critique'; 'The Neo-Gandhian Critique'; 'The Hindutva Critique'; 'The *Matam* of First Nations'; and 'Subaltern Critiques: Cornerstones as Tombstones'.

52. *Keshavananda Bharati vs Kerala* 1973 [4] SCC 225.

53. Mehta (2002, pp. 185, 207, 204). Also see Rudolph and Rudolph (1987: Ch. 3, pp. 103–26) and Austin (2000), Part II, 'The Great Constitutional Confrontation: Judicial *versus* Parliamentary Supremacy, 1967–1973', pp. 171–292.

54. See Government of India, Ministry of Law, Social Justice and Company Affairs, *Processual Justice to the People: Report of the Expert Committee on Legal Aid*, New Delhi, 1973 (V.R. Krishna Iyer, Chairman); *Report on Judiciary: Equal Justice–Social Justice*, New Delhi, 1978 (P.N. Bhagwati, Chairman).

The scholarship on this topic included Baxi (1983); Dhavan (1984); Galanter (1982). The phrase 'epistolary jurisdiction' is Baxi's. See Baxi (1983, p. 14).

55. One of his earliest works was an article in the *Journal of the Indian Law Institute*. See Galanter (1962).

56. For the rearguard action in defence of Nehru's scientific worldview, see Haksar *et al.* (1981, pp. 6 and 7). For an analysis of the content of the 'scientific temper' debate and its context, see Wang (2001, pp. 170–81).

57. According to John Mark Hansen,

the design they employed was, on multiple counts, the first of its kind in political science. They interviewed some 300 party officials, officeholders, and election activists. They gathered data on sex, age, length of residence, and citizenship for 5000 voters from the records of the Elections Commission. And, most novel, they drew a 'representative sample' of 6000 nonvoters,

sent a small army of students to interview them, and punched the results into Hollerith cards.

Non-voting, they found, traced to 'indifference and intertia', to illness and absence, to legal and administrative obstacles, to disgust with politics, and to a startling finding in the aftermath of giving women the vote in 1920—personal disbelief in the propriety of women's participation in politics. Equally startling was the discovery that non-voting by Blacks was due in large measure to what appeared to be deliberately created administrative obstacles. Hansen (1997, pp. 582–6) the quotation is at p. 583.

58. As a result of the revolt within the APSA led by the New Caucus for Political Science in 1967, by 2006 there were thirty-seven self-governing organized sections, each representing an epistemic community. For the meaning of the term 'epistemic community' and its application in international relations, see Haas (1992). For a more general discussion of epistemological pluralism, see Toulmin (2001).

59. Kaufman-Osborn goes on to give his gloss to what he calls 'the net result', 'a sort of unreflective compromise that tolerates [sic] the haphazard [sic] multiplication and formalization of new areas of political inquiry...' (p. 46). At the same time that he deprecates the 'multiplication...of new areas inquiry', Kaufman-Osborn mocks political science's claim to be a 'genuine science' as a Panglossian tale, giving as an example the introduction to Goodin and Klingemann (eds) (1996).

60. See Lipset (1959) for a proposition and supporting evidence which strongly suggested that democracy should be a failure in India. On almost every statistical measure of the 'requisites of democracy' (per capita income, literacy, industrialization, urbanization), India stood at or near the bottom; yet it was, and of course has continued to be, a democracy.

61. *Economic and Political Weekly,* 14 December 2002, p. 5003.

62. We say help fund because state governments had to share in the funding of ICSSR-supported centres. For details on the dates of establishment, location, and mandate see Chandel (2003).

63. The exception was the CSDS, Delhi, discussed below, which was established in 1963.

64. The CSDS at Delhi and the Centre for Studies in Social Sciences (CSSSC) at Calcutta, of which more below, were outstanding exceptions.

65. Many Social scientists hope that the recent appointment of Andre Béteille, one of India's most distinguished sociologists as Chair of ICSSR would revitalize the institution.

66. Uma Shanker Phadnis, told Kothari about 'a place called the Indian Adult Education Association (IAEA), located on Indraprastha Estate, which had all the space in

the world but did not know what to do with it and where I could...consider setting up the centre I had in mind' (ibid., pp. 37–8). CSDS later shifted to Delhi to its present location near the University of Delhi at 29 Rajpur Road.

67. The talented risk-takers became leading scholars. They included Kothari's friend, Gopal Krishna, who helped convert the IAEA's large space, Bashiruddin Ahmed, D.L. Seth, Ramashray Roy, Ashis Nandy, Ghanshyam Shah, Anil Bhatt, Rishikesh Maru, and H.R. Chaturvedi, Maru and Chaturvedi 'are no more', but of those who have left the Centre, all 'are today [2002] known figures and either heads of institutions and senior professors at major places of learning' (ibid., pp. 38–9).

68. Samuel Eldersveld's interest in Indian politics was an exception to the determined parochialism of most American behaviourists, starting with those at the Survey Research Center, whose focus was resolutely on American electoral behaviour.

Lloyd Rudolph spent the summer of 1958 on a Social Science Research Council grant arranged by V.O. Key at the Survey Research Center's Institute on Analysis of Electoral Behaviour. He tried, without much success, to get help in analysing the data from a random sample survey of voters in Madras on 'Political Literacy and Political Attitudes', which he and Susanne Rudolph in collaboration with the Indian Institute of Public Opinion had carried out in March 1957. Thanks to Yogendra Yadav, these data are now deposited in CSDS's data archive. Our survey was among the first random sample surveys conducted in India. An account of our survey research experience and some of our findings can be found Rudolph and Rudolph (1958).

69. Kothari found himself swept up in the surge of ambitious projects that comparative studies spawned at many American universities. Almond wanted to collaborate with the CSDS on a study that would be along the lines of the 'civic culture' study that he and Sidney Verba had recently produced. See Almond and Verba (1963). Like Almond, Phillip Jacob at the University of Pennsylvania was looking for collaboration on a cross-national value survey.

70. The first study we have been able to locate was of the first general election; see Kogekar and Park (eds), (1956). Another early study was co-edited by Weiner and Kothari (1965).

71. In 1978, Iqbal Narain and others brought out a comprehensive evaluation of state and national election studies. See *Election studies in India: An Evaluation*, Report of an ICSSR [Indian Council of Social Science Research] project, Bombay: Allied Publishers.

72. These included Sheth (1975); Ahmed and Eldersveld's (1978) major voting study based on the intellectual resources of CSDS; Weiner and Field's (1974–7) four-volume study funded by the US National Science Foundation; Ramashray Roy's formidable study of the process and criteria by which the Congress party selected its candidates, 'Election Studies: Selection of Congress Candidates', Part 1, 'The Formal Criteria', Part 2, 'Pressures and Counter Pressures', Part 3, 'Claims and Counter Claims', and Parts 4 and 5, 'Structure of Authority in the Congress', *Economic and Political Weekly*, 31 December 1966, and 7 and 14 January and 11 February 1967. W.H Morris Jones, representative of the best of the institutionalist perspective, abandoned it to collaborate with Biplab Dasgupta in a relentlessly quantitative, district by district exercise (1975). The Dasgupta/Morris-Jones study showed that while some socio-economic variables correlated with party voting behaviour at the constituency, district, and occasionally the state level, correlations washed out when attempted at the national level. Indian diversity defeated the search for national regularities.

A wide array of American and British scholars were attracted by the amount, richness, and challenge of Indian electoral data: Palmer (1975); Blair (1979); Sisson and Vanderbok (1983); Brass (1969) and (1986); Manor (1978). Later, Gould and Ganguly, as editors and contributors, asked ten scholars to analyse and explain the dynamics and outcomes of the ninth (1989) and tenth (1991) national elections. See Gould and Ganguly (eds) (1993).

Beginning in 1993, when he joined the CSDS, Yogendra Yadav has taken the lead in studying, interpreting, and explaining electoral politics in India. From 1996, he has designed and coordinated the National Election Studies, the largest series of academic surveys of the Indian electorate. His many articles in the *Economic and Political Weekly*, *The Hindu*, composite books, and elsewhere can be found at his website. www.csds.in/faculty-yogendra-yadav.htm.

73. Subsequent editions, Harper Torchbooks/Harper and Row, 1962; New Brunswick, NJ, Transaction Publishers [Social Science classic text series], 2001).

74. Social systems are anthropomorphized; they have 'needs' related to survival, system maintenance, and viability. The four functions specified are adaptability; goal attainment; integration; and pattern maintenance.

The pattern variables that define actor orientation and are said to distinguish tradition and modernity are: affectivity and affective neutrality; particularism and universalism; diffuseness and specificity; ascription and achievement; expressiveness and instrumentality. For a critique of the dichotomous view of tradition and modernity and a view of social change based on adaptation, see 'Introduction' to Rudolph and Rudolph 1983 (1967).

The Committee on Comparative Politics' valorizing of Anglo-American political culture in Almond and Verba (1963) and in Pye and Verba (eds) (1965), can be sorted under the shadow of neo-colonial interpretation.

For a recent critique of the ways the self-other relationship was understood in comparative politics and international relations see Susanne Hoeber Rudolph (2005).

75. There are seven functions, four input functions and three output functions: input functions were (a) 'political socialization and recruitment'; (b) 'interest articulation'; (c) 'interest aggregation'; (d) 'political communication' and the 'output functions' were (e) 'rule making'; (f) 'rule application' and (g) 'rule adjudication' p. 17.

76. A lot of this research appeared in the eight volumes sponsored by the SSRC Committee on Comparative Politics. The last volume edited and contributed to by Binder (1971) repudiated the structural–functional paradigm in the name of contingent change and cultural and historical specificity.

77. That Kothari in this book was in the grip of Almond's structural-functionalism can be seen from a claim in *Memoirs* that he had modified Almond and Coleman's concept of the 'politics of aggregation' with 'the conceptualization of intermediate aggregation' (p. 68).

78. For example, Lipset (1960) used the 'best available statistical information' to show that there is a correlation between countries with high level of industrialization and urbanization, literacy rates and educational levels, and 'stable democracy' (pp. 45ff). That India, with 20 per cent of the world's population, didn't manifest these features, and yet had proved herself to be a 'stable democracy' suggested that alternative paths were available.

79. See *New York Times*, 16 February and 22 March 1967; Stern (1967).

80. According to the 'Memorandum From the Central Intelligence Agency to the 303 Committee', dated 22 June 1966, Subject: The Asia Foundation: Proposed Improvement in Funding Procedures,

The Asia Foundation [TAF], a Central Intelligence Agency proprietary, was established in 1954 to undertake cultural and educational activities on behalf of the United States Government in ways not open to official US agencies. Over the past twelve years TAF has accomplished its mission with increasing effectiveness and has, in the process, become a widely known institution, in Asia and the United States. TAF is now experiencing inquiries regarding its sources of funds and connections with the U.S. Government from the aggressive leftist publication, Ramparts.... Some immediate defensive and remedial measures are required (US State Department, *Johnson Administration, Foreign Relations 1964–1968, Volume X, National Security Policy*. Published 15 August 2002).

81. For some of the causes of and justifications for the Emergency, see Rudolph and Rudolph (1987, pp. 117, 222, 137, 294, 301–2, 324).

82. For Paul Brass's polemic against political scientists who failed to see the failures and oppressions of Nehru's developmental state, see Brass (2006).

83. For our experience of the Emergency, see Rudolph and Rudolph (1977)·

84. He acquired an international reputation in these years because of his role in the peace movement. He helped found and edit *Alternatives*, a journal dedicated to articulating and realizing a peaceful egalitarian world order.

85. Namboodiripad recognized the 'pre-capitalist' character of Brahmin landlords in his home region of Malabar and elsewhere in what came to be the state of Kerala. Pre-capitalist formations in Kerala had, he wrote,

a social and caste aspect.... Caste is a very important factor in the development of the kisan [peasant] and agricultural labour movement.... Landlordism is not only an economic category; it is also social, cultural, and political. For instance, in terms of caste, in the old system of landlordism, the dominant castes were the caste Hindus and Syrian Christians, the caste Hindus in particular, and among caste Hindus, Namboodiris in particular (Ramachandran 1998).

86. For a discussion of the SNDP, see Rudolph and Rudolph (1967, p. 125).

87. The book was frequently reprinted, was re-issued in 1995, and reprinted in 2001 and 2004.·

88. Rudolph and Rudolph (1960) and Rudolph (1965). Rudolph and Rudolph (1967) dealt extensively with identity politics in the form inter alia of caste associations as 'para-communities', intentional associations which combine features of ascriptive and voluntary associations.

89. Included in Kothari's 1970b edited volume is an essay by one of the early scholars of caste associations, Robert L. Hardgrave, Jr. See Hardgrave (1966) and (1968). Another early scholar of caste associations, in addition to those included in Kothari's book, Eleanor Zelliot on 'The Mahars of Maharashtra' and Carolyn Elliott on 'the Reddis and Kammas of Andhra', is Harold Gould, whose 'The Adaptive Functions of Caste in Contemporary Indian Society' was published in 1963.

90. Chandra (2004) where she argues that India is a patronage-democracy. See also Jaffrelot (2003).

91. An extensive literature on Dalit politics has developed over recent decades.For a recent overview of this literature with an extensive bibliography see Eva-Maria Hardtman (2009). Persons who have helped shape the field include Zelliot (1992) and Pai (2002).

92. See Rudolph and Rudolph (2006: 77 and 90, n 59), where Article XVIII of Gandhi's 1920 Congress constitution dealing with linguistic Provincial Pradesh Committees is discussed.

93. See Thirumalai (2005).

94. For a critique of and a constructivist alternative to primordial readings of identity, see Rudolph and Rudolph (1993).

For the constructivist turn in international relations scholarship, see Wendt (1999), where Wendt observes that of late,

> students of international relations have increasingly accepted two basic tenets of 'constructivism': [1] that the structures of human associations are determined primarily by shared ideas rather than material forces, and [2] that the identities and interests of purposive actors are constructed by these shared ideas rather than by nature (p. 1).

95. We think particularly of the other political scientist of the collective, Sudipta Kaviraj, but also of those in the collective who deal with political questions, such as Shahid Amin, David Arnold, David Hardiman, and Shail Mayaram.

96. Some estimate of the influence of the postcolonial and subaltern paradigms on the intellectual climate of the 1990s can be gained from Gyan Prakash's assessment in a lead article for an American Historical Review Forum (1994).

> To note the ferment created by Subaltern Studies in disciplines as diverse as history, anthropology, and literature [political science was not mentioned] is to recognize the force of recent postcolonial criticism. This criticism has compelled a radical rethinking of knowledge and social identities authored and authorized by colonialism and Western domination.... The dissemination of Subaltern Studies, beginning in 1982.... [poses a challenge] not only in South Asian studies but also in the historiography of other regions and in disciplines other than history (pp. 1475–6).

97. Guha, a Gramscian Marxist academic intellectual, migrated from India to the UK in the 1960s, and subsequently to Australia. He currently lives in Vienna, Austria.

His first book, *The Rule of Property for Bengal*, was first published in 1963. His 1982 essay in the first number of *Subaltern Studies*, 'On Some Aspects of the Historiography of Colonial India', set the movement's agenda.

He wrote that the term subaltern referred to 'the demographic difference between the total Indian population and all those whom we have described as the elite'. His goal, according to Amalendu K. Chakhraborty, was to write into history

> the hegemonic consciousness and political agenda of Indian peasants, urban factory workers, plantation laborers, and rural millenarian visionaries—loosely defined [by the Subaltern Studies Collective] as *subalterns*, whose revolutionary anticolonial and

antibourgeois political voices, they contend, were suppressed in Indian historiography, first by colonial writers and then by the Indian nationalists who owed their origin and world view to the West (see Chakhroborty's review of Guha 1998, p. 375).

98. Chatterjee, like Subrata Mitra, another leading scholar of Indian politics, took his PhD at the University of Rochester. Chatterjee and Mitra studied with William Riker, who can be credited with introducing rational choice theory and analysis into political science. Unlike Mitra, who has straddled schools of analysis, Chatterjee abandoned his training in international relations, nuclear war strategies, and rational choice theory soon after returning to his home place, Calcutta, in 1972. He returned in the immediate aftermath of the Maoist uprising of 1969–71, in which many of his college friends were involved, and a few were killed. Chatterjee became an autodidact, initially turning his attention to agrarian class structure and state violence. In 2006, he held appointments as Visiting Professor of Anthropology at Columbia University and Director of the Centre for Study in Social Sciences, Calcutta.

99. Two essays by Sudipta Kaviraj not discussed in our text, but which have contributed to scholarship on the state in India, are 'The Modern State in India', in Doornbos and Kaviraj (eds) (1997), and Kaviraj (1992). Chandhoke (1995) also made a major contribution to the literature on the state.

100. The book is constituted by two of Nandy's most brilliant essays, 'The Psychology of Colonialism: Sex, Age and Ideology in British India', and 'The Uncolonized Mind: A Post-Colonial View of India and the West'.

101. There are many challenges to the view that there were no states in pre-colonial India. Muzaffar Alam's and Sanjay Subramanyam's extended 'Introduction' to their edited volume *The Mughal State 1526–1750*, 1998 and many of the essays that follow spotlight the shortcomings of Guha's Hegelian reading of state formation and, as a result, reveal an enormous lacuna in Guha's Marxist-style reading of Indian history. We take a different view of state formation in India in Wallace (ed.) (1985).

102. Hegemony was defined as a form of rule grounded in active consent on the part of those being ruled. Active consent was produced by institutions and practices. Even those classes not directly in power consented to the way in which society was ruled; rule was not based on sheer force. Guha seems to observe regretfully, even resentfully, that European States can govern via hegemony, not dominance, by consent, not coercion.

For a critique of Marx's use of the category 'peasant', see Rudolph and Rudolph (1965), Part One, 'Traditional Structures and Modern Politics: Caste', 'Marx, Modernity, and Mobilization', pp. 17–28.

103. This quotation and all subsequent quotations from Partha Chatterjee, except those attributed to identified books or articles, are from 'Interview with Partha Chatterjee', conducted by Nermeen Shaikh of Asia Source, A Resource of the Asia Society at www.asiasource.org.news/special_reports/chatterjee.cfm. Last accessed on 10 June 2006.

104. A phrase borrowed from Mitter (1992). The monstrous effect of colonial modernity may be an expression of an Indian version of 'Occidentalism', the demonization of the colonial other.

105. For a defence of the use of the phrase 'our postmodern era', see Lloyd I. Rudolph (2006).

106. For a conceptual account of colonial hybridity and an examination of how it affected the life of a particular person, see Rudolph et al. (2000).

REFERENCES

Ahmed, Bashiruddin and Samuel J. Eldersveld. 1978. *Citizens and Politics: Mass Political Behavior in India.* Chicago: The University of Chicago Press.

Alam, Muzaffar and Sanjay Subramanyam. 1998. *The Mughal State 1526–1750.* New Delhi and New York: Oxford University Press.

Almond, Gabriel. 1960. 'Introduction: A Functional Approach to Comparative Politics', in Gabriel Almond and James S. Coleman (eds), *The Politics of Developing Areas.* Princeton, NJ: Princeton University Press, pp. 3–64.

Almond, Gabriel and James S. Coleman (eds). 1960. *The Politics of Developing Areas.* Princeton, NJ: Princeton University Press.

Almond, Gabriel A. and Sidney Verba. 1963. *The Civic Culture: Political Attitudes and Democracy in Five Nations.* Princeton, NJ: Princeton University Press.

Appadorai, Angadipuram. 1992. *Indian Political Thought through the Ages.* New Delhi: Khama Publishers.

————. 1973. *Documents on Political Thought In Modern India.* Bombay and New York: Oxford University Press.

————. 1971a. *Indian Political Thinking in the Twentieth Century: From Naoroji to Nehru.* Madras: Oxford University Press.

————. 1971b. *Political Ideas in Modern India: Impact of the West.* Bombay: Academic Books.

Appleby, Paul. 1953. *Public Administration in India: Report of a Survey.* New Delhi: Manager of Publications.

Apter, David. 1998 [1996]. 'Comparative Politics, Old and New', in Robert E. Goodin and Hans-Dieter Klingemann (eds), *A New Handbook of Political Science.* Oxford and New York: Oxford University Press.

Arora, Balveer and Douglas V. Varney (eds), 1995. *Multiple Identities in a Single State.* New Delhi: Konark Publishers.

Austin, Granville. 2000. *Working of a Democratic Constitution: The Indian Experience.* New Delhi: Oxford University Press.

————. 1966. *The Indian Constitution.* New York and New Delhi: Oxford University Press.

Barker, Ernest. 1944. *The Development of Public Services in Europe, 1660–1930.* London and New York: Oxford University Press.

Basu, D.D. 1999. *Shorter Constitution of India.* 12th edn, Agra, Nagpur, New Delhi: Wadhwa and Company.

————. 1994. *Introduction to the Constitution of India.* 16th edn, New Delhi: Prentice-Hall of India.

Baxi, Upendra. 2006. *The Future of Human Right.* New York and New Delhi: Oxford University Press.

————. 2002. 'The [Im] possibility of Constitutional Justice: Seismographic Notes on Indian Constitutionalism', in Zoya Hasan, E. Sridharan, and R. Sudarshan (eds), *India's Living Constitution: Ideas, Practices, Controversies.* New Delhi: Permanent Black, pp. 31–63.

————. 1983. 'Taking Suffering Seriously: Social Action Litigation Before the Supreme Court of India', *Social Justice Reporter.*

————. 1980. *The Supreme Court and Politics.* Lucknow: Eastern Book Company.

Béteille, Andre. 1965. *Caste, Class and Power: Changing Patterns of Stratification in a Tanjore Village.* Berkeley: University of California Press.

Bhabha, Homi K. 1994. *The Location of Culture.* London and New York: Routledge.

Binder, Leonard. 1971. *Crises and Sequences in Political Development.* Princeton, NJ: Princeton University Press.

Bjorkman, James Warner. 2007. 'Public Law 480 and the Policies of Self-Help and Short-Tether: Indo-American Relations, 1965–68', in Lloyd I. Rudolph and Susanne Hoeber Rudolph (eds), *The Making of US Foreign Policy Towards South Asia.* New Delhi: Concept, pp. 359–425.

Bjorkman, James Warner and Het Ram Chaturvedi. 1994. 'Panchayati Raj in Rajasthan: The Penalties of Success', in Karine Schomer et al. (eds), *The Idea of Rajasthan: Explorations in Regional Identity, Vol II: Institutions.* New Delhi: Manohar, pp. 117–58.

Blair, Harry W. 1979. *Voting, Caste, Community, Society: Explorations in Aggregate Data Analysis in India and Bangladesh.* New Delhi: Young Asia.

Brass, Paul R. 2006. 'How American Political Scientists Experienced India's Development State', in Lloyd I. Rudolph and John Kurt Jacobsen (eds), *Experiencing the State.* New Delhi and New York: Oxford University Press, pp. 110–38.

————. 1986. 'The 1984 Parliamentary Election in 1984', *Asian Survey,* 26 (6), pp. 653–69.

Brass, Paul R. 1974. *Language, Religion and Politics in North India*. London and New York: Cambridge University Press.

_____. 1969. 'Political Participation, Institutionalization, and Stability in India', *Government and Opposition*, 4(1), pp. 25–53.

Chakrabarty, Bidyut. 2007. *Reinventing Public Administration: The Indian Experience*. Hyderabad: Orient Longman.

Chakrabarty, Dipesh. 2000. *Provincializing Europe: Postcolonial Thought and Historical Difference*. Princeton and Oxford: Princeton University Press.

Chandel, Sunil Singh. 2003. *Information Services in Academic Libraries*. Jaipur and New Delhi: Rawat.

Chandhoke, Neera. 1995. *State and Civil Society*. New Delhi: Sage Publications.

Chandra, Kanchan. 2004. *Why Ethnic Parties Succeed: Patronage and Ethnic Head Counts inIndia*. Cambridge: Cambridge University Press.

Chatterjee, Partha. 2002. 'Institutional Context of Social Science Research in South Asia', *Economic and Political Weekly*, XXXVII(35), pp. 3604–12.

_____. 1999. *The Partha Chatterjee Omnibus: Nationalist Thought and the Colonial World, The Nation and Its Fragments, A Possible India*. New Delhi: Oxford University Press.

Coupland, Reginald. 1944. *The Indian Problem: Report on the Constitutional Problem*. New York, London: Oxford University Press.

Crick, Bernard. 1967 [1959]. *The American Science of Politics: Its Origins and Conditions*. Berkeley and Los Angeles: University of California Press.

Dewey, Clive. 1993. *Anglo-Indian Attitudes: The Mind of the Indian Civil Service*, London and Rio Grande: The Hambledon Press.

Dhar, P.N. 1995. 'The Early Years', in Dharma Kumar and Dilip Mookherjee (eds), *D. School: Reflections on the Delhi School of Economics*. New Delhi: Oxford University Press, pp. 7–23.

Dhavan, Rajeev. 1984. 'Managing Legal Activism: Reflecting on India's Legal Aid Programme', typescript.

_____. 1978. *Selection and Appointment of Supreme Court Judges: A Case Study*. Bombay: N.M. Tripathi.

_____. 1977. *The Supreme Court of India: A Socio-legal Critique of its Juristic Techniques* (Foreword by Lord Denning). Bombay: N.M. Tripathi.

_____. 1976. *The Supreme Court of India and Parliamentary Sovereignty: A Critique of Its Approach to the Recent Constitutional Crisis*. New Delhi: Sterling Publishers.

Dhavan, Rajeev and Christie Davies (eds). 1987. *Only the Good News: On the Law of the Press in India*. New Delhi: Manohar Publications.

Dhavan, Rajeev and Christie Davies (eds). 1986. *Litigation Explosion in India*. Bombay: N.M. Tripathi.

_____. 1979. *President's Rule in the States* [prepared under the auspices of the Indian Law Institute]. Bombay: N.M. Tripathi.

_____. 1978. *Censorship and Obscenity*. London: M. Robertson and Totowa, NJ: Rowman and Littlefield.

Easton, David. 1969. 'The New Revolution in Political Science', *The American Political Science Review*, LXIII(4), pp. 1051–61.

_____. 1953. *The Political System: An Inquiry into the State of Political Science*. New York: Alfred Knopf.

Finer, Herman. 1949. *Theory and Practice of Modern Government*. New York: Henry Holt and Company.

Frankel, Francine. 1978. *India's Political Economy, 1947–1977: The Gradual Revolution*. Princeton, NJ: Princeton University Press.

_____. 1971. *India's Green Revolution; Economic Gains and Political Costs*. Princeton, NJ: Princeton University Press.

Friedrich, Carl J. 1950 [1937]. *Constitutional Government and Democracy: Theory and Practice in Europe and America*. Boston: Ginn and Company.

Galanter, Marc. 1984. *Competing Equalities: Law and the Backward Classes in India*. Berkeley: University of California Press and New Delhi: Oxford University Press.

_____. 1982. 'Patterns of Legal Services in India', mimeograph.

_____. 1962. 'The Problem of Group Membership: Some Reflections on the Judicial View of Indian Society', *Journal of the Indian Law Institute*, IV (July–September).

Gandhi, M.K. 1997, 'Hind Swaraj', in Anthony J. Parel (ed.), *Hind Swaraj and Other Writings*. Cambridge, UK: Cambridge University Press, pp. 1–121.

Gandhi, Rajmohan. 1989. *India Wins Errors: A Scrutiny of Maulana Azad's India Wins Freedom*. New Delhi: Radiant Publishers.

Gilbert, Irene A. 1972a. 'Autonomy and Consensus under the Raj: Presidency [Calcutta]; Muir [Allahabad]; M.A.O. [Aligarh]', in Susanne Hoeber Rudolph and Lloyd I Rudolph (eds), *Education and Politics in India: Studies in Organization, Society, and Policy*. Cambridge, MA: Harvard University Press and New Delhi: Oxford University Press, pp. 167–71.

_____. 1972b. 'The Organization of the Academic Profession in India: The Indian Educational Services, 1864–1924', in Susanne Hoeber Rudolph and Lloyd I Rudolph (eds), *Education and Politics in India: Studies in Organization, Society, and Policy*. Cambridge, MA: Harvard University Press and New Delhi: Oxford University Press, pp. 319–41.

Gilmour, David. 2005. *The Ruling Caste: Imperial Lives in the Victorian Raj*. New York: Farrar, Straus and Giroux.

Goodin, Robert and Hans-Dieter Klingemann (eds). 1996. *A Handbook of Political Science*. New York: Oxford University Press.

Gould, Harold. 1963. 'The Adaptive Functions of Caste in Contemporary Indian Society', *Asian Survey*, 3(9), pp. 427–38.

Gould, Harold and Sumit Ganguly (eds). 1993. *India Votes: Alliance Politics and Minority Governments in the Ninth and Tenth General Elections*. Boulder, CO: Westview Press.

Guha, Ranajit. 1997. *Dominance without Hegemony: History and Power in Colonial India*. Cambridge, MA: Harvard University Press.

Haas, Peter. 1992. 'Epistemic Communities and International Policy Coordination', *International Organization*, 46(1), pp. 1–35.

Hardgrave, Robert L. 1970. *India: Government and Politics in a Developing Nation*. New York: Harcourt, Brace & World.

Hardgrave, Jr. Robert L. 1968. *The Nadars of Tamilnad: The Political Culture of a Community in Change*. Berkeley: University of California Press.

———. 1966. 'Varieties of Political Behavior among the Nadars of Tamilnad', *Asian Survey*, 6(11), pp. 614–21.

Hardtman, Era-Maria. 2009. *The Dalit Movement in India: Local Practices, Global Connections*. New Delhi: Oxford University Press.

Harrison, Selig. 1960. *India: The Most Dangerous Decades*. Princeton, NJ: Princeton University Press.

Hasan, Mushirul. 1993. *India's Partition: Process, Strategy and Mobilization*. New Delhi and New York: Oxford University Press.

Haksar, P.N., R. Ramanna, P.M. Bhargava. 1981. 'A Statement of Scientific Temper', *Mainstream*, 19(47), pp. 6–10.

Hansen, John Mark. 1997. 'Harold F. Gosnell, Political Scientist, Obituary', *PS: Political Science and Politics*, 30(3), pp. 582–7.

Huntington, Samuel P. and Jorge I. Dominguez. 1975. 'Political Development', in Fred I. Greenstein and Nelson Polsby (eds), *Macropolitical Theory: Handbook of Political Science, Vol. 3*. Reading, MA: Addison Wesley, pp. 1–114.

Jaffrelot, Christophe. 2003. *India's Silent Revolution: The Rise of the Low Castes in North Indian Politics*. Delhi: Permanent Black.

———. 1996. *The Hindu Nationalist Movement and Indian Politics, 1995–1990*. London: Hearst and Company.

Jalal, Ayesha. 1985. *The Sole Spokesman: Jinnah, the Muslim League, and the Demand for Pakistan*. Cambridge and New York: Cambridge University Press.

Jayal, Niraja Gopal. 1999. *Democracy and the State: Welfare, Secularism, and Development in Contemporary India*, New York and New Delhi: Oxford University Press.

Jenkins, Rob. 1999. *Democratic Politics and Economic Reform in India*. Cambridge: Cambridge University Press.

Jennings, Sir Ivor. 1953. *Some Characteristics of the Indian Constitution*. Madras and New York: Oxford University Press.

Kapur, Devesh John P. Lewis, and Richard Webb. 1997. *The World Bank: Its First Half Century*, Washington DC. The Brookings Institution.

Kaufman-Osborn, Timothy V. 2006. 'Dividing the Domain of Political Science: On the Fetishism of Subfields', *Polity*, 38(1), pp. 41–71.

Kaviraj, Sudipta. 1997. 'The Modern State in India', in Martin Doornbos and Sudipta Kaviraj (eds), *Dynamics of State Formation: India and Europe Compared*. New Delhi: Sage Publications, pp. 225–50.

———. 1992. 'The Imaginary Institution of India', *Subaltern Studies, VII*, New Delhi: Oxford University Press, pp. 1–39.

Keith, Arthur Berriedale. 1936. *A Constitutional History of India, 1600–1935*. London: Methuen, & Co.

Kogekar, S.V. and Richard L. Park (eds). 1956. *Reports on the Indian General Election, 1951–1952*. Bombay: Popular Book Depot.

Kohli, Atul. 1990. *Democracy and Discontent: India's Growing Crisis of Governability*. Cambridge: Cambridge University Press.

Kothari, Rajni. 2002. *Memoirs: Uneasy is the Life of the Mind*. New Delhi: Rupa & Co.

———. 1970a. *Politics in India*. Boston: Little Brown.

———. 1970b. *Caste in Indian Politics*. Hyderabad: Orient Longman.

Kramnick, Isaac and Barry Sheerman. 1993. *Harold Laski: A Life on the Left*. New York: Allen Lane/Penguin Press.

Lipset, Seymour Martin. 1960. *Political Man: The Social Basis of Politics*. Garden City, NY: Doubleday.

———. 1959. 'Some Social Requisites of Democracy: Economic Development and Political Legitimacy', *American Political Science Review*, 53(1), pp. 69–105.

Madan, T.N. 1994. 'On Critical Self-Awareness', in his *Pathways: Approaches to the Study of Society in India*, New Delhi: Oxford University Press.

———. 1975. 'On Living Intimately With Strangers', in Andre Béteille and T.N. Madan (eds), *Encounter and Field Experience: Personal Accounts of Field Work*. New Delhi: Vikas, pp. 131–56.

Mahajan, Sucheta. 2000. *Independence and Partition: The Erosion of Colonial Power in India*. New Delhi: Sage Publications.

Manor, James. 2000, 'Wyndraeth Humphreys Morris-Jones', *The Journal of Commonwealth & Comparative Politics*, 38(1), p. 6.

———. 1997. 'Parties and the Party System', in Partha Chatterjee (ed.), *State and Politics in India*. New Delhi: Oxford University Press, pp. 92–124.

———. 1978. 'Where Congress Survived: Five States in the Indian General Election of 1977', *Asian Survey*, 18(8), pp. 785–803.

Mansingh, Surjit. 2003. *Historical Dictionary of India*. New Delhi: Vision Books.

Masaldan, P.N. 1965. *Planning and the People: A Study of Political Participation in Planning in U.P.* New York: Asia Publishing House.

———. 1962. *Planning in Uttar Pradesh: A Study of Machinery for Coordination of the State's Development*. Bombay: Vora.

Mathew, George. 1996. 'Panchayati Raj in India', in Kuldeep Mathur (ed.), *Development Policy and Administration in India*. New Delhi: Sage Publications, pp. 200–24.

Mehta, Pratap Bhanu. 2002. 'The Inner Conflict of Constitutionalism: Judicial Review and the "Basic Structure"', in Zoya Hasan, E. Sridharan and R. Sudarshan (eds), *India's Living Constitution: Ideas, Practices, Controversies*. New Delhi: Permanent Black, pp. 179–206.

Merriam, Charles E. and Harold F. Gosnell. 1924. *Non-Voting: Causes and Methods of Control*. Chicago: The University of Chicago Press.

Misra, B.B. 1990. *The Unification and Division of India*. New Delhi: Oxford University Press.

Mitter, Partha. 1992. *Much Maligned Monsters: A History of European Reactions to Indian Art*. Chicago: The University of Chicago Press.

Morris-Jones, W.H. 1957. *Parliament in India*. Philadelphia: University of Pennsylvania Press.

Morris-Jones, W.H. and Biplab Dasgupta. 1975. *Patterns and Trends in Indian Politics: An Ecological Analysis of Aggregate Data on Society and Elections*. Bombay: Allied Publishers.

Namboodiripad, E.M.S. 1962. *The National Question in Kerala*. Bombay: Allied Publishers.

Nandy, Ashis. 1983. *The Intimate Enemy: Loss and Recovery of Self Under Colonialism*. New Delhi: Oxford University Press.

Narain, Iqbal and P.C. Mathur. 1982. *Political Science in India: State of the Discipline and Agenda for the Future*. New Delhi: University Grants Commission.

Narain, Iqbal. 1978. *Election Studies in India: An Evaluation*, Report of an ICSSR [Indian Council of Social Science Research] project, Bombay: Allied Publishers.

Nayar, Baldev Raj. 1990. *The Political Economy of India's Public Sector: Policy and Performance*. Bombay: Popular Prakashan.

Nehru, Jawaharlal. 1981[1946]. *The Discovery of India*. New Delhi: Oxford University Press.

Noorani, A.G. 1970. *India's Constitution and Politics*. Bombay: Jaico Books.

Pai, Sudha. 2002. *Dalit Assertion and the Unfinished Democratic Revolution: The Bahujan Samaj Party in Uttar Pradesh*. New Delhi, Thousand Oaks, and London: Sage Publications.

Palmer, Norman D. 1975. *Elections and Political Development: The South Asian Experience*. Durham, NC: Duke University Press.

———. 1961. *The Indian Political System*. Boston: Houghton Mifflin.

Pandey, Gyanendra. 2001. *Remembering Partition: Violence, Nationalism, and History in India*. New York: Cambridge University Press.

Park, Richard. 1967. *Indian Political System*. Englewood Cliffs, NJ: Prentice Hall.

Park, Richard and Irene Tinker (eds). 1959. *Leadership and Political Institution in India*. Princeton, NJ: Princeton University Press.

Parsons, Talcott. 1953. *The Political System*. New York: Knopf.

Parsons, Talcott and Edward Shils (eds). 1951. *Toward a General Theory of Action*. Cambridge: Harvard University Press.

Prakash, Gyan. 1994. 'Subaltern Studies as Postcolonial Criticism', *American Historical Review*, 99(5), pp. 1475–90.

Pye, Lucian and Sidney Verba (eds). 1965. *Political Culture and Political Development*. Princeton, NJ: Princeton University Press.

Pylee, M.V. 1962. *India's Constitution*. Bombay and New York: Allied Publishing House.

———. 1960. *Constitutional Government in India*. Bombay and New York: Allied Publishing House.

Raj, K.N. 1995. 'The Delhi School of Economics', in Dharma Kumar and Dilip Mookherjee (eds), *D. School: Reflections on the Delhi School of Economics*, New Delhi: Oxford University Press.

Ramachandran, V.K. 1998. 'Talking About Kerala: A Conversation with E. M. S. Namboodiripad, April 28, 1992', *Frontline*, 15(9), 25 April–8 May.

Rau, B.N. 1963. *India's Constitution in the Making*. Bombay and New York: Allied Publishers.

Retzlaff, Ralph. 1963. 'The Problem of Communal Minorities in the Drafting of the Indian Constitution', in R.N. Spann (ed.), *Constitutionalism in Asia*. Bombay and New York: Asia Publishing House.

Riesman, David. 1958. *Constraint and Variety in American Education*. Garden City, NY: Doubleday Anchor Books.

Roy, Ramashray. 1966, 1967. 'Election Studies: Selection of Congress Candidates', Part 1, 'The Formal Criteria',

Part 2, 'Pressures and Counter Pressures', Part 3, 'Claims and Counter Claims', and Parts 4 and 5, 'Structure of Authority in the Congress', *Economic and Political Weekly*, 31 December 1966, and 7 and 14 January and 11 February 1967.

Rudolph, Lloyd I. 2006. 'The Road Not Taken: The Modernist Roots of Partition', in Lloyd I. Rudolph and Susanne Hoeber Rudolph (eds), *Postmodern Gandhi and Other Essays: Gandhi in the World and at Home*. New Delhi: Oxford University Press and Chicago: The University of Chicago Press.

_____. 1965. 'The Modernity of Tradition: The Democratic Incarnation of Caste in India', *The American Political Science Review*, LIX(4), pp. 975–89.

Rudolph, Susanne Hoeber. 2005. 'Presidential Address, The Imperialism of Categories: Situating Knowledge in a Globalizing World', *Perspective on Politics*, 3(1), pp. 5–14.

Rudolph, Lloyd I. and Susanne H. Rudolph. 2006. *Postmodern Gandhi and Other Essays: Gandhi in the World and at Home*. New Delhi: Oxford University Press, and Chicago: The University of Chicago Press.

_____. 2003. 'Engaging Subjective Knowledge: How Amar Singh's Diary Narratives of and By the Self Help Explain Identity Politics', *Perspectives on Politics*, 1(4), pp. 681–94.

_____. 1993. 'Modern Hate: How Ancient Animosities Get Invented', *The New Republic*, 22 March, pp. 24–9.

_____. 1987. *In Pursuit of Lakshmi: The Political Economy of the Indian State*. Chicago: The University of Chicago Press.

_____. 1985. 'The Subcontinental Empire and the Regional Kingdom in Indian State Formation', in Paul Wallace (ed.), *Region and Nation in India*. New Delhi: Oxford & IBH Publishing Co.

_____. 1977. 'Jaipur Notes', *The University of Chicago Magazine*, LXIX(4), pp. 359–88.

_____. 1960. 'The Political Role of India's Caste Associations', *Pacific Affairs*, 33(1), pp. 283–97.

_____. 1967. *The Modernity of Tradition: Political Development in India*. Chicago: The University of Chicago Press.

_____. 1958. 'Surveys in India: Field Experience in Madras State', *Public Opinion Quarterly*, 22(3), pp. 235–44.

Rudolph, Susanne Hoeber, Lloyd Rudolph, and Mohan Singh Kanota. 2000. *Reversing the Gaze: Amar Singh's Diary, A Colonial Subject's Narrative of Imperial India*. New Delhi: Oxford University Press.

Seervai, H.M. 1967. *Constitutional Law of India: A Critical Commentary*. Bombay: N.M. Tripathi.

Sheth, D.L. (ed.). 1975. *Citizens and Parties*. Bombay: Allied Publishers, CSDS Occasional Papers 2.

Shils, Edward. 1961. *The Intellectual between Tradition and Modernity: The Indian Situation*. The Hague: Mouton & Co. Publishers.

Sisson, Richard and William Vanderbok. 1983. 'Mapping the Indian Electorate: Trends in Party Support in Seven States', *Asian Survey*, 23(10), pp. 1140–58.

Spann, R.N. 1963. Constitutionalism in Asia. Bombay and New York: Asia Publishing House.

Srinivas, M.N. 1998. 'Itineraries of an Indian Social Anthropologist', in his *Indian Society through Personal Writings*. New Delhi: Oxford University Press, pp. 1–23.

_____. 1996. 'Indian Anthropologists and the Study of Indian Culture', *Economic and Political Weekly*, 16 March.

Stern, Sol. 1967. 'A Short Account of International Student Politics and the Cold War with Particular Reference to the NSA, CIA, etc.', *Ramparts*, March, pp. 29–39.

Taylor, Charles. 1994. 'The Politics of Recognition', in Amy Gutmann (ed.), *Multiculturalism: Examining the Process of Recognition*. Princeton, NJ: Princeton University Press, pp. 25–74.

Thirumalai, M.S. 2005. 'Language Policy in the Motilal Nehru Committee Report, 1928', Vol. 5 (May), http. www.languageinindia.com.

Toulmin, Stephen. 2001. *Return to Reason*. Cambridge, MA: Harvard University Press.

Varma, S.P., Iqbal Narain, C.P. Bhambhri. 1968–70. *Fourth General Election in India*. Bombay: Orient Longman.

Wang, Huiyun. 2001. *Discourses on Tradition and Modernization: Perspectives on Gandhi and Sun Yat-sen*. New Delhi: Maadhyam.

Weiner, Myron. 1979. 'Social Science Research and Public Policy in India—II', *Economic and Political Weekly*, 22 September.

Weiner, Myron and Rajni Kothari. 1965. *Indian Voting Behavior: Studies of the 1962 [fourth] General Elections*. Calcutta: Firma Mukhopadhayay.

Weiner, Myron and John Field. 1974–7. *Electoral Politics in the Indian States*. New Delhi: Manohar.

Wendt, Alexander. 1999. *Social Theory of International Relations*. Cambridge, UK: Cambridge University Press.

Wolin, Sheldon. 1969. 'Political Theory as a Vocation', *American Political Science Review*, LXIII(4): 1062–82.

Zelliot, Eleanor. 1992. *From Untouchable to Dalit: Essays on the Ambedkar Movement*. New Delhi: Manohar.

38 Data and the Study of Indian Politics*

Steven I. Wilkinson

Since the early 1990s, there has been a dramatic increase in the availability of data on Indian politics and society. Many national and state-level government departments and agencies now routinely make available online data and reports that used to be available only in printed format, and then only to the researcher with access to officials, a good library, or the patience to make repeated trips to government offices. The Indian Election Commission, for instance, now provides detailed election results on its website, as well as an archive of all post-Independence Lok Sabha and Vidhan Sabha returns, and a digest of current election law, codes of practice, candidates' declarations, and commission decisions.[1] For those with access to the web, there is no longer a need to use the older printed collections of election data that were so important in the past (Butler *et al.* 1995; Singh and Bose 1986–94). The Government of India has also made the various parliamentary, ministry, agency, judiciary, state, and district websites easy to find, by creating national web portals (goidirectory.nic.in/, and http://indiaimage.nic.in) that link to all these other sites.

In addition to these Central and state government initiatives, the boom in the economy and the massive expansion of print, television, and internet media have both fed and helped create a massive new appetite for information on society, economy, and politics. Existing bodies, such as the National Council of Applied Economic Research (NCAER), the Centre for Policy Research (CPR), and the Centre for the Study of Developing Societies (CSDS) in New Delhi, the Institute for Social and Economic Change (ISEC) in Bangalore, and the Centre for Development Studies (CDS) in Trivandrum, are doing more studies, polls, and surveys than ever.[2] Some of the key information and analysis from CSDS data collection and surveys, in particular, has come out in an important edited issue of the *Journal of the Indian School of Political Economy*.[3] There is a new and encouraging trend among various centres within South Asia to undertake comparative surveys of all the countries in South Asia, enabling scholars to see how well India is doing compared to Pakistan, Sri Lanka, Bangladesh, and

*I thank Devesh Kapur for his very helpful comments on an earlier draft of this chapter.

others in terms of indicators such as support for democracy, gender equality, and the level of trust in state institutions (*State of Democracy in South Asia* 2008). There has also been a massive expansion in the number of private polling companies and consultancies providing data on the Indian economy and consumer trends, some of it in GIS formats, which allow the graphic display of information on maps of states, districts, or towns.[4]

International organizations such as the International Monetary Fund (IMF) and World Bank, and aid organizations such as the British aid agency, Department for International Development (DFID), have also commissioned a growing number of surveys, polls, and case studies that are of tremendous interest to the researcher on Indian politics and society. The IMF and World Bank both make much of their economic data and research on India available online, along with important internal documents relating to their country strategies. Both DFID, as well as the independent Overseas Development Institute (ODI) in London, have established excellent web portals that make their own research as well as commissioned research on poverty, gender, and development issues in India available in one place.[5] Some of these papers, for instance those relating to the factors that influence local development spending and beneficiaries, are of great relevance to political researchers, as it turns out that these studies show just how much of the spending is for political purposes, rather than the stated development or social welfare goals of these programmes (Singh *et al.* 2003; Mooij 2003).

Together with these government and institutional resources, a growing number of academic centres outside India that focus on poverty, development, gender, and (by necessity) the politics of public goods provision within South Asia have been started over the past decade. Existing centres of research excellence on these issues, such as the ODI in London, the Institute of Social Studies in the Hague, and the Institute of Development Studies at the University of Sussex have been joined by these new research-producing centres and institutes such as the Earth Institute at Columbia University and the MIT Poverty Action Lab, which has made the results of large-scale randomized surveys of teacher and school performance in India available

on its website.[6] Some widely available research websites, such as that of the National Bureau of Economic Research in the USA, also contain a large number of pre-publication research papers on Indian development.[7] And the Center for the Advanced Study of India at the University of Pennsylvania has a large number of papers, talks, and other links of interest to those interested in contemporary Indian politics and society available on its website.[8]

Apart from these more formal institutions, there are also a large number of non-governmental organizations (NGOs) both inside and outside India that produce a massive range of studies, data, and links that are of great interest to the political researcher. The Peoples Union for Civil Liberties, for instance, has an enormous amount of information on social justice issues on its website (www.pucl.org/), while there are also many NGOs that focus specifically on particular groups' grievances, such as the National Campaign on Dalit Human Rights (http://www.ncdhr.org. in/) and the All Indian Christian Council (http:// indianchristians.in/news/). In addition to NGOs, we are also seeing the beginnings of Western-style political polling and data analysis companies, which can deliver—for a price—targeted demographic and other information to political candidates.[9] The range of topics and groups these thousands of NGOs cover is simply too vast to even sketch briefly here.

To be sure, there remain some important gaps in terms of data coverage. In terms of formal electoral politics, for instance, we have several obvious needs, most of which have been identified by Yogendra Yadav and Alistair McMillan in an excellent 2002 survey of data resources in Indian politics (Yadav and McMillan 2002). First, they point out that there is as yet no good information on roll-call votes in the Lok Sabha or the Vidhan Sabhas that would enable us to study which way members of these representative institutions vote, and why. Such studies have long been done for Western Europe and the USA, and are increasingly being undertaken for other regions of the world, such as Latin America and Eastern Europe, and they also need to be carried out for the world's largest bureaucracy. Second, we need more information about elections below the level of Vidhan Sabha polls: municipal elections, block and district elections, and the new panchayat elections that have followed the passage of the Seventy-second and Seventy-third Amendments. Who gets elected to these institutions? Are the politicians elected to these bodies always linked to Member of Legislative Assembly (MLAs) and Member of Parliament's (MP) patronage machines—as some case studies suggest—or do the panchayats and similar bodies provide a new arena for other political movements to flourish? At present, as Yadav and McMillan point out, these data (as well as new booth-level voting figures available since the 2000 elections) are held by the individual state Election Commissions, rather than the Election Commission of India (ECI), and they make a convincing argument in support of the fact that the data needs to be made more widely available through a central archive, perhaps hosted by the ECI.

There is also a huge gap in data coverage on such things as the composition of ministries in the Vidhan Sabhas (A.B. Kohli has fortunately largely met this need for the Lok Sabha) (Kohli 2000) as well as party histories, splits, defections, and so on, which are of obvious importance in explaining political outcomes such as which states, districts, and sectors of the electorate get government spending and which do not. At present it is possible, but only with a massive amount of effort, to reconstruct such data by using the Lok Sabha Secretariat's *Journal of Parliamentary Information*, combined with newspaper sources and government gazettes, but a central source for such information would be of immense value for students of Indian politics.[10]

THE KEY ISSUE OF DATA RELIABILITY AND QUALITY

However, an even more important issue than such obvious gaps in coverage, I will argue in this chapter, are the less obvious concerns about data quality and reliability. For the individual researcher, the growing availability of vast amounts of public and private data and research, much of which can be easily downloaded from the web, has its costs as well as its many obvious benefits. Most importantly, there is the issue of how to discriminate between good and bad data when confronted with such massive information overload. The hard work of gathering data from

contacts and fieldwork in the past had great value, because it forced researchers to speak to the people who generated the data and therefore made them much more aware of its problems and imperfections. The person who now downloads data remotely is less aware than in the past of what has been left out—which data are less robust than they appear, and which vital data or alternative explanations are not included, or included only in a partial or misleading way. As a result, the researcher may imagine that he or she is conducting a more rigorous or scientific study of a particular area—on the presumption that more data equals a more robust study—when in reality he or she is just building greater pseudo-scientific edifices on data that is, in reality, incapable of supporting the findings or theories that are generated.

Most data are, after all, far from being unfiltered reflections of social reality. As Devesh Kapur and Yoshiko Herrera have explored in a fascinating article on data quality in the social sciences, the belief systems of those who provide the raw data, as well as the capacity of the state and various financial, political, and social incentives to misrepresent or manipulate the numbers, all have a profound effect on data quality (Herrera and Kapur 2007). Numbers, in other words, often do not mean what we think they do. In the case of financial data, for instance, we might think that a rise in a state's Fiscal Self Reliance Indicator (FSRI)(the ratio of states' own revenue receipts to their revenue expenditure) is automatically a good thing. However, as Archana Dholakia has pointed out, a rise in this number might also mean that states are manipulating their financial data in order to bring about an illusory 'improvement' in this indicator to impress the Finance Commission, which has begun to use the FSRI as an indicator of states' progress on fiscal reform. To artificially improve their FSRIs, some states transferred revenue expenditure to their 'capital expenditure columns' so as to reduce the apparent size of their deficits, while others created special purpose financial vehicles (SPVs) on which to offload various debts and expenditures (Dholakia 2005).

In the remainder of this chapter, I want to highlight some general issues concerning the quality of data on Indian politics and society, as well as some ways in which the individual researcher might better assess the quality of the data that he or she uses. Elsewhere, I have already provided an extensive treatment of the weaknesses of data on riots (Wilkinson 2006: Appendix A), so here I will focus on issues concerning data quality and reliability in three other areas: data on crime; data on caste, language, and identity; and data on development spending. In each of these three areas, the official data are a lot less reliable than they appear; however, exploring the reasons for this unreliability can tell us a lot about contemporary Indian politics.

DATA ON CRIME

Indian crime data, published each year in *Crime in India* as well as in the various state reports on general administration and the police, are used extensively in research on political outcomes (Nayar 1975; Kohli 1990).[11] The problem with many of these data, however, as any Indian involved in a court case or one who needs to file a First Information Report (FIR) at a local police station knows, is that they are often of questionable quality, and that they often greatly underestimate the true rate of crime.[12] There are several issues. First, it is well established that many cases go unreported because many members of the public are reluctant to have any contact with the police, whom they fear. In a 1996 survey in Delhi, a city generally regarded as one with one of the better police forces, 60 per cent of the public said that they would not personally report a crime, relying instead on friends and relations to secure redress.[13] Second, it is well-established that many policemen demand bribes to register police cases, a fact that obviously depresses crime statistics even further: one survey in Varanasi in the 1970s found that 64 per cent of those who had sought the police's help had themselves been asked for money, and that 89 per cent of all respondents 'felt that the police were a corrupt lot and moved only when bribed'.[14] Third, especially since Independence, there have been professional incentives for police officers to minimize crime figures in order to make their performance and that of their political masters look better than it is.[15] Policemen are frequently transferred or otherwise punished for allowing crime rates to go up in their districts, and are therefore under implicit

(and at times explicit) pressure to not record particular crimes, or any crimes at all.

How much of a difference do all these factors make to the quality of crime data? N.S. Saksena, a senior Indian police officer who made several attempts in the 1960s to reduce the 'burking' (concealment) of crime, estimated that the proportion of cases registered to the number of crimes committed ranged from as low as 15–20 per cent in the case of thefts of cattle or bicycles, to as much as 80 per cent in the case of murders. His own attempt to improve the reporting of burglary in Uttar Pradesh—which involved testers being sent to police stations and increased punishments for the non-registration of crimes—found that official burglary figures went up by 100 per cent almost immediately, only to drop again when the officials concerned with anti-burking changed positions.[16]

More recently, beginning with a survey in Mumbai in 1992, a few studies have been carried out in an attempt to assess the true rates of crime and levels of under-reporting through victimization surveys, in which the numbers of people who reported having been victims of robbery, burglary, and similar incidents, can be compared with the percentage of the population which actually succeeds in registering such crimes in the official statistics. These surveys make for sober reading. A survey of victims of crime in Madurai, Coimbatore, Trichy, and Chennai in the late 1990s found under-reporting rates close to 100 per cent for consumer fraud and corruption, 79 per cent for theft, 58 per cent for robbery, and 48 per cent for burglary (Chockalingam 2003). Among victims of sexual assault, where the stigma of reporting is great, and victims often rightly perceive the police to be unconcerned with treating sexual offences as serious, the percentages were much worse: only 4 per cent of victims of sexual offences and 24 per cent of sexual assault victims reported these offences to the police (ibid.: 123–4).

As a result of all these problems, Indian crime statistics for most categories of crime represent only a small proportion of the actual number of crimes that take place. The Director of India's Home Intelligence Bureau, tongue firmly in cheek, pointed out in the early 1960s that

Whereas crime in the United States of America, United Kingdom, Japan, etc. which have very well organized and well developed law enforcement agencies, has shown a steady increase of 4 to 5 per cent per year, in India over the last decade crime figures have remained more or less steady though the population has increased by over 20 per cent.[17]

The tendency to under-report crimes seems to have accelerated quite sharply since Independence. In Uttar Pradesh, for instance, there were 335.5 Indian Penal Court (IPC) crimes per 100,000 in the decade 1905–14, but only 86.9 crimes in 1955–60, and only 73.2 in 2004 (Saksena 1967: 200–18, Table 1.6).[18] And, because the political and state capacity factors that influence crime reporting change a great deal from state to state and from regime to regime (or even month to month), the tendency to under-report is not constant over time and place, which unfortunately prevents us from simply computing the likely rate of crime using the *Crime in India* underestimates as a basis (Drèze and Khera 2004: 335–52).[19]

DATA ON CASTE, RELIGION, AND LANGUAGE

Data on caste, religion, and language are used in most academic research on Indian politics, as well as in many spheres of public policymaking. Caste data are necessary for the implementation of government and state caste reservations, reserved electoral districts for Scheduled Castes (SCs) and Scheduled Tribes (STs), and special category spending programmes directed at 'weaker sections', such as SCs or Most Backward Castes (MBCs). Language data help determine minority rights to education in their own language at the primary and secondary levels, as well as their rights to communicate with officials in that language. And data on religion, while apparently of less bureaucratic significance—because of the constitutional ban on discrimination on the grounds of religion—are nonetheless vitally important for many public policy debates. Even collecting data on religious minorities as a separate category is highly controversial, especially given the long history of divide and rule politics that used such religious data to apportion benefits between Hindus, Muslims, and Sikhs during the colonial

period. When the Sachar Committee on the status of Muslims tried in 2005–6 to collect data on the number of Muslims in the armed forces, it faced a furious political backlash, not only from the Bharatiya Janata Party (BJP), but also from the Communist Party of India (CPI), the Forward Bloc, and many military officers opposed to data that they thought might serve to 'communalize' the military.

The important thing to remember when using data on many ethnic identities is that they often represent not social 'facts' and identities that are unchanging, but that they are the outcome of what is frequently a highly complex, politicized, and biased process of data generation. The difference in the percentage of people in a particular caste or language category between one census and another, for instance, may reflect political incentives and strategic decisions to identify as a member of one group or another, as much as a 'real' increase or decrease in a group's population.

Some of the biases in the data are, it is true, less the outcome of politics than simply of an unavoidable attempt to capture the enormous linguistic, religious, and caste heterogeneity of India within a manageable set of categories in a particular census or survey. The 1891 census, for instance, generated more than 2.3 million caste names of various types, which had somehow to be simplified into a manageable set of aggregated categories for the census tables (Dirks 1992). Census officials argued then, and argue today, about how to aggregate similar sounding names, and whether groups need to reach a certain threshold size to merit inclusion in census tables or survey questions. More recently, the People of India project in the 1980s and 1990s did an initial survey that generated 68,000 separate castes, which, in the interests of manageability, they then simplified to 7300 castes, of which only 4635 castes were included in the final volumes.[20]

Much of the census and survey data we see *is*, however, the outcome of politics, of deliberate decisions by the state to carry out surveys using particular categories and not others, or even to not carry out surveys on some issues or with the use of some categories at all. It is also the outcome of individual and organizational responses to the questions being asked in a particular political situation, as groups of people decide that their material or social or political goals will be best served by providing one answer from their repertoire of possible identities rather than another.[21]

One good example of how politicians and bureaucrats decide which information to collect and how to aggregate it, and which categories are to be considered important, comes from the Indian census information on caste and language.[22] In order to promote Hindi after Independence, the linguistic category of 'Hindustani'—which emphasized the commonalities between the Persianized and Sanskritized styles of the north Indian vernacular—was downgraded, and then finally abandoned in 1971. In 1975, the Indian census decided that 48 separate answers to the question 'what language do you speak?' in the 1971 census would be aggregated in the published tables under the general category of 'Hindi'. So, only 70 per cent of those recorded as speaking Hindi in the 1971 census had actually given Hindi as their language:[23] the rest had recorded such answers as Banjari/Bhojpuri (23 million), Rajasthani (13 million), and Bundelkhandi (1.7 million).[24]

Another good example of the politicization of data is, of course, data on caste. In 1949, in the belief that not collecting and cross-tabulating caste data would help moderate caste prejudice and caste consciousness, the Dar committee recommended that caste data should no longer be collected by the Indian census, except for the constitutionally protected SCs and STs.[25] Since then, for many academic and bureaucratic purposes, scholars and officials have been forced to rely on extrapolations from the 1931 census, despite the many probable changes due to migration and differential birth rates, not to mention changes in government and individual identifications. There have been attempts to reintroduce caste data for other groups into the national census, most recently before the 2001 census, on the grounds that such data is vital for public policy implementation (Deshpande and Sundar 1998). However, precisely because of the vital nature of caste data, some groups and their leaders—for example 'creamy layer' groups within the lower castes—may prefer not to have detailed and accurate data available, which might diminish their claim to reservations or other forms of government

assistance. In Kerala, for instance, opposition from several backward-caste groups was key in preventing an economic caste survey from being carried out after it was first proposed in April 1995 (Vijayanunni 2003: 10–11).

On the other side of the equation, individuals and groups have many obvious incentives to misrepresent their identities or highlight only one of their multiple identities to the census or surveys. Historically, many Indians have 'Sanskritized' themselves by claiming a higher caste status in the census, for instance as happened after the 1901 census sought to rank castes. As the historian Nicholas Dirks tells us:

> When H.H. Risley adopted a procedure to establish precedence in the 1901 Census, caste became politicized all over again. Caste associations sprang up to contest their assigned position in the official hierarchy, holding meetings, writing petition, and organizing protests. By 1931, some caste groups were distributing handbills to their fellow caste members to tell them how to answer questions about their religious and sectarian affiliations, as also their race, language and caste status. (Dirks 1992: 68)

More recently, though, as programmes have been implemented to assist backward and lower castes, individuals have greater incentives to formally claim a lower-caste status to the government, even if this formal claim does not necessarily have an effect on their social caste practices. Examples of this kind of formal attempt to claim a higher status—cases where individuals represent themselves as lower caste to gain entrance to schools or colleges in the reserved category,[26] to get a reserved job, or to stand for a reserved seat in the Vidhan Sabha[27]—are ubiquitous, and are often highlighted in the media by those who dislike reservations in general and are out to discredit them. There are also cases where people misrepresent their religion in order to be eligible for reservations: because Para 3 of the President's Constitution (Scheduled Castes) Order, 1950, restricted reservations to Hindus, some Christian Dalits declare their stated religion to be Hindu in the census so as to be eligible for SC reservations.

Organized political movements can also have a huge effect on the accuracy of census data. For example, a movement by the Arya Samaj in Punjab to block an attempt at partitioning Punjab along linguistic grounds led to a majority of Hindu Punjabi speakers in Punjab declaring themselves as speaking 'Hindi' rather than 'Punjabi' in the 1961 census. As a result of this movement, the proportion of Punjabi-speakers dropped to below a majority of the population for the first (and only) time: from over 60 per cent in previous Punjab censuses to 41 per cent in 1961 (Brass 1974: 293–7). There are many other examples of this type of politically driven shift in the proportion of individuals in particular language or caste categories: the Jat Mahasabha in Rajasthan, for instance, was highly effective in getting both the BJP and the administration of Ashok Gehlot to support the declaration of the community as backward in the late 1990s and early 2000s, in a clear bid to gain that caste's political support.

Individual responses to census questions about people's 'true' caste, religious, or linguistic identity vary based on census rules (that require people to list only one religion, or three languages rather than all religious identities or languages that might apply), local understandings of identities, and the perceived costs and benefits of answering one way rather than another at a particular time.[28] These considerations sometimes make it very difficult to compare data on one group at one time with data on the same group at another, and also make it difficult to simply presume from the census data which the socially and politically meaningful identities in the country are.

One example of the problems that can arise when we wrongly assume that ethnic data now or in the past are somehow not the result of politics, and truly independent of many of the economic or political outcomes we wish to explain, is a recent article by Abhijit Banerjee and Rohini Somanathan.[29] Banerjee and Somanathan claim to demonstrate the negative effect of ethnic (caste) heterogeneity on public goods provision, a topic of intense interest for development economists. To guard against the possibility in their statistical analysis that the heterogeneity measure they use might be the *result* of political competition over public goods provision rather than its cause, the authors use caste data from the 1931 census, which they argued was largely independent of the outcome

they wish to explain because first, there was not much public goods provision before the 1970s and 1980s, and second, the 1931 census reflected identities prior to large-scale political mobilization over caste, such as the Dravidian movement.

Unfortunately for the authors' inferences and statistical analysis, caste identities in the 1931 census were emphatically *not* independent of political competition over government spending. The new elected provincial assemblies created in 1919 controlled such important spending areas as local government, public works (for example, sanitation), and education, and although the sums involved were not as large as after Independence, they seem to have been more than enough to engender fierce political competition, much of it along caste lines.[30] Nor was caste competition over such goods prior to 1931 the relatively insignificant factor assumed by Somanathan and Banerjee. In Madras, as Eugene Irschick and others have explored at length, the non-Brahmin Justice Party instituted large-scale caste reservations in the early 1920s that profoundly changed the caste composition of government employment, as well as the ways in which public expenditure was administered. It also changed the very size and composition of the groups themselves, as castes that had previously resisted the label 'backward' now had an incentive to have themselves declared as such in order to be eligible for large-scale job reservations: the number of officially recognized 'non-Brahmin' castes in Madras shot up from 45 to 245 by the mid-1920s as a result (Irschick 1986: 33–7).

The idea, therefore, that the authors have successfully tackled the endogeneity problem in their essay by choosing an indicator of ethnic identity (caste from 1931) that is not related to the outcomes they wish to explain seems mistaken, and possibly creates serious problems for their identification strategy.

DATA ON DEVELOPMENT SPENDING

The Indian state spends huge amounts of money on both physical infrastructure (roads, public works, and so on) and various projects aimed at improving citizens' lives through better healthcare, education, and other similar ends. Various government statistics then detail the amounts spent, the numbers of people helped, and the amount of jobs, infrastructure, clinics, or subsidies provided. These data are important for politicians to detail their achievements and concern for the ordinary voter, for bureaucrats and those in the development field who want to demonstrate their achievements and justify their positions, and are also useful for those people who study development, and are interested in how much, in terms of inputs (money, schools, healthcare, education), it takes to have an effect on poverty reduction.

The problem, however, is that the official data are often unreliable. The Central and state development spending regimes are subject to a lot of rent-taking along the way, and at each stage the people involved have every incentive to overstate the degree to which the money provided is really being spent for the stated purpose, and to which policy goals are actually being achieved. What we have often lacked, however, are good systematic data on whether the money is actually being spent as it should. Are the roads really built? Are job programmes or direct subsidies really reaching their intended targets? Are teachers really teaching?

There have always been some sources—in addition, of course, to the rich vein of qualitative research—that have raised questions about the accuracy of official data on development spending. The Indian government's own office of the Comptroller and Auditor General(CAG)—a constitutional body charged with overseeing government expenditure—provides invaluable evidence, albeit in often dry and understated language, of the extent to which there is often a gap between stated expenditures in government data and the reality at the state and district levels. The CAG's auditors tell us, for instance, that 73 per cent of the money meant to provide scholarships for SC/ST students in Andhra Pradesh from 2002–7 was diverted by local officials for other purposes, or else lost to corruption. The auditors also tell us that publicly-owned companies in Gujarat and elsewhere are rife with what appear to be inexplicable over-payments to outside contractors, who often have not done work of the required standard; the extremely

high consumption of fuel by company vehicles; bad handling of finances; and the unusual choices of vendors that ought to be ineligible.[31] For anyone interested in the inefficiencies of SOEs and the political economy of rent-seeking, the CAG reports are a goldmine of information.

In the past few decades, the CAG's work has been supplemented by a large number of new studies and surveys done by the reinvigorated Programme Evaluation Organisation (PEO) in the Planning Commission, as well as by development economists, aid organizations, and NGOs, which directly measure the extent to which development spending inputs are really being made, as well as the extent to which development outputs such as education, health, and poverty levels have improved as a result.

The Planning Commission studies in particular are an exciting and often untapped resource for political researchers, because they directly survey beneficiaries of poverty reduction schemes about the way the schemes are run, and how beneficiaries are chosen. We find out, for instance, that according to a study in 1997, *none* of the states participating in the 100-crore per annum Border Area Development Programme (BADP) are following the programme rules on what can and cannot be funded, and that actual access to safer water had not improved, despite the fact that states utilizing the BADP had reported improved access to safe water in 19 per cent of the sampled villages (Indian Planning Commission 2006: 45–53). We also find out that huge numbers of recipients of jobs under the 4000-crore per annum Jawahar Rozgar Yojana and Employment Assurance Programmes (approx. $1 billion US) are in fact too well-off to meet the programme's income requirements, and that in many villages, the lack of need for the jobs the programmes provide leads to the money being spent on unnecessary capital expenditures.

These are two programmes picked at random— similar stories could be told in many areas of the state's development expenditure, some of which are explored in a fine critique of current development spending programmes by both the Planning Commission itself and in an important article by Devesh Kapur and Partha Mukhopadhyay.[32]

CHECKING THE RELIABILITY OF DATA: SOME SIMPLE SUGGESTIONS

To end this brief discussion of data on Indian politics, I would like to suggest several ways in which users of data might assess the reliability of the information they use with a more critical eye.

The most basic rule of all is to cross-check the data one is using with other data sources that measure the same thing, or that are expected to be highly correlated with the data one is using, for instance as Angus Deaton, K. Sundaram, and Suresh Tendulkar did when they compared poverty with consumption estimates (see the discussion below). If there is a large discrepancy between these different sources, that cries out for further investigation.

The best sources against which to yardstick are direct surveys by agencies that appear to have no axe to grind, rather than data collected by agencies that seem to have an obvious interest in under or over-reporting. So for data on human development, for instance, it makes sense to compare the official state data on education, health, and so on, with sources such as the National Council of Applied Economic Research (NCAER) Human Development Reports for North and South India (NCAER 2001; 2003), as well as with the empirical papers done at the Massachussets Institute of Technology (MIT) and elsewhere that directly measure (with unannounced random visits to village schools) the extent to which students and their teachers are actually at school on any particular day (around 40 per cent are absent, as it turns out).[33]

For data on the prevalence of corruption, it is important to not only rely on official corruption and prosecution figures reported by the Central Bureau of Investigation (CBI)—which needs the permission of state governments in order to proceed with an investigation and prosecution—but also to look at independent surveys. Several NGOs have recently pioneered the use of citizen surveys that measure the bribes actually demanded and paid by members of the public. The best-known of these surveys, conducted initially by Samuel Paul and the Public Affairs Centre in Bangalore in 1993, for instance, found out such interesting facts as that 33 per cent of people had paid 'speed money' (an average of Rs 1850 per transaction) to get permits through the Bangalore development authority, and that 71 per cent of the poor people in the sample had to make three or more visits to government offices to even have a hope of getting their business completed (Paul 1993). The gap between such survey data and the official data on investigations and prosecutions provides a very valuable insight into the many political, bureaucratic, legal, and social factors that prevent a more aggressive state effort to punish the corrupt, as well as the problems with official data.

A second general principle is always, when confronted by large year-to-year jumps or declines in figures, to check if the difference is a real one, or whether instead it reflects either a typographical error (the list of errata printed at the beginning of many older government documents is seldom checked by many readers who use the data inside), or a change in coding procedures. The most notable instance of this kind of definitional change is probably the case of the Indian government National Sample Survey (NSS) data on the proportion of the population in poverty, which dropped substantially from 36 per cent to 26 per cent after a new method of determining those in poverty was introduced in the 1999–2000 NSS. This immediately raised suspicions that the new method had been introduced by the NSS in order to lower the proportion in poverty, and deflect criticism of the incumbent BJP's liberalization policies.[34]

Large increases may sometimes be the result neither of different coding rules or a 'real' increase, but simply that of improvements in the reporting rate. This is the case in several Indian states, where efforts have been made, at various times, to improve crime reporting. As the Indian Police Commission acknowledged, 'Whenever a genuine effort was made to register all crime—in Uttar Pradesh in 1961–2, and 1970–1, in Delhi, in 1970 and in Haryana in 1977–8, the figures showed such fantastic jumps as were impossible with any normal increase in one year.'[35] The political fallout of such efforts, however, has made them increasingly rare.

The most important way to assess data quality is to speak to the people who generate and know the data. My own fieldwork conversations prevented me from using problematic data, and helped me to understand the weaknesses of the data I did use. For instance, while researching riots in India, I was interested in how riot incidents were reported and how the formal statistics on riots were generated. I spoke to several officers with knowledge of crime data. One told me, 'If you look at the trend then riots are going down, but larger riots are taking place. There may be 15 incidents in one riot...a whole chain of events may be [categorized as] one riot.' He went on to say that in some cases where there was no obviously aggrieved party, 'the police thinks its better not to record'.[36] Interviews like these with other officials convinced me that we needed another data source on communal riots than the official figures, which I then went on to collect in collaboration with Ashutosh Varshney.[37]

Another example of how interviews can provide vital information on the reliability of data comes from this same research project on violence. I wanted to estimate how the level of formal associational density in each town might be related to violence, so I was initially interested in collecting data on registered associations in Uttar Pradesh. However, when I went to speak to an official in Lucknow familiar with the registration of associations, he explained the various ways in which official figures might be wrong: from aggregation and calculation issues, to the far more significant biases introduced by the fact that formal registration at that time (1995) delivered various subsidies, a fact that was likely to inflate the number of associations, as well as make the formally registered ones unrepresentative of associational life more generally, because one would expect 'connected' associations to be disproportionately well-represented in official figures. So I decided not to use the official data on associations for that reason.

The availability of data on Indian politics is enormous, but I have tried to show that there are certain key questions that can usefully be asked of all kinds of data before deciding whether to use it, and how: what are the incentives to under- or over-report? How are the categories selected or defined, and how have these changed over time?[38] How well do data correlate with data with which they ought to be positively or negatively related? And how can interviews and secondary sources such as articles, books, and op-eds help us understand the data better?

NOTES

1. http://www.eci.gov.in/.

2. The CSDS, especially through work archived or indexed on its Lokniti website (www.lokniti.org), is at the forefront of research on contemporary politics. CDS Trivandrum's important work on development has been made easily available in pdf format online at http://www.cds.edu/.

3. *Journal of the Indian School of Political Economy*, XV (1&2), 2003, contains several excellent analyses of Indian party politics in the states from 1990–2003, as well as a 300-page statistical supplement, drawing from the CSDS database, which provides data on elections for the Lok Sabha and Vidhan Sabhas since Independence. The introductory essay to this special issue, by Yogendra Yadav and Suhas Palshikar, also provides two valuable tables that show their calculations of the effective number of parties in each state by votes and seats in Indian states since Independence.

4. For example, ML Infomap and Radiant Informatics, both in New Delhi, provide political as well as other data in GIS formats.

5. http://www.research4development.info/index.asp.

6. The websites are available at www.odi.org.uk, (ODI) http://www.iss.nl/ (ISS), and http://www.povertyactionlab.com/ (MIT).

7. www.nber.org.

8. http://casi.ssc.upenn.edu/.

9. See, for example, www.infoedge-india.com.

10. http://www.parliamentofindia.nic.in/jpi/December 2000/CHAP-8(sl).htm. Last accessed on 13 March 2004.

11. Kohli uses official data on riots as an indicator of 'a dramatic increase of political violence in India' (1990, p. 6).

12. Data on murders are, for obvious reasons that have to do with the difficulty of concealing the bodies and the disappearance of victims from family and friends, likely to be more reliable than other crime data. The various problems with Indian crime data are explored in some depth in Saksena (1986). My exploration of this topic here owes a great deal to several valuable discussions with the late Mr Saksena in 1995.

13. Survey by the Centre for Image Management Studies, reported by UPI on 6 July 1996, and available online through the India News Digest.

14. Survey figures are from Srivastava (1972). See also *Report of the Punjab Police Commission 1961-62*, pp. 10–12.

15. The 1979-81 Indian Police Commission noted that:

Since the crime situation is discussed every year on the floor of the state Legislatures primarily on the basis of crime statistics, state Governments in the majority of cases are also interested in presenting a rosy picture of crime incidence. Therefore, the state Governments and the senior police officers frequently connive at under-reporting of cases (*Eighth and Concluding Report of the National Police Commission*, Government of India, May 1981, 61.37 p. 8; see passim sections 61.37–46, pp. 8–11).

A member of this commission, N.S. Saksena pointed out elsewhere out that the 1903 UP Police Regulations had specifically warned against using any numerical targets in assessing police performance, as these encouraged dishonesty (Saksena 1996, pp. 151–2).

16. Interview, August 1995.

17. *Report of the Punjab Police Commission 1961–62*, p. 15.

18. Saksena arrived at his estimates by sending test complainants to police stations and counting the number of cases actually registered.

19. Jean Drèze and Reetika Khera find that crime rates 'are not well correlated across different types of crime', which I infer to be not only because the true rates are different, but also because the incentives for under-reporting vary so much over time, space, and category of crime.

20. Personal communication from M. Vijayanunni, former Census Commissioner of India, 27 March 2003, and *People of India* survey

21. For a broader comparative review of the politics of census categorization, the best source is Kertzer and Arel (2002).

22. An excellent book on the political factors affecting data on language and religion is Brass (1974).

23. Actually, somewhat less than 70 per cent, since 'Haryanvi' speakers and Hindi speakers were lumped together.

24. Personal communication from M. Vijayanunni, former Census Commissioner of India, 27 March 2003.

25. Caste data are collected at the national level by the Census of India only for the SCs and STs, which together constitute around a fourth of the population. Caste data have also been collected for some states by commissions looking at caste inequality, but these commissions use very different data collection procedures from time to time and place to place. See Panandikar (1997).

26. See the case of the Velma caste landowner's son in Andhra Pradesh, who got entry to Osmania medical college as a 'Kappula Verma' in 1981 in *N. Bhuvaneshwar Rao, petitioner vs Principal, Osmania Medical College, Hyderabad, All India Reporter 1986 AP 196*, July, pp. 196–204.

27. The election of Telugu Desam MLA, C. Joga Rao, from Yellavaram ST reserved constituency was overturned for this reason in March 1987 (*Journal of Parliamentary Information*, June 1987, p. 239).

28. In addition, agents of the state may not aggregate the data in a way that reflects the answers that individuals give. Jo McGowan, for example, describes her argument

with a local census official in Dehra Dun, who initially refused to record that she and her children were a different religion (Christian) from her (Hindu) husband, and refused to list her husband's mother tongue as Punjabi, insisting to her that 'We are all Indians; we all speak Hindi'. McGowan (2001, pp. 8–9).

29. Abhijit Banerjee and Rohini Somanathan, 2001, 'Caste, Community and Collective Action: The Political Economy of public Good provision in India', unpublished paper available at http://econ-www.mit.edu/files/503. Subsequently published in 2007 as 'The Political Economy of Public Goods: Some Evidence from India', *Journal of Development Economics*, 82(2), pp. 267–528; see esp. p. 301.

30. Although only 3 per cent of the population could vote in these assembly elections, a much wider segment of society had a political interest in the elections, and in lobbying these assemblies over policies and the provision of public goods.

31. Audit Report (Civil), Andhra Pradesh For the Year 2006–7, Chapter III, pp. 43–4. Downloaded from http://www.cag.gov.in/index.php. Last accessed on 13 March 2009. *Audit Report (Commercial) Gujarat for the year 2005-06*, downloaded from http://www.cag.gov.in/html/cag_reports/gujarat/rep_2006/com_cont.htm.

32. 'Sisyphean State: Why Poverty Programs in India Fail and Yet Persist', paper presented to the American Political Science Association, Chicago, August 2007.

33. Esther Duflo collects her own and co-authored papers on her website: econ-www.mit.edu/faculty/eduflo/.

34. Although, in a fascinating sequel to this controversy, economists Angus Deaton, K. Sundaram, and Suresh Tendulkar separately determined—using expenditure measures that proxied for poverty measures and were comparable with the pre-1999 dataset—that there *had* actually been a significant drop in poverty from 1993–4 to 1999–2000, from 36 per cent to 28 per cent, which the 1999–2000 methodology had helped to uncover. Deaton (2002) accessed online at http://www.imf.org/external/pubs/ft/fandd/2002/06/deaton.htm. Last accessed on 13 March 2009.

35. *Eighth and Concluding Report of the National Police Commission*, Government of India, May 1981, Sec. 62.9, p. 15.

36. Interview with a retired IPS officer, 8 September 1995.

37. For details of this joint dataset, see Appendix A in Wilkinson (2006) as well as the Appendix to Varshney (2002).

38. I should note here that many constructivist social scientists would spend much more time than I have in giving a deeper epistemological critique of the very categories and labels that are used by government departments and private

generators of data, focusing on how these categories and labels may be produced by the very processes we wish to use these data to understand (the endogeneity issue discussed above with reference to Banerjee and Somanathan's work), how the data may be highly contested and problematic, and how the data may not capture the salient aspects of the process—the intensity of ethnic preferences, for instance— that we wish to understand. See Wedeen (2002) for a discussion of some of these critiques.

REFERENCES

Banerjee, Abhijit and Rohini Somanathan. 2007. 'The Political Economy of Public Goods: Some Evidence from India', *Journal of Development Economics*, 82(2), pp. 267–528.

_____. 2001. 'Caste, Community and Collective Action: The Political Economy of public Good provision in India', unpublished paper available at http://econ-www.mit.edu/files/503.

Brass, Paul. 1974. *Language, Religion and Politics in North India*. Cambridge: Cambridge University Press.

Butler, David, Ashok Lahiri, and Prannoy Roy. 1995. *India Decides: Elections 1952–1995*. New Delhi: Books and Things

Chockalingam, K. 2003. 'Criminal Victimization in Four Major Cities in Southern India', Forum on Crime and Society, 3 (1–2), downloaded from www.unodc.org/pdf/crime/forum/forum3_note3.pdf. Last accessed on 13 March 2009.

Deaton, Angus. 2002. 'Is World Poverty Falling?' *Finance and Development*, 39(2).

Deshpande, Satish and Nandini Sundar. 1998. 'Caste and the Census: Implications for Society and the Social Sciences', *Economic and Political Weekly*, XXXIII(32), pp. 2157–9.

Dholakia, Archana. 2005. 'Measuring Fiscal Performance of States: An Alternative Approach', *Economic and Political Weekly*, XL(31), pp. 3421–8.

Dirks, Nicholas B., 1992, 'Castes of Mind', *Representations*, Vol. 37, pp. 56–78.

Drèze, Jean and Reetika Khera. 2004. 'Crime, Gender, and Society in India: Insights from Homicide Data', *Population and Development Review*, 26(2), pp. 335–52.

Herrera, Yoshiko and Devesh Kapur. 2007. 'Improving Data Quality: Actors, Incentives and Capabilities', *Political Analysis*, Vol. 15, pp. 365–86.

Indian Planning Commission. 2006. *Compendium of Reports Volume IV, 1999–2006*, New Delhi: Ministry of Planning, available at http://planningcommission.nic.in/reports/peoreport/peoevalu/peo_cesc.pdf. Last accessed on 13 March 2009.

Irschick, Eugene. 1986. *Tamil Revivalism in the 1930s*, Madras: Cre-A.

Kapur, Devesh and Partha Mukhopadhyay. 2007. 'Sisyphean State: Why Poverty Programs in India Fail and yet Persist', paper presented to the American Political Science Association, Chicago, August.

Kertzer, David I. and Dominique Arel (eds). 2002. *Census and Identity: The Politics of Race, Ethnicity, and Language in National Censuses*, Cambridge: Cambridge University Press.

Kohli, A.B. 2000. *Councils of Ministers in India: Independence to 13th Lok Sabha*. New Delhi: Reliance.

Kohli, Atul. 1990. *Democracy and Discontent: India's Growing Crisis of Governability*. New York: Cambridge University Press.

McGowan, Jo. 2001. 'Lies, Damn Lies and Statistics', *Commonweal*, 128(14).

Mooij, Jos. 2003. 'Smart Governance? Politics in the Policy Process in Andhra Pradesh', available at www.odi.org.uk.

NCAER (National Council of Applied Economic Research). 2003. *North India: Human Development Report*, New Delhi: Oxford University Press.

_____. 2001. *South India: Human Development Report*. New Delhi: Oxford University Press.

Nayar, Baldev Raj. 1975. *Violence and Crime in India: A Quantitative Analysis*. New Delhi: Macmillan.

Panandikar, V.A. Pai (ed.). 1997. *The Politics of Backwardness*. New Delhi: Konark.

Paul, Samuel. 1993. 'Making Voice Work: The Report Card on Bangalore's Public Services', http://econ.worldbank.org/docs/513.pdf.

Saksena, N.S. 1986. *Law and Order in India*. New Delhi: Abhinav Printers.

_____. 1967. 'A 60-Year Review (1905–1964) of concealment of Crime in Relation to Burglary Cases in Uttar Pradesh', *Proceedings of the Sixth Police Science Congress*, Bhubaneswar, Orissa, pp. 200–18 and *Crime in India 2004* Table 1.6 downloaded from http://ncrb.nic.in/crime2004/cii-2004/Table%201.6.pdf. Accessed on 13 March 2009

Singh, Vikas, Bhupendra Gehlot, Daniel Start, and Craig Johnson. 2003. 'Out of Reach: Local Politics and the Distribution of Development Funds in Madhya Pradesh', available at www.odi.org.uk.

Singh, V.B. and Shankar Bose. 1986–94, *Elections in India*. New Delhi: Sage Publications.

Srivastava, Saraswati. 1972. 'Public Image of the Police', *Journal of the Society for the Study of State Governments*, V(3 & 4), pp. 243–63, pp. 252–6.

South India: Human Development Report. 2001. New Delhi: Oxford University Press.

SDSA Team. 2008. *State of Democracy in South Asia: A Report*. New Delhi: Oxford University Press.

Varshney, Ashutosh. 2002. *Ethnic Conflict and Civic Life*. Yale: Yale University Press.

Vijayanunni, M. 2003. 'Caste and the Census of India', unpublished paper presented at Duke University South Asia Seminar.

Wedeen, Lisa. 2002. 'Conceptualizing Culture: Possibilities for Political Science', *American Political Science Review*, 96(4), pp. 713–28.

Wilkinson, Steven I. 2006. *Votes and Violence*. New York: Cambridge University Press.

Yadav, Yogendra and Alistair McMillan. 2002. 'On Data Sources in Indian Politics', unpublished paper presented at a conference at the University of Michigan, July.

Contributors

KANTI BAJPAI is Professor in the Politics and International Relations of South Asia, affiliated to the School of Interdisciplinary Area Studies and the Department of Politics and International Relations, University of Oxford.

SANJIB BARUAH is Professor of Political Studies at Bard College, Annandale-on-Hudson, New York and Honorary Professor at the Centre for Policy Research, New Delhi.

AMRITA BASU is Associate Dean of the Faculty and Paino Professor of Political Science and Women's and Gender Studies at Amherst College.

AMITA BAVISKAR is Associate Professor at the Institute of Economic Growth, Delhi.

PARTHA CHATTERJEE is Professor at the Department of Anthropology, Columbia University.

NEERA CHANDHOKE is Professor at the Department of Political Science, University of Delhi.

STUART CORBRIDGE is Professor of Development Studies and Head of Institute at the Development Studies Institute, London School of Economics and Political Science.

JEAN DRÈZE is Honorary Professor at the Department of Economics, Delhi School of Economics, University of Delhi.

SUMIT GANGULY is Professor of Political Science, the Director of the India Studies Program, and holds the Rabindranath Tagore Chair in Indian Cultures and Civilizations at Indiana University.

RAMACHANDRA GUHA is the author of, among other works, *Environmentalism: A Global History* and *India after Gandhi*. He lives in Bangalore.

GOPAL GURU is Professor at the Centre for Political Studies, Jawaharlal Nehru University.

JOHN HARRISS is Professor of International Studies and Director at the School for International Studies, Simon Fraser University.

ZOYA HASAN is Professor of Political Science at the Centre for Political Studies, Jawaharlal Nehru University.

VERNON HEWITT is Senior Lecturer in Politics at the Department of Politics, University of Bristol.

CHRISTOPHE JAFFRELOT is Senior Research Fellow at the Centre d'Etudes et de Recherches Internationales (CERI-Sciences Po).

NIRAJA GOPAL JAYAL is Professor at the Centre for the Study of Law and Governance, Jawaharlal Nehru University, New Delhi.

ROB JENKINS is Professor of Political Science, Hunter College, New York and The Graduate Center, Associate Director, Ralph Bunche Institute for International Studies, City University of New York.

SURINDER S. JODHKA is Professor of Sociology at the Centre for the Study of Social Systems, Jawaharlal Nehru University.

DEVESH KAPUR is Associate Professor of Political Science, University of Pennsylvania.

SUDIPTA KAVIRAJ is Professor of South Asian Politics and Intellectual History, and Department Chair at the Middle East and Asian Languages and Cultures, Columbia University.

SUNIL KHILNANI is Starr Foundation Professor and Director of South Asia Studies at the School of Advanced International Studies (SAIS), The Johns Hopkins University.

ATUL KOHLI is David K.E. Bruce Professor of International Affairs and Professor of Politics and International Affairs, Princeton University.

ANIRUDH KRISHNA is Associate Professor of Public Policy and Political Science, Sanford Institute of Public Policy, Duke University.

JAMES MANOR is Emeka Anyaoku Professor of Commonwealth Studies at the Institute of Commonwealth Studies, University of London.

ALISTAIR MCMILLAN is a Senior Lecturer in the Department of Politics, University of Sheffield.

PRATAP BHANU MEHTA is President and Chief Executive at the Centre for Policy Research, New Delhi.

UDAY S. MEHTA teaches political theory and is the Clarence Francis Professor in the Social Sciences at Amherst College.

SUBRATA K. MITRA is Professor and Head of the Department of Political Science at the South Asia Institute, University of Heidelberg.

BISHNU N. MOHAPATRA is Programme Officer, Governance, The Ford Foundation, New Delhi. He formerly taught at the universities of Delhi and Kyoto, and Jawaharlal Nehru University.

DILIP MOOKHERJEE is Professor of Economics at Boston University.

RAHUL MUKHERJI is Associate Professor at the South Asian Studies Programme, Faculty of Arts and Social Sciences, National University of Singapore.

SUDHA PAI is Professor at the Centre for Political Studies, Jawaharlal Nehru University.

MALTE PEHL is Assistant Professor of International Studies at the College of Charleston, USA.

SHIRIN M. RAI is Professor of Politics and International Studies and Director of the Leverhulme Trust Programme on Gendered Ceremony and Ritual in Parliament, University of Warwick.

LAVANYA RAJAMANI is Professor at the Centre for Policy Research, New Delhi.

ANUPAMA ROY is Associate Professor at the Centre for Political Studies, Jawaharlal Nehru University, New Delhi.

LLOYD I. RUDOLPH is Professor Emeritus of Political Science, University of Chicago.

SUSANNE HOEBER RUDOLPH is William Benton Distinguished Service Professor Emerita, University of Chicago.

ARGHYA SENGUPTA is Research Associate at the Centre for Policy Research, New Delhi.

ASEEMA SINHA is Associate Professor at the Department of Political Science, University of Wisconsin-Madison.

E. SRIDHARAN is Academic Director at the University of Pennsylvania Institute for the Advanced Study of India (UPIASI), New Delhi.

ARUN R. SWAMY received his PhD from the University of California (Berkeley) and currently lives and works in Los Angeles.

STEVEN I. WILKINSON is Nilekani Professor of India and South Asian Studies and Professor of Political Science and International Affairs at Yale University.

YOGENDRA YADAV is Senior Fellow at the Centre for the Study of Developing Societies, Delhi.

Index